A HISTORY OF BAROQUE MUSIC

A
HISTORY
OF
BAROQUE
MUSIC

George J. Buelow

INDIANA UNIVERSITY PRESS
Bloomington & Indianapolis

This book is a publication of
Indiana University Press
601 North Morton Street
Bloomington, IN 47404-3797 USA

http://iupress.indiana.edu

Telephone orders   800-842-6796
Fax orders   812-855-7931
Orders by e-mail   iuporder@indiana.edu

Manufactured in the United States of America

Library of Congress Cataloging-in-Publication Data

Buelow, George J.
   A history of baroque music / George J. Buelow.
    p. cm.
  Includes bibliographical references (p.) and index.
  ISBN 0-253-34365-8 (cloth : alk. paper)
    1. Music—17th century—History and criticism. 2. Music—
18th century—History and criticism. I. Title.

ML193.B76 2004
780'.9'032—dc22   2003025348

1 2 3 4 5 09 08 07 06 05 04

In Memoriam: Professor Martin Bernstein (1904–1999)
Teacher, Mentor, Friend

Contents

Contents

A HISTORY OF BAROQUE MUSIC

INTRODUCTION

Baroque as a Historical Concept

OF ALL THE TERMINOLOGY BORROWED from art historians as labels for periods of music history, none has been more troublesome in its vagueness if not its inappropriateness than the word Baroque. From its origins in the sixteenth century as a technical and descriptive term for irregularly shaped pearls (in Portuguese *barroco*), to its popularization in English-language jargon meaning variously strange, distorted, extravagant, and so on, the word has frequently changed meaning and has found ever-wider applications. Early in the twentieth century it was still a novelty in musical historiography, usually thought best reserved in music for the works of J. S. Bach, Handel, and Domenico Scarlatti. By the end of the century it was assumed to define that period as well as music of the entire seventeenth century and to include musical styles by composers as individual and often separated by decades chronologically as Monteverdi, Carissimi, Lully, Purcell, Schütz, Corelli, Vivaldi, Rameau, Telemann, as well as the Scarlattis, J. S. Bach, and Handel. Is it possible to describe the music of a period following the Renaissance and preceding eighteenth-century Classicism as Baroque? Is "baroque" a valid concept for music history? What are the origins of this label in musical historiography?

Baroque was first related to music in France in 1734, when an unidentified critic in *La Mercure* said of a ballet in Rameau's *Hippolyte et Aricie* (1733):

> It ran through every trick with speed, unsparing of dissonances without end, sometimes two notes were persistently repeated for a quarter of an hour. There was much noise, force, humming; and when by chance two measures were encountered that could have made a pleasing melody, there was a quick change of key, of mode, and of meter. Continually, it was sadness instead of tenderness. The uncommon had the character of the baroque, the spirited of din. Instead of cheer, restlessness, and never any graciousness, nor anything that could reach the heart.[1]

Baroque apparently had its earliest musical associations with Rameau's operas, for which at this time he was often criticized for supposed lapses of musical taste in comparison to Lully. In 1739 Jean-Baptiste Rousseau commented in a letter that Rameau's *Dardanus* had led Rousseau to write a humorous ode containing the line, "distillers of baroque chords of which so many idiots are enamored."[2]

Nonmusical references, though rare, occur from at least 1701. In one instance Saint-Simon describes a recent ecclesiastical appointment as "baroque," meaning bizarre.[3] And the *Dictionnaire de l'Académie* of 1740 defined baroque as a figure of speech meaning irregular, bizarre, uneven. In 1746 the French philosopher Noel Antoine Pluche divided contemporary music into the Baroque and the *chantante,* the latter emphasizing beautiful melody and song, while the former was ineffective melodically because of extreme tempos, chords, and ornaments.[4] Baroque in this context stood for a style of French music opposed to the popular *chantante* or *galant* style; it was music of virtuosity, of complex, striking dissonances and exceptional modulations.

In 1753 Jean-Jacques Rousseau accused the Italians of writing music that was "bizarre and Baroque,"[5] and later, in his *Dictionnaire de musique* (Paris, 1768), appeared his well-known definition:

> Baroque music is that in which harmony is confused, charged with modulations and dissonances, in which the melody is harsh and little natural, intonation difficult, and the movement constrained.[6]

To some French writers of the later eighteenth century there was a definable Baroque music. It was music that sought primarily to explore extreme emotions, that had a dramatic expressivity, which to some critics seemed bizarre and even distorted. It was music apparently lacking the balance and control typical of the French *galant* style, that did not have the melodic clarity of the French *air*. It was eighteenth-century Italian music especially, but it could also be French. It was Rameau's music as distinguished from Lully's. This was not, however, the concept of the Baroque to be adopted by twentieth-century musicology but, rather, another quite different one developed in the late nineteenth century by art historians.

Even before the mid-nineteenth century, Baroque was known to art historians, for it was the authority and eloquence of the Swiss scholar Jacob Burckhardt who imposed the term Baroque on an art-conscious world. His usage was pejorative, meaning for him a decadent or corrupt Renaissance style, especially as found in later-sixteenth-century architecture, a period in which he believed the classic perfection of Renaissance art had disintegrated into a Baroque style. Burckhardt's student and successor at Basel University, Heinrich Wölfflin, legitimized the word "baroque" for art historians, as a style he conceived of as characteristic of seventeenth-century art. Unlike his teacher, Wölfflin, in his book *Renaissance and Baroque* (1888), established positive style characteristics of Italian art and architecture based particularly on developments in seventeenth-century Rome. Wölfflin hypothesized distinctive style contrasts between the art and architecture of the Renaissance and the Baroque in his *Kunstgeschichtliche Grundbegriffe* of 1915. These consisted of styles developing from (1) the linear to the painterly, (2) from plan to recession, (3) from closed to open forms, (4) from multiplicity to unity, and (5) from clarity to obscurity.

In a period with enthusiasm for a *Zeitgeist* philosophy of the arts, Wölfflin's views were soon taken over by German musicology and first applied by Curt Sachs in his article *Barockmusik* (1919).[7] Here Sachs identified musical style traits parallel to Wölfflin's five categories, for example, seeing the blurring of melodic lines by ornamentation as a musical concept similar to "painterly" style, or musical echo as similar to the use of shadow versus light in Baroque architecture. These and other more or less artificial and unconvincing similarities between the two arts seem today to yield little that is helpful to an understanding of musical styles.

The most influential attempt to establish the Baroque in music as a valid label for a period of related stylistic developments was Manfred Bukofzer's *Music in the Baroque Era* (1947). His thesis governing his belief in a "Baroque era" stated:

> . . . a musical era receives its inner unity from the music style and can be historically understood only in terms of stylistic development. It is for this reason that in the present history of baroque music the stylistic approach has consistently been adopted.[8]

But Bukofzer's difficulty with the concept of a unified baroque era is apparent in the following:

The music of the baroque era covers such contrasting figures as Monteverdi and Bach, Peri and Handel. What these composers have in common seems rather insignificant in the light of what separates them. Yet what they share are, besides minor traits, the recitative and the continuo, two fundamental devices of baroque music. In their artistic application, however, the differences are again more important than the similarities. Only the internal history of the baroque era can offer a satisfactory explanation of the striking developments that unfold in the span between Gabrieli and Handel.[9]

This was a standard German view of periodicity in history, based on the belief that one unified Baroque style existed, which, as Bukofzer's work shows by its organization, developed dynamically from simple to more complex, early to late, in stages labeled early, middle, and late Baroque. These phases in Baroque style development, according to Bukofzer,

must be kept in sight if the gap between Monteverdi and Bach is to be discussed. . . . the comparison of renaissance and baroque music has shown that the baroque era as a whole differs from the renaissance era much more fundamentally than early, middle, and late baroque styles do among themselves. In spite of their particular qualities, the three styles are linked together by the inner unity of the period which comes to light only in a comparison on a higher level.[10]

Yet Bukofzer does not make clear what the "inner unity" of the period was, nor what he means by his proposal to compare these styles on a "higher level."

Baroque music, therefore, has stood for a variety of concepts: in eighteenth-century France for an Italian-influenced music of composers, including Rameau. The usage is largely pejorative, implying excessive emotionalism, exaggeration, even ugliness. In the nineteenth century, Baroque was joined to other style terms borrowed by music historians from art historians. Here the appealing association of music with art and architecture received its strongest definition. With Bukofzer the Baroque was defined as a single, unified style, even though neither Bukofzer nor writers to follow in his footsteps have offered arguments to prove that one overall style or style concept gives inner unity to all music written from the ending decades of the sixteenth century through to the third or fourth decades of the eighteenth century.

Clearly, "baroque" has lost any specific style-relevant meaning for music. Nevertheless, the retention of the term seems unavoidable in its companionship with the other period designations, Medieval, Renaissance, Classic, and Romantic. These describe no more or less than rather artificial divisions in continuing historical developments in musical culture. As with the other arts, music does not suddenly abandon distinctive aspects of one stylistic paradigm for another, and therefore it is impossible to establish exactly when one so-called period begins and another ends. The Baroque in music certainly has roots in the late Renaissance, and the so-called late Baroque occurs in what must be considered an already advancing stage of the Classic period. Throughout this book, "Baroque" will be employed frequently to identify the general historic period, but as a term it must be considered style neutral, for a period beginning in the later decades of the sixteenth century, encompassing the seventeenth century, and overlapping and dying out in the developing stages of music in the eighteenth century.

A Paradigm for Baroque Music

The following paradigm of Baroque music serves as a foundation for this book. Even though not every detail of such an outline can be examined, the paradigm itself serves to

TABLE I.1.

A Paradigm for Baroque Music (c. 1580–1730/40)

I. Philosophical/Theoretical	II. Formal Concepts	III. Style Characteristics	IV. Social/Political

1. Humanism: Cultivating Greek theories relating words and musical expression. Music as rhetoric. Text domination of musical styles, forms, sonorities.	1. Monody—song;
	  a. air (strophic)
	  b. madrigal
		1. Basso continuo: new emphasis on outer parts—two/three part textures. Structural primacy of the bass.	1. Court and aristocratic domination of music, musicians (absolutism). Sacred and secular music.

2. Rationality of music and emotional expression. Development of theories of the Affects. The Affects as a basis of all musical expression. *Musica pathetica*.	2. Opera/Oratorio/Passion:
	  a. recitative
	  b. aria-types
	  c. overture, other instrumental forms
		2. Melodic domination of textures. Popularizing of melody (*bel canto*).	2. Church:
			  a. Northern Europe, Protestant church music traditions of polyphonic styles of Renaissance and the influence of the Protestant chorale. Introduction of new expressive styles of Italy. Interaction of 2a with III/6abc.

3. Cartesian theory of the emotions.	3. Concerted musical structures:
	  a. vocal (*cori spezzati*)
	  b. instrumental/vocal combinations
	  c. instrumental concerto grosso
	  d. solo concerto
		3. Solo song (aria, duet, recitative).	b. Renewed vigor of Catholic church music. Role of the Counter Reformation.

4. *Musica theoretica*. Continuing importance of number as a basis of (German) music theory. Theocentric music theory.	4. Cantata (from monody).	4. Development from intervallic to chordal sonorities.	3. Expansion of nonaristocratic society (bourgeoisie—middle classes).
5. Theories of musical styles.	5. Dance, dance forms, suite.	5. Decline of modal parameter, tonal experimentation, diatonic achievement.	4. Growing popularism in music. Venetian opera and its imitation. Home entertainment forms. New forms of solo and ensemble music. Keyboard music for amateur consumption.

6. Theories of musical styles.	6. Ostinatos (bass), harmonic formulas (variations).	6. Contrapuntal styles:
		  a. Roman—Franco—Netherlands (*stile antico* or *prima prattica*) [I].
		  b. Northern European Franco-Netherlands style *prima prattica* [I].
		  c. Venetian polychoral style, or *prima prattica* [II]. Motivic counterpoint.	

7. Continuing vitality of contrapuntal doctrine.	7. Chamber sonata/Church sonata (trio textures).	7. Expressive dissonance in contrapuntal texture:
		  a. melodic dissonances
		  b. *seconda prattica*	

8. Theory and practice of performance. Treatises and instruction manuals for professional and for amateur.	8. Sacred Music: Mass Motet (see under "style," interaction of old and new contrapuntal procedures). Also cantus firmus, including the chorale.	8. Concerted vocal and instrumental sonorities. Textural contrasts by sonorities.	

9. Introduction of tempered tunings.	9. Keyboard, other instrumental formal conceptions:
	  a. ricercar/canzona
	  b. improvisational forms
	  c. variation techniques
	  d. fugue
		9. Developing instrumental/vocal idioms—with some interchange.	

10. Thorough-bass as the basis for compositional doctrine.	10. Formal structures based on rhetorical concepts.	10. Trio textures for instrumental music (see 1 and 2).	
11. Music theory for the educated amateur (*galant homme*).		11. Dance and dance-based music, vocal and instrumental, solo and ensemble. Dance rhythms.	
		12. Developing concept of "national" or geographical, regional musical temperaments and styles.	

remind readers of a synthesis of musical developments on several different levels, or from several different perspectives. Rather than to suggest that there is an artificial unity to all music developments in the Baroque, the paradigm emphasizes that for the history of Western music culture from circa 1580 to circa 1740 there was a multiplicity of achievements, of approaches to musical style, a variety of focuses determined by musical as well as societal forces.

As the chart shows, music in the Baroque can be viewed from at least four different focuses: (1) concepts of philosophy and the theory of music; (2) new formal procedures, which in themselves are interconnected to (3) new or transformed musical styles; and (4) causal relationships between music, social, and political institutions. What this paradigm underscores is the error of thinking of a Baroque era with a unified style development across the face of Europe with its diversity of societies and political institutions. During this very long span of historical time, a diversity of styles developed. There was the creation of a vast amount of music, and there is no conceivable way to view music of the Baroque as developing from the simple to the complex, from experiment to climactic achievement. Monteverdi was not a primitive composer when compared to Handel; Schütz's genius stands independent and equal to that of J. S. Bach's; Purcell's music is not less mature than Handel's. Indeed, the number of gifted composers living in the Baroque period must give pause to anyone who would attempt to "unify" this extraordinary outpouring of musical achievements.

PART I

THE

BAROQUE

IN THE

SEVENTEENTH

CENTURY

CHAPTER ONE

The Renaissance in Transition: Origins of New Musical Concepts

The Historical and Cultural Context

DURING THE SECOND HALF of the sixteenth century European sensibilities toward the arts including music began to change. Why this happened, why one culture begins to fade and another to develop, remains one of the mysteries of human existence for which we seem to find only inconclusive answers. Despite the often-stated belief that the "Baroque" began in 1600, nothing could be further from the truth. Those aspects of change from what had been characteristic of the High Renaissance in the arts took place slowly, and the accumulated force of those changes became apparent at different times in art, architecture, literature, and music. There is no universal agreement when the Baroque era began, and no evidence to suggest that it occurred as a synchronic development. The origins of the new directions taking place in European culture would seem to lie at least partly in the social and political upheavals already shaking the foundations of European civilization in the late Renaissance and continuing through the seventeenth century.

The repercussions of Martin Luther's Reformation early in the sixteenth century created a profound schism in the Christian world and threw Europe into a continuous turmoil. This produced misery and armed violence on a scale unimagined until then. A seemingly endless series of wars began in the late sixteenth century between Spain and the Netherlands, which would soon engulf much of the Continent. It climaxed in the conflagrations usually labeled the Thirty Years' War (1618–1648). The Spanish, who in the sixteenth century had become a dominating world power, accumulating vast resources of wealth from the New World, began an inevitable decline of influence, although not without a considerable struggle. The Habsburg rulers, seated in Vienna, made their most powerful thrust into North Europe to establish a political hegemony, and with success almost within reach, failed. France, until the seventeenth century, fraught with religious dissension and political weakness at its governmental center, began a development, which culminated during the reign of Louis XIV, to become through statesmanship and costly wars the most powerful political and cultural force on the Continent. Italy, though divided into numerous independent or semi-independent states, often dominated by Spain, France, or Austria, had within its center the Roman states. These had the invested power of the Catholic Church and the Pope. Radiating out from this center was the papal determination to wage war against the Protestant revolution. The Counter Reformation of the sixteenth and early seventeenth centuries became the most successful of all the wars in this crisis-ridden time. Its victories reclaimed the minds and spirits of a significant portion of the European population previously loyal to Luther and Calvin.

Considering the degree of instability among the significant political powers and the enormous financial drain on them by prolonged warfare, destruction, and death in parts of central and northern Europe, it is remarkable that the arts survived as they did. Yet the first half of the seventeenth century produced major cultural achievements in all of the arts that had their conceptual origins decades before the turn of the century. In the visual arts the Baroque has been called the Age of Grandeur.[1] Despite the political and religious turmoil during the period, much of Europe witnessed a triumph in the arts. The heritage of the Renaissance remained the catalyst, and especially in architecture the Renaissance foundations in place by the second half of the sixteenth century affected the future evolution of the monumental Baroque seen typically in churches, palaces, and other public and private buildings and monuments. Although terms such as serenity, balance, and "Classicism" often describe achievements in the Renaissance visual arts, these characteristics were frequently modified or even distorted to create new, more dramatic and expressive tendencies involving color, movement, unresolved linear tensions, for example, in the works of sixteenth-century masters such as Titian, Correggio, Michelangelo, Veronese, and Tintoretto. These late-sixteenth-century manifestations of a new dynamism in the arts parallel the new vigor in the attitudes of the spiritual leaders of the Catholic Church toward the arts. Especially but not exclusively in Rome, a large number of new churches were already completed in the late sixteenth century. They suggest the validity of considering the Baroque monumental, at least in architecture.

Faced with its greatest crisis, the Protestant revolution and its threat to the stability of the Catholic Church, papal edict created the Council of Trent, held between 1545 and 1563. This extraordinary assembly of bishops met for eighteen years to argue about methods for resolving the complex issues of faith and church dogma that were challenged and often condemned by the Lutherans. A less important although not insignificant question also examined by the Council and the subsequent Commission of Cardinals was the role of music in the liturgy and the appropriate style as related to the sacred texts of that music. Clearly the Council was a major generating force for a revival of Catholic faith, leading subsequent popes to renew all aspects of their church, including a vigorous program to build new places of worship.

Significant to this Catholic revival were the religious orders, especially the Jesuits formed in 1540 by the Spaniard Ignatius Loyola. Other orders such as the Oratorians, Dominicans, Augustines, and Carmelites, as well as many bishops, were inspired by the reawakening religious fervor to build churches. Especially in Rome the churches that still dominate the cityscape today date largely from the period extending from the late sixteenth century to the first half of the eighteenth century. This unique revival of Catholicism, often labeled the Counter Reformation, made Rome the center of an outpouring of new art and architecture. The concept of the church as a place of quiet devotion, where the faithful witnessed the rite of the Mass from a distance, was revamped. As a result of the Counter Reformation, the Catholic Church embraced new methods to attract former and new worshipers of the faith. A new dynamism shook the very foundations of the Church hierarchy. Music could not be immune to these changes.

Roman architects such as Gianlorenzo Bernini (1598–1680) and Francesco Borromini (1599–1667) created sacred theaters, churches of eloquent dramatic spaces filled with visual movement forcing an interaction between the outside world and the interior. They modified or abandoned the strict symmetries, simple forms, straight lines, balances, and overall serenity of Renaissance structures. Rather, they favored curving lines, undulating walls, the dynamism of the oval in place of the perfect symmetry of the circle. The church façades are infused with emotional expression by turning away from the one-dimensional Renaissance form of church entrances that now are often molded like sculptures. Three-dimensional employments of pilasters and columns are combined with walls opened up with niches that twist in and out in agitated curving lines. Yet the rhetoric of these buildings makes its full impact only in the splendor of the interiors with their massing of architectural, sculptural, and painterly affects. Here one meets a theatrical and emotional experience that for the largely nonliterate congregations gave their eyes and their souls an experience unparalleled in previous Christian edification.

Just as the forces emanating from the Council of Trent vitalized architecture during the Counter Reformation in Italy, similarly the other visual arts also were affected. The increase in new churches and the renovation of others created a demand for an outpouring of frescoes, paintings, sculptures, and the other decorative arts. As with architecture, general stylistic approaches to sacred art were already established in the sixteenth century, but now they sought to simplify the message while intensifying the emotional impact of each canvas or sculpture. In the century that saw the development of opera, it is not surprising that for Italian artists it was the drama of the subject that gave focus to their creativity. To take only one example, the works of Caravaggio (1573–1610) were typical of the new art of realism and passion. His religious works, although based on Renaissance themes such as The Martyrdom of St. Matthew, The Conversion of Saul, The Crucifixion of St. Peter, The Entombment, and others, all unite a degree of classical form to powerful theatrical statements using naturalistic figures. The focus of his paintings is usually obtained through the control of chiaroscuro—the dramatizing of the subject by intense highlights and concomitant shadows. His naturalistic figures, often using ordinary peasants and others from the lower classes as models, gave his figures immediately recognizable expressions of pain, exhaustion, elation, sensuality. His is an art that suggests to us a psychological motivation of its figures.

Many are the other artists who contributed to this new dynamism: Peter Paul Rubens (1577–1640), with his gigantic canvases depicting the life of Maria de Medici for the Luxembourg Palace in Paris, and the *Descent from the Cross* in Antwerp Cathedral; the Dutch landscape and genre painters such as Frans Hals (c. 1585–1666) and Jan Vermeer (1632–1675); the greatest Dutch seventeenth-century master, Rembrandt van Rijn (1606–1669), best known for his strikingly individualistic portraits often cast in mysterious darkness with a few spots of light, enigmatic and strange, seething with inner emotions. In Spain there were Velázquez (1599–1660) and Murillo (1617–1682), and in France Georges de La Tour (1593–1652), whose canvases make extraordinary dramatic statements by the bold use of light and dark. At the same time there were two French artists living in Rome, Nicolas Poussin (1594–1665) and Claude Lorrain (1600–1682), who helped to define the French love of Classicism both in their portraits and historical paintings. Poussin often returned to antiquity for themes taken from Ovid and Tasso. He was fascinated by the way gesture, facial expression, pose of figures could capture emotions, and his efforts to categorize his methods later became a doctrine formalized by the French Académie.

The creative world in which music developed in the seventeenth century also was a century of new intellectual horizons as well as one giving serious challenges to established ideas and orders. In science and philosophy new discoveries led to exceedingly rapid changes in both how the world was viewed and how it would function scientifically, socially, politically, and humanly. Eventful discoveries occurred in astronomy, geology, geography, mathematics, physics, chemistry, biology, anatomy, and physiology. Science led the field, showing the way into a new world, while religion, challenged doctrinally as well as philosophically, began to lose the primacy of control over the minds of men and women. Sometimes, the clash of wills between science and religion was momentous, as when Galileo Galilei (1564–1642) agreed with the Copernican view that the planets revolved around the sun and not the earth, a view condemned by the Catholic Church as heretical and not conforming to biblical evidence. Yet, through the development of the telescope by Galileo, Kepler, and Newton, a new scientific and unsettling comprehension of the universe came about that ultimately would lead in the late twentieth century to the exploration of outer space.

In philosophy, too, a renewed vitality of the human intellect results in an outpouring of writings by seventeenth-century writers. Many were concerned with creating new philosophies of ethics and knowledge as the old verities of religious doctrine became weakened or destroyed. In France, René Descartes became one of the most influential writers of the first half of the century. He pursued an array of investigations including mathematics, physics, astronomy, anatomy, physiology, psychology, metaphysics, epistemology, ethics, and theology. One of his most influential works was *Les passions de l'âme* (1646), in which he presented a rational and seemingly clear and scientific statement to aid in the understanding of the emotions (affections) so that by rational means they could be expressed in the arts, including music. In England Francis Bacon (1561–1626) developed the inductive method by which nature would be studied by experience and experimentation in order to formulate universal laws. And Thomas Hobbes (1588–1679), like Descartes, analyzed the emotions and their influence on all human activity. However, it was John Locke (1632–1704), the greatest philosophical mind of the century, whose *Essay Concerning Human Understanding* is considered the most important book leading to modern psychology.

Lastly, one must not overlook the enrichment to the seventeenth century. In Italy, a brilliant legacy of poetry originated in the late sixteenth century that nourished a large body of music. It includes the works of Giovanni Battista Guarini (1537–1612), particularly his *Il pastor fido* (1585), and Giovanni Battista Marini (1569–1625). The latter's highly colorful, often heightened sexual imagery led to the coining of the term *marinismo*. Especially significant was the epic poem *Gerusalemme liberata* (1547) by Torquato Tasso (1544–1595), which was the source of inspiration for a great number and variety of musical settings. In Spain Cervantes (1547–1616) inaugurated the "golden age" of literature, especially with his *Don Quixote* (1604), and other major Spanish writers included Lope de Vega (1561–1635) and Calderón (1600–1681). Even richer literary achievements came from France. Foremost among the many writers were Molière (1622–1673), the genius of French theatrical comedy, as well as the tragedies of Pierre Corneille (1606–1684), the classical dramas of Racine (1639–1699), and the fables of Jean de la Fontaine (1621–1695). And in England lived that nation's greatest poet: John Milton (1608–1674), as well as John Dryden (1631–1700), Daniel Defoe (1659–1731), and at the end of the century, Alexander Pope (1688–1744) and Jonathan Swift (1667–1745).

This brief sketch suggests that in every area of human intellectual endeavor the seventeenth century witnessed an outpouring of new ideas, discoveries, and art works of lasting significance. It was the beginning of a new world, even if politically there seemed to be evidence to the contrary in many corners of Europe. Considering the ferment taking place in the sciences and the arts, it can come as no surprise that in the same century music, too, would undergo profound changes of forms and styles, changes as important to the future of the art of music as anything having taken place in previous centuries.

TABLE 1.1

Some Sixteenth-Century Sources of "Baroque" Musical Developments

I. Humanism	II. Italy	III. Northern/Southern Europe	IV. France	V. England
Pan-European development, with a particular focus in Northern Italy. Revival of Platonic philosophy, Aristotelian ideas about the arts, especially music. The search for a renewed musical vitality related to textural expressiveness, based on Greek/Latin ideas of rhetoric and oratory. Evolving theories of poetic and musical affects. Rise of Italian Platonic, other forms of Academies. The Bardi "Camerata" *Academie de poésie et de musique,* 1570. *Pléiade* (Baïf). *Vers mesurés.*	Franco-Netherlands polyphony: Roman, so-called *Prima prattica* [I]. *Coro spezzato*—Polychoral style combining vocal and instrumental sonorities. North Italian with Venice as a center: *Prima prattica* [II]. Mannerist polyphonic madrigal, with expressive, freer dissonance treatment. Beginning of so-called *Seconda prattica* (Wert, De Rore, Marenzio, Luzzaschi, others). North Italian, especially Florentine *Intermedii.* Spoken dialogue with various musical forms including solo songs. Dance, social and as musical forms. Transfer of vocal counterpoint to keyboard and instrumental ensembles. Origins of improvisational keyboard styles. Early independent instrumental forms and styles. *Basso generale.* **c. 1580–1607/8** Florentine experiments: solo song, expressive recitative. Contrapuntal madrigal to solo madrigal. *Favole in musica* (Peri, Caccini, da Gagliano, Rinuccini). Viadana, *Cento concerti ecclesiastici* (1602). Monteverdi, Book V madrigals with basso continuo. Da Cavalieri, *Rappresentativo* (1600). Monteverdi, *Orfeo* (1607).	Franco-Netherlands Polyphony: Mass/Motet, Senfl/Isaac, etc. Lassus (in Munich), Palestrina (de Kerle). Polyphonic Lied. German reformation Chorale (Lied). Polychoral style (Hassler) Humanism in Lieder (Celtes, Tritonius). Calvinist Psalter (Marot—Bourgeois). Theocentric orientation of musical thought.	Franco-Netherlands polyphony: Mass/Motet/Polyphonic Passion. Parisian Chanson. Baller de cour (*Ballet comique de la Royne,* 1581). Air de cour. Instrumental Fantaisie. Lute/harpsichord music. French organ music. *Musique mesurée.* French Psalter (Goudimel, Le Jeune).	English polyphonic tradition: modifications of Franco-Netherlands style. Latin sacred music (Byrd, Tallis). Italian/English madrigal composers. Verse Anthems. Keyboard Virginals music. Instrumental Fantasia. Consort music. The English Masque.

The Musical Context

A complexity of musical developments emanated from the second half of the sixteenth century, influencing and at times determining the new directions of music after the turn of the century. The Baroque was the logical consequence of Renaissance culture. Indeed, one of the characteristics of some seventeenth-century music is the retaining of Renaissance attitudes toward composition. An overview of sixteenth-century developments influencing the formation of new musical forms and styles is illustrated in Table I.1. Whereas much of this information will be discussed in appropriate places later in the book, some aspects of Renaissance thought and musical practice leading into the Baroque of the seventeenth century must precede those discussions.

Humanism

Beginning in the middle of the fifteenth century and for more than two centuries Italians pursued a search for their cultural roots in the ancient civilization of Greece. The rediscovery of the major classical writings in Greek and Latin by philosophers, orators, scientists, architects, poets, and music theorists led to an intellectual renewal among Italians that changed the collective knowledge of the West forever and established what we know as the humanistic basis of the Renaissance. Although it was an Italian development, its influence spread throughout Western society, and its impact was as vital to the changing cultures of France and other transalpine countries as to the Italian states. For music, humanism meant a thorough reexamination of the theories of music and the goals to which composers of music should aspire. It revived theoretical writing about music, and led to an outpouring of Renaissance music treatises and lively debates in Italy and elsewhere as to the true purpose of music. Not only did the new ideas derived from antiquity, especially Plato and Aristotle, overthrow most of the Medieval concept of music, but they became the sources out of which grew the precepts formulating further and drastic changes in music that can be considered to be the origins of Baroque music.

Evidence mounts to suggest the growing viewpoint early in the sixteenth century that music must return to the expressiveness of the ancient Greek music. Plato's statements (in the *Republic* 3) that words are the most important among the three elements of music also including rhythm and melody, "being the very basis and foundation of the rest," occur (apparently for the first time) in 1533 in a treatise on education by Bishop (later Cardinal) Jacopo Sadoleto.[2] Another prelate, Bishop Bernardino Cirillo Franco (c. 1500–1575) wrote, in a letter of 1549, thoughts about sacred music he says have been on his mind for many years:

> . . . music among the ancients was the most splendid of the fine arts. With it they created powerful effects that we nowadays cannot produce either with rhetoric or with oratory in moving the passions and affects of the soul. With the power of song it was easy for them to drive a wise mind from the use of reason and bring it to a state of madness and willfulness. By this means it is said that the Lacedaemonians were incited to take up arms against the Cretans; that Timotheus was roused against Alexander; that a young man of Taormina was induced to set fire to his house in which his beloved was concealed; that in the sacrifices of Bacchus people were roused to frenzy; and similar effects.[3]

By the end of the sixteenth century, humanistic studies in music largely abandoned the relevance of Medieval music theory and seriously challenged the domination of the Franco-Flemish contrapuntal style. Almost all of the important works of Greek music theory had been studied or translated into Latin. In addition to *De institutione musica* by Boethius, already familiar to the Middle Ages, they included the *Music* of Aristides Quintilianus, *De musica* of Plutarch, the *Musica* and *Harmonics* of Ptolemy, St. Augustine's *De musica*, Cleonides' *Musical Introduction* (*Eisagoge harmonike*), Aristoxenus' *Elementa harmonica*, and many others.[4] However, familiarity with this corpus of knowledge was largely limited to specialists, and much of it was unpublished and often in private hands. Very few specialists among musicians were capable of understanding the contents of these works and were dependent on secondary literature, which, as Palisca points out, was frequently unreliable.[5] Nevertheless, the growing debates regarding the true nature of music coalesced into two central topics: (1) was "modern" (i.e., contemporary) music or ancient music preferable, and (2) what was ancient Greek music and how could it be restored to contemporary practice.

These debates provoked a dramatic revision of the philosophical and theoretical context of music within the ancient structural division of the liberal arts. Since antiquity, music had belonged to the Quadrivium with arithmetic, geometry, and astronomy, whereas music theory was essentially a theory of number. In the humanists' search for the fabled expressivity of Greek music, two influential works on rhetoric and oratory seemed to hold some answers. Cicero's *De oratore* and Fabius Quintilian's *Institutio oratoria* both emphasized the control of emotions in orations. Cicero taught students to become effective speakers by varying their voices according to the emotions = affects they wished to arouse in their audiences. Quintilian, like Plato and Aristotle before him, emphasized the similarities between music and oratory, and asked that music be composed to excite generous feelings and to calm disordered passions. He classified the affections and gave instruction how the voice could be used to achieve the desired affect. Rhetorical doctrines would be joined to new approaches for composing music to expressive texts, and with this new goal music is shifted from the Quadrivium to the Trivium, or *artes dicendi* (grammar, rhetoric, and dialectic), of the seven liberal arts. Rhetorical concepts became part of compositional theory and appeared with various modifications and adaptations with some consistency throughout the Baroque in correlation with theories for achieving affective musical expression.

From the last decades of the sixteenth century the issue of textual clarity and poetic expressiveness in music led several writers to state that the music of the sixteenth century failed because contrapuntal intricacies obscured the meaning and affective potential of the music. Repeatedly it was stated that only the ancient Greeks had created such music and it was not contrapuntal. This, these writers believed they knew from comparing contemporary music with the effectiveness of Greek drama, which they thought was sung throughout. The condemnation of polyphony and the experimentation with homophonic textures became an important stylistic development at the end of the century. Needless to say, these writers did not have a single example of ancient Greek music that they could interpret to prove their thesis. This did not, however, prevent them from seeking a new style of music comparable in its effectiveness with what they thought Greek music achieved.

Musical Experimentation and Innovation at the End of the Sixteenth Century

The second half of the sixteenth century witnessed a bewildering variety of experimentations and new approaches to composing. This reflects the turmoil among composers and theorists as they confronted the challenges to the previously accepted principles of contrapuntal style, the *ars perfecta* of the Franco-Flemish polyphony, and the burgeoning innovative attempts to create a new style or styles of greater musical expressivity. Some writers, for example, Nicola Vicentino (1511–c. 1576), believed the unique expressive power of ancient

Greek music resulted from their modes and especially the chromatic and enharmonic *genera* which he claimed to have rediscovered. His treatise, *L'antica musica ridotta alla moderna prattica* (Rome, 1555), discards the unity of the ecclesiastical modes in favor of enriching scales with foreign tones for expressive purposes. In setting expressive texts that move from joy to full sorrow or death, "a composer can depart from the scale of the mode and enter into another, because he will not be obligated to the tone of the response, but his only obligation will be to give life to those words, and with harmony to show its passions, whether bitter, sweet, cheerful, sorrowful, according to the subject."[6] To find a practical means to perform in the three genera of the ancient Greeks Vicentino invented a new keyboard instrument, the *arcicembalo,* that divided the octave into thirty-seven microtonal steps on two keyboards.[7] The attempt to establish affective qualities of modes occurred with some frequency in sixteenth-century music treatises, and it would continue in various forms throughout the Baroque period and beyond. Vicentino's experiments, however, were quickly forgotten.

The growing division between composers pursuing the reasoned order of contrapuntal practice, and composers seeking innovative means to express the conceits of words, can be seen with particular clarity in changing character of the sixteenth-century madrigals. In the first half of the century the madrigal already dominated secular music in Italy, and is exemplified in the works of Verdelot, Festa, Arcadelt, Willaert, and Willaert's student Cipriano de Rore. The composers before Willaert generally employ a style Einstein has described as "polyphonic animation, though without ever leaving [a] homophonic basis,"[8] in others words, predominantly chordal textures but written with a sensitivity to contrapuntal voice leading. Musical phrases corresponding to poetic lines are usually clearly marked by cadences. Willaert, however, composes in a much stronger imitative style, closely related to his polyphonic sacred works, somber but intensely expressive of their Petrarchan texts. Beginning with the madrigals of Rore (first book for four voices, 1542, and for five voices, 1550) innovations are found that are directly related to making text settings more dramatic. Rore's "seminal influence," as Maniates so pointedly summarizes,

> is his attitude toward poetry. Rore achieves what seems to be a new and miraculous symbiosis of word and tone. Every single device departs from a basic aesthetic of imitating and representing every minute image and emotional connotation of the text. Counterpoint versus homophony, serene diatonicism versus dynamic chromaticism, traditional versus radical dissonance treatment, quiet versus agitated rhythms and tempos, consistent texture versus soloistic disintegration, homogenous sonority versus extreme ranges, and so on—all are called into play to depict the words.[9]

More than one writer beginning with Monteverdi praised Rore's music as the source of the "second practice."

The last three decades of the century included a large variety of madrigal types. Of particular relevance to musical changes growing out of a humanistic search for a musical style that would be committed to textual expression are the madrigal composers, who used extreme musical techniques for this purpose. These madrigals, sometimes referred to as Mannerist,[10] seek overt pathos, extreme emotional statements, especially the pathetic. One concurs with Einstein's observation that "at the end of the sixteenth century music may be said to have fallen into two categories—the pathetic and the pastoral: one might even say that it took refuge on these safe paths. The pathetic and the pastoral become a convention and remain so for nearly two centuries."[11] These conventions help to define the Baroque period, and composers such as De Wert, Marenzio, Luzzaschi, Gesualdo, and certainly Monteverdi must be considered among the founders of seventeenth-century Italian Baroque music. Their madrigals use extravagant musical conceits such as extreme high and low tessituras, difficult intervallic leaps, sudden tempo changes, complexity of texture changes from the polyphonic to the homophonic to the purely declamatory, and frequent chromatic experimentation, all wedded to textual expressiveness.[12] Gesualdo, it is well known, experimented with the most radical uses of chromaticism and startling harmonic passages involving unprepared dissonances, irregular resolutions, and angular voice-leading, often inspired by the violent nature of the poetry. There is no need to decide whether Gesualdo's eccentric, avant-garde madrigals are an end result of Mannerism or logically the outcome of the Renaissance composers' continuing experimentation with the application of the chromatic genus to music composed in the last decades of the century. It is, however, evident that Gesualdo's style is the most radical attempt by any composer to imitate the sense of words through harmonic means. His technique, though innovative, is also an end result of a long development, not a beginning. His extreme chromatic style destroyed the madrigal from within, as textual continuity and overall affective meaning are largely lost in the isolation of individual words and phrases produced with the extremes of disjointed progressions and the most anguished passages of dissonances.

The *cori spezzati* and the Concertato Style: The Gabrielis

Baroque music of the seventeenth century has many roots in the musical achievements of the Renaissance, among them were the development and rapid establishment of vocal works for more than one chorus utilizing an antiphonal style. Formerly, historians believed the composing of music for two or more choirs was largely associated with Venice and began with the innovations of Adrian Willaert (c. 1490–1562), the *maestro di cappella* at the basilica and ducal chapel of St. Mark's between 1527 and 1562. His publication of eight *Salmi spezzati* for two choirs in 1550 was seen as the beginning of the practice. Zarlino, in *Le institutioni harmoniche* (all editions, 1558, 1562, 1573, and 1589), associates Willaert with the practice and includes an extended discussion of the *coro spezzato* as does Vicentino in his *L'antica musica ridotta alla modern prattica* (1555). It was believed that St. Mark's double choir lofts provided a unique opportunity for composers to write music for two or more choirs separated by acoustical space.[13] However, the cultivation of sacred polychoral music was not only a Venetian phenomenon. Many churches had double choir lofts. And there is evidence to show similar stylistic developments among several Franco-Flemish composers, although the major impact of the *cori spezzati* (separated choirs) appears in the works of Italians employed in the regions to the north and west of Venice. Sacred works, particularly psalm settings, for double-choir technique can be traced back at least to the late fifteenth century. The impetus leading to the concept probably arose from the practice of antiphonal psalmody. By the 1560s, polychoral music is prevalent in German and Austrian sources, and the Munich court under Lassus's direction as Kapellmeister (1553–1594) heard an enriched repertory of this style of music that had significance for later Venetian developments. Lassus composed for double choirs in his Latin dialogues, psalms and psalm-motets, Magnificats, Masses, and other liturgical forms. Also in Rome, Palestrina and Victoria were among several composers to utilize double-choir techniques.[14] In Rome, as in Venice and elsewhere, music for two or more choirs became immensely popular. In part this was the result of seeking means to provide adequate tonal resources in the very large churches and perhaps also to create feelings of grandeur and even theatricality in the post–Tridentine Church.[15] The polychoral style of these composers varies in part as the result of text emphases. In essence, it relies on various degrees of antiphonal writing between the choirs that is either imitative or often homophonic. Subtlety and variety of how the two choirs interact, with a flexible and colorful employment of the sonorities the medium provides, are usually the goal of works in the multiple choir style.[16]

Although not originating in Venice, it was on that unique island state that the polychoral style found its most gifted exponents, Andrea Gabrieli and his nephew Giovanni. In their works sacred polychoral compositions reached a perfection that influenced many contemporary and subsequent Baroque composers. Alongside the conservative "Palestrinian" contrapuntal style (to be labeled "prima prattica" by Monteverdi), the polychoral works of the Gabrielis became another compositional style that, from our perspective, was equal to a second form of *prima prattica*. Of additional significance, the Gabrielis' polychoral works also established the ingredients for the important Baroque musical idiom of the *concertato* in which solo voices, chorus, and instruments are variously combined.

Andrea Gabrieli (c. 1533–1585),[17] Venetian by birth, spent some time early in his career in southern Germany. In 1562 he joined Lassus, who became an influential friend, and a group of musicians to accompany Albrecht V of Bavaria to the crowning of the emperor, Maximilian II, at Frankfurt am Main. He maintained important connections in Augsburg with the Fuggers and Archduke Karl at Graz. In 1566 he was appointed first organist for life at St. Mark's, and quickly was recognized as a major figure in Venetian music. His large compositional output includes many madrigals and other secular vocal music, important keyboard works, and numerous sacred compositions. None of his large-scale multichorus compositions were published during his lifetime, and our only source for them is from the collection brought out by Giovanni Gabrieli: *Concerti di Andrea, et di Gio. Gabrieli organisti della Sereniss. Sig. di Venetia. Continenti musica da chiesa, madrigali, & altro, per voci, & stromenti musicali, a 6, 7, 8, 10, 12, & 16* (Venice: A. Gardano, 1587).[18] Included here by Andrea are twelve concertos for two choruses, four for three choruses, and one for four choruses.

Although Andrea has often been left in the shadow of his more famous nephew Giovanni, it was the uncle who pioneered the new, Venetian, approach to sonority and compositional technique in his large, mostly ceremonial, sacred polychoral works. Many of the two- and three-chorus works employ a form of vocal-instrumental arrangement that heightens the coloristic impact of different sonorities. For example, *Jubilate Deo* contrasts the first chorus (*coro superiore)* of two sopranos, an alto, and a tenor with a second chorus (*coro grave*) of an alto, two tenors, and bass. The three-chorus *Deus misereatur*[19] shows these distinctions even more clearly, one chorus of conventional distribution of parts, soprano, alto, tenor, and bass (which Giovanni labels *Capella*), another of high tessitura, and a third of low tessitura. Although all the chorus parts are texted, nevertheless it is clear that instruments were required for support and also to play some of the parts for which the range was awkward if not very difficult for the voices. In works for three (and one for four) choruses, the high and low choruses probably used a solo voice for the "cantus," with instruments on the remaining parts, thereby increasing further the tonal contrasts. The performance practice for this kind of music was discussed as early as 1618 by Michael Praetorius,[20] where he suggests only one of the choruses must sing all parts, the others presumably employing instruments. The Gabrielis' concept of the *cori spezzati* influenced many composers of the seventeenth century, perhaps most important, Heinrich Schütz. The very usage of the Italian noun "concerto," from the verb *concertare*—to unite or combine contrasting groups of players or singers and the sonorities they produce into a harmonious ensemble—underscores the new compositional process, the *concertato* style,

EXAMPLE 1.1   Andrea Gabrieli, *Deus misereatur nostri*

EXAMPLE 1.1 (*continued*)

that had developed during the last decades of the sixteenth century and found its ultimate fruition in the works of both Gabrielis.

Andrea Gabrieli's polychoral compositions employ exceedingly diverse compositional techniques. In some instances the complexity of imitative textures indicates that the goal of grandiose sonorities at times replaced the advantage of textual clarity. This is most common at the conclusion of a concerto in tutti passages. For example, in the setting for three choruses of *Deus misereatur nostri* (Psalm 66/67), the final phrase, "et metuant eum omnes fines terrae," receives an imitative setting throughout all twelve parts (see Example 1.1). More frequently, however, the textures are solidly homophonic with some enlivening by contrapuntal voice leading. This aggressively chordal approach aids in the comprehension of the words.

Andrea Gabrieli's concertos, in comparison to earlier composers' multiple part writing, differ markedly in his concept of spatial organization and the variety of methods employed

EXAMPLE 1.2   Giovanni Gabrieli, *Virtute magna/ Alleluia*

for the interaction between choruses and the achievement of continuous musical growth. This growth relies on a strong if uncomplicated sense of tonality with frequent cadences, and an interweaving of short thematic motives attached to text phrases in what one writer calls a mosaic-like method.[21] The motives are used in a variety of compositional techniques which testify to the composer's musical imagination.[22] The potentialities of this concertato style may be seen in the concertos of his Venetian contemporary, Claudio Merulo (1533–1604), a style that would be developed by his student Hans Leo Hassler (1562–1612), and especially by his nephew. In the polychoral works of Giovanni Gabrieli (c. 1552–1612), there is evidence not only of the absorption of his uncle's stylistic innovations but also the use of that concertato style in new ways that stylistically clearly move beyond the Renaissance and into a new period, the Baroque.

After his earliest education, which must have included musical guidance from his uncle, Giovanni Gabrieli followed his uncle's own example and spent a number of years beginning in 1575 or earlier in Munich at the court of Duke Albrecht V. He remained there at least until 1579 where he would have enjoyed an association with Lassus and the stimulation of one of the major musical organizations in Europe. He became organist and principal composer at St. Mark's in 1585 for which he wrote many ceremonial works in the large polychoral format. His extensive catalogue of compositions also includes a rich variety of ensemble and keyboard compositions as well as secular madrigals. In addition to publishing the anthology of his uncle's concertos in 1587, which also contained five of his own compositions, he published the significant collection of his polychoral compositions, *Sacrae symphoniae . . . senis, 7, 8, 10, 12, 15, & 16, tam vocibus, quam instrumentis* (Venice, 1597). This was followed by the posthumous second volume, *Symphoniae sacrae . . . liber secundus, senis, 7, 8, 10, 11, 12, 13, 14, 15, 16, 17, & 19, tam vocibus, quam instrumentis* (Venice, 1615). Here, "symphoniae" means the same as "concerto" in the earlier works, compositions bringing together vocal and instrumental forces.

The *Sacrae symphoniae* of 1597 represent the climactic achievement in the Venetian polychoral tradition. Whereas a number of Giovanni's compositions for multiple choruses resemble similar works of his uncle, as well as those of contemporaries such as Giovanni Croce (c. 1557–1609) and Giovanni Bassano (c. 1558–1617), others enlarge and tighten the form and deepen the musical expressiveness of the sacred polychoral concerto. Many of them are brilliant achievements in vocal-instrumental sonorities, and, despite the frequent emphasis on homophonic textures, contrapuntal complexity becomes more prevalent. Formal cohesiveness has a new significance. The employment of *alleluia* refrains are often used, rondolike, to bind together these long and at times intricate compositions, and repetitions and also developments of motivic phrases can be extensive. The concertos of Giovanni Gabrieli have a rhythmic vitality infrequently found in earlier polychoral works. Dotted rhythms at times dominate textures and serve as motives joining choruses together or as formal patterns used variously in a composition as in this Alleluia passage from *Virtute magna* (see Example 1.2).

In *Omnes gentes,* Giovanni Gabrieli's only concerto for four choruses in the 1597 publication, he reaches the ultimate realization of the *cori spezzati* and the motet style of the Renaissance. Here, in the combination of chorus, instruments, and solo voices (not indicated by the part books but certainly inherent in the textures, voice ranges, and descriptions of performance practice[23] at St. Mark's), Gabrieli achieved a brilliance of spatial sonorities and a grandeur of musical architecture (see Example 1.3).

Three years after Gabrieli's death his second volume of sacred symphonies appeared. These works testify to the magnitude of changes that occurred in concepts of musical composition as the seventeenth century began. The *Symphoniae sacrae* of 1615 no longer belong to the Renaissance. Giovanni Gabrieli not only lived through these tremendous cultural changes but also proved his adaptability to the new spirit and brought the Venetian musical tradition into line with the new musical styles that had burst forth in Italy (see Chapter 2).

The Basso Continuo

When Hugo Riemann gave the title of *Der Generalbass-Zeitalter* to the Baroque section of his *Handbuch der Musikgeschichte* (Leipzig, 1922), he raised in importance above other aspects of Baroque music the compositional importance of the thorough-bass. All Baroque ensemble music demands an improvised realization by a keyboardist or player of another chord-producing instrument (such as lute, theorbo, gamba, etc.) of a supportive chordal texture derived from the harmonic structure of the bass line. This aspect of performance practice emphasized the universal Baroque partiality for a musical polarity between the bass and the melodic line or lines. (Riemann's title, however, is misleading, because there is not only a large, Baroque solo literature without thorough-basses but also the thorough-bass

EXAMPLE 1.3   Giovanni Gabrieli, *Omnes gentes*

EXAMPLE 1.3 (*continued*)

continued to be used by composers well into the eighteenth century.) As with other elements of musical style raised to great importance in Baroque music, the concept of the basso continuo appeared in the final decades of the Renaissance, although the practice of improvising accompaniments for vocal music from a bass line undoubtedly originated much earlier.

The first documented development that led to the practice of the basso continuo was organ basses. Organ basses gave a practical solution to an organist's need to find a solution to the problem of accompanying sacred music. Three factors necessitated a solution: (1) the growing complexities of sacred vocal music in which there were usually two or more choruses; (2) the frequent need for the organist to supply the missing vocal parts when singers were absent; and (3) the difficulty an organist had in determining the exact nature of the harmonic fabric from only the part books, which necessitated the time-consuming practice of preparing some kind of keyboard tablature or another form of a written-out accompaniment. The earliest preserved though undoubtedly not the first organ bass was included in the forty-voice motet of Alessandro Striggio, *Ecce beatem lucem,* performed at the Munich court in 1568 for the marriage of Duke William V of Bavaria to Renate of Lorraine. The explanation given in the manuscript bass part states that the bass was derived from the lowest voice parts in order to support the harmony, and that they should be played on organ, lute, cembalo, or viols, that is, as an early example of the organ bass practice.[24] Organ basses appear in print only at the end of the *cinquecento* and bear various descriptive names such as *spartitura* or *partitura* (referring to their characteristic use of bar lines), and also *basso generale, basso per l'organo, basso seguente,* and *basso principale.*[25] The first printed organ bass appears to be one published by Vincenti to a set of double-chorus motets of Giovanni Croce: *Spartidura [sic] delli motetti a otto voci* (Venice, 1594). The bass from each chorus is printed on two separate staves one above the other, and occasional indications of a sharp or flat above the notes specify major or minor triads. Another form of the organ bass appears in the *Concerti ecclesiastici a otto voci* (Venice, 1595) by Adriano Banchieri (1569–1634), also published by Vincenti. Here a *spartitura* is extracted from the first chorus only. The bass and above it the superius are printed on separate staves. Occasional directions such as *à 4* or *à 8* alert the accompanist to the number of parts in the vocal texture. Accidentals over both parts also help to signal major or minor triads. A note in the bass part advises that the missing *spartitura* to Chorus II can be formed by taking the *cantus* and *bassus* from that chorus and adding them to the printed *spartitura* at those places marked *à 8.*

Many organ basses continued to be published well into the early seventeenth century. They are usually of one of two types: (1) they draw the organ bass from the vocal basses, or (2) they are examples of *basso seguente,* that is, instrumental basses constructed from the lowest sounding notes of the vocal texture. None of these examples, however, possess independence from the vocal writing nor are they continuous when the lowest voice part or parts are silent. The idea of an organ part composed as a continuous bass = *basso continuo* first appeared in the *Cento concerti ecclesiastici* (Venice, 1602) by Lodovico Grossi da Viadana (1564–1645). In the important preface to this collection Viadana used the phrase *con il basso continuo* for the first time and asserted that the technique was his *nova inventione,* a claim repeated in the theoretical literature throughout the seventeenth and eighteenth centuries. Actually, as the early history of organ basses suggests, Viadana did not invent the basso continuo but, rather, gave a somewhat wider application and a name to the practice already inherent in the developing organ basses. The collection of motets, which Viadana claims were successful when performed in Rome five or six years earlier (c.

1596), are for one to four parts and are written in Renaissance polyphony. The basso continuo, although continuous, does not always have independence from the lowest vocal part. In others—for example, the two-part *Duo seraphim clamabant*—the basso continuo is free of the vocal lines and indicates to some extent that Viadana built vocal counterpoint on a harmonic foundation. In such pieces to remove the basso continuo is to destroy the harmonic organization, leaving the music to disintegrate, something that never occurs if an organ bass would be omitted in performance. The preface to Viadana's collection includes the earliest set of rules for realizing a thorough-bass accompaniment, the first in an outpouring of guides and treatises to dominate a large part of the theoretical writings about musical performance and composition in the seventeenth and eighteenth centuries.[26]

Music and the Theater: Precursors of Baroque Opera

The invention of opera was a unique innovation that helped to define the beginnings of the new musical era. Or, more precisely, it was the achievement at the end of the sixteenth century of a melodic style for the singing of poetic texts with a narrative function that made opera possible. The *stile rappresentativo* or *stile recitativo* was a momentous development leading to a conceptual breakthrough as to music's unrealized potential to achieve a new relationship with dramatic texts and to give to words an enhanced emotional expressiveness. A staged play that is sung throughout was the ultimate result in Western culture of centuries of artistic combinations of words, music, and frequently dance. Evidence, even if fragmentary, shows that various kinds of dramatic activity involving music can be found as far back as the early Christian centuries and even earlier. The Christian church, whose liturgy is in itself a highly dramatized ritual with music, developed other forms of dramatic ceremony, the most common being dialogue tropes of the introit of the Mass. The eventual growth of a large Medieval repertoire of liturgical dramas, some six hundred texts, focused largely on the Easter and Christmas religious celebrations but with others also taken from Old Testament subjects (*The Play of Daniel*), The New Testament (*The Conversion of St. Paul*), and the lives of the saints. They were sung throughout, largely in chant, but many also with nonliturgical music. Nonliturgical plays, especially mystery plays, with incidental music also were popular throughout Europe.

In the Renaissance lavish court entertainments further joined together the performing arts for numerous social occasions. There was the pageantry of elaborate processions with highly decorated wagons, as well as sung, danced, and mimed entertainments between courses of elaborate banquets. In Italy the court *mascherata,* in England the masque, and in France the early ballets all combined singing, playing, dancing, scenery, costumes, and various kinds of scenic splendor. They often were heavily infused with symbols from classical mythology and tied to political figures and events. The components of these forms of court entertainment would become essential aspects of the new operatic form. Especially in northern Italy one sees an increase in the appreciation for musical-theatrical entertainments, establishing a cultural climate leading finally to the tentative acceptance of sung plays at the end of the sixteenth century.[27]

Most important for opera in these developments was the *intermedio* and the pastoral. Already in Ferrara in the late fifteenth century *intermedii* divided the acts of classical drama. These plays, in five acts, were performed without the modern convention of the closing and opening of a curtain between acts. Four intermedii were needed between the acts and later two more before and after the play. These interpolated entertainments, at first without any unified theme or connection to the play, served to clarify the divisions of the play by suspending the action and probably also by giving audiences a sense of the compression of time that took place between acts. Madrigals were composed specifically for *intermedii* in sixteenth-century comedies. Philippe Verdelot, for example, provided them for Machiavelli's comedies *Clizia* (1525) and *La mandragola* (1526). *Intermedii* gave rich opportunities for musical-theatrical experimentation. Tantalizing is the description of an *intermedio* performed in Naples in 1558 after the second act of *Alessandro* by Alessandro Piccolomini. Cleopatra arrives by boat, stands and performs a series of stanzas "in a style midway between singing and reciting, with the instruments softly intoning rather than playing after each verse, which resulted in great gracefulness and majesty." This and other similar, even earlier, observations all suggest that attempts to develop a style midway between spoken language and song were made long before Galilei and the Florentine Camerata composers claimed to have invented the recitative style.[28]

As the *intermedii* became increasingly popular, they grew more extravagant, and took on an independent dramatic content with themes from the pastoral and mythological allegory. This is particularly evident in exceptionally elaborate *intermedii* composed for major events in court life, with those recorded for the Florentine Medicis the most splendid. At the marriage of Don Francesco de' Medici and Queen Johanna of Austria, the comedy by Francesco d'Ambra, *La Cofanaria*, was performed in 1565 with *Intermedii* by Giovanbattista Cini. This would appear to be the first example in which the *intermedii* were integrated into the plot of the comedy. The music for the first, second, and fifth *intermedii* was by Alessandro Striggio and for the third, fourth, and sixth, by Francesco Corteccia. The descriptions of the *Intermedii* give a picture of extraordinary stage machinery and opulent costumes and sets.[29] Alessandro Striggio composed music for two subsequent Florentine *intermedii*, the first in 1567–1568 to celebrate the christening of the first child of Francesco, and, in 1569, *La vedova*, for the arrival at court of the Archduke of Austria. In both instances, descriptions stress the elaborateness of the stage scenery and machinery, and the prominent role for vocal and instrumental music. Striggio's vocal music was primarily in madrigals in five or six parts, although evidence suggests these were often sung as solo compositions with the support of a visible or invisible ensemble, thus anticipating the concept of monody.[30]

The dramatic pastoral of the late Italian Renaissance was one of the fructifying poetic inventions to influence early Baroque musical developments, particularly opera but also the cantata. Indeed, pastoralism plays a dominant role as a musical and dramatic *topos* throughout the Baroque.[31] The *favola pastorale* has clear roots in the ancient eclogues and satyr plays, which introduced the Arcadian setting and personae—shepherds, satyrs, nymphs. A number of early Renaissance plays invoked the aura of pastoralism:

> . . . the world of the pastorale was that of a legendary Golden Age . . . —still unspoiled by the artificial needs and rules of social life and still blessed with innocence, naturalness, and freedom—men and women, that is, shepherds and nymphs, were not only happier than in the world we know, but also endowed with a spontaneous feeling for beauty and a natural gift for artistic expression, poetry and music. The nostalgic dream for a utopia of perfect happiness thus becomes the aesthetic vision of an idealized world. . . .[32]

This is already true, for example, in Poliziano's *Favola d'Orfeo* and Niccolò da Correggio's *Cefalo* (1487). While there is some disagreement as to the origins of the dramatic pastoral, most writers stress the significance in this development of Agostino de' Beccari's play *Il sacrifizio*, produced at Ferrara in 1554.[33] Here the emphasis on lyric poetry and opulent settings is enriched with music by Alfonso dalla Viola (c. 1508–c. 1573). He composed a solo bass, strophic invocation, to Pan, sung to the accompaniment of a *lira*. The music, in a simple recitative-like declamation, is essential to the dramatic action. In addition there are chordal ritornellos for this scene and also a four-voice canzona for the finale.[34] The dependence on music becomes a feature of distinction for the late Renaissance pastoral. The distinguished historian of Baroque Italian literature, Giovanni Maria Crescimbeni, stated that the pastorals "were the first dramas that were completely ornamented with music, and . . . they were represented on the stage by singers and not by actors; and they earned both the greatest applause and following." Other pastorals followed but none as famous and popular as Torquato Tasso's *Aminta* (Ferrara, 1573) and Guarini's *Il pastor fido* (completed by 1585).

Both Tasso and Guarini required music within their pastorals. Prologues and epilogues as well as *intermedii* between the acts, all integral to the drama, were sung and at times danced. In 1590 Tasso allowed his friends Laura Giudiccioni and Emilio de' Cavalieri to produce *Aminta* at Corsi's palace in Florence, perhaps with music by Cavalieri. One scene in Guarini's play, the *Giuoco della cieca* (blind-man's bluff), was composed by Luzzasco Luzzaschi; in 1592 music was to have been composed by Giaches de Wert and Francesco Rovigo, and another version survives by G. G. Gastoldi. The same scene served for a pastoral entertainment in Florence in October 1595, with music by Cavalieri and verse by Laura Guidiccioni. *Il pastor fido* provided models for various early opera librettos, creating a vogue for pastoral subjects during the Baroque. In addition, Guarini's pastoral poetry provided a source of texts, subjects, and characters for madrigals, monodies, and cantatas in Italy, Germany, and England into the eighteenth century.

CHAPTER TWO

Baroque Innovations in Italy
to circa 1640

The Camerata and Monody

AMONG THE SEVERAL THREADS woven together in a tapestry of new musical styles, one of the most important to the future development of music at the turn of the seventeenth century was the revitalized interest in solo song. As with so many aspects of the new in music perceived in Italian musical culture as the new century began, the origins of the "new" solo song literature are traceable back into the Renaissance and, indeed, even further and deeper into the very cultural matrix of Western civilization. The experiments in Florence led at first by Count Giovanni de' Bardi (1534–1612) and a small group of aristocrats, professional musicians, and amateur musicians aimed for a rediscovery of a style of solo singing older than modern Western civilization. It was from ancient Greek culture that the Camerata sought to reinvent this type of song. And their pursuit of an idea influenced by the humanistic studies of the late Renaissance is among the more remarkable and successful experiments in the history of music.

The Camerata met informally in the salon of Bardi from approximately 1573 to the end of the 1580s or even as late as 1592 when Bardi left Florence for Rome. At about this time Jacopo Corsi (1561–1602) became the principal patron of the arts in Florence outside of the Medici court. He maintained a form of public academy, perhaps to rival Bardi's, to which were invited distinguished members of the literary and musical arts. Regular members of this informal group were Ottavio Rinuccini (1562–1621) and Jacopo Peri (1561–1633), central figures involved in the development of the concept of opera.

Attending the Camerata, according to Bardi's son, Pietro, were "the most celebrated men of the city. . . . Thus the noble Florentine youth was raised with great advantage, occupying themselves not only in music but in discourses and instruction in poetry, astrology, and other sciences, which brought mutual profit to such beautiful conversations."[1] The only musicians who can be identified as belonging to the group are Vincenzo Galilei (late 1520s–1591), Giulio Caccini (1550–1618), and Piero Strozzi (c. 1550–1609). Caccini's remark, in the preface to *Le nuove musiche,* that the foremost musicians of the town were in attendance, suggests other musicians such as Alessandro Striggio, Cristoforo Malvezzi, Emilio de' Cavalieri, and Francesco Cini also may have participated. Caccini is the only contemporary to give the title of "Camerata" to Bardi's meetings.[2]

Enjoying the favor of Grand Duke Francesco I, Bardi was responsible for organizing many of the court festivities including several *intermedii.* He was reputed to have been an excellent composer although very few of his madrigals are extant, and he was a distinguished poet. His knowledge ranged widely from literary and scientific subjects, to sports and the military. It was, however, his particular interest in the music of ancient Greece that nourished many of the discussions taking place at his home. Around 1563 Bardi became the patron of Vincenzo Galilei, Florentine theorist, composer, lutenist, singer, and teacher, whom Bardi sponsored in studies with Zarlino. Subsequently, in the 1570s, Galilei and Bardi made concentrated efforts to define ancient Greek music and to contrast it with their perceived weaknesses of contemporary works, in particular the polyphonic madrigal. They were greatly aided in these endeavors by contacts with Girolamo Mei (1519–1594), an editor of Greek texts formerly from Florence, who spent some thirty years in Rome pursuing archival research into ancient Greek sources.

Between 1572 and 1581 Mei wrote more than thirty letters[3] to Galilei and Bardi that would become the primary source of Galilei's and Bardi's understanding of how Greek music differed from modern practice. The impact of these communications was decisive in leading to the early experiments, especially by Galilei, with monody. Mei had studied all of the available ancient musical treatises on music, and in 1573 he completed his four-book treatise on the Greek modes, *De modis musicis antiquorum*. His knowledge of Greek music, however, extended far beyond the Greek tonal system, and both Bardi and Galilei, in realizing Mei's authority, quickly bombarded him with questions. Mei's first letter to Galilei[4] has pivotal significance in the development of Baroque musical concepts. For it apparently gave Bardi and those connected with the Camerata not only the first solid evidence as to the nature of Greek music but also promoted Mei's opinion that Greek music was more effective in its ability to express the emotions contained within poetic texts than the polyphonic music of contemporary composers.

Mei believed polyphonic music failed because it could not convey the feelings of texts from composer to listener. His reading of ancient Greek sources convinced him that this was not true in ancient Greece, and he concluded that Greek music, whether choral or solo, was monodic, that is, single line melody:

> What chiefly persuaded me that the entire chorus sang one and the same air was observing that the music of the ancients was held to be a valuable medium for moving the affects, as witnessed by the many incidents related by the writers, and from noticing that our music instead is apt for anything else. . . .

Furthermore, Mei rationalized that voice ranges were specifically related to various affects, unlike modern polyphonic style, and if the ancients had sung

> several airs mixed together in one and the same song, as our musicians do with their bass, tenor, contralto, and soprano, or with more or fewer parts than these at one and the same time, it would undoubtedly have been impossible for it to move vigorously the affects that it wished to move in the hearer, as may be read that it did at every turn of the accounts and testimonials of the great and noble writers. . . .
>
> It appears to be clear enough, then, for the reasons given, that the music of the ancients was a single melody and a single air, however many or few voices were singing. . . . [E]veryone sang one and the same air in one simple tonos and in the best airs with a small number of steps [*corde*] in such a way that with its descents and ascents the voice did not go at all beyond the natural confines of the affect that the words wanted to express.

Mei's hypothesis was only a hypothesis, because he had no actual music that could prove his theory. Yet, his extensive knowledge of ancient writings persuaded members of the Camerata, who were searching for a new and emphatically more expressive form of music, quickly to accept his premises. Around 1578 Bardi addressed to Caccini a discourse on ancient music and singing, incorporating many of Mei's ideas but also proposing to reform vocal music.[5] This brief document is the first fruit of the Florentine Camerata to redefine the style of vocal music. Unlike Mei, however, he is not a proponent of unaccompanied monody but, rather, seeks to reestablish music as the Greeks employed it, supporting the recitation of poetry and moving listeners to the various passions found in the words. Rather than a monodic performance, he recommended singing to the accompaniment of instruments. He urged Caccini to give up the modal system and to replace it with the Greek tonal system.

In 1581 Galilei published *Dialogo . . . della musica antica e della moderna,* which he dedicated to Bardi,[6] and in part is based on Mei's concepts. Bardi's influence, however, is also present both in the imaginative *Dialogo* taking place between Bardi and Piero Strozzi and by Galilei's support of Bardi's belief that poetry should be sung to simple airs. Much of the content is devoted to Galilei's condemnation of composers who set texts in contrapuntal style, thus failing to imitate the emotions contained in the words. His solution closely followed Mei's: single melodies of narrow range, placed in high, middle, or low register as required by the affect. Rhythms were based on the poetry. Contrary to Mei, Galilei believed the melodies should be accompanied by simple chords, largely triads. He immediately set about experimenting with such melodies, composing Lamentations and Responses for Holy Week, and the Lament of Count Ugolino from Dante's *Inferno.* The latter was performed before the Camerata in 1582.[7] Unfortunately none of these earliest examples of what later were called monodies are extant.[8]

Caccini, no doubt influenced by Bardi's encouragement, also began to experiment with writing solo songs over a continuo bass. At least three of his early monodies, from the 1580s, are included in his famous collection *Le nuove musiche* of 1602.[9] This landmark publication established a major even if short-lived genre of vocal composition intimately connected with the new spirit of musical expressiveness generated in Florence by the Camerata.[10] Caccini divides his collection of twenty-two songs between twelve *madrigali* and ten *arie,* and includes the final chorus from his music for the pastorale by Gabriello Chiabrera, *Il Rapimento di Cefalo,* which had been performed as had Peri's *L'Euridice* at the wedding festivities for the marriage of Henry IV of France with Maria de' Medici. The distinction between madrigals and arie is significant: a madrigal, as its name suggests, is through-composed, with a highly expressive, free, arioso vocal line over a usually slow-moving bass that has little independence from the melody. The latter often has expressive and unprepared melodic and harmonic dissonance relationships with the bass, and, of course, remains largely true to the prosody and rhetorical expressiveness of the text. Two examples from Peri's monodies illustrate the affective power he drew from dissonances: In Example 2.1a, the concluding measures of *O durezza di ferro,* the vocal line leaps from a dissonance into a dissonance on *Duro aspettar* (harsh waiting), and concludes with a remarkable passage of repeated Cs sounding almost entirely dissonant against the accompaniment for *che mi conduci a morte* (that leads me to death). In Example 2.1b, from *Uccidimi, dolore,* the first word, *Uccidimi* (slay me), has an unresolved suspension sounding C natural against the C sharp of the bass that "slays" the tonal logic of the progression.

The accompaniment improvised by the singer, most frequently to a lute, theorbo, chitarrone, or later to the newly popular guitar, was deliberately chordal in contrast to most song arrangements of the previous century, when some attempt was usually made to retain a contrapuntal ordering of the parts. In Caccini's preface he offers invaluable suggestions as to how the singer is to interpret and especially to ornament the vocal lines. This detailed discussion of performance practices for the solo madrigals is an innovative aspect of the collection, which Caccini would expand upon through examples in a second collection of

EXAMPLE 2.1   Peri, *Le varie musiche* (1607)

a. from *O durezza di ferro*

b. from *Uccidimi, dolore*

monodies published twelve years later: *Nuove musiche e nuova manier a di scriverle.*[11] See Example 2.2 from this collection, the opening to the monody *In tristo umor,* in which extensive ornamentation is applied to most of the text. Clearly, this method of vocal technique and performance was crucial to the effectiveness of these songs.

In contrast, the arias are strophic songs repeated for a number of stanzas of a text. These can be simple, unornamented tunes, often with interesting rhythms including hemiolas and suggesting at times canzonettas and dance forms. Caccini, however, also includes three that are examples of strophic variation. Both the madrigal and aria types of monodies are important stylistically and formally to the music of the earliest examples of operas, and the strophic arias continued to have an influence on later opera as well as in the development of the cantata.

Within a decade following Caccini's *Nuove musiche* and other earliest monody collections[12] a flood of more than two thousand monodies appeared in some two hundred music books that were composed by court musicians and numerous amateurs, many of them wealthy aristocrats. This repertory is a keystone in the formation of seventeenth-century Italian music that is largely unknown, unpublished, and unstudied.[13] Some famous performers such as Francesco Rasi (1574–after 1620) also published their monodies. For the

EXAMPLE 2.2   *In tristo umor,* from *Nuove musiche* (1614)

most part the poetry is restricted to sentiments of the pastoral tradition. Especially the madrigals focus on love, love anticipated, love rejected as the recurrent themes of the majority. The poetry of Ariosto (*Orlando furioso*), Tasso (*Gerusalemme Liberata*), and Petrarch's sonnets frequently were used, as were the texts of Florentine nobleman and member of the Camerata, Ottavio Rinuccini. But most frequent are the poems of Guarini, Chiabrera, and Marino. The popularity of this sophisticated music developed largely at the major North Italian courts, but although Florence was the original center of its development, the interest there dissipated soon after 1620. In Rome the monodic concept was quickly adopted for sacred music, but it was in Venice that most of the published monodies appeared. As far as can be determined, however, Caccini, Caccini's daughter Francesca, da Gagliano, Peri, Rasi, and d'India were among those who achieved some of the most consistent and effective monodies composed during its rather short history and before the concept of the solo madrigal was transformed to become the Italian cantata and the monodic style infiltrated sacred music and the earliest operas.

The Beginnings of Opera

The remarkably fruitful musical innovations in Florence resulting from the Camerata and those influenced by it and also from Corsi's informal academy are all interrelated. Exactly how monody, *stile rappresentativo* (*stile recitativo*), and *favola in musica* (= opera) originated, who first "invented" the concepts and made the first musical trials, cannot be determined with any exactness. As has been shown, all of these new musical concepts grew out of the lengthy humanistic debates about the relationship of language to music and how music can be more effectively involved with expressing the emotions of language. One of the threads in this complexity of developments was spun by Emilio de' Cavalieri (c. 1550–1602), who had been brought from his native Rome to Florence in 1588 by Grand Duke Ferdinand I to supervise the musical establishment of the Medici court. He was in charge of the extraordinary *intermedi* for the marriage of the Grand Duke to Christine of Lorraine in 1589 with a dazzling group of other artists, including Giovanni de' Bardi, who wrote some of the poetry and originated the allegorical plan, the poets Ottavio Rinuccini, Giovanni Battista Strozzi, and Laura Guidiccioni, and the composers Malvezzi, Marenzio, Caccini, Peri, as well as Cavalieri. The following year Cavalieri collaborated with Laura Guidiccioni to compose music for two small pastoral plays, *Il satiro* and *La disperatione di Fileno*. A third *pastorella*, *Il giuoco della cieca*, adapted from Guarini's *Il pastor fido* by Laura Guidiccioni, was performed in Florence in October 1595. At a banquet honoring the wedding of Henri IV of France and Maria de' Medici, Cavalieri performed his *La contesa fra Giunone e Minerva*, to a poem by Guarini. None of the music to these works has been preserved. Of considerable significance, however, are the preserved settings by Cavalieri of two portions of the *Lamentations of Jeremiah,* one for the private chapel of the Medici at Pisa in 1599 and the other for the Chiesa Nuova in Rome, probably early in 1600. These lamentations indicate Cavalieri's employment of various solo forms with bass that are "monodic" and imply that they may be the earliest known representation of the experiments carried on by Galilei under the influence of Mei.[14]

Cavalieri stood firm in his belief that he was the first to create a dramatic new vocal style in these works. He is contradicted by Rinuccini who in his dedication to the Queen of France of his libretto of *L'Euridice,* dated 4 October 1600, states that he and Peri were the first to revive the ancient manner of reciting in singing. Caccini, always anxious to promote his own significance in these new musical developments, writes in the preface to his setting of *L'Euridice,* dated 20 December 1600, that he had already used this style fifteen years previously. Only Peri, in the preface to his *L'Euridice,* disagrees with his own librettist and acknowledges Cavalieri's claim, saying it was he who "before any other of whom I know enabled us with marvelous invention to hear our kind of music upon the stage."[15] However, Peri continues by saying he had already used this style "in another guise" in 1594, for the composition of *Dafne,* on which he collaborated with Jacopo Corsi. In a letter of 10 November 1600, Cavalieri writes in anger to the duke's secretary about Rinuccini's claim:

> He [Rinuccini] acts, as you can see, as if he had been the inventor of this way of representing in music [questo *modo di rappresentare in Musica*], never before found or invented by anyone. . . . I know that Rinuccini has gone head over heels into making everyone think he is more than most have been inclined to believe. . . . I sense that with this publication he hopes to be employed by the Queen in France as a secretary or some other such fancy. Indeed, I spoke to him about all this, for it seemed to me that he had done me wrong. Because this [style] was invented by me, and everyone knows this, and I find myself having said so in print. Now whoever sees the libretto of the Ranocchino [little frog] will consider me a liar.[16]

The reference to having "said so in print" refers to the statement by Alessandro Guidotti, the editor, in his dedication to Cavalieri's *Rappresentatione di anima et di corpo . . . per cantar recitando* (Rome, February 1600),[17] and no doubt dictated by the composer, that prior to these three pastorals "such a thing had never been seen or heard by anyone." Cavalieri, he said, sought to imitate "that style with which it is said that the ancient Greeks and Romans used on their stages and in their theatres to move the onlookers to various affects."[18] Nino Pirrotta has observed "the gist of the whole story seems to be that each contestant was deeply convinced of his own right to the priority he claimed and either failed to see the differences between his accomplishments and those of his rivals or else was afraid that the slightly different claims made by others might dim his own precious personal glory."[19] Another interpretation is possible. For the first time, after decades of learned discussions and elementary experiments, each of these composers surely recognized the breakthrough they had made out of the past, whether or not they envisioned the eventual forms of the new musical-dramatic concept. Even though the highly popular combining of text and the musical arts in *intermedii* would continue for some decades at major court festivities, the seed that was now planted, a play sung throughout, was without precedent. Certainly each of these talented musicians would comprehend the significance and potentialities of the concept. It is not surprising that each hoped to lay claim to his "new invention," the first in more than a century of musical developments.

The first known example of such a work sung throughout was *Dafne* composed by Jacopo Corsi and Jacopo Peri to Rinuccini's libretto. It was performed at Corsi's palace in 1598 with several other performances there and also, in 1599, at the Pitti Palace. Except for six brief passages from the score, however, the rest of the score does not survive.[20] The first preserved score, therefore, is Cavalieri's *Rappresentatione di anima et di corpo,* heard in Rome in the oratory of St. Mary in Vallicella (Chiesa Nuova). It is also the first printed score with a figured bass. The text, a sacred morality play, was fully acted out in the oratory of the church, the first in a tradition of sacred operas to become popular in Rome in the seventeenth century. It has, however, a strong relationship to earlier Florentine *sacrae rappresentazione,* and also to the *lauda* tradition. In fact, nearly all of scene 4 in act I, regarding the conflict of body and soul, was taken from a lauda book of 1577 used in Philip Neri's oratory.[21]

Musically, Cavalieri's work does not fully sustain his claim that he had preceded both

Peri and Caccini in the invention of a new style of reciting words in singing. Like the two *L'Euridices,* Cavalieri's work has a similarity of musical forms: instrumental ritornellos, tuneful madrigal choruses, songs in dance meters, and strophic songs. Some of the choruses in canzonetta style were danced, for example, the concluding *ballo.* But the recitatives are not similar to those found in Peri's or Caccini's impressive works. Cavalieri's have a some- what monotonous effect on the drama, at least in comparison to Florentine monody and its application to the recitative style. This is in part the result of the excessive regularity of the poetry in rhyming couplets and almost entirely set in lines of seven accents (*settenario*). There is little relief from the duple meters made obvious by the basso continuo beating out two or four bass notes to the bar. (Triple meters are largely confined to choral sections.) Dissonances are conservative and left almost entirely to the continuo realization. Lastly, the "recitatives" are predictable rhythmically, being tied to the bass line rhythms, and they often repeat phrases, further emphasizing the repetitiousness of the poetic couplets. Example 2.3, from the seventh scene of act II, illustrates all of these problematic stylistic character- istics.

Peri's *L'Euridice,* to Rinuccini's elegant libretto, was presented as one of several enter- tainments featured in October 1600 during the celebrations honoring the marriage of Maria de' Medici (niece of the Grand Duke of Tuscany) to King Henry IV of France. The event was one of the most important political marriages of the seventeenth century, although it was by proxy as King Henry did not attend, being immersed in a war in Savoy at the time. *L'Euridice* was performed in a small hall of the Pitti Palace on 6 October, as a present to the queen from Jacopo Corsi (who played harpsichord in the small instrumental ensem- ble), and with Cavalieri supervising. Peri, in the introduction to the printed score, reports that some of the music sung by those "dependent on Caccini" (i.e., his students and family members) was composed by him.[22] *L'Euridice,* however, was not the major musical event of festivities, for two days later occurred a lavish production of *Il rapimento di Cefalo,* libretto by Chiabrera with music largely composed by Caccini (lost except for the final scene included by the composer in his *Nuove musiche*). With elaborate scenery and some one hundred musicians taking part, it was performed before an audience of thirty-eight hundred. Unlike Peri's work, *Il rapimento di Cefalo* was in the mode of the spectacular intermezzi for which the Florentine court had earlier been famous. Its significance was quickly forgotten. Peri's work, however, had made an impact. It was performed a number of times, and the score was published a second time in 1607. Caccini, clearly intimidated by Peri's success, rushed to compose his own version of Rinuccini's text, and managed to publish it in January 1601, about a month before Peri's publication. Its sole performance took place at the Pitti palace in December 1602.

The *stile recitativo,* also called *stile rappresentativo,*[23] a style of "reciting in singing," receives its first definitive form in Peri's opera, and he describes in some detail in his preface to *L'Euridice* how he arrived at its compositional features, from which the following extract is taken:

> I decided that the ancient Greeks and Romans (who, according to the opinion of many, sang their tragedies throughout on the stage), used a harmony which, going beyond that of ordinary speech, fell so short of the melody of song that it assumed an intermediate form. . . . Therefore, rejecting every other type of singing heard up to now, I set myself to discovering the imitation necessary for these poems, and I decided that that type of voice assigned to singing by the ancients . . . could in part speed up and take an intermediate path between the suspended and slow movements of song and the fluent, rapid ones of speech, thus suiting my intention. . . . Similarly, I realised

EXAMPLE 2.3   *Rappresentatione di Anima et di Corpo*, act II, scene 7

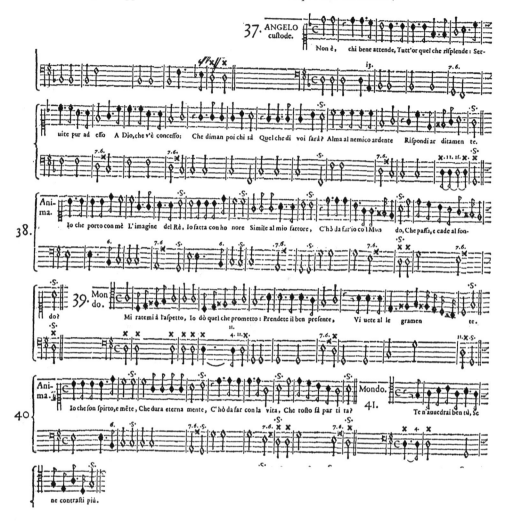

that in our speech some words are intoned in such a manner that harmony can be founded upon them, and that while speaking we pass through many others which are not intoned, until we return to another capable of movement to a new consonance. Taking note of these manners and accents that serve us in grief, joy, and similar states, *I made the bass move in time to these, now faster, now slower, according to the affect, and I held it firm through the dissonances and consonances until, passing through various notes, the voice of the speaker arrived at that which, being intoned in ordinary speech, opens the way to a new harmony.* [Emphasis added][24]

This gives a clear explanation of Peri's method of inventing a vocal style that would be true to the rhetoric and diction of a text and that would have a degree of structural coherence. While highly declamatory, this earliest form of recitative also was subtly expressive. The bass line moved for the most part only for accented syllables of the text (usually the penultimate at ends of lines) or to stress through harmonic color particularly expressive words or phrases. Passages of neutral narration, therefore, are highly syllabic and monotonal, but texts for dramatic monologues and emotional reactions to events or conflicts use subtle expressive devices in part based on madrigalian harmonies and in part on a style of melodic freedom and beauty rooted in the creation of monody. Particularly successful dramatic recitatives are found, for example, in Dafne's description of Euridice's death, Orfeo's lament on hearing that account, *Funeste piagge ombrosi* sung before the gates of Hell, and his plea to Pluto for the return of Euridice. Peri's achievement can be fully understood only with a detailed analysis of word/tone relationships of the entire work.[25] Example 2.4, an excerpt from that plea to Pluto, illustrates a few of Peri's techniques in this new recitative style.

EXAMPLE 2.4   *L'Euridice,* scene IV, Orfeo pleads to Pluto

Mira, Signor, dhe mira
Com'al mio lagrimar dolce sospira
Tua bella sposa, e come dolci i lumi

Rugiadosi di pianto a me pur gira.
Mira, Signor, dhe mira
Quest'ombre in torno, e quest'oscuri Numi:
Come d'alta pietà vint'al mio duolo

Parche ciascun si strugga e si consumi.[26]

Look, Lord, see
How at my weeping
Your beautiful wife sweetly sighs, and how sweetly
Her eyes, dewy with tears, turn to me.
Look, Lord, see
The shades around you, and the dark infernal Gods
How with great pity, conquered by my grief,
Each one languishes and is consumed.

In contrast, Caccini's *Euridice* is a much less adventuresome work. This can be shown by comparing his setting of the text in the previous example with Peri's. Caccini's recitatives tend to be more continuous, with fewer expressive phrase fragments, less rhetorical emphasis through rests, and very little exploitation of dissonances. Within the restrictions of the harmonic language employed by both composers, Caccini's is more conservative. An important distinction in Caccini's setting is the attention he gives to writing out the necessary and often elaborate ornamentation that, as he had stated in *Nuove musiche,* he believed was the responsibility of the composer.

Although these experimental court entertainments by Peri and Caccini did not lead quickly to an outburst of similar compositions, the Florentine performances did not go unnoticed. In the next three decades a number of operas were composed for court performances in Florence, Mantua, Bologna, and especially Rome.[27] Few of the scores are preserved, but among those that are Marco da Gagliano's *Dafne* (Mantua, 1608) was popular among his contemporaries and seems particularly indebted to Peri's achievement who along with Corsi had earlier composed their setting of Rinuccini's text for performances at the Palazzo Corsi in Florence during Carnival 1597/98. The most significant composer to turn his compositional genius to early opera was, of course, Claudio Monteverdi (see Chapter 3), especially his own immortal interpretation of the Orpheus legend, the *L'Orfeo* (Mantua, 1607), and one year later *Arianna.*

Opera in Rome

For most of the first four decades of the century performances of operas were limited to private entertainments at the aristocratic courts. The new Florentine style came to Rome in 1600 with Cavalieri's *Rappresentatione.* During Carnival 1606 Aggazzari produced with the help of young students at the Seminario Romano his *dramma pastorale, Eumelio,* also a morality play in monodic style. A sacred opera, *David musicus,* was composed for the Roman Seminary in 1613 by Ottavio Catalani. In 1620 the Florentine composer Filippo Vitali performed in Rome a secular opera, *Aretusa.*[28] Of greater significance is the only surviving opera by Domenico Mazzocchi (1592–1665), *La catena d'Adone,* performed in Rome at the Palazzo Conti in February 1626. The libretto was by Ottavio Tronsarelli.[29] In a listing of the airs and choruses in the work, Mazzocchi states: "There are many other semi-arias scattered throughout the work, which break the tedium of the recitative [*Vi sono molt'altre mezz'Aria sparse per l'Opera, che rompono il tedio del recitativo*].[30] Mazzocchi's expression of the "tedium of the recitative" is apparently the first indication that composers had begun to seek ways to relieve the continuous sung recitation that burdened the musical interest of many of the recitatives in Florentine works. Exactly what "*mezz'Aria*"—semi- or half-aria—meant to Mazzocchi remains unclear, although evidence of subsequent Roman operas suggests the infusion into recitative of more arioso passages, lyrical phrases of varying length over more active bass lines, and also songs with strophic texts such as canzonette.[31] Also extant from this period is a *favola boschereccia, Diana schernita* (Rome, 1629) by Giacinto Cornacchioli. But it was especially during the reign of Cardinal Matteo Barberini as Pope Urban VII (1622–1644) that opera became a somewhat regular aspect of cultural life in Rome. And it was in the palaces of the Pope's nephews, Cardinal Francesco, Cardinal Antonio, and Don Taddeo, that opera often was a spectacular feature of lavish carnival entertainments.[32] Eight operas were composed for Barberini performances up to 1644, all to librettos by the Roman prelate Giulio Rospigliosi (later Pope Clement IX). They are:

1631	*Sant'Alessio,* favola in musica, Stefano Landi (Rome, 1632, rev. 1634)[33]	
1633	*Erminia sul Giordano,* dramma musicale, Michelangelo Rossi (Rome, 1633)[34]	

1635	*I Santi Didimo e Teodora,* dramma musicale, Stefano Landi or Virgilio Mazzocchi
1637	*L'Egisto* or *Chi soffre speri,* commedia in musica, Virgilio Mazzochi and perhaps Marco Marazzoli (MS extant)
1638	*San Bonifatio,* dramma tragico per musica, Virgilio Mazzocchi (MS extant)
1641	*La Genoinda* or *L'innocenza difesa,* dramma tragico per musica, attributed to Virgilio Mazzocchi
1642	*Il palazzo incantato,* dramma musicale, Luigi Rossi[35]
1643	*Il Sant'Eustachio,* Virgilio Mazzocchi (MS extant)

The librettos indicate a significant change in dramatic direction from the pastoral plays of Florentine opera, with texts adapted from the lives of saints, from Tasso's *Gerusalemme liberata* (*Erminia sul Giordano*), from Boccaccio (the comedy, *Chi soffree speri*), and from Ariosti (*Il palazzo incantato*). These operas were performed in several places in Rome, but most of them were heard at the famous theater of the Palazzo Barberini alle Quattro Fontane, with a capacity of thirty-five hundred. The excellence of the composers and the availability of several scores provide considerable evidence of the changing stylistic characteristics of opera in Rome during the 1630s and 1640s.[36] In summary, these changes include: (1) three-act divisions, usually with a prologue (*La Genoinda,* as an exception, has five acts); (2) because of a papal ban on women appearing on stage, soprano parts usually were sung by castratos; (3) significant emphasis was placed on choruses (although not in the comedy *Chi soffre speri*), and, in several of the Barberini operas, the chorus serves as the act finale; (4) the recitative, although still modeled on the Florentine concept, includes significant lyrical passages, usually of short duration, that can be considered embedded ariosos, and much of the recitative tends to use longer passages of rapidly repeated tones than was typical of the Florentine operas; (5) solo songs (arias in the seventeenth-century meaning) as well as duos and trios become increasingly frequent, usually written to strophic texts; (6) instrumental passages, extended sinfonias, are employed, and many of the operas include important instrumental music for dances; and (7) Roman operas required the construction of costly machinery to create extravagant visual effects.

Landi's *Sant'Alessio* takes precedent as the first opera on a historical subject and is one of the first concerning the life of a saint. It has lengthy instrumental *sinfonias* preceding each of the acts and numerous ensembles and choruses. Rossi's *Il palazzo incantato* demonstrates just how far opera had developed from its Florentine origins. The text gives opportunity for a great range of emotions from the tragic to the comic. Whereas the opera remains strongly rooted in the recitative style, the musical weight of the work is clearly focused on lyrical arias, songs, and arioso passages. There are numerous solo ensembles as well as choruses and many dances. The influence of this form of Roman opera on Venetian opera (beginning in 1637) is clear. Almost all of the style characteristics of the first Venetian operas were imported from Rome.

Secular Vocal Music

The innovations in secular music in the first decades of the seventeenth century are reason enough to think of a new period in music history. Not to be overlooked, however, is the substantial carry-over into the new century of musical genres and styles of the late Renaissance. Although this has long been recognized in regard to the continuity of style in some of the sacred music of the seventeenth century, less recognition has been given to forms of secular vocal music, particularly the unaccompanied polyphonic madrigal. As

Bianconi reports, there is a marked falling off of first editions of polyphonic madrigals between 1600 and 1650, but the number of new editions remains impressive through 1620: between 1601 and 1610, 157 new editions; between 1611 and 1620, 118 new editions. Subsequently, from 1621 to 1650 only twenty-eight new editions are known.[37] Of course, the form of the madrigal did change; the impact of the basso continuo had a marked effect on the madrigal, particularly as seen in the works of Monteverdi, for example, in the considerable variety of styles, genres, and media in his Sixth Book of 1614. Gesualdo's most experimental madrigals in the last two books appeared in 1611 and all six books were published in score in Venice in 1613. Yet the role of the polyphonic madrigal was clearly on the wane, and one reason is suggested by Pietro della Valle who in 1640 complained about the madrigal that

> Today, not so many are composed because the practice of singing madrigals is in little use, nor is there any opportunity for them to be sung, because people now like better to hear free singing from memory with instruments in hand than to see four or five companions singing around a table with the book in hand, which seems too scholarly and academic.[38]

The era of amateur musicians singing madrigals for their own pleasure was largely to be replaced by professional singers performing before some form of audience. This, too, had been initiated in the previous century with the exceptional appearances of virtuoso singers at the Italian courts, including the famous *tre donne* of Ferrara. The initial popularity of the new monodic forms, the solo madrigal and aria, and the early development of operatic recitative supplied fertile ground for a succession of new solo vocal forms in the first half of the century. These song forms, lyrical in nature, largely developed out of the "arias" of the monodists. The growing emphasis on a new lyricism would bring new vitality to music and would change the concept of vocal music for succeeding centuries.

Arias were settings of strophic texts, most commonly in the first quarter of the century short, lively pieces with the character of the canzonet in triple or duple time. They often were based on the principle of strophic variation and frequently employed regularly moving bass lines in quarter notes, the so-called walking bass. Alessandro Grandi published his *Cantade et arie* (c. 1620),[39] famous for its first known use of the word *cantata*. It contains only one "cantata," the last piece in the collection, *Amor giustitia,* which is atypical of the early type, being through-composed, and repeating the opening phrase as a refrain three times. Early cantatas usually are songs on strophic texts with lyrical melodies that develop, as do arias, over either strict or free repetitions of the same bass, at times using preexistent harmonic plans with bass lines such as the Romanesca and the Ruggiero. These are in effect ostinato bass variations, a distinctive genre of music that at this time becomes popular among composers and quickly is established as one of the distinctive genres found in all types of Baroque music. Stefano Landi's *Arie a una voce* (Venice, 1620)[40] are typical of such arias composed with considerable ingenuity over what seem to be original bass lines. Many of these collections of solo (or at times duo) songs indicate they can be accompanied on the Spanish guitar and in some they give symbols for the guitar tablature, confirming the growing popularity of that instrument throughout the Italian peninsula.

Another Venetian, the singer Barbara Strozzi (1619–1664 or later), was apparently the only woman, besides Francesca Caccini, to compose significant secular chamber music in seventeenth-century Italy.[41] Five of her published collections (opera 2, 3, 6, 7, 8) include various solo vocal forms, a large number of which are labeled cantata.[42] These all are distinguished by the multisectionalism of recitative, arioso, and aria. However, other works, such as the lamentos and a serenata, also have the same characteristics, and even some of the "arias" are cantata-like in their length and diversity of vocal styles.

Rome was at the center of the development of the cantata. Particularly the almost three hundred cantatas of Luigi Rossi (c. 1597–1653) are pivotal to the achievement of this particular vocal form. His cantatas show the development of an Italianate lyrical vocal style, often loosely described as *bel canto,* that will dominate in various guises Italian vocal music for succeeding centuries. The cross-fertilization with Roman opera is apparent. From the short *ariette corte,* to the longer and more developed multisectional works (*aria di più parti*),[43] Rossi's cantatas are for the period unique in the variety of formal organization. There are also a small number of laments largely in recitative style. The *ariette corte* generally fall into four types: binary, rondo, ternary, and rounded binary. The longer works are through-composed and have no particular forms, but require individual description, as a series of recitatives, ariosos, and arias. It is the latter type that suggests the fundamental model for the multimovement cantatas of the last half of the century. The cantata *Non più vilta,* for example, has four arias, two recitatives, with one aria repeated as a refrain within the cantata:

Aria 1: *Non più vilta*
Aria 2: *Sono i pianti*
Rec. 1: *Un amante negletto*
Aria 3: *Non si lamenti*
Aria 2: *Sono i pianti*
Rec. 2: *Si preggia una spietata*
Aria 4: *E più possibile*

Sacred Music

An immense amount of sacred music appeared in Italy between 1600 and 1640. The richness and variety of that music, a great deal of which has never been studied nor published in modern editions, emphasizes how distorted and skewed our modern view of Baroque music has become. Although the innovations of the early monodists and opera composers were a driving force of most Italian music in this period, it was in sacred rather than secular music that these influences received their most numerous, early applications. Indeed, sacred music in the post–Council of Trent era and in the midst of the still relevant spirit of the Counter Reformation was in a sense reborn, and the progeny made up a most varied and prodigious output of sacred music hardly equaled in any future historical period. Yet the examination of sacred music in the seventeenth century usually takes second place to the emphasis on the new musical innovations in secular music occurring at the same time.[44]

A defining premise of Baroque music, the concept of style consciousness, was first established by developments in sacred music at this time. The *stile antico,* music written after 1600 according to the contrapuntal style most closely associated with the works of Giovanni Pierluigi da Palestrina (c. 1525–1594), remained for the Baroque in Italy as well as in North Europe a valid even if antiquated style of sacred music in contrast to those works composed in the "new" style or *stile moderno.*[45] Composed almost entirely for the great churches of Rome including St. Peter's, St. John Lateran, and the Pope's official musical establishment, the Sistine Chapel (Cappella Pontificia), Palestrina's music initially influenced a number of Roman composers (such as Soriano, the Anerios, the Naninos, and Gregorio Allegri).

But this strict contrapuntal style with its origins believed to be in the sacred works of Palestrina was preserved during the Baroque and into later centuries as a distinctly sacred musical style. Monteverdi, for example, wrote his three preserved mass settings in a form of the *stile antico,* and Johann Sebastian Bach in the late 1740s still found this style relevant to sections of the B Minor Mass.[46] Frequently this style was used within multimovement sacred works as an affective contrast to sections in contemporary styles. Further preserving and idealizing the nature of the so-called Palestrina style was its codification for instructional purposes by a number of theorists, culminating in Fux's *Gradus ad Parnassum* in 1725. And, whereas any discussion of sacred music necessarily focuses on the new stylistic and formal achievements at the beginning of the seventeenth century, it should not be overlooked that Palestrina's sacred works were available and still performed in the churches of Italy throughout the century.[47]

The new forms of sacred music can be loosely classified into the following types: (1) monodies for solo voice or voices and continuo, (2) small-scale works for few voices in the concertato style with or without accompanying instruments, and (3) large-scale concertato works including those based on the Venetian *cori spezzati* style of Giovanni Gabrieli. One impetus for several new forms of sacred music came from the Florentine experiments with a new style of text settings. The concept of composing music for one or more solo voices supported only by a bass line on which an accompaniment was improvised had an appeal that soon made striking inroads into Italian churches, and for two reasons. One was economic: few churches except those of cathedral status and several ducal chapels could financially support large numbers of musicians as soloists, instrumentalists, and choruses. The provincial and parish churches as well as most of the charitable confraternities seldom had sufficient funds for large performance groups, and this was particularly true in a period of economic decline in Italy in the early seventeenth century. They welcomed a form of musical worship requiring limited resources. Second, the very concept of a monodic composition in which melody is raised to pre-eminence over contrapuntal technique brought a new vitality to church ritual and new meaning and appreciable emotional expressiveness to sacred texts. Many in the Church supported the infusion of a style of music that was quickly to become more Italian in its melodic appeal and unquestionably more secular in its stylistic origins.[48]

Significant evidence has been cited that shows the earliest extant examples of monodic writing—to sacred, not secular, texts—are found in Cavalieri's two settings of the Lamentations of Jeremiah and also his Responses for Holy Week.[49] These combine chorus, ensemble, and monodic sections. The latter show evidence of more than one monodic style: (1) expressive, especially by using chromaticism; (2) lyrical, or more song-like; and (3) declamatory, found largely in the Lamentations (Rome, 1600).[50] Example 2.5, from the first lesson for Holy Thursday (Pisa, 1599), exemplifies the expressive style with its chromaticism, minor seconds, and expressive melodic passages, as on *et lacrimae et lacrimae ejus.*[51]

[Beth:] Weeping, she has cried in the night, and her tears were on her cheeks. There is none to comfort her among all them that were dear to her.

Cavalieri's Lamentations, however, were never published and could have had no widespread influence on sacred music in the early seventeenth century. Rather, it was Viadana's Op. 12, *Cento concerti ecclesiastici* (Venice, 1602), that had a major impact on composers of sacred works in Italy and later in northern countries.[52] It was republished several times,

EXAMPLE 2.5   Cavalieri, First lesson for Holy Thursday (Pisa, 1599)

including a German edition by Nikolaus Stein (1609), and second (1607) and third (1609) volumes followed. The fame of this collection as the first sacred publication to include a basso continuo has overshadowed its significance in the history of sacred music. According to the composer the work was intended as a practical body of sacred music for any number of singers from one to four. The basso continuo made possible the performance of a musical text even if any one voice type was lacking. The solo motets can claim to be the first published sacred music reduced to a single voice and a bass line, conceived, as Roche says, "as the result of a ruthless paring down of part-music."[53] With these examples the motet for solo voices would soon become a major form of liturgical music in Italy and later in northern Europe. Stylistically the Viadana solo motets in melodic phrasing and with frequent *passaggi* are without the new musical features of Florentine monody, but for the most part suggest sixteenth-century contrapuntal writing for single voice over a bass line that is more vocal than instrumental. In those for bass voice, the basso continuo doubles the bass line, and this also occurs frequently in those for tenor as well. Some imitation between bass and solo part occurs, especially at the beginning of phrases. Structural cohesion occurs through some phrase repetitions and rather simple phrase variation, as can be seen in *Quem vidistis pastores* (see Example 2.6).[54]

Equally significant are the motets for two and three parts. Those in four parts are most conservative with predominantly imitative textures. The three-part motets, however, show the beginnings of the Baroque duet form over the continuo bass (which here is sung), with two parts often moving in parallel thirds. These also have more prolonged formal designs including refrains and varieties of rondos replacing the cohesiveness of the abandoned imitative textures. Although Viadana's concertos are conservative stylistically, they bring a new musical approach to sacred music, at the opposite pole to the grandeur of the multi-chorus works established in Venice by the Gabrielis, and they remained popular when the performing forces were available to composers.

Monody continued to be part of the divergences of sacred musical styles. The conservative style of Viadana's works became a model particularly among Roman composers such as Giovanni Francesco Anerio (c. 1567–1630), Agostino Agazzari (c. 1580–1642), and Gio-

EXAMPLE 2.6   from Viadana, *Cento concerti ecclesiastici: Quem vidistis pastores*

EXAMPLE 2.6   from Viadana   (*continued*)

vanni Bernardino Nanino (c. 1560–1618), and the latter's student Antonio Cifra (1584–1629), who carried Roman conservatism to his position in Loreto. Decidedly up-to-date, however, were the *Arie devote* (Rome, 1608)[55] of Ottavio Durante, eighteen sacred Latin and two Italian texts set for solo voice (or duet for those with a texted bass), and figured basso continuo. These works, the earliest of their type to be published, are similar to the solo monodies of Caccini, whom Durante praises in a lengthy and important preface which includes the decidedly "modern" statement that *"alle Arie si permette qualche lizenza nel contrapunto per causa degli affetti."* Unlike Caccini's monodies, however, these have very elaborate vocal *passaggi*, as the excerpt from the *Magnificat tertii toni* in Example 2.7 shows. Other early printed collections of sacred monodies include Bartolomeo Barbarino's *Il primo libro de mottetti . . . decantarsi da una voce sola* (Venice, 1610—a second volume followed in 1614), Lodovico Bellanda's *Sacre laudi a una voce, per cantar et sonar nel organo, chitarone overo simili istromenti di corpo* (Venice, 1613), as well as those by Biagio Tomasi.[56]

More prevalent were the small-scale sacred concertatos for two, three, and four parts. Duets and trios became the most popular of these forms. Among the many composers contributing to the small-scale concertato and other developments in sacred vocal music

EXAMPLE 2.7 from Durante, *Arie devote*

EXAMPLE 2.7 *(continued)*

Monteverdi, of course, stands supreme. Equally distinguished and particularly influential in the second decade of the century, however, were the sacred works of Alessandro Grandi (1586–1630). He composed a large number of new forms of sacred music typifying the explosive developments affecting sacred music in Italy. First employed in Ferrara in 1617, he joined the choir at St. Mark's in Venice, directed by Monteverdi, subsequently becoming the latter's deputy in 1620. In 1627 he went to Bergamo as choir director at St. Maria Maggiore, where three years later he died of the plague.

The popularity of the first five books of his motets (published between 1610 and 1620) is evinced in their frequent republication. In the early duets Grandi remains largely unaffected by the recent Florentine attempts to abandon contrapuntal artifice, and these works often employ two parts in imitative and canonic textures over a basso continuo.[57] The motet, *Hodie nobis de caelo,* from Book I (1610) shows Grandi's appreciation of the various textural and structural contrasts available within the limited resource of two equal voices. Each of the three sections proceeds differently: first stanza introduced by the first voice, the second by the second voice, the third with both parts in imitation. Later duets, for example, his *Anima Christi* for two tenors from the fifth book of motets (1619), show a new attitude toward the treatment of both melodic parts as well as having more varied bass lines. The vocal parts are clearly divorced from polyphonic style and are related to the new styles of dramatic recitative and more tuneful melodies. In the fourth and fifth books a number of the motets are based on the highly sensuous texts from the *Song of Songs,* and in several instances, are composed as dialogues between man and woman. The clarity of the music underscores the declamation of the text. It is text clarity and interpretation that underlies the motivation of most of a significant number of composers of small-scale concertatos, and their success in this endeavor is frequently claimed in their published works. In Rome, for example, where the new form of the few-voiced motet was also explored by a number of composers,[58] Agostino Agazzari, in charge of music at the German Jesuit College, exclaims in the preface to his *Sacrae laudes* (1603):

> The new style, which if I do not deceive myself, I employ in the composition of the motet follows the general mood [of the text]; so that one is able to sing and expound the words ardently (the true purpose of the concerto) I have dared to declare my mind concerning the performance of this my new work, the fruit of years' labors.[59]

Few-voiced concertato motets flourished in large numbers, especially in northern Italy, and included works for one, two, or three parts, but also four, five, or six parts. In what would be an extensive list of composers contributing to this motet repertory one must include in addition to Grandi, who excelled in all these forms, Giovanni Francesco Capello (fl. 1610–1619), Ignazio Donati (c. 1570–1638), Giovanni Rovetta (1595/97–1668), Tarquinio Merula (1594/95–1665), and Giovanni Antonio Rigatti (c. 1613–1648).[60] Grandi also introduced the new genre of "motetti con sinfonie di violini" in three volumes during the time he was Monteverdi's assistant at St. Mark's. The significance of his innovation was to bring together the instrumental trio sonata and sacred vocal forms. The potential for textural and formal variety grew from simple introductory and intermediary sinfonias to various types of interactive scoring between instruments and voices, at times in the guise of a type of *cori spezzati*. The implication for the future of Baroque sacred music was immense, as Italian sacred music influenced other European regions for at least a century.

The early decades of the seventeenth century did not entirely ignore the notable achievements with *cori spezzati* techniques by Giovanni Gabrieli, particularly those large-scale works in his posthumously published second volume of *Symphoniae sacrae* (1615). In few places, except for Venice, were churches frequently able to fund the large performing forces required by such works. The significant exception was Rome where early in the century several composers employed polychoral techniques in vocal works that forecast the development of a "colossal Baroque" style of the mid-century.[61] Elsewhere, the use of concertato textures on a large scale, when composers had the opportunity, were most often applied to psalm texts and the Magnificat, less frequently to the Mass Ordinary. These texts were most often long and offered less verbal imagery and overt emotionalism than was typical of most motets. Large-scale settings for more than one chorus had less need for specific text interpretation and fluctuating affective expression, and the concerted medium gave variety and color to what were of necessity often long and largely syllabic compositions. In place of the by now somewhat out-of-date and expected contrasts between separate vocal ensembles, composers began to employ numerous contrasts between solo parts, solo ensembles, choral ripienos, and various instrumental solos and groupings.

The dimensions of the two-choir psalms of Gabrieli were expanded by composers to three, four, or five choirs early in the century. Exactly how these apparently huge vocal ensembles were performed is illuminated by the advice Viadana gives in his *Salmi a quattro chori* of 1612, which can be summarized as follows:[62]

> The first choir, in five parts, is placed with the main organ. It is the principal choir, and consists of five good singers who should sing in the modern manner, with confidence and boldness. No other instrument except for the organ (and if wished) a *chitarrone*, plays with this choir.

> The second choir, in four parts, is the *cappella*, "the nerve system and very foundation of good music." This choir requires at least sixteen singers.

> The third choir has four high parts. The first soprano is very high and played by cornet or violin, the second by up to three good sopranos, the third (alto), a mezzo-soprano part requires several voices, with violins and curved cornetts; also the tenor is sung by several voices, with trombones, and with violins and organ an octave higher than usual.

> The fourth choir has four parts. The top part, a very low alto, sung by several voices, with violins and curved cornetts an octave higher; the second part is in a tenor register, sung by a number of voices, with trombones; the third part is a baritone, with good voices or trombones with violins. The bass is always low, sung by deep voices with trombones, double-bass viols, bassoons, and the organ an octave lower than usual.

Equally significant are Viadana's further comments:

These psalms may be sung by just the first two choirs. However, for a really fine performance in the modern manner, they may be sung in any number up to eight choirs, by doubling the second, third, and fourth. There is no danger of error in doing this, for the whole performance depends on good singing in the first choir of five parts. The conductor must stand with the first choir, watching the organist, controlling the movement of the music and giving entries to the voices. In the ripieno sections he will turn to face all the choirs and will raise his arms to indicate that all are to perform together.

The separate musical functions of the two choirs, as defined by Viadana, are not usually maintained in subsequent decades. From various prefaces and other printed instructions what becomes obvious is the desire of composer and publisher alike to give church performers almost total freedom to choose, according to individual musical conditions, how these works will be performed. In general, emphasis is placed on solo voices for the first choir versus a ripieno ensemble of voices and various instruments as a ripieno second choir. These two basic groups then can be expanded in numerous ways to create additional choirs. For example, Ignatio Donati, in his impressive and sole collection of grand concertos, *Salmi boscarecci* (1623), in six parts, enumerates a remarkable variety of possible performance arrangements:

(1) The work in six parts may be sung by soloists (using the first six part books). None of these parts may be omitted.

(2) The second set of six books, called *ripieno*, contain six more voice parts, to be sung *in concerto*, and six instrumental parts, three low, three high. Some or all of these vocal and instrumental parts can be used to make another ensemble in the choir stalls; one may double the voices that sing the ripieni only in passages marked tutti.

(3) If one wishes to form additional ensembles, one may put the two sopranos, alto, and bass of the first six books with the organ, the first tenor with the low instruments as the second ensemble, and the second tenor [*quinto*] with the high instruments as a third ensemble. If additional copies of the part books are available, one can add two further ensembles in the same way. Soprano parts may be sung by tenors; voices may be doubled in tutti passages. One may use the last six books to create a fourth ensemble to sing in the tutti.

(4) One may use the second six books for both voices and instruments. Take note that where it says solo, only the singer sings without any instruments, and where it says trombone or violin, only the instruments should play. They sing and play together in unison in passages marked tutti.[63]

The result of the considerable subsequent experimentation with various combinations of vocal and instrumental forces was the "mixed concertato," in which the musical separation of each choir is amalgamated into a grand ensemble with a variety of frequently more complex musical textures freely employing vocal and instrumental solos, solo ensembles, and various tutti combinations. It was Monteverdi more than other composers who excelled in his psalm settings in the mixed style, as seen in the posthumous collection, *Selva morale* (1641), containing works written in the last decades of his duties at St. Mark's. Other Venetian composers, undoubtedly influenced by Monteverdi, who composed in the large-scale, mixed concerto were Giovanni Rovetta and Giovanni Rigatti. Large-scale Mass settings, although less frequently composed, are important as testimony to the influence of new musical influences on even the traditionally most conservatively treated liturgical texts. Grandi composed at the very end of his career a *Messa concertata* (1630), and Rovetta dedicated his Mass of 1639 to Louis XIII of France, an example of the type of ceremonial Mass to be composed for special occasions well into the eighteenth century.

Keyboard Music

The enormous impetus given to all forms of instrumental music in the second half of the sixteenth century continued unabated into the next century. In part this development consisted of the emancipation of instrumental music from vocal music. Significant contributions to Renaissance forms of keyboard music were made in Italy by Marco Antonio (c. 1490–c. 1560) and Girolamo Cavazzoni (c. 1525–after 1577), Annibale Padovano (1527–1575), Claudio Merulo (1533–1604), and Andrea Gabrieli.[64] In the early seventeenth century, the greatest expansion of instrumental repertories was composed for keyboard instruments, both organ and various forms of clavichord and harpsichord. For the most part the forms of early Baroque keyboard music grew out of their Renaissance models and included: (1) dances, including variations on dance melodies; (2) variations on vocal songs and plainchant; (3) variations on ground basses and chordal patterns; (4) improvisatory forms, including preludes and toccatas; and (5) contrapuntal forms, including the ricercar, the fantasia, and the canzona.

Among significant additions to keyboard repertory (largely for organ) in Italy early in the century are the toccatas, shorter *intonazioni,* ricercars, and canzonas of Giovanni Gabrieli. Other composers of more or less standard forms of keyboard music included Giovanni Paolo Cima (c. 1570–1630), Adriano Banchieri (1568–1634), Ascanio Mayone (c. 1565–1627), Giovanni Maria Trabaci (c. 1575–1647), and Giovanni Salvatore (?–1688). The greatest Italian composer of keyboard music, however, was Girolamo Frescobaldi. Although also a major composer of sacred and secular vocal music, Frescobaldi's immense fame in the seventeenth and the eighteenth centuries was based both on his keyboard works and on his reputation as an organist and teacher.

Frescobaldi was born in Ferrara in 1583; he died in Rome in 1643. In Ferrara he became a student of Luzzasco Luzzaschi. Frescobaldi came to Rome probably around 1601 and began a career that included various rewarding positions with the Roman aristocracy and the princes of the Church. Except for a brief period at Mantua and a somewhat longer appointment as court organist at Florence between 1628 and 1634, his entire career took place in Rome. For five months in 1607 he was organist at the Basilica of St. Mary's in Trastevere. Beginning in 1608 he came to St. Peter's as organist for the Cappella Giulia, a position he retained for the rest of his life while also serving as organist at other Roman churches during much of his career.[65] The brilliance and uniqueness of his keyboard artistry are frequently praised in contemporary accounts that spread widely throughout Europe. The Florentine composer and writer on music, Severo Bonini (1582–1663), made the following observation about Frescobaldi in his *Discorsi e regole* (completed by 1649–1650):

> Signor Girolamo Frescobaldi . . . has made an anatomy, as they say, of music by having discovered a new manner of playing the *gravicembali* in particular. As everyone knows, this manner has been adopted by the entire world so that today no one is regarded highly who does not play according to his style. Testimony to his worth is given by the universal reputation and renown that he enjoys, and by his manuscripts and published works . . . all demonstrating a marvelous skill.[66]

Frescobaldi published eight collections of keyboard works, which were known in reprints and copies throughout Europe into the next century:

Il primo libro delle fantasie a quattro (Milan, 1608)

Toccate e partite d'intavolatura di cimbalo (Rome, 1615)

Ricercari, et canzoni franzese fatte sopra diversi oblighi in partitura (Rome, 1615)

Il primo libro di capricci fatta sopra diversi soggetti, et arie in partitura (Rome 1624)

Il secondo libro di toccate, canzone, versi d'inni, magnificat, gagliarde, correnti, et altre partite d'intavolatura di cimbalo et organo (Rome, 1627)

Fiori musicali di diverse compositioni, toccate, kirie, canzoni, capricci, e recercari in partitura a quattro (Rome, 1635)

Toccate d'intavolatura di cimbalo et organo, partite di diverse arie et corrente, balletti, ciaccone, passachagli [with Aggiunta] (Rome, 1637)

Canzoni alla francese in partitura (Venice, 1645)[67]

As the titles indicate, Frescobaldi composed keyboard works in all of the standard forms inherited from the sixteenth century. Influences of earlier keyboard composers are clearly present, but Frescobaldi, in absorbing and amalgamating previous stylistic and formal procedures, created what can be considered the first major keyboard oeuvre in music history. This was accomplished not only because of the high level of his compositional craft but also because of his keyboard virtuosity, which underlies much of his music.

Typical for the early seventeenth century, Frescobaldi's keyboard works fall into fairly clear types: contrapuntal works, either monothematic or multithematic; and the polar opposite of the former, the toccatas employing the greatest freedom of keyboard techniques and formal organization. There are dance forms and variations on various types of subjects such as plainchant, popular tunes, and bass patterns. The techniques of variation, however, figure prominently in most of these forms. In the first publication, the *Fantasie* of 1608, are his most uncompromising explorations of keyboard counterpoint. They were published in keyboard partitura (i.e., each part has a separate staff). The title had no specific meaning at this time and is used here as a substitute for ricercar. There are twelve pieces organized by mode and the number of simultaneous subjects, that is, three ricercars each with one, two, three, and four subjects. The subjects are treated in all of the usual contrapuntal techniques and with rhythmic and melodic variation. They give striking evidence of Frescobaldi's youthful command of the art of counterpoint.

The two publications of 1615, the *Ricercari et Canzoni* and the *Toccate e Partite, libro primo*, exemplify the dualistic keyboard styles of Frescobaldi in their first maturity. The ten ricercars and five canzonas are also printed in keyboard *partitura*. All but the first two ricercars have a prescribed *obligo*, that is, a musical or prescriptive requirement setting limits to the form of the composition. For example, ricercars IV, VI, VII, and X are all constructed around ostinatos formed by solmization patterns of four to six tones. The *obligo* of ricercar V requires the composer to avoid stepwise motion (*Obligo di non uscir mai di grado*), and ricercar IX must have "four subjects." Sectionalism is created by changing textures, varying emphasis placed on contrasting thematic content, and the placement of punctuating cadences. The five canzonas all begin imitatively with a thematic idea marked by the conventional long, short, short (dactyl) rhythm of earlier canzonas. The sections vary and in some there is the introduction of new material, while in others each major section employs a variation of the original theme. In only the first canzona does the opening section not return in the concluding one.

The *Toccate e partite* of 1615 are published in keyboard score and the title states they are intended for harpischord, although they are equally playable on the organ, which was included in the title of the revised reprint of 1628. Previous composers such as Andrea

Gabrieli, Luzzaschi, Quagliati, and Merulo all composed toccatas. And from the somewhat mechanical figurations and loose structure of those by Gabrieli, to those of considerable sophistication by Merulo, the toccata rapidly became the ideal keyboard outlet for an attempted representation of the improvisatory artistry of gifted keyboardists. It was with Frescobaldi, however, that for the first time the toccata revealed the idiomatic, brilliant, and often idiosyncratic keyboard styles of this composer and performer unfettered by the necessity of contrapuntal development. His toccatas are his most original and the most representative compositions of the new and more dramatic spirit energizing the music in the Baroque period. They are works in which rhetorical gestures and the passions of the soul (*affetti*) dominate, as the composer emphasizes in his own important preface to the toccatas of 1615 and the revised and expanded edition of 1616.[68] Frescobaldi compares the manner of playing his toccatas to madrigal performances. The toccatas "must not be subject to [the dictates of] beat, such as is observed in modern madrigals. These, however difficult, are made easier [in performance] by means of a beat now languid, now fast, likewise sustained in mid-air in accordance with the affections and the sense of the words." He continues "in the toccatas, I have taken care not only that they be abundantly provided with different [keyboard] passage work [*passi*] and affects, but also that each one of the said passages can be played separately. The performer is thus under no obligation to finish them all but can end where he thinks best."[69] Two examples will illustrate some of the stylistic characteristics of the toccatas (see Example 2.8). Here as with most of the toccatas, the opening tends to have few if any long passages of sixteenth or thirty-second notes. In his advice to the performers in his preface Frescobaldi is specific as to the manner of playing the opening measures: "The beginnings of toccatas should be played adagio and with arpeggios. The *ligature* and *durezze* [suspensions and dissonances], also in the middle of the composition, will be played together [i.e., not arpeggiated], so that the [sound of] the instrument not be empty; these notes [of the suspensions and related dissonances] shall be replayed at will by the performer."

The opening six measures have one affect inherent in the minor mode, several dissonant suspensions, and the interplay between the hands of short trill figures. The opening consists of a set of varied repetitions of the descending bass line of measures 1 and 2. Measure 7 begins as if it too will continue the same varied repetition of the opening figure, but the affection changes as the first G major triad is reached in measure 8 and rapid passagework and longer trills begin to dominate the texture.

The majority of the toccatas in this book end as in Example 2.9[70] with a considerable buildup to the conclusion through rapid passagework, here combined with a contrast between sixteenths and triplet eighths. Tonally, a conflict between A minor and F major is maintained until the dramatically effective final cadence, which begins with the surprising leap to the B flat in the bass with its major seventh suspension.

In 1624 Frescobaldi published in keyboard partiture his next work, twelve capriccios composed on "various subjects and airs." Whereas with one exception they employ imitative counterpoint, the capriccios are less strict in procedure, lighter in mood, and frequently have figurations and textures associated with toccatas. Each of the twelve is different and each shows Frescobaldi at the height of his imaginative compositional powers. The first two, composed on the ascending (ut, re, mi, fa, sol, la) and the second on the descending (la, sol, fa, mi, re, ut) hexachord, are long, multisectional works resembling variation canzonas. The fourth capriccio also uses a solemization theme, well known in the Renaissance (la, sol, fa, re, mi). There are works on "airs," three to unknown tunes, "la Bassa Fiamenga"and "la Spagnoletta," and a third, the only one without imitative counterpoint, a set of five variations on "Or che noi rimena." For the capriccio on the "Ruggiero" Fres-

EXAMPLE 2.8   Frescobaldi, opening of *Toccata Quinta*

cobaldi constructs what is remarkably close to a four-subject fugue by dividing the ruggiero bass into four segments. No. VIII explores "cromatico con ligature al contrario," a study in chromaticism with the suspensions, contrary to contrapuntal rule, resolving up instead of down, certainly a capricious idea![71]

No. VIII (see Example 2.10) entails a stunning contrapuntal exploration of dissonances (*durezze*). The three unifying motives are all stated in the first two measures, the ascending line in the soprano against the descending line in the alto, plus the leap of a sixth in the bass. The flow of the piece is continuous with only one cadential pause (approximately at midpoint in measure 22).

For the keyboardist, No. XI (see Example 2.11) is both the most challenging and unusual: "Capriccio with the *obligo* to sing [!] the fifth part, without playing it, always with the *obligo* of the prescribed subject." It is both a capricious whim and also a test of the performer's musicianship. Because the entrances of the *soggetto* are not indicated in the music the keyboardist must determine where the fifth given part—a c c b d c b a—can be introduced correctly into the four-part contrapuntal texture. Finally, the most playfully

EXAMPLE 2.9   Frescobaldi, conclusion to *Toccata Ottava*

EXAMPLE 2.10   Frescobaldi, opening of Capriccio VIII

EXAMPLE 2.11   Frescobaldi, opening of Capriccio XI

amusing of these capriccios is No. III, "sopra il cucco," in which the minor third D–B sounds as a soprano ostinato throughout the composition. Additional minor third "cuccos" frequently are introduced into the contrapuntal texture, including one section (mm. 38–44) in which the entire texture consists entirely of "cuccos." It is a long composition (166 measures) with numerous sections, at times lightly contrapuntal, at times dancelike, at times toccata-like, which shift back and forth between duple and triple meters. In the capriccios Frescobaldi transforms the still relevant contrapuntal tradition of Roman sacred vocal music, which he had applied somewhat rigorously in his early fantasias, ricercars, and canzonas. At a time when much of Italy was immersed in the *stile moderno,* which began in Florence with its rejection of counterpoint, Frescobaldi remained true to the compositional principles of music that had survived for centuries. However, he also found ways to adapt and reinvent contrapuntal practice in a new, expressive style. In its emphasis on the affects and rhetorical declamation, Frescobaldi's keyboard music also was the consequence of the "new music" of the early seventeenth century.

Two more keyboard publications appeared, the second book of Toccatas in 1627 and the *Fiori musicali* in 1635. In addition, the revised edition of the first book of toccatas published in 1637 included a "supplement" of nine new pieces: a mixture of four "ballettos" with correntes and passacaglias in two and a ciaconna in a third; a capriccio in six variations based on the ruggiero bass and a superimposed *soggetto;* a *capriccio* "fatta sopra la pastorale," and one "sopra la battaglia." The more significant composition is the "one hundred partite [variations] on the passacaglia." This is one of the great sets of variations created during the Baroque period. The majority of the variations, actually numbering 118, are two measures long and are based on two different harmonic progressions: a "passacaglia" with basic harmonies being I, minor V6, IV, V, I (often on the descending tetrachord bass), and a "ciaccona" with a basic harmonic pattern of I, V, vi, I, IV, V, in which vi is frequently replaced with III or IV. The 326 measures are organized into several contrasting sections created in part by modulations, changes of meter, and the alternation between the passa-caglia and ciaccona harmonic patterns. The organization always moves progressively to new and different concepts of varying the simple two harmonic series, and Frescobaldi has a seemingly inexhaustible supply of ideas to create ever new inventions on such simple harmonic material. The *Cento partite sopra passacagli,* perhaps the composer's last major creation, belongs among the most memorable compositions of this type to be composed in the Baroque which includes the later works by François Couperin, Buxtehude, and J. S. Bach.

The 1627 collection includes six harpsichord toccatas related to those in the 1615 collection but with some modifications; two pedal toccatas for organ; two toccatas indicated to be suitable for performance during the Elevation of the Mass; and one further exploration of a toccata with "dissonances and suspensions." The rest of the collection is a mixture of types of pieces: six canzonas, five gagliardas and six correntes, and a set of works meant for church performances. These include *alternatim* versets for the Magnificat as well as hymns for important occasions of the liturgical year. There are variations on the "Aria detto Balletto" and "Aria detta la Frescobalda," as well as a keyboard setting of Arcadelt's madrigal, "Ancidetemi pur." The *Fiori musicali,* Frescobaldi's last and most famous work, is devoted almost entirely to liturgical organ music. It, too, is printed in keyboard partitura. Three organ Masses are included, but only for the Kyrie, Christe, Kyrie. In many of these rather short settings the plainchant is given as a cantus firmus largely in whole notes. The other free pieces in the volume are all related to the three Masses and illustrate Frescobaldi's keyboard art in its utmost refinement. The toccatas are specified to be heard before the Mass, during the Elevation, and before two ricercars. Canzonas are placed after the Epistle and after the Communion. One ricercar is placed before the Offering and two after Credos. Curiously, the third Mass concludes without organ movements for the Communion but, rather, substitutes two capriccios on Italian folk songs, *Bergamasca* and *Girolmeta.* With these exceptions and the compositions to follow the Elevation, all of the other pieces other than the Kyries are placed where a movement of the Proper of the Mass would normally be performed. It would seem probable that these organ pieces were meant to substitute for the customary music of the Proper, a practice for which instrumental music had been employed and published from at least the turn of the century.[72]

CHAPTER THREE

Claudio Monteverdi (1567–1643)

NOTHING MORE CLEARLY contradicts the legitimacy of rigidly delineated historical periods in music than the musical achievements of Claudio Monteverdi.[1] He lived almost his entire life within three North Italian cities: Cremona (where he was born 15 May 1567); Mantua, at the Gonzaga court; and Venice, the great island republic. Monteverdi grew up in the vibrant culture of the late Renaissance, and he reached musical maturity and significant musical stature before the Florentine experiments in monody and the *stile recitativo* had coalesced into the earliest Baroque music, including the first operas.

Yet Monteverdi went on to accomplish some of the most important early advances in the development of opera, writing what is often considered the first major work in that form, *Orfeo* (1607), and also having had a great success with his second opera, *Arianna* (1608). Today he is usually remembered for his three extant operas (*Arianna* is lost except for the famous *Lamento*), including the final two, *Il ritorno d'Ulisse* and *L'incoronazione di Poppea,* and for his madrigals published in nine volumes. He is frequently called the inventor of the modern style of dissonance practice (the *seconda prattica*), and invariably judged the most important figure in the history of Baroque music before Heinrich Schütz.

However, Monteverdi's art was nurtured in a musical environment that was more conservative than experimental. He learned from his teacher Marc' Antonio Ingegneri (c. 1547–1592) his knowledge of composition, especially counterpoint, and worked with such polyphonic forms as madrigal, canzonetta, and the few-voiced motet. Although later he absorbed monodic concepts of style as developed by Peri, Caccini, Cavalieri, and others, he never completely gave over his compositional style to what might be considered the experimental modernity of the Florentines. There are many aspects to Monteverdi's genius, but foremost among them are his refusal to abandon the fructifying resources of contrapuntal practice, and his never-ending search for new means to bring formal logic to his designs for secular and sacred compositions.

With the exception of his operas and other dramatic-oriented works, including several ballets, Monteverdi's career as a composer is anchored in the traditional forms of Renaissance music, secular and sacred. These include the madrigals, as well as a number of sacred works, three preserved Masses, solo and choral motets, and psalm settings, among which is the publication of the *Vespers of 1610.* In the madrigals as well as in the sacred works, Monteverdi created a highly instructive series of compositions using traditional styles as well as the newest techniques of his day. It is in his adaptation of the foundations of late Renaissance style, joined to more progressive contemporary demands of taste of his later career, that his music preserves its greatest instructive value.

The Madrigals

Monteverdi composed some two hundred madrigals known through their publication in nine books, the first early in his career in 1587, and the last, posthumously, in 1651. A detailed analysis of the madrigals, which can only be sketched here, provides a study of the composer's shifting stylistic achievements in this intimate Renaissance form. From works that suggest Monteverdi's spiritual roots in the music of composers such as Marenzio, Luzzaschi, and Wert, he turned to experiment with and to refine the newest concepts of musical style and expression: monody, the vocal concertato, recitative, affective dissonances, and the basso continuo. Few composers have left us as clear a picture of their musical maturation as Monteverdi in his madrigals, and this picture is even more fascinating because we witness the composer influenced by and also influencing the winds of musical change in the early seventeenth century.[2]

On the title page of Monteverdi's first book of madrigals he proclaims himself "discepolo dei Sig. Marc'antonio Ingigneri [sic]." However, there is little in the musical style of these pieces to connect pupil and teacher, and the more likely models are to be found in the madrigals of other late Renaissance masters such as Marenzio and Luzzaschi. The poetry, with a few exceptions, is undistinguished, a characteristic that will quickly change for the better in later books. Many of these twenty-one madrigals are rooted in the style of the Italian canzonetta (Monteverdi had published a book of canzonettas in 1584). However, these madrigals already show Monteverdi's propensity for refined musical treatment of texts, and therefore, most of them amalgamate the canzonetta's lighthearted, homophonic, reduced voice textures with more expressive, usually dissonant, treatment of such emotion-laden words as "dying," "martyrdom," "afflicted heart," and so on. Perhaps the best example of the steady influence of the canzonetta is found here in the three-part madrigal to a text of Antonio Allegretti, "Fumia la pastorella," "Almo divino raggio," "Allora i pastor tutti." Most of the madrigals have an A:B:B form (the second half of the poem and its musical setting repeated). There is considerable employment of motivic devices for structural reasons, including an incipient feeling for the basso ostinato (as for example in the first madrigal, *Ch'io ami la vita mia nel tuo bel nome*). Among those most successfully joining canzonetta elements with such Renaissance madrigalian devices of dissonance and chromaticism are: *A che tormi il ben mio, La vaga pastorella,* and the justifiably well-known setting of a Guarini text, *Baci soavi e cara.*

The second book of madrigals appeared three years later in 1590, and already evidence exists of Monteverdi's emerging musical style. Unlike the earlier collection, this one presents settings of distinguished poets, especially Tasso, whose words furnish inspiration for nine of the twenty-one madrigals.[3] These continue to be predominantly influenced by canzonetta textures and sentiments. But Monteverdi projects noticeable coolness to text expression by avoiding in most instances overly dissonant or chromatic underscoring of words normally associated with such madrigalisms. Here the emphasis is more often on the clarity of text setting. This suggests, perhaps, that the composer was already aware of the polemical arguments involving the relationships between words and music, best described by the spokesmen of the Florentine Camerata but also a topic of debate in other northern Italian academies. Musically these madrigals show Monteverdi considerably influenced not only by Marenzio but especially by Giaches de Wert, and at least one, the famous *Ecco mormorar l'onde,* is modeled on Wert's *Vezzosi augelli in fra le verdi fronde* (*Eighth Book of Madrigals,* 1586).[4]

Canzonetta-like madrigals are illustrated by *Non giacinti o narcisi* (5), and *Intorno a due vermiglie e vaghe labra* (6). But a growing sense of Monteverdian sound stands out in several, for example, the descending melodic phrases moving in patterns of thirds (see Example 3.1).

No madrigal better captures Monteverdi's maturing sense of structure, form, and above

EXAMPLE 3.1   Monteverdi, *Bevea Fillide mia* (3), mm. 58–68

all a new Italian lyricism than *Ecco mormorar l'onde*. The Tasso text paints a vibrant Nature picture, in which the beauty of dawn is used as a conceit to have the power to revive the burned-out heart of every lover:

Ecco mormorar l'onde
e tremolar le fronde
a l'aura mattutina e gli'arboscelli,
e sovra i verdi rami i vagh'augelli cantar
   soavemente,
a rider l'oriente.
Ecco già l'alba appare
e si specchia nel mare,
e rasserena il cielo,
e imperla il dolce gielo
e gl'alti monti indora.
O bell'e vagh'aurora,
l'aura è tua messagiera, e tu del'aura

ch'ogn' arso cor ristaura.

Now the waves murmur,
and the boughs and shrubs tremble in
   the morning breeze,
and on the green branches the pleasant
   birds sing softly
and the East smiles;
now dawn already appears
and mirrors herself in the sea,
and makes the sky serene,
and impearls the fields,
and gilds the high mountains.
O beautiful and gracious Aurora,
the breeze is your messenger, and you
   the breeze
which revives each burnt-out heart.[5]

EXAMPLE 3.2   Monteverdi, *Ecco mormorar l'onde,* mm. 1–6

Monteverdi's musical interpretation is almost totally removed from the previous idiom of madrigalist pinpointing of specific textual conceits. Rather, here it is mood more than anything else, and the mood projects simplicity, lyrical phrases, and frequent emphasis on the vocal colors of individual voice parts, in which duet and trio textures predominate. The well-known opening uses a declamatory style for the lowest ranges of alto, tenor, and bass (see Example 3.2). This musical mood is placed against the high voices, as they sing the lines "a l'aura mattutina e gli'arboscelli." When the "pleasant birds sing softly" no madrigalian twittering, no coloraturas occur but rather a lyrical duet set against a static harmonic support (see Example 3.3).

Even more striking is the setting for the penultimate phrase, "l'aura è tua messagiera, e tu de l'aura." The melody was prized by the composer as evidenced in its appearance in later works.[6] This already forms a typically Monteverdian passage: a duet texture with a

EXAMPLE 3.3   Ibid., mm. 30–36

EXAMPLE 3.4   Ibid., mm. 72–85

lyrical, memorable turn of melodic phrase, a descending line set against a slow-moving, descending bass that gives not only harmonic support, but supplies the rhetorical antithesis implied by the poetry. Such passages in countless guises occur in much of Monteverdi's later music, both secular and sacred.

In 1590 Monteverdi came to the artistically prestigious court at Mantua, appointed violist in the Duke's instrumental ensemble. Within two years, the Third Book of madrigals appeared, published in Venice with a dedication to his new employer, Vincenzo Gonzaga. Although they have many of the same stylistic features of the first two books, these twenty madrigals show a continuing experimentation with and greater emphasis on declamatory musical rhetoric, dramatic melodic material, intensive development of motivic counter-point, coloristic effects of harmony (although less so than in later books), and also frequent reductions of the five parts to trio textures for the upper parts. These were probably influenced by a trio of women vocalists engaged at the Mantuan court, perhaps in com-petition with the famous group of "*tre dame*" at the Estense court at Ferrara. Nine of the madrigals are set to poems by Guarini, who had close ties with Mantua, and the two three-part madrigals are settings from Torquato Tasso's *Gerusalemme liberata: Vattene pur crudel/ Là tra'l sangu'e le morti/ Poi ch'ella in sè tornò*—Armida's curse on Rinaldo as he leaves her, from the Sixteenth Canto; and *Vivrò fra i miei tormenti/ Ma dove, O lasso me/ Io pur verrò là dove sete*—Tancredi's lament at the tomb of Clorinda, from the Twelfth Canto.

EXAMPLE 3.5   *Vattene pur crudel,* mm. 1–10

The Tasso settings in particular display the influence of Wert's madrigal style. He had been *maestro di musica* at Mantua and continued to live there in semiretirement until his death in 1595. Monteverdi, inspired by the dramatic tone of these texts, strove to match them musically by writing a highly emotional, serious, often poignant music, considerably removed from the lighthearted, lyrical, canzonetta-like pieces of so much of the earlier volumes. This new style for Monteverdi has been linked to Wert's own musical settings of Tasso and has been labeled "heroic."[7]

The opening of *Vattene pur crudel* shows a characteristic declamatory setting found in many of the madrigals in Book III. Here the trio texture of upper voices is dramatically charged by the explosive use of a leap of a minor sixth on the word "crudel." This dramatic recitative-like style may have roots in a late Renaissance practice of reciting epic verses, especially Ariosto's *Orlando furioso.* It suggests yet another influence leading to new melodic styles associated with monody and recitative at the turn of the seventeenth century. The three *partes* of the madrigal scene frequently utilize this kind of declamation, often in homophonic passages such as in Example 3.6.

More lyrical madrigals in this book, somewhat similar in style to that already established in Book II with *Ecco mormorar l'onde,* are in the majority of cases composed to texts by Guarini, next to Tasso the most famous contemporary Italian poet and known especially

EXAMPLE 3.6 Ibid., mm. 30–38

for his *Il pastor fido*. These include: *O dolce anima mia dunqu'è pur vero, Stracciami pur il core, Se per estremo ardore, O primavera, gioventù dell'anno,* and *Perfidissimo volto*. Here as elsewhere in the collection, Monteverdi's command of motivic counterpoint lies at the heart of the expressive style. For example, in *Perfidissimo volto,* the first twenty-five measures are composed out of a fabric of just three motives.

The popularity of this madrigal book undoubtedly helped spread the composer's reputation, for it was reprinted in 1592, 1600, 1604, 1607, 1611, 1615 (with an added basso continuo), and 1621. For some unexplained reason, Monteverdi's normal pacing of publishing madrigals about every two years stops, and Book IV does not see publication in Venice until 1603. The reason may have been simply that he was too busy with court duties, and had traveled considerable distances twice in the duke's retinue. Also, he married the singer Claudia Cattaneo in 1599. Or perhaps the disarray of the Italian musical world, as has been suggested,[8] might have held Monteverdi back while he absorbed and perhaps even witnessed many of the new musical events taking place. He could not have been unaware of the Florentine experiments nor uninterested in the first operatic experiments by Peri, Caccini, and Cavalieri. The times were indeed musically more uncertain than at any previous period in Monteverdi's career, and these uncertainties opened up challenges and opportunities for new and imaginative treatments of text and music. Monteverdi would not be left on the sidelines in these matters, even if (as far as is known) he never expressed himself in writing about the new stylistic forces emerging around him.

Only two years separate the publication of Book IV (Venice, 1603) from Book V (Venice, 1605), and in these two collections Monteverdi reaches the apex of his achievement in developing a personal style within the expressive possibilities of the Renaissance concept of the madrigal. The works in these two volumes do not appear to be published in a chronological order, and a number of them display differences of style that must be the result of their composition at different times over the period of some eleven years since the publication of Book III.[9] Both books include works known to have originated in the late 1590s, as they were attacked by Artusi in two treatises made famous by these criticisms: *L'Artusi, overo Delle imperfettioni della moderna musica ragionamenti dui* (Venice, 1600), and *Seconda parte dell'Artusi overo Delle imperfettioni della moderna musica* (Venice, 1603). These attacks generated Monteverdi's defense of his compositional style in the preface to the Fifth Book, comments later expanded on in a letter by his brother, Guilio Cesare, printed in the *Scherzi musicali* (1607), which established the composer's celebrated stylistic concept of the *seconda prattica*.

The title page of Book IV lists Monteverdi for the first time as *maestro della musica* at the Mantuan court. However, his dedication honors the Accademia degli Intrepedi at Ferrara, and he comments that earlier he had hoped to present the volume to the Duke of Ferrara, Alfonso Il d'Este, who died in 1597. In a warmly complimentary tone, Monteverdi praised his colleagues in Ferrara and expressed his fondness for that court—none too subtle an allusion, perhaps, to his growing dissatisfaction with his position at Mantua.

Book IV contains twenty madrigals; Book V, nineteen. The largest number in them are set to poems by Guarini, many taken from his *Il pastor fido*. In Book IV an exception is *Sfogava con le stelle un inferno d'amore* by the Florentine poet and librettist Rinuccini and, in Book V, two settings by Boccaccio, *Io mi son giovinetta* and *Quel augellin che canta si dolcemente*. (Both books include several texts that remain unidentified as to author.) The musical accomplishment in these madrigals stands out in almost every piece, and no summary or typical example can explain why these madrigals are Monteverdi's first masterworks. The perfections are multidimensional: form, musical imagery, rhetorical expressiveness, vocal coloration, and harmonic control. The goal of text expressiveness and clarity pushed Monteverdi's style in the direction of simplifying textures. A cursory examination of the two books shows in almost every piece a predominance of homophonic, declamatory writing, sometimes in two or three parts, but also often in five parts. The extreme example, often cited, occurs in *Sfogava con le stelle,* in which for textual as well as structural reasons, parts of the poem are indicated to be sung in the *falso bordone* manner, and Monteverdi shows only the chord to which all five parts are to recite the text.

Often the stylistic simplicity can be explained by Monteverdi's purpose of expressing word-inspired moods, which from a twenty-first-century viewpoint seems to suggest an impressionistic use of vocal sounds. In such instances, contrapuntal interest declines or is eliminated. In Example 3.7, *A un giro sol de'belli occhi,* the following passage with its static harmony creates the musical equivalent of "Ride l'aria d'intorno, E'i mar s'acqueta ei venta"—"The surrounding air laughs, and the sea and wind quiet down."

Of the twenty madrigals in Book IV only four have poems longer than ten lines, and brevity seems also to be Monteverdi's goal in most of these compositions. The textual

EXAMPLE 3.7 *A un giro sol de'belli occhi,* mm. 8–15

brevity enables one to see how Monteverdi creates musical forms, since the musical structures are of necessity based on repetitions of text lines. To choose but one example, *Sí,
ch'io vorei morire* demonstrates much about the originality and new spirit of these madrigals.

The text by an unknown author[10] is a typical erotic scene, thinly disguised in late-
sixteenth-century conventional language. The lover's kiss, his passionate reaction, are all
that sustain the poem, but Monteverdi created from these lines a miniature gem of musical
eroticism. Because the opening line of text also closes the poem, a musical refrain is implied.
What could not be anticipated was Monteverdi's formal design for the rest of the madrigal,
which can be illustrated by the following breakdown of text according to the musical
sections:

Sí, ch'io vorei morire	A (three times)
Ora ch'io bacio, amore	
La bella bocca dei mio amato core	B
Ahi, cara e dolce lingua	
Datemi tanto umore,	
Che di dolcezza in questo sen m'estingua!	C
Ahi, vita mia	D
	D
	D
a questo bianco seno	Ea (three times)
Deh, stringetemi fin ch'io venga meno!	Eb (two-part descending)
	Ea
	Eb (three-part descending)
	Ea
[with bass]: Ahi bocca, ahi baci, ahi lingua	Eb (two-part descending)
Ahi bocca, ahi baci, ahi lingua;	
i'torn a dire	F
Sí, ch'io vorei morire	A

Among the musical features to be noted is the total lack of conventional madrigal-isms—word paintings. Monteverdi has interpreted this brief text solely in terms of its emotional content, giving musical substance to the lover's feelings at his moment of erotic bliss. The opening line, "Sí, ch'io vorei morire" (A) is stated in five-part homophony with a characteristic Monteverdian descending melody that includes an unresolved leading tone (the resolution is "exchanged" to the *quinto* part), the effect of which is to further accent the word "morire." These three statements descend to a point of rest before the action to follow. Immediately with "Ora" (now), the cross-relation of C sharp to C and the leap of the minor sixth in the tenor vitalize the music, raise anticipation, which is realized by the subsequent ascending passage (B) for "now I kiss the mouth of my dear heart." The physical sensation of that act, the rising eroticism of the kiss, is quite explicitly suggested by the passage C, with its melodic motive involving a second that clashes repeatedly in suspensions in all of the parts imitatively, bringing together the extraordinary three-note "tone clusters." As these tensions are released and the lover collapses on his partner's breast, the music also descends quietly for a temporary pause (m. 38). But the real musical and emotional goal of the madrigal is yet to come. The outburst of "Ahi, mia vita" (D), repeated two times leads directly to that climax (E). The complex series of repetitions involves the next two lines. "A questo bianco seno"—"on this white breast"—comes in three passionate outbursts, each slightly altered musically, and these are followed each time by "Deh, stringetemi fin ch'io venga meno"—"Oh, embrace me until I collapse." The first time the line involves a two-part contrapuntal passage in suspensions, the second time, a three-part (lower voices) ascending passage, and the third time, a repetition of the first two-part passage, but with the addition of rhetorical outbursts in the bass part—"Oh mouth, oh kisses, oh tongue." This line then is repeated to bring the scene to its climax, followed by a repetition of the opening line, "Yes, I should like to die."

This madrigal, except for the parts of greatest emotional fervor (E section), is largely composed in a declamatory style. Yet the effect remains of a musical and emotional passion that reminds one of the erotic moments between Nero and Poppea in Monteverdi's last opera, *L'incoronazione di Poppea,* written some forty years later.

With Book V Monteverdi reached a point in his career where he found it necessary to acknowledge in his publication his changing perception of musical developments. Already noted was the fame of this book as created by Artusi's accusation that the composer had used dissonances incorrectly. This led to Monteverdi's defense of a musical style that he contrasted with Renaissance polyphonic practices, a new practice that he labeled the *seconda prattica.* As important as this propagandizing for new music was for the history of music, even more important was Monteverdi's adoption in Book V of a basso continuo part. This he acknowledges on the title page can be employed for all of the madrigals, but it is obligatory only for the final six: *Ahi, com'a un vago sol cortese giro; Troppo ben può questo tiranno amore; Amor, se guisto sei; T'amo mia vita; E così a poc'a poco torno farfalla;* and *Questi vaghi concenti.* For the first time, in two of these, Monteverdi expands the traditional five-part texture: to six parts in *E così a poc'a poco torno farfalla,* and nine parts (double chorus of five plus four voices) in the final madrigal. Even more unexpected in the latter is the inclusion of two instrumental sinfonias.

Most of the texts from the first part of Book V come from Guarini's *Il pastor fido.* The volume opens with Mirtillo's first monologue, *Cruda Amarilli,* followed by Amarilli's lament, *O Mirtillo.* Undoubtedly both are placed at the beginning of the set because Artusi had made them if not controversial, at least popular. These are followed by two large cycles: *Ecco Silvio,* a dialogue of Silvio and Dorinda from Act IV, and *Ch'io t'ami,* a monologue by Mirtillio in Act III. These as well as those at the end of the book with obligatory continuo parts are all highly dramaticized musical realizations and suggest a theatrical representation, whether intended or not. Stylistically, the *a cappella* madrigals are even more intensely declamatory than those of Book IV, and Monteverdi seems often on the verge of the recitative style itself.

But even with the progressive stylistic tendencies identified in Book IV and the first half of Book V, one is not prepared for the change of concept found in the six continuo madrigals. Although these have been criticized in the past as rather conservative and less radically new than those to be found in later books, nevertheless this judgment overlooks the fundamental changes of style that the basso continuo enabled Monteverdi to achieve. It freed him in terms of harmonic texture and enabled him to write long, lyrically phrased melodic lines for one or more voices that need not be supported harmonically through imitation or part writing in other voices. This same melodic freedom offered Monteverdi the opportunity to write much more virtuosic, embellished solo melodies (for example, see *E così a poc'a poco*). Also, from a dramatic standpoint, the continuo support of a solo voice enabled the composer to distinguish dramatic roles, with responses between a solo voice and an ensemble of voices effectively suggesting characters in rhetorical responses. These various effects of solo or a few parts versus a larger ensemble, to which in subsequent books were added instruments as well, belong to the seventeenth-century concept of the *concertato* madrigal.

These newfound freedoms of compositional textures and organization also brought new problems. But Monteverdi met the challenges and his music succeeds with the greatest originality of formal organizations. Many of the new elements of the continuo madrigal already appear in the first of these in the Fifth Book, *Ahi, com'a un vago sol cortese giro:*

1. Ahi, com'a un vago sol cortese giro	Ah, at one pretty and graceful turn
2. de duo begli occhi, ond'io	of two lovely eyes, whence I

3. soffersi il primo e dolce stral d'amore,	was wounded by the first sweet arrow of Love,
4. pien d'un novo desio,	full of new desire,
5. sì pronto a sospirar torna il mio core!	how quickly my heart sighs once again!
6. Lasso, non val ascondersi, ch'omai	Alas, it is no good to hide, for now
7. conosco i segni che'l mio cor m'addita	I recognize the signs that my heart shows me
8. de l'antica ferita;	of the old wound;
9. et è gran tempo pur ch'io la saldai.	and it is long indeed since it was healed.
10. Ah, che piaga d'amor non sana mai!	Ah, a wound of Love is never cured![11]

The poem is without refrain, but Monteverdi, for formal and expressive purposes, chooses to use the final, moralistic line as a refrain. The repetitions of this line suggest a rondolike structure. "Ah, che piaga d'amor non sana mai" is stated completely five times, following line 5, line 8—two more times, once by the duet, once by the full ensemble. After a repetition of line 9, the full ensemble repeats the refrain again with each of the "Ah" openings increased in musical-rhetorical impact. Other levels of structural cohesion exist in melodic, rhythmic, and harmonic spheres. Harmonically the madrigal is freely modal with strong tonal elements. But most important to observe for the future development of Monteverdi's style is the degree to which harmonic patterns built on strong basses aid the overall logic of the composer's music. The following schematic representation of the harmonic block repetitions in this piece provides such an example of his planning:

A (Lines 1–5) mm. 1–7 = 8–15 = 15/22–23 (compressed)
B (Line 10) mm. 24–32
C (Lines 6–8) mm. 33–45

B mm. 46–51 = 24–32 (transposed)
D (Line 9) mm. 52–55

B mm. 56–61 = 24–26/30–32

B mm. 62–64 = 24–26
mm. 65–73 (varied repetition and development)

D mm. 74–77 = 52–55

B mm. 78–80 = 24–26
mm. 81–86 = 27–31

Cadence mm. 87–89 = 31–32

While the slow-moving bass lines in this and other continuo madrigals appear to suggest the style promulgated by the Florentine monodists, an overview of Monteverdi's works demonstrates that he invariably employs strong harmonic basses in both his monodic and recitative styles—unless, of course, the musical/rhetorical circumstance suggests such a static musical foundation.

In 1607 Monteverdi's first opera, *La favola d'Orfeo,* was performed in Mantua, where one year later his second opera, *L'Arianna,* received its premiere at court celebrations following the wedding of Francesco Gonzaga and Margaret of Savoy. In addition, Monteverdi's ballet, *Il ballo dell'ingrate,* was given for that occasion. Also in 1607, the *Scherzi musicale* appeared in Venice in an edition by his brother Giulio Cesare Monteverdi. In 1610 Monteverdi published the famous *Vespers* in a volume also including a six-part Mass. In 1612 Vincenzo I died and his successor, Francesco II, released Monteverdi and other court musicians from their positions. One year later Monteverdi became *maestro di capella* at St. Mark's in Venice, where he remained for the rest of his life. Therefore between the publication of the Fifth Book of madrigals and the Sixth Book in 1614, Monteverdi had experienced exceedingly productive but also often difficult years. The last three volumes of madrigals, which he supervised in publication, include works of considerable variety, reflecting numerous musical developments of Monteverdi's own style, but also the rapid pace of musical changes taking place in early-seventeenth-century Italy.

Book VI of madrigals, although published after Monteverdi's arrival in Venice, was still the product of his years in Mantua. The collection is dominated by two substantial laments, the great and famous five-part madrigal version of Arianna's monologue from the opera *Lasciatemi morire* and the *Lagrime d'amante al sepolcro dell amanta* (Tears of the Lover at the Tomb of his Beloved), the former opening the book perhaps because of the fame the lament had achieved already in 1614. The five-part texture may suggest some of the power of the original as it occurred in the opera, since the only surviving fragment of the opera is a monodic (voice and continuo) version of this lament which cannot reveal the dramatic and musical expressiveness of the work.[12] These, like the two madrigals to texts by Petrarch (*Zefiro torna* and *Ohimè, il bel viso*), are unaccompanied.

Together with Guarini and Chiabrera, a new poet is introduced, the well-known seventeenth-century Italian Giambattista Marino, and his poetry inspires the accompanied madrigals including *Presso un fiume tranquillo* (a "dialogue" in seven parts), *A Dio, Florida bella; Batto qui pianse Ergasto; Qui rise Tirsi;* and *Misero Alceo.* These concertato madrigals display a fuller realization of techniques already seen in Book V, such as in *Ahi, com'a un vago sol cortese giro.* The opening of *A Dio, Florida bella,* for example, illustrates emphases on solo song, dialogue, and response between solo voices and fuller textures.

It is, however, in Book VII, entitled *Concerto Settimo libro de madrigali a 1, 2, 3, 4, & 6 voci, con altri generi de canti* (Venice, 1619), that the new concertato style finds its fullest and most varied realizations. The largest group consists of duets over a continuo bass, early examples of the trio texture basic to Baroque concepts of ensemble music. Among these, four feature two sopranos and have the most elaborated virtuosic writing (see especially *O come sei Gentile*), one is for two altos, but the majority—eight—are for two tenors, including a remarkably dramatic setting, *Interrotte Speranze.* A few are for three voices and instrumental bass, and two for four voices. *Con che Soavità* has an unusual scoring for soprano and nine instruments; one is for six voices, two violins, and two flutes (*A quest'olmo, a quest'ombre*). Two atypical works in the form of recited letters are written in what Monteverdi calls the *genera rappresentativo e si canta senza battuta,* that is, in the dramatic recitative style sung without measure (i.e., without beating time). Finally, this colorful melange of vocal styles closes with a ballet, *Tirsi e Clori,* sung as well as danced, for five voices and an array of instruments.[13]

With the exception of the two works in recitative style, the collection is decidedly modern in its heavy emphasis on vocal duets, a popular development in music Monteverdi must have noted in the works of such contemporaries as Grandi, da Gagliano, and d'India.[14] No matter how much the individual works vary in their approach to texts, the one element that stands out is the new, more popular, often tunefulness of the melodic style plus an extroverted exploration of vocal beauty and virtuosity. It suddenly appears as if here for the first time Monteverdi places total emphasis on the Italianate joy of vocal lyricism, long phrases, sensuous dissonances, all remote from the last vestiges of Netherlands contrapuntal line and a less inherently emotional vocal style.

At the age of seventy-one, Monteverdi published his final book of madrigals,[15] the extraordinary Book VIII: *Madrigali guerrieri et amorosi con alcuni opuscoli in genera rappresentativo, che sarrano per brevi episodii fra i canti senza gesto* (Venice, 1638) (Madrigals of Love and War with some small works in the recitative style that will be for brief scenes for singers without acting). The volume is by far the largest of the madrigal collections and has a heterogeneous makeup with an astonishing variety of types of works, including large multivoice settings with instruments, smaller quartets, trios, and duets, two sung ballets, and two decidedly theatrical pieces. The volume establishes a landmark in the history of Baroque music and the developing sense of new musical styles characteristic of the period, and Monteverdi proclaims in his famous preface that he had discovered a new style, a new concept of rhythmic emphasis of certain "warlike" affects:

> I have reflected that the principal passions or affects of our mind are three, namely anger, moderation, and humility or supplication; so the best philosophers declare, and the very nature of our voice indicates this in having high, low, and middle registers. The art of music also points clearly to these three in its terms "agitated," "soft," and "moderate" [*concitato, molle,* and *temperato*]. In all the works of former composers I have indeed found examples of the "soft" and the "moderate," but never of the "agitated," a genus nevertheless described by Plato in the third book of his *Rhetoric* in these words: "Take that harmony that would fittingly imitate the utterances and the accents of a brave man who is engaged in warfare." And since I was aware that it is contraries which greatly move our mind, and that this is the purpose which all good music should have—as Boethius asserts, saying, "Music is related to us, and either ennobles or corrupts the character"—for this reason I have applied myself with no small diligence and toil to rediscover this genus.
>
> After reflecting that according to all the best philosophers the fast Pyrrhic measure was used for lively and warlike dances, and the slow spondaic measure for their opposites, I considered the semibreve, and proposed that a single semibreve should correspond to one spondaic beat; when this was reduced to sixteen semiquavers, struck one after the other, and combined with words expressing anger and disdain, I recognized in this brief sample a resemblance to the passion which I sought, although the words did not follow metrically the rapidity of the instrument.
>
> To obtain a better proof, I took the divine Tasso, as a poet who expresses with the greatest propriety and naturalness the qualities which he wishes to describe, and selected his description of the combat of Tancred and Clorinda [*La Gerusalemme liberata*, xii, 52–68] as an opportunity of describing in music contrary passions, namely, warfare and entreaty and death. In the year 1624 I caused this composition to be performed in the noble house of my especial patron and indulgent protector the most illustrious and Excellent Signor Girolamo Mocenigo, an eminent dignitary in the service of the Most Serene Republic, and it was received by the best citizens of the noble city of Venice with much applause and praise.
>
> After the apparent success of my first attempt to depict anger, I proceeded with greater zeal to make a fuller investigation, and composed other works in that kind, both ecclesiastical and for chamber performance. Further, this genus found such favor with the composers of music that they not only praised it by word of mouth, but, to my great pleasure and honor, they showed this by written work in imitation of mine. For this reason I have thought it best to make known that the investigation and the first essay of this genus, so necessary to the art of music, came from me. It may be

said with reason that until the present, music has been imperfect, having had only the two genera—"soft" and "moderate."[16]

It was in 1624 that Monteverdi's experiment with a concitato—agitated—style was first heard in the Venetian palace of his patron, and the work, *Il combattimento di Tancredi et Clorinda,* forms one of the two compositions in Book VIII in the "genera rappresentativo" (the other being the *Lamento della Ninfa* for soprano and a trio of two tenors and bass). Although Monteverdi says these works are performed without gesture, the score to the *Combattimento* gives indications as to how the two characters should act out (or did act out in 1624) their combat. Musically the piece is divided between long passages of recitative for narrator and the two protagonists and the action-filled descriptions of combat in which the *concitato* style is used. Not only are rapid repetitions of a note involved but also reiterations of brief figures imitating the blows of the swords, the sounds of horses' hoofs, and warlike trumpet figurations.

Book VIII is divided, as the title suggests, between madrigals of war (or perhaps the battle of the sexes in modern parlance) and madrigals of love. Each part ends with a ballet, the first part with *Volgendo il ciel,* written for Emperor Ferdinand III, to whom the volume is dedicated, and the second part with *Ballo delle ingrate* to a text by Rinuccini and originally performed at Mantua in 1608. The *concitato* style, which often seems a little naive in its effect, works best in the large-scale pieces such as *Altri canti d'amor,* opening the book, and composed for six voices, six string parts, and basso continuo, and also the striking *Hor ch'el ciel e la terra* (Petrarch) for six voices, two violins, and continuo. The *madrigali amorosi* generally are more intimate and first among Monteverdi's supremely beautiful and inspired madrigals. There is a considerable variety of types of pieces: the aria-like *Ninfa, che scalza il piede,* for solo tenor; and among the duets, *Mentre vaga Angioletta* (Guarini), set to a poem praising music, in which Monteverdi gives two tenors some exceedingly virtuosic vocal writing. Among the trios, the most masterful and significant is the *Lamento della Ninfa—Non havea Febo ancore,* for two tenors and bass, plus a soprano "solo." This is the second of the pieces Monteverdi describes as in the *genera rappresentativo.* The text, in three parts, is by Rinuccini. Part I, for a trio of men's voices, narrates the dramatic situation: a nymph leaves her abode, "sorrow was visible on her face, and frequently her heart expressed itself in a deep sigh. Thus lamenting for her lost love, she walked about mindlessly, trampling down the flowers." Part II, then, is her lament, with inserted asides by the three shepherds. It is a highly affective, dramatic recitative, composed to a descending minor tetrachord ostinato in the continuo (see Example 3.8).

Part III concludes with a short, moralizing postlude for the three tenors. Such laments over a descending tetrachord ostinato bass became prominent musical conventions for Venetian opera and for vocal chamber music in succeeding decades. Monteverdi's setting, which brilliantly solves the challenge of a repeating four-note bass pattern, uses syncopations, phrases that overlap the bass pattern, suspensions, and poignant dissonances. The unrelieved repetitions of the ostinato, which is often in conflict with the vocal line, and the sad but beautiful vocal writing are factors making this lament, if not the first of its type, certainly the most successful and influential in the first part of the seventeenth century. It would be difficult for contemporaries of Monteverdi not to have been influenced by the concept, and the numerous and similar laments, for example, in Cavalli's operas, seem to grow directly from Monteverdi's achievement.[17] Here is a madrigal in name only, breaking the mold, and highly operatic in its style. The emotion-laden text and its affective realization achieve a controlled, yet personal emotional expression that places it in the main-

EXAMPLE 3.8 Ostinato from the *Lamento*

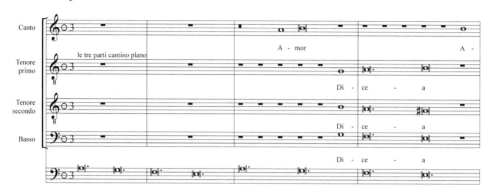

stream of developing musical styles during the first half of the seventeenth century. The madrigals of Book VIII in spirit as well as form have no roots in the Mantuan period. The value of Monteverdi's extraordinary creative output in madrigal form is not just artistic. Few composers have left such a legacy of traceable musical development (the string quartets of Haydn are another rare example).

The Operas

Monteverdi's *Orfeo* occupies a pivotal place in the early history of opera. As has been shown, this was not the first experiment with the new concept of combining continuous music with drama; however, Monteverdi's musical achievement towers above those earlier works by Peri, Caccini, and Cavalieri. Prince Francesco Gonzaga, first son and heir to Vincenzo, apparently requested that Monteverdi compose an opera. The prince belonged to a group of gentlemen amateurs in Mantua, the Accademia degli Invaghiti, and he probably wished to present Monteverdi's first opera to the Accademia during Carnival season 1607.[18] The librettist, Alessandro Striggio the Younger (a diplomat and poet, son of a composer), was also a member of the same academy. Poet and composer alike were undoubtedly familiar with the exceptional musical events that occurred in Florence in 1600, including Peri's *L'Euridice.* Striggio's libretto has many similarities with Rinuccini's, and Monteverdi's music reflects in various ways, often subtle, his knowledge of Peri's score.[19]

The same great myth, with its immortal tale of the power of music to overcome death itself, lies at the basis of both opera librettos. Well known from antiquity in versions found in Virgil's *Georgics* and Ovid's *Metamorphoses,* it was revitalized by new settings in the Renaissance. The source of the Rinuccini libretto, Angelo Poliziano's play *La favola di Orfeo* (1480), was still well known at the end of the sixteenth century. Aristocratic audiences in Florence as well as in Mantua would have been well versed in its story.[20]

Monteverdi's score treats the myth with richer musical details than Peri's. This comes partly from his incorporation into his *favola in musica* an amalgam of musical elements both traditional and new. The traditional elements are derived primarily from the *intermedio* of Renaissance entertainments, including dances, strophic songs, and especially madrigals. Also reflecting the nature of the musical portions of Renaissance dramatic presentations is Monteverdi's use of a large number of instruments,[21] which he says were used at the first performance in Mantua 24 February 1607 (a second performance was ordered by Duke Vincenzo and occurred on 1 March).

Striggio and Monteverdi probably worked together in preparing the libretto, for it displays careful planning to enable Monteverdi to focus primarily on the drama as it centers on Orpheus. The five acts[22] are balanced in various ways: the first two take place in a pastoral setting, the fields of Thrace; three and four in the Underworld, at its entrance in act III, in Pluto's realm in act IV; act V returns to the scene of the opening two acts. Following a traditional Prologue, sung by the allegorical figure of Music, the succeeding acts center either on an action taken by Orpheus or on his reaction to a dramatic development. Striggio's text gives ample opportunities for a variety of styles and types of music. Each act ends with a madrigalian chorus, while other ensembles are integral to each of the acts. There are places for dancing (the famous sung *ballo* in act I, *Lasciate i monti,* and the final *moresca* at the end of the opera). Instrumental ritornellos are used to divide strophes of songs, to tie together scenes into acts, and at significant points to relate acts to each other. The strophic songs contain the lyricism of the score (Orpheus's *Vi ricorda o bosch'ombrosi* in act II is one of the best), but they also furnish a basis for two of the most important dramatic moments: the centerpiece of the opera, Orpheus's plea to Charon (*Possente spirto*) in act III, to allow him to cross the River Styx to enter Hades, is a famous example of virtuoso singing based on a series of four strophic variations over an ostinato bass. Here Monteverdi published not only the basic melody, but also a highly ornamented version to guide singers in the performance. The first Orpheus, Francesco Rasi, was among the most gifted singers of the time and this example may suggest his own performance. More importantly, it offers an invaluable key to vocal performance practice. Another set of strophic variations on an ostinato bass line occurs at the second dramatic highpoint of the work, Orpheus's song as he leads Euridice from the Underworld in act IV (*Qual honor*). These overtly lyrical sections in stricter formal designs give a natural musical outlet for Orpheus, the greatest of all musicians.

For the new concept of the *stylo recitativo* Monteverdi drew from his experiences with the madrigal the means for greater musical expressivity than had characterized the works of Peri and his Florentine contemporaries. First among the madrigalian elements was Monteverdi's utilization of harmonic colorings for word emphasis. In *Orfeo* one frequently senses a harmonic drama that is at times as important as melodic design. However, he also showed an unusual sensitivity to the role of melodic shape, and the use of lyrical phrases in the recitatives often makes the passages into ariosos. Other expressive means in the recitative include the use of sequence (as such rather rare in Florentine recitatives) and rhythmic vitality and contrasts, to underscore rhetorical impulses that often further strengthen the immediacy of emotion. Many passages in *Orfeo* use these and other musical refinements to join music powerfully to the text. None is more illustrative of this aspect of Monteverdi's opera than the scene in act II when Orpheus learns from a Messenger (Sylvia, one of Euridice's companions) that his wife has died from a snake bite.

The force of impact of this tragic announcement is felt strongly because the previous music of the act has been continuously joyful. Orpheus and his companions have been celebrating his previous wedding night. He begins with an arioso, *Ecco pur ch'a voi ritorno/ Care selve e piaggi amate.* The melody is catchy, the rhythm invigorating. The same is true of the following music, to a strophic text, which is divided up into songs first for a solo singer, then for two in duet, and finally for a choral ensemble. This prepares the scene for Orpheus's well-known four-strophe song, *Vi ricorda o bosch'ombrosi,* in which he remembers the torments of his previous life and the utmost joy of the present. Continuing in this mood, a shepherd adds another joyful song, *Mira deh mira Orfeo,* in which he urges Orpheus to continue his singing.

Suddenly the flow of melody is stopped, and on a bass note progression from C to C sharp the Messenger enters with the memorable line, "Ahi, caso acerbo, ahi fat'empio e crudele, ahi stelle ingiuriose, ahi ciel avaro" (Ah, bitter event, ah impious and cruel fate, ah stars ill-designing, ah, avaricious heaven). Each of the outbursts on "Ahi" begins high in range, and the passage then plunges down into unprepared dissonances with the bass and its chordal realization.[23] This poignant outburst will become a refrain, repeated twice in this scene, once at the end in a vocal ensemble version. Many details of Monteverdi's recitative techniques are found in this passage: for example, the employing of distantly related tonal centers—A minor for the Messenger pitted against the F major of the shepherd; sequential melodies, as in Orpheus's questions, "D'onde vieni? ove vai? Ninfe che porti?"; also, a famous use of harmony for dramatic impact occurs in the announcement of Euridice's death by the Messenger: "la tua belle Euridice" to an E major chord which is cut off by Orpheus's interruption of "Ohimè che odo?" in a progression of G minor to C minor, first inversion. The Messenger completes her announcement with "La tua diletta spose" again to E major, but plunging into A minor for "è morta." Orpheus responds "Ohimè" stopping on a D major chord. Struck dumb by what he has heard, his D major chord never resolves to an anticipated G minor until the end of the scene when he finally speaks again with "Tu se'morta."

The long intervening description by the Messenger of how Euridice died encompasses many of the devices of musical and rhetorical relationships, tonal resources, melodic motives, unprepared dissonances, rhythmic activity, silences in the vocal line, bass movements both tonal and chromatic, vocal range, and more. At the end of the scene Orpheus resolves to follow Euridice into the abyss of the Inferno, and, in bidding farewell to the earth, sings one of the most moving lines of the opera, "A dio terra, a dio Cielo, e Sole a dio" (Farewell earth, farewell Heaven, and Sun, farewell).

The marriage of Francesco Gonzaga to Margherita of Savoy required new works from Monteverdi to honor the event. The Mantuan court undoubtedly expected the festivities to equal if not outshine in splendor those that had occurred at the Medici court in 1600. In the fall of 1607 Monteverdi began the composition of two works, both to librettos by Ottavio Rinuccini: a ballet, *Il ballo delle ingrate* (later published in Book VIII of the madrigals); and his second opera, *Arianna*. The latter was first performed on 28 May 1608. Court documents report a great success, and especially the lament of Arianna was singled out as so moving that there were no ladies in the audience who did not shed a few tears. The loss of this score is irreparable. It was Monteverdi's most famous dramatic composition, partly because of the beauty of the famous lament. Monteverdi himself thought he had achieved in the opera a new way to imitate in music emotionally elevated speech. He revised the opera in 1620 for a proposed repetition in Mantua and also a second time for the opening work of the Teatro San Moisè in Venice in 1640. The lament became the source of numerous imitations by other composers, and as late as the 1640s one writer commented that there was not a house in Italy having a harpsichord or theorbo that did not possess a copy of the Lament.[24] As has been pointed out, Monteverdi himself capitalized on the fame of his lament, which he thought the most fundamental part of the opera, by arranging it as a cycle of madrigals in six parts (Book VI). A solo version for soprano was published in 1632, and even later, in the *Selva morale e spirituale* (Venice, 1640), he published a sacred parody for soprano, *Pianto della Madonna sopra il Lamento d'Arianna*.

Subsequent to Monteverdi's move to Venice to become *maestro di cappella* at St. Mark's he continued an involvement with the Mantuan court on several theatrical projects. Most of these were left in various stages of incompleteness. They include the operas *Andromeda* (1618–1620) and *Licori finta pazza innamorata d'Aminta* (proposed for Mantua, 1627, but not composed except for a part of the first act).[25] Also the *favola marittima, Le nozze di Tetide* begun in 1616 was not finished. An eclogue with ballet, *Apollo,* is lost. The only remaining Mantuan dramatic work is the ballet, *Tirsi e Clori* (1616, published in Book VII of madrigals). An opera composed in Venice and performed at the Palazzo Mocenigo, *Proserpina rapita,* is lost except for one trio, *Come dolce oggi l'auretta* (in *Madrigali e canzonette,* 1651).

The loss of so many important dramatic works makes impossible a study of Monteverdi's changing concepts of dramatic style. With the exception of *Combattimento di Tancredi e Clorinda* (1624), the only Venetian dramatic works preserved are the final two operas, *Il ritorno d'Ulisse in patria* (1640) and *L'incoronazione di Poppea* (1643). Another Venetian opera, *Le nozze d'Enea con Lavinia,* and a ballet, *La vittoria d'Amore,* both from 1641, are also lost.

Il ritorno d'Ulisse, based on Homer's epic, is preserved anonymously in a score in Vienna.[26] It is still not well known, overshadowed by *L'incoronazione di Poppea*. Yet it shares with *Poppea* Monteverdi's late Venetian style, a rich composite of musical forms and styles. This includes, of course, the dramatic recitative first achieved in *Orfeo,* but further enriched with considerable flexibility of interactions between musically heightened speech and lyrical arioso and aria-like passages. Stunning examples of this occur in the lament of Penelope in act I, and in the same act the awakening of Ulysses (scene 7).

Penelope's lament seems to some extent to be modeled on the 1608 *Lamento d'Arianna*. It presents, however, an excellent example of the late Venetian style of Monteverdi as it is adapted to the dramatic recitative of the lament. The lengthy text is divided into three parts, separated by brief comments by Penelope's nurse, Ericlea. Each part uses various means to lend formal unity, and the entire lament is held together by the use of two different refrain texts and music. The range of the voice part helps to indicate emotional climaxes. Some of the text is underscored by madrigalisms, including sudden harmonic dissonances and unexpected tonal shifts. In Part III the recitative style is broken by a brief strophic song. Also in Part III both refrains sum up dramatically as well as musically the entire scene. The overall textural and musical structure has the following organization:

PART I:
a (mm. 1–9)	Di misera Regina
b (mm. 10–27)	l'aspettato non giunge
c (mm. 28–45)	Scorsero quattro lustri
d (mm. 46–61)	Ulisse, Ulisse accorto e saggio
e (mm. 62–66)	REFRAIN 1—TU SOL DEL TUO TORNAR
Ericlea (mm. 67–72)	Infelice Ericlea

PART II:
a (mm. 73–86)	Non è dunque per me varia la sorte
b (mm. 87–90)	REFRAIN 2—TORNA DEH TORNA ULISSE
c (mm. 91–98)	Deh torna Ulisse
d (mm. 99–106)	a l'anima affannata
e (mm. 107–10)	così per tua difesa
f (mm. 111–14)	REFRAIN 2—TORNA DEH TORNA ULISSE
Ericlea (mm. 115–20)	Partir senza ritorno

PART III:
a (mm. 121–33)	STROPHIC SONG-LIKE—Torna il tranquillo al mara
b (mm. 134–42)	L'huomo qua già ch'é vivo
c (mm. 143–48)	REFRAIN 1—TUO SOL DEL TUO TORNAR
d (mm. 149–55)	che mentra porti empie dimore
e (mm. 156–60)	REFRAIN 2—TORNA DEH TORNA ULISSE

Many musical details contribute to Monteverdi's affective setting of this text. For example: Much of the first part of the opening section is written around E, as Penelope in grief and almost lifeless barely manages to utter her words. A sobbing figure, descending melodic seconds interrupted by rests (*suspiratio*), closes each of the sections of this part. At the end of the part this figure is drawn out in repetitions descending from B flat to D. There are in this part many repetitions to sixteenths in the midst of slower note values giving a feeling of Penelope's agitated state. Refrain 1, with its rising sequence embodying the increasing emotion of Penelope, reminds one of a quite similar passage in *L'Orfeo* at the end of Orpheus's "Tu se'morta" to the words "A Dio terra, a dio cielo, e Sole, a dio." In Part II, Penelope stirs out of her grief and the recitative energetically rises from the low E to the first climax on the highest note D of the entire lament. Refrain 2 is introduced, Penelope's touching plea for Ulysses to return home, underscored by Monteverdian use of startling harmonic shifts, here between D7 and E, and the clash of the tritone. The following long passage of text is divided by cadences, two on D and then one on F, just before the return of Refrain 1. Part III opens with a suggestion of a strophic song, as Penelope reflects poetically on other kinds of returning found in Nature. This is broken off when she considers the human condition: the spirit may soar to heaven, but the body quickly returns to dust. Refrain 1 is repeated and there is a brief concluding recitative passage leading to the final and touching Refrain 2.

In contrast to this lament is the next scene in which Penelope's maid, Melanto, and her lover, Eurimaco, sing variously of love. The entire scene is lyric, largely in varieties of song, beginning with a series of solos for each of the two characters. These are followed by various duet passages, beginning with "De'nostri amor concordi sia pur la fiamma accesa." Virtuoso singing symbolizes "flames," and concordant melodies in parallel thirds and sixths remind one of similar writing in the last books of Monteverdi's madrigals. For the refrain "dolce, dolce mia vita," a lyrical suavity is in part the result of the lilting triple meter, and the passage is constructed on a basso ostinato. The climax of the scene, as the lovers promise to be faithful, uses recitation tones to bring their words as close as possible to musical speech.

What is considered to be Monteverdi's greatest operatic masterpiece, *L'incoronazione di Poppea* (The coronation of Poppea), with a libretto by Busenello, was first performed at the Venetian Teatro SS. Giovanni e Paolo during Carnival season, 1643.[27] Its plot is exceptional in that it is based on actual Roman history and historical personages. As explained in the Prologue, the story consists of a contest between Virtue and Fortune. Love acts as the catalyst generating a game of life in which the number of human tragedies horrifies. Emperor Nero lusts for the beautiful Poppea, and wishing to make her his queen plots to rid himself of his wife, Octavia. This leads to the latter's unsuccessful plan to murder Poppea, to Octavia's self-debasement and banishment from Rome, and to the suicide of Seneca, the court philosopher who had opposed Nero's actions. Court life is pictured as degenerate, perhaps a topic directed to the tastes of the aristocratic republic of Venice. The libretto totally lacks morally redeeming features. Vice triumphs over loyalties and morality. However, Monteverdi clearly found inspiration in a text based entirely on the strongest human emotions, especially erotic love, and at age seventy-five he created a masterpiece.

Even more than in *Il ritorno d'Ulisse* the vocal writing is marked by fluid changes between recitative style and lyrical, at times, florid aria-like solos and especially duets. A particularly Venetian feature (also found in *Il ritorno d'Ulisse*) places emphasis on the number of solos and duets composed to ostinato basses.[28] There are intensely dramatic monologues, for example, the two laments of Octavia, "Disprezzata Regina" from act I, and her farewell to Rome from act III, "A Dio Roma."

The score typifies Monteverdi's late style, as found in his madrigals as well as his Venetian sacred music, especially in its emphasis on song. Many are the examples in the score, for example, in act I, scene 3, as Nero prepares to leave Poppea after a night of love. Overshadowing the recitative passages are a series of short songs and duets of indelible erotic beauty, culminating in the sensuous "A Dios."[29] This same kind of lyricism flavored with sensuousness underscores the duet between Nero and Lucano, "Or che Seneca è morto," act II, scene 5. Having forced Seneca to commit suicide, the last obstacle to banishing Octavia from Rome has been removed. Nero and his intimate friend Lucano, a poet, rejoice in the beauties of Poppea. They sing—"cantiam"—first in a virtuoso duet. This is followed by a duet in triple meter, followed by more embellished singing, now in praise of Poppea's lips, "to which India and Arabia dedicated their pearls and offered their perfumes." In this extraordinary section, as Lucano sings an ever-more intense and elaborate song, over a descending tetrachord ostinato bass, Nero becomes transfixed, able only to utter with ever-greater emotional intensity, "Ahi, destin" (Oh, what destiny!). Finally he seems to collapse in frenzied ecstasy. The explicitness of the emotion driving Nero here is expressed musically in what must be a uniquely powerful passage for Venetian opera of this period. The scene closes with a short but melodically ravishing song in which Nero compares Poppea's lips to precious rubies and his heart to a diamond, the gems of Love.

The score of *L'incoronazione di Poppea* fully justifies a thorough study as the first great opera of the seventeenth century. If in *Orfeo* Monteverdi adapted the Florentine experiments in setting theatrical texts to music so as to produce a more varied and musically compelling opera, then in *Poppea* he demonstrated that in old age, with the experience of years of service to the Venetian republic and its musical tastes, he could again infuse into the still new operatic concept musical and dramatic values of unequaled mastery.

The Sacred Works

The earliest known compositions by Monteverdi, published in Cremona when he was fifteen, were sacred motets in three parts, *Sacrae cantiunculae tribus vocibus* (1582). These are stylistically conservative, perhaps taken from among the young student's best contrapuntal exercises in Roman (Palestrina) style. A collection of madrigals to sacred texts, *Madrigali spirituali a quattro voci* (Brescia, 1583), is lost except for a copy of the bass part. No further evidence of composing sacred music exists until 1610 when Monteverdi published his two-part collection containing a six-part Mass and music for Vespers, including the Vesper Psalms in *concertato* style, motets for solo voices, and two settings of the Magnificat.[30] The volume is dedicated to Pope Paul V, and seems intended to prove to him and Roman musical circles his abilities in both the *prima* and *seconda prattica,* perhaps with a hope for an appointment in the Eternal City. It is an extraordinary and complex collection of styles, a testament to Monteverdi's comprehensive command of the total craft of composition as it was practiced in the first decades of the seventeenth century.

The Mass in parody form is based on ten *fughe,* short themes or subjects that Monteverdi extracted from a motet of Nicolas Gombert (c. 1495–c. 1560), *In illo tempore.* The *fughe* appear at the head of the Mass in the Venetian print, suggesting that Monteverdi wished to demonstrate the textbook nature of his craft.[31] The complexity of the contrapuntal textures, with their almost unrelieved overlapping imitation, is astonishing, and looks back before the so-called late-sixteenth-century Palestrina style to earlier Renaissance techniques. Several writers perplexed by the intricacies of the setting have declared the Mass as unsuccessful.[32] Despite the obviousness of Monteverdi's demonstration proving he could compose in the strict contrapuntal idiom and in parody form, there lie within this grandiose work elements that not only sound "modern" but also distinctly Monteverdian. There is the compelling use of dynamic sequences, especially leading to climaxes, highly repetitive phrases, often descending chains of thirds, a strong harmonic organization around C major (C Ionian), and carefully constructed vocal climaxes based on reaching the highest point in the range of the part.

Some idea of the awesome technical accomplishment by Monteverdi in this Mass can be seen by examining the Kyrie. Kyrie I is based entirely on the first Gombert *fuga.* The subject is heard immediately in imitation on the dominant. Various rhythmically altered forms occur, including augmentation. Elaboration of the subject occurs already in measure 5 to allow a descending scale to move through the fifth from G to C. This scale and expanded forms of it are used in sequential patterns to bring Kyrie I to a close, pitted as they are against the subject itself in augmentation. The tendency for textures to move from high to low, noticeable in this movement, seems to be a particular feature of a considerable portion of Monteverdi's sacred musical style.

The Christe uses *fuga* IV. Its inversion is stated immediately both on the tonic and dominant in all the voices except for the *Sextus.* The inversion becomes the more important form of the subject. As with Kyrie I, Monteverdi extends the subject, and he uses his newly composed second half, with its dotted half-note and quarter-note pattern (in modern notation), as a prominent motive in its own right. Beginning in measure 18 this idea shares the thematic texture with the subject and finally overwhelms it as the movement comes to an end.

Kyrie II is based on *fuga* II. In a typical Monteverdian gesture of melodic style, he immediately develops from within the subject the pattern of descending thirds. In this instance, as in the Christe, the rhythmic pattern of a dotted half-note and quarter-note, inherent in the subject, takes on a form of its own as a countermotive to the pattern of descending thirds (m. 16). This development from within the original subject brings the Kyrie to a richly sonorous conclusion. The sudden intrusion of the triad on B flat within the omnipresent C major is in itself a device of significance for the overall unity of the Mass, for it appears in most of the movements, usually to textual references to Christ or God.

The Vespers music, the second half of the publication of 1610, is a compilation of forms of Italian music that would have been well known at a court such as Mantua. The variety of kinds of music, from large concertato compositions for a number of voices and instruments to solo motets, monodic in character, can best be seen in a descriptive listing of the contents:

1.	Domine ad adiuvandum	responsory	six voices (SSATTB) and six instruments and continuo
2.	Dixit Dominus	psalm	six voices (SSATTB) and six instruments and continuo
3.	Nigra sum	motet	solo voice (T) and continuo
4.	Laudate pueri	psalm	eight voices (SSAATTBB) and organ
5.	Pulchra es	motet	two solo voices (SS) and continuo
6.	Laetatus sum	psalm	six voices (SSATTB) and continuo
7.	Duo seraphim	motet	three solo voices (TTT) and continuo
8.	Nisi Dominus	psalm	ten voices in two choruses (STTTB) and (SATTB) and continuo
9.	Audi coelum, verba mea	motet	first for solo voice (T) and continuo with the effect of echoes, and then six solo voices (SSATTB) and continuo
10.	Lauda Jerusalem	psalm	seven voices (SSAATBB) and continuo
11.	Sonata sopra "Sancta Maria, ora pro nobis"	sonata	solo voice (S) and eight instruments and continuo
12.	"Ave, maris stella"	hymn	eight voices in two choruses (SATB) and (SATB) with continuo and instrumental ritornellos à5 (SSATB) and continuo
13.	"Magnificat" I	canticle	seven voices (SSATTBB) and six instruments with continuo
14.	"Magnificat" II	canticle	six voices (SSATTB) and continuo

The simpler and musically similar setting of Magnificat II was probably intended for performance at the Vigil, while the elaborately enlarged version would have been performed on the feast day itself. The four motets for solo voices stand in place of the antiphons normally associated with the psalm, and their inclusion may reflect Monteverdi's understanding of the freedoms allowed in the liturgy at Venice. The motets are solo monodies, written in the new dramatic recitative and aria styles. The first two are set to texts from the Song of Solomon. The principle of melodic variation underlies all four motets, and each has a considerable amount of vocal ornamentation, but it is especially elaborate in *Duo seraphim.*

The five psalms, as well as the Hymn, *Ave, maris stella,* and the instrumental sonata with the opening phrase of the Litany of the Saints—*Sancta Maria, ora pro nobis*—all involve the formal procedure of cantus firmus settings. But in every movement the technique is varied and no two psalm settings are similar. The opening respond, *Domine ad adiuvandum,* is a surprising parody of the Toccata to the composer's opera, *Orfeo,* against which the text of the respond is chanted in falsobordone. The structures of the psalms are each intriguing in their diversity of means.[33] For example, *Laetatus sum* for six-part chorus and solos with continuo relies on a pattern of bass formulas to help organize the nine verses and Doxology of the text as follows:

VERSE	BASS TYPE
1.	I
2.	II
3.	I
4.	III
	IV
5.	I
6.	II
7.	I
8.	III–IV
9.	I
Doxology	II–IV

The total character of the 1610 collection suggests Monteverdi's desire to prove that he was accomplished in all styles and forms of sacred music. There is an especially rich combination of these in the Magnificats, particularly in the version scored for soloists, chorus, and obbligato instruments.[34] Here is a setting of the Magnificat rooted in the past: each of the thirteen movements is based on a Magnificat plainchant (Tone I). However, around this cantus firmus Monteverdi composed a variety of vocal and instrumental compositions reflecting the most recently adopted sacred music styles, for example, monodic solos, duos of considerable virtuosity (*Et exultavit, Suscepit Israel,* and especially the *Gloria patri* with its echo effects), antiphonal writing for two choruses (*Et misericordia*) or instrumental groups (*Sicut locutus est*), and instrumental duets against a vocal cantus firmus (*Deposuit potentes de sede*).

As *maestro di cappella* at St. Mark's in Venice, Monteverdi undoubtedly composed a large body of sacred compositions, a substantial portion of which must be lost. Those that have been preserved appear, in addition to a scattering of works in various collections, in the *Selva morale e spirituale* (Venice, 1641), the last works to be published during the composer's lifetime, and the posthumous collection *Messe a quattro voci, et salmi a una, due, tre, quattro, cinque, sei, sette, & otto voci concertati, e parte da cappella, & con Letanie della B.V.* (Venice, 1650). The forty pieces in the *Selva morale* suggest in their variety of texts and forms Monteverdi's wish to preserve the widest variety of his achievements in sacred music. The collection begins with five sacred madrigals. A four-voiced Mass for chorus follows. The next four pieces are included as possible substitutions for sections of the Mass, written in modern style: *Gloria a 7 voci* (SSATTBB) "concertata con due violini e quattro viole da brazzo overo 4 tromboni quali anco si pono lasciare se occoresce l'acidente"; *Crucifixus* "a quattro voci" (ATTB); *Et resurrexit,* "a due soprani o tenori con due violini"; *Et iterum,* "a 3 voci: basso et due contralti concertato con quattro tromboni o viole da brazzo quali si ponno anco lasciare." There are fourteen psalm settings, seven hymns, two Magnificats, six motets, and Monteverdi's parody setting of the *Lamento d'arianna* as *Pianto della Madonna.* The collection of 1650 organized and published by Vincenti, although smaller in scope, has a somewhat similar organization: a Mass for four-part chorus, thirteen psalm settings, a Magnificat in seven parts, and a Litany of the Blessed Virgin for six voices.

These compilations are a prodigious testament to Monteverdi's genius. The styles and forms are numerous, and the psalm settings alone exhibit an amazing variety of means to organize texts of numerous verses. Indeed, these works as well as his other sacred composition await a comprehensive study.

CHAPTER FOUR

The Baroque in Italy from circa
1640 to circa 1700

Opera in Venice

THE ESTABLISHMENT AND DEVELOPMENT OF OPERA in Venice,[1] in historical perspective, was a seminal achievement of the musical Baroque. Venetian opera provided an extraordinary stimulus to composers both in leading them to new forms and styles of music as well as in providing previously nonexistent career opportunities in opera houses. As the first overtly popular musical genre, as created in Venice, opera gave birth to self-renewing musical/dramatic concepts that have ever since characterized opera history.

The Republic of Venice was unique among the Italian states: it was ruled by a small number of aristocratic families whose wealth and power was based on commerce, not a hereditary lineage or, as in the case of the Roman states, the rule of the Church. Although the seventeenth century witnessed the decline of Venice politically, the city retained its myth of power through lavish and often ceremonial displays of art and music.[2] For more than a century the annual Carnival celebrations (beginning on St. Stephen's Day—26 December—and customarily ending on Shrove Tuesday, preceding the beginning of Lent) had caused up to a doubling of the population with crowds of pleasure seekers from all classes of monied foreign visitors. With its emphasis on the masking of identities, the mixing of classes and nationalities, and the deemphasis on social status, Carnival crowds came with the expectation of venues for entertainment. What at first was a wondrous new theatrical experience quickly became a commercial success, and in subsequent years the demand for new operas by a paying public rapidly increased. Of equal significance to the creation of opera was the well-established Venetian love of spoken theater. This required the construction and maintenance of several theaters in the city, which, with some structural modifications, became readily available for opera performances.

The historic first Venetian performance of an opera occurred during Carnival in 1637 at the San Cassiano theater.[3] It was *Andromeda* by Benedetto Ferrari (1604–1681), the librettist, composer, and oboe player, with music by Francesco Manelli (1595/7–1667). They brought a small traveling company from Rome in which the composer and his wife Maddalena Manelli sang while, of the seven singers covering the twelve roles, five were soprano castratos employed in Venice as choristers at St. Mark's. The music to *Andromeda*, in a prologue and three acts, is lost, but the printed libretto includes a lengthy description of the production, including the amazing visual effects created by the stage machinery and the dazzling beauty of the costumes, features that in the development of opera in Venice would become ever more extravagant. For example, the opera began as

> the curtain disappears. The scene was entirely sea. In the distance was a view of water and rocks so contrived that its naturalness (although feigned) moved the spectators to

doubt whether they were in a theatre or on a real sea-shore. The scene was quite dark except for the light given by a few stars which disappeared one after another, giving place to Aurora who came to make the prologue. She was dressed entirely in cloth of silver with a shining star on her brow, and appeared inside a very beautiful cloud which sometimes grew large and sometimes small and, oh lovely surprise!, circled across the sky on the stage. . . . Then Juno came out on a golden car drawn by her peacocks, blazing in a coat of gold with a superb variety of jewels on her head or in her crown. . . . Then Mercury appeared before her. This personage was and was not in a machine. He was, since flying, impossible not to admit it; he was not, since one saw no other machine but that of a flying body. . . . In a moment one saw the scene change from a sea scape to a wood so natural that it carried our eyes . . . to real snowy heights, real flowering countryside, a regal spreading wood, and unfeigned melting of water. . . . [4]

The success of *Andromeda* was immediate and led during the next five years to performances of a growing number of operas,[5] which required the opening of new opera theaters. By 1678 Venetian Carnival audiences had seen 150 operas in nine different theaters: St. Cassiano, 1637; SS. Giovanni e Paolo, 1639; St. Moisè, 1640; Novissimo, 1641; SS. Apostoli, 1648; St. Apollinare, 1651; St. Salvatore, 1661; St. Angelo, 1676; and St. Giovanni Crisostomo, 1678. It would be wrong, however, to believe nine theaters functioned during any one season, because accounts show that seldom were more than four active at one time, and more usually only two.

The commercial success of Venetian opera depended on the success of three factors involving ownership, management (an impresario), and artistic imput into the enterprise. The theaters belonged to the major noble families of Venice such as the Tron, Grimani, Capello, and Giustinian, who owned the land and buildings as secure investments, and who had built new theaters or in some cases restored or adapted old theaters formerly used for *comedia dell'arte* troupes. They took no active role in presenting operas but, rather, rented out their theaters to impresarios, who invested their own capital, or that of a group of investors. The impresario, together with his investors, when they were included, covered all the expenses of the productions, and hoped to reap the profits coming from three sources: the rental of the boxes (the most important architectural feature of these theaters); second, the sale of individual fees for the benches on the main floor; third, entrance tickets charged to everyone entering the theater, including the box holders. Seldom, except in the earliest years of opera, was the impresario a member of the performing group. The librettist was responsible for the costs of printing of the libretto, but he also received the profit from their sales. The boxes in most theaters were constructed in several levels one on top of the other. The lowest level was reserved for members of the highest social class. Boxes were often rented not just annually, but in perpetuity, and the boxes became an extension of the owners' homes and places of social entertainment.

The origins of a Venetian form of opera are easily traced but also obscure. As has been shown, the concept of opera originated in Florence at the turn of the seventeenth century. It was Florentine, *favole in musica,* in which the libretto and its rhetorical effectiveness were joined to a form of almost continuous dramatic recitative. Monteverdi, who also figures prominently in the history of Venetian opera, expanded the musical variety and richness of this earliest concept of opera in *Orfeo* and *Arianna.* There are song and song-like passages, as well as a number of vocal ensembles and instrumental ritornellos. Yet the concept remains a play set to music in which the text is supreme and expressed in singular refinements of musical recitative directed to the privileged and small audiences of aristocrats. By mid-century, Venetian opera evinces little if anything of this concept. This development, however, is made obscure because most of the important early musical sources are not extant. For some fifty operas composed for Venice between 1637 and 1650 music exists for only twelve and by just three composers: Monteverdi (two), Cavalli (nine), and Sacrati (one).[6] None of the earliest works by Manelli, Ferrari, or Cavalli exist.

It can be assumed that the musical origins of Venetian opera lay in early Roman opera. Indeed, the first opera heard in a public theater in Venice was performed by a small touring company from Rome. Roman opera, like its Florentine model, was also a private affair heard in the palaces of the princes of the Church. But as has been recounted (see Chapter 2), Roman composers almost immediately sought to relieve the "tedium of the recitative" of Florentine opera with various lyrical insertions of arioso passages and many more strophic songs. These very style characteristics become a basic feature of the music in those Venetian operas, although it would seem from the earliest librettos of these operas (i.e., before 1640) that they had much less lyricism than was characteristic of Roman scores. This conclusion is based on Rosand's examination of the librettos in which she finds in the poetry little indication of anything but recitative.[7]

Claudio Monteverdi, one of the greatest composers of opera in the seventeenth century, who lived in Venice since 1613 when he became the *maestro di cappella* at St. Mark's, undoubtedly was a significant force in the development of opera in Venice. Regrettably here, too, crucial Monteverdi sources are lost: *Proserpina rapita* (1630) and *Le nozza d'Enea con Lavinia* (1641). His two greatest works, *Il ritorno d'Ulisse* (1640) and *L'incoronazione di Poppea* (1643) are themselves examples of the changing stylistic character of Venetian opera. In the former, Monteverdi, although still focused on dramatic recitative, adds numerous lyrical ariosos and arias, often adapting for these purposes the somewhat conservative recitative poetry of the librettist Giacomo Badoaro. In the latter with a libretto by Gian Francesco Busenello, the remarkable richness of the lyrical sections, both in the ariosos and the arias, stands out as a masterful amalgamation of his dramatic recitative and the new influences of Venetian music, influences that had also been strongly reflected in his late madrigals and Venetian sacred music (see Chapter 3).[8] *Poppea* should be viewed, however, as the capstone to Monteverdi's own uniquely great development as a composer of opera, as it had little influence on the future of opera in Venice or elsewhere.

For three decades until the 1660s, the dominating figure in Venetian opera was Pier Francesco Cavalli (1602–1676).[9] As a boy he was employed as a soprano in the cappella of St. Mark's, which established what would be a close association with Monteverdi. In 1639 he became principal organist at St. Mark's. In the same year he made his debut as an opera composer with *Le nozze di Teti e di Peleo* and until 1668 (with *Eliogabalo* which was never performed) Cavalli composed one, sometimes two operas for almost every season.[10] Of more than thirty works created during this formative period of opera, twenty-eight are extant, the largest corpus of opera scores by one composer surviving from the seventeenth century.[11] Because those that are preserved span Cavalli's entire career as Venice's most important opera composer, they document the evolution of the opera form well into the 1660s. This evolution depended on and was influenced by the several outstanding poet-librettists with whom Cavalli worked, including G. F. Busenello, G. B. Faustini, G. A. Cicognini, and N. Minato. Particularly significant is the evidence these operas give of Cavalli's changing concept of the relationship between recitative and vocal lyricism.[12] For this development he promoted a gradual enriching of the poetic structure of the libretto with texts adaptable to greater formal closure. And because lyrical pauses in the dramatic flow of the recitative text, whether short or long, usually stop the forward pace of the action, the increasing and, ultimately, dominating recourse to arioso and aria diminished the goal of verisimilitude that had guided poets and composers of earlier opera. The most important reason for this changing concept of both libretto and its musical realization was the growing demand of Venetian audiences for a greater focus on the singers' vocal artistry and a diminishing interest in the dramatic content of the text.[13]

Cavalli's operatic works spanning some three decades contain, in addition to various types of recitative,[14] a rich array of vocal forms almost defying classification. The librettos for Cavalli's earliest operas by Persiani and Busenello emphasize recitative texts but provide places for lyricism in a number of strophic texts and more rarely independent quatrains. The feature of strophic texts would dominate Venetian librettos for several years, although the manner in which composers treated them varied widely. For example, in *Didone* (1641), Cavalli received a libretto with twenty-six strophic texts, but he set only twelve of them as strophic arias, eight as strophic recitatives, and four as a mixture of recitative and aria. He changed or ignored the strophic texts in two. Nothing better illustrates Cavalli's artistry and early sensitivity to a text, and his unwillingness to create long, multistrophe arias (repeating the same music for each strophe) than act 3, scene 3 in *Didone*. For the seven strophes in which Enea bids farewell to Didone, Cavalli uses expressive recitative for the first four strophes, and aria in the form of a lullaby (*Dormi, cara Didone, il Ciel cortese non ti faccia sognar l'andata mia*—Sleep, dear Dido, may kind Heaven keep you from dreaming of my going) for the fifth and sixth strophes, although with the penultimate line of each as recitative. The last strophe returns to recitative.[15] The melting of recitative into or out of arioso or aria is characteristic of many of Cavalli's operas, but an increasing emphasis on aria becomes clear as Cavalli's career develops in the 1640s and 1650s.

The shifting of weight from dramatic recitative to passages of vocal lyricism advanced markedly in Venetian opera because librettists such as Faustini, Cicognini, and Minato continued to expand the potential for arioso and aria composition. Faustini, in particular, who wrote ten librettos for Cavalli, endowed his texts with characters and plots allowing more formal music, for example comic servants, including the much-loved stutterer, indulgent heroes and heroines immersed in the grand emotions of love or despair, and plots often focused on confusing disguises, which enabled characters to act and think unrealistically and disconnected to their own characters. Popular into the second half of the century was the epigrammatic arioso placed at the end of a recitative and often serving for the exit of a character. Other conventions include the sleep scene, mad scene, the closing love duet, and, most noteworthy, the popular lament found in most of Cavalli's operas.

Two basic aria forms, with numerous variations, dominate Cavalli's operas: the bipartite (AB and ABB') and the ternary (ABA), the last being the true precursor to the da capo aria. Both types originate in the poetic form of recitatives, especially those that included refrain lines in strophic texts. For example, strophic texts frequently end with a refrain or an epitomizing set of lines. If the rhetorical substance warranted it, the first part of the text would be set as a recitative (A) and the concluding refrain as lyrical melody (B). The expressiveness of the aria was quickly expanded by the repetition and modification of the B section (ABB'). ABA arias appeared early in Cavalli's works, and usually they were very short and given to comic characters. In earliest form, the A was a refrain that introduced and concluded a B passage of recitative. In these there was little or no contrast of musical style between the sections. Soon, however, a contrast of styles was introduced; changing meter, a different melody, contrasting harmony. In *Doriclea* (1645), in the aria *Udite amante* (Hear lovers, hear), act 1, scene 5, the form is considerably expanded to dimensions that would become more frequent in the second half of the century.[16]

Exactly what kind of small orchestral ensemble accompanied the voices is not entirely

EXAMPLE 4.1 Cavalli, *Erismena,* act 2, scene 7

clear, but its size would have been determined by the size of the theater. For a ten-year period from 1639 all but one of the extant operas have five-part string textures, and Cavalli returns to five-part textures between 1662 and 1666. Three-part textures dominate in the period from 1650 to 1657. Only four operas have a four-part texture.[17] In addition to strings one or more harpsichords, lutes, and oboes would usually be present for the continuo part, and the occasional use of brass instruments could be required by the librettos.

As a gifted singer himself, Cavalli understood the nature of the human voice and how to employ it in all its varied effects including simple, comic patter-songs, affective laments, and lyrical, sensuous, flowing vocal lines of original beauty. His vocal writing is predominantly simple and syllabic but at the same time often remarkably expressive of the affects. Elaborately ornamented vocal lines are infrequent. When melismatic passages occur, they may give emphasis to picturesque words. Others, however, are purely musical and form the lyrical flow and elegant shape to vocal lines, as illustrated by the passage from *Erismena* (1655) in Example 4.1.[18]

Cavalli's melodies often have simple motivic structures and tend to be a composite of unequal and unbalanced phrase structures, as in the passage from the duet for Medea and Giasone in *Giasone* (1649) in Example 4.2.[19]

First among the conventional aria types that audiences apparently relished in Venetian opera was the lament. It was an expression of a mournful or tragic text sung as a monologue by a main character, often just before the resolution of the drama in the third act. Many in Cavalli's operas are multisectional and combine dramatic recitative and aria sections. Especially striking is the frequent use for the aria of an ostinato bass, some form of passacaglia, and perhaps most common the descending tetrachord. The meter is frequently in three, the harmony often dissonant, the text in places repeated for rhetorical emphasis.[20] This rhetoric is usually enflamed with violent contrasts of emotion often arising from desperation. The tradition of lament settings originated in the late sixteenth century and was popularized by Monteverdi, whose *Lamento d'Arianna,* from his opera of 1608, was

EXAMPLE 4.2   Cavalli, *Giasone,* act 3, scene 2

widely imitated by other Italian composers in various chamber cantatas. It also was Monteverdi who established the formal as well as expressive potential of ostinato basses, in both his sacred and secular works. Cavalli's laments run a gamut of musical organizations. Many forms of ostinato are used, including the descending tetrachord that is found in several variations. As a chromatic descending tetrachord it lends particular poignancy to Climene's lament from *Egisto* (1643) (Example 4.3[21] gives the first eleven of nineteen variations).

For these most poignant arias Cavalli often strengthens the affect by adding string parts throughout. In Example 4.4, Alessandro's lament from *Eliogabalo* (1668,[22] one of Cavalli's last operas and never performed), the strings supply an additional texture of dissonances and rhythmic syncopations. The slightly varied tetrachord ostinato modulates from A minor to C major, a technique often used by the composer.

The fascination of composers and audiences alike for bass ostinato variations established one of the popular formal conventions of the Baroque, which continued throughout subsequent music history, including twentieth-century jazz and other popular musics. Descending tetrachords as well as other forms of ostinatos became a prominent feature of French as well as German and English music, and few composers in subsequent centuries could resist their fascinating musical potentialities.

Cavalli, of course, was not the only composer of Venetian opera in the seventeenth century. Other important opera composers to the end of the century include the singer and composer Giovanni Antonio Boretti (c. 1638–1672), Antonio Cesti (1623–1669), Domenico Freschi (1634–1710), Domenico Gabrielli (1659–1690), Giovanni Legrenzi (1626–

EXAMPLE 4.3   Cavalli, *Egisto,* act 2, scene 3

1690), Francesco Lucio (c. 1628–1658), Carlo Pallavicino (c. 1640–1688), Antonio Sartorio (1630–1680), Pietro Andreas Ziani (c. 1616–1684), and the latter's nephew, Marc' Antonio Ziani (c. 1653–1715). Whereas the development of opera in Venice grew out of a popularization of the original aristocratic court form, another more radical form of popularization further altered the musical character of opera by the close of the century.

In 1674 the impresario of the San Moisè theater, Francesco Santurini (the younger), drastically reduced by a little more than half the price of an entrance ticket. The move was decisive in stimulating the faltering attendance at the opera by middle-class patrons, and competition forced the other houses to follow suit. This gave a renewed vigor to opera

EXAMPLE 4.4 Cavalli, *Eliogabalo,* act 1, scene 13

in Venice, in part shown by the greater opera activity at San Cassiano, San Moisè, the Teatro Vendramino at San Salvatore, SS. Giovanni e Paolo, and also the opening of new theaters: Sant'Angelo in 1677 and San Giovanni Crisostomo in 1678 (although the latter did not reduce ticket prices and became the sole opera theater catering especially to the high society of the ruling classes).

Venetian *drammi per musica,* that initially were entertainments for crowds of participants from all social levels attending the annual Carnival celebrations in Venice, immediately were transferred to numerous cities across the Italian peninsula. It became, as Bianconi observed, "the only form of entertainment . . . both cultivated on a national scale and accessible to a public that is not exclusively intellectual."[23] Opera theaters were supported as in Venice by the impresario system or unlike Venice continued as a court function, but by the end of the century even aristocratic courts turned over to impresarios the running of their theatres that were opened to a paying public. Because performances in Venice were limited to the months of the Carnival period, many touring companies of performers then took their Venetian operas to other parts of Italy. And as Venice attracted such a remarkably diverse, temporary population for Carnival, the enthusiasm for this new form of entertainment was taken home with the visitors, not only to Italy but also to municipal and other cultural centers of Europe. Thus operas that had attained popular success in Venice repeated these successes many times over in other places. This often required that these operas be adapted both to different stage facilities and the expectations of changing audiences. The process inevitably brought change and growth to the very nature of the Venetian *dramma per musica.* As one example, Cavalli's *Giasone,* first performed at the Teatro San Cassiano in January 1649, was subsequently performed in Milan (1649), Florence (1650), Lucca (1650), Naples (1651), Bologna (1651), Piacenza (1655), Palermo (1655), Livorno (1656–57), Vicenza (1658), Ferrara (1659), Genoa (1661), Ancona (1665), Venice (1666), Reggio Emilia (1668), Rome (1671), Naples (1672), Bologna (1673), and Bergamo (before 1676).[24]

As opera became the artistic property and vehicle for commercial success of the singer, and as audiences focused largely on the beauty and virtuosity of singers, came the demand for composers to give more and more emphasis to arias. By the end of the century opera had been transformed from its heavy dependence on dramatic recitative with periodic insertions of arioso and aria passages to works in which arias defined the very meaning of opera. And not surprisingly singers began the practice of inserting unrelated solo arias into operas to satisfy both their own desire to win acclaim from audiences and because audiences expected the practice, especially because many operas were frequently repeated in different seasons. Some writers have criticized or regretted what they see toward the end of the century as a decline in the artistic and dramatic standards of Venetian opera.[25] Although the extant scores of operas from the last decades of the seventeenth century have yet to be examined in any comprehensive study, it is clear that the theory of a decline or disintegration of a musical form is invalid. Rather, the developments taking place in opera in seventeenth-century Italy demonstrate better than perhaps any other musical development the impact of society on music. Opera became a popular art form in Venice, and throughout its continuing history has almost always succeeded as a popular musical art. It is this fact that has enabled opera to remain a valid musical form through numerous changes of stylistic concepts through the centuries and to the present day.

The Oratorio

Together with the cantata and opera, the oratorio is the third major vocal genre to develop in Italy out of the achievements of the Florentine monodists and creators of a new concept of text/musical relationships. One cannot, however, speak with any definitiveness of "oratorios" as a distinct genre until the 1640s. Even then oratorio-like works often are not so labeled and can have a variety of titles such as *historia, melodrama,* cantata, dialogue, concerto, and motet.[26] The oratorio is the last of numerous types of sacred music linking together some form of dramatic presentation of a biblical or other sacred text with music. Although some of these forms undoubtedly influenced the creation of the oratorio, many others going back to the Middle Ages clearly are unrelated except insofar as they also sought to vivify and dramatize biblical texts. It was the impetus of the Counter Reformation that gave new life to these practices. In the mid-sixteenth century the Italian saint and religious leader, Filippo Neri (1515–1595), began to gather in Rome a group of laymen for religious discussions and prayer. They met in the oratorio, that is, the prayer hall, of a church. He introduced the singing of *laude spirituale* as a regular feature of these meetings. In 1575 Pope Gregory XIII officially recognized Neri's lay community as the religious order of the Congregazione dell'Oratorio, and granted them the church of St. Mary's in Vallicella, which would later be replaced by the "Chiesa Nuova," as it is still known today. Music quickly became a significant factor in attracting participants to these spiritual exercises, and what began as congregational performances were soon expanded to include professional musicians and later only professionals. In the second half of the seventeenth century the name of the prayer hall became synonymous with the music performed there.

While little is known of the music heard in Roman oratories in the first decades of the seventeenth century, it is certain that the performance of Cavalieri's *Rappresentativo di Anima e di Corpo,* in the oratorio of the Vallicella in February 1600, would have been an exceptional occasion and not unrelated to the development of the oratorio. Performed as part of Holy Year events, this unique sacred entertainment[27] introduced to a Roman audience not only the new monodic style but also incorporated the features of the laude, dramatic dialogues, choruses, and instrumental ritornellos and sinfonias. And early in the century appeared many collections of sacred (as well as secular) madrigals incorporating dramatic dialogues, written in the still new recitative style.[28] Among the most interesting of these collections is one by Giovanni Francesco Anerio (c. 1567–1630), *Teatro armonico spirituale* (Rome, 1619), dedicated to Filippo Neri and St. Jerome, the latter patron saint of the first Oratorian church, St. Girolamo della Carità. Many of the madrigals in this collection bear the title *dialogo* and four of them are extensive compositions lasting between sixteen and twenty minutes: *Dialogo dell'Anima, Dialogo del Figliuol Prodigo, Dialogo di David,* and *Dialogo della Conversione di San Paolo.*[29] In length and in some stylistic characteristics these can be considered close models for the earliest labeled oratorios. These and others in the collection were clearly intended for performances in the oratories of both S. Girolamo della Carità (the collection was dedicated to Oratio Griffi, director of music at that church) and also at the Chiesa Nuova. They are scored for soloists, chorus, and figured organ continuo bass. Both the dialogues *del Figliuol Prodigo* and *della Conversione di San Paolo* contain descriptive passages for an ensemble of string and wind instruments. All four of these dialogues have a contrapuntally based madrigal style but also are influenced by aspects of the recitative and arioso styles of the monodists.

By 1640 Rome's musical life had been considerably enriched with the expansion of church services involving music separated from church ritual such as the celebration of Mass or vespers which were usually performed in winter and during Lent. Pietro delle Valle (1586–1652), a major figure in the cultural life of Rome, reports of his delight in hearing excellent music in the oratories of St. Maria dell'Orazione e Morte, St. Girolamo della Carità, the Chiesa Nuova, and St. Maria della Rotonda.[30] And in a type of travel guide for Rome, Pompilio Totti's *Ritratto de Roma moderna* (Rome, 1638),[31] these oratories also are recommended to visitors for their musical events. Music also became more important at the Chiesa Nuova when in 1640 Borromini's architecturally distinguished new oratory was completed to the left of the church, where to this day music is still performed.

Two forms of oratorios were composed by the middle of the seventeenth century: the *oratorio volgare,* with texts in Italian, and the *oratorio latino.* Both had similar musical and functional origins in the previous decades, but they depended stylistically on the development of opera occurring at the same time. The *oratorio volgare* became the most popular type in the later part of the century, while the Latin form is particularly important for those written by the greatest of oratorio composer of the mid-century, Giacomo Carissimi (1605–1674). The practice already established by the Oratorians in the sixteenth century of separating two musical sections by a preached sermon was retained in the *oratorio volgare.* Latin oratorios, including all of Carissimi's, generally are in one section only.

Examples of the earliest oratorios in Italian are few in number. The first to be considered an oratorio is a large-scale, undramatic work for chorus, soloists, and basso continuo, the *Coro di Profeti* by the Roman Domenico Mazzocchi (1592–1665), composed for the Feast of the Annunciation and performed in the oratory of the Chiesa Nuova. It is tentatively dated before 1638.[32] Others include a *Dialogo* for the Feast of the Purification by Pietro Delle Valle, who also refers to it in correspondence as his *Oratorio della Purification,* the earliest known reference to oratorio meaning the musical composition. There are two by Carissimi, *Oratorio della Santissima Vergine* and *Daniele;* an anonymous work with the same title; two by Marco Marazzoli (c. 1602–1662), *Per il giorno di Resurrettione* and *San Tomaso;* and two anonymous works until recently attributed to Luigi Rossi, *Giuseppe* and *Oratorio per la Settimana Santa.*

Carissimi became the *maestro di cappella* at the German College in Rome in 1629 and remained until his death in 1674. The German College was founded by the Society of Jesus in 1552 as a center to train German students for the priesthood. In succeeding centuries this Jesuit college and its church, Sant' Apollinare, became famous throughout Italy and Germany for the excellence of its musical performances.[33] Between 1650 and 1660 Carissimi also had a working relationship with the oratorio of the SS. Crocifisso of San Marcello, attended by aristocratic families of Rome. It was here, for Lenten services, that many of Carissimi's Latin oratorios were composed. He also held a second position of considerable importance as the *maestro di cappella del concerto di camera* of Queen Christina of Sweden, where many of his secular cantatas as well as sacred works were probably performed.

All of Carissimi's manuscripts, originally deposited in the German College, have disappeared. Copies from the seventeenth and early eighteenth centuries are found across Europe with invaluable collections in Hamburg and Paris (where they were probably brought by Carissimi's student, Marc-Antoine Charpentier). These copies, however, give no proof that Carissimi himself used the terminology of oratorio or *historia*. This has led to a great deal of discussion concerning which of his works should be classified as oratorios, especially as Carissimi also wrote a large number of Latin dialogues (dialogue motets). Using Smither's classification,[34] thirteen works can be considered Latin oratorios:

1. Baltazar
2. Ezechia
3. Diluvium universale
4. Dives malus
5. Jephte
6. Jonas
7. Judicium extremum
8. Judicium Salomonis
9. Abraham et Isaac
10. Duo ex discipulis
11. Job
12. Martyre
13. Vir frugi et pater familias

The first eight include dialogues as well as narrative passages, and their texts are based on biblical stories. It is unknown who created the texts. Among the thirteen *Jephte* was the best known in the Baroque and it remains so today. The last five are shorter and less consistent in character. Numbers twelve and thirteen are not based on the Bible, and they together with number eleven do not employ narration. None of these, unlike most of the first eight, emphasize choral writing.

Carissimi's oratorios absorb the most modern developments of music of the early seventeenth century, most especially the concertato choral style pioneered by the Gabrielis and the recitative, arioso, and aria styles of early opera. They are an eloquent validation of the theories and practices developed by the Florentine monodists that required music to place primary emphasis on the rhetorical dynamics of language. Therefore, the various styles of music used to present the texts are with no exceptions uncomplicated. The heart of these works are the forms of recitative, most often in "simple" recitative (*recitative semplice*)[35] for the longer passages of narration accompanied by the continuo with rudimentary harmonies. These are given to the *historicus* (*testo* in the Italian oratorios), as well as other characters in the drama. More intensely expressive are the passages of varying length sung in arioso style. These employ a much richer language of dissonant melodic leaps, suspensions, and cross-relations, effective silences (rests), and subtle repetitions of expressive melodic phrases. Some of these passages occur at climactic points and next to

EXAMPLE 4.5 Carissimi, *Jonas,* "Justus es, Domine," mm. 234–61

the choruses are the most memorable parts of the oratorios. One such arioso is the great lament of Jephte, "Heu, heu mihi!" which has been called "one of the most moving pages of the whole century."[36] Another, the exceedingly moving lament from the same work, is sung by Jephte's daughter at the climax of the work, "Plorate, colles, dolete, montes." Equally compelling in its affective music is the prayer of Jonas from inside a great fish (see Example 4.5[37]):

Justus es, Domine,	You are just, Lord
et rectum judicium tuum,	and Your judgment [is] right.
potens es et voluntati tuae non est qui possit resistere.	You are powerful and no one can resist You.
Projecisti me in profundum maris, et fluctus tui super me transierunt.	You threw me into the deep sea, and Your waves passed over me.
Justus es, Domine . . .	You are just Lord . . .
sed cum iratus fueris,	but after your anger,
misericordiae recordaberis	You remembered Your mercy.

Placare, Domine, ignosce Domine,	Be gentle, Lord, forgive, Lord
et miserere.	And be merciful.

The example, the first of the three strophes, typifies Carissimi's expressive monodic style. Each strophe is set off by a concluding refrain ("Placare, Domine") ending with a twofold "miserere" with affective leaps of the diminished fifth. The opening leap into the dissonant G sharp, the shifts from major to minor, the conventional word painting such as on "profundum" and "super me," the sequential repetitions of motives, and the rests placed for rhetorical effectiveness are all common means by which Carissimi underscores the affective impact of the text.[38]

Formal arias are not common in the oratorios (which is also true of operas of the period), but aria style is employed for short passages, at times leading into choruses. When arias occur they are most frequently in binary (AB, ABB') or strophic forms. Duets are also occasionally employed, and they can be imitative, although more frequently the two voices move in parallel thirds and sixths. Instruments are not important to the character of these oratorios, and instrumental parts except for the continuo are found in only nine of the thirteen oratorios. The sources do not specify the instruments but, rather, indicate two instrumental lines in treble range and at times one bass part. When instruments are indicated, they have short sinfonias at the beginning and brief ritornellos within the works.

The personal imprint Carissimi placed on the new oratorio concept was primarily achieved by the considerable variety of choruses in all of the works except for *Job*. This emphasis on choral passages is not characteristic of the oratorios by Carissimi's contemporaries. And it was this emphasis that established a model for the oratorio valid throughout its subsequent history. The choruses are at times descriptive, for example, the storm in *Jonas,* or they can represent characters in the drama such as the powerful contrasts in the chorus of the Just and Sinners in *Judicium extremum.* Each oratorio usually ends with a climactic chorus with varying messages: to praise God, to expand on the theme of the work previously stated, as in *Jephte,* or to conclude the story, as in *Jonas.* In some of these works the relatively limited role of the chorus was likely intended for the three or four soloists. In longer works, the numerous and often contrasting types of choruses were undoubtedly performed by multiple voices to a part, for example, the five-part chorus in *Baltazar,* the six-part final chorus in *Jephte,* double choruses in *Jonas* and *Dives malus,* and triple choruses in *Judicium extremum* and *Diluvium universale.*

The choral writing tends to be predominantly chordal, but this does not mean that many of the most effective choruses are not without a variety of contrapuntal textures. For example, the rich texture of the concluding double chorus to *Jonas,* "Peccavimus Domine," depends on contrapuntal variety including suspensions, points of imitation, and subtle rhythmic contrasts between the eight parts. In perhaps Carissimi's greatest chorus, the concluding lament to *Jephte,* with its built-in, descending tetrachord, is a fugal exposition of extraordinary affective pathos based on that tetrachord. In contrast, many of the primarily narrative choruses are purely chordal, based on the text rhythms, and often repetitions of the same chord in what Heinrich Schütz called *stylo recitativo.*[39] The antiphonal writing of somewhat greater sophistication, with overlapping entrances between choruses, has its legacy in the polychoral style of the Venetian composers. Harmonically, as in the solo portions of the oratorios, the vocabulary is usually rather simple, although not without expressive chromaticism when required by the text. Carissimi's musical language was quite sophisticated,[40] and this clearly was recognized by those who distributed copies of these works throughout Europe, and in the praise he received from writers, such as Kircher:

Giacomo Carissimi, a very excellent and famous composer . . . through his genius and the felicity of his compositions, surpasses all others in moving the minds of listeners to whatever affect he wishes. His compositions are truly imbued with the essence and life of the spirit.[41]

Carissimi has dominated all historical writings about the oratorio. This is certainly the result of the exceptional quality of his works. But another factor is the almost total lack of editions for works by Carissimi's contemporaries and successors. A few oratorio-like works are known by both Domenico and his brother Virgilio Mazzocchi. They were published in *Sacrae concertationes binis, ternis, quinis, octonis, novenisque vocibus, . . . pro oratoriis modis musicis concinnatae* (Rome, 1664)—Sacred Concertos in 2, 3, 5, 8, and 9 Voices, Composed in Musical Ways . . . for Oratories—which includes seven "dialogues" that resemble Carissimi's oratorios in general form and style.[42] The collection also includes one dialogue by Virgilio Mazzocchi. As the title makes clear, they were composed for performances in Roman oratories. Several Latin oratorios as well as some with Italian texts have been ascribed to Marco Marazzoli (c. 1602/5–1662). Other Latin oratorios by Roman composers that are extant include three by Francesco Foggia (1604–1688) and two by Bonifazio Gratiani (1604/5–1664). Graziani's oratorios are significant for apparently being the first from this period to be in two parts.[43]

The novelty of the new expressive and dramatic musical styles brought into the oratories of Roman churches was spread, in part through the activities of the Oratorians, to many Italian cities as well as into northern Europe. The ever-increasing numbers of oratorios composed both by well-known and less-known composers in the later seventeenth century can be documented largely through the preservation of the printed oratorio librettos. Unfortunately, relatively few scores of these works have been preserved. In Rome, performances of oratorios began to take on the character of entertainments, although sermons were still preached between the two parts of the works. Before the turn of the next century oratorios were frequently heard in the previously mentioned oratories, as well as the oratory of San Giovanni dei Fiorentini, in educational institutions such as the Clementine College, and also in the secular surroundings of several great palaces of Rome.

Among the outstanding composers of Roman oratorios were Alessandro Melani (1639–1703), Bernardo Pasquini (1637–1710), Alessandro Stradella (1639–1682), and Alessandro Scarlatti (1660–1725)—see Chapter 5. Of the four surviving oratorios by Melani, *Il sacrificio di Abel* (also known as *Abele* and *Il fratricidio di Caino*), a substantial work in two parts with a libretto by Bendetto Pamphili, has only the four parts for Eve, Adam, Abel, and Cain, and no chorus. First performed in 1678, it is strongly lyrical both in arias and ensembles, and includes several effective laments.[44] Almost all of Pasquini's Roman oratorios are lost. His *Sant'Agnese,* which is extant, may have had a Roman performance in 1671.[45] Among Stradella's six preserved oratorios, *San Giovanni Battista* has deservedly remained his best known.[46] It was performed for the confraternity of the Florentines in the oratory of San Giovanni dei Fiorentini in 1675. Typical for the period, the work is in two parts, has five solo parts but no *testo* and a small role for a chorus. Unusual for the third quarter of the seventeenth century is the division of the orchestra into concerto grosso and concertino ensembles. These are variously used either separately or in combination in the arias. Allegedly, Stradella said he thought this his finest work composed to that date. The fame of *San Giovanni Battista* extends to a movement-by-movement commentary by Charles Burney written more than one hundred years later. Burney opines that "Stradella has introduced a greater variety of movement and contrivance in his oratorio, than I ever saw in any drama, sacred or secular, of the same period."[47]

Stradella's oratorio, unlike anything composed in the 1660s, testifies to the rapid changes that had occurred in the style and character of oratorios. These changes come directly from opera in which Stradella also excelled. They consist largely of an alternation of recitatives and arias, sometimes joined together. The recitatives are at times simple but also frequently highly dramatic in arioso passages. The arias, which tend to be rather short, are in several forms, most often binary but also through-composed and strophic. Several employ "motto" beginnings, in which the melody of the vocal opening is presented first in the preceding ritornello. Particularly operatic in character are the many difficult melismatic passages, and especially the parts for Herod and his daughter require considerable virtuosity, for example, Herod's "rage" aria *Tuonerà tra mille turbini.*" Some of the arias have a distinctive lyrical beauty providing examples of the new vocal style and technique that was already a distinctive characteristic of Pan-Italian operatic music. Impressive, too, is the prevalence of contrapuntal textures and fugal imitation in both the instrumental and vocal parts. This is particularly evident in the several dialogue duets, none being more remarkable than the concluding one between Herod and his daughter ("Che martire, che tormento"/ "Che gioire, che contento"), in which the daughter rejoices in St. John's death, and in contrasting music Herod simultaneously laments his action and comments "Men giocondo giorno il mondo non vede" (the world has never seen a more unhappy day).

Other significant centers where oratorios became a prominent aspect of musical life were Bologna, Modena, Florence, and Venice. In Bologna the Oratorians, established as early as 1615, were recognized by Pope Gregory XV in 1621 as the Bologna Congregation of the Oratory. Their permanent church became the Madonna di Galliera. The city was one of the great musical centers among the Papal States, and a close connection existed between it and Rome. Roman composers of oratorios are frequently identified in lists of oratorios performed in Bologna. Oratorios were heard not only in the oratory of the Madonna di Galliera but also in the many churches of other religious societies including the great church of San Petronio, as well as in several Bolognese academies and private palaces. The earliest extant libretto for an oratorio performed in Bologna in 1659 is for *La morte di S. Gioseppe* by Maurizio Cazzati (c. 1620–1677), *maestro di cappella* at San Petronio. At the nearby city of Modena numerous oratorios were presented, in large part by Bolognese and Roman composers. The duke, Francesco II d'Este (1660–1694), seemed to favor oratorios and in large part through his support more than one hundred oratorios were heard in Modena between 1680 and 1691. Among the few that remain are *Santa Dimna, figlia del re d'Irlanda* by Flavio Carlo Lanciani (1661–1706); *Santa Maria Maddalena dei pazzi* by Giovanni Lorenzo Lulier (c. 1662–1700); and *La Maddalena a'piedi di Cristo* by Giovanni Bononcini (1670–1747).[48]

A major Bolognese composer of oratorios whose works also were heard in Modena was Giovanni Paolo Colonna (1637–1695), *maestro di cappella* at San Petronio after 1674. Of his thirteen known oratorios, six are extant, including *Il Mosè, legato di Dio e liberator del popolo ebreo,*[49] performed in Modena in 1686, and *La caduta di Gerusalemme,* performed in Modena in 1688.[50] Another Colonna oratorio performed in Bologna in the oratory of the Madonna di Galliera around 1679 is *Salomone amante.*[51] The libretto is exceedingly worldly, concentrating on King Solomon's adulterous relationships outside his marriage (including one liaison with the Pharaoh's daughter). The line of demarcation between the secular world of opera and of the sacred world of oratorio disappears. There are a number of oratorios that focus on erotic sexual relationships (such as those concerning the biblical stories of David and Bathsheba, Samson and Delilah, and Adam and Eve), giving rise to the classification *oratorio erotico*. Another significant albeit neglected Bolognese composer of almost two dozen oratorios was Giacomo Antonio Perti (1661–1756), who served as *maestro di cappella* at San Petronio for sixty years from 1696. Nine of these were composed before the turn of the century and all of them deserve a comprehensive study.[52]

The origins of the oratorio in Florence, as John Hill has shown, extend back into the sixteenth century. Here, perhaps not in Rome, did the practice seem to originate to give dramatic renderings of sacred stories in monodic song and with costumes and action. These were part of religious assemblies held by the lay confraternity of the Compagnia dell'Arcangelo Raffaello, established for the purpose of giving a religious education to adolescent boys not expected to enter the clergy. The company's history begins in the fifteenth century, but particularly at the end of the next century and into the seventeenth there were documents indicating a thriving commitment to accompanied singing and the dramatic enactment of simple scenes. Among the adult members of the company were some of the important names among the Florentine monodists, including Giulio Caccini, Jacopo Corsi, Marco da Gagliano, and Jacopo Peri. Few of these works can be identified except by genre, but they include laude, dialogues, and madrigals. There can be little doubt that the genesis of the new musical styles employed in monodies and the first operas had another testing ground in the performances of such music at the religious ceremonies of this lay confraternity.[53]

Beginning in the 1660s and through the eighteenth century Florence had a large group of oratorio composers, mostly natives of the city. Many of them composed for San Firenze, the church of the Florentine Congregazione dell'Oratorio di San Filippo Neri. Oratorio performances were a major focus of musical life in the city during these two centuries, with between twenty-two and thirty-seven given monthly by the Oratorians and additional ones by the other lay confraternities. As in Rome they were a feature of winter musical life, usually with an oratorio performance every Sunday and on selected feast days during the winter period from All Saints Day to Palm Sunday. They were free but open only to the male public, in conformity with church doctrine requiring the separation of the sexes at religious functions. Unfortunately, almost none of these works remain because the entire music library of the Oratorians before 1750 has disappeared, leaving a serious lacuna in the history of the oratorio in Italy.[54]

In Venice in 1662, the Oratorians were granted by the Senate the oratory church of St. Maria della Consolazione (known as della Fava). In 1667 an oratory was built where, in December, the first "oratorio in music" was heard.[55] Through the eighteenth century St. Maria della Fava became a focus of oratorio performances, with over one hundred works identified through their printed librettos. The popularity of oratorios is also seen in their performances in large numbers at the four *ospedali* (dei Mendicanti, della Pietà, degli Incurabili, and dell'Ospedaletto), the charitable institutions that treated the sick or gave educations to homeless children.

The Cantata

The *cantata da camera,* the least comprehensively studied of the new vocal forms developing in the seventeenth century,[56] had its origins in Rome. The historical study of the cantata presents insurmountable problems because of the vast numbers of works composed during the Baroque and because after the earliest period very few cantatas were published, a fact remaining true today.[57] Vocal chamber music performed in the intimacy of the private homes of the wealthy quickly became the most popular form of social entertainment. The modest performing forces, for one or at times two or three voices, accompanied by the realization of the basso continuo part (rarely a pair of solo strings), required only relatively modest financial outlay. The popularity of these entertainments depended on the established reputations of the singers, and the cantata became just as important a means as opera by which singing careers succeeded or failed. As was true of the development of the oratorio, cantatas also underwent simultaneous changes of style and form as they were inserted in Roman and Venetian opera.

The earliest Roman cantata development is evident in works by Alessandro Grandi and especially in some three hundred cantatas by Luigi Rossi. Other significant Roman contemporaries composing cantatas included Carlo Caprioli (1615/20–1692/95), Antonio Francesco Tenaglia (before 1620–after 1675), Marco Marazzoli (with 379 cantatas extant), and Mario Savioni (1606/8–1685). It is Carissimi's cantatas, however, that are best known from this period.[58] The exact number of them remains uncertain, but 126 are clearly by him and probably another 19 as well. Of these, 109 are for solo voice, 27 for two voices, and 9 for three voices. Similar to the earlier secular monodies, the texts of the cantatas focus almost entirely on the subject of the trials and tribulations of the lover who has been rejected by a cruel woman.

Carissimi's cantatas, unlike those written later in the century, have a considerable variety of forms. While they are closely influenced by the texts, which usually have contrasting sections of narrative free verse suggesting recitative and strophes as arias, the musical results can be much more varied. Over half are composite forms made up of a succession of recitatives, ariosos, and arias, although often the distinction between arioso and aria is blurred. The variety of structures includes numerous types of arias (ABB', ABA or ABA', AB, AABB, strophic, rondo, strophic variation).[59] Most prevalent are ABA or ABA' and two-part forms. Several cantatas have strophic variations and a few are written entirely as dramatic ariosos. While the cantatas in general are written with musical moderation, they are also distinguished by Carissimi's musical-rhetorical art by which the affective pathos of a text is expressed not only in melody and harmony, but also in the variety of musical emphases given to richly figurative texts. Unlike the oratorios, his cantatas can be more adventuresome in the dramatic expressivity of their melodic and harmonic language, with various dissonant melodic leaps, chromaticism, unusual shifts of tonality from major to minor, and at times to more distantly related keys. See Example 4.6, the opening section from "Ahi, non torna."[60]

Ahi, non torna, et io mi moro	Ah, you do not return and I die
quel tesoro	that treasure
che stancato ha i miei sospiri.	who has exhausted my sighs.

The vocal writing in this example is very dramatic, midway between arioso and aria, arioso because of the fragmentation of some of the melody by rhetorically expressive rests and disjunct and frequent dissonant motives; aria-like because of the strong element of repetition for both text phrases ("Ahi, non torna, et io mi moro," "quel tesoro, che stancato ha i miei sospiri"). The fluctuating emotions of this abandoned lover are stressed by a tonality that moves between F minor and major ("mi moro" to "quel tesoro"), by the tormented cries of "ahi, non torna," twice to a diminished fifth, and a cross-relation between voice and bass (mm. 7–8). There is the effective modulation from F to E flat minor sustained over three measures with falling and syncopated bass notes (to stress "stancato ha"—exhausted), and in its repetition from C to B flat minor. A brief recitative section

EXAMPLE 4.6   Ibid., "Ahi, non torna," mm. 1–18

is followed by the repetition of the opening line of text made more frenetic by the reiterations of "et io mi moro" to minor seconds and made into gasps by the intervening rests and finally the dying line descending from C to F with the Phrygian color of a Neapolitan sixth (see Example 4.7, m. 33).

One factor making Carissimi's cantatas popular was the vocal beauty of so many of their arias. In these, singability, mellifluous phrases, seemingly quite simple in construction, all depend on the vocal artistry of the singer. With the cantatas of Carissimi and his contemporaries, as well as in the operatic repertory quickly spreading throughout Italy, there arose a concept of vocal melody bearing the unmistakable stamp of the Italians. It was a singular musical development, and its continuing development became one of the glories of Italian music history.

Among Carissimi's contemporaries, Antonio Cesti made the most important additions to the solo cantata repertory. While Cesti is better known as a composer of operas, including his grand five-act *Il pomo d'oro* for Vienna, he wrote a significant number of cantatas of which some sixty remain (including several duets). Although apparently he did not have direct contact with Roman composers, his cantatas seem to be influenced by those of Rossi and Carissimi with whom he was compared. The cantatas that are accessible for study show some similarities with Roman cantatas of the period.[61] Cesti's, however, have distinguishing features. There is still the flexibility of recitatives moving directly into aria or aria-like passages. However, Cesti's recitatives are simpler, seldom as dramatic as those found in the

EXAMPLE 4.7 Ibid., mm. 25–34

cantatas of Carissimi. Most of them have slow-moving basses over which the voice part is made up of fewer dissonant leaps and has more triadic motives and considerable tone repetition, in other words, *recitativo semplice*. There are fewer types of arias, and strophic, AB, and ABA forms dominate.[62] Most distinguishing, however, is the overall simplicity and flowing lyricism of most of the arias, the majority of which are in lilting 3/2 meters that remind one of Cavalli's Venetian opera arias, as in Example 4.8, from the cantata "Languia già l'alba":[63]

Mi dipinge amabil sorte	So agreeable a vision foretells
vision così gradita	a happy fate for me;
il germano della morte	death's own brother
mi congiunge alla mia vita	joins me to my life.

Alessandro Stradella lived in Rome for about a decade (c. 1666–1676). His contributions to the oratorio have been noted, but he was also a prolific composer of cantatas; about 200 exist.[64] These generally have the same characteristics of other mid-century Italian cantatas, including the considerable variety of formal organization. Many of them are accompanied by strings, and in at least two cases, perhaps the earliest examples, recitatives are also accompanied.[65] He also composed some cantatas on a larger scale, often divided into two parts and for more than one singer and an ensemble of instruments. These usually were labeled serenatas. Not surprising for a successful composer of operas and oratorios, many of Stradella's cantatas are similar to highly dramatic scenes from an opera, for example, Medea's impassioned cry to stop the gods from carrying out her own wish for the death of unfaithful Giasone in *Già languiva la notte,* Nero's laughter as Rome burns in *L'incendio di Roma,* and Seneca's preparation for suicide in *Se Nerone lo vuole.*[66]

Among other important composers of Italian cantatas should be cited Giovanni Legrenzi, Bernardo Pasquini, and Giacomo Antonio Perti. Finally, the history of the Italian cantata in the seventeenth century would be incomplete without the name of Agostino Steffani (1654–1728). Although living into the next century, Steffani composed the majority of his music before 1700. He wrote few solo cantatas; however his eighty-one chamber duets are central to the history of Italian secular vocal music with an influence reaching into the next century and including the music of Keiser, Handel, and Telemann.[67] The chamber duet, a special form of the cantata, came into significant popularity in the second half of the seventeenth century, although all of the composers who have been described as

EXAMPLE 4.8 Cesti, *Languia già l'alba,* "Mi dipinge amabil sorte"

contributing to the history of the Roman cantata also wrote some duets. Composers in Bologna following Cazzati's *Duetti per camera,* Op. 66 (Bologna, 1677), also composed a number of duet books. Steffani was born in Castelfranco near Padua. However, except for his period of study in Rome with Ercole Bernabei between 1672 and 1674, Steffani's career was entirely north of the Alps at the courts in Munich, Hanover, and Düsseldorf.

Steffani's duet cantatas, which have been compared to Corelli's trio sonatas in their significance to music history, were disseminated throughout Europe in an enormous number of copies. They were important for the spread of Italian vocal concepts and to the establishment of Italian formal procedures outside of Italy. The diversity of forms reflects the state of vocal chamber music from the middle of the century.[68] Some resembling madrigals from early in the century are largely through-composed for both voices. Another type consists of "aria" duets, in which da capo forms predominate (the work will often end with a repeat of the opening duet). In some, the sequence of movements will include solo arias, while recitative sections are infrequent. The third type of duet is more typical of solo cantatas with an alternation of solo arias or recitatives with duet movements. The recitatives frequently end with an extended passage of arioso. Two main features of these duets stand out for their historical significance: (1) the operatic vocal style, Italian vocal lyricism, and frequent reliance on lengthy melismatic passages included for their display of virtuosity; and (2) the outstanding demonstration of contrapuntal techniques realized in the two-part vocal writing combined with the harmonic support of the continuo bass. (This emphasis on contrapuntal textures indicates a strong influence of German composers.) In Example 4.9,[69] the entire opening measures of the duet "E perché non m'uccidete"

EXAMPLE 4.9   Steffani, "E perché non m'uccidete"

EXAMPLE 4.9 *(continued)*

consist almost entirely of a contrapuntal development of the two highly expressive motives stating and repeating the opening two lines of text. The continuo bass also has contrapuntal interest and the highly charged text is appropriately expressed with numerous suspensions, especially in the climactic last eight measures of the example.

This is an important step forward from the vocal duet writing found in Venetian opera and the oratorio in which the two parts usually proceed in parallel thirds and sixths. By the end of the century, the lingering distrust of counterpoint established by the Camerata and observed by many early-seventeenth-century composers had largely vanished. Steffani's duets show great contrapuntal skill. And the same stylistic development occurs at this time in Italian chamber music, especially the trio sonata. Thus, on the threshold of the eighteenth century, Italian composers have prepared the way for continuing musical changes of form and style that would influence most of the next generations of European composers. Steffani's chamber duets are an inseparable part of the self-renewing process of compositional styles in the Baroque of the early eighteenth century.

Instrumental Music

Instrumental music in countless forms has always existed in Western culture as it has in other contemporary and earlier cultures. And although Western civilization from the Middle Ages through the seventeenth century was dominated by vocal music, instrumental forms had grown progressively more prominent in succeeding generations, the result of changes in society and the invention of printing. By the end of the sixteenth century instrumental music had been largely emancipated from vocal music, and especially Italian publishers issued a significant volume of music for instruments.[70] This music consisted of various types: vocal music, such as chansons, madrigals, lieder, motets, and Masses, arranged for instruments; arrangements of pre-existing melodies, especially plainchant, for keyboard instruments; variations, including those on ground basses and recurring chordal progressions; ricercars, fantasias, and canzonas; preludes, preambles, and toccatas in an idiomatic style for solo instruments; dance music; and songs composed for lute and solo voice. Most of the ensemble music could be performed by more than one arrangement of instruments and even music for the keyboard and plucked strings was playable on a variety of instruments. As has been seen with vocal music at the turn of the seventeenth century, composers of instrumental music at this time also continued to employ many of these sixteenth-century forms. However, the radically new concept of monody and the invention of the basso continuo quickly led to significant modifications and ultimately new types and forms of instrumental music. The result was an immeasurable volume of instrumental music that was a major legacy created by Italian composers by the end of the century. The most significant aspects of that legacy in the seventeenth century will be examined in the categories of chamber and keyboard music.

Chamber Music

The instrumental equivalent to the cantata for one or two voices and continuo became the "trio" sonata.[71] The gradual formalizing of a "trio" sonata concept took place in Italy during the seventeenth century, until at the end of the century a somewhat stereotypic but classic form was created by Arcangelo Corelli (see Chapter 5). Confusion in the musicological literature has long existed as to the correct labeling of the "trio" sonata and other solo works for from one to four melody instruments. The problem arises when the harmonic continuo instrument is or is not included in the work's description.[72] It is preferable to adapt a consistent terminology as is usually found in the seventeenth-century sources of North Italian composers. Accordingly, the harmonic continuo instrument is not included in the numerical designation: Sonatas *à2* and *à3* were performed by two and three melodic instruments with a continuo instrument usually giving harmonic support. One of the instruments *à3* could be a tenor or bass that participated in the imitative texture (and required a separate part book). Usually in this case the continuo instrument doubles and often simplifies the lowest part. Even with this attempted standard of classification a lack of consistency occurs when the continuo bass has a dual character, at times giving only harmonic support and at other times in the same composition participating in the contrapuntal texture.

The rapid growth of instrumental ensemble music for solo instruments precludes any successful summary. The variety of opposing trends, the regional spread of composers, the often conflicting stylistic and formal achievements and, regrettably, the scarcity of available sources all impede an examination of instrumental music for small ensembles.[73] Yet by the 1630s this music had spread throughout the Italian peninsula and across the Alps to Italianate courts such as those at Vienna, Munich, and Dresden. Looking back to the first decades of the new century one finds that many ensembles continued to be written for varying numbers of instruments, with four and eight being most frequent. The canzona texture continued to be the most popular, and it would become a primary model for the developing instrumental sonata. Often the Renaissance practice continued, which left open the choice of instruments to be employed and also permitted arranging these "trio" compositions for organ solo. It is of relevant importance that the development of the "trio" sonata throughout the century was most often achieved by composers who were organists and who were skilled in contrapuntal practices. Through the first half of the century a frequent designation of instruments for performing these works was *violino o cornetto,* and only after the 1630s did a true violin idiom begin to take the place of music playable by violin or cornetto. Disconcerting also to those wishing uniformity in place of inconsistency are the varied titles applied to this music during most of the century with canzona, sinfonia, and sonata being the most common but not by any means mutually exclusive.[74]

The earliest known work of any significance for three solo instruments appears in the *Concerti ecclesiastici* (Milan, 1610) by Giovanni Paolo Cima (c. 1570–1630): *Sonata a tre per il violino, cornetto, e violone.*[75] There is no continuo part but, rather, a partitura giving the three instrumental parts in score. Features of this forerunner of the "trio" sonata in the first decades of the century include the organization into six continuous subsections, a texture based on antiphonal rather than linear counterpoint, and soloistic statements of the thematic material with the two treble parts usually paired against the bass.

Until the 1630s, however, Venice was the center of developments for instrumental music as it was for vocal music. Here Biagio Marini (1594–1663) published his Op. 1, *Affetti musicale* in 1617, the first Venetian work consisting entirely of instrumental works for small ensemble. It contains sinfonias, canzonas, sonatas, and dances for one or two violins or cornetti and bass. Another early Venetian collection is Dario Castello's two books of *Sonate concertate in stile moderno* "to be played on organ or harpsichord with various instruments" (Venice, 1621–1629). Twenty-four of the twenty-nine pieces are for combinations of less than four instruments. Features of the new Venetian *stile moderno* found in Castello's sonatas include sectionalism based on the most dramatically rhetorical musical contrasts. Startling alternations of affect occur by frequently changing textures, tempos, and dynamic levels. These "patchwork" sonatas of individual sections also have subsections of greatly contrasting music. The goal of raising the passions so evident in vocal music is shared by this instrumental music as well. Another characteristic of Venetian "trio" sonatas are notated passages of elaborate virtuosity. Allsop observes that Venetian chamber works are intrinsically related to the polychoral works of Giovanni Gabrieli. Although reduced to a few parts, they still employ antiphonal rather than strictly polyphonic textures. Based on the Gabrielian style, the Venetian *stile moderno* sonata relies on a rather limited range of textures. These are:[76] *motivic dialogue*—often set off by a rest, exchanged between the two instruments; *antiphonal statement*—the same technique as above, but based on longer subjects; *alternate solos*—lengthy solo passages stated alternately by each instrument; and *parallel movement*—extensive employment of parallel thirds between treble instruments. With so much emphasis on antiphonal style, it is to be expected that another feature of Gabrieli's music, the echo, would also be a common feature in these chamber works.

Among minor composers in Venice publishing examples of few-voiced chamber works up to the 1630s was Giovanni Battista Riccio. In the Veneto, further adaptations of the Venetian *stile moderno* sonata were made by Biago Marini (who returned to Brescia from Venice in 1620). His particular accomplishment was to establish the genre of solo sonata with continuo, with advances in violin technique including double stops.[77] Solo sonatas appear first in his Op. 1, *Affetti musicali* (Venice, 1617). Among the composers writing "trios" at the Mantuan court were Giovanni Battista Buonamente (?–1642) and the Mantuan monk, Giuseppe Scarani. It was, however, Salamone Rossi (1570–c. 1630) who made significant contributions to instrumental chamber music.

Rossi has, with some exaggeration, been viewed as having "established" the trio sonata, "the classic medium of baroque chamber music."[78] He published four impressive books containing 116 instrumental pieces, almost all of them in trio texture. Books I (1607) and II (1608) consist largely of *sinfonie* and *gagliarde* for two violas and chitarrone, while Books III (1623) and IV (1622) add *corrente* and *brandi* to the *sinfonie* and *gagliarde* and "various sonatas."[79] Book IV is to be played by two violins and chitarrone (or another similar instrument). In the four books, the sinfonia and gagliarda are most numerous, but they are almost always short pieces averaging between 20 and 30 measures. In the last two books, however, the sonatas, because they tend to be considerably longer, dominate and reflect a more contemporary aspect of the solo instrumental works. There are six sonatas in free form and thirteen in variation form based on bass tunes or patterns. The variation sonatas are somewhat more virtuosic than the free ones, but in all of them the musical style is decidedly conservative. There is little musical contrast between the sections of what are usually binary forms with the most conventional use of dissonances. Nor does one find any apparent influences of the more radical and dramatic Venetian *stile moderno*. Except for their trio texture, there is no connection between Rossi's sonatas and those written by composers later in the century. Yet these are true trios, with two melody instruments in duet contrasted to a continuo bass that supports but seldom shares in the musical developments of the upper parts (see Example 4.10[80]).

At Modena, Marco Uccellini (c. 1603–1680), composer and priest at the Estense court, stands out as a major figure among instrumental composers of the century. He published eight collections of instrumental music (the first, Op. 1, is lost). Seven books published between 1639 and 1667 contain free and variation sonatas as well as sinfonias and many dances. The *Sonate over canzoni*, Op. V was the first publication to consist almost entirely of solo violin and continuo compositions.[81] As a violinist, Uccellini placed some significance on expanding violin technique, often using fifth and sixth positions and indicating bowing slurs, tremolos, and scordatura. Particularly in the *à2* works his writing exhibits a more characteristic violinistic style than has generally been true in earlier Italians, with rapid passagework, including arpeggios, in sixteenth and even thirty-second notes, and a whole catalogue of rapid figurations. Also noteworthy is the growing importance of sequential repetitions of motives and the expanding employment of keys (such as C minor, B flat major, E flat major, B minor, and A major). While the sonatas consist of a series of subsections, these are given order and relationships through the procedures of variation, progressive diminution, and occasional repetitions of sections.

By mid-century, North Italian and Roman composers began to view the instrumental sonata as a succession of stylistically predetermined sections. This stage of formal organization foretells the standardization of movements of the Corellian sonatas to appear at the end of the century. The Cremonese organist Tarquinio Merula (1594 or 1595–1665) published four books of canzonas, the first in 1615 for *à4* ensemble, but the later ones (1632?,

EXAMPLE 4.10   Rossi, from Book IV, Sonata quarta

1637, and 1651) all give emphasis to *à2* and *à3* textures.[82] The 1637 book, Op. 12, is entitled: *Canzoni over sonate concerte per chiesa e camera a due et a tre.* This is the earliest known reference to works suitable for "church" or "chamber" performance, and the designation is quite rare in mid-century collections. Interesting is the fact that the designations are connected to the canzonas, disproving the frequent assumption that canzonas and sonatas were suitable solely for church performances. Although no rigid pattern of sections is found, a scheme, largely for *à3* compositions, tends to be an opening fugue/tripla (implying a faster tempo), a duple homophonic/sequential section, followed by an imitative section, and a closing coda that often has a thematic relationship with the opening fugue. Book IV (1651) canzonas, while more violinistic in string writing, are also less strictly contrapuntal. When the opening section begins imitatively, it seldom has fugal characteristics, because the parts frequently become antiphonal or one melody supported by simple figurations in the remaining parts. Texture in *à2* works avoids fugal structure and relies heavily on harmonically accompanied melodies in dialogue.[83] Most significant, perhaps, is the clear avoidance of a Venetian patchwork style, for the sections tend to be lengthy and even with meter and texture changes they fit together without extreme contrasts.

The fame of Maurizio Cazzati (1616–1678) resides in his major vocal and instrumental works composed while *maestro di cappella* at San Petronio in Bologna (1657–1671). His earlier career, however, included positions at Mantua, Bozzolo, Ferrara, and Bergamo. Among his ten instrumental collections four contain sonatas in *à2* and *à3* textures and encompass some twenty-eight years of sonata history (Op. 2, 1642; Op. 8, 1648; Op. 18, 1656; Op. 55, 1670). Here, too, well-defined sections of contrasting tempo and at times meter occur in various forms. Op. 2 shows a preference for fugue, tripla, slow section, da capo. In the Op. 18, the preference is for a fugal movement, a *grave,* a fast *tripla,* and a duple imitative closing section.

Giovanni Maria Bononcini (1642–1678), the first of the distinguished musical family that includes his sons Giovanni and Antonio Maria, was the last important seventeenth-century composer of chamber music whose entire career was spent in Modena. He was probably a student of Uccellini, and in 1673 became *maestro di cappella* of the cathedral. Bononcini was the author of *Il musico prattico* (Bologna, 1673), an important treatise on counterpoint having considerable influence for decades after his death. Of his fourteen *opera,* the first nine as well as the twelfth are string chamber works divided between dances, most of which are presented as *sonate da camera* and *sonate da chiesa.*[84] The dances, variously organized into suites, are among the last in the century still meant for dancing. The sonatas da chiesa are contained in three collections: Op. 1, *Primi fruitti del giardino musicali,* Op. 6, *Sonate da chiesa a due violini,* and Op. 9, *Trattenimenti musicali.* Some development of structure is apparent in these collections. Half of the sonatas in Op. 1 have clear four-movement divisions, four have five movements, and two three movements. The majority retain the earlier formal repetition of the opening movement as the conclusion often accredited to Merula. The later sonatas of Op. 6 employ somewhat more standardized forms with fugue–tripla–slow section–imitative finale being predominant, but with the alternative slow first movement still frequent. The first two collections are for two violins and continuo bass, the third set for two violins, bass, and basso continuo. Bononcini's sonatas, both da camera and da chiesa, have a strong personal character. In part this is the result of his melodic style and musically interesting contrapuntal textures. In the da chiesa sonatas the fugal writing has a marked formal regularity of expositions and strong, violinistic themes, at times of considerable length. The contrapuntal developments employ a fully realized application of sequences, a technique that had been developing during the seventeenth century in Italian music and now became a basic element of musical style for the Baroque period.

Giovanni Legrenzi (1626–1690), a major contributor to opera and sacred music, also composed significant instrumental music during the sixth and seventh decades of the century. More than half of his career took place in Venice. For a decade he was an organist in Bergamo, where he would have had associations with Merula and Cazzati, both employed in Bergamo at the same time. While in Bergamo he published two collections of sonatas: *Sonate à2 e 3,* Op. 2 (1655), and *Sonate da chiesa e da camera . . . à3,* Op. 4 (1656). A third volume of sonatas, Op. 8 (1663), was published while he was in Ferrara and his last volume, *La Cetra,* Op. 10 (1673) after he had settled in Venice. These four collections contain sixty-three sonatas for scorings of various numbers of solo instrumentalists, the trio ensemble being favored. Op. 4 also includes various dances. Legrenzi achieves a personal style that perhaps for the first time in the seventeenth century justifies calling his instrumental music a high achievement of a "middle" Baroque period. He was a master of contrapuntal textures, with exceedingly individualistic, "memorable" thematic ideas for strings that established a stylistic norm influencing composers of violin music for decades and even later attracting composers including J. S. Bach and Handel. Some characteristics of these string melodies are their vital rhythmic energy especially across barlines, effective wide leaps such as octaves, emphasis on triadic figures, and at times repeated notes. Many begin as an extended upbeat, which further impels the melody forward, and all of these and other melodic devices quickly fix the theme in the listener's memory. Example 4.11[85] illustrates several of Legrenzi's typical fugal subjects:

a. Sonata "La Zabarella" à tre, Op. 2, No. 1
b. Sonata "La Benaglia," Op. 4, No. 3
c. Sonata "La Bevilaqua," Op. 8, No. 8
d. Sonata "La Bonacossa," Op. 8, No. 9
e. Sonata "La Boiarda," Op. 8, No. 10
f. Sonata seconda a due violini, Op. 10, No. 2

His command of the tonal structures of his sonatas surpasses the more elementary organizations of his contemporaries. Undoubtedly one of the major composers of Italian opera, Legrenzi was served by the passionate, as well as the tragic, melodic characteristics of Venetian opera in personalizing his instrumental works. Many of his adagios are clearly modeled on operatic *lamentos*. Structures in the first three collections are most often in three sections, but usually these have frequent contrasting interior subsections of shifting meters and tempos. For example, Sonata 6 in Op. 4 (*La Pezzoli*) has three contrasting sections in which the middle consists of four brief subsections of contrasting texture and tempo (although no change of meter, which is somewhat unusual). Only in the last collection composed in Venice is there a marked tendency to expand the sonatas into four distinct parts.

Among the other seventeenth-century Italian composers of chamber sonatas, one of the major figures was Giovanni Battista Vitali (1632–1692) in Bologna. Bologna was second only to Rome in its patronage of music. Some 150 churches existed by 1700, and there was an especially significant support for instrumental music. Among its churches the great Basilica of San Petronio was a particularly influential center for both vocal and instrumental music in the century.[86] The appointment of Maurizio Cazzati at San Petronio in 1657 led to an expansion of the *cappella* to some thirty-three musicians. Cazzati's student, Giovanni Battista Vitali, a singer and performer on the violoncino (an early form of the violoncello) at San Petronio, was also a member of the Accademia Filarmonica. This important catalyst to the study and performance of music was founded in 1666 by musicians in the city. These influences helped to make Bologna a center of sonata creativity in the late seventeenth century.

Vitali published twelve collections of violin music. Most of these contain important collections of dances, including the *Sonate da camera,* Op. 14 (1692) published posthumously by his son Tomaso. The sonatas are found mainly in three publications, *Sonate a due violini,* Op. 2 (1667), *Sonate a due, tre, quattro, e cinque,* Op. 5 (1669), and *Sonate da chiesa a due violini,* Op. 9 (1684).[87] Even more than Legrenzi, Vitali was an outstanding contrapuntalist.[88] In the first two collections the emphasis was placed on *à2* (two violins and continuo) scoring, but also including a few for two violins, violone, and continuo and for four or five instruments. For the late collection, published in the year of Corelli's Op. 1, the scoring is entirely *à2*. There is in the first two collections clear evidence of a development toward structural regularity, with the most common formula found in Op. 5 being four movements: I, allegro (fugue); II, grave; III, 3/2 largo; and IV, grave—allegro. An important change appears in the *à2* sonatas, in which Vitali no longer avoided extensive contrapuntal writing as had been the case in earlier composers' works. Op. 9 exhibits most often a pattern of alternating movements of slow/fast or the reverse, with five and six movements employed most frequently. Slow introductions to the opening fugue occur and the internal movements usually alternate grave and tripla (fast) tempos. Subject themes in

EXAMPLE 4.11   Excerpts from Legrenzi's sonatas

a. Sonata "La Zabarella" a tre, Op. 2, No. 1

b. Sonata "La Benaglia," Op. 4, No. 3

EXAMPLE 4.11 (*continued*)

c. Sonata "La Bevilaqua," Op. 8, No. 8

d. Sonata "La Bonacossa," Op. 8, No. 9

EXAMPLE 4.11 (*continued*)

e. Sonata "La Boiarda," Op. 8, No. 10

f. Sonata seconda a due violini, Op. 10, No. 2

Vitali's fugues are even more than in Legrenzi's broadly evocative of the developments of Italian violin technique, and they reflect a concept of Italian string music to reach its greatest perfection in subsequent evolving of the Italian orchestral concerto.

Notable developers of the solo sonata in Bologna were Pietro degli Antonii (1639–1720), Domenico Gabrielli (1659–1690), and his student Giuseppe Jacchini (c. 1667–1727).

Antonii published in his Op. 1 (1670) and Op. 3 (1671) collections of paired dances. Op. 4 (1676) and Op. 5 (1686) are for solo violin and continuo bass in several sections. Significant in these works is the prominence of slow sections written with the pathos and style of operatic arias.[89] Gabrielli and Jacchini are important for having written some of the first sonatas for cello.

Keyboard Music

In the second half of the century, no Italian composer of keyboard music achieved the fame of Frescobaldi. Less than a dozen composers can be identified for whom keyboard music has been preserved. Among them probably the most significant are: Bernardo Storace, Gregorio Strozzi (c. 1615–after 1687), Fabrizio Fontana (?c. 1610–1695), Luigi Battiferri (1600/10–1682 or later), and Bernardo Pasquini (1637–1710).[90] Clearly, a considerable repertory of organ and harpsichord music remains to be discovered or is lost.

An impressive collection of keyboard works, perhaps the first to be preserved from the second half of the seventeenth century in Italy, is by an unknown composer of southern Italy, Bernardo Storace: *Selva di varie compositioni d'intavolatura per cimbalo ed organo* (Venice, 1664). The collection, in keyboard score, is not unlike other known keyboard publications in Italy during the latter half of the century. The emphasis is on variations employing such standard themes as the *passo e mezzo, Romanesca, Spagnoletta, Monica, Ruggiero, Folia, Passacagli, Ciaccona,* and *Balletto.* There are also two correntes, two toccatas with canzonas, two ricercars, and a pastorale, for a total of twenty-three compositions. Four separate sets of variations on the passacaglia give an impressive indication of this composer's ability. Possibly inspired by Frescobaldi"s "100" variations on the passacaglia formula, Storace creates more than three hundred variations on the same bass.[91] In addition to contrasts of meter and mode, these short two- or four-bar variations are an encyclopedic demonstration of southern Italian keyboard styles and techniques. What make these variations and much of the rest of the keyboard pieces in the volume impressive are the musical vitality, imaginative treatment of keyboard figurations, and sense of structural logic that separate Storace's art from the routine and often conventional keyboard writing of his contemporaries. One would like to know more about this composer.

Another important collection of keyboard pieces from southern Italy is the *Capricci da sonare cembali, et organi,* Op. 4 (Naples, 1687) by Gregorio Strozzi. Here, too, the collection is made up largely of conventional keyboard forms, printed in partitura, including contrapuntal capriccios, ricercars, and sonatas, dances, variations on the romanesca and passacaglia, and another intabulation of Arcadelt's *Ancideteme pur.* The first capriccio is perhaps one of the last of countless settings of the hexachord ut, re, mi, fa, sol, la in nine contrasting sections. The ricercars employ two, three, or four themes simultaneously, a technique reminiscent of Frescobaldi's fantasias. Most interesting are the four toccatas. Here Strozzi seems liberated from contrapuntal constraints, and composes exuberantly, with brilliant keyboard figurations between the hands, numerous indications of trills, and instructions such as *arpeggiando, gruppeggiando, accentando,* and *stretto.* The collection of twelve ricercars (Bologna, 1669) by the Ferrarese organist Luigi Battiferri, are contrapuntal studies for organ worthy of his teacher. There is a double fugue on two *soggetti* and some have four, five, or six subjects, which Johann J. Fux, the Viennese composer and famous theorist (*Gradus ad Parnassum*), is known to have copied. Another similar collection of *Ricercari* (Rome, 1677) by Fabrizio Fontana also has a close relationship with Frescobaldi's fantasias.

For the largest number of keyboard works by an Italian at the end of the seventeenth century, one turns to Bernardo Pasquini. He spent his entire adult life in Rome, becoming organist at St. Maria Maggiore in 1663 and one year later also at St. Maria in Aracoeli. He was well known as a virtuoso harpsichordist for Prince Giambattista Borghese, and he frequented the musical circles of the Colonnas, Pamphilis, Ottobonis, and Queen Christina of Sweden. He was equally famous as a teacher and composer of numerous operas, oratorios, motets, and cantatas. Unfortunately, a great deal of his music is lost including much of it for keyboard. Most of the latter that remains is found in four autograph manuscripts prepared for his nephew, Bernardo Felice Ricordati.[92] These include eleven works in the usual array of contrapuntal studies, thirty-five toccatas (at times called tastatas), twenty-two variation sets, seventeen suites, twenty-two arias, and various single dances. Most unusual are twenty-eight sonatas, fourteen for one harpsichord and fourteen for two harpsichords, notated only as figured basses. The contrapuntal pieces are rather routine, with excessive repetitions of mostly conventional subjects and little variety in episodic sections. The toccatas are elementary in their harmonic and melodic content, frequently with very long passages of the simplest kinds of keyboard figures and runs. Harmonies are decisively diatonic and with almost no chromaticism and no unusual modulations. Most of them consist of only one section, in contrast with the multisectional characteristics of earlier composers' toccatas. Of greater musical interest are the suites and also some of the variations. Pasquini seems to be the first composer in Italy to write suites in two, three, or four related movements in the same key. The majority begin with an alemanda and include a corrente, and conclude with a giga. There are no sarabands. The forms are binary with each section repeated. In these short dance forms Pasquini clearly is writing for the harp-

EXAMPLE 4.12   Pasquini, Alemanda from F major suite

sichord. The textures are open, in freely inventive motivic counterpoint that often has the character of the French *style brisé*. The melodies are simple but with a considerable variety of lyrical ideas (see Example 4.12[93]). They suggest the more popular melodic writing of the opera composer, and more than any other music by this composer reflect the change that has come to Italian musical style at the end of the century.

CHAPTER FIVE

Arcangelo Corelli (1653–1713) and Alessandro Scarlatti (1660–1725)

AT FIRST GLANCE it would appear that Arcangelo Corelli and Alessandro Scarlatti have little in common except as contemporary Italian composers of the late seventeenth century. Indeed, they are related most significantly as opposites, but their musical accomplishments taken together effectively summarize much of what was achieved in music in Italy by the end of the seventeenth century. Corelli was from northern Italy, born on 17 February 1653 in Fusignano, a town between Bologna and Ravenna. He studied violin in Bologna, which as has been shown, was a center for the development of instrumental music. As far as is known Corelli wrote no vocal music, and almost all of his compositions are preserved in just six published collections: four of string chamber music, one of solo violin sonatas, and one of concertos for string orchestra. Each contains twelve compositions. During the final quarter of the seventeenth century, Corelli lived in Rome where he became one of the most celebrated among violinists and teachers. His patrons included Queen Christina, later Cardinal Pamphili, and finally Cardinal Pietro Ottoboni. Corelli's works were sold throughout Europe in great numbers of reprints and arrangements, selections, and pastiches for various instruments and even for voice. Op. 1 had 39 editions before the end of the eighteenth century; Op. 2, 41; Op. 3, 37; Op. 4, 39; Op. 5, 36. In addition, numerous manuscript copies were circulated.[1] The concerti grossi, Op. 6 (1714) quickly became models for an outpouring of concertos by composers such as Geminiani, Gasparini, Venturini, and Castrucci. In England, Corelli's chamber sonatas and the Op. 6 concertos remained throughout the eighteenth century the most popular of those by any composer including Handel. Corelli was highly honored by being buried in the Roman Pantheon (St. Maria della Rotonda).

Alessandro Scarlatti was born in Palermo, Sicily, at the opposite end of the Italian peninsula from Fusignano on 2 May 1660. From the age of twelve he lived in Rome, where he received musical training by unidentified teachers, although possibly including Carissimi. His career was divided primarily between Rome and Naples. In Rome, Scarlatti found support from many of the same patrons as his contemporary Corelli. Scarlatti's first patron was Queen Christina of Sweden, who employed him as her *maestro di cappella*. Other influential Roman nobles were the cardinals Benedetto Pamphili and Pietro Ottoboni. He was also music director of St. Gerolamo della Carità. In 1684 he became the *maestro di cappella* for the Spanish viceroy in Naples. For eighteen years, Scarlatti wrote an enormous number of vocal works, operas, serenatas, oratorios, and cantatas. It was these works that established Scarlatti as a famous composer in Italy and in much of the rest of Europe. It is this vast corpus of music that makes him the most representative Italian composer of vocal music at the end of the seventeenth century. By 1702, however, in part as a result of the result of the War of the Spanish Succession, Naples no longer seemed a secure place for his court position. His hope to serve Prince Ferdinando de' Medici in Florence did not materialize, although Scarlatti wrote a number of important works for the prince including oratorios, other church music, and at least four operas (lost). At the end of 1703, he accepted the somewhat inferior post in Rome as assistant music director at St. Maria Maggiore, and perhaps also entered the service of Cardinal Ottoboni. In 1704 he was raised to *maestro di cappella* at St. Maria Maggiore and became very active writing music for his patrons, now including also the Marquis Francesco Maria Ruspoli. In 1709 Scarlatti returned to his old position in Naples and he remained for a decade. In 1718 he was again in Rome where for four years he produced the last of his operas. He retired to Naples in 1722. He died three years later, and was buried in the Cecilia chapel at St. Maria di Montesanto. Clearly, previous judgments of Scarlatti as a founder of a "Neapolitan School" in the eighteenth century have misread the composer's accomplishments. They are, whether as cantatas, oratorios, or operas, the crowning achievements of these musical forms in Italy for the latter half of the seventeenth century and the first decades of the eighteenth century. And they demonstrate for the most part that Scarlatti's musical roots were anchored in Roman and Venetian musical developments.

Corelli's Chamber Sonatas

Corelli was the first composer to achieve fame and some degree of immortality solely based on instrumental music. No other seventeenth-century composer's reputation rested on such a small number of compositions as Corelli's. Only a handful of his published works exist in addition to the six *opera.*[2] It would seem, however, from various accounts of Corelli's career in Rome as violinist and composer, that a large number of his compositions were not published in his lifetime and were subsequently lost. This fact destroys the long-held myth that Corelli gave for publication everything he had composed.

Corelli is generally considered to be a "classicist" among his contemporaries, a label that has merit if it means one who seeks perfection—idealization of forms and styles. Although in Rome from at least 1675, Corelli did not publish his first sonatas until 1681. Op. 2 followed four years later in 1685, Op. 3 in 1689, and Op. 4 in 1694. He composed slowly within self-determined formal and stylistic limitations, and he frequently revised his works before allowing them to be published. In a letter of 1708, Corelli refers to feelings of inadequacy as a composer and that "after many and extensive revisions I have hardly had the confidence to expose to the public the few works which I have sent to the press."[3] The idealization of formal order is paramount in the five *opera*, for each contains twelve sonatas. The first four *opera* alternate two books of church sonatas (Opp. 1 and 3) with two books of chamber sonatas (Opp. 2 and 4). Op. 5 contains six solo violin church sonatas, five chamber sonatas, and the famous capstone to his chamber music, the variations on the *folia*. There are twice twelve statements of the folia bass (variation 20 is repeated). Even his last and posthumous publication of orchestra concertos, Op. 6, consists of twelve works, eight in church style, four in chamber style.

The two books of church sonatas are all *à3*, that is they have a bass part that, with notable exceptions, participates in the development of the thematic materials of the two violin parts. These sonatas are given the alternative scoring of two violins, and either violone or archlute with bass for organ; and the chamber sonatas, two violins, and either violone or harpsichord. One well-known feature of the sonatas is their four-movement, slow–fast–slow–fast structure, even if only about half of the sonatas exhibit this feature. While the stylistic parameters of the sonatas are limited, which for the most part sets them apart from the chamber sonatas of his contemporaries and predecessors, there are strong suggestions of influences from both Bologna and Rome.[4] Overlooked generally is the significance of Palestrina on Corelli's works, an influence that can be traced to Corelli's contrapuntal studies with Matteo Simonelli (c. 1618–1696), a well-known Roman composer and singer in the Cappella Sistina.[5] The rebirth of contrapuntal style in Italian music has been discussed earlier. With Corelli there is every indication that one of the goals of his chamber sonatas was to achieve an integration and balance between the contrapuntal and the homophonic of dance textures on the foundation of a basso continuo and its diatonic harmony. Even while Corelli pointedly separates church sonatas from chamber sonatas, at the same time he employs forms and styles of the church sonata in his chamber works, and forms and dance styles of the chamber sonatas in his church works.

Other evidence of the limitations Corelli placed on his works are: the limited ranges for the instruments, with violins never exceeding third position; most of the individual movements of relatively short duration; and no extreme virtuosity. The harmony is severely diatonic, avoiding any emphasis on chromaticism with the notable exception of a single fugue subject in Op. 1, No. 11 (see Example 5.2a).

Within these "classic" parameters, however, the result remains forty-eight sonatas of considerable variety. It has been suggested that Corelli's goal was to create in the four *opera* something akin to a set of *Kunstbücher*, four volumes presenting every facet of the composer's art and craft in encyclopedic dimensions.[6] Each opus becomes a musical monument and is dedicated to one of his supportive Maecenas: I. Queen Christina of Sweden, II. Cardinal Pamphili, III. Duke Francesco II of Modena, and IV. Cardinal Ottoboni.

The church sonatas, like the chamber works, have such a considerable variety of movements that no selection of examples can convey the richness of ideas. The most common organization consists of a slow duple–a fugue–a slow triple–and an imitative triple finale. Another aspect of the contrasts between movements is that each has a different affect. Some of the church sonatas open exceptionally with improvisatory-like displays of violin virtuosity over long-held pedal basses, for example, in Op. 1, No. 4 and No. 9, and in Op. 3, No. 6 and No. 12. No. 12 in particular was certainly meant to open the last sonata in the series with a brilliant and difficult technical display by the violinists. Most typical, however, are the opening grave movements. These are not simply slow introductions but independent movements having serious and even poignant expressiveness. They are a distinctive contribution by Corelli to the trio sonata concept. For example, the Grave from Op. 3, No. 6[7] is a microcosm of Corelli's most searing emotionalism (see Example 5.1).

In motet style, in three-voice imitation, the movement begins with a leap of a minor sixth, an *exclamatio* typical of polyphonic motets but also a frequent device in monodies with sad or tragic words. The three strings imitate the affective power and beauty of the voice. The structure is typical of these opening movements, an AAB, with the second A in the dominant. The writing is "Palestrinian" in its careful preparation and resolution of dissonances, and this employment of dissonances is Corelli's characteristic means for achieving this type of expressiveness. Few bars are without suspended dissonances of the seventh or Corelli's favorite ninths (only in the opening statement, in its repetition at the dominant, and in the cadences of resolution are they omitted). The B section (m. 10) is one of continuous increase of dissonant tensions created by suspensions. Each of the strong beats has a dissonance. They begin to accumulate in bar 14 as the two violins move to their upper range and the climactic bars 16 and 17 consist of the highest note in violin I, a minor second between the violins and a ninth between the second violin and the bass. This peak

EXAMPLE 5.1 Corelli, *Grave* from Op. 3, No. 6

of tensions quickly relaxes into more suspensions and a surprising collapse of the harmony into a Neapolitan sixth in bar 17.

The concept of *Kunstbuch* has particular meaning when examining the frequently highly imitative second movements, which are usually classified simply as fugues. Most of them are "fugal," with the conventional opening statement of a theme or subject, but the treatments of the subject vary greatly in structure and style, and many defy any codification. Corelli provides a cross section of imitative procedures applicable to the trio sonata texture drawn from a number of sources.[8] A few samples of the opening section (see Example 5.2) will illustrate some of the varieties of themes and approach found in these fugal compositions: 2a, a two-part structure with the only chromatic theme in the sonatas; 2b, canzona-like two-part imitation without bass participation; 2c, violinistic patterns inherent in harmonic progression; 2d, a subject of motivic and rhythmic strength.

The internal slow movement in triple meter found in the majority of the church sonatas, more than any other movement, has roots in the operatic vocal style of the mid-century. The adagio tempo and the slow expressive duet writing of the two violins, with

EXAMPLE 5.2

a. Corelli, Op. 1, No. 11

EXAMPLE 5.2 (*continued*)

b. Corelli, Op. 1, No. 12

EXAMPLE 5.2 (*continued*)

c. Corelli, Op. 3, No. 5

d. Corelli, Op. 3, No. 9

EXAMPLE 5.3   Corelli, Op. 3, No. 7, third movement

numerous expressive suspensions of sevenths and ninths, all have a common bond with slow triple arias in Venetian opera and in the numerous cantatas generated by the same vocal and stylistic influences. It would not be difficult to imagine words of a *lamento* applied to many of these movements, including the one in Example 5.3.

The last movements are usually of substantial length, most frequently in simple or compound triple meters, and many of them suggest dance movements, especially the gigue. Some, especially in Op. 3, have the dance characteristic of binary form. The writing is at times fugal, although the majority are more or less homophonic with imitative openings and interior passages. Many of them, in part because of the quick tempos and considerable

EXAMPLE 5.4 Corelli, Op. 3, No. 5, last movement

passagework, are among the technically challenging movements of these sonatas. Example 5.4 is a typical giguelike movement with no true imitation except for the opening presentation of the theme in the three parts.

The church sonatas' overall stylistic unity is contained in their contrapuntal character, most especially in the various fugal movements. The chamber sonatas, in contrast, achieve their unity by emphasizing dance forms and a generally bass-supported, homophonic idiom. They are true *à2* sonatas in which, with few exceptions, the bass part does not participate in the musical development of the two violin parts. In many movements, however, "walking" or in some instances "running" basses lend considerable musical interest to the strong concentration of musical ideas in the first violin with support and sometimes antiphonal responses by the second violin.[9] Op. 2 has seven sonatas in four parts, four in three parts, and one set of variations on the *ciaconna*. Op. 4, in contrast, stresses the three-movement form for seven sonatas with only five in four movements. In Op. 2 every sonata includes an allemanda, as well as other dances from among the corrente, sarabanda, gavotta, and giga. Op. 4 gives greater emphasis to the corrente in eight sonatas, while the allemanda remains the next most important dance in seven of the sonatas. Except in three works, all the sonatas of Op. 2 begin with a preludio, as does each sonata in Op. 4. Notably, all of the preludes are slow (Op. 4, No. 6 and No. 10 have slow–fast–slow preludes) with textures that are much more contrapuntal, at times in three true parts, which clearly introduces church sonata style into these chamber works. For example, the prelude in Example 5.5 imitates the slow, triple meter movements of the church sonatas.

EXAMPLE 5.5   Corelli, Op. 4, No. 8, *Preludio*

SOLO VIOLIN SONATAS, OP. 5

While not the first published collection of solo violin sonatas, Corelli's Op. 5, published in 1700, six years after his final set of chamber sonatas, were the most frequently performed in the eighteenth century. They are divided into six church and five chamber sonatas, concluding with the famous twenty-four variations on the *folia*. These twelve compositions for "violin and violone or harpsichord" became models for violin sonatas written in England and the rest of Europe. In addition, they served and still serve students as valuable technical studies.[10] As with the chamber sonatas, their popularity resulted from the perfection of their formal and stylistic character and the particular lyrical beauty of their slow movements. Technically, the solo sonatas incorporate everything Corelli expected of a violinist, including

EXAMPLE 5.6   Corelli, Op. 5, No. 2, *Grave*

a number of challenges such as rapid bowing technique; playing contrapuntal movements with pure intonation, especially with the long passages of double stops in fugues; realizing passages of triple and quadruple stops in "arpeggio"; passages of *bariolage* (alternating open strings and stopped tones); over-the-strings passages; and *detaché*.[11]

The formal emphasis is on five movements, for all of the church sonatas and two of the chamber sonatas. Three of the latter group are in four movements. All of the church sonatas begin with a slow and expressive first movement followed by a fast fugue. Movements three through five alternate either slow–fast–fast or fast–slow–fast. Except for Sonata No. 4, all of the slow movements are in a triple meter and closely resemble similar movements in the church trio sonatas. Sonata No. 1 ends with a fugue, and all the others with a giga (sonatas 3 and 5) or a dancelike finale. All of the central fast movements (except for No. 5) are etudelike, with rapid passagework either in continuous eighths or sixteenths. The five chamber sonatas begin with a preludio, and continue with a group of dances chosen from the allemanda, sarabanda, corrente, gavotta, and giga. Only in the fifth sonata are the dance titles eliminated except for a concluding gavotte.

A number of sources, both printed and manuscript, indicate that Corelli himself and subsequent performers often added elaborate ornamentation to these sonatas. These include the important publication of Etienne Roger and Pierre Mortier (1710) and its reprint by Walsh and Hare, (c. 1711).[12] The publishers comment that "the ornaments are given for all the Adagios as Corelli wished them to be played." For example, the opening *Grave* and the third movement of Sonata No. 2 are given as in Examples 5.6[13] and 5.7.

CONCERTI GROSSI, OP. 6

From the late sixteenth century, "concerto" was a ubiquitous term that could stand for any combination of voices with instruments. It could mean an instrumental ensemble or an orchestra. Also inherent in the term was often the concept of contrast between a solo group and the entire ensemble or *tutti,* as was already the case in those large works for two or more choirs by Giovanni Gabrieli and his contemporaries. There are numerous applications to musical forms of this concept of contrast in vocal as well as instrumental music in the seventeenth century. Some time after the middle of the century the term *concerto grosso* began to be applied to the large instrumental ensemble of a composition in contrast to its "concertino" or little ensemble usually of solo instruments. Apparently it was Alessandro Stradella who first specified this type of divided ensemble in arias of his oratorio *San Giovanni Battista,* in other vocal works, and in instrumental pieces such as a *Sinfonia a violin i e bassi a concertino e concerto grosso distinti.* By the end of the century *concerti grossi* is applied, although with some inconsistency, to the composition itself, as with Giuseppe Torelli's *Concerti grossi,* Op. 8 (Bologna, 1709), and Corelli's *Concerti grossi con duoi violini e violoncello di concertino obligati e duoi altri violini, viola e basso di concerto grossi ad arbitrio che si potranno radoppiare,* Op. 6 (Amsterdam, 1714).

The publication by Etienne Roger in 1714 of Corelli's final opus appeared two years after the composer's death. The dedication to the Electoral Princess of Hanover is dated 3 December 1712, just one month before Corelli's death. As a posthumous publication, it remains uncertain exactly when Corelli composed and put into order the concertos. The great variety of pieces within these works and the somewhat uneven quality of some of them suggest they were written over a period of many years. Verification of this comes from Georg Muffat's preface to his sonatas in concerto form, *Armonico tributo* (Salzburg, 1682), which reported he had heard concerti grossi by Corelli while he was a student in Rome at the beginning of the 1680s. This documentation apparently makes Corelli's concerti the earliest known examples of the concerto grosso.

The twelve concertos of Op. 6 are divided between eight in "church" style and four in "chamber" style. The distinction, however, between the two types is even less clear than with the trio sonatas. Many of the movements of the church concertos are dancelike, although rarely so designated. Concerto No. 4 is without a fugue, and three of the movements are binary with repeated sections. Concerto No. 8, the last of the church type, is inscribed "fatto per la notte di natale" (the famous Christmas concerto) and ends with an atypical movement, *pastorale ad libitum,* which probably originated for a performance in church on Christmas Eve. The number of movements varies between four and eight. The

EXAMPLE 5.7   Corelli, Op. 5, No. 2, *Adagio*

first two concertos have what seems a fairly old-fashioned, canzona-like series of short sections alternating fast and slow tempos. With the exception of No. 4, all of the church style concertos include a fugal movement, although only one, No. 2, places it second after a slow opening movement.

The essential sonority of the concertos is a continuous musical texture highlighted by contrasts of soft (concertino) versus louder (combining concertino and concerto grosso). Corelli has in effect simply expanded the texture of his chamber sonatas by adding an orchestral ensemble of four parts that has almost no independence of thematic content. Often the orchestral tutti continuously doubles the solo ensemble (see Example 5.8). At other times it adds weight to cadential figures. It never sounds alone without the soloists.

Although Corelli's string writing is not virtuosic, the concertos do include more pas-

EXAMPLE 5.8   Corelli, Op. 6, No. 11, *Preludio*

sages of rapid string technique than the chamber works. Most of the writing consists of short scale passages and especially broken chord figurations. Only in the twelfth concerto does the first violin have a lengthy solo (see Example 5.9).

Of considerable difficulty are a number of the continuo bass parts with rapid and continuous sixteenth-note passages (see Example 5.10). Many of the slow movements, usually of rather short duration, serving as a connecting link to two longer movements, are similar. Almost entirely nonthematic and homophonic, they depend on the striking sonorities of dissonances and strong harmonic progressions to create a dramatic affect of

EXAMPLE 5.9   Corelli, Op. 6, No. 12, 2d movement

EXAMPLE 5.9 (*continued*)

tensions and surprises. They frequently end with a Phrygian (IV6) to V cadence leading into the next movement (see Example 5.11).

Corelli was a luminary among musicians working in Rome at the end of the seventeenth century. As a teacher his influence was widely spread by numerous students including well-known violinists such as Castrucci, Gasparini, Geminiani, Somis, and Anet. The perfection of his musical compositions was unique, although it needs to be remembered that he was not the only composer of chamber sonatas or concerti grossi at the end of the

EXAMPLE 5.10   Corelli, Op. 6, No. 11, *Allemanda*

seventeenth century. Familiarity with Corelli's musical style suggests that he was to an extent responsible for solidifying and perfecting a lingua franca, an Italianate concept of instrumental music for strings that appealed to as many non-Italians as Italians for decades. This musical "language" may seem now to be filled with clichés of motive patterns, simple harmonic progressions, conventional dissonant passages, and rather obvious string techniques. However, the enormous popularity of his music in Corelli's lifetime and subsequently proves the contrary.

EXAMPLE 5.11 Corelli, Op. 6, No. 10, *Adagio*

Vocal Chamber Music of Alessandro Scarlatti

With the chamber cantatas, as with the operas and oratorios, Alessandro Scarlatti was the culminating composer of Italian vocal music of the seventeenth century.[14] The exact number of cantatas written by Scarlatti remains unknown. With a total of at least six hundred works for which authorship is largely certain and more than another one hundred possibly by him, he was not only the most prolific and greatest writer of cantatas but also the composer who brought the Italian cantata of the seventeenth century to its musical perfection.[15] The enormous number of cantatas testifies to the role this vocal form played in the aristocratic society that employed Scarlatti. The cantata for solo voice or voices with a continuo accompaniment, and at times the addition of one or two solo winds or strings, became at the end of the century the most popular form of musical entertainment in the palaces of the wealthy. Scarlatti, who served the greatest Maecenas of Rome and Naples, thrived upon their constant demands for new cantatas for these concerts, at times called *conversazioni* or *accademie*. And it is in the cantatas that the full range of Scarlatti's musical genius is preserved. While subsequent composers also contributed to the Italian cantata, it was Alessandro Scarlatti who defined the form in all of its parameters through its declining popularity in the following century. He was, however, seldom an innovator, and his cantatas, like his other music, reflect the achievements of Italian composers of the seventeenth century. Earlier composers, especially Luigi Rossi and Carissimi, but also Cavalli, Stradella, Pasquini, Legrenzi, and Pietro St. Agostini, were all part of Scarlatti's musical inheritance.

Unfortunately, Scarlatti's cantatas, this treasury of music invaluable for the study of the Italian cantata at the end of the seventeenth century, still have not received a comprehensive examination. The reason for this significant lacuna in the history of Italian music lies in musical scholarship's failure to initiate a representative edition of his vast number of works, which now are available in a mere scattering of practical editions.[16] One can, therefore, describe only some of the general characteristics of this music and some of the developments in Scarlatti's concept of the chamber cantata. Except for a few with two voices, all of the cantatas are for one voice, most often for soprano, and the great majority of these are accompanied only by continuo. The poetry is for the most part conventional, most frequently describing the pains (less often the joys) of love, largely between Arcadian figures, such as the dominant presence of Clori, Tirsi, Mitilde, Dorinda, and Fileno. Some of the texts have topics taken from Classical mythology, Roman history, and contemporary events. Others have humorous or sacred subjects.

Three significant periods of cantata composition stand out in Scarlatti's career: in Rome before 1684; his return to Rome from Naples, 1703–1708; and his last years spent largely again in Naples from 1722. To be expected, the earliest cantatas resemble mid-century forms of the major Roman cantata composers, particularly Carissimi. Those that can be examined have a large variety of forms. These may include a particular emphasis on arioso passages within recitatives, prominent occurrences of strophic arias often composed on ground basses, and both textural and musical refrains. Several arias or ariosos may not be separated by intervening recitatives. From the earliest examples, recitatives are usually pointedly expressive of the rhetoric of the texts, through melodic motives, harmonic and tonal surprises, and emphases on appropriately expressive or pictorial words by coloratura passages.

After a lengthy period in Naples and a brief interlude in Florence, where in both places Scarlatti's compositional activity centered on opera, he returned to Rome in 1703. Here he composed numerous cantatas as well as important sacred works, including oratorios. The cantatas and their texts, with notable exceptions, became quite stereotyped in form. Usually limited to two recitatives and two da capo arias, these cantatas are more limited in scope of poetic content and musical duration. Recitatives characteristically have unrhymed strophes in seven and eleven syllables, while arias have rhymed verses within one poetic meter. A frequent characteristic of the arias is for the opening basso continuo theme to be taken up at the entrance of the voice as the thematic basis of the A section. What they do not lack is an inexhaustible source of melodic ideas. Scarlatti's vocal style is not closely related to the broadly lyrical, long-phrased "bel canto" melodies of later Neapolitan cantata and opera composers. Phrases tend to be shorter, contrapuntal interest with the bass line is marked, and vocal virtuosity if present at all is usually restricted to coloraturas expressive

EXAMPLE 5.12   Alessandro Scarlatti, *Care fila in cui d'Amore*

of an important word in the text. See the opening of the second aria in the cantata, *Elitropio d'amor* (see Example 5.12[17]).

Scarlatti's final years spent in Naples produced a number of cantatas that have been described as experimental, especially in view of the unusually complex harmonic language.[18] Now there is a tendency if not a development in Scarlatti's cantatas toward a more overt employment of chromatic harmonies. This would appear to be the result of the composer's continuing efforts to find stronger affective means to express powerful textural emotion. The Dresden court Kapellmeister, Johann David Heinichen, criticized Scarlatti in this regard, calling his harmonies extravagant, which, when part of a composer's musical style, could please only "bizarre amateurs." He suggests no other composer except for d'Astorga had imitated Scarlatti.[19] Heinichen includes one of Scarlatti's "extravagant" cantatas in his treatise (*Lascia, deh lascia al fine di tormentar mi*), and gives detailed, bass note by bass

EXAMPLE 5.13   Alessandro Scarlatti, *Quell'idol' infedele*

note, instructions for an accompanist to realize a continuo accompaniment from the cantata's bass line. His purpose, he states, is that once an accompanist can master similar
"difficult and irregular styles," then he will certainly have nothing to fear from other
common and regular compositions.[20] Example 5.13 gives the opening to the B section from
the second aria of Scarlatti's cantata (*Ti basti amor crudele*[21]) used by Heinichen, which
illustrates the composer's bold chromatic harmonies.

THE ORATORIOS

Scarlatti composed at least thirty-two oratorios between 1679 and 1720, most of them for
Roman churches or private performances for his aristocratic patrons but with several also
heard in other Italian cities including Florence, Venice, and especially Naples. At least
twenty-two are extant.[22] The oratorios reflect as do the cantatas and operas the changing
state of Scarlatti's formal musical development beginning with his first musical training and
experiences in late-seventeenth-century Rome. In all three vocal genres a noticeable transformation of his style takes place from early to late works. Among the early oratorios the
first, *Agar et Ismaele esiliati,* is typical of Roman forms of oratorio evolving from the works
of composers such as Carissimi and Stradella.

Composed for a private performance in 1683, probably in the Pamphili palace, it is
based on a libretto adapted by Giuseppe de Totis from the Old Testament story of Abraham's banishment of Ishmael and his mother Agar into the desert (from *Genesis*). In the
customary two parts, the oratorio is essentially operatic in form and style. *Agar et Ismaele*
is a highly successful dramatic and musical setting by the young Scarlatti. It is scored for
string orchestra and five voice parts. There are no da capo arias, but the work has a
considerable variety of vocal forms: these include duets and a trio; ABA and strophic
melodies in which the second strophe is usually connected by an instrumental ritornello
based on the vocal material; a number of continuo arias, several on ostinato basses, and
arias in 3/2 and slow moving melodies whose popularity goes back as far as early Roman
and Venetian opera. There also are arias of high drama and of considerable dimensions
accompanied by the orchestra. The vocal writing in some instances is quite virtuosic in
employing coloratura, although in general the vocal style is less challenging technically. The
recitatives can be characterized as *semplice,* but this does not fully convey Scarlatti's ever-
careful attention to melodic variety, harmonic tensions, and the dramatic impact of the
text. Through expressive melodic motives, dissonant harmonies, effective vocal leaps and

EXAMPLE 5.14   Alessandro Scarlatti, from *Agar et Ismaele,* Part I

a. Chi non sa che sia dolore

b. Solo il nome han di tormenti

EXAMPLE 5.14 (*continued*)

c. Ma qual'hor per vie nascose

arioso passages, the recitatives are an essential component to the overall effectiveness of the oratorio.

The focus of the libretto places a central emphasis on tragic, lamenting texts that contain some of the work's most powerful music. This is true of Abraham's lament at the close of Part I, a three-strophe text, which the composer divides into three arias in different styles: (1) on an ostinato bass that supplies the motto opening for the voice part. The vocal line frequently interrupted and with embellished passages especially on *dolor, tacer,* and *costanza;* (2) a 6/2 aria with continuous bass line (perhaps suggesting the flow of tears emphasized in the text); and (3) a continuous bass and vocal line, with *affano* affectively stressed by breaking the melodic line with rests (see Example 5.14a–c).

A decade later Scarlatti composed *La Giuditta,* which had performances in Naples in 1693, in Rome at the Collegio Clementino in 1696, and subsequently also in Vienna and Florence. Although still partly reflecting Scarlatti's youthful oratorio style, with frequent ostinato basses, ritornellos between two strophes, as well as conclusions to arias, there is a marked advancement in dramatic scope in part the result of the much more interesting vocal styles. Also, the four-part string ensembles frequently add concertato textures to the arias. In a few instances instrumental color is enlivened by adding trumpets or recorders. In Ozias's *Se la gioia non m'uccide,* the aria becomes a three-part concertato for solo violin and cello, with voice and continuo (see Example 5.15).

Many of the arias are expanded in structure. While the *da capo* is not employed, most of the arias have some form of ABA, with the B section often a separate aria in itself. And the scene between Judith and Holofernes leading to his decapitation is impressively controlled in its suspenseful treatment of the recitatives and a magnificent aria as Judith hesitantly contemplates the sleeping Holofernes before striking the fatal blow. The "Naples" *Giuditta* is the first of Scarlatti's major oratorios.

An exceptional example of Scarlatti's concept of the oratorio is illustrated by *Davidis*

EXAMPLE 5.15 Alessandro Scarlatti, from *La Giuditta,* Part II

pugna et victoria, performed in the Roman Oratorio del SS. Crocifisso, 6 March 1700. The libretto, the only one set by Scarlatti in Latin, gives a greatly simplified version of the biblical story of the battle between the Philistines and Hebrews in which Saul becomes terrified of the giant Goliath, who is slain by the victorious David. There is a *testo,* and apparently a unique employment in the Scarlatti oratorios of a double chorus of eight parts. Two such choruses appear in each part, for eight voices and four additional, independent lines for the two violins and two alto lines of the orchestra. The textural sumptuousness of the choral passages, undoubtedly requiring extended rehearsals, was perhaps made possible by the availability of greater financial support for church celebrations during the Jubilee Year of 1700. While in general the oratorio is similar in styles and forms to earlier

EXAMPLE 5.16 Alessandro Scarlatti, from *Davidis pugna et victoria,* Part II

EXAMPLE 5.16 (*continued*)

oratorios, these choruses must have been exceptional in their dramatic impact, for example, at the end of Part II when the first chorus representing the defeated Philistines cries out in defeat, *Heu, heu, sodales,* and the chorus of Hebrews responds with their jubilant shouts of *Victoria* (see Example 5.16).

In contrast to the large-scale form and dramatic content of *Davidis pugna et victoria* is an oratorio for two voices and instrumental ensemble, *Humanità e Lucifero,* written in 1704. It was performed in Rome at the Collegio Nazarino in September to observe the feast day of the Virgin Mary. In two brief parts of less than an hour of music, which probably were enriched with recited poems written for the occasion, the music has a beguiling simplicity and a rich variety of musical settings of the arias. Humanità, sung by a soprano, relates of the birth of Mary and the impending defeat of Lucifer through the power of goodness of Mary and her future gift to the world. Lucifer, a tenor, proclaims he shall persevere, but is soon defeated by Humanità's prediction that he will fall before the mighty will of Mary who, through her son, will bring peace and love to the world. All of the arias have da capo form and are variously accompanied by the string ensemble and frequent contrasts between tutti passages and solo writing for violin, trumpet, or sopranino recorder. The vocal writing has few challenges except for some coloraturas usually reserved for final syllables of a quatrain. The melodic ideas have arresting variety and are strongly profiled. Overall, the work, which could be considered a dramatic cantata, has a freshness and charm that reveals Scarlatti's growing mastery of the smaller dramatic vocal forms.

That mastery, undoubtedly achieved in part by Scarlatti's immersion in operatic composition, is exemplified in *Cain overo Il primo omicido*. Performed in Venice in 1707 and again in Rome in 1710, this example of Scarlatti's mature oratorios employs an anonymous libretto effectively dramatizing "the first murder," the death of Abel at the hands of Cain (Genesis 4:1–16). Six singers are required for the roles of Adam, Eve, Cain, Abel, the Voice of God, and the Voice of Lucifer. The two-part framework and the conciseness of the music now seem standard for Scarlatti's oratorios. The orchestra consists of a four-part string ensemble with continuo that is expanded at times with one or two solo violins and solo cello. In addition to the three-part sinfonia at the opening, the orchestra also has independent passages to introduce the characters of Lucifer and God. Also conventional, of the twenty-two arias and five duets all are in da capo form, and only three of the arias and one of the duets are not accompanied by some form of instrumental ensemble. The recitatives are *semplice* except for those of the Voice of God, which are accompanied. There is a change in Scarlatti's compositional style regarding bass lines. Regular bass ostinatos are largely eliminated except for a few arias in which a freely modulating form of ostinato-like rhythmic pattern occurs. Bass lines in general are much simpler than in previous oratorios, supportive but not partaking of the contrapuntal texture. At times there are purely harmonic basses; at others, simple "walking" basses; at others, fragmented bass lines. Most notable are the arias in which the bass line is eliminated entirely, for example, in Eve's moving lament, *Sommo Dio, ne'l mio peccato de' miei figli habbi pietà* (see Example 5.17).

Contrapuntal interaction between the voice or voices and the accompanying instruments is the outstanding feature of the great variety and expressivity of the arias, most frequently between the voice and unison violins over the continuo. This oratorio's musical success lies in part in Scarlatti's ability to express within standard, late-seventeenth-century forms a large variety of affects such as laments, sicilianos, pastorals, dance forms, and expressions of joy, and to create through his music real characters entangled in a primordial drama from the Bible.

THE OPERAS

On the autograph of his last opera, *La Griselda*, Scarlatti stated that it was his 114th! If indeed this actually refers to operas composed and not also to other kinds of theatrical works such as serenades, it would suggest that almost half of his operas have been lost and are unknown even by title. Of the eighty-five titles of known operas, only thirty-six seem to exist today in complete scores, and of these only nine have been published in scholarly editions.[23] His enormous achievement with operas spans almost his entire career. They were written primarily for performances in Rome and Naples, some for Florence and Venice, although many of them were often repeated in other cities. One, *Pyrrhus and Demetrius*, first performed in Naples in 1694, was heard at London's Haymarket Theatre in 1708. As with the cantatas and oratorios, the operas give similar witness to this composer's develop-

EXAMPLE 5.17 Alessandro Scarlatti, from *Cain overo Il primo omicido*

ing concepts of dramatic form and content. The inexhaustible inventiveness and extraordinary musical variety of Scarlatti's operas assure his distinction as the greatest Italian composer of the form in the late seventeenth century.[24]

Scarlatti's fame was quickly established with his first opera, *Gli equivoci nel sembiante*. It was presented during Carnival season, 1697 for a private performance in Rome, but through the influence of Queen Christina it was almost immediately repeated 12–14 February at the theater of the Collegio Clementino. Other private performances followed during the year. *Gli equivoci nel sembiante* became one of his most successful operas and was heard in many Italian cities such as Bologna, Naples, Siena, Ravenna, probably Palermo, as well as in Vienna.[25] It is a simple pastoral opera for four singers and four-part string ensemble. Characteristics of Scarlatti's early operas, all in three acts, include the brevity of most of the arias. These frequently are written to modulating basso ostinatos. Continuo arias are in the majority (about 60 percent) to those accompanied by the string ensemble (about 40 percent). Many of the arias have introductory and at times concluding ritornellos. Often for the many strophic texts, the first aria is repeated after an intervening ritornello for the second strophe. There are no da capo indications, but arias are often ABA with the repeated text and music written out in the score. Motto beginnings are frequent, and the vocal writing has few technical challenges. The aria *O mio ben* from act I illustrates a typical modulating ostinato bass, the motto beginning, and the motivic melodic line characteristic of Scarlatti's vocal writing from this period (see Example 5.18).[26]

The earliest surviving *dramma per musica* by Scarlatti is *Il Pompeo*, performed in the Teatro Colonna in 1683. Even after moving to Naples, Scarlatti wrote additional operas commissioned for Roman performances, including *Rosmene* (1686), *Gli equivoci in amore overo La Rosaura* (1690), and *La Statira* (1690). The latter, with a libretto by Cardinal Ottoboni, reopened the Tordinona theater on 5 January 1690, after the theater had been closed for years by papal edict. This opera, like others considered to be *drammi per musica*, is based on a free interpretation of some aspect of ancient history, in this instance concerning events after the defeat of the Persians by Alexander. *La Statira* is in the grand manner appropriate for the festive occasion of its premiere. Each of the three acts has three or four elaborate scene changes, many using machines, and act II ends with an earthquake. The cast requires three sopranos, alto, two tenors, and bass, and large numbers of extras for crowd scenes. The orchestra is still the string ensemble, but with trumpets added for moments of military pomp. The orchestra has prominence because it not only takes part in many of the arias in the concerted manner, but also plays ritornellos at the ends of arias or between the first and second strophes. There are also accompanied recitatives. While some of the arias are accompanied by continuo only, and are often brief, the majority of them have expanded forms, most of which are now da capo (or *dal segno*). Ostinato basses are almost entirely absent. The vocal writing, especially for the character of Alessandro, requires greater agility than that found in previous operas.

During his years in Naples, between 1684 and 1702, Scarlatti composed the greatest number of his operas, perhaps as many as seventy.[27] Only three are accessible in Grout's modern editions: *Massimo Puppieno* (1695), *La caduta de' Decemviri* (1697), and *Eraclea* (1700). They share in general with the Roman works the same formal and musical features (*Eraclea* is preserved without the recitatives). *La caduta de' Decemviri*, however, is the most interesting musically of the three. It was first performed in the Teatro San Bartolomeo in December 1697. As with Scarlatti's earlier operas, the arias are almost entirely in da capo form, and about two-thirds of the sixty-one arias are either accompanied by continuo alone or continuo with an added part for unison violins. A majority of the arias are in expanded

EXAMPLE 5.18   Alessandro Scarlatti, from *Gli equivoci nel sembiante,* act I

forms, although many of them with only continuo accompaniment are brief (around twenty measures or less). Unusual in this opera is the number of arias in 12/8, suggesting the *siciliano,* although not so called by Scarlatti, and many of them have fast tempos and are not dancelike. Particularly noteworthy, this seems to be Scarlatti's first opera to replace the old Venetian introduction of a slow movement followed usually by a fast section and a dance form with an overture in three parts: allegro, slow in triple meter with prominent use of suspensions, and a final, two-part dancelike movement in 12/8. This type of overture becomes the standard Italian *sinfonia* and is found in all of Scarlatti's later operas. Also significant is the emphasized status of the comic servant roles, which are given separate scenes and whose melodic style is very similar to patter-songs, sung quickly with numerous

EXAMPLE 5.19   Alessandro Scarlatti, from *La caduta de' Decemviri,* act I

pauses and repetitive motives all to emphasize the comedy of the scene (see Example 5.19). This musical style became a feature of the developing comic intermezzos in Naples and numerous buffo arias in the second half of the eighteenth century.

Between 1702 and 1709, Scarlatti again lived largely in Rome, although he continued to submit to Prince Fernando at least four operas (now lost) in hopes of gaining an appointment at the Florentine court. In 1707 *Mitridate Eupatore,* one of two operas he composed for Venice, was presented at the Teatro Grimani di S. Giovanni Crisostomo. It is the only opera preserved during this interim period before Scarlatti returned to Naples. Designated a *tragedia per musica,* and in five acts, *Mitridate* shows the final formal design toward which Scarlatti had been advancing in early works: scenes consisting of a simple and regular alternation of recitatives and arias, the formal pattern to dominate *opera seria* through much of the eighteenth century. Another tendency that can be noted already in

EXAMPLE 5.20   Alessandro Scarlatti, from *Tigrane*, act II

previous operas, the gradual reduction of the number of continuo arias, has the end result that in this opera there remain only three short arias; all the rest have a considerable variety of instrumental accompaniments.[28] Perhaps influenced by the Venetian audience for which it was composed, *Mitridate,* in contrast to preceding works, is more serious in its focus, less slanted toward popularizing of melody, and enriched with many slow arias of great pathos.

Scarlatti's final productive years with opera began with his return again to Naples in 1709, where for a decade he composed another eleven works as well as two for Rome. The Neapolitan works include *La principessa fedele* (1710), *Scipione elle Spagne* (1714), *L'amor generoso* (1714), *Tigrane* (1715), *Carlo re d'Allemagna* (1716), *Il trionfo dell'Onore, commedia in musica* (1718), and *Il cambise* (1719). The two Roman operas were *Il ciro* (1712), and *Telemaco* (1718). Among the Neapolitan works several authors have singled out *Tigrane,* about which Grout says it "is one of the greatest, if not the very greatest of Scarlatti's

EXAMPLE 5.21   Alessandro Scarlatti, from *Marco Attilio Regolo,* act II

EXAMPLE 5.22 Alessandro Scarlatti, from *La Griselda,* act III

EXAMPLE 5.22 (*continued*)

operas."[29] The developments are all a continuation of the forms and styles Scarlatti had established in his previous scores. Arias follow recitatives at the ends of scenes, the continuo aria has disappeared, and there is a fine variety of types of instrumental accompaniments. In general the aria forms are greatly expanded, and include among them a number of types. There are two slow 12/8 *sicilianos,* one in particular with a concerted accompaniment for violins, cello, and lute solo, omitting the bass line except for ritornello passages (see Example 5.20). There is also a noticeable increase in the dramatic impact of recitatives, especially because many of them are *accompagnato.*

The last operas were composed after 1718 when he again went to Rome for a period of three years. These include *Marco Attilio Regolo* (1719) and *La Griselda* (1721) as well as two others that have not survived. Although Scarlatti's operatic style remains largely similar to those of the previous decade, they have distinctions. The vocal writing in both is decidedly more difficult largely because of many long embellished passages, for example, in the aria in *Marco Attilio Regolo,* "Tutta sdegno ho l'alma in petto" (see Example 5.21).

In both operas, the majority of arias have accompaniments for strings in which the two violins and violas are usually independent of the vocal line and have considerable contrapuntal variety. In both, but most pronounced in *La Griselda,* there is an emphasis on a significant modification of texture. The continuo part is frequently omitted (see Example 5.22), and when it is not, Scarlatti indicates *solo,* thus eliminating the harmonic realization of the continuo line. The effect is twofold: the contrapuntal interplay between voice and strings is placed in strong relief and the normal, omnipresent bass-focused sonority is absent. Two conventional aspects of Baroque musical style are replaced by what may be considered characteristics of a newly developing style of eighteenth-century music.

Although Scarlatti's cantatas, serenades, oratorios, and operas are the most significant of his contributions to late-seventeenth-century Italian music, it should not go unnoticed that he also composed a considerable amount of music in other genres. His sacred music includes ten Masses, the *Passio Domini Nostri Jesu Christi secundum Joannen* (c. 1680), a large number of motets, the *Lamentazioni per la Settimana Santa* (Florence, 1706), and the twenty-seven *Responsori per la Settimana Santa* (Florence, 1708). Instrumental works are few in number. Most important are the twelve concerti grossi (1715), *Six concertos in seven parts, for two violins and violoncello obligato, with two violins more a tenor and thorough bass* (London, 1740), and six concertos for harpsichord and orchestra. There is a small group of chamber sonatas, and also solo toccatas and other miscellaneous pieces for keyboard. It is, however, the vocal music that made Alessandro Scarlatti the most gifted and representative Italian composer appearing at the end of the seventeenth century. This is true, although his influence was negligible as far as the succeeding developments in the next century were concerned. And although he did not create a Neapolitan operatic style, undoubtedly his long and successful position in Neapolitan operatic life helped significantly to establish Naples's importance for the future of Italian opera. Regrettably, because his enormous output is still largely unavailable for study and performance, he remains undeservedly obscure in the pantheon of the great contributors to the history of Italian music.

CHAPTER SIX

The Baroque in France

MUSIC IN SEVENTEENTH-CENTURY France developed on a foundation of four major factors, and these explain in large part the uniqueness of the French Baroque musical styles. Three of these factors were transmitted from the Renaissance: First, in France, as in Italy, intellectual ferment led to sustained studies of humanism and especially to the establishment of neo-Platonic academies. One subject of overriding fascination intrigued the French as it did the Italians, that is, what was the nature of ancient Greek music? Second, for more than a century, the dance had been the central focus of aristocratic culture, and it remained at the epicenter of all cultural developments taking place in France during the Baroque. Third, there was a substantial body of Renaissance solo songs with lute accompaniment, *chansons,* but labeled *airs de cour* for the first time in a collection published in 1571 by Adrian LeRoy. Fourth, the political changes occurring in the French nation led to the absolute authority of the king, and with Louis XIV, all the arts were brought under his personal control. Together with the extraordinary display of royal power and glory reflected in the palace he created at Versailles, sumptuous in every parameter, music too became a means to demonstrate the cultural superiority of France over Italy and to convince other European countries of France's political supremacy. Also, the arts, especially ballet, enabled the king to impose a deliberately ceremonial lifestyle at court in which he was the focus of the ever-present and obsequious nobility.

At no other time in history has music been created within as rigid a framework of artistic control. This control was exercised to proclaim the power and *gloire* of the king and at the same time to restrain composers from straying from stylistic parameters that would allow French music to be infected with other musical styles. The efforts to create a purely French music were remarkably successful even though the new musical influences of the period were Italian. How composers of the great age of the Sun King subsumed Italian musical elements into their music is in itself a complex and still inadequately understood development.

Before one can examine musical developments in France in the seventeenth century, it is necessary to outline those important influences on music that had already been established in the preceding century. By the mid-sixteenth century, considerable discussion among literary figures centered on music of the ancient world. These groups were strongly influenced by Italian academies of the mid-century, especially those that had grown out of Ficino's fifteenth-century Florentine academy. A group of poets known as the Pléiade, including Pierre de Ronsard, were instrumental in urging writers to base their works on Classical forms and meters. Another member, Jean-Antoine de Baïf (1532–1589), joined with a musician, Joachim Thibault de Courville (d. 1581), *joueur de lyre du roi,* to create a new music that would reestablish a close connection between music and text and would recreate the effects of ancient music. Their solution was *"vers et musique mesurés à l'antique."* Using the quantitative metrical patterns of Greek and Latin, they imposed on the French language

EXAMPLE 6.1   Mauduit, *Sus: tous ses servants, bénissez le Seigneur*

a concept of accents in which long syllables would receive long notes, and short syllables, short notes.

Another distinction of *musique mesurée* was its elimination of contrapuntal independence in individual parts and the use of a homophonic texture, whether vocal or instrumental, that rigorously maintained the rhythmic accentuation of the melody. As with Italian musical experiments at about the same time, these French intellectuals hoped to compose music with the expressive power of ancient Greek music, the *ethos,* that they knew from ancient sources Greek music possessed. In order for Baïf to convey his theories of music to Parisian intellectuals he established, with the support of Charles IX, the *Académie de poésie et de musique* in 1570. Three years later, Henri III gave continuing support by renaming the group as the *Académie du Palais.*[1] Concerts of *musique mesurée* were given in Baïf's home in great secrecy, and little is known of the actual music heard at that time. Some of the music was published later, and at least two gifted composers, Claude Le Jeune (c. 1528/30–1600) and Jacques Mauduit (1557–1627), composed a number of secular and sacred works in this style. The opening measures to the latter's setting of Psalm 133 in Baïf's *vers mesuré* translation show the musical result of this homophonic and rhythmically controlled style (see Example 6.1[2]).

The opening lines of *Eau vive, source d'amour,*[3] an *air de cour* attributed to Mauduit and composed to a text by Baïf in *vers mesuré,* illustrate the same concern for a metrical setting of the words with notes in a 2:1 ratio (see Example 6.2).

French inquiries into neo-Platonic humanism in the sixteenth century were as important as those occurring in Italy, to which they were interrelated. Direct influences of Baïf

EXAMPLE 6.2 Mauduit, *Eau vive, source d'amour*

and his academy on later developments of French music, however, remain obscure because so little of the musical results are preserved. But the spread of French humanism can be documented well into the seventeenth century through the establishment of new academies and also the teachings of the French Jesuits. Among the latter was the distinguished philosopher and music theorist Marin Mersenne (1588–1648). A priest in the Order of Minims, his cell at the monastery on the Place Royale in Paris was a meeting place for the leading writers, scientists, and musicians from around 1620. His numerous treatises were encyclopedic and strongly neo-Platonic in philosophy. The *Traité de l'harmonie universelle* (Paris, 1627) transmits much of what we know about the earlier French humanist achievements and remains our best guide to the state of musical knowledge in the first decades of the seventeenth century.

The Ballet de Cour

By the mid-sixteenth century, social dancing assumed a new ceremonial and entertainment importance within aristocratic society. Mascarades, which at times combined poetry, music, dancing, and various athletic contests, were performed before groups of nobles, and often concluded with the king and queen dancing the final entrée. The frequent contacts between the nobility of France and Italy led to expanding and enriching these entertainments, in part the result of the influence of the sumptuous *intermedii,* presented at the Florentine court. It was, however, during the regency of Catherine de' Medici and her son Charles IX that the pageantry and opulence of danced spectacles attained a new significance in France. In 1572 Baïf's academy was first involved in planning the fête for the wedding of Henry of Navarre with Marguerite of Valois. Entitled *Paradis d'amour,* it was held in the Salle de Bourbon at the Louvre and consisted of an elaborate dramatic plot, scenery representing Paradise and Hell, singing (poetry by Ronsard), and dancing. The three royal brothers danced a complicated ballet lasting over an hour.[4] For Baïf and his academy, as for dance theoreticians of the seventeenth century, ballet's central importance was its fusion of music, poetry, dance, and drama. Not only did this make ballet an equivalent form to ancient Greek drama but also the best medium by which to evoke sentiments and passions in spectators. In addition, ballet took on strong neo-Platonic symbolism, and was energized by the concept that dancing enabled the participants to imitate and benefit from the harmony of the spheres.

The record of ballets danced at the Valois court is scanty, and with one exception none of the music is preserved. The exception is the famous *Ballet comique de la Reyne,* performed in the grand hall of the Palais du Petit-Bourbon, 15 October 1581. The festivities were occasioned by the marriage of Marguerite of Lorraine, the queen's sister, to the Duc de Joyeuse, the favorite of King Henri III, and a financial backer of Baïf's academy. The work is usually called the first "ballet de cour" because it unites dance, poetry, and music in a unified dramatic whole. The impresario of the production was Baldassare da Belgioioso (who had Frenchified his name to Baltasar de Beaujoyeux), a fine Italian violinist who had served as valet de chambre to Catherine de' Medici, and later also in the same capacity to Henri III. The production used lavish scenery, dancers, soloists, a large orchestra, and chorus. The choruses especially indicate the influence of Baïf in their *musique mesurée* style. The ballet was filled with mythological and astrological symbolism, and used the story of the sorceress Circé to suggest the struggle of the king over the evils of religious strife and war in his search for a lasting peace. The political message was combined with philosophical and moral themes, and the total artwork was indeed a model for the development of the ballet de cour in the seventeenth century.[5]

The period between 1581 and 1610 (the death of Henri IV) continued to see ballet performances at court and elsewhere in aristocratic circles, although little of the music has been preserved.[6] Of particular interest is *Le ballet de Monsieur de Vendome* performed in Paris in 1610, which for the first time is said to have experimented with sung recitative in place of spoken texts. Because Caccini and his family performed at court in 1604–1605, it is often assumed this was the origin of experimentations with more Italianate approaches to singing styles. Because the music is unknown, the nature of such influence cannot be determined, and subsequent French vocal works, as in the *airs de cour,* show no specific impact of the *stile recitativo* on French composers.

When Louis XIII (1601–1643) assumed the throne of France in 1613, he substantially strengthened the role of music in court life. Known for his talents as a dancer, he also was an amateur composer of sacred music and at least one ballet, *Ballet de la Merlaison* (1635). He supported a large musical establishment for the royal chapel and made permanent the chamber ensemble, the *Vingt-quatre violons du roi.* In the first two decades of the century alone some one hundred ballets were danced at court, and to be able to dance was considered essential for social acceptability and political success. Most of these had no overall dramatic organization, but strongly resembled the Italian *mascharata* with numerous entrées of little or no relationship to a central poetic idea.

The grotesque and burlesque often predominated as subject matter, as titles often suggest, for example, *Ballet des vieilles sorcières* (1604), *Ballet d'Andromède exposé au monstre marin* (1606), *Ballet des sorciers et diables* (1608), *Ballet des Amazones* (1608), *Ballet des Ivrognes* (1609), and *Ballet des Singes* (1612). In 1617 Louis XIII chose the *Ballet d'Armide, ou La délivrance de Renaud,* in which he would dance a major role, a subject based on Tasso's *Gerusalemme Liberata* (1575). This work returned to the concept of a single plot and was perhaps the most extravagant production yet to be seen at court. Pantomime, vocal récits, numerous danced entrées, and a grand ballet at the end were staged with elaborate scenery and costumes.[7] A concert opening the ballet was conducted by Jacques Mauduit, formerly a member of the Baïf academy, with an ensemble consisting of sixty-four singers, twenty-eight violins, and fourteen lutes. The récits were composed by Pierre Guédron (after 1564–1619/20). The king chose to dance the role of the demon of fire, according to François Durand, the poet responsible for the work:

> He knew well that it is the property of fire to purify unrefined bodies and to unite homogeneous and similar things, separating gold and silver from all other less noble and less rich material, just as it is his Majesty's principal desire to remind all his subjects of their duty, and to purge them of all pretexts for disobedience. . . . he recognizes that fire cannot be imprisoned or circumscribed except by natural limits, just as he can be limited only by divine power and by his own will, and that the spirits which are nearest to God among the celestial hierarchies, being called seraphim, signify warming fire. He must also affect a quality agreeable to God himself, since he is the nearest and the best loved by him among men.[8]

Other dramatically unified ballets followed, including the *Ballet de Tancrède* (1619) and *Ballet de Psyché* (1619). Court ballets were the central focus of the reign of Louis XIII, although in subsequent decades they became more and more *ballets à entrées,* with the emphasis on pageantry, pantomimes, and separately choreographed parts. The threefold purpose of these works, court entertainment, glorification of the monarch, and interpretations of significant political events involving France, more or less coalesced in most of them. A pattern was established that would remain as the foundation for the future development of court ballet during the reign of Louis XIV.

Air de Cour

In 1571 Adrian LeRoy published a collection of solo songs with lute accompaniment entitled *Livre d'air de cours miz sur le luth.* This was the earliest appearance in print of the term *air de cour,* which LeRoy states in his preface he had given to the type of song usually called a *voix de ville* (vaudeville).[9] The work is dedicated to the Comtesse de Retz, an active participant in the Académie du Palais, which had originated with Baïf and Courville. These simple songs are arrangements of polyphonic *chansons,* similar to several earlier collections published by Attaingnant and Phalèse. No other collection of solo-voice *airs de cour* appeared in the century, although the descriptive title was given to collections of polyphonic songs with textures predominantly homophonic and with an emphasis on the upper part. There is considerable literary evidence that the French court favored solo song with lute accompaniment from at least the second half of the sixteenth century. The appearance of simple, metrically free melodies, with the French texts set to quantitative accents, suggests a continuing influence of *musique mesurée.* It also indicates that in France, as in Italy, musicians sought more and more the effectiveness of the solo voice with a homophonic accompaniment for poetry rather than the intricacies of contrapuntal textures.

The importance of the *air de cour* stands out because of the major impact this melodic concept had on French music for at least the next 150 years. It is one of the elements of musical style that readily defined French Baroque music. During the seventeenth century, the *air de cour* was an essential element in the *ballet de cour,* including those of Lully. Lully's *tragédies lyriques* model their airs on this French melodic style, as do the *récits* of the seventeenth-century French motet. Well into the eighteenth century, there is an omnipresent influence of the *air de cour* in the general melodic style of both sacred and secular vocal and instrumental music. As a genre, the *air de cour* was well established early in the seventeenth century, and, among the many composers of these songs, the most important were Gabriele Bataille (c. 1575–1630), Antoine Boësset (1586–1643), Pierre Guédron (after

EXAMPLE 6.3 Moulinié, *Enfin la beauté que j'adore* (first half only)

1564–1619/20), and Étienne Moulinié (c. 1600–after 1669). The poetry, written with court tastes in mind, is usually sentimental and becomes increasingly *précieux*. The poet most often used was Philippe Desportes, although numerous other writers such as François Malherbe, Honorat de Racan, Saint-Amant, Théophile de Vau, Jacques Davy Du Perron, Honoré d'Urfé, and Tristan l'Hermite appear frequently in various published collections. There is a degree of variety among the airs, although most of them maintain a coolness of approach to emotion and a degree of simplicity of melodic line that distinguish their French style. All of them are strophic, some are light in mood, with clear outlines and in regular rhythms. More characteristic are those in which musical meter plays little if any importance, and rhythmic organization tends to be achieved by placing long notes at the interior caesura and ends of lines, leading to an unavoidable monotony, and perhaps influenced by the theories of Baïf's academy. Many of these *airs,* however, have a subtle and distinctive expressiveness, melodies of considerable freedom of rhythmic design and long-phrased curves, sentimental indeed, but with artistic merit of high quality, for example, Moulinié's *Enfin la beauté que j'adore* (see Example 6.3[10]).

(This *air de cour* is from Moulinié's *1er livre d'airs de cour avec tablature de luth* [Paris: P. Ballard, 1624]. Étienne Moulinié served the king's younger brother, Gaston d'Orléans, as director of music from 1628. After the latter's death in 1660 Moulinié became the director of music for the estates of Languedoc. This example is typical both of the simple elegance of his *airs* and also of the characteristic French free style of melody often achieved in a limited vocal *ambitus*. Barlines would be useless in this free-flowing melodic style in which the composer has organized the musical stresses according to the accent given to the words of the text.)

The last collection of Moulinié's *Airs de cour à 4 parties* was published in 1668, and the second half of the century saw a continuing output of numerous collections of *airs* by many composers. Between 1658 and 1694, Ballard issued thirty-eight volumes of *Airs de différents autheurs à deux parties,* but without naming either composers or poets. Two of the most distinguished among composers of *airs* after 1650 were Bénigne de Bacilly (c. 1625–1690), famous also for his treatise on singing, *Remarques curieuses sur l'art de bien chanter* (1668), and Michel Lambert (c. 1610–1696). The latter collaborated with Lully (who would marry Lambert's daughter) on three court ballets, for which he supplied short vocal sections. Lambert was famous in Paris as a singer and voice teacher, and he was held in particular esteem by Louis XIV. While much of his music is lost, at least three hundred *airs* remain in prints and manuscripts. In a variety of forms—binary, rounded binary, dances, on chaconne basses, and as dialogues—Lambert's *airs* not only show the supreme refinement of this vocal genre but also are indicative of the interrelationship between the solo *air* and the vocal forms in the operas of Lully.

Italian Opera at the French Court

It would be a mistake to think France was ever isolated from Italian culture. Not only had French armies invaded Italian lands in the sixteenth century and brought back both art and artists to enrich French estates but also twice within less than a century a queen of France was a Florentine Medici—Catherine, who married Henri II, and Maria, wife of Henri IV. Both served as Queen Regent during the minority of their sons, Catherine during 1560–1563, and Maria, 1610–1617. The latter, who was the grandmother of Louis XIV (1638–1715), had a particularly significant influence on all aspects of court life, including the arts during the first half of the seventeenth century. Giulio Caccini and Ottavio Rinuccini came to Paris in the entourage of Maria de' Medici in 1602, introducing the new Italian concept of song and singing to court audiences. Often overlooked, too, is the frequency with which French singers went to Italy to learn their art of singing, including the Italian style of embellishments. Of perhaps even greater Italian influence was Cardinal Jules Mazarin (Giulio Mazzarini), minister of France and virtual king during the youth of Louis XIV. As an Italian with strong connections to Rome and the Barberini family, he clearly wished to bring Italian opera to Paris, perhaps partly for nostalgic reasons, but also for self-aggrandizement and state political power.

The Rome connection led Mazarin at the end of 1643 to invite Marco Marazzoli, composer in the employ of the Barberinis, to produce a theatrical work for Anne of Austria, Louis XIV's mother. He continued activity at the court by writing chamber cantatas for the queen until he returned to Rome in 1645. His service to the court was recognized by receiving a yearly pension from the government for life. During this same period the famous alto castrato and composer Atto Melani (1626–1714) won great favor at court, suggesting that the Italian style of singing had become popular with some members of the French nobility. Mazarin was responsible for bringing the Italian genius of stage machinery, Giacomo Torelli (1608–1678), to Paris in 1645. He designed with new technical ingenuity stage machinery used at the theaters in the Hôtel de Petit Bourbon and also the Palais Royal.[11]

Torelli created the machines for *La finta pazza,* based at least in part on the work by Francesco Sacrati, with new ballets added at the ends of each act, which was performed in December 1645 by a distinguished cast of Italian singers. It was the first Italian opera given a public performance in France.

In 1645 the Barberini family were forced into exile and settled in Paris, where they lived until 1653. Their household included Abbé Francesco Buti, their secretary and a poet who became superintendent of the Italian artists. Italian domination on court culture was now at its strongest. In February 1646, Mazarin arranged a performance of Cavalli's *Egisto,* although it achieved no real success with the small aristocratic audience. Undeterred, Mazarin invited Luigi Rossi to come to Paris in June 1646 to undertake the most grandiose opera production yet to be heard in Paris. The exceedingly elaborate sets and machinery were created by Torelli. As has been described, Rossi was a leading composer of vocal music in Rome, with close associations with the Barberini family. During the year he spent in Paris not only did he compose *L'Orfeo,* the first Italian opera written specifically for Paris, but also numerous cantatas for the queen, assisted as harpsichord accompanist for recitals of Italian singers, and collaborated during the summer of 1646 with French musicians for various entertainments at Fontainebleau.

L'Orfeo was performed several times at the Palais Royal beginning on 2 March 1647 with the libretto by Abbé Buti. The cast included several castratos including Marc' Antonio Pasqualini and Atto Melani. This work is a major achievement in opera history, an example of Roman opera successfully promoting Italian opera style at the French court. In three acts, the librettist has expanded the original plot of *L'Orfeo* with a large number of mythological characters, and expanded and enlivened the tragedy with considerable satirical and comic scenes. Written four decades after Monteverdi's first opera based on the same myth, Rossi's work exemplifies the rapid developments in operatic style taking place in Rome and undoubtedly also influencing the beginnings of Venetian opera. Although Rossi's style is sometimes said to have been influenced by French musical taste, it might be more accurate to see in this opera a strong determining factor on French dramatic music before Lully. The score, while retaining the essence of the *style rappresentativo* in its recitatives, has a great deal of flexible and lyrical interactions between recitative and arioso, aria, and dance songs, some of them based on the Italian love of the basso ostinato. Rossi's *L'Orfeo* has a large number of duets and other solo ensembles, as well as several choruses, all stylistic aspects generally conceded to be Italian and Roman in origin, but that became highly characteristic of French opera as later achieved by Lully.

The enormous costs involved in producing *L'Orfeo* became a political target for the Parisian parliamentary faction known as the Fronde, intent on establishing a constitutional monarchy and attacking Mazarin and his highly visible efforts to establish an Italian influence at court. Following a period of considerable political unrest, Mazarin returned to supreme power at court in 1653 and immediately renewed his determination to Italianize court music. In 1654 the Roman composer Carlo Caproli (before 1620–after 1675) came to Paris for performances at the Petit Bourbon of his opera *Le nozze di Peleo e di Theti* (libretto by Buti). Louis XIV, who was sixteen, made Caproli *maître de la musique du cabinet du Roy.* The king danced in the ballets at the conclusion of each of the scenes with music by several composers, including Lully, who had recently entered court service. The grafting of the *ballet de cour* on Italian opera is a development of no small importance, as it diluted the Italian nature of opera and established the French national passion for the dance. The climax of Mazarin's efforts, however, came when he commissioned Francesco Cavalli to compose an opera for the wedding celebrations in 1660 of the king to the Spanish infanta,

Maria Theresa. The work, *Ercole amante* (libretto also by Buti), was unfinished in July 1660 when Cavalli arrived in Paris. The construction of a new theater at the Tuileries palace, where the performances were planned to take place, also was unfinished. Cavalli substituted his *Xerxes,* revised from three to five acts, with ballet *entrées* with music by Lully interspersed between acts. It was performed in a temporary theater constructed in the Louvre palace. The commissioned work was not heard until 7 February 1662, almost a year after Mazarin's death. As with *Xerxes,* Cavalli's music found little support from the audiences, although the magnificence of the staging and the ballet insertions were popular. The opera lasted six hours, and each act ended in a ballet with Lully's music. The final ballet was entitled the *ballet de sept planètes,* recalling the popularity of astrological themes that had often been used for the *ballet de cour* from the beginnings of the century. The king himself appeared as Pluto, Mars, and of course in his favorite symbolic guise as the Sun.

Sacred Music

The nature of sacred music in France during the long period following the assassination of Henri IV (1610), which included the regency of his widow, Maria de' Médici, Richelieu as prime minister, the reign of Louis XIII (d. 1643), and the assumption of absolute power by Louis XIV in 1661, remains out of focus. In part the picture is made unclear by the state of religion in France, with the unresolved tensions between Catholics and reformed Protestant Huguenots. The Catholic or Gallican church continued in an uneasy relationship with the Holy See in Rome. At the same time a small but powerful segment of supporters led by the Jesuits struggled to bring French Catholicism into a closer conformity with Rome and the precepts of the Council of Trent. Although numerous manuscript and printed sources of French sacred music remain, little has been published or has been subjected to intensive examination. As is always the case with France, the study of musical developments outside of Paris is problematical because of the lack of available sources, even though the great cathedrals and churches in other population centers as well as the various aristocratic courts maintained important musical establishments.[12]

The first decades of the seventeenth century witnessed little change in the Renaissance forms and styles of polyphonic sacred music composed in France. There was no sudden break with traditions and no apparent desire to be influenced by the latest musical innovations occurring in Italy. The works of composers such as Philippe de Monte and especially Lassus dominated the taste of French composers of the Latin Mass. Indeed, Lassus's Masses continued to be published in Paris into the next century. Among the several known composers continuing the Franco-Netherlands compositional style into the new century, Eustache DuCaurroy (1549–1609) exemplifies in many of his preserved works the conservatism typical of sacred music in this crossover period between centuries. Four Masses are lost, but his five-part *Missa pro defunctis* for the funeral of Henri IV was printed by Ballard in 1636 and remained a traditional work for the obsequies of royalty at St. Denis into the eighteenth century. It is written largely in the *stylo antico,* and with some employment of paraphrase techniques in individual sections. The opening to the *Virga tua* (Psalm 23:4) responsory-gradual used in the Parisian churches gives an indication of the conservative contrapuntal textures favored by DuCaurroy (see Example 6.4).[13]

In his two volumes of motets, psalms, and Te Deums, *Preces ecclesiasticae* (1609), many of the works are composed for two choirs with an emphasis on dialogue techniques between the groups. In some of these there appears to be a plan to contrast an ensemble of solo voices with a second that is for chorus, a feature of French sacred music to grow in popularity and later to characterize the *grand motet* of the second half of the century.

EXAMPLE 6.4 DuCaurroy, *Virga tua*

Although strict contrapuntal techniques still dominate, there is also evidence of Du-Caurroy's employment of Baïf's principles of *vers mesuré à l'antique,* with sections of homophonic textures in rhythms of long and short note values; see the opening of *Vox Domini super aquas* (Psalm 28:3–9) from the *Preces ecclesiasticae* (see Example 6.5).[14]

French composers of masses and other sacred works such as motets continued in the first decades of the century to write conservatively with contrapuntal artifice in the *stylo antico;* for example, the following whose works are known to survive: Jean de Bournonville (c. 1585–1632), Pierre Lauverjat (?–after 1625), Charles d'Ambleville (?–1637), and André Péchon (c. 1600–after 1683). During the period encompassed by the reign of Louis XIII, however, distinct stylistic changes are found in the works of a new generation of composers. An emphasis on syllabic textual settings weakens and often eliminates any contrapuntal control of textures, and there develops a clear tendency toward tonality. The growing employment of double choruses, often with dialogue settings between a solo voice and a tutti chorus, suggests the probable influence of the Italian concertante style. In some instances, French sacred music becomes quite dramatic.

The most original adoption of these new techniques was achieved by Guillaume Bouzignac (before 1587–after 1642), who lived in the south of France, mainly in Grenoble and

EXAMPLE 6.5   DuCaurroy, *Vox Domini super aquas* (Psalm 28:3–9) from the *Preces ecclesiasticae*

the Languedoc.[15] In his Masses, motets, and psalms, all contained in two manuscripts and largely dating between 1628 and 1643, Italian influences of the madrigal composers, perhaps even Catalan music, seem present. His works are intensely rhetorical, with the emphasis on clarity and the meaning of the words. At times a chorus recites a text to a single chord, at others words are given affective meaning through melodic figures and striking harmonic progressions, while polyphonic textures are usually exceptional. A distinctive feature of many of his motets is the use of a solo narrative voice set against choral responses. Some of these works suggest techniques of the oratorio, which characterize the later works of Carissimi and Charpentier. Bouzignac's *Ecce homo* for five-part chorus and tenor solo dramatizes the scene of Jesus before Pilate. In *Tu quis es?*, the double choir of eight voices presents the dialogue of St. John in the desert. As the opening section illustrates, the music is purely dramatic, the reiterated and harmonically static *Tu quis es?* (who are you?) alternating with the responses of the "voice" (see Example 6.6).[16]

The Annunciation is dramatized in *Ave Maria,* with the angel Gabriel sung by a solo soprano in dialogue with a four-part chorus. In *Dum silentium,* one of Bouzignac's most extraordinary compositions, the Nativity scene is created in almost impressionistic sounds, with the mysterious musical "silence" of the night broken by the solo soprano voice of the angel and the responses of the shepherds.[17] Despite the paucity of information regarding Bouzignac's life and career, his music strongly suggests that he was a major figure in the development of seventeenth-century French sacred music.

Several other composers before mid-century can be identified as working in somewhat more progressive sacred musical styles, even if seldom with the boldness and originality of

EXAMPLE 6.6   Bouzignac, *Ecce homo,* "Tu quis es?"

EXAMPLE 6.7   Du Mont, *Tristitia vestra*

Bouzignac. They include Nicolas Formé (1567–1638), Étienne Moulinié (c. 1600–after 1669), Jean Veillot (d. 1662), and Thomas Gobert (d. 1672). As with Bouzignac's works, these composers achieved innovations with the double choir, in effect establishing a tradition of French Baroque sacred music. Gobert, in a letter to the Dutch diplomat, poet, scientist and musician Constantijn Huygens, describes the *grand choeur* as always in five parts and sung by many voices, and the *petit choeur* as composed only for solo voices.[18] This concept of concerted contrasts between a solo ensemble and a chorus marks the basic performance practice of the *grand motet*.

The sacred works of Henry Du Mont [de Thier] (1610–1684) span the period encompassed by Louis XIV's minority and more than two decades of this king's royal chapel. Du Mont's name is, therefore, the first among several to be closely associated with the sacred musical monuments created for the Sun King. De Thier was the original Walloon family name, which he changed to the French equivalent in the 1630s. When Du Mont arrived in France in 1638 he would have found sacred music remarkably conservative, for in his native Flanders Italian music of the early seventeenth century had already been accepted in Flemish churches. Du Mont would have learned of the *style recitativo* and its attendant basso continuo as the accepted practice of Roman and Venetian composers. It was the few-voiced concertato motet of the Italians that Du Mont adapted to his own sacred style, and it was Du Mont who apparently first introduced the trio texture of two solo voices and continuo in the form of the *petit motet,* which would become the most popular form of sacred music during Louis XIV's *grand siècle*. He also became a leading composer of the *grand motet* (this will be examined in Chapter 7). In 1652 Ballard published his *Cantica sacra,* the first music by a French composer to be printed in France with a basso continuo, the part printed separately and with figures. Several of the pieces also have an obbligato solo string part. Eighteen of the motets are for two voices, five for three, and twelve for four voices. Although there is a wide variety of vocal settings, the collection as a whole clearly emphasizes clarity of texts, simple contrapuntal writing, most often in duets, and a considerable stress on homophonic passages. Many have distinctive Italian stylistic qualities,

EXAMPLE 6.8 Du Mont, *Deposuit potentes*

even an echo duet, *In lecturo meo,* remarkably suggestive of similar works by composers such as Monteverdi and his generation. The opening of the motet *Tristitia vestra,* from Du Mont's *Cantica sacra,* exemplifies the trio texture in his music. Slow two-part counterpoint, with conventional dissonances made possible by the functional harmonic bass in the continuo, alternates for a rhetorical emphasis of the text with a quicker syllabic setting of the *Alleluya* (see Example 6.7).[19]

Five years later Ballard published Du Mont's *Meslanges à II. III. IV. et V. parties, avec la basse-continue,* a major collection of both secular chansons and sacred works, dedicated to the Duke of Anjou, the king's brother, and Du Mont's employer. The first part includes eighteen three-voiced chansons in contrapuntal style, prefaced by overture-like instrumental movements for two viols (an additional viol part was published in 1661). The imitative vocal writing of some textural complexity in what are probably early compositions is contrasted to the sacred compositions that further explore the style already established in the

EXAMPLE 6.9   Du Mont, *Jubilemus*

Cantica sacra. In the *Deposuit potentes* from his Magnificat *du Vème ton* the trio texture is maintained, for the vocal bass is largely a duplication of the continuo's harmonic function (see Example 6.8). The expressive melismas on *et exaltavit* are infrequent examples of vocal gestures similar to those found in Italian settings of sacred and secular vocal music.[20]

When imitative textures are employed they seldom continue in three real parts, and much of the time the counterpoint lapses into characteristic homophonic writing for all parts. Even with imitation the textures are opened up to permit clarity of the text. There is an emphasis on duet writing, and the melodic style is simple, at times like the *air de cour,* at times in the form of an arioso suggesting the particular concept of melody found in French *récits.* The close of the motet *Jubilemus* illustrates Du Mont's achievement of a style that became basic to French sacred vocal music for the decades of Louis XIV's reign (see Example 6.9).[21]

Sacred music in the first half of the seventeenth century in France included a number of other forms and styles other than Masses and motets. Plainsong was popularized and perhaps demeaned in numerous settings in fauxbourdon. A substantial number of psalm compositions were based on the paraphrases in French published in 1648 by Antoine Godeau. And there were a variety of works described as spiritual canticles as well as settings of French translations of Latin hymns. Much of the music of a definite simplicity was aimed at the large number of new religious orders and their convents including the Carmelites and the reestablishment of the Jesuits and their Collège de Clermont. This included collections of parodies of well-known *airs de cour.*

The Baroque in France during the Reign of Louis XIV

When Louis XIII died in 1643, his son Louis XIV (1638–1715) was only five years old. During his minority France was ruled by the regency of his mother, Anne of Austria, and by Cardinal Jules Mazarin, first minister. Only on the death of the latter on 9 March 1661 did Louis XIV assume absolute power and in so doing would become France's greatest king. Court culture that had dominated the arts since the Middle Ages remained at the center of most Baroque art as well. And north of the Alps and the Pyrenees, it was the court of Louis XIV that became the supreme model by which to judge all aristocratic life. By 1680 the Sun King, as he became known, had swept aside most of the political power of Europe, crushed the Habsburgs, and made France the first superpower of modern Europe. His brilliance in organizing the armed forces of France, which he led in innumerable battles, resulted in a series of military victories, and although they cost French society dearly, they made him the most admired and feared ruler of the second half of the seventeenth century.

The king's great passion for the arts, especially for music and the ballet, raised court culture to levels unknown previously or subsequently. He was from childhood well trained in music, on string instruments, keyboard instruments, and guitar. Like his father, he was a superb dancer, especially praised for his brilliant realizations of the branle and courante. From the age of twelve until 1670 Louis XIV danced in and made the ballet de cour a central focus of court entertainment. Indispensable for the king's passion for music and dance was the fortuitous appearance at his court of a young Italian, whose gifts for music were second only to his friendship with the young king. Jean Baptiste Lully would soon not only dominate music at Louis's court but also would become the most influential name in the history of seventeenth-century French Baroque music.

Jean Baptiste Lully (1632–1687)

Born in Florence, Giovanni Battista Lully was brought to France in 1646 to serve as chamber valet to the Princess de Montpensier, cousin to the king, and to tutor her in Italian. He quickly excelled in musical studies provided by her court at the Tuileries, becoming a virtuoso violinist and an accomplished dancer. These talents attracted the attention of the king, who was six years younger than Lully, and in 1653 he appointed Lully *compositeur de la musique instrumentale.* This began Lully's remarkable association with the king, becoming his confidant and virtual dictator of all musical activities for the royal establishment and for the nation. Already during Carnival celebrations of 1653 he had gained intimate association with the fourteen-year-old king by joining him in the dancing of the *Ballet de la Nuit* (vocal music by Jean de Cambefort) together with the court composer (and Lully's future father-in-law) Michel Lambert and Molière. At first Lully composed only the instrumental sections of the ballets, which was a traditional arrangement, but as early as February 1656 he composed the entire score for the *Ballet de la Galanterie du Temps* for a commission by Cardinal Mazarin, which was presented before the king and queen at the Louvre palace. The role of a *galant* was danced by the king. The score (which is lost) was performed by the *petits violons* also known as the *petite bande,* a group of sixteen players (later twenty-one), an offshoot of the famous "24 violons du Roi" established by Louis's father, and placed under the control of Lully. He demanded a new performance discipline that included the removing of traditional and excessive ornamentation and improvisation. The results would soon become famous throughout Europe as an important stage in the growth of the modern orchestra. The airs in this ballet were in Italian and sung by Italian artists employed by the court. Before 1661, Lully's melodic style was essentially Italian.

THE BALLETS DE COUR

Lully is known to have composed all or parts of twenty-eight court ballets, all but two of them between 1653 and 1670. With few exceptions they were composed in collaboration with Isaac de Benserade (1613–1691), court poet who supplied the textbooks as well as verses for the sung *récits* (solos, duos, trios, and quartets) and choruses. These were usually published in *livrets* and distributed to the audiences. During the approximately two decades in which Lully composed ballets he not only made important changes in the concept of the genre but also used the experiences to develop his own musical style, gradually abandoning the Italianate aspects and formulating what would soon be recognized as a French musical language. The small quantities of music preserved from his early ballets, for example, for the *Ballet de l'amour malade* (1657), demonstrate with what success he had absorbed the French style of the various dance forms.[22] The orchestra is divided into the usual French form of five string parts: two for violin, two for viola, and a *basse de violon.* The *ouverture* has the characteristic two-part form in which each section is repeated, and the first part has some employment of dotted rhythms. It is on this model of an instrumental introduction that Lully developed his later French overture form and style. The *ouverture* to his *Ballet d'Alcidiane* (1658)[23] has a somewhat more characteristic Lullian "French overture" form: dotted rhythms often preceded by upbeat flourishes of eighth notes and a B section that begins with imitation, though as is true in the second parts of most of Lully's overtures the result is not, as is often stated, fugal.

The *Ballet de la Galanterie,* like the *Ballet d'Alcidiane,* also includes *récits* in both Italian and French for the Prologue and the concluding scene. In the guise of comedy, the contrast of Italian and French vocal styles is made the theme of a dialogue between a French and an Italian musician, which opens the *Ballet de la Raillerie* (1659). Here the "L'Italienne" mimics in song the art of the French and "La Musicienne" does the same for Italian song. The French singer criticizes the long melismas characterizing Italian vocal art and the Italian voices her dislike of the languorous style of French airs. French style appears to be victorious in this ballet.[24]

Together with Benserade, Lully experimented in various ways to bring more dramatic consistency to the court ballets, diminishing and, finally, in the *comédies-ballets,* eliminating the conventionalities of a series of danced *entrées* with little or no dramatic continuity. The innovations and maturing of Lully's musical style developed together with his growing position of influence with the king. In 1661 he was appointed *surintendant de la musique et compositeur de la musique de la chambre,* replacing Cambefort who had died, and the next year he became *maître de la musique de la famille royale.* For the period through 1670 Lully composed two and sometimes three ballets a year, which received performances at the various royal palaces in Paris at the Tuileries, the Louvre, and Palais Royale; at Fontainebleau; Vincennes; Saint-Germain-en-Laye; and, beginning in 1663, at Versailles. The latter, which had been the hunting lodge of his father, became the passion of Louis XIV's life, and beginning in 1661 he instituted a series of massive reconstructions and expansions he did not live to see completed. The king did not move his court permanently to Versailles until 1682, but during the intervening years used the building and its extraordinary formal gardens for special celebrations, including ballet performances.

THE COMÉDIES-BALLETS

The integrating of a spoken comedy with musical and dance elements from the ballet de cour originated with the French playwright Molière. For court festivities at Fouquet's palace of Vaux-le-Vicomte in 1661 a comédie-ballet by Molière, *Les fâcheux,* was performed, the dances by Pierre Beauchamp. Molière explained in the preface to his work, "in order not to break the thread of the play by these *intermèdes,* we decided to link them with its subject as best we could and to make a single thing of the ballet and the play." This led to a nine-year collaboration between Molière and Lully that achieved ten comédies-ballets: *Le mariage forcé* (1664), *Les plaisirs de l'île enchantée* (1664), *La Princesse d'Elide* (1664), *L'Amour médecin* (1665), *La pastorale comique* (1667), *Le Sicilien, ou L'Amour peintre* (1667), *Intermèdes pour George Dandin* (1668), *Monsieur de Pourceaugnac* (1669), *Les amants magnifiques* (1670), and *Le bourgeois gentilhomme* (1670). They also created together with Pierre Corneille and Quinault the tragédie-ballet *Psyché* (1671).

The comédies-ballets are among Lully's major achievements, and in their splendid union of Molière's spoken text with dance, and with solo, ensemble, and choral singing contain the musical-dramatic essence of what Lully will achieve in his tragédies en musique. He has subsumed his Italian musical origins into a style that can only be heard as French. The airs are related to those found in his ballets de cour, songs based on the style of the air de cour, usually in binary form with limited range, wedded to the textual rhythms, and with subtle and affective dissonances and frequent cadences. There are also dance songs based on an instrumental dance they either precede or follow. Of particular importance is Lully's use of recitatives in the comédies-ballets. Even though they appear infrequently, since most of the text was spoken, they give evidence of Lully's developing command of a type of French recitative that will be one of the most important and characteristic features of his tragédies en musique. For example, see the following recitative dialogue from *Les amants magnifiques* (Example 6.10).[25]

Lully's perfected form of the French overture prefaces several of these works, for example, *Les amants magnifiques* and *Le bourgeois gentilhomme.* Each of the two large sections now has typical stylistic features: the opening is in duple meter, majestic, somewhat slow, with dotted rhythms and often with upbeat flourishes. It is repeated. The second part, in triple or compound meter, is faster than the first and usually begins with imitative entries. Contrary to many definitions of Lully's overture form, this section is not fugal and in the ballets as later in the operas may not maintain any form of an imitative texture. This part is also repeated. Some of the overtures, especially from the later operas, end with a return to a slow section resembling the opening part, although not necessarily using the thematic materials of that section. In general, the instrumental writing in the dances as well as in the *ritournelles,* symphonies, and other introductory pieces is stamped with Lully's style. What Lully must soon abandon in the tragédies en musique, however, is his superb sense for musical comedy found throughout these works, with perhaps the most hilarious example being the "Turkish ceremony" from *Le bourgeois gentilhomme.*

EXAMPLE 6.10   Lully, *Les amants magnifiques*

TRAGÉDIES EN MUSIQUE

Despite the various attempts to introduce Italian opera at the French court, and despite the presence of Italian musicians at court through the 1660s, opera received no apparent royal support following Mazarin's death in 1661, until 1672 when Lully himself turned his attention to it. The first success with French opera, however, did not come from Lully. *Le triomphe de l'Amour sur des bergers et bergères* would seem to be the first French *comédie en musique.* Composed by Michel de La Guerre to a text by Charles de Beys, it was performed for the king at the Louvre in 1655 and revived as a stage work with scenery in 1657. The music is lost. A counterclaim for being first was made by the French poet and librettist, Pierre Perrin (c. 1620–1675).[26] In collaboration with the composer Robert Cambert (c. 1628–1677) they produced their *Pastorale,* which was performed in the home of M. de la Haye at Issy in April 1659. Perrin described his text for this simple, five-act stage work as the "première comédie françoise en musique." Its considerable success led Cardinal Mazarin to arrange a court performance at Vincennes, and subsequently Perrin and Cambert prepared an opera, *Ariane, ou le mariage de Bacchus,* intended for but not performed at the wedding festivities of Louis XIV and the Infanta of Spain. In 1669 the king awarded Perrin a privilege giving him sole rights over twelve years to establish "academies of opera" in France. On 3 March 1671, Cambert and Perrin finally opened their Académie de musique with their new opera, *Pomone,* at the Jeu de Paume de la Bouteille theater in Paris. The music is only partially preserved (overture, prologue, act I, and the opening to act II).[27] *Pomone* had a considerable success with performances over seven or eight months. In February or March 1672 Cambert produced a second opera, *Les peines et les plaisirs de l'amour.* By this time, however, Perrin was imprisoned for debts that would destroy his career, and Cambert collaborated with the playwright Gabriel Gilbert.[28] The run for this new opera ended on 1 April 1672 when the king closed the theater. Lully had bought the rights of the original privilege from the imprisoned Perrin and the new company was named the Académie royale de musique. With the support of Louis XIV and the new patent or royal privilege, Lully and his descendants gained absolute power over the nation's musical theater.

To establish quickly his new theatrical endeavor, Lully created a pastoral pastiche from earlier works, *Les fêtes de L'Amour et de Bacchus,* which was performed on 15 November. Beginning with *Cadmus et Hermione* the following year he composed one opera a year (except in 1681), for a total of thirteen. All but three of these *tragédies en musique* (later in the eighteenth century referred to as *tragédies lyriques*) employed librettos by the poet Philippe Quinault (1635–1688). Lully had agreed that each work would be performed first before the king and his court, although for about half of them court performances occurred after the first public performances in Paris. Beginning in 1674 the king made available to Lully without charge the theater in one of the wings of the Palais Royal in the Rue St. Honoré. Although none of the musicians in the employ of the court were permitted to perform in the public presentations of the works, the king did allow the scenery and machines built for the court performances to be used without charge for the Académie performances.

The history of French opera begins with Lully's thirteen *tragédies en musique.* In them, he achieved a consummate amalgamation of French theatrical language, with singing, the dance, and elaborate spectacle that would remain the only form and style of opera to flourish in France up to the Revolution.[29] Although these operas result in part from Lully's adaptations of aspects of Italian musical style, they are based on the most French of dramatic achievements, the theater of Corneille, and this foundation enabled Lully to overcome the long-held prejudice of the French against sung dramatic representations they had experienced from Italian composers. As an oeuvre, the importance of the *tragédies en musique* lies beyond the musical achievement. The Lully operatic canon created an autonomous French musical-dramatic style believed to represent the magnificence and superiority of French culture. Lully's operatic music established an aesthetic code that quickly became the basis for numerous treatises arguing for the pre-eminence of French music over Italian.[30]

All of the operas are in five acts, as were French dramas, and each begins with an independent Prologue meant to glorify the king and the state. Although the king is never mentioned by name, the action of the Prologue is allegorical and its reference to the greatness and the brilliance of his glory, whether in affairs of war or peace, is never left in doubt. The success of these works resulted as much from Lully's librettist as from his musical creativity. It is important to remember that for his audiences, it was foremost the dramatic setting of the text that mattered. Therefore, one cannot begin to understand the achievement of Lully without comprehending the achievement of Quinault. While Quinault's *livrets* are original in conception, they synthesize numerous dramatic and ceremonial aspects of the ballet de cour, the pastorale, the *comédie-* and *tragédie-ballets,* even Italian opera as well as French spoken theater. Except for the last three, all of the operas are based

The *Tragédies en musique*[31]

LWV	Title	Libretto	First performance
49	Cadmus et Hermione	Quinault, after Ovid: *Metamorphoses*	Paris, Jeu de Paume de Béquet, ?10 Nov. 1672
50	Alceste, ou Le triomphe d'Alcide	Quinault, after Euripides: *Alcestis*	Paris, Opéra, 19 Jan. 1674
51	Thésée	Quinault, after Ovid: *Metamorphoses*	St. Germaine-en-Laye, 11 Jan. 1675; Paris, Opéra, April, 1675
53	Atys	Quinault, after Ovid: *Fasti*	St. Germaine-en-Laye, 10 Jan. 1676; Paris, Opéra, April, 1676
54	Isis	Quinault, after Ovid: *Metamorphoses*	St. Germaine-en-Laye, 5 Jan. 1677; Paris, Opéra, Aug., 1677
56	Psyché	T. Corneille, after Apuleius: *The Golden Ass*	Paris, Opéra, 19 April, 1678
57	Bellérophon	Corneille, after B. de Bovier de Fontenelle, after Hesiod: *Theogeny*	Paris, Opéra, 31 Jan. 1679
58	Proserpine	Quinault, after Ovid: *Metamorphoses*	St. Germaine-en-Laye, 3 Feb. 1680; Paris, Opéra, 15 November 1680
60	Persée	Quinault, after Ovid: *Metamorphoses*	Paris, Opéra, 17 or 18 April 1682
61	Phaéton	Quinault, after Ovid: *Metamorphoses*	Versailles, 6 Jan., 1683; Paris, Opéra, 27 April, 1683
63	Amadis	Quinault, after Montalvo adapted by N. Herberay des Essarts; *Amadis de Gaule*	Paris, Opéra, 18 Jan. 1684
65	Roland	Quinault, after L. Ariosto: *Orlando furioso*	Versailles, 8 Jan. 1685; Paris, Opéra, 8 or 9 March 1685
71	Armide	Quinault, after T. Tasso: *Gerusalemme liberata*	Paris, Opéra, 15 Feb. 1686

on mythology, while the final three concern legends of chivalry. The themes of all of the works are always the same: the vicissitudes of love between mortals and the gods and the concept of *gloire,* the glory of the state. A number of the librettos include a heroic figure easily identified with Louis XIV himself. The king is known to have taken a great interest in which texts Lully should employ, making personal choices for *Amadis, Roland,* and *Armide.*

Lully's operatic form has been described somewhat misleadingly as a type of *Gesamtkunstwerk,* or "total art work," in which all of the musical and theatrical elements are combined for the purpose of the drama. These include the *récits* (a term meaning simply solo vocal passages)—consisting of recitatives and various solo and ensemble airs—choruses, introductory instrumental passages (overture, ritournelle, prelude) as well as descriptive *symphonies,* dances that are often combined into ballets, especially the self-contained though dramatically integrated *divertissements.* Elaborate scenery and intricate stage machinery are also vital components of these operas. The dramatic core of the *tragédie en musique* lies in the recitatives that tend to make up at least 50 percent of each work. Based on Quinault's *vers libre,* that is, on poetic lines of varying lengths, the various forms of recitative are characterized by their freedom and subtleness of their component styles, wedded to the rhetorical expressiveness of the words. These recitatives depend on the singer's ability to bring the words to life. Lully, who had already had considerable experience in the development of recitative styles in his ballets, is quoted as saying that his recitatives were made only for speaking. And he claimed to have based his knowledge of French declamation on a study of the actors of the French tragedy, especially the famous "La Champmeslé" (Marie Chevillet).

Lully's recitative is exceedingly complex and therefore cannot be described in a simple formulation. And because the composer's operatic style, including the recitative, underwent a continuous development, generalities about any aspect of these operas can be misleading. *Récitatif simple* and *récitatif mesuré* are the usual terms to describe forms of Lully recitative.[32] The former describes a recitative that is declamatory, often in fluctuating meters, and is meant to be sung with a freedom and the rhetorical emphasis inherent in the text itself. The latter, which suggests greater lyricism and tends to be in regular meters, can be related to the Italian concept of *arioso*. The strength of his recitative style is its unpredictability. It is frequently difficult to determine when a recitative becomes an air or when an air has moved into a more declaimed style. The genius of Lully lies in part in his awareness that recitative can be dull, and in the best of his music despite the long passages of narration, one seldom needs to wait long for a lyrical phrase or phrases or a complete air. It seems likely that this concept of a recitative that constantly moves between poles of strict declamation and various forms of lyricism is modeled on the recitative in Cavalli's Venetian operas, two of which Lully would have learned to know intimately during their performances at court for which he wrote the ballet *intermèdes*. The frequent changing of meter in the recitatives has been a puzzle that is still not entirely solved. Many of the metrical changes, such as C to 3/4, are Lully's method of handling the differences in lengths of text lines. Others, however, such as the juxtaposing of 2 and C or 3 and 3/2, probably require changes in tempo.[33]

Undeniably, the French character of Lully's operas depends partly on the care with which he observed the dramatic, accentual, and durational qualities of the French language in the recitatives. Musically, however, it is the song element that defines the purity of the French sound of these works. The *airs* occur in a considerable variety of types and vary widely in length and dramatic significance. Unlike the Italian employment of arias in operas that usually interrupt time and dramatic development, the French *air* invariably is imbedded in and belongs to the dramatic flow of time. It is always, however, cast in a vocal style that has its origins in French vocal music from at least the end of the Renaissance and was highly developed in the *air de cour*, the *chansons à boire*, and brunettes of the first half of the seventeenth century.

The vocal forms remain similar if not the same, most often as rondeaus, binary types, and sometimes a ternary ABA. The variety of binary forms frequently results from the quatrain structure of the text (A = two lines, B = two lines), but Lully adapts these to a number of musical versions such as AAB, AABB, ABB, and ABb or AABb. The last type is especially common, in which the Bb pattern illustrates the repetition of the B text but with different music. The binary *air* also can be adapted to texts of more than four lines. Many varieties of the *air* are joined to recitative texts, for example, the rondeau-like A–recitative–A–recitative–A. And of course numerous free forms of *air*- like songs fill the *récits* of these works, including those written over ostinato basses. Many binary *airs* are either dance songs (in which the singing precedes or follows an actual dance) or are in dance rhythms. The *air* also occurs as solo ensembles, the duet being the most common. Except for infrequent melismas on some words for added rhetorical emphasis, the *airs* are generally syllabic and true to textual accent and cadence. The frequent regularity of the rhythmic accompaniment, especially in triple meters, either in the continuo or, at times, in a modest two-part string or wind obbligato, gives the majority of the *airs* a lilting and at times popular tunefulness. Range is usually very limited, although for dramatic outbursts sudden leaps into a higher register are always very effective.

The considerable use of choruses in Lully's operas lends a distinctiveness that became a defining characteristic of French opera well into the nineteenth century (for example, the "grand operas" of Meyerbeer). Some acts tend to be dominated by choral writing (for example, act III of *Isis*) and many are filled with brief choral exclamations as part of the continuous dramatic dialogue. Choruses often are participants in the drama, as in the combat scene of act I of *Thesée;* at other times they give expression to universal emotions to be shared by the audience, such as the dirgelike refrain in *Alceste,* "Alceste est morte" (act III, scene 4), or at the moment of the murder of Sangaride by Atys (act V), the moving chorus of Phrygiens, "Atys, Atys luy-même fait périr ce qu'il aime." The various *divertissements* usually include major choral writing and often end with a danced and sung chaconne of considerable length; see, for example, the conclusion to *Amadis.* Although the employment of various forms of ostinato bass lines was already a characteristic of earlier seventeenth-century Italian music, for example, in Monteverdi, Cavalli, and Rossi, the magnitude and frequent grandeur of Lully's chaconnes and passacaglias has often led to the false conclusion that this technique was Lully's innovation. The writing for chorus is generally homophonic, either for five-part ensemble of two sopranos, haute-contre, tenor, and bass, or for the *petit choeur* of the upper three parts. Exceptional instances of contrapuntal writing stand out usually for their subtle and gentle expressiveness, such as the "Sleep" chorus in *Atys* (act III). An exceptional example of choral innovation is the "shivering chorus" from *Isis* (act IV), the fame of which brought it to Henry Purcell's attention who adapted it for the frost scene in his *King Arthur.*

Orchestral music is another crucial element defining Lully's operatic genre. He had, of course, considerable experience writing for instrumental ensembles in the court ballets, and the operas are greatly enriched by the variety of these instrumental pieces. The "French" overture, already crystallized in form for some of the *comédies-ballets,* prefaces each opera, and it became not only one of the earliest of independent orchestral forms but also would be used by composers for at least a century after Lully in various contexts. In this development, especially by German composers such as J. S. Bach and Handel, the second part of the overture becomes distinctly fugal, unlike those by Lully. Scenes most often are introduced by preludes or *ritournelles,* frequently but not always rather brief, that establish the mood or affect of the ensuing vocal music. Instrumental dances, of course, are prominent in the operas—minuets and gavottes the most common—but the whole range of dance forms are represented, especially in the *divertissements.* These *symphonies* also can be descriptive of the action, for example, slumber scenes, demon dances, storm music, or battle music. Lully's Paris Opèra orchestra was, like the chorus, divided between a *grand choeur* and a *petit choeur.* The *grand choeur* usually (there is some disagreement) consisted of six soprano violins (*dessus de violon*), twelve alto and tenor violins or violas (*haute-contre, taille,* and *quinte*), six basses (*basses de violon*), and the continuo. In addition, oboes and bassoons often doubled the outer parts. Some scores require trumpets perhaps played by two of the wind players. The *petit choeur* consisted of two violins (*dessus de violon*), two bass viols (*basses de viols*), perhaps a contrebasse, a harpsichord, two theorbos, and continuo. The continuo instruments included harpsichord, theorbos, *basse de violon,* and bass viols.

SACRED MUSIC

Because Lully never held an official position with the royal chapel, he had limited opportunities for composing sacred music. His six *Motets à deux choeurs pour la chapelle du Roi* were published by Ballard in 1684 at the explicit request of the king. According to Lully's introduction to this volume, addressed to the king, these *grands motets* were composed for exceptionally solemn sacred observances (such as royal births, deaths, marriages) when the musicians of the king's chamber and those of the royal chapel were joined together. Another five motets for two choirs remain unpublished in various manuscripts.[34] In addition to these eleven large-scale motets, Lully also composed ten or eleven *petits motets*.[35] These are works of intimate character, for three solo voices and continuo (two have an introduction with an added violin), perhaps written for a convent. The vocal writing is exceedingly expressive and prominently imitative, suggesting a late style of Lully that is less frequently found in his large sacred works. The grand motets employ a large group of performers with a six-part orchestra consisting of first and second violins, three viola parts, basse de violon, and a continuo bass for organ. The usual arrangement of voices is made up of the *petit choeur* for two sopranos, haute contre, tenor, and bass, which at times is reduced to the five solo voices, and the *grand choeur* that omits the second soprano and doubles the bass parts with the inclusion of a baritone.

The large number of performers—one report in the *Mercure galant* of the *Te Deum* performance in 1679 says 120 took part—and the frequently massive homophony of the writing create a grandeur and sonic splendor reflecting the royal image cultivated by the king of France at Versailles. The main role of the orchestra, which for some performances added winds and brass, was to double the choral parts. However, in addition to the introductory and at times intermediate *symphonies,* the orchestra also signaled larger structural divisions with *ritournelles*. The usual continuo support for the solo *recits* is often supplemented by the orchestra, sometimes in full ensemble, other times as bass and two treble instruments. In addition to the prominent *récits* in a vocal style similar to that found in the *tragédies en musique,* it is the concertato effects of small vocal ensemble pitted against the large chorus that adds great vitality to these works. While they are generally homophonic, Lully does use points of contrapuntal interest, especially for particularly moving texts requiring expressive dissonances, as, for example, in the opening of the Lacrymosa from the *Dies irae* (see Example 6.11).

The grand motet became one of the major sacred vocal forms during the ancien régime. Although Lully wrote relatively little sacred music, his success at court with the grand motet undoubtedly influenced other composers, contemporaries such as Du Mont, and those to come after Lully. The *Miserere mei Deus* of 1664, which the king and his court are known to have favored, is among his most successful. For a performance at an official funeral in 1672, Madame de Sévigné recorded her well-known comment that during the *Libera me* "all eyes were filled with tears. I do not believe any other music to exist in heaven." The style of the *récits* at times comes closer to the more expressive vocal writing of Italian composers, with affective dissonances, some chromaticism, rhetorically emphatic vocal lines, and frequent textural variety contrasting imitative writing with homophony. More characteristic of the grandeur associated with Lully's motets is the *Te Deum,* which because of the text is a sprawling work of over twelve hundred measures. Very long passages for choral homophony and emphatic diatonicism lend a certain monotony to the music that is not present in the *Miserere.* However, the brilliance of the orchestra with its trumpets and timpani and the impassioned rhetorical drive of the double choruses wedded to the triumphant text of praise to God—and, by analogy, to the king—create a standard of politicized musical style unequaled before or perhaps since.

EXAMPLE 6.11 Lully, *Dies irae*

Music for the Chapelle Royale

Because the king favored the low Mass (*Messe basse solennelle*), which included the *grand motet* (also the *petit motet*), this form of sacred music dominated the Chapelle Royale not only during Louis XIV's reign but also up to the Revolution. These motets were performed while the Mass itself was read by the priest. In their musical extroversion and theatricality and because their texts (taken from the psalms, sequences, *Magnificat, Te Deum,* and newly written sacred Latin poetry) were seldom related to the liturgical year, the *grands motets* often took on the character of a sacred concert. The institution of the Chapelle Royale belonged to the church of the king's choice, at first in various ones in Paris, then at Saint Germain-en-Laye, and finally at both Versailles and Fontainebleau. Prior to 1663 two musical directors or *sous-maîtres* were responsible, for six months each, for all of the chapel music. (The title of *maître* was an honor held usually by a church dignitary such as a bishop.) In 1663 Louis XIV divided these duties among four *sous-maîtres:* Thomas Gobert (d. 1672), Pierre Robert (c. 1618–1699), Gabriel Expilly (c. 1630–c. 1690), and Henry Du Mont. By 1683, all four had retired, and the king ordered a competition to choose the new *sous-maîtres.* From the thirty-five competitors, those gaining the positions included the insignificant composers Nicolas Coupillet (d. after 1713) and Guillaume Minoret (c. 1650–1717), the former secretary and assistant to Lully, Pascal Collasse (1649–1709), and the major figure of Michel-Richard Delalande (1657–1726). Among those not chosen (including Paolo Lorenzani, Guillaume-Gabriel Nivers, Jean Rebel, and Henry Desmarets) was Marc-Antoine Charpentier (1643–1704), who was said to be too ill to participate in the final competition. However, he received a generous pension from the king, officially in gratitude for his services to the dauphin.

Among the four *sous-maîtres* appointed in 1663, it was Du Mont and Robert who were the most gifted and prolific composers of the grand motet, and who created a repertory of works not unlike those of Lully, although the question of influence, if any, remains unclear. Du Mont's twenty grand motets were published posthumously in 1686 but no doubt were composed during his two decades serving the Chapelle Royale. These are important works by a composer who, as has been shown, did not entirely shun Italian influences of musical style. The motets are tightly structured in their smoothly developing connections between the various episodes of instrumental *ritournelles,* solo and ensemble *récits,* and the interchanges with both *petit* and *grand choeurs.* Frequently both solo ensemble and choral passage textures are enlivened contrapuntally as well as by the concerted effects between solo voices and the large chorus. The melodic writing can have a decidedly lyrical if not passionate expressiveness born of highly expressive texts, as, for example, in his *Magnificat.*

Similar to Du Mont's *grand motets* are the twenty-four by Pierre Robert published, as was the case with those of Du Mont (and Lully), by Ballard in 1684 at the command of the king. Robert's motets have significance in the development of this sacred form. In apparent distinction to both Lully and Du Mont, his motets greatly expand the importance and complexity of the *récits* for the solo ensemble. Not only are they longer, with developments of short motives on fragments of the text, but also they show considerable interest in contrapuntal textures. The *petit choeur* is dived into eight parts (two each, sopranos, altos, tenors, and basses), and are combined frequently into a series of solos, duets, trios, and quartets. Whether the lively contrapuntal interest is a new stylistic feature, or perhaps a reflection of Robert's commitment to older Franco-Flemish techniques, is difficult to ascertain with the lack of availability of most of his motets. Du Mont and Robert undoubtedly helped to develop the distinctive conception of the *grand motet* by Delalande, the outstanding member of Louis XIV's Chapelle Royale at Versailles.

Michel-Richard Delalande

Of the four *sous-maîtres* appointed to the Chapelle Royale following its competition in 1683, Delalande quickly became the king's favorite. In 1695 he became *maître de musique de la chambre,* and by 1714, with the retirement of the last of the other three *sous-maîtres,* he gained total control of the chapel music. Although he wrote a considerable amount of secular music, ballets and divertissements, airs, and instrumental *symphonies* extracted from the ballets and divertissements (such as the *Sinfonies pour les soupers du Roi*), it is the composition of over seventy *grands motets* (of which sixty-four survive) that distinguishes Delalande as a major if still much-neglected composer of the French Baroque and the creator of what might be called the Versailles motet style. Not only were these works favorites of Louis XIV and Louis XV, but also they continued to be sung in the chapel until the crushing of the ancien régime in 1792. Further emphasizing the popularity of the motets, they became a regular feature of the repertory of the public *Concert spirituel* established in 1725. For the next forty-five years these concerts gave more than 590 performances of some 41 different *grands motets*.[36]

Three major sources preserve these works: the Philidor manuscript copy of twenty-seven motets in ten volumes made in 1689–1690, forty motets in twenty volumes published in Paris, 1729, and a mid-eighteenth-century copy of forty-one motets, the Gaspard Alexis Cauvin collection. Comparisons of the same motets found in the Philidor collection with versions in later sources indicate that Delalande methodically revised many of his motets to conform to his changing style, which seems heavily indebted to increasing Italianate influences. These changes involve the adapting of shorter and more loosely structured *récits* into independent and often elaborate solo or ensemble movements; at times the altering of the predominantly homophonic style of choruses into a much more polyphonic style with obbligato instruments; and the enriching of the orchestra's role from simply doubling the choral voices to frequently becoming musically quite independent. A new style of lyricism and expressiveness permeates Delalande's motets, bringing his music into the new century, and the richness of this music depends on the extraordinary amalgamation of types of music. The official and pompous court style is still present but also Italianate arias and solo ensembles with elaborate vocal virtuosity, and forms based on phrase repetitions, walking basses, and other continuo basses with familiar Italian rhythmic gestures can be found. The older arioso-like *récits* are replaced with clearly structured arias, many of them in some type of ternary form. Perhaps what is most enriching in the motets is Delalande's contrapuntal diversity, various imitative discourses, and notable fugal writing often with striking countersubjects. At times these brilliant movements concluded with a grand pause in preparation for a homophonic and usually slow final cadential passage that recall the same technique used later by Handel in his oratorios. The discrete sectionalism of the motets cast them very much in the image of the Italian cantata.[37]

Marc-Antoine Charpentier (1643–1704)

Of all the stars forming the galaxy of composers of the French Baroque in the seventeenth century, none is brighter than Marc-Antoine Charpentier. Although he never achieved an appointment at the Sun King's court, which obviously restricted opportunities for composing secular music, Charpentier's greatness as a composer of a considerable variety of music was recognized by his contemporaries who valued him as the most gifted contemporary of Lully. Of all the French composers from the mid-seventeenth century, Charpentier is the one who most overtly embraces concepts of expression and style of the Italians. His Italian proclivities no doubt came from the years spent in Rome in the 1600s, where, according to the *Mercure galant*, he was a pupil of Giacomo Carissimi. It is Charpentier who is usually credited with introducing the concept of the Italian oratorio into France. In Paris, Charpentier's career began in the employ of the nobility, including the *grand dauphin* (the king's oldest son) and as music teacher to the Duke of Chartres (the king's nephew), who later became the Duke d'Orleans (in 1701) and Regent of France between 1715 and 1723. Charpentier also wrote music for Molière's troupe, but his reputation was soon established as a composer of church music. Many of his sacred works were written for the principal church of the Jesuits in Paris, St. Louis (today known as Saint-Paul–Saint-Louis), and in his last five years as *maître de musique* of the Sainte-Chapelle, a church position of importance second only to that of the royal chapel at Versailles.

Charpentier, while not unimportant for his secular works (discussed later), was perhaps by the demands of his occupation primarily a composer of sacred music. His very large output of 471 sacred compositions of various forms remains to be examined in comprehensive detail and only general observations are possible here. Among these works there are eleven masses, four sequences, thirty-seven antiphons, nineteen hymns, ten Magnificat settings, nine settings of the Litany of Loreto, fifty-four lessons and responsories for Tenebrae services, four Te Deums, eighty-four psalm settings, and 207 motets, some of which are of such a dramatic nature as to be considered oratorios or *histoires sacrées*.[38] Charpentier's music was almost completely forgotten for two centuries, and it was particularly fortunate that his own extensive collection of autograph scores, contained in twenty-eight large volumes of the *mélanges autographes,* have been preserved and are now in the Bibliothèque nationale at Paris.

Charpentier's highly personal and exceptionally varied style initially grew out of his Italian training. The influences, in addition to that of Carissimi, would have been composers active in mid-century Rome such as Domenico and Virgilio Mazzocchi, Francesco Foggia, Orazio Benevoli, and Luigi Rossi. A Mass in sixteen parts by Francesco Beretta, *Missa mirabiles elationes maris,* was copied by Charpentier, to which he added a number of observations concerning strengths and weaknesses of the composer's counterpoint.[39] Contemporary criticism charged the composer with employing overt and unpleasant Italianisms, false relations, various single and double suspensions, and particularly a strikingly rich dissonance treatment including augmented chords, major sevenths, ninths, and even augmented octaves. As with the example set by his teacher, Charpentier's music often is powerfully rhetorical, in which the very substance of the music arises out of the poetic and dramatic qualities of the text. In many works, especially the *histoires,* Charpentier fully assimilates Italian recitative practices, and many of his vocal compositions display characteristics of Italianate melody, including lengthy melismas for expressive or colorful purposes. His music is strongly tonal, often with sequential bass patterns moving by fifths or thirds that also suggest the Italian practice of the mid-century.

It would be misleading, however, to overlook the most important achievement of Charpentier's music: his amalgamation of the contemporary French style as established by Lully with his own. Like the music of his great contemporary Delalande, most of Charpentier's works are clearly French. They remain true to the elements of the dance and the air de cour melodic style. The "Versailles" *grand motet* style, in its grandiose and pompous character, is often found in his Te Deums (especially the well-known one in D major, H. 146), many of the motets, and Magnificats. The Charpentier orchestra normally remains the same as Lully's, five string parts doubled with winds (and added trumpets and timpani for majestic works) for the *grand choeur* with a soloistic *petit choeur* of two treble parts and a bass part. At times, however, the string section of the orchestra is reduced to four parts.

THE "ORATORIO"

Among Charpentier's manuscripts is a copy of Carissimi's *Jephte,* and it is evident that Charpentier not only introduced the concept of the Roman oratorio into France but also was the only French composer of his generation to compose in the genre. Even though the term may have had some currency in late-seventeenth-century France (Brossard defines it in his *Dictionnaire de musique* of 1703), it was never used by Charpentier and his contemporaries. The relationship with Carissimi's Latin works in semidramatic form originating in the Latin dialogues is clear. As is true with Carissimi's works, Charpentier's vary greatly in length. Very few of them are extended in length such as his best-known work, *Judicium Salomonis* (H. 422), as well as *Judith sive Bethulia liberata* (H. 391), and the lovely Christmas work, *In nativitatem Domini canticum* (H. 416). Charpentier used a variety of designations for oratorio-like works including *motet, historia, canticum, dialogus,* and *méditation.* Hitchcock[40] prefers the label "dramatic motet," because none of the French composer's works had the function of Carissimi's—performed at oratory meetings—but, rather, as motets for church services. The texts are largely anonymous adaptations of biblical passages often with prose insertions. Many of them draw on highly dramatic and favorite passages to be used by composers throughout the Baroque, in addition to *Judith,* including *Historia Esther* (H. 396), *Filius prodigus* (H. 399), *Mors Saulis et Jonathae* (H. 403), and *Josue* (H. 404).

His thirty-five dramatic motets vary greatly not only in length but also in style and performing forces. Some are composed as *petit motets* for vocal trio and two violins or recorders and continuo, for example, *In resurrectione Domini Nostri Jesu Christi* (H. 405). Many of the dramatic motets characteristically feature the best and most striking elements of Charpentier's style: stunning choruses in the tradition of his *grand motet,* a superb sense of melodic expressivity, and an impressive emphasis on instrumental music. The orchestra in some works is expanded to include flutes, oboes, and bassoons, and in *Caecilia virgo et martyr* (H. 397) two four-part orchestras are required. The long narrative passages for solo voice or voices also are similar to the expressive recitative of his other sacred works with frequent shifts from intensely rhetorical, Italianate declamation to passages in the style of the French *air.* The intensity of the dramatic element is also dependent on Charpentier's remarkable harmonic language, its coloristic dissonances and employment of chromaticism. Perhaps nothing better illustrates the latter characteristics than the passage in the first part of the non-biblical *Pestis Mediolanensis* (The Plague of Milan, H. 398; see Example 6.12) describing the plague with the choral refrain *Clamabant aegrotantium ora, suspirabant morientium pectora, et non erat auxiliator*—"Cries rose from the mouths of the sick, sighs from the breast of the dying, and there was no one to help."[41]

Sacred Works by Charpentier's Contemporaries and Later Composers

Sacred music by French composers written through the first half of the eighteenth century includes a considerable repertory that can in most cases only be cited, as little research has been directed to it. Among the many composers of distinction were: Guillaume-Gabriel Nivers (c. 1632–1714), Louis-Nicolas Clérambault (1676–1749), Jean-Baptiste Moreau (?1656–1733), Pascal Collasse (1649–1709), Louis Marchand (1669–1732), Daniel Danielis (1635–1696), Henry Desmarets (1661–1741), Guillaume Poitevin (1646–1706), Jean Gilles (1668–1705), and especially André Campra (1660–1744) and François Couperin (1668–1733). Significant contemporaries of the latter two also include Sébastian de Brossard (1655–1730)—author of the first French music dictionary—Nicolas Bernier (1665–1734), Jean-Baptiste Morin (1677–1745), Jean-Joseph Mouret (1682–1738), and, finally, Jean-Philippe Rameau (1683–1764).

André Campra, born in Aix-en-Provence, spent the early part of his career in southern regions of France including Arles and Toulouse, before coming to Paris in 1694. He was *maître de musique* at Notre Dame until 1700 when he began his highly successful connection with the Académie royale de musique. In 1723 he received a court appointment as one of *sous-maîtres* of the royal chapel. In his lifetime and subsequently Campra was best known for his theatrical works, especially the *opéra-ballet,* but also for his continuation and adaptation of the Lullian *tragédie en musique.* His sacred music written both for Notre Dame and the royal chapel, the majority of which remains without modern editions, is a distinguished and important contribution to French music history. His most extensive sacred composition is a superb *Messe des morts* for five-part chorus, soloists, and orchestra, probably a late work but of uncertain date. It is, like many of the motets, distinctly

EXAMPLE 6.12   Charpentier, from *Pestis Mediolanensis* (ed. H. Wiley Hitchcock)

influenced by Italian musical style, lilting solo and duet melodies, rhetorically impulsive full choral outbursts, rhythmically simple imitative writing and strong walking basses, yet retaining the nobility and grandeur characteristic of the Versailles *grand motet*.

Campra published four books of *petits motets,* I. (1695), II. (1699), III. (1703), and IV. (1706), with a total of forty-six solo vocal works with continuo for one to three voices in which one or two violins or flutes are added at times. Only in Book III does Campra remark in the title that he has included *"un autre motet, á maniére italienne, á voix seule, avec deux dessus de violons,"* a reference to "O dulcis amor." All four books, however, are often suggestive of the Italian cantata and include vocal as well as continuo writing that reflects contemporary Italian style. There is considerable textual repetition, passages of florid melismatic as well as intensely expressive writing. In the fourth book, da capo airs appear frequently. Even in the first book many of the solo motets are oriented toward the highly expressive vocal recitative of the Italians of the middle of the century as, for example, the

EXAMPLE 6.13 Campra, Salve Regina

opening of the fourth motet, Salve Regina with its expressive silences, dramatic exclamations, and sensitive melismas on words such as *Salve, lachrimarum valle,* and the typical rhetorical conceit of rests breaking up both melody and bass for the "sighs" of the line *Ad te suspiramus* (see Example 6.13[42]).

A fifth book of motets appeared in 1720. After Campra's appointment to the royal chapel, he published in 1737 and 1738 two collections of psalms in the Versailles style of the *grand motet.* Versailles, however, had lost its centrality to royal splendor, for, following the death of Louis XIV in 1715, a regency was established with Philippe Duke d'Orléans, who returned the court to Paris, where it remained until Louis XV began his reign in 1722. Even then Versailles never again regained its control over all new French music.

Secular Music after Lully until the End of the Regency

TRAGÉDIE EN MUSIQUE

The death of Lully in March 1687 did not end his extraordinary influence on the subsequent history of French music, especially the *tragédie en musique.* Lully had not only established a uniquely politicized and suprapersonal style of music, which shaped the taste for music at the court of France for some thirty years. In his domination over music, his ruthless suppression of younger talented contemporaries, and a dictatorial control of all public performances of theatrical scores, he managed even after death to lay a heavy hand on the future of music in France until well into the eighteenth century. His operas continued to be performed, although with frequent modifications and additions by other composers, at the Académie Royale on a yearly basis as late as 1779. There were frequent performances outside of Paris in Marseille and Lyon and less often in other provincial centers. Numerous secular and even sacred parodies of Lully's airs were published throughout the eighteenth century.[43]

Lully had prepared several composers to administer performances of his works at the Académie: his son Louis (1664–1734), Pascal Collasse (1649–1709), Jean Françoise Lallouette (1651–1728), Henry Desmarets (1661–1741), and Marin Marais (1656–1728). Collasse had worked closely with Lully for years and was responsible for completing acts II and III of Lully's last *tragédie en musique, Achille et Polyxène.* He held major appointments at Versailles, as one of the *sous maîtres* in the royal chapel, and also as a court composer. His efforts to succeed as a dramatic composer included *Thétis et Pelée,* the only one of several stage works to remain in the repertory for the Académie into the second half of the eighteenth century. Henry Desmarets succeeded with only one out of his six operas, *Didon* (1693). Marin Marais, best known as the most important composer of the French school of bass viol, collaborated with Lully's son Louis on the opera *Alcide* (1693), and composed three other operas of which *Alcyone* (1706) had the greatest and longest-lived success and has one of the earliest uses of a double bass in a French operatic score.

Charpentier was apparently unable to overcome the insurmountable obstacles imposed by Lully barring him from contributing to music at court, and only six years after the latter's death did he finally gain access to the Académie Royale de Musique. Nevertheless, he wrote music for the theater during most of his career even if handicapped by Lully's restrictions placed on the number of musicians permitted to participate in any dramatic work. After Lully and Molière ended their partnership, Charpentier became Molière's new collaborator, contributing a major score of incidental music to his final play, *Le Malade imaginaire* (1673). He also created scores for other plays presented at the Comédie-Française, for example, *Circé* by Thomas Corneille. He composed a large number of pastorales, many for Mlle de Guise, including *Actéon,* and two attractive Christmas pastorales. Two one-act works that are operatic in content are *Les plaisirs de Versailles* (early 1680s) and *Les arts florissants* (1685–1686).

His career as a composer of dramatic music ended with three major *tragédies en musique,* each in five acts with a prologue and including all the diverse musical forms characterized by Lully's operas. These were *Celse Martyr* (1687, music lost); *David et Jonathas* (1688), presented in the theater of the Jesuit College Louis-le-Grand; and *Médée* (1693) for the Opéra. *Médée* with a libretto by Thomas Corneille was greeted with disdain by Lully partisans for its Italianisms, especially in its harmonic audacity, and the work survived only ten performances. It is, however, his greatest dramatic achievement and its style is generally a continuation as well as a considerable enrichment of Lully's own dramatic musical style. Emotional intensity derives from subtle psychological insights. Highly original orchestral colorings, choruses of grandeur, and a considerable variety of types of solo vocal music while rooted in the earlier concept of *tragédie lyrique* are much more than mere imitations; rather, they intensify and personalize Lully's concept of dramatic vocal music.

A milestone in the development of the *tragédie en musique* was reached with Rameau's first dramatic opera, *Hippolyte et Aricie* (1733), a work that remains true to Lully's concept of the form but abandons a subservience to Lully's stylistic domination. Several composers preceded Rameau in the continuing development of the operatic genre. First among them was Campra with eight major works, including *Tancrède* and *Idoménée;* also six operas by André Cardinal Destouches (1672–1749), including *Amadis de Grèce, Omphale,* and *Sémiramis,* and *Jepthté* by Michel Pignolet de Montéclair (1667–1737).

OPÉRA-BALLET

By the last decade of the seventeenth century the sun began its inevitable decline at Versailles. Major defeats on the battlefield, economic crisis, and the aging and ill king all brought about a lessening of influence from Versailles on the arts in France. The king no longer attended public musical events, and the courtiers began to look elsewhere, in the town houses in Paris and in the country châteaux, for fashionable and new musical entertainments. Although Lully's works remained a staple of the Académie Royale in Paris, audiences sought new forms of entertainment responsive to changing tastes of the pleasure-seeking public. The inherent French love of the dance that had long been placed in a secondary role in the *tragédie en musique* again became the focus of a new genre, the *opéra-ballet.*[44]

André Campra and the poet Houdar de la Motte, beginning with their *L'Europe galante,* first performed at the Paris Opera in October 1697, are credited with having created this genre. It is distinguished as consisting of a prologue and four acts, each of which is composed of a single and different action presented in *divertissements* of songs and dances. The acts do not have a continuous dramatic development, and the only unifying factor for the work is contained usually in the title, which suggests some general theme or overall idea. A source of this genre was the formal structure of the *ballets à entrées* from the earlier seventeenth century. What was new in the *opéras-ballets* was the choice and tone of topics for the actions that no longer concentrated on mythology or allegory but, rather, on more contemporary themes. For example, in the prologue to Ballard's full score (1724) of *L'Europe galante,* La Motte gave the following explanation of the work:

> We have chosen those Nations that are most contrasting and that offer the greatest potential for stage treatment: France, Spain, Italy and Turkey. We have followed what

is normally considered to be characteristic behavior of their Inhabitants. The *Frenchman* is portrayed as fickle, indiscreet & amorous. The *Spaniard,* as faithful and romantic. The *Italian,* as jealous, shrewd & violent. Finally, we expressed, within the limits of the stage, the haughtiness and supreme authority of the *Sultan* and the passionate nature of the *Sultanas.*[45]

Eighteen *opéras-ballets* fitting this definition were performed at the Académie Royale, beginning with Campra's first work in 1697 through the year of Rameau's first composition in this genre, *Les indes galantes* of 1735:

Title	First performance	Composer	Librettist
1. *L'Europe galante*	24 October 1697	Campra	La Motte
2. *Le Triomphe des Arts*	16 May 1700	La Barre	La Motte
3. *Les Muses*	28 October 1703	Campra	Danchet
4. *Les Fêtes vénitiennes*	17 June 1710	Campra	Danchet
5. *Les Amours déguisés*	22 August 1713	Bourgeois	Fuzelier
6. *Les Fêtes de Thalie*	19 August 1714	Mouret	La Font
7. *Les Fêtes d'l'été*	12 June 1716	Montéclair	Pellegrin
8. *Les Ages*	9 October 1718	Campra	Fuzelier
9. *Les Plaisirs de la campagne*	10 August 1719	Bertin de La Doué	Pellegrin
10. *Les Fêtes grecques et romaines*	13 July 1723	Colin de Blamont	Fuzelier
11. *Les Eléments*	29 May 1725 (1st perf. 22 Dec. 1721 [Tuileries])	Destouches	Roy
12. *Les Stratagèmes de l'amour*	28 March 1728	Destouches	Roy
13. *Les Amours des Dieux*	14 September 1727	Mouret	Fuzelier
14. *Les Amours des Déesses*	9 August 1729	J. B. Quinault	Fuzelier
15. *Le Triomphe des sens*	5 June 1732	Mouret	Roy
16. *L'Empire de l'amour*	14 April 1733	de Brassac	Moncrif
17. *Les Grâces*	5 May 1735	Mouret	Roy
18. *Les Indes galantes*	23 August 1735	Rameau	Fuzelier[46]

Responding to the changing tastes of French audiences during the Regency, the *opérasballets* contain nothing of the tragic and little of the pompous associated with the official taste of the *grand siècle.* Rather each act tends to have a fast pace, short scenes with a number of brief Italianate *ariettes* leading to *divertissements* of dances. The music is almost always light and gracious in style. Further indication of the decline of the *tragédie en musique* as a relevant force at the Parisian opera was the introduction of comedy into the *opéras-ballets,* first in Campra's *Les fêtes vénitiennes.* This ballet also includes two *cantates,* bringing together the Italian da capo aria with French recitative and dance. This is not surprising, because by this time the French cantata had become one of the newest and most popular musical forms resonating in the chamber music entertainments throughout France.

THE FRENCH *CANTATE*

The *cantate française* had a brief but impressive popularity. Appearing toward the end of the reign of Louis XIV, it was at the height of its popularity in the 1720s, and continued to be composed up to the Revolution. Some eight hundred works were created during this period. Most of the French composers of the period composed them.[47] There is no evidence that the term was known in France in the seventeenth century, and, as late as 1703, in the first edition of Brossard's *Dictionnaire,* he does not apply it to French music. (In the third edition, *cantate française* does appear, with Brossard's comment that they have begun to appear in recent years.) Jean-Jacques Rousseau, in his *Dictionnaire de musique* (1767), points to the Italian origins of the genre and describes it as "a type of short lyric poem, which is sung with accompaniment, and which, although written for the chamber, should receive from the musician the warmth and the gracefulness of imitative and theatrical music."

Cantatas consisted of a series of movements, most often three recitatives and three arias, sung in alternation. This poetic form was established by Jean-Baptiste Rousseau (1671–1741), whose twenty-seven texts were composed numerous times. While most of the texts are anonymous, other well-known poets who wrote them included Houdar de la Motte, Pierre Roy, and Antoine Danchet. With a few exceptions all the *cantates françaises* were secular, with themes of love largely although not exclusively drawn from myth. Probably before 1700, in the salons of Paris and the châteaux of the royalty, cantata-like compositions were performed, although there is little evidence in extant music. Charpentier's famous work of 1683, *Orphée descendant aux enfers,* often considered the earliest French cantata, seems to be related more to the concept of a dramatic *scena,* with an element of the oratorio in its moralistic conclusion.[48]

The earliest cantatas in the French language were published by Ballard in 1706 and 1707, six cantatas (*cantates françaises*) in each of two separate volumes. Each consisted of six cantatas (five for one voice, one as a duo) by Jean-Baptiste Morin (1677–1745). In about 1701 Morin worked for Philippe III, Duke of Orléans and future Regent, who was known for his love of Italian music. Morin makes clear his own commitment to Italian style by stating in the preface to this volume of cantatas: "I have done all that I can to retain the sweetness of our French style of melody, but with greater variety in the accompaniments and employing those rhythms and modulations characteristic of the Italian cantata."[49] Morin's recitatives show the infusion of Italian style, with longer held bass notes, more rapid declamatory melodies, and an avoidance of mixed meters that had characterized the recitative in French vocal works since Lully. The result is something of a compromise between Italian and French approaches to setting declamatory texts. The airs, however, are more influenced by the lyrical expansiveness of the Italian cantata of the later seventeenth century, although still retaining the French *douceur.* The most Italianate features, however, can be seen in the *devise* or motto openings in which a continuo melodic fragment or phrase becomes the opening music of the voice part, and also in the sequential and frequently rapid basses in clearly instrumental figurations that, by opposing the melodic structure of the voice part, create interesting musical tensions. Another clear Italian influence was the introduction of instrumental ritornellos, especially the use of the violin obbligato and the growing importance of Italian string figurations.

The remainder of Morin's cantatas, Op. 6 with six works, were published in 1712. Four volumes of cantatas appearing between 1706 and 1714 were by Jean-Baptiste Stuck—who published under the name of Batistin (1680–1755)—an Italian composer of German descent also employed by the Duke of Orléans. In dedicating his work to the duke he commented he had made the "attempt to join the taste of Italian music with French words." In these early collections of cantatas composers obviously were anxious to stress the adaptation of Italian musical style to French words. This is noted most strongly but with obvious concern in the preface to André Campra's first volume of French cantatas (1712):

> As cantatas have become the fashion, I thought, after entreaties from several persons, that I ought to present to the public some of my fabrication. I have tried, as much as I am able, to mix the delicateness of our French music with the vivacity of Italian music: perhaps those who have abandoned completely the taste of the former will not approve of the manner which I have treated this small work. I am persuaded as much as anyone of the merit of the Italians, but our language could not tolerate certain things that they allow. Our music has some beauty that they cannot help admiring,

and trying to imitate, although it is neglected by some of our French composers. I have dedicated myself above all, to conserve the beauty of melody, the expression and our manner of reciting, which according to my opinion is the best.[50]

The very rich output of cantatas, still little known today, was produced by more than two dozen composers, many of whom were major figures in the history of French music of the eighteenth century. In addition to three books by Campra, cantatas of musical significance include seven books by Nicolas Bernier (1665–1754), including Book V (1715) containing works performed as evening entertainments in the gardens at the famous chateau of the Duchess of Maine and entitled *Les nuits de Sceaux, concerts de chambre ou cantates françaises à plusieurs voix en manière de divertissements.* These are hybrid works for soloists, chorus, and a larger instrumental ensemble made of many individual movements including dancing and choral singing. Elizabeth Jacquet de La Guerre (1659–1729), who was perhaps the first woman to achieve professional status as a composer, published two unusual volumes of sacred cantatas (1708 and 1711) in addition to a book of secular ones (undated). Other composers writing significant books of cantatas before 1730 are Michel Pignolet de Montéclair (1667–1737), André Cardinal Destouches (1672–1749), Colin de Blamont (1690–1754), Louis-Nicolas Clérambault (1676–1749), Joseph Bodin de Boismortier (1691–1755), Jean-Joseph Mouret (1682–1738), and Jean-Philippe Rameau (bap. 1683–1764).

It was Clérambault, however, who gained greatest success and popularity with his cantatas. Twenty of his twenty-five cantatas were published in five books between 1710 and 1726. They range widely, subsuming stylistic characteristics found in most of the cantatas written in the previous decade, from works of intensely dramatic expression such as *Medée* and the masterful *Orphée* to others of simple lyrical charm. Many of them have expanded forms involving ritornellos and rather elaborate writing for the violin bordering on the Italian concerto. However, the range of styles depending on both French and Italian elements is considerable, and it is impossible to define in a few words the richness and complexity of ideas that characterize his music.[51]

After Rameau had reestablished the *tragédie en musique* in Paris in 1733, the popularity of cantatas rather quickly waned. Fewer cantatas were composed after the third decade, and a shorter form, the *cantatille,* usually consisting of two very short recitatives and two or three airs, gained a certain popularity through mid-century. In these works the spirit of the Baroque has faded and the Rococo stands out, light, sometimes more florid, avoiding dramatic intensity. Among the important composers of the *cantatille* were Jean-Joseph Mouret and Louis Lemaire (1693 or 1694–c. 1750).

THE *CONCERT SPIRITUEL*

Musical life in Paris centered not only in the palaces of the royal family. Private concerts took place in the homes of the wealthy aristocrats and the middle class. Antoine Crozat (1655–1738) gave concerts at his home for several years beginning in 1715, and he joined with a number of wealthy Parisians to establish the *Concert Italien* from 1724, for which only professional musicians performed in a subscription series at the Tuileries palace. The success of this venture led to the establishment of the *Concert spirituel* in 1725, which became until the last decade of the century a major focus of nonoperatic public concerts. It was founded by Anne Danican Philidor (1681–1728), son of the composer and royal music librarian André Danican Philidor *l'aîné.* At first, concerts consisted usually of instrumental works and sacred works with Latin texts, and they were held on religious holidays when the Paris opera was closed. Later, secular works with French texts, especially cantatas, were introduced. The first concert took place on Passion Sunday, 18 March 1725, with instrumental music and two grand motets by Delalande (who as has been mentioned was the most performed of all the composers programmed for these concerts), and the "Christmas Concerto," Op. 12, No. 8 of Corelli. Performances, for which admission was charged, took place until 1784 in the Salle des Suisses in the Tuileries palace, a gift of Louis XV. The singular importance of the *Concert spirituel* rests in the opening up to concert audiences of the sacred repertory and in presenting a very large and varied repertory of new music. In subsequent years these concerts became a major force in presenting instrumental works, especially solo concerts.

Baroque Instrumental Music in France

LUTE AND KEYBOARD COMPOSERS

The lute dominated private music-making in aristocratic chambers as well as the homes of the bourgeoisie long before the seventeenth century. In France, as in all of the European countries, the lute was a preferred instrument both for solo entertainment as well as for the accompaniment of solo songs, especially for the *air de cour*. The intimate relationship of performer and instrument, its subtle, intense expressivity, and the richness of its sound made the lute the ideal means to convey the most personal of the affects. Lute virtuosos were prized members of court life. The instrument's popularity, however, began to fade by the middle of the seventeenth century as the harpsichord rather quickly replaced it both as a solo and also accompanying instrument. Yet, harpsichord music developed as a continuation and imitation of many of the stylistic traits characteristic of lute music.

At the turn of the seventeenth century, French lute music is exemplified by two major collections: *Le trésor d'Orphée* (Paris, 1600) by Anthoine Francisque (c. 1575–1605), and the encyclopedic *Thesaurus harmonicus* (Cologne, 1603) by Jean-Baptiste Besard (c. 1567–after 1617).[52] The seventy pieces in *Le trésor* consist largely of dances including *passemèzes et pavanes, gaillardes, branles et gavottes, courantes, voltes,* and *ballets*. Besard's enormous publication of some four hundred pieces by twenty-one composers contains, in addition to transcriptions of some vocal pieces, many improvisatory preludes and fantasies, also numerous examples of dances such as *passamezzi, gaillardes, branles, ballets, allemandes, courantes,* and *voltes*. Robert Ballard, son of the founder of the Parisian printing firm, dedicated his first book of lute pieces (1611) to Maria de' Medici, regent of France, who appointed him *maître de luth* at court and teacher of the lute to the young Louis XIII. Ballard's work as well as Besard's not only preserves a considerable repertory of dances from the *ballets de cour,* but also shows a changing concept of style from the typical Renaissance emphasis on full strummed chords and virtuosic passagework to homophonic, ornamented dances that begin to reveal a concern for creating some textural variety between melody and bass line. These pieces display many characteristics of ornamentation of the *air de cour,* and establish the important concept of the *stile brisé*. The *stile brisé* is the most idiomatic feature of seventeenth-century lute technique. Its purpose is to simulate polyphonic writing by means of broken arpeggios. Consecutive notes suggest contrapuntal lines that appear and disappear within chordal textures. A large number of ornaments are required for both the melodic and expressive emphases of the inner parts. These features also became an essential stylistic feature of French harpsichord and organ music.

Among other distinguished French lutenists in the first and second decades of the century were René Mesangeau (late sixteenth century–1638) and Charles Bocquet (c. 1570–before 1615), and in the third decade, François Dufaut (before 1604–before 1671), François

EXAMPLE 6.14   Gaultier, *Orphée* from the eleventh suite

de Chancy (d. 1656), Vincent (c. 1580s–after 1643), and another Vincent (c. 1610–after 1661), and particularly the Gaultiers, Ennemond (1575–1651), known as "le vieux Gaultier," and his cousin Denis (1603–1672). Their music continues the tradition of miniatures of refinement and frequent melancholy, further defines the specific character of the various dances, and explores subtle and enriching harmonic colorings, all aspects of style to be adopted by the harpsichord composers. Both Gaultiers often give fanciful titles to their pieces, and Denis Gaultier at times composes music descriptive of his titles. They are among several composers in the same period who develop the new concept of the *tombeau,* an expressive allemande honoring the death of a friend or illustrious person.

The major monument to lute composition in the century is Denis Gaultier's *La rhétorique des Dieux* (Paris, c. 1652), fifty-six short dances grouped tonally into twelve suites plus a closing *Tombeau de Monsieur de L'Enclos,* a friend and well-known lutenist in Paris.[53] The manuscript is beautifully illustrated with plates based on drawings of the painter Le Sueur. The allegorical basis of the collection is taken from Classical antiquity, and the work is clearly meant for an informed and initiated audience. Each suite uses a different tonality (although given the names of the Greek modes). Following the opening *La dédicace (Dedication),* most of the movements refer to a god or goddess: *Phâeton foudroyé (Phaeton Thunderstruck), Le Panegirique (The Panegyric* [in praise of Mercury]), *Minerve (Minerva), Ulisse (Ulysses), Andromède (Andromeda), Atalante, Mars superbe (Proud Mars), Appolon orateur (Apollo the orator), Diane au bois (Diana in the woods), Circé, Orphée (Orpheus), Narcisse (Narcissus),* and *Junon ou La Jalouse (Juno or the Jealous One).* Example 6.14, *Orphée* from the eleventh suite (Mode Ionien), contrasts the free rhythmic notation of the lute tablature with the attempt to transcribe the music for a keyboard realization. The freedom of voice-leading and the frequent open textures are all characteristic of lute technique.

Beginning around the middle of the century lute players and their music lost much of their popularity. Important stylistic achievements, however, remained and became an integral part of the music composed by the French *clavecinistes.* Around 1650 a number of distinguished harpsichordists produced a major repertory of French *clavecin* music that would influence all composers for the harpsichord through at least the first half of the eighteenth century. The *clavecin* repertory of the seventeenth century is very large, and only a few of the major composers and their works can be cited here.[54] The first to give artistic distinction to the growing emphasis on harpsichord music was Jacques Champion de Chambonnières (1601 or 1602–1672). His fame was both as a composer and a player. He held positions at the courts of both Louis XIII and Louis XIV, and performed frequently in the Parisian homes of the wealthy. Mersenne, in the introduction to his famous treatise, *Harmonie universelle,* refers to Chambonnières's harpsichord technique with "it can be said that this instrument has met its ultimate master."[55] In addition, his influence was powerfully felt by most of the next generation of French harpsichordists whom he either taught or sponsored, including Louis Couperin (1626–1661) and his two brothers, François "the elder" (c. 1631–between 1708 and 1712) and Charles (1638–1679), Robert Cambert (c. 1627–1677), Henri D'Anglebert (1635–1691), Nicolas-Antoine Lebègue (1630–1702), Jacques Hardel (d. 1678), and Guillaume Gabriel Nivers (c. 1632–1714).

Chambonnières is represented by about 145 keyboard pieces, the majority of which are preserved in volume 1 of the Bauyn MS (Paris, Bibliothèque nationale, Vm7 674–75), and in two volumes printed by the composer in 1660 containing sixty pieces.[56] The Bauyn MS organizes the various dances according to tonality, but with little apparent regard for suggesting actual suites. The two printed volumes, however, each contain suites organized by tonality, although they are considerably different in content and numbers of dance movements. Only three do not include an initial allemande, two or three courantes, and a sarabande. Some end with another dance such as a gaillarde, carnaris, gigue, or minuet. A few bear descriptive if illusive titles such as allemande *La rare,* courante *La toute belle,* gigue *La vilageoise,* or sarabande *Jeunes Zéphirs.* The published volumes give a substantial number of indications for applying ornaments to the notes, and Chambonnières was one of the first of the *clavecin* composers to publish a table of explanations for the symbols he applied to his music, in the first volume of *Les pièces de Clavecin* (Paris, 1670).

These are in the best sense of the word elegantly refined miniatures, binary dances rarely extended in length. The one notable exception is the pavane *L'entretien des Dieux,* which in its length, rich contrapuntal texture, expressive harmonies, and superbly expressive melodic lines seems appropriately inspired by the concept of "the conversation of the gods." The "broken style" reflective of lute technique makes possible a constantly moving texture, more or less contrapuntal, depending on the dance. The allemandes tend to be the richest in textural expressiveness, although most of the dances have some contrapuntal interest. The courantes are usually written in a compound 3/2 6/4 meter, which lends them an interesting, unstable rhythm of conflicting two and three accents to the bar. The simplest and often most elegant are the sarabandes. The prevailing rhythm is either with a dotted first note, or at times the dotted note on the second beat. Even here the textural movement of the accompaniments creates a constant energy and flow beneath the simple but by no means uninteresting melodic content (see Example 6.15).

Louis Couperin was the first member of the Couperin dynasty to distinguish himself as a composer both of harpsichord and organ works. He and his two brothers came to Paris from Chaumes in the province of Brie between 1650 and 1651, and Chambonnières was instrumental in establishing them in Paris. The two main sources (the Bauyn MS and the Parville MS at the University of California, Berkeley) preserve for Couperin's *clavecin* music more than one hundred pieces.[57] As with Chambonnières, the largest number are in dance forms: courantes, sarabandes, allemandes, gigues (in order of decreasing numbers).

EXAMPLE 6.15   Chambonnières, Sarabande

Similarities to the keyboard works of his mentor are obvious. Most of the dances are relatively brief and in binary form, and the style of some of the dances, especially the sarabandes, is comparable. However, Couperin's works show a new and rich variety of inventiveness and expressiveness, and in this regard he is perhaps the most outstanding *clavecin* composer before his uncle François *le grand*. He treats the harpsichord much more dramatically than Chambonnières, often emphasizing for coloristic purposes the uppermost and lowest range of the keyboard. Sonorities are made powerful by thickly scored chords and pungent dissonances including sevenths and ninths. The vitality of many of the works is the result of an exceedingly lively, rather contrapuntal texture between the parts. Much more than Chambonnières, Couperin's music surprises by its sudden flashes of unexpected originality. For example, the Allemande in G minor is unlike any of the same dance forms by Chambonnières (see Example 6.16).

In addition to the dance forms, there are twelve chaconnes/passacaglias, most of which are in strict rondeau form with the opening or *grand* couplet of the ostinato returning unchanged except usually for its final statement. Quite different is the powerful *Passacaille* in G minor, which has forty four-measure variations on the minor and then major descending tetrachord on G.[58] Perhaps most famous among his works are the twelve *préludes non mesurés,* keyboard pieces suggesting in their notation—entirely in semibreves and with curious wavy lines implying groupings or phrasings of notes—a type of improvisatory composition (see Example 6.17). Similar unmeasured preludes occur in the keyboard works of other contemporaries such as D'Anglebert and LeRoux. Some writers believe these works come closest to the style of the toccatas by the German composer-keyboardist Johann

EXAMPLE 6.16   Louis Couperin, Allemande in G minor

Froberger. The latter is known to have been in Paris in 1652 to give a highly acclaimed concert. As his fame preceded him, he undoubtedly met with other *clavecinistes* in the city such as the Couperins. One of Couperin's preludes is inscribed "*à l'imitation de Mr. Froberger.*"[59] This prelude and one other are in three large sections in which the middle one is fugal, stylistically similar to Froberger's own contrasting sections in his toccatas.

Among other important *clavecinistes* before François Couperin are Nicolas-Antoine Lebègue (c. 1613–1702) and Jean-Henri D'Anglebert (1635–1691). Lebègue published two *livres de clavecin* in 1677 and 1687.[60] They are very much in the same style as the works of Chambonnières and Louis Couperin. More interesting are the harpsichord pieces by D'Anglebert published in 1689[61] in a large miscellany that includes four suites, a number of transcriptions of overtures, dances and other instrumental selections from Lully's operas, five organ fugues on the same subject, an organ Kyrie in four parts based on three plainchant subjects, and a short treatise concerning the principles of accompanying. The suites all contain the standard order of allemande, courante (two or three), sarabande, gigue, with an unmeasured prelude beginning each of the first three. Following the gigue, a variety of other dances appear. Suite three concludes with variations on the long-popular *Les folies d'Espagne,* and suite four with the *Tombeau de Mr. de Chambonnières.* D'Anglebert's music is heavily ornamented with a larger variety of types than in previous composers. (His own table lists twenty-nine different *agréments*—ornaments). It is generally agreed that his works

EXAMPLE 6.17 Louis Couperin, Unmeasured Prelude No. 3 from the Parville MS

are among the finest composed by a French composer in the seventeenth century. They grow out of the style and forms he learned from his teacher Chambonnières, but are also richer in contrapuntal textures and eloquent harpsichord sonorities.

François Couperin, *le grand* (1668–1733)

The Couperin dynasty produced distinguished French musicians for almost two centuries. Louis Couperin, the uncle of François, was the first. His brother Charles, father of François, succeeded him as organist at St. Gervais church in Paris, where François, his cousin Nicolas, and a succession of heirs continued the family tradition of organists at St. Gervais into the nineteenth century. François Couperin stands out, however, not just as the greatest musician in this illustrious family but also as one of the major figures in French music history. In addition to his position as organist at St. Gervais, he was appointed one of the four organists to the king in 1693, sharing the duties at Versailles with Lebègue, Nivers, and Buterne. Couperin did not officially become *Ordinaire de la musique de la chambre du roi pour le clavecin* until 1717 when Jean-Baptiste-Henri d'Anglebert died. However, his activities at court during the last years of Louis XIV's reign were numerous, including those of court composer, especially of chamber music, participation in concerts at Versailles and other royal palaces, and the composing of sacred music for the royal chapel. Much of Couperin's life was taken up with teaching at Versailles and in Paris, where he was recognized as one of the most famous teachers of harpsichord and organ. It was these activities coupled with his numerous court responsibilities that probably explain the relatively small size of his compositional output.[62]

ORGAN WORKS

In addition to Couperin's harpsichord pieces preserved in four published volumes, his music includes two works for organ, important chamber works, and secular and sacred vocal compositions. Although he was an organist at St. Gervais for forty years, his only compositions for this instrument, the two organ Masses, are early works from 1690 when he was twenty-two. Both of them had a liturgical function. The first and most impressive of the two, *à l'usage ordinaire des paroisses pour les fêtes solemnelles,* may have been written for use at St. Gervais. It follows the established practice of alternating keyboard couplets for the odd verses of the Kyrie, Gloria, Sanctus, Benedictus, and Agnus Dei with the singing of plainsong. In this case, it is *Cunctipotens genitor Deus* (Mass IV) that serves as the cantus firmus in the first and third Kyrie couplets, and the first of the Gloria, Sanctus, and Agnus Dei. The second organ Mass for abbey churches, *propre pour les Convents de Religieux et Religieuses,* is without a cantus firmus, and the individual movements are mostly smaller in musical scope than the first Mass. The range of techniques and styles in both works is particularly impressive considering Couperin's age when composing them. Already there is a mature command of contrapuntal techniques in the fugues and dialogues. And numerous examples give evidence of the amalgamation of the contrapuntal to the harmonic that characterizes the greatest part of his harpsichord pieces. Throughout, one finds a simplicity and grace of melodic design and a frequent recourse to dance rhythms that defines Couperin's musical style. Most notable in both Masses are the Offertories, which have unprecedented lengths. In the first Mass, the Offertory begins as a lengthy C major prelude with the dignity and strength of a French overture. This is followed by a serious fugal section in C minor with chromaticism and aggressive dissonances suggesting Italian influences. This in turn is succeeded by a brilliant fugal gigue again in C major.

VOCAL WORKS

Couperin's vocal works, although also small in number, have considerable importance. Secular songs are limited largely to a *Recueils d'airs sérieux et boire* published by Ballard in 1697 and 1712. Much more substantial and still little known are the sacred works. Publications included three sets of verses from Psalms 118, 84, and 79 published in 1703, 1704, and 1705, the *Leçons de tenèbres à une et à deux voix,* circa 1714–1715, and some twenty-seven motets.[63] Couperin is also credited with having composed twelve *grand motets,* which are lost. Not only do the sacred works suggest in their range of styles a source of his instrumental melodic style, but also the variety, dramatic intensity, and the lyrical exquisiteness of many of the motets, especially the *Leçons,* preserve a landmark of French Baroque sacred vocal composition. The sacred works were composed during the final years of Louis XIV's reign, 1685–1715. During this period Delalande also held a court appointment. It is probable that both Delalande as well as Charpentier had an influence on the development of Couperin's sacred style. More important, perhaps, than his two contemporaries was the impact of Italian stylistic concepts, even if still contained within French parameters of balance, elegance of text setting, a fondness for duets in parallel thirds and sixths, and ostinato basses. The motets are composed for from one to three solo voices and basso continuo, with solo and duet being predominant. Seven require two obbligato violins, one—*Salvum me fac Deus*—also two flutes. While there is still a suggestion of the *air de*

EXAMPLE 6.18   François Couperin, *Regina coeli laetare*

cour and Lullian melodic style in many of the solos, Couperin's melodies frequently are energized by vigorous phrases of dynamic intervallic leaps, sequences, and brilliant melismatic passages of rhetorical impact. *Regina coeli laetare*[64] is an example of an almost entirely Italianate motet, with its leaping melodic lines, typically Italian rhythmic motives, regularly paced basses, and sequential patterns (see Example 6.18).

Passages of Italian *recitativo semplice* are frequent in these motets. And many of the airs exhibit an Italian regularity of melodic phrase structure, often, as in the example from the Elevation, *O misterium ineffabile*,[65] because Couperin repeats the same rhythmic pattern for several phrases (see Example 6.19).

Couperin's greatest achievement in sacred music is his *Leçons de Ténèbres*. Several French Baroque composers wrote settings of the prescribed verses from the *Lamentations of Jeremiah*, including Bouzignac, Michel Lambert, Charpentier, Delalande, and Bernier. Meant to be sung in convents at Matins on Thursday, Friday, and Saturday of Holy Week, they consisted of three lessons for each day. Couperin published only the three for the first service,[66] and if he did complete the remaining six lessons they have been lost. Despite the simplicity of settings—soprano and continuo with viol for the first two and two sopranos for the third lesson—Couperin's music soars to unprecedented heights of dramatic vocal writing. The intensity of the lamentations of Jeremiah inspired Couperin to his most affective vocal expressiveness. The tradition, originally, of singing ornate plainchant melismas on the Hebrew letters preceding each division of the text is extended by the composer

EXAMPLE 6.19 François Couperin, *O misterium ineffabile*

into extraordinary vocalises (only the first Hebrew word of each lesson is actually a variation on the appropriate plainsong). Here the Italian vocal exuberance is combined with French ornamentation to achieve a vocal style of power and beauty not equaled in any of Couperin's other vocal works (see Example 6.20[67]).

    a) from *Leçon* I: *Beth*
    b) from *Leçon* II: *Vau*
    c) from *Leçon* III: *Caph*

    The Latin texts in each *Leçon* are composed either in free declamatory *récitatif* or arioso passages that frequently resemble Italian aria-like forms of long phrases. The serious and often lamenting nature of the texts allows Couperin opportunities to write passages of moving and tragic sadness within a variety of forms. Each *Leçon* contains memorable passages, which are exemplified by the closing section to the first *Leçon*, a setting of the refrain *Jerusalem, Jerusalem, convertere ad Dominum Deum tuum* (Jerusalem, Jerusalem, return to the Lord thy God) (see Example 6.21[68]).

EXAMPLE 6.20

a. François Couperin, from *Leçon* I: *Beth*

b. François Couperin, from *Leçon* II: *Vau*

c. François Couperin, from *Leçon* III: *Caph*

EXAMPLE 6.21 François Couperin, from *Leçon* I: *Jerusalem, Jerusalem*

INSTRUMENTAL CHAMBER WORKS

Couperin composed two types of instrumental chamber works: those for solo instrument and continuo and those for a trio ensemble. To the first group belong the suites entitled *Concerts royaux* (Paris, 1722)—playable on harpsichord, although Couperin suggests they can also be performed by violin, flute, or oboe with viol and bassoon. This set of four *concerts* was continued with nine more in *Les goûts-réunis ou nouveaux concerts* (Paris, 1724). This volume also included the important trio entitled *Le Parnasse, ou L'apothéose de Corelli*. Couperin's final published work was for solo bass viol and continuo, *Pièces de violes avec la basse chifrée* (Paris, 1728). Further compositions in trio form are the famous *Concert instrumental sous le titre d'Apothéose composé à la memoire immortelle de l'incomparable Monsieur de Lully* (Paris, 1725), and four trios in *Les nations: sonades et suites de simphonies en trio* (Paris, 1726). The four works in *Les nations* each consist of a *sonade* followed by a suite of dance forms. Three of the four *sonades* are reworked versions of earlier compositions, originally bearing titles different from their versions in *Les Nations:* I. *La françoise = La pucelle*, II. *L'espagnole* = *La visionnaire*, IV. *La piemontoise* = *Astrée*, but for the third *sonade* he composed a new work entitled *L'impériale*.

In these works more than in any other genre Couperin proclaims his commitment to the enriching of French music with Italian style. This is emphasized in the title of the second collection of solo *concerts* labeled *Les goûts-réunis;* and also *L'apothéose de Corelli* is a large sonata in the style of the sonata da chiesa. The *Concert . . . à la memoire immortelle d'l'incomparable Monsieur de Lully* is an elaborate instrumental "drama," program music of a type, with subtle touches of humor. Apollo comes to Lully in the Elysian Fields and gives Lully his violin and his place on Parnassus, all to music appropriately French in style. Corelli and the Italian Muses welcome Lully in a typical sonata da chiesa movement, while Lully thanks Apollo in a French sarabande, with considerable ornamentation. After Apollo "persuades Lully and Corelli that the reunion of the French and Italian tastes should achieve perfection in music," a very French *Essai en forme d'Ouverture* gives the first violin line to Lully and the French Muses and the second to Corelli and the Italian Muses. The work concludes with *La paix du Parnasse,* an Italianate trio sonata uniting the French and the Italian Muses and their leaders on the two violin lines.

Couperin associated his art from the beginning with the goal of bringing Italian stylistic traits into French music. In the significant preface to *Les Nations* he relates that the first *sonade* in the collection (*Les Françoise*) had actually been written much earlier, sometime probably in the 1690s, under an Italianized form of his name. This *sonade,* he continues,

> was the first that I composed and had been the first composed in France. Its history is curious: charmed by those [sonatas] of Corelli, whose works I shall love as long as I live, just as I do the French works of Monsieur de Lully. I ventured to compose one myself and had it performed in the concert series where I had heard those of Corelli. Knowing the keen appetite of the French for things new and foreign in all things, and being unsure of myself, I did myself a favor by resorting to a little white lie.[69]

He pretended that a relative of his had been in the service of the King of Sardinia from whom he had received the *sonade* by a new Italian composer. The *sonade* had great success, and he composed others under his Italianized name. Two years earlier, in the preface to *Les goûts-réunis,* Couperin had already taken his stand regarding the continuing discussions in France arguing for the superiority of French style over the Italian:

> The Italian and the French tastes have for a long time shared the Republic of Music (in France). For myself, I have always highly regarded the things which merited esteem, without considering either the composer or nation; the first Italian sonatas that appeared in Paris more than 30 years ago, and that encouraged me to start composing some myself, to my mind wronged neither the works of M. de Lully, nor those of my ancestors, who will always be more admirable than imitable. And so, by a right which my neutrality gives me, I remain under the happy influence which has guided me until now.[70]

Lully had been dead since 1687 and Louis XIV since 1715. The greatest bastions defending the purity of French taste were no longer either in place or relevant. François Couperin had a leading role in legitimizing *Les goûts-réunis,* and nowhere can this been seen to better advantage than in his instrumental ensemble music and his keyboard works.

WORKS FOR HARPSICHORD

Couperin published four books of harpsichord music, the first in 1713 and subsequently in the years 1716–1717, 1722, and 1730. They contain 240 harpsichord pieces, a repertory of music of the highest inventiveness and musical quality. They bring to a climax the development of French harpsichord style, become a landmark in the history of keyboard music, and establish Couperin as one of the great composers of the French Baroque. Each book is divided into *Ordres,* a term Couperin adopts in place of suites. The number of *ordres* varies in the four books (I = 5, II = 7, III = 7, IV = 8), and each *ordre* can include as few as four and as many as twenty-three separate pieces, with those in seven or eight movements most frequent. While an *ordre* contains features of a suite, it is not a suite. The usual dances of the suite may not always be present, and these *ordres* usually contain other dances, although not so named, as well as a kaleidoscopic array of freely composed pieces with fanciful titles.

The first book, which Couperin waited until he was forty-five to publish, is the least consistent in its contents, and clearly includes a miscellany of pieces Couperin had written much earlier, many probably originating as teaching material. Only in this book does the suite design remain partially intact. The first, second, third, and fifth *ordres* all include a standard succession of dances: allemande, two courantes, sarabande followed by a gavotte and gigue in the first, a gavotte, menuet, canaries, passepied, and rigaudon in the second, a gavotte and menuet in the third, and only a gigue in the fifth. The remainder of each *ordre* continues with an array of pieces with various titles, some descriptive, some names of known personages, many of unclear or unknown meaning. For example the *Troisième ordre* places pieces after the menuet with the following titles: *Les pélerines, Les Laurentines, L'Espagnolette, Les regrets, Les matelotes Provençales, La favorite, La lutine.* Subsequent books abandon the suite of dances entirely, and, while dances still appear, they are almost always in the guise of a titled composition.[71] In his preface to Book I, Couperin comments:

> I have always had a subject in mind when composing these pieces—subjects suggested on different occasions. Thus the titles correspond to ideas I have had; I hope I may be excused from explaining them further. But since, among the titles, there are some which appear to indulge my own vanity, I should add that the pieces they describe are types of portraits which have sometimes been judged quite lifelike when I performed them, and that any flattery in the titles is intended for those memorable originals I wished to depict rather than for the copies I made in these musical portraits.

The pieces are often heavily laden with ornaments (*agréments*) which are not superfluous embellishments but, rather, are integral to the expressive content as Couperin emphasized in the preface to Book III:

> I am always surprised (after the great care I have taken to indicate the appropriate ornaments for my pieces, which are rather completely explained in my description of my playing method known by the title *L'art de toucher le clavecin*) to hear persons who have learned these pieces without following my rules. This is an unpardonable oversight, the more so because it is entirely improper to add whatever ornaments one wishes. I affirm that my pieces should be executed exactly as I have marked them, and that they will never make the correct impression on persons of true taste so long as the performer does not observe to the letter all that I have marked, adding and removing nothing.

To aid the performer in the proper execution of these *agréments* he published an extensive table of symbols and their interpretation in Book I. This table, together with his *L'art de*

EXAMPLE 6.22 François Couperin, opening section of *La Mézangére*

toucher le clavecin (Paris, 1716), were not only essential for the proper performance of his keyboard music but also established for the first time a standardization of symbols for the French practice of embellishment.

Some of the characteristics of the *clavecin* music by Couperin's predecessors are retained in his pieces. The *ordres* are unified by a single tonality, although with alternations between major and minor modes. (An exception to this arrangement occurs in the twenty-fifth *ordre,* which begins in E flat major, and continues in C major and minor.) Only three forms constitute all 240 pieces: the binary, the rondeau, and the passacaglia and chaconne. The binary occurs most frequently, although the rondeau becomes more prominent in the later *ordres* and serves for many of the more extended pieces. Despite the overall similarity of structure for so many individual pieces, the variety of musical ideas and the enormous range of emotional—affective—values is extraordinary. The heart of Couperin's style consists of three major elements: harmonic order and expressiveness, texture, and melodic invention.

All the pieces grow out of a clear tonal organization, with the harmonic structure as well as melodic figurations a realization of the harmonies of the real or implied bass line. Probably because much of the music is based on dance styles there is a general tendency to organize structure in four- and eight-bar phrases. While sections can be longer, there is seldom a lack of frequent interior cadences. Couperin's harmony can be exceedingly rich in dissonances for appropriate expression of an affect, which are often placed in the richest middle and low registers of the harpsichord. As is true of his younger German contemporary, Johann Sebastian Bach, Couperin achieves in many of these pieces a rich amalgamation of the harmonic and the contrapuntal, combined in a freely flowing texture, except in the most homophonic of dances. The brilliance of his contrapuntal technique with its

EXAMPLE 6.23   François Couperin, opening of the *Passacaille* in B minor

clear harmonic definition can be shown in the predominantly two-part counterpoint of a large number of these works. It is often pointed out that Couperin employs the *stile brisé* or what he refers to in several pieces as the *stile luthé,* commonly considered to be an important stylistic innovation adapted from lute music by seventeenth-century French *clavecin* composers. For example, from Book II, *La Mézangére,* Couperin identifies the texture as "*Luthé*" (see Example 6.22).

Couperin's melodic invention is inexhaustible and explains the vitality and diversity sustaining the frequent repetitiveness of the forms. The expressive scope seems to span the entire melodic resources of French music from Lullian ballet and opera to Couperin's own musical generation, from lucid diatonicism to anguished chromaticism. There are noble melodies of the opera overture, majestic sarabande themes, folklike and pastoral tunes, popular dance melodies, and numerous inherently witty keyboard jokes. In addition to the intimately lyrical, in the tradition of the popular *brunettes,* there are many based on motivic ideas that are developed throughout the pieces, often involving the harpsichordist in athletic keyboard leaps and arpeggios. The famous *Rossignol-en-amour* (Book III) is an ideal example of the Baroque decorated vocal line. Rhythmic variety and a decidedly coloristic use of the sonorities of the harpsichord in its upper and lower ranges all lend to Couperin's melodies an originality unequaled by those *clavecin* composers who preceded him.

Couperin's last book of harpsichord pieces appeared just three years before his death in 1733. Most of his keyboard music was composed during the Regency, and this fact has often colored critical opinion about Couperin's art. It has been called *galant* or Rococo, and words such as "miniatures," "trifles," "lacking in seriousness" have all been attached to his music. Of course, this is music meant to entertain small audiences of the aristocracy, and most of the pieces are in themselves of short duration. But it is a critical error to suggest Couperin's works avoided all that was serious and lacked depths of expression that

EXAMPLE 6.24   François Couperin, *Passacaille* in B minor, mm. 142–47

explored wider musical dimensions. Each of the *ordres,* beginning with Book II, takes on a definite musical character of its own. Even the shorter pieces, such as the several allemandes, have an intensity and dramatic power that could never be viewed as a "trifling" (for example, *La Raphaéle,* Book II). And the opening to the twenty-third *ordre* (Book IV), *La Audacieuse,* with its dotted rhythms and interacting textures, is as noble and intense as any Lullian overture. Finally, one need only hear the three monumental passacaglias/chaconnes to realize the inaccuracy of such a critical viewpoint. The first, *La Favorite* (Book I), in C minor, is a chaconne written in typical French rondeau form. The four-measure theme with a descending chromatic tetrachord bass returns after five intervening *couplets* (episodes), which are also related to the chaconne bass. This elegant and grand keyboard work is overshadowed by the *Passacaille* in B minor from Book II, one of two of Couperin's greatest keyboard works. In 174 measures, the B minor passacaglia with a bass that ascends by a chromatic fifth supports a powerfully dramatic theme (see Example 6.23).

Eight *couplets* continue the inexorable development of the work, climaxing in the intense seventh *couplet* with its powerful sonorities of dissonances and suspensions (see Example 6.24).

The architectural grandeur and passion of this piece places it alongside the achievements of Couperin's greatest Baroque contemporaries, not least of those being J. S. Bach. No less monumental and even longer than this work and with a distinct originality of concept is the passacaglia, *L'amphibie,* from Book IV. Unlike the former two, this is not in rondeau form but, rather, a series of variations, at times rather loosely connected to the ground bass of a passacaglia of some complexity consisting of two eight-bar themes. The passacaglia does not return intact until the end of the work, although, in the succeeding variations, it always seems to exist in some suggestion of its original statement. It is tempting to see in these something of the character variation technique to be developed in the next century by composers such as Beethoven, Schumann, and Brahms. However one describes these passacaglias, they stand as eloquent testimony to Couperin's compositional genius as the last of the great composers of the French Baroque.

CHAPTER SEVEN

Sacred Music in Northern and Southern Europe and Austria in the Seventeenth Century

At the beginning of the seventeenth century, musical developments in the northern and central German states, as well as in the Netherlands, were profoundly influenced by the diverse political and religious animosities and a constant condition of war throughout the region. Much of the chaos that developed during the first decades of the century, known generally as the Thirty Years' War, concerned the efforts of the Habsburg emperor and the Catholic Pope to regain the German lands that had followed Martin Luther in establishing the Protestant religion. The Protestants also had their internal conflicts, and already in 1563 the northern Netherlands had broken with the Protestants to establish the Calvinist church. Within the second decade of the century all of the major and many of the minor powers of Europe—Austria, Spain, France, England, Bohemia, Hungary, the German states, Denmark, Sweden, and even Turkey—became entangled in a series of wars of unprecedented devastation in much of central and northern Europe.

The development and distinction of sacred music in most of the central and northern German states originated in 1517 when Martin Luther (1480–1546) nailed his famous ninety-five criticisms of the Mother Church on the door of a church in Wittenberg. This was the spark leading to the Protestant Reformation and to the collapse of religious solidarity in Europe. It also inspired the Counter Reformation emanating from Rome. Both of these religious and political developments created the foundation on which Baroque sacred music flourished. When Luther broke with the Catholic Church, he set off a series of chain reactions leading to an ever-widening split between the church denominations and an ever-greater contrast between the cultures of North and South Europe.

Luther and the Protestant Chorale

The profound impact Luther had on German sacred music is a subject of enormous scope that can be given here only in its basic essentials.[1] Luther had a university education and substantial musical training. He played the lute, composed, and participated in singing in his own home. He claimed Josquin as his favorite composer and admired the polyphonic style of the Netherlanders. Ludwig Senfl was a friend with whom he frequently corresponded. He gave music the highest place of honor next to theology, and welcomed all forms of music into his church, including plainchant and works by Catholic composers. It was this openness to all forms of earlier music that were absorbed into Protestant church music that laid the basis for its developing richness and changing nature into the eighteenth century. For Luther, there was a theology of music that enabled one to sing the praises of God, and through the singing of sacred texts to better understand God. He believed music could build piety, and would help to spread God's word. Luther, alone among the several religious reformers, was the only one to place such emphasis on the role of music in the liturgy.

A fundamental innovation of Luther's reforms grew out of his belief in what he called a congregation of priests, an active congregation that would take a central role in the church service. In his *Formula missae* (1523) he stated: "I would like also that we had many German songs, which the people can sing during the celebration of Mass or along with the Gradual and along with the Sanctus and Agnus Dei." Almost immediately he expanded what had already become something of a tradition in the Catholic liturgy of the congregational hymn, creating the congregational chorale (*Gemeinlied*). Luther never advocated banishing Latin from his reformed liturgy, and he created both a vernacular and a Latin form of the Mass. Indeed, one of the characteristics of the Protestant service was Luther's insistence that it be adapted in various ways to the needs of the individual churches and areas adopting Protestantism. However, the Latin form was intended for cathedrals and collegiate bodies, while the *Deutsche Messe* (1526) was used by smaller congregations with little or no knowledge of Latin.

Beginning almost immediately Luther and his circle of advisors began to gather together a repertory of sacred songs in German. This emphasis on German songs, including German folk and art song, quickly gave what would become an enormously large repertory of chorales a distinctive national character. The first chorale books appeared in 1523–1524, including Johann Walter's influential and subsequently enlarged *Wittenberger Geystliche gesangk Buchleyn*, with thirty-eight German and five Latin compositions for three to five voices. These are all *cantus firmus* settings, and of the thirty-eight German chorales, thirty-six place the melody in the tenor, the other two in the discantus. While several subsequent chorale books also place the melody in the tenor in a contrapuntal texture, many printed just the single melodic line, for example, *Das Klugsche Gesang-Buch*, published under the direction of Martin Luther in Wittenberg in 1529 (only a reprint of 1533 is extant). Luther is credited with composing, or in some cases arranging or adapting previous melodies and texts of thirty-six chorales, including such pillars of the Lutheran Church as *Aus tiefer Not schrei ich zu dir; Ein feste Burg ist unser Gott; Jesu Christus, unser Heiland; Nun komm der Heiden Heiland; Von Himmel hoch da komm ich her;* and *Christ lag in Todesbanden.* In their search for a large depository of melodies, the early Protestant composers not only created new melodies but also arranged melodies from many different sources:

1. Liturgical melodies, especially hymns of the Catholic Church
2. Sacred songs in German from the pre-Reformation period, hymns and other songs used in church and at home
3. Popular, that is, social music and folk songs. Texts were usually changed or rewritten creating a large repertory of *contrafacta*
4. Pre-Reformation German sacred lieder, pilgrim songs, *Leisen,* sacred songs of the Minnesinger and Meistersinger, songs of penitence, Crusade songs, and sacred folk songs.[2]

The repertory of chorales grew steadily in the sixteenth century. One of the most important collections was *Newe deudsche geistliche Gesenge. Mit vier und fünff Stimmen für die gemeinen Schulen* published by Georg Rhau in 1544. It includes 123 chorale settings, most in polyphonic style with the cantus firmus in the tenor. Already some two hundred hymn books were published in the first half-century of the Reformation. Johannes Keuchenthal's *Kirchen Gesenge latinish und deudsch,* which appeared in 1573, was the first to order the chorales *de tempore* (i.e., according to the church year). The second half of the century witnessed an outpouring of hymn books in cantional style, that is, simple, four-part homophonic settings with the chorale melody in the top part, such as Lucas Osiander's 1569 hymn book *Fünffzig geistlicher Lieder und Psalmen mit vier Stimmen auff contrapunctsweise.* This was composed, according to Osiander, for schools and churches, "so that the entire Christian congregation can sing along." Protestant hymnbooks retained this style through succeeding centuries. A considerable variety of regional publications began to appear that retained Luther's chorales and those authorized by him, but also many new chorales, texts as well as melodies. Especially the addition of many contrafacta varied among the publications, causing the local repertories of Protestant chorales to fluctuate widely.

The chorale texts and their music not only possessed powerful religious authority, but for the Protestant clergy as well as the congregation they were as sacred as the Bible itself. Chorale texts were seen as interpretations of the Bible and the chorale melodies were as liturgical as Gregorian chants, many of which Luther had retained in his reform of the Mass. Chorales became the central source and inspiration of a vast repertory of music serving the Protestant church, and for more than two hundred years they were adapted to traditional as well as new forms of sacred music.

North German and Dutch Sacred Vocal Music in the Seventeenth Century

Older musical traditions remained a powerful force for musical continuity in northern Europe in the seventeenth century. In contrast to Italy, innovations at the turn of the century had introduced a new concept of the expressive power of music and had placed alongside the centuries-old traditions of polyphony new styles of the multivoiced concertato, monody, and opera. German composers would not remain immune to new forms of Italian music, but at no time in the development of Baroque music in the seventeenth or eighteenth centuries would they entirely abandon polyphony. Throughout the sixteenth century, little difference can be seen between Catholic and Protestant music, and it was the authority of Luther himself who left the Protestant liturgy open to Catholic music. The preponderant musical style remained that of the Franco-Netherlands composers. The chorale as cantus firmus quickly became ideally adaptable to its formal procedures and led to motetlike works based on chorale and other sacred melodies. Lassus, who held the post of Kapellmeister at Munich beginning in 1556, was and continued to be one of the powerful musical influences affecting German composers during and beyond the second half of the sixteenth century.

The first fertile wave of new musical concepts from Italy came from Venice. The polychoral style of Andrea and Giovanni Gabrieli was quickly imitated by both Catholic and Protestant composers. A long-lived tradition of German musicians making the arduous trip to Venice for study began as early as the 1580s when both Gregor Aichinger (1564/65–1628), a Catholic, and Hans Leo Hassler (1564–1612), a Protestant, became pupils of the Gabrielis. The awareness of the Venetian style of the Gabrielis was widespread in Germany by the end of the sixteenth century, primarily through their published works but also through German compositions employing the Venetian style. The odyssey undertaken by Germans to study in Venice continued into the eighteenth century. Other German composers writing music in Venetian style included Adam Gumpelzhaimer (1559–1625), Hieronymus Praetorius (1560–1629), and, of particular significance, Michael Praetorius (1571–1621). Hassler wrote most of his polychoral sacred works when serving the Catholic Fuggers in Augsburg. He composed his two significant works for the Protestant church after becoming director of town music in Nuremberg in 1601: *Psalmen und christliche Gesänge, 4 vv, auff die Melodeyen fugweiss componiert* (1607), and *Kirchengesänge: Psalmen und geistliche Lieder, auff die gemeinen Melodeyen, 4 vv, simpliciter gesetzt* (1608).[3] The latter contains sixty-eight chorales in simple, four-part, and musically sensitive settings. The contents include the most important traditional chorales for Sundays and the major sacred festivals as well as chorale settings of psalm and catechistic texts. The *Psalmen und christliche Gesänge* employ a conservative polyphonic style that relates them to the later sixteenth century. These "chorale motets" derive motives or phrases from the chorale melody that are imitated in each of the four parts. In some of the motets, the cantus firmus remains largely intact in one or more of the parts.

Michael Praetorius

Michael Praetorius (Schultheiss) was the cardinal figure in the development of Protestant sacred music in Germany in the early seventeenth century. This was the result of his intense devotion to organizing and enlarging the music available for the Protestant liturgy. He composed and published an immense repertory of music largely made up of an extraordinary variety of works employing more than twelve hundred chorales. There is also a considerable repertory of new compositions for Latin texts retained in the Protestant services. Although much of this music was composed while Praetorius lived in the small ducal town of Wolfenbüttel, his fame and musical guidance were widely influential throughout the Protestant lands. He was also the author of the *Syntagma musicum* (3 vols., 1614–1619), which, together with Mersenne's *Harmonie universelle* (1636/7), preserves the most important sources of information about the theory and practice of music for the century.

Praetorius was born in Creutzberg, a Thuringian town just north of Eisenach, where his father was a Lutheran minister. Little is known about Praetorius's education, and it appears he was largely self-taught as a composer. He started his profession as organist in Frankfurt an der Oder. In 1595 he began a fruitful career in Wolfenbüttel in the service of Duke Heinrich Julius of Braunschweig-Wolfenbüttel, first as organist and in 1604 as court Kapellmeister. When his patron died in 1613 Praetorius was invited by the Elector of Saxony to the Dresden court to serve in the capacity of Kapellmeister. He remained for two and a half years. It was undoubtedly here that Praetorius first came into actual contact with the new musical styles emanating from Italy that would influence his late works, especially the *Polyhymnia Caduceatrix et Panegyrica* (1619). Praetorius began a period of several years in which he traveled to many Protestant centers such as Halle, Magdeburg, Sondershausen, Kassel, Leipzig, Nuremberg, and Bayreuth. At this time he came to know both Schütz and Scheidt. In many of these places he advised on church musical matters, examined organs, organized church performing groups (*capelle*), and often directed performances. He returned to Wolfenbüttel in 1620 and died a year later.

Of the twenty volumes published by Praetorius,[4] only one, *Terpsichore* (1612), contains secular music and is a collection of French dances. No survey of Praetorius's compositional output in the other nineteen volumes can adequately suggest the variety and significance of this music for the German Protestant church in the post-Reformation period. In addition, Praetorius as teacher enriched his publications with a wide variety of pertinent advice on performance practices of continuing value today. Some indication of the magnitude of his accomplishment may be conveyed by the following brief descriptions for each work:

I–IX. *Musae Sioniae, oder, Geistliche Concert Gesänge, über die fürnembste, Herrn Lutheri und anderer Teutsche Psalmen,* in nine volumes (1605–1610), the composer's monumental achievement. The first four volumes contain eight-part double chorus (as well as several twelve-part triple chorus) arrangements of chorales. These chorale motets present an encyclopedic overview of late-sixteenth-century imitative techniques that draw on motives from the chorales. There is also interspersed homophonic writing, especially in the responsorial interchanges between double and triple choruses. Part V consists of 166 compositions, most of which are multiple settings of German chorales for the major church holidays in from two to seven parts, as well as compositions employing German translations of texts in Latin appropriate for the Matins, the Mass, and Vespers. Included are examples by Johann Walter, Raselius, de Wert, and Gesius. Most of the chorales appear in several settings of varying degrees of difficulty. For example, *Nun bitten wir den heiligen Geist* has seven versions: one in two parts, two in three parts (first with the chorale in the top part, second with chorale in the bass), a four-part homophonic arrangement, and one each in four, five, and six parts, the latter being an extensive motet with seventy-five measures. Parts VI–VIII are in simple four-part cantional homophony, and Part IX consists of chorales arranged in *bicinia* and *tricinia* textures.

X. *Musarum Sioniarum: motectae et psalmi latini . . .* (1607). Fifty-two Latin compositions in from two to twelve parts in sixteenth-century style, for the Lutheran service, as well as a Lutheran Mass, and a Magnificat. In the index, Praetorius indicates the places in the church calendar where these motets and psalms would be appropriate. Also included are compositions by Aichinger, Händl, Porta, and Palestrina. Indications in the scores specify contrasting sections between solo and choral passages and places where organ and instruments should double the voice parts.

Volumes XI–XIV form a group, each giving Praetorius's compositions based on texts in Latin still employed in the liturgy.

XI. *Missodia Sionia, continens cantiones sacras, ad officium, quod vocant summum ante meridiem in ecclesia usitatas . . .* (1611). In two to eight parts, polyphonic settings for the Mass Ordinary, Collects, Prefaces, various Amen and Gloria intonations, and songs for Compline.

XII. *Hymnodia Sionia, continens hymnos sacros XXIV. anniversarios selectos . . .* (1611). 138 Latin hymns in three to eight parts, designated by church calendar. Seven hymns are arranged for organ.

XIII. *Eulogodia Sionia, continens cantiones sacras in ecclesia conclusionis loco ad dimissionem usitatas . . .* (1611). In two to eight parts, motet settings of the Benedicamus Domino and the response *Deo dicamus gratias*. Also present are arrangements of Luther's version of the *Regina coeli laetare* and Salve Regina.

XIV. *Megalynodia Sionia, continens canticum B. Mariae Virginis, Magnificat, 5, 6, & 8. voc. super Ut Re Mi Fa Sol La, & quaedam madrigalia ac motectas . . . accommodatum . . .* (1611). Magnificat compositions, including instructive examples of those with chorale insertions for Christmas and Easter performances. Many are parodies composed to madrigals and motets, some by Marenzio and Lassus.

XV. *Terpsichore, musarum aoniarum quinta . . .* (1612). The first and only one published of several volumes planned to contain instrumental music, this one consisting of important examples of French dances.

XVI. *Kleine und Grosse Litaney, Zusambt dem Erhalt uns Herr bey deinem Wort . . .* (1613). Praetorius gives a history of the Litany together with appropriate examples showing how to perform the lesser and greater forms. An arrangement of the chorale *Erhalt uns Herr bei deinem Wort*, in eight parts for two choruses, is in simple homophonic style enabling congregational participation in singing this final hymn of the Sunday service.

XVII. *Urania oder Urano-Chorodia. Darinnen XVIII der fürnembsten, gebreuchlichsten Geistlichen Teudtschen Kirchen Gesänge . . .* (1613). Arrangements of nineteen of the most well-known chorales for two, three, and four choruses, in simple homophonic style with the chorale in the top part "so that also the congregation in the church can sing the chorale at the same time."

XVIII. *Polyhymnia Caduceatrix et Panegyrica . . .* (1619). Forty chorale concertos in the polychoral style of Giovanni Gabrieli, Praetorius's most modern vocal collection. For one to twenty-one parts, which are divided in from two to six choruses, and for the first time in his music including a basso continuo.

XIX. *Polyhymnia exercitatrix seu Tyrocinium musicum harmonicum . . .* (1619). Fourteen exercises to train young voices in the Italian ornamented singing style. Latin psalm texts and German chorales for two to eight parts divided into three groups, one for boys, one for adults, one for instrument with basso continuo.

XX. *Puericinium. Hoc est trium vel quatuor puerorum, trium pluriumve adultorum & quatuor instrumentorum concentio . . .* (1619). Similar to the preceding work, fourteen chorales for instruction in three groups: one for three or four boys, one for adults, and one for instruments with basso continuo.

The astonishing achievement with Latin and German sacred music underscores Praetorius's devotion to Luther's innovative musical reforms placed at the heart of Protestantism. In effect, Praetorius recomposed almost the entire corpus of Protestant sacred music, much of it originating in the Reformation itself. Because he was actually able to realize his extraordinary publications project of twenty volumes, and because he traveled extensively among the major German cities and courts, he had the means and access to instruct other Lutheran church musicians how to employ his works in their churches. Praetorius also was a teacher, and his publications include copious instructions meant to help his peers learn how to perform his music. Most of his advice is based on principles of Renaissance imitative polyphony, and this fact highlights the difficulty in considering him a "Baroque" master. As with many early-seventeenth-century composers whose music is rooted in the sixteenth century, Praetorius is another one whose art was nourished by the past and who carried these principles of composing into the new century.

Although he never traveled to Italy, Praetorius was well informed about musical developments in Venice. In his late works, most especially the *Polyhymnia Caduceatrix et Panegyrica,* he commits his music to those new musical styles established by the Gabrielis and Monteverdi. These motets in two to six choruses of instruments and voices were obviously only intended for performing ensembles in the great churches and aristocratic chapels. Praetorius says they contain "various new forms and styles of concerted music, each of which includes a basso continuo." Numerous performance instructions precede each work, and references are included to his lengthy analytical discussion of twelve types of polychoral compositions found in *Syntagma musicum,* Part III, Chapter 8. Praetorius joins the chorale to the brilliant Venetian style that combines various groups of sonorities, instrumental as well as vocal, choral as well as solo. Vocal and instrumental writing is often ornamented with Italianate diminutions. They are also applied to the chorale melodies, although Praetorius usually supplies an unornamented version for German singers untrained in Italian vocal styles. Each concerto is meant to illustrate a different solution to using these large and varied forces with chorales. There are massive homophonic passages for all of the performing groups, individual solos, and open textures in which short motives are imitated back and forth between parts. Declamatory chordal passages approach the concept of recitative as do those found in Schütz's *Psalmen David* published in the same year. Because of the presence of chorales and considerable emphasis still on imitative textures these concertos make something of a conservative musical impression. However, the new spirit of the Italian innovations in sound and style is present. The complex and often grandiose settings shift attention away from the simple context of sacred word and melody to chorales immersed in colorful sonorities and constantly changing textures. Praetorius, according to his own comments in *Syntagma musicum,* planned to recompose much of his earlier work in light of these new polychoral innovations.[5] Italian musical inroads into the north of Europe now became a major factor for the future of German music.

Sweelinck and Sacred Vocal Music in the Netherlands

Swiss reforms of the Lutheran church in the sixteenth century had restrictive consequences for composers of sacred music. John Calvin (1509–1564), founder of Genevan Calvinism, banned from his church all polyphony, the use of instruments, and singing from the altar. This was true in German regions as well as the Dutch Netherlands, which had adopted Calvinism. The only sounds of music in the Calvinist church service became unaccompanied unison singing in the vernacular by the congregation. The texts were limited to the Bible, and the psalms made the central source for the congregational hymns. The Genevan Psalter in French, begun by Clément Marot under the guidance of Calvin and completed in 1562 by Théodore de Bèze, became the official Calvinist source for metrical translations of the psalms. It appeared in a great number of translations, editions, and musical arrangements throughout the century.

Jan Pieterszoon Sweelinck (1562–1621), the most important Dutch composer in the early seventeenth century, famous as organist and teacher, is best remembered for his secular vocal works and major keyboard compositions. Although organist at Amsterdam's Oude Kerk, he composed little sacred music because he was restricted by the tenets of the Dutch Calvinist church. His two major collections of sacred music, ... *des psaumes de David nouvellement mis en musique à 4, 5, 6, 7, 8 parties,* in four volumes (1604, 1613, 1614, 1621), and the *Cantiones sacrae* (1619)[6] were both composed for performances outside of his church.

The *Psaumes de David* contains 153 psalm compositions (three in two versions) employing the Marot and de Bèze French texts. In their highly expressive settings and their artful employment of the various contrapuntal techniques these are clearly not "Calvinist" works. Sweelinck probably composed them for influential Amsterdam citizens who performed music in private groups including a Collegium musicum. Volume II, for example, is dedicated to eight men Sweelinck calls "philomuses," "who come together to join their voices in a sweet musical concert." The composition of these four volumes was spread out over Sweelinck's entire career. Each psalm is composed in the sixteenth-century polyphonic style and is based on the melody for the text as it appeared in the Genevan Psalter. Many are chorale motets with the entire hymn given usually in either the cantus or tenor. For multiverse settings, the tune usually migrates to a difference voice. The majority of the psalms, while clearly stressing the hymn, are composed in a multiplicity of contrapuntal designs in which the chorale is arranged for specific types of motivic and phrase interplay. Clarity of text is achieved by preventing the overlapping of different text lines in the confluence of phrases or motives in the several parts. Frequent homophonic sections also serve text clarity. Madrigalisms and other text emphases common to sixteenth-century sacred and secular polyphonic style are found throughout these richly inventive and beautiful compositions.

The *Cantiones sacrae* are dedicated to a young Catholic friend of the composer, Cornelis Plemp, and contain thirty-seven motets in five parts with a basso continuo on texts from the Catholic Vulgate and liturgy. The writing in comparison to his psalm compositions is decidedly simpler, in part because of the lack of a cantus firmus. Textures, while basically contrapuntal, remain largely in five parts, with few significant examples of concerted repetitions between the parts. There are few rhythmic complexities, and almost no rapid or ornamented melodic passages. The text for these reasons is particularly emphasized, frequently with homorhythmic statement in all the parts. These are pieces clearly meant to be less challenging for performers, but there is also the apparent influence of Venetian choral idioms from the end of the sixteenth century.

Johann Hermann Schein and Samuel Scheidt

In the first major German history of music, *Historische Beschreibung der edelen Sing- und Kling-Kunst* (1690), Wolfgang Caspar Printz named Schein, Scheidt, and Schütz "the three best composers in Germany."[7] All three were born in the mid-1580s, knew each other, and worked in the same area of Germany (Leipzig, Halle, and Dresden). Schein and Schütz were close friends. Subsequent history has, of course, raised Schütz to the pinnacle of greatness, especially as the supreme creator of German sacred music in the century (see Chapter 9). Schein and Scheidt were, however, equally significant in the development of sacred music in the first half of the seventeenth century and, unlike Schütz (as far as we know), also created major repertories of instrumental music.

Johann Herman Schein (1586–1630) was born in Annaberg, south of Chemnitz. At thirteen, he entered the Hofkapelle of the Elector of Saxony in Dresden as a soprano. He received musical instruction from Rogier Michael, Kapellmeister at the court. It was important for his future development as a composer that at the Dresden court he was able to hear and study a large and varied repertory of German, Latin, and Italian music. Schein's subsequent education in music and the humanities was excellent, first at the electoral school at Schulpforta (1603–1607) and subsequently in law and the liberal arts at the University of Leipzig (1608–1612). In 1615, he became Kapellmeister to the court at Weimar, and one year later succeeded Sethus Calvisius (1556–1615) to the post of Thomaskantor in Leipzig, thus becoming another in a distinguished line of musicians to precede Johann Sebastian Bach in that position.

Schein's sacred works are found in five collections: I. *Cymbalum Sionium sive Cantiones sacrae, 5, 6, 8, 10 & 12 vocum* (1615); II. *Opella nova, geistlicher Concerten, mit 3, 4, und 5 Stimmen* (1618); III. *Fontana d'Israel, Israelis Brünlein, auserlesener Krafft-Sprüchlin altes und newen Testaments, von 5 und 6 Stimmen . . . auf eine sonderbar Anmütige Italian Madrigalische Manier* (Leipzig, 1623); IV. *Opella nova, ander Theil, geistlicher Concerten, mit 3, 4, 5, und 6 Stimmen* (Leipzig, 1626); and V. *Cantional oder Gesangbuch Augspurgischen Confession . . . mit 4, 5, und 6 Stimmen componiret* (Leipzig, 1627).[8] The *Cymbalum Sionium* was published just as Schein took up his duties at Weimar. The collection of thirty motets, divided between texts in Latin and German and largely from the Bible, has a variety of styles. Many suggest a compositional period perhaps as early as his student days. There are pieces in five vocal parts (with two sopranos) and also polychoral works in eight and twelve parts. Some are clearly based on sixteenth-century imitative techniques, while others have considerable emphasis on homophonic textures and closer attention to clarity of text settings.

The *Cantional oder Gesangbuch Augspurgischen Confession* appeared three years before Schein's death, and it is his major contribution to the Protestant hymnal. Composed to replace the earlier hymnal by Calvisius, it contains 286 hymns (313 in the revised edition of 1645 by Schein's successor, Tobias Michael), most of them part of the Leipzig repertory of the St. Thomas and St. Nikolaus churches. With the exception of a few in five or six

EXAMPLE 7.1   Schein, *Nun lob, mein Seel, den Herren*

parts, the majority of hymns are composed in four parts in typical cantional style, with the tune in the upper part. Schein added figures to the bass part, forming a continuo part "for organists, instrumentalists, and lutenists." He usually gave the hymns a new harmonization, sometimes composed a new melody, and included many in multiple settings. Schein contributed more than sixty new hymns, some of them on the subject of death. These were in part brought about by the deaths of his entire family, a reflection of the rampant spread of war and disease in this period.

Both the *Cymbalum* and the *Cantional* are collections of works rooted in the styles and purposes of the sixteenth century. The other three collections of sacred music, however,

EXAMPLE 7.2   Schein, *Aus tiefer Not schrei ich zu dir*

vividly show how much the musical tide had turned under the influence of Italian music and the growing importance of giving greater rhetorical-musical interpretations to texts, characteristics that mark the true beginnings of the German Baroque. On the title page to the first volume of the *Opella nova,* Schein states these "sacred concertos" were composed in the "current, customary Italian invention." Largely settings of Lutheran chorales, the thirty concertos are mostly for two solo voices and accompanying basso continuo. A few add a tenor and one or two additional instrumental parts. The great historical significance of the work rests in part on the influence of Viadana's *Cento concerti eccelisastici,* which was first published in Germany in 1609. As in Viadana's concertos, Schein's two vocal parts are dependent for harmonic continuity on the continuo realization (and Schein recom-

EXAMPLE 7.3   Schein, *Die mit Tränen säen*

EXAMPLE 7.3 (*continued*)

mends that the performer of the organ, theorbo, or lute consult Viadana's rules for guidance). A second bass part is intended for bassoon, trombone, or viola grossa. The writing is lightly imitative at times, solidly homophonic in others. The chorale is usually broken into motives or phrases that alternate between the two parts (see Example 7.1[9]). This style can no longer be called *prima prattica,* and these concertos are more artistic interpretations rather than faithful presentations of the chorales.

Other chorale melodies are varied, usually for affective emphasis, into more expressive figurations, as in the following setting for *Aus tiefer Not schrei ich zu dir.* In this composition almost the entire concerto has incessant overlappings of the two parts to impart the impassioned pleading to God (see Example 7.2[10]).

A second collection of sacred music, one of the masterworks of German choral music of the first half of the seventeenth century, is Schein's *Fontana d'Israel—Fountain of Israel, A little spring of Israel chosen from Select proverbs in the Old and New Testament. [Composed] in a special, graceful Italian madrigal style.* These five-voice, sacred madrigals with a basso continuo duplicating the lowest voice part reach new heights of affective emotion and text interpretation. They adapt the principles of word expression originating with Italian composers of the madrigal, especially Monteverdi, and apply new techniques of German musical-rhetorical figures. The opening to Schein's *Die mit Tränen säen* (see Example 7.3)[11] is a memorable employment of the chromatic scale to express the affect of "sowing tears."

Each text obviously was chosen for the marked affective content of the words. In several of the pieces one finds outcries of pain or pleading, for example, the opening of *O Herr, ich bin dein Knecht,* in which the opening evocation from Psalm 116 infuses the texture with the cries of "O Lord" (see Example 7.4[12]).

The thirty sacred madrigals deserve to be studied for the word/tone relationships. Perhaps the most chilling and moving of all of these examples occurs in *Da Jakob vollendet hatte,* as the son weeps over the remains of his father. Seldom have parallel chords of the sixth expressed such sadness and desolation (see Example 7.5[13]).

The second part of the *Opella nova* was Schein's last collection of sacred music. The combining of influences from Italy and the important innovations of the *Fontana d'Israel* now are achieved with an even greater emphasis on word-inspired music. Only eleven of the thirty-two concertos are arrangements of chorales. They are similar in style to those in Part I. Many of the concertos have important instrumental ensembles serving for introductions, ritornellos, and concerted ensembles with vocal parts. These are particularly important in those concertos that in effect are partly or entirely accompanied monodies. The sound of the motets takes something from Praetorius's large-scale concertos, especially the *Polyhymnia.* Schein, however, has absorbed much more faithfully the Italian stylistic ambience. These motets are for the most part large works in form and in style. Homophonic, homorhythmic choruses contrast with sections of motivic, multivoiced textures, instrumental ritornellos with solo monodies, and instrumental obbligatos combined with solo voice. All these features separate Schein's last sacred works from any that preceded them. And most interesting is how closely Schein has come to the concept of sacred music for which Schütz is well known.

Samuel Scheidt (1587–1654) lived his entire life in Halle, except for a brief period around 1608 when he was Sweelinck's student in Amsterdam. It was as an organist that he developed his career, first in 1609 as court organist to the Margrave Christian Wilhelm of Brandenburg, and in 1628 as director of music and organist at Halle's Marktkirche. At the Brandenburg court he had contact with and became a friend of Michael Praetorius, who

EXAMPLE 7.4   Schein, *O Herr, ich bin dein Knecht*

EXAMPLE 7.5   Schein, *Da Jakob vollendet hatte*

EXAMPLE 7.5 *(continued)*

served briefly as Kapellmeister. Around 1620 Scheidt himself was made court Kapellmeister while remaining court organist, and in the following years he composed much of his sacred vocal music. After 1625 Halle suffered the catastrophe of occupation and destruction by forces of the Thirty Years' War, and Scheidt's court position became moribund. Only in 1638 under the new court administration of Duke August of Saxony did Scheidt return to his former position. Both in life as in posthumous reputation Scheidt is known foremost as an organist who composed a major repertory of keyboard music. However, he also made a significant contribution to German sacred music in three important collections: I. *Cantiones sacrae* (1620); II. *Pars prima concertuum sacrorum, adjectis symphoniis et choris instrumentalibus* (1622); and III. four volumes of *Geistlicher Concerten* (1631, 1634, 1635, 1640).[14]

Scheidt's sacred music developed similarly to Schein's, and perhaps even more than the latter was much influenced by Michael Praetorius. Like Schein's *Cymbalum Sionium,* Scheidt's *Cantiones sacrae* contain polychoral motets (with one exception) all in eight parts divided four plus four. Except for the two clarino parts in *In dulci jubilo,* there are no indications for instrumental accompaniment nor is there a basso continuo part. This does not mean, of course, that organ and other instruments would not have doubled or even substituted for the vocal parts in performances. Almost a third of the thirty-nine motets are set to Latin liturgical texts (except for the devotional hymn *O Domine Jesu Christe*), and about half are contrapuntal arrangements of chorales, many of which strongly resemble similar works by Praetorius in his *Musae Sioniae.* As with Praetorius, Scheidt employs a great variety of contrapuntal procedures that are often interrupted by homophonic blocks of sound either in all eight voices or in antiphonal passages between the two choruses.

EXAMPLE 7.6   Scheidt, from *Herr, unser Herrscher*

One, a setting of Psalm 148, *Lobet ihr Himmel der Herren,* is composed entirely in block chords in which one chorus echoes the words and music of the other. Motets not based on chorales and using biblical texts in Luther's translation have somewhat more and imaginative forms of madrigalisms and other word emphases than the chorale settings. Most of the motets are large, complex pieces with rich and often grand sonorities clearly composed for a professional choir such as was maintained by the Margrave.

The *Concertus sacri* follow the *Cantiones sacrae* in less than two years (the preface is dated September 1621), but these twelve sacred concertos for from two to eight and twelve parts belong to the new century. They bear some resemblance to Praetorius's *Polyhymnia Caduceatrix,* although the multiple part writing is less complex. With the exception of the psalm *Herr, unser Herrscher* (see Example 7.6),[15] all the concertos are to Latin texts, including two Magnificats, and a *Missa brevis* based on *Herr, unser Herrscher.*[16] Instruments are employed for opening "symphonies," interior passages, indicated doublings of voice parts, and for obbligato passages with vocal sections. The majority are composed in eight parts in double chorus textures, with one chorus frequently given to an instrumental ensemble. There is an apparent plan by Scheidt to make each of these concertos different in its instrumental/vocal organization, and within a concerto there are frequent changes of ensemble. Many sections are in what is often described as monodic style for one to three solo voices accompanied by the basso continuo (see Example 7.7). These are, however,

EXAMPLE 7.7   Scheidt, from Missa brevis super *Herr, unser Herrscher*

usually written in an imitative style and even solo lines do not have the freedom of melodic contour and development associated with Italian monodies.

Scheidt planned that the *Geistlicher Concerten* would be published in six volumes, but the fifth and sixth although composed never appeared and they have not been preserved in manuscript. The 115 concertos in the four volumes are mostly in two and three parts with basso continuo, while some have four, five, or six voices. With a few exceptions, the

EXAMPLE 7.8   Scheidt, *Erbarm dich mein, O Herre Gott*

EXAMPLE 7.8 (*continued*)

texts are in German. The largest number are arrangements of chorales, which in Volume III are arranged according to the church calendar, including Magnificats for Christmas, Easter, and Pentecost. A large number of these few-voiced concertos are actually reduced versions of concertos in many parts and choruses. In the index to all six volumes (in Volume II), Scheidt states that "these concertos have also been composed by me . . . with eight and twelve voices, two, three, and four choruses, with symphonies and all sorts of instruments." He expresses hope that someone would publish them "to the glory of God," but wartime conditions undoubtedly discouraged such an enormous project when church and court choirs were for the most part disbanded.

The sacred concertos together with the chorale arrangements of Praetorius and Schein are the outstanding examples of the inexhaustible variety of music inspired by the Protestant ongoing development of the congregational hymn. Scheidt's compositions are conservative in their adaptation of stylistic features of contemporary Italian music, and the strong contrapuntal foundation of his music is seldom absent. This feature of Scheidt's music composed in the second and third decades of the seventeenth century must reflect the conservative preferences of the congregations that he served. Indeed, Scheidt felt the need in one of the concertos, *Erbarm dich mein, O Herre Gott* (see Example 7.8), to add an explanation in the part books as to why his music was so heavily laden with chromaticism and dissonances, saying "that some *Dissonanten* in this psalm are composed on purpose because of the text."[17]

Other German Composers of Sacred Vocal Music

The extraordinary demand in church and at home for new music for worship that was central to Lutheran orthodoxy resulted in a huge output of sacred music by a long list of seventeenth-century German composers. Kapellmeisters and organists employed by towns and cities and at the many aristocratic courts in the many largely independent German states all contributed, usually in great quantities, to a continuing demand for such music. Some of the composers are famous—certainly Praetorius, Schein, Scheidt, and especially Heinrich Schütz are the most important—and their works established most of the forms and styles of sacred music employed by other composers for the century. But many remain more or less obscure, and the sum total of their prolific productivity of sacred music defies a comprehensive summary. The following acknowledges some of these composers who so greatly enriched German Baroque music of the seventeenth century.

In the North the two Hanseatic cities, Hamburg and Lübeck, with their several splendid churches, had a rich tradition of supporting sacred music. In the former, the music in the churches was the responsibility of the cantor, who also directed music at the Johanneum, a famous Latin school for boys. In the seventeenth century Hamburg employed two distinguished cantors: Thomas Selle (1599–1663) and Christoph Bernhard (1628–1692). In addition, the city was widely known for its organists in the four main parish churches. Selle's music, which remains largely unresearched, exists in his *Opera omnia* manuscript containing 89 Latin and 193 German texted works in sixteen part-books and three volumes of tablature.[18] His significance is well established for the development of the Passion, having composed a St. Matthew (1636) and a St. John Passion (1643). The latter is an early example of the oratorio Passion, in which the biblical text is not recited continuously but is broken up by the insertion of contemplative passages on various sacred texts. Selle employs recitative, interludes for six vocal and six instrumental parts, and a five-part vocal ensemble placed distant from the organ and another four-part chorus at the organ. Further adding to the colorful variety, he suggests different accompanying instruments for each of the soloists.

Bernhard's posthumous fame was largely the result of his musical treatises, especially the *Tractatus compositionis augmentatus,* a major source regarding the division of music into church, theater, and chamber styles, and the definition of various musical-rhetorical figures.[19] In Dresden he was a favored student of Schütz and may also have studied with Carissimi during one of two visits to Rome. Only one of his sacred works, *Geistliche Harmonien* (1665), was published, not unusual at this time when most Protestant church music was available only in manuscripts. It includes twenty concertos with German texts for one to four voices and basso continuo, and for many the addition of two violins.[20] Although generally similar to the *Kleine geistliche Concerte* and the *Symphoniae sacrae* by Schütz, they have an individuality of melodic style. Unpublished works by Bernhard, mostly in the Düben collection,[21] include a Mass and a dialogue and concertos mostly to Latin texts, some for one to three voices and others on the grand scale with choruses for voices and instruments. Many of Bernhard's concertos exhibit the growing tendency to compose what have been called concerto-aria cantatas that reflect the well-established form of the Italian cantata. In these, the composer divides his musical setting into distinct, contrasting sections for multiple voices and for solos in recitative and aria styles that at times are separated by instrumental ritornellos. Bernhard's sacred concertos testify to his melodic gifts, which are often demanding for the voice with long melismatic passages of musical-rhetorical emphasis and aria-like sections in seventeenth-century operatic style most often in 3/2 meters. He employs numerous examples of various musical figures to underscore the affective emphases of his texts. Bernhard's successor at the Johanneum was Joachim Gerstenbüttel (c. 1650–1721), whose large output of sacred vocal music is lost except for thirty-one works in the Bokemeyer manuscript collection.[22]

In Lübeck as in Hamburg organists dominated the performance and composition of sacred music. The most important of those to precede Buxtehude was Franz Tunder (1614–1667). Appointed organist at the Marienkirche in 1641, he remained in that position until his death, when he was succeeded by his son-in-law Buxtehude. Tunder's known vocal works number only seventeen, but they are important examples of the absorption of modern Italian forms.[23] Three chorale settings, *Helft mir Gottes Güte preisen, Wend ab dein Zorn,* and *Ein' feste Burg,* are German chorale cantatas, with a varied setting of the tune for each verse. The Latin texts are composed variously for a small ensemble of a soloist with four- or five-part string ensemble, one or two vocal and instrumental soloists, or large vocal ensembles with instruments. Although there are frequent imitative passages, the overall style is homophonic and at times in large ensembles very declamatory. There is both beauty and intense expressivity to his melodies, especially in the solo passages that are often in a free arioso style. The various ensemble works are filled with powerful, even explosive musical-rhetorical gestures creating an intense sense of musical oratory.

Dieterich Buxtehude (c. 1637–1707)

Among the most important North German composers of sacred music in the second half of the century was Dieterich Buxtehude, born c. 1637, probably in Helsingborg (then Danish, now Hälsingborg in Sweden) where his father, of German origin, was organist at St. Mary's church.[24] His son's early life, training, and career were spent largely between the Danish cities of Helsingborg and Helsingør (on the Danish mainland of Jutland). Buxtehude, who succeeded Tunder on the latter's death in Lübeck in 1667, became organist at the Marienkirche in April of the following year, a position he retained for the rest of his life. He also held the position of Werkmeister, the church's secretary, business manager, and treasurer. Buxtehude's contemporary as well as posthumous fame rests on his great talents as an organist and as a composer of organ music. It was this, probably, that attracted the young J. S. Bach to make his famous trip from Arnstadt to Lübeck in October 1705, where he remained for some four months. He also may have investigated the possibility of succeeding Buxtehude, who at this time was sixty-eight, at the Marienkirche.

Buxtehude was widely known for having reestablished Tunder's practice of giving *Abendmusik* concerts at the Marienkirche. These Buxtehude presented at 4 P.M. on the last two Sundays in Trinity and the final three Sundays in Advent. The music to these sacred texts (unfortunately all lost) was oratorio-like, with works in five parts, one for each of the Sundays. Although a considerable portion of Buxtehude's vocal music is lost, the 122 extant works outnumber his organ works for which he is best known. Two sources hold most of the vocal works: the collection made by Buxtehude's friend, Gustav Düben (1629–1690), Kapellmeister to the Swedish king and organist at the German church in Stockholm,[25] and a manuscript in tablature from the Lübeck city library (Mus. a 373).[26] Because Buxtehude was employed as organist and not as cantor at the Marienkirche, the question arises for what purpose these 122—out of surely many more lost vocal works—were composed. It was the cantor's responsibility to prepare the music for the Sunday service. Some of Buxtehude's works belong to special services such as weddings and funerals. Others were performed during Communion, and many of the texts have clear references to specific feasts within the church year. Also, there is no compelling reason to doubt that the cantor himself, Jacob Pagendarm, might have requested works from Buxtehude, or that some of the music was included in Buxtehude's *Abendmusik*.[27] While still something of a mystery, whatever the occasions for the sacred vocal works, they stimulated Buxtehude to compose some of the most beautiful and distinctive sacred music within the German sphere toward the end of the seventeenth century.

About two-thirds of the texts to these works are in German, about one-third in Latin. They are either biblical, especially from the psalms, or strophic poems from hymns and sacred songs composed without their given melodies or chorales using text and melody. These types of texts are employed in forms characteristic of German sacred music at the end of the seventeenth century: (1) the aria; (2) the concerto; and (3) chorale settings, all in their broadest definition. Both the concerto and aria are found in Buxtehude's chorale compositions, and they are also integral to what can be considered a prototype of the German sacred cantata. The majority of Buxtehude's vocal works begin with an instrumental introduction, often labeled sonata or at times sinfonia. These ensembles frequently have a significant part within the compositions as ritornellos or concerted with the voices and can be scored for just two violins and continuo or up to as many as five string instruments, and at times including bassoons. On rare occasions cornetts and trumpets are required.

For each of these formal types, Buxtehude employed a rich variety of compositional techniques. While general observations can be made concerning his works, it is in the variety of details that the greatness of this music lives. Forty-one works can be classified as arias. They are all composed to strophic texts. Only thirteen of these are for just solo voice with two violins and continuo.[28] Half of the others employ two or three singers and instruments, varying in number from two violins and continuo to *Mein Gemüt erfreuet sich,* Bux 72,[29] for SAB, eighteen instruments, and continuo. Seven have even larger ensembles, especially Bux 110, *Wie wird erneuet, wie wird erfreuet,* for six soloists and sixteen instruments and continuo.

The strophic poetry influences structure in a variety of ways. The strophes are often emphasized by being separated by ritornellos. At times a refrain text and its music are repeated, at others the same music is used for succeeding strophes. Chaconne basses are found in two arias (Bux 62 and 70), but more frequently a bass for an entire strophe is retained for variations in the upper part or parts for some or all of the subsequent strophes. For example, Bux 14, *Dein edles Herz,* employs the same bass for verses one, two, three, four, six.[30] Bux 58, *Jesu, komm mein Trost und Lachen,* has, except for the opening sinfonia, the same bass part for all thirteen movements.[31] In general, and this is also true of the concertos discussed below, the melodic writing is particularly attractive in its lyricism and more popular style and tunefulness. This perhaps reflects the influence of the sacred song literature but also Buxtehude's familiarity with Hamburg opera arias. There is frequent attention paid to the rhetorical emphasis of words through the use of common musical figures. Recitatives, however, are rare. When they occur, most of them tend more to arioso than to simple recitative style. Phrases are clearly marked and simple rhythmic patterns often contribute to melodic form. While Buxtehude's vocal style can be melismatic, especially for the stressing of certain words, with notable exceptions the vocal difficulty is not great. Similarly, while arias in two, three, or four parts frequently have passages with contrapuntal textures, Buxtehude's style tends in general to be solidly homophonic.

The concerto is the other major vocal form, with twenty-seven extant. A majority are for solo voice and an instrumental ensemble; others are scored for two, three, and four voice parts. The texts are largely biblical and are divided between the German and Latin languages. The concertato style is the defining characteristic and results in a variety of ways for instruments and voice or voices to interact. Indeed, in general these concertos are unique in formal structure. Most are composed in sections, created by changes of meter, tempo indication, or instrumental ritornellos. The vocal part usually is divided into musical phrases to agree with textual phrases, and these alternate or overlap with repetitions of the motives or phrases in the instrumental parts. Another contrasting type consists of arioso or aria-like passages for solo or ensemble voices. A few of the concertos employ a solo instrument concerted with a solo voice, at times involving considerable virtuosity, for example, in Bux 64, *Jubilate Domino,* for viola da gamba and alto.[32] Others, such as Bux 71, *Lobe den Herrn, meine Seele,* pit a tenor voice against a large ensemble of three violins, two violas, and continuo, producing a concerto of considerable textural variety and contrasts.[33]

Buxtehude's extant vocal works include only sixteen settings of chorales. Half consist of straightforward harmonizations in four voice parts with various concertato effects, sometimes simply separating chorale strophes, at others interrupting the chorale line with concerted insertions related to text repetitions. Among the most impressive of these chorale compositions and combining features of aria and concerto is Bux 60, *Jesu, meine Freude,*[34] scored for violins I and II, bassoon, SSB, and continuo. After an extensive three-part instrumental sonata, the six strophes of the chorale are treated variously: I and VI, instruments and voices in a cantional-like harmonization with instrumental passages between lines of the text; II and V, continuo aria for soprano without the chorale melody; III, aria for bass with chorale fragments within the new melody and with full ensemble participation; IV, a freer paraphrase treatment of the chorale for the voices and ensemble. Among other remaining vocal works that mix elements of aria and concerto are four dialogues (Bux 36, 61, 111, 112). There are a few compositions in strict counterpoint, for example, Bux 76, *Mit Fried und Freud ich fahr dahin*, three canons, and Bux 114, a *Missa alla brevis*, consisting of a Kyrie and Gloria in *stile antico.*

At least fifty other North European composers of music have been identified, in addition to Selle, Bernhard, Gerstenbüttel, Tunder, Theile, and Buxtehude.[35] The music of many of these composers is largely lost, or sometimes only one work remains. Many, however, remain identifiable by dozens of compositions, largely unresearched, especially, as Webber emphasizes, of composers from eastern areas of North Germany. The following composers are particularly worthy of further research: Crato Bütner (1616–1679), organist at Danzig; Balthasar Erben (1626–1686), Kapellmeister at Danzig; Kaspar Förster (1616–1673), Kapellmeister in Denmark and Danzig; Johann Philipp Förtsch (1652–1732), Kapellmeister at the Gottorf court; Christian Geist (c. 1646–1711), organist at the courts at Stockholm and Copenhagen; Johann Valentin Meder (1649–1714), cantor at Reval and Riga, Kapellmeister at Danzig; Georg Österreich (1664–1725), Kapellmeister at Gottorf court, singer at Wolfenbüttel; Augustin Pfleger (c. 1635–1686), Kapellmeister at Gottorf court; Christian Ritter (1645/50–after 1717), organist, vice-Kapellmeister at Stockholm court; Johann Vierdanck (c. 1605–1646), organist at Stralsund; Julius Johann Weiland (d. 1663), at Wolfenbüttel court; and Christoph Werner (1617/18–1650), cantor at Danzig.[36]

Among the many composers of sacred music in the Thuringian-Saxon regions of Germany, four may be singled out for their major achievements: Andreas Hammerschmidt (1611/12–1675), Johann Rudolph Ahle (1625–1673), Sebastian Knüpfer (1633–1676), and Johann Schelle (1648–1701), the last two the immediate predecessors of Johann Kuhnau and J. S. Bach as cantors at St. Thomas in Leipzig. Hammerschmidt served his entire career as an organist, first in Saxon Freiburg and from 1639 in Zittau. His prolific output of more than four hundred compositions is largely in sacred vocal forms characteristic of the mid-seventeenth-century German Lutheran church. Hammerschmidt's music, often apparently influenced by works by Heinrich Schütz, who was his friend, received warm praise from the latter in a dedicatory poem printed in the former's *Chormusic auff Madrigal Manier: fünffter Theil Musicalischer Andachten,* 5–6 parts, basso continuo (Freiberg and Leipzig, 1652–1653). The four previous volumes of "musical devotions" consisted of: I. sacred concertos, 4 parts, basso continuo (1639), II. sacred madrigals, 4–6 parts and chorus ad lib. of 5 parts, basso continuo (1641), III. sacred symphonies, 1, 2 parts, 2 violins, cello, basso continuo (1642), IV. sacred motets and concertos, 5–10, 12 and more parts, basso continuo (1646).[37]

These works contain a mélange of characteristic forms of sacred vocal music from this period: concertos for few voices, sacred madrigals, motets, and concertos for large numbers of parts. The fifth volume, motets for five or six voices, is modeled on Schütz's motet collection, the *Geistliche Chormusik.* Hammerschmidt also contributed to the genre of sacred dialogue with two publications: *Dialog, oder Gespräche zwischen Gott und einer gläubigen Seelen, ersten Theil,* 2–4 parts, basso continuo (Dresden, 1645)[38] and *Geistliche Dialogen ander Theil,* 1 and 2 parts, violin, cello, basso continuo (Dresden, 1649). He was one of a few composers at this time (others being Johann Georg Reuschel, Christoph Peter, and Johann Theile) to compose Latin Lutheran *missae breves.* Hammerschmidt's *Missae V. VI. VII. IIX. IX. XI. XII. et plurium Vocum . . .* (Dresden, 1663) with fifteen *missae breves* (and one with the Sanctus) is the largest printed collection of Lutheran masses from the mid-century. As is characteristic of most of Hammerschmidt's music, these concerted masses for instruments and a varying number of voices are composed almost entirely in a simple and largely homophonic style, characterized by considerable repetition of motives for blocks of text setting, frequent recourse to rapid, recitative-like chordal passages, and almost no chromaticism. For infrequent imitative sections, thematic ideas avoid sixteenth-century techniques and depend largely on conjunct, diatonic character. It is important to recognize that the composer conceived his Mass compositions as suited to choruses of limited resources and capabilities, provincial churches and schools rather than major court or city church *cappella.*[39]

Johann Rudolph Ahle's career was as organist largely at the St. Blasius church in his hometown of Mühlhausen. His son, Johann Georg (1651–1706), also a composer but of more importance historically as a theorist, succeeded his father at St. Blasius. He, in turn, was succeeded by the young J. S. Bach in 1707. Johann Rudolph Ahle's large compositional output consists almost entirely of works in the major forms of Protestant music popular in Thuringia-Saxony. As with Hammerschmidt, who was an influence, Ahle's music also shows a decided popularizing tendency in its style.[40] Among his works are numerous sacred songs based on texts from the Bible as well as those of such significant poets as Johann Franck, Martin Opitz, Johann Rist, and Ahle himself. These include four sacred *Arien* collections for a choir of four or more voices or for solo voice with basso continuo and an accompaniment of four violas (1660–1662). The best known still of these sacred songs is *Es ist genug.* Several collections of concertos range from those for two voices, *Himmelsüsse Jesu-Freude* (1648), to others for larger numbers of parts, up to twenty or more parts in the third part of the *Neu-gepflantzter-Thüringischer Lustgarten* (1665). Not everything by Ahle is in simple styles. For example, there are chorale concertos such as *Zwingt der Saiten in Cithara* (1665), an extensive work for six instruments—two violins and four trombones—three voices, and continuo, which freely employs the chorale, *Wie schön leuchtet der Morgenstern,* with the text for the sixth verse. Elaborate textures are based on motives from the chorale, and Ahle achieves a fantasia-like setting for each chorale line with concerted instrumental insertions, florid scales, canon, contrapuntal textures as well as climactic homophony and dramatic rhetorical emphases. Like Hammerschmidt, Ahle also published monodies in the *Musikalische Frühlings-Lust* (1666) and as sacred dialogues in his *Geistliche Dialoge aus Sonn- und Festtags-Evangelien* (1648).

The careers of Knüpfer and Schelle closely resemble those of Hammerschmidt and J. R. Ahle, in that they also devoted themselves almost exclusively to composing Lutheran church music in Latin and German. Knüpfer was Thomaskantor as well as director of music for Leipzig between 1657 and 1676; his successor was Schelle, who served in the same capacities until 1701. In these forty-four years, German Lutheran church music of the seventeenth century had reached an important consolidation of stylistic and formal characteristics found in both of these composers' works.[41] They excelled in multisectional, motetlike settings for chorus, most often for five parts, solo ensembles, and a large component of instruments. The orchestra often is quite large, at times having two or three violins and viols, bassoon with continuo, to which are added variously clarinos with timpani, cornettos, and trombones. Many employ chorale texts and often their melodies. Massive homophonic passages contrast with intricate polyphony and sections for solo voice or ensemble. In effect, these bear most of the characteristics of what a few decades later will usually be labeled sacred cantatas.

Sacred Vocal Music in Southern Germany and Austria

In the seventeenth century the Habsburg Empire in Austria, and the contiguous regions of influence to the north and south, espoused types of sacred music that reflected the resurgent power of the Catholic Church. In the previous century a period of church reforms briefly had inspired Protestant sacred music, but this was largely eradicated by the Counter Reformation in the early seventeenth century. It was the renewed vitality of Catholicism and also the proximity of Italy to Habsburg lands that quickly led to the introduction of traditional as well as new Italian musical innovations. Italian musicians had already traveled north across the Alps in increasing numbers in the late Renaissance. And they would bring with them many of the Italian compositional forms and practices. Of equal significance for the spread of Italian music was the devotion of the Habsburg rulers to Italian music. Three of them were educated musicians and composers: Ferdinand III (1608–1657, emperor from 1637), Leopold I (1640–1705, emperor from 1658), and Joseph I (1678–1711, emperor from 1705). Archduke Ferdinand, the future emperor Ferdinand II, as ruler of Inner Austria at Graz from 1596 toured Italy, seeking out musicians such as Giovanni Croce and Giovanni Gabrieli at Venice. Venetian music clearly formed the basis of his musical tastes. Already in 1604 he had employed the Italian singer and composer Bartolomeo Mutis (c. 1575–1623), the earliest musician employed at a court in the North to compose and publish the new Florentine type of secular monodies.[42] Ferdinand's Kapellmeisters at Graz were Italian, as were composers such as Francesco Stivori (c. 1550–1605), Giovanni Sansoni (1593–1648), and Alessandro Tadei (c. 1585–1667). The latter was a student of Giovanni Gabrieli. Another composer and famous trumpet player at the court, the German Georg Poss (c. 1570–after 1633), had been trained in Venice. Choirbook sources preserved from Ferdinand's Graz reign contain considerable polychoral music by composers with Venetian backgrounds including, in addition to Tadei and Stivori, Giovanni Croce, Baldassare Donato, Claudio Merulo, Annibale Padovano, Giovanni Priuli, and Gregorio Zucchini.[43]

When in 1619 Archduke Ferdinand was crowned Holy Roman Emperor, he moved the court and his entire musical establishment to Vienna. This in effect ended the long domination of the imperial court by Franco-Flemish musicians, and initiated more than a century of Italian domination of music in the imperial city.[44] Vienna, now established as the capital of the Habsburg Empire, quickly spread its influence throughout the realm. Not unlike Paris and Versailles for France, Vienna led the way for the Empire in all political, social, and artistic matters. The *Hofkapelle* during the reign of Ferdinand II (1619–1637) would employ some 120 singers and instrumentalists, the majority being Italians.[45] The Kapellmeisters were Giovanni Priuli (c. 1575–1626), who began his service in Graz, followed by Giovanni Valentini (1582/83–1649), both represented by extant sacred works that help to define sacred musical styles in the first half of the seventeenth century in southern Germany, Vienna, and at several other courts of the empire.[46] That style was predominantly influenced by the Venetian choral works of Giovanni Gabrieli, a style we have concluded can be viewed as a second form of *"prima prattica"* for composers of sacred music at the beginning of the Baroque period before it was largely replaced by the small-scale concertato motet. This influence dominates Priuli's *Sacrorum concentuum;* Book I (1618) containing "sacred concertos" with organ basses for one chorus is in four to seven parts and for two choruses in eight parts.[47] The writing is conservatively contrapuntal, with dominating imitation of head motives and longer contrapuntal phrases. Those for two choruses exhibit typical Gabrielian textures of strong homophonic passages and pregnant rhythmic phrases between the alternating choruses. However, the originally designated *prima prattica* of sixteenth-century polyphonic style also remained a seminal force in Vienna[48] as did the concertato style for both large vocal and instrumental forces and small solo vocal concertos with continuo and often obbligato instruments. The preserved works of both Priuli and Valentini give ample testimony to these conclusions.

Priuli, for example, in his late *Missae . . . quatuor, sex, & octo vocibus concinendae, cum basso totius operis pro Organo, si placet* (1624), includes five Masses, three in four parts, one in six parts, and one in eight voices. They contain an alternation of the *prima prattica* style of polyphony with considerable homophonic writing, the latter probably indicating an influence of Venetian polychoral writing. In an earlier Mass written in Graz but also used later in Vienna[49] the music is representative of the so-called colossal Baroque. Sixteen parts are divided among four choirs, reflecting the Venetian practice of making one choir a vocal *cappella* and the other three each performed by one voice and three appropriate instruments. Another collection of Masses also published in 1624, *Missae . . . octo, novemque vocibus atque etiam instrumentis musicis concinendae,* are more characteristic of seventeenth-century works by Giovanni Gabrieli, in *cori spezzati,* as well as modern concertato Masses with obbligato instrumental parts. The same distinctions of style are evident in the sacred works of Valentini.

More interesting from the view of the impact of new stylistic trends by Italians on sacred music are the small-scale motets for one or more voices by both Priuli and Valentini. Their earliest known examples appear in a collection published in Venice by Giovanni Battista Bonometti, *Parnassus musicus Ferdinandaeus* (1615).[50] About half of the composers in the collection were employed in Graz; others, including Monteverdi, were from Italy. Priuli's motets appear to be conservative, still wedded to imitative procedures of the *prima prattica* by alternating parts in imitation over a basso continuo. Solo passages of simple monody employ melodic writing of limited expressiveness, with few lyrical phrases, and those usually seem unaffected by the meaning of the text. Chromaticism is rare, and sequential development is largely absent.[51]

In contrast, the motets by Valentini are richer musically and clearly moving toward an Italianization of his sacred motet style. This can be seen in Valentini's works in the *Parnassus musicus Ferdinandaeus.* Melodic lines, although still constrained by imitation, are less rigid or predictable in shape than those by Priuli, which were still based on older polyphonic practice. Harmonic language begins to become richer in its expression of the text, and sections in triple meter have an integrity of line that does not break into motives.[52] Profound changes in Viennese sacred music are immediately apparent in Valentini's *Sacri concerti* (Venice, 1625). Most of the texts of the twenty-one motets contain extreme emotional images found in Marian antiphons and in Counter Reformation Latin poetry. Valentini resorts to various madrigalian expressive devices, an emphasis on musical-rhetorical figures, and—especially to be noted—perhaps the first appearance in Viennese sacred music of a form of simple recitative. One Salve Regina brings immediately to mind the elaborate florid vocal style in Monteverdi's *Vespers of 1610.* Set in virtuoso concerto style, each of the four voices (Canto I–II, Tenor I–II) toss motivic fragments back and forth among themselves. The music fully embraces a luxuriant form of vocal virtuosity found in madrigals, such as Monteverdi's late works, as well as in his Venetian sacred music.[53]

The Italian domination of the Viennese court was virtually complete by the end of the century. The Italian language had largely replaced German at court and among the educated classes. The influence of the Counter Reformation emanating from Rome shaped much of court life, most especially the richness and elaborateness of sacred services. Under Emperor Leopold I (1640–1705), a composer of distinction, sacred dramatic works became a feature of court religious services. These included oratorios based on Italian models and *sepolcri,* several composed by Leopold himself, and by Italians in Vienna such as Valentini (music lost), Giuseppe Tricarico (1623–1697), Antonio Bertali (1605–1669), the prolific Antonio Draghi (1634/35–1700),[54] Giovanni Battista Pederzuoli (?–after 1691), Giovanni Felice Sances (c. 1600–1679), and Pietro Andrea Ziani (1616–1684). The distinction between the various forms of sacred music dramas is often unclear, but the form of a *sepolcro,* although similar to the oratorio, is uniquely characteristic of Viennese court ritual. Performed during Lent, it is distinguished from oratorios by usually having only one formal part, no *testo,* and the theme limited to the Passion and Crucifixion of Christ. These works were performed with scenery, costumes, and, unlike the oratorio, with action. The scenery usually focused on or even was limited to the holy sepulcher of Christ. Other terms often used in place of *sepolcro* were *azione sacra, azione sepolcrale,* and *rappresentazione sacra.*

Other Austrian contributions to sacred music took place especially at Salzburg and Innsbruck. The latter was capital of the Tyrol province until 1665 when the Habsburg emperor Leopold I assumed control after the death of the last member of the Tyrolean Habsburg line. Periods of concentrated attention to sacred music at Innsbruck, for example, during the reign of Archduke Ferdinand II (1567–1595), were followed by periods of reduced musical forces. Only one name of significance belongs to Innsbruck's history of sacred music in the first half of the century, Johann Stadlmayr (c. 1580–1648). A German, he worked first in the services of the Archbishop of Salzburg, and in 1607 Archduke Maximilian II appointed Stadlmayr Kapellmeister in Innsbruck where he remained until his death. His importance as a composer of sacred music was emphasized by Wolfgang Caspar Printz in his work of 1690, *Historischen Beschreibung der Edelen Sing- und Klingkunst,* in which Stadlmayr is praised as one of the major composers of the seventeenth century. A similar opinion by Praetorius appears in his *Syntagma musicum* III. As late as 1732 his name appeared with a citation of some of his works in Walther's *Musicalisches Lexicon.* A significant number of his works were published in his lifetime including Magnificats,[55] Masses, Introits, antiphons, Vesper psalms, and hymns. Numerous works appear in various anthologies, and others remain in manuscript in monastic archives such as at Kremsmünster and Bressanone (Brixen). As with many composers straddling the end of the sixteenth century and the beginning of the new century, Stadlmayr wrote rather conventional music both in sixteenth-century imitative counterpoint, which is frequently interspersed with solid chordal passages, and later in Venetian textures of polychoral works for two and three choirs.

Salzburg enjoyed a rich tradition of sacred music from the Middle Ages. As the seat of the prince-archbishops, sacred as well as secular music received the support of the archbishop for his court and for the city churches through the centuries. Among the composers in Salzburg early in the first half of the seventeenth century were Johann Stadlmayr, Peter Gütfreund (also known as Pietro Bonamico; c. 1580–1625), and Stefano Bernardi (c. 1585–1636). Bernardi, a Veronese composer and theorist, was one of the first to bring the new Italian concerto style to Salzburg. He composed a Te Deum for twelve choirs (lost) for the consecration of the new cathedral in 1628. But as has been seen with sacred works elsewhere in Austrian regions, sixteenth-century polyphony remained a potent stylistic feature of Salzburg's church music into the eighteenth century.[56] Another composer contributing to sacred music in the city was Abraham Megerle (1607–1680), a student of Stadlmayr, and Kapellmeister to the prince-archbishop between 1640 and 1651. He stated he had composed more than two thousand sacred works, most of which are lost.[57] Among his surviving works is *Ara musica,* with over one hundred compositions for the church year. Here the mid-century mixture of musical styles stands out with solo works with continuo to various vocal and instrumental compositions for up to twenty-four parts. Polychoral music clearly remained a significant aspect of the sacred service of Salzburg cathedral.

During the second half of the century, sacred music in Salzburg was composed for the most part by Andreas Hofer (1629–1684) and Heinrich Biber (bap. 1644–1704). The latter's subsequent fame as the greatest violin virtuoso of his time and as composer of instrumental music has overshadowed the importance in Salzburg of his sacred music. Hofer's preserved works include two published collections: *Salmi con une voce, e doi violini, e motetti con e senza violini* (1654), fifteen solo works with continuo, either voice with two violins or three solo voices; and *Ver sacrum seu flores musici* (1677), eighteen offertories, one for eight voices and three instruments, the rest for five-part chorus (mostly CCATB) with two violins and either violas or trombones. Works remaining in manuscript include a *Dixit Dominus,* a Magnificat, two Te Deums, Offertories, and a Mass for eight-part double chorus and instruments. Others are for choruses of five or six parts with instruments.[58]

The only published sacred work by Biber is his *Vesperae longiores ac beviores unacum litaniis Lauretanis* (1693), containing twenty-nine psalms and a *Litaniae Lauretanae,* for SATB soloists, four-part ripieno chorus doubled by one cornetto and three trombones, two violins, two violas, and organ continuo. A small amount of other Vespers music is contained in manuscript. Six Masses, two Requiems, and some miscellaneous works such as Offertories, a Salve Regina and a Stabat Mater are also preserved. In addition, as Eric Chafe's monograph and catalogue indicates,[59] there is a small amount of sacred music of uncertain authorship possibly by Biber. The most important and famous among these works is the *Missa Salisburgensis,* which formerly was widely attributed to Orazio Benevoli and incorrectly dated to around 1628. For a number of convincing reasons Chafe concludes that Biber is the probable composer,[60] and its origins in the second half of the century. The score contains a large ensemble including two eight-part choirs; two groups of two violins and four viole; a group of two oboes, four flutes, and two clarinos; one or two cornettos and two trombones; two additional groups of four trumpets and timpani; and organs and basso continuo.[61] The indications of some sixteen solo sections would have found ideal positioning in Salzburg cathedral with its four balconies for musicians built onto four massive pillars supporting the dome at the crossing.[62] This work, like many of Biber's double chorus works, was clearly intended for celebratory music for Salzburg cathedral. They, as well as other mixed ensembles of instruments with multiple choruses, gave rise to the decidedly misleading concept of a "colossal" Baroque in music. Although the performing forces are large in a work like the *Missa Salisburgensis,* they are not "mammoth."[63] Biber's sacred music is rich in stylistic and sonic contrasts: *stile antico* choruses with instrumental doublings, double chorus antiphony, with contrasting instrumental groups doubling, solo vocal sections for one voice, duets, and up to eight soloists, at times with elaborate concerted sections for violin and a frequent dependence on trumpets for brilliant affects. His sacred music contains outstanding examples of the amalgamation of vocal and instrumental styles that occurred in the later seventeenth century from Venice and Rome in the south to Vienna, Salzburg, and the major centers of sacred music in the north.[64]

Keyboard Music

Sacred keyboard music composed for organ is one of the glories of the Baroque in Germanic lands. The roots from which this vast repertory of organ music received sustenance were anchored in the Reformation and the newness and vitality of the Protestant chorale with its central position in the reformed liturgy. The seventeenth century witnessed significant technical changes and improvements in the instruments themselves, and in tandem composer-organists continuously developed improved techniques for playing the instruments. An important catalyst for the evolution of a distinctly Protestant organ music came from Sweelinck. Although famous for his many keyboard works (see Chapter 8), he was unable to perform chorale-based organ works in the Calvinist service, and therefore he composed very few organ chorale compositions.[65] However, it was his development of a technically advanced organ keyboard style, influenced especially by the music of English virginalist composers, that became the foundation of the keyboard style characteristic of most German organ music. Scores of German organists traveled to Amsterdam to become his students and subsequently many were responsible for the transplanting of Sweelinck's achievements with the organ to their native lands.

Among the places where organ music developed in the seventeenth century none was more important than Hamburg. A city with impregnable defenses and an official political neutrality, Hamburg prospered while many of its neighbors suffered greatly during the long period of wars afflicting North Europe. It was a city of wealth, fortuitously situated on the Elbe River, with a vital economy based on its access to ships and barges from the North Sea and also central and east European regions. Its mixed citizenry of various nationalities and a large conservative Protestant ethnic population devoted much of its financial resources to culture and especially music in the churches. The four main parish churches, the Petrikirche, Nikolaikirche, Catherinenkirche, and Jakobikirche, played a central role in the city's musical culture, and the excellence of the organists employed by these churches gave the city a particular musical distinction. The Hamburg composer and theorist Johann Mattheson described Sweelinck as the "creator of Hamburg organists."[66] They included Sweelinck's students Jacob Praetorius (1586–1651) at the Petrikirche, Heinrich Scheidemann (1625–1663) at the Catharinenkirche, and Ulrich Cernitz (1632–1654) at the Jakobikirche. In addition, the Sweelinck influence was continued by Matthias Weckmann (?1616–1674), organist in 1655 at the Jacobikirche who was a student of Praetorius, and Johann Adam Reincken (1623–1722), a student of Scheidemann who was his successor at the Catharinenkirche in 1663.

The first to establish Sweelinck's influence in Hamburg was Jacob Praetorius, son of the famous Hamburg organist Hieronymus Praetorius (1560–1629). Little of his music remains; there are six chorale preludes, including *Durch Adams Fall ist ganz verderbt*.[67] Although incomplete, it gives strong evidence to Praetorius's organ techniques in a fantasia-like setting. More important are the six cantus firmus settings of the Magnificat tones I, II/VIII, III, IV, VI, and VIII, discovered in 1964,[68] in which annotations in the music indicate that some of the music parodies his father's organ Magnificats. Each Magnificat setting is divided into three verses (except for tone III, which has four). The music exhibits a rich variety of keyboard techniques from straightforward homophony and lightly contrapuntal passagework, to brief or longer imitative sections, and many fine examples of keyboard techniques of scales and rapid passages in various figurations, broken chords, and short motives alternating between the hands.

As with Praetorius, the sacred organ works of Heinrich Scheidemann fall into the categories of multisectional variations on chorales and other church melodies. Of Sweelinck's students, Scheidemann's works survive in greatest number and they substantiate a leading organ composer in Hamburg. There is an especially fine collection of cantus firmus variations on the eight tones of the Magnificat.[69] Scheidemann's organ style is virtuosic, using the forms and many of the keyboard patterns established by Sweelinck. The Magnificat settings, each in four verses for manuals and pedals, employ the tonal and technical resources of the North German Baroque organ for compelling and often brilliant sonorous display. The tones of the Magnificat usually appear either in the top or the bass of the keyboard manuals or in the pedals. In contrast to Praetorius's extant compositions, contrapuntal imitation suggestive of the ricercar and fugue drives much of Scheidemann's compositions. Organ sonorities become exciting both by the repetition of simple figurations between the organ's keyboard manuals and the *Rückpositiv* and also by the frequent brilliance of the keyboard virtuosity, with cascading scales, arpeggios, and other keyboard figurations. Equally significant are the twelve organ intabulations on melodies by Lassus, Hans Leo Hassler, Hieronymus Praetorius, and Giovanni Bassano, and thirty-five chorale preludes, most of them composed as multimovement variations on the chorale and several of which appear in more than one version.[70] Many of the techniques of variation found in organ chorale settings composed as late as those by J. S. Bach are present in these pieces. There are *bicinia* and those in three and four parts in which the chorale is placed against ornamented counterpoint. In some the melodic variation of the chorale can be elaborate and in a few instances the tune is broken up into fragments that are repeated with echo effects between the organ and the *Rückpositiv*. Other preludes in two parts for the manuals allow the chorale to migrate between the hands. Most impressive, however, are the choral fantasies in three parts for two manuals: *Vater unser in Himmelreich* II, *In dich hab ich gehoffet, Herr* I, and the greatly extended *Jesus Christus, unser Heiland* I[71] in four parts for organ, *Rückpositiv,* and pedals, which form an instructive compendium of chorale variation techniques from North Germany at or near mid-century.[72]

Neither of the second-generation Hamburg organists was born locally: Weckmann came from near Mühlhausen in Saxony and went to Dresden to become a favored student of Schütz, and Reincken, possibly of Dutch or Alsatian birth, was from the Netherlands. Both, however, had a major impact on Hamburg's musical life. Only eight chorale preludes are generally accepted to be by Weckmann.[73] They are somewhat more conservative in expressive techniques than Scheidemann's and closely resemble the chorale variations by Sweelinck. Two of Weckmann's have considerable length and employ canons in individual movements (*Es ist das Heil uns kommen her,* and *O lux beata trinitas*). In both there also are innovative examples of a chorale employed as a cantus firmus in long notes against what might be considered a "countersubject" developed imitatively through the entire variation (the first three variations of *O lux beata trinitas,* and the first and last of *Es ist das Heil*). It is perhaps not surprising that Weckmann, as a student of Schütz, would have placed considerable stress on contrapuntal ingenuity in his chorale preludes.

Reincken, the most famous of the Hamburg organists in the second half of the century, was organist at the Catherinenkirche for almost sixty years. He lived to be just short of one hundred, and his organ music as well as his keyboard artistry undoubtedly had a profound influence on J. S. Bach's own organ music and virtuosity, beginning as early as his student years in nearby Lüneburg.[74] It is especially regrettable that only two examples of his organ chorale preludes are extant: *Was kann uns kommen an für Not* and *An Was-serflüssen Babylon*.[75] Especially the latter is a virtuoso composition, a great organ chorale fantasie of more than 300 measures. Each phrase of the chorale or a motive is extracted, varied more than once and often so elaborately that the melody itself is swallowed up in the figurative patterns. The artistic or if one will the entertainment emphasis of this kind of organ virtuosity overshadows the religious sanctity and symbolic meaning of the chorale. It was the Hamburg organists who led the way toward such a virtuosic keyboard style being adopted in large measure throughout Germany, most spectacularly, of course, by J. S. Bach. Other important North German organists not active in Hamburg whose sacred keyboard music is largely lost include Melchior Schildt (1592/93–1667), another Sweelinck student who was organist in his home city of Hanover and earlier at the Danish court and also Wolfenbüttel; Franz Tunder, Buxtehude's distinguished predecessor at Lübeck;[76] and Delphin Strunck (1601–1694), organist at Wolfenbüttel, Celle, and Braunschweig.[77]

Samuel Scheidt, also a Sweelinck student, produced for the early seventeenth century a major repertory of sacred organ music in his three-volume *Tabulatura nova* (1624).[78] As the title suggests, it was the first German keyboard publication to employ open score (a separate staff for each part) instead of German organ tablature in letter notation. The first two volumes contain in random order various forms of keyboard music including eleven works based on Protestant chorales, seven on Latin hymns, one on a psalm text, nine Magnificats, a Kyrie and Gloria, and a Credo. Only two of these are not chorale variations but, rather, chorale fantasies: *Fantasia super Ich ruf zu dir* and *Allein Gott in der Höh*. Volume III consists of settings of chant and chorale melodies intended for the Lutheran Mass and Vesper services: settings of a Kyrie and Gloria, a Credo, a psalm, nine Magnificats, and six Hymns. The concept for these organ preludes derives from Sweelinck's development of his keyboard variation techniques. Scheidt employs a great variety of contrapuntal settings for the melodies. Each of the chorale preludes states the entire melody as a simple cantus firmus of sustained tones or, in some instances, either as an embellished melody or as a series of motives derived from the chorale. The settings can be in two-, three-, or four-part contrapuntal designs such as figural counterpoint, imitative counterpoint, double counterpoint, and canon. The chorale often migrates through all of the parts, which adds variety to the many multiple verse sections. Scheidt does not attempt to reflect the affective meaning of the chorale texts in his preludes. Rather, they are technical demonstrations of great prowess, even when the writing at times relies on the stereotypical patterns of keyboard figurations characteristic of most of the German organ music of the first half of the seventeenth century.

However, the apex of the North German development of chorale-based and other forms of organ music before Bach was achieved by Dieterich Buxtehude in Lübeck. His forty-seven chorale settings make up the majority of his organ works, and they fall into the three fundamental types: chorale preludes (thirty-two works), chorale variations (six works), and chorale fantasies (nine works).[79] The preponderance of chorale preludes reflects the required usage of such pieces as preludes to the singing of the chorales by the congregation. Buxtehude's form of the preludes is simple in design: the chorale tune as cantus firmus in the top part, accompanied by two middle parts (for the left hand), and a pedal bass.

The results, however, are rich in compositional variety. The concept of the *stylus phantasticus* dominates, and there is a singular variety and freshness of compositional techniques in these preludes. Largely absent is any suggestion of the predictable and stereotypical forms of variation and embellishment of Sweelinck. The chorale melody often is embellished with

EXAMPLE 7.9a   Buxtehude, Chorale *Nun bitten wir den Heiligen Geist*

Italian vocal embellishment in mind, as is seen in comparing the opening two lines of the chorale *Nun bitten wir den Heiligen Geist* with the organ prelude (Bux 209) (see Examples 7.9a[80] and 7.9b[81]).

Most noteworthy is Buxtehude's infusion of affective meaning into the preludes as related to the chorale text, making each setting different in character. Figuration, harmony, and texture combine to give a rhetorical interpretation to the chorale melody. *Durch Adams Fall ist ganz verderbt* (Bux 183) (see Example 7.10)[82] is an example of Buxtehude's affective response to this early Reformation chorale text, which tells of the original sin and fall of Adam. The curious bass passage of falling fifths separated by silence underscores the "fall" of Adam, and the dissonances and chromatic passages create the dominant affect of sadness or perhaps the pain of sin. In this organ prelude as in many of the others Buxtehude's affective treatment of the chorales seems likely to be the model on which Bach himself developed his form of text-expressive chorale preludes.

Each of the nine chorale fantasies demonstrates different facets of Buxtehude's art of keyboard improvisation, and in some he achieves the most original and innovative settings of sacred melodies among all of the German organ composers of the seventeenth century. The grandest and most extensive of the nine examples are *Nun freut euch, lieben Christen* (Bux 210), and two based on chants: *Magnificat primi toni* (Bux 203), and the longest and most remarkable on *Te Deum laudamus* (Bux 218). In it the composer's "fantasy" is stimulated by four phrases from the *Te Deum:* "Te Deum laudamus," "Pleni sunt coeli et terra," "Te martyrum," and "Tu devicto mortis aculeo." These four sections are preceded by a forty-three-measure *Praeludium.* The tones of the Te Deum, as with the notes of a chorale in the other chorale fantasies, are used to inspire long sections of imaginative and usually virtuosic music. The melodies are seldom heard as a complete cantus firmus, and most of the variations are based on a free incorporation of motives or fragments of motives into

EXAMPLE 7.9b Buxtehude, *Nun bitten wir den Heiligen Geist* (Bux 209)

the variations. At times the tune is entirely lost. In some sections it seems to hover somewhere in the variation; at others times it comes forth clearly to reestablish its authority
within the complex matrix of the old and the new which is inspired by the old. These are
organ works to test and challenge the keyboard technique of the performer and to give the
congregation an unmatched musical experience emanating from the sonic wonders of a
North German baroque organ such as was heard in St. Mary's church in Lübeck.

Organ works incorporating chorales and other sacred melodies become much less prev-

EXAMPLE 7.10   Buxtehude, *Durch Adams Fall ist ganz verderbt* (Bux 183)

alent in prints and in manuscript copies in the latter half of the seventeenth century, and very few composers seem to have made a significant contribution to these forms of organ music while being well known for substantial bodies of secular keyboard works. However, a few names stand out for their significance. Georg Böhm (1651–1733) was the famous organist at the Johanniskirche in Lüneburg from 1698 until his death. The eighteen extant organ compositions based on chorales are important contributions to the history of chorale-based organ works because of the quality of their imaginative treatment of the chorales and the variety of the forms of variation techniques. In addition, there is likely relevance of Böhm's organ music as an influence on the young J. S. Bach, who was a student in Lüneburg beginning in April 1700.

Böhm may be the first to add the form of the keyboard partita to the standard forms of organ chorale variations. "Partite" by Böhm's time had both the meaning of a series of variations on a given bass pattern or melody (i.e., Frescobaldi's *Partite cento sopra il Passachagli*, or Reincken's *Partite diverse sopra . . . "La Meyerin"*) and the more recent connotation of a suite of dances. Böhm's partite are a form of chorale variations, but the distinction with chorale variations, which he also composed, lies in the degree to which each variation preserves the integrity of the chorale melody. In general, the chorale variation lies in the top voice of the keyboard texture. Unlike the innumerable freedoms of contrapuntal textures, register, harmony, and motivic breakup of melodic phrases characteristic of chorale variations, Böhm's chorale partite retain both the harmonic and formal structure of the chorale, which is almost always recognizable within the variation patterns.[83] In the chorale variations, Böhm's style, while reflecting some of Buxtehude's own virtuosic figurations, tends to be less difficult technically. A notable distinction, however, is the degree to which the French style of keyboard ornamentation is applied to the chorale, for example, in the first of his two settings of *Vater unser in Himmelreich*[84] (Example 7.11).

Among the composers of sacred organ music working in the central regions of Germany one name towers over everyone else during the second half of the seventeenth century: the Nuremberg composer Johann Pachelbel (1653–1706). His career as organist included several important positions, first in Eisenach, and subsequently in Erfurt and Stuttgart. In 1695 he was invited by the authorities of his native city to become organist for Nuremberg's most important church, St. Sebald, where he remained until his death. More than seventy chorale preludes and ninety-four Magnificat fugues by Pachelbel are preserved.[85] Among the chorale preludes several are short chorale fugues with the subject limited either to the first or at times the first and second phrases of the melody. With the exception of three two-part settings (bicinia), the majority of the preludes employ the chorale in simple half notes either in the soprano or bass part against which Pachelbel works out a variety of keyboard counterpoints, sixteenth-note figurations usually being dominant in the three-part pieces while eighth notes make up the prevailing texture in the four-part pieces.

A unique form of Pachelbel's chorale preludes begins as an opening section with a chorale fugue on the first phrase of the melody, which is then connected by a transition to a separate section containing a three- or four-part setting of the entire chorale melody. The purpose of these compositions remains unclear. Seiffert suggested that these organ pieces did not involve congregational singing but, rather, were used by Pachelbel for the organ recitals he gave at Erfurt. Apel, however, believed the congregation could have joined the organist in singing the chorale tune in its entirety as it appeared in the second section. This would not seem practical, however, for not only the various lengths of the transitional section between the two parts would leave the congregation unclear as to when to begin to sing but also organ passages between the individual lines of the chorale would leave the congregation equally unsure when to continue the chorale melody.[86] Pachelbel's sacred organ music preserves an extensive and richly instructive repertory of forms of chorale variations typical of later-seventeenth-century organ music in central and southern Germanic regions. All of the chorale forms are similar in their dispassionate interpretation of the chorale melody, and there is no effort as had already begun to occur by North German composers to interpret the meaning and affect of the chorale melody and its text. Their

EXAMPLE 7.11 Böhm, *Vater unser in Himmelreich*

interest and significance lies in the brilliance and variety of the contrapuntal art as Pachelbel adapted it to the organ keyboard.

Another important contributor to keyboard music was Pachelbel's younger contemporary and Handel's teacher in Halle, Friedrich Wilhelm Zachow (1663–1712). In addition to a small number of cantatas, forty-four chorale preludes are extant, works of contrapuntal craftsmanship, for the most part shorter and technically less challenging than those of other contemporary German keyboard composers.[87] Most of them would seem to be typical of the type of introductory prelude preceding the congregation's participation in singing the melody. The types of treatments of the chorales resemble those of Pachelbel, such as chorale fugues and cantus firmus settings with the melody usually in the soprano or bass within a three- or four-part texture. A few of them place an emphasis on greater virtuosity, albeit fairly conservative in keyboard figurations. The longest and most interesting of these is *Jesu meine Freude* as a set of twelve variations.

CHAPTER EIGHT

Secular Music in Northern and Southern Europe in the Seventeenth Century

The Establishment of Opera

THE UNPRECEDENTED INVENTION OF "OPERA" in Florence at the beginning of the seventeenth century soon spread to other Italian courts and cities, especially to Rome, and then to Venice in 1637, where the first public opera theater was established. Operatic entertainment became another of the Italian Baroque musical innovations admired and emulated at the German/Austrian courts. In the first half of the century there is little documentation verifying significant operatic activity north of the Alps. In succeeding decades, however, evidence of operatic interest in these regions reflects the strong ties existing between various German and Austrian courts and Italian courts and cities, particularly Venice. It frequently has been suggested that the first German opera was *Dafne,* composed in 1627 for the Dresden court by Heinrich Schütz to a libretto by Martin Opitz. The music is lost and recently doubts have been raised as to the nature of this work and whether it was actually operatic in form.

After 1630 a number of courts in the German/Austrian regions welcomed transplanted Italian opera as a new form of musical entertainment, particularly suitable for celebrations such as the crowning of a new sovereign, birthdays, marriages, and so on. Many of these performances are known by title alone, which makes difficult the classification of them as operas. In the earliest stages, various kinds of dramatic presentations were in vogue, for example, plays with musical insertions, intermezzos between acts of spoken text, dramatic ballets, and other more unusual combinations of singing, dancing, and acting. Before mid-century, opera performances occurred only sporadically within various court festivities. In southern Germany, a strong tradition developed of including vocal music in Jesuit school dramas that often were performed not only in churches but also in their schools and at times at courts.

Early in the developing popularity of opera, suitable theaters were largely nonexistent, and provisional stages frequently had to be erected in the halls of palaces or, in the summer, in parks and other open spaces. The first theater constructed specifically for opera in Germany opened in Munich in 1651. The first opera (actually a dramatic cantata), *L'arpa festante,* was performed there in August 1653 to honor a visit by the Emperor Ferdinand III to the Bavarian court. The composer and librettist was Giovanni Battista Maccioni (d. c. 1678). This initiated one of the important beginnings of largely Italian-dominated opera developments in central Europe. Contributing to it in the seventeenth century was the German Johann Kaspar Kerll (1627–1693), Munich court Kapellmeister between 1657 and 1673, and also the Italians Ercole Bernabei (1622–1687), his son Giuseppe Antonio Bernabei

(?1649–1732), and Agostino Steffani (1654–1728). The latter spent much of his early career in Munich where his first known opera, *Marco Aurellio,* was performed in 1681. Steffani was one of a number of important Italians to influence operatic developments not only in Munich but also throughout much of Germany during the century. His later appointments included writing operas for the first permanent opera company in Hanover from 1688.

The Saxon capital of Dresden also quite early established dramatic stage performances. In addition to his *Dafne,* Schütz composed a dramatic ballet with songs, *Orpheus und Euridice* (1638). A significant landmark in Dresden's opera history was the first performance of an Italian work in North Germany, *Il Paride,* by the multigifted castrato, Giovanni Andrea Bontempi (1625–1705).[1] It was given in November 1662 during celebrations for the marriage of the daughter of the elector of Saxony to the Margrave of Brandenburg. In five acts, *Il Paride* is a grand festival opera in Venetian opera tradition, with ballets at the end of acts (not included in the score). Its arioso solos are accompanied by two violins and continuo. Strophic songs and strong basses, a few of which are ostinatos, also reflect Venetian practice.

Not until 1667 did Dresden open its first opera house with *Teseo,* libretto by Giovanni Andrea Moniglia, composer unknown.[2] In 1672, *Dafne,* performed at the Dresden Comoedihaus, was a collaboration between Marco Gioseppe Peranda (c. 1625–1675) and Bontempi, who may also have adapted Opitz's libretto originally used by Schütz.[3] It would appear, as the earliest fully preserved German opera, to have led the way to the subsequent flourishing of opera in Germany. Its style is still somewhat focused on the Venetian characteristic of recitatives as well as numerous, usually short ritornellos, serving as preludes, interludes, and postludes (in two unspecified instrumental parts and bass). Of great interest, however, is the German lyricism that dominates many scenes in songs, often strophic, that tend to approach the style of folk music and suggest music written for German Singspiels. But a German influence on opera in Dresden was short-lived. The Elector Johann George III, determined to establish an Italian opera in Dresden, brought Carlo Pallavicino (c. 1640–1688) to the city in 1685 for that purpose. Pallavicino produced his *La Gierusalemme liberata* in 1687, and his last opera, *Antiope,* with the third and last act completed by N. A. Strungk, was performed posthumously in 1689.

German opera became an important new form of entertainment after 1650 at smaller court cities and towns, for example, in the Thuringian cities of Altenburg, Coburg, Eisenberg, Gotha, and Weissenfels. Especially in the latter city opera performances were an established tradition into the eighteenth century. Other German court towns also had intermittent court festivities featuring operas, such as Stuttgart with works by Johann Sigismund Kusser from 1662, Halle from 1663, Ansbach, served briefly by Johann Wolfgang Franck, from 1673, as well as Hanover, where Agostino Steffani was composer. A significant center of operatic activity developed at the court of Brunswick (Braunschweig)-Wolfenbüttel, at the latter town until 1690 and subsequently in Brunswick. There the Rathaus was converted in 1690 into a fine opera theater, and a rich variety of works were staged including those by Lully as well as by Italians such as Antonio Giannettini, Antonio Draghi, Alessandro Scarlatti, Agostino Steffani, and Carlo Francesco Pollarolo. German operas included those by Kusser, Johann Philipp Krieger, and Reinhard Keiser. Although these were performances for the Wolfenbüttel court and paid for by Duke Anton Ulrich, he made them accessible to the public that wished to purchase tickets, a tradition lasting well into the next century.

It was, however, in Hamburg that the most important operatic activity began to flourish, from 1687 when the first public opera house outside of Venice was established. The moving force in this development was the Hamburg patrician and lawyer Gerhard Schott. He engaged the Italian architect Girolamo Sartorio to build an opera theater at the city's Gänsemarkt, in approximately the same location as the current Hamburg State Opera. The first Hamburg operas were often based on biblical themes, for example, Johann Theile's *Der erschaffene, und gefallene und auffgerichtete Mensch [Adam und Eva]*. Sacred operas clearly were meant to soften the criticisms of various church officials in Hamburg who vigorously condemned operas as sinful entertainment. Other composers presenting their operas in Hamburg during the seventeenth century included, in addition to Theile, Nicolaus Adam Strungk, Johann Philipp Förtsch, Johann Wolfgang Franck, and Johann Georg Conradi. The latter's *Die schöne und getreue Ariadne* (1691) is especially important as the earliest score to survive from the Hamburg repertory.[4] The music has a cosmopolitan mixture of Venetian, German, and French musical styles in which the French spirit dominates almost all the music except for the recitatives. From its opening French *Ouverture* to the lengthy closing *Passacaille* with seventy-eight statements of a conventional four-measure descending tetrachord, sung and probably also danced, Conradi displays substantial familiarity with French operatic achievements.[5]

Outside Italy, the earliest operatic activities took place in Salzburg, where the Archbishop Marcus Sitticus introduced significant cultural and economic ties with Italy. Opera was performed at his court from 1614. He also established the Steintheater in the gardens of the summer residence at Hellbrunn just outside the city. In 1619 the new emperor, Ferdinand II, attended a performance of an *Orfeo* at the Salzburg court. And it was the emperor's Italian wife, the Mantuan princess Eleonora Gonzaga, who brought to the Viennese court her love of Italian culture, and who introduced the concept of *Invenzioni*. These were dramatic presentations usually combining singing and ballet. During Ferdinand's reign an influx of Italian composers and performers streamed into the Habsburg capital, and they would dominate Viennese musical life for at least two hundred years.

Dramatic music performed at court during Carnival season and various special celebrations in the first half of the seventeenth century was seldom specified as to types. Performances usually took place in a large public room in the Hofburg, although for the marriage in 1631 of the Crown Prince Ferdinand to Maria Anna of Spain an opera, *La caccia felice,* was staged in the great chamber of the Imperial Diet for Lower Austria.

The arts in Vienna, especially music, received particular encouragement and support during the reign of Leopold I (1658–1705), who in his own right was a composer of some distinction. His first love was opera, and for his marriage in 1666 to Margarita of Spain he had constructed a large theater in the "Cortina" of the Hofburg, which was designed by Lodovico Burnaccini. Here, in July 1668, the performance of Antonio Cesti's famous five-act opera *Il pomo d'oro*, libretto by Francesco Sbarra, received a sumptuous production. Probably because of its extended length of some eight hours it was divided into two parts and performed on two separate days. Johann Schmelzer composed the ballet music. The elaborate scenery in twenty-three different stage sets for the production, the costumes, and machines, which became the talk of Europe, were by Burnaccini.[6] While the music is very much in the Venetian operatic style, the work is exceptional in its five acts, large orchestra, and an enormous cast of more than forty singers and numerous supernumeraries. Since the music to the extant acts first appeared in a modern edition by Guido Adler,[7] *Il pomo d'oro* has exemplified the grandeur and extravagance of Baroque court opera.

During the forty-seven-year reign of Leopold I, opera as well as other forms of musical-dramatic works such as oratorios and sacred representations dominated musical life at the Viennese court. In addition to Cesti's operas, many scores were presented by composers such as Antonio Bertali (1605–1669), Pietro Andreas Ziani, and especially Draghi. The latter composed a large number of operas and oratorios, many of them in collaboration with the emperor, who often contributed arias and sometimes entire scenes. In 1683 the court theater in the Cortina was torn down as a fire hazard. Until 1697 operas were again presented in provisional settings in the Hofburg and elsewhere on the grounds, as well as at various palaces of the Habsburg family, for example, at the summer estate, La Favorita (known today as the Theresianum), of the empress. In 1700 the great hall of the Hofburg was restored as the imperial opera theater under the supervision of Francesco Galli-Bibiena, and opened with Draghi's *Alceste* and *Il fato monarchico,* the first of several operas by Johann Joseph Fux (1660–1741). At the same time an opera by Carlo Agostino Badia (1672–1738), *Diana rappacificata con Venere e con l'Aurora,* became the first opera performed at Schönbrunn, the newest summer palace of the emperor. By the end of the seventeenth century, with the steady stream of operas, oratorios, and *rappresentazione sacrae* performed largely for the aristocracy, Vienna became known throughout Europe as the most important and influential center for developing styles of Italian dramatic music in the Germanic regions.

Court opera also appeared sporadically in other Habsburg cities during the century, for example, at Linz, where the first known opera performance there took place in 1677 with Antonio Draghi's *Hercole acquistatore dell'immortalità,* presented for the birthday of the empress. When the emperor traveled north, as, for example, to Augsburg during the Christmas season of 1689–1690, two operas were given in the house of the Fuggers. Salzburg, too, continued to be a center of court opera through the support of the prince-bishops. Among those operas known to have been composed for such occasions are works by Andreas Hofer, Georg Muffat, and Heinrich Ignaz Biber. The latter's score, *Chi la dura la vince* (?1690–1692), is the only opera known to survive from this period in Salzburg.

The Development of the German Lied

"Music began with singing." [8] From times immemorial the human voice has been a dominant feature of cultures from the most primitive to the most sophisticated, from the most ancient to the most recent. The origins of the German lied evolved from the earliest records of German music, particularly the courtly lyrics sung by the minnesingers during the extended period between the twelfth and fourteenth centuries. In the early Renaissance, German vocal music, both sacred and secular, became largely wedded to the polyphonic practices from France and the Low Countries. Collections of polyphonic lieder from the second half of the fifteenth century, such as the *Lochamer Liederbuch, Schedelsches Liederbuch,* and the *Glogauer Liederbuch,* [9] established a consistent love of polyphonic textures that would often characterize German music throughout much of its history. In these collections the polyphonic *Tenorlied,* in three or four parts, dominated German vocal forms well into the mid-sixteenth century. Examples from the fifteenth century include those by the German Heinrich Finck, the Austrian Paul Hofhaimer, and the Flemish Isaac, whose career fluctuated between Italy and Austria. Polyphonic treatment was also characteristic for the great outburst of chorale melodies established by the early composers of the Protestant Reformation.

By the last decades of the sixteenth century, Italian songs and texts became widely known in Germany and Austria, and they would influence and change the traditional German lied forms. Particularly the early-seventeenth-century Italian development of the continuo accompaniment would radically affect German and Austrian song composers. It was, however, also the familiarity with Italian poetic forms such as the villanella that began to attract German composers. For example, Hans Leo Hassler's first published work was the *Canzonette* of 1590, simple homophonic songs composed to Italian texts, as were his set of Italian madrigals from 1596. In the same year he published *Neue teutsche Gesäng nach Art der welschen Madrigalien und Canzonetten* (New German songs in the style of Italian madrigals and canzonettas). The title "new German songs" became a commonplace label for German composers of lieder in the early seventeenth century. The Italian influences in Schein's *Musica boscareccia* (published in three parts, 1621–1628) are especially telling. The texts are based on the Italian pastoral tradition, and while the lieder are all for two sopranos and a bass, the latter is texted but also figured. As has been found with his sacred vocal works, these lieder begin to give evidence of expressive musical/rhetorical treatment of individual words and phrases. Among Schein's recommendations for performance options is the suggestion that it was appropriate to have just one soprano sing, the second part given to violin or flute, and both accompanied only by an instrumental continuo. Here, then, is confirmation that the concept of the German continuo lied is at hand.[10]

Johann Nauwach (c. 1595–c. 1630), who spent most of his brief life at the Dresden court, is credited with being the first to publish such lieder in Germany.[11] His two collections of songs are *Libro primo di arie passeggiate à una voce per cantar e sonar nel chitarrone et alti simili instrumente* (Dresden, 1623) and *Erster Theil teutscher Villanellen mit 1, 2, und 3 Stimmen auf die Tiorba, Laute, Clavicymbel, und andere Instrumenta gerichtet* (Dresden, 1627). Nauwach, beginning in 1612, spent six years studying in Turin and Florence where he became familiar with Italian vocal music. His first collection, consisting of through-composed madrigals, is indebted to the works of the Italian monodists such as Caccini, including a heavily ornamented version of the latter's famous *Amarilli*. For the origins of the German lied the *Teutscher Villanellen* (only a few of which are true villanellas) has special importance. Among the various types of Italianate and older German song types in two and three parts with strophic texts, eight works have historical significance as the earliest published solo continuo songs in German. *Ach Liebste, lass uns eilen* is a typical example with some resemblance to Italian monodic practice (see Example 8.1[12]).

The future of the German continuo lied, however, would depend on greater musical and poetic talents than are found in the extant songs by Nauwach. It was the Königsberg [now Kalinningrad] poet and composer, cousin of Heinrich Schütz and friend of Hermann Schein, Heinrich Albert (1604–1651), known as the father of the German lied, who gave substance and musical values as well as a definite "German" character to the developing tradition of German song. This was exemplified by his extraordinary publication in eight volumes of *Arien* between 1638 and 1650 containing 170 sacred and secular songs.[13] As was true of many of the lied composers, Albert's songs are composed to excellent poetry by the influential Martin Opitz (1597–1639) and especially to the poems of Simon Dach (1605–1659), one of a group of poets belonging to the Königsberg "school." At least eighteen songs are to poems by Albert himself. The songs, largely strophic, are for solo voice and continuo. Most of them originated for performances at local events such as weddings, funerals, and for the enjoyment of the composer's friends. Their great popularity is reflected in many of them being transformed into chorales but also republished in song collections by other composers and in numerous pirated editions. Albert at times composed texts to musical settings suggesting the influence of the Italian cantata and even the madrigal. In these texts repetition and some suggestion of recitative are present as well as rhetorically expressive melodic figures and chromatic colorations. In such instances Albert seemed indifferent as to how these specifically text-related interpretations did not always agree with unrelated texts in the other strophes of a poem.[14]

During the seventeenth century the number of German continuo lied composers rapidly increased. In the North, in addition to Albert, a contemporary of some significance

EXAMPLE 8.1   Nauwach, *Ach Liebste, lass uns eilen* (2d and 3d verses omitted)

was the Hamburg cantor Thomas Selle (1599–1663) and his collection of monodic songs *Monophonetica, hoc est, Allerhand lustige und anmutize Frewden-Liedlein* (1636). Just as the Königsberg composers found lyrical inspiration in poets such as Opitz and Dach, the stimulus for song composition in the Hamburg region was the several major collections of poetry for both sacred and secular songs by the German theologian, poet, and composer Johann Rist (1607–1667). Secular texts are found in such significant publications as *Des edlen Daphnis aus Cimbrien Galathee* (1642), *Das edlen Daphnis . . . besungene Florabella* (1651), and *Neuer teutscher Parnass* (1652). Some of these secular poems were composed by Rist, but the majority were set to music by minor composers such as Michael Jacobi (1618–1663), Peter Meyer (fl. 1640–1678), and Heinrich Pape (1609–1663).

In central Germany it was Adam Krieger (1634–1666) who was outstanding in furthering the musical significance of the German lied. He was a student of Scheidt at Halle, held the position of organist at the Nicolaikirche in Leipzig, and after 1657 completed his short life as composer and organist at the Dresden court of Johann Georg II. Krieger published only two collections of *Arien,* the first with some fifty lieder in 1657 which is lost,[15] and the second, *Neue Arien in 6 Zehen eingetheilet* (Dresden 1667, enlarged in 1676), containing sixty lieder.[16] The poetry is by Krieger, although it is thought some of the melodies are taken by the composer from other sources to which he added new words. The variety of texts ranges from student drinking songs to love songs of joy or despair.

Those in the *Neue Arien* are of considerable variety although they all are strophic, with ritornellos for five strings and continuo separating the strophes. In a few cases the strophes are through-composed. Most are for one voice, but others have settings for from two to five voices. There is a distinctive flow and structure in phrases to the melodic lines composed over the continuous figured basses of the continuo. It is the character of the melodies that is new. It seems Italian, although largely it sounds German. The music is wedded to the texts in sentiment and at times in melodic figurations. One, "Die unfreundliche Mopsa—Der verliebte Dafne,"[17] structurally suggests an Italian cantata, beginning with a symphonia and dividing the nonstrophic text into duets and solos for the two characters. Another example of cantata-like structure and the most powerful example of Krieger's affective musical language is "Adonis Tod bringt mich in Not"[18] (see Example 8.2).

Besides Krieger, other composers from central Germany adding significantly to the lieder repertory included Andreas Hammerschmidt, Georg Neumark (1621–1681), and Constantin Christian Dedekind (1628–1715). Hammerschmidt, best known for his numerous sacred vocal works, composed in three parts the significant *Weltlicher Oden oder Liesbesgesänge* (I and II, 1642–1643) for one and two voices—one frequently a violin obbligato— and continuo.[19] These short two-part strophic songs are simple in structure and largely syllabic text settings. Many are dancelike and include the earliest known vocal setting in German music of a sarabande. Part III, entitled *Geist- und Weltlicher Oden und Madrigalien* (1649), is for one to five voices and continuo. Most of these are in two or three vocal parts with continuo. Only the last two, which are in madrigal style, employ either four voices and continuo (in number twenty-nine) or in that last one two violins, three voice parts, and continuo (which actually makes six parts). Here the lied as such is abandoned with a lengthy, imitative vocal setting, composed over a basso ostinato.

Neumark was a poet as well as a novelist. His most important collection of continuo songs was *Fortgepflanzter musikalisch-poetischer Lustwald* (1657), with eighty-five lieder for solo voice, two violins, and continuo. Before settling in Weimar in 1656 as court poet he made extensive travels in Germany that gave him numerous contacts with other composers and poets including Heinrich Albert and Simon Dach. Dedekind was another poet and composer who spent a major part of his life at the Dresden court, first as a bass singer and later as director of the court orchestra. His invaluable contributions to the German lied include the enormous collection of 146 sacred and secular solo songs and canzonettas with continuo, the *Aelbianische Musen-Lust* (1657).[20] The songs are composed to texts identified as by more than twenty German poets and include such distinguished writers as Dach, Finckelthaus, Fleming, Neumark, Opitz, Rist, Schirmer, and Dedekind himself. There is a great variety of texts set to various forms of song styles. The largest number are syllabic settings, with only a few passing tones or short melismas over the continuo bass for the most part giving only simple support harmonically and rhythmically. Dance rhythms are frequent, especially the sarabande, and many of the songs begin with tunes that are either quotations from or imitations of chorales. Rhetorically expressive melodies, however, are not absent, and for many of the songs Dedekind has composed melodies and harmonies of beautiful expressiveness suggesting some Italian influences, for example, in his lied *Der wahren Tugend Gegenstreit rührt von der Erden Eitelkeit*, with its expressive melodic leaps, melismatic passages, and also harmonic tensions[21] (see Example 8.3).

The great outpouring of secular songs with continuo in Germany, however, would soon end. By the 1670s song collections were mostly changed in content. More frequently based on French dance types, they became filled largely with excerpts from the newly popular operas and Italian cantatas. A few minor poets continued to create poems for

EXAMPLE 8.2 Krieger, "Adonis Tod bringt mich in Not"

sacred song collections. The secular lied for a brief period found acceptance in the early operas (often called *Liedoper*), especially those performed in Hamburg. In this city Mattheson, singer, composer, prolific journalist and musical scholar, complained, as did many other writers, that in music nothing is more wretched and tasteless as having the same melody (in strophic songs) constantly repeated to different texts.[22] The Italianate song, that is, the quickly popularized *da capo* aria, would quickly dominate German opera.

EXAMPLE 8.3   Dedekind, *Der wahren Tugend Gegenstreit rührt von der Erden Eitelkeit*

Keyboard Music in the First Half of the Seventeenth Century

Music for keyboard instruments flourished in the seventeenth century with the number of major and minor composers far exceeding those who wrote for keyboard instruments in any other historical period. Partly this occurred in Germanic lands because of the great improvements being made in the sound and size of organs and also in the continuing improvements in the refinement of construction for harpsichords. The magnitude of the keyboard literature from the seventeenth century is such that it can only be dealt with here by surveying some of the works by its most important and defining composers. The secular nature of this music is largely obvious for harpsichord music, somewhat less so for organ music. Here will be discussed only that organ music that is without a cantus firmus based on chorales or other sacred melodies.

As was indicated in the previous chapter, keyboard music development in the seventeenth century owes much of its stylistic distinction to English virginalist composers and their influence in the Netherlands, especially on Sweelinck's keyboard compositions.[23] It is, therefore, with Sweelinck that this survey begins. Regrettably, none of his keyboard works are preserved in his own manuscripts, which at times makes decisions of authenticity difficult. However, some two dozen sources remain, some of more importance than others and many copied by Sweelinck's students, among whom were such distinguished German composers as Andreas Düben, Samuel and Gottfried Scheidt, Paul Siefert, Jacob Praetorius, and Heinrich Scheidemann. And with few exceptions, all of the keyboard pieces can be performed on either organ or harpsichord. Those that are believed to be authentic fall into three major groups: (1) twelve sets of variations on popular tunes and dances, (2) thirteen fantasias and one ricercar, and (3) fifteen toccatas and two preludes.[24]

The English influence on Sweelinck is clearly apparent in his variations. Several of the tunes have English origins and also were used for variations by English composers, including John Bull and Orlando Gibbons. One of Sweelinck's variations is based on the famous *Pavana Lachrimae* of John Dowland, and another, *Pavana Philippi*, is a new arrangement of a pavanne by Peter Philips. The variation techniques are predominantly homophonic in four-part textures with (1) the unaltered tune supported by chords in either hand, (2) the ornamented tune similarly supported by chords, (3) the tune in the lower part, or (4) the tune embellished by rapid passages in eighths or sixteenths. However, some of the individual variations have expressive contrapuntal textures, for example, in the beautiful settings within *Mein junges Leben hat ein End* and *Pavana Lachrimae*.

His thirteen fantasias also show English influences with some keyboard writing similar to that of Italians such as Andrea Gabrieli and Claudio Merulo. The fantasias are studies in imitative counterpoint and employ a considerable variety of contrapuntal techniques. Each one opens with a subject, which is repeated throughout the composition and is combined with secondary themes that can also be developed. Most of the fantasias have three large sections in which the subject appears first in opening form or in inversion, then in augmentation, and in the third section in diminution. Many of these fantasias are large, dramatic, and technically exciting displays of contrapuntal ingenuity and keyboard virtuosity. Four of them are distinguished by being composed, no doubt for organ, "in the manner of an echo." A threefold division is maintained, an opening in imitative style, a middle section with a playful display of echo textures, and a third section as a toccata. The fifteen toccatas vary greatly in length but are largely based on the same organizing principle: a slow homophonic or at times imitative section followed by rapid eighth- or sixteenth-note passages. It seems implicit in some of his toccatas that one of their purposes was as teaching pieces. Sweelinck's influence was mainly felt by his students in Germany. However, his keyboard works did introduce into the seventeenth century a new concept of how to compose for the keyboard, at once more technically challenging and significantly more interesting musically.

German keyboard music, especially in the first half of the seventeenth century, was dominated by organ compositions based on Protestant chorales. However, a considerable amount of secular keyboard music also was composed throughout the century, even though much of it remains largely inaccessible for study, existing in numerous unpublished manuscripts most often written in keyboard tablature.[25] Even some of the most important of these composers have had only small portions of their oeuvre published in modern editions.

Another composer of secular keyboard music in the first half of the century was Samuel Scheidt (1587–1654), who was born and died in Halle. His *Tabulatura nova* has been examined in the previous chapter in regard to its sacred keyboard compositions. This *magnum opus* also includes in the first two volumes a variety of secular keyboard works, fantasias, dances, variations on popular songs, fugues (which could be labeled fantasias), canons, and two called Echo. The emphasis in these secular pieces, which are strongly influenced by Sweelinck, is on contrapuntal ingenuity. The impression gained from many of them, especially the variations and fantasias, is a severity of style in which an almost mechanical application of repetitive figurations and imitations dominates. While the textures are usually contrapuntal, missing are the interesting and often beautiful interweavings of the four parts found in Sweelinck. Many of the compositions simply disguise the four parts in essentially homophonic accompaniments. It is not surprising perhaps that the secular keyboard works never rise to the musical and expressive beauty of his sacred works inspired by melodies and texts of the Protestant chorales. Other less significant composers of secular keyboard music from central Germany include Johann Erasmus Kindermann (1616–1655)[26] from Nuremberg, Christian Michael (c. 1593–1637), organist of the Leipzig Nicolaikirche, and Johann Klemm (c. 1595–1659 or later), an organist at the Dresden court whose only published work, *Partitura seu Tabulatura italica,* presents a collection of thirty-six fugues in two to four voices and in the twelve modes, printed in open score.

The center for North German developments in organ music was Hamburg, and among the several important organists employed in this city's many churches, the most outstanding and prolific was another Sweelinck student, Heinrich Scheidemann (c. 1591 or earlier–1663).[27] He replaced his father as organist at Hamburg's famous Catherinenkirche in the 1620s where he remained until his death. His prominence comes from an accumulation of some one hundred extant keyboard works. While his reputation remains centered on his many sacred organ compositions, especially the chorale preludes, he also composed a number of secular pieces for harpsichord as well as for organ. They consist of thirty-six ornamented keyboard intabulations[28] and fourteen praeambulae, fugues, fantasias, mascaratas, toccatas, dances, and variations.[29] Scheidemann's works in various forms reflect a mixture of influences, especially from Sweelinck. Yet, in contrast, Scheidemann's keyboard works are less complex and technically challenging, and, as Mattheson observed, "easier to play" (*liessen sich leicht spielen*).[30] Technically, for example, one seldom finds long outbursts of passages in sixteenths so characteristic of Sweelinck's works. Also, Scheidemann's textures are much more idiomatic for the two hands on a keyboard, often with the four-part counterpoint reduced to parallel vertical combinations of two and three parts, which subverts any impression of vocal polyphony. Evidence of Sweelinck's influence is certainly present in the traditional forms, albeit few in number, composed by Scheidemann such as the Toccatas in C and G, the Fantasia in G, and the particularly impressive Praeambulae.

Works that can be assigned to the harpsichord are much fewer than those for organ. However, these, too, stand out as significant in comparison to any other extant harpsichord music by other North German students of Sweelinck. Among pieces showing influence of Sweelinck are the variations on *Betrübet ist zu dieser Frist.* English influence, probably conveyed by examples from Sweelinck, is found in Scheidemann's intabulation of Dowland's *Pavana Lachrimae.* A brilliant set of variations on a Gaillarda in D minor also reflects English keyboard style as do the variations on an English Mascarata in G minor, and the intabulation of Anerio's *Mio cor, se vera sei salamandra.* There appear to be varied English, Italian, and French influences in the several allemandes and especially in the fifteen courantes, half of the latter having separate variation movements. Particularly piquant is Scheidemann's command of the French *style brisé* technique in maintaining a three-part keyboard texture in the dances. Scheidemann's greatness as a composer unquestionably lies in his organ works with a cantus firmus in which he established a distinctive and enduring North German concept of sacred organ music. However, his secular pieces for harpsichord or organ were widely known in North Germany and are preserved in some twelve sources,[31] suggesting that they were admired for their uncomplicated technical demands and the vitality and inherent musicality of his musical ideas.

Keyboard music in the southern region of Germany was largely influenced by Italian keyboard composers such as Gabrieli and Merulo. Among the few significant composers of secular keyboard music are Hans Leo Hassler (1562–1612), Christian Erbach (1568/73–1635), and Johann Ulrich Steigleder (1593–1635). Only Steigleder's keyboard works show signs of developing a true keyboard style belonging to the seventeenth century, while Hassler and Erbach both wrote primarily in sixteenth-century keyboard style. Hassler's and Erbach's works fall into the traditional categories of toccatas, ricercars, fugues, and canzonas.[32] Steigleder's only secular keyboard collection, the *Ricercar tabulatura* (1624), replaces the former traditional modal designations by modern key designations. The twelve ricercars have a considerable contrast of individual treatments and originality of musical ideas. Most unusual of these ideas is found in No. 3 in F, where the central section consists of sixty-three measures of a motive suggesting a bird call (cuckoo) in a wide variety of contrapuntal environments.

Keyboard Music in the Second Half of the Seventeenth Century

There was a significant increase throughout Germanic lands, now also including Austria, in the number of gifted and widely popular composers of keyboard music in the second half of the seventeenth century. And a number of these composers' careers and influence extended into the final decades of the Baroque in the eighteenth century. The accumulated repertories of secular keyboard works are numerous and have been described in various articles and monographs in greater detail than can be achieved in the following survey.

The fame of the North German "school" of organ composers continued and was the focus of the music composed by seven organists: Franz Tunder (1614–1667), Matthias Weckmann (?1616–1674), Johann Adam Reincken (1643–1722), Vincent Lübeck (c. 1654–1740), and the three "Bs" of North German Baroque organ music: Georg Böhm (1661–1733), Nicolaus Bruhns (1665–1697), and the incomparable Dieterich Buxtehude (c. 1637–1707). Works by Tunder, organist at the Marienkirche in Lübeck, consist of nine chorale preludes and six keyboard pieces without cantus firmus: five preludes (one a fragment) and a canzona in G.[33] The preludes, like those of Scheidemann, have a three-part structure, toccata, fugue, postlude, that has considerable importance in later organ works, especially those by Buxtehude, where the formal design becomes greatly dramatized and expanded.

Weckmann's early career was enriched by his years at the Dresden court where he was a student of Schütz who sent him to Hamburg, 1637–1640, to become a student of Jacob Praetorius. Subsequent years were spent as organist, first at the Dresden court, and then for periods at Magdeburg, at Nykøbing on the Danish island of Falster, and back again to the Dresden court. It was here that at the desire of the Elector the keyboard contest took place between Weckmann and Froberger, as reported by Mattheson.[34] The contest resulted in a lifelong friendship and in developing musical influences between the two composers. In 1655 Weckmann became organist at Hamburg's St. Jacobi church. Much of Weckmann's music is lost, and there has been considerable debate concerning the authenticity of some of his keyboard music. Solid evidence confirms that of his keyboard music without cantus firmus there remain a praeambulum, a fantasia, and a fugue all in D; six toccatas; five canzonas; a set of five suites (although not labeled as such) with four dances each (two arranged in the order allemande, courante, sarabande, and gigue; two as allemande, gigue, courante, and sarabande; and one as allemande, gigue, [courante, ?lost], and sarabande); and four variations based on a secular tune, *Die lieblichen Blicke*.[35] Only the praeambulum, fantasia, and fugue include a pedal part and are obviously organ works. The remaining pieces can be played on either organ or one of the stringed keyboard instruments, although the toccatas seem especially suited to the sustaining ability of the organ.

The keyboard music, although limited in number and forms, gives strong evidence of

Weckmann's compositional gifts. There are many indications of an advancement in the earlier concepts of keyboard style. The toccatas are rich in exploring new potentials of the keyboard and what seems to be a new level of improvisatory command of the instrument. One might conjecture that these may be among the first organ/harpsichord works to have a dramatic, even theatrical excitement about them that can be described as "baroque." The rapid passages are seldom routinely worked out, and in numerous ways they are made exciting by their division between the hands and the rich harmonic support as the fingers move back and forth between the keyboards. The forms vary; three preserve the now conventional division into a slow, improvisatory opening followed by an imitative or fugal section, and a short postlude. Others substitute for the fugue imaginative and often dramatic sections of contrasting textures between the hands. This occurs especially in a passage marked *adagio* in the Toccata in A minor where a combination of numerous dissonant chords and progressions, elements of a lament as well as recitative, preserves a passage of Weckmann's most expressive, indeed almost operatic, secular keyboard music. The five suites illustrate clear evidence of Froberger's influence on Weckmann, in their open, *stile brisé* keyboard textures, and even in organizing the movements with Froberger's original design placing the gigue as the second dance.[36]

A central figure in the history of organ music in Hamburg was Johann Adam Reincken. He was a student of Scheidemann, the organist at St. Catharine's, whom Reincken succeeded in 1663. From the paucity of existing sources, it appears Reincken composed very little keyboard music. However, his fame as an organ virtuoso and improviser attracted the young J. S. Bach, who attended Reincken's performances a number of times while he was a student in Lüneburg. Subsequently, he performed for Reincken, who praised Bach's extraordinary improvisational ability on the great organ of Reincken's church. Only twelve harpsichord works are known to exist: eight suites with the standard four dances; three sets of variations, including one on *Die Mayerin* of Froberger; and a very long (154 measures) toccata. The suites are superbly crafted for keyboard performance with intriguing figurations and unusual off-beat motives and conflicting rhythmic patterns between the hands. Most of the gigues are fugal and in 12/8 measures, and probably influenced many of Bach's gigues which they resemble. The suites are clearly the product of a virtuoso performer who brought great imagination to the keyboard, although none of them is especially difficult.

Another organist who enjoyed great fame in Hamburg, but for whom little keyboard music remains, was Vincent Lübeck. As organist at Hamburg's Jakobikirche, with its famous Schnitger organ, his reputation was widely established both as a performer and a teacher. His entire extant oeuvre consists of two chorale preludes; seven preludes and fugues; the *Clavier-Übung* consisting of a Praeludio, fugue, a suite of four dances; and a chaconne based on the chorale *Lobt Gott ihr Christen allzugleich*.[37] The organ preludes and fugues are also compositions of a virtuoso, although the figurations and scale patterns of the preludes and the subjects of the fugues tend to be somewhat routine with unimaginative materials having less compelling originality than has been found in the other Hamburg keyboard composers' works.

The finest North German contributions to keyboard music in the second half of the seventeenth century belong to the works of Georg Böhm and Dieterich Buxtehude. Böhm, a well-educated musician who studied at the University of Jena between 1684 and 1693, then spent five years in Hamburg, although no records document his experiences in music there. It seems probable that Reincken became a significant influence on Böhm's growth as an organist, a talent that was soon famous throughout the region when he became the organist at the Johanniskirche in Lüneburg. Here the question remains how he and the fifteen-year-old student J. S. Bach became acquainted. No evidence suggests a teacher-student relationship, although it is clear that Bach and Böhm developed a lasting friendship that must have included Bach's rapid growth as an organist and as a composer of keyboard music. It is also probable that it was Böhm who introduced Bach to Reincken.[38]

The works of Böhm, in addition to considerable vocal music, also include for keyboard chorale partitas and chorale preludes for organ, and free forms for clavier. These consist of four preludes (and fugues), a Capriccio in D major, another prelude, possibly part of a Suite in F major, and eleven suites.[39] These works suggest, perhaps for the first time, a serious endeavor by a composer of significantly original talent to synthesize into his music developments in keyboard music coming from northern, central, and southern Germany, from France, and from composers such as Froberger and Buxtehude. Six of the suites have the usual order of the four dances: ACSG. The others contain a variety of exceptions: No. 2 in D major, the longest and most impressive of the suites, begins with an Ouverture, continues with Air, Rigaudon and Trio, Rondeau, Menuet, and Chaconne. No. 6 in E flat major omits the Gigue, and No. 8 in F minor substitutes a Chaconne for the Gigue. No. 9 in F minor lacks a Gigue, and No. 10 in G major opens with a Prelude. Melodic figurations and stylistic connotations of *stile brisé* often seem based on Froberger's suites. However, the inclusion of *agréments* and the remarkable variety of pieces contained in Suite No. 2 are the result of influences from French keyboard music. This suite may be an early if not the earliest example for keyboard of a French overture, and suggests a possible origin for the concept of J. S. Bach's Partita in D major, BWV 831.

The preludes in form are similar to many composed by other North German organists. The first two in C major and A minor have the characteristic sections of prelude, fugue, and short postlude. The D minor Prelude is similar except that it includes two short fugues that are thematically related. The G minor Prelude is very different, surprising in the context of a prelude for the period, and even somewhat strange. It begins with a prelude of seventy-eight measures in 3/2 of four-part chords in half notes, predominantly with octaves in the left hand. They rise through the keyboard range, fall back and rise again. For the most part, the triads are consonant but at times form unexpected dissonances. During about half of this section the bass obsessively reiterates octaves on the tonic, the dominant, or the lower seventh degree. When these stop the tone repetitions appear in the top part, creating an overall affect intensely dramatic, melancholic, and even threatening (see Example 8.4a). The fugue also has a theme that is neither bold nor typical, descending, but subdued and joyless (see Example 8.4b). The postlude is formed by a continuous series of broken chord arpeggios in the right proceeded by single chordal tones in the left hand (see Example 8.4c).

Regrettably, the secular organ works of Nicolaus Bruhns are almost entirely lost and give all too little evidence of his compositional achievements. All that remains are three preludes and fugues, two in E minor (see Example 8.5), one in G major, and perhaps another one in G minor, the authenticity of which remains unclear.[40] He was a student of Buxtehude, and spent his entire short career as organist in Husum. Not surprisingly, the preludes suggest influences coming from Buxtehude in their emphasis on pedal techniques and various keyboard figurations. Only the Prelude and Fugue in G major is an exceptional work in scope and musical intensity and conveys something of Bruhns's compositional originality. There are two fugues. The first employs a conventional descending chromatic scale. The second, however, has a decidedly original and totally unconventional fugue subject that suggests something of the spirit of many of J. S. Bach's subjects.[41]

The most influential composer and performer among North German organists, as the

EXAMPLE 8.4a   Böhm, G minor Prelude, Fugue, and Postlude

EXAMPLE 8.4b, c

b.

c.

seventeenth century progressed toward its end, was Dieterich Buxtehude. His impact on most of the organists from that region was substantial, and not the least significant was the seminal importance his artistry as a performer and his organ compositions had for the development of Bach's talents as an organist and a keyboard composer. Bach's awareness of Buxtehude, probably through his earlier connections with Reincken and Böhm, and his courageous decision to walk the 250 miles from his church job in Arnstadt to Lübeck to meet—and probably to study with and play for—Buxtehude is the most compelling and illuminating story from the young Bach's life. The impact of Buxtehude on Bach was clearly all-encompassing.[42] Given permission to be away from Arnstadt for four weeks, Bach overstayed his leave in Lübeck to about sixteen weeks from mid-October 1705 to early February 1706. An intimate knowledge of Buxtehude and his music inspired Bach.

EXAMPLE 8.5   Nicolaus Bruhns, Prelude in E Minor

He became Buxtehude's spiritual and musical successor and grew to become the greatest composer for the organ of the German Baroque.

In addition to the forty-seven organ works based on chorales (discussed in Chapter 7), Buxtehude's keyboard works are preserved in substantial numbers: twenty-six preludes (praeludiae), including two toccatas and a praeambulum, all of which combine extensive improvisatory styles with fugues; eight canzonas and three fugues; three ostinato works (a passacaglia and two ciacconas); and for harpsichord nineteen dance suites and six sets of variations mostly on well-known tunes. The central focus of Buxtehude's greatness in the secular organ keyboard works lies in the preludes, compositions that actually are toccatas in multiple sections with one or more fugues. Buxtehude took advantage of the great organ in Lübeck's Marienkirche with its numerous, colorful stops on the three manuals, and especially those for the pedal keyboard. No one before Buxtehude, and only Bach after him, demanded such virtuosity on the pedal keyboard, and the tremendous sonorities erupting from the bowels of the organ contribute to a formidable affect of *gravitas* and sonic majesty.

There is no formal precondition for the preludes, and each one is different, revealing Buxtehude's apparently inexhaustible imagination for inventing anew figurations, fugue subjects, contrapuntal textures, and harmonic surprises. While the preludes all tend to reflect by this time the established formal plan of praeambulae and toccatas, that is, the contrast between freely invented keyboard virtuosity and contrapuntal sections in fugal style, many of Buxtehude's preludes are on a considerably larger scale. They include two or three fugues, outbursts for full (*pleno*) organ chords, emphasis on pedal passages, and much more. The freedom of form relates directly to the prevalent Baroque concept of the *stylus fantasticus,* defined by Johann Gottfried Walther as "belonging to instruments and is a form of composing totally free from all restrictions."[43]

In the central region of Germany during the second half of the seventeenth century a number of contributions were made to the development of keyboard music. Among the more significant names are several for whom little remains of their keyboard compositions. These include members of the Bach lineage: Heinrich Bach (1615–1692), J. S. Bach's great uncle, and the former's two sons Johann Christoph Bach (1642–1712) and Johann Michael Bach (1648–1694).

Towering above other composers, however, was the Nuremberg organist and composer Johann Pachelbel (1653–1706). His career as organist was developed over a wide area that took him first to Vienna in 1673 as deputy organist of St. Stephen's Cathedral. Four years later he moved to Eisenach in 1677, then to Erfurt in 1678, to Stuttgart in the south in 1690, to Gotha near Eisenach in 1692, and back to Nuremberg as organist at the St. Sebaldus church in 1695. These extensive travels gave Pachelbel a variety of opportunities to study developments in sacred and secular music. (For his significance as a composer of sacred keyboard works, more than sixty chorale preludes, and the ninety-five *Magnificat* fugues, see Chapter 7). His extant secular keyboard works include, in addition to the widely popular Canon (and gigue) in D major, sixteen toccatas, seven preludes, three ricercars, six fantasias, twenty-six fugues, six chaconnes, seventeen suites, and the famous *Hexachordum Apollinis,* variations on six arias (songs) (Nuremberg, 1699). This wide variety of forms and types of keyboard music influenced his numerous students and later their students as well. J. S. Bach learned of Pachelbel's works primarily from Bach's oldest brother, Johann Christoph, a Pachelbel student for three years.

Most of the keyboard works, the preludes, fantasias, ricercars, and toccatas are for organ, with pedal parts.[44] They tend, with notable exceptions, to be rather short and infrequently more than thirty-some measures. The best of them, though often employing stock keyboard figurations, are seldom routine works without affective impact. For example, the dramatic and extended Praeludium in D minor opens with a long solo pedal passage, an extensive development for the keyboard of a brief motive taken from the pedal part, followed by a section of cascading arpeggiated triads and another of three-part writing for manuals and pedal. It concludes with crashing, alternating triads in the manuals, and a rapid passage in thirds and sixths over a pedal.

Of Pachelbel's six chaconnes, the masterwork among them is in F minor,[45] with twenty-two variations on the most common of ground basses, a four-bar descending tetrachord for pedal in F Dorian, which is repeated. This supports a simple and somewhat melancholic 4 + 4 bar melody for the manuals (see Example 8.6).

All of the twenty-two variations maintain the eight-bar structure, but at times, and especially beginning with variation 14, changes are made to the last four bars. Each variation employs various figures, keyboard textures, and at times compelling dissonances in the part writing. Yet this is not a typical monumental Baroque chaconne. It would be inappropriate to perform it with the full plenum resources of an organ. There is an element of quiet beauty that distinguishes this great chaconne and gives strong testimony to Pachelbel's musical sensitivities. Even more intimate musically are the variations in Pachelbel's best-

EXAMPLE 8.6   Pachelbel, Chaconne in F Minor

known keyboard work, *Hexachordum Apollinis* (1699). It is dedicated jointly to Ferdinand Richter (1651–1711) in Vienna and Dieterich Buxtehude. The title page specifies the work is for organ or cembalo, although the individual movements are clearly composed with harpsichord textures in mind. Six apparently original melodies, instrumental rather than vocal in style, are in the keys of D Dorian, E minor, F major, G Dorian, and A minor, but the "hexachord" pattern is curiously abandoned with the sixth melody that, although with a key signature of B flat, is actually in F minor. The melodies, labeled "arias," are followed by six variations, except for the second, which has five, and the sixth, inscribed "Aria Sebaldina"—probably a reference to the St. Sebaldus church—which has eight. The variations are simple in design, all of them retaining the essential melodic and bass structure tones embedded in various patterns of figures, arpeggios, broken chords, and runs. The textures are in two or three parts. And there is a degree of elegance and sophistication in these charming pieces that is not immediately obvious in the apparent but misleading simplicity of the keyboard style.

Also from Nuremberg and significant composers of instrumental, vocal, and keyboard music were the Kriegers, Johann Philipp (1649–1725), and his younger brother Johann (1651–1735). Johann Philipp's career began as organist at the margravine court in Bayreuth in 1669. In circa 1673 (the date is uncertain) he began an extensive tour of Italy, where he met most of the outstanding Italian composers of the period. From 1677 he served as chamber musician and chamber organist at the court of Saxe-Weissenfels in Halle-on-Saale. In 1680 he became court Kapellmeister in Weissenfels, where he remained until his death. Although Krieger was a prolific composer of instrumental music, eighteen operas, and apparently some two thousand cantatas, his keyboard music is almost totally lost, with just three pieces remaining, a toccata, fugue, and a passacaglia with five variations.[46] The younger brother, however, is represented by various keyboard works. There are two published collections: the *Sechs musicalische Partien* (1697), each partita made up of the usual four dances: allemande, corrente, sarabanda, gigue—two of the gigues being followed by a minuet; and *Anmuthige Clavier-Übung* (1699), which includes preludiae, ricercars, fugues, an individual fantasia, two toccatas, and a chaconne. Johann Krieger's keyboard music exhibits a scholastic tendency, is strong in contrapuntal artifice, but often is more routine than inspired by fresh musical ideas. Many of the pieces suggest they may have been meant for teaching purposes.

Another composer of significant keyboard works from central Germany was Johann Kuhnau (1660–1722), keyboardist, author (of *Der musikalische Quacksalber*), lawyer, scholar, linguist, and Bach's predecessor as cantor at the Thomasschule in Leipzig. He was a composer of much sacred music, especially cantatas, but he remains best known for his keyboard pieces, published in four sets. *Neuer Clavier-Übung, erster Theil* (1689) and *anderer Theil* (1692) both consist of seven suites of dances, those in the first in major keys, in the second in minor keys. *Frische Clavier Früchte* (1696) has seven sonatas—another sonata in B flat, included in Part II of the *Neue Clavier-Übung*, is generally thought to be the earliest sonata for a stringed keyboard instrument to be published in Germany or Austria.[47]

The fourth and best-known volume is the *Musicalische Vorstellung einiger biblischer Historien* (1700),[48] that consists of six multimovement "sonatas," a type of program music, each preceded by a prose description of an incident from the Old Testament illustrated in the music: *The Battle between David and Goliath; Saul cured by David through Music; Jacob's Wedding; Hezekiah, Sick unto Death and Restored to Health; Gideon, Saviour of Israel; and Jacob's Death and Burial.* In Kuhnau's informative introduction, he states that his purpose in these compositions, among other things, was to demonstrate how keyboard music, without the benefit of a poetic text, could capture the emotional states (the affects) emanating from an action or the description of a character. The various sections of each sonata bear Italian subtitles as clues to the particular emotional state or action described by the music. The keyboard music in all four collections tends to be quite simple both melodically and, on the whole, harmonically. The rather naive programmatic details of the fourth collection are, however, sustained by a rich variety of rhythms and especially textures: massive chords, often in both hands, motivic interplay in the manner of the *style brisé*, poignant dissonances, rapid toccata-like passages, and fugal sections.

Keyboard music was important not only to composers in southern Germany but also those in Vienna. In addition to native Austrians several German as well as Italian composers came to Vienna. They were especially prominent at the Viennese court where they were supported by the enthusiasm for music of the Austrian emperors Ferdinand III (1608–1657) and Leopold I (1658–1705). The most widely known and most influential of these keyboard composers was Johann Jakob Froberger (1616–1667). Froberger's career is not well documented. He was born in Stuttgart. More than once he was in Vienna, first around 1634. Court documents affirm that in 1637 Froberger was employed as organist by Emperor Ferdinand III who financed his study with Frescobaldi in Rome. Froberger was again at the Viennese court from April 1641 until October 1645. For the next eight years specific facts about his whereabouts are vague although it is probable he had returned to Rome and traveled also to Brussels, Paris, Dresden, and England. In April 1653 he again returned to Vienna as court organist, remaining there until 1658. Froberger's final years were spent in retirement in Germany (today Haute-Savonne in France) at the estate of Princess Sibylla of Württemberg-Mömpelgard (today Montbéliard) at Héricourt (near Belfort), where he died in May 1667.

Except for two sacred vocal works, all of Froberger's extant compositions are for the keyboard.[49] They are composed for clavier, that is, either organ or string keyboard instruments. The only exceptions are two toccatas for organ, which are specified *da sonarsi alla levatione,* to be played in church during the Elevation of the Host. The greatest portion of Froberger's *oeuvre* is in forms largely derived from his teacher Frescobaldi. There are twenty-five toccatas, fifteen ricercares, six fantasias, six canzonas, and sixteen capriccios. The fantasias and ricercars are scholastic exercises in strict contrapuntal designs. Slow-moving subjects in *alla breve* style, largely in whole and half notes, are worked out in the *prima prattica* derived from sixteenth-century Italian sacred polyphony. The canzonas and capriccios are fugal genres, multisectional and formed from successive variations of the opening subject. Most of the canzonas are in three sections, while the capriccios range from unified wholes to works in two, three, four, and six parts. Both genres employ lively fugal subjects, often with leaps and interesting rhythmic patterns lending vitality and at times brilliance to the contrapuntal display. If Adlung was correct in stating that Bach held Froberger in "high esteem,"[50] it was likely because of the excellence of Froberger's thematic invention in these works.

The toccatas, notated on a treble staff of six lines and a bass staff of seven, although having characteristics of Frescobaldi's works, differ in being organized into large contrasting sections. An opening, improvisatory display, with long-sustained chords on pedal notes leading into brilliant runs, arpeggios, and other keyboard figurations, with exposed dissonant clashes, is juxtaposed to a section of imitative counterpoint, which may or may not be interrupted at least once by the return, usually abbreviated, of the opening section. As in other fugal forms, the succeeding contrapuntal sections are usually variations on the first subject.

Froberger's historical importance has always been related largely to his thirty harpsichord suites. In part, this resulted from the mistaken belief that he was the first to organize a series of dances in one tonality and with the standard eighteenth-century arrangement of allemande–courante–sarabande–gigue. However, Froberger's own autograph volumes presented to Emperor Ferdinand III, one from 1649 and the other 1656, do not substantiate this belief. The suites in the earlier volume each have three dances arranged allemande–courante–sarabande, except for Suite No. 2, which concludes with a gigue. The second autograph contains only four-movement suites, each arranged in the order allemande–gigue–courante–sarabande. Only in an Amsterdam publication of *10 Suites de Clavessin,* published some forty years after the composer's death, are his suites, according to the editors Mortier and Roger, "put into a better order," by always ending with the gigue. Unfortunately, Guido Adler, editor of the suites for the *Denkmäler der Tonkunst in Österreich,* regrouped the dances of the suites to end with the gigue, conforming to this preconceived pattern not found in the original Froberger sources. Among the suites his most famous is the *Partita auff die Mayerin,* a set of variations on a popular melody. Particularly impressive are three keyboard laments, on the deaths of Emperor Ferdinand III, his son Ferdinand IV, and for the death of Froberger's friend, Monsieur Blancheroche.

The dance movements are in symmetrical binary forms, largely homophonic, but employ the *style brisé* of the French lutenists to suggest contrapuntal independence of parts. There is some evidence here of the variation suite found in earlier instrumental dance collections by German and Austrian composers, but thematic connections are obvious only between the allemandes and courantes, and in the latter this relationship is normally limited to the opening bars. Whereas individual dances often resemble those by Louis Couperin and Chambonnières, Froberger expands significantly the expressive dimensions of the allemande. They are filled with interesting keyboard figures moving between the two hands that obscure the four-square meter found in most French examples. The courantes, although some also emphasize interior part-writing, are usually more oriented toward the highest part. The sarabandes resemble most closely the French models on which they are based. Usually in 3/2 meter, they have conservative melodies confined within a rather narrow range. But they are not inexpressive, especially when they have the support of affective dissonances. Most of the gigues begin with conventional imitative entries which, however, often lapse into more homophonic textures in dotted rhythms. Froberger's suites as a whole afford striking evidence of the French influence on the style and form of mid-seventeenth-century keyboard music. However, the German penchant for intensity of expression, lively textures, and colorful harmonic tensions transforms the French models into suites that for almost a century provided the basis for further development of the suite in Germany.

Other significant composers of keyboard music active in southern Germany and Austria were: the Italian Alessandro Poglietti (?–1683), who lived in Vienna; Johann Kaspar Kerll (1627–1693), a Saxon whose career was pursued variously in Brussels, Rome, where he studied with Carissimi, and especially Vienna and Munich; and Georg Muffat (1653–1704), French by birth and a student of Lully, who in 1678 became organist and chamber musician to the Archbishop of Salzburg. This appointment was interrupted early in the 1680s by Muffat's travels in Italy, including his study in Rome with Pasquini. He returned to Salzburg in 1682, and in 1690 was appointed Kapellmeister to the Bishop of Passau.

Poglietti's keyboard music includes, in addition to twelve ricercares and other keyboard pieces, a significant number of works with pictorial and programmatic content. These include a type of suite depicting "the revolution in Hungary"; a cycle dedicated to the Emperor Leopold I; "Rossignolo" (The Nightingale), in which various musical instruments are imitated; a canzona and capriccio "Concerning the Cries of Hens and Roosters"; a "toccata made on the Siege of Philippsburg on the Rhine"; and, in his pedagogical work *Compendium oder kurtzer Begriff und Einführung zur Musica* (1676), themes for various capriccios imitating the songs of birds and other sounds. Kerll's secular keyboard works (he also composed eight Magnificat settings) include programmatic works, a *Capriccio sopra'il cucu* and a *Battaglia,* as well as eight toccatas, six canzonas, a ciaccona and passacaglia, and four suites with the standard four dances. Suites 3 and 4 also have a movement of variations on each of the dances.[51] Georg Muffat's singular contribution to German organ music is the *Apparatus musico-organisticus* (1690), which he presented to Emperor Leopold while they attended in Augsburg the coronation of Leopold's eldest son Joseph as Holy Roman Emperor. It contains twelve toccatas, a ciaccona, a passacaglia, and an aria entitled *Nova Cyclopeias harmonica* and a set of variations entitled *Ad malleorum ictus allusio,* related somehow to the concept describing sounds of a hammer and anvil. The toccatas in structure though not in sound are indebted to Frescobaldi. They are formed by a continuity of five or six contrasted sections supported by a prevalence of pedal parts, in which there is free virtuoso passagework, imitative and fugal sections, and adagio sections of motives moving in a mosaic of brief imitations between the hands. French influence is suggested by the numerous indications for ornaments and also, as in Toccata 7, by opening with rapid scales sweeping upward that imitates the opening of a French overture.

Lastly, the keyboard works by Johann Joseph Fux (1660–1741), although few in number, should not be overlooked. As a distinguished Austrian music theorist and composer of operas and sacred vocal works, the remaining keyboard pieces,[52] all of which come down to us only in copies of students and others, provide an important connection with Austrian keyboard music and such composers as Johann Joseph Froberger, Ferdinand Richter, and his students Gottlieb Muffat and Georg Wagenseil. The seven extant keyboard works of Fux include four suites (*Parthie*) each with a different arrangement of dances, an Ouverture with seven dances, and especially noteworthy a grandly imposing Ciaccona of 231 measures with 334 four-bar variations on the four-measure descending tetrachord on D.

CHAPTER NINE

Heinrich Schütz (1585–1672)

THE MOST SIGNIFICANT GERMAN BAROQUE MUSICAL achievement through the mid-seventeenth century belongs to the approximately five hundred preserved works by Heinrich Schütz.[1] With the exception of his first published volume, a collection of nineteen Italian madrigals (1611), Schütz's extant compositions are largely sacred vocal works, written primarily for devotional services at the courts of Dresden and Copenhagen. Schütz was one of the most famous composers of his century, widely known partly as the result of his position as Kapellmeister at the court of Dresden, but also by the publication of a substantial amount of his music printed under his own supervision during his lifetime. Schütz's music, although seldom performed in succeeding centuries, was never completely lost sight of, and in the twentieth century it became the focus of an almost cult-like attention, especially in Germany.

Born in Saxony in 1585 in what today is Bad Köstritz, he moved with his family soon thereafter to Weissenfels. His musical gifts, especially as a singer, came to the attention of Landgrave Moritz of Hessen-Kassel. He obtained the parents' permission to bring the young boy to Kassel as a singer in 1595, where he also continued his general education. Following his parents' wishes, however, he entered the University of Marburg in 1608 to study law. Landgrave Moritz, who was attracted by Schütz's musical abilities, convinced Schütz's parents to accept financial support for their son's travel in 1609 to Venice for study with the aged Giovanni Gabrieli. Although Schütz was uncertain at first of his talent as a composer, his relationship with Gabrieli became immensely fruitful. It lasted not the originally planned two years, but was extended to three until Gabrieli's death in August 1612. As Gabrieli's disciple, Schütz mastered the compositional techniques of the Venetian school of composers, and transported to northern Europe many aspects of early-seventeenth-century Italian music. It was these Italian musical developments that Schütz subsequently adapted to form his own uniquely German musical style.

Schütz's first publications were *Il primo libro de madrigali* (Venice, 1611), SWV 1–19, and the *Psalmen Davids sampt etlichen Moteten und Concerten* (Dresden, 1619),[2] SWV 22–47. The madrigals were dedicated to Landgrave Moritz, but musically they attest to his achievements as a student of Gabrieli. They are a mature collection of nineteen madrigals, all in five parts except for the last one (*Vasto mar, nel cui seno*), for double SATB chorus. Retrospective in style, they incorporate the best techniques of madrigalian expressiveness going back to late-sixteenth-century masters such as Wert and Marenzio, as well as Monteverdi. Nevertheless, these pieces, mostly interpretations of well-known poems by Marino and Guarini, amply reveal Schütz's sensitivity to text-oriented expressiveness, and to the underlying foundation of late-sixteenth-century harmonic and contrapuntal structural forces. The display of contrapuntal ingenuity and the employment of expressive dissonant treatment clearly indicate to what an extent Schütz had mastered a solid technical command of Italian compositional practices. The element of contrapuntal textures appears as an important early indication of a trait in Schütz's compositional process that he will seldom abandon in later music. Indeed, Schütz taught his contemporaries how to create a new, distinctly seventeenth-century musical style from principles of linear part-writing that were an essential aspect of Italian as well as Franco-Netherlands musical craftsmanship of the preceding century.

Schütz returned to Germany in 1613 and after a period as organist at Landgrave Moritz's court at Kassel, he was summoned in August 1615 to the Electoral court of Johann Georg at Dresden. Here he acted as Kapellmeister, although without receiving the official designation until 1618. In effect, Schütz was commanded to attend the musical establishment of the Elector in Dresden, and Landgrave Moritz relinquished Schütz's services with reluctance. However, throughout his career, Schütz retained close personal and professional connections with the Kassel court and its personnel, seen particularly in the fact that he presented copies of a majority of his works to Kassel, where many are still preserved, while much of his music originally preserved at Dresden as well as Copenhagen would subsequently be lost in fires.

In the spring of 1619 Schütz published his Op. 2, the *Psalmen Davids*, SWV 22–47, which appropriately was dedicated to his new patron Johann Georg. Twenty of the twenty-six compositions set complete psalm texts. They are arranged for from eight to twenty parts, with eight in the majority of cases. In the preface Schütz says he composed them in the "Italian manner" learned from "my dear and world-famous preceptor, Giovanni Gabrieli, while I lived with him in Italy." The Venetian style of the concerted polychoral motet forms the basis of these early but mature works, some of which were probably composed in Venice shortly before Schütz's return home. The variety of performing forces is unusually rich, perhaps unique to that time in sacred music published in Germany. The scoring calls for two *cori favoriti*—two solo groups of singers and/or instrumentalists—which in many of the compositions are reinforced by one or two *Capellen*[3]—choruses of less well trained singers or instrumentalists. Thus, the music has no fixed scoring since, as the composer states in his preface,[4] several different combinations of voices and instruments are permissible: when *Capellen* are found in addition to *cori favoriti*, they must be omitted entirely or played by instruments alone. Normally the *Capellen* written in high tessitura are for instruments alone, although Schütz says if singers are available who can perform the parts, "so much the better." In some instances he suggests also that the *cori favoriti* may each be performed by a single solo voice with instruments taking the remaining parts. All of these options make the music variously adaptable to local musical establishments in the churches of the German states, for probably only in the large and musically excellent Kapelle at Dresden could these psalms have been performed in their richest and most complex possible combination of voices and instruments. The polychoral disposition of these pieces receives further emphasis by Schütz's suggestion that the *cori* and *Capellen* be separated spatially into two groups of performers.

Because of the inherent flexibility Schütz envisioned for them, modern editions of these large compositions appear to require greater forces than is actually necessary. For example, the opening of the psalm *Herr, unser Herrscher*, SWV 27 (see Example 9.1), appears to require three choruses, doubled by instruments in at least the case of the *coro capella*, plus instruments for the *basso continuo*. However, the high range of the upper parts for the *Capella* suggests instruments only. Furthermore, the entire *coro capella* might be eliminated, and the two *cori favoriti* sung by soloists, with only a continuo accompaniment, or with perhaps solo instruments doubling the voices. Indeed, Schütz himself recommends the possibility of using violins and cornettos in the upper chorus, trombones and other instruments in the lower chorus, and one singer only for each chorus.

EXAMPLE 9.1   Schütz, *Herr, unser Herrscher* (SWV 27)

Although the stylistic heart of these psalm settings lies in the Venetian school of polychoral music, the differences that define Schütz's own style in this formative stage are numerous. In the preface, Schütz states that his "psalm settings employ a recitative style (which, so far, has remained almost unknown in Germany) and . . . there is no style better suited to the composition of the psalms—the large amount of text being recited in continuity and without an abundance of repetitions." Recitative style here means a simple, rhythmically homophonic, verbally clear, and accentually correct ensemble presentation of the texts. It has frequently been observed that in the *Psalmen Davids* we find a key to Schütz's music: it is word-shaped, absolutely rhetorical both in a faithfulness to German language accentual patterns, but also in the many ways in which Schütz derives musical figures, musical accents, and musical interpretations from words. While the music in this collection is often decisively homophonic and rigorously antiphonal, there is also prevalent

EXAMPLE 9.2   Schütz, *Ist nicht Ephraim mein teurer Sohn* (SWV 40)

another aspect of Venetian musical style, and that is the continuing vitality of contrapuntal designs.

For example, the touchingly beautiful opening of the famous motet from this collection, *Ist nicht Ephraim mein teurer Sohn* (Is not Ephraim my dear son—Jeremiah 31:20), SWV 40, is strongly rooted in imitative contrapuntal flow (see Example 9.2). Equally poignant, though utilizing traditionally prepared and resolved dissonances, is the opening to SWV 42, *Die mit Tränen säen* (They that sow in tears—Psalm 126:5–6) (see Example 9.3). As in many psalm compositions, this reflective and slow-moving contrapuntal passage is opposed to the parallel and contrasted text line, *werden mit Freuden ernten* (shall reap in joy), using Schütz's "recitative style"—simple homophonic declamation repeated several times between the two choruses.

There is in the *Psalmen Davids* a variety of musical ideas inspired either by the rhythm of the poetic line or the rhetorical emphasis on individual words or longer phrases of text. Each of these works repays close analysis as a demonstration of Schütz's early style. One such example, Psalm 84, *Wie lieblich sind deine Wohnungen*[5] (How lovely is Thine own

EXAMPLE 9.3   Schütz, *Die mit Tränen säen* (SWV 42)

dwelling place), in SWV 29, shows some of these stylistic features. Schütz gives the rather long psalm text a musical structure based on a division into thirteen verses. Major sectional climaxes usually combine both choral groups, which in themselves consist of a "high" vocal ensemble (coro I) and a "lower" vocal ensemble (coro II). These structural divisions are shown below by the horizontal lines dividing groupings of verses:

1. Wie lieblich sind deine Wohnungen,
Herre Zebaoth
2. Mein Seel verlanget
und sehnet sich
nach den Vorhöfen
des Herren,

How lovely is Thine own dwelling place,
Thou Lord of Hosts!
My soul desires and longs

for the courts of the Lord's temple,

	Mein Leib und Seele freuet sich in dem lebendigen Gott. 3. Denn der Vogel hat ein Haus funden und die Schwalbe ihr Nest dass sie Junge hecken, nämlich deine Altar,	My body and soul rejoice in the living God. Even the bird has found a home and the swallow her nest where she raises her young, namely at Thy altar,
IA	Herre Zebaoth, mein König und mein Gott. 4. Wohl denen, die in deinem Haus wohnen die loben dich immerdar, Sela.	Lord of Hosts, My king and my God. Happy are they who live in Thy house ever singing Thy praise, Selah.
IB	5. Wohl den Menschen die dich für ihre Stärke halten, und von Herzen dir nach wandeln.	Happy are men whose strength is in Thee and from their hearts turn to Thee.

II	6. Die durch das Jammerthal gehen
	und graben daselbst Brunnen.
	7. Und die Lehrer werden
	mir viel Segen geschmücket
	Sie erhalten einen Sieg
	nach dem andern,
	dass man sehen muss
	der rechte Gott sei zu Zion.
		As they go through the valley of woe
		and they themselves dig a stream.
		And the teacher will be adorned with
		   many blessings
		They obtain one victory after the other,
		
		so that one sees the true God is in
		   Zion.

III	8. Herr Gott Zebaoth, höre mein Gebet, vernimms, Gott Jakob, Sela. 9. Gott, unser Schild, schau doch siehe an das Reich deines Gesalbten. 10. Denn ein Tag in deinen Vorhöfen ist besser, denn sonst tausend.	Lord of Hosts, Hear my prayer, Listen, God of Jacob, Selah. God our shield, behold look upon the realm of Thine anointed. For one day in Thy temple court is better than a thousand elsewhere.

IV	11. Ich will lieber der Tür hüten in meines Gottes Hause, denn lange wohnen in der Gottlosen Hütten. 12. Denn Gott der Herr ist Sonn und Schild, der Herr gibt Gnad und Ehre. Er wird kein Gutes mangeln lassen den Frommen.	I would rather be keeper of the door in the house of my God, than to live for long in the tents of the godless. For God the Lord is son and shield, The Lord gives mercy and honor. He will keep no good thing from the pious.

13. Herr Zebaoth, wohl dem Menschen, der sich auf dich verlässt.	O Lord of Hosts, blessed is the man who trusts in Thee.

To be observed are the variety and subtleties of sonorities derived not only from the separation of a higher and lower ensemble, but also from the employment of three basic textures within these groups and in combinations: (1) homophonic; (2) homophonic—antiphonal; and (3) polyphonic. Lines 1 and 2 each begin with the strikingly beautiful, textually appropriate ("wie lieblich") chords with chromatic inflections. There is an even more intense choral passage on "Mein Seel verlanget" (m. 15). Often Schütz arrives at sectional climaxes by adding textures and parts. For example, the psalm opens homophonically, line 2 is set polyphonically, and line 3 (m. 39) progresses homophonically, polyphonically, antiphonally (homophonic), and finally in eight parts in a combination of the homophonic and polyphonic for the conclusion of this section. Line 4 (m. 65) begins homophonically in eight parts and then becomes antiphonal between choruses over a simple cadential (I–V–I) progression. Line 5 (m. 79) continues the antiphonal texture, but for "von Herzen dir nach wandeln," all of the eight parts "wander" in polyphonic texture for the first major point of arrival. Line 6 (m. 101) continues the polyphony in Chorus II, using appropriate chromaticism for "Die durch das Jammerthal gehen," but this abruptly stops for line 7, "Und die Lehrer werden mir viel Segen geschmücket, Sie erhalten einen Sieg nach dem andern," for which the composer employs antiphonally the "recitative" or declamatory style he had cited in his preface as previously almost unknown in Germany. This line is brought to its conclusion with a texture of antiphonal motivic repetitions together with a simple but emphatic melody in whole notes in the lowest voice of each chorus. Lines 8, 9, and 10 are developed into the central climax, set as *falsobordone* with all eight voices reciting the text to a single chord, perhaps inspired by line 8, "Herr Gott Zebaoth, höre mein Gebet." Lines 9 and 10 are each placed a tone higher for an increase in musical excitement. The final three lines have a similar contrast of textures until the work concludes, again with all eight parts involved with the final cadential passage.

Other elaborate settings of psalm texts were apparently written for a planned though never published second part to the *Psalmen Davids*. A substantial number of additional similar psalm compositions remained in manuscript.[6] Psalm texts also appear frequently in other collections, and there are Schütz's simple four-part settings in Cornelius Becker's *Psalmen Davids, hiebevorn in teutsche Reimen gebracht* (Freiburg, 1628, reprinted 1640, and a revised edition in 1661). However, Schütz's most impressive single setting of a psalm was completed in the final years of his life, which he referred to as his *Schwanengesang* (Swan Song), Psalm 119, and its companion pieces, a setting of Psalm 100, *Jauchzet dem Herrn*, and a German Magnificat, *Meine Seele erhebet den Herrn*. Psalm 119 stands as an encyclopedic compendium of Schütz's compositional achievement within this type of music, originating in his earliest career, and first published in the *Psalmen Davids*. With 176 verses, Psalm 119 is the longest in the Psalter, and Schütz created with this text eleven motets of sixteen verses each. Until recently thought lost, the *opus ultimum* was published for the first time just prior to the four hundredth anniversary of Schütz's birth.[7]

Schütz remained officially active as Kapellmeister at the Dresden court for more than forty years. However, during the turbulent period of the Thirty Years' War (1618–1648), when the impoverishment of court financial resources decimated the music establishment, Schütz frequently was absent. In 1628 he again went to Venice. In 1634 he spent a year as Kapellmeister to King Christian IV in Copenhagen where he would return in 1642–1644.

In 1639 he served Georg von Caldenberg at Hanover and Hildesheim as Kapellmeister, and he also had a fairly lengthy association with Duke August of Brunswick-Lüneburg at his court in Wolfenbüttel.

During his long career fourteen works were published, a surprisingly large number considering the uncertainties of the political and economic times. These prints, most supervised in preparation by the composer, include collections of smaller pieces as well as individual, large-scale works. In the latter category are: *Historia der frölichen und siegreichen Aufferstehung unsers einigen Erlösers und Seligmachers Jesu Christi* (Dresden, 1623), SWV 50; and *Musicalische Exequien* (Dresden, 1636), SWV 279–281. In addition, a partial print was issued (recitative portions only) for the *Historia, der . . . Geburth . . . Jesu Christi,* SWV 435. Other large-scale works remained in manuscript: *Die sieben Wortte unsers lieben Erlösers und Seeligmachers Jesu Christi,* SWV 478, and three Passions, all from the year 1666, according to Matthew, SWV 479, Luke, SWV 480, and John, SWV 481.

Printed collections of smaller motets, psalms, and other sacred texts consist of *Cantiones sacrae* (Freiberg, 1625), SWV 53–93; *Symphoniae sacrae* (Venice, 1629), SWV 257–276; *Erster Theil kleiner geistlichen Concerten* (Leipzig, 1636), SWV 282–305; *Anderer Theil kleiner geistlichen Concerten* (Dresden, 1639), SWV 306–337; *Symphoniarum sacrarum secunda pars* (Dresden, 1647), SWV 341–367; *Geistliche Chor-Music* (Dresden, 1648), SWV 369–397; *Symphoniarum sacrarum tertia pars* (Dresden, 1650), SWV 398–418; *Zwölff geistliche Gesänge* (Dresden, 1657), SWV 420–31; and the four-part settings of all the psalm texts in the Becker version, referred to above, published in 1628, 1640, and in an enlarged edition (Dresden, 1661), SWV 97–256.

Many compositions are lost,[8] including Schütz's setting of Rinuccini's libretto *Dafne* in a translation by Opitz, performed at Torgau on 13 April 1627 for the marriage of Landgrave Georg II of Hessen-Darmstadt and Princess Sophia Eleonora of Saxony; and an "opera-ballet," *Orpheus und Euridice,* to a text of Buchner, for the marriage of Prince Johann Georg and Princess Magdalena Sybilla of Brandenburg, at Dresden on 20 November 1638.

The *Cantiones sacrae,* the first collection of sacred pieces to be published after the *Psalmen Davids,* show a significant contrast in musical style. The *Cantiones sacrae* was one of two collections Schütz wrote to Latin texts (the other being the *Symphoniae sacrae,* Part I). Thirty-five four-part motets are grouped in either pairs or larger sets, written to texts taken largely from a well-known Latin prayer book by Andreas Musculus (*Precationes,* first published in 1553), based on biblical sources, the writings of St. Augustine, and other sacred texts. In addition, the set closes with five four-part Grace settings (*Tischreden*). Schütz dedicated the work to Prince Hans Ulrich Eggenberg, a convert to Catholicism, who was a prominent political figure at the Viennese court of the emperor. In the preface Schütz comments that the pieces in part are from an earlier period of composition, and in part are in a new style. He blames his publisher for being forced to add a continuo part, preferring that the organist would fill out all of the voices, that is, in a realization more contrapuntal than chordal. However, he also reports that he has added at the end of the collection compositions requiring a role for a more independent continuo part (motet 32 and those of Psalm 6, Nos. 33–35).

No other collection reveals the Schütz so wedded to creating intensely subjective responses to the texts, most of which are exceedingly penitential or otherwise highly personal and reverent reflections of a Christian commentator. Whereas some writers have emphasized the new in these pieces—the monodic style of melodies, sections in chordal antiphony, duet texture—nevertheless the majority exude a masterful technique of contrapuntal in-

EXAMPLE 9.4   Schütz, *Ego dormio, et cor meum vigilat* (SWV 63)

genuity. Many of them suggest Schütz's intimate familiarity with the late-sixteenth-century musical styles of Lassus and German composers of sacred music. The *Cantiones sacrae* have justifiably been called "sacred madrigals," because of the intensely word-inspired musical settings and a frequent recourse to various musical-rhetorical emphases of vividly pictorial or emblematic words and phrases. A number of the motets open with a musical juxtaposition derived from the rhetorical conceit of the text. For example, SWV 63, *Ego dormio, et cor meum vigilat* (see Example 9.4), has two distinct and combinative musical units, one for "I sleep" and a second for "my heart keeps watch," that is, is "awake."

More madrigal-like but similar in its antithetical construction is the opening of SWV 68, *Sicut Moses serpentem in deserto exaltavit,* with the opening four-note motive on *Sicut Moses* (just as Moses) constantly placed in contrasted combination with the word-inspired scalar passage usually in parallel thirds or sixths on *serpentem in deserto exaltavit* (lifted up the serpent in the wilderness) for the first fourteen measures of the motet (see Example 9.5).

EXAMPLE 9.5   Schütz, *Sicut Moses serpentem in deserto exaltavit* (SWV 68)

Despite Schütz's annoyance because he was required by his publisher to add a continuo part, most of the forward-looking motets clearly require the sustaining of a continuo realization as, for example, the solo and duet textures in SWV 84, *Ecce advocatus meus,* and throughout the three-part setting of Psalm 6 (SWV 85, 86, 87). One finds solo and other noncontrapuntal textures that musically demand support from a continuo part and that bespeak strongly of Schütz's adaptation of the new monodic style of Italian composers, as in Examples 9.6 through 9.8.

In the period from 1629 to 1650 Schütz composed several major collections of music which, with two exceptions, demonstrated his mastery of the Italian few-voiced concertato style. He arrived in Venice in November 1628, in part to escape the hardships and dangers of the Thirty Years' War, but also to obtain instruments for future court use as well as copies of new music printed in Italy. While in Venice he experienced firsthand recent stylistic changes in Italian, especially Venetian, music composed by Monteverdi, but also

EXAMPLE 9.6   Schütz, opening of *Domine, ne in furore tuo arguas me,* SWV 85

by Alessandro Grandi. Later Schütz returned to his homeland imbued with new musical ideas he would adapt to works required by his employment at the Dresden court. In his preface to the *Symphoniae sacrae I* Schütz comments on what he found in Venice:

> Staying in Venice with old friends, I found the manner of musical composition somewhat changed. They have partially abandoned the old church modes while seeking to charm modern ears with new titilations. I have devoted my mind and my powers to present to you for your information something in accordance with this artistic development. . . .[9]

The first volume of *Symphoniae sacrae* (Venice, 1629), SWV 257–276, takes its title, in an act of further homage by Schütz, from the well-known collections of sacred motets by

EXAMPLE 9.7   Schütz, opening of *Quoniam non est in morte,* SWV 86, Part II

Andrea and Giovanni Gabrieli. Subtitled "his second ecclesiastical opus" (*Cantiones sacrae* was the first), this is the last work in which Schütz employs Latin texts throughout. These twenty "symphonies" consist of a variety of solo part settings (three to six parts plus continuo), of which *Fili mi, Absalon* (SWV 269) for four trombones—or two violins and two trombones—and bass voice is the most famous. The texts are biblical: the psalms, Song of Songs, and other Old and New Testament passages.

Stylistically what is new is the reduction of performing forces to achieve sonorities more typical of chamber music. The prominent involvement of instruments, with an array of coloristic choices, including violins, gambas, flautino (descant recorder), fiffaro (shawm), cornetto and cornettino (zinks), bassoon, trumpets, and trombones, while perhaps reminiscent of earlier Venetian instrumental music, are used by Schütz in a variety of formal and expressive possibilities. These include introductory and intermediary "sinfonias," as ritornellos and sometimes as distinctive, nonrecurring passages serving as interludes and shaping the formal divisions of a text. Instrumental color also serves various expressive purposes; for example, in the dark trombones of the powerful lament, *Fili mi, Absalon;* similarly for the expression of night, the three bassoons or gambas in *In lectulo per noctes,* SWV 272 (Upon my bed by night) and also *Invenerunt me custodes civitatis,* SWV 273 (The watchman found me). Cornettos (or cornetto and trombone) are the obvious choice for *Buccinate in neomenia tuba,* SWV 275 (Sound the trumpet).

EXAMPLE 9.8   Schütz, Psalm 6, SWV 87, Part III, mm. 8–17

EXAMPLE 9.8 (*continued*)

The voice and instrumental parts are so arranged as to form a progressive accumulation of parts: Nos. 1–6 for three parts; 7–12, four parts; 13–17, five parts; and 18–20, six parts. It would, however, be misleading to emphasize too greatly a profound Italian influence on these works, for in most ways the music is emphatically Schützian in style. Most of the concertos display his continuing mastery of contrapuntal procedures, whether in short motivic imitations or in more expansive fugal passages. Modality controls the harmonic forces in most of the pieces. Although there is a prominent use of duet writing, it seldom sounds Italian, nor reminds one of Monteverdi, Grandi, or other masters of the new duet techniques developed at the beginning of the seventeenth century. Also absent is any suggestion of Italianate melodic lyricism, for the melodic structures are strongly rhetorical, often rhythmically expressive of word accents, and frequently use typical musical-rhetorical devices for word emphasis. Most characteristic of this composer's mature style, however,

EXAMPLE 9.9a   Schütz, *Cantabo Domino in vita mia*, SWV 260, mm. 17–22

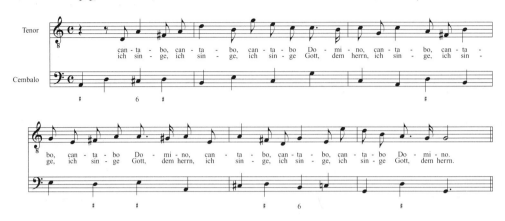

are the many triadic and other short and disjunct melodic structures. See Examples 9.9a, 9.9b, and 9.9c, and perhaps the most dramatic melodic idea of this type at the opening of *Fili mi, Absalon*, Example 9.9d.

In 1634 Schütz left for Copenhagen to withdraw from the greatly deteriorating conditions at the Dresden court, which was seriously threatened by the accelerating war in Saxony. He was appointed court Kapellmeister to King Christian IV, and he remained in Denmark until the spring of 1635. In the subsequent December, Prince Heinrich Posthumus von Reuss, a friend and patron, died, and Schütz was commissioned by the widow and children to compose his most impressive funeral composition, Op. 7, the *Musicalische Exequien* (Musical Exequies), SWV 279–281. Although frequently labeled the "first German Requiem," the text is unrelated to the ecclesiastical form of the Requiem. Rather the Exequies are, as the title suggests, a burial service: Parts I and II for the actual church service, and Part III for the funeral procession to the grave site. The texts were chosen by Posthumus himself, and these various biblical lines were, according to Schütz's preface, engraved on the sides and cover of Posthumus's sarcophagus.

Part I, *Concert in Form einer teutschen Begräbnis-Missa* (Concert in the Form of a German Funeral Mass), is the longest of the three, scored for six voices (SSATTB), but with the option for an additional six-part chorus for those sections marked *Capella*. The form is a freely conceptualized German Mass, opening with a "troped" Kyrie and followed by a quasi-Gloria in nine verses and eight insertions of German chorale strophes, with the

EXAMPLE 9.9b   Schütz, *Venite ad me*, SWV 261, mm. 21–25

EXAMPLE 9.9c Schütz, *Jubilate Deo omnis terra,* SWV 262, mm. 1–14

EXAMPLE 9.9d Schütz, *Fili mi, Absalon*, SWV 269, mm. 43–53

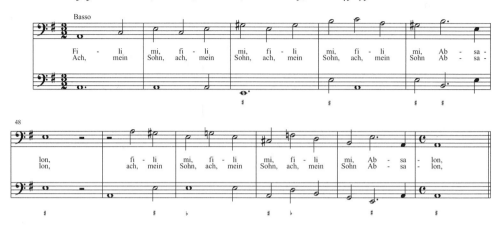

chorale melodies freely and impressively varied. The Kyrie employs the *Capella* "tuttis" for the three lines of the German form of the Kyrie text (*Herr Gott Vater im Himmel, erbarm dich über uns; Jesu Christe, Gottes Sohn, erbarm dich über uns; Herr Gott heiliger Geist, erbarm dich über uns*). Each line is preceded by a related biblical passage. As in the Gloria, the nontutti sections are most frequently composed for two solo voices in rigorous counterpoint, often canon, with the melodies simple but powerful in their expression of text accents and meanings. Here, even more than in the *Symphoniae sacrae I,* Schütz adapts the Italian concept of monody and solo ensemble writing to achieve a personal and unique style of "sung speech."

Part II, a funeral motet and companion to the funeral sermon, *Herr, wenn ich nur Dich habe* (Lord, if I only have Thee), is for a SATB double chorus with or without organ. The writing is almost entirely antiphonal and chordal, rather reminiscent of the music found in the *Psalmen Davids*. Part III is the most moving in its musical poetry, an original setting of the *Nunc Dimittis* (Luke 2:29–32, Song of Simeon), *Herr nun lässet Du deiner Diener in Frieden fahren* (Lord, now allow thy servant to depart in peace). A five-part choir (AATTB), according to Schütz, "near the organ" is joined to a three-part ensemble (SSB) of two seraphims and a "Beata anima cum seraphinis," which should be placed some distance away from the main chorus. This trio sings the text beginning *Selig sind die Toten* (Blessed are the dead). As a processional motet, Schütz, rather than leading the remains to a grave, carries the spirit of Heinrich Posthumus to heaven with the voices of angels. The music is sublimely effective, one of the composer's masterworks, and though an occasional composition, it justified his pride in his accomplishment by its publication and his stamping of it as his Op. 7.

The most extensive and in some ways most complex collection of sacred works written by Schütz during his middle years was published as the *Kleine geistliche Konzerte* (Small Sacred Concertos): Op. 8, volume I (1636), SWV 282–305, and Op. 9, volume II (1639), SWV 306–337. The publication dates do not necessarily indicate the period of composition, for at least part of volume I was probably composed while Schütz lived in Copenhagen. Circumstances that led to publishing these pieces were, according to Schütz's own words, that "the laudable art of music, among the other liberal arts, has not only greatly declined but at some places has even been completely abandoned, succumbing to the general ruination and disorder which unhappy war is wont to bring in its train."[10] Schütz offered those remaining church music organizations a number of "small," that is, few-voiced sacred concertos, requiring, with one exception, only a continuo accompaniment. To the extent that the ravages of the Thirty Years' War inspired Schütz to publish these volumes, one can attribute social and political pressures to the creation of a particular masterwork. However, the *Kleine geistliche Concerte* are more than that, for they stand as the culmination of Schütz's stylistic adaptation of Italian monodic and few-voiced solo concerto styles, already initiated in 1602 with the publication of Viadana's *Cento concerti ecclesiastici.* The *Kleine geistliche Konzerte* are Schütz's most important achievement in this concept of sacred music that had developed out of the musical revolution occurring in Italy at the turn of the seventeenth century.

The two volumes contain fifty-six pieces, nine for solo voice, twenty-one for two voices, nine for three, eleven for four, and six for five parts. Individual pieces vary greatly in combinations of parts, in length, in types of formal organizations, and in styles of setting the words. The key to all of the settings is contained in Schütz's indication for the first composition in the first volume, SWV 282, *Eile mich, Gott, zu erretten* (Hurry God, to save me): *"In Stylo Oratorio."* This means these concertos are to be sung with the expressive force and freedoms associated with spoken orations, with impassioned sermons from the pulpits of contemporary Protestant churches. Therefore, much of the musical style depends on a combining and often subtle eliding of recitative and arioso or aria-like sections. Words are, as with almost all of Schütz's music, the inspired font of his musical invention.

In both volumes Schütz continues to draw heavily on his texts from the psalms (for twenty-two compositions). Some come from the Old and New Testaments, several from Protestant chorales, two from the Meditations of St. Augustine, and others, such as the *Veni, Sancte Spiritus,* from venerable Latin sacred texts retained for the Protestant service. Musically, duet textures are most frequent even in works composed for three, four, or five parts, which suggests Schütz's fondness for this popular compositional style of his Italian contemporaries. Words often are sung over slow-moving continuo basses. This style, however, is frequently placed in contrast to lively and dramatically paced bass lines. Usually the strength of the bass lines reveals the almost ever-present force of contrapuntal organization continuing to sustain and inspire Schütz's style. Most of the compositions are modal, and many of them contain startling dissonances, perhaps none as expressive as those in the final measures of the four-part *Siehe, mein Fürsprecher* (See, my advocate) (see Example 9.10).

Vocal styles are too varied to be reduced to any one description. Both books are organized to proceed from simple solo pieces, through duets, trios, quartets, to end in quintets, with the longest and most complex piece concluding each book. Book I ends with the eighteen-verse setting of the chorale *Ich hab mein Sack Gott heimgestellt* (To God have I entrusted all), SWV 305; Book II with the extended five-part concerto *Aufer immensam, Deus, iram* (Take away, O God, Thy anger), SWV 337. Nevertheless, the second volume contains more pieces that employ larger structures and more difficult vocal writing. For example, the two-part *Sei gegrüsset Maria* (Be blessed, Maria), *Ave Maria,* SWV 333–334, approaches the content and length of an oratorio. The elaborately difficult vocal writing of *Veni, Sancte Spiritus* (Come Holy Spirit), SWV 328 (see Example 9.11), is only one example of a highly embellished style of writing found in a number of the works from Book II. Even a cursory examination of these volumes suggests that Schütz aimed to publish

EXAMPLE 9.10 Schütz, *Siehe, mein Fürsprecher,* SWV 304, mm. 83 to end

works that would meet the needs of almost all of the churches of the period still able to perform music, from the simplest solo concertos, to elaborate five-part compositions involving singers with considerable vocal ability.

Schütz's fondness for antithetical musical statements derived from contrasting or opposing textual ideas is found throughout the collection. Sometimes, as in *Fürchte dich nicht* (Fear thee not), SWV 296, the rhetoric of the text is interpreted not only in contrasting thematic ideas, but also with changes of meter (see Example 9.12). The same technique appears in the well-known *Ich liege und schlafe* (I lie and sleep), SWV 310. Even more Baroque, in its use of the descending chromatic melody, is *Wann unsre Augen schlagen ein* (When our eyes are closed), SWV 316, which places the chromatic "sleep" figure in antithesis to the next line, *so lass das Herz doch wacken sein* (then permit still our heart to be awake), with extended passages of lively eighth-note melismas.

EXAMPLE 9.11   Schütz, *Veni, Sancte Spiritus*, SWV 328, mm. 19–25

One example from among many to illustrate Schütz's mastery of musical-textual re-lationships in his simplest and yet most effective style can be seen in SWV 317, *Meister, wir haben die ganze Nacht gearbeitet* (Master, we have toiled all night). Here the recita-tive style pervades and every note counts in its expressive setting of this text (from Luke 5:5), as Simon Peter and Andrew tell Christ: "Meister, wir haben die ganze Nacht gear-beitet" (Master, we have toiled all night) "und nichts gefangen" (and caught nothing) (see Example 9.13a), "Aber auf dein Wort" (But at your word) "will ich das Netz aus-werfen" (I will throw out the net) (see Example 9.13b). Rhetorical pauses after "caught nothing" stress the point, and the growing embellishment for each repetition of "net" strengthens the imagery each time until a melisma is fully unfurled musically in the final measures.

EXAMPLE 9.12   Schütz, *Fürchte dich nicht*, SWV 296, mm. 1–12

During the years 1642–1644, Schütz once again joined the Copenhagen court, and during these years a major part of his next important publication, the *Symphoniae sacrae*, Part II, SWV 341–367, was written. These twenty-seven "German Concertos," as they are subtitled, were published in Dresden in 1647 and dedicated to Christian V of Denmark. They are composed for one, two, or three voices with an accompaniment of two instrumental parts for violins or other like instruments (except for SWV 344, in which the composer suggests several other instruments to alternate with the violins). Schütz's informative introduction implies that the popularity of his first book of sacred symphonies in Germany, even if in some places their Latin texts were translated into German, served as an incentive to publish his new volume set entirely to German verses. Furthermore:

> it was especially a prevailing lack of acquaintance in Germany with the modern Italian manner, its style of composition and performance (which the keen judgment of Signor Claudio Monteverdi in the preface to his Eighth Book of Madrigals described as a final perfection of music) that led me to give it into print. Experience has shown (to relate the unhappy truth) that the modern Italian manner and its style of composition, with new refinements involving shorter note values, has neither rightly suited many of us Germans not trained in this tradition, nor met with proper understanding . . . and that pieces written in this style have been poorly rendered and mistreated as if in defiance of their language, so that they caused nothing but annoyance and disgust to the intelligent listener or even to the composers themselves.[11]

He also suggests that those German musicians not familiar with the Italian style found in these works seek out instruction before "they attempt performing one or the other piece in public, and that they might not mind obtaining some private practice, so that they as well as the author might not be subjected, without his fault, to undeserved censure rather

EXAMPLE 9.13a   Schütz, *Meister, wir haben die ganze Nacht gearbeitet,* SWV 317, mm. 1–18

than approbation." Schütz honors Monteverdi by adapting the latter's *Armato il cuor* and *Zefiro torna* (both from the *Scherzi musicali* of 1632) in *Es steh Gott auf,* SWV 356. Also, he employs what Monteverdi believed was the "final perfection of music," the agitated style or *stile concitato*. Rapid reiterations not only of single tones but also of declamatory passages in figurations of various kinds, triadic patterns, and instrumental motives lend to many of these concertos a livelier and more excited style than was found in the earlier work.

Considering the enormous variety of the few-voiced concertos in this second volume of *Symphoniae sacrae,* their modernity, and ostensible pedagogic purpose of spreading an understanding of Italian musical idioms in Germany, Schütz's next published collection one year later, the *Geistliche Chormusik* (Dresden, 1648), SWV 369–97, comes as a stunning surprise. Dedicated to the city fathers of Leipzig, Schütz presented the collection to the St. Thomas church choir, formerly directed by his friend Johann Hermann Schein. As the composer's ultimate exploration of the motet style, these twenty-nine pieces in five, six, and seven parts represent one of the major musical-didactic accomplishments of the German Baroque. In another of Schütz's invaluable prefaces, he explains that his music was conceived to show German composers the art of contrapuntal composition without a

EXAMPLE 9.13b   Ibid., mm. 25–46

continuo support. Deemed by him "the hardest nut to crack," Schütz expresses a fear that young composers were becoming ignorant of this time-honored compositional discipline, now being immersed in the Italian concerted style—a style that Schütz himself bore considerable responsibility for introducing into his own country. Although all of Schütz's music has an intrinsic contrapuntal basis, nevertheless, in his few-voiced sacred concertos his writing grew progressively less so, as the continuo support opened up ever greater freedom to individual voice parts. However, a musical propensity that was rooted in Schütz as it was in most German composers for the contrapuntal style, a *prima prattica,* and the *Geistliche Chormusik,* like Bach's *Die Kunst der Fuge,* speaks with unexcelled eloquence of this fact.

The *Geistliche Chormusik,* of all of Schütz's collected volumes of sacred music, deserves detailed analysis as a sourcebook of stylistic achievements distinguishing Schütz's genius from that of his German and Italian contemporaries. The music displays a dazzling array of compositional features. It seems as if here Schütz wished to demonstrate not simply that music can be composed without a continuo part but, rather, that all features of musical style known to him, from his Italian studies as well as his knowledge of the Franco-Netherlands and German masters, could be drawn together as an inexhaustible source of techniques serving his vivid interpretations of sacred texts. There hovers over many of these motets the Venetian musical achievements of the Gabrielis: the antiphonal style, the solid, blocklike chordal climaxes, the instrumental techniques and rhythmic innovations. This musical heritage is often placed in contrast with older Renaissance concerns for long-line polyphonic flow and frequent imitations of word-inspired musical motives. There are monodic settings, for example, *Du Schalksknecht* (Thou Wicked Servant), SWV 397, for tenor and six-part, low tessitura instrumental accompaniment in ricercar style, and similarly *Auf dem Gebirge hat man ein Geschrei gehöret* (A Cry Was Heard on the Mountain), SWV 396, for two altos and five low tessitura instruments. *Herzlich lieb hab ich dich, O Herr* (From the Depths of My Heart I Love Thee, O Lord), SWV 387, for six parts freely paraphrases the chorale melody for New Year's, with largely homophonic declamatory writing, at times varied with antiphonal alternations between the parts. From among the many passages illustrating Schütz's virtuosic command of polyphony one might refer to the opening of *So fahr ich hin zu Jesu Christ* (Thus I Journey Forth to Jesus Christ), SWV 379, with the imitative entries *recto* and *contrario* to emphasize the text conceit of "I journey forth" (see Example 9.14).

Another example of expressive contrapuntal writing is found in *Die mit Tränen säen* (Those Who Sow Tears), SWV 378,[12] in which in the opening measures the typically Schützian motive and the subsequent metrical and motivic contrasts underscore "Those who sow tears," versus "Will harvest with joy" (see Example 9.15). This motet ends with a concerto-texture adaptation of the contrapuntal style, on the line *Und kommen mit Freuden und bringen ihre Garben* (And they come joyously and bring their gifts).

Among the several motets that exemplify a combination of older polyphonic style with Venetian antiphonal and homophonic writing, as well as the monodic and "excited" styles of contemporary Italian practice, is Schütz's funeral motet *Das ist je gewisslich wahr* (This Is Assuredly True), SWV 388, composed for the funeral of Johann Hermann Schein (in the earlier extant version, SWV 277), and symbolizing the poignant relationship of Schütz's *Geistliche Chormusik* with the St. Thomas choir and its former choirmaster. Here, in perfect harmony and balance, exist these several styles, each in turn perfectly attuned to musical interpretations of the text.

Two years after the conclusion of the disastrous Thirty Years' War, Schütz published his final collection of sacred concertos, volume III of the *Symphoniae sacrae* (Dresden, 1650), SWV 398–418. The volume is dedicated to the Elector Johann Georg, as was Schütz's first collected volume as Saxon Kapellmeister. In a petition accompanying his presentation, Schütz makes a moving plea to be allowed to retire from his duties because of "old age, failing eyesight and strength,"[13] a plea that apparently fell on deaf ears. This last collection of "sacred symphonies," perhaps influenced by Schütz's hope for a restoration of larger

EXAMPLE 9.14   Schütz, *So fahr ich hin zu Jesu Christ,* SWV 379, mm. 1–13

forces in the Dresden Kapelle, returns to the concept of sonorities found in the *Psalmen Davids.* These concertos are scored for three to six voice parts with two instrumental parts, for violins "or similar instruments." In addition most include an optional *complementum* of four parts, which may be omitted, sung, performed by instruments, or by combining voices and instruments. Exceptional indications are found for other instrumental combinations, and even additional choirs occur, as in the most famous piece in the collection, *Saul, Saul was verfolgst du mich* (Saul, Saul, Why Dost Thou Persecute Me),[14] SWV 415. However, except for this particular piece, the collection as a whole remains relatively unknown, even though it contains a storehouse of almost every musical achievement made by the composer over more than a thirty-year career. The concertos usually have substantial instrumental sections including opening sinfonias. Solo sections are predominantly monodic, while the polyphonic sections display most aspects of Schütz's command of the contrapuntal technique within various stylistic applications. As is characteristic of his output since the *Psalmen Davids,* the words inspire an intense and profound musical-poetic re-

EXAMPLE 9.15   Schütz, *Die mit Tränen säen,* SWV 378, mm. 1–15

sponse. Here Schütz achieved the ultimate realization of mid-seventeenth-century German sacred music, devout in sentiment, rhetorical in its creative impulses.

In addition to the set of sacred songs, *Zwölff geistliche Gesänge,* Op. 13 (Dresden, 1657), SWV 420–31, as well as an expanded and revised third edition of the four-part settings of the Psalter, published as *Psalmen Davids jetzund . . . auffs neue übersehen, auch . . . vermehret* [Op. 14] (Dresden, 1661), SWV 97–256, the remaining important portion of Schütz's preserved compositions includes the five *historiae* and the somewhat hybrid work combining elements of Passion and oratorio, *Die sieben Wortte . . . Jesu Christi* (The Seven Last Words of Jesus Christ), SWV 478, of uncertain origin and date. This rather brief but strikingly dramatic work is scored for SATTB, continuo, and two unspecified concerted instruments (perhaps violins). The *Seven Last Words* has an opening and closing five-part instrumental Symphonie and is contrasted to the other *historiae* by its highly expressive recitative. The final words of Christ on the Cross, for Tenor II, illustrate how profoundly moving this climactic moment becomes, with the text from the Bible: *Eli, Eli lama asabthani* (see Example 9.16).

EXAMPLE 9.16   Schütz, *Die sieben Wortte, Jesu Christi*, SWV 478

Connecting the words of Jesus are recitative passages for the Evangelist composed variously for soprano, alto, first tenor, or SATB quartet, and passages for the two thieves. The first and last verses of the chorale *Da Jesus an dem Kreuze stund,* in five-part motet style, open and close the composition.

The five *historiae* come both early and late in Schütz's career. The importance of this form of liturgical-musical tradition, rooted in the Middle Ages, had particular significance for the Protestant church. And Schütz's works stand at the end of this tradition, leading to but not influencing the later form of the oratorio Passion, as created by J. S. Bach. Schütz's *Historia der frölichen und siegreichen Aufferstehung . . . Jesu Christi* (Story of the Resurrection of Jesus Christ) (Dresden, 1623), SWV 50 was composed for the Easter season, to be performed "in the chapels or chambers of Princes, for spiritual Christian edification." This is a richly varied score composed to a text derived from the four Gospels. It uses two ensembles: I. The Evangelist complement, with an accompaniment of instruments (including the possibility of an improvising quartet of viols); II. Music for Christ, the three Marys, Angels, Cleophas, the High Priests, Apostles, etc. The Evangelist's role is sung largely as psalm-tone recitation written in plainsong notation. Most of the other parts, including that for Jesus, follow the German tradition of being set as duets, although trios are employed for the Three Marys and the High Priests. A six-part chorus (SSATTB) opens the *Historia* and a double chorus (SATB + SATB and the voice of the Evangelist), in the style of the *Psalmen Davids*, brings the Resurrection Story to a close. Unlike the three historias written in old age, this one has dramatically compelling music, Italian in its emotionalism, but characteristic of Schütz in the uniqueness of its melodic and contrapuntal styles.

The best known of these *historiae* is the Christmas Story, *Historia, der freuden und gnadenreichen Geburth Gottes und Marien Sohnes, Jesu Christi* (Dresden, 1644), SWV 435, which was first performed probably already around 1660. In 1664 the composer published only the accompanied Evangelist's part, omitting the choruses, ensembles, and aria-like sections because, in his words, "outside of well-appointed princely choirs these inventions would hardly achieve their proper effect." The remaining portions of the work, the ten concertos for voices and instruments, were available only in the form of manuscript copies. Even for these, Schütz suggests that some church choirmasters might wish to make adaptations (presumably to simplify performances) or even substitute newly composed music. The text is drawn from the Gospels of Matthew and Luke, and the score is thoroughly modern both in its usage of the recitative style for the Evangelist and the various concerted techniques in the *intermedios*. The latter are especially attractive as Schütz adapts his style to the nature of the texts. He seems particularly led by the Christmas story toward a popular, often pastoral style, and the frequently severe musical rhetoric of much of his oeuvre is replaced here by music of charm, even humor, and lovely poetic imagery.

Last to be mentioned is the important set of three Passions, the *Historiae* according to St. Matthew, SWV 479, St. Luke, SWV 480, and St. John, SWV 481, first performed in Dresden in 1666 (a first version of the St. John had been performed already on 4 March 1666). Moser describes what he calls Schütz's "threefold journey through the Passion history" as "the crown of Schütz's lifework."[15] All three are ritualistic, even archaic compositions for unaccompanied (i.e., without continuo) solo recitation and *a cappella* choral insertions. The recitation is composed to unmeasured notation, which appears to imitate Gregorian formulations; however, the style is subtly modified by Schütz to attain expressivity through musical motives, melismas, and other means of expressive vocal writing, bringing the Passion dramas to life. The *turbae* show the stamp of the aged master, in their brief but frequently dramatic outbursts at the points of greatest tension and tragedy in the passion narrative.

Each of the three Passions are individualized by mode: the St. Luke Passion in Lydian, the St. John in Phrygian, and the St. Matthew in Dorian G minor. Furthermore, each Passion concludes with a polyphonic setting of a chorale: the St. Luke with "Wer Gottes Marter in Ehren hat" (the ninth verse of "Da Jesus an dem Kreuze stund"); the St. John with "O hilf, Christe, Gottes Sohn" (the eighth stanza of "Christus der uns selig macht"); and the St. Matthew with "Ehre sei dir, Christe, der du littest" (the last verse of "Ach wir armen Sünder"). The St. Matthew concludes with a remarkably progressive and bold harmonization for the Kyrie, Christe, Kyrie Eleison, of which Moser concludes "here Schütz has the courage to present modernisms he never employed before. . . . It is a movement in which every note written by the eighty-year-old magician discovers new continents."[16]

CHAPTER TEN

English Music during the Stuart Reign, the Commonwealth, and the Restoration

THE GREAT QUEEN ELIZABETH I died in 1603, Shakespeare in 1616, and the incomparable William Byrd at eighty in 1623. Almost all of the music to be composed in the first decades of the seventeenth century grows out of musical achievements that took place during the reign of the last Tudor monarch. Among her most notable achievements was the completion of the Reformation begun by her father, Henry VIII, and the establishment of the national Anglican Church. As with Luther's similar separation from Catholicism on the Continent, the results had profound significance for the future of sacred music as well as a catastrophic effect on political developments in the nation. Unlike France with its powerful and stable governments of Louis XIII and XIV, England experienced a century of political upheavals that by mid-century seriously affected English institutions and culture and led to the temporary abandonment of royal rule. The monarchy itself, one of the greatest sources of support for music, was in constant turmoil and conflict with parliament. Seven different rulers were heads of state in the seventeenth century. The following summarizes this political scenario:

1603: James I (VI of Scotland), son of Mary Queen of Scots and cousin of Elizabeth I of England, succeeds to the throne (Jacobean court)

1625: Charles I ascends the throne (Caroline court). This begins a period of tumultuous conflicts between the king and parliament

1629: (March): The king dissolves parliament

1642: Civil war breaks out between Royalists and parliament

1649: Charles I is executed, after a rump trial by a military junta. The Commonwealth is established. Oliver Cromwell is its "protector"

1658: Cromwell dies

1660: The Restoration of the throne. Charles II becomes king

1685: James II (Catholic) becomes king. Protestant forces revolt against the Catholic king in "The Glorious Revolution." James II flees the country

1689: Mary (daughter of James II) and William III of the Dutch House of Orange (and son of eldest daughter of Charles I) jointly crowned as William III and Mary II. She died in 1694; he died in 1702

English music in all of its diversity began to develop a national character even before the Elizabethan period, but the second half of the sixteenth century solidified the elusive stylistic aspects of those "English" qualities in a great outburst of music. It was a period especially of secular music. The madrigal imported from Italy was recreated into an English concept, and vocal forms such as consort songs and other polyphonic songs flourished. Instrumental music for lute, cittern, bandora, for consorts of strings, virginals, all were composed in great numbers and these forms continued without interruption into the seventeenth century. The court masque and incidental music for theater were other outlets for many composers. And while as a result of the Reformation the Catholic ritual was officially banned, some composers such as Byrd continued to compose Latin sacred works for private services.[1] The texts and the music for the Anglican Church were largely prescribed by *The Book of Common Prayer*, first authorized in 1549, and revised in 1559 during Elizabeth I's reign. In parish churches music was almost entirely limited to the congregational singing of psalms in English translations to metrical arrangements of the appropriate tunes. In cathedrals and collegiate churches, as well as in the Chapel Royal, the music of the sacred ritual was divided into two types: services and anthems.

Sacred Music before 1644

The form of the service underwent several revisions during the sixteenth century, but remained essentially an adaptation and compression of the component parts of the Catholic divine service. It was divided into three parts, which, although retaining their Latin names, were usually sung in English with texts drawn from *The Book of Common Prayer:*

I. Morning Prayer (based on Latin Matins, Lauds, and Prime)
    Venite exultemus (O come let us sing unto the Lord). Set only by the early composers
    Te Deum laudamus (We praise Thee, O God)
    Benedictus
    Jubilate Deo (O be joyful in the Lord)
II. Evening Prayer (Evensong) (based on Latin Vespers and Compline)
    Magnificat anima mea Dominum (My soul doth magnify the Lord)
    Nunc dimittis servum tuum Domine (Lord, now lettest Thou thy servant depart in peace)
III. Holy Communion (Mass), from Elizabeth's reign; of the five Latin parts usually only two were composed:
    Kyrie (Lord have mercy upon us)
    Credo (I believe in one God)

In addition to psalms, preces and responses are sung at Morning and Evening Prayer. Composers could set just the morning service, evening service, or communion service, or combine them into compositions of greater scope as "complete services" with each movement in the same key. A short service refers to compositions that are essentially note against note, without text repetitions, and sung responsorially. Verse service usually referred to compositions in which the texts were sung by solo voices with contrasting choral passages supported by organ accompaniment. Similarly, verse anthems, which were motets in English, were also composed for solo voice or voices alternating with choruses accompanied by organ or other instruments. In contrast, full anthems placed emphasis on choruses, but could also include soloists, and usually some form of instrumental accompaniment. But in the developing forms of the anthem in the seventeenth century, especially after the Restoration, these distinctions were often considerably varied.

Until the Long Parliament banned *The Book of Common Prayer* in 1644, composers of sacred music continued generally to employ the polyphonic idiom that had characterized the outpouring of works from the previous century and into the seventeenth century by composers such as Christopher Tye (c. 1505–before 15 March 1573), Thomas Tallis (c. 1505–1585), John Shepphard (c. 1515–1558), Robert White (c. 1538–1574), William Byrd (c. 1540–1623) and his student Thomas Morley (1557 or 1558–1602), John Bull (1563–1628), Edmund Hooper (c. 1553–1621), Alfonso Ferrabosco II (before 1578–1628), Adrian Batten (1591–1637), John Amner (1579–1641), and Michael East (c. 1580–1648). William Byrd was of course the greatest connecting link between the Elizabethan Renaissance and the beginning of the Jacobean period.[2] His compositional style was also essentially based on imitative counterpoint, but with a technical brilliance and expressive textual achievement distinctly superior to his contemporaries. With the *Gradualia* of 1605 (a second volume in 1607) he published his last major work of Latin sacred music including Masses and Office Propers and more than one hundred motets for Catholic services that must have been private. He also composed major works for the Anglican Church, including two complete Services, as well as verse and full anthems.

The continuing tradition emanating from Byrd for sacred music influenced the works of Thomas Weelkes (1576–1623), Orlando Gibbons (1583–1625), and another of Byrd's students, Thomas Tomkins (1572–1656). Best known today for their madrigals, their sacred music shares a common bond in sixteenth-century imitative contrapuntal practices, but that infrequently exhibits madrigal-like rhetorical emphases of individual words. Weelkes's career was as a cathedral organist, first at Winchester and beginning in 1602 at Chichester. He was a prolific writer of Services. Four of them are verse Services, four full Services. With the exception of one short Service for Matins, none of them are preserved completely. None of some forty full and verse anthems were published in his lifetime. Of the twenty-three verse anthems, only five are preserved intact; thirteen of the full anthems are complete. The full anthems are also conservative in their contrapuntal writing, at times for six or seven parts, and they achieve a grandeur and majesty of sound that is English in character and becomes a distinctive aspect of English sacred music into the next century. For example, see the seven-part *O Lord, Arise, into Thy Resting Place,* and *O Lord, Grant the King a Long Life,* or the six-part *Gloria in excelsis Deo.*[3] Closer to the spirit of the madrigal are the full anthems, *O Jonathan* and *When David Heard/O My Son Absalom,* moving laments on the biblical text from 2 Samuel. Many of the anthems close with Amens that illustrate Weelkes's exceptional contrapuntal skills, for example, the seven-part Amen from *O Lord, Grant the King a Long Life* (see Example 10.1). Weelkes clearly represents one of many composers in England who composed during a period of transition between what is considered the Renaissance and the Baroque. His verse anthems in melodic style and forms remain committed to Byrd's compositional practices. Solo vocal melody is not often inspired by word imagery. It remains broadly thematic, but neutral and far removed from madrigalian lyricisms.[4]

Orlando Gibbons has been called the "last of the great Elizabethans."[5] He was a popular composer in the early seventeenth century, especially for his Anglican Services and anthems. But his distinction among English composers of the period also rests on madrigals, and on both solo keyboard and ensemble instrumental music. He became an organist to the Chapel Royal and in 1623 added the duties as organist at Westminster Abbey. His church works consist of a large body of some forty anthems (fifteen Verse, the rest Full), a Short Service and a Second [Verse] Service. As is true with Weelkes, many of Gibbons's anthems display brilliant contrapuntal textures. This is especially apparent in his full anthems, for example, the extraordinary six-part *Hosanna to the Son of David,* or the musical

EXAMPLE 10.1   Weelkes, from *O Lord, Grant the King a Long Life*

excitement produced by the contrapuntal interplay in *O Clap Your Hands,* and its second part, *God Is Gone Up with a Merry Noise.*[6] These and other full anthems also possess the quality of grandeur one associates with English sacred music of this century. There is, however, in some of the verse anthems a contrasted style, in which Gibbons aims for greater simplicity and clarity of the texts. Many of the verse anthems have rather long solo or duet sections, and even in the latter instances points of imitation are often staggered rather than continuous. It also can be noted that many of the chorus entrances are particularly homophonic, again giving clarity to the texts. Although Gibbons is at times considered to be a conservative composer, these aspects of his anthems suggest a trend away from Renaissance techniques of contrapuntal artifice to the growing tendency in the seventeenth century, no doubt influenced by the madrigal, toward emphasis on textual intelligibility. A good example of this is found in the opening to *Blessed Are All They.*[7] Although the opening solo verse is surrounded by a contrapuntal texture for instruments, the melody is simple and rhetorically emphatic. The chorus response is almost completely homophonic (see Example 10.2). Even more dramatic in its use of solo writing is *This Is the Record of John.*[8] Here St. John's words are set as an alto solo with an instrumental accompaniment. The dramatic choral responses are reserved for the words of the priests and Levites.

Of the three composers discussed here, Thomas Tomkins lived the longest, witnessing the disaster inflicted on the Anglican Church by the Puritans during the civil war. He was

EXAMPLE 10.2   Gibbons, from *Blessed Are All They*

Master of the Choristers at Worcester Cathedral until 1646 when services were discontinued. Early in his career he also joined the choir of the Chapel Royal, and in 1621 was appointed an organist of the Chapel Royal.[9] Tomkins was the last of the pre-Restoration composers employing the compositional techniques of his teacher William Byrd. His sacred works are numerous and, although none of them were published in his lifetime, they were collected together, probably by his son Nathaniel, and published in 1668 as *Deo sacra et ecclesiae anglicanae.*[10] In addition to five Services, there are ninety-four anthems, divided between forty-one verse and fifty-three full forms, twenty-six anthems for men's voices, and five metrical psalm-tunes. Some two-thirds of the anthems employ psalm texts. Tomkins's contrapuntal mastery is exhibited particularly in the full anthems, for example, *Behold I Bring You Glad Tidings* in ten parts, and especially in *O Praise the Lord All Ye Heathen* for twelve parts. The verse anthems have a remarkable variety of combinations of solo voices employing from one to eight parts. The choruses can be simple in homophonic textures or involve complex polyphony. The melodic style is anchored in a neutral response to the rhetorical dynamics of his texts. Excepting rather conventional text emphases (so-called word painting), Tomkins's music, as was true of the music of most of his predecessors and contemporaries, required thematic points of imitation, and these are more concerned with rhythm, melodic shape, and dynamic motion than with individualizing the expressiveness of individual words. But these essentially Renaissance ideals would finally become largely archaic, as England entered a period of political and social turmoil brought on by civil war.

Sacred Music after the Restoration

The reestablishment of the Stuart monarchy, when Charles II ascended to the English throne in 1660, ended the Puritan ban on Anglican Church services and allowed for a progressive renewal of sacred music. It had been a dark period of almost two decades for sacred music and its supporters. Choirs were disbanded, many organs were removed or destroyed, and composers and performers lost their positions. In addition, theaters where many composers and performers had participated in incidental music to plays were closed. Yet it must not be thought that music disappeared from English life. Secular music was encouraged by the Puritans, and it presented composers with abundant outlets for their art. The masque, chamber music, orchestral works, and a great variety of songs and madrigals all were outlets for composers to continue developing their musical styles, often strongly influenced by music originating in Italy. Some composers of Anglican Church music survived the Commonwealth and took up composing again after 1660, often changing little in their earlier contrapuntal style. Best known of these composers was William Child (1606 or 1607–1697), organist at St. George's Chapel, Windsor, who later joined the Chapel Royal as organist and served three royal households: Charles II, James II, and William and Mary. His large output of Services and anthems in some exceptional instances shows influences of Italianate ideas such as declamatory chordal passages and solo passages approaching recitative style. Not to be overlooked is the substantial survival of pre–civil war sacred music by composers such as Byrd and Gibbons, and others, which had an influence on later composers.

A change of musical styles did impact sacred music after 1660, as the forms of verse, full anthem, and Services now were treated by a new generation of composers familiar with musical developments on the Continent. For the first time English sacred music became contemporary in the context of seventeenth-century musical innovations and can be viewed as having characteristics of the Baroque. Of course, many of these innovations were already present in the secular music of the earlier transitional decades. Most significant for the future of Anglican music was the demand by Charles II that the Chapel Royal composers write a new kind of sacred music to conform to his tastes that had been formed in France and elsewhere. His favorable impression of music heard at the French court led to his decision, clearly inspired by Louis XIV's "vingt-quatre violons du roi," that the Chapel Royal have a private band of twenty-four strings to take part in church services and court entertainments. The king also provided for the Chapel choir boys to be trained in new methods of singing, and made Captain Henry Cooke (c. 1615–1672) the first Master of the Children. Cooke was the first composer of anthems for the restored Chapel Royal. He also seems to be the first to compose verse anthems with string parts and continuo, establishing the pattern of an opening Symphonia and short ritornellos between the full and verse sections. But his fame was more as a singer and choir trainer. For example, John Playford, in *A Brief Introduction to the Skill of Musick* (1664), praised Cooke for his excellence in singing in the Italian manner, including improvisation of embellishments. The boys under his tutelage were taught Italian songs, and among these children were Michael Wise (c. 1647–1687), Robert Smith (c. 1648–1675), and William Turner (1651–1740), as well as the three major composers of the Restoration: Pelham Humfrey (1647–1674), John Blow (1649–1708), and the greatest among them, Henry Purcell (1659–1695).

To this group must be added Matthew Locke (1621/23–1677), noted composer of chamber music and dramatic music. He also wrote motets and anthems, and published the first known English rules for realizing a figured bass, *Melothesia, or, Certain General Rules for Playing upon a Continued-Bass* (1673). Locke became acquainted with Charles II during the civil war, and lived for a period in the Netherlands during Charles II's exile there. At this time Locke converted to Catholicism. In 1660 Charles II appointed him private composer-in-ordinary to the king, composer of wind music, and composer for the band of violins. He was also organist in the Catholic chapels of the king's consort, Catherine of Braganza, and the Queen Mother Henrietta. His Catholicism prevented him from becoming a member of the Chapel Royal. Locke's sacred music, while not extensive, consists of some sixty extant sacred works including over thirty anthems, responses to the Ten Commandments, motets, hymns, songs, and canons in Latin. The fifteen Latin motets, perhaps performed in either of the Catholic chapels or for the king's "private music," or as some evidence suggests at the music school at Oxford, are beautiful chamber compositions written for modest resources: usually one to three solo voices (with a few for four or five voices), and most for two or three strings and basso continuo. Nothing remains of pre-Restoration sacred musical style. Textures, while at times imitative, are not methodically contrapuntal, and vocal lines are often distinctly melodic, in regular phrases organized in tonal harmony. One of the finest of these motets is the setting of the first nine verses of Psalm 136/137, *Super flumina Babylonis*.[11] The two-part "Sinfonia" for three strings and basso continuo opens with an Italianate duo over the bass with both sections appropriately emphasizing chromaticism to reflect the sadness of the text, "By the waters of Babylon, there we sat down and wept" (see Example 10.3). Following a contrasting section in triple meter, the text is set largely in a recitative style, part simple, part more arioso in character, as, for example, the opening lines of the text (see Example 10.4).

Locke's thirty-two extant anthems, about half in verse form, are with some exceptions written for a chamber ensemble of two to five voices with basso continuo.[12] However, one, *Not unto Us, O Lord,* has eight parts, and another, *When the Son of Man Shall Come,* has six parts and three parts for string instruments. Most remarkable of the anthems is *Be Thou Exalted Lord . . . The King Shall Rejoice in Thy Strength,* for three four-part choirs, and a band of three violin parts, viola, and bass viol. The exceptional number of performers was

EXAMPLE 10.3 Locke, from *Super flumina Babylonis*

EXAMPLE 10.4 Ibid.

no doubt occasioned by the anthem's celebratory role as "A Song of Thanksgiving for His Majesty's Victory over the Dutch" in 1666. Its emphasis on homophonic textures and brief concerted passages of imitation between the three choirs all suggest the Venetian practices attributed to the Gabrielis and perhaps the grand motets of Lully. Other features of the developing form of the anthem influenced by Charles II and beginning with Cooke are solo vocal passages placed in contrast with full ensemble writing and dancelike passages in triple meter. Only a few of the verse anthems add strings and are early examples of what have become known as symphony anthems. In these instances, an introductory "Symphony" and interior ritornellos occur, and in some, instruments also accompany vocal parts as in *The Lord Hear Thee in the Day of Trouble* (see Example 10.5).

Humfrey and Blow were the most important composers of sacred music during the Restoration to precede Purcell.[13] Despite Humfrey's early death at twenty-seven, and the small body of music he composed, he was one of the major talents contributing to English sacred music. He served as a chorister in the Chapel Royal until the end of 1664 when he was sent abroad by the king for study in France and Italy. He returned in October 1667 and was appointed a Gentleman of the Chapel. He also became composer for the violins and in 1672 Master of the Children of the Chapel Royal. No record of Humfrey's European experiences exists, and this fact together with the evidence in his music places in considerable doubt the often-stated premise that there are significant French and Italian influences in Humfrey's music. His vocal music does not sound French and the instrumental style has little to compare to Lully's instrumental works. (Despite claims to the contrary, Humfrey is not known to have studied with Lully.) There are, however, obvious and not surprising relationships in style to the sacred works of both Cooke and Locke. And clearly Humfrey absorbed by way of earlier English secular music the Italian concept of recitative style into his overall dynamic approach to text expressiveness.

Humfrey's sacred music consists of a Service in E minor, several sacred songs, and eighteen anthems, two of which are of doubtful authenticity.[14] Another, *I Will Always Give Thanks,* known as the "Club" Anthem, was composed in three sections by Humfrey, Blow, and Turner. The anthems are rich in affective responses to the texts, the majority of which are penitential. In several, there are new ways to achieve formal cohesion, not only by clearly organized tonalities but also by using repetitions of the opening symphony or the internal ritornellos to tie together the verses of the text. Choruses are mostly in simple, homophonic textures; solo ensembles have little counterpoint, except for points of imitation for successive vocal entrances. The key to Humfrey's importance lies in the particularly dramatic and expressive settings of the texts. This is found both in a form of recitative to be recognized as peculiarly English and also in lyrical passages with regular phrase structures involving text repetition and often in triple meter that become airs in all but name. For example, the following "air" from *Have Mercy upon Me O God* (II) (see Example 10.6).

Although a comprehensive evaluation of Blow's music will be attainable only with a more complete publication of all of his sacred works, the following summarizes what appears particularly significant in Blow's sacred works. Many of them favor the alto, tenor, and bass voices (often in pairs), and prominent solo parts with wide ranges are frequent for one or two basses, reflecting the court's pleasure in renowned bass soloists such as John Gostling.

John Blow was the most respected as well as most prolific composer of Restoration sacred music. His early training was under Cooke in the Chapel Royal. In late 1668 he became organist at Westminster Abbey, the first of a large number of official positions that established his primacy among his contemporaries, including King's Musician for the

EXAMPLE 10.5 Locke, from *The Lord Hear Thee in the Day of Trouble*

EXAMPLE 10.5 (*continued*)

Virginals (from 1669), Gentleman of the Chapel Royal and Master of the Children, the latter succeeding Humfrey, and Composer-in-Ordinary for voices at court (all from 1674), Organist of the Chapel Royal (from 1676), and Master of the Choristers at St. Paul's Cathedral (1683–1703). Blow was a teacher of Purcell and their careers ran largely in parallel to Blow's sacred music, many Services, and some ninety-two full and verse anthems. Blow also composed a very large amount of secular music, numerous odes, songs, many works for organ and harpsichord, and one dramatic work, *Venus and Adonis*. In quantity and generally in quality, Blow was a major figure of the English Baroque, even if his musical gifts cannot be compared to those of Purcell. His posthumous reputation was seriously damaged by the bitter personal attack on him by Charles Burney, who concentrated on perceived "crudities" in Blow's harmony and part-writing.[15]

Blow composed all three types of anthems: twenty-four full, forty verse, and twenty-

EXAMPLE 10.6 Humfrey, from *Have Mercy upon Me O God* (II)

eight symphony anthems (plus a few of doubtful authenticity).[16] There is in these anthems a great variety of approaches to texts that often reflect practices established by Locke and Humfrey but also suggest influences on Blow from his contemporary Purcell. Blow's anthems run the whole gamut of possible forms and expressions, and frequently achieve a grandeur reflective of a royal ethos. For example, the monumental anthem for eight largely contrapuntal parts and string ensemble for the coronation of James II, *God Spake Sometime in Visions*,[17] emphasized and developed the importance of formal cohesion beyond his predecessors by using forms of repetition of the opening "Symphony," by a variety of ritornellos, and by concluding solo passages with an instrumental repetition of the vocal melody that leads to a full choral statement of the melody. There are instances of motive use and alternating sections of verse/full sections. Textures can consist of simple homophony, recitative-like passages, solo and ensemble sections of extended melodies, and, especially to be noted, contrapuntal writing of some complexity, albeit seldom obscuring the perception of the text. This recourse to contrapuntal textures reflects the continuity of pre-Restoration compositional practice at the Chapel Royal as well as at many of the cathedrals. Fugal procedure is frequently suggested by subject answer entrances on the tonic and dominant, although a true fugue rarely occurs. There is a decisive emphasis on dancelike music in triple meter. Outstanding is Blow's care in reflecting language accents and structure in his melodic lines, and the musical/rhetorical emphases given to the words. For example, the expressive power of the passage from *I Said in the Cutting Off of My Days* can be seen in Example 10.7.[18]

Blow achieved a consummate mastery of the musical styles characteristic of Restoration sacred and secular music. Whether or not his "crudities," in Burney's view—such as fondness for augmented chords, cross-relationships, "incorrect" voice-leadings, and some very startling simultaneous dissonances—are examples of his original and slightly eccentric approaches to text settings or simply errors of a careless or inattentive composer no longer seems significant. He was admired in his lifetime for his musical achievements and he remains one of the two major figures in English Baroque sacred music.

Secular Vocal Music

As with sacred music, English secular vocal music in the seventeenth century continued an unbroken development in both quantity and quality from the precedents originating

EXAMPLE 10.7 Blow, from *I Said in the Cutting Off of My Days*

in the Elizabethan period. This enormous amount of vocal music can be divided loosely into several types: (1) madrigals; (2) lute songs; (3) declamatory (monodic) songs; (4) miscellaneous forms such as dialogue, glee, and catch; and (5) vocal music in the court masque, ode, and earliest attempts at opera. It was especially in secular vocal music that the inevitable influence of new Italian concepts of music found enthusiastic acceptance. In part, the musical culture of the "Elizabethan Age" is characterized by the influx of Italian music, particularly the madrigal. And English composers transformed the Italian madrigal style into an unmistakably English musical repertory. Although copies of Italian madrigals appear in manuscript collections from at least two decades earlier, the first large anthology of Italian madrigals was published in England in 1588, *Musica transalpina*, edited by Nicholas Yonge. The largest number of madrigals in this collection were by the elder Alfonso Ferrabosco and Marenzio. The latter also has the majority of madrigals in the next madrigal anthology, *Italian Madrigalls Englished* published by Thomas Watson in 1590.[19]

The history of the English madrigal belongs to the Renaissance.[20] The style reaches its perfection in the early seventeenth century in the works of three composers: Thomas Morley, Thomas Weelkes, and John Wilbye (1574–1638).[21] Morley, the most influential composer among the English madrigalists, was the synthesizer of English sensibilities for tunefulness and lighthearted charm out of Italian style and techniques. His published works include the first set of *Canzonets, Or Little Short Songs to Three Voices* (1593), and, the following year, *Madrigalls to Foure Voyces*. Both collections emphasize Morley's mercurial style, with only a few settings of narrative and serious texts. His madrigals are the ideal realization of vocal chamber music. They focus on giving the singers the greatest musical and entertainment fun. This comes from the interactions of the parts, their uncomplicated but brilliantly evocative contrapuntal sections, and their sometimes dramatic, sometimes humorous explorations of "madrigalisms"—Morley's inexhaustible musical representations of textual conceits. He also popularized in *First Booke of Balletts to Five Voyces* (1595) the Italian form of the *balletti* best known from the works of Gastoldi. Many of Morley's compositions are modeled on Italian works. *The First Booke of Canzonets to Two Voyces* (1595) also appeared in an Italian edition (now lost). In *The Triumphes of Oriana to 5 and 6 Voices* (1601), Morley collected and published a major collection of madrigals by twenty-three composers to honor his queen. He achieved a degree of lasting fame with the musical treatise *A Plaine and Easie Introduction to Practicall Musicke* (1597). Both Weelkes and Wilbye, while continuing to follow the madrigal tradition of Morley, deepen and further intensify many of their musical settings of texts. Next to Morley, Weelkes published in three books the greatest number of madrigals: *Madrigals to 3, 4, 5, & 6 Voyces* (1597), *Balletts and Madrigals to Five Voyces with One to 6 Voyces* (1598), and *Madrigals of 5 and 6 Parts, apt for the Viols and Voices* (1600). Examples of expressive chromaticism, harmonic experimentation, and some preference for texts of sad or tragic affect enrich Weelkes's madrigals. Contrapuntal textures are important, a fact emphasized in the publication of 1600, which Weelkes states are "apt for Viols and Voices." The finest madrigals by an English composer are by John Wilbye. They are contained in just two books, *The First Set of English Madrigals to 3,4,5, and 6 Voices* (1598) and *The Second Set of Madrigals to 3,4,5, and 6 Parts* (1609). These contain both madrigals in the lighter style of Morley as well as in the serious mold of Weelkes. Wilbye is outstanding in the Italian approach to text expression, turning these insights into exceptional interpretations of English texts. Like Weelkes, his compositional technique is contrapuntal but employed carefully so as not to obscure the text. A number of the madrigals include solo-songs similar to those associated with the lute ayre. And reflecting later Baroque approaches to text settings, some of Wilbye's most serious madrigals are not divided into sections but set the entire poem of somber mood that evokes a single affect.

The first decade of the seventeenth century witnessed a steady decline in the popularity of the English madrigal. Orlando Gibbons's only book of madrigals "apt for Viols and Voyces" appeared in 1612, and Thomas Tomkins published one book of madrigals (songs) in three, four, five, and six parts in 1622. Several less important composers continued to publish them, including Thomas Bateson (c. 1570/75–1630), Michael East (c. 1580–1648), and Francis Pilkington (c. 1570–1638). The last publication of madrigals appeared in 1632, *Madrigals and Ayres,* in two to five voices, by Walter Porter (c. 1587/95–1659), a student of Monteverdi. Here one finds the Baroque transformation of the madrigal concept, with figured continuo basses, introductory toccatas, sinfonias, and ritornellos. The concertato style prevails and the spirit is Monteverdian. Recitative, solo, duet, and dialogues are found as are virtuoso vocal passages. The English madrigal is no more.

The solo song with lute accompaniment flourished at about the same time as the English madrigal and as its more intimate solo counterpart. Lute songs had been preceded from about the middle of the sixteenth century by songs accompanied by a consort of four viols. The most important and largest collection of consort songs was by Byrd: *Psalmes, Sonets, & Songs* (1588). However, the vogue for consort songs soon faded, probably in part because the viol consort was no longer as popular among amateur musicians. Collections of lute songs (ayres) suddenly appeared in print and had an enormous vogue with amateur musicians for about two decades when, as with the madrigal, they quickly lost significance as the solo-song took new directions.[22]

The popularity of the ayre with lute accompaniment began with John Dowland (1563–1626)[23] and his *First Booke of Songes or Ayres* (1597). Reprinted three times, it was followed by three additional books: *Second Booke of Songes or Ayres* (1600), *Third and Last Booke of Songs or Aires* (1603), and *A Pilgrimes Solace* (1612).[24] Dowland traveled widely in France, Germany, and Italy, and in France he converted to Catholicism. His awareness of recent European musical developments cannot be doubted. The English ayre, of which he was the greatest exponent, is related to the French *air de cour* and the Italian monody, but Dowland's melodic style is innately English. He published most of his ayres both as solos with lute accompaniment and as part songs. In the latter the alto, tenor, and bass parts were printed on the page opposite to the cantus and facing different directions on the page. This enabled the performers sitting around a table to perform from a single copy.

His ayres are often quite simple with mostly strophic settings in two sections, the second being shorter and usually repeated. The texts of these are most frequently about either the joys or tragedies of love. Many, however, have a variety of treatments, for example, the through-composed, poignant, and exceptionally beautiful expressiveness joining voice and lute in "I Saw My Lady Weep" (see Example 10.8). There are dance songs, some of which were originally instrumental pieces to which words were added, for example, "Flow My Tears" (Book II), which is based on Dowland's famous *Lachrimae* pavan. The lute accompaniment can be homophonic, but frequently it has freely flowing (*style brisé*) counterpoint with highly expressive dissonances and shifting tonal centers that add great beauty to the vocal line. Among Dowland's finest ayres are those of sadness and despair. Some of these, particularly in the last book (*A Pilgrimes Solace*), begin to incorporate stylistic features of Italian monodies. In "Welcome, Black Night," the discontinuous, dramatic parlando vocal line, static basses, and largely homophonic accompaniment all suggest an adaptation of Italian monodic style and introduce a new stage of development of the song leading to the declamatory air (see Example 10.9).

EXAMPLE 10.8   Dowland, "I Saw My Lady Weep" (Book 2)

EXAMPLE 10.8 (*continued*)

eyes, in those fair eyes where all per-fec-tions keep. Her face was full of woe,

full_____ of woe; But such a woe, be-lieve me, as

wins more hearts Than Mirth can do with her, with her en-tic - ing parts.

In addition to Dowland, a number of other composers[25] also published ayres during the two decades these songs flourished. The most prolific composer of these was the poet and musician Thomas Campion (1567–1620). His ayres are contained in five volumes: Philip Rosseter's *Booke of Ayres* (1601), which contains twenty-one ayres by Campion; *Two Bookes of Ayres* (c. 1613), of which the first is devoted to religious songs; and *The Third and Fourth Bookes of Ayres* (c. 1617). Campion was a well-known poet who used his own verses exclusively. His ayres are light and strophic, many of the best in triple time, and predominantly short (between ten and twenty-five measures). The longest is the last ayre in Book

EXAMPLE 10.9   Dowland, "Welcome, Black Night" (Book 4)

IV, *Fain Would I Wed,* a series of variations on a passamezzo-type bass. Melodies have a clear-cut, two-part form, in which either the second part only is repeated (ABB), or others in which in addition to the second part the melody of the first part is restated for the second half of the text (AABB). Campion's melodies are careful to observe the metrical structure of his texts, and they are most often in clear phrase structures and predominantly conjunct and tuneful. The lute accompaniments are almost entirely homophonic. The texts themselves focus on love, sometimes humorously bawdy, but in the first book of the circa 1613 collection there are deeply felt religious ayres that at times resemble hymns.

Printing books of lute-ayres ended in 1622 with Attey's *First Booke of Ayres,* but the form itself had not died. Both the strophic, light ayre and its outgrowth, the declamatory ayre, appear in numerous manuscript collections. Most important among the composers are Alfonso Ferrabosco, Nicholas Lanier (1588–1666), Henry Lawes (1596–1662) and William Lawes (1602–1645), and John Wilson (1595–1674), but a host of less well known as well as unidentified musicians also contributed.[26] Frequently the ayre became an important part of both masques and plays, especially after the Restoration. Most of these ayres were written as melodies with unfigured basses. The singer would improvise on the bass a chordal accompaniment for one of the several appropriate instruments such as lute, theorbo, guitar, or harpsichord. Lanier, a singer, lutenist, and artist, as early as 1613 was performing at court and became a lutenist in the King's Musick in 1616. His songs indicate he was a significant innovator in realizing the declamatory form. For a court masque by Campion in 1613 he composed and sang "Bring away the sacred tree," which may be one of the earliest declamatory ayres. It circulated in later sources with the text "Weep no more my wearied eyes" (see Example 10.10).[27] Another "song" widely circulated in England for some forty years was "Nor com'st thou yet, my slothful love." Roger North[28] says that Lanier wrote this "recitativo" shortly after returning from Italy in 1628. The text relates the tragedy of Hero and Leander. The following excerpt emphasizes the extent to which Lanier adopted the

EXAMPLE 10.10   Lanier, "Weep no more my wearied eyes"

declamatory elements in Italian recitative, although the regular bass movement is not characteristic of Italian style (see Example 10.11).

The most important and productive song composer after 1630 and preceding the Restoration was Henry Lawes, whose extant songs number more than four hundred. He set the poetry of the most prominent poets of his time: Carew, Herrick, Lovelace, Suckling, and Milton, for whose play *Comus* he wrote five songs. He contributed songs to a number of plays and court masques in the 1630s. It would seem likely that the development of declamatory songs was nurtured by the growing popularity of plays and masques with their song components. In 1626 Lawes became Gentleman of the Chapel Royal and in 1631 a musician in the King's Private Music. Many of his best songs were written for the court. John Playford published three books of his *Ayres and Dialogues* in 1653, 1655, and 1658, as well as many individual songs in his various miscellanies between 1652 and 1669. Lawes's ayres, including many of those that are declamatory, are strophic. This at times necessitates modifying the vocal line for the subsequent stanzas without structural parallelism to conform with the differences in prosody. The declamatory songs of the 1630s are especially effective in their absorption of the rhetorical subtleties of the texts. Words and their inflections in speech generate melodic details and rhythms. Punctuation marks lead to cadences and affect the unequal lengths of phrases. Various conventional dissonances underscore appropriate words, but there are also dissonances in the vocal lines that pass through harmonic structure without preparation or resolution. Lawes comes somewhat close to the guiding principles of the Italian monodists, but at the same time creates a melodic style appropriate to English verse. The second stanza of "When thou, poor excommunicate" (by Thomas Carew)[29] demonstrates some of these characteristics of dramatic rhetoric, melodic realizations of speech inflections, breaking the flow of the lines with rhetorical pauses, and the regrouping of the lines of the poem for affective emphasis, as can be seen by comparing the original stanzaic form (see Example 10.12).

EXAMPLE 10.11   Lanier, from "Nor com'st thou yet, my slothful love"

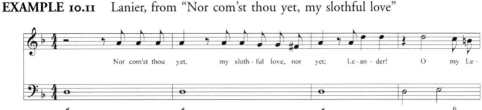

> Then shalt thou weepe, entreat, complaine
>   To Love, as I did once to thee:
> When all thy teares shall be as vaine
>   As mine were then, for thou shalt be
> Damn'd for thy false Apostasie.

Lawes's brother William, who was and remains better known as an instrumental composer, continues to be somewhat in the shadow of Henry as a composer of songs. More than two hundred songs both sacred and secular are extant, but only a small number are currently in print. Those that are published have the same variety of forms and excellence of text settings found in his brother's ayres. Some indication of his success was the long-lived popularity of his song set to a poem by Robert Herrick, "Gather your rosebuds whilst

EXAMPLE 10.12   Henry Lawes, from "When thou, poor excommunicate"

you may" (see Example 10.13). It was also arranged as a part-song, and appeared in instruction books such as *Musicks Recreation: On the Lyra Viol, Musick's Delight on the Cithren,* and *Synopsis of Vocal Musick,* and in many editions of Playford's *Introduction to the Skill of Musick.*

In addition, William Lawes contributed vocal music to many plays and court masques. His vocal music appears to have had the same popular success as his brother's. Both brothers composed a number of dialogues, a form of vocal chamber music with a lengthy history in both France and Italy. Especially in Italy their popularity soared with the establishment of the recitative style. Most of the Italian composers of the early seventeenth century, including Monteverdi, Carissimi, and Stradella, wrote dialogues, which became dramatic scenes between two singers taking the roles usually of figures from pastoral plays but also from mythology and the Bible. Good examples of English dialogues in the new recitative style were composed by many of the composers of ayres: Lanier's "Tell me, shepherd, dost thou love?," Ramsey's "Howl not, you ghosts and furies, while I sing," Hilton's "Rise, princely shepherd, and be arbiter," Henry Lawes's "As Celia rested in the shade," and William Lawes's "Charon, O Charon! Hear a wretch oppres'd."[30]

Throughout the Commonwealth period, with theaters closed, organs silenced, and the Court exiled, music for the home, and the middle class as well as aristocrats, prospered. In addition to providing music for professional musicians, there was a ready market for amateurs. That market, for example, was the focus of numerous vocal and instrumental publications by John Playford (1623–1686). His *Select Ayres and Dialogues* (1652; later editions, 1653, 1659, and 1669) was of major significance. It included songs for one or two voices with continuo, pastoral dialogues also with continuo, and three-part ayres or glees by major composers, especially Henry Lawes, and others of lesser significance. Also becoming popular for private entertainments at home, in taverns, and other venues of private gatherings were catches, usually with humorous or bawdy texts, canons, and rounds. They

EXAMPLE 10.13   William Lawes, "Gather your rosebuds whilst you may"

1.Ga - ther your rose - buds whilst you___ may,   Old   time   is   still   a -
2.The glo - rious lamp of heav'n the___ sun,   The high - er   is   a -

fly - ing;   For that same flow'r that smiles to - day,   To - mor - row will be dy - ing.
get - ting,   No soon - er will his race be___ run,   And near - er is to set - ting.

quickly became popularized with the series entitled *Catch that Catch Can,* edited by John Hilton in 1652, with several later and enlarged editions.

The popularizing of ayres and songs was given further momentum with the restoration of King Charles II, and the reopening of the theaters in 1660.[31] This can be seen in the title to Playford's collection of songs appearing in five volumes between 1673 and 1684: *Choice Ayres, Songs & Dialogues to Sing to the Theorbo-Lute, or Bass-Viol being most of the newest Ayres and Songs, Sung at Court and at the Publick Theatres. Composed by Several Gentlemen of His Majesties Musick, and others.*[32] Here one finds songs by successful composers of the Commonwealth period such as John Banister (c. 1624/25–1679), William Gregory (?1624–1691), Pelham Humfrey, Matthew Locke, Alfonso Marsh (1627–1681), and Robert Smith. They not only found success with their songs at Court but also were among many composers creating a major song literature for Restoration plays. Among these composers Humfrey stands out as having both a refinement of taste and some depth of expression. As with the other song composers, short, strophic, triple-time pieces dominate, many based on contemporary dance rhythms. Fewer declamatory songs were composed, and some of them are coupled with a second tuneful section. There is a surfeit of songs based on poetry referring to nymphs and shepherds of pastoral plays and a quality of superficiality underlying the simple tunefulness of many of these songs.

In the final decades of the century, English song literature was dominated by John Blow and the unique talent of Henry Purcell. They overshadow all other song composers including Thomas Farmer (d. 1688), James Hart (1647–1718), Robert King (c. 1660–1726), and William Turner (ii) (1651–1740). It was inevitable that Blow as a song composer would suffer critically when compared to the extraordinary achievements in that genre of his student, Henry Purcell.[33]

Blow composed more than 120 songs, all appearing in various anthologies such as Playford's *Choice Ayres.* Blow published fifty of them in the collection *Amphion Anglicus* (London, 1700),[34] and this provides a good cross section of the many types and forms of his songs. There is considerable variety, with an emphasis on long declamatory forms and duets. Many have accompaniments of strings, rarely recorders, and at times they end with a chorus. The longer ones resemble cantatas in their contrasting sections and indications of tempo changes. The musical repetitions for strophic songs are usually written out. Blow shows the same interest in ostinato basses as Purcell, although Blow's usage does not employ a consistent repetition of the pattern, and often they are modulatory. In this collection, at least, there are very few dance songs, and only four dialogues. The majority of the songs are serious in affect. His music is at times idiosyncratic and certainly experimental. Although such traits as unusual dissonances, cross-relations, and augmented melodic leaps are hardly new to English music, Blow does experiment with tonal organization, harmony, and melodic phrase structures. These do not always seem to be successful, but such typical characteristics of the composer's style cannot be simply attributed to ignorance or an inadequate training in composition.

Also typical of Purcell is Blow's frequent use of highly embellished vocal lines clearly meant for virtuoso singers, for example, the flowing "recitative" passage from Blow's memorable and deeply moving tribute, *Ode on the Death of Mr. Henry Purcell* (1696), to the poem by John Dryden (see Example 10.14[35]).

EXAMPLE 10.14   Blow, from *Ode on the Death of Mr. Henry Purcell*

Too few songs of Blow have been published in practical editions for singers, and there is no adequate discussion of Blow's achievement as compared to Purcell's. Purcell's achievements in song as in everything else he composed are incomparable (see Chapter 11). This in no way means one must ignore the works of his contemporaries or criticize them with standards applicable only to his genius. John Blow was recognized by his contemporaries as an outstanding composer of his generation. We can do no less in our examination of his extensive accomplishments.

Instrumental Music

Instrumental music in the first half of the seventeenth century also reflects the extraordinary musical achievements of the Elizabethan Age. As with vocal music, instrumental composers and their music extend the English Renaissance into the new century. Consort music, solo lute music, and keyboard music were already highly developed by the last decades of the preceding century, and many of the composers were active well into the new century. All of this music responded to the great demands for intimate musical entertainments for performers especially, and at times for small audiences within the privacy of court life and in the homes of the aristocracy and a wealthy middle class. What was a true form of chamber music began as a very sophisticated art and became a popular music in the best sense of the concept.

Consort Music

Dominating English chamber music through to the early years of the Restoration was the consort ensemble. Consorts were made up either of instruments of one family, such as recorders or viols, or were "broken," that is, made up of a group of different instruments. For much of the first half of the seventeenth century, the viol consort was very popular. A "chest" of viols consisted usually of a treble, tenor, and a bass or two of each. The music for these ensembles can be divided into several categories: (1) cantus firmus compositions; (2) the fantasia or fancy; (3) variations, including those of improvisatory character on grounds; (4) dance forms often entitled aires (or ayres); and (5) dances grouped into suites or "fantasia-suites."

The origins of consort music and its long-lived characteristic style were in the imitative contrapuntal vocal music of the Renaissance. As is true of other aspects of early-seventeenth-century English music, William Byrd again showed the way with his own viol music: cantus firmus settings on a plainsong hymn, a *Miserere*, and the *In Nomine* melody,[36] the latter continuing to be used by English composers as late as Henry Purcell. Byrd's fantasias, probably from the 1590s, and especially a late one *à6* in his *Psalmes, Songs, and Sonnets . . . Fit for Voyces or Viols* (1611), indicate the degree of contrapuntal sophistication that had become characteristic of this rapidly developing major instrumental form of the Jacobean decades. The end of the sixteenth century saw a great increase in all forms of viol music as song accompaniments, dances, cantus firmus settings of plainchants, and especially various popular songs. The largest repertory, however, was for pieces having the ubiquitous title of "fantasia" or "fancy." There are also those that can be called fantasia-suites, consisting of a proper fantasia followed by alman and galliard. These all share the same general stylistic feature of two to six parts written in counterpoint. Points of imitation, at times more motivic than thematic, create a continuous flow of melody. Thematic unity was seldom a consideration. Sections can be formed by cadences or a change to a new thematic idea. Both the substance of the melodic material and the challenge of the imitative textures, which in fantasias for four, five, or six parts can become intimidating, led to a repertory of extraordinary musical vitality, emotional variety, and for the performers the pure joy of participating in these musical conversations and, indeed, orations.

Among the important first generation of composers writing consort music were Thomas Morley, Orlando Gibbons, John Coprario, that is, Cooper (c. 1570/80–c. 1626), Alfonso Ferrabosco II, Thomas Lupo (1571–1627), William Brade (1560–1630), Richard Dering (c. 1580–1630), John Ward (c. 1589–1638), and Thomas Tomkins.[37] Coprario's ninety extant fantasias for from three to six parts provide a body of consort music representative of the early decades of the century. Those in five and six parts are imitations of and in some cases transcriptions of his madrigals. The three- and four-part fantasias are highly sectionalized with a variety of points of imitation. These are fairly common subject types found in late-sixteenth-century polyphony with their considerable stepwise motion, little rhythmic variety, and few distinctive motivic figures. Some of Coprario's fantasias employ subjects more specifically instrumental in character.[38] This development toward idiomatic instrumental writing is an important characteristic of the more than fifty consorts for viols by the influential Alphonso Ferrabosco II. Quickly, consort works became richer in both the variety of thematic materials and in the increasing emphasis on string techniques and enriched musical textures. These characteristics occur in subsequent composers, for example, those by Thomas Lupo. In the six-part fantasia seen in Example 10.15,[39] points of imitation are less well defined as the textures become a maze of short motives in a variety of rhythmic conflicts between the parts.

Of particular significance is the consort music of Orlando Gibbons. Forty-two works include thirty-three free fantasias, four based on the *In Nomine;* four dances; and a set of variations on a popular melody, "Go from my Window."[40] While a number of the fantasias continue the late-sixteenth-century style of a continuous texture of overlapping points of imitation, there is a sense of innovation and continuity of dramatic development. Thematic ideas are highly individual and instrumental in character. Many of the fantasias have sections contrasted by texture and notational values, others by shifts from duple to triple time. Dance underlies some of the music and a few employ popular tunes. Particularly interesting is Gibbons's employment of the double bass (a violone with a contra-A as the lowest string). In those three-part fantasias for double bass, bass, and treble viol, and those in four parts with a bass viol added, the treble part has the opportunity at times to move between three and four octaves above the lowest notes of the texture and in effect to create a new sense of musical space. In addition to Gibbons, the consort works of Thomas Tomkins are also important. They include fifteen three-part fanatasias, several dances for four, five, and six viols, and four fantasias for six viols.[41]

Other composers of consort music during the Jacobean and Carolinian periods include Michael East and William White (1571–1634). Of particular significance are the works of William Lawes and John Jenkins (1592–1678). Lawes, musician-in-ordinary to Charles I, despite his tragic death at forty-three, while fighting in the king's service during the civil war, composed a vast amount of music.[42] Among the hundreds of extant pieces in almost every musical form of the period, there are thirty-nine works for viol consorts in four, five, and six parts, including fantasias, In Nomines, pavans, and aires (stylized dances, usually almans). The *Royall Consort* from 1630 has sixty-seven dances arranged into large suites of dances ("Setts"), the basic group consisting of an alman, a corrant, and ending with a saraband.[43] Other dances variously inserted include the paven, galliard, and Morris. They are scored for two trebles, tenor, and bass with continuo. A second version changes the scoring to two trebles, two basses, and continuo for two theorbos. This seems to be the earliest

EXAMPLE 10.15   Lupo, from Fantasia in D

EXAMPLE 10.15 *(continued)*

English example of the suite-form, which subsequently will be expanded with the addition of the jig.

Lawes's fantasias are made up in sets in three or four movements with various groupings of fantasies, aires, and In Nomines. As became common practice in the Jacobean period, a chamber organ part supports, usually duplicates, the string texture, and at times fills in the harmony. Lawes's fantasias and related dances and aires still have a regard for the earlier contrapuntal forms achieved by other composers such as his teacher Coprario. Yet Lawes is a distinctly original composer whose works are part of the developing new spirit of the century, which can be seen to have been influenced by Italian music. The differences are apparent in the themes of his fantasias: some are introspective phrases, some simply brief motives, while others have strong affective impact, instrumental rather than vocal in character, at times with startling harmonic content. Themes can be varied in the course of a fantasia, and contrasts of style, homophonic passages versus intricate counterpoint, rather than continuity mark the various sections. There is frequent *concertato* interaction between parts, and bold, often innovative harmonic surprises.

John Jenkins's career experienced the turmoil of Stuart rule, the Commonwealth, and the beginnings of the Restoration. He was the most famous and highly praised English composer of consort music of his time. He composed about one thousand works (the majority still unpublished), largely for instruments and including more than one hundred for viol consorts. Of these, forty-six employ four, five, or six viols with organ, and are the culmination of Jacobean consort music in this form and style.[44]

While no source gives dates for these works, it is generally agreed they were composed before the Commonwealth. In the fantasias, Jenkins continues to be true to his heritage of composers such as Coprario, Ferrabosco, Lupo, Ward, and others, in using a mostly conservative contrapuntal texture in which fugal imitation remains the essence of the style. Nevertheless, within that style he created a variety of forms. These include: (1) fugues followed by a number of contrapuntal sections based on new points of imitation that may follow without break or at times be separated by a contrasting "interlude" such as harmonic sonorities in long note values or sprightly dance rhythms; (2) imitative pieces in two large sections; and (3) monothematic pieces in which the theme often may be modified, may appear in augmentation, or has added to it new secondary motives. Especially noteworthy is the considerable range of expressiveness from work to work and often within a composition. There are noble, stately pieces; joyful ones in which the contrapuntal interactions of the parts are like brilliant conversations; themes of rhetorical power whose hidden potential Jenkins realizes in flowing lyricism and a rich organization of tonalities, especially with strong key contrasts. There are also many somber, pensive, serene fantasias, and a considerable emphasis on the minor modes. Jenkins's viol consort works are the last of a magnificent creative achievement that burst forth in England from the end of the sixteenth century and for the most part ended with the Restoration.

In addition to the large repertory of fantasias for viol consorts, there was also a diverse and extensive amount of viol music, at times in combination with instruments of other kinds. The amount and variety of this literature can only be summarized here. Mention has been made of the continuing tradition of variations on a cantus firmus, especially the In Nomines and other plainsongs. Particularly popular was the practice of variations, called divisions, on a ground bass. Christopher Simpson (c. 1605–1669) defined the nature of the practice in *The Division-Violist* (London, 1659), "division viol" referring to an instrument smaller than a bass but with the same tuning. Although the practice was often improvisatory, composers also wrote out the divisions for their music. Jenkins composed a number for two division bass viols and organ, and the technique of writing elaborate passages of "divisions" appears in consort music by many composers in addition to Simpson and Jenkins. The latter as well as Simpson, Coprario, and William Lawes also composed a small but important consort repertory for lyra viols. Music for the instrument occurs in some eighteen printed English sources and more than fifty manuscript sources. A lyra viol apparently did exist as a slightly modified bass viol, but playing the "lyra-way" usually meant to perform from tablature rather than staff notation, which could be done on any standard bass viol. The greater distinction for this music was the numerous unusual tunings required for lyra viol music.[45]

Besides consort fantasias, another significant form of viol music was the so-called fantasia-suite (a term of recent scholarship), which appears first in the twenty-four works for one or two violins, bass viol, and organ by Coprario, the earliest known English contrapuntal music to require violins.[46] These are three-movement suites, opening with a fantasia, and followed by an alman and galliard. William Lawes retained his teacher Coprario's three-movement form in his sixteen fantasia-suites for one or two violins, bass viol, and organ.[47] The violin writing is frequently bold and striking in its thematic originality, totally instrumental in style. The organ parts are substantial, usually independent of the string writing, and enrich the overall musical weight. Both Coprario and Lawes wrote these pieces for the court of Charles I. Jenkins, however, wrote many of his fantasia-suites in the 1640s and 1650s mostly for wealthy amateurs. His three-movement form often replaces the galliard with a coranto.

Jenkins developed the genre further in a set of nine suites for treble, two division basses, and organ, which presented the string players with virtuosic difficulties of technique and ensemble.[48] In another set of seven suites, the form is reduced to two movements, a fancy followed by an ayre. The ayres are elaborate, abstract dances. The fancies vary between three, four, or five sections of contrasting music. In these the organ, although written rather sketchily and requiring filling out, has a prominent role and employs concerted techniques and solo interludes.[49] There is a distinct emphasis on a more popular instrumental style. In most of these works the opening is based on a subject, usually a brief, simple phrase and not always carried through the section. This follows without interruption a section of divisions for all three parts, the greatest technical challenge of the work. Divisions are also featured in the ayres. The next section is often a homophonic movement in triple meter that is followed usually by another imitative concluding section in duple meter.

Finally, during the period from the end of the Commonwealth to the Restoration, consort music reaches both its ultimate development and formal transformation in the five consorts by Matthew Locke: *Duos for two Basse Viols* ("For Several Friends"), *The Little Consort of Three Parts*, *The Flat Consort* ("For my Cousin Kemble"), *The Broken Consort*, and *The Consort in Four Parts*.[50] The ten suites in the *Little Consort* each contain four movements: pavan, ayre, courante, and saraband, binary dances for two trebles and a bass. The five suites in *The Flat Consort* (all except the fifth one in a "flat" key) for treble, alto, or tenor viol and bass in Nos. 1 and 2, and for treble and two division basses in Nos. 3, 4, and 5, are works of greater scope. The first two contain six movements: fantazie, courante, fantazie, saraband, fantazie, and jigg with a coda. The remaining three have four movements: fantazie, courante, fantazie, and saraband with a coda. The opening fantazies serve as impressive, multisectional introductions to the suites contrasting slow, stately sections with imitative and more homophonic sections. *The Broken Consort* has two separate parts, the first of which probably dates from 1661. It contains six suites each made up of four movements with the order of fantasia, courante, ayre, and saraband and with the instrumentation of two trebles and bass (autograph parts also exist for three theorbos to duplicate the bass part). Part II is not consistent in its arrangement of movements. Each begins with a pavan and is followed by four (in No. 4, five) movements of ayres, courantes, galliards, and in single instances a saraband, a chicona, and a jigg. The six suites in *The Consort in Four Parts*, although without specific indication as to instruments, appear to be for an ensemble of viols: treble, alto, tenor, and bass. These also have a regular makeup of an initial fantazie in several sections, followed by a courante, ayre, and saraband. While these four-part viol consorts reflect on the past, they are at the same time removed from the past in their much simpler textures and their reliance on more popular dance movements. They are a fine summation of the English consort music prior to mid-century, even as composers moved forward to a new musical attitude of less complexity that left behind the intricacies of the late Renaissance "golden age" of English music.

Following the Restoration, composers of ensemble music, with the exception of Purcell, largely abandoned the style and instrumentation of the viol consort, although, of course, among many musicians the tradition of private viol consort performances continued. In part, the changes in music were the result of court tastes encouraged by Charles II's love of French music formed during his years of exile in France. His appointment of the controversial Louis Grabu (d. 1694) as composer to the king in 1665 and a year later as Master of the King's Music seemed based entirely on Grabu's French origins and as an exponent of Lully's music. Arrangements of French music, especially excerpts from Lully's *ballets de cour* and operas, were frequently heard at court for the king's band of twenty-four violins but also elsewhere. French dances such as the bourrée, branle, gavotte, and minuet soon dominated dancing in the social scene. Lully's *Cadmus et Hermione* was a major event when heard in London in 1686, and arrangements of instrumental music by Lully became plentiful, as, for example, in John Playford's *Apollo's Banquet* (1669 and additional editions to 1701). English instrumental ensembles began to imitate Lully's orchestral style, including the French overture. Also the characteristic melodic style of the French composers, with its greater tunefulness, regular phrase structure, and distinctly articulated forms, influenced a new generation of composers. Perhaps the most obvious musical influence of the French on English composers was the at times excessive use of dotted rhythms.

London, however, was quickly becoming a cosmopolitan city and not only French musicians but also Germans, Netherlanders, and Italians added to the changing musical environment. A number of English musicians circulated between their homeland and the Continent as did their music, for example, the violists and composers Henry Butler (d. 1652) who served at the court of Philip IV of Spain, and William Young (d. 1662), violist at Innsbruck, both of whom composed sonatas for various combinations of solo violins and bass viols. German and Italian musicians had been coming to England from early in the century. In the 1620s the German violist Ditrich Stoeffken (later as Theodore Steffkin, d. 1673) was in London, and joined the Private Musick of Charles I where he became admired for the brilliance of his solo playing and for his compositions. He returned to Germany during the Commonwealth, but took up his former position at the court of Charles II. Another German, Thomas Baltzar (c. 1631–1663) dazzled London audiences with his violin technique, his playing in the highest register of the violin and in multiple stops. The Moravian composer Gottfried Finger (c. 1660–1730) served in the Catholic chapel of James II from 1678, and composed considerable instrumental music including sonatas for bass viol, for recorders, and two violins all with continuo, as well as considerable incidental music for London plays. The invasion of England by Italian musicians reached its climax in the next century, but it was already under way with the arrival after 1670 of Nicola Matteis (after 1713). He was the first to bring to England the sound and concept of Italian violin playing, one writer calling him "a second to Corelli." A large number of his publications for violin and continuo were all published in London. Also an influence on the growing interest in Italian music was Giovanni Battista Draghi (c. 1640–1708), composer and keyboardist, who came to London as part of James II's unsuccessful plan to establish opera.

Keyboard Music

Keyboard music of the first decades of the seventeenth century, like all other major forms of English music at that time, had its roots in the sixteenth century, especially in the Elizabethan period. The early sixteenth century saw the development of distinctive organ settings of plainsongs for the Mass and Office. These remained the basis of much keyboard music, for example, as found in the early Elizabethan *Mulliner* manuscript. Also included are free contrapuntal forms labeled voluntary, fancy, or fantasia. Little keyboard music, however, seems to have developed until the end of the century, when another manuscript, *My Ladye Nevells Booke* (c. 1591), was devoted exclusively to keyboard pieces by William Byrd.[51] He led the way at the end of the Renaissance for what became a remarkable outpouring of music for harpsichord and virginals.[52] Clearly Byrd was the founder of the so-called virginalist school subsequently joined in the early decades of the next century by a number of composers, most importantly John Bull, Giles Farnaby, Orlando Gibbons, and Thomas Tomkins. Since most of the music was never published, knowledge of this significant body of English keyboard music is derived largely from manuscripts. An exception is *Parthenia, or the Maydenhead of the First Musicke that Ever was Printed for the Virginalls* (1612–13). Among the many manuscripts is the remarkable collection known as the *Fitzwilliam Virginal Book,* previously assumed by William Barclay Squire to have been copied by Francis Tregian (1574–1617), which contains nearly three hundred pieces by most of the major English keyboard composers.[53]

The majority of the ninety-five known pieces by Byrd[54] are dances, the most frequent being pavans and galliards, but almost every other type of keyboard form is also found: the imitative fantasia (or fancy), the freely improvisatory prelude, variations on popular songs, on plainsong and solmization syllables, on grounds, and the multimovement programmatic "battle" pieces. These works established a keyboard style for harpsichord (virginals) that in its cultivation by Byrd's successors had a decisive influence on keyboard music on the Continent, first and foremost on Dutch composers such as Sweelinck. Byrd's pieces both short and long are idiomatic for the keyboard and leave behind earlier keyboard transcriptions of vocal works. While most of the dances and settings of songs are homophonic, nevertheless Byrd's consummate contrapuntal artistry lies within many of the accompanying parts. No other aspect of his keyboard pieces is more impressive or more significant historically than the predominant recourse to variations, many of great length and complex developments. Byrd was the first to demand a keyboard technique of substantial virtuosity, replete with a considerable application of embellishments, which must have challenged the many Elizabethan amateurs as well as professional performers. Whereas his variation techniques possibly were influenced by the Spanish composers of *diferencias,* Byrd's stand apart with their greatly enriched forms and imaginative musical ideas and, many of them, by their exciting and climactic conclusions resulting from the steadily increasing brilliance and the technical difficulty of the keyboard figurations.

In general the keyboard works by John Bull stay within the parameters of Byrd's stylistic achievements. Bull was an eminent keyboard virtuoso who early in his career was organist at Hereford Cathedral, soon became a member of Queen Elizabeth's Chapel Royal, and received a Doctor of Music degree from Cambridge. He was organist to James I, and had a reputation as a fine organ builder. His several travels in Europe brought him international fame as a keyboardist, and he certainly helped to introduce the music of the English virginalist composers on the Continent. In 1613, because of a sexual scandal, he fled England for Belgium, where he remained and, after 1617, was organist at Antwerp cathedral. There are some two hundred keyboard works by Bull, a large number of them undoubtedly intended for organ, even if they were also suitable for harpsichord.[55] These include sets of cantus firmus and free figuration variations on plainsongs such as the *In nomine, Miserere, Salvator mundi, Salve Regina,* and others. Bull's contrapuntal prowess is amply demonstrated in the settings of solmization syllables *ut, re, mi, fa, sol, la.* The several fantasias are less contrapuntal than Byrd's and illustrate the greater emphasis on highly innovative keyboard figurations. Pavans and galliards continue to be the most common dances, but there are also a number of almans and corantos. Bull's inventiveness in using the keyboard stands out especially in his secular works where variation techniques predominate. Comparison of Byrd's twenty-two "Walsingham" variations with Bull's thirty variations on the same tune[56] confirms an increased intensity in Bull's virtuoso style. His variations are much richer in techniques that employ new and often difficult figures, for example, parallel thirds and sixths for each hand, rapid figurations containing repeated tones, various leaping figures antiphonally repeated between the hands, arpeggiated chords simultaneously in both hands, conflicting rhythms between the hands, and passages in which the hands must cross.

Among the other significant "virginalist" composers Giles Farnaby (c. 1563–1640) is the least consistent in the quality of his works. Of the fifty-three pieces known to have been composed by him, almost all appeared in the *Fitzwilliam Virginal Book,* a testimony to their popularity.[57] Farnaby was a joiner (woodworker) by trade, a composer as a hobby. His compositional skills were uneven, especially in contrapuntal technique. Many of the pieces are dances, some called jigg, toy, spagnoletta, and mask. His keyboard techniques are largely the same as Bull's but without the difficulties of virtuosity. Of greater significance are the keyboard works of Orlando Gibbons, the popularity of which is reflected in their numerous manuscript sources. The usual variety of pieces are found among the forty-five that survive:[58] preludes, fantasias, pavans and galliards, almans, corantos, and several variations on popular tunes and grounds. The third and last significant member of this trio forming the virginalist school was Thomas Tomkins. Many of his pieces were written between 1646 and 1654, at the very end of the English keyboard tradition. Among the seventy-three pieces preserved are many for organ based on liturgical melodies. There are also the usual dance forms and variations.[59] Much of the keyboard style reflects the past, and with exceptions seems remarkably conventional. As a student of Byrd, perhaps Tomkins found reflective pleasure at the end of his life in working with the forms and techniques of the earlier, most inventive period of English keyboard music.

The composing of keyboard music in general and especially works for organ almost totally ceased during the Commonwealth. Thus, the exuberant achievements of the "virginalist" composers ended. The destruction of church organs was a deciding factor, although organs in private homes were not uncommon. With the Restoration, foreign dance music became a major focus of English musical life, even though there is evidence of a developing keyboard style among English composers, a large number of them unknown today. Those who can be identified include Albertus Bryne (c. 1621–1668), Matthew Locke, William Lawes, Richard Portman (d. 1656), Edward Lowe (c. 1610–1682), Henry Purcell, and, most important in number of works, John Blow.[60] While little of his harpsichord music has been published, there is an edition of forty-five organ voluntaries and psalm settings. These are serious, mostly contrapuntal works in fugal style and with very little display of keyboard virtuosity.[61]

Solo Music for Lute and Other Tablature Instruments[62]

The lute was the dominant solo instrument in Europe from 1500 to around 1700, and its popularity is well documented in all the major European regions with the exception of Spain where the guitar and vihuela de mano were preferred. The lute was known at the Tudor court of Henry VIII (who together with his children played the instrument), where it was performed primarily by Flemish and French artists. The earliest manuscript evidence of English lute music comes from shortly before mid-century. The greatest period for English lute music was from around 1590 through the first two decades of the new century. However, a continuing interest in lute music remained until the Restoration when the playing of solo lute music in general came to an end. The lute was not, of course, the only instrument whose music was written in tablature. Reference has been made to the popularity of the lyra viol. But other plucked string instruments include the cittern, which originated in Italy, while the bandora and orpharion had English origins. These three instruments, however, had wire strings rather than those of gut. In the second half of the century, at the court of Charles II, the five-course guitar was introduced by the outstanding Italian composer and guitarist Francesco Corbetta,[63] and the instrument remained popular in England well into the eighteenth century.

The lute repertory is large, containing some sixteen hundred pieces. Little of this music was published and most of the extant sources are in manuscripts. The earliest English instructions for lute were two published in 1568 and 1574, and based on the now lost French source by LeRoy, *Brève et facile Instruction pour apprendre la tablature, à accorder, conduire et disposer la main sur le Luth* (1567). Another, *A New Booke of Tabliture,* was published by William Barclay in 1596. An important lute method appeared in 1603, *The Schoole of Musicke,* by Thomas Robinson. The only other English lute publication of the first part of the seventeenth century is Robert Dowland's *Varietie of Lute-lessons* (London, 1610), which includes in addition to pieces by Italians, French, and Germans also those by English composers including Robert and his father John Dowland.

The greatest and most influential composer of lute music during the "golden age" unquestionably was John Dowland. Some seventy-five pieces survive of established authenticity (plus some sixteen others of uncertain ascription), which present examples of innovation and variety of forms and styles unmatched by his contemporaries. While famous for his melancholic pieces, especially the widely copied and varied *Lachrimae* pavan, Dowland's favorite form was the galliard. He also composed almans, jigs, corantos, and settings of songs, and popular tunes. Many of them appear in various arrangements and adaptations. There are seven superb contrapuntal fantasias;, two of them are exceptional being based on a six-note chromatic figure that in "Forlorne Hope" descends and in "Farewell" ascends. Other significant contributors to solo lute music from this period include Daniel Bacheler (1572–1619),[64] Francis Cutting (fl. 1571–1596), and Robert Johnson (ii) (c. 1583–1633).[65]

Music for solo lute in the period leading up to the Commonwealth exhibits two distinct styles. One reflects a few English composers' continuing love for the old contrapuntal style with emphasis on thematic development and employment of the full range of the instrument as found in lute fantasias and pavans. Most unusual among examples of this type are those found in a manuscript by John Wilson (1595–1674),[66] thirty fantasias with varying styles composed in all the major and minor keys. Some are short and homophonic; some, however, are imitative and motivic, not unlike ricercars, and in several the writing is highly chromatic. The second style resulted from seminal changes in lute music coming from the steadily increasing influences of French composers and performers. At the court of Charles I, his consort Queen Henrietta Maria had come from France with her retinue. In 1625 Jacques Gautier (d. before 1660), a highly successful French lutenist, entered the queen's service as well as did other French singers/lutenists; and outstanding French lutenists such as Ennemond Gaultier (1575–1651) and René Mesangeau (d. 1638) were also in England at this time. Another French lutenist, Jean Mercure (c. 1600–before 1661), was established at the court of Charles I in 1641, and was one of several bringing the free-voiced texture and heavily ornamented *style brisé* of the French lutenists and keyboardists to England. It was this new element of lute style that quickly brought about significant changes in English lute music.

Little lute music survives after 1660, and there are few evidences of a continuing interest in the instrument. There is the Burwell lute tutor from between 1660 and 1672, and as the last published source of English lute music the famous if largely retrospective work of Thomas Mace, *Musick's Monument; or, a Remembrancer of the Best Practical Musick* (London, 1676). Part II, entitled *The Lute Made Easie,* is important for the practical details regarding the instrument, and a method and simple pieces for developing a technique. Mace's emphasis is largely on the style of English lute performance developed earlier between 1620 and 1640.

The English Court Masque and Early Opera

The English court masque originated at the Tudor court and in the seventeenth century became a complex theatrical form of entertainment involving elaborate costuming, dancing by masqued courtiers to a specific choreography, in a hall of a palace decorated with appropriate scenery related to the allegorical or mythological theme of the work, with spoken dialogue, songs, and instrumental music. This combination of spectacle, dancing, vocal and instrumental music, while demonstrating some obvious influences from the Italian *intermedio* and the French *ballet de cour,* nevertheless became a uniquely English tradition in design and purpose. Masques were performed to honor and to entertain the sovereign and the attending court audience. Of great importance, they served a political purpose in impressing by their lavishness foreign ambassadors and other dignitaries. Masques were also a feature of the seasonal festivities by the four law societies of the Inns of Court. But their popularity also led to numerous masques created for performances in the homes of aristocrats, and they were frequently included as part of stage plays, for example, in the works of Shakespeare. And the masque had a defining influence on the development of Restoration semi-opera and early English opera.

The development of the masque reached the apex of its popularity during the reigns of James I and Charles I.[67] The brilliance of these masques resulted largely from the gifted team of poet, dramatist, and masque librettist Ben Jonson (1572 or 1573–1637) and architect and stage designer Inigo Jones (1573–1652). The former achieved a structural coherence and a dramatic unity for what was a collection of diverse forms of poetry, music, and spectacle. Jonson's masques were meant to entertain but also to instruct, and were a means to propagandize the role of the court by illuminating the greatness and wisdom of the king who was protector of English society. Jones, the outstanding English architect of the period, was essential to the development of the masque as a theatrical event. He was both stage and costume designer, creator of stage machinery, producer, and at times coauthor of masques. The Jacobean court masques were usually organized into a loose structure of contrasts:

(1) procession, (2) allegorical speech or dialogue, (3) anti-masque songs and dances, (4) discovery of the scene of the masque, (5) song I, (6) entry dance I of the masquers and descent to the floor, (7) song II, (8) main dance II of the masquers, (9) song III, (10) revels with the audience, (11) song IV, (12) return to the stage and final dance III of the masquers or grand chorus.

The dances were performed by courtiers, not by professionals. For revels these dancers went to the audience to choose noble ladies for social dancing which could last for hours. The masque singers were male professionals. The anti-masque, first introduced by Jonson in 1609, presented comic or grotesque dances, pantomime, spoken burlesques, singing, and dancing all created by professionals involving low humor, bizarre low-class characters, and pantomimes of animals, witches, and various other magical figures.

Masques were seldom performed more than once, after which the work was essentially abandoned. The ephemeral nature of the masque handicaps any attempt to fully evaluate these works as musical-theatrical totalities. A large number of masque texts are preserved, but almost nothing remains of something like a score giving the music for the songs and dances, a script specifying speeches and the action, or a description of the choreography of the dances. Masque songs by the important composers such as Alfonso Ferrabosco (ii), John Coprario, Thomas Campion, and Nicholas Lanier survive in printed and manuscript collections. They are usually similar to the lute songs published at the time, often by the same composers, and can be light dance songs, or more serious declamatory melodies with affective harmonies. These subsequent publications of masque songs, however, are usually in the conventional form of ayres as melody and a bass for realization by lute. In the masque texts, indications often state that songs were sung in various vocal and instrumental ensembles in several parts.

The dances, which form the masque's most important musical and entertainment elements, are also preserved in many prints and manuscripts. They usually give titles to the dances that might suggest the work from which they have been taken. However, the attempts to extract these dances and to attribute them to actual masques have seldom been convincing, primarily because the titles are often generic and could have come from a number of different works.[68] The various collections of dances often contain tunes of triteness, patched together out of common musical motives. Many of the sources give the dances in only two parts, for example in British Library, Add. MS 10444 (containing 138 dances). Others have arrangements in five and six parts that may be similar to arrangements used in masque performances. Significant collections include John Adson's *Courtly Masquing Ayres* (London, 1621),[69] and the one by William Brade, a violinist and violist who resided mostly in Germany, *Newe ausserlesene liebliche Branden, Intraden, Mascharaden, Balletten, All'manden, Couranten, Volten, Auffzüge, und frembde Tänze . . . ; Mit fünf Stimmen: Auff allerley musicalischen Instrumenten, Insonderheit auff Fiolen zugebrauchen* (Hamburg, 1617).[70]

The instrumentalists were drawn from the King's Musick, a large and diverse group divided into ensembles for each of the component parts of the masque. "Loud" music was played by wind instruments—oboes and sackbuts—to announce the arrival of the king and/or the beginning of the masque. It also was used for transformation scenes (to cover the sound of machinery), as well as at times in the anti-masque. In the latter, all kinds of unusual or eccentric instruments could be introduced to provide strangeness or "rude" music, including various percussion instruments, folk instruments, bagpipes, and anything else that would contrast with the normalcy of sound appropriate to the masque proper. Here the conventional accompaniment for dances was the five-part violin band. Lutes accompanied songs and were often used in large numbers, usually twelve, and at times also were used to accompany dancing.

Masques continued to dominate Charles I's court entertainments, although very little of their music remains. At least some of the music in the masques of William Lawes is preserved for his three works: James Shirley's *Triumph of Peace* (1634), and William Davenant's *The Triumphs of the Prince d'Amour* (1636) and *Britannia triumphas* (1638).[71] Another important aspect of the history of the masque for which little music remains are those works performed away from court, at times for the royal family, at times in the homes of the nobility. The most famous of these was the masque to Milton's *Comus* performed at Ludlow Castle in 1634, but for which only five songs by Henry Lawes exist.

The advent of the Commonwealth and the closing of the theaters largely ended the masque tradition. A few were written for private performances and particularly as a form of school dramas. Most important of the former was Shirley's *Cupid and Death,* created to entertain the ambassador of Portugal in March 1653. Another private performance in 1659 employed a revision, preserved only in Locke's manuscript, which is the only complete score to a masque written before the Restoration.[72] Sections of music by Christopher Gibbons from the first version were retained by Morley, who composed new music for much of the work. *Cupid and Death* has particular significance because it contains the greatest number of lengthy recitatives known in English staged drama to this time.

The question of the influence of Italian monody and recitative styles on English music has generated considerable speculation.[73] References to employing recitative do suggest that as early as 1617, in Lanier's masque *Vision of Delight*, Delight "spake in song (stylo recitativo)." In another masque also by Ben Jonson performed the same year, *Lovers Made Men,* reportedly "the whole Maske was sung (after the Italian manner) stylo recitativo by Master Nicholas Lanier, who ordered and made both the Scene and the Musicke." These comments however, appear only in the folio of Ben Jonson's works published much later in 1640, not in the edition of 1617, and no music survives. Another proposed candidate for having composed the earliest recitative has already been cited, Lanier's lament, *Hero and Leander,* of uncertain date but some time after 1628 with no source earlier than the Restoration. Yet it has been shown that as early as the first decade of the century Dowland was composing airs, for example, *Welcome Black Night,* in a monodic style that appears to imitate the Italian style.

English composers were certainly knowledgeable about the musical innovations of the Italians, both from travel to the Continent and also from Italian musicians in England. Many composers of airs wrote dramatic melodies that are usually described as "declamatory," which often appears to mean "recitative in an English manner." The search for Italian-style recitatives in English music of the seventeenth century music is futile, not because English composers avoided the new style, but because the concept itself as wedded to the Italian language could not be applied to the English language. The goal of most English composers of recitatives, as with the Italians, was to compose music for affective texts, to support but also to illuminate the meaning of the words with musically enriched declamation. English poets often contrasted the Italian language to the English, none better than John Dryden, when reflecting on the difficulties of writing recitative in English:

All, who are conversant in the *Italian,* cannot but observe, that it is the softest, the sweetest, the most harmonious, not only of a modern Tongue, but even beyond any of the Learned. It seems indeed to have been invented for the sake of Poetry and Musick: the Vowels are so abounding in all Words, especially in the Terminations of them, that excepting some few Monosyllables, the whole Language ends in them . . . the natural harshness of the *French* or their perpetual ill accent, [can never] be refin'd into perfect Harmony like the *Italian.* The English has yet more natural disadvantages than the *French;* our original Teutonique consisting most in Monosyllables, and those incumber'd with Consonants cannot possibly be freed from those Inconveniences.[74]

It was one of the stunning achievements of English composers in the seventeenth century to have found within the idiomatic aspects of their language a potential for musical expression, enabling Henry Purcell to create one of Western civilization's great repertories of song.

The Restoration of Charles II witnessed a rapid development of theater in London, and it was in theatrical works that the masque was absorbed along with a great deal of song, dance, and instrumental music. As for opera, which by the end of the century flourished in many of the capitals of Europe, England had almost none. William Davenant (1606–1668), dramatist, theater manager, and poet, is usually credited with having written the first English opera, *The Siege of Rhodes,* with the vocal music by Henry Lawes, Henry Cooke, and Matthew Locke. It had a private performance at Rutland House in September 1656 and later at the Cockpit in Drury Lane in 1658, but the music does not survive. The two operas known to have been heard in London resulted from the command of Charles II. He brought French composer Louis Grabu (? fl. 1665–1694) to court, where he directed and composed additional music for Robert Cambert's and Perrin's opera *Ariane, ou Le mariage de Bacchus* performed at the Theatre Royal, Drury Lane, on 30 March 1674 to celebrate the marriage of James, Duke of York (the future James II) to Mary of Modena. It was the first all-sung opera performed by professionals in England (music is lost). Grabu also composed music for Dryden's opera *Albion and Albanius,* produced at the Dorset Garden theater in 1685 as part of celebrations for the continuation of the reign of the Stuarts. The death of Charles II and the political upheaval created by Monmouth's Rebellion contributed to the opera's failure. Purcell's *Dido and Aeneas* (before December 1689) stands out as the unique exception as England's greatest opera of the century.

As a compromise to English taste, a new form, the semi-opera, appeared in 1673 at the new Dorset Garden theater. It was conceived of by the actor-manager Thomas Betterton together with the playwright Thomas Shadwell and composer Matthew Locke. Semi-operas brought together the Restoration play, the Jacobean masque with a combination of spoken texts for main characters and song and dance for minor characters, and elaborate stage scenery and machinery. In 1674 Shakespeare's *Tempest* was presented with great success as a semi-opera with music by a committee of composers including Pelham Humfrey, Locke, and others. In 1675 *Psyche,* adapted by Thomas Shadwell from the French, was composed by Matthew Locke. The most significant works are those with music by Henry Purcell: *Dioclesian, King Arthur,* and *The Fairy-Queen.*

CHAPTER ELEVEN

Henry Purcell (1659–1695)

THE PREVIOUS CHAPTER related the significant musical developments occurring in seventeenth-century England. In examining the achievements of Henry Purcell, there is little new to add. His musical style and its forms and techniques would all appear to reflect most of what was achieved in English music before he began his career. However, Henry Purcell was peerless in talent and temperament. It was the originality of his genius, the uniqueness of the musical invention he brought to bear on the traditions and conventions of English music in which he was trained, that made Purcell one of England's greatest composers. It is astonishing to contemplate the potency of his creative power, which in the brevity of only seventeen years between 1678 and his death produced a catalogue of works containing in addition to string ensemble works and keyboard music, twenty-four odes and welcome songs, sixty-five verse and full anthems, more than 230 songs, over fifty catches, as well as *Dido and Aeneas,* and music for the Restoration theater, including semi-operas such as *King Arthur, The Fairy-Queen,* and *The Indian Queen.* Yet it has only been in the final decades of the twentieth century that Purcell's musical greatness became better known. With the exception of the masterful *Dido and Aeneas,* a few of the Cecilian odes and church anthems, a handful of the songs, and a little of the ensemble instrumental and keyboard music, the glories of Purcell's music were largely ignored or forgotten along with the largest amount of seventeenth-century English music.

Purcell's life appears to have been preordained for music since both his father (also named Henry) and his uncle Thomas were singers with important positions in the Chapel Royal. The composer's brother Daniel (d. 1717) was an organist and also a composer. Like other members of his family, Henry Purcell spent his entire life in the service of the kings of England during the Restoration. The very few recorded facts concerning his life give us little more than milestones in that career. As a boy he joined the Chapel Royal choir, trained at first by Captain Henry Cooke and after 1672 by Pelham Humfrey. When his voice broke in 1673, requiring he leave the choir, he became assistant to John Hingston, keeper of the keyboard and wind instruments at court. The following year Purcell was the tuner of the organs in Westminster Abbey, and for the two subsequent years he worked as a copier of organ parts to choral music sung in the Abbey. In 1677 he succeeded Matthew Locke as composer for the court violins, and in 1679 he followed John Blow, who had also been his teacher, as the Abbey organist. In 1682 he became one of the organists of the Chapel Royal and in 1683 Purcell succeeded John Hingston as keeper of the king's instruments. In 1685 King James II appointed him court harpsichordist, and his royal appointments were renewed by the new king, William III.

Purcell's music has stimulated a great deal of commentary regarding which musical influences affected his style. Basically, Purcell was a conservative composer deeply rooted in English music growing out of the sixteenth century and, as has been shown, characteristic of all of the major composers to precede Purcell. His own training was exposed to powerful influences from the teaching and music of Humfrey, and especially Blow, and his associations with Locke, John Jenkins, and William Child. Foreign influences can be identified, and their integration into his own musical style becomes one of the fascinating aspects of his music.[1] However, the primary characteristic of Purcell's music is almost always dependent on contrapuntal textures. Equally important to his vocal style was the remarkable relationship between his musical ideas and the sound and structure of the English language. This symbiotic union of the phonology of the language and the sung word is difficult to explain, but it is a basic element in what can be called the Purcellian sound. Also fundamental to those distinctive characteristics of his vocal music is Purcell's employment of an extensive variety of musical-rhetorical techniques that so frequently underscore the affective and musical impact of his dramatic texts.

Instrumental Music

Purcell's instrumental music is more extensive than catalogues usually reveal. The reason is that the largest number of his important and innovative works for instruments appear in his vocal music as overtures, introductions, ritornellos, and dances. A modest number of keyboard pieces are extant. Many are arrangements of songs and other music from Purcell's plays and semi-operas as well as music by other composers, probably originating in part as teaching pieces. Instrumental works for string ensembles vary between the famous Chacony in G minor, several pavans, and the significant sets of fantasias and sonatas. The fantasias all originate around 1680 and are usually viewed as intensive studies by Purcell to become familiar with the strict contrapuntal style of pre-Restoration composers. In addition to the Fantasia on a Ground for three instruments and continuo and the Fantasia on One Note for five viols, there are twelve major consort works: three in three parts, nine in four parts, as well as a six-part and a seven-part In nomine. This is music based on what would have been viewed by this time as an archaic style. The viol consort had largely been replaced by the violin family of instruments. And Purcell eschews any emphasis on those popular dance forms found in most Restoration string music. No other composer around 1680 would have considered the long-favored practice of contrapuntal settings of the In nomine as relevant. And the fantasias themselves besides their contrapuntal textures have little that resemble such recent string ensemble music as that of Matthew Locke. Each of the fantasias consists of a varying number of contrasting slow and faster sections in which the essential compositional style is imitative, with a vigorous display of various forms of contrapuntal artifice. This is not, however, characterless contrapuntal technique. Among the best of the fantasias there is an individuality of affective expression uniquely Purcellian even at this early stage of his creative life. And in such a contrapuntal *tour de force* in prima prattica style as the In nomine in seven parts there breathes a grandeur and intensity of expression that has little connection to this style's origins in the sixteenth century (see Example 11.1[2]).

Why Purcell wrote these works is unknown. One can speculate that in part they were retrospective studies in the contrapuntal style that had dominated English music before the Commonwealth but had been largely lost by the effects of the civil war and the ban on church music. Purcell, however, created much more than exercises. Many of the fantasias are miniature dramas leading the consort players from the serious and at times sad or tragic slow movements to the technically brilliant miniatures in the "brisk" sections. For example, in Fantasia No. 5 in B flat major (Z536),[3] how much eloquence and painful affect fill the opening ten measures as the music collapses into chromatic descent following the surprise of the A flat seventh in the first measure, only to soar by chromatic steps through the

EXAMPLE 11.1 Purcell, In nomine in 7 parts (conclusion)

EXAMPLE 11.2   Purcell, Fantasia No. 5 in B flat major (Z536)

penultimate measure, with an intensity tightened by the minor second in measure seven, the minor ninth in measure eight, and the parallel tritones in the upper parts into the next measure (see Example 11.2[4]).

Several of the fantasias have a ricercar-like character, as seen in the opening to the Fantasia No. 7 in C minor (Z538), in which the two thematic motives in the opening measure largely dominate the movement by alternating or overlapping in a seamless flow of three- and four-part counterpoint (see Example 11.3[5]).

In contrast, the twenty-two trio sonatas for two violins, viola da gamba, and continuo for organ or harpsichord, probably composed sometime early in the 1680s, demonstrate Purcell's integration of recent developments in string ensemble compositions into his own style. His first published work was the twelve sonatas of 1683. Another ten appeared posthumously in 1697. The first set includes a preface by Purcell, which has remained famous for the following statement:

> . . . for its author, he has faithfully endeavour'd a just imitation of the most fam'd Italian Masters; principally, to bring seriousness and gravity of that sort of Musick into vogue, and reputation among our Country-men, whose humor, 'tis time now, should begin to loath the levity, and balladry of our neighbours.

Two questions arise from these comments: Who are the "neighbours" whose music is characterized by "levity, and balladry," and who are the most famed Italian Masters that Purcell wishes to imitate to bring seriousness and gravity of that music into vogue? It is

EXAMPLE 11.3 Purcell, Fantasia No. 7 in C minor (Z538)

generally agreed that the "neighbours" refers to the French. As to "the most fam'd Italian Masters," the most perceptive opinion is probably correct in suggesting Roman composers of string ensemble music of the mid-seventeenth century: Cazzati, Legrenzi, Vitali. Also important are the sonatas (called *simfonie*) attributed to Lelio Colista (although some of them are actually by the Roman violinist Carlo Ambrogio Lonati). Colista's instrumental works seem to have found particular appreciation in Restoration England, although they existed only in manuscript copies.

Sorting out Italian stylistic elements in Purcell's music involves both speculation and

EXAMPLE 11.4   Purcell, from Sonata No. 5 in A minor (Z794)

uncertainty.[6] And the sonatas are so diverse in structure as to resist generalization. They consist of four, five, and, exceptionally, six movements, usually distinguished by contrasting tempos and styles. At least one and often more dance movements in triple time are included, although without identifying labels. Many aspects of Purcell's fantasias and pavans remain, such as the elaborate contrapuntal movements employing augmentation and inversion techniques. Also, very Purcellian, *recte* English, remains the frequent use in the slow sections of stark, unprepared dissonances, false relations, and chromaticism (see Example 11.4[7]). However, the Italianate two-part violin texture over the bass opens up the contrapuntal matrix to greater clarity than found in the fantasias. Also Italian style would appear to be the basis of frequent uses in imitation of simpler but longer themes (see Example 11.5a[8]) and others frequently with strong scalar or intervallic profiles and vigorous rhythmic energy (see Examples 11.5b[9] and c[10]). These characteristics are found especially in movements labeled "canzona." Other thematic ideas, however, remain very much in Purcell's musical language, as in the typical dotted rhythms so characteristic of his style. Of particular significance for the future development of Purcell's compositional achievement is the chaconne Sonata No. 6 in G minor (Z807)[11] on a five-measure descending minor sixth: G F E flat D C B flat C D G, of French character, repeated forty-four times. Also of interest is the interior structure achieved by dividing the chaconne into sections marked

EXAMPLE 11.5a Purcell, from Sonata No. 8 in G major (Z797)

by the infrequent coming together of the upper parts in a cadence with the ostinato bass. This technique of overlapping of the upper parts on an ostinato formula became a significant characteristic of Purcell's numerous ostinato settings.

Sacred Music: The Church Anthems

The sacred music of Purcell consists of some seventy anthems, thirty-seven sacred solo and ensemble songs, a morning and evening Service, a Magnificat and Nunc Dimittis, and the Te Deum and Jubilate in D for Cecilian celebrations in 1694. Considering the short span of Purcell's creative life, this is an extraordinary amount of music. Together with the large number of sacred anthems by his teacher and contemporary John Blow, their great corpus of sacred music stands together as the summit of English Baroque church music developed over more than a century. The earlier description of anthems as either full or verse remains, although with some modification. Full anthems for chorus only and no strings or independent continuo can be modified to add solo voices as well. The verse anthem for solo voices with some choral insertions (often at the midpoint and conclusion) and continuo but no strings is the most common form composed by Purcell. This, too, appears modified as the "Symphony" anthem for solo voices, chorus, continuo, and a string ensemble of varying sizes.

Purcell's works were largely composed for performances at the court of Charles II, a

EXAMPLE 11.5b   Purcell, from Sonata No. 1 in B minor (Z802)

few dating probably from as early as the late 1670s. Not many were written after 1689 and the accession to the throne of William and Mary. The decisive influence on Purcell's anthems was Charles II's demand that his Chapel Royal have music less serious than formerly and of French character. It should be tuneful, with perceptible metrical emphases as in dances, and with the lightness of French style. He required a string ensemble to join the Chapel Royal musicians. As with other influences on Purcell's music, these new ideas were integrated into his own style, enriching but not overshadowing other stylistic elements that were decidedly Purcellian and English. The texts for Purcell's anthems are almost entirely from the Psalter, the Collects of the Book of Common Prayer, and the Authorized Version of the Bible. Most of them offered the composer words of expressive power

EXAMPLE 11.5c   Purcell, from Sonata No. 3 in A minor (Z804)

and imagery ideally suited to Purcell's command of the musical-rhetorical potential of his music.

An overview of the anthems substantiates the fact of Purcell's developing musical style. Among those that would appear to be his earliest anthems, originating in the late 1670s and early 1680s, many illustrate Purcell's contrapuntal prowess. Outstanding examples are to be found in verse anthems such as *Hear Me, O Lord* (Z13A and B), *Blessed is he whose unrighteousness* (Z28), the ten-part *Blow up the trumpet in Sion* (Z10), *Bow down Thine ear* (Z11), *Let mine eyes run down with tears* (Z24), and *Save me, O God* (Z51).[12] The latter opens with an example of five-part imitative counterpoint that defeats any possibility of text clarity and resembles many of the more or less dense textures found in the consort fantasias (see Example 11.6).

Purcell's early delight in the musical challenges of imitative techniques is also evident in this anthem's concluding five-part canon for "and mine eyes have seen his desire upon mine enemies." Full anthems are in the minority in Purcell's output. Many of them illustrate a close relationship to a *stile antico* with the bass accompaniment *basso sequente,* and Purcell's most complex contrapuntal techniques. Among these, which are probably from between circa 1680 and 1682, are *Hear My Prayer, O Lord* (Z15), *Lord, how long wilt thou be angry* (Z25), *Thou art my God* (Z35), *O God Thou hast cast us out* (Z36), *O Lord God of hosts* (Z37), and the profoundly beautiful funeral sentences written for the funeral of Queen Mary (from the Book of Common Prayer), *Man that is born of woman* (Z27), *In*

EXAMPLE 11.6   Purcell, from *Save me, O God* (Z51)

the midst of life (Z17A and B), and *Thou know'st Lord, the secrets of our hearts* (Z58B and C). In particular, *In the midst of life,* with its extreme chromaticism and dissonances for the affect of "the bitter pains of eternal death," seems even more retrospective in style and technique (see Example 11.7).

Others among the early anthems, however, indicate that one of Purcell's developing aims was to assure text comprehension. This was achieved by various techniques such as frequent passages in homophony, the reduction of the number of parts, especially in solo verse sections, and by beginning contrapuntal movements with lengthy subjects usually expressing musically the text's rhetorical or affective meaning. These stand alone at the outset and subsequently avoid frequent overlapping of parts except where the text is aligned in all or most of the parts, as in Example 11.8.

During the period between circa 1682 and 1685, Purcell devoted his composing for the Chapel Royal almost entirely to the composition of fifteen verse anthems with string en-sembles. Many of these are considerably expanded in various formal designs and have

EXAMPLE 11.7 · Purcell, from *In the Midst of Life* (Z17A)

superb solo and ensemble sections. Most begin with a "symphony" for four-part string ensemble. The form, resembling superficially the French overture, usually has two sections, the first of which is slow and in duple meter and the second faster, dancelike, and in triple meter. The first section often emphasizes dotted rhythms. Seldom, however, does Purcell's music suggest a close imitation of French instrumental style. The symphony may return later in the work, most often at the center of the work. The string ensemble often has ritornellos, especially at the close of vocal solos or ensembles, and in rare instances the violin serves as an obbligato accompaniment to vocal sections. In addition to the standard SATB chorus, most of the verse sections are for alto, tenor, and one or two basses, but one omits the tenor and only two add two sopranos (boy trebles). One of these, *Praise the Lord, O my soul, and all that is within me* (Z47), divides the six singers into two ensembles (SST/TBB). In effect, the two groups often are scored as a divided ensemble not unlike the *cori spezzati* familiar from the earlier Venetian practice.

This great variety of forms and combinations of the voices gives these anthems their outstanding musical richness. There is a notable increase in dotted rhythms in the instrumental and vocal writing, at times generated by words related to affects of joy, gladness, praise, triumph, etc., but in other cases more or less neutral in affect and used either as a general stylistic component or to give rhythmic emphasis to melismatic passages. The

EXAMPLE 11.8   Purcell, from *Out of the Deep* (Z48)

reverse rhythmic "snap" of sixteenth to dotted eighth note is also a common means for achieving dynamic emphasis to individual words and melismatic passages.

The greatness of Purcell's anthems, as of all his vocal music, lies in its inexhaustible variety, dramatic intensity, and vocal beauty. Whether as dramatic recitative, arioso, or song forms, the language of the texts, the imagery and emotional content, and the sound of the words inspired Purcell to numerous forms of musical discourse that are a crowning achievement of seventeenth-century Baroque music. The Chapel Royal clearly included singers of exceptional abilities, for the vocal writing is often challenging, both in range and technical aspects such as long melismatic passages. Purcell took particular delight in the exceptional bass voice of John Gostling (c. 1650–1733), who joined the Chapel Royal in 1679. There is a noticeable emphasis on the bass part in many of these anthems, especially when the texts suggest an extensive male vocal range, as in *They that go down to the sea in ships* (Z57) (see Example 11.9).

EXAMPLE 11.9   Purcell, from *They that go down to the sea in ships* (Z57)

My heart is inditing (Z30), an anthem composed in 1685 for the coronation of James II, was performed at the end of the ceremony with the crowning of his queen, Mary of Modena. It is an exceptional work for an exceptional occasion and was performed in Westminster Abbey, which offered Purcell, in addition to the singers and the twenty-four violins of the Royal Chapel, some twenty boys and forty-eight men, none too many considering the great vaulted space of the Abbey. The occasion, the place of performance, and the great assembly of English society motivated Purcell to compose a work of eloquence and majesty. The scoring is larger than found in other sacred works: four-part strings employed throughout, eight-part chorus (SSAATTBB) and eight soloists (SSAATBBB—at places reduced to six or seven parts). The long opening two-part symphony (each part repeated) is followed by the chorus in eight-part counterpoint, which with such a large number of voices heard at the ceremony would have made a powerful effect. The texture quickly resolves to grandiose homophonic writing, which in general is true of other sections that have initial contrapuntal passages. The solo verse sections tend to be largely homophonic or antiphonal responses between homophonic groupings of the parts. Several of the sections emphasize the frequent inclination of Purcell to favor, when appropriate, dotted rhythms (already heard in the second part of the symphony). The verse following the repeat of the symphony, "Harken, O daughter, consider, incline thine ear," is especially beautiful in its combination of contrapuntal elegance and antiphonal repetitions. The return of the chorus with massive block chords for "Praise the Lord, O Jerusalem" in retrospect seems "Handelian," which raises the frequently pondered question as to the possible influence on Handel of Purcell's sacred vocal works.

The number and to some extent the quality of Purcell's anthems decline after 1685. This would appear to result from the growing disinterest of the sovereign in the Chapel Royal during the reigns of both James II and William and Mary. Purcell returns to the verse anthem without instruments in a little more than half of the eighteen composed between 1686–87 and 1694, while the remainder continue to employ strings. Many of the verse anthems are rather short, and are marked by the greater reliance on long melismatic passages in the solo writing, for example, the passage for alto and bass from *O give thanks unto the Lord* (Z33), composed in 1693 (see Example 11.10).

Such lengthy passages of vocal embellishment were routinely employed by Purcell in some of the late anthems to extend movements with brief texts in which word and phrase repetitions are apt to be more extensive. Several of these last anthems are, however, among the finest Purcell composed. One of them is *O sing unto the Lord* (Z44), of exceptionally large dimensions in thirteen sections and rich in various compositional techniques. Composed in 1688, its grand musical content suggests a performance for a major court event. The opening symphony is unusual in that, unlike most of the others, it avoids even the superficial characteristics of a French overture. It is largely homophonic and without a trace of dotted rhythms. It closes with five measures that create a slower effect by changing from a duple meter of eighth notes to one of half notes, and the harmony is suddenly more dissonant. The impression is not unlike the brief second movements in Italian concertos. The third movement is very Italianate with a lightly imitative texture and the stress on the

EXAMPLE 11.10   Purcell, from *O give thanks unto the Lord* (Z33)

upper two parts supported by a "walking" bass. The chorus is particularly prominent, unlike its function in most verse anthems:[13]

(a) Verse: bass, with continuo, eight measures—"O sing unto the Lord"

(b) Chorus: with strings, fifteen measures—"Alleluja"

(c) Verse: bass with continuo, ten measures—"Sing unto the Lord all the whole earth"

(d) Chorus: with strings, fifteen measures—"Alleluja"

(e) Strings [ritornello]: twenty-eight measures

(f) Verse: four parts with continuo, twenty-one measures—"Sing unto the Lord and praise His name"

(g) Verse: four parts with strings, twelve measures—"Declare his honor to the heathen"

(h) Chorus: with strings, thirteen measures—"Glory and worship are before Him"

(i) Verse: soprano and tenor with continuo (ostinato bass), forty-two measures—"The Lord is great"

(j) Ritornello based on preceding ostinato, thirty-seven measures

(k) Verse: five parts, twenty measures—"O worship the Lord"

(l) Verse: bass alternating (adding onto) chorus, twenty-three measures—"Tell it out among the heathens"

(m) Verse: five parts, joining onto the chorus, fifty measures—"Alleluja"

EXAMPLE 11.11   Purcell, from *Blessed are they that fear the Lord* (Z5)

Finally, not to be overlooked is the particularly beautiful anthem, *Blessed are they that fear the Lord* (Z5). It was composed, probably as a royal commission, early in 1688 for the Thanksgiving "appoint'd to be in London & 12 miles round, . . . for the Queen being with Child." The form combines the usual aspects of a conventional two-part symphony, and a setting of Psalm 128 in a combination of ensemble and solo verses, with only three measures for chorus in the conclusion of the "alleluja." The unusual if not unique feature of the anthem is the use of a recurring two-measure motive, "O well is thee," always sung to the same pitches by two boy trebles in parallel thirds (see Example 11.11). It interrupts the first solo bass passage three times: "for thou shalt eat the labour of thine hands," "and happy, happy, happy shalt thou be," and "Thy wife shall be as the fruitful vine." It concludes the following passage for alto, "thy children like the olive branches round about thy table," and also the bass verse, "the Lord thy God from out of Sion shall so bless thee." Lastly, the two sopranos with the first four notes of the motive begin an antiphonal section with the two lower parts of alto and bass in which "O well is thee" is repeated several times before the passage continues with "and happy, happy shalt thou be." Do the two boy sopranos sing as angels or perhaps as unborn children? Their assurances are, in the psalm, clearly directed to the king, but might they also express in Purcell's setting assurance of good health to the queen? Whatever the interpretation, the musical effect is magical and mysterious, and Purcell has created an unusual Baroque affect of strangeness added to beauty.

Odes and Welcome Songs

Purcell's twenty-four odes and welcome songs, while not all of the same high quality, include a large number of his most mature and musically imperishable masterworks. With a few exceptions they were composed for specific court celebrations with a focus solely on members of the royal family. The reorganization of the Chapel Royal by Charles II gave Purcell an excellent group of soloists as well as a strong chorus. The royal string band was at times supplemented with brass and woodwinds. Whereas one might think a composer would be less enthusiastic about composing overtly political sentiments often couched in bombastic and obsequious poetry, clearly the results indicate Purcell relished these opportunities to compose for the king and his family. The custom of performing odes at court had been limited in the 1660s and 1670s only to celebrating the New Year and the king's birthday. In the 1670s these were composed largely by John Blow who continued to share responsibilities for various odes once Purcell joined the court and when occasions requiring celebratory music were expanded.[14] Purcell's twenty-four odes and welcome songs fall into six distinct categories:[15]

Welcome songs for Charles II:

Welcome, Vicegerent of the mighty King (Z340)	1680
Swifter, Isis, swifter flow (Z336)	1681
The summer's absence unconcerned we bear (Z337)	1682
Fly, bold rebellion (Z324)	1683
From those serene and rapturous joys (Z326)	1684

Welcome songs for James II:

Why, why are all the muses mute? (Z343)	1685
Ye tuneful muses, raise your heads (Z344)	1686
Sound the trumpet, beat the drum (Z335)	1687

Birthday odes for Queen Mary II:

Now does the glorious day appear (Z332)	1689
Arise, my muse (Z320)	1690

Welcome, welcome, glorious morn (Z338)	1691
Love's goddess sure was blind (Z331)	1692
Celebrate this festival (Z321)	1693
Come, ye sons of art, away (Z323)	1694

Miscellaneous odes related to royal family:
What shall be done in behalf of the man (Z341)	1682
(welcome song, Duke of York)	
From hardy climes (Z325)	1683
(marriage ode, Lady Anne and Prince George of Denmark)	
Who can from joy refrain (Z342)	1695
(birthday song for Duke of Gloucester)	

Odes for St. Cecilia's Day (November 22nd):
Welcome to all the pleasures (Z339)	1683
Laudate Ceciliam (Z329)	1683
Raise, raise the voice (Z334)	1683
Hail! bright Cecilia (Z328)	1692

Miscellaneous odes for other occasions:
Celestial music did the gods inspire (Z322)	1689
(for Mr. Maidwell's School)	
Of old, when heroes thought it base (Z333)	1690
(the "Yorkshire Feast Song")	
Great parent, hail (Z327)	1694
(Centenary celebration, Trinity College, Dublin)	

Purcell wrote one or more odes for every year between 1680 and 1694 except during the year of revolution in 1688. They consist largely of welcome songs for Charles II and James II, and especially exquisite birthday odes for Queen Mary. In these fifteen years one witnesses changes in compositional procedures and style until Purcell, at the height of his creative powers, reaches his musical maturity. The odes begin in concept where the anthems end. They are in superficial ways patterned on the anthems' forms: each ode retains an opening symphony, usually in two parts, and a succession of solo, ensemble, and choral movements. In most of the odes, however, the forms are considerably enlarged, instrumental ritornellos and accompaniments have greater impact, and the vocal and choral writing is extended and often enriched contrapuntally. The declamatory solos, especially for tenor or bass, become more unrestrained in melismatic embellishments. Most of the odes contain one or more solos or duets composed to a basso ostinato, or a modulating basso ostinato,[16] which by this period had become signature forms for the composer. The odes are, understandably, brighter, and for the most part more joyful and sensuous than the church anthems.

The welcome songs for Charles II, as the earliest group of odes by Purcell, contain various experiments in a variety of organizational forms, instrumental styles, and key contrasts. These are obvious already in the first ode, *Welcome, Vicegerent*. The symphony itself is unusual for its inconsistent and shifting styles in both the first and second sections. The first brief section consists of three duet passages of contrasting styles for two violins over mostly descending lines in the two lower parts. The second section is canzona-like with dotted figurations that are interrupted by four-part chords separated by rests. The opening chorus repeats the second section of the symphony as accompaniment, creating a movement in seven independent parts. Although this creates a particularly successful unity between the opening symphony and the first vocal music, Purcell never again repeated this experiment in later odes. The verse, *Ah! Ah! mighty Sir,* for alto, bass, and continuo, concludes

EXAMPLE 11.12   Purcell, from *Welcome, Vicegerent of the mighty King* (Z340)

with a ritornello that is based on just the final six measures of the duet. The next section, a short homophonic chorus for *But your blest presence now,* is followed by another and much longer ritornello. The tenor verse, *Your influous approach our pensive hope recalls,* has choral echoes answering the second half of each solo phrase. The attractive tune, *Music, the food of love,* has a choral reprise of each 12-measure segment of the melody as: aA:bB (see Example 11.12). And the melody is repeated another time by the following ritornello setting. These tuneful songs in triple meter occur frequently in the odes and resonate with many of Purcell's popular songs, especially those written for the theater.

All of the welcome songs for Charles II are replete with innovative features that warrant close study. The symphony to *What shall be done,* while retaining a suggestion of the French overture in the first part, gives in the second part a fine example of Purcell's wedding of the Italian canzona to English violin practice. *Swifter, Isis, swifter flow* employs Purcell's first use of recorders as well as an oboe, instruments to gain prominence only in the late birthday odes for Queen Mary and St. Cecilia's Day. The ode of 1682, *The summer's absence unconcerned we bear,* opens with a bass solo with a range of more than two octaves, undoubtedly for John Gostling as are similar ones in other odes, and in "All hearts should smile," there is a suggestion of French vocal style in the lilting duet in parallel thirds for two trebles in triple meter to appear frequently in later odes. In the same ode two solos are sung over ostinato basses: the first is for alto, "And when late from your throne heaven's call you attend" to the simplest and most venerable of ostinatos, a descending tetrachord in C major in dotted half notes, which is repeated for the following choral version sung to the last two verses of the text.

More complex and an example of the evolving form of Purcell's treatment of ostinato basses is the alto solo, "These had by their ill usage drove the beauteous nymph long since away." Here the running bass in eighth notes moves between the D minor tonality, its dominant and relative major. For each tonal area the four-measure ostinato changes the pattern, though not so radically as to disturb the impression of a continuous ostinato bass. As with many of the solo movements in the odes, this one also reuses the same bass for the concluding string ritornello.

The finest of Charles II's welcome songs is *Fly, Bold Rebellion*. The especially frank political text by an unidentified poet makes specific allusions to the recently foiled Rye House Plot in which several prominent aristocrats and Whigs, including the king's illegitimate son, the Duke of Monmouth, plotted the murder of the king. The affair was but the last of a long series of attempts to remove Charles from the throne and to prevent the succession of his Catholic son, James. Purcell created a musical testament to the sovereign's victory over his Protestant enemies, even though the text has little elevated poetry and includes such lines as:

> Fly, bold Rebellion, make haste and be gone!
> Victorious in counsel great Charles is returned
> The plot is displayed and the traitors, some flown
> And some to Avernus [i.e., Hell] by Justice thrown down.

or even more uncompromisingly partisan:

> Come then, change your notes disloyal crowd,
> You that already have been too loud
> With importunate follies and clamours;
> 'Tis no business of yours
> To dispute the high powers,
> As if you were the government framers;
> But with heart and with voice
> Join all to rejoice
> With welcomes redoubled to see him appear,
> Who brings mercy and peace
> And all things to please
> A people that knew not how happy they are.

There is not a routine piece in this work, and the vocal and instrumental writing is exceptionally beautiful. The symphony continues with the same form as employed in the first of the welcome songs, a slow section with dotted rhythms followed by a joyful canzona in 9/8. The ode develops with notable continuity aided by the formation of large sections in the same tonality and by devices such as inserting connecting continuo passages between sections and instrumental ritornellos that reprise and enrich the music of the solo movements. In this ode Purcell has successfully achieved a formal plan that logically as well as musically places structural emphasis on large musical blocks out of what could have been composed previously as brief and unconnected segments. The structure in this case can be divided into four large divisions:

Ia.	Quintet (AATBB): "Fly, bold rebellion" and ritornello Bass solo: "The plot is displayed"	All in F major
b.	Chorus: "Then with heart and with voice prepare to re-joice"	
c.	connection by continuo bass	
IIa.	Alto solo: "Rivers from their channels turned" and ritornello	D minor
	Chorus: "For Majesty moves" connects to	
b.	Bass recit.: "If then we've found the want of rays"	D minor
c.	Tenor solo: "But Kings like the sun" with ritornello	B flat to C major
d.		A minor to C major
IIIa.	Verse (SSA): "But Heaven has now dispelled" and ritornello	F major
	Verse (ATB): "Come then, change your notes"	
b.	Chorus: "But with heart and with voice"	F minor
c.		F major
IVa.	Alto solo: "Be welcome then, great Sir" and ritornello on ostinato bass	
	Verse (SSAATBB): "Welcome to all those wishes fulfilled" +	
b.	chorus	F major

Among the odes, the late ones, especially the six for the birthdays of Queen Mary (30 April) and also *Hail, Bright Cecilia,* are Purcell's greatest achievements in this form. A summary fails to convey the richness of ideas, formal variety, and the musical energy that impels these works. And only an examination of them in their entirety will reveal the originality of Purcell's genius. No two are alike, although with few exceptions they share many features. Most of the six birthday odes have very large dimensions. Structurally, Purcell modifies forms found in the earlier odes and invents new ones to achieve a musical continuity through blocks of music often more extensive than in earlier odes. Dramatic recitatives are less frequent than airs and lyrical solo ensembles. There are, however, several examples of form that Purcell takes from opera: the sequence of short recitatives followed by lyrical solos or ensembles. All of these odes usually rely on the pattern of rounding out solo music with ritornellos, either arranging for strings the entire music or repeating some section of the preceding vocal work, often the final one. And many of the solo ensembles are restated immediately and impressively by chorus.

New to the last two odes is another operatic practice, that of introducing a vocal number with a ritornello based on it. Also a significant development in these odes is the expansion of the instrumental ensemble to underscore the royal ambience of the music with oboes, recorders, trumpets,[17] and, in the last ode, drums. The opening symphony also undergoes major changes. The first section no longer has any musical dependence on French style. For example, *Now does the glorious day appear* (1689) and the two following odes begin with an Italianate, imitative first section in which the strings suggest royal trumpet, heraldic motives. The second section of the symphony remains canzona-like in its rather simple contrapuntal textures. But the final ode, *Come ye sons of art* (1694), is completely original and in its sectionalism perhaps reflects the developing Italian opera overture. The first section consists of a progression of slow homophonic chords, and the second section is contrapuntal with three contrasted subjects: the first opening with a

EXAMPLE 11.13   Purcell, from *Celebrate this festival* (Z321)

gesture of a dotted quarter and two sixteenths and continuing with eighth notes. The second subject consists of a series of triplets on the second and fourth beats of the 4/4 measure with intervening rests, giving rise rather astonishingly to cross rhythms of two against three between the parts. A third subject presents a simple scale progression of quarter notes on the strong beats of the measure. A third section follows with antiphonal passages of sixteenth-note figures, and a concluding fourth section contains an intense adagio focused on the two violin parts over a descending chromatic bass.

The last two birthday odes and the final Cecilian ode, *Hail, Bright Cecilia,* are Purcell's finest works in any genre except for the masterworks for the theater. *Celebrate this festival* is in contrast to *Come ye sons of art,* longer and more complex, constructed in numerous small sections moving through several keys. Vocally there is an emphasis on the soprano voice, but all of the other ranges have significant music replete with extensive melismatic passages. Among the impressive passages for soprano is the solo, "Let sullen Discord smile, Let War devote this day to Peace" (see Example 11.13).

Probably the longest solo movement in all of Purcell's choral works is the bass, da capo aria of 130 measures with trumpet obbligato, "While for a righteous cause he arms." Among Purcell's many ingenious ostinato bass settings stands out "Crown the altar, deck the shrine," a da capo song with its mesmerizing four-bar bass in triple meter (see Example 11.14).

Come, come ye sons of art, the final birthday ode for Queen Mary, together with *Hail, Bright Cecilia,* are the only choral compositions by Purcell to retain their popularity in performances and subsequently in recordings. The former fully deserves its enduring reputation. Inspired by the topical nature of the text with its focus on music, Purcell created a somewhat shorter, simpler, but exceptionally tuneful ode with emphasis on solo voices. The form is again organized into blocks of music, but these are much less complex than in earlier odes, for in this case there are only three large sections that follow the remarkably innovative symphony: In D major the opening ritornello for strings and oboes introduces

EXAMPLE 11.14   Purcell, "Crown the altar, deck the shrine"

the tune of the alto solo and continuo; the same melody is repeated, set for trumpets, oboes, strings, and chorus; the splendid duet for two altos, "Sound the trumpet," employs the voices in delightful fashion imitating trumpets and oboes and exalting over the joys of music against an ostinato continuo part; and closing this section a repeat of the opening chorus.

The middle section begins in D minor and modulates to A minor and A major before returning to D major. It begins with another alto solo with an ostinato continuo bass, "Strike the viol, touch the lute," which is concluded with an instrumental arrangement of the same for strings and recorders; a bass solo follows with string ensemble, "The day that such a blessing gave," concluding with a choral version of the same; an elaborately embellished solo for soprano, "Bid the virtues, bid the graces," is followed by "These, these, are the sacred charms" for bass with an equally captivating ostinato continuo bass. The brief, short third section returns with a dancelike duet for soprano and bass, "See Nature, rejoicing, has shown us the way," and concludes the ode with a brilliant recapitulation of the music for chorus, trumpets, oboes, drums, and strings. In *Come, come ye sons of art,* Purcell created a technically perfect union of melodic inspiration and supreme craftsmanship. In 1694 he had reached the ultimate command of his art. As is the case with another unique musical genius, Mozart, one can hardly imagine where this genius would have taken Purcell if he had not died the following year.

Music for the Theater

Besides church anthems and court odes, the other focus of Purcell's creativity was the extensive corpus of music written for the Restoration theater. Beginning with Charles II's reign and continuing until the ascension of Queen Anne in 1702, the London public theaters produced around 600 plays. These were supported by the court and attended largely by aristocratic society. Most of these plays depended greatly on music, both in a continuation of court masque traditions of singing and dancing, and also for solo songs, ensembles, choruses, and independent musical-dramatic scenes. They required music before the drama began, between the acts, and music to create and support dramatic effects. In some more or less exceptional works, the amount and significance of the music led to their being described as "semi-operas" or "dramatick" operas.[18]

Before 1689 Purcell's contributions to the theater were limited largely to a few solo songs and duets, the exception being music assumed to be by Purcell for Nathaniel Lee's

Theodosius, which premiered in 1680. However, in the remaining years of his life Purcell's music for the theater dominated his output with works for some fifty staged productions. Among these are four semi-operas, *The Prophetess, or The History of Dioclesian* (1690), *King Arthur, or The British Worthy* (1691), *The Fairy-Queen* (1691), based on Shakespeare's *A Midsummer Night's Dream, The Indian Queen* (1695), final masque by Daniel Purcell, and Purcell's only opera, *Dido and Aeneas.*

The only known performance of *Dido and Aeneas* was, according to the preserved libretto,

> An Opera, Perform'd at Mr. Josias Priest's Boarding School at Chelsey. By Young Gentlewomen. The Words by Mr. Nat. Tate. The Musick Compos'd by Mr. Purcell.

Therefore, it was performed privately by amateurs, although no indication is supplied as to who sang the various male roles, including that of Aeneas. Generally, it is agreed this performance took place in 1689,[19] making it the earliest of Purcell's dramatic works and one that would later be viewed as his greatest. Two distinguished writers on Purcell's *Dido* have described it as being "the greatest operatic achievement of the English seventeenth century,"[20] or even more telling, "one of the greatest operas composed between Monteverdi's lifetime and Mozart's."[21] Not to be overlooked, however, are the influences shaping the work. There can be little doubt that Purcell's through-composed setting was influenced by Blow's earlier *Venus and Adonis* and probably the London performance of Lully's *Cadmus et Hermione* in 1686. The most obvious influences come from the Stuart court masque, in the several dance scenes, the solo airs followed by chorus repetitions, the anti-masque element of the witches, and the long-developed tradition, refined by a number of English composers, that created a decidedly English style of setting words to music. This being said, *Dido and Aeneas* has exceptional power and beauty encompassed in about an hour's music set to a better-than-serviceable poetic text. It has become a landmark in the history of Baroque opera.

Tate's greatly simplified adaptation of the fourth book of Virgil's *Aeneid,* often severely and unfairly criticized, was ideal not only for its purpose as a school play but also for the focus of its musical development. In the simplest and yet most powerful emotional parameters of a tragedy the affects are few, but for an audience also the most compelling: love, deception, hate, death. Purcell's affective musical language in places transcends musical techniques and creates human emotions that while Baroque in concept are eternal in their power. Most remarkable is how simple the musical means are to achieving the musical drama.[22] Unforgettable is Purcell's humanization of a Baroque cliché, an ostinato bass made of the descending chromatic tetrachord, for Dido's great lament, "When I am laid in earth." The recitative leading into the lament, "Thy hand, Belinda; darkness shades me," portrays Dido's anguish in a passage descending an octave through seconds (the *passus duriusculus* of rhetoricians). Purcell's genius with ostinato basses also is illustrated in three other pieces: "Ah, Belinda," "The Triumphing Dance," and "Oft she visits."

The many choruses throughout are largely in simple homophonic textures, but they display Purcell's melodic and rhythmic style at its finest. Each one has musical individuality and is memorable: the echo chorus, those for the sailors and witches, and the most moving of all, the final chorus, which begins as a four-part canon: "With drooping wings ye Cupids come, and scatter roses on her tomb."

Of no lesser importance are several of the recitatives. Except for a few that are short and perfunctory in their need to tell quickly some aspect of the story, the substantive

EXAMPLE 11.15   Purcell, from *Dido and Aeneas*

passages of "recitation" are in fact declamatory airs as found in the English masque and Purcell's odes, but they are often made intensely dramatic by musical and rhetorical means. For example, clear tonal organization, embellished words of particular moment, and motive repetitions all add to the power of the first-act recitative between Dido, Belinda, and the "Second Woman." The emotional uncertainty caused by Dido's crisis of conscience after she has met and become attracted to Aeneas is conveyed in the potent musical affect for the concluding line, "Mean wretches' grief can touch," begun with a leap of a minor sixth and continuing with a soaring line building in tension by seconds and ending with two falling minor sixths on "I fear" and "I pity," in the final measures (see Example 11.15).

Recitatives of different and equally compelling affect are those with string accompaniment for the sorceress with her witches in act II. With their static basses and highly repetitive vocal lines they are as close as anything Purcell wrote to Italian recitative style, yet the effect remains unambiguously Purcellian.

Entombed in a number and variety of plays, both tragic and comic, for the London stage is a large amount of music by Purcell that has never been heard since Purcell's death in its proper context and perhaps never will be. There is little likelihood that most of these Restoration works will ever again have an accepting audience. For most of the some fifty plays, Purcell's contribution was minor—a song or duet or two—although even those vocal pieces are invaluable contributions to the Purcell canon. About a dozen plays contain somewhat more extensive music, including *Circe* (Davenant); *A Fool's Preferment, or The Three Dukes of Dunstable* (D'Urfey after Fletcher's *The Noble Gentleman)*; *Amphitryon, or the Two Sosias* (Dryden); *Sir Anthony Love* (Southerne); *Oedipus* (Dryden and Lee); *The Double Dealer* (Congreve); *The Maid's Last Prayer, or Any rather than Fail* (Southerne); *The Libertine* (Shadwell); *Timon of Athens* (Shadwell after Shakespeare); *Bonduca, or The British Heroine* (Fletcher after Beaumont); and *The Rival Sisters, or The Violence of Love* (Gould).[23]

After *Dido and Aeneas* Purcell's most significant "operatic" music is found in the four semi-operas written between 1690 and the year of his death. All have memorable music, though *King Arthur* and *The Fairy-Queen* are the greatest among them for the quality and extensiveness of the music. They have also had revivals. In its somewhat convoluted history the text of *King Arthur* by Dryden was originally conceived as a second part to the laureate poet's *Albion and Albanius* with music by the French-trained, Catalan composer Louis Grabu (fl. 1665–1694). Performed in London in 1685, it survived for only six performances. Subsequently Dryden chose Purcell for his considerably expanded "second part" or sequel. Considering the subject, it is not surprising that *King Arthur* is a political opera immersed in perceived allusions to the tense political period between the death of Charles II and the reign of William and Mary.[24] More significant is the work itself, the only major work by Purcell for the stage not based on a previous play, and the composer's most popular success, with frequent performances following its premiere and at least two revivals before the composer's death. It continued to have performances, although variously and often drastically reworked, in the eighteenth century.[25]

Contributing to the work's continuing popularity in the eighteenth and succeeding centuries was the famous "Frost Scene," the masque in act III, which at times was performed separately as an entertainment during Purcell's lifetime and judged to be one of Purcell's finest works. Its popularity resulted not only from the spectacular stage scenery but also from its grand originality, the strangeness or one might say the "baroqueness" of the music. The stage is transformed into a frozen landscape, a symbolic representation of Emmeline's frozen horror at seeing the lecherous Saxon magician, Osmond. Cupid appears in a machine and awakens the Cold Genius, commanding him to "awake, and winter from thy furry mantle shake." This aria is a most unusual and original realization of Purcell's musical imagination, a Baroque setting of extravagant affect, a *tour de force,* in the words of Curtis Price, who continues:

> Its purposely antiquated chromatic style, reminiscent of Locke's and Blow's bizarreries, helps to paint a picture of the hoary Genius. Yet the carefully calculated, occasionally abstract harmonies are profoundly moving, as they twist a feeling of awe into a vision of agonizing death.[26]

The four-part string setting indicates wavy lines under each part, as do the voice parts, suggesting some form of playing and singing that would imitate shivering or freezing,

EXAMPLE 11.16   Purcell, from *King Arthur*

although exactly how instrumentalists and voices were to realize the effect remains unclear. Purcell may have borrowed this technique from Lully, who has similar indications for a "shivering chorus" in the fourth act of *Isis*. Purcell's score, however, is far removed from Lully's in the intensity of the affect, the passionate rising line of the bass, and the extraordinary chromatic harmony of the pulsating chords (see Example 11.16).

However, the overt seriousness of affect for this music abruptly shifts to comic tones with Cupid's aria, "Thou doting fool, forbear! What does thou mean by freezing here?," and the Cold Genius's pompous response: "Great Love, I know thee now: Eldest of the gods art thou." The "shivering" music returns, this time for a chorus of Cold People, but without the intensity of chromatic harmony or the passionate vocal lines of the previous passage. The music for act IV, some of which is lost, consists of two exceptional pieces. The first, "Two daughters of this aged stream," is for two sopranos as sirens who "shew themselves to the Waste," and tempt Arthur to be lured into their arms. The act closes with a long sung and danced passacaglia on the subject of love, fifty-seven variations on a simple four-bar ostinato on a descending tetrachord and its inversion with ritornellos and vocal solos, duets, trios, and choruses. The effect strongly suggests French influence, especially the danced and sung *grand ballet* found at the end of Lully's operas.

The music for act V is the weakest in the entire work, even though it contains the jewel among all the music in this semi-opera. This masque begins following the defeat by Arthur of the Saxon king Oswald. Merlin says to Arthur, "For this Day's Palm, and for thy former Acts, Thy *Britain* freed, and Foreign Force expell'd, Thou, Arthur, has acquir'd a future Fame. . . ." He waves his wand, and the scene changes to reveal the British Ocean in a storm. Once the winds are calmed in a bass aria, "Ye Blust'ring Brethren," the scene changes again to reveal an island rising, on which Britannia is seated "with Fishermen at her Feet." The texts of less than Dryden's greatest poetry are a miscellaneous and largely jingoistic group glorifying Britain as the Queen of Islands, its pastoral land, and its commerce. Venus sings a hymn to Britain, "Fairest Isle, all Isles Excelling, Seat of Pleasures, and of Loves." For this clearly jingoistic moment Purcell, one of the great melodists in music history, created this most memorable melody (see Example 11.17).

EXAMPLE 11.17   Purcell, from *King Arthur*

The Fairy-Queen was Purcell's third "opera," first performed at the Dorset Garden theater in May 1692. A second version with additional music was given in February 1693. It was based on a radical revision by an unknown author of Shakespeare's *Midsummer Night's Dream,* in which four of the five acts conclude with masques of extravagant and costly stage effects. These contain Purcell's consistently most effective and beautiful music for the stage, superior to the music in his other dramatic stage works. However, unlike *King Arthur,* these masques are not interrelated with the spoken text, which is largely Shakespeare's. Rather, they reflect on the dramatic content of the spoken dialogue, supply allegorical and symbolic pieces. They stand independent of the action and do not move the continuity of the play forward. Nevertheless, the transitions from play to each masque are prepared by the text, often by taking a cue from Shakespeare's own call for music.

The musical richness found in *The Fairy-Queen* includes an emphasis on instrumental music, consisting, in addition to introductory ritornellos to songs and choruses, some twenty-five independent pieces. There are many dances, often based on English folklike rhythms and tunes, act tunes, preludes, considerable French-influenced music including the French overture in act III called a symphony, "while the swans come forward," and a typically Lullian chaconne of the final act. To complete the focus on national styles, Purcell includes a superb Italian-type symphony at the opening of act IV.

There is little in the music added to the second version of act I that is particularly interesting or necessary for revivals of the work. The "Scene of the Drunken Poet," in which the fairies torment a poet by pinching him, relies on the already popular Venetian operatic penchant for creating hilarity for an audience by having a character sing in exaggerated stuttering. The music of the second half of act II (the first vocal music of the 1692 version), set in fairy land, responds to Titania's request to her band of fairies: "Sing me now to sleep and let the sentinels their watches keep." The masque begins with eloquent vocal pieces for Night (soprano), Mystery (soprano), Secrecy (countertenor), and Sleep (bass), a landmark of vocal and expressive beauty in seventeenth-century opera history. In this glorious quartet the first movement stands out because of its originality. The ritornello for muted violins and viola without continuo weaves in close imitation an undulating and descending theme in half notes of ethereal peace and uncanny quietness that makes it almost possible to "feel" night as it falls on the scene. The affect of the music is continuous throughout this song of exceeding simplicity, but there are also passages of subtle and expressive emphasis of the text (see Example 11.18).

The masque for act III follows a lengthy scene adapted from acts II, III, and V of Shakespeare's play. The most important event occurs as Titania awakes; she sees Bottom with an ass's head, and immediately falls in love with him. She calls her fairies to entertain her lover, and the scene changes to a great wood with a river and a bridge formed from two dragons. The masque's central theme is love, and it begins with a threefold arrangement of another of Purcell's memorable tunes, "If love's a sweet passion," as a prelude for strings, as a continuo air for soprano, and as a choral response with orchestra, each with variations of harmony and texture. Following dances for fairies and anti-masque savages (or "green men," according to the score for the first production), the masque takes a sudden turn to low comedy in the dialogue of Coridon and Mopsa. The latter protects her virtue as Coridon insists they "merrily, merrily play, and kiss, and kiss, and kiss the sweet time away." The musical dialogue between these two country characters is very funny as they respond back and forth between pleading and refusal. And if the language is somewhat indecorous, it provides welcome relief to the unreal world of fairyland. The last air, "A thousand, thousand ways we'll find to entertain the hours," for countertenor followed by

EXAMPLE 11.18   Purcell, from *The Fairy-Queen*

a choral reprise demonstrates another significant development in Purcell's music for this work.

The masque concluding act IV again is initiated by Titania's call for music, and requires another complex change of scene to a "garden of fountains." "A sonata plays while the Sun arises." The four seasons enter with attendants, and the opening music is an air, "Now the night is chas'd away, all salute the rising sun," and a chorus, "'Tis that happy, happy day, the birthday of King Oberon," both composed to one of Purcell's inimitable ostinato basses, a descending tetrachord composed in leaping octaves. The masque now becomes a celebration of the four seasons. Phoebus, that is, Apollo, God of the Sun, is welcomed in a chorus of royal pomposity with trumpets, oboes, and kettledrums. Each of the seasons is given a contrasting air: spring (soprano), summer (bass), fall (tenor), and winter (bass). Winter is composed almost entirely to the chromatic scale on A, which at the opening ritornello descends in the strings three octaves. The masque concludes with a repeat of the opening chorus for Phoebus, "Hail, hail great parent!"

The act V masque also requires an elaborate stage set, a Chinese Garden filled with an extraordinary variety of plants, animals, fountains, and architectural structures, established with no real connection to the play dramatically or musically, not even to Oberon's introduction: "Now let a new transparent world be seen, all Nature joins to entertain our Queen. Now we are reconcil'd all things agree to make an Universal Harmony." A Chinese man and woman dominate the scene, adding some delightful visual exoticism for the audience's entertainment. The music is focused for the most part on simplicity and directness of appeal. For example: the Chinese man begins with a da capo, continuo air, "Thus, the gloomy world," sung in duet with a trumpet and in the "A" section to a two-measure bass ostinato, which is dropped for the "B" section. This bears the "classic" stamp of Purcell's simple yet most delightfully entertaining music. Two arias for soprano, "Hark, how all things in one sound" (for the first woman) and the following "Hark, the echoing air" (for the second woman), impress with the vocal difficulties of their extended melismatic passages. The second, in addition, challenges the singer to imitate, very much in Italian concept, trumpet melodic style. Firmly in French tradition, the masque concludes the opera with a chaconne, a "Grand Dance of Twenty-four Persons," including the Chinese man and woman and a final chorus with trumpets and strings, "They shall be as happy as they're fair; Love, Love shall fill all, all the places of care."

A comprehensive examination of the music of the greatest English composer of the Baroque remains to be achieved. Further insights into his musical legacy require a knowledge of Purcell's more than two dozen Catches, and more than two hundred songs, the largest number of them written for the theater. There also are some forty sacred (devotional) songs, including the sublime "Tell me some pitying angel" (Blessed Virgin's Expostulation). The fecundity of Purcell's creative inventiveness remains unexplained—that so much music of imperishable greatness could be composed over such a short lifespan.

CHAPTER TWELVE

Spain, Portugal, and Latin America

Rui Vieira Nery

The Iberian Peninsula: The Seventeenth Century

An "Indigenous" Baroque in Iberian Music

THE FIRST THING to bear in mind when applying the concept of Baroque to the history of music in the Iberian Peninsula is that no radical musical changes conveniently located around the year 1600 occur simultaneously in Spain or Portugal, unlike Italy, be it in terms of new musical genres, of new compositional techniques, of new theoretical assumptions, or of new aesthetic principles. Indeed, when viewed from a distance, Iberian music at the beginning of the seventeenth century seems instead to emphatically affirm its unrelenting adherence to the Mannerist polyphonic tradition of the previous century, which is then at the very peak of its local development: Tomás Luís de Victoria publishes his final opus, the *Officium defunctorum,* already in 1605, to be followed by such major monuments of Spanish *prima prattica* counterpoint as Sebastián de Vivanco's *Motetes* (1610), Aguilera de Heredia's *Canticum Beatissimae Virginis* (1618), or López de Velasco's *Libro de misas* (1628), whereas the three main Portuguese polyphonists who are already in full activity around the turn of the century—Duarte Lobo, Manuel Cardoso, and Filipe de Magalhães—will only have their works printed throughout the following four decades, from 1605 to as late as 1648.

General surveys of European music history have often taken the simplistic view that this apparent prevalence of the "classical" polyphonic models in the works of Portuguese and Spanish composers well into the first half of the new century, at a time when opera, accompanied monody, early sonata forms, and *concertato* writing were already in full development in Italy and elsewhere in Europe, could only mean an ultraconservative artistic attitude (if not a state of actual stylistic stagnation), as well as an overwhelming and anachronistic predominance of Palestrina's style in the Peninsula, long after its gradual rejection by his Italian successors. This verdict is to a great extent a part of the Romantic construction of the so-called dark legend regarding the Iberian Counter Reformation. It was a product of mostly nineteenth-century Northern European, Protestant historians only too willing to depict Catholic Spain and Portugal as backward-looking countries. They were viewed as stubbornly rooted in a Medieval world and fiercely opposed to the specific model of economic and cultural development that had characterized these authors' own countries and that they considered, in a typical Darwinian evolutionist view, as the only valid path to civilizational progress in the history of Western Europe as a whole.

A closer look at Iberian music of this period, however, will undoubtedly reveal that its essential component of continuity coexisted with an intense process of internal transformation. This goes back to at least the 1530s and 1540s, when Spanish composers such as Luys de Milán, Alonso Mudarra, or Luys de Narváez were already publishing monodic songs with a chordal accompaniment for the six-course vihuela. Milán inserted over his *tientos* and *fantasias* for this same instrument explicit indications of tempo alterations and of expression, anticipating several of the Baroque *affetti*. And Diego Ortíz included in his 1555 *Trattado de glosas* for the viols instructions on how to improvise on the harpsichord a harmonic realization of a ground bass in long durational values, supporting the melodic, virtuosic line of the solo viol. Similarly, as seen below, both the vocal polyphonic settings and the keyboard works of the Iberian musicians of the first decades of the seventeenth century include, under a surface of ceremonious respect for the conventions of the *prima prattica,* an increasing number of features that reflect the same basic concerns characterizing many of the more blatant innovations of their Italian contemporaries.

These innovative features are not constant throughout the repertory, and the same composer may use them in a particular piece and go back to "classical" counterpoint in the next one. Some authors are clearly more interested in experimenting than their colleagues, and some musical genres lend themselves more easily than others to such experimentation. As a matter of fact, the situation is not altogether different from what happened in Italy in the same period, if we consider, for instance, the case of Monteverdi working simultaneously on his final Baroque operas and on such a masterpiece of *prima prattica* composition as the Mass in the *Selva morale e spirituale*. Rather than a period of stagnation dominated by an acquired routine of artistic production and reception, the first three or four decades of the seventeenth century seem to represent in Iberian music an era of enormous creative vitality, in which all the principal composers struggle to demonstrate their individuality by offering a personal synthesis of tradition and innovation, combining a polyphonic idiom which they still consider as the basis of the very identity of the Peninsular musical tradition with a plethora of new, daring compositional features.

Thus said, when can we begin to speak of Portuguese and Spanish music of the seventeenth century as "Baroque" music? An answer to this question may vary, depending on whether we choose to consider in isolation the local emergence of each of the new technical procedures associated with our knowledge of the Italian Baroque—accompanied monody, basso continuo, concertato writing, or the early trio sonata, for instance—or instead decide to take into consideration the perpetuation of the typical features of the sixteenth-century Peninsular tradition of polyphonic writing. In fact, several of the "progressive" traits of the Italians can be found in Iberian music, as we said, as early as the mid-sixteenth century, whereas *prima prattica* sacred works are still being composed, copied, and performed in Madrid or Lisbon as late as the 1720s and 1730s. For at least some forty years into the seventeenth century, Baroque idioms occur increasingly in the context of musical composition in the Peninsula, but ultimately as the result of an attitude of individual experimentation that can be still associated primarily with the late-sixteenth-century Mannerist worldview, rather than with the systematic, formalized, rationalist approach that, properly speaking, will eventually characterize the Baroque.

It is safe to say, nevertheless, that somewhere between 1640 and 1650 the music of Spain and Portugal shares already most of the new basic concerns of musical composition that gradually emerged in Italy since the beginning of the century. A few of them were the result of a direct artistic exchange with Italy, as the Spanish crown controlled large Italian territories, particularly those of the wealthy Kingdom of Naples. And manuscript and printed repertory, as well as musicians, circulated widely between the two regions. Others were the result of a "domestic" evolution within Iberian polyphony itself. In both cases, however, the result was a synthesis that corresponded to the specific cultural context of the two Iberian monarchies as well as of their vast colonial empires, rather than to a passive, cosmopolitan adoption of the Italian style.

We can speak, therefore, of an "indigenous" Baroque in the music of the Peninsula, evolving gradually throughout the first few decades of the seventeenth century, parallel to the survival of many features of the Mannerist polyphonic tradition, reaching its maturity around the central decades of that century and *lasting*, as we shall see, until at least the early years of the following one. In order to be properly understood, this new stylistic period in Iberian music—which corresponds to an era of acknowledged artistic splendor (*el siglo de oro,* or "the golden century") in various other creative fields, such as painting, literature or the theater—must, of course, be judged on the basis of its own features, rather than measured exclusively according to the Italian patterns. Viewed as such, in all its specificity, it will undoubtedly emerge as yet another fundamental original contribution of the Peninsula toward the global heritage of the European Baroque.

Latin Church Music

Much of the music written in the Peninsula in the seventeenth century is intended for liturgical use and is performed in a vast and complex network of religious institutions, at the top of which are the various royal chapels of the kings of Portugal and Spain, the private chapels of the first rank of the high nobility, the main cathedrals, and the wealthiest convents and monasteries in both countries. Each of these institutions has a *capilla* (chapel), a permanent ensemble of professional musicians headed by a *maestro de capilla* (chapel-master) and typically consisting of some twelve to sixteen singers distributed through the four polyphonic ranges, as well as of one or two organists, one or two harpists, and a wind ensemble of variable dimensions and composition but which tends to include recorders, shawms, sackbuts, cornets, and *bajones* (an early form of the bassoon). In many cases, such as those of the Flemish Chapel at the service of the Spanish kings or the cathedrals of Seville, in Spain, or Évora, in Portugal, for instance, the soprano parts are sung by choirboys trained in music as well as in the humanities at a school attached to the chapel. Those schools are thus responsible for the training of many of the professional singers and cha-pelmasters who are later hired by other chapels.

Chant is still an essential part of the musical liturgy. As the Tridentine reform failed to impose a unified chant repertoire on the universal Church, several Spanish and Portu-guese dioceses proudly maintain their own specific monophonic traditions, and in certain cases their chant books even deviate from the official texts of the Roman Breviary and Missal of Pius V, especially in regard to the choice of psalm and *Magnificat* antiphons. With the few exceptions discussed later, Office items are usually sung in chant, as are Mass propers, except for those belonging to the Requiem Mass. As chant singing is considered to be within the reach of any trained clergyman these items are generally not part of the repertory of the chapel, which is reserved for the performance of polyphony.

COMPOSITIONAL TECHNIQUES

Imitative counterpoint in the sixteenth-century tradition is still the predominant style of Iberian polyphony in the first decades of the new century. The established modal system, as well as "classical" dissonance handling, cadence patterns, *cantus firmus* elaborations, and parody and paraphrase techniques are strictly taught in cathedral schools and explained in great detail by treatises such as Domenico Pietro Cerone's *El Melopeo y Maestro* (1613), which became the most influential theoretical reference in Spanish and Portuguese music throughout the seventeenth century. Practical models of the Renaissance and Mannerist contrapuntal legacy, furthermore, are quite familiar to all music students, as the Peninsular church repertoire, with the exception of the peculiar genre of the sacred villancico, is to a great extent cumulative: in any particular ceremony newly composed works may be performed along with the established masterpieces of early-sixteenth-century authors such as Josquin, Escobar, or Peñalosa, as well as with those of Morales, Ceballos, Guerrero, or Victoria. Even when printed editions for this earlier literature are no longer available, local chapelmasters will frequently have them copied in new choir books covering the needs of their chapel for the whole liturgical calendar, often side by side with their own new compositions.

Under this surface of reverential adherence to past *prima prattica* models, however, mature composers feel free to experiment with a vast gamut of innovative idioms that ultimately lead to growing changes in the established polyphonic style, but from within a continuous tradition rather than against it. Most of these innovations are justified by a concern for effective emotional expression and word painting that had always been "unofficially" encouraged by the Counter Reformation theologians and church authorities in Portugal and Spain. Thus, for instance, well in keeping with the precedents of a Guerrero or a Carreira, we witness a rather free use of dissonance and modulation that increasingly breaks away from the purity of Renaissance modality and tends to affirm a new major/minor duality.

The contrapuntal texture itself undergoes a considerable evolution. The traditional association of soprano and tenor as the leading pair of voices within the polyphonic ensemble tends to be gradually replaced by a new structural pairing of the treble voice with a bass line unmistakably preharmonic in nature, full of constant leaps of fourths and fifths and following a growing logic of chordal attraction and resolution. The introduction of the basso continuo greatly reinforces this particular aspect. "Vertical" V–I and IV–I cadences, devoid of the usual 7–6 and 4–3 suspensions, tend to replace the "horizontal" perfect and plagal *clausulae,* respectively. The balanced imitation of all four or five contrapuntal parts often gives way to new, unorthodox techniques, including irregular, pseudo-canonic imitation involving only the head motive of the theme or even just its rhythmic figuration, as well as the opposition of pairs of voices, each pair in parallel motion at the third or sixth (see Example 12.1). Moreover, the polyphonic even flow is frequently broken into contrasting sections, some of which present a texture similar to that of the Italianate accompanied monody and trio sonata.

In connection with these innovations, melodic design also changes significantly. Composers seek to explore the rhythmic patterns implied in the prosody of the text, especially in proparoxytones such as "Dominus" or "Virginis," for instance, usually set to triple-meter dotted figurations. The melody is now frequently broken into comparatively smaller cells separated by rests, with monosyllables such as "tu" or "non" often being treated as interjections uttered homophonically by all voices (see Example 12.2). Characteristic figurational themes are repeatedly used in sequences within the same voice, besides serving for imitation between various parts. By contrast, complex coloratura patterns, sometimes employing dotted rhythms and sextuplets, begin to appear systematically in the 1630s (see Example 12.3).

Polychoral writing was already a favorite of Peninsular composers from at least the late 1560s, as seen in Victoria's many eight-part psalm settings of 1576 to 1600 and in his twelve-part *Laetatus sum* of 1583. Seventeenth-century composers in Spain and Portugal—from Cererols in Barcelona to Comes in Valencia, Patiño and Capitán in Madrid, D. Pedro de Cristo in Coimbra, or Rebelo in Vila Viçosa—develop this tradition to its extreme, writing

EXAMPLE 12.1 Diogo Dias Melgaz, *Salve Regina,* mm. 19–27, in *Opera omnia,* ed. José Augusto Alegria. Lisbon: Calouste Gulbenkian Foundation, 1978, pp. 158–59

EXAMPLE 12.2 Juan García de Salazar, *Hei mihi*, mm. 67–78, in *Lira sacro-hispana*, Vol. IV, ed. Hilarion Eslava. Madrid: M. Salazar, 1869, pp. 78–79

a significant number of works for eight voices in two choirs, twelve voices in three choirs, or even larger ensembles. By the middle of the century the typical vocal distribution for such works is SSAT SATB for the two-choir pieces, or SSAT SATB SATB for three-choir ones, always with basso continuo, and frequently even with a separate continuo part for each choir. Continuo realization, although often indicated only as *acompañamiento,* is usually assigned to either the organ or the harp, supported by a *bajón* or a bass viol.

Not all polychoral works are based on an even distribution in four-part choirs, however, and composers such as Mateo Romero or Juan Bautista Comes are particularly fond of combining various choirs of irregular dimensions, forming ensembles of seven, nine, or thirteen parts, in several instances with one or more of the participating choirs composed of just one or two solo voices with continuo. Obbligato instrumental parts may be employed within these ensembles, with numerous instances of one of the choirs consisting of

EXAMPLE 12.3 João Lourenço Rebelo, *Lamentation Jeremiae Prophetae*, mm. 95–102, in *Psalmi tum Vesperarum, tum Completorium*, Vol. IV, ed. José Augusto Alegria. Lisbon: Calouste Gulbenkian Foundation, 1982, p. 708

a solo voice and three instrumental lines, in contrast with one or more choirs with the opposite distribution (see Example 12.4). With relatively few exceptions, however, these obbligato parts are not attributed to specific instruments, which leaves the choice of the instrumentation to the chapelmaster, according to the variety and ability of the players available in his ensemble. The mid-seventeenth-century manuscripts of the Portuguese Augustinian monastery of Santa Cruz, in Coimbra, are particularly rich in information about instrumentation, usually indicating various combinations of wind instruments.

With all its possibilities of concertato effects of opposition between one or more so-loistic voices and the full ensemble, as well as between contrasting choirs, polychoral writing

EXAMPLE 12.4 João Lourenço Rebelo, *Lauda Jerusalem*, mm. 45–48, in *Psalmi tum Vesperarum, tum Completorium*, Vol. II, ed. José Augusto Alegria. Lisbon: Calouste Gulbenkian Foundation, 1982, p. 282

offers Peninsular composers an ideal space for daring innovation in many of the areas in which the Italian Baroque is simultaneously experimenting, albeit in different musical genres. Heavily employed in Latin sacred music, it will, nevertheless, find a particularly adequate repertory in the sacred villancico, where it will be often associated with theatrical effects related to the plot of the text.

LATIN POLYPHONIC GENRES

The Iberian polyphonic repertory sung in Latin covers the three main categories found elsewhere in Catholic Europe: Mass ordinaries, motets, and settings of certain Office items.

The Mass ordinary, as a large-scale musical structure with a rich internal variety of textual and dramatic situations, is clearly the favorite genre for Iberian sacred polyphonists. It can be treated according to all the compositional styles described above, from "classical" four-part counterpoint to massive polychoral settings with up to twenty voices and obbligato instrumental parts. Parody and paraphrase techniques are still to be found in the first half of the century (namely in the Portuguese Fr. Manuel Cardoso's parody elaborations on motets by Palestrina as well as in the works of the composers of the Madrid Flemish Chapel) but tend to be ultimately replaced by polychoral writing. A particularly interesting subgenre is that of the *Misa de batalla* (battle mass), of which a remarkable example was left by the Catalan Joan Cererols. Thematically it is based on the traditional motives of Jannequin's chanson *La bataille de Marignan,* with its colorful musical depiction of the sound effects of a battlefield: infantry marches, cavalry charges, cannon shots, sword clashes, trumpet calls, fife and drum fanfares, drum rolls, and so on. Requiem Masses, on the contrary, are considered such solemn music that they remain solidly anchored on a more conservative *prima prattica* contrapuntal tradition.

In the first half of the seventeenth century the motet is still widely cultivated as an optional liturgical piece, usually drawing on excerpts from the text of one or more of the proper items of the Mass in which it is inserted. Except for the gradual introduction of the basso continuo, it tends to remain based on a four- to five-part contrapuntal setting, with a strong emphasis on the dramatic treatment of the words. Frequently it makes copious use of the traditional late-sixteenth-century expressive devices such as chromaticism and dissonance, and alternates imitative writing with declamatory homorhythmic passages. From the 1650s on, however, the number of motets greatly diminishes but for those needed for the penitential seasons of the liturgical year, such as Advent and Lent, as the sacred villancico in the vernacular tends to replace this genre as the preferred optional item in most other feasts in the church calendar.

Matins of Christmas and Holy Week (particularly those of Palm Sunday and of Maundy Thursday to Holy Saturday) continue to be extremely important occasions for liturgical practice, and lead to a considerable number of polyphonic settings of their Responsories and Lessons, as well as of the four Passions, with particular emphasis on those of Matthew and John. Whereas the tradition of the previous century was to set polyphonically only the passages of the Synagogue (especially the *turbae,* or *bradados*) and leave the remaining sections of the Passion in chant, mid-seventeenth-century Portuguese and Spanish composers begin to experiment also with contrapuntal treatment of the sections of the Evangelist and even with those of Christ. Except for these particular feasts, however, the evening Office hours—Vespers and Compline—now seem to acquire a predominant role in public liturgy, and the psalms, particularly those for Sunday and Marian Vespers, as well as the solemn canticle of the *Magnificat* become a favorite genre for Peninsular composers. They are quite clearly intended to produce a Baroque effect of monumentality and together with the Mass ordinaries constitute the prime sacred genre for experimentation with polychoral writing. Other Office items to be set polyphonically include a few Hymns and Sequences, as well as the great Marian antiphons.

IMPORTANT CENTERS OF SACRED MUSIC

For over a century, ever since the time of Emperor Charles V, the Spanish kings had at their service two separate royal chapels, the capilla *flamenca* (Flemish chapel), which originated in the private ensemble of Franco-Flemish musicians brought to Spain by Philip the Handsome in his capacity as Duke of Burgundy, and the *capilla española* (Spanish chapel), properly speaking, which had resulted from the integration of the former Castillian and Aragonese royal chapels of Isabella and Ferdinand. By the beginning of the seventeenth century, following the death of the chapelmaster Philippe Rogier in 1598, the Flemish Chapel is headed by the latter's favorite disciple, the Liège-born Matthieu Rosmarin (c. 1575–1647)—or, as he is best known in the Peninsula, Mateo Romero, "El Maestro Capitán." The repertory of this institution continues the old tradition of elaborate counterpoint developed by a distinguished lineage of Franco-Flemish polyphonists at the service of the Spanish Crown, going back to Nicolas Gombert, Georges de la Hèle, and Rogier. Besides being himself a revered master of imitative counterpoint, Capitán was admired for his skill in polychoral composition, as well as in villancicos and *tonos humanos,* and when he retired in 1634, he had accumulated various sources of income that made him a considerably wealthy man for a professional musician of his period.

At the time of Romero's retirement his chapel already had a mixed staff, its choir boys all from Spain rather than from the Netherlands, and Philip IV decided to merge the Flemish and Spanish chapels into a single institution, under the new chapelmaster Carlos Patiño (1600–1675). A former disciple of Alonso Lobo at the cathedral of Seville, Patiño became the most influential personality in Spanish musical life, excelling in all polyphonic genres, from the traditional *stile antico* to the new Baroque works for various choirs, and from the secular song with continuo to theater music.

Spanish sacred music was still based, nevertheless, on the polyphonic chapels and schools of the country's wealthiest cathedrals, in which some of the main Iberian polyphonists were active as composers and conductors as well as often in charge of teaching and managing their institution's music archives. According to the available income for the musical establishment in each of these cathedrals at a given time, their ability to attract the best musicians to their service—and thus also their place in the ranking of musical centers in the country—may have varied. This established between them an informal hierarchy, which explains why the typical ascending career of a talented musician implies constant moves from one institution to the next until he reached a stable position at the highest level available to him (an extreme case is that of Diego de Pontac [1603–1654], who successively held positions at Granada, Santiago, Zaragoza, Valencia, and Madrid.) Among the most prestigious institutions of this kind that became associated with influential composers were the cathedrals of Barcelona (Joan Pau Pujol, 1570–1626), Málaga (Estêvão de Brito, c. 1575–1641), Salamanca (Sebastián de Vivanco, 1551–1622), Seville (Fr. Francisco de Santiago, c. 1578–1644), Valencia (Juan Bautista Comes, 1582–1643), Zamora (Juan García de Salazar, d. 1710), and Zaragoza (Fr. Manuel Correia, d. 1653). Of the composers mentioned, the Valencian Comes is most likely to be the one who acquired the most undisputed artistic reputation in his lifetime, especially in the realm of the sacred villancico in which he explored most effectively all the compositional innovations of his time.

To these main cathedrals should be added a few great monastic houses with either a tradition of carefully selecting and training their own musicians from an early age—as with the Abbey of Montserrat, in Barcelona, where Joan Cererols (1618–1676) was active for several decades—or with a large enough income to afford a permanent chapel of first-rank singers and instrumentalists, such as the royal monastery of the Descalzas Reales (Barefoot Clarist nuns), with Gabriel Díaz Bessón (c. 1580–1638) and Sebastián López de Velasco (c. 1584–1659) among its chapelmasters, or that of the Encarnación, both in Madrid.

Portugal was for sixty years (1580–1640) part of a dual monarchy under the king of Spain, but the fact that during that time the Portuguese Royal Chapel almost never had the opportunity to perform for the sovereign did not diminish its reputation, mostly because of the presence of two highly qualified chapelmasters, the Aragonese Francisco Garro (to 1623), and his successor, the Portuguese Filipe de Magalhães, who retired in 1641. After the restoration of Portuguese independence, in 1640, the Lisbon Royal Chapel greatly benefited from the fact that the new king, John IV (1603–1656), was the former Duke of Braganza, a formidably wealthy music amateur, who even before ascending to the throne had an essential role as a generous sponsor of music and musicians in his country as well as in Spain. Among the various aspects of his lifelong devotion to music, John began to assemble—and continued to do so in his new capital—what is still considered to be the largest European music library of his time in his ducal palace of Vila Viçosa. Although the collection was destroyed in the Lisbon earthquake of 1755, the 1649 printed Part I of its catalogue lists around two thousand prints and four thousand manuscripts, which represent as little as a third of the total contents of the library at the time of its collector's death. The king is known to have called the musicians of his chapel every morning to have them sight-read the new music that he had received from all over Europe. This ensemble differs from most other Iberian chapels in that it was not only restricted to the repertory of its routine liturgical duties but also had the opportunity of singing through a vast music literature that may not have been heard elsewhere in the Peninsula in this period.

John's favorite Portuguese composer was João Lourenço Rebelo (1610–1661), a wealthy aristocrat who had access to all the resources of the king's music library and could thus freely try his hand at many of the modern compositional techniques represented in the collection. His 1657 anthology of polychoral psalms, printed in Rome at the sovereign's expenses and assembling pieces composed from as early as the late 1630s, can be seen as the first major work of an unmistakable Baroque character by a Portuguese polyphonist.

Outside the circle of the Royal Chapel or of the private chapel of the Dukes of Braganza, the main institution dealing with sacred music in Portugal was the cathedral of Évora, at whose school a particularly gifted teacher, Manuel Mendes (c. 1547–1605), trained successive generations of outstanding polyphonists, including the future chapelmasters of the Royal Chapel itself: Filipe de Magalhães (c. 1571–1652), of Lisbon Cathedral; Duarte Lobo (?1564-9–1646); and Fr. Manuel Cardoso (1566–1650) of the Lisbon Carmelite convent. The latter three composers were responsible for ten choir books published either in Antwerp by Plantin or in Lisbon by Craesbeeck, a disciple of the Flemish printer, between 1605 and 1648. These volumes were intended for widespread use in cathedrals and large churches, and therefore preserve only the strictest *stile antico* side of the artistic production of their authors rather than the more innovative features the latter are known to have used in other compositions written for more sophisticated artistic circles, such as that of the king's own private performances. They nevertheless document many of the original characteristics of the Évora school, with its taste for elaborate contrapuntal settings (Lobo) and expressive handling of dissonance and chromaticism (Cardoso, Magalhães). Among the later representatives of this school, Diogo Dias Melgás (1638–1700) must be mentioned for his skillful combination of *prima prattica* tradition and Baroque harmonic innovation.

Other Portuguese religious institutions with a significant activity in the field of Latin sacred music in the seventeenth century were the cathedrals of Lisbon, Braga, Elvas, and Viseu, as well as the two great Augustinian monasteries in the country, Santa Cruz in Coimbra, and São Vicente in Lisbon, both of which produced a considerable extant repertory of polyphonic music covering all the genres discussed earlier.

THE SACRED VILLANCICO

If there is a seventeenth-century polyphonic genre that is exclusive from the Peninsular and Latin American world, it is the sacred villancico, a kind of religious song in the vernacular performed within a Mass or Matins, which was itself a transformation of one of the most characteristic genres in the Spanish and Portuguese secular songbooks of the previous two centuries. It is difficult to say precisely when this type of secular song first made its way into the Catholic liturgy, but by the 1570s it was already a steady component of some of the church ceremonies celebrated in those festivities of the liturgical calendar of a more joyous nature, such as Christmas.

Musically, the old secular villancico followed an ABBA structure not unlike that of the medieval *virelai,* in which the first A corresponded to a two- to three-line *estribillo* (refrain), and each of the *coplas* (stanzas, or verses) of the poem was then distributed through a B section of the music that was heard twice (the *mudanza,* or change) and a return to the music of the original A (the *vuelta,* or return). Poetically, the final line of the text of the *vuelta* could be the same as the one in the *estribillo.* By the beginning of the seventeenth century this earlier soloistic form had been expanded to adapt to the choral medium of its new performance context and obeyed the following pattern of alternation between soloists and choir:

Estribillo		*Mudanza*	*Vuelta*
Introdución	Responsión	Coplas	
A	B	c	B, or A and B
(soloists)	(choir)	(soloists)	

The soloistic *introdución* (introduction) usually consists of a section for one to four voices, the text of which often implies some degree of dialogue between them, and is followed by a choral *responsión* (response). Both sections together replace the traditional *estribillo,* alternating with a variable number of successive *coplas* sung again by one or more soloists. The repeat of the *estribillo* can be done entirely or in some instances reduced to just the *responsión.* And when the number of *coplas* justifies it, several of them can be sung in a row before the return to the complete or partial rendition of the refrain. Although at first the majority of the works had strophic *coplas,* regardless of the quantity of these soloistic verses, the development of the genre tends to lead to a different musical treatment of each one of them or to the combination of both systems. In fact, as the seventeenth century progresses, there seems to be a considerably growing freedom in each composer's approach to these general formal boundaries except for the required presence of a choral refrain in alternation with solos of various types. Moreover, the *responsión* tends to be set polychorally, often involving all kinds of internal contrasts of texture, whereas the soloistic sections offer excellent occasions for experimenting with monodic and trio writing. Thus, even more so than the Latin repertory, the sacred villancico soon became a particularly apt vehicle for stylistic innovation in Iberian music.

Villancicos—or *chanzonetas,* as they frequently were referred to in the first half of the century—could be sung at Mass, particularly during the Elevation of the Host, but their predominant context of performance appeared to be the Office hour of Matins, in which they were inserted after each of the nine Lessons distributed along the three Nocturnes, probably replacing the Latin Responsories, which originally fulfilled that function. Just as the final Responsory in the third Nocturne of Matins could be omitted and replaced by a Te Deum in solemn feasts, the same could happen to the final villancico, which means that for any given feast we can find a series of either eight or nine villancicos.

Although in principle Matins were intended as the first Office hour of the day, celebrated at sunrise on particularly important feasts, it could be moved to the previous evening and performed around midnight. The first and foremost occasion for which villancicos were composed was, therefore, Christmas Eve, after Midnight Mass. But soon villancicos were composed for the feasts of the Immaculate Conception (8 December) and the Epiphany (6 January), as well as for Corpus Christi and the various festivities of the Virgin Mary and of the saints. As early as the first few decades of the seventeenth century, villancicos are clearly the predominant optional item in the polyphonic music repertory of the liturgy in the Peninsula, far superseding in that function the motet, which was reserved for penitential feasts. The 2,285 villancicos listed in the 1649 printed catalogue of the music library of John IV of Portugal, and by practically all the important Iberian composers of the time, were distributed throughout the liturgical year in the following way:

Feast	No. of Works	Percentage
Christmas	1,004	43.93
Corpus Christi	522	22.84
Marian Feasts	236	10.32
(Immaculate Conception	71)	
Epiphany	147	6.63
Easter	20	0.87
Other feasts of Christ	12	0.52
Feasts of Saints	308	13.50
(John the Evangelist	47)	
John the Baptist	35	
Augustine	24	
Jerome	17	
(Anthony	14)	
Other feasts	36	1.37

The joyous nature of all these celebrations allows for the choice of very lighthearted texts that in many instances preserved some of the original flavor of the sixteenth-century secular villancico, with only some minor concessions to the new liturgical context. Thus, Christmas villancicos often portrayed popular characters such as shepherds and peasants, who experienced all kinds of rather mundane situations while on their way to Bethlehem to adore the newborn Christ, while Marian "chanzonetas" offered a display of gallant praise of female beauty applied to the Virgin, and Corpus Christi pieces tended to describe the

EXAMPLE 12.5   António Marques Lésbio, *Ayrecillos mansos,* villancico, mm. 1–15, in *Vilancicos portugueses,* ed. Robert Stevenson. Lisbon: Calouste Gulbenkian Foundation, 1976, p. 49

"celestial banquet" represented by Holy Communion in terms of the most conspicuous gluttony (see Example 12.5).

The texts frequently seek to represent the various popular types of Portuguese and Spanish society, including not only those of the rural population of each Peninsular region but also ethnic minorities such as the Gypsies and Moors or African slaves. Each of these social groups is evoked in terms of its specific accent and vocabulary, as well as of its

EXAMPLE 12.6   Anon., *Sã qui turo zente pleta,* negro, mm. 23–31, in *Vilancicos portugueses,* ed. Robert Stevenson. Lisbon: Calouste Gulbenkian Foundation, 1976, p. 154

regional and/or ethnic traditions of music and dance, albeit in a stereotyped and often blatantly biased way. Even though Castillian was the predominant language (used for more than 92 percent of the villancicos in King John's library, for instance), texts in Portuguese, Galician, Basque, regional dialects, and early forms of African Creoles, Spanish, and Portuguese also appear, quite regardless of the nationality of each composer. This same taste for "exotic" color led composers constantly to make use of the characteristic rhythmic features of popular genres of Peninsular songs and dances, including, among many others, the *folía,* the *jácara,* or the *chacona.* For the same reason, the villancicos designated as *negros* or *guineos* often employed dance rhythms and responsorial features that even today can be recognized as part of African musical traditions (see Example 12.6).

This multilingual content and the theatrical nature of many of the texts were among the reasons mentioned against this genre by conservative opponents such as Domenico Pietro Cerone, who accused them in 1613 of "transforming the house of God into a theater" and of deviating the minds of the congregation "from real devotion to mere entertainment," although the Neapolitan theorist recognized that the announcement of villancicos would fill any liturgical ceremony, even with people who would otherwise miss church "even on prescribed days." For over a century, however, such bitter criticism does not seem to have had any effect on the attitude of the Iberian ecclesiastical authorities, who considered this genre as a particularly efficient way of encouraging church attendance on the part of their congregations.

Villancicos for each particular celebration in a given cathedral or royal chapel were usually written by the chapelmaster himself, who could be temporarily released for this purpose from at least part of his remaining duties, and were in principle intended just for that single occasion, or at least for the exclusive use of that institution. Although there is in fact evidence of some instances of multiple use and circulation, they tend to be copied hurriedly in sets of small-size, highly perishable, paper part-books, which explains why a large percentage of this music disappeared once it fell out of musical fashion. Nevertheless, a considerable legacy of villancicos survives in Iberian and Latin-American archives, together with small printed libretti containing all the texts sung at a particular feast. These were often published, probably for distribution at the ceremony itself, so that the congregation could follow the performance of new works. Pedro Ruimonte's *El Parnaso Español de madrigales y villancicos* (Antwerp, 1614) remains the only known example of a collection of printed sacred villancicos in this period.

Practically all the prominent Iberian composers in the seventeenth century wrote villancicos, but among those who were particularly famous for excelling in this genre were the director of the Madrid Flemish Chapel, Mateo Romero; the Spaniards Gabriel Díaz Bessón, Carlos Patiño, Juan Bautista Comes, Juan Hidalgo, Cristobal Galán, and Sebastián Durón; and the Portuguese Fr. Francisco de Santiago, Gonçalo Mendes Saldanha, Fr. Manuel Correia, and António Marques Lésbio. Latin America, as we shall see, also produced an extensive repertory of this kind. In fact, the intense musical exchange between the Iberian models and the Amerindian and Afro-American musical traditions that took place all over the Spanish and Portuguese colonies in the New World may well have had, in turn, a considerable influence on the evolution of the Peninsular villancico, particularly in such characteristic subgenres as the *negro*, the *negrilla*, the *guineo*, or the *indio*, or in works that include the rhythmic patterns of the new dances originating in the Americas (the *cumbé*, the *zarambeque*, and possibly even the *zarabanda*).

SECULAR SONG AND THEATRICAL MUSIC

Tono humano

The development of the Baroque secular song in the Peninsula is so closely related to that of the sacred villancico that the word *tono* is often used interchangeably to designate both genres, with the added qualification *al divino* (in the "divine," or sacred manner) or *al humano* (in the "human," or secular style) to identify each of them, respectively. The main difference lies, of course, in the absence of choral writing in the *tono humano* repertory, but soloistic music is remarkably similar in these two contexts, mostly because the sacred villancico incorporates, as we have seen, a strong component of popular music and dance in its semitheatrical attempt to portray the various popular types of Spain and Portugal.

The seventeenth-century secular song goes back to the double tradition of the polyphonic songbooks, started more than a century earlier with the *Cancionero del Palacio,* and of the solo villancicos and romances with instrumental accompaniment published in the vihuela prints of Milán, Narváez, and others, from 1536 on. The old distinction between the villancico, with its recurring refrain, and the strophic romance had disappeared in the meantime, however, and the term *romance* was now applied indifferently to works both with and without refrain, and with the most diversified formal design, being almost a synonym of *tono* in this new context. Other frequent designations for the same genre include *tonada* (or *tonada humana*), *solo* (or *solo humano*), *tonillo, chanzoneta, letra, baile,* or *jácara,* all of which just refer to the same generic reality of a secular song for one to four parts, with or without an instrumental accompaniment.

Throughout the first half of the century this repertory was compiled in several songbooks now preserved in various countries, including, among others, the two at the Madrid National Library (*Romances y letras a tres voces* and *Libro de Tonos Humanos*), two in Spanish private collections (*Tonos castellanos—B* and the *Cancionero de Onteniente*), and those belonging to the Library of the Ajuda Palace (Lisbon), the National Library of Torino, the Casanatense Library (Rome), and the Bayrisches Staatsbibliothek (Munich)—the latter assembled by the copyist of the Spanish Royal Chapel, Claudio de la Sablonara. To these manuscript sources must be added a print, the *Libro segundo de tonos y villancicos* (Rome, 1624), by Juan Arañes, private musician of the Duke of Pastrana, Spanish Ambassador to the Holy See.

Composers represented in these collections include the inevitable Mateo Romero, as well as Juan Blas de Castro, Gabriel Díaz Bessón, Carlos Patiño, Juan Bautista Comes, Juan Hidalgo, Álvaro de los Ríos, Juan del Vado, the Catalan Joan Pau Pujol, and the Portuguese Manuel Machado. Ranging from two to four parts, these songs usually include tuneful melodies and lively dancelike rhythms, and tend to favor dialogue between the upper parts, parallel motion at the third or sixth, and homophonic declamation of energetic rhythmic figurations rather than imitative counterpoint (see Example 12.7).

From the mid-seventeenth century, the Iberian secular song appeared mostly in the form of works for one or two voices with basso continuo or guitar accompaniment, frequently extracted from scores intended for the various genres of theatrical music—incidental stage music, opera, or zarzuela. The outstanding quality of the songs of José Marín (1619–1699), joining expressive text handling, refined melodic design, and the use of such popular dance patterns as the *canarios* or the *pasacalles,* must be stressed in the context of a vast manuscript repertory that has as yet not been the object of the systematic study it deserves.

Although several Portuguese composers who worked in Spain distinguished themselves in the field of the *tono humano,* particularly Manuel Machado, the fact that there was no court in Lisbon until 1640 and that John IV, who rose to the throne of Portugal in that year and died in 1656, was almost exclusively interested in sacred music does not seem to have allowed for the development of this secular genre in the country during the first two-thirds of the seventeenth century. Immediately afterward, the local and foremost poet and writer of the 1660s, D. Francisco Manuel de Melo, published a few of his texts that had been set to *tonos* and gives the name of each of the composers responsible for the setting. But none of the musical settings of these poems has been found. An incomplete collection of part-books of what seems to have been a series of *tonos humanos* for four voices and continuo is at this point all that remains to exemplify the late blooming of this genre in Portugal in the final third of the seventeenth century.

EXAMPLE 12.7   Carlos Patiño, *A bailar zagalejas,* final section, mm. 1–11, in *Las obras humanas de Carlos Patiño,* ed. Danièle Bécker. Cuenca: Instituto de Musica Religiosa de la Diputación Central, 1987, pp. 134–35

INCIDENTAL MUSIC, OPERA, AND ZARZUELA

The Peninsular theater had a long-standing tradition of stage music, including, from the early sixteenth century, playwrights such as Juan del Encina in Spain and Gil Vicente in Portugal. By the beginning of the seventeenth century, both the sacred *autos sacramentales* and the secular *comedias,* performed in any of the various *patios* (courtyards) of the major Iberian cities where theaters were allowed to function, usually opened with a *tono* for four voices and continuo known as *cuatro de empezar* (literally "four-part opener"), sometimes followed by a *loa* (laud). Besides incidental songs or dances that might be inserted in the dramatic action itself, successive acts could be separated by musical interludes called *bailes* or *entremeses,* and the performance there could end with a musical *fin de fiesta* ("end of feast").

Literary sources show that this tradition of combining the spoken theater with music in an informal way, to a greater or lesser extent according to the number and quality of the musicians available, or in some cases to the musical talent of the actors themselves, continues throughout the century. Only an in-depth comparative study of the extant Spanish songs and dramas of the period may, however, allow one eventually to establish concordances leading to the identification of such links between both repertories, even if it is clear that a part of this combination may have been improvisatory in nature and had disappeared without leaving any written musical evidence.

Opera, in the strict sense of a drama entirely set to music, was introduced in the Peninsula in 1627, with the staging of *La selva sin amor* at the Coliseo del Buen Retiro, the theater at the royal palace of Madrid. Although the libretto was by the great Spanish dramatist Lope de Vega, the performance can be considered a mere "cosmopolitan" operation on the part of the young King Philip IV, with music (now lost) and sets by two Italians—the composer Filippo Piccinini and the stage designer Cosimo Lotti, respectively—and most likely under the influence of the Papal Nuncio, Giulio Rospigliosi, who had been the librettist for some of the operas of Stefano Landi while moving in the circle of the Barberini family in Rome. The experiment did not have a sequel for more than thirty years, even if Lope de Vega himself praised the performance enthusiastically in the preface to the later edition of his play.

A second similar attempt, entirely produced by Spanish artists and in keeping with the general trends of Iberian music of the time, took place in 1660 with the presentation of two new operas, both with texts by the most prestigious playwright of Spain, Pedro Calderón de la Barca: *La púrpura de la rosa* (17 January) and *Celos aún del aire matan* (5 December), dealing with the Classical myths of Venus and Adonis and of Cephalus and Procris, respectively. The special occasion for these performances may have been the celebration of the peace treaty between Spain and France and of the ensuing marriage of the French King Louis XIV with the Infanta Maria Teresa. We have lost the music of the first work, but the score of *Celos,* by Juan Hidalgo, survives, alternating lengthy but highly expressive recitatives with triple-meter strophic arias (several of which are based on traditional Spanish dances, such as the *jácara* or the *seguidilla*) and with occasional brief choruses. No instrumental parts survive, except for the continuo, but it may be assumed that they were improvised according to the well-established principles of the *contrapunto concertado* that had been explained and exemplified in the music theory of the Peninsula from the mid-sixteenth century.

The success of these Calderonian operas is attested to by the fact that they were repeatedly produced at court in the following few decades, but the next Spanish work in this genre (and the first to bear the name "opera" in its descriptive title) was not presented until 7 February 1700, when Sebastián Durón's *La guerra de los gigantes* was first performed at the court of Charles II. The score offers a written-out orchestration for trumpet, two violins, and bass, and this ensemble was frequently called on to perform *ritornelli* between the various *coplas* in an aria, as well as purely instrumental sections, including the final minuet. In comparison with Hidalgo, Durón employs shorter recitatives, more complex aria patterns, and more numerous choruses for the principal characters themselves rather than for any mythological characters external to the main dramatic action (see Example 12.8).

In the near absence of a continuous tradition of true opera sung throughout (only four titles in almost eight decades), the Spanish court seems to have experimented also with a mixed genre following similar patterns to those of the English semi-opera, with a combination of spoken dialogue with elaborate operatic recitatives and arias attributed to the gods, and semipopular songs given to the mortal characters. This type was exemplified by the settings of Calderón's plays *La fiera, el rayo y la piedra* (1652), *Fortunas de Andrómeda y Perseo* (1653), *Fieras afemina amor,* and *La estatua de Prometeo* (both of the early 1670s), all of which with music probably by Hidalgo.

Nevertheless, it was in a lighter genre that theatrical music of a new kind fully estab-

EXAMPLE 12.8 Sebastián Durón, *Salir el Amor del mundo*, Diana's aria, mm. 1–14, in José López-Calo, *Historia de la musica española: 3. Siglo XVII.* Madrid: Alianza Editorial, 1983, p. 193

lished itself in the Peninsula in the mid-1650s, when the Marquis of Heliche was in charge of producing plays at the theater of the royal palace of La Zarzuela, near Madrid, for the entertainment of the king and the court. In 1657 and 1658, respectively, he presented two new plays by Calderón—*El golfo de las sirenas* and *El laurel de Apolo*—both under the descriptive title of "fiesta de La Zarzuela," although the latter ended up, in fact, being performed at the theater of the palace of Buen Retiro. The music for these works has not survived, but the librettos show that they consisted mostly of spoken dialogue with interspersed songs and choruses as well as with the usual introductory *loa* and possibly also with a musical conclusion. Still, in 1658 a similar play, *Triunfos de Amor y Fortuna,* by dramatist Antonio de Solís, was also produced at the Buen Retiro, and a few of its songs have survived, although the earliest zarzuela for which we possess a complete score is *Celos hacen estrellas,* with text by Juan Veléz de Guevara and music by Juan Hidalgo. The number of zarzuelas performed at the various royal palaces and soon also in public theaters grew constantly until the end of the century, with texts by Veléz de Guevara, Francisco de Avellaneda, Augustín de Salazar, Antonio de Solís, and later by José de Cañizares. Music appeared to be mostly by Hidalgo until his death (1685) and then by his younger contemporaries Cristobal Galán, Juan de Navas, and the young Sebastián Durón, who opened an impressive career in this genre with *Salir el amor al mundo* (1696), on a text by Cañizares.

Although the Évora Public Library owns several scores of late-seventeenth- and early-eighteenth-century zarzuelas (and even that of Hidalgo's opera *Celos aún del aire matan*), and archival documents list several Spanish *comedias* performed at the Lisbon court from the 1660s on, no evidence has yet been found concerning the musical component of the latter or suggesting that any Portuguese composer prior to the eighteenth century may have tried his hand at a complete score in the new theatrical genres. However, a recently identified early-seventeenth-century manuscript in the Braga Public Archive contains a large number of *bailes* and songs specifically intended as incidental music for the theater, and among the composers represented in the collection, besides many of the above-mentioned Spanish authors, are Portuguese musicians of the turn of the century such as António Correia and José Leite da Costa.

ORGAN MUSIC

In the early decades of the seventeenth century the Iberian organ did not undergo any radical changes with regard to the innovations that had been introduced from the 1570s and 1580s, that is, a tendency toward an increase in the number and variety of stops (including the use of several large-scale, bright reed stops, such as "trombetas" and "clarines," besides the traditional principals and mixtures) and the introduction of the split keyboard. The latter was certainly the most original characteristic of the Spanish and Portuguese instruments in comparison to their equivalents in other European countries, and this consisted in a break between the keys of central C and C sharp, each half of the keyboard operating a different ensemble of stops. Contrasts of timbre that usually demanded two keyboards could thus be obtained on a single manual as long as the range of the contrasting parts did not go over the above-mentioned break. Pedal keyboards were generally absent or reduced to a few keys that might be used only for pedal-points or cadences.

By the middle of the century, Peninsular organs became larger, with a wider variety of reed stops, some of which were placed in swell boxes ("en eco"), although no evidence exists of the use of gradual *crescendo* or *decrescendo* effects but, rather, to the mere opposition of fully contrasting dynamic levels. The choice of the halved stops assigned to each half of the keyboard seems to have resulted mostly from the wish for variety of tone color instead of from a fully balanced conception of the whole range of the instrument according to the northern European or Italian organ-making traditions. Thus, left-hand stops may in fact sound higher than those of the right side of the keyboard, or vice versa, and others, for instance, will produce a melodic line doubled at the upper twelfth. External, horizontally placed reed stops "en chamade" may have been used since the 1620s or 1630s and became the general rule in the second half of the century, when they were often added to earlier instruments.

The Iberian keyboard repertory of the early seventeenth century is still formally presented as being intended for any of the keyboard instruments available at the time—organ, clavichord, or harpsichord—as well as for other harmonic instruments such as the vihuela or harp. In fact, however, the growing predominance of an idiomatic writing for the organ, specifically intended for several of the characteristics described above, soon became evident. The composers working in the 1610s and 1620s—Bernardo Clavijo del Castillo, Sebastián Aguilera de Heredia, and Francisco Peraza, among others—basically developed the legacy of the great sixteenth-century local masters, such as Antonio de Cabezón and António Carreira, who had excelled at the service of the Spanish and Portuguese Royal Chapels, respectively. The two most significant monuments of this development can be found, however, in the printed collections of the Portuguese Manuel Rodrigues Coelho (*Flores de Música,* 1620) and the Spaniard Francisco Correa de Arauxo (*Facultad Organica,* 1626).

In both cases, the predominant form is that of the "tiento," the Iberian equivalent to the Italian *ricercare,* based on a four- to five-part imitative texture, often lasting for more than two hundred measures. Coelho, who ended his career as organist to the Portuguese Royal Chapel in Lisbon, wrote mostly plurithematic tientos, with a wealth of thematic, motivic, and merely figural material freely presented throughout successive contrasting sections, several of which make use of highly virtuosic passages in triplets or dotted rhythms, not unlike those employed in the works of the English virginalists or of Sweelinck. As to Correa de Arauxo, who spent most of his life in the service of the convent of San Salvador in Madrid, he seems to be particularly fond of monothematic writing, following the tra-

EXAMPLE 12.9 Pedro de San Lorenzo, *Obra de primer tono de mano yzquierda,* mm. 90–95, in *Obras selectas para órgão,* ed. Gerhard Doderer. Lisbon: Calouste Gulbenkian Foundation, 1974, p. 49

dition of Cabezón. His remarkably free use of dissonance, with frequent clashes of unprepared seconds and sevenths, led him to develop the specific subgenre of the "tiento de falsas," similar to the Italian *durezze e legature,* in which an innovative, daring harmonic language breaks away from the rules of modal counterpoint and opens the path to many aspects of Baroque tonality. Correa also presented several examples of variations on sacred and secular well-known melodies (*Dexaldos mi madre, Todo el mundo en general, Guárdame las vacas,* or Lasso's *Suzanne un jour,* on which Coelho also left four sets of virtuosic diminutions), and the preface to his *Facultad Organica* is a precious source of information regarding such issues as ornamentation, rhythmic *inegalité* (or "buen ayre"), and fingering.

Correa de Arauxo included in his collection several "medio registros," tientos based on the new device of the split keyboard in which one of the voices of the contrapuntal texture is placed entirely in one of the halves of the keyboard, whereas the remaining parts are written within the other half, thus allowing for a contrasting registration between both sides. The *medio registro* can be "de tiple" (soprano), "de alto," or the "de bajo" (bass), according to the part that is isolated from the remaining polyphonic texture, and later composers used this particular genre to explore all kinds of concertato contrasts between solo and tutti, in a process that paralleled many of the similar experiments taking place in Italian instrumental music at the same time (see Example 12.9).

A characteristic genre of organ music developed in the Peninsula from the mid-seventeenth century is the so-called batalla, a battle-piece that was probably performed at Mass during the Elevation of the Host as a sort of musical representation of the mystical struggle between Good and Evil. Like its vocal equivalent, the "misa de batalla," it makes use of the theatrical motives of Jannequin's *La bataille de Marignan* in its attempt to portray the sound effects of the battlefield. The growing number and variety of bright reed stops in the Iberian organ helped the choice of tone colors for this musical portrayal, which must have had an extremely effective dramatic impact on the congregations assembled in the local cathedrals (see Example 12.10).

Besides these soloistic genres, the organ was called on to play for various moments of

EXAMPLE 12.10   Fr. Diogo da Conceição, *Batalha do quinto tom,* mm. 18–35, in *Livro de obras para órgão,* ed. Klaus Speer. Lisbon: Calouste Gulbenkian Foundation, 1967, p. 147

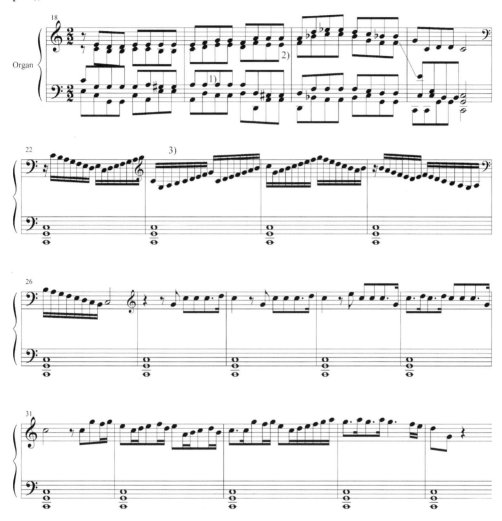

the liturgy, either doubling the choir or, at certain occasions, replacing it altogether. In fact, one of the tests to which organists were submitted when applying for a church position was to play four-part *vocal* polyphony at first sight, directly from a choir book. Extant regulations for most cathedral chapels in the Peninsula specifically state that the organ must take part in the performance of several polyphonic items, especially the Kyries, the Magnificat, and other canticles, Marian antiphons such as the *Ave maris stella* or the *Salve Regina,* and hymns such as the *Pange lingua.* In some cases the organist may have doubled the full choir, or he could play a four-part accompaniment to a vocal psalm-tone, but in many other instances he replaced the voices completely, and the keyboard sources of this period contain a large number of versets intended for that purpose.

No organ music after Correa de Arauxo's book seems to have been printed in Portugal or Spain for the rest of the seventeenth century, but a considerable number of manuscripts assembled in both countries during that period have reached us, assembling a large repertory that obviously circulated all over the Peninsula, as well as in Latin America, regardless of the nationality or the actual area of activity of each composer. Among the most influential authors represented in those handwritten sources were the Aragonese José Ximénez (1601–1672) and Pablo Bruna (1611–1679), as well as the Portuguese Pedro de Araújo (fl. 1662–1705) and Diogo da Conceição (fl. seventeenth century). These and other composers, many of whom are known for only a few works each, employed all the genres described above—the tiento, the medio registro, the batalla, and the various types of versets—and developed such idiomatic Baroque features as stock virtuosic passages, modulatory repetitions of long phrases, melodic sequences, hemiolas, and irregular metric patterns, building a highly idiomatic organ literature that simultaneously parallels but stands apart from the French, German, and Italian repertories.

The peak of this development can be found in the works of Juan Bautista Cabanilles (1644–1712), for most of his long life organist at the cathedral of Valencia. His formidable reputation in his lifetime and afterward was shown by the large number of extant copies of his compositions, among which a particularly extensive collection assembled by his disciple Josep Elías, who significantly opened it with the Latin heading *"ante ruet mundus quam surget Cabanilles secundus,"* or "the world will crumble before a second Cabanilles appears." In his music, sinuous chromaticism and harsh dissonance are often employed to create chiaroscuro effects as well as to achieve emotional expression and dramatic tension. He was a master of imitation and of contrapuntal elaboration on a cantus firmus, and also experimented with Italianate toccata-like writing as well as with energetic dance patterns, especially in his sets of virtuosic variations on Spanish popular "pasacalles," "paseos," and "gallardas."

OTHER INSTRUMENTAL MUSIC

Besides the organ, the soloistic instrument to receive the largest compositional output in the Peninsula is clearly the five-course guitar, which in fact will become known all over Europe as the "Spanish guitar." Already described in 1555 by the theorist Juan Bermudo, it superseded both the six-course vihuela and the four-course guitar, and it remained the standard instrument of its family in Spain and Portugal throughout the seventeenth century. As the guitar became an increasingly favorite instrument (in 1677 Ruíz de Ribayaz said that "even the children of Madrid know it and play it"), there was an expanding market for pedagogic treatises as well as for basic repertory dedicated to it, which explains why Juan Carlos Amat's introductory treatise entitled *Guitarra española de cinco órdenes,* originally published in Barcelona in 1596, was the object of various editions until at least 1639.

In 1624 Juan Arañes published in Rome his above-mentioned collection of polyphonic *tonos* and villancicos both in mensural vocal notation and in an easy system of *zifra* for the guitar, and two years later Luis de Briceño gave in his *Metodo muy facillissimo para aprender a tañer la guitarra* (Paris, 1626) not only specific instructions on the technique of strumming chords (*rasgueado*) but also the basic chord progressions for an extensive series of songs and dances adapted to the instrument: among others, *romances, letrillas, folías, zarabandas, gallardas, chaconas,* and twelve *pasacalles.* As for Nicolau Doizi (or possibly Dias) de Velasco, who served the Spanish Viceroy in Naples and the King of Spain in Madrid and was known as the "Portuguese Orpheus" and the "Lusitanian Amphion," he was the author of the *Nuevo metodo de cifra* (Naples, 1640), one of the first theoretical sources by an Iberian musician to explain the system of basso continuo realization.

Francisco Guerau's *Poema harmonico* (Madrid, 1694) in many ways culminated this evolution, with a series of virtuosic *pasacalles* of unsurpassed technical difficulty, contrapuntal elaboration, refined ornamentation, and sheer beauty. Guerau's extant documentary sources constantly mention the guitar as an essential element of musical life in the Peninsula in the following decades, and the *alfabeto* was often used in music manuscripts, generally in connection with the accompaniment of secular vocal music. It was, however, only in 1674 that a new influential manual was published in Zaragoza, the *Instrucción de música sobre la guitarra española* by Gaspar Sanz, with such impact that it was reprinted eight more times by 1697. Sanz, a guitar virtuoso who traveled in Italy and entered the service of Philip IV's illegitimate son, Don Juan de Austria, begins by giving detailed instructions on how to string, fret, and tune the instrument, how to master the techniques of the *rasgueado* (strummed chords) and *punteado* (plucked strings), and how to realize a continuo. He proceeds to offer a long collection of his works, distributed by tonality according to an order of growing difficulty for the performer: traditional dances from Spain (*canarios, zarabandas, villanos, marizápalos, folías, españoletas, jácaras, chaconas, matachines,* and thirteen magnificent sets of *pasacalles*) as well as modern dances from France (*allemandes, courantes, sarabandes, gigues*), and even a *capricho arpeado* that is clearly influenced by the French *prélude non mesuré*.

If Guerau's music demands outstanding technical skills, various manuscript sources of the end of the century provide the amateur with a large repertory of accessible songs and dances. That is the case with Antonio de Santa Cruz's manuscript anthology wrongly entitled *Libro de vihuela,* and with the three Portuguese guitar tablatures preserved at the Coimbra University, the Lisbon National Library, and the Gulbenkian Foundation, in which we find also the first notated examples of African (or most likely Afro-Brazilian) dances such as the *cumbé* or the *paracumbé.*

The guitar is also one of the instruments discussed in the *Luz y Norte musical* (Madrid, 1677) by Lucas Ruíz de Ribayaz, together with the harp, an instrument that in the meantime acquired a considerable importance in continuo realizations in church, chamber, and theater music, after being for decades associated with mere adaptations of the keyboard and vihuela repertory. Ruíz was indeed the first author to publish a number of interesting *folías, jácaras,* and *pasacalles* specifically intended for the harp. A few years later another important work for this instrument, printed in two volumes in 1702 and 1704 but written in the course of the previous thirty years, as the author himself declared in his preface, was Diego Fernández de Huete's *Compendio numeroso de zifras armonicas.*

If the soloistic literature for keyboard, guitar, or harp is well represented in the Peninsula, the Iberian seventeenth-century repertory for instrumental ensembles, on the contrary, is extremely scarce. This situation contrasted sharply with the intense activity of instrumental performance that we know to have taken place in Portugal and Spain during this period, as Cerone's 1613 *El Melopeo* describes in great detail, and as is shown by the specific instrumentation indicated in many manuscript sources of Latin sacred works, villancicos, and *tonos.* The most likely explanation for this is the perpetuation of the often-stated sixteenth-century practice of adapting for instrumental ensemble performance any suitable vocal or keyboard work, with the musicians reading directly from the original source without needing a written transposition.

There are, nevertheless, a few significant exceptions to this rule, starting with Bartolomé de Selma y Salaverde's *Primo libro de canzoni, fantasie & correnti* (Venice, 1638), which contained, in the tradition of Diego Ortíz, a number of highly virtuosic works for one to four instruments and basso continuo. The mid-seventeenth-century manuscripts of the

EXAMPLE 12.11 Fr. Teotónio da Cruz, *Concertado a 3,* mm. 1–11, in Rui Vieira Nery, "New Sources for the Study of the Portuguese Seventeenth-Century Consort Music," *Journal of the Viola da Gamba Society of America* XXII (1985), p. 22

monastery of Santa Cruz (Coimbra) also contain almost one hundred examples of one- to four-part contrapuntal elaborations on a *cantus firmus* that are undoubtedly instrumental in nature. They are designated as *tonos concertados* or simply *concertados* and are attributed to Augustinian composers of the 1630s and 1640s such as D. Teotónio da Cruz, D. António da Madre de Deus, and D. João de Santa Maria (see Example 12.11).

Finally, Francisco José de Castro's *Trattenimenti armonici da camera a tre, due violini, violoncello o cembalo* (Bologna, 1695), a somewhat Corellian collection of sonatas, seems to contain few Spanish traits besides the composer's nationality, as Castro was entirely Italian trained as a musician, and in some way he simply anticipated in his work the coming switch to the Italian taste that will take place in Iberian music in the first few decades of the eighteenth century.

Spain and Portugal: The First Half of the Eighteenth Century

THE PENETRATION OF THE ITALIAN MODELS

Charles II, the last Spanish king of the dynasty of Austria, died childless in 1700, having chosen Philip of Bourbon, Duke of Anjou and grandson of Louis XIV of France, as heir to his crown. This choice was challenged by the Austrian Archduke Charles of Habsburg, and all the major European powers became involved in a lengthy and brutal military confrontation, the War of the Spanish Succession. The conflict ended with the confirmation of Philip V's accession to the throne, albeit in exchange for the loss of practically all non-Iberian Spanish possessions in Europe, including Milan, Naples, Sicily, Sardinia, and the Netherlands. However, once in power, Philip proved to be an innovative ruler, open to the new political and ideological theories of the Absolutist state and interested in modernizing his kingdom and opening it to Europe.

Similar ideas were adopted by the young Portuguese King John V, who came to the throne in 1707. Portugal had been at war with Spain for more than six decades, after recovering its independence in 1640. The public finances were exhausted, but John benefited not only from the effects of a definitive peace with the neighboring country but also particularly from the discovery of gold mines in Brazil. They provided the Portuguese Crown with immense wealth it had not known since the golden age of the spice trade with India in the fifteenth and early-sixteenth centuries.

Both countries were now ready to intensify their intellectual and cultural exchange with the rest of Western Europe, breaking the isolationist trend that had characterized, to a great extent, the Counter Reformational Iberian tradition for over a century and a half. Rather than being seen abroad as the proud mainstays of a fundamentalist Catholic resistance against secular rationalist humanism, the two Peninsular sovereigns now wanted to project a cosmopolitan image of modern rulers according to the mainstream European tendencies of the period. They did this at various economic, political, and institutional levels, but they were especially keen with regard to the artistic patterns adopted by their courts.

The considerable changes that took place in Spanish and Portuguese music throughout the first half of the eighteenth century and that corresponded, most of all, to the massive penetration of the models of the Italian Baroque can only be understood in the context of this larger political framework. The two courts took the lead in this process of stylistic change, starting with their own Royal Chapels. As the Absolutist system reinforced the role of the aesthetic choices of the court as the model for the local urban elites all over the country, the musical life of Portugal and Spain tried to adapt as fast as possible to the new artistic fashions.

It was not a simple or immediate process, however. During much of the first quarter of the century the music institutions and musicians who were caught in this transition sought simultaneously to acquire an increased awareness of the imported cosmopolitan models and to integrate them into the local Peninsular traditions in a somewhat balanced way. To some extent, they just quickened the pace of the process of assimilation and local reelaboration of the new European musical trends that had already characterized much of the previous half-century. The haste with which such efforts were conducted produced a variety of blatantly hybrid solutions: works still bearing modal ascriptions but increasingly tonal in their harmonic language; polyphonic compositions in strict imitation but with violin and oboe obbligato parts; villancicos written in the form of a cantata, with a succession of arias and recitatives; organ tientos inserting graceful trio-sonata textures into otherwise solemn imitative works.

The ultimate imposition of the Italian models, achieved mostly though the gradual hiring of Italian composers, singers, and instrumentalists by the principal musical institutions of the two countries and their colonies, took place from the mid-1720s. Still, many musical genres, especially those with a popular appeal, such as the zarzuela and other types of theatrical music, or the guitar and keyboard repertory, reflected some combination of Iberian and Italian characteristics.

Portugal is a much smaller country, and the fact that the overwhelming power of the state was not balanced by other social agents with some degree of economic autonomy able to serve as significant patrons of the arts—either large aristocratic estates or wealthy bourgeois families, for instance—appears to have quickened this process of assimilation of the Italianate musical taste by the Portuguese musicians. John V's choices had greater repercussions on the musical life of his country than those of Philip V of Spain.

CHURCH MUSIC

When Philip V ascended to the Spanish throne, the chapelmaster of the Madrid Royal Chapel was Sebastián Durón (1660–1716), one of the most distinguished Peninsular composers of his generation. In 1701, after the reforms introduced by the new sovereign, the institution had a choir of fourteen singers and an orchestra of fourteen instruments including strings, trumpets, and *bajones,* as well as four organists, two harpists, and one archlute player. This was the musical staff that Durón had at his disposal and that corresponded to the performance needs of the sacred music, most of which were still written for the two-choir and continuo ensemble inherited from the previous century, in a few cases with obbligato instrumental parts but rarely with a full orchestral accompaniment. Durón was nevertheless accused by the traditionalist circles of the Spanish musical life of being responsible, during his tenure in office, for an excessive penetration of the Italian style, both in the general repertory of the chapel and in his own compositions.

But in 1706 Durón made a serious political faux pas: when the Habsburg pretender to the Spanish throne, the Archduke Charles, temporarily conquered Madrid on 25 July, the composer led the Royal Chapel in a welcoming ceremony that, quite understandably, caused the wrath of the opposing party. The Bourbon armies took the capital back a few days later and Durón felt he had no other choice but to go into exile, settling in France for the rest of his life, although Philip V did not officially replace Durón as chapelmaster until the composer's death.

Durón's successor was José de Torres y Martínez Bravo (c. 1670–1738), who in 1702 had published the first Spanish treatise on the realization of figured bass, the *Reglas generales de acompañar,* based on the Bolognese Lorenzo Penna's 1672 *Li primi albori musicali per principanti.* Torres's growing enthusiasm for the Italian style was shown in the evolution of his own writing, as he gradually began to use violins, oboes, and continuo on a systematic basis in his sacred music, and later adopted the recitative-aria pattern for the soloistic sections in it. Under his direction, the Royal Chapel's orchestra increased the number of strings and oboes, constituting a full Baroque orchestral ensemble by at least 1715.

On Christmas Eve 1734, a fire destroyed the music archives of the Royal Chapel. Torres was in charge of acquiring new music for the ensemble, which contributed even more to the renovation of the repertory, as there was no effort to obtain new copies of the traditional seventeenth-century music literature that constituted the basic fare of the chapel in the past. Torres's own works formed the nucleus of the new music library, together with those of Antonio Literes, of José de Nebra, and of two Italian composers who had been introduced by Philip V's second wife, Queen Isabella Farnese: Filippo Falconi and Francesco Courcelle, or Corselli. If Literes, who became particularly well known for his zarzuelas, was somewhat more faithful to the Iberian tradition than any of the other composers involved, it is quite evident that by the mid-1730s the Spanish Royal Chapel had adopted wholeheartedly the new Italianate Baroque taste in sacred music.

When José de Torres died in 1738, the new royal chapelmaster was Courcelle, an Italian composer from the Duchy of Parma, like the new queen, but of French ancestry. He left more than three hundred works of sacred music, several of which are with orchestra, and various operas to libretti by Metastasio. Both genres show a clear Neapolitan influence. Indeed, when asked in 1751 by King Ferdinand VI to draw up a list of composers whose works should be copied to enlarge even further the archives of the Royal Chapel, his choice included the names of Alessandro Scarlatti, Francesco Durante, Leonardo Leo, and Pergolesi.

Another influential figure associated with the Spanish Royal Chapel in this period was José de Nebra (1702–1768), the institution's first organist and later vice-chapelmaster, who also was heavily involved after the fire of 1734 in the composition of the chapel's new repertory. Although de Nebra was particularly famous for his numerous theatrical scores, he also was the author of almost one hundred works of sacred music, many of which had a full orchestral accompaniment. When Ferdinand VI's wife, Maria Barbara of Braganza, died in 1758, Nebra composed a monumental Requiem Mass and Office of the Dead.

In Portugal, at John V's request, various papal decrees transformed the Royal Chapel into the wealthiest and most prestigious religious institution in the country. At its head was the Archbishop of Lisbon himself, with the new dignity of patriarch and precedence over all the remaining bishops in the kingdom. Thanks to the apparently inexhaustible resources of the Brazilian gold mines, the Portuguese embassy in Rome was entrusted with the mission of hiring the very best musicians available at the papal curia, no matter the cost. The most extraordinary—and expensive—acquisition was that of Domenico Scarlatti, who in 1719 left the splendid position of chapelmaster of the Cappella Giulia to accept a similar office at the Portuguese Royal Chapel. And many other virtuoso singers and players were similarly hired. In 1728, Walther's *Musikalisches Lexikon* listed the members of the chapel's string orchestra (seven violins, two violas, two cellos, and a double bass, all foreigners, plus a Portuguese organist, Carlos Seixas), and by 1730 the chapel choir consisted of as many as thirty singers, all from Italy, to which should be added the players of the *Charamela Real,* the king's wind ensemble.

Scarlatti's presence in Lisbon became, of course, a pillar in the new musical establishment of the court. He arrived in the Portuguese capital in November of 1719 and remained there until the end of 1729, with a possible absence in 1724, when Quantz met him in Rome, and yet another one in 1728–29, when again he went to the papal city to celebrate his marriage to Maria Catalina Gentili. He returned to Lisbon on 29 December 1729, and only then left for Madrid to join his pupil, the Portuguese Infanta Maria Barbara of Braganza, who had just married the crown prince of Spain, the future Ferdinand VI.

Scarlatti remained in Spain until his death. His duties at the Portuguese court included directing all the sacred music performed at the Royal Chapel, choosing the repertory, and determining the recruiting policy of the institution, an area in which there can be little doubt that his personal reputation was decisive in attracting to Lisbon the plethora of distinguished musicians assembled under his authority. As a composer he does not appear to have dedicated himself intensely to the writing of sacred music for this ensemble, although three of his liturgical compositions for voices and continuo—a *Te Deum,* the motet *Te gloriosus,* and the psalm *Laudate pueri*—survive in the archives of the Lisbon cathedral.

In 1713 a music school was attached to the Royal Chapel, the Seminario da Patriarcal, which had a major role in the training of Portuguese professional musicians for over a century. A few years later, three of the best students from this seminary—António Teixeira, João Rodrigues Esteves, and António de Almeida—were sent to Rome to pursue advanced studies in composition on a royal scholarship. On returning to Lisbon, they in turn became important to Portuguese musical life, as well as respected pedagogues.

The musical model imported from Italy by John V was, therefore, that of the Roman "colossal" style of Orazio Pitoni, well represented, for instance, in António Teixeira's monumental twenty-part *Te Deum* written for the Italian church of Lisbon, Nossa Senhora do Loreto. On a smaller scale, both the Mass for eight voices and the Magnificat by Rodrigues Esteves demonstrate the same strict handling of compact imitative writing (see Example 12.12), albeit occasionally combined with florid coloratura lines. By contrast, Almeida, whose greatest triumph while in Rome was achieved with his oratorio *La Giuditta* (1726), was more influenced by the tradition of Stradella, and once back in Lisbon he in fact dedicated much of his energy to operatic composition, albeit without ever abandoning the field of sacred music altogether. To these composers should be added the organist and vice-chapelmaster of the Royal Chapel, Carlos Seixas, who displayed in his extant liturgical works the same gifts of melodic invention and expressive writing that characterized his keyboard sonatas.

One of the most interesting aspects of John V's role in the evolution of Portuguese church music is the fact that some of his personal choices in music affected not only the Royal Chapel but also the whole country. His intense dislike of the traditional sacred villancico, which he considered barbaric and provincial, and as such impossible to reconcile with the new cosmopolitan image he wanted to forge for the arts in his country, moved him to the extreme of forbidding this genre altogether, first at his chapel (1717), then in the entire kingdom (1723). Such a radical decision was never accepted in Spain, where the villancico was still quite fashionable until the middle of the eighteenth century, even if frequently subject to a considerable Italian influence, and only thereafter gradually moved from the liturgical repertory of the main ecclesiastical institutions into the popular tradition.

One area of Peninsular sacred music that is still far from having been properly studied is that of the chant repertory of this period. Both Philip V of Spain and John V of Portugal paid considerable attention to the official imposition of the Roman melodies and the suppression of local chant variants, and throughout the first half of the eighteenth century most Spanish and Portuguese cathedrals spent large amounts of money in the copying of new chant choir books that often explicitly claimed to be faithful to the practices of the papal choir. Curiously enough, we find in some of those "reformed" chant books a number of rather spurious additions to the original melodies, such as florid soloistic cadenzas with operatic coloratura inserted at cadential points, and some sources also suggest the use of unorthodox performance practices such as four-part harmonizations and basso continuo accompaniment.

EXAMPLE 12.12 João Rodrigues Esteves, *Magnificat,* mm. 166–72, in *Obras selectas,* ed. Gerhard Doderer. Lisbon: Calouste Gulbenkian Foundation, 1980, p. 211

OPERA AND STAGE MUSIC

On 25 August 1703, Philip V celebrated the birthday of his first wife, Maria Luisa of Savoy, with a performance of at least part of an opera at the Coliseo del Buen Retiro theater. The work was entitled *Il pomo d'oro,* but it is not clear whether or not this was a revival of Cesti's 1668 score. The Italian company invited to produce this performance, known in Madrid as the *Truffaldines* because of the name of one of the "commedia dell'arte" characters involved in the plot of the above-mentioned opera, remained active in Madrid.

After a few further productions at the Buen Retiro, in 1703 the Truffaldines rented a new theater at the Calle de Alcalá. Their enormous success with the local audiences and the fact that they were exempt from paying the traditional taxes to the city's hospitals led the two traditional companies of Spanish theater officially licensed in Madrid to complain bitterly to the king about what they considered a form of unfair competition, but to no avail. By 1708, the Italian company was established in the *corral* (patio) of Los Caños del Peral, where it remained, under the protection of the queen herself, until 1714.

In 1716, following the death of Maria Luisa and the second marriage of the king to the Italian Princess Isabella Farnese, a new Italian operatic troupe was already at work in the same theater, protected first by the Duke of Alberoni, brother of the all-powerful Spanish Prime Minister, and later by the Marquis Anibale Scotti. The company accompanied the court to Seville during the five years (1728–33) of residence of Philip V in that city, and later to Aranjuez and La Granja. Meanwhile, in 1735–37 the theater of Los Caños del Peral was used by a company of Spanish singers who performed Italian operas translated into Spanish, in an effort to regain the favor of the public and of the court.

However, the theater was demolished and lavishly rebuilt in 1738 in the Italian style, as a royal establishment in which the Italian company performed in succession a series of operas by Hasse—*Demetrio, Demofoonte, Siroe,* and *La Clemenza di Tito* (all with librettos by Metastasio)—as well as two anonymous compositions: *Artaserse,* again with a libretto by Metastasio, and *La fé en las traiciones,* on a Spanish text by Jerónimo Gilli.

In 1737, the arrival of Carlo Broschi, that is, Farinelli, one of the most famous castrati in Europe, had direct consequences in this operatic life of the court. Invited by Queen Isabella Farnese, who hoped the singer's talent would have a positive effect of Philip V's chronic depression, Farinelli quickly gained the sovereign's complete confidence, so much so that he was exempt from submitting to the authority of any other person or institution in the country but the king and queen. Given lavish support from 1738 until his departure from Spain in 1759, he produced a new operatic season at the remodeled Coliseo del Buen Retiro, with a large orchestra and a cast of first-rate Italian singers, which included *bel canto* luminaries such as Anton Raaf, Pio Fabri, and Caffarelli. The operas presented were usually by Courcelle, Corradini, and Mele, often based on Metastasian libretti.

When Philip V died, in 1746, and was succeeded by his son, Ferdinand VI, Farinelli's role as producer of operatic entertainment for the court was even further reinforced by the new monarch and Queen Maria Barbara of Braganza. Until Ferdinand's own death, in 1759, his budget for the Fiestas Reales ("royal feasts") he presented either at the Buen Retiro or at the king's summer palaces made the Spanish court one of the most sumptuous centers of opera production in Europe. Although Domenico Scarlatti was fully active at the Spanish court from 1729 and had earlier had considerable success with the operatic genre, he was never involved in opera productions while in Spain, either before or after the arrival of Farinelli. Scarlatti's role in the musical life of the court seems to have been limited to his activity as a keyboard virtuoso, composer, and teacher.

John V of Portugal was not as directly interested in opera as his Spanish neighbor. If the first opera performed in Portugal—*Il Don Chischiotte della Mancha,* with music by an anonymous composer—was given at the royal palace of Ribeira in 1728, and even repeated there several times in the following years, only six more operas were produced at court until the monarch's death in 1750. Three of these were by the Portuguese composer Francisco António de Almeida: *La pazienza di Socrate* (1733), *La finta pazza* (1735), and *La Spinalba* (1739), written in a style not unlike that of his Roman oratorio *La Giuditta* (see Example 12.13).

Various operatic *serenate* commemorating festive events concerning the royal family

EXAMPLE 12.13   Francisco António de Almeida, *La Giuditta,* Oloferne's aria, "Date trombe il suo guerriero," mm. 33–37, in *La Giuditta,* ed. Jaime Mota, Fernando Bessa Valente, and Jorge Alexandre Costa. Oporto: Fermata, 2000, p. 100

were nevertheless presented at court with significant success. Until 1728 Domenico Scarlatti was heavily involved in the composition of many of these, as testified by the reports of the papal nuncio in the Portuguese capital during those years, and so was Almeida after the Italian master's departure to Spain.

The sovereign's concern with putting an end to all artistic genres he considered old-fashioned led him in 1727 to forbid the traditional Spanish and Portuguese comedies presented every year for the benefit of the Lisbon All-Saints Hospital. Starting in October 1731, however, various performances of operatic *serenate* were allowed in improvised theaters set in private residences of Lisbon, and in December 1735 an Italian opera company headed by the violinist Alessandro Paghetti was authorized to give public performances at the Academia da Trindade, starting with Schiassi's *Farnace.* In 1738 the company was established in the new theater of the Rua dos Condes, where until 1742 it performed twenty-five *opere serie* by composers such as Schiassi, Leonardo Leo, Rinaldo di Capua, and Pergolesi.

A second public theater in Lisbon, the Teatro do Bairro Alto, presented from 1733 various puppet-operas with texts by the Jewish playwright António José da Silva—among them *Esopaida* (1734), *Os encantos de Medeia* (1735), *Anfitrião* (1736), *As guerras de Alecrim e Manjerona* (1737), and *As variedades de Proteu* (1737)—with music by António Teixeira. The texts are highly satirical in nature and may have contributed to the playwright's arrest, trial, and execution by the Portuguese Inquisition in 1739. Teixeira's music consists mostly of recitatives and arias in the *buffo* style, alternating with the spoken dialogue, showing the overall Italianate taste that one would expect from a Roman-trained composer. The fact that this kind of theater may have appealed particularly to the middle classes, rather than to the aristocratic elite, did not lead him to use any of the traditional types of Iberian songs and dances.

In 1742 John V suffered a heart attack and was partially paralyzed thereafter until his death in 1750. Dominated by terrible religious fears, and convinced by his confessor that his condition was a punishment for his personal sins and those of the country, the monarch forbade all forms of public entertainment in Portugal, as a form of collective, national atonement. For the next eight years, opera, the theater, and dancing, whether in public or private spaces, were completely forbidden in the entire Portuguese territory, much to the annoyance of the crown prince, the future King Joseph I, who will in due time become an enthusiastic protector of operatic performances.

In Spain, however, where none of these drastic decisions is in effect, the public continues to favor the traditional Spanish zarzuela as an alternative to the Italian opera. Although Sebastian Durón's exile prevents him from writing new works for the Madrid stages after his Spanish opera *La guerra de los gigantes,* his influence continued to be felt in the works of his successors. António Literes (*Con musica y por amor, Acis y Galatea, Hasta lo insensible lo adora* and *El estrago en la fineza*) and José de Nebra (*Amor aumenta el valor, Venus y Adonis, Viento es dicha de amor,* and various comedias on the lives of saints) were two of the most prolific authors in this genre, usually to texts by playwrights José de Cañizares or Antonio de Zamora. But some of the Italian composers active in Madrid in the first half of the eighteenth century, such as Jaime Facco, Antonio Duni, and particularly Francesco Coradini, also distinguished themselves in the zarzuela, thus producing an even greater contact between Peninsular and Italian musical idioms in the Spanish theatrical music of the time. To these should be added the many *autos sacramentales* with music by José de Nebra.

In fact, it is due to a great extent to the zarzuela and other similar types of popular theater that the traditional Iberian dance and song patterns inherited from the seventeenth century survived through the first half of the eighteenth century, even if in a permanent dialogue with the Italian operatic Baroque style. By the last third of the century, when the new Classical and pre-Romantic aesthetic trends point again toward the constitution of an idiomatically Spanish art music, it was in this urban stage music, rather than in any direct inspiration from the musical traditions of the rural areas, that composers tended to find their source material.

INSTRUMENTAL MUSIC

Iberian keyboard music in the early years of the eighteenth century was still strongly influenced by the legacy of Cabanilles and of the organ repertory tradition of the previous century. The organ anthologies assembled by the Catalonian Antonio Martin i Coll (c. 1660–c. 1740) in the years 1706–1709 under some very Baroque-sounding names—*Flores de Musica, Pensil deleitoso, Huerto ameno* I and II, and *Ramillete oloroso*—represent a perfect example of this period of transition, as they contain traditional Iberian dances and songs (Folía, Villano, Canarios, Marizápalos, Vacas), tientos and *fabordones,* French minuets and sarabandes, and Italian songs and instrumental pieces, including adaptations of movements from Corelli's Op. 5. The old and the new, the local and the international are brought together into the same manuscripts but side by side, without any stylistic mixture.

A different case is that of another organist from Catalonia, Josep Elías (c. 1678–c. 1755), who was Cabanilles's favorite disciple. Having collected his works in 1749 under the revealing title *Obras de órgano entre el Antiguo y el Moderno estilo* ("organ works between the old and the modern style"), Elías not only wrote individual pieces in each of the various styles but also combined traditional and innovative features within the same multisectional compositions. If some works remained faithful to the contrapuntal organ tradition, in many other pieces systematic fugal writing gave way to a free manipulation of the thematic material, often sequential rather than imitative. Unexpected modulations take us to remote keys, while virtuosic figuration can be combined with sustained pedal-notes (see Example 12.14). A similar approach was adopted by the Aragonese Miquel López (1669–1723), trained as an organist and choirmaster at the Escolanía de Montserrat, and the Basque Joaquín

EXAMPLE 12.14   Josep Elías, *Tocata de contras quinto tono*, mm. 57–64, in *Liber Organi: Orgel musik des spanischen Barock*, ed. James Wily. Mainz: Schott, 1966, pp. 34–35

Oxinagas (1719–89), organist of the cathedrals of Burgos and Bilbao and later of the Spanish Royal Chapel.

But although the Peninsular tradition of organ building reached its peak as the century progressed, with larger and more powerful instruments replacing previous ones or being installed for the first time even in relatively small churches and convents, and organists remained fundamental participants in the musical liturgy, the solo keyboard repertory switched gradually to the orbit of the harpsichord. The many forms with which the organ composers experimented around the turn of the century also were replaced by the predominance of the single-movement, bipartite sonata—usually under the designation of *tocata*—and, to a lesser degree, by the minuet.

The presence of Domenico Scarlatti in Lisbon and Madrid may have in many ways contributed to these changes, as his duties included teaching harpsichord to the Infanta Maria Barbara of Braganza, for whom many of his keyboard works were undoubtedly intended. Furthermore, we know that John V of Portugal himself greatly enjoyed hearing Scarlatti's keyboard music and had his personal secretary order copies of it at various times. It should be stressed, however, that the most representative keyboard composers active in Portugal and Spain in the first half of the eighteenth century had already completed their musical education and were full-pledged professional musicians by the time Scarlatti arrived in the Peninsula. So the influence that the Italian master undoubtedly exerted over them must be considered as part of a much wider and more complex process of stylistic evolution, and not a simple phenomenon of imitation. In fact, Scarlatti's direct influence, as a forerunner of many of the innovations of the Classical style, is much more clearly felt in the works of later Iberian composers, such as Antonio Soler, for instance, than in those of his immediate contemporaries.

Vicente Rodríguez (d. 1760), who successfully competed for the office of organist of the cathedral of Valencia after the death of Juan Bautista Cabanilles in 1712, exemplifies this transition. He wrote a few battle-pieces for the organ, but his most important keyboard works were the thirty harpsichord sonatas contained in his *Libro de tocatas para cimbalo*. In this collection he employed a highly virtuosic figuration that presupposes a complete technical mastery of the instrument, but he also excelled in expressive melodic design, rarely combined with any purely contrapuntal elements.

A particularly original personality in this context was the Portuguese Carlos Seixas (1704–1742), who at the early age of sixteen was already organist of the Lisbon Royal Chapel. Of the seven hundred keyboard sonatas attributed to him in a biography published shortly after his death, more than one hundred survive, and these cover a vast range of compositional choices, some of which are extremely innovative. Seixas was far more interested in the melodic flow of his works than in purely contrapuntal writing or in modulatory experimentation. His sonatas often present a wealth of thematic and motivic material, thus considerably extending the sheer dimensions of the form, and in some cases engage in so much motivic development immediately after the central double bar that the result is a tentative tripartite structure. His phrasing tends to be metrically irregular, and his melodic design is frequently intensely lyrical in the slow movements, at times suggesting similarities with the German *Empfindsamkeit* of his time, but it can also be graciously ornamental, evoking instead the *style galant*. Rarely requiring the Scarlattian hand-crossing, Seixas's sonatas can nevertheless be quite demanding technically (see Example 12.15). His Concerto in A Major for harpsichord and string orchestra is one of the earliest examples of a solo keyboard concerto in Europe.

Sebastián de Albero (1722–1756), like Oxinagas and Nebra an organist of the Spanish

EXAMPLE 12.15   Carlos Seixas, *Sonata in G minor,* mm. 44–51, in *80 Sonatas,* Vol. II, ed. Macario Santiago Kastner. Lisbon: Calouste Gulbenkian Foundation, 2d/1992, p. 180

Royal Chapel, differs from Rodríguez and Seixas by maintaining a closer connection with the Spanish seventeenth-century polyphonic tradition in the keyboard repertory. Rather than the harpsichord, Albero was particularly attracted to the expressive dynamic of the clavichord, or at a later stage, of the new pianoforte. His two main collections of works are in the *Treinta sonatas para clavicordio* and the *Obras para clavicordio y pianoforte.* The latter are particularly interesting in that the contents always follow the sequence *Recercata– Fuga–Sonata.* The recercata, a form that goes back to the sixteenth-century legacy of Diego Ortíz, here is an improvisatory prelude suggesting in some cases the influence of D'Anglebert's *préludes non mesurés,* which Albero, born not far from the frontier with France, may have known in his student years. The fugues are based on a free circulation of the thematic material through all the voices, with the main theme accompanied in each presentation by thinner or thicker harmonic textures, without a strict polyphonic structure. The sonatas combine the overall requirements of the bipartite form with a concern for expressive modulation and chromaticism.

The interest in the new pianoforte on the part of Iberian musicians, as shown in Albero's late sonatas, can be traced back to 1732, when the first printed set of works for the instrument, Ludovico Giustini da Pistoia's *Sonate da cimbalo di piano, e forte,* was dedicated by the composer to a Portuguese prince, the Infante D. António, younger brother of John V.

In addition to the keyboard instruments, the guitar was still a central instrument to the context of chamber music in the Peninsula. The series of distinguished Iberian guitarists of the previous century continued with Santiago de Murcia, the author of the last printed tablature for this instrument, the *Resumen de acompañar la parte con la guitarra* (Antwerp,

1714). A second volume, entitled *Pasacalles y obras para guitarra*, was ready for publication in 1732 but remains in manuscript, and a third was the Mexican *Codex Saldivar no. 4*, mentioned later. The first two volumes witnessed the growing influence of French dance music, especially the second, written after Santiago de Murcia had contact in Belgium with important French guitarists such as Visée, Campion, and Lecocq. The third, with all its pieces of a popular flavor, reflected the general trend in the evolution of the Spanish guitar in the mid-eighteenth century, a transition from the sophisticated tradition stemming from the vihuelists, two hundred years earlier, to a relatively "lowbrow" popular repertory.

The violin became a prominent staple of most musical genres in Portugal and Spain, constituting a sort of timbric hallmark of modernity, but the development of a chamber music repertory for strings in the Peninsula occurred mostly in the second half of the century. A significant exception to this rule is a recently discovered manuscript by Pedro Lopes Nogueira (fl. 1720), a virtuoso in the Portuguese Royal Chamber, containing more than one hundred preludes, fantasies, and other compositions for solo violin that are at once extremely demanding from the technical point of view and highly original in the Iberian context.

Latin America

The main problem one faces when attempting to survey the development of music in Latin America in the seventeenth and eighteenth centuries is the obvious disproportion between the wealth of all kinds of extant musical sources and the relatively small amount of fundamental research and scholarly publications now dedicated to it. Although this situation is rapidly improving, with a growing number of Latin American academic institutions, state-sponsored research programs, and well-trained musicologists taking the lead in the study of their own musical traditions, we are still at a very early stage of rediscovery. The results of such a study are fundamental, first of all, for establishing a comprehensive awareness of the cultural identities of the Spanish- and Portuguese-speaking countries of Central and South America. But, as our knowledge of this field increases, it also illuminates many aspects of our global view of European early music as well, especially with regard to the issues of performance practice.

In fact, the full dynamics of circulation of the models of production and reception of Baroque music as a whole, and the specific role of the Iberian Peninsula in that context in particular, can be properly evaluated only when one realizes that in the seventeenth and eighteenth centuries Europe was already but a part of a much larger musical complex in which Latin America played an impressive role in terms of the sheer size of the repertory created and performed in it, and of the intensity of its musical life. Seen in this perspective, Spain and Portugal are no longer the mere westernmost, somewhat "exotic" periphery of a European music scene only too often explained on the exclusive basis of what happens in the Italian–French–German triangle but, rather, a fundamental link in the exchange of artistic and aesthetic models between the two sides of this Euro-American development.

The concept of exchange is indeed essential for the understanding of this phenomenon. At the first stages of the colonization process, the two Iberian crowns merely sought to transpose to their new American territories the same artistic patterns adopted in the Peninsula, that is, in connection with the imposition of the Catholic religion, which is a key element in the new colonial order. Music—both in the form of chant and of polyphony—played an important role in the work of missionaries, as well as in the liturgical ceremonies performed in the churches and cathedrals that were rapidly erected in all urban centers of any consequence, often over the ruins of the pre-Columbian temples. But the musical models imported from Europe quickly began to be reprocessed in the framework of the cultural interaction between the Iberian rulers and the local Amerindian populations, and this interaction expanded even further with the arrival of large quantities of African slaves who brought into the Latin American complex their own songs and dances. The Iberian matrix remains the predominant element in the musical life of the Portuguese and Spanish colonies in the Americas, but throughout the seventeenth century the results of the local interaction with Amerindian and African traditions gradually reached the Peninsula, where their fresh, "exotic" appeal led to their incorporation into the very model that Spain and Portugal ultimately sent back to the New World. Certain genres, such as the sacred villancico, which even in its original Peninsular context was particularly keen on absorbing multilinguistic and multiethnic elements, offered a particularly fertile soil for such cross-cultural exchanges.

MEXICO AND THE CARIBBEAN

The highly centralized nature of the Aztec empire forced the Spanish colonial authorities to adopt an administrative pyramid that closely mirrored the ecclesiastical hierarchy established in the new viceroyalty of New Spain ("Nueva España"), extending from present-day Florida to Guatemala, and including the Caribbean islands. The viceroyalty was divided into large administrative provinces called *audiencias*. By the end of the sixteenth century, the archbishop of Mexico City already had primacy over six bishops; this system was based on a network of wealthy cathedrals established throughout the whole territory.

Cathedral music in New Spain followed the model used in the Peninsula, with chapels each including, by the beginning of the seventeenth century, a chapelmaster, a choir of boy sopranos and professional adult singers, several wind players, and at least a harpist and one or two organists. Locally trained Indian musicians were sometimes hired, especially as instrumentalists, but the leading positions in this organization tended to be reserved for musicians born and trained in Spain or Portugal, who benefited from their knowledge of the repertory performed at court or at the great Iberian cathedrals. Even when locally composed works, either by Mexican- or European-born composers, ultimately became predominant in the liturgical ceremonies, large quantities of copies of Old World music continued to be imported by the local cathedral chapters and other church authorities, in a conscious effort to keep up with the current musical tastes of the Peninsula.

Mexican Cathedral Music in the Seventeenth Century

By the beginning of the seventeenth century, the chapelmaster of Mexico City cathedral was Juan Hernández, who served in this function until 1620. He has been tentatively identified with the otherwise unknown Juan de Lienas, the author of several polyphonic masses and motets in the so-called Carmen Codex, copied in the final years of the previous century. If so, Hernández can be considered an excellent representative of the "classical" polyphonic tradition of Morales and Guerrero, with strict imitative textures of four to five parts in a purely modal framework.

The same tradition of elaborate *prima prattica* composition can be found in the works of the most distinguished of Hernández's immediate successors, Francisco López Capillas, who served as organist at the Puebla cathedral before becoming chapelmaster in Mexico City from 1654 to 1673. López shows a particular compositional skill in all kinds of elaborate contrapuntal techniques, from parody mass writing to florid paraphrases of hexachordal themes, and from full imitation to the use of a chant cantus firmus in long durational values in one of the voices (see Example 12.16).

EXAMPLE 12.16 Francisco López Capillas, *Magnificat,* "Gloria Patri," mm. 1–15, in *Tesoro de la musica polifónica en Mexico,* ed. Jesus Bal y Gay. Mexico: Instituto Nacional de Bellas Artes, 1952, p. 48, as reproduced in Gérard Béhague, *Music in Latin America: An Introduction,* Englewood-Cliffs, N.J.: Prentice-Hall, 1979, p. 14

After the tenure of José de Loaysa y Agurto (1676–88), Antonio de Salazar, who had been chapelmaster of the Puebla cathedral from 1679, applied for the same position in Mexico City and was hired after a thorough public examination in all fields of composition and music theory. His compositional output includes some impressive polychoral Latin works and a number of lively villancicos that were among the attractions of Christmas Matins in the Mexican capital. In office until 1715, he not only strengthened the musical staff of the chapel but also reorganized the musical archives of the cathedral, commissioning new copies of works by his predecessors as well as by important Iberian composers, and thus consolidating the seventeenth-century repertory performed at this institution.

The second most important center of sacred music in the viceroyalty of New Spain during the seventeenth century was the cathedral of Puebla. In 1606 the position of chapelmaster was given to the Portuguese composer Gaspar Fernandes (c. 1570–1629), a former student of the Évora cathedral music school who had already had the same responsibilities at Guatemala City cathedral. As he had done in Guatemala, Fernandes assembled several choir books of polyphonic compositions by various New and Old World authors in order to provide the Puebla chapel with the necessary repertory for the full liturgical year. But Fernandes is mostly known for his impressive autograph collection of some 250 sacred villancicos now preserved in the Oaxaca cathedral archives. Expanding the typical compositional conventions of this genre, he experimented with all kinds of different formal solutions, and drew largely on the Amerindian and Afro-American traditional musical idioms to write his *indios* and *negros* (or *guineos*), villancicos on texts in Nahuatl and African early Creoles of Spanish, respectively.

After Fernandes's death in 1629, the position of chapelmaster was filled by Juan Gutiérrez de Padilla (c. 1590–1664), who had been his predecessor's assistant since 1622. Gutiérrez is mostly known for his eight-part Masses and motets, many of which were assembled in the Puebla choir book XV by order of the cathedral chapter. His handling of the double-choir texture is particularly effective, with either homophonic declamation of energetic rhythmic motives in all voices or antiphonal opposition between the two choirs (see Example 12.17). He also was the author of a considerable number of villancicos covering all

EXAMPLE 12.17   Juan Gutiérrez de Padilla, *Mirabilia testimonia tua,* mm. 143–46, in *Juan Gutiérrez de Padilla: Mirabilia testimonia tua,* ed. Ivan Moody. London: Venderbeeck & Imrie, 1989, p. 20

the different types within this genre, and often based on texts by a Mexican nun, Sor Juana Inés de la Cruz (d. 1695), who remained the most influential Spanish-speaking sacred poet in Latin America until well into the eighteenth century.

Gutiérrez de Padilla greatly benefited from the patronage of the enlightened Bishop Juan de Palafox y Mendoza, who arrived in Puebla in 1639 and immediately endowed his cathedral with a lavish income for its musical establishment, in addition to founding in the city the first public library in the New World. He was able to afford to hire a large ensemble of the best singers and instrumentalists, and by the mid-seventeenth century the Puebla cathedral even surpassed Mexico City in the scope and quality of its sacred music. One of the most acclaimed successors of Gutiérrez was Miguel Matheo de Dallo y Lana (?c. 1650–1705), who also set to music a considerable number of villancico poems by Sor Juana Inés de la Cruz and whose works even crossed the Atlantic and reached the musical archives of the Peninsula.

None of the other dioceses in the viceroyalty of New Spain could compare with the two above-mentioned cathedrals as centers of sacred music. After a period of some significance in this field, which lasted until the early years of the seventeenth century, Guatemala cathedral lost much of its importance, which it did not regain, if only partially, for more than a century. Occasional documentary evidence identifies several chapelmasters at the Oaxaca cathedral, including, in the 1670s, a Zapotec Indian, Juan Matías, and later, in the 1690s, one Mateo Vallados. Nevertheless, the bulk of the present-day holdings of the Oaxaca archives appear to have been copied by the eighteenth century, with the exception of the Gaspar Fernandes villancico collection, which must have been brought from Puebla at some point after the Portuguese composer's death.

The Arrival of the Italian Models

Antonio de Salazar's successor as chapelmaster of Mexico City cathedral in 1715 was his favorite student, Manuel de Zumaya (c. 1678–1755), the first American-born musician to ascend to the leading position in a cathedral chapel of the first order in the New World. Zumaya was by then already a well-known composer, as he was the author of the first opera performed in the Mexican capital, *La Partenope,* on an Italian libretto by Silvio Stampiglia that eventually also was set, albeit in a modified version, by Handel. Performed at the palace of the Viceroy of New Spain, the Duke of Linares, on 1 May 1711, to celebrate the birthday of King Philip V, this experiment does not seem to have had any direct effect, and the music is now lost, although the libretto printed for the occasion survives.

From an early stage of his career Zumaya was subject to a strong Italianate influence, which suggests that the new repertory of that same nature adopted at the Madrid court had by then arrived in the colony. Some of Zumaya's numerous villancicos still preserve many of the traditions of the genre inherited from the previous century, but others were composed in the style of a sacred cantata, with clear-cut recitatives and arias, often of a florid, virtuosic nature. Similarly, if some of his Latin sacred works remained faithful to the polyphonic heritage, in his polychoral Masses, for instance, he tended to adopt whole-heartedly the conventions of the "modern" style, the melodic writing entirely structured according to the regular rhythmic patterns and the symmetric phrase design of the Italian *cuadratura,* even when he sought to maintain a solemn, relatively conservative atmosphere (see Example 12.18).

The reasons that led Zumaya to abandon his position in 1739 and to move to Oaxaca, where in 1745 he became the local cathedral chapelmaster, are not clearly known, but, judging from the number of his works now preserved in the Oaxacan archives, this change did not affect in any way his intense rhythm of composition or the quality of his music. A new chapelmaster of the Mexico City cathedral was not appointed until 1746, and even then on an interim basis only for another three years. The position then was given to Ignacio Jerusalem, an Italian composer who had been composing and conducting the music for the performances of the city's Coliseo Nuevo theater from 1742. Until his death in 1769, Jerusalem produced an immense musical output that includes over two hundred pieces of sacred music, often with full orchestral accompaniment. Large-scale homophonic textures in the "massive" Baroque tradition alternated with florid coloratura arias of a *style galant* flavor and with virtuosic violin obbligato writing.

The first half of the eighteenth century witnessed the development of other centers of sacred music in New Spain. In Guatemala, Manuel José de Quiroz was appointed cathedral chapelmaster in 1738 and sought to acquire copies of a large repertory that included traditional seventeenth-century villancicos as well as "modern style" cantatas by Iberian (Té i Sagau, Francisco José Coutinho) and Italian composers (Astorga, Galuppi, Pergolesi, and

EXAMPLE 12.18   Manuel de Zumaya, *Misa de tercer tono,* "Credo," mm. 24–26, *Misas de Manuel de Sumaya,* ed. Aurelio Tello. Mexico: Instituto Nacional de Bellas Artes, 1986, p. 183

Porpora). In the same year, a newly established college for orphan girls in Valladolid, the Colégio de Santa Rosa, began to assemble a considerable collection of villancicos for small vocal ensembles, frequently with obbligato violins and continuo.

Little as yet has been studied of the theatrical repertory performed at the Coliseo Nuevo, operating in Mexico City from 1735. At least three manuscript tablatures for various plucked string instruments reached Mexico by the mid-seventeenth century or were copied locally. The most important of these sources is the so-called *Codex Saldívar No. 4,* a large collection of guitar works by the Spanish virtuoso Santiago de Murcia, who may have spent the final years of his life in New Spain in the 1730s. It presents the typical contents of the guitar tablatures of the late-seventeenth-century Iberian tradition, with its characteristic mixture of old Iberian dances and passacalles, Afro-American rhythms such as those of the *cumbe* and the *zarambeque,* French *contredanses,* and Italian instrumental pieces including various transcriptions of Corelli sonata movements. Such a repertory, together with the information concerning theatrical performances, suggests that in the first decades of the eighteenth century there was an intense activity of secular music in the Mexican capital, both in the domestic sphere and in the new public context of urban sociability.

PERU AND NEW GRANADA

The second great administrative subdivision of the Spanish empire in the Americas was the viceroyalty of Peru, replacing at first the former monarchy of the Incas but quickly assuming control over all the Spanish possessions in South America through its various *audiencias.* Although the former Amerindian capital, Cuzco, "the city of the Incas," remained a fundamental urban center throughout the sixteenth century, the viceroys established a new capital in Lima, "the city of the Kings," which was to become the heart of cultural and artistic life in the viceroyalty. Nevertheless, important cities such as Bogotá, in the *audiencia* of New Granada ("Nueva Granada," corresponding to present-day Panama, Venezuela, Ecuador, and Colombia), and La Plata (now Sucre), in the *audiencia* of Charcas (mostly the equivalent to modern Bolivia), soon also possessed significant poles of sacred music in their respective cathedrals, closely followed by those of Quito, Trujillo, and Caracas.

More so than in the case of New Spain, by the beginning of the seventeenth century musical life in Peru, despite Lima's gradual predominance, was thus based on a multicentered system that allowed for a widespread circulation of artists and repertory, similar to the one existing in the same period in Spain. A good example of that circulation is the career of Gutierre Fernández Hidalgo (c. 1547–1623), a distinguished polyphonist in the strict "classical" contrapuntal tradition, who served as chapelmaster, in succession, at the cathedrals of Bogotá (1684–86), Quito (1586–89), and La Plata (from 1589 to his death). The Bogotá archives preserve several of his psalm, *Salve,* and *Magnificat* settings, for up to six parts in rigorous imitation.

In 1612 Estácio de la Serna, who had previously been the first organist of the Lisbon Royal Chapel, was appointed chapelmaster of the Lima cathedral. Neither he nor his immediate successors in this position for more than half a century left any compositions in the local archives, either at the cathedral or at the rich music collection of the Seminary of San Antonio Abad, but all documentary evidence shows that the musical establishment of the cathedral was greatly reinforced in that period, both in terms of income and of the number and quality of the musicians hired. In 1631, Juan Pérez Bocanegra, a Franciscan friar, published in Lima his *Ritual Formulario,* a handbook of instructions for liturgical ceremonies in which he inserted the first piece of polyphony to be printed in the New

World, an anonymous four-part sacred song on a text in the Quechua language, intended as a processional hymn to be sung by Indian parishioners as they enter a church (see Example 12.19).

In 1674 the office of chapelmaster was given to Juan de Araujo (1646–1712), who was born in Spain and arrived in Lima as a young man, pursuing his studies at the city's university. Two years later, however, he abandoned this position for reasons that were never absolutely clear and after a brief sojourn in Panama he settled in La Plata, where he became the cathedral chapelmaster from 1689 to the time of his death. In his many villancicos, Araujo went beyond the established stereotypes of the genre and demonstrated a subtle lyricism and an impressive technique of handling the Baroque expressive *affetti,* which explains the reason why he received at La Plata what was probably the highest salary of a professional musician in Latin America, and why his works were still performed by different New World chapels more than seven decades after his death.

EXAMPLE 12.19 Anon., *Hanapchac,* mm. 1–10, in Robert Stevenson, *Music in Peru.* Washington: Pan American Union/General Secretariat of the Organization of the American States, 1959, pp. 47 and 50.

Araujo's successor as the Lima chapelmaster was Tomás de Torrejón y Velasco (1644–1728), another Spaniard who came to Peru in 1667, in the retinue of the new viceroy, the Count of Lemos. An aristocrat by birth, Torrejón enjoyed at the viceroyal court a gamut of privileges quite beyond those of a mere cathedral musician, and in fact accumulated various official positions in the administration that granted him a substantial income. Besides his duties as chapelmaster he was also the main figure in the musical establishment of the court of the count, who had various first-rate musicians at his service, including, for a few years, the distinguished Spanish harpist and composer of instrumental music Lucas Ruíz de Ribayaz.

In 1701, while at the peak of his fame, Torrejón received a double large-scale commission from the new viceroy of Peru, the Count of Moncloa. Early in that year he composed the polychoral music for the Office of the Dead celebrated at the cathedral on the occasion of the death of King Charles II. But he also wrote an opera for the local commemoration of the eighteenth birthday of the young Philip V, the first Bourbon king of Spain, and the celebration of the latter's accession to the throne as a consequence of the War of the Spanish Succession. Moncloa's well-known record of faithful service to the House of Habsburg made him the potential object of considerable suspicion on the part of the new Spanish government, and these lavish commemorations were to be a public demonstration of his allegiance to the new Bourbon dynasty, thus the need to include in the program nothing less grand than the first performance of an opera in the New World, and one especially commissioned for this purpose.

The libretto was none other than that of *La purpura de la rosa,* by Pedro Calderón de la Barca, the same text that had been set by Juan Hidalgo as one of the two operas by this composer performed in Madrid in 1660, which commemorated the signing of the Peace of the Pyrenees between Spain and France. Because those earlier operas also commemorated the marriage of Philip V's grandparents—Louis XIV of France and the Spanish Infanta Maria Teresa—and because *La purpura* evoked indirectly the genealogical legitimacy of the Bourbons' claim to the Spanish crown, such a choice had clear political motivation. An introductory *loa* praising the young sovereign was added to the original libretto, and Torrejón, who may have attended the performance of Hidalgo's opera as a young man belonging to the minor court nobility, adopted a style not unlike that of the older Spanish composer: alternation of choral responses with solo sections and a copious use of strophic arias (*tonadas*), rather than recitatives, as a musical support of the dramatic structure.

Although evocative of the tradition of Hidalgo, the music of *La purpura* also shows close affinities with Torrejón y Velasco's own style, as adopted in his many lighthearted, energetic villancicos found in most South American archives. In his later works the influence of the new Italianate style becomes more evident, although without ever leading to a break with the composer's previous manner. His Latin compositions, judging from the few extant examples, tend to be of a more austere, polychoral nature, with an expressive use of dissonance and a few instances of virtuosic melodic writing.

But if Torrejón was, in many ways, a forerunner of the introduction of the "modern" style in Peru, the Italian models soon arrived in Lima in a more direct way, through the presence of the Milanese composer Roque Ceruti (c. 1683–1760), brought in by the new viceroy, the Marquis of Castell do Ríus, in 1708. Later in that year Ceruti was called upon to write the music for a new opera, *El mejor escudo de Perseo,* on a libretto by the Marquis himself. From then on, even if Torrejón was still the chapelmaster of the cathedral, the

Italian Ceruti became the central figure in the musical life of the Peruvian court. After a brief absence in Trujillo, from 1720 to 1728, on the death of the older master, Ceruti inherited Torrejón's position as the head of the Lima cathedral chapel.

By this time the Italian models predominated entirely in the music of the viceroyalty, as in that of New Spain and in the Peninsula itself. Ceruti's influence, particularly evident in the quasi-operatic style of his Latin sacred works and villancicos, and in the fact that he is the first chapelmaster to hire violins for the permanent staff of his cathedral, must have constituted a decisive factor in that trend. But other local composers follow the same patterns, including the cathedral's organist and later Ceruti's successor as chapelmaster, José de Orejón y Aparicio (1706–1765).

This evolution is also evident in other musical centers. In 1747, for instance, an Augustinian monk from Cuzco, Fray Esteban Ponce de León (d. 1750?), composed a short operatic *serenata* entitled *Venid, venid deydades,* celebrating the appointment of the new Bishop of Paraguay, and, in spite of the sacred nature of the ecclesiastical position involved, the text is an Arcadian dialogue between mythological characters and the music is a series of recitatives and arias in which at least one of the movements is a French-style minuet.

In the meantime, in 1718 the *audiencia* of New Granada became a new autonomous viceroyalty directly submitted to the Spanish Crown. The chapelmaster of the Bogotá cathedral was by then José Herrera (c. 1670–1738), who succeeded José de Cascante, the holder of that position for almost fifty years, in 1703. Herrera's sacred production is another revealing example of an author caught between the time-honored Iberian polyphonic tradition of the seventeenth century and the new Italian influences.

THE "JESUIT REPUBLIC"

Throughout the sixteenth century the viceroyalty of Peru expanded into the interior of South America, particularly to the rich silver-mining region of Potosí, then known as High Peru, and to the Río de la Plata (literally "the river of silver"). Although new cities were established, such as Córdoba, Asunción, and Buenos Aires, these areas constituted a frontier territory without any major urban centers that could boast of an artistic life comparable to that of Lima or Bogotá. Beyond them there was still an immense region populated by various Amerindian tribes independent from the authority of either the Spanish or the Portuguese crowns—among them the Chiquitos and Mojos in the northern zone, currently part of Bolivia, and the Guaranis in an area mostly located now in Rio Grande do Sul (Brazil) and Paraguay.

The Jesuit missionaries were the first to penetrate this inner territory and to achieve the conversion of Chiquitos, Mojos, and Guaranis, who were incorporated into the Jesuit "Province of Paraguay," politically submitted to the king of Spain and part of the viceroyalty of Peru. In 1609, however, the Spanish Crown, while maintaining some degree of authority over the region through one of the viceroyalty's administrative circumscriptions, the *audiencia* of Charcas, granted its direct administration to the Jesuits, forbidding the admission of any other Spanish or foreign subjects into the territory. Further legislation increased the autonomy of the province, as long as one-third of all its agricultural production was delivered to the Crown.

The administrative system established by the Jesuits is based on villages, or "reductions" (*reducciones*), in each of which up to seven thousand Indians are concentrated, under the authority of two priests but preserving to some degree their traditional social and political hierarchy. By the end of the seventeenth century, there are some thirty such reductions in the area of the Guaranis, with as many as 150,000 inhabitants, plus ten similar villages in the region of the Chiquitos and Mojos. In all of them, the celebration of the Catholic liturgy, with a strong musical component, was an essential part of the daily life of these communities.

Anton Sepp, an Austrian Jesuit who arrived in the missions of Paraguay in the early 1690s, describes in great detail these musical activities. Elementary music education was given to Indian children together with basic religious and literary tuition, and those among them who showed particular gifts in this field received advanced training, either in vocal or in instrumental music. Music manuscripts were copied systematically to ensure the availability of the repertory to all villages, and all sorts of musical instruments were made by local craftsmen, including flutes and shawms, viols and theorbos, harps, and even pipe organs.

As most missionaries, like Sepp himself, came from Switzerland, Austria, or southern Germany, it is not surprising that the European repertory mentioned in his reports was by composers from the German-speaking area, including Schmelzer, Biber, and the chapel-master of the Augsburg cathedral, the Swiss Melchor Gletle. No Iberian authors are ever mentioned, as the Jesuits seemed to be particularly interested in adopting an international artistic language of their own rather than stressing the artistic connections between the regions under their direct administration and those included in the Spanish or Portuguese viceroyalties to which the former nominally belonged.

Sepp's reports and the other Jesuit sources very rarely—if ever—mentioned the work of Amerindian composers. We must bear in mind, however, that the political goal of such descriptions was to present the local populations as merely passive recipients of cultural patterns that had to be handed over to them by the missionaries and in regard to which the Amerindians excelled as gifted copyists and performers but were unable to ever reach the level of artistic creation—thus justifying the permanent authority of the Jesuits rather than that of just a temporary teaching function. In fact, the very efficiency and widespread nature of the musical training described in these documents must necessarily have led to the emergence of local composers as well as of performers. The absence of their names in all documentary sources can only be understood not only as part of that systematic, prejudiced underestimation of the creative powers of the Amerindian musicians but also as a consequence of the same collectivistic ideals of life in the perfect Christian society that led to the almost complete omission of the names of the local Jesuit composers themselves in those same reports.

Music in the Amerindian Archives

One remarkable exception to this rule of anonymity is that of Domenico Zipoli (1688–1726). Born in Prato (Tuscany), he pursued his musical studies in Florence (1707) under the local cathedral chapelmaster, Giovanni Maria Casini, later in Naples with Alessandro Scarlatti, and finally in Rome (1710) under Pasquini. After starting a brilliant career as a composer in the Roman musical circle, with several vocal and instrumental works (including a collection of *Sonate d'Intavolatura* for organ and harpsichord printed in 1716), he suddenly decided to become a Jesuit, and by late 1716 he was already in the society's college in Seville, from where he sailed the following year to Buenos Aires. Established in Córdoba as a student of theology at the local Colégio Mayor, he died in 1726 without having yet taken his final religious vows.

EXAMPLE 12.20 Domenico Zipoli, *Chapie Zuichupa* ("Thank you, our Lord"), mm. 1–5, in *Cantos chiquitanos,* ed. Piotr Nawrot. La Paz: Editorial Verbo Divino, 2000, pp. 59–60

None of Zipoli's European compositions have survived in New World copies, except for a somewhat simplified version of part of his printed book of keyboard sonatas, but the musical archives preserved by the Chiquitos and Mojos contain a significant number of works attributed to him, often in multiple sets of parts copied throughout the eighteenth century, several decades after the composer's death. These range from a large-scale setting of Vespers for the feast of Saint Ignatius to various smaller works, some of which seem to have been composed originally on a Latin text but were later translated into one or another of the Amerindian languages of the region.

The style of these compositions is quite different from both Zipoli's own early manner and that of the cathedral music of the viceroyalties of Mexico or Peru. Although the melodic writing can be rather elaborate and technically demanding, especially in the soloistic passages, the polyphonic structure is free from any particular contrapuntal or modulatory complexity and tends to produce a homorhythmic effect based on a choice of fundamental harmonic functions (see Example 12.20). This approach, understandable in a context of collective choral singing such as the one established in the Jesuit reductions, characterizes much of the extant repertory from these missions throughout the eighteenth century. This makes some of the attributions to Zipoli somewhat doubtful, especially as the various sets of parts for the same works may contradict each other, with at least one instance in which the pieces in question are in fact by Michel Corrette. The prestige of the young Zipoli and the fascination with his adventurous arrival in the New World, leaving behind him all the fame and glory of his early career in Italy, may have gradually created a myth leading to a generalized attribution of sacred music to the Tuscan composer by later copyists, on the basis of mere hearsay.

The musical archives of the Jesuit college in Córdoba no longer survive; neither do those of the thirty reductions of the Guarani region. More than eight hundred musical compositions are preserved in the Bolivian region, particularly in the central archive of the Chiquitos in Concepción. The large majority of these works are anonymous, but there are pieces by Corelli and Vivaldi, as well as by yet another Jesuit, Martin Schmid, a Swiss architect and musician who arrived in the region in 1729 and had a decisive role in the overall organization of musical life in the reductions of Bolivia.

Particularly interesting are the three extant sacred operas, one in Spanish (San Ignacio) and two in the Chiquitan language (San Francisco Xavier and El Justo y el Pastor, the latter only partially preserved). They are but a few examples of a tradition of sacred theatrical performances that is described by many documentary sources and that may have had its roots in the very early years of the Jesuit missionary work in the region. Reports such as Anton Sepp's also mention the use of dances used in church on Corpus Christi and other joyful feasts of the liturgical calendar, and in fact the opera *San Francisco Xavier* ends with a very simple minuet for two treble instruments and continuo that may correspond to a final stage of that tradition of sacred dances (see Example 12.21).

With the treaty of Madrid, signed in 1750, Spain handed over to Portugal the sovereignty over the area of the Guarani reductions in exchange for the colony of Sacramento (Uruguay). Forced to abandon their territory, the Guaranis fought a desperate war against the joint armies of the two Iberian crowns. When the Jesuits were ultimately expelled from the Portuguese (1759) and Spanish (1767) possessions, the economic and social system that had served as the basis for almost two hundred years of intense musical activity disappeared, and the former "Province of Paraguay" was fully incorporated into the general administrative system of the viceroyalties. The fact that the Chiquitos and Mojos maintained a living tradition of preserving, copying, and performing this repertory is undoubtedly one of the most fascinating phenomena of the Baroque legacy in Latin America.

BRAZIL

As we have seen, the Spanish Crown adopted in Latin America, from the very beginning, a model of colonization that had to do not only with its own previous experience of a powerful state ruling over a complex mosaic of different ethnic, linguistic, and cultural entities in the Peninsula as well as in Italy and in the Netherlands, but also with the already highly centralized nature of the Aztec and Inca empires it had conquered. The Portuguese settlements in Brazil, by contrast, were part of a colonial strategy that at least throughout the sixteenth century was still centered on the spice trade with India, even though in the first half of the seventeenth century the latter had lost much of its previous splendor. Rather than building an empire penetrating deeply into the continental heart of Brazil, Portugal established along the coast of its new territory a string of outposts that could serve as the basis for a growing maritime trade involving the local natural products and also an increasing number of African slaves.

As these outposts developed into larger cities, their ecclesiastical institutions became

EXAMPLE 12.21   Anon., *Taquiruus Atoña,* minuet in *Opera San Francisco Xavier,* ed. Piotr Nawrot. La Paz: Editorial Verbo Divino, 2000, p. 143

more numerous and wealthier. The first Brazilian bishopric, created in Bahia in 1551, remained, however, the only one in the colony for more than a century; for only in 1675 were new dioceses established in Olinda (Pernambuco), Maranhão, and Rio de Janeiro, to be followed in 1720 by that of Pará. Cathedral music, which was so prominent in the colonial society of Hispanic America since the early sixteenth century, was therefore conducted on a comparatively much smaller scale in Brazil for more than two hundred years, well into the mid-eighteenth century.

Nevertheless, we know of several chapelmasters appointed from 1559 to the cathedral of the Brazilian capital, Bahia, including, in 1661, a native of the Brazilian capital itself, Joaquim Correia, who was therefore the first American-born musician to become the head of a cathedral chapel in the New World. One of his successors in the same position, Fr. Agostinho de Santa Mónica (1633–1713), a Paulist hermit from Lisbon who served as chapelmaster at the Bahia cathedral for over twenty years at the turn of the century, is known to have composed many polyphonic Masses, Vespers psalms, and responsories and lamentations for Holy Week and the Office of the Dead. In 1728, a manuscript report mentions the performance of a *Te Deum* in the cathedral by "four choirs of musicians, including the very best singers and instrumentalists." Throughout the seventeenth century, similar chapels were established in various wealthy churches in other cities, and ecclesiastical documents frequently mention the performance of polyphony, although they very rarely specify the authors or works involved.

By contrast, various orders erected large-scale religious houses all over the territory. First came the Jesuits, who conducted much of the early missionary work, often using vocal and instrumental music as a key vehicle of indoctrination. They also founded several colleges that were for two centuries the mainstays of public education in Brazil and in which sacred music was one of the disciplines of the core curriculum taught. In the 1580s the Carmelites, the Franciscans, and the Benedictines arrived, followed in the 1610s by the French Capuchins and, then later in the seventeenth century, by the Mercedarians, the Theatines, the Oratorians, and the Augustinians. Of these, the Benedictines seem to have been the religious order more intensely devoted to providing elaborate polyphonic music to the liturgical ceremonies of their great monasteries of Rio de Janeiro, Olinda, and Bahia, in the latter of which the acquisition of a printed choir book with works by Duarte Lobo is documented around 1660.

The same source refers to the performance of "chançonetas," or villancicos, in the monastery, a practice to which sources regarding other ecclesiastic establishments also allude, namely the above-mentioned reports by the Jesuit Father Anton Sepp, in the 1690s. An early-eighteenth-century biography of Fr. Agostinho de Santa Mónica lists several "tonilhos," yet another designation of this genre, among his extant compositions. The full scope of the sacred repertory in use in Portuguese churches thus seems to have been adopted also in the colony as soon as the local institutions acquired the human and material resources to afford it, and certainly by at least the early to mid-seventeenth century.

As the Brazilian colonial society expanded and prospered in the late seventeenth and early eighteenth centuries, a growing network of laymen's brotherhoods began to play a decisive role in the promotion of sacred music. Ranging from exclusive associations that recruited their members within the upper class of wealthy landowners and merchants to the various local *irmandades* of Our Lady of the Rosary, formed by blacks and mulattos, these brotherhoods became powerful sponsors of religious music, not only in the context of the church ceremonies themselves but also as part of various processions and other devotional outdoor traditions.

Recent researches in the archives of the Inquisition have uncovered significant data concerning musical practice in the circuit of the wealthy families of sugar cane plantation owners in Rio de Janeiro in this same period, as well as a growing demand for professional teachers and performers of instruments such as the harp or the bassoon, both in the secular and the ecclesiastical circles of the city. Several texts by the Brazilian satirical poet Gregório de Matos (1623–1696) repeatedly allude to almost all of the different genres of dance music—many of which are African influenced—represented in the Portuguese manuscripts compiled for the Baroque guitar around the turn of the century, which suggests that this repertory was also widely cultivated in Brazil.

Sadly, no music copied in the seventeenth century has survived in Brazil; the earliest extant sources apparently date from the 1720s and 1730s. They consist of a collection of manuscripts found in the region of São Paulo, in the small town of Mogi das Cruzes, and two further sources in the province of Minas Gerais—a codex in a private collection in Piranga, and a set of the late-seventeenth-century Passions by Francisco Luís in Mariana.

EXAMPLE 12.22   Anon., *Pueri Hebraeorum*, mm. 1–8, in Paulo Castagna, "O 'Estilo Antigo' no Brasil, nos séculos XVIII e XIX," in *A Música no Brasil Colonial*, ed. Rui Vieira Nery. Lisbon: Calouste Gulbenkian Foundation, 2001, p. 177

Much of the repertory preserved in these manuscripts, at least, is of Portuguese origin, and consists of four-part polyphony in *stile antico* (see Example 12.22).

Concordances between these and later Brazilian eighteenth-century copies of polyphonic music with Portuguese manuscripts and prints allow us to identify a few works by composers dating as far back as the late sixteenth century, such as António Carreira, D. Pedro de Cristo, Fr. Manuel Cardoso, Francisco Martins, and Francisco Luís. The fact that in none of these compositions the author is mentioned apparently suggests that the Brazilian church authorities were mostly concerned with assembling and spreading a basic corpus of polyphonic repertory suited for the routine needs of the liturgy, regardless of any purely "artistic" concerns, and that this goal was still accepted even in the second half of the eighteenth century, when it coexisted with the "modern" aesthetic trends of the Italianate *stile concertato* newly imported from the Portuguese court. The manuscripts from Mogi das Cruzes include the single surviving example in Brazil of a villancico in the vernacular, *Matais de incêndios,* possibly intended for Christmas.

That the best Brazilian musicians in the first half of the eighteenth century were thoroughly trained in the established music theory of the period is quite clear from the extensive Arte de Canto de Órgão by Caetano de Melo Jesus, a two-volume manuscript survey of all theoretical issues of polyphonic composition, including a debate on the proper use of accidentals in which the chapelmasters of the main churches of Recife (Inácio Ribeiro Nóia), Olinda (Inácio Ribeiro Pimenta and Manuel da Costa Rego), and Rio de Janeiro (António Nunes de Siqueira) demonstrate a level of proficiency quite similar to that of their peers of the Lisbon, Évora, and Coimbra cathedrals. It is difficult to state, however, when concertato writing was adopted by Brazilian composers. A Lisbon-born Carmelite friar, Fr. Antão de Santo Elias, who took his vows at his order's convent of Bahia in 1697, is mentioned in a 1737 biography as the author of numerous compositions of sacred music "with various instruments," information that the same source usually provides only in the case of works in the new style, but even if we accept this added meaning to such a reference it is not clear whether he composed them while still in Brazil or already after his return to Portugal.

The earliest known example of a Brazilian piece in the "modern" style is thus an

EXAMPLE 12.23 Anon., aria "Se o canto enfraquecido," mm. 26–35, in *Recitativo e Ária para José Mascarenhas,* ed. Maria Alice Volpe and Régis Duprat. São Paulo: Universidade de São Paulo, 2000, pp. 94–95

anonymous laudatory ode dedicated in 1759 to a magistrate from Bahia, *Heroe, egregio, douto, peregrino,* with an accompanied recitative leading to a da capo aria in keeping with the standard Neapolitan taste of the period (see Example 12.23). But the full bloom of the various indigenous schools of sacred music that represent Brazil's massive contribution to the Latin American musical scene in the colonial period occurred only in the second half of the eighteenth century and reached its peak by the time of the arrival of the Portuguese royal family to Rio de Janeiro in 1808, at a time when the Napoleonic armies were occupying Portugal. Even though the productive system of music in Brazil at that time still by and large coincided with the Baroque institutional model, the aesthetic and technical idioms meanwhile adopted by the Brazilian composers—like those of their Portuguese colleagues of the same period—by then had moved into the post-Baroque universe, thus placing them outside the boundaries of the present study.

CHAPTER THIRTEEN

Baroque Music in Eastern Europe

Music in Croatia

Ennio Stipčević (*Zagreb*)

AT THE TURN OF THE sixteenth and seventeenth centuries, the Croatian lands were shaken by grave political problems: the Ottomans established their power in the eastern regions, while the Habsburgs and Venetians reigned over most of northern and coastal Croatia. At the beginning of the seventeenth century the territory of Croatia, governed by the Viceroy (*ban*) appointed from Vienna, was smaller than ever before or after. During the sixteenth and seventeenth centuries—*plorantis Croatiae saecula duo,* as they were called by the historian Pavao Ritter Vitezović in his 1703 poem—a large part of the Croatian nobility was directly involved with the military operations, and one can often see in their portraits the motto "Arte et Marte."[1] That was a time when the sound of galloping cavalry replaced the sound of gentle Renaissance music, and when few musicians enjoyed even the occasional patronage of nobility or praise in the bourgeois drawing rooms. With the exception of Dubrovnik, which was a free city state with a developed cultural heritage, Croatian musicians could have found secure employment almost exclusively in religious institutions.[2]

This was a reason so many Croatian musicians, who spent time during the seventeenth and eighteenth centuries working abroad, often followed their names by an indication of their origin. Among them were Vinko Jelić (1596–1636), *Fluminensi sancti Viti* (of Rijeka), who worked in Alsace, in the service of Archduke Leopold, and published in Strasbourg three collections of *sacri concerti.* His sacred concertos indicate progressive musical orientation, great variability of tempo (often marked with *presto, tardi, tardissimo, allegro, allegrissimo*), melodic invention, and emotive sensibility in interpretation of the text.[3] Hieronimus Talonus (fl. 1625–30), *Polensis* (of Pula in Istria, not Poland, as supposed Robert Eitner), worked as the *maestro di cappella* at Albano Cathedral near Rome and published two collections of sacred music (*Armonicus Parnassus,* Rome 1628; *Motecta psalmi vespertini,* Rome 1629), both in rather conservative style.[4] Damjan Nembri (1584–c. 1648) of Hvar, a Benedictine monk of Italian origin, had spent most of his life in the Monastery of St. Giorgio Maggiore in Venice. In 1640 he published a collection of three- to eight-voice Masses, which did not survive, and *Brevis et facilis psalmorum quatuor vocibus modulatio* (Venice 1641), consisting of six four-part Vesper psalms. Nembri was a master of polyphonic technique, very inventive in the organ continuo. His psalms do not resemble the rich vocal-instrumental pieces performed in the mid-seventeenth century at the basilica of St. Mark. In fact, these psalms show, in some aspects, the influences of the older Monteverdi's 1610 collection (*Sanctissima Virgini Missa . . . ac Vesperae pluribus decantandae*).[5] Giovanni Sebenico (Ivan of Šibenik) (1630-40–1705) was an active singer and *maestro di cappella* in Turin and Venice; while in London he held the post of Master of the Italian Music at the court of King Charles II and played the organ in Queen Catherine's private chapel. He left a few church compositions, but none of his three operas survived.[6] Francesco Usper

414

(c. 1560–1641) of Poreč, a student of Andrea Gabrieli, was a prominent Venetian composer. He published five collections, all in Venice, and was most versatile in his instrumental compositions (Alfred Einstein declared Usper's "Sinfonia prima" from *Compositioni armoniche* to be the forerunner of the concerto grosso).[7] True, the music composed by these and other emigrants largely exceeds in quantity and quality music produced in Croatia at the time. In this respect, Vitezović's reference to the "two weeping centuries" in Croatian history was not merely a poetic figure.

The second half of the sixteenth century in Croatia was marked by the appearance of the highly developed polyphonic music, both sacred and secular. Even the earliest printed Croatian polyphonic compositions—madrigals by Andrija Petrić (Patrizio), madrigals and motets both by Julije Skjavetić (Giulio Schiavetto) and Lambert Courtoys—show its closeness to developed European music centers, such as Venice, Rome, Vienna, and the influence of the Netherlands School. The fact that the Renaissance polyphonic music of the Netherlands reached Croatia is little known. It seems that the Croatian coast was the farthest southeastern point in Europe reached by Renaissance Dutch polyphony and Franco-Flemish music.[8]

True, printed music manuals and printed books were in lively circulation between the two Adriatic coasts since the end of the fifteenth century, and native musicians sometimes got hold of anthologies coming from the more distant north European centers of printing. But in Croatia, music publications were not printed in any systematic manner before the mid-eighteenth century, when manuscripts began to be gradually superseded by printed works. Therefore, a great part of Croatian Renaissance and Baroque music was published outside of the country, mostly in Venice. The Renaissance heritage was the original and most important starting point for musical activity in the first decades of Seicento. The inclusion of musical art as a theme for discussions in Renaissance academies, in Istria and Dalmatia, its presence in theoretical works and in practice in the theater—all this played its part in the lively but also specific reception of various early Baroque models.

The contribution of writers, philosophers, and playwrights to the development of the musical life can be best judged from the activities of the learned societies, called "accademie." The *Accademia dei Concordi* (Akademija Slóžnih) from Dubrovnik, probably the oldest association of Croatian writers, brought together intellectuals whose ideas on various subjects discussed in their midst have survived in print. They used to meet at the Sponza Palace, famous for its Gothic-Renaissance architecture, and the idyllic gardens and parks of the Dubrovnik country houses. The topics that the *Concordi* used to discuss must have included the art of music, a subject included, for example, in books written by Nikola Gucetic (Nicolo Vito di Gozze) (ca. 1549–1610) and in *Irene, ovvero della bellezza* (Venice 1599, 2nd ed. 1604) by Miho (Michale) Monaldi (1540–1582). The latter discourse was the first published systematic study in aesthetics by a Croatian author. Monaldi dedicated his entire "Dialogo ottavo" to the art of music, presenting his neo-Platonist idea of the relation of speech and music, and giving special attention to the theory of meaning in music.[9] Less innovative was *Dialogo con brevità a cantar canto figurato* (Venice, 1619) by Giorgio (Juraj) Alberti (b. 1604) of Split, which was made for local use. It was the aim of this small volume to offer basic information about ways of *cantare con tantà liberta & sicurezza solfeggiando.* It is not surprising that the text lacks originality because, as the front page tells us, Alberti was a *giovane d'anni quindeci,* thus only fifteen years of age when the book was published. More originality was shown by Juraj Križanić (Crisanius, 1618–1683), whose visionary Pan-Slavism and a desire to reunite the Eastern and Western churches urged him to undertake his many voyages from Rome and Vienna to Moscow and Siberia. Among his enormous literary output, which remained almost entirely in manuscript, there were also a few texts on music theory. Especially interesting is his *Asserta musicalia* (Rome, 1656), a treatise comprising only fifteen pages but filled with great intellectual and theoretical potential, consisting of twenty numbered assertions dealing with different fields and aspects of musical art. This was also the only text Križanić was able to publish in the course of his adventurous life.[10]

The Croatian reception of contemporary operatic works offers a valuable insight into the status of Baroque innovations in Croatia, including the fact that *Aminta* (1581) by Torquato Tasso and *Pastor fido* (1580) by Giovanni Battista Guarini were translated in Croatian very early (Dubrovnik poet Dominko Zlatarić published his translation in Venice in 1580, thus one year before the Italian original). As early as the sixteenth century, Italian pastorals contributed to the development of Croatian and Italian poetry, which could be used by the new generation of Baroque composers. The first printed Croatian translation of an opera libretto was *Euridice* (Venice, 1617), written in Italian by Ottavio Rinuccini and translated by Paskoje Primović from Dubrovnik.[11] Working on his translation Primović used the Italian libretto along with the printed scores composed in 1600 by Jacopo Peri and Giulio Caccini. Primović's *Euridice* was to be recited and sung, in part also accompanied by instruments (as indicated by the stage directions). However, the Dubrovnik performance ended up as a spoken "tragicomedy" with some musical accompaniment.

Primović's translation inaugurated the finest Croatian tragicomedies of the period. Some of the leading playwrights, such as Ivan Gundulić (1589–1638) and Junije Palmotić (1607–1657), also translated libretti from the Italian. They were aware of the Baroque poetics of *imitazione della parola*, which strived for a unique fusion of poetry and music. However, this direction was not followed in Croatian theaters. The relation of word and music in the early Baroque theater was reflected in Bartol Kašić's *Sveta Venefrida* (*St. Winifred*), a "triumph of purity," written in 1627, at the time when Kašić was the Father Superior of the Jesuit Residence in Dubrovnik. *Sveta Venefrida* is crammed with diverse sounds, from shrieks, weeping, and chanted prayer to music proper, including choruses with instrumental accompaniment. However, these hypertrophied staging requirements were the reason why Kašić's *Trionfo* was never performed and was known to contemporaries and followers only in manuscript. After this early enthusiasm for Italian Baroque libretti, in the course of the eighteenth century Croatian theater generally rejected all music that was not strictly a function of the performance.[12] It should be noted, however, that Dalmatia sporadically found a place for theatrical performances in Italian language, some of which were filled with musical numbers.[13]

It is quite evident that the strongest new cultural impulse came from Italy. But the main and most reliable financial supporter of musical art was the clergy. Three church orders were especially important for the development of the Baroque in Croatia: the Jesuits, Paulists, and Franciscans. The Jesuits brought unprecedented luxury and monumentality into the musical life; new organs were built and instrumental ensembles and small orchestras constituted for the needs of church services. In addition, along with the Franciscans and Paulists, the Jesuits relied on pious folk songs in their missionary work. Just how industriously meticulous and serious-minded the Jesuits were when they drew up a Counter Reformation program can be seen in Bartol Kašić's Croatian translation of *Rituale romanum Pauli V. Pont. Max (. . .) Et Urbani VIII. auctoritate recognitum* (Paris 1635),[14] the very first printed translation of *Rituale romanum* in vernacular. Kašić's translation included choral tunes faithfully transported from the original edition, and it played an important role in musical-liturgical service rites in Croatian lands until the beginning of the nineteenth century. The liturgy in vernacular language as well as in Latin was one of specific quality of musical culture in Croatia since the Middle Ages.[15]

Practicing *contrafactum,* Jesuits cleansed folk songs from the texts they considered "dirty" and "lascivious," and wrote new theologically approved texts. By cultivating and writing down folk tunes in order to introduce them into church services, the Jesuits indirectly embraced the influence of opposed Protestant ideological matrices, earlier absorbed into these Croatian tunes.[16] Jesuit writers, such as Nikola Krajačević (1582–1635), Juraj Habdelić (1609–1678), and Juraj Mulih (1694–1754), made it very clear that some of these folk melodies would have to be cleansed of their "dirty" and "lascivious" texts, with new religious texts substituted. In his book *Pervi otca našega Adama greh* (*The First Sin of Our Father Adam,* Graz 1674), written in the Baroque kajkavian (North Croatian) dialect, Habdelić said that these folk songs should not be banned from social events. He believes that both the master and his peasant should sing merry songs "but only such as existed among honest and God-fearing folk in old times, pious, honest and praising God in His glory."[17]

The largest manuscript collection of seventeenth-century church songs is the *Pavlinska pjesmarica* (Pauline Songbook), a part of a larger *Pavlinski zbornik* (Pauline Collection, manuscript dated to 1644, *HR-Zu* R3629), containing about fifty pious songs, mostly in the kajkavian dialect of the Croatian language and some in Latin.[18] The songs stem mostly from the central European folkloristic and religious repertory, some of them going back to Medieval times. A large number of these songs were later included in the collection *Cithara octochorda seu Cantus Sacri Latino-Sclavonici in octo partes, pro diversis anni temporibus distributus* (printed in three editions, Vienna, 1701, 1723; Zagreb, 1757),[19] which confirms the constancy and strength of the tradition of writing manuscripts within the church. Some folk songs from these songbooks were copied into manuscripts and reprinted in later editions.

The Franciscans were a preaching order that had always remained in touch with the common people.[20] They were rarely as learned as the Jesuits and unlike many Paulists they were not recruited from noble families. The Franciscan manuscript songbooks deliberately dispensed with theatrical effects. Even the general constitution of the Franciscan order expressly banned polyphonic singing at church services and chose the organ as the only instrument allowed in church. Until the second half of the eighteenth century all other instrumental music was officially forbidden in Franciscan services, which does not mean that these rules were not broken and that the organ was not occasionally replaced by a small orchestra. It must be emphasized, however, that the foremost musical activity of the Croatian Franciscans was to copy music from older sources and adapt it to the local reproductive potentials.

The Croatian bourgeoisie and nobility could not afford to offer financial security to choral and instrumental ensembles for any extended period of time. Dubrovnik was the only city where the art of music could flourish unsuppressed.[21] From the fourteenth to nineteenth century the Governor's *cappella* existed there, whose main function was to appear at public celebrations. In other towns along the coast (even on islands such as Hvar, Korčula, or Vis) and in North Croatia (Zagreb, Varaždin, Osijek), professional musicians were occasionally hired to play at public celebrations. Indeed, it was this secular element contributed by the ordinary citizens and the common folk that created a variety and liveliness of Baroque music. Even a brief glance at the archival materials dealing with property and inheritance shows that musical instruments such as the guitar, lute, violin, and harpsichord were quite common in private homes.

In the seventeenth century, however, the cathedrals were still the focal points of a varied musical life. The *maestro di cappella* was in charge of the vocal and instrumental ensemble, saw to it that the repertory was up to date, and that musical scores were available, often composing some music. If a church had an organ, this was in itself an indicator of the higher musical level within the community, because organs were expensive to buy and service. In spite of so much, and some of it quite recent, war destruction, a large number of Baroque organs are still preserved in Croatia.[22] Although the oldest records concerning organ playing go back to the fourteenth century, the art of building organs in Croatia reached a high level of excellence only in the eighteenth century. One of the best known organ builders of that time was Pietro Nacchini (Petar Nakić, 1694–c. 1796),[23] born in the village Bulići near Benkovac in Dalmatia. He was an outstanding innovator who influenced the craft both in Dalmatia and Venice, and some of the most notable and busiest master organ builders in Italy and Austria learned their craft in his workshop in Venice. An estimate is that he built about 350 organs, most of them in Italy and about a dozen in Istria and Dalmatia. Although in Nacchini's homeland finances were meager, organ builders who found employment abroad made a very decent living. In Croatia the musicians who played for the city—*piffari, hornisti, timpanisti*—usually also held other jobs. Indeed, it was difficult to be a professional musician in Baroque Croatia.

In the first decades of the seventeenth century, Baroque innovations quickly reached Dalmatia owing to its close relations with Italy. Two Italian musicians were active in Croatia for a long period of time. Gabriello Puliti (c. 1575–1542/43) from Montepulciano[24] was a Franciscan friar and organist who moved to Istria in 1604. He served as an organist and instrumentalist in Trieste, Muggia, Capodistiria (Koper), and Albona (Labin), and composed at least thirty-six volumes of secular and religious music, including almost all the musical forms except the opera: Masses, motets, psalms, madrigals, *mascheratas,* instrumental compositions. Tomaso Cecchini (1580/85–1644), "Veronese"[25] was active in Dalmatia from 1603, and as *maestro di cappella* of the cathedrals in Split and Hvar composed twenty-seven volumes of varied music. Puliti and Cecchini published their music mostly in Venice, and some of their pieces were also included in anthologies of their time. Thus, it was mostly because of these two competent and very productive composers that Istria and Dalmatia were a part of the early Baroque musical scene of Europe.

These music anthologies compiled by Puliti and Cecchini in Croatia are completely different, although both composers were receptive to early Baroque experimentation. Cecchini's early music is close to the Florentine monody; Puliti, before coming to Istria, composed religious polyphonic music in late Renaissance style. Later, after the two composers were acquainted with the modest local performance potentials and simple tastes, their music became much less demanding. This can be concluded just by looking at the title pages of their music, indicating that certain madrigals or motets could be "accomodati per qual si voglia stromento" (adapted to available instruments), were "facili per cantare" (easy to sing), "comodi, facili ad ogni cantore" (adaptable and easy for every singer). That local singers had problems even with this music is clear from Puliti's remark addressed to the musicians in his collection *Lilia convalium Beatae Mariae Virginis libro terzo delli concerti a una voce* (Venice, 1620): "Essendomi stato detto d'alcuni che questi miei Motetti sono alquanto difficili, io gli rispondo che l'ho composti solo per quelli Virtuosi, che sanno ben Cantare, & non per quelli che strapazzano il mestiere. State sani" (As I have been told by some that these motets of mine are somewhat difficult, I answer them that I composed them only for virtuosi who can sing well, not for those who fail in the execution).

On the front page of the collection *Armonici accenti voce sola per cantar nel chitarrone & in altri stromenti musicali . . . op. 24* (Venice, 1621), Puliti signed himself as "Maestro di

EXAMPLE 13.1   Puliti, *Donna ingrata senza Amore*

Cappella & Organista nella Chiesa maggiore di questa Nobil Terra vostra d'Albona," and dedicated it to the noble family Negri of Labin. This was neither the first nor the only collection dedicated to the Negri family. In 1612, when he served as the organist of Trieste cathedral, Puliti devoted his collection *Ghirlanda odorifera... cioe mascherate a tre voci* to Tranquilo Negri, the military officer from Labin actively involved on the Venetian side in the war against the Habsburgs, a poet, and the author of the comedy *Anima d'intrico* (performed in 1633).[26] *Armonici accenti* consists of eight relatively short monodic madrigals and two three-part *a cappella* madrigals, dedicated to Antonio Bragadino and Agnesina Negri on the occasion of their wedding. These homophonic madrigals (written by the Istrian poets Giambattista Brati and Ottonelo de' Belii) are close to the canzonetta form, and provide precious musical evidence of wedding songs performed in the bourgeois and noble homes of Istria and Dalmatia. The monodic madrigals have a simple, popular form. The strophic structure of melody results from the structure of the text written in stanzas. There is a rather consistent coincidence between the *ababc* rhyme and the meter, which most usually follows the pattern 2 + 3 + 2 + 3 (*ritornello:* 2 + 3). The melody is so freely and inventively developed that the composer's consistent adherence to patterns is not felt as an encumbrance. Thus, the madrigal *Donna ingrata*, which was composed on the basis of the popular *Ruggiero-bass* melody, provides a good example of clear structure with a likable melody (see Example 13.1).[27]

Like Puliti, Cecchini acquired friends and patrons in his local area, dedicating to them his printed works; his collections include monodies, madrigals and canzonettas for several voices, psalms, motets, instrumental sonatas, and at least four books of Masses. The prolific composer introduced a number of innovations into the music of Dalmatia. In fact, his *Amorosi concetti: Madrigali voce sola facili per cantare e sonare nel clavicembalo chitarone o liuto, libro primo* (Venice, 1612) was the earliest collection of Baroque compositions written for the Croatian milieu, and was dedicated to the Capogrossi brothers. A few years later, some members of the Capogrossi family were accused of being heretics, along with the Split Archbishop Marcantun de Dominis (1560–1624). It appears that, because of his ties with De Dominis and the circle of his Split supporters, Cecchini moved to Hvar in 1614, where he remained until his death.[28]

In *Amorosi concetti, libro primo* (Venice, 1612) and *libro terzo,* Op. 7 (Venice, 1616)— the second book did not survive—the influence of G. Caccini's *Le nuove musiche* is obvious. These collections show how the new achievements of early Baroque monody quite quickly found their way to the Croatian coast. Solo singing with instrumental accompaniment could easily accommodate the strong tradition of Renaissance lute music and poetry.[29] But, during his career as a composer, Cecchini moved toward increasing simplification; he passed from up-to-date attitudes that distinguished his early works to the predilection for a marked stylistic immediacy associated with light performing requirements. The specific synthesis of the *stile antico* and the *stile moderno* is perhaps best shown in his liturgical works, especially in the book of Masses. Not just in his early 1617 collection[30] but also later in *Il terzo libro delle messe ariose,* Op. 19 (Venice, 1624), *Missae tribus, quatuor, quinque et octo vocibus,* Op. 22 (Venice, 1627), and *Cinque messe a due voci . . . et vinti due motetti a voce sola . . . con otto sonate per gl'istrumenti, bassi & soprani* (Venice, 1628) (all in Biblioteka Jagiellonska, Krakow), Cecchini showed an ability to adapt modern expression to the modest local performing possibilities. For instance, in one of his eight-voice Masses from 1627, it is possible to recognize Palestrinian-type counterpoint in the opening sections of the *Kyrie* and *Gloria,* while the *Credo* is written in the choral *da cappella* style, in which the melodic development of the individual lines is completely sacrificed to the vertical, harmonic development in a lively rhythm (see Example 13.2).

By contrast, his eight sonatas from 1628 were written for liturgical use, and they have some significant features in common with Giovan Battista Riccio's *Divine lode musicali,* a collection of motets and canzonas in three books (Venice, 1612–20), although on a small scale and with the utmost simplification. There is a similar insistence on the succession of short sections based on the opening subject and contrasting sections in triple meter, but Cecchini uses the less radical components (see Example 13.3).[31]

Ivan Lukačić (c. 1587–1648) from Šibenik achieved a fine synthesis of European influences and local traits in his only collection, *Sacrae cantiones* of one- to five-voice motets with organ continuo (Venice, 1620). This collection was unknown for centuries, until the Croatian American musicologist Dragan Plamenac found it and brought it to light in 1934. This gave Lukačić the fame of the "father of Croatian music" and the most notable older Croatian composer.[32] Lukačić's talent was recognized already by his contemporaries: returning to Split after several years of music education in Italy, he was offered high church and music functions (he was superior of the Franciscan monastery and *maestro di cappella* at the Split cathedral). Some of his compositions from *Sacrae cantiones* were included in anthologies printed in northern Europe (the third volume of J. Donfrid's anthology *Promptuarium, musicum,* Strasbourg, 1627, contains five, and J. Reininger chose one motet for his 1626 anthology, *Deliciae sacrae musicae,* published in Ingolstadt).

A total of twenty-seven compositions in the *Sacrae cantiones* collection were probably written during Lukačić's studies in Italy. They show a strong influence of the early Baroque expressiveness of Venetian liturgical music, whereas the restrained expression can be accounted for by a similarity with the North Italian Franciscan composers, such as Giacomo Finetti (whose name is mentioned on the title page). Nevertheless, *Sacrae cantiones* was intended primarily for the local audience, that is, for the expectations of the clergy and

EXAMPLE 13.2 Cecchini, Credo

EXAMPLE 13.2 (*continued*)

EXAMPLE 13.3   Cecchini, *Sonata prima* from *Cinque Messe* (Venice, 1628)

superiors in Split. Their melodic inventiveness is usually within the parameters of a more restrained expression, lacking any sentimental figures or ornamental cadenzas. Characteristic of his monodic motets are clear melodic lines and simplicity of harmonic flow. The three-part *Domine, puer meus* contains a fine dramatic dialogue between Christ, the narrator, and centurion, organized like an early type of the oratorio. Lukačić's ability to synthesize different musical expressions can be seen in his four-part *Quam pulchra es,* composed in the form of rondo: the triple *tutti* refrain on the words "Quam pulchra es" is homophonic,

EXAMPLE 13.3 (*continued*)

EXAMPLE 13.3 *(continued)*

while the solo interludes abound in *espressivo* figures. In this motet the juxtaposition of solo and choral sound functions as a fusion of the traditional *prima prattica* and new *seconda prattica* style (see Example 13.4).

As a counterpoint to the Baroque virtuosity of composers such as Puliti, Cecchini, and Lukačić were simple, unpretentious, easily memorized *Kirchenlieder* provided with a Baroque touch by the church writer Atanasius Jurjević (Georgiceus, c. 1590–c. 1640), the *consiliere* and interpreter for the Slavic people of the kingdom at the court of Ferdinand II of Habsburg. His songbook *Pisni za najpoglavitije, najsvetije i najveselije dni* (Songs for the Most Important, Holiest, and Most Joyful Days; Vienna, 1635), the first printed songbook in Croatian with notes, consists of twelve religious monodic tunes with unfigured continuo, written for the use of common folk.[33]

It seems that Croatian became the language of musical instruction only in the mid-eighteenth century. At that time students ceased to write their lecture notes in Latin or in Italian, and their textbooks began to be written in Croatian, introducing the native language into presentations and discussions of music theory, harmony, and even of some beginnings of musical aesthetics. In 1770, the Slavonian Franciscan Josip Pavišević (1743–1803) wrote a manual of music theory in Croatian, and Ivan Velikanović (1723–1803) dedicated two chapters to music in his book *Upučenja katoličanska* (Osijek, 1788; this is in fact a rather free translation of a work originally written by the French author Francesco Amato Pouget). Mihajlo Šilobold Bolšić (1724–1787) usually wrote in his native kajkavian Croatian dialect, but when he published a textbook on Gregorian chant for the seminarians of the Zagreb Chapter, he chose the Latin language (*Fundamentum cantus gregoriani seu choralis*, Zagreb, 1760). Latin was at that time undoubtedly still the predominant language used in scientific publications.[34]

However, it should be noted that the very first music books were printed around the middle of the eighteenth century in Zagreb: the third edition of the mentioned gargantuan anthology *Cithara octochorda* from 1757; Šilobold Bolšić's theoretical treatise from 1760, and the 1764 collection of passions in the kajkavian dialect of Croatian language *Muka i smert Kristuševa* (The Passion and Death of Christ) by Toma Zakarija Pervizovic. In fact, during these years music activity in the Zagreb cathedral reached its peak.

EXAMPLE 13.4   Lukačić, *Quam pulchra es* from *Sacrae cantiones* (Venice, 1620)

EXAMPLE 13.4 (*continued*)

Under the influence of constant military activity against the Ottoman invasion, migrations, and changes in population structure, the thinning ranks of literate or educated men concentrated their efforts to keep alive the Croatian national identity. The composers and musicians were faced with very precise tasks created by the historical situation. The listeners—which at the beginning of the eighteenth century were almost synonymous with the church congregation—needed to hear music they recognized and whose textual message they understood. Such music was often anonymous, as can be seen in the music transcribed and adapted by Franciscan priests, which was mostly unsigned, accompanied only by the formula "ad maiorem Dei gloriam." The Franciscans left behind manuscripts of one-part church tunes, which were probably sung to the accompaniment of the organ and perhaps occasionally sung in several parts.

About 1750, the Superior of the Franciscan Province, Josip Janković, commissioned in the Venetian monastery San Francesco della Vigna codices for the monasteries in Slavonia and Srijem, and the scribes Joseph Maria, Constantin, and Bartolomeo Cordans wrote a number of almost identical codices for both northern Croatian and Dalmatian monasteries. These liturgical books were continuously used until the church reforms of 1776 and 1785, when they were replaced by unified *Singmessen*.[35] Of course, not all Franciscan musicians shared the same sources: at the beginning of the eighteenth century, the cathedral in Split was still an important music center, with a professional choir and *maestri di cappella* such as Gaetano de Stephanis (c. 1660–c. 1710), whose *Messe a quattro voci* (Venice, 1700) was dedicated to the "celebre metropolitana di Spalato," and Carlo Antonio Nagli (c. 1680–1756), who left one *Messa concertata* for choir and small orchestra.

In northern Croatia, the music written by the Franciscans is the oldest and best music of the Baroque period. Furthermore, in the early decades of the eighteenth century the Franciscan codices written throughout Croatia—from the north (Medimurje and Hrvatsko Zagorje), through the east (Baranja, Slavonia, Srijem, and western Bosnia), to the south (Dalmatia)—had a rather uniform repertory and style. In no way relegated to spontaneous improvisations of local parish priests, in the first half of the eighteenth century songbooks for church and monastery use were prescribed by church dignitaries. Among the scribes, miniaturists, and composers one should mention Frane Divnić (1612–93) and Petar Knežević (1719–1768) in Dalmatia; Filip Vlahović-Kapušvarac (c. 1700–1755), Franjo Vukovarac (fl. 1722), and Matija Jakobović (fl. 1725) in Slavonia; and Ladislav Šebelić (fl. 1710–36) in Hrvatsko Zagorje. Kapušvarac was a poet, as well as copyist and illuminator of several codices written for Slavonian Franciscan monasteries (dated in 1719, 1720, 1730, 1737). His activity is typical of the North Croatian Baroque music of that time, modest and adapted to nonprofessional church singers. By contrast, *Cvit mirisa duhovnoga* (Flower of spiritual scent; Venice, 1726, and a few later editions) by Toma Babić (1680–1750), was one of the most popular Baroque books with prayers and songs, which are still remembered today in oral tradition.

In contrast to religious music, the secular musical life deteriorated greatly, and began to revive only in the second half of the eighteenth century, with the rise of the middle classes and the recovery of the nobility, when almost simultaneously in the northern and southern parts of Croatia patrons reappeared and music could again enjoy financial support.

Orchestras supported by the patrons were formed and often led by excellent musicians, mostly foreigners, and music again became professionalized. The patrons promoted the European musical repertory (music by Italian, German, Austrian, Czech, and Hungarian composers survived in church archives and in some private collections), but were often great patriots who inaugurated the political climate of the early nineteenth century. The rise of aristocratic families such as the Patačić, Drasković, Erdödy, Prandau, Kulmer, Bathany, and Janković during the second half of the eighteenth century, and the appearance of new ideas among the nobility and the middle classes are indicative of the new thinking brought by the Enlightenment.

Croatian music in the seventeenth and early-eighteenth centuries was characterized by the variety of its Mediterranean and central European characteristics. In difficult historical circumstances, the efforts of the religious orders to keep music alive often crossed the narrow limits of liturgical music, becoming an important element of cultural life. By contrast, Baroque music for the middle class and for noble families shows dynamic features in its variety and scope.

Music in Slovenia

Metoda Kokole (*Ljubljana*)
edited by Zdravko Blazekovic

Although only recently established as a sovereign state, in the past Slovenia was (except for an interlude of seven decades in the twentieth century) culturally, economically, and politically fully integrated with Western Europe. Slovenian territory had been incorporated into the Holy Roman Empire early in the Middle Ages and belonged until 1918 to the Habsburg monarchy. In the seventeenth and eighteenth centuries, the region was administratively divided among the Inner-Austrian Archduchies of Styria and Carinthia, the Duchy of Carniola, and the County of Gorizia with its free city of Trieste—the hereditary Habsburg lands lying in close proximity to the *Terraferma veneta* and the Adriatic possessions of the *Serenissima*—part of which, especially the coastal towns of Koper (It. Capodistria), Izola (It. Isola), and Piran (It. Pirano) with their hinterland, now also belongs to Slovenia.[36] The Slovenian capital Ljubljana, in the early seventeenth century a small provincial town of about seven thousand inhabitants, was the seat of the regional administration of Carniola, which encompassed the major part of today's Slovenia, and from 1461 also was the seat of a bishopric. Ljubljana's geographical position stimulated a peculiar blend of diverse cultural influences coming from the Latin southwest, the Germanic north, the Hungarian northeast, and the Slavic southeast. Until late in the eighteenth century, the former two currents were dominant. During the Baroque era, the city and its surrounding regions were largely multilingual. In addition to scholarly Latin, the languages Slovenian, German, and Italian were spoken interchangeably.

The evolution of Baroque music in the Slovenian provinces corresponds closely with the fundamental historical and stylistic changes taking place elsewhere in Europe. It began relatively late, around 1600, and a Baroque idiom persisted until around 1770. In spite of the relatively modest output, performances in Ljubljana of both sacred and secular Baroque music are fully documented.[37]

The number of Slovenian-born musicians active at home increased during the Baroque period, although opportunities were still very limited. Some of them, following the example of Jacobus Handl-Gallus in the sixteenth century, sought their fortune elsewhere in Europe. The elements of the nascent Baroque, for example, could be found in the works of Gabrijel Plavec, born in Carniola during the last quarter of the sixteenth century and active in Mainz, where he died in 1642. Plavec's most important work is the collection *Flosculus vernalis sacras cantiones, missas aliasque laudes B. Mariae conteniens* (Aschaffenburg, 1621) for three to ten voices with basso continuo.[38]

In the period immediately preceding the Baroque, the Slovenian lands were strongly marked by the Protestant movement but, as the religious freedom lasted only a few decades, the development of sacred music following German examples was suspended in its initial phase. At the same time, the professed Lutheran utilitarianism impeded the absorption of more advanced Italian forms. However, other religious confessions did not impede the Slovenian Protestant nobility and bourgeoisie from displaying a marked interest in Italian music, for they are known to have been familiar with the composers Cipriano de Rore, Giacomo Gorzanis, and Claudio Merulo.[39]

From about 1598, the Counter Reformation movement also marked the beginning of a new era in the Inner-Austrian provinces of Carinthia, Carniola, and Styria. All Protestant preachers and cantors were expelled, and any cultural heritage tinged with Lutheranism was systematically destroyed, including a number of printed books in Slovenian that had been published since the early 1550s. The main local agent was the Jesuit Order, which established its outpost in Ljubljana as early as 1597.[40] The Jesuits in Ljubljana were fully supported by the Archduke Ferdinand of Habsburg, the future Holy Roman Emperor Ferdinand II, a fervent supporter of the Counter Reformation movement. In 1595, Archduke Ferdinand took over the government of the Inner-Austrian provinces and then resided in the Styrian capital Graz. As a devout Catholic, Archduke Ferdinand was particularly fond of sacred music, especially Italian.[41] The role of Graz as the center of dissemination of Italian music in Inner Austria is particularly well illustrated by the anthology *Parnassus musicus Ferdinandeus,* dedicated in 1615 to Archduke Ferdinand, which was acquired for Ljubljana cathedral.

The repertory performed at Ljubljana cathedral can be surveyed through the *Inventarium librorum musicalium ecclesiae cathedralis labacensis,* compiled between 1620 and 1628 by order of Tomaž Hren, which lists a complete inventory of the cathedral's music.[42] Hren was at that time Prince-Bishop of Ljubljana and from 1614 also an Inner-Austrian Deputy, in which capacity he moved to Graz where he came into direct contact with the latest Venetian music cultivated by the court musicians. Indeed, some of the published musical anthologies listed in the *Inventarium* may have been brought from Graz to Ljubljana by the bishop himself after the relocation of the court chapel from Graz to Vienna. One such example are the still extant six *Chorbücher,* copied by the Graz tenor Georg Kuglmann,[43] and at least one of them, a book of litanies, was personally presented by Kuglmann's son to the bishop in 1616.[44]

The *Inventarium* lists 317 items written by at least three different hands.[45] The inventory, in its core compiled in 1620, is divided into several sections: *missae,* motets or *sacrae cantiones, cantus concertati cum basso generali,* psalms, madrigals, and instrumental compositions. In the course of the first revision of the inventory that took place after 1620 missing works were marked on the margin with a note *deest* or *desunt.* The repertory listed in the *Inventarium* is indeed remarkable in its scope and variety, reflecting the cosmopolitan musical aspirations of Ljubljana early in the seventeenth century. Apart from the names of several celebrated Renaissance composers,[46] it lists a number of more recent compositions that already contained early Baroque elements. These included motets in *stile concertato, madrigali concertati,* and instrumental compositions by composers such as Agazzari, Finetti, Grandi, Rossi, Banchieri, Caccini, Puliti, and Posch. Some of the most interesting entries include Alessandro Grandi's *Madrigali concertati* (1615), Francesco Turini's *Madrigali* (1621); Biagio Marini's *Musiche di camera* (1624); and Isaac Posch's *Musicalische Tafelfreudt* (1621). Two examples of early forms of oratorio—*Dialogo concertus a 6, 8 voci cum basso* by Agostino Agazzari and *Madrigali e dialoghi a 6 voci* (1598) by Francesco Stivori—are also included. It is, of course, indicative that, in contrast to the more German-oriented sixteenth-century lists, this inventory contains primarily works by relatively contemporaneous Italian composers.

The *Inventarium* lists by name a substantial number of musicians from the Graz court, such as Giovanni Valentini, Reimondo Ballestra, Pietro Antonio Bianco, Simone Gatto, Heinrich Pfendner, Francesco Stivori, Alessandro Tadei, Lambert de Sayve, Batrolomeo Mutis, Georg Poss, and Giovanni Priuli, and their presence is easily explained. The documentary evidence indicates, for example, that Ballestra was actually invited by Prince-Bishop Hren to Ljubljana in 1611 and spent one month there.[47] The same section also includes two items by Alessandro Grandi and as many as five by Giacomo Finetti, an Italian composer of small-scale motets who enjoyed special popularity in northern Italy as well as north of the Alps.[48]

Furthermore, it is of particular interest that the *Inventarium* mentions two copies of Giulio Caccini's *Euridice* (probably the second printed edition that came out in Venice in 1615). It seems unlikely that Caccini's score was acquired in duplicate for the sole purpose of being included among the music prints in the cathedral collection. Because forces for a performance of such a piece were available in the town,[49] it is tempting to speculate about its actual staging in Ljubljana at some point around 1620. This would be the earliest performance of Caccini's masterpiece outside Florence. For the lack of unequivocal evidence this must, however, remain only an attractive hypothesis.

In the cathedral's collection were also entered works by Isaac Posch, the only active local composer. Posch was apparently born around 1591 in the Austrian town of Krems an der Donau.[50] In 1597 he came to Regensburg, where he remained in the city's humanistic Protestant school, the *Gymnasium poeticum,* until fall 1606 or spring 1607. As a foreign alumnus, Posch was entitled to extracurricular instruction in music from the current cantors Andreas Raselius, Paul Homberger, and Leonhard Pfaffreuter. We still do not know where Posch spent the period between 1607 and 1614, when—according to the preface to his first-known printed work, *Musicalische Ehrenfreudt*—he became the organist to the Carinthian Provincial Estates in Klagenfurt. As such, he was probably active among the Protestant nobility, especially his patrons, who were members of the Provincial Estates.[51] It seems that he worked on a more or less freelance basis and depended for his living on occasional earnings rather than on a regular salary.

From 1617 to 1622 Posch was frequently in Carniola, where he was temporarily employed as organ builder by the Franciscan monastery of Ljubljana and by Prince-Bishop Hren. In 1617–18, he was repairing musical instruments for the Prince-Bishop in his residence in Gornji Grad (Oberburg in Lower Styria). In 1618, he published the collection of ensemble instrumental dances entitled *Musicalische Ehrenfreudt* in Regensburg.[52] The composer signed the dedicatory letter in Ljubljana on New Year's Day 1618 and sent it by a courier to Regensburg. The volume was dedicated to the Carinthian Provincial Estates, which supported the project financially. In 1620 Isaac Posch dedicated his second instrumental collection, *Musicalische Tafelfreudt,*[53] to his other patron, the Carniolan Provincial Estates, who also were the dedicatees of his eight motets published in February of the following year. In 1621 he built in Ljubljana an organ for the Franciscan church and published in Nuremberg his *Musicalische Tafelfreudt*. In 1622 he repaired an organ at Ljubljana cathedral. Posch died between 24 December 1622 and 31 March 1623. On 4 June 1623 his widow dedicated his collection of small-scale Latin motets, *Harmonia concertans,* to the Carinthian nobleman Melchior Putz, a counselor to Ferdinand II of Austria, and the collection was printed in the same year by Simon Halbmayer of Nuremberg.[54]

The first two music collections of three surviving—*Musicalische Ehrenfreudt* (1618) and *Musicalische Tafelfreudt* (1621)—include ensemble instrumental dances that reveal traditional German forms and were intended for performances at banquets and wedding festivities. The first collection contains forty-nine four-part compositions divided into four *balletas,* intended expressly to accompany aristocratic meals, and fifteen groups, or suites, each made up of three dances, *gagliarda* (in the last three cases *couranta*)–*Tanz*–*proportio,* to be performed either then or for dancing afterward.

Posch's collection is historically important because it is one of the latest examples of printed music that explicitly mention dance. This gives an indirect clue that similar compositions by other composers also were intended for practical purposes.[55] In his suites Posch combines duple and triple meters—which create an alternation of slow and fast movements—and bases to some extent the three dances included in the suite on the same motivic material. The groupings of dances are comparable with the similarly structured variation suites contained in the collections of Johannes Thesselius (1609),[56] Paul Peuerl (1611),[57] and Johann Hermann Schein (1617).[58] The characteristic feature of these variation suites is that individual dances are thematically related. Last but not least, Posch's dances are—according to the use of clefs in the four-part instrumental texture—the earliest known example of a scoring for a string quartet, even before Thomas Simpson's *Taffel-Consort* of 1621.[59]

The four- and five-part dance movements of Posch's *Musicalische Tafelfreudt* (1621) include some recent stylistic innovations coming from the south. They have musical textures strongly reminiscent of the earlier Anglo-German style of William Brade, Thomas Simpson, and Valentin Haussmann, with some traits of contemporaneous Italian innovations. The collection contains nine pairs of five-part instrumental *paduanas* and *gagliardas,* and twelve pairs of simpler four-part *intradas* and *courantas.* The compositions were intended for any kind of string instruments. Noteworthy among the four-part *intradas* is number eleven, which the composer entitled *Ludit Author Chromaticè,* alluding in this way to the relatively dense chromatic writing of this piece that undoubtedly surpassed the practice of the time. The five-part *paduanas* and *gagliardas* are formally and musically complex pieces. A couple of them also have, quite uncommonly for the time, dynamic markings for piano and forte.

Posch's only vocal volume, the *Harmonia concertans* (1623), consists of Latin motets for one to four voices with an organ continuo (*Partitura*). There are no fewer than twelve solo motets that are very advanced in their expression. Considering that the collection was brought out by a Protestant printer in Nuremberg in 1623, this is an exceptionally large number. Among Posch's duets three are for equal voices, a popular combination in Italy during the 1620s, as well as three motets for the combination of soprano and bass. The motets for three and four voices are for the most part written in a more traditional style, although Posch, interestingly, tried to reduce the number of vocal parts by substituting instruments for them. In six cases the actual vocal scoring of the three- and four-part motets is equivalent to that of a duet (*Magnificat, Ego dormio, Hodie Christus natus est, Alleluja, Dum complerentur,* and *Haec est dies*). He further minimized the incidence of traditional four-part texture by utilizing a rondolike form with a *tutti* refrain and solo episodes (motet *Jubilate Deo*).

The title page of his *Harmonia concertans* refers directly to Italian models, describing Posch's motets as "Cantiones Sacrae, quas Concertus Itali vocant." In his introduction for performers, Posch was even more explicit, referring directly to Lodovico Grossi da Viadana. However, Posch goes some distance beyond this model in structure and the expressive qualities of his music, reaching the newer style exemplified by the small-scale sacred concertos of Alessandro Grandi and Giacomo Finetti, the *Parnassus musicus Ferdinandeus* motets by the Graz court musicians Giovanni Priuli and Giovanni Valentini, and even the shorter motets of Claudio Monteverdi.[60]

Posch's music as a whole, and his sacred concertos in particular, are excellent examples of the dual German and Italian stylistic allegiance so characteristic of the Slovenian lands, which was held in high esteem already during his lifetime. Most popular were apparently his small-scale motets, a number of which managed, amid the social and economic devastation of the Thirty Years' War, to be included in printed anthologies such as *Deliciae sacrae musicae* (1626), the *Fasciculus primus . . .* (1637), and *Fasciculus secundus geistlicher wolklingender Concerten* (1638). It is significant that Posch is cited in the preface to the *Fasciculus primus* among the Italian composers.[61] A number of his motets were also copied for practical use in local churches in Saxony.[62] Isaac Posch was one of those *Kleinmeister*—in the most positive sense of the term—working in this genre, who through their influence throughout the German-speaking lands paved the way for Schütz's masterpieces in the same genre.

The cultural history of the northern part of Istria, that now is part of the Republic of Slovenia, forms a special chapter in the Slovenian history of music. In the seventeenth and eighteenth centuries, this geographic area was under the Venetian jurisdiction and, therefore, not directly connected with the rest of the territory populated by Slovenians. Koper—appropriately called *caput Istriae*—was from the thirteenth to the eighteenth century the capital and the administrative center of the Venetian Istria, populated by the Slavic people in the hinterland and mostly Italian- (viz. Venetian-)speaking people in the urban centers.

The cultural life in Koper and Piran in the sixteenth century was especially marked by the foundation and activities of two learned academies, the *Accademia dei Desiosi* (1553–54) and its successor the *Accademia Palladia* (1567–1637). The members of these academies met to discuss philosophical and ethical topics as well as poetry and medicine. It is telling that their *favole pastorali* called also for music accompaniment. The most prominent figures among the *Palladians* were Giulio Belli and Girolamo Vida, the author of *Cento dubbi amorosi* and *Sileno*, a dialogue with musical *intermedii*.[63]

The important centers of sacred music included the chapel attached to the cathedral in Koper, the chapel of the parish church of San Giorgo in Piran, and chapels at many monasteries. Among the foremost musicians of the cathedral in Koper were Francesco Bonardo, Silao Casentini (c. 1540–1594) from Lucca, and Niccolò Toscano (c. 1530–1605). In 1610 the chapelmaster in Koper was Jacopo Loschi, who was succeeded in August 1614 by the Italian composer of some importance Gabriello Puliti. The latter kept this post with short interruptions until 1624. Other seventeenth-century *maestri di cappella* included Iseppo Paulazzi, a native *sacrestario;* Antonio Julii (Giulio), a Minorite friar from Padua; Francesco Volpi; and Iseppo Quirini. In the same period the chapel of the Church of San Giorgio in Piran hosted Marco Petener (in 1579), Giovanni Donato Cabalus (in 1608), Papo Fonda (in 1616), Pellegrino del Senno (1623–26), and Zuane Chierego (from 1629). The acquisition of new music from Venice for the chapel testifies to the high level of musical life in Koper.[64]

The organists of the cathedral were almost exclusively priests or members of religious orders—the majority of the latter came from the local convent of Franciscan Conventuals, the Minorites. The most notable member of this order was the "organist of the Cathedral in Koper," Gabriello Puliti (c. 1580–1644), a prolific composer of thirty-six sacred and secular works in various musical forms, such as secular madrigals, *mascherate,* instrumental pieces, and sacred motets, psalms, and Masses, printed between 1600 and 1635.[65]

The earliest surviving music of Gabriello Puliti, who was born in Montepulciano near Arezzo in Tuscany around 1580, is in two collections of traditional five-part motets and psalms, printed in Parma and Milan in 1600 and 1602. From 1604, when he is recorded to have resided at the Minorite monastery in Pula, he apparently remained in Istria until his death in 1644. During three periods he lived in Koper (1606–1609, 1614–20, 1622–24), where he composed, in his capacity as the cathedral organist, a collection of custom-made madrigals, *Baci ardenti* (1609), dedicating it to Archduke Ferdinand of Inner Austria, then residing in Graz. On the title page of this collection Puliti is referred to for the first time as the *accademico armonico detto l'Allegro,* indicating that he was a member of an Italian academy.

Puliti's second stay in Koper, between 1614 and 1620, was the most productive and advanced phase of his compositional endeavors. In 1614 he published two collections of sacred music. His *Psalmodia vespertina* with psalms for four equal voices and continuo—dedicated to Jakob Reinprecht, the Abbot of Stična Monastery (Ger. Sittich) in Carniola—was apparently written to fulfill the needs of the Cistercians of Stična. The other collection coming out in that year was a collection of motets for one to three voices and organ, *Sacri concentus.* A year later his *Lunario armonico* was printed, a volume of three-part villanelle. The next extant opus is No. 20 from 1618, which is the first of his five volumes of monodic motets, *Pungenti dardi spirituali.* Op. 21 is lost, but the two volumes printed in 1620 are preserved: the *Lilia convallium* and the *Sacri accenti.* Puliti returned to Koper in 1622 and remained there until 1624, when he published a volume with two Masses.

Closest to the early Baroque idiom are Puliti's monodic motets of 1618 and 1620. The motets of *Sacri accenti* are in a strict relation to the liturgical calendar of the Koper bishopric; two motets were even destined for the feasts of the city patron San Nazario and the locally much-venerated Santa Orsola. Gabriello Puliti made a substantial contribution to the musical life in Koper not only as an organist but also as an active composer who responded to the musical needs of the Istrian *capoluogo.*

Whereas in Ljubljana the introduction of new musical forms had in the early Baroque phase been stimulated primarily by the bishop and the secular nobility, the musical activity during the middle phase (1630–1700) centered on the Jesuit College. Particularly significant for the growth of musical production and reproduction in the Carniolan capital were the theatrical performances of its students. By the mid-seventeenth century, these plays gradually adopted characteristics of the contemporary Italian operas, and thus paved the way for the forthcoming visits of Italian operatic groups in Ljubljana.[66]

By contrast, we also know that as early as 1660 the governor of Carniola, Count Wolfgang Engelbert Auersperg (1610–1673), the brother of the emperor's prime minister Johann Weichard Auersperg and a notable promoter of Italian culture in Ljubljana, had a certain *Comedia italiana in musica* staged in his garden pavilion.[67] The performance was organized during the official state visit of the newly crowned Holy Roman Emperor Leopold I to his hereditary lands.[68] The staging of an opera, sung in Italian by local performers, in Ljubljana at this relatively early date does not, however, come as a surprise, in view of the geographical proximity of Venice, then the prime center of operatic art. Moreover, there is some evidence that Carniolan nobles had a strong interest in Italian culture.[69]

The most conspicuous musician associated with the Jesuit college in Ljubljana was Janez Krsnik Dolar, *Carniolus Lithopolitanus,* born around 1620 at Kamnik near Ljubljana.[70]

After his elementary schooling in Ljubljana, he left for Vienna, where in 1639 he entered the Jesuit order. From 1645 to 1647 and from 1656 to 1658 he was engaged at the Ljubljana Jesuit College and contributed to the musical life in the Carniolan capital. Later he worked in Györ, Passau, and Vienna. All of his surviving compositions, known only in transcriptions, probably date from the last ten years of his residence in Vienna. Apart from sacred music (three Masses and psalms), he also wrote instrumental sonatas and *balletti*.[71] Dolar died in 1673 in Vienna, where from 1661 he had been the music director of the Jesuit church Am Hof.

Dolar's compositions should be evaluated side by side with the works of his contemporaries in Vienna, such as Bertalli, Schmelzer, Kerll, Draghi, and Biber. Nevertheless, the Carniolan composer seems to have been substantially influenced by contemporary Italian style, which he could have absorbed during his stay in Ljubljana. At a time when composers were still frequently resorting to the so-called *stile antico*, Dolar incorporated in his works all the stylistic elements of the middle Baroque idiom. The distinction between vocal and instrumental parts is evident, and the contrasts of *soli* and *tutti* are clearly emphasized. The movements of his Masses are linked with instrumental sonatas that bring the musical material from the preceding vocal movement. A characteristic example is his *Missa Viennensis* for four four-part choirs with sixteen soloists, and an ensemble of string and brass instruments with related soloists and organ. All the movements except sonatas and the Benedictus require all the performers. Dolar's *Missa Viennensis* is therefore an example of the colossal polychoral style introduced to Vienna by Orazzio Benevoli. It represents Dolar's most brilliant composition and places him among the important composers of the Viennese circle.

In the second half of the seventeenth century the cultural life of the Venetian coastal area of today's Slovenia slowly declined. The main music centers were still the chapels of the cathedral in Koper and especially Minorite monasteries in Koper and Piran. The only musical figure of the time deserving mention was Antonio Tarsia (1643–1722), born in one of the foremost Koper noble families.[72] Little is known about his early schooling, except that he sang as a boy in Koper cathedral, and in 1662 he was appointed the organist there. He apparently retained this post until 1710. His preserved manuscript compositions date between 1674 and 1718 and are mostly liturgical and comprise seven autograph Mass movements, ten psalms, a number of motets, a sequence, and some nonliturgical compositions including an interesting dramatic dialogue. The style of his compositions develops from early Baroque monodic writing to the developed Baroque idiom in his later compositions. However, in general, his music is deliberately traditional and local and does not exhibit the contemporary modern trends of Venetian composers.

At the beginning of the eighteenth century, Baroque music in Slovenian lands entered its last productive phase. The Jesuit college was still one of the principal promoters of musical life in the capital. Among the most important composers to contribute music for the Jesuit plays and religious services were Janez Jurij Hocevar (1656–1714), the musical director of the theater and a composer of at least five school dramas; Marijan Cadez (d. 1718); and Mihael Omersa (1679–1742). The latter two were both composers of lost oratorios.

However, early in the eighteenth century, Italian cultural influences prevailed and determined the late Baroque idiom for decades to come. Following the example of similar associations in Italy, as early as 1693 Ljubljana acquired its own learned society, the *Academia operosorum*.[73] Moreover, in 1701 two of its members initiated the creation of a specialized music academy, after Italian examples: the *Academia Philharmonicorum Labacensium*.[74] This music academy not only was the earliest music institution of the kind in Slovenian territory but also was among the earliest exclusively music academies to be established within the confines of the Holy Roman Empire.

The *Academia Philharmonicorum* was founded in 1701 by Johann Berthold von Höffer (1667–1718), a nobleman from Ljubljana. Its statutes, the *Leges,* printed in Ljubljana the same year, provide valuable information on its structure, admissions policy, and required activities. Initially, its full members numbered only fifteen musically educated noblemen. Soon, however, they also accepted musical amateurs. The maximum number of *philharmonici* was, however, limited to thirty-one. In addition to the yearly performances on the feast of St. Cecilia (the patron saint of the Academy), the activities of the society were twofold—music-making in private homes (*exercitium musices inter parietes*), and public performances (*actus publicus*). Particularly elaborate was the music program for the yearly summer regatta on the Ljubljanica River, which obviously followed Venetian examples.

Unfortunately, we lack more specific information regarding the musical repertory of the *Academia Philharmonicorum.* But, according to available sources, it included—in addition to the works of contemporary European composers—compositions of its own members. Only some of the titles and authors' names have been recorded. Among the local composers were Janez Gasper Gosel (d. 1716) and Wolfgang Conrad Andree Siberau (1688–1758). Apparently they wrote sacred and secular, vocal and instrumental music. Among their compositions were oratorios, litanies, Masses, psalms, cantatas, serenades, and sonatas. It is particularly important to note the popularity of oratorios. Some preserved libretti indicate that the music for them was written in the late Baroque Italian style. The foremost composer of this genre was the academy's founder, Johann Berthold von Höffer. In the first two decades of the eighteenth century, he composed at least three oratorios, although only the libretto for his oratorio *Patientia victrix in amico Iob* (1716) is preserved.

Closely bound up with the history of the *Academia operosorum* (and therefore also with the *Academia Philharmonicorum*) is the early history of the Seminary Library of Ljubljana, founded in 1701 by three high-ranking clergymen and leading *Operosi:* the Prince-Bishop of Ljubljana, Ziga Herberstein; the provost Janez Krstnik Preseren; and the cathedral dean, Janez Anton Dolnicar. The Seminary Library also contains a notable collection of 235 Italian opera libretti from the seventeenth and eighteenth centuries, many of them donations from its first librarian and other highly educated nobles from Ljubljana.[75] According to Sartori,[76] the collection includes twenty-seven *unica,* while another ten libretti—five of them German translations of familiar Italian operas (*Aëtius,* 1732; *Craesus,* 1723; *Demetrius,* 1733; *Jason,* 1733; and *Ornospade,* 1727)—are not listed in Sartori, and therefore they are presumably *unica* as well. There are also ten bilingual libretti issued for the productions in Klagenfurt, Graz, Ljubljana, and Brno. Most of the libretti on the list were printed for productions in Italy, 102 in Venice alone. Interestingly, fewer than half that number, forty-eight, were originally intended for performances in Vienna, mostly at the imperial court (nearly 50 percent of them date from the last two decades of the seventeenth century). Five pieces were published specifically for the productions in the Carniolan capital, Ljubljana (*Il Tamerlano,* 1732; *Euristeo,* 1733; *Artaserse,* 1740; *Rosmira,* 1740; and *Didone abbandonata,* 1742).

It is true that, for the most part, these Italian operas mentioned above were never performed in Ljubljana, but the *Operosi* and other benefactors who donated their libretti to the Seminary Library obviously appreciated this kind of music, and must have attended operatic performances elsewhere in the Holy Roman Empire and in northern and central Italy. Thus, Carniolan music lovers of the Baroque period undoubtedly contributed to the formation of a cultural climate favorable to operatic performances in their homeland.

The final phase of the Baroque in Slovenian lands was characterized by the increased number of Italian operatic groups that arrived in Ljubljana in the middle of the preceding century, but that encouraged the local production of operatic works only in the first half of the eighteenth century. The first documented opera by a Carniolan composer was *Il Tamerlano* (1732) by Giuseppe Clementi de Bonomi, the music director in the private chapel of the Carniolan vice-dominus.[77] This *tragedia per musica* was again staged in the palace of Count Thurn-Valsassina, viz. Della Torre e Valsassina. However, the libretto, which was published only in Italian and was printed by Girolamo Savioni in Venice, does not specify either the occasion or the exact date of the performance. Count Franz Anton Siefried Thurn-Valsassina (1668–1741), to whom the opera was dedicated, was then the vice-dominus, a powerful administrator of the imperial estates in Carniola, and according to the flattering dedication of his musical director also one of the most generous patrons of arts and sciences in the province. The librettist is not named; however, the text closely follows the text by Agostino Piovene.

After 1732 operatic performances in Ljubljana were not staged in a private setting of aristocratic palaces but in public places that were presumably accessible to much larger audiences. However, a strong operatic tradition during the Baroque period started only with the regular operatic productions of the Mingotti company in the 1740s, which opened a new chapter in the history of the Italian operas in Ljubljana.[78] A list of thirty-four Italian productions recorded between 1732 and 1797 gives the impression that Italian opera companies were the most active in Ljubljana during the 1740s, primarily because of the famous impresarios Angelo and Pietro Mingotti, who brought to Ljubljana at least five operas: *Artaserse* and *Rosmira* by Johann Adolf Hasse, *Didone abbandonata* by Domenico Sarri, *Il Demetrio* by an unspecified composer, *Il mercato di Malmantile* by Domenico Fischietti, and the comic intermezzo *Pimpinone e Vespetta* by Tomaso Albinoni.

However, the popularity of Italian opera in Carniola seems to have reached its peak in 1765, when a new building for the Provincial Theater was constructed in one of Ljubljana's main squares (later Kongresni trg). The first opera to be produced there in 1766 was Galuppi's *L'amante di tutte,* mounted by an impresario from Prague, Giuseppe Bustelli, who also was responsible for the three productions of 1769: *Il cavaliere della piuma, La contadina in corte,* and *Il ciarlone.* The impresario of the 1773 productions—*La locanda* by Giovanni Bertati, *L'amore senza malizia* by Bernardino Ottani, *La buona figliuola* by Niccolò Piccinni, and *Il carnovale* by an unspecified composer—was Gaetano Pecis, and Giuseppe Bartolini produced in 1787 a performance of *Li due castellani burlati* by Vicenzo Fabrizi. After 1668 performances by German groups considerably increased.

In the third quarter of the eighteenth century, economic, social, and cultural conditions in Slovenian lands underwent a radical transformation. The *Academia Philharmonicorum,* which, at its peak in the preceding decades, was the principal promoter of the new musical forms in Slovenia, lost its momentum by the middle of the century and ceased to exist by 1769. Four years later the Jesuit Order also was dissolved and Lenten processions were prohibited. Hence, Ljubljana was suddenly deprived of both institutions that had for decades favored its manifold musical life. The Baroque period in Slovenian music history had thus abruptly reached its conclusion in the wake of the ill-fated administrative reforms of Emperor Joseph II.

Music in Russia (Ukraine)

Claudia Jensen (*Kirkland, Washington*)

If concepts defining Baroque are difficult to specify for Western and central European music, what might they mean in a Ukrainian or, especially, a Muscovite context?[79] The chart in the Introduction (Table I.1) attempts to pin down some of the stylistic fingerprints of the era, based on a core of four areas: concepts of philosophy and theory; new formal procedures; new or transformed musical styles; and the complex interrelationships between music and society. This approach, unlike some earlier evaluations, emphasizes diversity over an artificially imposed unity, and an abundance of stylistic choices over an evolutionary view of music from simple (early) to complex (late). Even within this generous scheme, however, one must pause when considering how best to fit the music of the sprawling Muscovite state into these categories.

In many ways, Muscovy itself defies rigid categorization. Seventeenth-century Russia witnessed tremendous change in virtually every aspect of its culture and society during this period. The Romanov dynasty, which would last for nearly three hundred years until another cataclysmic century, was established at the beginning of this period. With the increasing stability of the new dynasty following decades of terrifying upheaval around 1600, the state developed strongly in military and economic power, increasingly confined the peasantry to the land where they would be retained until the reforms of the 1860s, and witnessed a wrenching schism within its church, a break promulgated by no less a figure than the patriarch himself. Muscovy's ties to the West, considerable even during the sixteenth century, were immeasurably strengthened as a result of the decades of ultimately victorious wars with Poland at the beginning of the century, and with Sweden at the beginning of the next; in between, Muscovy united with Ukraine, a virtual conduit of information from and about the West.

Muscovy was not isolated during this period; there were nearly constant diplomatic and economic contacts with most of the European powers throughout the century. The tsars made particular efforts to keep abreast of Western events and had summaries of Western newspapers drawn up from the beginnings of the century, and a regular mail service, beginning in 1665, also kept the flow of information constant. Yet Muscovite music remains little studied in the West, its culture more a Churchillian "enigma wrapped up in a mystery" than it probably was to contemporary Europeans.

How then does Muscovite music fit into our conceptions of the Baroque? It is a particularly knotty question, especially when one considers one of the few commonly known—perhaps, unfortunately, the *only* known—anecdotes from this period and this place. This is a story told by Adam Olearius, a Holsteiner who visited in the 1630s and 1640s. He describes the incomprehensible sight of his Russian hosts rounding up five wagonloads of musical instruments in the city of Moscow—and burning them![80] The story is inconceivable in any city to the west of the Russian capital and serves only to distance an already distant and difficult culture. But the story also may serve as an object lesson, pointing out the unique dichotomies of Muscovite music and the unique ways in which this music might be understood in the context of the Western Baroque.

Idiomatic instrumental writing, the use of basso continuo, and the elaboration of complex instrumental forms are certainly part of our understanding of the Western Baroque and feature prominently in Table I.1 of this study. Burning wagonloads of instruments clearly does not fit within these parameters. Yet the Russians were certainly not trying to destroy every instrument in the capital; as Miloš Velimirović observes, five wagonloads from a city of one hundred thousand or more, at any rate, suggests a somewhat lackadaisical attitude at best.[81] The instrumental bonfire represents one of the final attempts, long futile, to destroy an idea, the association between the pagan past and the musical instruments by which this past was expressed. This must be understood within a stricture not encountered in most European contexts: the complete absence of musical instruments in Russian Orthodox church services. The Russian authorities were not attempting to ban all instrumental music—and Olearius might have kept in mind the many occasions on which he was serenaded by Muscovite instrumentalists—but simply those instruments that, by their long association with the pagan past, represented a continuing challenge to the authority of the church.

How then might Muscovite music be fitted into at least some of the categories of the Baroque? The answer is, in many ways, each of which must be understood within the complex framework of Muscovite culture of the seventeenth and early eighteenth centuries. Muscovite musicians equaled their Western comrades in their desire for a clear philosophical or theoretical framework for their music. They were not focused on humanism as an organizing ideal, although humanistic ideas, particularly from rhetoric, did permeate musical thought, especially in Ukraine and later in Muscovite court culture as a whole in the last third of the century. In writing monophonic and polyphonic works, Muscovite and Ukrainian musicians worked within a strong theoretical framework, using both long-standing procedures for liturgical music as well as more recently borrowed terms and concepts drawn from Western practice. For both styles, they produced a variety of notation and composition treatises intended for specialists as well as students. Although monody, one of the central stylistic elements of Baroque musical language, does not apply to the Muscovite context, we do see an exploration of concerted musical structures, often highly complex and subtle. And the domination of music and musicians by courts and the aristocracy, so much a part of the Western musical experience during this period, is crucial to an understanding of Russian music in the seventeenth century. In the early eighteenth century, under Peter the Great, the growing audience for music and the expansion of that audience to include amateur performers, particularly among the aristocracy, mirror developments in Western culture. The generous variety by which contemporary scholars understand all of Baroque music allows, even requires, us to bring Muscovy back in from the cold.

MUSIC OF THE CHURCH TO MID-CENTURY

The choirs associated with the tsar and the patriarch, called the *gosudarevy* and *patriarshie pevchie d'iaki,* were elite groups, the most skilled, the most highly trained, and certainly the most visible musical figures in Muscovy throughout the seventeenth century.[82] Their histories go back to the sixteenth century and perhaps even earlier; the Moscow patriarchate was established only in 1589, but the sovereign singers existed as an organized group associated with the grand dukes of Muscovy and with various monasteries and church hierarchs throughout the sixteenth century, with at least one reference suggesting an even earlier period of organization.[83] Their ultimate origins, of course, stretch back to the time of the conversion to Christianity, late in the tenth century, when emissaries from Constantinople sent to Kiev all the necessities for the new converts: liturgical books, clerics, and singers.[84] One of the outstanding and fortunate characteristics of these singing groups was their detailed hierarchical organization, which permits us to trace the development of the ensembles as a whole, and of individual members as they moved through the ranks.

Although the evidence from the earliest period of their organization precedes the Baroque, the basics of their hierarchy were already well established in the sixteenth century and would be maintained throughout the seventeenth. The separate choirs were subdivided into ranks or groupings called *stanitsy.* In the 1570s, at the time of their full development under Ivan IV (Ivan the Terrible; r. 1533–84), there were nearly thirty men in the sovereign singers, divided into five ranks, with another handful of unattached singers. Members came from many different geographical areas, a pattern that was to hold through the seventeenth century as well. Other ecclesiastical hierarchs had their own singers, generally smaller groups. The ensemble associated with the Chudov monastery around this period, for example, had nine singers, as did the Iosifo-Volokolamsk monastery two decades later. But there were nearly thirty Novgorodian singers in mid-century, reflecting the city's important and influential traditions in the field of church singing.[85]

This structure was broken somewhat during the turbulent period known as the Time of Troubles, when the ruling Rurikid dynasty was extinguished and civil war, as well as invasion from Poland, brought calamitous disruption to all areas of Muscovite life. The election of Mikhail Romanov to the throne in 1613 brought a measure of peace, reflected, among other areas of Muscovite culture, in the restoration of the singing ensembles. As S. G. Zvereva points out in her excellent survey of this period, during the first half of the seventeenth century the ensembles exhibited both great stability as well as obvious planning for gradual, controlled evolution. The primary singers, especially early in Mikhail's reign, were the experienced men from the ensembles of the last century, many of whom had been members for many decades; one Ivan Fyodorov, for example, sang in the group for nearly fifty years.[86]

One of the most important aspects of their duties was teaching youngsters, who, in their turn, would be expected to work their way up the ladder and teach their own students, providing for a smooth transition in the case of the retirement or death of an older singer. In addition to the sovereign and patriarchal singers, the court establishment also included singers attached to the tsarevich, Aleksei Mikhailovich; they performed along with the sovereign singers, although they were designated as belonging to the tsarevich (*tsarevichevye pevchie d'iaki*). Musical instruction was also provided not only to young singers but also to the young Aleksei Mikhailovich himself, who was taught by the leader of the sovereign singers' first *stanitsa*. As the older singers of the reestablished ensembles retired during the course of the 1630s to 1650s, new performers were promoted or imported from other cities, particularly Novgorod, a development that, as we shall see later, was to have an important impact on the repertory of these organizations. The membership of the sovereign and patriarchal ensembles toward the end of the first half of the century again reached around thirty or so singers each. By the end of the century, this figure would more than double.

Because the groups were so highly and hierarchically organized, we can glean a great deal of information about them from the abundant payment records surviving throughout the century. A singer's rank in the choir was an important measure of his talent, experience, and, not coincidentally, his salary. Although each singer's rank is generally listed in the records, even in its absence the various *stanitsy* are listed as units, with all of the singers of the first rank listed together, all of the second rank, and so forth. The singers were well paid, the sovereign singers from the tsar's Privy Chancery and the patriarchal group from the Patriarchal Treasury. They received yearly salaries in the range of five to ten rubles, more as the century progressed, and they were fed frequently, if not daily, at the court's expense. Their housing was provided, as was a clothing allowance. These benefits sometimes continued to the family even after the singer himself had died.

The particular case of the singer Elisei Gavrilov gives us a sense of a typical career. He is mentioned as early as 1658 as one of the sovereign singers. The next year, we learn that he was in the fifth rank, a fairly lowly position perhaps indicating that he was still in training. By the mid-1660s, he had moved up to the second rank, and in 1669 he performed one of the ensemble's unfortunately frequent duties: singing at a royal funeral, in this case for Tsar Aleksei Mikhailovich's first wife, Maria. He remained in the choir throughout the

1670s and 1680s, when the choirs were reorganized and attached to various Kremlin churches. He died after decades of service in 1701.[87]

The singers themselves apparently wrote out musical manuscripts, especially in the first part of the century.[88] In the second part of the century, we find records for a special group of scribes who worked, as the documents always specify, at "a little house by the river" along with the bookbinders. The scribes, like the singers, worked for many years at their jobs. Potap Maksimov, for example, spent twenty-five years there in the 1660s to 1680s, collecting an annual salary of ten rubles.[89]

What kinds of music did the sovereign and patriarchal groups sing and where did they sing it? Their most important function was to sing at worship services at which either the tsar or the patriarch was present. Often the two groups combined forces, dividing themselves into ensembles standing to the right or the left of the *kliros,* an elevated area on either side of the iconostasis. The right-hand group was the more prestigious and was uniformly taken up by the sovereign singers or, if a single ensemble was performing, by the first *stanitsa.* When ecclesiastical hierarchs from outlying cities came to Moscow, they brought their own singers, who also might join in services, and whose names and ranks are duly noted in the payment books. They also sang in funerals and memorial services. For these services, the singers would generally have performed monophonic chant, which in the first half of the seventeenth century was represented by a complex and growing network of styles and notations, as discussed below.

Although royal and patriarchal worship services are certainly not to be considered private, the ensembles did have what might be considered public appearances in the yearly cycle of religious processions and liturgical dramas in which the singers played important roles. This is where they would be most likely to have been seen by the Moscow public at large. The most important of these public ceremonies were the Epiphany and the Palm Sunday processions. Both of these ceremonies should be understood in a variety of ways, each highlighting the complex and changing Muscovite court culture of the seventeenth century. They not only provided for a public display of the monarch's humility before church and Christ, as Paul Bushkovitch notes in his study of the Epiphany ceremony, but they also served to illustrate his formidable secular resources, particularly in the Palm Sunday procession, where, by mid-century, the bowing multitudes consisted of the state's armed musketeers, the *strel'tsy.*[90] It would have been impossible to conceive of such a ceremony without the presence of the *pevchie d'iaki,* and even the young trainees of the patriarchal ensemble had assigned roles in the procession. The singers also had roles in lesser processions, for example those honoring visiting church dignitaries.[91]

The most important and elaborate of these public religious ceremonies, however, was the annual production of a liturgical drama, the story of the three boys in the fiery furnace from the Old Testament Book of Daniel, generally referred to in Muscovite sources simply as the Play of the Furnace (*Peshchnoe deistvo*).[92] This production involved extensive singing by both men and boys, and the singers were kept busy not only with their elaborate costumes and props, but with teaching the young singers their roles. The patriarchal singers seem to have borne the responsibility for the drama, and contemporary documents record their work in teaching and producing this event over the course of many years, beginning in the second quarter of the sixteenth century and continuing through the mid-seventeenth century. The play represents a confluence of influences typical of Muscovite society: from Byzantium, where a similar drama was also known; from the West, the probable source of some of the more spectacular theatrical effects (the descent of the angel and the apparently vast quantities of artificially produced flames for the furnace); and finally from age-old folk traditions, with which *skomorokhi*, itinerant secular musicians reminiscent of *jongleurs* or *Spielmänner* in the West, were associated—they took the roles of the evil Chaldean jailers in the play. Although productions were abandoned around mid-century, the Play of the Furnace must also be considered an important forerunner of the first court theater, which emerged in the 1670s, at the end of Aleksei Mikhailovich's reign (r. 1645–76).

The singers would have been well versed in a variety of chant styles in the first half of the seventeenth century, for the period of the mid-sixteenth to mid-seventeenth century marks an expansion, even an explosion, in monophonic chant styles and notations. It is also beginning in the late sixteenth century, at the time of the proliferation and consolidation of the various singing ensembles, that we begin to have substantial information about individual singers and singing styles. The period of the Western Baroque brings us into the middle of these far-reaching changes, and we shall consider several interrelated developments: a brief survey of the basic vocabulary and approach of Russian liturgical chant; the development around 1600 of a variety of monophonic singing styles, concurrent with the rise of the singing ensembles discussed above; and finally, the development of polyphonic singing, which was widespread in Russian Orthodox lands in the seventeenth century, and its impact on singers, notations, theory, and musical style. Overarching all of this is one of the basic tenants of Orthodox church music: it is unaccompanied by instruments and is therefore receptive to, or more accurately, predicated upon, the texts themselves. Changes in these texts, as we shall see, resulted in major changes in Russian liturgical singing.

The basic chant style of the Russian church was the *znamennyi* chant (from *znamen'*, or sign, referring to its neumatic notation). The ultimate roots of this style and its notation are Byzantine; as Vladimir Morosan says, it was "born out of intricate, virtuosic improvisations on the basic fabric of the Byzantine melos."[93] And, like the interrelated chants of the Greek and Latin churches to the west, Russian chant is based on a series of melodic formulae or patterns, organized into eight modes, a system taken from the Greek singers and ecclesiastics who brought the new religion to tenth-century Kiev. In the period of the Baroque, more than six hundred years later, Kiev and its singers and musical traditions were leading influences in Muscovite musical thought. The other great influence was from the northern city of Novgorod, a tradition absorbed into the Muscovite sphere when Novgorod came under direct Muscovite control during the reign of Ivan IV in the mid-sixteenth century. These two cities, both with significant ties to the West (Novgorod was a member of the Hanseatic League, and Kiev and much of Ukraine were part of the Polish-Lithuanian orbit well into the seventeenth century), formed two important and controversial sources of musical and liturgical authority for Muscovy.

Beginning around 1600 there were significant changes in Russian liturgical singing and notation. As early as the mid-sixteenth century, we begin to see a great variety in the types of chant mentioned in sources. The *znamennyi* chant itself was divided into two types, called *bol'shoi* (great) and *malyi* chant (the term means lesser or small, and refers to a less elaborate style), and other new types are mentioned as well. The well-known series of hymn settings (*stikhiri*) by the singer Fyodor Khrestianin are examples of *bol'shoi* chant, which is highly ornate and melismatic, with a wide melodic range and large leaps. Kazan chant seems to be associated with Ivan IV's singers (he took the city of Kazan in 1552) and Greek chant emerged in the mid-seventeenth century in Muscovite sources and has a distinctive melodic profile: an almost recitative-like character, with relatively simple, direct melodic lines, often with few leaps and careful use of dissonance. The style seems to have derived from that of Greek singers in Moscow in mid-century.[94]

The most important of the newer styles is *demestvennyi* chant, which apparently originated in the previous century. Its origins are controversial, but its name is believed to have come from the term *demestvo*, indicating a singer of exceptional skills, and the style itself is ornate and difficult. *Demestvennyi* chant has its own notational symbols and its pieces do not follow the patterns of the traditional eight modes.[95]

Although it may be convenient to create a kind of periodization of Russian chant by using various types of notation as general indicators, recent scholarship has shown that the situation is far more fluid and complex than this notational shorthand indicates. The notational innovations around 1600 by the Novgorodian Ivan Shaidur seem to represent, as Miloš Velimirović says, the first of several codifications whereby Russian neumes were interpreted as representing specific pitches rather than designating intervallic space. Shaidur used special signs written in red ink (thus called *kinovarnye pomety*, or cinnabar signs) to indicate pitch, based on a system of four trichords. As Velimirović notes, this system strongly resembles Western hexachordal arrangements and was probably derived from them.[96] The succeeding reforms are more difficult to date. Recent scholarship, primarily by N. P. Parfent'ev, indicates that reforms traditionally associated with Aleksandr Mezenets in the third quarter of the century actually occurred earlier, perhaps even more or less simultaneously with the Shaidur signs. This innovation involved using signs in black ink (*pomety, priznaki*) to specify pitch. Parfent'ev's studies of manuscripts from the first half of the century show that this innovation seems to be connected with the important monastic center of Zvenigorod in the 1640s or earlier, and that it was fairly widespread before the official correction of liturgical books at the church councils of the 1650s and 1660s. These changes were codified by the Second Commission in 1669 (and published in a treatise entitled *Izveshchenie o soglasneishikh pometakh* [Report about the most agreeable markings] in late 1670), but by then, events had overtaken these belated efforts at notational reform. Not only was Western, five-line staff notation well known in Ukraine by this time (Muscovites called it Kievan notation), but it was known in Muscovite lands as well, and gave rise to a type of manuscript called a *dvoznamennik*, which lined up neumatic and staff notational systems.[97]

The church commissions represent an important turning point in Russian Orthodox liturgical music, not so much for the proposed notational reforms, but as evidence of significant, oftentimes wrenching, changes to the liturgy and its musical expression. The reforms were spearheaded beginning in 1653 by Patriarch Nikon, a powerful force in the early years of Tsar Aleksei Mikhailovich's reign, who counted on this influence for his reform efforts. As his musical and liturgical authorities, Nikon relied on the educated clerics of Ukraine, long an important source for Muscovy's musicians. Throughout the 1650s, Ukrainians singers were a highly visible presence at court as they came, were brought, or were ordered north to Moscow.[98] The church was indeed ripe for reform, as singing practices had become, in places, lax to the point of unintelligibility. In the mid-seventeenth century, documents describe the practice of simultaneous singing—not polyphony, but cacophony:

> At that time . . . great confusion entered into the Holy Church, since contrary to the Rule and the Church order, they began to perform church singing not in one voice, but in two, three, and six voices, not understanding one another; and from the priests and clergy themselves there arose in the holy churches a very strange noise and goat-bleating, since the singers on both kliroses would sing the Psalter and other church hymns without waiting for the other to finish and shouting all together. . . . [99]

Changes in the language itself also prompted Nikon's efforts, necessitating extensive revisions in the musical realizations of these texts.[100] Nikon overreached himself, however, when his efforts met with resistance; in the eyes of some Muscovite clergy, Nikon's Ukrainian authorities were tainted with the heresies of the West, to which they were closely tied not only geographically but through the Uniate Church, and the patriarch did himself no good when he resigned, waiting in a fit of pique to be recalled by the malleable young tsar. But Aleksei, by this time, was not quite so young and not so malleable. Nikon was not called back, although his reforms were pushed through. The results of these reforms, as Richard Wortman describes, "were the cultural and political equivalent of the original conversion to Christianity. Ruthlessly enforced, they alienated large numbers of those faithful to the 'Old Belief,' who resisted or immolated themselves rather than submit to what they perceived as a foreign heresy."[101] The commissions were called to navigate the twin minefields of musical/textual reform and musical notation. As we have seen, although the Second Commission finally issued a report in the early 1670s, it was far too late by that time to be concerned with nuances of neumatic notation. The old notation survives in the Old Believer (or Old Ritualist) communities scattered throughout the world today. Their resistance is familiar to Westerners through Musorgskii's opera *Khovanshchina*.

The Ukrainian singers in Moscow would have brought with them a tradition of liturgical music different in many important respects from that of their Russian hosts. Ukraine's long-standing association with Western musical traditions, via Poland, is very clear in the travel diary of Paul of Aleppo, who accompanied and recorded the visit to Muscovy of Macarius, Patriarch of Antioch, in the mid-1650s. In the city of Uman', roughly 120 miles south of Kiev, for example, Paul described the music he heard, which included the use of the organ: "In this church are lofty pillars; with galleries looking over the choir, in which the musicians stand, and sing from their musical books to the organ, making with it a noise that emulated thunder." In the city of Sakoka, Paul made a similar observation: "Above the Great *Narthiks* are Galleries; with balustrades, looking over the choir, in which the singers stand and chaunt to the organ." Paul's descriptions are supported by a musical source linked to Uniate practice which contains figured bass notation underneath Cyrillic liturgical texts.[102] The music of the Uniate practice was thus strikingly different from the unaccompanied singing of the Muscovite Orthodox tradition.

Another important Ukrainian musical tradition, one that was to flower in Muscovy as well, was polyphony, especially choral polyphony. This was particularly important in the Orthodox brotherhoods (*bratstva*) in Ukraine, which served as musical bastions against the encroaching traditions of the West, stimulated by (especially Jesuit) efforts as part of the Counter Reformation. Sources from late in the seventeenth century confirm this; for example, Bishop Simeon of Smolensk was chastised for his use of Western-style polyphonic singing, whereupon he replied simply that his parishioners were used to it, and without it they would be bored. The extent of this choral polyphony in lands to the west and southwest of Moscow is indicated by a listing of musical manuscripts at the L'vov *bratstvo* from 1697, which includes hundreds of large-scale polyphonic works set to liturgical texts.[103]

Exactly when polyphonic chant settings and, later, choral polyphony were introduced into Muscovite practice is not known, but apparently before the importation of Ukrainian singers in the 1650s, although their skill in polyphonic singing was certainly an important consideration. Even before their arrival, however, there is evidence of polyphonic chant settings, generally in two and three parts, in Russian practice, and this evidence goes back into the sixteenth century. Some scholars believe that in an oral tradition, the practice may stretch back even earlier. The texts most frequently set polyphonically were proper hymns for major feasts and texts of the Divine Liturgy, and they are found in widely dispersed Muscovite manuscript sources. The musical and notational styles are quite varied. There are both simple and highly melismatic polyphonic settings (especially of *demestvennyi* chant), written using *znamennaya, demestvennaya,* and later, staff notation, although the precise method of transcribing the neumatic polyphonic notations is controversial.[104] The style is called *strochnoe* singing, from the term *stroka,* or line. The fixed chant melody, the cantus firmus, was called the *put',* or path, and the added voices were called the *verkh* (upper or top) and the *niz* (lower or below). Along with influences from Ukraine, Novgorodian singers also seem to have figured prominently in this bourgeoning polyphonic practice. As Zvereva points out, it is precisely in the 1630s, when Novgorodian singers were so important in the reformed and restabilized Muscovite ensembles, that we see widespread performance of *strochnoe* singing in Muscovy. We know that this style was already important in Novgorod, because a *chinovnik* (a book recording liturgical practice) from the city's Cathedral of St. Sophia written circa 1630 shows extensive use of polyphonic singing.[105]

One of the most important documents recording the early use of polyphonic singing in Muscovy is a listing made by the sixteen-member choir of Simon, Archbishop of Vologda and Belozersk. In 1666, these singers listed all of the pieces they knew and the parts they sang. In this smallish, northern ensemble, somewhat removed from the larger and more important singing ensembles of the tsar and patriarch, almost all of the singers knew at least two parts, usually adjacent lines, and a few singers knew all of the parts. All of the three singers who knew only one line sang the cantus firmus. Their listing also indicates a wide repertory representing many types of liturgical singing. This information meshes with evidence from other sources; we know that singers tended to specialize in one or two parts and that they were replaced by singers with similar specialties. Thus, an ensemble could perform a wide variety of polyphonic music, from four-part *demestvennyi* settings to smaller, two- or three-part settings, because each singer knew several of the lines and the choir could reconform itself as necessary.[106]

The period from the mid-sixteenth to the mid-seventeenth century was thus one of enormous change in the most fundamental elements of liturgical music, particularly notation and the expansion of the repertory, both in terms of monophonic styles and with the addition of polyphonic performances. The sovereign and patriarchal singers constituted one of the important elements of continuity, although they, too, were almost entirely reformed after the upheavals of the Time of Troubles, introducing practices and even singers from the important centers of Novgorod and Kiev. They were involved in every aspect of liturgical singing: performance, worship, notational reform, and the public ceremonies of state in the form of the annual processions and, particularly, the Play of the Furnace. In many of these profound musical changes, we see influences, usually filtered through Ukrainian practice, from the West and this holds true also for the musical life of the tsar's court in the period of the Baroque.

SECULAR MUSIC: THE COUNTRYSIDE AND THE COURT

In his account of his travels in Russia, Adam Olearius provides us with the vivid image of the burning of wagonloads of musical instruments, which were regarded as heretical and unclean through their long association with the *skomorokhi,* the itinerant entertainers of old Muscovy.[107] But Olearius's treatise also lets us know how feeble a gesture that bonfire really was. The *skomorokh* tradition dates back to some of the oldest Russian written documents from the eleventh century. In Olearius's time, these entertainers still preserved their ancient associations with instruments, games, dances, and songs, all of which were regarded as scandalously evil, literally devil-inspired, by the clergy. Indeed, the *skomorokh* tradition represented a continuing challenge to the authority of the church, a challenge that the clergy apparently had little power to overcome. The document produced following the church council of 1551, presented in a series of chapters arranged as questions and answers, shows the continuing and unsuccessful efforts to combat the *skomorokhi* centuries after the conversion to Orthodoxy. Chapter 41 of the report, for example, reads: "At secular [!] weddings, poets and musicians and *gusli* players and merry-makers perform and they sing profane songs. And when the couple then goes to the church and the priest meets them with the cross, all of these profane performances roam before them, and the priest can not stop or forbid them."[108] (The *gusli* is an ancient Slavic instrument, somewhat resembling a psaltery; it is held upright on the lap and plucked.) This persistent association with secular entertainment is documented in Olearius's book, where he includes pictures of *skomorokhi* playing musical instruments (the *gusli* included) and giving puppet shows.

In some ways, the seventeenth-century clergy seemed willing to tolerate these associations; Guy Miege, who wrote the account of the Earl of Carlisle's embassy to Moscow in 1663–64, recounts the riotous behavior of *skomorokhi* in connection with the Play of the Furnace: "In the 18. of December we saw that strange representation, that is annually made by the Moscovites of the fiery furnace.... The Persons [apparently *skomorokhi;* the other performers were members of the patriarchal singing ensemble] that act in it are disguised, and their beards rubbed over with honey, their hats of wood with which they run up and down the streets, and with wild fire in their hand burn the hair or beard of any body they meet, with great insolence."[109] There was indeed a certain amount of overlap between the sacred and secular traditions, which comes out particularly strongly in the use and depiction of musical instruments. On the one hand, certain musical instruments, like the psaltery, harp, or trumpet, figure prominently in biblical texts, particularly in the Book of Psalms. In Russian sources, King David is depicted, as he is in the West, surrounded by instruments; he himself sometimes holds a *gusli*. On the other hand, the *skomorokhi,* as representatives of the secular past, were often associated with specific types of instruments, particularly wind instruments (especially the pipelike *svirel*) and a bowed string instrument called a *gudok*. They, too, played the *gusli,* however, and the various depictions of this instrument— as King David's instrument of God or the *skomorokh* instrument of the devil—demonstrate the ambiguous role of musical instruments in Russian society.[110]

The *skomorokhi* were not the only ones to carry this "outlander" association with musical instruments, for accounts of the pretender to the throne during the Time of Troubles, the False Dmitrii known to Westerners through Musorgskii's *Boris Godunov,* consistently mention his grossly inappropriate use (to Orthodox ears) of music and musical instruments. The account by the Dutch merchant and traveler Isaac Massa, for example, details the elaborate orchestra made up of imported musicians for the wedding feast of Dmitrii and his Polish bride. It cannot be a coincidence that Massa reports later that most of the musicians were killed when Muscovite forces overthrew Dmitrii.[111]

Although intense interest on the part of Russian scholars and collectors in their own rich folk music was a development of the late eighteenth century, the historical record provides a few remnants and clues to other kinds of secular music of this early period. A handful of seventeenth-century sources preserve what might be termed historical songs, that is, pieces with texts reflecting contemporary events. The most famous collection of this type is that associated with the Englishman Richard James, who was in Moscow in 1619; apparently the collection of texts was written at his request. It includes song texts reflecting the disruptions of the Time of Troubles (for example, the suffering of Godunov's daughter and Filaret Romanov's return from Polish captivity). There are also songs about other events of importance: the uprising of Stepan Razin in mid-century or, earlier, songs about Ivan IV.[112]

If we return to Olearius's account, however, we see the important flip side of the coin: the development in the seventeenth century of elaborate court ceremonies drawing heavily on the participation of court-sponsored instrumental musicians. In this, the Muscovite court is clearly and closely linked to Baroque practices of the West, and it is no coincidence that this period witnessed nearly continuous diplomatic exchanges at a variety of levels between the Tsar's court and those of Europe. The Muscovite court, too, had specific musical requirements and a specific set of instrumentalists considered appropriate for these tasks. State-sponsored fanfare music was used in Moscow throughout the seventeenth and early-eighteenth centuries for events of grandeur, particularly for diplomatic receptions. Diplomats' accounts throughout the century describe being accompanied by the sounds of Russian trumpeters and percussionists, often not to their liking. Guy Miege, in his chronicle of the Carlisle mission, had a typical reaction, setting out the different set of instruments used for state fanfares in Muscovy:

> . . . and for their Musique there were so many Trumpets, Kettle-drums, Howboys, and other such instruments of War, which they had disperst in parties thorow all their Troops, that for two miles we were in no want of Musique. But they having battered our ears with one continued aire above two hours together all the way as we marcht, the noise of those Instruments which at first had delighted us with their melody, became now obstreperous and troublesome.[113]

Foreign delegations also brought their own instrumentalists with them, and in a few instances there is evidence that they interacted with Russian musicians. Miege's report hints that on occasion, such interaction may have taken place on an informal footing: "Our Musique was most commonly at Dinner," he says, "at which time there was nothing to be heard but Trumpets and viols, whose delightful and agreeable Harmony, did sometimes so charm the Russes, that it drew great Company of them to hear it. And indeed the Musique was very good, being managed by one of the best experienced Musicians of England, who from time to time composed new airs."[114] Muscovite diplomats abroad also took along a quantity of musicians sufficient to create the proper impression. The English description of Pyotr Potyomkin's visit in 1681–82 notes that: "The Czars Trumpetts & Kettle Drums having one of them [a small boat] to themselves, with the Tilt taken off, that they might sound, as the Amb: desired, in their coming up."[115]

Organs and organists were another important musical element at court. This, too, was sponsored by the tsars beginning in the 1620s, when Mikhail Romanov (r. 1613–45) hired Western organists to perform and teach Russian students. It appears that keyboard instruments were known at court before this time, however, and may date particularly to the time of Tsar Ivan III's marriage to Sophia Paleologue, niece to the last Byzantine emperor. Sophia had been educated in Italy and she invited an organist to come with her to Moscow; he arrived in 1490, apparently without bringing an organ with him, implying that instruments were available in Moscow. A century later, the English diplomat Jerome Horsey, preparing for his return trip to Russia in 1586, wrote: "[I] had made my provicion of . . . organes, virgenalls, musicions . . . and other costly things of great value, according to my commissions," the requests apparently coming from the Muscovite side. Organists were a constant feature of court life through the seventeenth century, with special provisions made for the training of Russian students. In the 1660s Simeon Gutovskii, a Pole from Smolensk (a city that had recently been taken by the Russians), came to the tsar's court as organist and keyboard master. His career there spanned more than thirty years and, among his other activities, he helped build and transport an organ sent as a diplomatic gift from Tsar Aleksei Mikhailovich to the Persian shah in the early 1660s.[116]

Both of these traditions—the outdoor fanfares and the use of organs—spread from the court to the upper echelons of Muscovite society. Olearius himself was serenaded by the private trumpeters belonging to the Morozov family, and in fact he concludes his story of the burning of the instruments by mentioning Nikita Romanov, the tsar's cousin, "who has a harmonium [*Positiv*] and many other instruments in his palace." Many high-ranking families owned organs, small, portable instruments of the sort depicted in Karion Istomin's *Bukvar* (Alphabet) of 1694, an early Russian primer, suggesting that the instrument must have been widely recognizable.[117]

Moscow's Foreign Quarter was another important source of knowledge about Western music and musical practice. The Foreign, or German, Quarter (*Nemetskaia sloboda*) had grown throughout the seventeenth century to number around two thousand, primarily northern Europeans who worked for the tsar in a variety of military and manufacturing capacities. Yet the Foreign Quarter was equally important for its culture, particularly during the last decade of Tsar Aleksei Mikhailovich's reign, in the 1660s and early 1670s. (Here again, Olearius's account is useful, for he describes Nikita Romanov as a "friend of the Germans.") A variety of elements came together in this period to create what has been termed the cultural renaissance of Aleksei's final decade. The first of these elements was the presence of the Foreign Quarter itself in Moscow; the second was its interaction with the highest levels of Muscovite society, including even the tsar himself. The third element was the presence in Moscow of an influential group of highly educated non-Muscovite Orthodox, for example, the poet Simeon Polotskii and others from lands to the west and south of Muscovy. The most important musical result was the creation of the court theater in the early 1670s.[118]

There are a number of important antecedents to the theater, reflecting these varied cultural influences. Muscovite liturgical drama of the late sixteenth and early seventeenth century, which was in turn influenced by both Western and Byzantine practice, is certainly an important theatrical forerunner. Muscovite envoys abroad were familiar with Western theater; Vasilii Likhachev gives a breathless account of his views of Florentine entertainments in 1660, and Pyotr Potyomkin, on a diplomatic tour of Spain and France in 1667–68, saw two productions in Paris, one by the Molière company and the other at the Théâtre du Marais. The continuing presence of foreign diplomats in Muscovy throughout the century was another factor; the Carlisle mission even produced a play (apparently with music) in their Moscow lodgings.[119] The Muscovite government, beginning particularly in the 1660s, sought Western specialists in theater and music along with their requests to find mining experts and military aides. The immediate catalyst for the tsar's court theater seems to have been a production of the Orpheus legend staged by resident foreigners under the supervision of Artemon Matveyev, the head of the diplomatic chancellery and the guardian of the tsar's lively second wife, Natalia Naryshkina. *Orpheus* seems to have been a lavish affair, with costumes, sets, a variety of entertainments (including the German *commedia*-like character Pickleherring), and vocal and instrumental music.[120] Immediately after this, the court (in the person of Matveyev) began in earnest to make preparations for their own theater. Although they attempted to bring instrumentalists and actors from abroad, the plays initially seem to have been performed by actors and musicians from Moscow itself, from the Foreign Quarter and its musicians alongside musicians in Matveyev's employ. Between 1672 and Aleksei's sudden death in 1676, about a dozen plays were produced, beginning with a long and elaborate production of the story of Esther (*Artakserksovo deistvo* [The Play of Ahasuerus]), which included singing and instrumental music among its ten hours' duration. The plays tended to become increasingly secular as the theatrical activities progressed, ending with productions, for example, on the story of Bacchus and Venus. Instruments, cues for songs, and even the phrase *intermedia,* signifying some sort of musical entertainment between acts, appear throughout these plays; most of the texts survive, although no music has been preserved.[121]

Music at the tsar's court in the third quarter of the seventeenth century was thus quite varied, ranging from the simple fanfares used to greet visiting diplomats to the elaborately staged theatrical productions employing a mixed instrumental ensemble (apparently strings, woodwinds, brass instruments, and an organ). But this was certainly not the only music the tsar and his advisors would have heard. Interest in polyphonic styles continued throughout this period, cultivated in particular by the composers and singers of the long-established vocal ensembles associated with the tsar, the patriarch, and other church hierarchs, resulting in a profusion of elaborate and skilled settings of liturgical, sacred, and some secular texts in the late seventeenth and early eighteenth centuries.

MUSCOVY'S LATE BAROQUE

The large-scale *a cappella* settings of the late seventeenth and early eighteenth centuries reflect the same variety of influences as does the theater: traditions of Muscovite Orthodoxy; traditions from Ukrainian Orthodox in Moscow, with their far more direct experience of Western musical, educational, and cultural practices; and influences from the West (often channeled through the Ukrainians). All of these influences are clearly evident in the two important compositional genres of this period: the *kant* and the *kontsert.* Together, these two types of composition are known as *partesnoe penie* (part singing), and they represent a polyphonic practice distinct from the earlier chant polyphony.

The names of both genres obviously reflect their Western origins. *Kanty* are the simpler of the two. In general, *kanty* are three-part strophic vocal compositions set to sacred texts, although secular texts become increasingly common as the century progresses. They are written in score in staff notation, apparently as *a cappella* works, although the melodic profiles of some of the bass lines suggest a role as harmonic support, and the bass parts are also differentiated by their often elaborately ornamented melodic lines; this may suggest an instrumental performance in some cases. The origins of the *kanty* stretch back to the beginnings of the seventeenth century in Ukrainian and central European hymn traditions, and many of the earliest Muscovite sources show strong musical and linguistic evidence of Polish and Ukrainian influences. They seem to represent a tradition of sacred domestic music-making, a tradition made explicit in the introduction to Simeon Polotskii's verse translation of the Psalter (1680), in which he says that he made his translation into Russian because, although many in Muscovy enjoyed singing from the Polish-language versified Psalter, they did not understand the texts. As he says, they appreciated these settings "only from the sweetness of their song." Polotskii's translations were set to music by one of the sovereign singers, Vasilii Titov, several years later; his settings circulated widely and for many years.[122]

Many *kanty* have been published, including the entire contents of a single source from Moscow in the 1680s. The repertory of this collection, which includes nearly two hundred *kanty,* shows many influences, from Polish and Ukrainian traditions, from Russian chant, and from folk practice. The works of several poets are represented as well, particularly that of the monk (later abbot) German of the New Jerusalem Monastery outside of Moscow

EXAMPLE 13.5 German, *Veseliia den i spaseniia dnes*

(the name is pronounced with a hard *g* in Russian; he died in 1682). One scholar who has focused intensively on this repertory, Olga Dolskaya, suggests that German also may have written some of the music to his texts. His style, in contrast to some of the dancelike Polish rhythms found elsewhere in this collection, suggests a musical process based on the continually unfolding motives typical of Russian chant composition. Texts by Simeon Polotskii, mentioned above, are also set in this collection. At least some of the repertory seems to have been quite well known. Although there has been no comprehensive study of the concordances of *kanty* found in Muscovite and Ukrainian sources, the rate would appear to be significant, with many pieces found in a variety of sources.[123]

The *kant* "Veseliia den i spaseniia dnes" (Today is the day of rejoicing and salvation) is typical of German's style. The opening motive, transcribed here as a quarter note followed by six eighth notes, permeates the work, particularly in the two upper voices, where it is eventually reversed (eighth notes preceding the quarter note) and finally elongated in the final phrase. The work's brief imitative passage is typical of the style, which is dominated by the consonant flow of parallel thirds in the upper parts. The motion of the bass is generally slower, and that voice functions here as harmonic support. The inseparable relationship between the chant-influenced text, commemorating the Resurrection, and the musical setting suggests that German was the author of both. He was the choirmaster at the New Jerusalem monastery for a time and wrote many *kant* texts, often featuring elaborate acrostics (see Example 13.5).[124]

The other important polyphonic genre, the *kontsert* (again, the name reflects the style's Western origins), is more elaborate and complex. *Kontserty* arose in Muscovy in the last half (particularly the last quarter or so) of the seventeenth century. The early examples are most often settings of texts from the Divine Liturgy for multiple voices (generally for four, five, eight, or twelve parts) although, as in the case of the *kanty*, secular texts appear at century's end. *Kontserty* circulated in part-books written in staff notation and, although the specifics of their performance in Muscovy are unclear, it is reasonable to assume that some of them were sung during the celebration of the Divine Liturgy. The extremely fragmentary iconographic evidence suggests performances by smaller rather than larger ensembles.[125] Surviving manuscripts generally show signs of frequent use, with corrections entered and even candle drippings on the pages. Many of the pieces are attributed and some of the composers were members of the sovereign singers. It is very probable that *kontserty* were performed by members of these large ensembles, as they would have had the specialized training and rehearsal time necessary to perform these large compositions. A total of around fifty composers are known from the second half of the seventeenth century, including Simeon Pekalitskii (d. after 1699), a Ukrainian cleric who traveled to Moscow on several occasions, Nikolai Kalashnikov and Fyodor Redrikov (both fl. c. 1680s–1700), and perhaps the most skilled and important composer of the time, Vasilii Titov (c. 1650–c. 1715).[126]

The *kontserty* are quite varied musically. Some use chant-related, or possibly chant-inspired, melodic fragments, while others seem to be entirely freely composed. They are generally large-scale pieces, often falling into several sections that are sometimes delineated by means of metrical changes; their composers were finely attuned to variances in texture, often alternating the full ensemble with a smaller, *kant*-like group. As Olga Dolskaya, one of the few Western scholars to explore this repertory, has noted, the fact that *kontserty*, as liturgical works, do not use musical instruments resulted in "an intuitive exploration of exceptional combinations of timbres and sonorities," and it is in these pieces that one begins to trace the distinctive Russian choral sound so well known to foreign visitors even in the early eighteenth century. Thus, as Dolskaya has observed, duplication of parts even in the largest of the *kontserty* is rare; instead, composers prefer to explore a working-out of a small musical motive which is woven throughout the fabric of the piece, in a manner she describes as echoing processes in Russian architecture and decorative arts, and certainly familiar from Russian Orthodox chant traditions. This approach is evident in some of Titov's best-known works, for example his twelve-part setting of "Angel vopiiashe" (The angel cried out), with its focus on textural distinctions, or "Vsekh skorbiashchikh Radoste" (O Thou joy of all the sorrowful), which treats melodic motives in a kind of ritornello fashion. *Kontserty* also include devices such as word painting, an approach familiar in the West.[127]

A closer look at Titov's "Vsekh skorbiashchikh Radoste," a twelve-part *kontsert*, demonstrates his intense focus on texture and its expressive possibilities.[128] The opening of the work, illustrating the word "vsekh" ("fseh," of all), features the full ensemble, each voice singing independently yet each simultaneously linked with the others through waves of parallel and contrary motion. The immediate repetition of the opening word (bar 4) is performed by the reduced ensemble, a *kant*-like grouping of three voices, which is immediately juxtaposed to the full group, exclaiming the word "radoste" (joy). This alternation between the large and small groups is repeated throughout the piece, with the full ensemble repeating the opening text as a kind of punctuation, underscoring the work's textual structure and creating a clear and ever-evolving musical scaffolding. Works like "Vsekh skorbiashchikh Radoste" were clearly conceived with a built-in progression of dynamics, dictated by the sense of the text itself and realized by the textural nuances of the musical setting (see Example 13.6).[129]

One of the hallmarks of Western Baroque thinking is the desire to establish a firm theoretical infrastructure for musical forms and styles, and the late Muscovite Baroque is no exception. For the *kontserty*, this theoretical base was set out by Nikolai Diletskii (d. after 1681), a Ukrainian theorist and composer who worked in Vilnius and Smolensk before coming to Moscow around 1677. Diletskii's work, the *Musikiiskaia Grammatika* (Musical

EXAMPLE 13.6   Titov, *Vsekh skorbiashchikh Radoste*

EXAMPLE 13.6 (*continued*)

Grammar, in three versions from 1677 to 1681) is a composition treatise, designed to teach youngsters the rudiments of music and the basic approaches to composing *kontserty*. Diletskii's theoretical infrastructure is Western, using hexachordal syllables and other terminology derived from Western practice. His approach to composition employs typically Baroque devices derived from rhetorical and grammatical practice and vocabulary, evident in the very title of the work itself. The content of Diletskii's treatise, like his career path (from Ukraine to Vilnius in Poland-Lithuania, and finally to Smolensk and Moscow in Muscovite territory), traces the important influences on Muscovite musical thinking in the late seventeenth century. In one important area, Diletskii anticipates Western theoretical developments. In a section on expanding a composition, entitled "On Amplification" (he uses the borrowed rhetorical term "O amplifikatsii" or the Russian "O razmnozhenii"), he explains that a work might be lengthened by passing a brief melody through all of the pitches or letters on what he calls the musical circle. He then gives as an example two short musical phrases, each presented literally on circular staves, progressing by fifths in each of the twelve major and twelve minor keys. This is the first written circle of fifths, antedating by several decades similar presentations by Johann David Heinichen (1711) and earlier theorists. Other, much briefer, Muscovite theoretical works use the terminology Diletskii presents in the *Grammatika,* and his theoretical precepts circulated, particularly among Russian church musicians, until the end of the eighteenth century and even beyond.[130]

Diletskii's work was clearly didactic in purpose, an aim underscored by an illustration in one surviving copy depicting a music master teaching several young men and boys seated around a table with pens, inkpots, and paper. Although there were apparently private singing ensembles (one version of Diletskii's treatise, for example, is associated with the powerful Stroganov family), the most likely source of both teachers and promising students would have been the sovereign and patriarchal choirs. In the last decades of the seventeenth century, these choirs expanded greatly to include seventy or more singers. They were split up in this period, assigned to various members of the royal family (this was during the reign of the young co-tsars Ivan and Peter) or to specific Kremlin churches. Indeed, the singers are omnipresent in the court records at this time, running errands, singing numerous memorial services, and performing their traditional duties for the tsar and patriarch.[131]

In addition to their poorly documented (but highly likely) performance of the new *partesnoe penie* styles, the singing ensembles continued to perform monophonic chant and there were experiments in printing this music.[132] Tsar Fyodor Alekseyevich, Aleksei's son and successor (r. 1676–82), is credited with composing a monophonic setting of the liturgical text "Dostoino est'" (It is meet and right), following a long line of tsars to whom musical compositions are ascribed. At his death, he left a large number of chant manuscripts, some of them inherited from his father. At the same time, he was familiar with the kind of mechanical and keyboard instruments that had been a fixture of the court since the time of his grandfather, and it was to Fyodor that Simeon Polotskii offered his rhymed translation of the Psalter. The Old Believers, of course, also continued traditions of monophonic singing, although far removed from Muscovite urban centers.

With this vital and multifaceted Muscovite musical life in mind, it is no surprise that the changes wrought by Peter the Great on the Russian musical scene should be regarded as more in degree than in kind. Peter, the lively son of Tsar Aleksei's lively second wife, certainly brought sweeping changes throughout all areas of Russian society, yet in music, his changes represented an intensification of the Western gaze already so prominent in his father's time.

The most visible aspect of Peter's use of music were the many large-scale processions, parades, and ceremonies marking important military victories and other events throughout his quarter-century reign (reigned as co-tsar with his half-brother Ivan 1682–89; reigned solely from 1689 to 1725). Music had long played an important part in Muscovite religious and diplomatic processions in Muscovy, and Peter built upon this familiar foundation. In some cases, a mid-seventeenth-century diplomatic reception and a Petrine-era victory parade even used some of the same kinds of music: trumpet fanfares and percussion flourishes. Peter's state ceremonials, on a much larger scale and far more frequent than in the past, also used the three-part *kant* style, but with important changes. The Petrine panegyrical *kant* and *vivat* were simple, fanfarelike works, some of which, judging by the character of the melodic lines, were certainly performed by instruments as well as voices. They are often repetitive (with multiple exclamations of the word *vivat*), sometimes featuring a concertato approach, appropriate for outdoor performance on specially erected victory arches. As Yurii Keldysh notes in his excellent survey of Petrine music, the texts of the panegyrical *kanty* refer specifically to the event being celebrated, and there were a whole series of such works written for Peter's long string of military victories, beginning with Azov in 1696 and marking especially the important victory over the Swedes at Poltava (1709). This genre was also used to note more intimate state occasions, for example, events celebrated by and for the royal family. Their texts were apparently composed, or compiled, by students and teachers at the Moscow Spiritual Academy, following traditions of poetry from the seventeenth century and including phrases taken directly from the Psalter. As Keldysh notes, examples from the 1720s on seem to include more Classical references in their texts. This is certainly in keeping with Peter's emphasis on education based on Western models, but also recalls the many Muscovites and, especially, Ukrainians in the seventeenth century whose education followed these same models.[133]

Kontserty also formed part of Peter's musical arsenal; again, he employed musical styles familiar from the past, but in new, public, even civic, contexts. Whereas most of the seventeenth-century *kontserty* are set to liturgical texts, especially texts from the Divine Liturgy, the Petrine-era *kontserty* often join with the *kant*-style pieces to celebrate military victories, again using texts specifically reflecting those events. Settings of liturgical texts continued during this period, however, and there is evidence that performance of all types of *kontserty* was widespread. Prince A. D. Menshikov, for example, received both singers and *kontsert* manuscripts from the collection of the tsar's sister, Natalia Alekseyevna, after her death; the collection included dozens of volumes of works, with pieces ranging from four- to forty-part *kontsert* settings.[134]

Other polyphonic pieces were being written at this time as well, and these styles have important links to the polyphonic chant settings of the seventeenth century. These works, too, were written for state occasions and victory celebrations. One of the most important composers of this period was Stepan Beliayev, a member of the court choir who came from a family of singers and who was acquainted with Peter, traveling with him on his path-breaking excursions to Western Europe in 1697–98. The choir, now named the court [*pridvornyi*] choir, was transferred to St. Petersburg and not only took part in the festive celebrations of military victories but also accompanied Peter on his various trips; the patriarchal singers remained in Moscow and were renamed the Synodal Choir in 1721. Other large monasteries and academies also had choirs, as did some individuals, for example, Menshikov, mentioned above.[135]

Monophonic chant was still performed and written in the early eighteenth century as well, especially in churches and towns outside of the large cities and estates, which did not have the resources for the complex, multivoice *kontserty*. Monophonic styles also played a role in victory celebrations; a number of monophonic pieces were commissioned for the various processions described above.

All of these styles come together in the celebrations marking the important victory at Poltava (1709), which ended the long series of battles of Peter's Northern War against Sweden. The musical celebrations for this victory were lavish, involving many composers, performers, and writers. V. V. Protopopov, in his important study of the Poltava festivities, describes the elaborate venues constructed for the musical elements: seven triumphal gates were set up in Moscow, through which Swedish prisoners (including many musicians) were paraded. A group of twenty-four Russian trumpeters and six percussionists opened the procession, which then wound through the arches; at each arch, the procession stopped, speeches were given, and musical compositions sounded. Many different styles of works were commissioned for the Poltava victory celebrations: a cycle of ten monophonic settings, which Protopopov suggests are arranged in a specific musical ordering that was to unfold as the celebration proceeded; various fanfarelike *kanty* and *vivaty* for three parts, of which over two dozen are extant; a four-part "Service of Thanksgiving for the Poltava Victory," probably written by Beliaev; and a twelve-part *kontsert* by Vasilii Titov. Protopopov also includes information on some polyphonic folklike songs with texts referring to Poltava.[136]

Apart from this very public display of music, Peter also focused on music in its social context. Although there is evidence that important families in the seventeenth century employed their own musicians and owned some musical instruments (keyboards, in particular), this aspect of musical culture was considerably intensified during Peter's time. The sources for Russian understanding of Western music and musical contexts were the same as in the previous century: Westerners in Russia and Russians abroad. The Russians who went abroad in Peter's time, however, were not only greater in number, but far more influential in the hierarchy of Russian culture, beginning with Tsar Peter himself, the first Russian tsar to travel to the West. In this context, works such as Pyotr Tolstoi's travel journal from his assigned study in the West in 1697–99 and the diary of the Holstein diplomat Friedrich Wilhelm von Bergholz covering his years in St. Petersburg in the early 1720s are particularly important.[137]

One of Peter's important, characteristically top-down reforms was the institution of the assembly, based on models he had learned about in the West. These were heavily regulated affairs involving specified behavior and activities at game playing (especially cards), the offering of refreshments, and dancing, all of which provided musical opportunities for performers both Russian and foreign. Wealthy citizens maintained their own instrumental ensembles. A. D. Menshikov, who inherited the large collection of *kontsert* manuscripts, also maintained an orchestra consisting of strings, trumpets or other brass instruments, oboes (used extensively in Russian military ensembles), and flutes. The musicians were both Russian and foreign, including some Swedish musicians taken prisoner at Poltava. Ensembles of this sort not only played for dances but also provided *Tafelmusik* to accompany meals and games, and serenade music for outdoor excursions. Members of the aristocracy hired musicians for their entertainment, and they also began to play musical instruments themselves, particularly keyboard instruments.[138]

Musical ensembles were also an important component of the theater in Peter's time. Aleksei Mikhailovich's court theater did not survive his death in 1676, but interest in the theater was revived at the Russian court by Peter's sister, Natalia Alekseyevna, and there was even an attempt at creating a public theater; in addition, there was a continual stream of Western entertainers and troupes in Russia during Peter's years. The interactions among these various groups are complex and are being explored in a series of works by Russian music historians. Although many of the specifics are cloudy, in general, there are four main threads one must consider. The first is the public theater set up by the German impresario Johann Kunst and, at his early death early in 1703, taken over by Hans Fürst. The productions were housed in a theater on Red Square in Moscow. The troupe was originally made up of foreigners from Kunst's German troupe, but early on, Russian students were added. Fürst headed this mixed group until 1706; its productions were in Russian and German. Tsaritsa Natalia Alekseyevna was also interested in theatrical productions and established a theater that ran from late in the first decade of the century for nearly ten years, and her influence constitutes the second main thread linking the various developments in early-eighteenth-century Russian theater. Although Natalia's was not a public theater in the sense of the Kunst/Fürst operation, it was far more extensive than a domestic, private enterprise; there are accounts of these productions by several foreign visitors. Lists of her theatrical personnel include the names of singers (Grigorii Basist [the bass], Grigorii Tenorist [the tenor], and so forth), including some with titles suggesting that they were church musicians. There also were instrumentalists, and the plays included singing as well.

As the recent research by L. M. Starikova indicates, the Kunst/Fürst and the Tsaritsa's theaters seem to represent a continuum, merging together at the time when the public theater closed and covering the period from 1702 to around 1717. Along with these two important ensembles, there were a number of foreign, especially German, entertainers in Moscow and St. Petersburg, particularly from the late teens through the 1720s. And finally, there was a strong tradition of school dramas, via Ukraine, which kept theater in the center of Russian musical life. The Ukrainian tradition dates to the seventeenth century, and in the early eighteenth century, this tradition was sustained in Moscow by the Moscow Spiritual Academy, which produced a variety of plays with singing and some instrumental music.[139] Ukrainians continued to play a vital and influential role in all aspects of Russian musical life, as evidenced by the Ukrainian-language version of Nikolai Diletskii's composition treatise, which survives in a copy from St. Petersburg, 1723. The music school established in the Ukrainian town of Glukhovo in the late 1730s continued this important tradition.

The early eighteenth century also witnessed the growth of other musical styles that were to form an important background to developments later in the century. The Russian court was interested in folk music at this time and employed Ukrainian *bandura* players (the *bandura* is a lute-shaped folk instrument with a flat, oval body). Visitors to the court and to private homes of the wealthy described this style of music and even cited some folk tunes they had heard in Russia. This was also the time of the beginnings of the lyric song, which was to play such an important role in the late eighteenth century; this tradition grew out of the lyrical *kant*.[140]

Although Peter's focus was on music in its state and social context, and particularly its role in large-scale public functions, the lively and varied musical and theatrical activities in his time demonstrate important continuities in the realms of monophonic and polyphonic church music, in the large-scale vocal *kontserty,* both sacred and secular, and in the linked traditions of instrumental music, theater, and ceremony. All of these developments in Russia would have been familiar to the tsars of the preceding century, and all were to have important musical consequences in the early Classical period.

Operatic life in the dual Russian capitals of Moscow and St. Petersburg began under Peter's successors, the Empresses Anna (r. 1730–40) and Elizabeth (r. 1741–61). The first opera performed in Russia was a production of Giovanni Ristori's (1692–1753) comic *Calandro* in Moscow in 1731, directed by the composer and performed by his Italian troupe. At about the same time, another Italian troupe arrived in St. Petersburg, where they performed *intermezzii*. The responsibility for more systematic, state-sponsored operatic productions was soon taken up by Francesco Araja (1709–c. 1770), who arrived in St. Petersburg at the invitation of the empress in 1735 armed with an operatic company and a repertory of *opere serie,* which he produced at intervals over the next decade at court; he eventually composed eight new *opere serie* for St. Petersburg, in addition to other, largely celebratory, works. (Araja was the first to collaborate with a Russian librettist and produce an opera in the Russian language, when, in 1755, he and the poet Aleksandr Sumarokov wrote *Tsefal i Prokris* [Cephalus and Procris].)[141]

These early performances in Russia reproduced the pattern of the first court operas in the West: intended for important occasions, they were special affairs, with limited performances for a select audience. Araja's operas, beginning with *La forza dell'amore e dell'odio* in 1736, were performed in this capacity. The situation soon changed. A multitude of performing troupes, individual singers, traveling instrumental virtuosi, and music teachers soon flocked to St. Petersburg and Moscow, and regular operatic performances in several different public (although generally state-sponsored or state-controlled) theaters were well established by mid-century, featuring performances in Italian, French, German, and, slightly later, English.[142] Russian singers and instrumentalists took part in these performances, laying the foundations for the important series of vocal and instrumental works written by Russian composers, and performed by Russian soloists, in the last third of the century. By the second half of the century, the impact on Russian and Ukrainian musicians was substantial. The composers Dmitrii Bortnianskii (1751–1825), Maksim Berezovskii (1745–1777), and Yefstignei Fomin (1761–1800) all studied in Italy. Fomin was elected to Bologna's Accademia Filarmonica in 1785, and both Bortnianskii and Berezovskii had *opere serie* performed in Italy while they were there. When Fomin returned home, he wrote a series of Russian comic operas; Bortnianskii wrote three *operas comiques* on libretti fashioned by Crown Prince Paul's Swiss librarian, Lafermière. It was also during the vibrant and varied years of mid-century that Russian instrumentalists were exposed to Western virtuosi and compositions, again laying the strong foundations for the emergence, later in the century, of the long and impressive Russian instrumental school. The traditions, evolutions, and developments of the Russian Baroque—like the Baroque elsewhere in Europe—represent ceaseless curiosity, creativity, and transformation of ideas from outside, forming an indispensable link to the institutions and styles of the Classical era.

PART II

THE BAROQUE

IN TRANSITION

CHAPTER FOURTEEN

Music in Italy

CENTURY LANDMARKS ARE CONVENIENT MEANS TO organize the historian's comprehension of the passage of time and the inevitable unfolding of historical events. But as has been experienced when the world moved from the twentieth to the twenty-first century, no sudden and dramatic changes immediately occurred in the new century. There will be differences between the two centuries, but they will take place slowly and variously, not at the stroke of midnight on 31 December 1999. So it is with all achievements of humankind including music. It has already been noted that a Baroque period in music began to develop in the decades prior to 1600, not, as so many music history students have been taught, at the beginning of 1600. And the end of the Baroque has been variously placed by historians as somewhere between 1715 and 1740. Musical developments achieved during the seventeenth century continued without pause at the entrance into the eighteenth century. But it was in this new century that the Baroque, clearly by mid-century and in most places even earlier, would be superseded by new musical styles, forms, and performance concepts.

Opera and the Comic Intermezzo

The profound influence of Italy in the history of music extends from the Middle Ages through the nineteenth century. The Baroque in particular is indebted to the extraordinary contributions made by Italians to music that affected composers and performers in most of Europe.[1] The Florentine invention of opera, and its rapid development, especially in Venice, is in many ways the most significant achievement to affect the overall history of music in the Baroque. Italian opera was a seminal musical force affecting almost all musical forms and styles beginning in the seventeenth and continuing through much of the eighteenth century. By the end of the seventeenth century, opera, predominantly by Venetian composers, was performed in many cities throughout Italy, but the primary operatic center remained Venice, although Naples soon became its equal.

In Venice the initial frenetic operatic activity in the first decades of the seventeenth century died down for a period of reduced productions and fewer theaters open. After 1670, operatic activity again increased with more theaters active, including the new Teatro Sant' Angelo (1677) and the Teatro San Giovanni Crisostomo (1678), as well as a number of less opulent halls devoted to opera performances. The concluding decades of the century witnessed many changes in Venetian opera.[2] These changes were the result of the gradual popularizing of opera demanded by a broader spectrum of social classes making up the audiences. Already noted was the increased emphasis on the singers' virtuosity demanded by audiences. This led to the separation of recitative and aria, with the latter becoming the focus of the drama. Arias became structured into the easily comprehended da capo form. And the new singing style also influenced new approaches to composing for the voice. The traditional continuo accompaniments, with string passages employed only for ritornellos, soon were largely replaced by a continuous orchestral accompaniment. This resulted in an enriched makeup of the orchestra by supplementing strings with solo oboes, horns, trumpets, and flutes. These solo instruments at times were given obbligato passages. The opening music for the instrumental ensemble developed into the three-movement form to be known as the Italian overture.

The most original music in Venetian and Neapolitan opera at the turn of the eighteenth century was composed for the comic intermezzo. The roots of this kind of music were planted early in Italian opera in which musical episodes by comic characters frequently occurred, often interrupting the primary development of the plot. These episodes were particularly characteristic of Venetian operas in the first half of the seventeenth century. By the mid-seventeenth century such scenes became integrated into the operas, usually involving stock characters such as a young manservant or pageboy, and a lascivious, designing old woman such as a nurse. Later in the century, reform-minded writers began to eliminate comic figures from their Venetian librettos, although not for some time from those performed in Naples where they remained popular. At the turn of the eighteenth century, comic intermezzos in Venetian operas became self-contained acts with separate plots performed at the ends of the three acts, and published separately or at the ends of the *opera seria* librettos. In effect, the practice led to creating two very different operas in one work. As these intermezzos were not related to the main libretto, they could be reused any number of times in different operas. By 1710 many were collected together and widely used by traveling troupes of performers.

The comic intermezzo became an integral part of *opera seria* early in the eighteenth century. Unlike Venetian intermezzos, those found in Neapolitan operas after 1720 usually were integrated into the drama. This was achieved by giving one or two of the comic characters significant roles in the main opera. While the conflict of comedy and tragedy would appear to be incongruous to audiences, Charles Troy[3] has shown that such insertions of comic scenes had practical as well as artistic merit. Often they were inserted just before a change of scenery, thus holding the audience's interest during the pause. Comic intermezzos also articulated the drama and provided a sense of time lapse before the principal scene action resumed. And, probably even more important, they continued the operatic convention of comedy that formerly had been a popular and integral part of Venetian librettos. Composers of the comic intermezzos, largely Italians, created a distinctive comic vocal style, the so-called *buffo* style that would continue to be employed by later composers of comic music such as Mozart and Rossini and others in subsequent centuries.[4]

Familiar characteristics of that style include: grotesque distortions of serious vocal technique such as ungraceful leaps, vocalizations conceived as parodies of heroic opera technique, also elaborate vocal ornamentation, stuttering (popularized in Venetian opera), overly rapid vocal articulation (or patter-songs), imitations of popular songs, the imitating of nonmusical sounds such as those of animals, as well as other onomatopoeic sounds such as the beating of a lover's heart. Librettos at times instructed singers to deliver their lines "laughing," "raving," "sighing," "with anger," and the composer often would include these effects in the vocal lines.

Early in the eighteenth century Italian composers began to reject what could be considered Baroque style characteristics. A case can be argued as to just how much of Venetian opera in the final decades of the seventeenth century was Baroque in spirit. The flourishing of the new intermezzo, with its clear emphasis on comedy, simplicity of style, and a cast of just a few soloists, is evidence enough that the Baroque was becoming passé. The works of Alessandro Scarlatti are exceptional in that, although they are usually classified as Neapolitan, they are more representative stylistically of late-seventeenth-century Roman opera traditions, even though Scarlatti spent the latter part of his career in Naples and had a decisive influence on Naples's reputation as an operatic center where the best works of Italian composers including Scarlatti were heard (see Chapter 5).

In fact, there has been no comprehensive study of the works of those Italian opera composers whose works were performed well into the first decades of the eighteenth century. They were not for the most part composing for Naples, but they had widespread, even international careers throughout Italy and also in northern European cities such as Dresden, Hanover, Munich, Vienna, and London. That Italian music had taken on an international character also can be seen in the acceptance by opera theaters in Venice of non-Italian composers. For example, Handel had a resounding success with his opera *Agrippina* peformed at the San Giovanni Crisostomo theater in December 1709, and Johann David Heinichen (1683–1729) in 1713 also had great successes at Venice's Sant' Angelo theater with two operas: *Mario* and *Le passioni per troppo amore.* The following Italians would seem to be the last to continue to compose operas in varying degrees of Baroque styles: Pietro Torri (c. 1650–1737), Carlo Francesco Pollarolo (c. 1653–1723), Agostino Steffani (1654–1728), Giacomo Antonio Perti (1661–1756), Alillio Ariosti (1666–1729), Antonio Lotti (1666–1740), Francesco Gasparini (1661–1727), Giovanni Bononcini (1670–1747), Tomasso Giovanni Albinoni (1671–1750/51), Giovanni Antonio Pollarolo (1676–1746), Antonio Maria Bononcini (1677–1726), Francesco Ciampi (c. 1690–after 1764), Giovanni Antonio Giay (1690–1764), and, lastly, Antonio Vivaldi (1678–1741).

While opera had importance in Naples as early as 1650, when most of the works performed were by Venetian composers, Naples as "the capitol of the world's music"[5] first became a reality around 1740. Its history, therefore, extended primarily beyond the Baroque period. However, Neapolitan operas were not immune to influences from the earlier decades of the century, and the most important of them was the changing nature of librettos. Essential to this reform were the poets Apostolo Zeno (1688–1750) and especially Pietro Metastasio (1698–1782). Zeno's importance to reform has perhaps been overstressed. He had little interest in music or the operatic dramatization of texts and his sole focus was on improving the literary excellence of texts, especially in organizing them into regular verse. He did remove comic elements and moved arias to the ends of scenes. His respect for history is shown in the careful citings he gave in the plot summaries of his Classical and Medieval sources.

Metastasio, however, was a towering influence in providing texts for late-seventeenth- and eighteenth-century operas, a literary figure described by contemporaries as the equal of Homer and Dante. He composed twenty-seven three-act, heroic *drammi per musica,* and these together with other theater works were given over a thousand musical settings. Some of them inspired as many as seventy different operatic versions.[6] All but three of the librettos were employed by composers for performances in Naples, and the majority of them were heard there in more than one musical version. The rather rigid structure of the Metastasian libretto with its precise formal patterns of recitative and aria, the latter formalized into the three-part da capo structure and in practice often an "exit" aria, led to these operas being embraced by the concept of *opera seria* that would dominate Neapolitan opera for the entire century. This is a remarkably rich post-Baroque musical development, which in itself changed the course of opera in the century. Though its music is not "baroque," exactly what this period of music should be labeled is uncertain. Suggestions have ranged from "galant" to "pre-Classical," or more recently to "early Classical."

Cantata and Oratorio

In no other musical form did Italian composers excel in such a volume of new music as the *cantata da camera*. Unfortunately the music still remains largely unknown, with few new editions of even significant examples of this vast repertory for study or performance. Cantatas, the most popular form of Italian chamber music, comprise the richest repertory of Italian vocal music in the seventeenth and eighteenth centuries. But the close interrelationships between the development of vocal forms and styles in opera and cantata are still not thoroughly examined. The history of the cantata in much of Europe during the seventeenth century was considerably enriched by Italian composers (see Chapter 4). The floodgates of cantata composition were opened by Italian composers, most spectacularly by Alessandro Scarlatti's seven-hundred-plus cantatas, but also including other composers such as Giovanni Bononcini, known widely throughout Europe, who composed more than two hundred cantatas; Antonio Lotti, more than seventy cantatas; Benedetto Marcello (1686–1739), more than 375 cantatas; and Nicola Porpora (1686–1768), over 130 cantatas. Others who contributed significantly to the Italian cantata were Tomaso Albinoni (1671–1750/51), with some forty-six solo cantatas, Emanuele d'Astorga (1680–?1757), with more than two hundred, and Antonio Vivaldi, with thirty-six.

The development of the cantata in the seventeenth century began in Rome as well as in Venice and other Italian musical centers.[7] It was, however, around 1670 that composers began to organize cantatas into various arrangement of recitatives and arias, which toward the end of the century fell into prescribed patterns of alternating the two vocal forms. The pattern of repetitions varied, but with recitative, aria, recitative, aria (RARA) becoming the most frequent. Many cantatas, however, also included additional recitatives and arias and others were made up of the simplest grouping of ARA. Alessandro Scarlatti's cantatas, with their assortment of numerous forms, variously organized recitatives including lyrical ariosos, chromatic harmonies, strong bass lines with melodic definition, and highly affective vocal melodies united to powerfully expressive texts, are the most Baroque. But they are already somewhat atypical of the direction cantata composers were moving toward with simpler forms, vocal styles, and harmonies. Some of Scarlatti's contemporaries, as well as almost every cantata composer to follow him, no longer emulated his distinctive style of Baroque expressivity.

As was true with opera, cantatas in the first half of the eighteenth century also reflected the transitional nature of musical developments of this period as Baroque musical characteristics faded away. The reform of the libretto and a development toward a greater simplicity of music underline the cantatas composed at this time. To a large extent cantatas take on a formulaic character. The arias invariably have a predictable three-part da capo form frequently initiated by a motto (*Devise*), in which the singer initiates the opening of the cantata with the first phrase of his or her aria, to be followed by the opening ritornello, and then the completion of the phrase by the singer. Another distinctive feature of many of these cantatas is the exceedingly elaborate vocal writing, suggesting that vocal virtuosity was one of the central attractions of this music for audiences. And, unlike Alessandro Scarlatti's cantatas, the later-eighteenth-century cantatas tend to have much reduced activity in bass lines. The popularity of these cantatas spread from Italy throughout Europe, in France, Germany, and England, and they were imitated by numerous composers. However, by the 1750s, the cantata form had become far less significant, and Italian composers largely resorted instead to supplying scenes from operas or various forms of opera arias and songs for the entertainment of chamber music audiences.

The oratorio, as with the cantata, flourished in Italy somewhat in tandem with the musical developments affecting changing perceptions of opera. And the earlier association of oratorios with sacred ritual was slowly eliminated in the seventeenth century as they became more and more operas without action and scenery. The close musical relationship of the oratorio to opera is apparent in the somewhat parallel musical development and stylistic changes occurring in the two forms and already identified in connection to the cantata. The frequent traveling of composers between the various musical centers in and outside of Italy developed a fairly consistent Italian vocal and instrumental style. And as is true for opera and the cantata, changes in the style and content of the Latin and Italian oratorio in the eighteenth century cannot be precisely dated as to when "new" musical features replaced the "old" or seventeenth-century concepts. By the first decades of the eighteenth century, however, vestiges of the older "baroque" features of these forms become less and less common, and a new stylistic label seems mandatory where they become "galant" or "pre-Classical."

In his study of the oratorio, Smither finds in contrast to the earlier oratorios the following as characteristics of the oratorios composed by Caldara in the second decade of the eighteenth century:[8] the orchestra is smaller, with an emphasis on upper register and restricted to two violin parts, continuo and cello. The continuo no longer maintains a linear part and often employs triadic lines. The harmonic rhythm is slow. The upper ranges of the vocal parts are also emphasized, with frequent omission of the bass voice. The arias are da capo, but with more prominent dance rhythms that favor the minuet and gavotte. More evident are repetitions of rhythmic patterns of measures and phrases. Aria accompaniments are simpler and the voice and violins often proceed in unison or parallel motion. Rare in earlier cantatas, arias now can be accompanied without the continuo and with only violins.

Regarding the oratorio in Venice, as previously noted, it was late to arrive as compared to other cities in Italy. The first reference to a Venetian performance of an oratorio (not identified) was in 1667 when one was performed at St. Maria della Consolazione (detta Della "Fava"). By the end of the eighteenth century more than five hundred oratorios are known to have been heard in Venice, although a discouraging lack of extant scores hampers any comprehensive history of the Venetian contributions to this musical form.[9] The Fava, understandably as church of the Order of the Oratorians, was the first center for oratorio performances in Venice, beginning in 1671 with several works by Legrenzi. During the remainder of the seventeenth century, over one hundred oratorios have been identified as being heard at the Fava. Three of Legrenzi's works are extant: *Sedecia, La morte del cuor penitente,* and *La vendita del cuor humano.*[10] Other important composers in addition to Legrenzi at the Fava oratory (works mostly lost) included Pietro Andrea Ziani, Giacomo Antonio Perti, Antonio Caldara, Leonardo Leo, and many others of lesser fame. However, the most important centers for oratorio performances were the four *Ospedali.* A major emphasis on oratorios began in the 1660s and 1670s (except for the Ospedaletto where oratorios began to be featured at the turn of the eighteenth century). Among composers of major reputation who wrote for these churches, often large numbers of oratorios, were Carlo Pallavicino, Antonio Lotti, Francesco Gasparini (thirteen works), Carlo Francesco Pollarolo, Baldassare Galuppi (twenty-four works), Antonio Gaetano Pampani (nineteen works), Ferdinando Bertoni (seventy works), Antonio Pollarolo, Pasquale Anfossi (twenty works), and Bonaventura Furlanetto (more than fifty works).

Chamber Music

It has been noted (see Chapter 4) that one of the major musical developments in seventeenth-century Italy was the chamber sonata for one, two, or three solo instruments and continuo. Although first composed in Venice, the rapid rise in the popularity of chamber sonata performances soon enlisted composers in other Italian cities, especially Rome and Bologna and then beyond Italy to various aristocratic courts such as at Vienna, Munich, and Dresden. As is true with many Baroque musical forms and styles that continued into the next century, the trio sonata underwent a series of transformations. By the mid-eighteenth century its form and style had lost most of the characteristics that earlier might have been labeled "baroque."

The most important influence on the Italian sonata composers was the achievements of Corelli. Among the many composers known to contribute to the sonata literature,[11] a few such as Albinoni and Vivaldi stand out both for their productivity and their musical achievements. The more than one hundred instrumental works by Tomaso Albinoni include around fifty-five chamber sonatas and suites. Most of them are contained in his published opera: Op. 1 (trio sonatas), Op. 2 (despite the title of *Sinfonie,* these are church sonatas and concertos), Op. 3 (suites entitled *Balletti*), [Op. 4](*sonate da chiesa*), Op. 6 (*Trattenimenti* [entertainments] *armonici per camera*), Op. 8 (six *balletti* [suites] and six *sonate a tre*), and, in manuscript, six *Sonate a tre*. Not surprising, perhaps, Albinoni's Op. 1, twelve trio sonatas, most closely show the strong influence of Corelli.[12] Of particular distinction among Albinoni's early chamber works is Op. 2, which alternates six church sonatas and six concertos scored for a five-part ensemble of two violins, alto and tenor violins, and cello plus continuo. The church sonatas consist of the traditional four movements, slow, fast, slow, fast, with the fast ones being fugues. Most of the fugal movements have strong and at times distinctive lyrical subjects. The slow movements are particularly beautiful, at times of noble melancholy and in other cases with melodic lines reflecting Albinoni's command of operatic lyricism.[13]

Besides Vivaldi, other significant contributors to the Italian chamber sonata during the first half of the eighteenth century include Francesco Maria Veracini (1690–1768), Giuseppe Tartini (1692–1770), and Pietro Antonio Locatelli (1695–1764). There are some forty violin sonatas by Veracini, twelve each in the manuscript collection of 1716, in Op. 1 (Dresden, 1721) and in Op. 2 (London, Florence, 1744). Although there are clear resemblances to aspects of Corelli's sonatas, there also are major distinctions suggesting the changes overtaking the concept of the chamber sonata. Veracini, for example, composes neither fugues nor dance movements, thereby making no distinction between church and chamber sonatas. Also not Corellian is his treatment of dissonances, either unprepared or with resolutions transferred from one part to another, and his preference for homophonic textures over contrapuntal ones. These are all intimations of a new pre-Classical tendency as is Veracini's preference to write in balanced antecedent-consequent phrases.[14] Equally representative of the kinds of changes taking place in the concept of musical form and style are the more than two hundred sonatas of Tartini[15] and some forty sonatas by Locatelli, who although an Italian from Bergamo and a student of Corelli, lived most of his life in Amsterdam.[16]

The Concerto

The orchestral concerto became a remarkable vitalizing factor in the character of late Baroque music and its reception throughout most of Europe. Because concertos presented new musical forms, styles, and textures, they energized and reshaped a considerable portion of the instrumental repertory during the 1720s and 1730s. Their stylistic and technical demands affected the very concept of orchestral sound and the nature of orchestral performance. And their relatively simple formal designs, at times piquant harmonies, and energetic rhythms found audience acceptance across the borders of national tastes. The orchestral concerto had its origins in both Bologna and Rome, beginning in Bologna with Torelli's early trumpet concertos but also his solo concertos in Opp. 6 and 8, and in Rome with the widely popular concertos grosso of Corelli. It was in Venice, however, that the Baroque orchestral concerto was truly born and nourished. And this was largely achieved in the works of two Venetian contemporaries, Tomaso Albinoni (1671–1750/51) and Antonio Vivaldi (1678–1741).

Albinoni's father was a successful Venetian stationer and a manufacturer of playing cards. Tomaso Albinoni remained a freelance musician throughout his life, was never employed as a violinist or composer, and until his father's death emphasized this status usually by describing himself on title pages of his music as a "Venetian dilettante" and (adding at times) a "violinist" ("musico di violino"). It is incorrect, however, to think that his use of "dilettante" or "amateur" implied a debasement of either his talents as a musician or his successes as a composer. Albinoni was widely known not only in Italy but elsewhere in Europe through his many operas. He claimed to have composed eighty-one operas, of which only five complete scores remain. In addition to composing for the Venetian theaters, his operas appeared on the stages of numerous other Italian cities including Bologna, Florence, Genoa, Rome, Verona, and to the north in Munich, Prague, Breslau (Wroclaw), Linz, and London. Albinoni's popularity was widespread in part because of the significant amount of his instrumental music that was published and republished, at first in Italy and quickly thereafter in Amsterdam by Estienne Roger and in London by Walsh.

Albinoni published fifty-nine concertos in five *opera* beginning in 1700 with Op. 2, which included—besides the six sinfonie—six concertos for two violins, alto, tenor, violoncello, and bass. These are orchestral concertos without soloists, although in 1701–1702 Roger reprinted them with the addition of "solo" and "tutti" indications. In sequence each sonata is followed by a concerto. Talbot observes[17] that these were the first concertos by any composer to become known in northern Europe. Bach made a copy of the second concerto and Johann Gottfried Walther transcribed the fourth and fifth concertos for organ. For these concertos Albinoni added a sixth part-book for a "violino de concerto," an orchestral first violin part distinct from the violino primo. These concertos usually have two and sometimes three violins doubling, and there are only two short solo passages for violin. Of greater musical significance are the four later collections of twelve concerti a cinque: Op. 5 (1707), Op. 7 (1715), Op. 9 (1722), and Op. 10 (1735–1736).

In Op. 5 Albinoni explored for the first time the evolving concept of the solo concerto by placing some emphasis on solo/tutti passages. Each of the twelve works is in three movements. The opening allegro movement is based on a motto theme, which is repeated, usually with insertions of solo passages from the principal violin. Second movements are in three brief sections, allegro, adagio, allegro. The adagio in three of the concertos is divided into three sections: adagio, presto, adagio, the presto being a brief technical display for solo violin. The final movements are highlights of these concertos with fugues of strong thematic identity. In their episodes solo passages for the principal violin are joined onto the fugal textures. In all of these concertos, as in all of Albinoni's concertos, the solo passages have little or no integration within the overall musical context in which they are inserted.

There are two *opera* devoted largely to concertos for oboes, Op. 7 (Amsterdam, 1715), the first oboe concertos by an Italian to be published, and subsequently Op. 9 (Amsterdam, 1722), dedicated to the Elector of Bavaria Maximilian Emanuel. Both collections consist of twelve concertos: four for one oboe and strings, four for two oboes and strings, and four for strings alone. Op. 9 is the stronger of the two collections, with outer movements of greater length and considerably more active writing for the inner parts. To be noted also, the four concertos with principal violin (i.e., without oboe) are the clearest examples among Albinoni's concertos of achieving true violin concertos having some virtuosity. Albinoni's final collection of twelve concerti *a cinque*, Op. 10 for strings (Amsterdam, 1735–1736), was seemingly unknown until three copies of the Le Cène edition came to light in the 1960s.[18] The fifty-nine concertos of Albinoni are a major contribution to the development of the Venetian concerto. It is remarkable and fascinating that his concertos were composed with such independence from those of his younger Venetian contemporary Vivaldi. While some few influences from Vivaldi can be noted in Albinoni's late instrumental works, these seem for the most part to be more reflections of a developing concept of a Venetian musical style also shared by other Venetian composers. There is little to compare with Vivaldi's concertos. Albinoni's are always more succinct, less complex formally in the first and third movements, and decidedly conservative in avoiding any lengthy displays of violin virtuosity for its own sake. Albinoni, who was a major composer of operas, was a superb creator of lyrical as well as dynamic melodies. His concertos lack the virile strength and stunning imagination of Vivaldi's works, and in that sense they are an end result of seventeenth-century concertos influenced by Corelli.

Antonio Vivaldi (1678–1741)

Vivaldi was the most original and prolific Italian composer in the first decades of the eighteenth century. He made many original contributions to the concept of the instrumental concerto and musical style, and he augmented Italian composers' developments of violin techniques and orchestration. Usually labeled a composer of the late Baroque, more accurately his music actually spans the period of musical changes leading from the Baroque into the pre- or early Classical age. In his own lifetime he was a controversial figure, the ordained "red-haired priest" (*il prete rosso*), who abandoned his responsibilities to his church to become a violinist, opera impresario, conductor, teacher of orphaned and abandoned girls at the Pio Ospedale della Pietà, and a composer of an extraordinary number of instrumental and vocal works.

Although handicapped from birth with what is usually described as an asthmatic condition, he travelled widely, especially in Germany and Austria, promoting his music. The concerts he directed for a number of years at the Pietà attracted Venetians as well as numerous foreign heads of state, diplomats, and aristocrats from various parts of Europe who returned home with the praise of Vivaldi's music on their lips. And he established relationships with publishers in northern Europe, especially Etienne Roger in Amsterdam, who through the publication of a large number of his works widely spread Vivaldi's influence north of the Alps. This influence had a particularly potent effect on other composers of instrumental music, including J. S. Bach. However, by the end of the eighteenth century, Vivaldi's fame had faded. It was not until the twentieth century, and especially because of the development of the LP and then the compact disc, that his instrumental music was rediscovered. Vivaldi's concertos became one of the most popular repertories of recorded classical music. It has been estimated that the instrumental music of no other composer has been recorded as frequently as Vivaldi's "Four Seasons" from Op. 8, *Il cimento dell'armonia e dell'inventione,* a claim that seems justified by the enormous number of different recordings of this one work found in the bins of CD shops everywhere.

The staggering number of instrumental and vocal works by Vivaldi prevents anything approaching a comprehensive description and analysis of his oeuvre. Here the goal is to survey his compositions with the intention of discussing a few that can be considered among some of the most significant compositions in the Vivaldi catalogue.[19] The instrumental music belongs in three categories: some five hundred concertos, ninety sonatas, and eighteen sinfonias.[20] The only music published in Vivalid's lifetime was instrumental, and appeared in thirteen *opera.*

Vivaldi like Albinoni was a prolific sonata composer. His career was initiated with thirty-six of his chamber sonatas issued in three publications: Op. 1 (1705), [12] *Suonate da camera a tre, due violini e violone o cembalo;* Op. 2 (1709), [12] *Sonate a violino e basso per il cembalo,* and seven years later, Op. 5 (1716), *VI Sonate, quatro a violino solo e basso e due a due violini e basso continuo.* There is also a set of 6 sonatas for violoncello and bass (Paris, c. 1739). The formal tendencies in the sonatas are conservative. Those of Op. 1 are traditional trio sonatas in chamber style in which the bass can alternate between cello and harpsichord. Beginning with a movement, usually in slow tempo, they continue with a group of dances all in the same key and in binary form. In some of the sonatas there is a mixing of church and chamber styles that results from interspersing between the dances one or two slow, nondance movements with some suggestion of Corellian influence. Vivaldi's tribute to Corelli stands out in the final movement of Op. 1, No. 12, with his variations on *La folia,* a work made famous by Corelli in his Op. 5 sonatas. The second set of twelve sonatas, Op. 2, are for solo violin and harpsichord. Op. 5 is the continuation of Op. 2 with sonatas 13–16 for one violin and figured bass and sonatas 17 and 18 for two violins and figured bass. There are a number of unpublished sonatas for solo instrument and continuo and also trio sonatas. Also to be noted is the important collection in manuscript of chamber sonatas preserved in the Central Library of Manchester.[21]

A large part of Vivaldi's far-reaching fame in his own time as well as in the twentieth and twenty-first centuries was generated by his concertos. The five-hundred-some concertos have an astonishing variety of instrumentations; for example, solo concertos with a variety of solo instruments, double concertos for two solo instruments equally varied in the choices of instruments. In lesser numbers there are also concertos for string orchestra and continuo, chamber concertos with three to six solo instruments and continuo, concertos for two string orchestras and soloist (s), and ensemble concertos with more than two solo instruments. Vivaldi published in nine *opera* eighty-four of his concertos, sixty of which are for one violin soloist, and the others for two or four violinists (in some with added cello), oboe, and transverse flute. Three of the concerto collections stand out for their exceptional content: Op. 3, *L'estro armonico* = harmonic fancy (or inspiration, or fire); Op. 4, *La stravaganza* = the extravagance; and Op. 8, *Il cimento dell'armonia e dell'invenzione* = the trial (or test) of harmony and invention.

Op. 3 was published in 1711 by Roger in Amsterdam, and soon was reprinted in London and Paris. It quickly established Vivaldi's European reputation. Adding to its fame was the subsequent arrangement by J. S. Bach of six of the twelve concertos in this collection: two for organ—Op. 3/8 in A minor and Op. 3/11 in D minor; three for harpsichord—Op. 3/7 in G major, Op. 3/9 in D major, Op. 3/12 in E major; and one for four harpsichords—Op. 3/10 in B minor. *L'estro armonico* became one of the most influential publications of instrumental music in the first half of the eighteenth century. It offered a rich variety of types of solo violin concertos filled with dazzling and often highly original virtuoso features, rhythmically vibrant movements, and surprising and often startling dissonances unknown in earlier Italian violin music. The twelve concertos, while still having some features recalling works of Corelli, Torelli, and Albinoni, are a source book of concerto experimentation.

Formally, the twelve concertos are with three exceptions in three-movement, fast, slow, fast form. The exceptions have brief slow introductions, or in one, two adagio transitions before and after the second movement. The twelve are arranged in groups of four, each group having a concerto for four solo violins, one for two solo violins, and one for one solo violin. The tonalities alternate between major and minor keys, except for the final three, where in order to end the last concerto in major the order becomes minor, minor, major. There is an extraordinary variety of movements in these concertos. The ritornello form of later Vivaldi—that is, a tutti opening with a memorable theme usually in three distinct sections, which reappears four or five times and ends the movement—is employed but usually in rather a rudimentary form in half of the twelve concertos. Two that stand out are in movements later arranged by J. S. Bach: Op. 3, No. 8, and the memorable model for Bach's four-harpsichord concerto from Op. 3, No. 10. Movements that at times begin with strong thematic identity frequently evolve as movements emphasizing violin concerto virtuosity.

The twelve concertos, Op. 4, entitled *La Stravaganza* (the extravagance) are violin solo concertos supported by an accompaniment of two violins and viola, with violoncello and organ continuo. The "extravagance" undoubtedly refers to the harmonic daring but also to the frequently unusual violin passagework in these concertos. Much more prominent than in Op. 3, they usually have strong ritornello openings which are repeated in part or totally in the course of a movement. Some of them, for example, Op. 2, No. 1, have ritornellos of thematic strength that defines the very character of a Vivaldian concept. The twelve concertos are grouped in pairs, one in major, one in minor, with the last two in major. Four of these concertos (Nos. 1, 4, 9, and 11) require a solo group of two violins and continuo, adding a violinist from the ripieno to join the soloist in several sections. The three-part concerto form is strengthened by the expansion of the scope and musical weight of the second movements that are without exception for a solo violinist usually with ripieno accompaniments. They are distinguished by their lyrical beauty. The second movement of Concerto 12 suggests an operatic aria based on a descending ostinato bass; another, Op. 4/2, exploits multiple stops on the violin, and Concerto 11/1 consists of a violin solo with cello accompaniment.

Of all Vivaldi's sets of concertos, Op. 8, beginning with its publication in 1725, has remained his most famous work because it includes *Le quattro stagioni*—"The Four Seasons"—a set of four programmatic concertos which are the most frequently performed, arranged, recorded, and even dramatized of all his music. Op. 8 was planned to emphasize programmatic music, a well-known concept for music going as far back as the Middle Ages. Of the twelve violin concertos, seven bear suggestive titles: "The Four Seasons," that is, Concerto No. 1, *La Primavera* (Spring); No. 2, *L'Estate* (Summer); No. 3, *L'Autunno* (Autumn); and No. 4, *L'Inverno* (Winter); and three others that are more descriptive than programmatic: No. 5, *La Tempesta di mare* (The Storm at Sea); No. 6, *Il Piacere* (Pleasure); and No. 10, *La Caccia* (The Hunt).

The music is based on the four anonymous sonnets that furnish the "program" and that Vivaldi attached to the first violin part. The events described by the sonnets are pointed out in the music by cues and in some places portions of the texts inserted over the notes. The close connection between the poems and the music would seem to demand that audiences must have the poems in hand in order to follow their musical realizations. This does not seem, however, to be entirely necessary, as the detailed program notes supplied by Vivaldi are often not made available to audiences nor for that matter in many recordings of the concertos. Many of the musical details are fairly obvious—birdcalls, running water, wind, storms with lightning and thunder—but others are not. Each of the four concertos is replete with stunning technical feats for the solo violinist, unusual harmonic passages, strange sounds that fascinate even if the programmatic explanation is sometimes unclear. This in itself may be one of the factors giving these unique Baroque violin concertos their unending fascination for audiences. Here is music that has meanings, is operatic but without texts, and the listener is challenged but also rewarded by creating his or her own interpretations of what this exciting and fascinating music expresses within the context of each listener's subjective relationship to the concept of each season.[22]

The great amount of instrumental music by Vivaldi has overshadowed until recently his vocal works. The amount is small; around fifty sacred works are extant as well as twenty-nine solo cantatas. Twenty-one scores of operas by Vivaldi also survive, some lacking one or more acts. Because most of these works were discovered in the Turin manuscripts, it was only after they began to be published in modern editions that performances were possible. Recordings of most of the sacred music and excellent research publications have also made the sacred vocal works accessible.[23] Most of the sacred works were composed by Vivaldi during his employment at the Pietà. This occurred especially during the period after 1713 when Gasparini, who had composed sacred works for the church, left on a sick leave but never returned. At the time Vivaldi held the position of *maestro de'concerti,* but the governors were so pleased with Vivaldi's compositions that they presented him with an annual bonus of fifty ducats for "an entire mass, a vespers, an oratorio, over thirty motets and other labors." The sacred music forms four categories: music for solo voice, for solo voices, for choir, and choir with added soloists. Among the most impressive of Vivalid's sacred music compositions are those for two concerted choruses and instrumental ensemble such as the *Gloria,* RV589; the *Beatus Vir,* RV597; the *Dixit Dominus,* RV594; and the *Salve Regina,* RV618. Also impressive are many of the works for solo voices, particularly the hymn *Stabat Mater,* RV621, an early work written for Brescia, and the psalm *Nisi Dominus,* RV608. Of Vivaldi's four known oratorios, regrettably only one survives: *Juditha triumphans devicta Holofernes barbarie,* RV644. It is a magnificent work, filled with a great variety of instrumental accompaniments and certainly one of Vivaldi's most appealing dramatic vocal scores. Its infrequent performances today are a great loss to all those who admire Vivaldi's inexhaustible musical genius.[24]

CHAPTER FIFTEEN

Opera at Hamburg, Dresden, and Vienna

Opera Developments before 1750

OPERA CONTINUED TO FLOURISH in Hamburg in the first decades of the eighteenth century. The vitality of the Hamburg stage was assured during the years 1696 to 1717 by the domination of works by Reinhard Keiser (1674–1739). Born near Weissenfels, Keiser's first successes as an opera composer were at the court of Brunswick-Wolfenbüttel, but by 1696 or 1697 he had moved to Hamburg where for twenty-one years he became the most important composer for the opera theater, and continued more sporadically through 1726. He was director of the Hamburg opera from 1703 to 1706. Of at least sixty-six operas, only nineteen mostly complete scores survive as well as portions of several others. Between 1696 and 1717 one can speak of an "age of Keiser" in Hamburg, when except for 1708 he composed at least one and sometimes several operas for the Gänsemarkt theater. The public approval of his music was recognized by many contemporaries. For example, the German composer and theorist Johann Adolph Scheibe commented that Keiser was "perhaps the greatest original genius in music that had ever appeared in Germany,"[1] and Johann Mattheson, distinguished composer, critic, lexicographer, and theorist, called Keiser the "*premier homme du monde*"[2] and "the leading man of the world."[3]

Keiser's operatic music was somewhat eclectic, combining features of both French and German music with the latter being the most prominent aspect of his scores. Whereas the arias are often Italian in design, there is hardly any suggestion of Italian vocal style in his works. Curiously, however, in 1703 Keiser's opera *Claudius* included eleven arias in Italian, and most subsequent operas performed at the Hamburg theater contained Italian texts that were translated into German in the librettos sold to audiences. It would seem that both composers and singers preferred the sound and singability of the Italian language. There are numerous uses of "popular" tunes of the period in North Germany. The operas are composed in an affective musical language both for recitatives and arias. Keiser was famous for his understanding of the human voice, and in both recitatives and arias he invariably found the means to express a text's emotional substance. Arias can be virtuoso display pieces, but many are in contrast melodies sensitive to the potential musicality of the texts. No less a composer than Handel found the beauty and strength of Keiser's melodies worthy of reuse or adaptation in his own works. Mattheson strikes the right note when he says of Keiser's achievements: "in the period in which he flourished, there was no other composer, especially in tender vocal pieces, who composed [music] so rich, so natural, so flowing, so attractive, and for the most part, so clearly, intelligently, and rhetorically."[4] Keiser was the first German opera composer to utilize the orchestra with originality and new dramatic effects. Colorful and expressive treatment of solo instruments, with subtle and affective concerted passages, interact with the voice, and extensive programmatic passages colorfully paint scenes and emotions inspired by the libretto.

Keiser's tenure as Hamburg opera's major composer ended in 1726. Georg Philip Telemann (1681–1767) had already become director of the opera in 1722. Telemann was Germany's leading and most prolific composer of the first half of the eighteenth century. More than any other composer of the period his music straddles the transformation of music from the Baroque to the Galant or pre-Classic period (see Chapter 18). Telemann composed some twenty operas for Hamburg, and was the last of the outstanding German composers contributing to Hamburg's Baroque operatic history. Audience support of the opera had severely diminished as spoken drama and visiting Italian opera troupes became the new attractions, and in 1738 the Hamburg opera was forced to close.

Except for Hamburg there were few other venues for opera in Germany/Austria that maintained continuous seasons of opera performances. As in the previous century, much of the operatic activity was sporadic, involved the support of small aristocratic courts, and was often limited to festive occasions. There is a significant trend, noticeable in the late seventeenth century, of performing Italian operas, which increased in the first half of the eighteenth century. Only in connection with major courts such as those at Munich, Dresden, and especially Vienna were opera companies usually maintained for a continuity of opera seasons supported by established orchestras and rosters of singers. As has been noted (see Chapter 8), Munich from 1653 had a long albeit not entirely continuous history of supporting Italian opera. The first opera house was completed in 1654. Between 1701 and 1714, the absence of the Elector Maximilian II Emmanuel from Munich (to serve as governor of the southern Netherlands) silenced opera performances at the court. But with his return, operas were again regularly performed, by an impressive group of Italian composers including Agostino Torri, Antonio Vivaldi, Alessandro Scarlatti, Tommaso Albinoni, Nicola Porpora, Giovanni Ferrandini, Francesco Pelli, Giovanni Porta, Giovanni Battista Pergolesi, Bernardo Alliprandi, and Girolamo Tonini.

Operas in Dresden during the first half of the 1690s had a prominent place in court festivities during Carnival. These, however, were abandoned when the new Elector, Friedrich August I (1670–1733),[5] dismissed the Italian company. Instead, he lavished his attention and considerable court expenditures on his love for the French theater. Between 1700 and 1705, a French theatrical troupe including dancers and musicians resided at court, and in 1708 a new French group of actors, dancers, and musicians were engaged, directed by the famous French dancer Louis de Poitier.[6] Through the urging of Crown Prince Friedrich August II, a new Italian opera company was established in 1717 with Johann David Heinichen appointed as Hofkapellmeister. This was only one aspect of the significantly enlarged component of singers and players added to the court between 1709 and 1719. The court orchestra became famous throughout Europe, and included distinguished musicians such as J. B. Volumier (c. 1670–1728), its leader, succeeded by J. G. Pisendel (1687–1755); F. M. Veracini, court composer and violinist; Christian Pezold (1677–1733), court composer and organist; S. L. Weiss (1686–1750), theorbist; J. D. Zelenka, composer and double bass player; P. G. Buffardin (c. 1690–1768), flutist; and Johann Christoph Richter (1700–1785), oboist.

This expansion of Dresden's musical forces was part of the enormous preparation for one of the most elaborate festivities staged in Europe during the first half of the eighteenth century. The celebrations honored the marriage of the crown prince to Maria Josepha, daughter of the Emperor Joseph I, a political union bringing together Saxony and Poland with the Habsburg Empire. After their marriage in Vienna on 20 August 1719, the wedding party traveled to Pirna on the Elba where on 24 September they boarded an enormous gondola and sailed to Dresden. In addition to numerous church, musical, sporting, and other kinds of elaborate entertainments, there were operas featuring the works of Antonio Lotti: *Giove in Argo, Ascanio, ovvero Gli odi delusi dal sangue,* and *Teofane.* Heinichen contributed a new opera, *Flavio Crispo,* whose performance in 1720 was canceled by the Elector when he dismissed the entire Italian opera ensemble after learning that Berselli and Senesino had created an embarrassing scene during rehearsal. Senesino accused the composer of ineptitude in setting the Italian text, tore up the music, and threw it at the composer's feet. Heinichen's opera has never been performed.

In 1726 Italian opera returned to the Dresden stage when the crown princess ordered the performance of Giovanni Alberto Ristori's comic opera *Calandro* to celebrate her husband's return from Warsaw. Another Ristori comic opera, *Un pazzo ne fa cento, ovvero Don Chisciotte,* based on Cervantes, was the musical centerpiece of the Carnival celebrations in the following year. In 1730 Johann Adolf Hasse, by then a widely famous composer of opera in Naples as well as Venice, was invited to come to Dresden together with his wife, the illustrious soprano Faustina Bordoni. Trained in Italy, a student of Nicola Porpora and Alessandro Scarlatti, Hasse had for seven years been court composer in Naples and also had great successes in Venice. He was appointed *maestro di cappella* of the Dresden court. His first opera for Dresden, *Cleofide,* was performed in the Dresden opera house on 13 September 1731, and over the next thirty-two years in Dresden Hasse performed some thirty-four of his operas.[7] While Hasse and his wife spent extended periods in Dresden, they were also frequently in Italy, often lived in Vienna, and at the end of their careers retired to Venice. Hasse was the premiere composer of *opera seria,* and he made the Dresden court opera internationally famous. His music was deeply rooted in early-eighteenth-century musical developments, and it left behind the concept of Baroque musical style. What remains of the Baroque is found in the elaborateness of the stagings, the magnificence of the costumes, and the spectacular vocal gifts of the stars of the opera stage, the Italian singers. However, when Friedrich August II died in 1763 and his son Friedrich Christian came to power, he eliminated all elaborate court extravagance and ordered Hasse's and his wife's services to the court to be cancelled. Dresden's Baroque Age had come to an end.

As has been shown, it was Vienna more than any other German city that had the most widespread reputation for fostering the musical arts during the seventeenth century, a tradition that continued without interruption into the new century. The strength of the Viennese court's commitment to music was in large part the result of a succession of four emperors all of whom were composers: Ferdinand III (1637–1657), Leopold I (1657–1705), Joseph I (1705–1711), and Charles VI (1711–1740). A figure central to the development of secular music and also sacred music at the Habsburg court in the first half of the eighteenth century was Johann Joseph Fux (1660–1741). Although as a composer largely neglected by general histories of music, and usually recognized almost solely for his major composition treatise, *Gradus ad Parnassum* (1725), Fux was a significant composer of music in which were combined features of both the Italian and Austrian Baroque. Employed from 1698 as imperial court composer and made Hofkapellmeister in 1715, he contributed during his forty-year career a large amount of sacred music (including ninety Masses and other sacred vocal works), thirteen oratorios and *componimenti sacri,* church sonatas, overtures and keyboard works, and twenty-two operas (five are lost). His most famous opera, *Costanza e Fortessa,* was composed for the coronation at Prague of Charles VI and his wife as king and queen of Bohemia and performed in 1723 with magnificent sets by Giuseppe Galli-Bibiena. The open-air theater was reported to hold four thousand spectators. Galli-Bibiena also designed the sumptuous staging for an open-air performance in 1716 of Fux's *Angelica vincitrice di Alcina* in Vienna's gardens of the Favorita.

Fux's position as court composer of oratorios and operas was overshadowed by two other composers, Francesco Conti (1681/82–1732) and even more so by Antonio Caldara. Conti, who was employed in 1701 as a virtuoso theorbist, became court composer in 1713. His large output of operas as well as intermezzos were written for the yearly Carnival season and also for birthdays and name days of the imperial family. His dramatic works were also heard in Germany, in Dresden, Hamburg, and Brunswick, in translations made by such notable figures as Keiser, Telemann, and Mattheson. Antonio Caldara was well known in Venice and Rome for his operas before he was appointed vice-Kapellmeister at the Viennese court in 1716. He was an astonishingly prolific composer, writing in addition to many oratorios and various forms of sacred church music some sixty operas for Viennese court, many of which were also performed in Salzburg and Graz. About a third of his operatic output was composed to librettos composed by the reformers of the opera libretto, Apostolo Zeno and, after 1730, Pietro Metastasio.

CHAPTER SIXTEEN

George Frideric Handel (1685–1759)

AMONG ALL OF THE NAMES OF Western civilization's greatest composers, George Frideric Handel deserves a special place of honor, not only as a famous composer of Baroque music but also for the imperishable genius of so much of that music. Yet, Handel's posthumous reputation is unique in music history. Although honored in his lifetime as England's greatest composer, he subsequently remained famous for only a handful of his oratorios, and even today his fame and popularity are largely based on a single composition, the oratorio *Messiah.*

In his lifetime Handel had, before composing *Messiah* in 1742, already composed more than one hundred cantatas, some forty operas, the oratorios including *Esther, Deborah, Athalia, Saul, Israel in Egypt;* the odes *Alexander's Feast, A Song for St. Cecilia,* and *L'Allegro, il Penseroso ed il Moderato;* numerous sacred and ceremonial vocal works; and a large number of keyboard, chamber, and orchestral compositions. Handel was not only the first independent, self-employed composer but also a leading musical personality of his age. His genius was rooted in German, French, Italian, and English musical styles from the turn of the eighteenth century, but he was, especially in his later works, more and more attuned to synthesizing these various styles. His late oratorios in particular advanced far beyond the traditions of Baroque music and in many ways approached the later concept of an "international" style characteristic of the Classic era.

George Frideric Handel[1] was born in the central German city of Halle, 23 February 1685. His sixty-three-year-old father, Georg, was surgeon and *valet de chambre* to the local court of the Duke of Weissenfels, located some twenty miles from Halle. Little is known about Handel's early life.[2] Although his father was opposed to a musical education for his son, apparently the Duke of Weissenfels became so impressed by the boy's talent that he urged his father to give his son professional music lessons. This led to engaging for this purpose Friedrich Wilhelm Zachow (1663–1712), organist at the Halle Liebfrauenkirche, and an important composer of church cantatas and organ music. Handel was about nine at this time, and Zachow became his only teacher. Handel learned from him the craft of composition, the procedures of counterpoint and harmony, the art of composing with chorales, and importantly, a lifelong curiosity about other composers' music. Zachow also trained Handel's extraordinary talent as keyboardist that later made him internationally famous. In 1702, at the age of seventeen, Handel entered Halle University planning to study law, apparently acceding to his late father's wishes. At the same time he became organist at the cathedral in Halle. During this period Handel met Georg Philipp Telemann, a student at nearby Leipzig, and so began a lifelong friendship between the two composers. Soon, however, Handel made the momentous decision to leave Halle, based no doubt on his goal of becoming a professional musician and learning more about the most singular of Baroque musical genres, the opera.

Sometime in the spring of 1703 he arrived in Hamburg, northern Europe's greatest metropolis, a thriving port on the Elbe River, and the only city outside Venice to have a public opera house. Here he found employment first as ripieno second violinist and later as harpsichordist and conductor in the opera orchestra. Among his new friends was Johann Mattheson (1681–1764), a gifted composer, whose later fame was established with a distinguished series of treatises and other music books that record an enormous amount of information about music in Germany in the early eighteenth century. Also significant were Handel's contacts with Reinhard Keiser, director of the Hamburg opera at this time, and a composer of some eighty operas for Hamburg and elsewhere. Keiser's music made an indelible impression on the young Handel, who resorted at times in subsequent years to using themes and motives by Keiser in his own compositions. Later in life Handel commented that in Hamburg he "composed like the Devil," although very little of his music can be traced back to this period.

Four operas were composed for the Hamburg Theater am Gänsemarkt: *Almira* (1705), *Nero* (1705), *Florindo,* and *Daphne* (1706, first performed, 1708),[3] but only the first one has been preserved in its entirety. As Handel's first opera and one of the earliest preserved compositions, *Almira* deserves close study. Even though Handel was quite inexperienced with the theatrical scene and had had no previous opportunity to write operatic music, *Almira*[4] reveals an inconsistent but generally interesting amalgam of Hamburg operatic styles, including a mixture of arias in German and Italian languages, numerous French dances, and an emphasis on short continuo arias and liedlike songs. Some of the arias are of greater complexity, employing oboe solos, sometimes in a concerted texture with the strings. In a few instances, as in the aria "Geloso tormento" (act I, scene 6), one finds a notable example of Handel's developing gift for creating dramatic and highly compelling vocal writing combined with an expertly concerted instrumental accompaniment.

Three years, however, proved more than adequate for Handel's operatic apprenticeship in Hamburg. He, like many of his countrymen before him, found the lure of Italy irresistible, and by the fall of 1705 he had left Hamburg, perhaps stopping first in Florence at the invitation of the Medici prince Ferdinando with whom Handel had become acquainted in Hamburg. By the beginning of the new year Handel had settled down in Rome. The next three years, though we are still uncertain at times concerning Handel's whereabouts, were decisive in his maturation as a composer. It was a period of great productivity. In addition to Prince Ferdinando de' Medici, for whom the young composer wrote his first Italian opera in the fall of 1707 (*Vincer se stesso è maggior vittoria* [HWV 5], but usually known as *Rodrigo*[5]), he met several princes of the Catholic Church. *Il trionfo del tempo e del disinganno* (HWV 46a), composed in Rome in early 1787, used a libretto by Cardinal Benedetto Pamphili. Handel also knew Cardinals Carlo Colonna and Pietro Ottoboni. The latter lavishly supported the arts in his Palazzo della Cancelleria, where Corelli had lived in residence and directed weekly concerts since 1690.

Many of Handel's Italian compositions resulted from the interest in him and his music by the Marquis (later Prince) Francesco Ruspoli, who employed Handel as house composer for his Rome palace and also his country estates during May–October 1707, February–May 1708, July–November 1708, and perhaps also during part of 1709.[6] Among his duties was the composing of cantatas for weekly concerts, called *conversazione,* on Sundays. Many were written to texts containing the poetic conceits of pastoral life that reflected the gatherings of the Arcadian Academy[7] at the Ruspoli palace, for example, the impressive cantata for two sopranos and string instruments, *Arresta il passo (Aminta e Fillide)* (HWV 83). Other solo and duo cantatas with instruments that may have been written during this Italian period include *Diana cacciatrice: Alla caccia* (HWV 79), and several major works which in their dramatic scope and intensity resemble operatic scenes: *Ah! crudel nel pianto mio* (HWV 78), *Armida abbandonata: Dietro l'orme fugaci* (HWV 105), and *Agrippina condotta a morire: Dunque sarà pur vero* (HWV 110). At least forty solo cantatas with continuo originated in the Italian period. These testify to Handel's quick transference to his music of Italian vocal and instrumental styles found in the music of such major Italian composers as Corelli, Alessandro Scarlatti, and Bernardo Pasquini. Indeed, since so little of Handel's pre-Italian music is preserved, the unproven possibility exists that the growing suavity, new lyricism—"*bel canto* techniques"—had already become part of Handel's developing vocal style even before he arrived in Rome. An excellent example of his dramatic and Italianate musical style composed almost immediately upon his arrival in Italy is found in the cantata *La Lucretia: O numi eterni* (HWV 145), written in Florence in late 1706 or early 1707.

For a performance in 1707 Handel composed *Il trionfo del tempo* (The Triumph of Time) (HWV 46a), often called his first oratorio, but more accurately described as a large-scale cantata, on an allegorical text by Cardinal Pamphili. In addition to numerous cantatas composed for Prince Ruspoli's Arcadian society, Handel wrote a number of sacred works in 1707 for Catholic services. These include the antiphons *Haec est regina virginum* (HWV 235), *Te decus virgineum* (HWV 243), and a *Salve regina* (HWV 241); and the motets *Coelestis dum spirat aura* (HWV 231), *O qualis de coelo sonus* (HWV 239), *Saeviat tellus inter rigores* (HWV 240). Psalm settings are represented by two versions of *Laudate, pueri dominum* (HWV 236/237) (the earlier of which may have originated in Hamburg), *Nisi Dominus/Gloria patri* (HWV 238), and composed as early as in April, *Dixit Dominus* (HWV 232). Some of these compositions have been connected to Handel's participation in a Vesper service under the patronage of Carlo Colonna at the Carmelite church of St. Maria di Monte Santo in Rome, in July 1707.

From among these Latin works, nothing compares to the setting of Psalm 109/110, *Dixit Dominus.* Many of Handel's already advanced techniques of composing for voices and orchestra appear here fully matured, and one must assume that we lack today other earlier works in the choral genre that would give witness to his rapidly advancing command of vocal and orchestral forces. The work is composed for five-part chorus and five-part string ensemble. Handel divides the text[8] into eight movements: five choruses, two solos, and one duet. The opening and final movements incorporate a cantus firmus based on an unidentified (or perhaps newly composed) Gregorian chant, an obvious acknowledgment of the Catholic liturgy in which the work was first performed.

Movement I provides a brilliant example of modern, Italian ritornello form, with virtuoso string writing and elaborate vocal ensembles. The concerted form popularized in the music of Corelli and other Italians provides the basic structure for Handel's setting of the opening verse. The other movements are rich in a variety of musical conceptions. Movement IV has particularly powerful homophonic passages and explosive chordal dissonances on "Juravit Dominus." A two-part contrapuntal texture suggestive also of later Handelian choral style gives expression in the next movement to "Tu es sacerdos in aeterum." Movement VI, "Dominus a dextris tuis," comes close to being a Corellian type of contrapuntal texture, with an exposition for solo voices in two-part counterpoint in continuous suspensions, followed by the same music for five-part ensemble.

The most striking and rhetorically inspired passage occurs for "conquassabit capita in terra multorum," with chordal reiterations of the "sa" of "conquassabit," the "blows" raining down on the heads. The penultimate movement, "De torrente in via, in via bibet, proterea exaltabit caput," is the affective and lyrical highlight of the work, with a melody of particular beauty in duo form, to which there are choral responses. The final movement is especially complex, in a large bipartite form, with difficult solo and choral passages seemingly more instrumental than vocal in style, sung against the same cantus firmus used in movement I. The work concludes with a long fugue for "et in saecula saeculorum, Amen." This movement, as is true of the first, is infused with exuberance and energy, with musical ideas that in their simplicity are nevertheless abstractly ingenious in their memorable qualities. In the choral genre, *Dixit Dominus* stands out as a major achievement of the Italian period.

Handel composed his first oratorio, which was commissioned by the Marquis Ruspoli, in 1708. Entitled *La resurrezione* (HWV 47), it is an *oratorio volgare* on a sacred text. The first performance occurred at Ruspoli's Bonelli palace on 8 April, Easter Sunday, and the expenses were considerable. Corelli conducted a large orchestra, singers included at the first performance the prima donna, Margherita Durastanti (who frequently sang for Handel in Italy), an elaborate stage was erected in the palace, and painted backdrops were created specifically to illustrate scenes from the oratorio. The text relates events taking place between the Crucifixion and the Resurrection, and with it Handel achieved some of his most original music to date. The form is in the Italian tradition of sacred oratorios in the vernacular, with arias separated by simple or accompanied recitatives. Handel was particularly successful in musical characterizations, for example of Mary Magdalene, St. John the Evangelist, and especially Lucifer. The scoring is frequently colorful, the music operatic in its dramatic intensities as well as its subtle expressiveness. Later, Handel drew on many of the arias or their thematic components for use in other compositions, just as he also reused many arias from the Italian cantatas. *La resurrezione* remains a musical treasure known to all too few audiences today.[9]

In the spring of 1708 Handel traveled to Naples, probably invited by the Duke of Avito. Here he composed the serenata *Aci, Galatea e Polifemo* (HWV 72), presumably for the ducal wedding celebrations on 19 July. Although based on the same mythological pastoral, it should not be confused with the later English masque *Acis and Galatea* (HWV 49), with which it has almost no musical connection. The earlier work is a small masterpiece, resembling a one-act opera, though undoubtedly not intended for staging. The music with few German overtones proves the assimilation of Italian musical styles that Handel had been accumulating with his writing of chamber cantatas in Rome. In *Aci, Galatea e Polifemo* there remain elements of his earlier Hamburg operatic works, such as the rich contrapuntal textures and unusual orchestral colors. However, the vocal writing is decidedly Italian, with much extended and more lyrical melodies than are found in the Hamburg opera, *Almira*. There is a change in style for vocal coloraturas that now are often of greater length, motivic diversity, and difficulty. Both in melodic construction and harmonic organization melodies show a wider range of affective responses to the texts. German popular lied types no longer occur, though some of the melodies might be described as popular Italianate tunes. There are fine trios for the three characters as well as impressive duets for Aci and Galatea. The death of Aci, "Versi già l'alma col sangue," exemplifies the expressive writing often found in the second movements of Italian instrumental concertos, with the pulsating string chords without continuo support, piercing dissonances, and a poignant vocal line. From the vocal writing in the *serenata* one concludes that not only had Handel learned a great deal about writing for the voice and how to use the Italian language effectively, but also that he had discovered the stimulation of writing for exceptionally gifted singers.

From Italy to London

For at least part of 1709 Handel lived at the Florentine court of his patron, Prince Ferdinand Medici. In early November he left, with a letter of recommendation to Prince Karl von Neuberg in Innsbruck, but rather than traveling immediately northward, he went first to Venice. Here, on 26 December 1710,[10] he presented the first of twenty-seven performances of the opera *Agrippina* (HWV 6) in the Teatro San Giovanni Crisostomo. Such a large number of performances of an opera by a non-Italian composer suggests a major success for Handel, and many years later John Mainwaring, his first biographer, reported (perhaps repeating Handel's own recollections):

> The theatre, at almost every pause, resounded with shouts and acclamations of *viva il caro Sassone!* and other expressions of approbation too extravagant to be mentioned. They were thunderstruck with the grandeur and sublimity of his stile: for never had they known till then all the powers of harmony and modulation so closely arrayed, and so forcibly combined.[11]

Yet this "grandeur and sublimity of his stile" was entirely retrospective musically, for *Agrippina* is almost entirely based on music borrowed from earlier works, much of it by Handel himself (especially his cantatas), but also with considerable music by Reinhard Keiser and others.[12] *Agrippina* is a particularly instructive example of Handel's practice of basing new works on borrowings from his own and other composers' music, a fact that has spawned a large and often critical literature beginning already in his lifetime.

Early in 1710 Handel left Italy, his goal probably to find employment as a court Kapellmeister in the German-speaking Protestant North. Innsbruck did not apparently interest him as a possibility, and he went on to Hanover where the Electoral court had long supported music, especially opera. The opera house received great praise for its superb machinery, and had seen performances of several operas by Agostino Steffani prior to Handel's arrival. On 16 June, the Elector of Hanover appointed Handel court Kapellmeister. However, Handel spent little time in his new position, for his duties seemed to carry little significance.[13] He was free to travel, and after a trip to Halle to visit his mother and a longer period at the court of the Elector Palatine at Düsseldorf, Handel set out for London.

He came to London most likely at the invitation of the nobility and perhaps also from Aaron Hill, the energetic director of the opera house at the Haymarket, the Queen's theater. The first decade of the eighteenth century saw a growing enthusiasm in London for Italian opera. In the years prior to Handel's arrival Bononcini had achieved a great success with his *Camilla*. Yet no comparable work was to follow until Handel produced *Rinaldo*. Rather, most of the operas in the interim were pasticcios, pieced together from various Italian works by hack arrangers.[14]

Rinaldo had its premiere on 25 February 1711, and a total of fifteen performances during the season, becoming Handel's most popular opera with fifty-three performances during his lifetime. It was the first Italian opera written specifically for the London theater. The libretto was a collaborative creation by Aaron Hill and Giacomo Rossi.[15] In part, the work's popularity resulted from spectacular staging effects and complicated machinery, including flying apparitions, dragons spouting fire and smoke, transformations, waterfalls, and much more. What surprised and even disconcerted the audience the most was the garden scene in act II for which a flock of sparrows was released on stage and then proceeded to fly out into the audience. The music of *Rinaldo* is heavily indebted to borrowings from preceding works, but usually with considerable recomposition of the adopted materials.[16] The score is stronger than *Agrippina* in its presentation of memorable melodies, such as *Caro sposa* and the famous *Lascia, ch'io pianga, mia cruda sorte,* or the virtuosic *Venti, turbini, prestate le vostre ali,* and *Or la tromba in suon festante.* The advance in Handel's understanding of the operatic theater is particularly evident at the close of act II with the accompanied recitative for the sorceress, Armida, *Dunque i lacci d'un volto,* followed by the lament aria, *Ah crudel* (with a striking orchestral accompaniment for solo oboe, bassoon, three-part violins, and solo cello).

The success of *Rinaldo* not only gave Handel immediate fame in London but also opened up for him various avenues to English society. At this point, as in his later life, much remains unclear as to how exactly he managed his career. He was introduced at court to Queen Anne, but by the end of the opera season in June he returned to Hanover to resume his official duties as Kapellmeister. Here, too, few facts are available as to these duties, but as the court opera was closed, he had no outlet for that aspect of his musical gifts.

In the fall of 1712 he returned to London, but this time to remain and eventually to become a British citizen. During the subsequent year he served Queen Anne more than once as composer, and apparently she was instrumental in obtaining Handel's dismissal from his Hanover position. In December 1713, he received an appointment to the queen at an annual pension of £200. Thus, it seems false to maintain that when in the Hanoverian succession Handel's former employer became King George I of England, Handel faced serious censure from the new monarch for having failed to return earlier to Hanover.[17] Nor is there any apparent truth to the often-told story that Handel was able to restore himself to the new king's favor only by writing the famous *Water Music.*

Between 1714 and his death in 1758 Handel served King George I and his successor George II, as well as other British nobles, especially in the earlier part of his career. However, for most of his life he was an independent composer, writing music for profit, either from ticket sales or the sales of published editions. Although he had failures, some of them serious, Handel succeeded not only financially but also by becoming England's most celebrated composer in the eighteenth century.

The Operas

After the success of *Rinaldo,* Handel must have viewed the London musical scene as ideal for establishing himself as an opera composer, and one of the few places in the world where such a career would be entirely free from the constraints imposed by a court appointment. In the first years in London he composed five operas: after *Rinaldo* was *Il pastor fido,* first performed November 1712; *Teseo,* January 1713; and *Amadigi,* May 1715. The fifth work, *Silla,* was composed in 1713, but details of its performance, if any, are uncertain.

Beginning in 1720, Handel's career focused on opera as the result of the establishment of the Royal Academy of Music in London by members of the nobility under the patronage of the king. It was conceived as the means to give Italian opera long-term financial support. Handel was named director, J. J. Heidegger, the manager, and Paolo Rolli, Italian secretary and librettist. All the operas were produced at the King's Theater, Haymarket. Handel's operas written between 1720 and 1728, when the Academy failed, were the following:

Opera	First Performance
Radamisto	27 April 1720
Muzio Sevola (only act III)	15 April 1721
Floridante	9 December 1721
Ottone	12 January 1723
Flavio	14 May 1723
Giulio Cesare	20 February 1724
Tamerlano	31 October 1724
Rodelinda	12 February 1725
Scipione[18]	12 March 1726
Alessandro	5 May 1726
Admeto	31 January 1727
Riccardo Primo	11 November 1727
Siroe	17 February 1728
Tolomeo	30 April 1728

Italian composers who had works performed during these eight years of the Academy were Amadei, Ariosti, Bononcini, Porta, and Domenico Scarlatti. In the first two years Bononcini's works dominated the seasons with seventy-one performances, in contrast to twenty-six for Handel's operas.[19]

Despite the failure of the Academy, Handel persisted in his career as opera composer by forming a partnership with Heidegger and establishing a so-called second academy between 1729 and 1734, for which he wrote:

Opera	First Performance
Lotario	2 December 1729
Partenope	24 February 1730
Poro	2 February 1731
Ezio	15 January 1732
Sosarme	15 February 1732
Orlando	27 January 1733
Arianna in Creta	26 January 1734

Already in the 1733–1734 season, Handel found himself competing with another opera enterprise, the "opera of the nobility," and in the summer of 1734 Heidegger rented the King's Theater to the nobility, forcing Handel to move his company to the new playhouse in Covent Garden. He was able to move back to the King's Theater in 1738, and in 1740–1741 he produced operas at the theater in Lincoln's Inn Fields. These peregrinations encompassed Handel's last years of operatic composition, during which time he produced:

Opera	First Performance
Oreste (pasticcio)	18 December 1734
Ariodante	8 January 1735
Alcina	16 April 1735
Atalanta	12 May 1736
Arminio	12 January 1737
Giustino	16 February 1737
Berenice	18 May 1737

The following at King's Theater:

Faramondo	3 January 1738
Alessandro Severo (pasticcio)	25 February 1738
Serse	15 April 1738
Giove in Argo (pasticcio)	1 May 1739

The following at Lincoln's Inn Fields:

Imeneo	22 November 1740
Deidemia	10 January 1741

Many of these works are among the imperishable creations of the lyric stage, and in no way are inferior to the operas of Monteverdi or Mozart. However, because Handel's operas are rooted in opera seria conventions, and because they are indelibly linked to those Italian vocal forms and styles, they were previously thought invalid for modern audience acceptance. The subjects are drawn from history and myth, and the majority are revisions of librettos previously used by other Italian composers. When given sensitive and technically accomplished performances in the theater, their musical values reveal a composer who was a supreme musical dramatist. Together with various Italianate influences, Handel brought to opera a unique blending of German elements of counterpoint, serious vocal expressiveness, harmonic richness, and highly original orchestral scoring. Few composers in the history of music equal Handel's melodic inventiveness. With approximately two thousand arias contained in his operas, which have as yet to be studied in their entirety, Handel's operas are a great monument to his melodic genius.

Based on the librettos, Handel composed operas of markedly distinctive dramatic character. While a rigid classification according to type would be misleading, there are at least three categories of operas discernible: (1) heroic, (2) magic, (3) "anti-heroic" or semiserious/satirical.[20] The largest group and the most typical of opera seria librettos are the heroic. In these all the characters are not only royal or noble, but they are treated solemnly, even grandiloquently. The plots, which do not focus at all on common people, usually consist of themes of love and dynastic politics. Among the twenty-six operas by Handel falling loosely into this category, *Radamisto, Giulio Cesare, Rodelinda,* and *Tamerlano* are among the finest. Also belonging to this group are three operas to Metastasian texts: *Siroe, Poro,* and *Ezio.*

Magic operas depend on illusion, sorcery, unreality to promote the dramatic twists and turns of the plot. Three of the composer's earliest London operas represent this type: *Rinaldo, Teseo,* and *Amadigi.* However, Handel's great magic operas, both based on Ariosto's *Orlando furioso,* are *Orlando* and *Alcina.* A third group of operas cannot be classified as simply under a single rubric, depending as they do on varying amounts of mockery, parody, satire, often aimed at the conventions of opera seria. Winton Dean labels them "anti-heroic" for want of a better term. Handel's earliest surviving scores, *Almira* and *Agrippina,* fit this type as do *Flavio, Partenope,* and also his last operas, *Serse, Imeneo,* and *Deidemia.*

While all of Handel's operas have conventional roots, literary as well as musical, based on opera seria, nevertheless his greatness as an opera composer lies partly in his imaginative adaptations of those conventions. His operas rely generally on the two basic ingredients of Italian opera seria: (1) the recitative and (2) the da capo aria. Despite the straightjacket limitations of these conventions—concentrating the action in half-sung, half-spoken descriptions and narrations in recitative mostly accompanied only by basso continuo, and the lyrical and emotional response to the action in the affect-laden da capo aria—in his best operas Handel employed countless ways to adapt the conventions, to bend them, shape them into more malleable, dramatically flowing structures. Handel, unlike many of his contemporaries, viewed opera as a drama in music in which characters are pitted against each other, and in the course of the action, they develop and often reveal themselves as more than stock characters of a familiar libretto text. Even though character development would seem alien to the rigid structures of recitative alternating with da capo arias (the latter further standardized by the anticipated exit of the singer), Handel found in these conventions the means to achieve great musical-dramatic expressions.

In his London operas, Handel tends to restrict the recitatives to greater brevity than in his earlier Italian works or as is characteristic of most works by his Italian contemporaries. While it is still customary to label recitatives of the period as *recitativo secco,* the term is misleading for most of Handel's works. The older term, *recitativo semplice,* remains the more appropriate. For as with Venetian composers of opera in the later seventeenth century, Handel's recitatives, even those with a simple continuo accompaniment, are almost always highly expressive musical settings of the recitative texts. Through the means of harmonic progression, dissonance colorings, strong melodic design relying on rhetorically expressive motives, leaps, sequential patterns, and rhythmic pacing, his recitatives are anything but the formulaic "dry," rapidly sung passages found especially in later-eighteenth-century scores.

Every opera provides instruction in Handel's mastery of setting recited language to dramatized melodic expression. For moments of greatest dramatic impact, such as climaxes before a critical denouement and scenes of intense emotion, no Baroque composer writes more powerfully in the accompanied recitative style. Some of Handel's finest musical and dramatic moments occur in these recitatives (often combined with ariosos or inserted arias), normally accompanied by the string ensemble but also at times using other instruments of the orchestra, for example: Caesar before the funeral urn of Pompeo (*Giulio Cesare* I/7), Alcina's "Ah! Ruggiero crudel" (II/8), Orlando's extraordinary mad scene (II/9), and one of the most compelling of all, the extended death scene by suicide of Bajazet in *Tamerlano* (III/10). The passage within this scene in which Bajazet informs his daughter he is dying stands out as a prime example of Handel's command of harmonic and tonal resources to express the most poignant of dramatic moments in an affecting passage of harmonies descending from F-sharp major through F minor, cadencing in E minor.

The da capo aria did not obstruct Handel's genius for dramatic handling of the form. For example, when the B section of a text allowed the composer to create a contrasting musical affect, the form took on a stunning capacity for drama.[21] Furthermore, because audiences held a general expectation that the A section would be repeated (with appropriate embellishments by the singers), Handel occasionally achieved a brilliant theatrical jolt by breaking off the aria at the end of the B section and moving dramatically into the scene. (This occurs, for example, in act I, scene 5 of *Ariodante,* when the title character's love duet with Ginevra is interrupted by the king at the end of the B section.) Similarly, audiences would notice the many instances of arias lacking B sections, often placed at intense moments of the drama and sometimes embedded into accompanied recitatives.

Of course, Handel's operas exhibit in their organization of arias the protocol of opera seria, which demanded that the leading female and male stars have more arias than the next pair of singers of lesser star quality. A third pair could, in their lesser roles, have as few as a single aria each or even no arias. Handel wrote for many of the most famous singers of his day. At least twice, in 1719–1720 and 1728, he traveled on the Continent in order to hire new singers. Especially during the first Royal Academy period his operas benefited from performances by such illustrious virtuosos as, for example, the sopranos Margherita Durastanti, Anastasia Robinson, Faustina Bordoni, Francesca Cuzzoni, and Anna Strada, the castratos Senesino, Matteo Berselli, Benedetto Baldasare, the tenor Francesco Borosoni, and the bass Giuseppe Boschi.

During the Covent Garden season of 1734/35 Handel composed two of his most important works, *Alcina* and *Ariodante*. The distribution of arias in *Ariodante* illustrates a typical division among the principal and secondary roles. There are thirty-one arias (including four duets) in three acts, divided among the parts as follows:[22]

	Number of Arias			
Role	*Act I*	*Act II*	*Act III*	*Total*
Ariodante (male alto)	2	2	2	6 + 3 duets (with Ginevra)
Ginevra (soprano)	3	2	2	7
Polissano (female alto)	2	1	1	4
Dalinda (soprano)	2	1	1	4 + 1 duet (with Lurcanio)
Lurcanio (tenor)	1	2	—	3
King (bass)	1	1	1	3

A dramatic development of character occurs in each of the acts achieved by the music, especially the arias. Already in act II Handel, with great economy of means, tightens the various characters' entanglements so effectively that one wonders how this tragedy with all of its mistaken conclusions can be resolved to the advantage of the hero and heroine. The arias illuminate character through a variety of conflicting emotional expressions so organized as to allow the audience to sense in the music a developing change dramatically in each character.[23] It is in the third act that the various threads of conflict, crisis, deceit, and human failings as well as noble reactions are revealed, and act III of *Ariodante,* as is true of all of Handel's final acts, rewards close study.

The English Church and Secular Music

Once settled in England, Handel's career would center on opera until 1741 and subsequently on the writing and performance of his oratorios. However, during his long career he also wrote a substantial body of vocal music for the Anglican Church, both for private services in the Chapel Royal and for public occasions. In addition, two important dramatic pieces in English originated early in his career in England, *Acis and Galatea* and *Esther.* Especially during the first years in England, while establishing his reputation and before the opening of the Royal Academy of Music in 1720, Handel composed a variety of sacred works. The first of these, the *Utrecht Te Deum and Jubilate,* was completed in January 1713, only months after his arrival in London. It was performed at St. Paul's Cathedral on 7 July that year, as court and nation gave thanks for the end to the War of Spanish Succession that had been accomplished by the Treaty of Utrecht.

What is remarkable about the *Utrecht Te Deum* is the immediately noticeable English, one is tempted to say Purcellian, sounds of the score. Before Handel's *Te Deum* became known, it was Purcell's *St. Cecilia Te Deum* that had usually been performed on such occasions. Much has been made of Handel's probable study and imitation of that score. Clearly Handel's work, as well as the music for the contemporaneous *Ode for the Birthday of Queen Anne,* does aim to create a decidedly English musical style, and probably Handel did examine Purcell's own works. In the *Te Deum,* Handel deliberately adapts his German musical heritage and his newly learned Italianate melodic style to English musical elements. But the *Utrecht Te Deum* is not simply an imitation of Purcell's work. The two scores placed side by side prove that the *Te Deum* text receives a more complex and expansive treatment by Handel. There is a Germanic emphasis on contrapuntal textures, especially fugal sections. See for example "All the earth doth worship Thee" or the decidedly "Handelian" treatment of "Thou art the King of Glory." Yet, even though Handel could not have had much proficiency as yet in the English language, there stands out a "Purcellian" clarity to his text settings. Many of the homophonic choruses in their grandeur and immediacy are surely Handel's first adaptations of the English anthem style that would fertilize the music in his late and greatest oratorios.

As in Italy where he had the good fortune to benefit from the patronage of noble families, so too in London did he find aristocrats to support him at the beginning of his career. From 1713 to 1716 he lived for the most part in Burlington House, Piccadilly, home of the Dowager Countess Juliana and her son, Richard Boyle, Earl of Burlington. He was an architect, a strong proponent of the Palladian movement, who cultivated a prominent salon for famous literary and artistic personalities. According to Hawkins, Handel assisted frequently at evening concerts, often performing his own music. "The course of his studies during three years residence at Burlington-house, was very regular and uniform: his mornings were employed in study, and at dinner he sat down with men of first eminence for genius and abilities of any in the kingdom."[24]

At some point in late 1716 or the first half of 1717 Handel composed one of only a few extant compositions in his native tongue, the Passion Oratorio, *Der für die Sünde der Welt gemartete und sterbende Jesus* (Jesus, who was martyrized and died for the sins of the world), to a well-known text by Barthold Heinrich Brockes.[25] The same text was also composed by Keiser, Telemann, and Mattheson, all Hamburg composers. Handel's work was also performed in Hamburg, perhaps as early as 1716, but definitely in 1719. It is not clear whether the composition of the same Passion text by these four famous German composers represented some kind of competition. However, Handel's Passion is an important even if seldom discussed major work. He drew upon it for a number of later compositions including *Esther*, *Deborah*, and *Athalia*.

In 1717 Handel entered the employ of the Earl of Carnarvon (who in April 1719 became the first Duke of Chandos), James Brydges, as composer-in-residence. According to Mainwaring,[26] Handel spent a part of two years at Brydges's newly built grand manor house at Cannons near Edgware, today on the northwest side of London. As with so many facts surrounding Handel's life, it remains uncertain as to the actual time he lived in the Cannons household. At intervals during this period Handel wrote an important corpus of music: 11 *Chandos Anthems*, the *Chandos Te Deum* in B flat, the masque *Acis and Galatea*, and the oratorio *Esther*.

James Brydges was Paymaster-General to the continental armies of Marlborough (during the War of Spanish Succession), and he amassed an enormous personal fortune by skillful graft and theft from the queen's treasury. The Cannons mansion, which was still unfinished during Handel's tenure there, was described as having a magnificence unequaled by most residences of the German princes.[27] The *Chandos Anthems* and *Te Deum* originated as music for the private worship of his patron. Since the chapel in the mansion was not completed until 1720, most of these works were performed in the adjacent, small parish church of St. Lawrence Whitchurch, Little Stanmore (which remains to this day). The duke employed only a small number of musicians in his household, and the available space for performance in the church was very limited. Handel's compositions exhibit these restrictions in their scoring: two violins, no viola, basso continuo, oboe, bassoon, soprano, tenor (sometimes in multiple parts), and bass, but no alto. This peculiarity of the vocal scoring suggests one reason for the unfortunate lack of performances today of these compositions by choral conductors. Handel himself recognized their worth by using many of them in other scores, for example, in his *Coronation Anthems,* other ceremonial works, and particularly in the oratorio *Deborah.* Some (for example, Nos. IV and VI) are based on earlier Chapel Royal anthems. While the actual dates and ordering of these compositions remain unclear, a letter by Brydges dated 25 September 1717 to Dr. John Arbuthnot (Royal Physician and friend of the literary greats of the day) indicates they were composed in pairs:

> Mr Hendle has made me two new Anthems very noble ones & Most think they far exceed the two first. He is at work for 2 more & some Overtures to be plaied before the first lesson.[28]

The titles and most probable order of composition of the first eight of the "Chandos" anthems, originating around the period of the last four months of 1717, are given here with the numbers as they appear in Chrysander's *Gesamtausgabe:*

Pair I:	Anthem 6A	*As pants the Hart*
	Anthem 4	*O sing unto the Lord*
Pair II:	Anthem 7	*My song shall be allway*
	Anthem 11A	*Let God arise*
Pair III:	Anthem 3	*Have mercy upon me, O God*
	Anthem 1	*O be joyfull in the Lord* (arr. from the *Utrecht Jubilate*)
Pair IV:	Anthem 2	*In the Lord put I my trust*
	Anthem 5A	*I will magnify Thee*

Somewhat later, at an undetermined date, Handel wrote also for Chandos the following three large-scale anthems:

Anthem 8	*O come let us sing unto the Lord*
Anthem 9	*O praise the Lord with one consent*
Anthem 10	*The Lord is my light* and the Te Deum in B-flat major

The texts are English translations, sometimes paraphrased, of the psalms, many taken from the *Book of Common Prayer.* With one exception (No. 9, *O Praise the Lord with One Consent*), all of them begin with an Italianate slow/fast instrumental piece, some of which he later included in instrumental works such as his trio sonatas, Op. 5. While there is some unevenness in the quality of a few of the individual movements, in general the *Chandos Anthems* maintain a high level of musical interest. Each work includes a mixture of arias and choruses—a few also include accompanied recitatives. There are examples of Handel approaching his later oratorio style. No. 6A, *As Pants the Hart,* has more than one adaptation of German fugal styles, as in the moving double fugue of the opening choral movement, and the typically Handelian, two-part subject of the final fugue, "Put thy trust in God," with half the theme ascending, the other half descending in suspensions. The chorus, "Snares, fire, and brimstone on their heads," from No. 2, *In the Lord Put I My Trust,* must have been in Handel's mind when twenty years later he composed "Fire mingled with hail ran along upon the ground" in *Israel in Egypt.*

In No. 8, *O Come Let Us Sing,* in the chorus "Glory and worship are before him, power and honour are in his sanctuary," there are blocklike choral statements of the entire line, followed by antiphonal reiterations of "power," "honour," "glory," and "worship" that anticipate similar treatment of such musical-rhetorical exclamations in later works, such as in *Messiah*. Also, as in subsequent works, this predominantly homophonic, antiphonal movement runs into a fugue for the text, "Tell it out among the heathen, that the Lord is King." Especially worthy of detailed study are anthems 9 and 11A (*O Praise the Lord with One Consent* and *Let God Arise*), among the finest in the collection. Here there are examples of musical-rhetorical pathos, hymns of great power, ceremonial, or what Paul Lang has called "dynastic," music[29] expressive of the English sense of nationality. This amalgamation of Italian instrumental style, German counterpoint, English anthems, and Handelian unique melodic inventiveness in the *Chandos Anthems* forms much of the musical substance to be developed further by Handel in his later odes and oratorios.

Throughout his career Handel would have occasions to compose other anthems and similar works for public ceremonies as well as private ones within the royal household. Of these, none stand out in their significance more than the four *Coronation Anthems*, written for the coronation of George II in Westminster Abbey on 11 October 1727. It was an honor for Handel, who had become a naturalized British subject in February of that year, to be commissioned to write music for the coronation (and apparently by the new king himself). His success was such that these four anthems further cemented Handel in the minds of the public as the most important living "English" composer. The anthems and their probable place in the coronation service[30] are: I. *Zadok the Priest* (second to be performed, for the ritual of the anointing of the king), II. *Let Thy Hand Be Strengthened* (first, following the recognition of the new king by the people), III. *The King Shall Rejoice* (third, at the crowning of the king), and IV. *My Heart Is Inditing* (fourth, for the crowning of the new Queen Caroline).

With the exception of the more intimate fourth anthem, these are Handel's most brilliant achievements in ceremonial music, meant to stir the assembly to the thrill of dynastic succession, to raise their emotions to fever pitch of praise and joy in the new king and the perpetuation of the nation through its new ruler. The music becomes almost elemental, with little contrapuntal artifice, and powerful effects through instrumental and choral sonorities. Especially brilliant are the uses of instrumental and vocal sound in *Zadok the Priest*, a work that has been performed at every subsequent coronation. The "alleluias" in this anthem as well as in *The King Shall Rejoice* are models of his compositional imprint to appear often in later choral compositions. Only in *My Heart Is Inditing* is the tone appropriately more intimate, being expressive of the crowning of Queen Caroline, who was and would remain one of the composer's greatest supporters. Here the contrasts between solo statements followed by choral restatements remind one of the English anthem tradition, and most likely the dancing figures of a dotted eighth and sixteenth for the movement with the text "Upon thy right hand did stand the Queen in vesture of gold, and the King shall have pleasure in thy beauty" reflect Handel's absorption of Purcell's similar stylistic treatment of rhythmic figurations for expressions of gladness and joy.

Handel gave honor to Queen Caroline again on the occasion of her funeral in 1737. *The Ways of Zion Do Mourn* is Handel's most German choral composition, and a major work in the anthem tradition. Other anthems by Handel include: *This Is the Day* (wedding anthem for Princess Anne and Prince William of Orange, 1734), *The King Shall Rejoice* (*Dettingen Anthem* for the victory at Dettingen, 1743), *How Beautiful Are the Feet* (anthem for the Peace of Aix-la-Chapelle, 1749), and *Blessed Are They That Considereth the Poor* (the so-called *Foundling Hospital Anthem*, 1749).

The Instrumental Music

Although Handel's greatness as a composer undeniably lies in his achievements in all the major vocal forms of his day, nevertheless the instrumental works make up a substantial[31] output beginning in his earliest student days. A few of these works are popular, but most of them are not widely known. They fall into three groups: I. keyboard music, II. chamber music, and III. orchestral works and solo concertos with orchestra. Much of the music is impossible to date precisely, as Handel frequently drew on earlier compositions, sometimes revising them, for inclusion in later publications. Like other popular composers of the eighteenth century, Handel suffered the problem of publication piracy—the issuing of his music without his approval. Also, it was not uncommon for unscrupulous publishers to print music with his name that he had not composed. These are among the reasons that cloud the authenticity of some of the instrumental works. One indication of Handel's remarkable fame is the enormous number of printed editions of much of his music, frequently in a variety of collections and often in many different instrumental arrangements. This is especially true of arrangements of arias and other music taken out of his operas and oratorios.[32] However, a substantial portion of the instrumental works remained in manuscript and were not published until the twentieth century.

KEYBOARD MUSIC

From the several published collections of his keyboard music (almost all for harpsichord) and the numerous individual pieces in printed anthologies and manuscript copies, the three most important publications appearing during Handel's lifetime are: (1) *Suites de pièces pour le clavecin* [first series] (London: J. Cluer, 1720); (2) *Suites de pièces pour le clavecin* [second series] (London, J. Walsh, 1733); and (3) *Six fugues or voluntarys for the organ or harpsichord* (London: J. Walsh, 1735). In his preface to the first collection of suites Handel remarks:

> I have been obliged to publish some of the following lessons because surrepticious and incorrect copies of them had got abroad. I have added several new ones to make the Work more usefull which if it meets with a favourable reception: I will still proceed to publish more reckoning it my duty with my small talent to serve a Nation from which I have receiv'd so Generous a protection.

Terence Best[33] presents, in arguments supporting his chronology of the keyboard music, the opinion that many of these works originated from early in Handel's career in Hamburg to about 1720. Although most of them were published only beginning in 1720, which reflected the increasing demand for his compositions, it seems unlikely that Handel wrote anything for solo keyboard after this period.

The keyboard collections combine both rather elementary and more mature pieces, but none of them suggest the stylistic advancement and sophistication of German keyboard works from the same period, for example, those by J. S. Bach. Some of Handel's works are undemanding technically because they originated at the beginning of his career, when such teaching pieces were aimed at amateur performers. Many of the works are almost skeletal in their simplicity and may represent a basic frame to which Handel applied his famous improvisational gifts. Some of the individual pieces, especially in the first series, are improvisatory in character, though not so demanding as to suggest Handel's own keyboard prowess. Taken as a whole, these pieces present almost every facet of keyboard music: multimovement suites of dances, sonatas in the style of Domenico Scarlatti, fugues, and variations on both melodic themes and chaconne basses.

The generally simple technical demands, however, must not be viewed as unworthy of Handel's genius. The music represents Handel's craft at a high level and demonstrates much of his melodic originality, rhythmic vitality, and overall musical appeal. It is, however, more effective in performance than its appearance on the printed page suggests, and it is more suited to the sharply defined sonorities of the harpsichord than to the softer and more blended tone of modern pianos.

Handel's suites do not follow any basic pattern of dance forms. Some of them contain only a few movements, often four in the sequence allemande, courante, sarabande, and gigue (or jig). Others are longer and without any prescribed regularity of design. For example, Suite No. 8 in G major in the second series consists of allemande, allegro, corante, aria, menuetto, gavotta, double, and gigue. Suite No. 2 in G minor in the same series includes a chaconne with twenty-one variations, and the first suite in B flat major has an "aria con variazioni" (to the theme later used by Brahms in his own Handel piano variations). Another set of variations in the fifth suite in E major in the first series later became known by the spurious title of the *Harmonious Blacksmith*.

The first series, however, does suggest that Handel meant to make a strong musical impression with the first published keyboard work that he himself had prepared. For in these eight suites there is the widest diversity of movements, several impressive improvisatory preludes, a fine overture, several fugues, and an overall richness of free-flowing keyboard textures. The variety of types of movements is suggested by their titles:

I. A major	II. F major	III. D minor
Prelude	Adagio	Allegro (fugue)
Allemande	Allegro	Allemande
Courante	Adagio	Courante
Gigue	Allegro (fugue)	Air and five variations
		Presto

IV. E minor	V. E major	VI. F sharp minor
Allegro (fugue)	Prelude	Prelude
Allemande	Allemande	Largo
Courante	Courante	Allegro (fugue)
Sarabande	Air and 5 variations	Gigue
Gigue		

VII. G minor	VIII. F minor
Ouverture	Prelude
Andante	Allegro (fugue)
Allegro	Allemande
Sarabande	Courante
Gigue	Gigue
Passacaille	

CHAMBER WORKS

Relatively few compositions by Handel for one or two solo instruments and basso continuo appeared in his lifetime. They are included in three collections published circa 1730 to 1739, and they would be frequently reprinted. The first and second collections had a curious publication history by being issued initially with French titles and ostensibly by the Amsterdam publisher Jeanne Roger. Thus, *Sonates pour un* [sic] *traversière, un violon ou haut-*

bois, con basso continuo came out around 1730; but the same music appeared two years later in London, printed from largely the same engraved plates, by John Walsh (the Younger) as *Solos for a German Flute, a Hoboy or Violin, with a Thorough Bass for the Harpsicord or Bass Violin,* to which a note was added; "This is more corect [*sic*] than the former Edition." The collection has been referred to as Handel's Opus I since Chrysander gave it that label in his edition.

A second work, trio sonatas for two melody instruments, appeared in the same fashion, first as a publication from 1730–1732 by Roger, Amsterdam, entitled *VI Sonates à deux violons, deux haubois ou deux Flûtes traversières & Basse Continue . . . Second ouvrage,* which came out in London from John Walsh with the same French title and again a qualifying note: "This is more Correct than the former Edition." For this work Chrysander added further confusion by publishing the pieces as *IX Sonatas or Trios for Two Violins, Flutes or Hoboys . . . Opera seconda.* He created a work of nine compositions by adding without explanation as Nos. 3, 8, 9 three trio sonatas (HWV 392–94) not found in the original publications but rather in unrelated manuscripts.

In 1739 Walsh published a second set of trio sonatas: *Seven Sonatas or Trios for two Violins or German Flutes with a Thorough Bass for the Harpsicord or Violoncello . . . Opera Quinta.* Lastly, three solo sonatas for flute were identified as by Handel in Walsh's collection of 1730 entitled *Six Solos for a German Flute and a Bass and two for a Violin with Thorough Bass for the Harpsicord or Bass Violin Compos'd by Mr. Handel, Sigr. Geminiani, Sigr. Somis, Sigr. Brivio.* However, these three pieces, HWV 374, 375, and 376, are of questionable authenticity.

Among the problems raised by the solo sonatas is the designation of the solo instrument. The titles to the original publications suggest that Handel did not care which instrument—violin, flute (or recorder), oboe—would be employed. However, the extant autographs show that usually Handel specified only one of these instruments, and undoubtedly it was the publisher who broadened the performance possibilities to encourage more sales. Another problem concerns the chronology of these works, which has been narrowed down more accurately through recent advances in paper and watermark studies. Questions of authenticity also plague these works. Table 16.1 gives the best overview of the sonatas according to the instrument originally intended by the composer, and locates them in the Chrysander edition and the *Händel Hallische Ausgabe.* The latter regrettably breaks up the original order of the solo sonatas as they appeared as a set so as to group them in volumes according to the solo instrument. Nineteen solo sonatas can be identified as authentic. These generally resemble in form the solo sonatas by Corelli and his students and followers. The majority are church sonatas, with four movements alternating slow, fast, slow, fast. The slow movements tend to be aria-like, while most of the fast sections are in binary forms. As is true of similar works by Italian composers, dancelike movements occur (especially gigues for final movements), and for some Handel indicates the dance style by such words as *Tempo di Menuet, Bourrée anglaise, Siciliana.* Several of the fast movements are fugal. Some contain just three movements, but two are expanded to five and one to seven movements.

The trio sonatas in the collections published as Opp. 2 and 5 contain much of Handel's finest chamber music, even though a good portion of the music was adapted or taken wholly from previous compositions. This is particularly true of the sonatas in Op. 5.[34] Although Handel had no reason to avoid reusing previous compositions, he usually chose carefully and for the new version created in a real sense a "new" work.

The six sonatas of Op. 2 (to which Chrysander added another three, HWV 342, 343,

TABLE 16.1   Sonatas for a Solo Instrument and Basso Continuo[35]

HWV No.	*Chrysander Identification (Published Works)*	*HHA Vol./No.*	*Approximate Date of Composition*
Violin Sonatas			
PUBLISHED			
361	Op. 1/3 (A major)	IV/4 (No. 1)	c. 1725/26
364a	Op. 1/6 (G minor)	IV/18 (No. 2)	c. 1724
	(Contemporary prints designate Oboe. Handel's autograph also recommends Viola da Gamba = 364b)		
368	Op. 1/10 (G minor)	IV/4 (No. 2) (authentic?)	c. 1730
370	Op. 1/12 (F major)	IV/4 (No. 3) (authentic?)	c. 1730
371	Op. 1/13 (D major)	IV/4 (No. 4)	c. 1750
	(Chrysander falsely added to his "Op. 1")		
372	Op. 1/14 (A major)	IV/4 (No. 5) (authentic?)	c. 1725/26
373	Op. 1/15 (E major)	IV/4 (No. 6) (authentic?)	c. 1725/26
MANUSCRIPT			
358	Autograph (G major)	IV/18 (No. 1)	c. 1707/1709
359a	Autograph (D minor)	IV/18 (No. 3)b	c. 1724
	(Earlier version of 359b = Op. 1/1)		
Oboe Sonatas			
PUBLISHED			
366	Op. 1/8 (C minor)	IV/18 (No. 7)	c. 1710/11
MANUSCRIPT			
357	Autograph (B major)	IV/18 (No. 6)	c. 1707/1709
363a	(F major)	IV/18 (No. 8)	c. 1712/16
	(Transposed to G major for violin sonata 363b)		
Flute (Traverso) Sonatas			
PUBLISHED			
359b	Op. 1/1b (E minor)	IV/3 (No. 2)	c. 1726/32
363b	Op. 1/5 (G major)	IV/3 (No. 5)	c. 1726/32
367b	Op. 1/9 (B minor)	IV/3 (No. 7)	c. 1726/32
374	Sonata XVI (A minor)	IV/3 (No. 9) (authentic?)	before 1730
	(Hallenser Sonata No. 1)[36]		
375	Sonata XVII (E minor)	IV/3 (No. 10) (authentic?)	before 1730
	(Hallenser Sonata No. 2)		
376	Sonata XVIII (B minor)	IV/3 (No. 11) (authentic?)	before 1730
	(Hallenser Sonata No. 3)		
379	Op. 1/1a (E minor)	IV/3 (No. 1)	c. 1727/28
	(Added by Chrysander to his "Op.1" from an autograph source—not found in the Roger/Walsh prints)		
MANUSCRIPT			
378	(D major)	IV/18 (No. 9)	c. 1707/1709
Recorder Sonatas			
PUBLISHED			
360	Op. 1/2 (G minor)	IV/3 (No. 3)	c. 1725/26
362	Op. 1/4 (A minor)	IV/3 (No. 4)	c. 1725/26
365	Op. 1/7 (C major)	IV/3 (No. 6)	c. 1725/26
369	Op. 1/11 (F major)	IV/3 (No. 8)	c. 1725/26
MANUSCRIPT			
367a	Fitzwilliam Sonata III[37]—Autograph (D minor)	IV/18 (No. 5)	c. 1724
	(Original version of 367b [in B minor])		
377	Fitzwilliam Sonata I—Autograph (B flat major)	IV/18 (No. 4)	c. 1724/25

344) are splendid compositions in typical church sonata form (No. 4, HWV 389, includes a fifth-movement gigue). The inherent three-part instrumental medium, always especially congenial to Handel's compositional ideas, enabled him to weave together beautiful lyrical textures in slow movements and exhilarating and technically demanding imitative or fugal fast movements. Melodically, rhythmically, structurally, most of these are mature, "Handelian" pieces. Only in the case of No. 2 in G minor (HWV 387) and No. 6 also in G minor (HWV 391) does the style seem less developed. In fact, No. 2 may be the earliest datable composition by Handel. On a copy of the score made for Charles Jennens (librettist for Messiah and other oratorios) he wrote: "Composed at the age of 14," or approximately 1700. Jennens could only have learned this fact from Handel himself. Op. 2, No. 2 presents an interesting example for comparison with the later works in the same collection—such as No. 1b in B minor (HWV 386b), No. 3 in B flat major (HWV 388), or No. 5a in G minor (HWV 390a). Unlike the latter ones, No. 2 is simpler in every parameter and convincingly a youthful achievement.

SOLO CONCERTOS AND ORCHESTRAL WORKS

Handel composed a considerable amount of orchestral music. Most of it, however, belongs to the vocal works as overtures, incidental music, and dance music. Instrumental music published separately or left in manuscripts not directly associated with the dramatic works is limited to solo concertos, especially those for organ. In addition to the two published sets of concerti grossi, there are various miscellaneous overtures, concertos, and other pieces, as well as his two most famous orchestral compositions: the *Water Music* and the *Music for the Royal Fireworks*.

Three concertos for oboe exist, two in B flat major (HWV 301 and 302a) and one in G minor (HWV 287). The second in B flat major is almost entirely arranged from movements in the *Chandos Anthems* and other movements largely found in the chamber works. The G minor concerto was first published in the mid-nineteenth century, based on a manuscript copy in the possession of the Leipzig firm of J. Schubarth, and apparently bearing the compositional date of 1703. Since the manuscript is lost and no other copy comes down from Handel's lifetime, the authenticity cannot be guaranteed. A single solo violin concerto in B flat major (HWV 288), which Handel entitled Sonata *à 5* on his autograph, originates from the Italian period. It is thought that the work may have been written for Arcangelo Corelli, whom Handel knew in Rome.

The London publisher Walsh issued three separate sets of six organ concertos each, all bearing in the title "for harpsichord or organ" as performance options. This was made possible because English organs with which Handel would be familiar did not include a pedal board (only one of the concertos in the third series, HWV 306 in B flat major, has indications for pedals), and probably had only a single manual. The organ concertos are all linked to Handel's oratorios and were composed by him for his own performances, usually during the pauses between the acts. Always the innovative entrepreneur, Handel devised this means to make his oratorio performances more attractive to his ticket-purchasing public, for he was justifiably famous as one of the greatest keyboard artists of his age.

Handel cooperated in the publication of only the first set, which appeared as Op. 4 in 1736 with the following title and notice by the composer: *Six Concertos For the harpsicord or Organ Compos'd by Mr. Handel . . . These six Concertos were Publish'd by Mr. Walsh from my own Copy Corrected by myself and to Him only I have given my Right therein. . . . NB. In a few days will be Published the Instrumental Parts to the Above Six Concertos* (HWV 289–

294). The second set came out in 1740 without opus number (HWV 295–300), and a third set was published posthumously in 1761 as Op. 7 (HWV 306–311). All three collections received many further editions in the eighteenth century as well as down to the present day. Some of the individual concertos, for example, Nos. 3–6 in the second series, are much less effective than the others, and were probably arranged from Handel's music by someone other than the composer. All of the organ concertos are actually arrangements from his music as well as other composers.[38] As vehicles to display Handel's improvisatory talent they often consist of simple musical textures with frequent indications of *ad libitum,* all suggesting places where he applied his improvisatory art. The organ concertos are in essence chamber works, meant for a small instrumental ensemble. They are unsuited to the large orchestral accompaniments and large organs of great tonal strength that are sometimes employed.

The Concerti Grossi

In 1734 Walsh issued a collection of six concerti grossi by Handel entitled *Concerti Grossi Con Due Violini e Violoncello di Concertino Obligati e Due Altri Violini, Viola e Basso di Concerto Grosso ad Arbitrio da G. F. Handel. Opera Terza* (HWV 312–317). The title utilizes the promotional value of the concerto grosso form, which was held in high favor by musicians in London even still for the works of Corelli and numerous imitators of his concertos and sonatas. Op. 3 is a continuation of the Walsh series of Handel instrumental publications beginning with the solo sonatas, Op. 1, and continuing with the trio sonatas, Op. 2. Although not specified in the title, these concertos also include parts for oboes in the *concertino* (also recorders in No. 1), which led later in the eighteenth century to the misleading title of "Handel's Oboe Concertos," even though these are not solo concertos for that instrument.

Handel probably had little if anything to do with their publication, and more likely it was Walsh who made the choices of music to be published as concerti grossi.[39] With the exception of No. 1 in B flat major, all of these concertos consist largely of movements borrowed from previously composed music. For example, No. 5 in D minor reuses music from the symphony in the *Chandos Anthem* No. 2 (for movements 1 and 2), and the sonata to *Chandos Anthem* No. 6a (for movement 4).[40] However, as is generally true for Handel's music, the quality of a work seldom suffers from these transferences from one work to another, and the six Concerti Grossi, Op. 3, represent an important landmark in the publication of Handel's instrumental music during his lifetime.

Op. 3, however, is overshadowed in importance by the magnitude of Handel's subsequent achievement in the concerto grosso form, the twelve concerti grossi, Op. 6, published by Walsh in 1740 as *Twelve Grand Concertos in Seven Parts for Four Violins, a Tenor Violin, A Violoncello with a Through Bass for the Harpsicord* (HWV 319–330). Title, opus number, the size of the collection, and instrumentation all imitate Corelli's famous set of concerti grossi. Handel's works stand as a magnificent companion to Corelli's, and they are in the direct line of development of this instrumental form that also includes Vivaldi's and Geminiani's concertos. Handel's are equal in their significance to Bach's *Brandenburg Concertos.* They were composed by Handel within a brief period of four weeks between 29 September and 30 October 1739. As is typical for Handel, many of them have relationships to thematic ideas from earlier works as well as to Gottlieb Muffat's *Componimenti musicali* (c. 1739); however, with the exception of No. 11 in A major (drawn largely from the Organ Concerto HWV 296A), these are mostly newly composed. And unlike Op. 3, Handel did oversee the publication of his *Grand Concertos.*

Each of the twelve is different, even if they all reflect the historical mold of a multi-movement instrumental form with a contrasting group of solo instruments (two violins in this case—two oboe parts in manuscript exist in the Manchester [England] public library with a string ensemble for the *ripieno*). Even in this regard, the concertos have exceptions. For example, No. 7 in B flat major does not have a *concertino* group. Also typical is the alternation of movements in a pattern of slow and fast tempos. All of the concertos except for No. 8 in C minor include a fugue. Individual movements comprise a compendium of Handel's instrumental styles, both as found in chamber music and the incidental music in his dramatic vocal works. One finds the French-styled overtures (No. 5 in D major and No. 10 in D minor); theme and variations, including the extensive variations for the musette in No. 6 in G minor, as well as those in Nos. 10 and 12. Two of the concertos have four movements, three have six, and seven have five movements. Most of the concertos are conservative tonally, seldom leaving the key of the opening movement, except usually to use the relative major or minor. Many of the slow movements contain some of Handel's most beautiful melodic achievements, frequently resembling the poignant and noble affects found in his operas and oratorios. The twelve concertos, in the scores, look deceptively simple and very conservative technically and musically, and although they have been mistakenly judged little more than imitations of the style of Corelli and his successors, they are anything but that. Their diversity of styles, forms, melodic inspiration, textural brilliance, rhythmic energies cannot be summarized in a few words. They repay close study, for they are not only an encyclopedic collection of Handel's instrumental achievements, but they are among the foremost monuments in the history of orchestral music.

The Orchestral Works

Two works for orchestra were published in Handel's lifetime, both of which resulted from his role as composer to the royal household and were to become famous among all of his instrumental music. They are the *Water Music* (HWV 348–350), a complex of individual movements of uncertain origin, published c. 1733/34, and the *Music for the Royal Fireworks* (HWV 351), published in 1749.

Boating on the River Thames was a popular summer recreation for aristocrats as well as commoners. Several contemporary references were made to Handel's involvement with the royal family's river party on 17 July 1717. The following report appeared in the London *Daily Courant*:

> On Wednesday [July 17th] Evening, at about 8, the King took Water at Whitehall in an open Barge, wherein were also the Dutchess of Bolton, the Dutchess of Newcastle, the Countess of Godolphin, Madame Kilmanseck, and the Earl of Orkney. And went up the River towards Chelsea. Many other Barges with Persons of Quality attended, and so great a Number of Boats, that the whole River in a manner was cover'd; a City Company's Barge was employ'd for the Musick, wherein were 50 Instruments of all sorts, who play'd all the Way from Lambeth (while the Barges drove with the Tide without Rowing, as far as Chelsea) the finest Symphonies compos'd express for this Occasion, by Mr. Hendel; which his Majesty liked so well, that he caus'd it to be plaid over three times in going and returning. At Eleven his Majesty went a-shore at Chelsea, where a Supper was prepar'd and then there was another very fine Consort of Musick, which lasted till 2; after which, his Majesty came again into his Barge, and return'd the same Way, the Musick continuing to play till he landed.[41]

Another commentary[42] stated that the fifty instruments involved were trumpets, horns, oboes, bassoons, flutes, recorders, violins, and basses. These reports are the only record that

Handel composed "water music." An earlier summer river party in August 1715 is also reported to have had music. However, no known evidence has connected Handel with its composition, even though this is the occasion when the famous legend concluded that with his music Handel restored himself to the good graces of King George I. A subsequent royal party in April 1736 with Crown Prince Frederick (future King George III) entertaining his fiancée, Princess Augusta of Saxony-Coburg-Gotha, also had music by an unidentified composer, perhaps Handel.

The contemporary published versions and manuscript sources suggest that Handel composed three different suites of *Water Music:* in F major for strings, horns, and oboes, in D major for strings, horns, and trumpets, and in G major for strings, flutes, recorders, and bassoon. It is, however, unknown whether these groupings of pieces by tonality were directly associated with any particular occasion, and since the autographs are lost, Handel's original compositional arrangements cannot be determined.[43]

Written for open-air performance, the *Water Music* contains uncomplicated, often boldly assertive music, with particularly successful uses of horn and trumpet, as for example in the famous hornpipe from the D major suite. In addition to a brilliant fanfare-type opening, this suite also includes a minuet, a movement marked *lentement,* and a bourrée. The F major suite, the largest of the three, begins with an overture, continues with two slow and two fast movements in alternation, has an air, minuet, bourrée, hornpipe, and concludes with a final movement in D minor. The G major suite with flutes and recorders, with its more intimate character and made up of dances (minuet, rigaudon, and country dances), suggests possibly dinner music or conceivably even dancing itself on the royal barge.

Handel's other popular orchestral work, *Music for the Royal Fireworks,* was commissioned by King George II to be performed as part of a gala open-air festivity in London's Green Park in April 1749 to celebrate the Treaty of Aix-la-Chapelle (concluded in October 1748). The treaty ended the War of Austrian Succession in which England had been involved since 1740. The king required "martial instruments" only, that is, winds, not an unwise request considering the vast open spaces involved. Handel resisted composing the score with strings, writing the music for nine trumpets, nine horns, twenty-four oboes, twelve bassoons, a contrabassoon, three pairs of kettledrums, and side drums. Later, however, he added string parts when his score was published in 1749.

A public rehearsal, for which tickets were sold, was held on 21 April in the Vauxhall Gardens on the opposite side of the Thames, which attracted twelve thousand persons. "So great a resort occasioned such a stoppage on *London Bridge,* that no carriage could pass for 3 hours."[44] The performance itself took place on the 27th, before the actual fireworks display. The fireworks in some instances failed to ignite properly, and burned part of a great structure that had been erected in the park, causing panic and injury among the vast crowds attending the celebration.

The suite in D major has six movements: a long ouverture in three sections, a bourrée, a siciliana labeled La Paix, an allegro entitled *La Rejouissance,* and two minuets. The outstanding opening movement is an exhilarating example of politically inspired music. It begins with blaring trumpets and horns, dignified dotted rhythms, the "royal" rhythms of the French overture, and a processional fit for the king. The following Allegro is filled with "warlike" sounds, fanfares, snarling oboes, all obviously meant to stir the blood of every patriotic English citizen.

The Oratorios

Not often in music history can a composer be credited with inventing a new musical form, but Handel was the exception, for he is acknowledged as having created the English oratorio.[45] These oratorios have little in common with the earlier Italian *Oratorio volgare*, including his own *La Resurrezione*. Handel, always the composer sensitive to financial necessity, found in the oratorio a means to circumvent the social and economic factors that had ended his previous successes with opera. The roots of the oratorios, largely written after 1730, lie in a number of English forms and styles, including the masque, ode, pastoral, semi-operas by Purcell, and also in Handel's earlier works for which no exact precedent existed. Several of them assured Handel's musical immortality, and they crystallized a concept of "English" choral style that would impede further developments of music styles in that county for more than a century.

Handel came to the idea of the oratorio from opera, and most of these works are highly dramatic. There were, however, other reasons unrelated to musical goals. His first opera, *Esther*, has only a slight connection to the later works and was an adaptation necessitated by threats of musical piracy. In 1732, in the midst of Handel's "second opera academy," a series of private performances were given in London of his Cannons *Esther*, originally labeled a masque. Prepared by Bernard Gates, master of the children of the Chapel Royal, the first took place in honor of Handel's birthday, 23 February, and subsequently on 1 and 3 March. The performances, it needs to be stressed, were presented without stage action as a type of sacred opera, and the production took place in the Crown and Anchor tavern in the Strand. In April, an unidentified promoter announced a performance of Esther, as "never Perform'd in Publick before." Someone had obtained a copy of the score and intended a pirated performance to reap the profits from what had become a much discussed and popular work in the city. Handel responded with the following announcement in the London *Daily Journal* of 19 April:

> By his Majesty's *Command.* At the King's Theatre in the Hay-Market, on Tuesday the 2d Day of May, will be performed, *The Sacred Story* of Esther: an *Oratorio in English.* Formerly compos'd by Mr. *Handel,* and now revised by him, with several Additions, and to be performed by a great Number of the best Voices and Instruments. N.B. There will be no Action on the Stage, but the House will be fitted up in a decent Manner, for the Audience.[46]

Handel defused public interest in the pirated version by circulating the news of his new version with a cast of important singers and a large instrumental ensemble. He did the same thing again only a month later when Thomas A. Arne gave an unauthorized performance of the masque *Acis and Galatea*. It is, however, the final sentence of the *Esther* announcement that holds greatest significance, preparing the audience for a condition of the performance that had resulted from an edict of the Bishop of London banning the acting out of biblical texts on the stage. The performance of the revised *Esther* had considerable success, undoubtedly noted by Handel, and thus the concept of the unstaged English oratorio, although unplanned, was born out of a need to protect his works from artistic piracy and the puritanical morality of a London church prelate.

In 1733 Handel experimented further with oratorios as a new vehicle for public performance, composing *Deborah*, a work that has not received much critical praise[47] and includes extensive borrowings from earlier works. Soon thereafter, *Athalia*, based on the Racine play, was composed for a performance in Oxford. It was perhaps intended as an expression of thanks for the honorary doctorate offered to Handel by the university, which for some unexplained reason he declined to accept. *Athalia* is Handel's first major oratorio and contains some superb, dramatically conceived music with fine choruses, an array of excellent arias, and a colorful use of the orchestra. It is only a short distance from *Athalia* to the great works of the ensuing decades beginning with *Saul* in 1738.

In 1734 Handel was forced to move his opera productions to a new theater in Covent Garden. Here, in 1735, he produced among others two of his finest operas, *Ariodante* and *Alcina*. But the season did not prosper, and he even filled out the subscription series with revivals of *Esther, Deborah,* and *Athalia.* In 1736 he composed only a single new opera, *Atalanta,* but added to the opera season as a novelty *Alexander's Feast,* a St. Cecilia ode on a text by John Dryden. This was given in oratorio fashion with Handel performing at the organ (as had become his custom during the intervals between acts of the operas).

In the fall of 1737 Handel suffered a serious illness variously described as a nervous breakdown or a stroke. The pressures on him as the result of the failing opera enterprise may have been responsible for the attack. He repaired to a spa at Aix-la-Chapelle (Aachen) for a cure, which was remarkably effective in a rather short time. He returned to London, remained committed to opera, and composed three more for the season of spring 1738: *Faramondo, Alessandro Severo,* and *Serse.* This season failed, and when he learned that advance ticket sales for the following season were inadequate to open the theater, he turned his creative energies again to oratorio: first *Saul,* composed in the summer of 1738, followed by *Israel in Egypt* in the fall. Perhaps he hoped these works would tide him over to a more propitious opera season, and one last time in 1740–1741 he presented new operas, *Imeneo* and *Deidamia,* only again to have no success. Finally, Handel ended some two decades of continuous operatic activity in London and turned completely to oratorios for the remainder of his career. As Table 16.2 shows, his compositional energies were quickly restored, and the oratorios from these years remain Handel's best-known and most significant legacy to music.

There is no typical Handelian oratorio, although many are similar in general musical design. He tried out various musical solutions throughout this phase of his career, and some of the works seem experimental. The largest number are based on Old Testament plots, telling biblical stories of personal and national tragedy developed dramatically through scene structure and three acts. Some are nondramatic, having no story line, for example, *Israel in Egypt* and *Messiah.*[48] Some are composed to texts arranged from major literary works, by distinguished writers such as Racine, Milton, Dryden, and Congreve. The dramatic oratorios show in their printed librettos that audiences were expected to imagine scenery, dramatic action, and the coming and going of characters. Incidental music often contributes to a sense of this kind of action. These facts have led to staging of some of the oratorios in more recent times, for example, the stagings of *Samson* in Europe and at various opera houses in the United States. There is no evidence that any oratorio of Handel's was ever staged in his lifetime or that he would have wished a staging of these works.

Handel composed an enormous volume of music in the oratorios, and all too little of it is familiar to audiences today (except perhaps in England). No summary can adequately treat the extensive variety and richness of musical ideas and compositional techniques, the superb handling of the textual drama, and the originality of the instrumentations. Even the librettos themselves have as yet not received a comprehensive study for what they could reveal about Handel's requirements for a libretto or about the intellectual climate in England at the time.[49]

Any discussion of the oratorios must focus on the choruses, because they are the

TABLE 16.2 The Odes and Oratorios

Work	Source of Text	Librettist	Year Composed	Place/Date of First Performance
1. *Esther*	Racine	?A. Pope and J. Arbuthnot	?1718	?Cannons, 1718
2. *Deborah*	OT: Judges v	Humphreys	1733	King's Theater, 17 March 1733
3. *Athalia*	Racine	Humphreys	1733	Oxford, Sheldonian Theater, 10 July 1733
4. *Ode: Alexander's Feast*	J. Dryden: Ode for St. Cecilia's Day, 1697	N. Hamilton	1736	Covent Garden, 19 Feb. 1736
5. *Saul*	OT: I Samuel xvii & II Samuel i	C. Jennens	1738	King's Theater, 16 Jan. 1739
6. *Israel in Egypt*	OT: Exodus xv, Prayer Book Psalter		1738	King's Theater, 4 April 1739
7. *Ode for St. Cecilia's Day*	Dryden	(Dryden)	1739	Lincoln's Inn Fields, 22 Nov. 1739
8. *L'Allegro, il Penseroso ed il Moderato* (Ode)	Milton (Parts I & II), C. Jennens (Part III)	C. Jennens	1740	Lincoln's Inn Fields, 27 Feb. 1740
9. *Messiah*	Bible & Prayer Book Psalter	C. Jennens		Dublin: New Music Hall, 13 April 1742
10. *Samson*	Milton	N. Hamilton	1741–42	Covent Garden, 18 Feb. 1743
11. *Semele*	W. Congreve	?	1743	Covent Garden, 10 Feb. 1744
12. *Joseph and His Brethren*	OT: Genesis xli–xliv, Acts II & III based on A. Zeno's *Giuseppe*	J. Miller	1743	Covent Garden, 2 March 1744
13. *Hercules*	Sophocles, *Trachiniae*, Ovid: *Metamorphoses* ix	T. Broughton	1744	King's Theater, 5 Jan. 1745
14. *Belshazzar*	OT: Daniel v, Jeremiah, Isaiah, Herodotus, *History* i, and Xenophon, *Cyropaedia*	C. Jennens	1744	King's Theater, 27 March 1745
15. *Occasional Oratorio*	Milton's paraphrases of psalms, excerpts from E. Spenser: *The Faery Queen, Hymn of Heavenly Beauty, Tears of the Muses*	N. Hamilton	1746	Covent Garden, 14 Feb. 1746
16. *Judas Maccabaeus*	OT: I Maccabees, and Josephus, *Antiquities* xii	T. Morell	1746	Covent Garden, 1 April 1747
17. *Joshua*	OT: Joshua	T. Morell	1747	Covent Garden, 9 March 1748
18. *Alexander Balus*	OT: I Maccabees	T. Morell	1747	Covent Garden, 23 March 1748
19. *Susanna*	Apocrypha	Anon.	1748	Covent Garden, 10 Feb. 1749
20. *Solomon*	OT: II Chronicles, I Kings v, and Josephus, *Antiquities* viii	Anon.	1748	Covent Garden, 17 March 1749
21. *Theodora*	R. Boyle, *The Martyrdom of Theodora and Didymus*	T. Morell	1749	Covent Garden, 16 March 1750
22. *The Choice of Hercules*	R. Lowth, *The Judgment of Hercules* (Glasgow, 1747)	T. Morell?	1750	Covent Garden, 1 March 1751
23. *Jephtha*	OT: Judges xi, and G. Buchanan, *Jephthes sive Votum* (1554)	T. Morell	1751	Covent Garden, 26 Feb. 1752

singular feature of these works. Various writers have commented upon the musical influences apparent in Handel's choral idiom: the choruses in Carissimi's oratorios, the choral style of Purcell, Italian concerto techniques, Venetian double chorus style, and especially German contrapuntal practices—fugue, cantus firmus, and chorale-based polyphony—as well as motet and cantata styles. Also to be remembered is that from his first years in England Handel had attuned his choral style to have a marked rapport with the English anthem.

Already in *Saul* (HWV 53), the first in a series of oratorio masterpieces, numerous threads of Handel's choral and contrapuntal techniques coalesce into a large variety of types of choruses. Following a multimovement overture, *Saul* immediately exploits the choral idiom in an Epinicion, a scene of pageantry in which the Israelites celebrate the victory of David over Goliath and the Philistines. The first chorus ("How excellent, Thy name, O Lord), for an unusually large orchestra (three trombones, two trumpets, timpani, oboes, bassoons, strings, and continuo), places the homophonic writing for chorus against contrasting orchestral material. As is frequent in the oratorios, this A section leads into an imitative section ("Above all heav'ns, Oh King ador'd"), which establishes a typical Baroque formal plan of contrasts, an A + B. The next chorus, similarly bipartite, begins with a brief concerted passage for chorus and orchestra ("The youth inspir'd by Thee Oh Lord") that connects to a fugue ("Our fainting courage soon restor'd"). The latter is a characteristic Handelian fugue in which subject and countersubject employ the simplest of means to be contrasted, deriving their musical distinctions from the text—the subject, with its drop of a fifth and rise by a sixth giving emphasis to "our fainting courage soon restored," and the countersubject illustrating "headlong drove the impious crew" with a descending "driving" scale through the interval of a thirteenth.

The Epinicion is rounded out by a return of the opening chorus, but this has been shortened for a concluding "Halleluja," one of Handel's most characteristic, even conventional types of choruses (often combined with "Amen" passages). This one is typical: two short motives, musically contrasted, are pitted together with intervening chords and quick melismatic passages. It is evidence of one aspect of Handel's genius that he was able to create so many memorable and different choruses from this kind of formulaic compositional technique.

Two additional choruses occur in act I. There is the irresistible welcoming song of the daughters of Israel, a dancelike hymn of joy scored for carillon and strings that gives rise to Saul's jealousy as the women praise David who has "his ten thousand slew," while Saul "hast thy thousands slain." The women are interrupted by the first of many compelling accompanied recitatives for Saul, "What do I hear? Am I sunk so low?," but he is quickly silenced by a return to the same chorus, this time with full orchestra including trombones and men's voices. The second chorus closes the act in the form of a standard type of fugue, "Preserve him for the glory of Thy name."

Act II begins with the famous choral chaconne, "envy eldest form of Hell," composed to a descending diatonic scale in eighths and a dotted rhythmic accompaniment in the orchestra. These thirty-four measures offer a microcosm of Handel's musical-rhetorical art. The chorus, caught up in the action (and not simply describing it), cries out in isolated shouts, sometimes also in concerted pairs of voices. The inexorable march suddenly halts for the warning: "Hide thee in the blackest night; virtue sickens at thy sight," in which "night" and "sickens" receive affective harmonic twists.

The second chorus illustrates a frequent type of chorus in which the music either repeats literally or reinterprets the preceding aria. "Is there a man, who all his ways directs, his God alone to please?" is based on the previous pastoral duet of Michal and David, "Oh fairest of ten thousand fair." The final chorus of the act, one of Handel's memorable creations, "Oh fatal consequence of rage, by reason uncontroll'd," again presents the chorus as participants, here reacting in horror and fright at having witnessed Saul's attempt to murder his own son Jonathan. The first section begins imitatively with anguished motives leaping down by diminished fifths for "Oh fatal." This is followed by a recitative-like treatment of the choral writing supported by insistent and agitated string passages for "with ev'ry law he can dispense; no ties the furious monster holds." The second section is fugal. Two subjects each have expositions, which are repeated. The first fugue projects the rhetoric of the text as the subject leaps down by a seventh in syncopation and is pitted against a countersubject of descending melodic thirds for "blindly, blindly he goes." The two themes interlock in cross-accents to suggest Saul stumbling blindly "from crime to crime," the force of which is intensified as the passage becomes increasingly chromatic. The second fugue is contrasted in its lyricism for "nor end but with his own destruction knows."

The third act of *Saul,* as is true of final acts of most of the oratorios (and operas), is climactic and a masterwork of musical and dramatic inventiveness. The opening part portrays the meeting of Saul with the Witch of Endor and the summoning of the prophet Samuel's ghost during which Handel employs simple and accompanied recitatives. The only aria in the scene, for the Witch as she calls forth Samuel, continues the intensity of the action in music of striking demonic power. The prophet Samuel rises to mysterious musical sounds made even stranger by the sounds of two bassoons.

The climax of the tragedy is introduced by a brilliant sinfonia meant to suggest the battle of Saul and Jonathan against the Philistines. The outcome is related to David by the Amalekite, who reports the death of father and son, proudly declaring he himself killed Saul and bearing his crown as a gift to David. David's response, in an aria of furious affect, is one of the more operatic in the entire work. The final part of the act, introduced by the famous Dead March, consists of a seven-section elegy on the death of Saul and Jonathan, filled by Handel with sadness and noble lamentation. Four choruses are combined with arias giving individual words of grief and reflection on the preceding events. The aria, with choral responses "fatal day," remains one of the composer's most vivid musical expressions of tragic mourning.

The oratorios to follow *Saul* as well as the delightful ode, *L'Allegro, il Penseroso ed il Moderato,* are rich, sometimes richer in choruses, many with innovations of form and purpose. Nor should one neglect to stress the central role of recitatives, both simple and accompanied, and the arias and duets that contribute to the overall dramatic success of these works.

Messiah, which to this day stands synonymous with Handel's fame and greatness, is in some ways uncharacteristic of Handel's other oratorios. Influenced both by the English anthem and the German passion, *Messiah* is based entirely on biblical texts, some from the New Testament. It is, however, nondramatic (it does not relate the life of Christ), and does not employ acting roles. Since the nineteenth century, *Messiah* has been considered mistakenly as a religious work for the church. Except for performances in the chapel of the Foundling Hospital, it was never performed in a church in Handel's lifetime. It is allegorical, presenting the struggle between Light and Darkness, Good and Evil, God and Man. Performances of *Messiah* after Handel's death have led to the false notion that his oratorios were meant to be performed by enormous orchestral and vocal forces, sometimes numbering in the hundreds if not the thousands. Furthermore, *Messiah* has become an icon of religiosity, part of church music traditions. Without diminishing the greatness of the work, however, one needs to understand that it has obscured Handel's importance as a composer of other vocal and choral music of extraordinary breadth and genius.

Handel's Borrowing Practices

Much more remains to be learned about how Handel composed. What has been known, even in his own lifetime, is his singular ability to reuse music he had already composed, and to adapt it, or even to recompose it into new compositions. Also well known is that he frequently resorted to using the music of other composers, most frequently motives and themes he found stimulating to his compositional inventiveness, but sometimes also entire movements. This fact has generated a large, critical literature, and beginning in the nineteenth century has led to accusations of plagiarism. Some writers have raised the issue of immorality, suggesting that Handel concealed the fact he had taken music from other composers. The charge has also been made that Handel was incapable of having an original musical (i.e., thematic) idea.

These are complex issues, but the following can be observed. First, no composer of the Baroque or earlier periods thought of composing primarily as an act of originality; for composers before the late eighteenth century, the concept of craftsmanship was equally important. This was especially true of German composers. Second, the centuries-old principle of resorting to pre-existing musical ideas played a significant part in the craft of composing. In addition, since Handel was a commercially oriented composer, and as much of his music (for example, the Italian cantatas) once performed would never be heard again, there could be no reason for him not to reuse the materials from these scores.

Yet the fact remains: Handel, more than we know of for any other composer, reused, adapted, and created new works out of old ones, and in the process borrowed from himself and other composers. What must now concern and occupy students of Handel's creative methods, however, are the conditions under which he borrowed these materials, what they were, and especially how he used them in later works. His oeuvre contains vast resources of music still to be studied from the viewpoint of Handel's compositional procedures. Until this is achieved, Handel's music and creative genius will not be fully comprehended.[50]

CHAPTER SEVENTEEN

Johann Sebastian Bach (1685–1750)

WITH JOHANN SEBASTIAN BACH, we encounter a composer from the first half of the eighteenth century who more than any other has held the world of scholarship and general music appreciation in awe up to the present day. Bach's career, as organist, church musician, and Kapellmeister, is largely indistinguishable from that of most of his predecessors and contemporaries in the Germany of the seventeenth and first half of the eighteenth centuries. His achievements, except for those works composed for instruction and a few at the very end of his career, were the products of his occupational responsibilities. His compositional techniques, which now are appreciated for their extraordinary innovations, were at times mistakenly viewed as conservative if not old-fashioned by some of his contemporaries. And this composer of modest background never left the central region of Germany after completing his formal education in Lüneburg. His contemporary fame rested for the most part on his abilities as an organist and harpsichordist, but he has been judged variously in the nineteenth and twentieth centuries as the "fifth Evangelist," as the greatest genius of Western art music, as an icon, perhaps *the* icon of music history. It is clear that no other composer of the Baroque period stands so completely rooted to his own times but paradoxically has become suprahistorical, a creator in music who is recognized as one of the few among the many to be venerated as having achieved a status of supreme greatness in Western cultural history.

No other composer had as unique a family lineage, which extended from the sixteenth into the early nineteenth century, with more than fifty Bachs who were actively engaged in the music profession. They included fiddlers, town musicians, organists, cantors, and members of musical establishments at both minor and major courts. Johann Sebastian became the greatest member of the Bach dynasty, but others also had distinguished careers, including his four sons, Wilhelm Friedemann, Carl Philipp Emanuel, Johann Christoph Friedrich, and Johann Christian Bach.[1] With some exceptions, generations of the Bach family, which was established by Veit Bach (d. before 1578), lived and worked in Thuringian territory bordered by Meiningen, Mühlhausen, Arnstadt, and Weimar. Bach also was employed in this region until his final positions took him first to Cöthen and then to the Saxon city of Leipzig in 1723.

A great deal of information has been established about Bach's life and career, and it will suffice here to note only the important landmarks that lend structure to an examination of Bach's achievements as a composer.[2] He was the eighth and last child born in Eisenach to Ambrosius Bach (1645–1695), a town musician, and Maria Elisabeth Lämmerhirt (1644–1694). Eisenach, lying at the foot of the Wartburg where Luther had translated the New Testament into German, was a town steeped in Protestant traditions. In a double tragedy for the young Bach, he lost his mother in May 1694 and his father in February 1695. Johann Sebastian and his older brother Jacob were taken to Ohrdruf to live with their older brother, Johann Christoph, an organist who had been a student of Pachelbel. Bach's earliest musical education is conjectured to have begun with violin lessons given by his father. Keyboard instruction was initiated with lessons from Johann Christoph. Bach entered the Ohrdruf Lyceum and progressed from the fourth to the first class with outstanding academic achievements, but shortly before his fifteenth birthday in March 1700 he left Ohrdruf for Lüneburg in northern Germany.

Here Bach would make singular progress as musician and composer. He had at the time an unusual treble voice, and the school of the Michaeliskirche gave him free tuition for becoming a member of the church's matins choir. He retained that position even after his voice broke and changed from his much-praised soprano to bass. At school Bach succeeded in what was essentially a preuniversity curriculum with emphasis on Lutheran theology, Latin, arithmetic, history, geography, German poetry, and physics. His musical education appears to have been less formal. There was the superb Michaeliskirche library of vocal music that must have enriched his experiences with the choir. Organs in Lüneburg at the Nicolaikirche and the Johanneskirche offered possibilities for instruction, especially at the latter where Bach undoubtedly came to know Georg Böhm. Furthermore, the metropolis of Hamburg was only some thirty miles to the north, where Bach could visit a cousin, Johann Ernst, and where he may have attended the famous Hamburg opera directed by Reinhard Keiser. Most important were his efforts to hear on more than one occasion the distinguished composer and organist J. A. Reincken (1623–1722) and the particularly outstanding organ in the Catherinenkirche. To the south of Lüneburg lay Celle, seat of Duke Georg Wilhelm, who had a strong fondness for French music. He maintained an orchestra largely of French musicians, which, according to the Bach's obituary, gave him "a thorough grounding in the French taste, which, in those regions, was at the time something quite new."[3] This experience, however, did not take place at the duke's Celle residence but, rather, in his recently built Lüneburg castle.[4] Bach left Lüneburg at some time in 1702 confident in his musical abilities and seeking employment. Success was not immediate. An attempt in July 1702 to become the organist in Sängerhausen failed, and nothing further is known of Bach's whereabouts until 4 March 1703, when he was paid as a lackey and violinist at the court at Weimar of Duke Johann Ernst. Opportunities also existed there for Bach to substitute as court organist.

The Five Stations of Bach's Career

Bach's career of forty-seven years was divided among five different positions. The specified requirements of each of these determined the forms of much of the music he would compose. In four of the five positions Bach's duties were focused on music for the Protestant church, both vocal music as well as organ works. While many occasions and also Bach's own creative interests produced a large body of secular music, it was only at the Cöthen court, which was Calvinist and did not permit any elaborate vocal or instrumental music, that he could concentrate almost exclusively on secular compositions.

Bach's professional career began as organist for the New Church in Arnstadt on 14 August 1703. His duties were light, and he began to compose organ works in significant numbers. But he had difficulties with rowdy students in the choir, and was criticized for confusing the congregation "by having hitherto made many curious variations on the chorale, and mingled many strange tones in it." The most important event occurring during this period was Bach's request to church officials for a leave to travel to Lübeck perhaps to study with Buxtehude and surely to hear him play the organ (a journey of some 260 miles he is said to have made on foot). He requested an absence of four weeks but stayed almost four months, leaving in October 1705 and returning in February 1706.

The experience of witnessing Buxtehude perform his organ music and direct his cantatas and oratorios must have been overwhelming. Here was a composer and performer worthy of emulation. Buxtehude had almost total freedom to compose; he was a virtuoso organist who traveled and taught numerous students. He was his own impresario who organized the widely famous *Abend-Musiken* at his church. He was a scholar-musician with a wide-ranging background in the theory of music, and he applied this knowledge in his own mastery of counterpoint. It was probably in Lübeck that Bach began to realize his own potential as an artist and composer. Did he resolve then to seek a position that would enable him to create music of the dimensions and depths of expression he had heard in Lübeck? Clearly, Bach's restless nature that left him ultimately dissatisfied with every position he would fill began with his return from Lübeck. Early in July 1707 he moved to Mühlhausen as organist at the St. Blasius Church. But again he became disappointed with the conditions of his employment, staying only until midsummer 1708, when he, with his new wife Maria Barbara, moved to Weimar as organist and chamber musician at the court of Duke Wilhelm Ernst.

Several organ compositions have been assigned to the period between 1703 and 1708, largely on the basis of style, early works mostly in the form of preludes or toccatas and fugues. Also, a number of organ chorale preludes in the so-called Neumeister Collection originate among Bach's earliest compositions.[5] In addition, there is Bach's programmatic clavier work, *Capriccio sopra la lontananza del suo fratello dilettissimo* (Capriccio on the departure of his most loved brother), BWV 992,[6] usually thought to be inspired by the departure in 1704 of Bach's brother Johann Jacob who went to Poland to join the army of Charles XII of Sweden as an oboist.[7] From the Arnstadt and Mühlhausen periods originate the first examples of Bach's compositions in the sacred cantata form. They include BWV 4, *Christ lag in Todesbanden* (extant only in Bach's revision made for Leipzig); BWV 131, *Aus der Tiefen rufe ich, Herr, zu dir;* a funeral cantata, BWV 106, *Gottes Zeit ist die allerbeste Zeit* (Actus tragicus); for the service in 1708 marking the Mühlhausen town council election, BWV 71, *Gott ist mein König;* and probably a wedding cantata, BWV 196, *Der Herr denket an uns,* and BWV 150, *Nach dir, Herr, verlanget mich.* There is no substantive explanation as to how Bach had arrived this early in his career to create vocal works of such sophistication and expressive beauty.

The nine years Bach and his growing family of children spent at the court of Weimar were exceedingly productive. Bach's compositional style reached distinctive maturity as he absorbed the recent Italian musical developments, especially the concerto form. In the ancient tradition of learning by copying music, Bach made transcriptions for organ (four) and for harpsichord (sixteen) of instrumental concertos, most notably by Italians (six by Vivaldi, one each by Alessandro and Benedetto Marcello, and Giuseppe Torelli), as well as one by Telemann and four by Prince Johann Ernst. Bach was employed as court organist, but he was also called *Cammermusikus* (chamber musician) in court documents and must have played violin or viola in the court orchestra that performed music by French and Italian composers.

The majority of Bach's organ works are assumed to have been composed at Weimar, although the almost total lack of original manuscripts makes a precise determination of their origins difficult. Of great significance was Bach's project to compose organ chorale preludes for the entire liturgical year. Entitled the *Orgelbüchlein,* the project was never completed.[8] In March 1714, the duke promoted Bach to the position of *Konzertmeister.* Of harpsichord music, it is now believed the so-called English Suites, BWV 806–811, probably were composed late in his Weimar tenure. His new responsibilities included composing a cantata once every four weeks for the ducal chapel, but regrettably from some forty Weimar cantatas only about twenty-two are preserved. Bach enjoyed rich and varied experiences composing and performing music at the Weimar court. In addition, he had a number of music students, and his fame as an authority on organs led to many engagements to oversee restorations and constructions of organs. It was a full life but Bach grew unhappy when he was passed over for the position of Kapellmeister, and he again realized the necessity to find a new court position, one that would advance him to the position of music director. In December 1717 Bach left Weimar for Cöthen, some sixty miles to the northeast, first having spent almost a month in the Duke of Weimar's jail, imprisoned and subsequently dismissed in disgrace by the duke, who apparently was enraged by Bach's demands to be released from his employ.

Bach must have arrived in Cöthen in high spirits. He had finally gained a position worthy of his abilities at a significant court, ruled by the young Prince Leopold. Leopold was twenty-three and a musician of considerable ability who had studied in Berlin, and made the Grand Tour of England, France, the Low Countries, and Italy. He was known to be an accomplished player of the violin, viola da gamba, and harpsichord. The court was Calvinist, so Bach's musical duties would be focused on secular and largely instrumental works. Although no church cantatas would be required, he did compose secular cantatas for royal birthdays, a marriage, New Year's celebrations, and so on, none of which have been preserved. Leopold increased his orchestra (which he referred to as a collegium musicum) to eighteen members, and also employed several singers. Bach could assume that he would be in charge of a major musical establishment, possibly well into the future. His creative energy supported the output of a major body of harpsichord and solo and ensemble instrumental works. Among the works documented as being composed in Cöthen are, for harpsichord, the Inventions and Sinfonien, BWV 772–801, the Chromatic Fantasie and Fugue, BWV 903, the Well-Tempered Clavier, Part I, BWV 846–869, and the French Suites for clavier, BWV 812–817. For solo violin there are the Three Sonatas and Three Partitas, BWV 1001–1006; for solo cello, Six Suites, BWV 1007–1012, and the Sonata for Solo Flute, BWV 1013. For violin and string ensemble is the Concerto in E major, BWV 1042. (The Double Violin concerto in D minor, BWV 1043, may be from Cöthen and the Violin Concerto BWV 1041 is now placed among the Leipzig works.) Finally, there are Bach's best-known works for orchestra, the six Brandenburg Concertos, BWV 1046–1051.

Bach made a remarkable career change in coming to Cöthen. It would appear to be the very antithesis of everything he had prepared himself for, and that he himself stated was the goal of his life, "to compose a well-regulated church music for the glory of God." It was in Cöthen that he gave up his remarkable career as organist, for which he would never again be employed—although it needs to be noted that in late 1720 Bach traveled to Hamburg to audition for the position of organist at St. Jacob's Church, which perhaps suggests he already had his first doubts about the stability of the Cöthen appointment. Bach immersed himself in the exciting musical life of a princely court, which had an excellent musical establishment of instrumentalists and singers. He could choose the music to be performed, take part in its performances, perform and study other composers' works, travel widely, give guest performances at other courts, and continue his career as an organ examiner. It was undoubtedly the most successful and personally satisfying period in his entire life.

That, however, would soon change, as personal tragedy again came to Bach with the death of his wife in July 1720. Bach had returned with Prince Leopold from the latter's visit to the spa at Carlsbad to find that Maria Barbara had died and was already buried.

Some sixteen months later, on 3 December 1721, he married Anna Magdalena Wilcke, daughter of a court trumpeter and also a talented singer. She was sixteen years younger than Bach and became his great supporter for life, stepmother to his four surviving children, mother to thirteen additional children, and one of the most important copyists of his music.

Now, apparently, all was no longer satisfactory for Bach. A year later he applied for the position in Leipzig previously held by Johann Kuhnau (who had died in June 1722), as cantor of Leipzig's Thomasschule, with related responsibilities as director of music for the city. The reasons for Bach's decision to leave Cöthen are unclear. It is usually stated that it was the result of the marriage of Prince Leopold to his cousin Princess Friderica, who had no interest in music and managed to break up the support of the prince for Bach's position as Kapellmeister. More recent information suggests that Bach's decision to leave Cöthen more likely involved the declining financial fortunes of the prince who had gone seriously into debt, which threatened the support of every aspect of the court's musical establishment, including Bach's salary. It is, perhaps, not unreasonable to think that the aftermath of Bach's sudden and tragic loss of his first wife led him to a serious reconsideration of his life and career. This introspection based on his faith in God would have underscored his failure at Cöthen to serve God as he had always planned. The opportunity to become cantor in Leipzig would have appeared to be the ideal, even preordained, solution for returning him to his long-held commitment to create well-ordered church music. It also would provide an opportunity for his sons to have a university education, something that their father had been unable to achieve.

The circumstances leading up to Bach's appointment in Leipzig have frequently been described, and are repeated here only in brief outline. In June 1722, five applications were received by the town councilors of Leipzig for the position of cantor at the Thomasschule. Among the five the preferred candidate was Telemann, thought to be the greatest composer in Germany at that time. After Telemann had threatened to leave Hamburg, the authorities refused to release him, but they gave Telemann (as he had requested) a substantial increase in pay. By December, five candidates remained in consideration, including Bach and Christoph Graupner, Kapellmeister at Darmstadt. The latter now became the choice of the council, but, as with Telemann, Graupner also was unable to obtain release from his position. Finally, the council members appointed Bach, not without some concern that he would not be a "cantor" in the sense that his main function was to be the instruction of the boys in the Thomasschule, both in regard to their musical education but also in academic subjects such as Latin. Indeed, Bach made it clear from the beginning that he had no interest in the academic side of the appointment. Arrangements, therefore, were made for a substitute, paid for out of Bach's pocket, to take on some of these responsibilities. On 7 February 1723 Bach came to Leipzig and successfully passed the required test of a candidate's abilities by performing at the Thomaskirche, before and after the sermon, two cantatas: *Jesus nahm zu sich die Zwölfe*, BWV 22, and *Du wahre Gott und Davids Sohn*, BWV 23. In April Bach received a cordial dismissal from the Prince of Anhalt-Cöthen, who arranged for Bach to retain his title of Kapellmeister to the court. Bach's election as cantor was approved on 5 May. On 22 May, the Bachs moved into the cantor's newly renovated apartment at the St. Thomas School. A week later, on Sunday, 30 May, Bach took up his duties, performing the first of his cantatas written for the two principal churches, BWV 75, *Die Elenden sollen essen*, at Nicolaikirche.[9]

In accepting the position at Leipzig, Bach's career took a step backward from the distinction of court Kapellmeister. Yet, as he knew, the cantorate at Leipzig over several centuries had been among the most important in Germany and had been occupied by musicians as famous as Johann Hermann Schein (1586–1630), Sebastian Knüpfer (1657–1676), Johann Schelle (1677–1701), and Johann Kuhnau (1660–1722). The cantor's post was truly a full-time job. Among his many responsibilities were teaching music and other subjects to the boys enrolled at the Thomasschule, giving individual music lessons, rehearsing and conducting the first choir at the Thomaskirche and the Nikolaikirche on alternate Sundays, overseeing the work of the organists and other musicians at those churches, and periodically supervising meals and having responsibility for school discipline. Other activities, for which he would receive extra payment, included attendance at weddings and funerals. Bach also held the responsibility, as director of music, to provide and usually to compose music for important civic occasions. In addition he assumed responsibilities between 1729 and 1741 for the collegium musicum, which had been organized in 1702 by Telemann.

Considering all of the duties Bach needed to fulfill for his contracted responsibilities, the extensiveness of his compositional output seems almost incomprehensible. At the forefront of his Leipzig achievements stand a staggering number of sacred vocal works, amazingly almost all written in the first six years at Leipzig. He was responsible for performing a cantata at the Hauptgottesdienst every Sunday and feast day in the year—except during the Lenten season and the last three Sundays in Advent. It is estimated that if, as the obituary states, he completed five yearly cycles of cantatas, each made up of some sixty works, he would have composed some three hundred cantatas, of which around 190 have been preserved. In addition, he composed five Passions (only the St. John and St. Matthew are preserved), three oratorios (the *Ascension,* BWV 11, *Christmas,* BWV 248a,[10] *Easter,* BWV 249), four short "Lutheran" Masses, a Magnificat, several motets. Later he also composed (largely arranged or adapted from previous compositions) the B Minor Mass, and miscellaneous vocal works for civic occasions, for collegium musicum readings, and for weddings and birthdays.

While the instrumental works from the Leipzig period are less numerous than those for voices, they are in no sense less important. Among those for instrumental ensemble composed in the period from the early 1730s into the 1740s are seven harpsichord concertos, BWV 1052–1059, all arrangements of earlier concertos, some of which are lost; three concertos for two harpsichords adapted from earlier concertos, BWV 1060–1062 (the last one from BWV 1043, concerto for two violins in D minor); two concertos for three harpsichords, from lost or unknown sources, BWV 1063–1064; a triple concerto for flute, violin, and harpsichord, BWV 1044; and a concerto in A minor, BWV 1065, an arrangement of Vivaldi's concerto, Op. 3, No. 10 (RV 580). Also credited to the Leipzig period are the four orchestral suites in C major, B minor, and the third and fourth in D major.[11] Keyboard works include the following:

Well-tempered Clavier, volume II, BWV 870–893
The *Clavier-Übung:*
    Part I, Six Partitas, published separately, 1726–1731, and as Op. 1 in 1731, BWV 825–830
    Part II, *Overture nach französischer Art,* BWV 831, and the *Concerto nach italiänischem Gusto,* BWV 971
    Part III, "consisting of various chorale preludes on the Catechism and other melodies," including the opening Prelude, BWV 552; the chorale settings and the concluding fugue, BWV 669–89; and four keyboard duets, BWV 802–805
    Part IV, "Aria with various [thirty] variations" (the *Goldberg Variations*), BWV 988

From the final years of Bach's life come three monumental instrumental works.

For organ: Canonic variations on *Vom Himmel hoch, da komm' ich her,* BWV 769
For flute, two violins, keyboard, and basso continuo: *The Musical Offering,* BWV 1079
The *Art of Fugue,* BWV 1080, left unfinished at Bach's death

It has been frequently observed that the total number of Bach's compositions do not begin to equal the output of contemporaries such as Telemann and Graupner. But what does distinguish Bach's music in contrast to that of his contemporaries is the unique quality of originality and perfection characteristic of each work. Exactly how to describe the genius of Bach's creativity has challenged and continues to challenge writers. No better brief attempt to describe Bach's musical mind has been expressed than those words by his son Carl Philipp Emanuel and his student Johann Friedrich Agricola that appear in Bach's obituary:[12]

If ever a composer showed polyphony in its greatest strength, it was certainly our late lamented Bach. If ever a musician employed the most hidden secrets of harmony with the most skilled artistry, it was certainly our Bach. No one ever showed so many ingenious and unusual ideas as he in elaborate pieces such as ordinarily seem dry exercises in craftsmanship. He needed only to have heard any theme to be aware—it seemed in the same instant—of almost every intricacy that artistry could produce in the treatment of it. His melodies were strange, but always varied, rich in invention, and resembling those of no other composer. His serious temperament drew him by preference to music that was serious, elaborate, and profound; but he could also, when the occasion demanded, adjust himself, especially in playing, to a lighter and more humorous way of thought. His constant practice in the working out of polyphonic pieces had given his eye such facility that even in the largest scores he could take in all the simultaneously sounding parts at a glance.

The Organ Music

As his obituary states, Bach was known far beyond the city of Leipzig as a great organist. Even though he never held another position as organist after Weimar, organ music was central to his life, and he composed organ music throughout his career. While it has been thought that the largest body of music for organ was composed at Weimar, new research suggests that a considerable part of these compositions originated earlier at Arnstadt and Mühlhausen, and probably even Lüneburg. The chorale partitas BWV 766–767, and the early version of BWV 768 in their characteristic Böhm style, seem particularly related to Bach's Lüneburg experience. His reputation as organist was partly built on a reputation as an expert in organ building and repair, and he frequently was employed to evaluate new as well as old organs, and to recommend repairs or builders. Many occasions arose in which the testing of an organ concluded with a public concert, from which his fame as a virtuoso spread widely. There are a number of documented organ performances by Bach including those in Hamburg, Dresden, Berlin, and Kassel. In addition, Bach apparently frequently was asked to perform for visitors coming to Leipzig for the annual fairs, and probably also by those students eager to hear Bach's virtuosity, just as Bach earlier in his life had gone to Lübeck to hear Buxtehude.

Bach's organ music was composed for various purposes: music for spiritual edification, for enjoyment of the performer as well as for the listener, and music for teaching purposes. To a separate category belongs music for the church, most of it based on Protestant chorales. Very little of his organ music can be related to a specific period in Bach's career. This is the result of the disappearance of most of the original manuscripts, the works being now preserved usually only in copies, many of them made by Bach's students. Attempts to assign places for the keyboard works in a specific chronology are, therefore, based on conclusions that cannot always be precise about the development of Bach's keyboard style.[13]

On the basis of new source materials from the Neumeister collection, which contains thirty-eight chorale preludes by Bach, thirty-three of them previously unknown, there is now important evidence to suggest that Bach had already developed his compositional skills as regards the organ chorale prelude before composing his first major organ work, the *Orgelbüchlein.* These early compositions cannot be dated precisely but some may actually have originated as early as Bach's years with his brother in Ohrdruf, and they are clearly pre-Weimar in style. Their stylistic connection with Bach's *Orgelbüchlein* is apparent, and two of the preludes appearing toward the end of the Neumeister collection (BWV 639, *Ich ruf zu dir, Herr Jesu Christ,* and BWV 601, *Herr Christ, der einig Gottes Sohn*) are also included in the *Orgelbüchlein.*[14]

Several of Bach's works bear instructive titles, for example, the composer's inscription to the opening page of his "Little Organ Book, in which a beginner at the organ is given instruction in working out a chorale in many diverse ways, and at the same time in acquiring facility in the study of the pedals, since in these chorales the pedals are treated wholly obbligato." Composed in Weimar probably during the years 1713–1716 (only the title page was written in Cöthen), Bach prepared the manuscript for 164 melodies by entering the chorale titles, each on a separate page. He completed, however, only forty-five preludes. It is clear from his title page that Bach composed this collection as instructional material for students, one of several such works that he compiled in his lifetime. What is remarkable about the *Orgelbüchlein* is the variety and depth of affective meaning contained in many of these chorale prelude miniatures. Most of them appear to be simple in design. The chorale is usually placed in the top part, in quarter notes or sometimes in half notes. Except for three in five parts, all the preludes are in four, with the top parts divided between the two hands, at times the left hand on a second keyboard. The variety of settings of the chorales depends on Bach's seemingly endless resources for inventing different contrapuntal textures to support the chorale and to unify the prelude. Eight preludes employ canon (double canon in *In dulci jubilo*); four between chorale and bass, two at the fifth in the right hand, one at the twelfth between left hand and right, and one between the bass and alto in right hand.[15]

Bach's greatness in his numerous settings of the Protestant chorale lies in his devout personal introspection into the texts of these basic melodies of the Protestant creed. True to Baroque aesthetic, he creates for each one a musical affect that expresses the meaning of each of these sacred texts. At times, the result is also pictorial in its rhetorical emphasis, such as the prevailing falling motive of a seventh as a type of ostinato that underscores the opening words of *Durch Adams Fall ist ganz verderbt,* or the joyous context filling *In dir ist Freude* with a bass motive that leaps with joy, and the incessant repetition of the opening motive for "In Thee Is Joy." In the *Orgelbüchlein* the most intensely moving and intro-spective preludes elaborately embellish the chorales and employ unexpected and highly expressive dissonances. Three of the preludes in this collection are exceptional in this regard: *Das alte Jahr vergangen ist, Wenn wir in höchsten Nöten sein,* and *O Mensch, bewein' dein'*

Sünde gross. The last of these remarkable works is perhaps best known. The total composition, melodic variation, ornamentation, range, textures, bass progressions, dissonant harmony, and even the rare performance indication for the final bar as *Adagissimo* testify to Bach's artistic maturity at the age of only thirty to give a musical-rhetorical interpretation in music equal to this profoundly moving text.

Applying the words of the first verse to the chorale tones demonstrates that hardly a single word is not given expressive accent by ornamentation, striking dissonances, harmonic progressions, or frequently affective melismas which threaten to and at times do burst the very structure of the chorale melody. Bach's immersion in the meaning of these words is also indicated by the fact he chose not to repeat the same music for the second "A" of the bar form. The contrast of the first six bars with the subsequent six bars, the first in reference to Christ, the second to the Virgin Mary, reveals considerable differences of expression given to the same chorale tones. It is, however, in measures twelve to the end of the B portion of the chorale that each word of the text is interpreted with all of the expressiveness of Bach's genius. In the penultimate lines, "[Christ] carried our sin's heavy burden" (*trug unser Sünden schwere Bürd*), the parallel-sixth chords moving by seconds give a sense of the "heavy" burden while the word "sin" is inundated with dissonance as the melismatic line soars above the chorale tone C to B flat, the highest notes of the setting. The melodic climax is balanced with the extraordinary harmonic progressions for the final line of text, "indeed for long on the cross" (*wohl an dem Kreuze lange*), as the chorale moves over a rising chromatic bass line as if pointing to the symbolic cross and then collapsing into a C flat chord as Bach indicates the final measure is to be played *adagissimo*, underscoring these final words with a passage of profoundest sadness (see Example 17.1):

EXAMPLE 17.1   Bach, *O Mensch, bewein' dein' Sünde gross*

Bach composed about 140 chorale preludes on some 90 melodies. Most are extensive compositions, many found in various manuscript copies such as the Kirnberger manuscript, BWV 690–713a. Also important sources for the chorale preludes are the eighteen so-called Leipzig chorale preludes, BWV 651–668, the six Schübler chorale preludes, five of which are Bach's transcriptions of movements from his cantatas, BWV 645–650, the organ chorale preludes published in Part III of the *Clavier-Übung,* BWV 669–689, and variations in canon on *Vom Himmel hoch, da komm' ich her,* BWV 769, published in 1748.

Of considerably more formal variety are some sixty-five organ works without chorales. Most of them challenge the organist with high levels of virtuosity, including many with difficult pedal parts, suggesting they were meant for public performances by Bach. The majority of them are paired compositions usually with some form of improvisatory piece entitled variously prelude, toccata, or fantasia. These are frequently coupled with a fugue, although individual movements of each type also exist, and it is not always certain Bach wished them to be coupled. From the Weimar period are five concertos transcribed and arranged by Bach for organ after concertos by Prince Johann Ernst (BWV 592 and 595) and Vivaldi (BWV 593 after Op. 3, No. 8 for two violins; BWV 594 after Op. 7, second collection, No. 5 for violin; BWV 596 after Op. 3, No. 11, concerto grosso). In addition, there are six trio sonatas, BWV 525 (E flat major), 526 (C minor), 527 (D minor), 528 (E minor), 529 (C major), 530 (G major), probably in part arrangements of chamber works that, according to Forkel, Bach arranged for his son Wilhelm Friedemann.

Despite the lack of a reliable chronology for these works, one can perceive a general development of Bach's keyboard style in some of these compositions.[16] The early influence of Georg Böhm in Lüneburg is apparent in the chorale partitas BWV 766–768, and French keyboard style would appear to have influenced Bach in the Fantasia in G major, BWV 572. Also probably early works are the fugues Bach arranged after Legrenzi and Corelli, BWV 574 and 579. The typical prelude, toccata, or fantasia plus fugue form developed in Weimar is as yet unachieved in the much looser Prelude and Fugue in D major, BWV 532, which consists of a short improvisatory praeludium, a longer alla breve, and a lengthy fugue with a simple and highly repetitive subject that resembles a theme by Pachelbel.

Although the dating is uncertain, Bach's great *Passacaglia in C minor* is generally considered to have been composed either late in the Mühlhausen period or early in Weimar.[17] Although Bach frequently employed ostinato bass forms, the organ *Passacaglia* is unique among his compositions. The first four measures of the theme are derived from the *Trio en Passacaille* by the French composer André Raison (before 1650–1719). Bach undoubtedly knew other passacaglias for organ by Pachelbel and Buxtehude, but his work expands the concept far beyond the probable models, creating a longer, more complex and sophisticated piece. While he apparently never composed another ostinato work for organ, its companion work is the extraordinary chaconne that closes the *Partita in D Minor,* BWV 1004 for Unaccompanied Violin.

The Passacaglia consists of twenty variations that are connected without pause, and as if it is the twenty-first variation, a grand fugue based on Raison's theme, to which Bach adds two countersubjects. In the fugue the theme is stated twelve times while always preserving the original intervallic structure (there are no "tonal" answers). Various analyses of the passacaglia have been suggested, each giving a different interpretation of Bach's formal design and seeking to relate and interrelate the individual variations into cohesive structural blocks. However, one can perceive a rather simple and yet majestic plan. It is based on two different ideas: one distinguishes distinct structural divisions and contrasts of textures and rhythms that generate musical tensions and relaxations. Significant in the growth of the structure are the frequent pairings of the variations. The other idea is created by a general development toward the climax with ever-increasing rhythmic activity and passages in smaller, more active note values. In this view the first ten variations lead to an interior climax. They are followed by the greatly contrasted and reduced texture of five variations in which the pedal part is silent and the passacaglia melody itself moves to the upper voices. With the arrival of the sixteenth variation the theme returns energetically in the pedals, and the last five variations develop to the climax, first with an ostinato figure alternating between the hands and then in a great climax incessantly doubled in both hands.

Bach's style rapidly changed and matured in Weimar, in part through the impact of his discovery of the music of Vivaldi and other Italian composers. His fascination with the new Italian concerted style would inspire him on many occasions in Weimar and later to arrange works by Venetian composers. Italianate traits (form, harmonic structure, rhythmic vitality) are subsumed rapidly into Bach's own complex style in his keyboard, orchestral, and sacred vocal music. The development of the typical two-part keyboard composition, with the opening more or less reflecting keyboard improvisational practice in contrast with contrapuntal restrictions of the fugue procedure, reaches the highest level of perfection in Bach's keyboard works. Each pairing of movements whether for organ or harpsichord becomes a unique solution to a simple concept of contrasts. No two of the organ works are alike, and each is a testament to Bach's unlimited resourcefulness of musical ideas and compositional techniques. They are magnificent if only inadequate glimpses into what made Bach the "world-famous organist."

Harpsichord Music

More than any other body of Bach's music, the works for harpsichord/clavichord are the source of his early reputation and remain a significant part of his continuing fame to the present.[18] Collections such as the *Inventions* and *Sinfonias* and especially *The Well-Tempered Clavier* are staples of piano pedagogy. Yet, Bach's harpsichord music of only some two hundred pieces comprises a distinctly small part of his entire output. In addition to the well-known harpsichord works, there are a substantial number of largely early compositions of miscellaneous types originating most likely during the Arnstadt and Weimar periods.[19] They include suites (sometimes labeled "overtures" or "partitas"), fugues, three-part "sonatas," and the better-known seven toccatas, BWV 910–916, which have at times been classified as organ music.

Bach's harpsichord music served two purposes: (1) to give pleasure to the performer recreating the music ("for the refreshment of the spirit of the amateur"—*denen Liebhabern zur Gemüths-Ergötzung*), or (2) for instruction. Bach favored the basic keyboard concept of the Baroque that fosters a rich variety of affective contrasts between paired compositions. A first-movement prelude in somewhat "free" form, at times improvisational in character, explores various keyboard styles or even imitates nonkeyboard styles. In these pieces, as with the similar organ pieces called variously prelude, toccata, fantasy (fantasia), we come as close as possible to the improvisational keyboard styles for which Bach was famous. The other half of the pair, the fugue, is in striking contrast and related to its prelude only by tonality. Bach's greatest achievement in this form was, of course, *The Well-Tempered Clavier* (WTC) in two books each with twenty-four preludes and fugues composed in all of the major and minor tonalities of the chromatic scale. Bach's title for the first volume again emphasizes the performance pleasure and the instruction that the music provides:

The Well-Tempered Clavier
or
Preludes and Fugues
through all of the tones and semitones
both as regards the tertia major or Ut, Re, Mi
and as concerns the tertia minor or Re, Mi, Fa
for the use and profit
of Musical Youth Desirous of Learning
as well as
for the pastime of those already skilled in this Study

No complete autograph manuscript exists for volume II. Rather, we have only copies dating from around 1742. Volume II, generally less well known to keyboard players than volume I, has a noticeable maturity and variety of forms as well as the exploration of new styles. The preludes in volume II are infinitely varied and often of greater formal size, including sonata form, and few repeat any aspect of those in volume I. Dance idioms are prominent in the preludes and the fugues, signified in part by the noticeable decline in 4/4 time that dominated the first book. The fugue writing in the two volumes is encyclopedic in its variety of styles and formal procedures. Codification of types of fugues becomes impossible, although a few typical models can be identified as common to all of Bach's instrumental and vocal fugal compositions: the alla breve fugue related to sixteenth-century vocal practice, with a theme and at times two themes emphasizing half and quarter notes and frequent emphasis on vertical textures, especially suspensions; the fugue with an emotionally intense, grave, or sad affect, usually slow in tempo and often employing chromaticism, what Johann G. Walther labeled *fuga pathetica*. There are also fugues with toccata-type subjects and others that imitate figurations suggesting instrumental string techniques, sometimes called *Spielfugen*.[20] The fugues, contained in the majority of Bach's works but especially in these two WTC collections and *Die Kunst der Fuge* composed at the end of his life, established an imperishable legacy supplying models and inspiration for composers that continues in the twenty-first century.

Bach composed three major sets of suites of dances.[21] There is no recorded evidence of Bach playing his solo keyboard music in public, although it seems probable that there would have been opportunities to perform for his royal patrons at Weimar and Cöthen, and for his collegium audiences in Leipzig. The extensive history of suite composition reaches back to the beginnings of and even prior to the Baroque, and Bach was familiar with many dance suites, certainly those of the French *clavicinistes* including Couperin, as well as of Froberger, Telemann, and other German and Italian composers. Of the three collections the English Suites are considered to be the earliest, originating probably in Weimar. The title is not Bach's and its origin is unknown. It was already applied to the collection in Forkel's time, who says they were known as "English" Suites "because the composer made them for an Englishman of rank."[22] As with the other two collections, the English Suites consist of the standard Baroque arrangement of six works, each in a different tonality, with the usual set of four dances, allemande, courante (two in Suite I), sarabande, and gigue, prefaced by a free form labeled "prelude," and expanded by an alternative dance inserted before the gigue.

However, each suite has a rich variety of styles, mixing Italian, French, and German traits. There are the more or less homophonic textures for dances such as the sarabandes, gavottes, and minuets, the considerable complexity of two- and three-part contrapuntal movements as in the allemandes, and at times fugal texture as in several of the gigues. Some of the contrapuntal writing is complex and awkward for the hands. Of importance for the insight they give into Bach's variation techniques are the two "doubles" for the second courante in Suite I and the suggested *agréments* for the sarabandes in Suites Nos. 2 and 3. The sarabande in Suite No. 6 is also given as a varied "double." Except for the "prelude" of the first suite, a fantasia movement in three-part counterpoint, the other "preludes" are the most exceptional and remarkable pieces in these suites. They tend almost to overwhelm the structure of the suites with very long compositions, concerto movements with da capo elements. Often fugal in part, they also feature thematic recapitulations, and extended passages of repetitious but never uninteresting instrumental figuration. They remind one of the orchestral techniques of contrasting tutti and solo textures imitated, for example, in the first and third movements of the *Italian Concerto* and also in the keyboard cadenza for the *Brandenburg Concerto,* No. 5.

In contrast to the English Suites, the French Suites (also with a title of unknown origin) are much simpler in the technical demands placed on the performer. None of them have introductory preludes. All of the dances could serve as teaching pieces, unlike the English Suites with their frequently difficult contrapuntal textures and especially the long and technically challenging preludes. The autograph scores for the first five of the French Suites appear in the *Clavier-Büchlein von Anna Magdalena Bach,* dated 1722, thus placing the compositions in the Cöthen period. However, these suites underwent numerous later revisions by Bach, and the sixth suite was most likely not composed before about 1725.[23] The French Suites, the first three in A, C, and B minor, the second three in E flat, G, and E major, for the most part are not only noticeably different from the English Suites, but they present a distinct change in Bach's developing keyboard style. With few exceptions the emphasis is on two-part counterpoint, except when a dance is composed as a melody with chordal accompaniment or in some instances when the texture is enriched to three parts, usually to add further harmonic support to the contrapuntal lines. Bach shows a new interest in *galant* textures, and in some of the suites places an emphasis on *galant* dances (for example, in Suites Nos. 5 and 6). There are only two true fugues, which are found in the gigues of the first and fifth suites, the latter standing out as the most technically brilliant and difficult keyboard writing in the collection. Several of the sarabandes are arioso-like, and their expressive melodies and chordal harmonies also reflect the influence of a *galant* style.

Bach's development of the keyboard suite is perfected in the third collection, the six Partitas. They inaugurate Bach's efforts to publish some of his own music. The first Partita, labeled Op. I, appeared in 1726 as:

Keyboard Practice (Clavier-Übung)[24]
consisting of
Preludes, Allemandes, Courantes, Sarabandes, Gigues,
Minuets, and other Galanteries
Prepared for the spiritual refreshment of music lovers
by
Johann Sebastian Bach
Actual Kapellmeister of Anhalt-Cöthen and
Directore Chori Musici Lipsiensis
Partita I
Published by the Author, 1726

The subsequent five were published one each year until all six were brought together and reissued as the *Clavier-Übung,* Part I in 1731. Here Bach transforms the concept of the dance suite. He clearly aimed to compose the six parts of his first *Clavier-Übung* with an eye both toward spreading his reputation beyond the confines of central Germany and also toward generating sales at the Leipzig trade fairs, which offered new opportunities for the dissemination of his work. However, it may also be true, as Schulenberg suggests, that Bach "must have felt compelled to issue something worthy of himself and of his reputation as Germany's greatest keyboard player."[25] Each partita, in reexamining the potentialities of the dance suite and its conventional array of dance types, is unique. The six suites all begin with a different type of movement and, except for No. 4, an original form not associated with dance suites that would raise the curiosity of a potential buyer: No. 1 (B flat major), Praeludium; No. 2 (C minor), Sinfonia; No. 3 (A minor), Fantasia; No. 4 (D major), Ouverture; No. 5 (G major), Praeambulum; and No. 6 (E minor), Toccata. In addition to the unexpected individuality in form and style of the opening movements, variety is the constant rule in these suites, both in the reinterpretations of the standard dances and also with the array of added dances. Each suite contains surprises that result from the new dimensions and meanings applied to traditional dance types.

Five of the six partitas have seven movements; only No. 2 has six, although it has other distinguishing features. It lacks a gigue, for which is substituted a "capriccio," a three-part fugue with wildly leaping tenths in the subject. The "alternative" movements also add considerable variety with emphasis on simple meters and *galant* dances: No. 1, two minuets; No. 2, a rondeau; No. 3, a burlesca and a scherzo; No. 4, a minuet; No. 5, tempo di menuetto and passepied; and No. 6, tempo di gavotta. There is a marked increase in length of the suites beginning with No. 4, which contains in addition to the extended ouverture a very long allemande, sarabande, and gigue. No. 5 also has an expanded opening, a praeambulum and an extensive gigue, while the sixth suite is the longest and the climax for the entire set with its magnificent toccata–fugue–toccata opening, an elaborately embellished allemande, an extensive courante, and a sarabande with equally stunning embellishments. The most impressive achievement, however, is the final gigue. It is a fugue of severe and one might say archaic contrapuntal style, with hardly a modulation from E minor. It is light-years removed from the gigue of the first suite, and is one of Bach's most original keyboard works, relentless in its constant dotted rhythm and its startling chromatic relationships between the parts. It exists, as does so much of Bach's music, with roots deep in the past but with elements that are not so much of his present as they are of the future (see Example 17.2).

Forkel attests to Bach's exceptional and widely known achievement with the *Clavier-Übung* I:

> This work made in its time a great noise in the musical world. Such excellent compositions for the clavier had never been seen and heard before. Anyone who had learnt to perform well some pieces out of them could make his fortune in the world thereby; and even in our times, a young artist might gain acknowledgement by doing so, they are so brilliant, well-sounding, expressive, and always new.[26]

Encouraged perhaps by the success of the Partitas, Bach in the 1730s and early 1740s continued the *Clavier-Übung* series with three additional volumes of keyboard music: Part II in 1735, an Italian Concerto in F major, BWV 971, and an Overture in B minor, BWV 831; Part III in 1739 with ten chorales for organ, BWV 669–689, paired settings for keyboard alone and also with pedals, all enclosed within the great *pedaliter* Prelude and Fugue (the

EXAMPLE 17.2   Bach, Partita No. 6, Gigue

so-called St. Anne) in E flat major, BWV 552. There are also four keyboard duets, BWV 802–805, which some writers believe were intended for harpsichord, although nothing in the music makes them unsuited for organ. Finally, Part IV in 1741, a collection of thirty keyboard variations based on the bass and its harmonies of a sarabande, known as *The Goldberg Variations,* BWV 988. Both Parts II and IV are specified as composed for a two-manual harpsichord.

The *Clavier-Übung* Part II contains two major keyboard works that transfer to the keyboard the two most significant and prominent forms of contemporary orchestral music. The Italian Concerto makes clear references in its three movements to the later Venetian concerto, especially the widely known works by Vivaldi.[27] The first movement is more succinct than the typical first movement of an Italian concerto, but the opening ritornello has much of the same thrust and thematic distinction of the Italian form. Contrasts in sonorities between "solo" and "tutti" are suggested by the indications of *piano* and *forte,* often divided between the two hands and the two keyboards. The second movement even more clearly imitates many of the second movements found in Vivaldi's concertos, which usually have a reduced scoring with an aria-like melody often with elaborate embellishments. The left hand in Bach's work has a constantly repeating four-note motive across the barline and continuous eighth-note repetitions in the bass. The right hand resembles an instrumental solo over this simple instrumental accompaniment, which Bach expands with lavish and exceedingly expressive embellishments (see Example 17.3).

The last movement, with its *presto* tempo, again in ritornello form, is both more brilliant and dancelike than the opening movement. Indications of tutti and solo contrasts usually extend over longer sections than in the first movement, and there is more contrapuntal interest, the latter element of style being decidedly not characteristic of the Vivaldian concerto.

The Overture in B minor, by contrast, is based on the most prominent musical representative of French national style, which by this time had become an international genre

EXAMPLE 17.3 Bach, Italian Concerto

employed not only for keyboard music but also for various other instrumental works such as orchestral suites and opera overtures. Bach's *Ouverture* is similar to the D major one that opens Partita No. 4. The slow, heavily dotted opening section has the same length and style. Both fugues are quite long, although the D major one is even longer. They are similar in their dancelike subjects, the Partita fugue in 6/8, the B minor one in 9/8. The latter, however, is distinctive in its Italian concerto-like episodes. The *Clavier-Übung* extends the length of the movement by repeating the entire opening section at the conclusion of the fugue. The added dances, two gavottes, two passepieds, and two bourrées are all simple, in two-part textures except for the bourrées. The jewel among these dances, however, is the sarabande. The style of a sarabande is suggested by the 3/4 meter and the frequent though very subtle stresses on the second beat. But there is no dancelike character. This sarabande is an eloquent and subdued expression of reflective or perhaps elegiac affect. Largely in four parts with frequent recourse to *style brisé* passages, the inner voices match and enrich the melody by their expressiveness. The gigue, unexpectedly, is followed by an inventive and humorous "Echo," a concerto-like binary movement in which forte "tutti" measures are quickly repeated by piano echoes suited to the second manual of a harpsichord.

The crowning glory of Bach's series of "keyboard exercises" is certainly the fourth publication, an extraordinary set of variations published in 1741:

Keyboard Practice
consisting of an
ARIA
with various variations for
harpsichord with two manuals
composed to refresh the spirits of music lovers
by Johann Sebastian Bach
Royal Polish and Electoral Saxon Composer,
Kapellmeister, and Director Chori Musici in Leipzig
Published in Nürnberg by Balthasar Schmid

The title of "The Goldberg Variations" originated with Forkel, who related how the former Russian ambassador to Saxony, Count Kaiserling, had asked Bach to compose some pieces that his harpsichordist Johann Gottlieb Goldberg could play for him during his long sleepless nights resulting from illness. The count expressed his delight in the variations by presenting Bach with a gold goblet filled with a hundred Louis d'Ors.[28] Curiously, there is no mention of either Count Kaiserling or Goldberg on the title page of Bach's score, which has suggested to some that the origins of the work as told by Forkel may not be true. The work itself, one of the great examples of keyboard variations, deserves its universal fame because of its unprecedented scope, craftsmanship, its formal organization, and the manifold variety of the individual variations. The basis for the variations is the opening "aria," a thirty-two-bar sarabande divided into two sixteen-bar sections, each to be repeated. Some writers have erred in describing the variations as composed on an ostinato bass. Although the bass notes often appear as a structural element in the variations, many of them vary the bass line, ornament it, place it on a beat other than the first, move it up into the other parts, or even eliminate it. Bach's variations are essentially harmonic, even if Bach uses substitute harmonies for those in the sarabande. It is one of Bach's remarkable achievements that the thirty variations remain so closely connected to the harmonic structure of the sarabande, and yet are also so often freed from restrictions of that harmonic plan.

Bach was focused, especially in his Leipzig years, on creating a structural logic in his works, and in the Goldberg Variations that logic is the essential feature. Its organization amalgamates several different formal procedures. Every third variation is canonic, beginning with a canon at the unison; the interval of imitation then is enlarged for each succeeding one: to the second, third, fourth, fifth, sixth, seventh, eighth, ninth, for a total of nine canons. At the midpoint of the work, variation 16 opens the second half of the thirty variations appropriately with a French overture. The Goldberg Variations consist of a compendium of Baroque keyboard styles and contrapuntal ingenuity. For example, one finds dances, highly ornamented variations (variations 13 and the profoundly melancholic variation 25), brilliant etudes with hand-crossing technique requiring two keyboards (variations 5 and 20), trio sonata textures (variation 18), fughetta (variation 10), *alla breve* texture (variation 22). The last variation is a quodlibet, in which Bach brings together two apparently well-known folk tunes, perhaps as a kind of "in-joke," although it remains unclear exactly what the joke was. The work concludes with a return to the opening sarabande.

However, in fact, Bach was not through with the work since, as was discovered in the mid-1970s, his own copy of the published work, which includes invaluable emendations to the printed score of ornaments and tempo and articulation indications, turned up in France. The stunning surprise was that Bach had appended a formerly unknown autograph addition entitled "Diverse canons upon the first eight notes of the preceding Aria's fundamental bass notes."[29] The manuscript gives the first eight bass notes of the sarabande with written and notational clues supplying the key to the realization of these fourteen "riddle" canons. At the bottom of the fourteenth canon Bach inscribes the abbreviation for "et cetera," suggesting that he believed these eight bass notes had the potential for an endless series of new canons. Here we have further evidence of the centrality of the canon to his creativity, a preoccupation with canonic form that appears throughout his music, especially in his late works such as the canonic variations on *Vom Himmel hoch* and the canons in the *Musical Offering*.

No examination of Bach's harpsichord music can fail to discuss his most unusual and, during his lifetime and later, one of his most popular keyboard works, the Chromatic Fantasie and Fugue, BWV 903. It was Forkel who summed up in a few words the character of this work: "I have taken infinite pains to discover another piece of this kind by Bach, but in vain. The fantasia is unique, and never had its like."[30] The original manuscript is lost, but there remain the extraordinary number of thirty-seven sources, many of them from late in the eighteenth century, that give testimony to the work's long-lived popularity.[31] There are a great number of versions of the work, and undoubtedly the evolution began with Bach himself, probably in Cöthen, and then continued with his sons and students. The changes to the score became especially prominent after 1750, and published editions began in 1802 and continued unabated through the twentieth century. Forkel's observation of the work's uniqueness is confirmed by the Fantasie, an extraordinary musical oration for the harpsichord that demonstrates Bach's immersion in undefined yet clearly passionate and overtly tragic affects, a *musica pathetica* that Walther defined as "eine die Affecten bewegende oder erregende Music" (music that moves or excites the affects).[32]

This Fantasie, although a free form related to keyboard improvisation, is given in its three distinct parts an increasingly dramatic and expressive structure. It begins simply with two measures of scale flourishes, followed by a section based on broken chords and the first intimations of the chromatic half step. A second section changes the style of the fantasy from scales and broken chords to arpeggios. These are written as three- and four-part chords for both hands, which the performer is asked to improvise as arpeggios. They move through predominantly dissonant harmonies. The complex third and final section is, as Bach indicates, a recitative of ever-increasing tensions and passionate affect. The falling chromatic second becomes the focus of the chordal outbursts that punctuate the recitative line. This same figure finally becomes the controlling musical force in the concluding bars as the harmonic and melodic textures descend through the entire D minor scale, each scale degree being harmonized with an extraordinary series of dissonant chords, a passage that is indeed "unique" in the works of Bach (see Example 17.4).

Out of what has been a musical journey through some of Bach's most dissonant and singularly stressful music, the fugue that is initiated with a subject of four chromatic notes restores a balanced and rational order of the contrapuntal style.

Chamber Music

Bach undoubtedly had many opportunities to perform chamber music to entertain the court at Cöthen and also during the Collegium concert series in Leipzig. It is regrettable that so much of this music appears to be lost, and the total remaining chamber music is very small. A good bit even of what has earlier been assumed to be chamber music by Bach now is considered to be spurious. Yet, what remains is by no means unimportant, for the works include the great unaccompanied violin sonatas and partitas, BWV 1001–

EXAMPLE 17.4   Bach, Chromatic Fantasie and Fugue, BWV 903

1006, and the unaccompanied cello suites, BWV 1007–1012. There are six remarkable sonatas for keyboard and violin, BWV 1014–1019, two sonatas for violin and continuo, BWV 1021, 1023, three sonatas for harpsichord and viola da gamba, BWV 1027–1029, two sonatas for flute and keyboard, BWV 1030, 1032, two flute sonatas with continuo, BWV 1034–1035, and the sonata (partita) for solo flute, BWV 1013 (composed in Cöthen). BWV 1027 is an arrangement of BWV 1039, a sonata for two flutes and continuo.

The unaccompanied violin works combine the formal elements of Italian church and chamber sonatas with an expanded and immensely enriched technical style of solo violin music. The concept is German. Earlier composers such as Biber, Johann Jakob Walther, and Nicolaus Bruhns all employed polyphonic writing in their solo violin music, including high positions and multiple stops that have prominence in Bach's works. However, solo violin music without a continuo bass line for realization was rare, and perhaps the first to compose solo polyphonic music for violin was the obscure Johann Paul von Westhoff (1656–1705) of Dresden, whom Bach probably met in Weimar in 1703. Later Westhoff also served the Weimar court between 1699 and 1705,[33] and his unaccompanied violin music may have influenced Bach. It is not known why Bach composed the solo violin works, although Forkel suggests that they as well as the cello solos became instructional examples highly prized by students to perfect their mastery of the instruments,[34] and this remains true to the present day.

Bach completed these works at Cöthen in 1720. The six alternate three sonatas with the three partitas, the former resembling the Italian church sonata with the alternation of slow and fast movements, while the partitas consist largely of the standard variety of dance types. There are, however, surprises. The three sonatas in G minor, A minor, and C major begin with a variety of preludes and fugues and the Sonata in G minor includes a siciliana. The preludes of the first two sonatas are introspective, highly embellished examples of violin improvisation at its most compelling. The second and third fugues are exceedingly long and with the exception of the famous chaconne at the end of the Partita in D minor, by far the most challenging music to be realized on the solo violin. The first Partita in B minor has a separate variation (double) for each of the four dances: allemande, courante, sarabande, and tempo di borea (bourrée). Both the sonatas and partitas have a variety of violinistic challenges that include in addition to multiple stops rapid cross-string technique (bariolage) and passages in high positions.

The capstone to Bach's achievements in these works is the concluding chaconne of the second Partita, a work that has never lost its fame as a grandiose composition based on the most improbable of musical circumstances: an enormous set of figurative and harmonic variations on an ostinato thorough-bass that would seem impossible on an instrument with four treble strings. The sixty-three variations evolve from the harmonic design of a continuo line (D, C sharp, D, B flat, G, A, C sharp, D, and its variations), just as an unstated but clearly evident continuo bass structures the other movements of the sonatas and partitas.[35] The Baroque in all the arts tends to strive for illusion, for achieving the impossible, and for creating the monumental, and this may also be seen in this example of Bach's innovative compositional genius. The Chaconne in its dazzling originality and musical grandeur leaves behind all previous stylistic and technical conceptions of music for violin.

The six suites for solo cello, BW 1007–1012, also originated during Bach's Cöthen period. Except for a few pieces composed by Bolognese composers early in the century, there was no precedent set for composing for solo cello. These suites are the equal of the solo violin works in originality and command of the technical limitations of the instrument. Each has the conventional movements of the sonata da camera: prelude, allemande, courante, sarabande, "optional dance," and gigue. In Suites No. 1 (G major) and No. 2 (D minor), the optional dance is the minuet; in No. 3 (C major) and No. 4 (E flat major), bourrées; and in V (C minor) and No. 6 (D minor), gavottes. The fifth suite introduces scordatura, tuning the A string down a whole tone, and the last suite calls for a cello with a fifth string, E above the A string.

In contrast to the violin works, these suites are somewhat less adventuresome in the technical demands placed on the performer. The overall impression is largely linear, with any apparent contrapuntal interest arising out of Bach's ability to create the impression of contrapuntal lines within the single melodic design. Because the cello is a bass string instrument, the harmonic structure of these suites is usually clearly derived from a more or less obvious bass (continuo) line. Many of the movements, but especially the preludes, are based on various typical string patterns that often suggest improvisations on the continuo bass structure. One must add, however, that this is made musically compelling by Bach's ability to find new variations for typical bass patterns. Multiple stops are rare in the first four suites, except in the sarabandes, but in the final two suites the prevalence of chordal passages increases markedly as does the overall technical complexity of many of their movements. The fifth suite in C minor is exceptional in that the prelude is actually a French overture. The stately opening in duple meter with dotted rhythms and frequent runs leading to the next downbeat is followed by a remarkable fugue in triple meter in which Bach creates the illusion of separate contrapuntal lines. Later, in Leipzig, Bach arranged this suite for lute, transposed to G minor (BWV 995).

Among the other chamber works, the sonatas for violin, viola da gamba, and flute with concertante harpsichord are among Bach's most original and incomparable instrumental ensemble achievements. Composition of them probably began in Cöthen and was completed in Leipzig. As with the solo violin and cello works, Bach again created an instrumental form for which there was no precedent: solo sonatas with written-out keyboard parts, in effect three-part contrapuntal compositions.[36] The first five of the six violin sonatas (in B minor, A major, E major, C minor, and F minor) have a regular, four-movement, slow, fast, slow, fast, "church sonata" form. The fast movements are largely fugues or highly imitative, often virtuosic pieces with blithesome themes in which concerted interplay between violin and harpsichord is notable. The slow movements contain some of Bach's most beautiful and profound essays in serious, sad, or lamenting affects. The variety of forms also include canon (No. 2, third movement), modulating ostinato (No. 3, third movement), and ritornello and da capo movements.

The origins of the sixth sonata in G major are complex, with two earlier versions preceding the final form as found in the manuscript copied by Altnikol. Of the five movements only the first two remain from the two earlier versions.[37] The inconsistencies with the previous five sonatas are several. Five movements instead of four, the ordering of the movements by tempo indications is changed from slow, fast, slow, fast to fast, slow, fast, slow, fast. While the first five retain the opening tonality for all movements except the third, the sixth sonata retains the opening tonality only in the last movement. Most unusual, however, is the third movement, an allegro for harpsichord solo, the longest movement in the sonata, in two sections, each repeated, and technically challenging. It is perhaps not unreasonable to see this harpsichord solo as serving Bach's desire to impress upon his collegium audience not only his command of the harpsichord but also to underscore Bach's belief so amply demonstrated in these sonatas as well as those for viola da gamba and for flute that he has emancipated the harpsichord from its bondage to the basso continuo.

Another work by Bach requiring an ensemble of instruments is the *Musical Offering* (BWV 1079). It is unique among Bach's oeuvre, and not a traditional chamber work, but its significance to Bach's instrumental works should not be overlooked. It is a composite collection of contrapuntal inventiveness with two ricercars (fugues), ten canons, and a concluding sonata *à3* for flute, violin, and basso continuo in four movements. The concept is as unusual as its origins, which are well known: Bach visited Potsdam near Berlin in May 1747 to visit his son Carl Philipp Emanuel, his wife, and their first child. C. P. E. Bach was harpsichordist to King Frederick the Great, in his own right a celebrated flutist who held frequent musical soirees in the royal palace. Bach's fame preceded him and the king invited him to hear the royal music-making. Almost immediately upon Bach's arrival the king presented him with his own "royal" theme on which Bach was asked to improvise a fugue. The king further asked that he also improvise a six-part fugue, for which Bach did not attempt to use the royal theme but rather employed one of his own composition. After he returned to Leipzig, Bach composed and had published on 1 October 1747 the expanded set of contrapuntal treatments of King Frederick's theme as a gift for Frederick. In the preface to the original edition, Bach stated that his focus and aim in composing the collection known as the *Musical Offering* were in "working out" in homage to Frederick the King's "right Royal theme more fully and then to make it known to the world."[38]

Orchestral Music and the Concertos

The orchestra as a major institution for public and private concerts developed late in the seventeenth century. In Bach's day there were no standards for what defined an orchestra, and many courts had small groups, often quite inadequately staffed from any point of view. Except at the more wealthy courts, orchestras in Bach's region of Germany were scarce and often changing in their personnel. The poor quality of these ensembles and the absence of others may have led Bach to avoid writing a great deal of music for orchestra. Yet, what remains is surely smaller in number than one would have expected and suggests that much of it must be lost. No orchestral music seems to survive, for example, from the Weimar period, even though Bach actively participated as concertmaster in that court ensemble. And there is very little orchestral music from the Leipzig period, although for many years Bach was director of the collegium musicum whose regular concerts at times must have included music for some form of orchestra. Bach's major employment of an orchestral ensemble is found in his cantatas and other large vocal works as well as in those related to his various concertos.

The four Overtures (or Suites), BWV 1066–1068, are the only surviving orchestral works not belonging to the concerto genre. The lack of autographs makes dating these works impossible. Only the first in C major may have been composed in Cöthen, while the other three probably originated in Leipzig where Bach could have composed them for his collegium concerts. Although clearly not planned as a set of overtures, they are all related by their brilliant adaptation of the French overture. Each of the four begins with the traditional two-part overture: a majestic, heavily dotted, and extensive opening movement in duple rhythm followed by a fugue and a concluding but varied repetition of the opening section. The French origins of Bach's concept stand out in the variety of dance movements and *galanteries* that follow the opening overtures, each group of dances being different: No. 1 (C major) Courante, Gavotte I and II, Forlane, Menuet I and II, Bourrée I and II, Passepied I and II; No. 2 (B minor) Rondeau, Sarabande, Bourrée I and II, Polonaise and double, Badinerie, a brilliant, concerto-like movement for solo flute; No. 3 (D major) Air (later in a popular arrangement for violin known as the "Air on the G string"),[39] Gavotte I and II, Bourrée, Gigue; No. 4 (D major) Bourrée, Gavotte, Menuet I and II, Réjouissance.

The first two overtures are somewhat similar in adding woodwinds to the ensemble, in the first two, oboes and bassoon, and in the second, solo flute. Also the fugues in the C major and B minor overtures have similar subjects that employ themes with regular rhythmic patterns clearly marking entrances throughout the fugues. Even more obviously related are Overtures No. 3 and No. 4, both in D major with three trumpets and timpani. The third adds two oboes to the strings and the fourth, three oboes and bassoon. The fugue subjects in the two D major overtures are also similar. In the first there is an almost continuous flow of eighth and two sixteenths patterns, with only one intervening contrast of leaping eighth notes. Even more continuous is the subject in the fugue of the fourth overture with its steady stream of triplet figures and almost no other defining melodic motive. The longest of the four fugues, it is a contrapuntal *tour de force* of instrumental virtuosity. Bach employed the opening two movements of this overture as the first movement of the Leipzig Christmas cantata, BWV 110, *Unser Mund sei voll Lachens*. The slow instrumental opening is followed by a remarkable adaptation for voices of the instrumental fugue. The text's emphasis on laughter (*Lachen*) suggests the reason for the ebullient affect Bach extracted from the instrumental fugue.

The Italian concept of the concerto became one of the defining forms of Baroque music attracting composers and audiences of all nationalities. From 1715, at least much of Europe, and most especially Germany, was awash in Italian instrumental music. It was widely imitated and developed until eventually it was replaced by the predominant orchestral form of the symphony. Bach, as has been noted, became interested in the new style of Italian music already in Weimar, especially as demonstrated in works by Vivaldi. He adapted concertos both by him and other composers for keyboard, and wrote a significant number of instrumental and solo concertos, the most notable being the six Brandenburg Concertos, BWV 1046–1051.

The title of these works, which is not Bach's, refers to those precious manuscript copies of six concertos for orchestra that Bach sent to the Margrave of Brandenburg in March 1721, together with a lengthy dedication[40] explaining the origins of his musical gift. Here he refers to a visit he made to Berlin two years earlier when he played for the Margrave, who requested that Bach send him some of his compositions. The resulting six concertos "avec plusieurs instruments"[41] have been called "the most inspired and complex concerti grossi of the baroque era."[42] While the dedication to the composite manuscript containing the six concertos is dated 1721, this does not suggest that in the preceding two years Bach had composed all of these concertos. It seems probable that the Brandenburg concertos had been written for and played by the orchestra Bach directed at Cöthen. Earlier versions of three movements from the first concerto are extant as a Sinfonia in F major (BWV 1046a), and there is also an earlier form of the fifth concerto with a much briefer harpsichord cadenza. The earlier forms of two of the concertos suggest the possibility that Bach may have included other existing works or their adaptations in those he presented to the Margrave. Although the six Brandenburg Concertos have some stylistic relationships with Vivaldi's works, they are, however, unique in the unprecedented variety of forms with no two instrumentations being alike:

I.	2 horns	II.	trumpet	III.	3 violins
	3 oboes		recorder		3 violas
	bassoon		oboe		3 cellos
	violino piccolo		violin		
	(tuned a minor 3rd higher)				
	+		+		+
	vls. I & II, vla., cello		vls. I & II, vla., violone		b.c. with violone
	b.c. with violone		b.c. with cello		G major
	F major		F major		
IV.	violin	V.	transverse flute	VI.	2 violas
	2 recorders		violin		2 violas da gamba
			harpsichord		
	+		+		+
	vls. I & II, vla., cello		vls. I & II, vla., cello		cello, violone
	b.c. with violone		b.c. with violone		b.c.
	G major		D major		B flat major

The six concertos can be viewed as organized into two groups of three, each with highly different characters: the more modern Italian concertos, Nos. 2, 4, and 5, and those with stronger German characteristics, Nos. 1, 3, and 6. The first concerto is a grand, festive composition with royal horns, and the fourth a vigorous example of competitive virtuosity between a solo violin and two recorders. Each group ends with the smallest grouping of instruments of the three, and they also lack a ripieno/solo contrast (though single instruments are still contrasted against the whole ensemble). Thus, two concertos in each group for a mixed set of instruments are followed by one for a homogeneous grouping of (solo?) strings alone. Also interesting is that the concertos begin with a work requiring the largest number of players, and this requirement diminishes through to the sixth concerto (thirteen, ten, eleven, nine, seven, and seven instrumental parts). Nos. 1, 2, and 4 employ in the first movements the concerto/ritornello form for more than one instrument in the solo group. No. 3 is a "concerto grosso" for solo instruments, while No. 5 in its opening movement approaches the condition of being the first original solo keyboard concerto, with ritornello form and (in its revised form) with a majestic harpsichord cadenza. No. 6 would also appear to be an adaptation of the concerto grosso form for solo instruments with the remaining parts serving as accompaniment. Only No. 1 has five movements in its final form (or seven movements counting the trios to the Menuet and Polacca). Nos. 1, 2, 3, and 5 all have opening movements with powerfully concentrated affects, while Nos. 4 and 6 have affects that are more relaxed and quieter.[43] Exactly what impression this stunning variety of instrumental works made on the Margrave is unknown. Bach's intention, it seems clear, was to send him a collection of instrumental works with the greatest possible variety of forms and instruments, hoping to impress his patron with the extraordinary richness of his musical inventiveness. It seems probable that Bach had already grown dissatisfied with his career at the Cöthen court, and that he saw this as an opportunity to establish himself as a potential candidate at the Margrave's court where music was regarded as having greater significance.

In addition to the Brandenburg Concertos there remain seventeen concertos for solo or a combination of solo instruments. Of those, very few are original works and not arrangements of pre-existent scores. Some or perhaps all of them may have been composed in Cöthen: they are BWV 1041, a concerto for violin in A minor, BWV 1042; a concerto for violin in E major; and BWV 1043, a concerto for two violins in D minor. These masterworks underscore the extent to which Bach had absorbed in Cöthen the Vivaldi model of the concerto into his now mature and distinctively original instrumental style.

Superficially, they are Vivaldian: vigorous opening movements cast in some form of ritornello structure; the middle movements slow with expressive melodies and ostinato basses (ostinato rhythm in BWV 1043); and final movements fast and dancelike (in Concertos No. 1 and No. 2). Here comparisons must end. The A minor concerto is closest to the Italian model with a substantial ritornello in the conventional three parts of *Vordersatz, Fortspinnung,* and *Epilog.* These thematic segments, however, consist of smaller melodic modules that are combined and developed variously in the solo sections and in the orchestral accompaniment. The ritornello returns are brief and never complete, but they are separated either by new solo material or by the solo violin developing material out of the ritornello. The first movement of the second violin concerto in E major is less complex and opens with a Vivaldian three-part ritornello. The movement has three clearly defined sections similar to a da capo form. The extensive central section, in C sharp minor, is strongly developmental as the solo violin provides elaborately embellished passages concerted against thematic material in the orchestra and taken from the ritornello. The movement concludes with a written-out repeat of the entire first part. The greatest divergence from the Italian first movement plan occurs in the concerto for two violins. Here the three-part ritornello is replaced by a fugue for the solo instruments and the orchestra, followed by a new subject in canon between the violins. These two themes dominate the movement, often with fugal and canonic writing between the solo parts.

The variety of musical forms characteristic of the first movements is also found in the third movements, each with a different one: a gigue in the first, a rondeau in the second, and for the third an extended concerted movement with cross-rhythms between the two solo violins and the orchestra, as well as extensive canonic and imitative passages between the solo instruments. The slow movements are similar to one another in their lyrical orientation. In the first and second concertos, Bach composes against unyielding and somber ostinato basses some of his freest and most beautifully structured and embellished melodies for the violin. The double concerto has, if that is possible, an even more beautiful movement, a largo with a continuous siciliana rhythm. The two soloists weave together a continuously flowing melody of exquisite calmness and peace hardly of the real world, Bach's or ours.

The remaining fourteen concertos probably were all assembled in Leipzig for collegium musicum concerts. With two exceptions, they originate as arrangements of previous concertos by Bach. Six solo harpsichord concertos, BWV 1052–1056 and 1058 are adapted from violin concertos. BWV 1057 is a harpsichord concerto with two recorders and strings based on the Brandenburg Concerto No. 4. There are also concertos for two harpsichords, original work unidentified, BWV 1060–1061, and another, BWV 1062, arranged from Bach's double violin concerto in D minor. Two concertos exist for three harpsichords, BWV 1063–1064, originals also unidentified. One concerto, BWV 1044 for flute, violin, harpsichord in A minor, was put together with arrangements from the Prelude and Fugue in A minor, BWV 894 for movements 1 and 3, and movement 2 from the D minor Organ Sonata, BWV 527. Also, a concerto for four harpsichords in A minor, BWV 1065, was adapted from Vivaldi's concerto for four violins in B minor, Op. 3, No. 10. Clearly, concertos were a very popular aspect of collegium concerts in Leipzig, and one of the attractions undoubtedly was the presence of Bach himself and his sons at the keyboards.

Vocal Works

THE CANTATAS

The number of cantatas composed by Bach cannot be accurately determined. According to the obituary prepared by C. P. E. Bach and Johann Friedrich Agricola, Bach composed five annual cycles (*Jahrgänge*) of church pieces for all the Sundays and feast days of the church year.[44] With approximately sixty cantatas per year, this suggests he wrote some three hundred cantatas, of which only around two hundred sacred cantatas survive today. The obituary, however, does not mention the extant cantatas originating in Mühlhausen or a number of cantatas composed in Weimar, many of which were reused for performances in Leipzig. The chronology of the extant works[45] indicates that Bach began his Leipzig tenure with an extraordinary outpouring of cantatas completing two cycles for the first two years. Evidence begins to dwindle for a third year, and little seems to remain of sacred cantatas for year four. One can account for forty-two new cantatas belonging to the first cycle; the second cycle (the chorale cantatas cycle) consists of about fifty works. Only forty-six works can be identified as part of a third cycle and just nine for the fourth cycle. No evidence remains of a fifth cycle, although some cantatas were still composed sporadically into the 1740s. According to the most recent tally of sacred cantatas composed by Bach, 194 works remain out of at least 295.[46] This number does not include Bach's secular cantatas nor those with sacred texts performed outside of the church liturgy, for example, at weddings, town council elections, funerals and memorial services, and so on.

The loss of more than 140 cantatas can best be explained by the fact that, upon Bach's death, his musical estate was divided primarily between his oldest sons and his wife. Forkel is again our witness in speaking of Bach's many unpublished vocal works: "The annual sets [the cantata *Jahrgänge*] were divided after the author's death between the elder sons, and in such a manner that Wilhelm Friedemann had the larger share because, in the place which he then filled at Halle, he could make the most use of them. In the sequel, his circumstances obliged him to part, by degrees, with what he had obtained."[47] Other documentary evidence, especially the inventory of C. P. E. Bach's estate, indicates he inherited the first cycle in alternating scores and parts, and the third cycle largely in scores with duplicate parts. The second cycle, the chorale cantatas, were divided between Anna Magdalena Bach, who received the parts and gave them to the St. Thomas School, and W. F. Bach who received the scores and duplicate parts.[48]

Even though only 194 cantatas remain, they make up the largest body of music Bach composed in any one form, consisting of some 1,270 individual movements. An understanding as to what this massive amount of sacred music means for the evaluation of Bach's musical genius and to the period of music history labeled the Baroque has been slow to be realized. By the mid-nineteenth century these works were almost totally forgotten. It was the audacity and courage of the Bach Gesellschaft's decision to publish all of Bach's music that saved the remaining cantatas from being lost and inspired Bach "revivals" that continue to the present day. Yet, it can be said that for most of the twentieth century very few of the cantatas became widely known. The change in interest came about by the enormous growth in post–Second World War Bach scholarship, the intensive study of Bach manuscripts, and the establishment of a new and better-informed chronology for the vocal works. Equally important was the development of the so-called early music movement and the invention of the LP record and later the CD. It hardly seems possible that before 1970 there was no complete recording of Bach's cantatas, but now there are three.

Bach gave the title of "cantata" only to his secular solo cantatas. For some types of cantatas he used "concerto," for others, "dialogus." Most of Bach's cantatas, however, bear no title, and they have become familiar to us by two different means: either they are referred to by the opening line of their text or, especially among Bach scholars and others who are knowledgeable, by the number given to each in sequence as they were published in the volumes of the original Bach Gesellschaft.[49]

Arnstadt/Mühlhausen Cantatas (1703–1708)

Examples of cantatas by Bach exist beginning with his career in Arnstadt/Mühlhausen and then from each subsequent position. Only in Cöthen were these works of necessity limited to secular cantatas. Six cantatas originate in Arnstadt/Mühlhausen, the earliest preserved examples of Bach's vocal music: BWV 4, *Christ lag in Todesbanden* (extant only in Bach's revision for Leipzig); BWV 106, *Gottes Zeit ist die allerbeste Zeit;* BWV 71, *Gott ist mein König;* BWV 131, *Aus der Tiefen rufe ich, Herr, zu dir;* BWV 196, *Der Herr denkt an uns;* and BWV 150, *Nach dir, Herr, verlanget mich.* They are composed in the seventeenth-century form, without recitatives or da capo arias, and with no suggestion of Italian influence on melodic form. Movements, which tend to be short, are usually more or less continuous.

BWV 71, *Gott ist mein König,* was composed for a church service in February 1708 celebrating the election of the Mühlhausen town council. The council printed both the score and parts, the only cantata published in Bach's lifetime that is extant.[50] Appropriately, it has the earliest example in a cantata of Bach's "festival" scoring, with three trumpets, timpani, two recorders and two oboes, bassoon, violins I and II, viola, cello, violone, and organ (with obbligato). The four-part chorus (*Coro pleno*) is contrasted in places with a reduction to a four-part solo ensemble. This is noteworthy in the final fugue, "muss täglich von neuem," in which the first exposition, beginning with four solo voices without instrumental doublings, is expanded to six voices with independent entrances by oboe I/violin I and oboe II/violin II. The second exposition is sung "tutti" as instruments are added progressively to the voice parts until finally chorus and orchestra all participate in the resonant climax of the fugue. This technique of progressively adding instrumental and vocal parts to create a fugal climax is found later in many of the Leipzig cantatas. The fugue in movement 3, "Dein Alter sei wie deine Jugend," also has important significance as apparently the earliest example of a new type of Bach fugue found in his early vocal compositions, the so-called permutation fugue, that is, a fugue without episodes, rather like a round, in which the subject is divided into sections and the subsequent answers exhibit the characteristics of invertible counterpoint:

Soprano subject A:	a	b	c	d	etc.			
Alto answer B:		a	b	c	d	etc.		
Tenor subject A:			a	b	c	d	etc.	
Bass answer B:				a	b	c	d	etc.

Among the other earliest cantatas, probably written in Arnstadt, perhaps for a Mühlhausen audition, BWV 4, *Christ lag in Todesbanden,* assumed to be composed for an Easter service, has become one of Bach's best known. Although the manuscript copies of the parts[51] belong to the Leipzig period, the music they contain has convincingly been proven to belong to Bach's earliest period of cantata composition. This is in part confirmed by the total absence of any of the characteristic features of the so-called Neumeister cantata form to be found in Bach's works beginning in Weimar. In this cantata, Bach employs the seventeenth-century form of chorale variations found, for example, in works by Buxtehude and Pachelbel. The cantata consists of a set of cantus firmus variations on all seven stanzas of Martin Luther's Easter chorale. They are preceded by a brief but highly expressive Sinfonia for two violins, two violas, and continuo with dark Lenten colors and, embedded in the first violin part, a reference to the opening phrase of the chorale. The highly structured format of the cantata will appear frequently in later works. (Italic type indicates the parts carrying the cantus firmus):

Verse:	I	II	III	IV	V	VI	VII
	Chorus	Duet	Solo	Quartet	Solo	Duet	Chorus
	SATB	*SA*	*T*	*SA*TB	*B*	*S/T*	SATB

The repetition of the same vocal forms as pairs on either side of the central movement (No. IV) creates a balanced structure or chiastic design analogous to the Christian symbol of the Cross that was favored frequently in Bach's sacred compositions. Each movement presents the chorale in a different context, which is based on Bach's masterful interpretation of key words and their musical-rhetorical emphasis. Assuming Bach composed this cantata about 1707–1708 when he was twenty-two or twenty-three, it is then a remarkable example of his musical maturity and the early stage in his development leading to the chorale cantatas composed in Leipzig.

Among the cantatas believed to have originated in Mühlhausen, BWV 106, *Gottes Zeit ist die allerbeste Zeit (Actus tragicus)* stands out clearly as the greatest achievement of a composer in his early twenties. It is the "work of genius as other great masters only seldom achieve and with which the 22-year old with one stroke leaves behind him all of his contemporaries. Indeed, one may say that Bach's art in succeeding years became still more mature but hardly more profound. The *Actus tragicus* is a piece of world literature."[52] The score is lost and the only source comes from the second half of the eighteenth century. The purpose of the cantata remains unknown, although previous suggestions that it was composed as a funeral service for the composer's uncle, Tobias Lämmerhirt, remain unconfirmed. The scoring for just two recorders, two violas da gamba, continuo, and a four-part vocal ensemble is unusual (perhaps influenced by similar combinations found in Buxtehude's works). It shares features with BWV 131, which is datable to 30 May 1707. Like this cantata, BWV 106 has no recitatives, employs a form of pseudo-ostinato basses in continuo arias, and has a curious melodic trait of frequent tone repetitions. There are the

EXAMPLE 17.5 Bach, *Gottes Zeit ist die allerbeste Zeit (Actus tragicus),* BWV 106

always surprising and somehow amusing "piano" final cadences in sections five and eight that also appear in BWV 131.

The text, which is drawn together from various passages in the Bible, is a highly effective dramatic construction, almost operatic, in which there is a progression from the inevitability of death, according to God's Law of the Old Testament, to the comfort and victory over death through Christ of the New Testament. These ideas are combined dramatically and musically in the powerful central section of the work, a grand theological antithesis depicting in music the confrontation of death and eternal life. A three-part fugue (alto, tenor, bass) initiates a dirgelike march over a walking bass. The subject expresses with its minor second and leap of a tritone the affect of sadness and pain of the text, which is repeated over and over again for "Mankind you must die" (Ecclesiasticus 14:7) (see Example 17.5).

The fugue is interrupted by the musical consolation of the soprano line: "Yes, yes come Lord Jesus" (Revelation 22:20), which is supported by the third musical element of this dramatic scene: the superposition over the voices of the funeral hymn *Ich hab' mein Sach Gott heimgestellt* heard in the recorders and viola da gamba. The fugue returns, is combined with the plea heard in the soprano part, as additional phrases of the chorale bear down on the voices. In one of the most moving passages in Bach's vocal works, the unrelenting progress toward the certainty of death stops as the fugue suddenly collapses. The chorus reaches the final "sterben" and the passage breaks down into a soaring three-part melisma in eighth notes first over a B flat and then an F pedal. The chorus ends on a V°/7 chord as the soprano enters on the D flat ninth with the syllable "Je-." The penultimate measure with the instruments silent except for the throbbing continuo pedal on F proceeds with a soprano melisma of a kind and beauty unknown otherwise in Bach that completes the word Jesus and concludes with one last "Herr Jesu." In the next measure, "Je- (with a trill) su" is sung in utter silence (see Example 17.6). It is a moment of great genius. Bach makes clear that those who had been making the fearful march to death had found Jesus and that death had been silenced, confirmed in the final measure by fermatas over whole note rests in all of the parts. This example of religious conviction merged into highly original musical imagination documents the profound development of the young Bach's command of his compositional talent and inspiration.

Weimar Cantatas (1714–1716)

The twenty-two extant sacred cantatas Bach composed in Weimar coincide primarily with the years 1714-1716.[53] They resulted because of the duties defining his new position as concertmaster, one of which was to compose a sacred cantata every four weeks for a service in the ducal chapel. The poetry for most of these works was written by Salomo Franck (1659-1725), Weimar court poet-in-residence. He was one of the most gifted German poets of the time and Bach obviously found his poetry especially appealing. His texts are greatly influenced by the reforms instituted by the Hamburg minister Erdmann Neumeister (1671–1756), who had been a student at the University of Leipzig and worked for a time in Weissenfels. Neumeister had introduced the term *cantata* for his cycles of sacred vocal texts, thus emphasizing their connection with recitative and aria forms of Italian opera and secular cantatas. Two of Bach's Weimar cantatas (BWV 18 and 61) are composed to Neumeister texts.

The most significant development found in the Weimar cantatas is Bach's first use of the Italianate recitative and aria forms. He appears immediately to fully command the resources of musical expression and design inherent in them. Bach composed simple recitatives with continuo accompaniment and about one-third of them as accompanied recitatives with an instrumental ensemble. Many of the simple recitatives include sections in arioso style. It is striking to what an extent Bach now focuses on all the various forms of text emphasis in the recitatives as well as in the arias. The latter include the conventional solo or duet parts accompanied only by continuo, but there are also many examples of adapting Italian aria types including ritornello structures with frequent da capo or dal segno repetitions. Half of the cantatas have six movements, most often with a conventional alternation of aria and recitative. However, several of the cantatas in their original form, before being revised for performances in Leipzig, have only one recitative or none at all (BWV 70a, 147a, 172, 186a). Often the vocal parts originate in the ritornello material itself. This frequently emphasizes that form of Bach's vocal style which is instrumental in character.

EXAMPLE 17.6 Ibid.

Nothing is more difficult concerning Bach's music than to define or explain his vocal styles. It is clear, however, that the heart of that style lies in Bach's commitment to give expressive realization to texts, to individual words of those texts, and to the affects that motivate their meaning. His solo vocal parts are seldom simply lyrical, and they are without the slightest resemblance to Italian *cantabile*. They are almost always highly dramatic and often filled with complex rhythmic motives and angular lines with wide leaps. Melismatic passages, some of extraordinary length, occur at times to give rhetorical emphasis to, or even to symbolize, a word, but at other times, they are an integral part of the melodic development.

Bach took significant advantage of his charge to compose cantatas by choosing to explore a large number of cantata forms. These first achievements with forms new to Bach proved to be invaluable for his great cycles of cantatas composed in Leipzig. This can be seen especially in the variety of choral styles he employed, including fugue, canon, ostinato variation, Italian concerto form, the French overture, and the older motet style. The many different instrumental ensembles employed in these cantatas probably reflect those instrumentalists available to Bach at the Weimar court, but they also suggest the composer's wish to experiment with a number of possible groups of instruments for these works. Some of the cantatas continue to employ the older French five-part string ensemble with two violas, some the conventional four string parts plus continuo. Others, however, have highly individual instrumental groups made up variously of recorders, oboes, bassoon, and trumpet that complement Bach's vocal settings of each text. Beginning in 1715 one finds Bach working toward Italianate scoring.

The variety of forms, styles, and musical inventions in these cantatas is beyond summarizing, but they are suggested just in the many different ways Bach begins these cantatas.[54] Only one (BWV 155) begins without any form of instrumental opening but rather as a recitative with continuo. The largest number of them begin with a vocal solo or duet, in the latter form, two (BWV 80a and BWV 185). There are three with arias for soprano (BWV 132, 165, 199), two for alto (BWV 54 and BWV 161), one each for tenor (BWV 163) and bass (BWV 162). Each of their instrumental accompaniments is different. Five cantatas open with independent orchestral movements: BWV 152, for recorder, oboe, viola, viola da gamba, and continuo in two sections that suggest the form of the French overture; BWV 82, labeled "sonata" for recorder, two violins, two violas, and continuo; and three labeled "sinfonia"—BWV 12, for oboe, strings, bassoon, and continuo; BWV 18, for two recorders, four violas, bassoon, cello, and continuo; and BWV 61, for oboe, two violins, two violas, continuo, and bassoon. Four cantatas in their original Weimar form begin with significant chorus movements: BWV 70a = 70, for trumpet, oboe, strings, bassoon, and continuo; BWV 61, a French Overture, the first slow section with an embedded chorale, the faster contrapuntal section in triple meter, for two violins, two violas, continuo; BWV 174 = 147a, with trumpet, bassoon, strings, and continuo; and BWV 186a, with oboe I/violin I doubling, oboe II/violin II doubling, taille/viola doubling, and continuo.

Leipzig Cantatas

For Leipzig, evidence indicates, Bach composed somewhere around 250 new sacred cantatas. This extraordinary assemblage of Bach's music contains a varied complexity of styles and forms, and a significant record of Bach's inventive genius. Unlike other exceptional musical achievements in a genre, for example, Beethoven's quartets or Mozart's piano concertos, Bach's cantatas still lack a comprehensive study from which one could draw a confident opinion as to what Bach had actually achieved.[55] Bach's unusual genius, which seemed to demand that he always seek new ways to compose in more or less traditional forms, suggests that each cantata, being a unique creation and requiring individual and intensive analysis, defies general synthesis. In Leipzig the cantata (or *Hauptmusik*) was placed in the liturgy after the Gospel and Creed and before the sermon. At times a second cantata or the second half of a longer cantata would be sung after the sermon, during the Eucharist. It was customary in Leipzig that the *Hauptmusik* or other major musical performance alternated Sundays between the St. Nicholas and the St. Thomas churches. On major feast days, the concerted music was heard at both churches, early in the morning at St. Nicholas, with the first choir of St. Thomas conducted by Bach, and later in St. Thomas with the second choir conducted by one of the prefects.[56]

The first cycle of church cantatas comprises works beginning with the first Sunday after Trinity, 30 May 1723, and ends on Trinity Sunday, 4 June 1724. A total of fifty-five cantatas are included in the cycle: forty-two new works[57] and thirteen that were repetitions and often extensive revisions of Weimar cantatas. The forty-two cantatas consist of between four and fourteen movements, almost half of them in six movements, six in seven movements, one in four, others in five, and exceptionally in eight, and nine, ten, twelve, and fourteen movements. A slight majority of these cantatas have the predominant feature of beginning with a major choral movement usually with an orchestra of strings and at times wind and brass instruments. Some are formed as two contrasting sections, the first more or less homophonic, the second a fugue or fugal. Others suggest various and distinctly Bachian procedures by which an instrumental ritornello is the basis of the entire movement, as is often also the case in the solo arias. However, there are a number of exceptions: fourteen cantatas begin with an aria (or duet) as the first movement or as the opening movement of the second part of the work. As is true of the cantatas beginning with a chorus these also usually continue with a conventional alternation of recitatives and arias or duets. All of the cantatas end with a four-part setting of a chorale, with instruments doubling the voice parts or having separate obbligato parts (in the first cycle especially).

The Protestant chorale, which has from almost the beginning been at the center of Bach's compositional career, as, for example, in the early Neumeister collection, gains exceptional prominence in the first Leipzig cycle. Not only does each cantata conclude with a chorale, but fifteen cantatas also have chorales embedded in new ways into the movements themselves. For example, the Cantata BWV 25, *Es ist nichts Gesundes an meinem Leibe*, opens with a grand movement of stunning contrapuntal virtuosity for instruments (three flutes, cornetto, three trombones, two oboes, and strings) and four vocal parts. Phrases of the chorale, *Herzlich tut mich verlangen*, are placed in the bass and highest instrumental part against a choral fugue, then against a second fugue, and finally over the two fugues now combined as a double fugue. A similar use of a chorale, *Dies sind die heil'gen zehn Gebot*, appears in Cantata BWV 77, *Du sollst Gott, den Herren, lieben*. In Cantata BWV 37, *Wer da glaubet und getauft wird*, the duet of the third movement is based on an elaboration of the chorale *Wie schön leuchtet der Morgenstern*. The third movement of BWV 44 has a simple continuo aria for tenor with continuo based on the chorale *Ach Gott, wie manches Herzeleid*. Similarly, movement three of BWV 166, *Wo gehest du hin?*, places the chorale *Ich bitte dich, Herr Jesu Christ* in the soprano part without elaborations against an independent part for the violins and viola in unison.

The most unusual setting of a chorale among this first cycle of cantatas is found in BWV 138, *Warum betrübst du dich, mein Herz*, which incorporates the chorale with this title in movements one, three, and seven. In the first the chorale phrases of verse 1, in four voice parts with independent instrumental passages, are separated by arioso passages consecutively by tenor and alto. In the third movement, the first three phrases of the second verse are again stated in four parts with instrumental doublings. They are also interrupted by a long recitative for soprano, followed by the final line of the verse. Movement 7 sets verse three with each of the four phrases accompanied and then separated by two oboes and two violins, the latter having elaborate passages largely in thirty-second notes. All of the other inserted chorale movements, both in the opening and interior movements, are equally diverse. And one is constantly engaged by Bach's sensitivity to the emotional substance of texts, and the variety of musical means he draws upon in these and other cantatas to give important words dynamic rhetorical and at times pictorial musical interpretations.

Bach initiated the second, the so-called chorale cycle of cantatas, on the first Sunday after Trinity, 11 June 1724. There seems to be no adequate explanation for this change of cantata form. Perhaps, growing out of Bach's greater immersion into the theological symbolism and musical power of the Protestant chorale in the vocal context of the first cycle, he was inspired to create something new: a cycle of cantatas in which the first movements become elaborate chorale-fantasias for chorus and instruments while the same chorale forms the final movements in a simple four-part arrangement. The appropriate strophes of the chorale text are composed verbatim in the first and last movements, but the interior movements, usually consisting of arias and recitatives, are composed to the remaining strophes written in paraphrased poetic forms. The literary achievement of these cantata texts is diminished only by the anonymity of the poet who has never been identified. The chorale cycle, consisting of thirty-nine works,[58] reaches its climax on 25 March 1725 (Sunday of the Annunciation) with one of Bach's greatest cantatas, BWV 1, *Wie schön leuchtet der Morgenstern*. The cycle is concluded with performances of the St. John Passion and Easter Oratorio, and with twelve additional cantatas, nine to texts by Christiane Mariane von Ziegler (1695–1760). Three of those are in the form of chorale cantatas.[59]

The general organization of these cantatas resembles those in the first cycle with most in six or seven movements, the former being in the majority. The recitatives and arias though similar in forms and styles to the first cycle display the same continuing determination of Bach constantly to find new musical approaches to composing their texts. The unique aspect of the chorale cantatas is, of course, the character, size, and musical weight of the opening chorale fantasias. The emphasis on a chorale melody usually in bar form, placed often in a complex contrapuntal texture, and preceded by a significant introductory section for instruments, frequently resembling the character of a concerto ritornello, all add up to movements of considerable length. This rich assortment of musical forces enables Bach to exceed himself in the overall originality and variety of these thirty-nine works. Some of them present the chorale in a largely homophonic four-part texture with the melody in the top part in long note values, while the remaining parts have some contrapuntal movement. Cantata BWV 20, *O Ewigkeit, du Donnerwort*, and Cantata BWV 99, *Was Gott thut, das ist wohlgethan*, are examples. The former is especially notable as it opens the cycle with an emphasis symbolically and musically on French overture form and style.

The chorale cycle ends with Bach's grandiose interpretation of Nicolai's chorale, *Wie schön leuchtet der Morgenstern*. It is a joyous chorale celebrating the annunciation of the birth of Christ, which is conveyed to Mary by the Angel Gabriel. The orchestra is large with two horns soaring into their high range, two oboes da caccia, two solo (concertante) violins plus the two violins and viola of the ensemble, and continuo. The opening ritornello has at least five contrasted melodic ideas. In keeping with the theme of the chorale, the movement is of great pastoral beauty, in a stable F major and with a lilting rhythm in 12/8. The chorale's bar form is strictly maintained. The A (A1) and B sections are in turn divided into three separate phrases which receive separate musical settings with the chorale in the soprano part. The last phrase of the chorale, "hoch und sehr prächtig erhaben" (high and most brilliantly raised up), sustains the inspired climax to the movement. Beginning with the bass part the voices in imitation build a pyramid of sound, as the ascending phrase climbs through the tenor and alto parts until it reaches the high F of the soprano, doubled by the horn for "*hoch*" of the chorale—just one of the many unforgettable moments in the chorale cantatas (see Example 17.7).

The great variety among these chorale cantatas involves almost all the elements of compositions concerned with text settings and instrumental forces. Text settings alone illustrate a multitude of different ways Bach gives musical emphasis and meaning to rhetorically significant words and phrases. For the opening chorale fantasia the regular instrumentation always includes the core four-part string ensemble and at least two oboes (or taille, oboe d'amore, oboe da caccia), often doubling violins I and II, and at times one or two flutes. Cantatas for the major feast days may expand these instrumental forces by adding horns, trumpets, timpani, and trombones. Each of the chorale fantasias is unique, and from among all of them a few may be singled out for their formal distinctions: Cantata BWV 38, *Aus tiefer Noth schrei ich zu dir,* is a motet reinterpreting the seventeenth-century style with the chorale in whole notes in the soprano part, while the lower parts doubled by instruments flow imitatively in half-note values. Cantata BWV 93, *Wer nur den lieben Gott lässt walten,* is exceptional in the way Bach allows the soprano part for the chorale cantus firmus to alternate chorale melody with sections of the fugal passages. In Cantata BWV 121, *Christum wir sollen loben schon,* again with instruments only doubling the parts, each line of the chorale in the soprano is preceded by three-part fugal exposition. BWV 78, *Jesus, der du meine Seele,* is one of a handful of Bach's cantatas to have become widely known, in part because of its extraordinary adaptation of the chorale to a chromatically descending passacaglia.

Approximately thirty-four new cantatas make up what appears to be a rather long cycle III. Assuming Bach began this cycle, as previously, on the first Sunday after Trinity, these cantatas would extend from 3 June into early 1727, with the end of the cycle uncertain.[60] A number of the cantatas appear to be lost. Those that remain, however, exhibit a rich variety of forms, including some that did not exist or were not prominent in Bach's earlier cantatas. The majority (nineteen) begin with a large chorus, including a few continuing in the form of the chorale cantata (BWV 3, 16, 27, 137, 177), while another twelve have an opening chorus usually of impressive structure and length (BWV 14, 17, 19, 39, 43, 45, 47, 72, 79, 102, 110, 187). Five are divided into two separate parts presumably performed before and after the sermon (BWV 17, 35, 39, 88, 102). The second largest form in this cycle has the conventional alternation of recitative and aria (duet) or aria and recitative movements (BWV 32, 55, 56, 57, 58a, 82, 84, 88, 151, 164, 168, 170), and particularly interesting is the number of solo cantatas: two for soprano (BW 52, 84), three for alto (BWV 35, 169, 170), one for tenor (BWV 55), and two for bass (BWV 56 and 82). Notable are six cantatas (BWV 35, 42, 49, 52, 146, and 169) that omit the opening chorus and replace it with an instrumental movement usually labeled "sinfonia." These are arrangements of instrumental concertos, the originals of which apparently are lost, except for BWV 146, which is the harpsichord concerto BWV 1052. Another distinction of these cantatas is the addition of organ obbligato parts to several (BWV 27, 35, 47, 49, 146, 169, 170). As in the earlier cycles the pieces that stand above all others in addition to the chorale cantatas are those first movements for chorus based on extraordinary craftsmanship. They usually begin with various fugal displays, sometimes in two-part forms in which the fugue is the second part, or in which fugal and other vocal styles such as imitation or solo passages are in various ways

EXAMPLE 17.7 Bach, Nicolai's chorale, *Wie schön leuchtet der Morgenstern*

EXAMPLE 17.7 (*continued*)

combined with fugal sections. Most impressive, perhaps, are BWV 3, 19, 39, 45, 79, 102, and 110.

Some scholars believe that Bach began a fourth cycle based entirely on the poetry of Christian Friedrich Henrici (1700–1764), who used the pen name of Picander. He was the poet for a large number of Bach's vocal works, including the St. Matthew Passion, and sacred as well as secular cantatas. Nine sacred cantatas (one a fragment) set by Bach remain from the years 1728–1729 (BWV 145, 149, 156, 159, 171, 174, 188, 197a), and if Bach did compose an entire cycle on Picander's poetry, the remainder must be assumed lost. Bach's devotion to composing new sacred cantatas waned after 1729. Composing sacred vocal works of large dimensions no longer was at the center of Bach's compositional efforts during the last two decades of his life. Evidence shows that he did repeat cantatas from the past on many occasions, and only a scattering of about twenty new cantatas remain. Almost all of these late cantatas begin with a chorus movement, and among them the chorale cantata continues to be favored. In most, however, Bach has replaced his previous use of poetry-based, paraphrased chorale verses with the actual texts in each of the movements (see BWV 97, 112, 117, 178, 192).

Bach's focus on composing cantatas was not limited to sacred works, for throughout his career, beginning in Cöthen, he composed a significant number of secular cantatas (many lost) for a wide variety of events. There are those dramatic scenes, the nearest Bach came to writing opera, such as BWV 201, *Geschwinde, geschwinde, ihr wirbelnden Winde—Drama per musica: Der Streit zwischen Phoebus und Pan;* BWV 205, *Zerreisset, zersprenget, zertrümmert die Gruft—Dramma per musica: Der zufriedengestellte Aeolus;* BWV 211, *Schweigt stille, plaudert nicht* (The Coffee Cantata); BWV 213, *Lasst uns sorgen, lasst uns wachen—Dramma per musica: Hercules auf dem Scheidewege;* BWV 212, *Mer hahn en neue Oberkeet* (The Peasant Cantata). Others were composed for weddings and to honor court occasions such as royal birthdays and name days, and so on (BWV 206, 207a, 208, 214, 215), funerals such as the ode for Christiane Eberhardine, Electress of Saxony and Queen of Poland, BWV 198, *Lass, Fürstin, lass noch einen Strahl;* and also to honor university professors such as Professor Korttens of Leipzig University, BWV 207, *Vereinigte Zwietracht der wechselnden Saiten—Drama per musica.*

THE MAGNIFICAT AND THE MOTETS

Martin Luther retained the Magnificat of the Catholic liturgy, the Canticle of the Virgin (Luke I:46–55), and in Leipzig it was sung in German at Vesper services, normally on Sunday afternoons. On major church holidays, however, such as Christmas, Easter, and Whitsunday (Pentecost), the Magnificat was sung in Latin as a major musical work in concerted style for chorus and orchestra. Bach copied out several Magnificats by other composers to be used in these special services, but only one of his has been preserved. This is the E flat Magnificat, BWV 243a, composed for Bach's first Leipzig Christmas service in 1723. It is the most elaborate work originating during his still early career, composed for five-part chorus and soloists, three trumpets and timpani, recorders, oboes, and strings. Reflecting a long-established Christmas tradition, Bach created a double chorus composition by inserting four German and Latin choral songs of praise: "Vom Himmel hoch," "Freut euch und Jubilieret," "Gloria in excelsis Deo," and "Virga Jesse floruit" (fragment). About a decade later Bach revised this "Christmas" Magnificat into a work appropriate for any Vesper service by removing the four inserted Christmas songs of praise, by transposing the work to D major, and making small changes in the instrumentation, especially replacing the recorders with the more modern transverse flutes (BWV 243).

Bach divides the Magnificat text into its twelve sentences, which inspired a succinct encyclopedia of contrasting musical movements: there are choruses in concertato style, a duet, a trio with the German Magnificat chorale as cantus firmus, a quartet, fugue and canon, a continuo aria, and other arias with contrasting instrumental accompaniments. Appropriate for the sacred nature of the text, no recitatives are employed. All but two of the movements (the opening "Magnificat" chorus and the soprano solo "Et exultavit") are concise and easily perceived statements of the affective and rhetorical substance of the words. The music has popular appeal. It is by turns joyful, exuberant, even humorous, as well as in some movements serious or contemplative. Although on a small scale, Bach's Magnificat gave his congregation a transporting initial demonstration of his compositional craft and musical imagination.

In Leipzig services, motets were sung as introits, usually chosen from the sixteenth-century motet anthology of Erhard Bodenschatz, *Florilegium Portense* (1618), and also for special occasions. Bach's eight preserved motets all are probably for burial services.[61] However, only BWV 226, *Der Geist hilft unser Schwachheit,* is so designated, for the funeral of Johann Heinrich Ernesti, rector of the Thomasschule in 1729. While formerly all were believed to have been composed in Leipzig, two motets now can be attributed to the Weimar period, BWV Anh. 159, *Ich lasse dich nicht,* and BWV 228, *Fürchte dich nicht.*[62] Five motets are in eight parts for double chorus, in addition to BWV Anh. 159, BWV 226 and BWV 228, also BWV 225, *Singet dem Herrn ein neues Lied,* and BWV 229, *Komm, Jesu, komm.* Two are for one chorus, BWV 227, *Jesu, meine Freude* (in 5 parts), and BWV 230, *Lobet den Herrn, alle Heiden* (in four parts).

THE PASSIONS

The statement in the obituary that Bach composed five Passions is not confirmed by those that have remained. His first passion setting written for Leipzig was the St. John, performed on 7 April 1724. Evidence of three subsequent versions exists for the years 1725 (30 March), 1728 (26 March) or 1732 (11 April), and 1749 (4 April). In 1726 Bach performed a St. Mark's Passion usually attributed to Reinhard Keiser,[63] a work Bach had previously used in Weimar in 1714. It is now known that the first performance of the St. Matthew Passion took place in Leipzig in April 1727, earlier than the previously accepted date of 15 April 1729. It was revived on 29 March 1736 and on two later occasions. A third Passion ascribed to Bach, the St. Mark Passion, was performed on 23 March 1731, but only the libretto by Picander survives. It has been conjectured that some of the movements in the St. John and St. Matthew Passions probably originated in Weimar, suggesting the existence of a fifth and now lost Passion. This could have been a Passion by Bach, known to have been performed at the palace church in Gotha in March 1717.[64]

The performance in some form of vocal setting of the biblical texts describing Christ's Passion originated in the first century of the Christian era. The earliest settings were intoned in chant formulas, and through the centuries new forms often developed. By the sixteenth century, a type of motet Passion evolved in which the entire biblical text of the Passion as recorded by one of the evangelists was composed in polyphonic style. The reformed liturgy established by Luther, retained for the Good Friday service; the tradition of performing a setting of one of the evangelist's Passion texts; the biblical words of the Evangelist and other speakers were sung monophonically on a passion tone while the crowd texts (*turbae*) were sung polyphonically. By the end of the seventeenth century the changing form of the Passion created a very new and expanded concept, usually called an "oratorio Passion," which became the basis for Bach's works. As is evident in his Passions, the form is greatly enlarged in its musical variety and dramatic scenario: (1) in addition to the Gospel, free poetic texts express personalized individual reactions to the biblical scene; (2) these texts are composed as recitatives and arias similar to those found in his cantatas; (3) instruments add to the dramatic expressiveness of the texts and to the variety of the scores; and, of particular importance, (4) the practice of inserting chorales already found in earlier Passions is considerably enlarged and becomes a focus of the congregation's immersion in the sacred drama.

The St. John Passion

Bach had been in Leipzig some ten months prior to the first performance of the St. John Passion during Vespers. Those ten months must have been extraordinarily full with his new duties for composing and for directing musicians in cantatas at the Nikolaikirche and Thomaskirche, becoming settled with his family, and fulfilling his obligations at the Thomasschule. The only period he probably had free to concentrate on this exceptionally important work, the most complex he had ever undertaken, was with the beginning of Lent on 20 February 1724. During the next five weeks, in addition to the Passion, he needed to compose only a cantata for the Feast of the Annunciation (25 March).

Bach reached a totally new dimension of musical creativity with the St. John Passion. The inspiration of the Gospel text, the potential for dramatic musical forms of chorus, aria, recitative, and chorale, and the incorporation of a significant orchestral ensemble enabled Bach to create a monumental musical and dramatic composition new for him and for the history of Baroque music. As was traditional, the Passion is divided into two parts, preceding and following a sermon. The author of the miscellany of borrowed poetry used in the nonbiblical text is unknown, although several of the arias (and in two instances the preceding ariosos) as well as the final chorus, "Ruht wohl, ihr heiligen Gebeine," are based on poetry found in the popular *Brockes Passion* composed by Keiser, Handel, Mattheson, and Telemann. The biblical narrative is employed word for word from the Gospel according to John 18:20 with two inserted additions from St. Matthew.

The opening chorus, *Herr, unser Herrscher,*[65] the exordium to the Passion text proper, in its magnitude and dramatic intensity had never previously been attempted by Bach. The Passion might be considered "operatic" except it is without any aspect of eighteenth-century operatic style. More appropriate, perhaps, would be to describe it as a form of "music drama." Although the first chorus is in a large da capo form, the B section, rather than contrasting with the first part, continues to develop and expand on it. The music expresses a crowd scene of unrelenting anxiety as the Faithful witness the events unrolling before them and call out to their Lord and Master (*Herr und Herrscher*) "to show in his Passion that he is triumphant as the true Son of God even in suffering the deepest humiliation" (*Zeig uns durch deine Passion, dass du, der wahre Gottessohn, zu aller Zeit, auch in der grössten Niedrigkeit, verherrlicht worden bist!*).

The scene begins *in medias res,* plunging into the score's turbulent affect expressed both instrumentally and vocally. There are three layers to the instrumental dimensions of the score: the two oboes (doubled in version IV by flutes) have almost continuously the most striking dissonant and at times chromatic passages. The two parts constantly cross and frequently leap into unprepared dissonances. The violins and violas have largely churning sixteenth-note figures, which at times are also taken over by the voices. The relentless drive of the whole movement lies in the continuous, throbbing, ostinato-like pattern of eighth notes in the bass. Into these intense and stressful instrumental textures, the four vocal parts portray the anxieties and fears of the crowd. They begin as four-part chordal exclamations on "Lord," separated by rests to emphasize their rhetorical impact. Except for passages in which the voices double the sixteenth-note figurations of the strings, the choral part is either fugal or canonic. This not only highlights the individuality of the crowd voices as they enter one by one, but also places the word *Herr* on the upper note of the octave leap beginning the imitation so as to be heard as a constant scattering of impassioned cries throughout the contrapuntal texture (see Example 17.8).

Bach proceeds with a rather compact dramatization of the Gospel text. The score is dominated by the Evangelist's narrations. In Part II, especially, the text requires a number of choruses (*turbae*), which Bach composes as a cycle of intensely dramatic, even violent imitative segments such as *Wäre dieser nicht ein Übeltäter* (If he were not a criminal), *Wir dürfen niemand töten* (We are not allowed to kill anyone), *Sei gegrüsset lieber Jüdenkönig* (Hail, King of the Jews), and the longer sections, even more terrible in their affect, *Kreuzige* (Crucify!), followed by *Wir haben ein Gesetz* (We have a law), *Lässet du diesen los* (If you let this man go), and *Weg mit dem, kreuzige ihn* (Away with him! Crucify him!). The contemplative interaction of the congregation as an integral part of the drama is achieved by the insertion of ten chorales in appropriate places within the developing tragedy of Christ's Passion.

There are few arias, only three in Part I and five in the longer Part II. Of these, one stands out because of its unusual, even archaic, use of the viola d'amore: *Erwäge wie sein*

EXAMPLE 17.8   Bach, St. John Passion

EXAMPLE 17.8 *(continued)*

blutgefärbter Rücken (Consider how his back, stained with blood), for just two violas d'amore, tenor, and continuo, the longest aria in the work and the only one in da capo form. In another, *Es ist vollbrach,* for strings, viola da gamba, alto, and continuo, Bach reaches new depths of desolate emotional expressiveness. The last words uttered by Christ as he died (in the previous recitative), *Es ist vollbracht* (It is accomplished), a six- (sometimes five-)note, plaintive, descending sixth, are heard against the doleful viola da gamba solo, creating a dirge of profoundest sorrow (see Example 17.9).

The opening solo for viola da gamba, to be performed *molt'adagio,* reiterates this motive in varied forms in a ritornello of desolate sadness, and the same motive pervades the duet between viola da gamba, tenor voice, and continuo in the A section. A short vivace B section with added strings follows: *Der Held aus Juda siegt mit Macht* (The hero from Juda ends his victorious fight). Victory is emphasized by trumpetlike D major triadic arpeggios in voice and strings. But these last only for a fleeting moment as the B minor adagio interrupts with *Es ist vollbracht* in the original form heard in the preceding recitative. The viola da gamba repeats the opening ritornello, and this simple aria of such profundity and lamentation ends with one last devastating repetition of *Es ist vollbracht.*

The final section of this Passion, focused on the burial of Jesus, relates the remaining portion of the Gospel text in recitative. In addition, there is an aria for bass and four-part chorus in the style of a chorale, *Mein teurer Heiland lass dich fragen/ Jesu, der du warest tot, Lebest nun ohne Ende* (My dearest Saviour, let me ask you/ Jesus, you were dead and now

EXAMPLE 17.9   Ibid.

live for ever), and another for soprano with a flute and oboe da caccia duet, *Zerfliesse, mein Herze, in Fluten der Zähren* (Dissolve, my heart, in floods of tears). The Passion ends with the chorus *Ruht wohl, ihr heiligen Gebeine, die ich nun weiter nicht beweine* (Rest well, Thy sacred bones, for which now I will no longer weep). Here the score seems becalmed in a gentle, exquisite peace, the chorus predominantly homophonic and emphasizing the rocking motion of half- and quarter-note values in 3/4 meter, while the flutes, oboes, and strings moving almost always in descending arpeggiated passages subtly underscore the fact of burial. The work closes with the chorale *Ach Herr, lass dein lieb Engelein am letzten End die Seele mein in Abrahams Schoss tragen* (O Lord, send your cherubs in my last hour to bear my soul away to Abraham's bosom), one among the many of Bach's great chorale harmonizations.

The St. Matthew Passion

How Bach's congregation reacted to his dramatized and significantly expanded musical interpretation of St. John's Gospel is unknown. Indirectly, some evidence suggests they would have been bewildered if not antagonistic.[66] The unprecedented originality and the extended length of this work could hardly have been met with total enthusiasm by the conservative Leipzig congregation. Yet, far from reducing the length of his second Passion, Bach made the St. Matthew at least an hour longer. This results not just because the Gospel text is longer, but rather because every aspect of the musical forms and styles of the earlier work have in one way or another been greatly enlarged. The St. John Passion became the working model for Bach. There were differences, especially the expanded and more dramatic account by St. Matthew of Christ's suffering and death. Also, the text is enriched immeasurably by the poetry of Christian Friedrich Henrici (known as Picander), in a unified libretto written with Bach's oversight. But it was Bach's unique ability to reinvent an existing work by finding a new and, in this instance, a greater potential for expressing the religious substance, the monumentality and profoundest emotions of the text, that opened the way leading from the St. John to the creation of the St. Matthew Passion, his greatest sacred and at the same time most human musical drama.

The label "monumental Baroque" often employed to describe architecture of the period is no less appropriate here. The St. Matthew is Bach's largest score, and employs two orchestras and two choruses with soloists drawn from the latter. These forces create the antiphonal nature of many sections, in the tradition of earlier Venetian practice, and add a broad spaciousness to Bach's score. As is true of the earlier Passion, the Exordium of the St. Matthew became the longest and most complex of all the movements in the work. It is an immense musical canvas of ideas and sounds.

The opening ritornello doubled by both orchestras is ponderous, with unceasing motion and with sinuous and chromatic contrapuntal imitations. These are placed against a steady pastoral rhythm in 12/8 of quarter and eighth notes for the Lamb of God. The Daughters of Zion (Chorus I) bring visionary witness to the scene of Christ bearing the Cross to Cavalry. In contrapuntal music based on the ritornello they ask for help from the chorus of "believers" in their lamentation and point to the bridegroom who is like a lamb while the second chorus punctuates with chord blocks on *Wen?* (Who?), *Wie?* (How?). At this moment of dramatic tension Bach expands the texture and further dramatizes and sanctifies this amazing scene by introducing a separate group of sopranos who sing the chorale *O Lamm Gottes unschuldig, am Stamm des Kreuzes geschlachtet*—the German troped version of the *Agnus Dei*. The exordium has become a gigantic chorale fantasy. Each of the following lines of the chorale is preceded by related commentary and injections from the choruses: "Behold his patience (*Geduld*)," with injections of *Was?, Was?* followed by the chorale line, "all time You were so patient, even though You were despised"; "Behold," *Wohin?*, "Behold our guilt," *Wohin?*, and the chorale line "All sin hast Thou borne, else we must have despaired"; and in both choruses, "Behold Him, out of love and graciousness, Himself carrying the wood of the Cross," and the final chorale line "Have mercy upon us, O Jesus." The scene closes with the return of the opening vocal music performed now by both orchestras and choruses.

The St. Matthew Passion is encyclopedic in its musical content, employing and often adapting many of the styles and forms of music previously known to Bach. The vastness of the drama is held together primarily by the Gospel text and the carefully calculated placement of arias, but musically Bach enriches the sacred story with levels of contrasting dramatic and lyrical music that add several additional formal structures to the overall continuity and climaxes. It is to be expected that Bach would set the text to music both from the Bible and the additional poetry of Henrici with exceptional clarity. But Bach is the master of text expression and interpretation. This is particularly evident in the numerous recitatives that are at the most basic level of the music drama. The two forms originating in opera, the simple[67] and accompanied, are for the most part divided between the Evangelist's narrations and Jesus' commentaries. The Evangelist's recitatives sung to the continuo bass line and its realized harmonies are filled with dramatic and rhetorical emphases— striking dissonances, unusual melodic leaps, words stressed by exceptional pitch levels, musical figures of pictorial word emphasis—which give this part a vividly real presence. By contrast, the recitatives of Jesus, until his abandonment on the Cross, are accompanied by a glowing sonority of string chords, variously interpreted as a "halo" of sound or as a sanctifying of the words. When the text requires it, a recitative can become an arioso, for example, the final, heart-rending words of Jesus on the Cross: "Eli, Eli, lama, lama asab-thani?" (No. 61a), or the Evangelist's moving melisma referring to Peter on "he cried bitterly" (No. 38b) (see Example 17.10a–b).

Among the factors making the St. Matthew more expansive and lyrically expressive than the St. John is the greater emphasis on arias and also the addition of a number of both lyrical and succinctly dramatic ariosos (Bach calls them recitatives) preceding ten of the fifteen arias. The arias make up the richest and most varied collection of aria types found in Bach's works. And their considerable variety of expression is perhaps even more remarkable considering the total absence of the affect of joy in them. The arias encompass the contemplative, often highly personal and frequently pietistic responses to the crucial events in the developing drama of the Gospel text. Four of them are dramatized as dialogues between the soloist (the voice of Zion) and the chorus of believers (Nos. 20, 27d, 30, and 60). In many of the arias there is for Bach a new element of lyricism, a noticeably more conjunct melodic style with little of the torturous and often rhythmically complex melodies of previous vocal writing. These melodies cannot be accused, as has been the case in other works, of being "instrumental" in style and complexity. For example, Bach never composed more affecting, lyrical, vocal melodies as in the final aria of the Passion, "Mache dich, mein Herze rein" (No. 65),[68] the ethereal beauty of "Aus Liebe will mein Heiland sterben" (No. 49), or the profoundly moving "Erbarme dich, mein Gott" (No. 39) with its compelling violin solo.

The fifteen chorales spread out through the Passion add another level of structural continuity to the work but also contribute both to its grandeur and its intimacy. The power of the opening chorale fantasia on *O Lamm Gottes unschuldig* (O guiltless lamb of God) has its counterpart in the final movement of Part I, another immense chorale fantasy, this one on *O Mensch bewein dein Sünde gross* (O Man, bewail your great sin). It was, un-doubtedly, the frequent interruptions of the dramatic action at appropriate moments by chorales simple in their four-part settings, but affecting in their richly subtle harmoniza-tions, that for Bach's congregation involved the most personal and pious reactions. The greatest structural and expressive role is given to Hans Leo Hassler's *Herzlich tut mich verlangen*, which became known as the Passion chorale and occurs five times with five different verses in the St. Matthew. Its most well-known verse, *O Haupt voll Blut und Wunden* (O head, full of blood and wounds), is heard at the moment following the beating of Christ and his condemnation to crucifixion. It is sung again with the verse *Wenn ich einmal soll scheiden* (When once I must depart) as Christ dies on the Cross. The multiplicity of affects this chorale creates for the congregation at this moment achieves the finest and

EXAMPLE 17.10a   Bach, St. Matthew Passion, no. 61a

EXAMPLE 17.10b   Ibid., no. 38b

most moving interpretation of a chorale melody Bach achieved in his lifelong involvement with Protestant chorales.

In this music of imperishable grandeur, Bach composed his greatest masterwork for the Protestant church and a landmark musical achievement in Western civilization. The story of Christ's Passion, the central doctrine of Christianity is, even when removed from its sacred and doctrinaire associations, one of the most moving and profound tragedies ever written. Bach, as a devout Protestant, presents his interpretation of this immense human tragedy from a singular perspective. At the same time, however, this magnificent even if tragic narrative remains alive and valid today, as it continues to inspire audiences on many meaningful levels that reach out into areas of thought and appreciation perhaps not even contemplated by the composer.

THE B MINOR MASS

Bach's monumental setting of the Mass Ordinary, known as the *B Minor Mass,* is a work of unparalleled greatness but also of paradoxes and unanswered questions. Unknown is Bach's purpose in composing (or adapting with parodies) the entire Ordinary of the Catholic Mass. Initially, only the Kyrie and Gloria were composed, and the remaining sections of the Mass Ordinary were completed more than a decade later in the last years of his life. This contributes to the B Minor Mass the character of a final musical and religious testament possessing a magnitude without comparison in music history.

It was the provocations arising from Bach's ever-growing dissatisfaction with his position in Leipzig and the recurring struggles with the Town Council that led Bach to compose the *Missa.* The circumstances are well known and need only to be outlined here. Almost from the beginning of his appointment Bach found himself at odds with the university regarding his post in the university church. Soon he also began to have various difficulties with the town council. By 1730, Bach was exasperated by the serious decline in performance conditions at the Thomasschule. This led in 1730 to his famous and highly critical letter to the authorities, the "Short but Most Necessary Draft for a Well-Appointed Church Music."[69] In it, he emphasized the lack of talented singers and instrumentalists at his disposal, and his inadequate budget, and he made significant and reasonable recommendations to improve his working conditions. By this time, however, Bach had lost the support of the council members who, complaining of his total indifference to his job, reduced his income.[70] He in turn gave up his intense preoccupation with composing sacred music and instead in 1729 became the director of the local collegium musicum. For their weekly performances, Bach shifted his efforts in composition to a steady stream of secular cantatas, concertos, and keyboard compositions, many of them arrangements of works written for Cöthen. Bach's discouragement and frustrations erupted in a long letter, one of the few of his to be preserved, to his school friend Georg Erdmann. Written in October 1730, Bach asks his help in finding a new position. The following excerpt of crucial lines reflects Bach's state of mind: "(1) I find that the post is not as remunerative as it was described to me, (2) many of the *accidentia* [incidentals] of the position have been withdrawn, (3) the cost of living is very high here, (4) the authorities are odd, and little interested in music, with the result that I must live with almost constant vexation, envy, and harassment, [and] I shall be compelled, with help from the Most High, to seek my fortune elsewhere."[71]

In February 1733, the Saxon Elector Friedrich August had died. In the subsequent spring Bach, in his continuing search for a new position, took the opportunity of establishing himself with the new Elector Friedrich August II by sending to him the performing materials for a five-voiced Mass, a *Missa brevis,* consisting of the Kyrie and Gloria. He approached the new ruler of Saxony with a revealing letter of dedication:

> My Most Gracious Lord, Most Serene Elector, Most Gracious Lord! To Your Royal Highness I submit in deepest devotion the present small work of that science which I have achieved in *musique,* with the most wholly submissive prayer that Your Highness will look upon it with Most Gracious Eyes, according to your Highness's World-Famous Clemency and not according to the poor *composition;* and thus deign to take me under Your Most Mighty Protection. For some years and up to the present moment I have held the *Directorium* of the Music in the two principal churches in Leipzig, but have innocently had to suffer one injury or another, and on occasion also a diminution of the fees accruing to me in this office; but these injuries would disappear altogether if Your Royal Highness would grant me the favor of conferring upon me a title of Your Highness's Court Cappella, and would let Your High Command for the issuing of such a document go forth to the proper place. Such a most gracious fulfillment of my most humble prayer will bind me to unending devotion, and I offer myself in most indebted obedience to show at all times, upon Your Royal Highness's Most Gracious Desire, my untiring zeal in the composition of music for the church as well as for the orchestra, and to devote my entire forces to the service of Your Highness, remaining in unceasing fidelity, Your Royal Highness's most humble and most obedient servant,
>
> Johann Sebastian Bach
> Dresden, 27 July 1733[72]

Only subsequent to a second request from Bach (in September 1736) did the Saxon Elector grant him the desired title of composer to the Dresden court. Several speculative suggestions have proposed when and where Bach's work may have been performed, but no solid evidence documents any contemporary performance of the *Missa* in Dresden or elsewhere.[73] Bach seems to have made no further effort to have his *Missa* performed. He did, however, continue to have interest in Latin Mass composition. This is indicated by the short *Missa* (or Lutheran Mass) settings composed (arranged is the better term, because they are largely parodies) around 1738: in A major (BWV 234) and G major (BWV 236) and probably those in F major (BWV 233) and G minor (BWV 235). The *Missa* score, however, was not forgotten, for around 1745 he borrowed three movements from its Gloria for the Latin-texted *Gloria in excelsis Deo* (BWV 191). This may have, as George Stauffer suggests, stimulated Bach to reconsider how his original *Missa* might be used in another way, and perhaps for the first time he thought of completing the entire Mass Ordinary.[74]

Bach scholars now generally agree that the B Minor Mass was assembled by the composer in the last two years of his life, most specifically in the period August 1748–October 1749.[75] The composite score (P 180, preserved in the Berlin State Library) is the only complete original source. It has led to considerable discussions as to what it tells us about Bach's intentions. The "score" is actually four separate scores, written in the composer's hand, bearing separate and numbered title pages, which specify required instrumentation and voices:

No. 1. Missa [Kyrie and Gloria][76]
No. 2. Symbolum Nicenum [Credo]
No. 3. Sanctus [Sanctus, without Osanna and Benedictus]
No. 4. Osanna/Benedictus/Agnus Dei et Dona nobis pacem [Osanna and Benedictus of the Sanctus, and Agnus Dei]

The original *Missa* now formed the first two parts of the Catholic Mass Ordinary. The remaining three parts, with a nontraditional division of the Sanctus text, are largely parody movements. Here Bach demonstrates his exceptional gift for choosing appropriate music to which new texts could be joined with sensitive concern for matching of the new text to the affective meaning of the music in the borrowed work. The technique of parody had become a central aspect of Bach's compositional practice in Leipzig with many new cantatas created from earlier Weimar ones or secular Cöthen cantatas, as well as the transferring of movements from some cantatas to the new texts of works such as the Christmas oratorio.[77] But it was in the B Minor Mass that he raised the technique to the highest level of compositional artistry. The following movements are the identified parodies based on earlier works by Bach.

1. from the Gloria
    "Gratias agimus tibi" = "Wir danken dir Gott," BWV 29/2 (1731)
    "Qui tollis" = "Schauet doch, und sehet" (A section), BWV 46/1 (1723)
2. from the Credo
    "Credo in unum Deum = Chorus "Credo in unum Deum" in G (c. 1747–1748?)
    "Patrem Omnipotentem" = "Gott, wie dein Name," BWV 171/1 (c. 1729)
    "Crucifixus" = "Weinen, Klagen, Sorgen, Zagen," BWV 12/2 (1714)
    "Et expecto" = "Jauchet, ihr erfreuten Stimmen" BWV 120/2 (c. 1728)
3. from the Sanctus
    "Sanctus" = "Sanctus," BWV 232 (1724)
4. from the Osanna/Benedictus/Agnus Dei
    "Osanna" = "Preise dein Glücke," BWV 215/1 (1734)
    "Agnus Dei" = "Ach, bleibe doch," BWV 11/4 (1735?)
    "Dona nobis pacem" = Double parody: repeat of "Gratias agimus tibi," which is a parody of "Wir danken dir Gott," BWV 29/2 (1731)

It is probable that other movements are also based on sources now lost. Indeed, several Bach scholars have postulated that many if not all the other movements are also parodies of previously composed music, and perhaps only the introduction to the Kyrie and the transitional bridge of the "Et expecto" are completely new.[78]

There is a phenomenal wealth of great music in this score, and it has a frequent complexity of the compositional process and also an immersion into symbolic references to Bach's intepretation of the ancient, sacred text. Numerous articles and several books have ventured to analyze and describe the B Minor Mass,[79] all challenged by the immensity, subtleties, and the mysteries of the work. Here, one can only suggest a few of the many unique aspects of Bach's *Opus ultimum*.[80]

The Kyrie

The Kyrie text is divided into standard three sections: Kyrie I, Christe, Kyrie II, and each section has three statements of the text. Bach views the text symbolically and stresses this view musically as a statement of the Christian Trinity: God the Father, Christ the Son, and the Holy Spirit. The tonalities of the individual movements form a B minor triad: I. B minor, II. D major, III. F sharp minor. The triad had been labeled the *Trias harmonica* by earlier theorists who perceived a sacred order in the perfection of the ratio 4:5:6 and quickly viewed the triad as the musical equivalent of the sacred Trinity. Enlarging on the concept of the individuality of each person of the Trinity, Bach created each movement in a distinctly contrasted style: Kyrie I, following a massive four-measure outcry of "Lord

Have Mercy," marked Adagio, with chromatic bass movement and stunning dissonance, continues with the grandest and most formidable of the three movements. A great five-part fugue built into a Baroque ritornello form results in a wonderwork that idealizes God in number, craft, design, and musical spaciousness. The Christe, a duet in eighteenth-century contemporary style, emphasizes the new element at the center of Christianity, the New Covenant, the New Testament. The Son of God, here as in numerous cantatas, is symbolized by a duet, the combination of Father and Son, and the latter number two in the Trinity. The two voices maintain the concept either of two voices in one with parallel thirds and sixths or one voice in two parts when in canon. The Kyrie II is composed in the old Renaissance style, the *prima prattica,* the purely contrapuntal, a remote and mysterious sacred sound recalling the effect and compositional style of Palastrina's Masses.

The Gloria

The Latin Gloria has, with the exception of the Greek Kyrie, the oldest Mass text, which brings together texts from two different sources: I. Song of Praise of the Angelic Host (Luke 2:14), and II. the "Laudamus" text, an ancient hymn of praise and petition to God united with the Gloria opening since time immemorial. The sudden change of affect created by the "Gloria in excelsis Deo" is abrupt and almost shocking. From the slow and stylistically remote Kyrie II in F sharp minor, one is plunged into a joyous, dancelike angelic concert in D major. It is German Baroque at its most typical. The somewhat conventional musical imagery for the heavenly music of angels is derived especially from the three trumpets and timpani parts. The five vocal parts together with brass, percussion, two flutes, two oboes, strings, bassoon, and continuo produce a vibrant and compelling sound. The ritornello form is almost unvaried in its repetitions, and the voice parts although beginning as a fugue quickly become lightly imitative and often exuberantly homophonic.

At measure 100, Bach surprises us again with another stunning change of affect for the second line of the Gloria, "et in terra pax hominibus bonae voluntatis" (And on earth peace, good will toward men). Heavenly music vanishes as the trumpets and timpani are silenced; the dancelike 3/8 meter becomes 4/4 (C). We are brought down to earth with the sudden shift of tonality to the subdominant G major, which is grounded by long pedal notes in the bass. A pastoral mood is invoked in the strings and voice parts by conjunct slurred note pairs in thirds and sixths. A permutation fugue with three expositions and two episodes on the same text returns to D major. The episodes are particularly powerful. In the first, the trumpets and timpani rejoin the chorus, giving powerful musical substance to the concept of peace descending on earth with a series of three descending chordal passages. An even greater rhetorical emphasis on this text occurs in the second episode. The chorus begins on D, reverses the motion of the homophonic texture, and ascends to a climax while the tenors, on arpeggiated triads on D, E, and F sharp, begin at the top of the triad, descend through the triad, and then leap up again to the upper octave. The movement ends with trumpets and timpani doubling the last entrance of the fugue in a final metaphor for the peace created by the union of Heaven and earth.

The second half of the Gloria text is formed by three choruses and three arias and a duet:

1. Aria (soprano) *Laudamus te*
2. Chorus *Gratias agimus tibi,* parody of "Wir danken dir, Gott" from Cantata 29
3. Duet (soprano I and tenor) *Domine Deus*
4. Chorus *Qui tollis,* parody of "Schauet doch, und sehet" from Cantata 46

5. Aria (alto) *Qui sedes*
6. Aria (bass) *Quoniam tu solus sanctus*
7. Chorus *Cum sancto spiritus*

The *Laudamus te* is a great song of praise and exuberant joy for both a virtuoso soloist and a violinist. Both voice and instrument raise their voices to Heaven to praise, bless, worship, and glorify the Lord. The difficult, rather operatic, part for the soprano, with its very long phrases, trills, and frequent melismas, lies unusually low for a soprano, and may have been composed by Bach for the famous soprano Faustina Bordoni, who possessed a similar range.[81] She was the wife of Johann Adolf Hasse, and both were employed by the Dresden court at that time. The *tour de force* of the aria, however, is the solo violin part, soaring into the upper positions in writing seldom seen in ensemble music of the Baroque. It was perhaps composed with Johann Georg Pisendel, the court Cappella's concertmaster in mind.

The following *Gratias agimus tibi,* a parody based on a chorus in Cantata BWV 29, is one of Bach's formidable choruses. The close general meaning of the texts in the original chorus with the parody is clear: Cantata 29, "We give thanks unto thee, O God/ and proclaim Thy wonders," and "Gratias," "We give thanks to Thee/ for Thy great glory." Stylistically, the chorus in older Renaissance counterpoint reminds somewhat of the Kyrie II. Its smoothly rising and falling first phrase in half and quarter notes and a second phrase dominated by eighth notes move in continuously imitative textures; at first the two themes are separated, but quickly they form a complex texture in double counterpoint. The wonder of this chorus, clearly derived from the text, lies in its sensation of continuous musical growth and the expansion of its affective power. The first theme always moves forward and directionally usually upward in the order of imitation of the parts. A climax is reached when the trumpets enter in canon with the first phrase, which four measures later joins a contrapuntal matrix spread over four octaves and in six real parts with the timpani heard for the first time as they support an entrance of the first phrase in the bass. At this point, the musical texture moves imitatively one more time from the lowest range until the trumpets enter again in canon doubling the thematic entries of the first phrase and giving another tremendous and stirring emotional lift with the combined sounds of voices, trumpets, and timpani.

The *Domine Deus,* with its textual references to the duality of God and Christ, is again a duet as is the "Christe," but it is scored quite differently for soprano I and tenor, with an exceedingly beautiful solo flute part, violins and viola muted, and the bass line pizzicato. As with the "Christe" there is similar musical treatment of the two vocal parts in canon versus the two parts in parallel intervals. The work is divided into a triune structure of thirty plus thirty plus thirty measures with a five-measure bridge leading into the following *Qui tollis.* The *Qui tollis* once again is a parody—with considerable revisions, of the opening chorus of Cantata 46, "Schauet doch, und sehet ob irgendein Schmerz." The chorus is transposed from the original D minor to the B minor tonality of the Kyrie. The sound of the *Qui tollis* is greatly changed from the original cantata movement with its two recorders, trumpet, two oboes, and strings replaced by the darker, less extroverted sounds of two flutes, strings, and a four-part chorus. The chorus, ending on the dominant F sharp, prepares B minor for the solo aria *Qui sedes* for alto, oboe d'amore, and strings.

This penultimate movement in the "Gloria" is one of Bach's strangest arias. The *Quoniam tu solus sanctus* is scored for bass, corno da caccia, bassoons 1 and 2, and continuo. It restores the mood of a "Song of Praise" with a powerful, almost pompous, virile affect.

The sound is unique among all of his works with the reliance on the bass voice, one horn, and two virtuoso bassoon parts. These instruments were chosen perhaps because of Bach's awareness of the virtuoso players employed at the Dresden court. The movement leads without pause into the final section of the "Gloria," the *Cum sancto spiritu in Gloria Dei patris*, and the heavenly music of the opening returns in a magnificent concerto-fugal composition of unequalled joy and majesty. It brings the Gloria to a resounding conclusion with perhaps Bach's most memorable climax, a crescendo in sounds, a grand anabasis, as the bass line and all of the voice parts move ever higher through seven measures for the final "Gloria Dei Patris, Amen."[82]

The Credo

Bach's composition of the Credo of the Mass Ordinary is an awesome demonstration of organizing music by combing Christian symbols and musical structure, and it is the greatest compositional achievement in his expansion of the Kyrie and Gloria into a *Missa tota*.

The Credo text, known as the Nicene Creed, is the ancient statement of beliefs of all Christians, going back to the first Council in Nicea in 325 A.D. where it was adopted and later expanded by a Council of Constantinople in 381 A.D. The Credo became the foundation of beliefs for the Catholic and later the Protestant faiths. This ancient standard of belief is central to Bach's entire work, and within these statements Bach reflects the centrality for Christians of the threefold belief in Christ's birth, death, and resurrection. Bach divides the text into nine parts, although the initial composing of the work was in eight parts. He must have realized the opportunity or desire to create the nine divisions for the Credo by separating from the "Et in unum Deum" the final lines of text, "Et incarnatus." This then placed the "Crucifixus" as the fifth and central movement where the tonality reaches its lowest point in the entire Mass, E minor, the lower dominant minor of B minor.

Each of the nine movements is overlaid with numerous symbolic references, only a few of which will be pointed out here. Of all nine movements, the first and the last two are the most remarkable in their originality, the forming of structural cohesiveness, and as a powerful rhetorical emphasis on their sacred symbolic content. The first, "Credo in unum Deum," is an imposing polyphonic statement in what was then considered the old style of imitative counterpoint, or *stile antico*, associated with composers of the Renaissance, especially Palestrina. Bach's use of the style here emphasizes the ancientness, the eternal value of the Credo text, and more than likely the universality of the Credo doctrine to all Christians. Over a continuous walking continuo bass Bach employs the five-part, unaccompanied (a cappella) chorus. In an extraordinary demonstration of Bach's contrapuntal prowess, each voice part states the Gregorian chant for Credo II in whole notes. After this is stated by each voice part, which then continues in free counterpoint, Bach adds two violin parts to complete seven statements of the Credo II chant. The entire procedure is repeated adding another seven statements of the chant. However, the fourteenth entrance, in the bass, now is presented in augmentation, doubling the length of each note, against which soprano II and alto add a separate layer of the chant in parallel sixths to which the two violins add the last two statements.

The "Patrem omnipotentem" follows immediately without pause, a joyous fugue derived from the chorus "Gott, wie dein Name, so ist auch dein Ruhm" of Cantata 171. Thus, from the *stile antico*, Bach startles us by plunging directly into the contrasting *stile moderno*. But, in a significant recomposition of the cantata fugue, he overlays the first three entrances of the fugue theme with insistent repetitions in block chords of the words "Credo in unum Deum," emphasizing the dual basis of Christian beliefs.

EXAMPLE 17.11   Bach, B Minor Mass

EXAMPLE 17.11 *(continued)*

The last two movements of the Credo again consist of a pair of choruses contrasting *stile antico* and *stile moderno* styles. Comparable to the opening Credo, the same form of setting is found in the Confiteor (I acknowledge one baptism), one of the eternal, universal values of Christianity. Again, the *stile antico* is employed in the same a cappella style, with the appropriate portion of the chant for this text from the same Credo II. It also appears in augmentation. This is joined by the 24-measure Adagio transitional bridge leading to the "Et expecto resurrectionem mortuorem," a brief passage of compelling affect, harmonic strangeness, and boldness. Emphasizing the place of the crucifixion in both baptism and eternal life, Bach returns abruptly at the Adagio indication to the bass motive of slurred, repeated bass notes that had dominated the "Crucifixus" movement until finally the entire harmonic foundation of the score sinks miraculously to the dominant of D major.

Then, with a blaze of D major and a burst of the full Baroque orchestra (three trumpets and timpani, two flutes, two oboes, strings, continuo) and the entrance of the five-part chorus, begins the most obviously *stile moderno* movement and completes the entire text of "Et expecto resurrectionem mortuorum et vitam venturi seculi. Amen." This is again a parody, based on the second movement of Cantata BWV 120, "Gott, man lobet dich in der Stille," with the text "Exult, all ye joyful voices rise, climb up to Heaven," words exactly matched by the affect achieved in Bach's music (see Example 17.11).

The Sanctus

Bach's great Sanctus for six voices, BWV 232, was composed for the Leipzig Christmas service in 1724. Some time later, as he considered expanding the Kyrie and Gloria movements into a *Missa tota*, he must have decided this Sanctus would become part of the new Ordinary. Indeed, it has been conjectured that it was this Sanctus that compelled Bach to create the complete Mass Ordinary. The binding of the Christian congregation with the angels before the throne of the Lord is achieved in a great extroverted expression of praise. As in the Gloria, the congregation joins in praise with words that are heavenly. Bach's Sanctus towers above all other settings of this text in its magnificence, in its tonal picture of an unknown world of mystery and splendor. In 1724, Bach had been particularly inspired by the biblical text:

Isaiah 6:1–4
In the year that King Uzziah died I saw the Lord sitting upon a throne, high and lifted up: and his train filled the temple. Above him stood the seraphim: each had six wings: with two he covered his face, and with two he covered his feet, and with two he flew. And one called to another, and said: Holy, holy, holy is the Lord of hosts; (Lord Zebaoth), the whole earth is full of His glory ["Sanctus, sanctus, sanctus Dominus Deus, Sabbaoth. Pleni sunt coeli et terra gloria tua," which in Bach's Latin version changes "gloria tua" to "gloria euis" to match the German translation, which changes "your glory" to "His glory"].

From this simple yet dramatic text of considerable visual potential Bach created a musical canvas, a vast Prelude and Fugue, by dividing the text so that the "pleni sunt coeli et terra gloria euis" becomes a fugue. It is a composition that presents a vision of musical form and meaning, which, in its spaciousness and spectacular power, places it among the great works not just of Bach but also of the German Baroque.

The Sanctus gives one of the intriguing demonstrations as to how Bach's works seem frequently to be influenced by number.[83] The composer found both inspiration and apparent delight in the picture of the seraphims (the highest order of angels) with their *six wings*. There is an obvious variety of ways that six fills the pages of this work. For example, the original five-part chorus has been expanded to *six parts;* the choral sonority is exceptional in that it is primarily made up of chords of the *sixth;* the timpani part intones a *six-note* ostinato twenty-one times; at measure 19 the three oboes and then the three strings (two violins and viola) have a curious ostinato passage of *sixth* chords repeating the same pitches *six* times as if actually counting out *six.* Or is this Bach's musical image of the six wings? Even more surprising is the *six-part* fugue. It begins in measure 48 (6×8). The fugue subject fills *six* measures, with the result that each entrance of the *six* voice parts will be at the distance of *six* measures. The fugue subject has twenty-four tones (6×4). In measure 78 (6×13), a new subject is introduced in the bass which will be repeated several times. Its significance is made clear only in the following Osanna.

Osanna/Benedictus, Agnus Dei including Dona nobis pacem
The fourth part of Bach's *Missa* is unorthodox in the splitting off of the "Osanna" and "Benedictus" from the Sanctus and adding them to the traditional fifth part of the Mass, the "Agnus Dei." The "Osanna" text from Matthew 21:9 presents the cries of the multitude as Jesus entered Jerusalem. The movement is a parody, which previously had been related to the opening chorus of the secular cantata "Preise dein Glücke," BWV 215. It is more accurate, however, to suggest that both the Osanna and the secular cantata BWV 215 are parodies derived from a chorus in the secular cantata "Es lebe der König, der Vater im Lande," BWV Anh. 11, for which only the text has been preserved. The scoring for the "Osanna" has the largest number of parts found in the Mass. The same complement of instruments remains as employed in the "Sanctus," and added to them is an eight-part double chorus, inspired no doubt by the "many voices" shouting out Osannas and by the traditional employment of a double chorus to represent the multitude of the heavenly host. The parts are arranged as an almost riotous exhibition of homophonic "shouts" within the contrapuntal texture between the two choruses.

Encompassed by the *da capo* repeat of the "Osanna" is the "Benedictus"—"qui venit in nomine Domine" (Blessed is he who comes in the name of the Lord), the line following the "Osanna" in Matthew 21:9. The aria is sung by a tenor with continuo and an obbligato solo part for which Bach does not indicate a choice of instrument. The range and stylistic character of the part suggest the possibility of flute or perhaps violin. In B minor, this quiet and structurally simple aria becomes an oasis of solitary introspection and quietness, that gives welcome relief from the excitement and sonic splendors of the "Sanctus" and the two statements of the "Osanna" surrounding the "Benedictus."

For Bach's concluding division of the Mass Ordinary, the "Agnus Dei, qui tollis peccata mundi," and the concluding line, "Dona nobis pacem" (Lamb of God, who takest away the sins of the world, and Give us peace), he returns again to the intimate aria style for the "Agnus Dei," and to a repetition of the movement from the Gloria for "Dona nobis pacem." The aria has long been known to be a parody based on "Ach bleibe doch, mein liebstes Leben," from the Ascension Oratorio, BWV 11. More recent examination of this thesis shows that, as in the case of the Osanna, the Agnus Dei and the aria from the Ascension oratorio are both derived from another aria, "Entfernet euch, ihr kalten Herzen" (Withdraw your cold hearts), from a wedding serenade, "Auf! Süssentzückenden Gewalt" of 1725 for which the music is lost.[84] The "Agnus Dei" in some ways recalls "Seufzer, Tränen, Kummer, Not" from the early cantata BWV 21. Both are impressive studies in affective dissonances, especially the so-called "saltus duriusculus," expressive melodic leaps of harsh dissonances such as diminished fifths, various sevenths and ninths, as well as chromatic inflections. Whereas the style of the Agnus Dei is more sophisticated and far less obvious than the one in Cantata 21, the stylistic connection with the early aria is interesting because, as Christoph Wolff has suggested, the "Agnus Dei" may be the final composition Bach composed before his death.[85] As is true of the "Qui tollis" and the "Crucifixus," the "Agnus Dei," in a duet with the violins, reminds the listener one more time of Christ crucified. It is a profoundly personal musical representation of passionate supplication by the individual Christian.

The "Great Catholic Mass" (the words are those of Bach's son, C. P. E. Bach, in his estate catalogue) concludes with a parody of second grade, a repeat of the "Gratias agimus tibi" with the new text taken from the third line of the "Agnus Dei." More than one writer has looked with a critical eye on the "Dona nobis pacem" and proposed various theories why Bach decided to complete his enormous work by repeating a movement from the Gloria, which had already existed as a movement from cantata BWV 29. The most obvious reason is that such repetitions of a previous movement at the end of the Mass Ordinary were common in earlier Masses, especially those performed in Dresden.[86] They were usually intended, as is surely the case in Bach's work, to give an encompassing structure to a work of numerous individual movements. But there is clearly more than that in Bach's repetition of the "Gratias." This is made obvious by the effect the "Dona nobis pacem" has on the listener's experience at the final crucial moment in this very long work. Perhaps the explanation of that effect must be an individual one, for each individual listener brings his or her own musical and religious conditioning to the B Minor Mass. It has to do somehow with the peace received from God and God's messenger, in this case, Bach. The music's magnificence, although note for note the same as heard in the Gloria, seems to have grown even more powerful and affecting. It is Bach's last statement of his belief in the glory of God. It is a statement made even more profoundly moving when one realizes it must be these final pages of the score that were in all likelihood the very last notes Bach set to paper.

The mysteries and unanswered questions about the B Minor Mass remain. But the evidence tells us much about this singularly monumental creation of the human mind. Bach finds in the Mass his own individual religious concepts in a mold of Christian idealism almost as old as Christianity itself. Nurtured in the spirit of the Reformation, he does not seem willing to accept the divisiveness and sectarian views of Christianity that festered and caused such untold misery still in the eighteenth century. Is this a Protestant Mass made comprehensible only through a Catholic heritage? Or perhaps is it a Catholic Mass made comprehensible only through a Protestant heritage? Even though Bach's religious beliefs and his work are incomprehensible without the Reformation, without Luther, and without seventeenth-century developments in sacred music, the Mass nevertheless probes deeper than that.

One should note that Bach avoids all congregational hymns throughout the work but not Gregorian chant. Was this because the chorale was not viewed as a universal statement of the sacred? Although Bach incorporates several cantata movements in the Mass, nothing has been chosen hastily or carelessly, and nothing that is taken into the Mass has been left untouched. There are no recitatives, the most obvious musical style representing the secular world of music. Five-part writing predominates even though this is generally rare in other vocal works by Bach and seems to reflect his general interest in aspects of Italian sacred vocal music.

It is as if Bach, from personal conviction and at the close of his own life, had been transformed to a belief in a universal Christian doctrine. There is really no other work, in this writer's experience, that in a fine performance comes so to life, to touch one's soul with the immediacy of a composer's profoundest outpourings of his own soul. Consider what are the greatest monuments to man's creative spirit, the foundations of our Western civilization, and Bach's B Minor Mass must be on that list.[87]

CHAPTER EIGHTEEN

Georg Philipp Telemann (1681–1767)

GEORG PHILIPP TELEMANN, the leading and most prolific German composer of his day, was more famous than either J. S. Bach or George Frideric Handel, both of whom were his friends. His reputation, however, was greatly debased in the nineteenth century, in part by the excessive critical reverence for Bach and Handel and the domination of German music by the great symphony and opera composers. Most damaging was the prevalent critical judgment that made frequent negative comparisons of Telemann's works with those of J. S. Bach. Only with the relatively recent appearance of recordings by "early music" groups of at least a representative number of Telemann's works from his vast output has it been possible to begin to reassess his significance in music history. Such a reassessment, however, has a long way to go before we will be able to discuss Telemann with anything like a comprehensive knowledge of his life and musical achievements.

The enormity of his productivity—he composed more than three thousand works, the majority not published—in itself prevents an adequate overview of the totality of his musical output.[1] Furthermore, we still are not well informed about the very nature of those compelling changes that affected musical forms and styles during the first half of the eighteenth century and were frequently central to Telemann's musical development. He soon achieved music that, although not in imitation of earlier Baroque music, also was not in the high Classical style that dominated the second half of the century. Frequent critical descriptions of Telemann's music as *galant,* or Rococo, or even early Classical simplify the complex and individualistic styles and forms that characterized his music composed during some sixty years. Although born during the Baroque, Telemann created instrumental and vocal music that incorporated significant changes in musical styles occurring in Europe in the first half of the eighteenth century. And his music soon reflected the impact of the Enlightenment that often influenced the musical preferences of audiences, especially those in Hamburg, where he lived and composed music for some forty years.

Telemann was born in Magdeburg on the Elbe in eastern Germany. Almost immediately he immersed himself in the study of music, despite the strong objections of his mother, learning singing, keyboard playing, and the principles of composition. He was an autodidact, teaching himself the recorder, violin, and zither. Already at the age of twelve he had composed an opera, *Sigismundus* (to Postel's libretto). He continued his studies at Zellerfeld from 1693 or early 1694, and from 1697 at the Gymnasium Andreanum in Hildesheim. During a number of visits to the courts nearby at Hanover and Brunswick he heard performances of the latest French, Italian, and "theatrical" styles, learned to play many more musical instruments, and became acquainted with the music of composers such as Steffani, Rosenmüller, Corelli, and Caldara. In 1701 Telemann went to Leipzig intending to study law at the university. However, his focus on law quickly dissipated as he became involved with composing music for the Thomaskirche and Nikolaikirche and, later, for his organization of a forty-member student collegium musicum. In 1702 he took over as musical director of the Leipzig opera house for which he would write many operas. In 1704 he obtained the joint positions of organist and music director at the Neukirche.

SORAU AND EISENACH

In June 1705, Telemann left Leipzig for Sorau in Lower Lusatia (now Zary in Poland) to become Kapellmeister to Count Erdmann II of Promnitz. The count favored French instrumental music, which gave Telemann his first incentive to study French style in the works of Lully and Campra. Telemann later judged he had composed two hundred "Overturen" while employed at Sorau, probably a reference to the number of French overtures and suites composed for that court. Of significance, too, for the subsequent development of his compositional style were his travels with the court to Krakow and Pless (now Pszcyna) in upper Silesia, where he became enthusiastic about Polish and Hanakian (Moravian) folk music, commenting "on its true barbaric beauty. . . . One can hardly believe what wonderful ideas bagpipers and fiddlers have when as often happens the dancing stops and they improvise. One could gather from them in eight days enough ideas for an entire lifetime. There is very much good material that lies hidden in this music, if one knows how to handle it properly. In due course I wrote a number of grand concertos and trios of this style which I clad in an Italian coat with alternating Allegros and Adagios."[2]

At some time, probably in 1707, Telemann moved to Eisenach, where in December 1708 he became Konzertmeister for the newly established court orchestra of Duke Johann Wilhelm of Saxe-Eisenach. The following August he was appointed Secretary and Kapellmeister and charged with performing church cantatas at court, which required him to bring singers to court who could also play violin in an instrumental ensemble. The first indication of Telemann's extraordinary compositional productivity is apparent in his comments that at Eisenach he composed large quantities of vocal music, numerous Masses, psalms, and other sacred works, twenty birthday and name-day serenatas, and fifty German and Italian cantatas. Some of this music was probably sent to Eisenach after Telemann was in Frankfurt. At Eisenach he also composed a large number of concertos for orchestra. A sign of Telemann's great success at Eisenach is reflected in the fact that, even after having accepted a position in Frankfurt in 1712, he later was made Kapellmeister for Eisenach *von Haus aus* (in absentia) from 1717 until 1730. He sent to Eisenach cycles of church cantatas every two years as well as other instrumental and occasional music. In his autobiography Telemann remarked he did not know how he had been persuaded to leave Eisenach, which is perhaps not quite true. He had begun to complain about his heavy responsibilities at the Eisenach court and the indifference of court members toward music. His disenchantment with court life is also reflected in his turning down a major offer from the music-loving and wealthy Dresden court. Artistic freedom, professional security, and dissociation from the whims of court rulers apparently led him to apply between late December 1711 and January 1712 to Frankfurt am Main for the vacant post of city director of music and Kapellmeister at the Barfüsserkirche.

FRANKFURT AM MAIN

Frankfurt was a free Imperial city without aristocratic domination and renowned for the celebrations surrounding the coronation of the Holy Roman Emperor in the Frankfurt cathedral. Telemann's contractual responsibilities required that he provide and direct music for the Barfüsserkirche as well as the Katharinenkirche, for which he wrote several annual cycles of church cantatas. Also he was required to compose music for civic occasions, give music instruction to six or eight schoolboys of his choosing, and supervise the teaching of singing in the Lateinschule. During Telemann's nine years in Frankfurt, his energetic and productive creativity continued with various musical projects and an ever-growing number and variety of new musical works. He assumed directorship and revived the collegium musicum of the Frauenstein society, an association of patricians and the bourgeoisie, which enabled him to present weekly and later biweekly public concerts. They were the beginning of regular public concert life in Frankfurt, and Telemann's devotion to public concerts subsequently became a landmark of his career in Hamburg. He later married (his first wife having died in 1711 in Eisenach) Maria Katharina Textor, daughter of a Frankfurt council clerk, in 1714. This permitted him to become a citizen of Frankfurt, a privilege he would retain by continuing to compose church cantatas for Frankfurt after he settled in Hamburg. In July 1721 the city of Hamburg asked Telemann to succeed Joachim Gerstenbüttel, who had died on 10 April that year and who had served the city as cantor at the Johanneum Lateinschule and as *director musices* of the city's five main churches. Telemann accepted the invitation and for the subsequent forty-six years in Hamburg he achieved his greatest musical successes, which established him as the most famous composer in Germany as well as in other parts of Europe such as England and especially France.

HAMBURG

By 1678 Hamburg had become the largest and richest city in northern Europe, the result in part of having escaped the ravages of the Thirty Years' War. Known as the Venice of the North because of the numerous canals intersecting the city, Hamburg since the Middle Ages was an imperial city-state and a member of the Hanseatic League. It became a great cosmopolitan port city on the Elbe River, the gateway to the North Sea and the innumerable trade routes by water to the four points on the compass. With its focus on trade and commerce, Hamburg attracted transient populations of sailors, merchants, diplomats, and all manner of other travelers. It also was a city of enormous intellectual vitality and an early center for the formation of Enlightenment philosophy. Its disparate population consisted of a mixture of wealthy burghers and numerous refugees who had fled the religious persecutions following the Thirty Years' War, with Dutch, Spanish, Portuguese, and Jews all contributing to the diverse character of the city and to the support of its cultural institutions. The Hamburg public was known for its love of music and its support for concerts and operas. Telemann expressed his delight in being in Hamburg when shortly after his arrival he wrote: "I do not believe that any place can be found which is more encouraging to the spirit of one working in this science [of music] than Hamburg."[3]

In 1678 Hamburg opened the *Oper am Gänsemarkt*, the first public opera house in any city outside Italy, and it was at the opera that Telemann probably gained his first impressions of the city. Telemann had been in Hamburg prior to receiving the invitation to be employed by that city. His comic opera *Die geduldige Socrates* was peformed at the Hamburg opera on 21 January 1721, and the composer undoubtedly attended rehearsals and performances. Even earlier he had traveled to the city for the performance of his *Brockes Passion* in 1718, which was repeated in 1719 and 1720. Telemann was officially made music director of Hamburg's main churches on 17 September 1721, and on 16 October was installed as cantor at the Johanneum. In his previous positions at Sorau and Eisenach he had already displayed remarkable productivity, and he was unfazed by the demands of his new responsibilities that required he compose two cantatas for the city's five main churches each Sunday, and a new Passion cantata each based on the Gospels in a four-year sequence. He provided special cantatas for induction ceremonies, the many civic ceremonies, and oratorios for church consecrations. Each year he also had to compose music for the entertainment of guests of the commandant of the Hamburg militia, which consisted of an oratorio and a serenata (the so-called *Kapitänsmusiken*). In May 1722 he became the director of the Hamburg opera, where he performed his own operas, of which some twenty-nine can be identified but only eight seem to have survived. He also composed operas for the Bayreuth court, where from 1723 to 1726 he held the appointment of Kapellmeister (in absentia).

A study of Telemann's compositional achievements and a comprehensive evaluation of his music as it contributed to the history of music in the eighteenth century are not only daunting to contemplate but in some crucial ways impossible to achieve satisfactorily. Considering the scope of Telemann's lengthy career, significant research into his life and works remains disappointingly minuscule. There still is no comprehensive biography of his life and works in any language, and the rather small amount of published research is largely in German.[4] Despite more recent efforts to publish Telemann's music, only a relatively small portion of his immense output is available today for study. An estimate of Telemann's compositional achievements can only be tentatively suggested, primarily because a large portion of his compositions have been either lost or not published. What can be summarized as the Telemann legacy, even if the data is incomplete, includes the following categories of works:[5] Sacred Music = circa seventeen hundred extant cantatas, including twenty complete annual cantata cycles (circa seventeen hundred lost church cantatas), fifty-two liturgical Passions (forty-eight lost); eight sacred oratorios; thirty-two psalms; sixteen motets; twenty Masses and sacred services. Secular Vocal Music = thirty-two wedding cantatas and serenatas (twenty-nine lost); circa fifty secular cantatas; at least twenty-nine operas (nine survive, although more that are lost is likely); 113 songs. Secular Instrumental Music = circa 125 orchestral suites; 125 concertos; forty-three quartets; 130 trios; eighty-seven solos; eighty for one to four instruments without bass; circa two hundred pieces for keyboard; and twenty-seven *Kapitänsmusiken* (each with an oratorio and serenata pairs; and twenty-nine lost).

TELEMANN'S STYLES

Frequently it has been observed that the period of music history known as the Baroque did not begin on the first day of 1600 (see Chapter 1) but, rather, resulted from several decades of musical developments and changes occurring toward the end of the sixteenth century. Similar circumstances occurred as the Baroque faded away between the end of the seventeenth century and the early decades of the eighteenth. In the first half of the eighteenth century some composers continued to compose in styles and forms of the previous century, while others turned to new concepts of musical composition. Bach and Handel, both of whom lived well into the middle of the eighteenth century, often have been characterized as the last composers of the Baroque, even though their music infrequently employed any of the new styles coming from Italy, France, or Germany. In Germany, it was Telemann, more than any other composer, who was recognized and celebrated for loosening the bonds of Baroque music, which led to new styles and forms in his German music.

Already at the beginning of his career at Sorau, Telemann showed enthusiasm for new stylistic innovations by using Polish folk melodies to compose concertos and trios, which he "clad in an Italian coat." However, developments in Telemann's style in these early compositions still cannot be accurately documented because the scores are either lost or if extant, remain unexamined and undated. From Telemann himself we have important statements defining his developing passion for music. In his autobiography published by Johann

Mattheson in 1718 he related how as a child he was devastated when his mother took away his instruments and forbade that he write another note of music. Nevertheless, at night he spent many hours with pen in hand, in a "lonely place" with his safely obtained instruments. In his thoughts, the following lines occurred to him:

> Singing is the fundamental of music in all things.
> Who applies oneself to composition
> must sing in his music.
> Whoever plays instruments must be experienced with singing.
> Therefore, one diligently imbues singing on young people.[6]

This youthful realization would become a foundation for Telemann's developing musical style. In his 1729 autobiography, submitted to Johann Gottfried Walther, Telemann commented: "What I have done with styles of music is known. First it was the Polish, then followed the French, church, chamber, and operatic styles, and [then] what is called Italian, which currently occupies me more than the others do."[7] Interestingly, there is no reference here to a "German" style.

As early as the first decades of the eighteenth century, Telemann began to compose in what became known and widely discussed as a "mixed" style. Johann David Heinichen (1683–1729), who was a fellow law student with Telemann at Leipzig, suggested in his monumental thorough-bass treatise (1728) that "a felicitous mélange of Italian and French taste would affect the ear most forcefully and must succeed over all the taste of the world."[8] Support for a new German mixed style also came from Johann Joachim Quantz (1697–1773), an admirer of Telemann's compositions, who suggested: "If one has the necessary discernment to choose the best from the styles of different countries, a *mixed style* results that, without overstepping the bounds of modesty, could well be called *the German style*, not only because the Germans came upon it first, but because it has already been established at different places in Germany for many years, flourishes still, and displeases in neither Italy nor France, nor in other lands."[9] The creation of a mixed style of music incorporating elements of French, Polish, and Italian music was a significant factor in the disintegration of Baroque musical concepts and the abandonment of many seventeenth-century German compositional practices.

Although the greatest amount of Telemann's music has not received a thorough overview regarding stylistic developments, those works available for examination, some of which have received analytic attention, allow for a tentative if incomplete description. Telemann scholar Steven Zohn has stated with justification that characterizing Telemann as a *galant*, Rococo, or even an early Classical composer is not justified by Telemann's known repertory.[10] Just how his music changed over the decades still needs to be documented in greater detail, but some characteristics stand out: he created idiomatic vocal forms that "sang," were sometimes reflective of German folk song and popular dance styles. His harmonic style, which remains to be more completely analyzed, is rich and not without some relationships to Baroque practices. Although criticized by some for avoiding contrapuntal textures, quite to the contrary Telemann's works frequently display vigorous and at times elegant counterpoint, as, for example, in his chamber works such as the *Nouveaux quatuors en six suites* (Paris, 1738). Also not to be overlooked are the numerous fugal movements in a large variety of works, the many overtures and concertos, the fugues for keyboard, and in vocal movements in the church cantatas and especially the large choral works.

The term *galant* so frequently applied to Telemann's music, even by the composer himself, is in itself problematic as to what it actually meant, or whether to various writers it could mean different things.[11] The composer generally employed the term to mean free of contrapuntal complexity, up-to-date—that is, modern—and other writers applied *galant* to homophonic textures, short melodic phrases, emphasis on diatonicism, and the "mixed style." Certain popular rhythms such as the Lombardic snap also were included in the context of the *style galant*. Admittedly, the term often had vague connotations and was one of several terms attempting to describe music in that unique period of musical developments following the Baroque era and preceding the Classical age for which no appropriate label has ever been established.

TELEMANN'S REPUTATION BEFORE 1767

In most of Europe during the first half of the eighteenth century, Telemann was one of the most highly regarded and widely known composers. His earlier positions as composer and performer at the courts at Sorau, Eisenach, and especially at Frankfurt am Main had already contributed to his growing reputation as a composer of the kind of music that seemed to resonate most favorably with audiences desiring more popular musical enrichments of traditional church services as well as for public concerts. That reputation was greatly magnified by his long career in Hamburg. Telemann grasped every opportunity to enlarge his audiences both for sacred and secular music. While his positions as teacher at the Johanneum, composer for Hamburg's five great churches, and director of the Hamburg opera all added luster to his reputation, he became remarkably successful financially as a composer because of his business acumen. It enabled him to develop sources of income from his composing and publishing that had seldom been employed by other composers, not even Handel, whose business sense was by no means inferior. Telemann had the foresight to realize that income from his official positions in Hamburg would be inadequate, and that he must find other ways to increase his financial well-being, thoughts no doubt prompted by his large family of children and his second wife who was neither prudent nor apparently concerned about creating large family debts. He had a number of confrontations with publishers and sellers of his texts for cantatas and passions, at times engaging in lawsuits with the municipal press.

Telemann was not, however, in danger of facing poverty. He received substantial honoraria as Kapellmeister at Large for the courts of Eisenach and Bayreuth. From Eisenach he also received an additional salary for serving as "correspondent" (i.e., reporter), supplying political and economic news to the court. In 1722 and for fifteen years he became the director of the Hamburg opera for a substantial annual salary until the theater closed in 1738. It was also in 1722 that Telemann learned of the death of Cantor Johann Kuhnau in Leipzig. The Leipzig town council, undoubtedly influenced by Telemann's earlier successes in Leipzig, was unanimous in choosing him from among several well-known musicians, not the least of them being J. S. Bach. Telemann informed the Hamburg Council of his desire to leave his Hamburg obligations, pointing out to them the advantages of the Leipzig position and the apparent lack of improved financial prospects in Hamburg. Telemann was asked to state what he would require to remain in Hamburg, and despite some unhappiness in the council, they granted a significant raise in his salary. Telemann declined the Leipzig post. In 1729 he also turned down an offer to become Kapellmeister to the St. Petersburg court, and remained in Hamburg for the rest of his life.

Public concerts became a tradition in Hamburg as early as the 1660s, performed in the refectory of the cathedral. Telemann further developed his well-known interest in giving public performances that required an admission fee. Among major musical events in Hamburg were Telemann's programs at the annual banquets for the citizen-captains, the so-called *Kapitänsmusik* performed first for a private audience and repeated for the public. For years he gave public concerts on Mondays and Thursdays at the Drill House, which had been built as a place for exercising the Hamburg city militia. It was also in the Drill House that Telemann gave public concerts of his cantatas that immediately followed their performances at the church service for which they had been composed. Similarly, performances of Passion settings and oratorios requiring admission fees also were presented by Telemann in other public buildings. Another significant endeavor of this extraordinary man was his money-making decision in 1725 to publish his own music, bringing out forty-three publications for which Telemann himself engraved the plates. In order to assure successful sales, he engaged agents in Berlin, Leipzig, Jena, Nuremberg, Frankfurt, Amsterdam, and London, and he also increased the distribution of his music through booksellers and friends.

Telemann's reputation spread throughout Europe. And many respected musicians/writers published in their works various forms of praise for this composer's works. Heinichen, as early as 1709, referred to Telemann as "world famous."[12] Words of praise are also found in Johann Adolph Scheibe's *Critischer Musikus* (Leipzig, 1745), as well as in more than one work by Johann Mattheson, the famous Hamburg composer, encyclopedist, commentator on various aspects of music, and Telemann's colleague and friend. In 1737 Telemann undertook a long-postponed trip to Paris, where according to his own comments he had a standing invitation from "various virtuosi there who had admired several of my printed works." He remained for eight months, established a royal publishing privilege to prevent the printing of pirated editions of his music, and had performed his most recent set of six quartets known as the *Nouveaux quatuors en six suites*.[13] He commented about their performance: "The wonderful manner in which these quartets were played would merit a description here, if only words were adequate to the task. Suffice to say that they caused the ears of the court and the city to be uncommonly attentive, and obtained for me in a short time an almost universal respect, which was accompanied by increased politeness."[14] French music was usually the backbone of Telemann's compositional style, and his emphasis on this style in his music was well known everywhere, but particularly in France. Scheibe commented that "Telemann was the first in Germany who generally made the [French] overture known in Germany, and who so excelled in this that one can say . . . with justification: as an imitator of the French, finally this foreigner himself has surpassed [them] in their own national music."[15]

TELEMANN'S POSTHUMOUS REPUTATION

Although Telemann's works continued to be extolled by many commentators well into the nineteenth century, nevertheless, as early as three years after his death, a new critical tone began to appear. Among the earliest and most severe criticism, which seemed to have established the tone and even the language for many future critics, was that of Christoph Daniel Ebeling (1741–1817), a German writer on music and a translator. It appeared in his *Versuch einer auserlesenen musikalischen Bibliothek* (Hamburg, 1770) in the article "Kritische Würdigung G. Ph. Telemanns vor allem als Kirchenkomponist." Among Ebeling's various criticisms of Telemann's music were: (1) "In his inordinate desire to declaim words correctly, he sacrifices the beauty of the melody. The instruments interrupt the flow of melody more often than they advance it, which is a great fault in all his work which he learned from the French."[16] (2) "He so loved tone painting that not seldom he applied it senselessly to a picturesque word or thought, and therefore so forgot the entire affect that he sank into child's play and wished to paint things that no music can express." (This particular criticism appeared in many subsequent critiques of Telemann's music.) (3) "Above all, he would be greater if it had not been so easy for him to write so unspeakably much. Seldom has one achieved many masterworks from a polygraph." (This, too, was a frequent charge against Telemann's music, as were the words *Vielschreiber*—voluminous writer, endless scribbler—and *polygraph* also frequently applied.)

It was in the nineteenth century that anti-Telemann voices began a concerted attack on Telemann's music, inspired to a considerable extent by an all-encompassing, passionate admiration for the works of J. S. Bach, but perhaps also influenced by an anti-French bias. Distinguished authors such as Philipp Spitta compared Telemann's cantatas unfavorably to those by J. S. Bach. A sampling of other writers of the century underscores the negative evaluation of Telemann's music that was established: Eduard Bernsdorf's article "Ausführliche kritische Würdigung G. Ph. Telemanns," in his *Universal-Lexikon der Tonkunst,* vol. III (Offenbach, 1861),[17] stated: (1) "His melody in arias and instrumental things . . . are very often stiff and dry, as if he is not emancipated from the hastiness of the composing and the stereotypeness of the style."(2) "He shares with many of his contemporaries an exaggerated preference for tone painting." (3) "One of the greatest 'Vielschreiber' that has even been, he no longer knew himself everything he had composed." In "Kritische Beurteilung G. Ph. Telemanns vor allem als Opern-und Kirchenkomponist," *Handbuch der von den ersten Anfängen bis zum Tode Beethoven's* (Leipzig, 1868), Arrey von Dommer believed: (1) "his search for originality misled him in younger years to unnaturalness," (2) "his inclination to tone painting frequently permitted him to put forth absurd trivialities that were entirely against the affect," (3) "He possessed beauty and flow of melody, but they were lost to him in the affectation of expression and the stiltedness of the declamation."

Many examples of such a critical bias reflecting a deep-seated admiration for Bach's achievements appeared, for example, in Carl Hermann Bitter's *Beiträge zur Geschichte des Oratoriums* (Berlin, 1872) in an article "Kritische Bewertung einiger Oratorien G. Ph. Telemanns."[18] Bitter published one of the first biographies of J. S. Bach in 1865, eight years before the first volume of Philipp Spitta's life of Bach. He devoted much of his career to Bach scholarship, discovered important documents regarding Bach's life and work, and "laid the foundation for Bach research with a historical-philological orientation."[19] Here are a few of his criticisms, especially regarding Telemann's Passions: (1) "What Sebastian Bach's great genius had achieved was undoubtedly unknown to him (Telemann). Otherwise his *Seelige Erwägens* [Passion] could hardly have been created." (2) "One would be simply astonished that a man of Telemann's undeniably great talent could allow himself to be carried away by such absurdities. But he was, when one shall judge on the basis of his music and his entire art and how he composed, clearly very vain. . . ." (3) "This work in itself can promote no interest. In the relationship to music history it plays an unsuccessful role. Yet it was much loved in the Hamburg of his time. It was still performed after Telemann's death in churches in its entirety before and after the sermon. From this one simply sees clearly with how little the Hamburg public was satisfied." (4) "So the looking back on Telemann's many years of service in Hamburg can only be regretted. His efforts were a failure and superficial." Hugo Riemann, in an article in his famous *Musik-Lexicon* (Leipzig, 1882), "Ausführliche kritische Würdigung des Komponisten G. Ph. Telemann," praised Telemann's success in that (1) "he composed his works with admirable quickness just as he required, as they demanded." (2) "His style was flowing, and correct. He mastered counterpoint." (3) "Yet, he lacked Bach's genuineness, depth, and profundity."[20]

Otto Wangemann, in an article in his *Geschichte des Oratoriums von den ersten Anfängen bis zur Gegenwart* (Leipzig, 1882), "Kritische Beurteilung der theatralischen Kirchenmusik G. Ph. Telemanns," criticizes Telemann for his operatic treatment of "Es ist vollbracht," but finds even more unacceptable a long (three-measure) melisma for the word "streiten": (1) "Can one imagine anything more unnatural? If the good Telemann already then had had an idea what Bach had already created, he would certainly have found it difficult to give out such nonsense." In the *Dictionary of Music and Musicians,* ed. Sir George Grove (London, 1895), Alfred Maczewski writes in his article on Telemann: (1) "In his own day he was placed with Hasse and Graun as a composer of the first rank, but the verdict of posterity has been less favourable." (2) "With all his undoubted ability he originated noth-ing [!], but was content to follow the tracks laid down by the old contrapuntal [*sic*] school of organists, whose ideas and forms he adopted without change. . . ." (3) "He was a highly-skilled contrapuntalist, and had, as might be expected from his great productiveness, a technical mastery of all the received forms of composition. . . . but these advantages were neutralised by his lack of any earnest ideal, and by a fatal facility naturally inclined to superficiality. . . ." (4) "His shortcomings are most patent in his church works, which are of greater historical importance than his operas and other music." (5) "The shallowness of the church music of the latter half of the 18th century is distinctly traceable to Telemann's influence, although that was the very branch of composition in which he seemed to have everything in his favour—position, authority, and industry." (6) "But the mixture of con-ventional counterpoint with Italian opera air, which constituted his style, was not calculated to conceal the absence of any true and dignified ideal of church music."[21]

Finally, at the opening of the twentieth century, one musical scholar, the distinguished Arnold Schering, in the preface to his volume of Telemann's works in the *Denkmäler deutscher Tonkunst, erste Folge,* vols. 29 and 30 (Leipzig, 1907), writes with insight into the nature and importance of Telemann's music that seems to have escaped most if not all previous critics. In speaking of Telemann's concertos, he points out: (1) "A classification of his concertos according to the order of movements or stylistic unity is impossible, for the number of experiments is great. The F major concerto clearly illustrates such experiment in the arrangement: Presto–Un poco grave–Allegretto–Scherzo–[Rondo]–Polacca–Min-uetto, as well as the peculiar insertion of the violin solo with the Doubles of the dance movements. The work is actually an orchestra suite with introductory violin concerto, and it was perhaps intended for an opportunity where it was meant to show the best side of the orchestra performers. This explains the strong instrumentation. To it in appropriate relationship stand the choice of themes, which when the full orchestra is employed are broad and imposing, and later in the solo parts are found to be more graceful. Many unusual mixtures of sounds and accompaniment effects were sought for, perhaps for the first time, and also metrical complications are not lacking." (2) "The spirit that lives in the work is, said in the sense of the time, absolutely progressive. Compared to concertos grosso and suites by Bach and Handel, Telemann's movements have a tendency toward folk mel-odies and harmony which perhaps are the result of blending Italian and French style elements. . . . At hand are also aspects which belong to the older art, certain modish melodic turns, the constraint of the thorough-bass and, above all, the lack of thematic development that just there today's critics most often miss where Telemann's themes approach the ex-pressiveness of the new times. . . . Telemann's style, as he documents it in this concerto, is a transitional style, which leads from the old Sebastian Bach period to a cantabile [style] in the second half of the eighteenth century."[22]

Telemann and the End of the Baroque

Telemann was an amazingly prolific composer. His critics were correct in that judgment (although labeling him a *vielschreiber* suggests they thought this expressed a negative criticism). It was inevitable that his massive productivity would at times produce music of varying strengths of originality and artistic success. A great number of his scores were composed in the heat of immediate need, and he had little or no assistance as far as is known to aid in the sheer physical efforts of creating or obtaining necessary texts, or in the immense efforts of composing and scoring his works—unlike the invaluable assistance J. S. Bach received from students and his family. The fact that Telemann was self-taught gave him significant freedom from the more rigid German discipline of composition based on venerable even if out-of-date compositional techniques. It is clear that at an early stage he decided that his music would avoid much of the complexities of earlier German music— music that would "sing" and that would appeal to audiences of various musical sophistication. In his autobiography (1731), sent to Mattheson, he confirmed his desire to compose with simplicity and that in church music "I not only endeavored to employ all instruments according to their individual qualities, but also with an intent for lightness, as I have almost always done in all of my other compositions." This idea inspired another poem from Telemann:

> For I am of the belief—
> A movement that contains sorcery in its lines,
> I mean, when the page contains many difficult passages,
> almost always makes music a burden,
> whereby one often notices plenty of grimaces.
> I say furthermore: one who can be of use to many,
> Does better than he who writes something only for the few;
> What is simply composed, now universally serves everyone:
> Therefore it will be best, that one remains with this [practice].[23]

From the beginning, Telemann developed a new and distinctive musical style focused variously on French chamber and orchestral works, Italian instrumental and vocal music, and also the colorful and largely unknown musical sounds he discovered in Poland.

What so many of his late-eighteenth- and nineteenth-century critics failed to recognize or to acknowledge was that Telemann realized more clearly than they could the fact that a new century had brought changes to European culture, and that included a turning away from the support of aristocratic patrons and a need to appeal to a general populace of music lovers such as existed in Hamburg. J. S. Bach largely ignored this fact until he became involved with his popular collegium musicum concerts in Leipzig. Handel recognized soon enough the new demands of societal change that led him to turn his attention from the aristocratic opera audiences and to seek out and find acceptance with the greater popularity of his sacred and secular oratorios. Telemann's critics seemed to believe that an appreciation of Telemann's new musical styles degraded or insulted the unique greatness of composers such as J. S. Bach, although interestingly neither Telemann's godson, Carl Philipp Emanuel Bach, nor his grandson, Georg Michael Telemann, failed to praise and perform his music with success long after Telemann's death.

It is unfortunate that so much of Telemann's music is lost or unavailable, especially the early works composed at Sorau, the sacred vocal music for Eisenach, the many operas for Leipzig that would give some indication of the sources of his musical style and perhaps those Baroque elements the young composer might have relied on as he developed his own non-Baroque idioms. Music history has long been viewed as a series of compartmentalized historical periods: Medieval, Renaissance, Baroque, Classic, Romantic, Modern, and now Postmodern. They have been particularly useful as historical landmarks for those who teach music history in colleges and universities. What has often been forgotten, however, is the obvious fact that such periodization idealizes historical facts that never existed. Historical developments are not formed from unified blocks of conceptualized musical styles. Although style developments have not been totally ignored in music literature, they have often taken second place to the notion of a single dominating style for a specific period.

Telemann was a pathfinder in music, an original, imaginative creator of musical forms and styles for the new age in which he became a composer. His vast number of compositions, many of them now becoming more available in publications and recordings, hold answers to significant and seldom answered questions regarding how music changed and developed in the eighteenth century, a century for which musical terminology is often vague and conflicting. Telemann's music includes examples of literally all of the forms of music not only prevalent in the first half of the eighteenth century but also many of the forms and styles developing after mid-century. His music is most frequently defined as being either *galant* or Rococo, or pre-Classical, or early Classical. One can conclude, however, that in various ways his music examines and illustrates all of these somewhat vague concepts in the multiplicity of forms he composed in such staggering numbers. It would be misleading to suggest that Telemann single-handedly ended the Baroque era in his music. This he certainly did not attempt. But what his music does substantiate is that he was one of music history's outstanding and gifted composers, one who clearly realized early in his career that music of the seventeenth century no longer had significant relevance for the new audiences of the age of the Enlightenment. The inevitable conclusion for Telemann was to understand that he must create new forms and styles of music that would find favor with the variety of audiences in Hamburg, music that would express the spirit of a new century in music. For this he had both the insight and the ability to compose a prodigious number of significant musical compositions, an ability making him by far the most famous and widely acclaimed composer of the first half of the eighteenth century.

Notes

INTRODUCTION

1. "Lettre de M.X*** à Mlle.*** sur l'origine de la musique," in *Le Mercure,* May, 1734, pp. 868–69, first cited by Georgia Cowart, *The Origins of Modern Musical Criticism* (Ann Arbor, 1981), p. 97.

2. *Correspondence de Jean Baptiste Rousseau et de Brosette,* ed. Paul Bonnefon (Paris, 1911), II, pp. 180–281.

3. Quoted from the *Mémoires,* in Bruno Migliorini, *Profili di parole* (Florence, 1968), p. 25.

4. Antoine Pluche, *Spectacle de la nature* (Paris, 1746), vol. 7. These French origins of the term are from "Baroque" by Claude Palisca in *Handwörterbuch der musikalischen Terminologie* (Wiesbaden, 1971–). See also his article for the "Baroque" in *The New Grove Dictionary of Music and Musicians,* 2d ed. (London, 2001), vol. 2, pp. 749–56.

5. In his "Lettre sur la musique françoise," *Oeuvres complètes* (Paris, 1826), vol. 14, p. 22.

6. Rousseau continues: "It seems as if this term comes from the *baroco* of the Logicians," a reference to one of the rarer syllogisms of Medieval logicians: the fourth mode of the second figure. This origin of "baroque" now is generally thought incorrect, although it was originally advanced by both Benedetto Croce, *Storia della età barocca in Italia* (Bari, 1929), and René Wellek, "The Concept of Baroque in Literary Scholarship," in *Journal of Aesthetics and Art Criticism* V (1946), pp. 77–106.

7. In *Jahrbuch der Musikbibliothek Peters,* 26 (1919), pp. 7–15.

8. *Music in the Baroque Era* (New York, 1947), p. xiii.

9. Ibid., pp. 16–17.

10. Ibid., p. 18.

I. THE RENAISSANCE IN TRANSITION

1. Victor-L. Tapié, *The Age of Grandeur: Baroque Art and Architecture,* trans. A. Ross Williamson (New York, 1961).

2. *De pueris recte instituendis* (Venice, 1533), cited in ibid., p. 14. Palisca adds that this important passage from Plato was later quoted by Johannes Ott, *Missae tredecim* (Nuremberg, 1539); Zarlino (*Istitutioni,* IV, p. 32); Giovanni Bardi, *Discorso mandato a Caccini sopra la musica e 'l cantar,* in Giovanni Battista Doni, *Lyra Barberina* (Florence, 1763), II, p. 244; Giulio Caccini, foreword to *Le nuove musiche* (Florence, 1601=1602); and Guilio Cesare Monteverdi, in preface to Claudio Monteverdi's *Scherzi musicali* (Venice, 1607).

3. From Aldo Manuzio, *Lettere volgari di diversi nobilissimi huomini . . . Libro terzo* (Venice, 1594), pp. 114–18. Translation by Lewis Lockwood in *Palestrina, Pope Marcellus Mass,* ed. L. Lockwood (New York, 1975), p. 11.

4. See Thomas J. Mathiesen, *Ancient Greek Music Theory: A Catalogue Raisonné of Manuscripts* (Munich, 1988), which in its comprehensive listing of manuscripts indicates the large number that originated in the fifteenth and sixteenth centuries.

5. Claude Palisca, *Humanism in Italian Renaissance Musical Thought* (New Haven, 1985), p. 50.

6. Translation by Tim Carter in *Music in Late Renaissance & Early Baroque Italy* (Portland, Ore., 1992), p. 53.

7. Vicentino's treatise was written to defend his position in a debate with Vicenti Lusitano, which he lost, on the role of the chromatic and enharmonic genera in contemporary practice. A judge in the debate, Ghiselin Danckerts (c. 1510–after 1565), a singer in the Sistine Chapel, left his own conservative views about contemporary music in an unpublished treatise, *Sopra una differentia musicale,* Bibl. Casanatense, Rome, MS 1880. The controversy encapsulates the growing split among practicing musicians and theorists. These fascinating documents give early evidence of the rejection of speculative theory as a guide to composing and of the employment of all musical means for the purpose of expressing the affects of texts. The controversy is discussed in detail in Claude Palisca, *The Beginnings of Baroque Music: Its Roots in Sixteenth Century Theory and Polemics* (Ph.D. diss., Harvard University, 1953).

8. Alfred Einstein, *The Italian Madrigal,* trans. Krappe, Sessions, and Strunk (Princeton, 1949), vol. I, p. 249.

9. Maria Rika Maniates, *Mannerism in Italian Music and Culture, 1530–1630* (Chapel Hill, 1979), p. 314.

10. See ibid., pp. 331–409 for a detailed examination of the concept of Mannerism and how it may help to define the madrigals written in the final decades of the sixteenth century.

11. Einstein, *The Italian Madrigal,* vol. II, p. 575.

12. Monteverdi's madrigals are discussed in Chapter 3.

13. The performance of sacred works for two or more choirs in San Marco remains a cloudy issue. Even as late as the end of the sixteenth century evidence proves that vesper psalm settings were not sung from the organ lofts above the choir but rather from the ground floor of the basilica, often from one of the two large pulpits placed on either side of the iconostasis (the large screen separating the sanctuary from the rest of the church). See David Bryant, "The *cori spezzati* of St. Mark's: Myth and Reality," in *Early Music History I* (Cambridge, 1981), pp. 165–86.

14. The author is indebted for these comments on the early history of double-choir music to the extensive study by Anthony F. Carver, *Cori Spezzati: The Development of Sacred Polyphonic Music to the Time of Schütz,* 2 vols. (Cambridge, 1988).

15. See Tim Carter, *Music in Late Renaissance & Early Baroque,* pp. 111–12.

16. Volume II of Carver's *Cori spezzati: The Development of Sacred Polyphonic Music,* includes complete scores of double choir works from the earliest examples through seventeenth-century German composers, including those by Phinot, Padovano, Lasso, Palestrina, and Victoria.

17. Revised dates according to Martin Morell, "The Biographies of Andrea and Giovanni Gabrieli," *Early Music History,* 3 (Cambridge, 1983), pp. 110–11.

18. The concertos are published in the *Edizione nazionale delle opera di Andrea Gabrieli,* series II, vols. 1 and 2 (Milan, 1989), ed. David Bryant.

19. Ibid., vol. 1, pp. 45 and 173.

20. Michael Praetorius, *Syntagma musicum,* III (Wolfenbüttel, 1618), pp. 91–92.

21. Carver, *Cori spezzati: The Development of Sacred Polyphonic Music,* p. 140.

22. See ibid., pp. 129–44 for an excellent discussion regarding Andrea Gabrieli's compositional achievements in the polychoral style.

23. Ibid., pp. 146–48 for a good summary of these performance practices.

24. *"Bassone cavata dalla parte più basse del 40, per sonar in mezzo del circolo con un*

trombone . . . per sostentamento della armonia per sonarsi con organo, liuto & cimbalo o viole."
The Florentine performance is reported in Massimo Troiano, *Dialoghi di Massimo Trojano: Nozze dello . . . Prencipe Guglielmo . . . Duca di Baviera; e . . . Renata di Loreno . . .* (Venice, 1569), p. 47. Troiano refers only to a forty-voice motet by Alessandro Striggio. Gustave Reese was the first to draw attention to the specific motet of Striggio in *Music in the Renaissance* (New York, 1954), p. 487.

25. The classic study of the early history of organ basses is by Otto Kinkeldey, *Orgel und Klavier in der Musik des 16. Jahrhunderts* (Leipzig, 1910).

26. Published with an English translation in F. T. Arnold, *The Art of Accompaniment from a Thorough-bass* (London, 1931), pp. 10–20.

27. The development of theater with music in the Italian Renaissance is discussed in a series of outstanding articles by Nino Pirrotta in *Music and Theatre from Poliziano to Monteverdi* (Cambridge, 1982).

28. The citation is from Pirrotta, p. 198. He also cites an earlier reference to a new concept of vocal style in a letter addressed to Pico della Mirandola around 1490 by Poliziano, author of the *Orfeo* play (c. 1480). In describing the singing by Fabio Orsini at a banquet, he says: "His voice was not entirely that of someone reading, nor entirely that of someone singing; both could be heard, and yet neither separated one from the other; it was, in any case, even or modulated, and changed as required by the passage. Now it was varied, now slowing down and now quickening in pace, but always it was precise, always clear and always pleasant." Ibid., p. 36.

29. Details given in ibid., pp. 176–82.

30. Ibid., pp. 194–96.

31. For a comprehensive examination of the influence of pastoralism on music, see Hermann Jung, *Die Pastorale: Studien zur Geschichte eines musikalischen Topos* (Bern and Munich, 1980).

32. Pirrota, *Music and Theatre from Poliziano to Monteverdi,* p. 264.

33. The various viewpoints concerning the development of the dramatic pastoral are discussed in Ellen Harris, *Handel and the Pastoral Tradition* (Oxford, 1980), pp. 16–25.

34. For a discussion of the literary background to Beccari's play and also dalla Viola's music, where the musical excerpts are printed in their entirety, see Henry W. Kaufmann, "Music for a *Favola Pastorale* (1554)," in *A Musical Offering: Essays in Honor of Martin Bernstein,* ed. E. H. Clinkscale and C. Brook (New York, 1977), pp. 163–82.

2. BAROQUE INNOVATIONS IN ITALY TO CIRCA 1640

1. Letter, Pietro de' Bardi to Giovanni Battista Doni (Florence, 16 December 1634); printed in Angelo Solerti, *Le origini del melodramma* (Turin, 1903), pp. 143–45.

2. In his dedication to Bardi in *L'Euridice composta in musica in stile rappresentativo* (Florence, 1600), fol. 2r, and again in the preface to *Le nuove musiche* (Florence, 1601 = 1602 n.s.), fol. Aiv. In Pietro de' Bardi's letter to Doni he also refers to the group as the Camerata.

3. See Claude Palisca, ed., *Girolamo Mei (1519–1594): Letters on Ancient and Modern Music to Vincenzo Galilei and Giovanni Bardi* (Rome, 1960, 2/1970).

4. Given in English translation in Claude V. Palisca, *The Florentine Camerata, Documentary Studies and Translations* (New Haven, 1989), pp. 56–77. Although the three extant copies of this letter are not addressed to Galilei, Palisca gives convincing evidence that Galilei was the recipient of the letter. Excerpts from this letter are all from Palisca's translation.

5. *Discorso mandato a Giulio Caccini detto Romano, sopra la musica anticha, e 'l cantar bene,* original text and English trans. in Palisca, *The Florentine Camerata,* pp. 78–89.

6. (Florence, 1581, R/New York, 1967); English translation of pp. 80–90 in O. Strunk, *Source Readings in Music History* (New York, 1950), pp. 302–22.

7. One preserved example of Galilei's monodic style appears in his manuscript, *Cosi nel mio cantar voglio essere aspro.* See the transcription by Tim Carter in *Jacopo Peri: His Life and Works* (New York, 1989), vol. II, pp. 367–69.

8. The term "monody" was not employed by the composers of what were solo madrigals. It was first used in the writings of Giovanni Battista Doni in the 1630s.

9. *Le nuove musiche* (Florence 1601 = 1602 n.s.). New ed. by H. Wiley Hitchcock (Madison, Wis., 1970). The three monodies are "Perfidissimo volto," "Vedrò'l mio sol," and "Dovrò dunque morire."

10. The title, which is best translated as "new musical compositions," suggests that Caccini had probably expected his work would be the first publication in the new style of solo vocal compositions. However, shortly before its delayed publication in July another book of monodies had appeared in March by Domenico Melli, *Musiche . . . composte sopra alcuni madrigali di diversi. Per cantare nel Chitarrone, clavicembalo, & altri instromenti* (Venice, 1602) with a content similar in musical concept.

11. Florence, 1614. New ed. by H. Wiley Hitchcock (Madison, Wis., 1978).

12. Including the books of monodies by Domenico Melli (1602), Bartolomeo Barbarino and Domenico Brunetti (1606), Lodovico Bellanda (1607), Francesco Rasi (1608), and Sigismondo d'India (in four books, 1609, 1618, 1621, 1623), and Jacopo Peri (1609), "Le varie musiche."

13. The only major study of the development of the monody in English remains the unpublished dissertation by Nigel Fortune, "Italian Secular Song from 1600 to 1653: The Origins and Development of Accompanied Monody" (Ph.D. Cambridge University, 1954), which is the source of much of the information about the monody given here. See also Fortune's introductory essay on the subject, "Italian Secular Monody from 1600 to 1635," *MQ* 39 (1953), pp. 171–95, and his "A Handlist of Printed Italian Secular Monody Books, 1602–1635," *Royal Musical Association Research Chronicles* III (1963), pp. 27–50. See also Jan Racek, *Stilprobleme der Italienischen Monodie* (Prague, 1965).

14. These are discussed by Murray C. Bradshaw in "Cavalieri and Early Monody," *Journal of Musicology* 9 (1991), pp. 238–53 and also in the introduction to his edition of Cavalieri's *Lamentations* in the series of the American Institute of Musicology: *Miscellanea 5, Early Sacred Monody. Emilio de' Cavalieri, Lamentations and Responsories of 1599 and 1600 (Biblioteca Vallicelliana MS o 31)* (Neuhausen-Stuttgart, 1990).

15. Translation from Peri's preface in Oliver Strunk, *Source Readings in Music History* (New York, 1950), p. 373.

16. Letter published in translation by Claude Palisca, "Musical Asides in the Correspondence of Emilio De'Cavalieri," *MQ* 49 (1963), pp. 353–54.

17. Giudotti's remarks are dated September 3, 1600, facsimile editions, ed. Francesco Mantica (Rome, 1912), with later facsimile editions published in Bologna and Farnborough, 1967.

18. Translation by Tim Carter in *Music in the Late Renaissance and Early Baroque,* p. 203.

19. Nino Pirrotta, *Music and Theatre from Poliziano to Monteverdi* (Cambridge, 1982), pp. 240–41.

20. See William V. Porter, "Peri's and Corsi's *Dafne:* Some New Discoveries and Ob-

servations," *JAMS* 18 (1965), pp. 170–96. Two of the excerpts are identified as by Corsi. The brevity of the musical passages makes any decisive evaluation of the work impossible. One of the excerpts is identified as in the recitative style and by Peri. It is given in Carter, *Jacopo Peri*, vol. II, ex. 12, pp. 377–78.

21. Lauda text is given in Howard E. Smither, *A History of the Oratorio*, vol. I (Chapel Hill, 1977), pp. 57–64, and p. 86. It is usually ascribed to Agostino Manni (1548–1618), a poet who joined the Oratory in 1577 and may also have been the author of Cavalieri's entire text.

22. Preface to Peri's *La musiche di Jacopo Peri, nobil Fiorentino, sopra L'Euridice del Sig. Ottavio Rinuccini, rappresentate nello sponsalizio della Christianisima Maria Medici, regina di Francia* (Florence, February 1601, n.s.): "Non dimeno Giulio Caccini (detto Romano) il cui sommo valore è noto al Mondo, fece l'aria d'Euridice, & alcune del Pastore, e Ninfa del Coro, e de' Cori, AL CANTO, AL BALLO, SOSPIRATE, e POI CHE GLI ETERNI IMPERI. E questio, perchè dovevano esser cantate da persone depende[n]ti da lui, le quali Arie si leggono nella sua composta. . . ."

23. For the first time in the title of Caccini's *L'Euridice: L'Euridice composta in musica in stile rappresentativo da Giulio Caccini detto Romano.*

24. Translation by Tim Carter in *Jacopo Peri, 1561–1633: His Life and Works*, pp. 152–54.

25. Recommended is Tim Carter's extensive discussion of Peri's opera in *Jacopo Peri, 1561–1633: His Life and Works*, pp. 157–204.

26. Translation by Tim Carter in *Jacopo Peri, 1561–1633: His Life and Works*, pp. 152–54.

27. For the history of opera before 1637, see Lorenzo Bianconi, *Music in the Seventeenth Century*, translated by David Bryant (Cambridge, 1987), pp. 170–80.

28. In the previous year Stefano Landi composed *La morte d'Orfeo* (Venice, 1619), an opera often cited as having been performed in Rome, although no evidence has ever been found to substantiate this claim. For excerpts from this opera, see Hugo Goldschmidt, *Studien zur Geschichte der italienischen Oper im 17. Jahrhundert*, vol. I (Leipzig, 1901), p. 188.

29. See the study by Wolfgang Witzenmann, "Autographe Marco Marazzolis in der Biblioteca Vaticana," *Analecta musicologica* 7 (1969), pp. 36–86; 9 (1970), pp. 203–94.

30. Cited from Stuart Reiner, "Vi sono molt'altre mezz'arie . . . ," *Studies in Music History: Essays for Oliver Strunk* (Princeton, 1968), p. 241.

31. The meaning of "aria" changes significantly between the sixteenth and later centuries. See Claude V. Palisca, "Aria in Early Opera," in *Festa musicologica: Essays in Honor of George J. Buelow* (Stuyvesant, N.Y., 1995), pp. 257–69, or Palisca's comprehensive study of the term under "Aria/air/ayre/Arie," *Handwörterbuch der musikalischen Terminologie*, ed. Hans Heinrich Eggebrecht (Stuttgart, 1971–).

32. Concerning the Barberini influence on culture in Rome, see the important study by Frederick Hammond, *Music & Spectacle in Baroque Rome: Barberini Patronage under Urban VIII* (New Haven, 1994), especially for the operas, pp. 183–253.

33. Facsimile ed. (Bologna, 1970). The published score is richly illustrated with the stage sets.

34. Facsimile ed. (Bologna, s.d.). Also with reproductions of stage sets.

35. Facsimile ed. (Bologna, s.d.).

36. A major study of Roman Baroque opera is Margaret Murata's *Operas for the Papal Court, 1631–1668* (Ann Arbor, 1981). I am indebted to her work for many of the observations made here regarding the musical substance of these operas.

37. Bianconi, *Music in the Seventeenth Century,* p. 2. By comparison, in the previous decade, 1591–1600, 271 first editions appeared.

38. In *Della musica dell'età nostra che non è punto inferiore, anzi è migliore di quella dell'età passata (1640),* given in Angelo Solerti, *Le origini del melodramma* (Turin, 1908), p. 171. Translation by Carter, *Music in Late Renaissance & Early Baroque,* p. 241.

39. The first edition is lost, and the second edition dated 1620 apparently is not extant. A facsimile of the 1626 edition is given in *Italian Secular Song: 1606–1636),* vol. 6, *Venice I: Books Published by Alessandro Vincenti,* ed. Gary Tomlinson (New York, 1986).

40. Facsimile ed. in *Italian Secular Song: 1606–1636,* vol. 3, *Rome and Naples,* ed. Gary Tomlinson (New York, 1986).

41. See Ellen Rosand, "Barbara Strozzi, *virtuossima cantatrice:* The Composer's Voice," *JAMS* 31 (1978), pp. 241–81.

42. Edited by Ellen Rosand in the series *The Italian Cantata in the Seventeenth Century,* vol. 5 (New York, 1986). It includes all of Opp. 2, 3, and 6 and selections from Opp. 7 and 8.

43. The terminology comes from Eleanor Calouri's important work on Rossi's cantatas, *The Cantatas of Luigi Rossi: Analysis and Thematic Index,* 2 vols. (Ann Arbor, 1981). A collection of Rossi's cantatas in facsimile are published in *The Italian Cantata in the Seventeenth Century,* vol. I, *Cantatas by Luigi Rossi,* selected and introduction by Francesco Luisi (New York, 1986).

44. A notable exception to the general lack of substantive studies of sacred music in the first half of the seventeenth century is Jerome Roche's *North Italian Church Music in the Age of Monteverdi* (Oxford, 1984).

45. Monteverdi in the preface to his fifth books of madrigals (1605) established a similar distinction between the *prima prattica* and the *seconda prattica* which stressed the contrast between the old Renaissance polyphonic techniques in which music was master of the words and the new madrigal style where words were master of the music. Monteverdi's concept is based primarily on the differences in employing dissonances and is not in fact an all-encompassing definition of "old" versus "new" musical styles.

46. See Christoph Wolff, *Der Stile Antico in der Musik Johann Sebastian Bachs* (Wiesbaden, 1968).

47. Relevant to the study of the *stile antico* tradition is: Karl G. Fellerer, *Das Palestrinastil und seine Bedeutung in der vokalen Kirchenmusik des achtzehnten Jahrhunderts* (Augsburg, 1929).

48. The origins and spread of new forms of sacred music in the early seventeenth century are a complex subject. One is encouraged to read the excellent work by Roche, *North Italian Church Music in the Age of Monteverdi,* especially the chapter "The Social and Geographical Context."

49. See Murray C. Bradshaw, ed., *Emilio De' Cavalieri: The Lamentations and Responsories of 1599 and 1600,* in *Miscellanea 5: Early Sacred Monody,* vol. 3.

50. These three types of monody were discussed by Giovanni Battista Doni, *Annotazioni sopra il Compendio de' generi e de' modi della musica* (Rome, 1640), pp. 60–62, 284, and 359.

51. Ibid., pp. 126–27.

52. The full title reads: *Cento concerti ecclesiastici a una, a due, a tre, & quattro voci. Con il basso continuo per sonar nell'organo. Nova inventione commoda per ogni sorte de cantori, & per il organisti.* To date no complete edition of this seminal work has appeared, nor have

volumes II and III. Volume I in *Monumenti musicali mantovani,* edited by Claudio Gallico, contains only the concertos for one part and continuo. The only monograph on Viadana is by Federico Mompellio, *Lodovico Viadana, musicista fra due secoli* (Florence, 1966), which includes a chronologically arranged catalogue of the composer's works.

53. Roche, *Northern Italian Church Music,* p. 57. See further his discussion of Viadana's *Cento Concerti,* pp. 51–58, to which the present author is indebted here for details of his discussion of Viadana.

54. Example from *Monumenti musicali mantovani,* pp. 24–25.

55. The complete title states: *Arie devote, le quali contengono in se la maniera di cantar' con gratia, l'imitation' delle parole, et il modo di scriver' passaggi, et altri affetti.* The work is dedicated to another of the great Roman clerics and maecenas, Cardinal Montalto.

56. Examples of sacred monodies by Barbarino and Tomasi appear in Roche, *Northern Italian Church Music,* pp. 68–69.

57. See Roche, "The Duet in Early Seventeenth-century Italian Church Music," *Proceedings of the Royal Musical Association,* xciii (1967–1968), pp. 33–50, which includes the examples cited here: *Hodie nobis de caelo* and *Anima Christi.*

58. See Graham Dixon, "Progressive Tendencies in the Roman Motet during the Early Seventeenth Century," *Acta Musicologica,* liii (1981), pp. 105–19.

59. Cited by Dixon, ibid., p. 108.

60. Roche, in *Northern Italian Church Music,* gives numerous other composers contributing to this genre.

61. See Dixon, *Progressive Tendencies in the Roman Motet,* pp. 116–19.

62. This important document concerning performance practices of multi-choir compositions is given in its entirety in English translation in Roche, *Northern Italian Church Music,* pp. 118–19.

63. Translation taken from the preface of Donati's work based on that in Martha N. Johnson, *A Critical Edition of Ignatio Donati's Magnificat Sexti Toni (Salmi Boscarecci, 1623)* (D.M. document, Indiana University, 1986), pp. 137–39.

64. See Brown, *Music in the Renaissance,* chapter 9, for a concise discussion of the growth of instrumental forms in the sixteenth century. The standard history of keyboard music up to 1700 remains Willi Apel's *The History of Keyboard Music to 1700,* trans. by Hans Tischler (Bloomington, Ind., 1972).

65. The outstanding study of Frescobaldi's life and works is by Frederick Hammond, *Girolamo Frescobaldi: His Life and Music* (Cambridge, Mass., 1983).

66. Severo Bonini, *Discorsi e regole, a Bilingual Edition,* trans. and ed. Mary Ann Bonino (Provo, 1979), p. 155.

67. See ibid., pp. 274–325, for a complete descriptive catalogue of all of Frescobaldi's publications and principal manuscript sources.

68. English translation in Bianconi, *Music in the Seventeenth Century,* pp. 95–96, which is adapted for the commentary from the preface cited below.

69. From *Il primo libro di Toccate d'intavolatura di cembalo e organo, 1615–1637,* ed. Etienne Dabellay, in Girolamo Frescobaldi, *Opere complete,* vol. 2 (Milan, 1977), p. 16.

70. Ibid. p. 32.

71. This and the next example are taken from *Il primo libro di capricci* (1624), ed. Etienne Darbellay, in Girolamo Frescobaldi, *Opere complete,* vol. 4 (Milan, 1984).

72. For a detailed discussion concerning this practice, see Stephen Bonta, "The Use of the Sonata da Chiesa," *JAMS* 22 (1969), pp. 54–84.

3. CLAUDIO MONTEVERDI (1567–1643)

1. The best shorter biographical-analytical study in English of Monteverdi and his music remains Denis Arnold's *Monteverdi* (London, 1963). The work by Leo Schrade, *Monteverdi, Creator of Modern Music* (New York, 1950), despite the curiously misleading title, is a valuable contribution to the study of Monteverdi and his music.

2. Gary Tomlinson, *Monteverdi and the End of the Renaissance* (Berkeley, 1987), provides an in-depth study of Monteverdi's madrigals.

3. Madrigal 17, *Crudel perche mi fuggi,* is often attributed to Tasso, although the text is by Guarini.

4. Discussed by Arnold, see pp. 56–58.

5. Translation cited by Tomlinson, p. 49, is from Luciano Rebay, *Italian Poetry: A Selection from St. Francis of Assisi to Salvatore Quasimodo* (New York, 1969).

6. See, for example, the Sanctus, mm. 34–38, in the six-part Mass of 1610.

7. The term is Tomlinson's from *Monteverdi and the End of the Renaissance.* See his extensive discussion of Wert's heroic style in relationship to Monteverdi's, pp. 58–72.

8. By Arnold, *Monteverdi,* pp. 61–64.

9. Tomlinson, pp. 98–111, makes some convincing deductions regarding the order of composition of the madrigals in Books IV and V.

10. Joel Newman, in a Communication to *JAMS* 14 (1961), pp. 418–19, has suggested the author to be Maurizio Moro. See also Tomlinson, pp. 110–11.

11. Translation from Tomlinson, pp. 154–55.

12. As Tomlinson, p. 138, reminds us, the original *Lamento d'Arianna* was not a true monody as performed in the opera, as it is known the accompaniment consisted of an ensemble of viols. That Monteverdi's *Lamento* was particularly popular is revealed also in the many imitations of it published subsequently by other composers. Monteverdi not only capitalized on it by arranging the *Lamento* for five-part madrigal ensemble but also adapted sacred words to the solo version (1623), published in the *Selva morale e spirituale* (1640) as *Iam moriar, mi Fili (pianto della Madonna sopra il Lamento d'Arianna).*

13. In a letter dated Venice, 21 November 1615, Monteverdi gives specific instructions for the performance of the ballet, which he suggests should include in the instrumental ensemble eight viole da braccio, a contrabass, a spineta arpata (harp-shaped spinet), and if possible two small lutes. See *The Letters of Claudio Monteverdi,* translation and introduction by Denis Stevens (Cambridge, 1980), pp. 107–108.

14. See John Whenham, *Duet and Dialogue in the Age of Monteverdi* (Ann Arbor, 1982), for a major study of the development of the vocal duet in the seventeenth century, including a large number of music examples.

15. Book IX was published posthumously in 1651.

16. Translation from Strunk, *Source Readings,* pp. 413–14.

17. The development of the lament in seventeenth-century music, based on the convention of a descending tetrachord, is traced by Ellen Rosand, "The Descending Tetrachord: An Emblem of Lament," in *The Musical Quarterly* 65 (1979), pp. 346–59.

18. Little is known about the compositional history or the first performance of *Orfeo.* The best discussion of these matters is by Iain Fenlon, "The Mantuan 'Orfeo'," in *Claudio Monteverdi, Orfeo,* ed. John Whenham (Cambridge, 1986).

19. Similarities between the Rinuccini/Peri score for *L'Euridice* and the Striggio/Monteverdi score for *Orfeo* have been commented on by several writers. See for example, Gary Tomlinson, "Madrigal, Monody, and Monteverdi's 'via naturale alla immitatione' ", in

JAMS 34 (1981), pp. 60–66; Barbara Russano Hanning, *Of Poetry and Music's Power: Humanism and the Creation of Opera* (Ann Arbor, 1980), ch. 3.

20. For a discussion of Poliziano's play, see Nino Pirotta and Elena Povoledo, *Music and Theatre from Poliziano to Monteverdi* (Cambridge, Mass., 1982), pp. 3–36.

21. The score was published twice, in 1609 and 1615. Monteverdi lists the instruments he employed, although the listing makes clear these were the instruments that had been used, not necessarily the ones that must be used. There are some omissions and discrepancies between his list and indications in the score proper. As Jane Glover points out, the list of instruments falls into three groups of sonorities: strings, brass, and continuo instruments. See her article "Solving the musical problems," in *Claudio Monteverdi, Orfeo,* ed. John Whenham, pp. 138–46. Monteverdi lists the following: duoi gravicembani [*sic*] (two harpsichords), duoi contrabassi de viola (two double basses), dieci viole da brasso (ten members of the violin family, probably first and second violins, first and second violas, and violoncello), un arpa doppia (double harp), duoi violini piccoli alia Francese (small violins transposing up an octave), duoi chitaroni (two chitarrone—actually three according to the score), duoi organi di legno (two organs), tre bassi da gamba (three bass gambas), quattro tromboni (four trombones—actually five), un regale (regal), duoi cornetti (two cornetti), un flautino alia vigesima seconda (soprano recorder—actually two), and in the opening Toccata, un clarino con tre trombe sordine (a clarino and two muted trumpets).

22. Although Monteverdi indicates act and scene divisions in the printed score, it is probable that the opera was given without pauses between the acts, in the same performance tradition as employed for Renaissance dramatic presentations. See John Whenham, "Five acts: one action," in *Claudio Monteverdi, Orfeo,* pp. 42–47.

23. If one examines this score in Malipiero's edition in the Complete Works, care must be taken in accepting the chordal realization of the continuo part. The chords are frequently contrary to the thorough-bass practice of the time, and often smooth out or eliminate the pungent melodic dissonances Monteverdi had intended.

24. By Severo Bonini in *Discorsi e regole sopra la musica de Severo Bonini,* ed. L. G. Luisi (Cremona, 1975). An analysis in some detail of the lament is given by Tomlinson in "Madrigal, Monody, and Monteverdi's 'via naturale alla immitatione," *JAMS* 34 (1981), pp. 86–108.

25. Previously thought to have been completed but lost. See Gary Tomlinson, "Twice Bitten, Thrice Shy: Monteverdi's 'finta' *Finta pazza"* in *JAMS* 36 (1983), pp. 303–11.

26. In the Vienna National Library. Because the score is not an autograph and differs widely from the preserved libretto for the Venetian performance, some writers have doubted its authenticity. More recent scholarship finds in the music powerful evidence confirming Monteverdi's authorship.

27. The date 1642 usually given for this opera does not take into account the Venetian calendar. *L'incoronazione* was performed during the Carnival season 1642/1643, which began on 26 December 1642.

28. Among such pieces is the final duet, "Pur ti stringo, pur ti godo," over a descending tetrachord, probably the most famous moment in the score. However, it now seems likely that Monteverdi did not compose the duet, the text of which does not appear in the libretto of the Venetian production of 1643. Both of the preserved scores are later versions subsequent to the composer's death, one in Venice, the other in Naples. The same duet text appears in operas by Benedetto Ferrari and Filiberto Laurenzi. The music for these operas, however, is lost. And since the Venetian copy of the score comes from Cavalli's

library, who made alterations in his copy, he too might have been the composer of this justifiably favorite duet in the opera.

29. Reprinted in *The Norton Anthology of Western Music,* ed. C. Palisca (New York, 1988), no. 70.

30. The title reads: *Sanctissimae Virgini missa senis vocibus ac vesperae pluribus decantandae, cum nonnullis sacris concentibus ac sacella sine principium cubicula accommodata* (Venice, 1610), which freely translated means: For the most holy Virgin, a Mass in six parts suitable for church choruses together with vespers for larger forces with some motets (*sacri concentibus*), both suitable for chapels or the apartments of princes.

31. The use of the ten subjects in the various sections of the Mass is shown in tabular form in Paolo Fabbri, *Monteverdi* (Turin, 1985), pp. 157–58.

32. For example, Arnold, in *Monteverdi,* p. 138, states: "The virility of Netherlandish rhythm and the bite of dissonance are both lacking and since Monteverdi refuses to make clear even such contrasts as exist between 'Crucifixus' and 'Et resurrexit', the result is a curiously emasculated work. . . ." Jerome Roche, "Monteverdi and the 'Prima Prattica,'" in *The New Monteverdi Companion,* ed. Denis Arnold and Nigel Fortune (London, 1985), p. 169, states: "the result is somewhat of a hotch-potch, not linked with anything else Monteverdi did, and falling short in several ways of being the perfect reincarnation of the music of the Netherlands master."

33. An excellent discussion of the Vespers, and the Mass of 1610, including considerable perceptive analysis of individual movements, is included in Jeffrey G. Kurtzman, *Essays on the Monteverdi Mass and Vespers of 1610,* Rice Universtiy Studies, vol. 64, no. 4 (Houston, 1978).

34. Kurtzman suggests that the large version of the Magnificat should probably be considered a parody by Monteverdi of his somewhat shorter version for six solo voices. See *Essays on Monteverdi's Mass and Vespers of 1610* (Houston, Tex., 1979).

4. THE BAROQUE IN ITALY FROM CIRCA 1640 TO CIRCA 1700

1. The history of opera in Venice in the seventeenth century has stimulated many published essays and books beginning already in the seventeenth century. The most comprehensive and indispensable is by Ellen Rosand, *Opera in Seventeenth-Century Venice: The Creation of a Genre* (Berkeley, 1991), to which this section is indebted. Also important is Simon Towneley Worsthorne, *Venetian Opera in the Seventeenth Century* (Oxford, 1954).

2. See Ellen Rosand, "Music in the Myth of Venice," *Renaissance Quarterly* 30 (1977), pp. 511–37.

3. Like most Venetian theaters, it bears the name of the parish in which it was situated.

4. From Worsthorne, *Venetian Opera,* pp. 25–27, which includes the entire scenario in English translation and also in the original Italian.

5. According to Rosand, *Opera in Seventeenth-Century Venice,* p. 2 (fn), to which the composers' names are added: one in 1638 (*La maga fulminata,* Manelli), three in 1639 (*Le nozze di Teti e di Peleo,* Cavalli; *Delia,* Manelli; *Armida,* Ferrari), five in 1640 (*Gli amori d'Apollo e di Dafne,* Cavalli; *Adone,* Manelli; *Il ritorno d'Ulisse in patria,* Monteverdi; *Arianna,* Monteverdi; *Il pastor regio,* Ferrari), five in 1641 (*Didone,* Cavalli; *Il ritorno d'Ulisse in patria,* Monteverdi; *Le nozze d'Enea e Lavinia,* Monteverdi; *La ninfa avara,* Ferrari; *La finta pazza,* Sacrati), and seven in 1642 (*La virtù de' strali d'Amore,* Cavalli; *Narciso ed Ecco immortalati,* ?; *Gli amori di Giasone e d'Isifile,* ?; *Sidonio e Dorisbe,* Fontei; *Amore innamorato,* Cavalli; *Alcate,* Manelli; *Bellerfonte,* Sacrati).

6. A score to Sacrati's *La finta pazza* has been discovered by Lorenzo Biaconi, but the facsimile of that score has as yet not appeared in the series Drammaturgia musicale veneta.

7. Rosand, *Opera in Seventeenth-Century Venice,* pp. 248–49. The librettos in question are for Ferrari's *Andromeda* and *La maga fulminata.* The poetry is in the standard recitative form of *versi sciolti,* with *settenario* (seven-accent) and *endecasillabo* (eleven-accent) lines. In the latter opera, however, especially for the comic charcter of the nurse, the occurrence of strophic texts, as well as closed sections with metric organization based on unusual combinations of lines (*versi misurati*) suggests some insertions of lyrical passages.

8. The relationship between the librettos and Monteverdi's use of them is examined in some detail in Rosand, *Opera in Seventeenth-Century Venice,* pp. 250–56.

9. Cavalli was his adoptive name. He was born in Crema as Pier Francesco Caletti, and was adopted by a Venetian, Federico Cavalli. Among many studies concerning Cavalli and his music, see Jane Glover, *Cavalli* (London, 1978).

10. Except in the years 1646/47/48, 1654, 1661, 1663, and 1667.

11. Preserved in the Contarini collection of the Biblioteca Marciana in Venice, which is discussed in Glover, *Cavalli,* pp. 65–72.

12. Frequently this form of vocal lyricism is given the label of *Bel canto,* despite the fact that the term is incorrect historically. *Bel canto* as a term somewhat vaguely describing certain elegant qualities of Italian vocal style did not appear in musical literature until the nineteenth century. Its introduction into musical scholarship for vocal style in the Italian Baroque began in the German literature, especially Robert Haas's *Die Musik des Barocks* (Potsdam, 1928), and was introduced into American scholarship by Manfred Bukofzer in *Music in the Baroque Era* (New York, 1947).

13. The changes in Cavalli's musical style summarized here is the central focus of Rosand's *Opera in Seventeenth-Century Venice,* especially pp. 256–386.

14. The first extensive study of recitative in Venetian operas is by Beth Glixon, "Recitative in Seventeenth-Century Venetian Opera: Its Dramatic Function and Musical Language" (Ph.D. diss., Rutgers University, 1985).

15. See Rosand, *Opera in Seventeenth-Century Venice,* pp. 467–72, for the music to this entire scene.

16. Ibid., pp. 514–17, for the aria.

17. Statistics from Glover, *Cavalli,* pp. 106–107.

18. From Rosand, *Opera in Seventeenth-Century Venice,* p. 539.

19. Ibid, pp. 492–93.

20. Important discussions of the operatic lament include Ellen Rosand's chapter "*Il Lamento:* The Fusion of Music and Drama," ibid., pp. 361–86; the same author's "The Descending Tetrachord: An Emblem of Lament," *The Musical Quarterly,* 55 (1979), pp. 346–59; and Lorenzo Bianconi, *Music in the Seventeenth Century,* trans. D. Bryant (Cambridge, 1987), pp. 204–19.

21. From Ellen Rosand, "Aria in the Early Operas of Francesco Cavalli" (Ph.D. diss., New York University, 1971), p. 119, which gives further examples of another ten laments.

22. From Glover, *Cavalli,* pp. 88–89.

23. Bianconi, *Music in the Seventeenth Century,* p. 190, from the important chapter "The Diffusion of Opera in Italy."

24. Ibid., p. 196, based on Bianconi's examination of the opera librettos. It is not possible to ascertain the degree of adaptation and change this opera sustained over almost thirty years of repeat performances.

25. For example, Worsthorne, *Venetian Opera,* p. 121, says "the quality of the scores rather declines as the composers have to yield to the claims of virtuoso singers." He fails to define his concept of "quality" and offers no specific musical evidence.

26. The most comprehensive study of the oratorio is by Howard E. Smither, *A History of the Oratorio,* vol. I: *The Oratorio in the Baroque Era, Italy, Vienna, Paris;* vol. II: *Germany and England* (Chapel Hill, 1977). Volume I includes an extensive study of "The Antecedents and Origins of the Oratorio." See also in Biaconi, *Music in the Seventeenth Century,* pp. 123–33.

27. What to call this work has generated considerable discussion. It is not the first oratorio, since the performers acted out the plot and wore costumes. It is closer to being considered a sacred opera, although its place of performance and the simplicity of most of its music weaken the appropriateness of such a label.

28. Smither, *A History of the Oratorio,* vol. I, pp. 96–117, examines a number of dramatic dialogues in some detail.

29. Ibid., pp. 126–42 for extensive comments and music examples from these dialogues.

30. Pietro delle Valle, *Della musica dell'età nostra che non é punto inferiore, anzi migliore di quella dell'età passata,* in Angelo Solerti, *Le origini del melodramma: Testimonianze dei contemporanei* (Turin, 1903), p. 176.

31. Cited in Smither, *A History of the Oratorio,* I, p. 159.

32. This oratorio-like composition and the others belonging to the earliest history of the *oratorio volgare* are discussed in detail in Smither, ibid., pp. 168–206.

33. The major study concerning the history of the German College and its musical achievements is by Thomas D. Culley, *Jesuits and Music, I: A Study of the Musicians Connected with the German College in Rome during the 17th Century* (St. Louis, 1970).

34. Smither, *A History of the Oratorio,* I, pp. 224–25. Titles are frequently different in the various manuscript sources. Those given here are by Smither, adapted by him from recent modern editions.

35. "Simple recitative" (*recitativo semplice*) was the seventeenth-century term given to recitative that is made up of many repeated tones, short scale passages, and simple triadic skips. *Recitativo secco* or "dry" recitative is employed only much later in the eighteenth century and is not used in this book.

36. Claude V. Palisca, *Baroque Music* (Englewood Cliffs, N.J., 1991), p. 127.

37. *Historia Jonas,* edited by Lino Bianchi, and published by the Istituto italiano per la storia della music (Rome, 1989), vol. XI.

38. A considerable literature discusses the use by Carissimi of "musical-rhetorical figures." The terminology and character of these figures are often used to explain such musical procedures as identified here in the passage from *Jonas.* The topic was first studied in depth by Günther Massenkeil, *Die oratorische Kunst in den lateinischen Historien und Oratorien Giacomo Carissimis* (diss. Mainz, 1952), and in the same author's article "Die Wiederholungsfiguren in den Oratorien Giacomo Carissimis," *Archiv für Musikwissenschaft* 13 (1956), pp. 42–60. There is, however, no solid evidence that Italian composers of this period knew a terminology that was employed primarily by German composers. And many of the figures so labeled are simple compositional techniques that have an obvious connection to rhetorical-musical stresses. For a general introduction to this subject, see George J. Buelow, *The New Grove Dictionary,* 2d ed., vol. 21, pp. 260–75, *Rhetoric and Music,* subheads "Baroque," "Musical Figures," "Affects."

39. In the preface to his *Psalmen Davids* (1619), pp. 262–70.

40. Manfred Bukofzer, in *Music in the Baroque Era* (New York, 1947), ensnared in his own viewpoint of the Baroque as developing from the simple to the complex, says, in perhaps his least felicitous phrase, that the choruses "by themselves seem primitive."

41. Athanasius Kircher, *Musurgia universalis* (Rome, 1650), I (book 1), part 3, p. 603; translation by Palisca, *Baroque Music,* p. 126.

42. These are discussed by Smither, *A History of the Oratorio,* vol. 1, pp. 247–49. A modern edition of these works is by Wolfgang Witzenmann, *Sacrae concertationes,* by Domenico Mazzocchi, in *Concentus musicus,* vol. 3 (Cologne, 1975).

43. For comments regarding Foggia's and Graziani's oratorios, see Smither, *A History of the Oratorio,* vol. 1, pp. 254–56. Two of Foggia's oratorios, *David fugiens a facie Saul* and *Tobiae oratorium,* as well as those of Graziani, *Adae oratorium* and *Fili prodigi oratorium,* are published in *The Italian Oratorio: 1650–1800,* vol. 1.

44. Published in *The Italian Oratorio, 1650–1800,* vol. 3.

45. Published in ibid., vol. 8.

46. See David W. Daniels, "Alessandro Stradella's Oratorio San Giovanni Battista: A Modern Edition and Commentary" (diss., State University of Iowa, 1963). Smithers discusses this oratorio in some detail in *A History of the Oratorio,* vol. 1, pp. 316–26. Further information concerning the oratorios is found in Carolyn Gianturco, *Alessandro Stradella, 1632–1682: His Life and Music* (Oxford, 1994).

47. Charles Burney, *A General History of Music,* 2 vols. (London, 1776–1789), ed. Frank Mercer (London, 1935), pp. 578–80.

48. The oratorios by Lanciani and Lulier are published in facsimile in *The Italian Oratorio: 1650–1800,* vol. 6; the Bononcini, in vol. 8.

49. Briefly discussed by Smither in *A History of the Oratorio,* vol. 1, pp. 327–32.

50. Printed in *The Italian Oratorio: 1650–1800,* vol. 5.

51. Ibid., vol. 4.

52. *Agar,* performed in 1689, appears in ibid., vol. 4.

53. For a detailed account of this significant development in Florentine music history, see John Hill, "Oratory Music in Florence, I: *Recitar cantando,* 1583–1655," *Acta Musicologica* 51 (1979), pp. 108–36.

54. See John Hill, "Oratory Music in Florence, II: At San Firenze in the Seventeenth and Eighteenth Centuries," *Acta Musicologica* 51 (1979), pp. 246–67.

55. From Denis Arnold and Elsie Arnold, *The Oratorio in Venice* (London, 1986), pp. 3–4. This monograph is the only study to date devoted to the history of the oratorio in Venice. It includes an invaluable appendix listing all the known titles of oratorios performed in Venice from 1662 to the end of the eighteenth century.

56. The only attempt to survey the history of the cantata was by Eugen Schmitz, *Geschichte der Kantate* (Leipzig, 1916).

57. Very helpful, however, for the study of the cantata in the seventeenth century is a series of sixteen volumes edited by Carolyn Gianturco and published by Garland (New York) of manuscripts in facsimile containing cantatas by twenty-six Italian composers.

58. See Gloria Rose, "The Cantatas of Giacomo Carissimi," *The Musical Quarterly,* 47 (1962), pp. 204–15.

59. These details of formal organization are from Rose, ibid.

60. From the *Istituto italiano per la storia della musica, Monumenti III,* vol. I: *Giacomo Carissimi, Cantate,* ed. Lino Bianchi (Rome, 1960), pp. 12–14.

61. Vol. 6 of the Garland Series, *The Italian Cantata in the Seventeenth Century*, includes eight of Cesti's cantatas edited by David Burrows. Burrows has also edited modern editions of seven cantatas in *The Wellesley Edition*, vol. 5 (Wellesley, 1963).

62. There are not, however, any da capo indications, which are misleadingly given in the Burrows edition.

63. In Burrows, *Wellesley Edition*, p. 19. Translation by Burrows.

64. A list of the cantatas is given by Gianturco in *Alessandro Stradella, 1639–1682*, pp. 251–55. See her extensive discussion of these works, pp. 77–139.

65. These earliest known examples of accompanied recitative are noted by Carolyn Gianturco in her volume of fifteen Stradella cantatas in the Garland series. The two cantatas in question are *Da cuspide ferrate* (No. 13) and *Crudo mar di fiamme orribili [Sopra l'anime del purgatorio]*, both sacred cantatas.

66. Nos. 12, 11, and 6 in the Garland volume.

67. The number of Steffani duets is according to the authoritative research of Colin Timms. See the introduction to his edition of *Twelve Chamber Duets* (Madison, 1987), vol. 53 in *Recent Researches in the Music of the Baroque Era*. See also Timms, "The Chamber Duets of Agostino Steffani (1654–1728), with Transcriptions and Catalogue" (diss.).

68. The classification of chamber duets is from the Preface to Timms's edition of *Twelve Chamber Duets*, which includes further valuable discussions of the texts and formal procedures of these works.

69. From Timms's edition, pp. 34–36.

70. For a useful survey of Renaissance instrumental music, see Howard M. Brown, *Music in the Renaissance* (Englewood Cliffs, N.J., 1976), pp. 257–71.

71. The most comprehensive study of the Italian trio sonata is by Peter Allsop, *The Italian "Trio" Sonata: From Its Origins until Corelli* (Oxford, 1992), to which this discussion is greatly indebted. The extensive background discussions concerning "Period, Place, and Personalia"; "The Instrumental Ensemble"; "Genre and Function"; and "The Composer in Society" are highly recommended as valuable additions to the limited examination of the trio sonata presented here. Also important material regarding the trio sonata is found in William S. Newman's pathbreaking *The Sonata in the Baroque Era* (Chapel Hill, 1959). All of the significant composers of Italian seventeenth-century violin music receive useful discussions in *Willi Apel, Die italienische Violinmusik im 17. Jahrhundert* (Wiesbaden, 1983), English trans. Thomas Binkley (Bloomington, Ind., 1990).

72. A thorough study of this terminology is presented by Niels Martin Jensen in "Solo Sonata, Duo Sonata, and Trio Sonata: Some Problems of Terminology and Genre in 17th-Century Italian Instrumental Music," in *Festskrift Jens Peter Larsen* (Copenhagen, 1972), pp. 73–101.

73. Allsop, p. 23, in reference to the great loss of sources, cites the startling figures that of some hundred or so composers of trio sonatas "only about twenty provide more than ten extant examples, and of these fourteen produced more than one collection—surely a meagre number given that the population of Italy by the end of the century was in the region of 13,000,000."

74. See Allsop, *The Italian "Trio" Sonata*, pp. 47–56. As the author points out, some scholars have held such strong views as to the implications of genre that they have actually changed the titles of works to conform to their views. See Bukofzer, *Music in the Baroque Era*, p. 53, who substitutes "sonata" for the *Sinfonia* of Salamone Rossi.

75. Modern edition by Eric Schenk, *The Italian Trio Sonata*, in *The Anthology of Music*, vol. 7.

76. Adapted from Allsop, *The Italian "Trio" Sonata,* pp. 87–88.

77. See Thomas D. Dunn, "The Sonatas of Biagio Marini: Structure and Style," *The Music Review* 36 (1975), pp. 161–79.

78. Bukofzer, *Music in the Baroque Era,* p. 53.

79. See *Salamone Rossi, Complete Works,* ed. Don Harrán, Part II: *Instrumental Works,* American Institute of Musicology (Neuhausen, 1995), including the editor's valuable introductions to the volume and to the individual books.

80. Ibid., pp. 9–10.

81. Facsimiles and transcriptions of Uccellini's music appear in F. M. Pajerski, "Marco Uccellini and His Music" (diss., New York University, 1979), vol. 2. See also the many examples appended to Allsop's valuable discussion of Uccellini in his *The Italian "Trio" Sonata,* pp. 116–23, exs. pp. 275–78.

82. Books I, II, and IV are published in *Opere complète di Tarquinio Merula* (Institute of Medieval Music, Collected Works, 7), ed. A. Sutkowski (Brooklyn, 1974–78).

83. For examples of the two contrasting textures, see Allsop, pp. 279–83.

84. The most important study of G. M. Bononcini is by William Klenz, *Giovanni Maria Bononcini of Modena* (Durham, N.C., 1962). Its particular value lies in some three hundred pages of transcriptions from Bononcini's publications and the detailed and insightful analyses of Bononcini's musical style.

85. Sonatas 12a and 12f are found in *The Instrumental Music of Giovanni Legrenzi,* ed. Stephen Bonta, Harvard Publications in Music, vols. 14 (1984) and vol. 17 (1992). Sonatas 12b, c, d, and e are found in *Sonate da chiesa, Op. 4, Op. 8,* ed. Albert Seay, *Le pupitre* (Paris, 1968).

86. See Anne Schnoebelen, "Performance Practices at San Petronio in the Baroque," *Acta Musicologica* 41 (1969), pp. 37–55.

87. A complete transcription is given by John Suess in "Giovanni Battista Vitali and the Sonata da chiesa" (Ph.D. diss., Yale, 1963), vol. 2.

88. Allsop, *The Italian "Trio" Sonata,* p. 165, states that an uncatalogued folio in a manuscript of biographies for members of the Accademia Filarmonica in the Biblioteca Communale, Bologna, describes Vitali as "advanced in counterpoint." His *Artifici musicali,* published in Modena in 1689, presents sixty compositions illustrating his ideas regarding instrumental counterpoint.

89. See Newman, *The Sonata in the Baroque Era,* pp. 138–39; also Apel, *Die italienische Violinmusik im 17. Jahrhundert,* pp. 172–75.

90. This list according to Apel, *The History of Keyboard Music to 1700,* pp. 681–703. The *Corpus of Early Keyboard Music,* published by the American Institute of Musicology, includes editions of music by Storace, Strozzi, Battiferri, and the complete keyboard works of Pasquini.

91. In the *Corpus of Early Keyboard Music,* vol. 7, pp. 65–107.

92. See *Bernardo Pasquini, Collected Works for Keyboard,* ed. Maurice B. Hayes, Corpus of Early Keyboard Music, vols. 1–7.

93. Ibid., vol. 2, p. 4.

5. ARCANGELO CORELLI (1653–1713) AND ALESSANDRO SCARLATTI (1660–1725)

1. See Hans-Joachim Marx, *Arcangelo Corelli: die Überlieferung der Werke: Catalogue raisonné* (Cologne, 1980).

2. See Hans-Joachim Marx (ed.), *Werke ohne Opuszahl* (=*Arcangelo Corelli, Historisch-kritische Gesamtausgabe der musikalischen Werke*), vol. 5 (Cologne, 1976).

3. Translation by Dennis Libby in "Interrelationships in Corelli," *JAMS* 26 (1973), p. 265 from a letter dated 1708 and published in Mario Rinaldi, *Arcangelo Corelli* (Milan, 1953), pp. 444–45.

4. These are discussed in Allsop, *The Italian "Trio" Sonata*, pp. 227–39.

5. Andrea Adami, in *Osservazione per ben regolare il coro dei cantori della Cappella Pontificia* (Rome, 1711), refers to Simonelli as "the Palestrina of the seventeenth century." The significance of the Palestrinian style for Corelli was first emphasized by Hans Joachim Marx. See, for example, his *Arcangelo Corelli . . . Catalogue raisonné*, pp. 12, 46.

6. This important view is contributed by Jürg Stenzl in his *Einleitung* to his edition of the *Sonate da Camera, Opus II und IV*, in Arcangelo Corelli, *Historisch-kritische Gesamtausgabe der musikalischen Werke* (Laaber, 1986), vol. 2, p. 15.

7. From *Les oeuvres de Arcangelo Corelli*, ed. J. Joachim and F. Chrysander (London, n.d.), vol. 2, p. 160. Examples from Op. IV are also from vol. 2, and Op. I from vol. 1.

8. See Allsop, *The Italian "Trio" Sonata*, pp. 230–32, concerning some of the likely influences on Corelli of other trio sonata composers both Bolognese and Roman.

9. It should be observed that Corelli specifies that these sonatas are to be performed by two violins and violone or harpsichord, not violone and harpsichord, an indication of performance practice seldom observed.

10. Francesco Maria Veracini found reason to write his *Dissertazioni del S[i]g Francesco Veracini sopra l'Opera Quinta del Corelli* (c. 1760), an intensive study of the works for which Veracini added more imitation and invertible counterpoint and expanded the use of motives, creating "greater formal unity and symmetry, and greater logic and consistency even to the point of becoming pedantic or academic," according to John W. Hill. See his *The Life and Works of Francesco Maria Veracini* (Ann Arbor, 1979), pp. 287–95.

11. See Sonya Monosoff, "Violinistic Challenges in the Sonatas Op. V of Arcangelo Corelli," in *Studi corelliani IV. Atti del quatro congresso internazionale*, ed. Pierluigi Petrobelli and Gloria Staffieri (Florence, 1990), pp. 155–63.

12. See Marx (ed.), *Catalogue raisonné*, pp. 176–77 and 322–23. Sir John Hawkins in his *General History of the Science and Practice of Music* (London, 1776) gives Corelli's Sonata No. 9 with the ornamentation of Corelli's student Francesco Geminiani.

13. The ornamented versions are given in the Joachim and Chrysander edition.

14. The belief, in part spread by Manfred Bukofzer, in *Music in the Baroque Era,* chapter 7, that Alessandro Scarlatti belonged to a "Late Baroque" misreads the nature of this composer's musical influences and achievements.

15. A catalogue by Giancarlo Rostirolla listing 705 cantatas by title, including those of "uncertain attribution," is given in *Alessandro Scarlatti* by Roberto Pagano and Lino Bianchi (Turin, 1972).

16. The American scholar Edwin Hanley gained control of the sources of Scarlatti's cantata during a lifetime of research. His general article on Scarlatti in *MGG*, vol. 11, cols. 1482–1506, remains the best introduction to this composer's achievements and includes the extraordinary catalogue of his works. It is the basis for all subsequent listings of Scarlatti's cantatas. See his "Alessandro Scarlatti's Cantate da Camera: A Bibliographical Study" (diss., Yale University, 1963). An important though out-of-date monograph remains E. J. Dent's *Alessandro Scarlatti: His Life and Works* (London, 1905; rev. ed. with additions by F. Walker, 1960).

17. Found in a large notebook in the university library of Pavia (Catalogue No. 423), and transcribed with three other cantatas from the same source by Giampiero Tintori, *4 Cantate* (Milan, 1958).

18. For example, see Dent, *Alessandro Scarlatti,* pp. 189–91, and Eugen Schmitz, *Geschichte der Kantate* (Leipzig, 1914), pp. 126–27.

19. Johann David Heinichen, *Der General-Bass in der Composition* (Dresden, 1728), p. 797 and foonote **.

20. Heinichen's practical demonstration is given with a realization of his instructions in George J. Buelow's *Thorough-bass Accompaniment according to Johann David Heinichen,* revised edition (Ann Arbor, 1986; paper, Lincoln, Nebraska, 1992), pp. 293–306.

21. Ibid., pp. 297–99.

22. See Rostirolla's catalogue in *Alessandro Scarlatti,* pp. 497–507. A complete, modern edition of the oratorios was initiated by Lino Bianchi, *Gli oratorii di Alessandro Scarlatii* (Rome, 1964–), which includes in the first five volumes: *La Giuditta* (i), *Agar et Ismaele esilati* (ii), *La Giuditta* (iii), *Cain overo Il primo omicidio* (iv), and *Davidis pugna et victoria* (v). The Latin Passion, *Passio Domini Nostri Jesu Christi secundum Joannem,* has been edited by Edwin Hanley (New Haven, 1955).

23. Donald Grout initiated a plan in cooperation with Harvard University to publish all of Scarlatti's operas. *The Operas of Alessandro Scarlattti,* ed. Donald J. Grout, includes: vol. 1, *Eraclea* (1974); vol. 2, *Marco Attilio Regolo* (1975); vol. 3, *Griselda* (1975); vol. 4, *La principessa fedele* (1977); vol. 5, *Massimo Puppieno* (1979); vol. 6, *La caduta de' Decemviri* (1980); vol. 7, *Gli equivoci nel sembiante* (1982); vol. 8, *Tigrane* (1983); vol. 9, *La statira* (1985). Unfortunately, no further volumes were published.

24. The best introduction to Scarlatti's operas remains Donald Jay Grout's *Alessandro Scarlatti: An Introduction to His Operas* (Berkeley, 1979), which has been drawn on for this discussion.

25. For more details regarding its performance history, see Frank D'Accone's commentary in his edition of *Gli equivoci nel sembiante* (Cambridge, Mass., 1982), pp. 6–9.

26. The following examples are taken from *The Operas of Alessandro Scarlatti,* Donald Jay Grout, General Editor: Ex. 5.18, volume VII, ed. Frank A. D'Accone; Ex. 5.19, volume VI, ed. Hermine Weigel Williams; Ex. 5.20, volume VIII, ed. Michael Collins; Ex. 5.21, volume II, ed. Joscelyn Godwin; Ex. 5.22, volume III, ed. Donald Jay Grout.

27. See Grout, *Scarlatti: An Introduction to His Operas,* p. 52.

28. Ibid., pp. 73–75.

29. Ibid., p. 81.

6. THE BAROQUE IN FRANCE

1. For a valuable discussion of Baïf's academy, see D. P. Walker, "The Aims of Baïf's *Académie de poésie et de musique,*" *Journal of Renaissance and Baroque Music,* I (1946), pp. 91–100.

2. Seven *Psaumes mesurés de Jean-Antoine de Baïf* originally were printed in Marin Mersenne's *Quaestiones celeberrimae in Genesim* (1623). A modern edition including this example was published by Henry Expert, in *Florilège du concert vocal de la Renaissance* (Paris, 1928), p. 1.

3. The version with lute accompaniment appeared in G. Bataille, *Airs de différents autheurs, mis en tablature de luth,* vol. III (Paris, 1611), and in a modern edition in A. Verchaly, *Airs de cour pour voix et luth (1603–1643)* (Paris, 1961), p. 28.

4. For a detailed description of this ballet, see Frances A. Yates, *The French Academies of the Sixteenth Century* (London, 1947), pp. 254–57.

5. A modern edition of the ballet with a translation of the texts by Carol and Lander MacClintock, and music transcribed by Carol MacClintock, is published by the American

Institute of Musicology (1971). Among the many discussions of the work, see especially Frances A. Yates, *The French Academies,* pp. 236–74, and Robert M. Isherwood, *Music in the Service of the King* (Ithaca, 1973), pp. 76–88.

6. Some of the instrumental music is preserved in the famous Philidor collection in the Bibliothèque nationale, Paris. See Margaret M. McGowan, *L'art du ballet de cour en France, 1581–1643* (Paris, 1963), pp. 49–67, and especially the appendix: *Sources des ballets de 1581–1643.* See also François Lesure, "Le recueil de ballets de Michel Henry," *Fêtes de la Renaissance,* I (Paris, 1956).

7. Several contemporary engravings showing scenes from the ballet are reproduced in McGowan, *L'Art du ballet de cour en France,* appendix.

8. François Durand, *Discours au vrai du ballet dansé par le roi* (Paris, 1617), pp. 5–6, translation in Isherwood, *Music in the Service of the King,* pp. 97–99.

9. The *Livre d'air de cours,* including the preface, is given in L. de la Laurence, A. Mairy, and G. Thibault, *Chansons au luth et airs de cour Français du XVIe siècle* (Paris, 1976).

10. Printed in modern notation with the lute part realized in keyboard notation, *Airs de cour pour voix et luth (1603–1643),* ed. A. Verchaly (Paris, 1961), pp. 144–45.

11. For details of Torelli's magnificent and technically original achievements with stage machinery, see Per Bjurström, *Giacomo Torelli and Baroque Stage Design,* 2d ed. (Stockholm, 1962).

12. The most important publications regarding sacred music in France before 1661 are by Denise Launay. See "Church Music in France, 1630–60," in *New Oxford History of Music,* vol. V: *Opera and Church Music 1630–1750,* ed. A. Lewis and N. Fortune (London, 1975), pp. 414–37; and especially her *Anthologie du motet Latin polyphonique en France (1609–1661)* (Paris, 1963).

13. E. DuCaurroy, *Missa pro defunctis quinque vocum,* ed. Michel Sanvoisin (Paris: Alphonse Leduc & Cie., 1993).

14. Printed in its entirety in Launay, *Antologie du motet Latin polyphonique,* p. 28.

15. None of Bouzignac's music was published during his lifetime. It is contained in two manuscripts, one at Tours, the other in the Brossard collection of the Paris Bibliothèque nationale, where only eleven works can be definitely authenticated as by Bouzignac. The distinctive originality of his style, however, enabled Denise Launay to ascribe another 125 of the works to him. See the article by Martial Leroux in the *New Grove Dictionary,* 2d ed., vol. 4, pp. 126–29.

16. Printed in its entirety in Denise Launay, *Antologie du motet Latin polyphonique,* p. 100.

17. Printed in Henri Quittard's edition in *SIMG* 6 (1904/1905), pp. 356–417.

18. W. J. A. Jonckbloet and J. P. N. Land, eds., *Musique et musiciens au XVIIe siècle: correspondance et oeuvres musicales de Constantin Hygens* (Leiden, 1882), p. ccxvii.

19. Published by Launay in *Antologie du motet Latin polyphonique,* pp. 132–46.

20. The Magnificat is from the edition by Launay in *Antologie du motet Latin polyphonique,* pp. 147–55.

21. From the edition of the *Meslanges* by José Quitin published by the Publications de la société liégeoise de musicologie (Liege, 1984), pp. 26–39.

22. Published with a facsimile of the *livret* in *Oeuvres complètes de J.-B. Lully,* Les Ballets, vol. 1, ed. Henry Prunières (Paris, 1930–39; repr. New York, 1966).

23. Published with a facsimile of the *livret* in *Oeuvres complètes de J.-B. Lully,* Les

Ballets, vol. 2 (Paris, 1933). This *livret* gives the names of the performers for all of the characters, including the king, other members of the court, and Lully.

24. See Denise Launay, "Les airs italiens et français dans les Ballets et les Comédies-Ballets" in *Jean-Baptiste Lully, Actes du colloque,* ed. J. de La Gorce and H. Schneider (Laaber, 1990), pp. 31–41.

25. Published in *Oeuvres complètes de J.-B. Lully. Les comédies-ballets,* vol. III (Paris, 1938), p. 176.

26. See Louis E. Auld, *The Lyric Art of Pierre Perrin, Founder of French Opera,* especially Part 1, "Birth of French Opera" (Henryville, Penn., 1986).

27. Published by J.-B. Weckerlin, *Chefs-d'oeuvre classiques de l'opéra français,* vol. II (Paris, 1881).

28. This opera, too, is preserved only in part: overture, prologue, and act I. See *Chefs-d'oeuvre classiques de l'opéra français,* vol. III (Paris, c. 1882).

29. There is still no comprehensive examination of Lully's operas. This writer is indebted especially to the section on Lully in James R. Anthony, *French Baroque Music from Beaujoyeulx to Rameau* (New York, 1974; rev. and expanded, Portland, Ore., 1997), pp. 93–120.

30. For example, the important work by Jean Laurent Le Cerf de la Viéville, *Comparaison de la musique italienne et de la musique française* (Brussels, 1704–1706).

31. This list by Lois Rosow is adapted from *The New Grove Dictionary of Opera,* ed. Stanley Sadie (London, 1992), vol. III, pp. 89–90.

32. These terms are from Pierre Estève's *L'esprit des beaux-arts* (Paris, 1753). Despite the more than half-century distance from Lully's creative life, the terminology retains relevance largely because of the extended period in France in which Lully's operatic style remained the only viable one for later composers.

33. See Lois Rosow's valuable studies, "The Metrical Notation of Lully's Recitative," in *Jean-Baptiste Lully, Actes du colloque,* pp. 405–22, and "French Baroque recitative as an expression of tragic declamation," in *Early Music,* October 1983, pp. 468–79.

34. As with much of Lully's music, the lack of a complete edition of his works prevents any full assessment of his achievements. Five of the six motets in the Ballard collection have been published in the *Oeuvres complètes de J.-B. Lully: Les Motets.* They are: Miserere (i), Plaude laetare (ii), Te Deum (ii), De profundis (iii), Dies irae (ii), but not the Benedictus. Only one of the five in manuscripts is published in this edition, Domine salvum fac regem (iii); the four remaining are: Exaudiat te, Notus in Judaea, O lachrymae, and Quare fremuerunt. The authenticity of another, Jubilate Deo, is disputed. The authorship by Lully is argued for by Lionel Sawkins who believes the work to be the composer's first grand motet. See "Lully's Motets: Source, Edition and Performance," in *Jean-Baptiste Lully, Actes du colloque,* pp. 383–403.

35. The exact number, sometimes given as thirteen, is uncertain since all are found in manuscripts where in some cases the attribution is unclear. To date, no complete edition has been published. See Catherine Massip, "Les petits motets de Jean-Baptiste Lully: de quelques problèmes d'authenticité et de style, in *Jean-Baptiste Lully, Actes du colloque,* pp. 155–64. The authenticity of ten seems certain: Anima Christe (in *Oeuvres complètes,* vol. III), Ave coeli munus, Dixit Dominus, Domine salvum, Laudate pueri, O dulcissime Domine, O sapientia in misterio, Omnes generationes, Regina coeli Loetare, and Salve regina mater. An eleventh motet, Exaudi Deus, may be by Lully.

36. According to Lionel Sawkins, thus making Delalande the most frequently per-

formed composer in the history of the series. See his article "Lalande and the *Concert spirituel*," in *The Musical Times,* 116 (April 1975), pp. 333–35.

37. Few motets have appeared in modern editions. Recommended for study is the edition by James R. Anthony of the *De Profundus* published by the University of North Carolina Press (Chapel Hill, 1980).

38. These statistics are based on the important complete catalogue of Charpentier's music by H. W. Hitchcock, *Les oeuvres de Marc-Antoine Charpentier: Catalogue raisonné* (Paris, 1982). See also his book *Marc-Antoine Charpentier* (Oxford, 1990).

39. The commentary is given in Claude Crussard, *Un musicien français oublié, Marc-Antoine Charpentier* (Paris, 1945), pp. 83–87.

40. See Hitchcock, *Charpentier,* p. 52, and also his "The Latin Oratorios of Marc-Antoine Charpentier," *Musical Quarterly* 41 (1955), pp. 41–65. The "H" numbers refer to Hitchcock's invaluable catalogue, *Les oeuvres de Marc-Antoine Charpentier: Catalogue raisonné* (Paris, 1982).

41. Marc-Antoine Charpentier, *Pestis Mediolanensis,* ed. H. Wiley Hitchcock (Chapel Hill, 1979).

42. André Campra, *Motets à I, II, et III voix avec la basse continue, [livre premier]* (Paris, 1695), in Fac-Similé Jean-Marc Fuzeau, *La musique Française classique de 1650 à 1800* (Editions J. M. Fuzeau, 1986), pp. 18–19.

43. The reception of Lully's music is documented in Herbert Schneider, *Die Rezeption der Oper Lullys im Frankreich des Ancien Régime* (Tutzing, 1982).

44. As James Anthony points out, the term "opéra-ballet" is seldom employed in sources of the early eighteenth century, and not even consistently after 1750, but rather became more common in nineteenth-century writings. See his "The French Opera-Ballet in the Early 18th Century: Problems of Definition and Classification, *JAMS* 18 (1965), pp. 197–206, and also "The Opéra-Ballet," in the same author's *French Baroque Music* (1997 edition), pp. 165–82.

45. The quotation is from James Anthony's *French Baroque Music* (1997 edition), p. 171.

46. This table is reproduced from Anthony, *French Baroque Music* (1997 ed.), p. 170. I am indebted to Anthony's valuable discussion of the *opéra-ballet* in ibid., pp. 165–82.

47. For a detailed discussion of the French cantata, see David Tunley, *The Eighteenth-Century French Cantata,* especially the 2d ed. (Oxford, 1997).

48. As Hitchcock concludes in his *Marc-Antoine Charpentier,* p. 77.

49. Full quotation cited in Tunley, *The Eighteenth-Century French Cantata,* 2d ed., p. 47.

50. André Campra, "Avertissement," *Cantates françoises,* book I (Paris, 1708), fol. 2r. Translation in Gene E. Vollen's *The French Cantata: A Survey and Thematic Catalog* (Ann Arbor, 1982), p. 14.

51. No better introduction to Clérambault's cantatas can be recommended than that found in Tunley, *The French Cantata,* 2d ed., pp. 120–49.

52. Published in fascsimile by Minkoff (Geneva, 1975).

53. The *Rhétorique des dieux* is available in a facsimile and transcription by André Tessier in *Publications de musicologie,* vols. VI–VII (Paris, 1932–33).

54. The definitive catalogue of this repertory is by Bruce Gustafson, *French Harpsichord Music of the 17th Century,* 3 vols. (Ann Arbor, 1979).

55. Marin Mersenne, *Harmonie universelle* (Paris, 1636–37), p. [Av-verso].

56. See *J. J. Chambonnières, Oeuvres complètes,* ed. Paul Brunold and André Tessier (Paris, 1925, repr. 1967).

57. See the excellent collected edition of Paul Brunold, *Pièces de Louis Couperin,* with an extensive revision by Davitt Moroney (Monaco, 1985). Moroney's long introduction is very informative and includes an invaluable discussion of how to perform Couperin's unmeasured preludes.

58. Ibid., no. 98, p. 148.

59. Ibid., no. 6, p. 56.

60. New edition published as *N. Lebègue: Oeuvres de clavecin,* ed. N. Dufourcq (Monaco, 1956).

61. New edition published in *Jean-Henri D'Anglebert: Pièces de clavecin,* ed. Kenneth Gilbert (Paris, 1975).

62. The most comprehensive study of François Couperin, his music, and the age of Louis XIV remains Wilfrid Meller's *François Couperin and the French Classical Tradition* (new ed., London, 1987).

63. The *Recueils d'airs sérieux et boire* and the psalm verses are published in the *Oeuvres complètes,* ed. Maurice Cauchie et al. (Monaco, 1933), vol. xi. The *Leçons de tenèbres* and 18 of the motets are found also in the *Oeuvres complètes,* vol. xii, and in the revised edition, ed. K. Gilbert and D. Moroney (Monaco, 1985), vol. v and supplement. The remaining nine motets are in the edition of P. Oboussier, *Neuf motets* (Paris, 1972).

64. Printed in *Neuf motets,* no. VI, pp. 37–38.

65. Printed in the *Oeuvres complètes* (1985), p. 45.

66. Couperin, however, inscribes them *"pour le mercredy"* (for Wednesday), reflecting the custom of the time to move up the first service from Thursday evening to Wednesday afternoon.

67. Printed in the *Oeuvres complètes* (1985), pp. 11, 21, 33.

68. Printed in the *Oeuvres complètes* (1985), pp. 19–20.

69. *Oeuvres complètes de Couperin,* IX: *Musique de chambre III, Aveu de l'auteur au public.*

70. *Oeuvres complètes de Couperin,* VIII: *Musique de chambre III,* preface.

71. The meaning of many of the titles can be deduced only in those cases where they represent something descriptive such as "the little windmills, "the sounds of war," "bagatelles," "the nightingale in love," or "harlequin"; or refer to known personages among the nobility or the students of Couperin. Many of the titles suggest amusing or even bizarre interpretations of subjects or people no longer identifiable. Wilfred Mellers, in his *François Couperin* (new version, 1987), includes appendix III, a valuable attempt to interpret the meaning of all of these titles.

7. SACRED MUSIC IN NORTHERN AND SOUTHERN EUROPE AND AUSTRIA IN THE SEVENTEENTH CENTURY

1. The literature on Luther and the Protestant Reformation is immense. The best study in English regarding Luther and the development of Protestant church music remains that of Friedrich Blume, in collaboration with Ludwig Finscher, Georg Feder, Adam Adrio, Walter Blankenburg, Torben Schouboe, Robert Stevenson, and Watkins Shaw, *Protestant Church Music: A History* (New York, 1974), especially pp. 1–124.

2. Ibid., pp. 14–51, for an extensive discussion of the origins of chorale texts and melodies.

3. Published in *Hans Leo Hassler: Sämtlicher Werke,* ed. C. R. Crosby, vols. VII (1965) and VIII (1966).

4. Modern edition published as *M. Praetorius: Gesamtausgabe der musikalischen Werke,* ed. Friedrich Blume and others (Wolfenbüttel, 1928–1940, 1960).

5. Michael Praetorius, *Syntagma musicum,* vol. III (Wolfenbüttel, 1619), p. 197.

6. Both published in *Jan Pieterszoon Sweelinck, Opera omnia,* by the Vereniging voor Nederlandse Muziekgeschiedenis.

7. Wolfgang Caspar Printz, *Historische Beschreibung der edelen Sing- und Kling-Kunst* (Dresden, 1690), p. 137.

8. Published in *J. H. Schein: Neue Ausgabe sämtliche Werke,* ed. A. Adrio, Arno Forchert and others (Kassel, 1963–?1986).

9. Ibid., vol. 4, p. 93.

10. Ibid., vol. 4, p. 75.

11. Ibid., vol. 1, p. 15.

12. Ibid., p. 3.

13. Ibid., pp. 66–67.

14. In *Samuel Scheidt Werke,* ed. G. Harms and C. Mahrenholz, vols. I–XII (Hamburg, 1923–62), vols. XIV–XVI (Leipzig, 1971–).

15. Ibid., vol. 15, p. 70.

16. Ibid., p. 81.

17. Ibid., vol. 9, p. 61, footnote.

18. In the Hamburg Staats- und Universitäts Bibliothek.

19. See the important examination of Bernhard's musical-rhetorical figures in Folkert Fiebig, *Christoph Bernhard und der stile moderno* (Hamburg, 1980).

20. In *Das Erbe deutscher Musik,* 1st series, vol. 65 (1972). A second volume of miscellaneous sacred works appears in the same series, vol. 90 (1982).

21. Gustav Düben (c. 1628–1690), Swedish organist and composer, was a member of the Swedish court orchestra and conductor and organist of the German Church in Stockholm. He is famous as a collector of some eighteen hundred musical manuscripts especially from the second half of the seventeenth century containing copies of music by many of the major composers for which original sources have been lost. The collection was given to the University of Uppsala in 1732 by his son.

22. A large collection of manuscripts preserved in Berlin, containing some eighteen hundred sacred and secular works collected by Georg Österreich at the Gottorf and Wolfenbüttel courts and subsequently by his pupil Heinrich Bokemeyer.

23. Published in *Denkmäler deutscher Tonkunst,* vol. 3 (1900).

24. The complexities involving Buxtehude's birth and national origins are fully discussed in the important book on the composer and his music by Kerala J. Snyder, *Dieterich Buxtehude: Organist in Lübeck* (New York, 1987), and this section is indebted to her work.

25. Preserved at the Universitetsbiblioteket at Uppsala.

26. In the Deutsche Staatsbibliothek.

27. See Snyder, *Dieterich Buxtehude,* chapter 3, "Lübeck: St. Mary's Church" for a comprehensive discussion of the church, its physical characteristics, organs, and musicians employed before and during Buxtehude's tenure.

28. See ibid., chapter 5, for Snyder's extensive discussion of the vocal works.

29. Bux indicates the number in the *Buxtehude Werke-Verzeichnis (BuxWV)* by Georg Karstädt, *Thematisch-systematisches Verzeichnis der musikalischen Werke von Dietrich Buxtehude* (Wiesbaden, 1974, 2d ed. 1985).

30. Published in volume 9, *Dieterich Buxtehude, The Collected Works,* ed. Kerala Snyder (New York, 1987), pp. 37–57.

31. Ibid., vol. 7, pp. 81–87.

32. Ibid., vol. 2, pp. 19–24.

33. Ibid., pp. 44–53.

34. Ibid., vol. 5, pp. 87–95.

35. See the important study by Geoffrey Webber, *North German Church Music in the Age of Buxtehude* (Oxford, 1996), which includes a valuable listing of all the extant compositions by these composers and their sources.

36. Ibid., pp. 198–206.

37. For selections from the first four parts of the *Musikalische Andachten,* see *DDT,* vol. 40.

38. Published in *DTÖ,* Jg VIII, vol. 16.

39. For an essential study of Hammerschmidt's Masses in the context of the mid-seventeenth century, see John Howard, "The Latin Lutheran Mass of the Mid-Seventeenth Century: A Study of Andreas Hammerschmidt's Missae (1663) and Lutheran Traditions of Mass Composition," 2 vols. (Ph.D. diss., Bryn Mawr College, 1983).

40. A cross section of the various types of Ahle's compositions are found in *DDT,* vol. 5.

41. A selection of Knüpfer's and Schelle's vocal works are found in *DDT,* vols. 58–59. A performing edition of six of Schelle's chorale cantatas, ed. Mary S. Morris, is found in *Recent Researches in the Music of the Baroque Era,* vols. 60–61 (Madison, Wis., 1988).

42. *Musiche a una, doi e tre voci* (Venice, 1613). Modern edition by Othmar Wessely and Erika Kanduth, eds., in *DTÖ,* vol. 125 (Graz, 1973).

43. Documentation from the important monograph by Steven Saunders, *Cross, Sword, and Lyre: Sacred Music at the Imperial Court of Ferdinand II of Habsburg (1619–1637)* (Oxford, 1995).

44. First observed by Ludwig Ritter von Köchel in *Die kaiserliche Hof-Musikkapelle in Wien von 1543 bis 1867* (Vienna, 1869).

45. See Appendix A, "Personnel of the Imperial Music Chapel under Ferdinand II," in Saunders, *Cross, Sword, and Lyre,* pp. 225–30.

46. The sacred works by these composers are examined in great detail in Saunders's monograph, with the added advantage of numerous music examples transcribed by the author. The few conclusions drawn here from Saunders are no substitute for reading his invaluable work together with examining the music.

47. Edited by Albert Biales in *Concentus musicus,* vol. II (Cologne, 1973). A second volume of the *Sacrorum concentuum* was published in 1619 with motets in ten and twelve parts.

48. Saunders (on p. 39) gives a list of works from Graz choir books used in Vienna, which contain considerable music by late-sixteenth-century composers including Palestrina and Lassus.

49. In manuscript A-Wn, Cod. 16702. The nine other Masses in the manuscript are also for sixteen parts.

50. For Priuli's motets, see Hermann J. Busch, ed., *Giovanni Priuli: Vier Generalbassmotetteen aus dem Parnassus musicus Ferdinandaeus* (1615), in *Musik alter Meister,* vol. 23 (Graz, 1970).

51. For example, see *Gustate et Videte* given in Saunders, *Cross, Sword, and Lyre,* pp. 251–56.

52. See Steven Saunders, ed., *Fourteen Motets from the Court of Ferdinand II of Hapsburg* (Madison, 1995). No. 1, "O Maria, quid ploras" and No. 2, "Vulnerasti cor meum" are examples of Valentini's early motets.

53. Ibid., pp. 295–306, for a modern edition of this Salve Regina. For more concerning the music of Priuli and Valentini, see the preface by Saunders to his *Fourteen Motets from the Court of Ferdinand II of Hapsburg.*

54. Smither, *A History of the Oratorio,* pp. 398–406, discusses as a representative Viennese oratorio Draghi's *Jepthe* (1687), with music examples.

55. See Hilde H. Junkermann, "The Magnificats of Johann Stadlmayr" (Ph.D. diss., Ohio State University, 1966); also her edition of selected Magnificats in *Recent Researches in the Music of the Baroque Era,* vol. 35 (Madison, Wis., 1980).

56. These remarks regarding Salzburg's sacred music in the seventeenth century are indebted to the invaluable study by Eric T. Chafe, *The Sacred Music of Heinrich Biber* (Ann Arbor, 1987); see especially pp. 53–69. See also his catalogue of Biber's works, pp. 227–64.

57. See Heinrich Albert, "Leben und Werke des Komponisten und Dirigenten Abraham Megerle" (Ph.D. diss., Munich, 1927).

58. See Miriam W. Barndt-Webb, "Andreas Hofer: His Life and Music" (Ph.D. diss., University of Illinois, 1972).

59. Chafe, pp. 230–86.

60. Ibid., pp. 56–58 and 63–66.

61. A facsimile of the *Missa Salisburgensis,* attributed to Benevoli, was edited by Laurence Feininger (Vienna and Salzburg, 1969).

62. See Chafe, p. 44, for the famous engraving showing a musical performance in the cathedral in 1682. These balconies no longer exist.

63. The concept of a "colossal Baroque" in analogy to Roman church architecture of the time entered American scholarship through Bukofzer's *Music in the Baroque Era.* See especially pp. 68–70, where he describes this Mass as bearing "testimony to the stupendous facility of spatial dispositions and, at the same time, the inflation of essentially modest music to mammoth dimensions."

64. Little of the sacred music has appeared in modern editions. Highly recommended is Chafe's detailed discussions of these works with copious music examples.

65. See Chapter 8 for a discussion of secular keyboard music.

66. Johann Mattheson, *Grundlage einer Ehren-Pforte* (Hamburg, 1740), p. 332.

67. See *Jacob Praetorius Choralbearbeitungen,* ed. Werner Breig (Kassel, 1974).

68. In the Clausholm fragments, also variously described as the Visby or Petri Tablature. See Henrik Glahn and Søren Sørensen, *The Clausholm Music Fragments* (Copenhagen, 1974).

69. Gustav Fock, ed., *Heinrich Scheidemann, Magnificat-Bearbeitungen* (Kassel, 1970).

70. The twelve intabulations are published by Cleveland Johnson, ed., *12 Orgelintabolierungen,* in 3 vols. (Wilhelmshaven, 1991), and the chorale preludes by Gustav Fock, ed., in *Heinrich Scheidemann, Choralbearbeitungen* (Kassel, 1967).

71. Ibid., p. 64.

72. For a comprehensive study of Scheidemann's organ music, see Werner Breig, *Die Orgelwerke von Heinrich Scheidemann, Beihefte zum Archiv für Musikwissenschaft.*

73. A ninth, *Ach wir armen Sünder,* is probably not Weckmann's. See Werner Breig, ed., *Matthias Weckmann, Choralbearbeitungen* (Kassel, 1979).

74. See Christoph Wolff, "Johann Adam Reinken and Johann Sebastian Bach: On the

Context of Bach's Early Works," in *J. S. Bach as Organist,* ed. George Stauffer and Ernest May (Bloomington, 1986), pp. 57–80.

75. Both chorale preludes are given by Willi Apel, ed., in *Adam Reincken: Collected Keyboard Works, Corpus of Early Keyboard Music* 16 (n.p., 1967).

76. See Klaus Beckmann, ed., *Franz Tunder, Sämtliche Orgelwerke* (Wiesbaden, 4th ed., 1985), which includes nine chorale preludes.

77. Chorale preludes included in Willi Apel, ed., *Delphin Strunck and Peter Mohrhardt: Original Compositions for Organ, Corpus of Early Keyboard Music,* vol. 23 (n.p., 1973).

78. Christhard Mahrenholz, ed., *Tabulatura nova, Teil I und II,* vol. 6; *Teil III,* vol. 7, in *Samuel Scheidt Werke* (Hamburg, 1954).

79. This and subsequent discussion about Buxtehude's organ music is indebted to Kerala J. Snyder's *Dieterich Buxtehude, Organist in Lübeck.* See her valuable listing of all the chorale melodies set by Buxtehude, pp. 496–501.

80. The chorale form as used in Lübeck, given by Snyder, ibid., p. 269.

81. Christoph Albrecht (ed.), *Neue Ausgabe samtlicher Orgelwerke,* vol. 5 (Kassel, 1998), p. 14.

82. Ibid., vol. 4 (Kassel, 1997), p. 18.

83. Three chorale partite are included in *George Böhm sämtliche Werke,* vol. 2, ed. J. Wolgast, rev. G. Wolgast (Wiesbaden, 1952): *Ach wie nichtig, ach wie flüchtig* (1), *Freu dich sehr O meine Seele* (8), and *Wer nur den lieben Gott lässt walten* (14). All of the organ pieces with chorales are included in *Georg Böhm, Sämtliche Orgelwerke,* ed. Klaus Beckmann (Wiesbaden, 1986).

84. Ibid., p. 138.

85. The chorale preludes were published in *Johann Pachelbel, Orgelkompositionen,* ed. Max Seiffert, in *DTB,* vol. iv/I (Leipzig, 1903), and in republication by Dover Publications (Mineola, N.Y., 1994). The Magnificat fugues are contained in DTÖ, VIII/2 (vol. 17), ed. H. Botstiber and M. Seiffert (1901).

86. For Seiffert's comments, see *DTB,* vol. iv/I, p. xiv. Apel's remarks are in *The History of Keyboard Music,* p. 657.

87. See *Gesammelte Werke von Friedr. Wilh. Zachow,* ed. Max Seiffert, *DDT,* erste Folge, vols. 21–22.

8. SECULAR MUSIC IN NORTHERN AND SOUTHERN EUROPE IN THE SEVENTEENTH CENTURY

1. Published in a fine facsimile edition in *Biblioteca musica Bononiensis,* Sezione IV, no. 126 (Bologna, n.d.).

2. The frequent attribution to Bontempi is doubtful.

3. Modern edition, Susanne Wilsdorf, ed., in *Denkmäler Mitteldeutscher Barockmusic,* Series II, vol. 2 (Leipzig, 1998).

4. The other early extant German operas are the Singspiel by Sigmund Theophil Staden, *Seelewig* [1644], published by R. Eitner in *Monatshefte für Musikgeschichte,* vol. 13 (1881), pp. 65–146; and Johann Wolfgang Franck, *Die drei Töchter des Cecrops* (1679), edited by G. F. Schmidt in *Archiv für Musikforschung,* vol. 4 (1938), p. 257.

5. The score to Conradi's *Ariadne* is found in the Music Division of the Library of Congress. See Buelow's article with several music examples from the score in "Die schöne und getreue Ariadne (Hamburg 1691): A Lost Opera by J. G. Conradi Rediscovered," *Acta Musicologica,* vol. 44 (1972), pp. 108–21.

6. The only score for the opera lacks acts III and V. Concerning a new source containing some music for these and the other acts as well as an important discussion of the work and its history, see Carl B. Schmidt, "Antonio Cesti's *Il pomo d'oro:* A Reexamination of a Famous Hapsburg Court Spectacle, *JAMS* 29 (Fall 1976), pp. 381–412.

7. *Denkmäler der Tonkunst in Österreich,* Jg. III/2 (Bd. 6) and Jg. IV/2 (Bd. 9) (Vienna, 1896–97).

8. Curt Sachs, *The Rise of Music in the Ancient World East and West* (New York, 1943), p. 21.

9. See Reese, *Music in the Renaissance,* pp. 632–38.

10. The importance of the secular vocal works of Johann Hermann Schein is discussed in some detail in R. Hinton Thomas's *Poetry and Song in the German Baroque: A Study of the Continuo Lied* (Oxford, 1963), pp. 21–33.

11. For the best discussion in English of Nauwach's music, see ibid., pp. 34–43.

12. Reprinted from Walther Vetter, *Das frühdeutsche Lied,* vol. II (Leipzig, 1928), p. 48. In addition, Vetter gives another six examples of Nauwach's songs.

13. Published in the *Denkmäler deutscher Tonkunst,* ed. Hermann Kretzschmar (Leipzig, 1935), vols. XII–XIII.

14. Regarding this and other aspects of Albert's songs, see Thomas, *Poetry and Song in the German Baroque,* pp. 44–52.

15. Although lost, most of the contents have been collected from other sources in H. Osthoff, *Adam Krieger* (Leipzig, 1929; reprinted 1970).

16. Published in the *Denkmäler deutscher Tonkunst,* ed. Alfred Heuss (Leipzig, 1905).

17. Ibid., p. 105.

18. Ibid., p. 16.

19. Published in *Das Erbe Deutscher Musik,* vol. 43, ed. Hans Joachim Moser (Mainz, 1962).

20. No modern edition exists. However, a facsimile of the edition of 1657 has been published by Gary C. Thomas in *Nachdrucke Deutscher Literatur des 17. Jahrhunderts,* vol. 47 (Bern, 1991). It includes an informative discussion of the work and its composer, the poets, and the lieder.

21. Reproduced from Hans Joachim Moser's *The German Solo Song and the Ballad* (Cologne, 1958), p. 2.

22. Johann Mattheson, *Critica musica* (Hamburg, 1722), part II, p. 100.

23. The major study of Sweelinck's keyboard works is Pieter Dirksen's *The Keyboard Music of Jan Pieterszoon Sweelinck* (Koninklijke Vereniging voor Nederlandse Muziekgeschiedenis, 1997).

24. Published in two volumes in *Jan Pieterszoon Sweelinck, opera ominia,* ed. Gustav Leonhardt, Alfons Annegarn, and Frits Noske (Amsterdam, 1968). Volume 1 also includes fourteen additional works of questionable authenticity.

25. An indication of the massive amount of organ and harpsichord music buried in unpublished manuscripts just from the first half of the seventeenth century is found in Lydia Schierning's *Die Überlieferung der deutschen Orgel- und Klaviermusik aus der ersten Hälfte des 17. Jahrhunderts* (Kassel, 1961).

26. See Apel, *The History of Keyboard Music to 1700,* pp. 387–88. Organ pieces from his *Harmonia organica* (Nuremberg, 1645) and thirty dances, including courantes, ballets, sarabandes, and allemandes, are found in the *Denkmäler der Tonkunst in Bayern* (Augsburg, 1924), vols. 21–24.

27. The usual date given for Scheidemann's birth is around 1595. Konrad Küster in

"Zur Geschichte der Organistenfamilie Scheidemann" in *Schütz-Jahrbuch* 22 (1999), p. III, gives a convincing argument for placing Scheidemann's birth before 1591.

28. See Cleveland Johnson, ed., *12 Orgelintavolierungen*, 3 vols. (Wilhelmshaven, 1990).

29. Twenty-eight pieces for harpsichord are included in Pieter Dirksen, ed., *Sämtliche Werke für Clavier (Cembalo)—Complete Harpischord Music* (Wiesbaden, 2000). Also there are *15 Preludien und Fugen*, Max Seiffert, ed., in *Organum, Vierte Reihe, Nr. 1 (Leipzig, n.d.)*. Thirteen Praeambulas, two fugues, two canzonas, a fantasia, and two toccatas are given by Werner Breig, ed., in *Heinrich Scheidemann Orgelwerke*, vol. 3 (Kassel, 1971).

30. In *Grundlage einer Ehren-Pforte* (Hamburg, 1740), p. 329; this in comparison to the organ works of Jacob Praetorius.

31. These sources are given in Dirksen, *Sämtliche Werke für Clavier*, p. 78.

32. The toccatas of Hassler are published in Stijn Stribos, ed., *Hans Leo Hassler Toccatas* (Hänssler-Verlag, 1985), and examples of his ricercar, fantasia, fugue, and canzona in Georges Kiss, ed., *Ausgewählte Werke für Orgel (Cembalo)* (Mainz, 1971). Erbach's works are edited by Clare G. Rayner in *Christian Erbach: Collected Keyboard Compositions*, vol. I: *Ricercars;* vol. III: *Fantasias, fugues, canzonas;* vol. IV: *Toccatas* (American Institute of Musicology, 1971, 1973, 1976).

33. Published by Klaus Beckmann, ed., in *Franz Tunder: Sämtliche Orgelwerke* (Wiesbaden, 1985).

34. Mattheson, *Grundlage einer Ehren-Pforte*, p. 396.

35. Published by Siegbert Rampe, ed., *Matthias Weckmann, Sämliche Freie Orgel- und Clavierwerke* (Kassel, 1991). There is also an important preface including the most recent examination of the questions of authenticity and the sources containing Weckmann's keyboard works.

36. Ibid., pp. 42–54.

37. The *Clavier-Übung*, Hilmar Trede, ed., published as *Klavier-Übung 1728* (London and New York, 1940). The organ works, published as *Vincent Lübeck Orgelwerke*, ed. Hermann Keller (London and New York, 1940).

38. For more regarding the important connection between Böhm and J. S. Bach, see Wolff, *Johann Sebastian Bach: The Learned Musician*, pp. 60–62.

39. Published in *G. Böhm: Sämtliche Werke: Klavier- und Orgelwerke*, vol. I, rev. ed. Gesa Wolgast (Wiesbaden, 1952).

40. Published in Michael Radulescu, ed., *Nicolaus Bruhns Orgelwerke*, 2 vols. (Vienna and Munich, 1993).

41. Apel in *The History of Keyboard Music*, p. 368, says of this subject that it "is one of the most original ideas in the fugue literature of the seventeenth century."

42. For a detailed discussion about Buxtehude's influences on Bach, see " 'First Fruits' and the Buxtehude Experience," in Wolff, *Johann Sebastian Bach: The Learned Musician*, pp. 92–101.

43. Johann Gottfried Walther, *Musikalisches Lexicon oder Musicalische Bibliothec* (Leipzig, 1732), p. 584. Johann Mattheson, in *Der vollkommene Capellmeister* (Hamburg, 1739), pp. 87–89, also discusses the importance of the concept. See the discussion of the Mattheson passage in Kerala J. Snyder, *Dieterich Buxtehude: Organist in Lübeck*, pp. 248–57.

44. These keyboard works are published in *Denkmäler der Tonkunst in Bayern*, Jg. IV (1) (1903).

45. Published in *Johann Pachelbel Ausgewählte Orgelwerke*, ed. Karl Matthaei, vol. I (Kassel, 1931), pp. 54–63.

46. The extant works of both Krieger brothers are contained in *Johann & Johann*

Philipp Krieger, Sämtliche Orgel- und Clavierwerke, vols. I and II, ed. Siegbert Rampe and Helene Lerch (Kassel, 1999).

47. See William S. Newman, *The Sonata in the Baroque Era* (Chapel Hill, 1959), p. 240.

48. All four volumes are published in *Denkmähler der deutsche Tonkunst,* vol. IV, ed. K. Päsler (Leipzig, 1901). The first three volumes also are published in facsimile, ed. L. Alvini, M. Castellani, and P. Paolini (Florence, 1995, 1996).

49. The complete keyboard works were published in the *Denkmäler der Tonkunst in Österreich,* ed. Guido Adler, Jg. IV/1, vol. 8; Jg. VI/2, vol. 13; Jg. X/2, vol. 21 (repr. Graz, 1959).

50. Jacob Adlung, *Anleitung zu der musikalischen Gelahrtheit* (Erfurt, 1758), p. 711.

51. All published in *Johann Caspar Kerll: The Collected Works for Keyboard,* ed. C. David Harris (New York, 1995).

52. Published in *Johann Joseph Fux: Sämtliche Werke, Serie VI/1, Werke für Tasteninstrumente,* ed. Friedrich Wilhelm Riedel (Kassel, 1964).

9. HEINRICH SCHÜTZ (1585–1672)

1. For a succinct biography of Schütz and an analysis of his compositions, see Basil Smallman, *Schütz,* The Master Musicians (Oxford, 2000).

2. SWV = *Schütz-Werke-Verzeichnis: Kleine Ausgabe,* ed. W. Bittinger (Kassel, 1960).

3. Schütz uses an archaic spelling for *Cappella,* the modern Italian form of the word for "chorus."

4. This preface is given in an English translation in the *American Choral Review* (October 1985), pp. 8–9.

5. A text that Johannes Brahms, who admired Schütz's music, made effective use of in the fourth movement of his German Requiem.

6. These individual Psalm compositions are published in the *Neue Ausgabe sämtlicher Werke* as *Einzelne Psalmen,* vols. 27/28, ed. W. Breig (Kassel, 1970, 1971).

7. In the *Neue Ausgabe sämtlicher Werke,* vol. 39, as *Der Schwanengesang. Des Königs und Propheten Davids 119. Psalm in elf Stücken nebst einem Anhang des 100. Psalms und eines deutschen Magnificats,* SWV 482–94, ed. W. Steude (Kassel, 1984).

8. A list of compositions presumed lost appears in *The New Grove North European Baroque Masters* (London, 1985), pp. 129–31.

9. Quoted from H. J. Moser, *Heinrich Schütz: His Life and Works,* trans. C. Pfatteicher (St. Louis, 1959), p. 128.

10. Moser, *Heinrich Schütz,* translated by Pfatteicher, p. 100.

11. For complete text in English translation, see "A Schütz Reader," *American Choral Review* (October 1985), pp. 25–26.

12. In many instances Schütz recomposed the same text, offering valuable opportunities for the study of his developing style. See, for example, the earlier setting of this text in the *Psalmen Davids,* SWV 42.

13. The document is found in *Gesammelte Briefe und Schriften,* ed. E. H. Müller (Regensburg, 1931), pp. 207–16.

14. See HAM, vol. 2, p. 36.

15. Moser/Pfatteicher, *Heinrich Schütz,* p. 660.

16. Ibid., p. 684.

10. ENGLISH MUSIC DURING THE STUART REIGN,
THE COMMONWEALTH, AND THE RESTORATION

1. The best in-depth summary of English music in the fifteenth and sixteenth centuries remains Gustave Reese's *Music in the Renaissance* (New York, 2d ed., 1959), pp. 763–883.

2. A valuable study of sacred music from the Reformation is by Peter Le Huray, *Music and the Reformation in England, 1549–1660* (Cambridge, 1978). See also Ian Spink's comprehensive *Restoration Cathedral Music: 1660–1714* (Oxford, 1995).

3. The anthems cited here are found in *Musica Britannica,* vol. XXIII: *Thomas Weelkes Collected Anthems.*

4. The best study for Weelkes remains David Brown's *Thomas Weelkes* (New York, 1969).

5. Edmund H. Fellowes, *English Cathedral Music* (London, 1941), p. 99.

6. These anthems are included in *Tudor Church Music,* vol. IV (Oxford, 1925).

7. In *Early English Church Music,* vol. 3: *Orlando Gibbons, Verse Anthems,* ed. David Wulstan (London, [1962]), p. 38.

8. Ibid., p. 179.

9. See Denis Stevens, *Thomas Tomkins, 1572–1656* (New York, 1967).

10. Published in a series of six volumes in *Early English Church Music,* ed. Bernard Rose (London, 1965–92).

11. This one and five others of the fifteen motets are included in *Matthew Locke, Anthems and Motets,* ed. Peter Le Huray, in *Musica Britannica,* vol. 38 (London, 1976).

12. Ibid., for the anthems cited here.

13. Not to be overlooked, however, are the many important composers employed in the cathedrals of England. See Ian Spink, *Restoration Cathedral Music, 1660–1714* (Oxford, 1995).

14. The sacred songs have not been published. The Service and anthems are contained in *Pelham Humfrey, The Complete Church Music,* vols. 1 and 2, ed. Peter Dennison, in *Musica Britannica,* vols. 34 and 35 (London, 1972). The question of authenticity of Nos. 4a, *Have Mercy Upon Me, O God,* and No. 6, *Hear My Prayer,* is discussed by Don Franklin in his review of Dennison's edition in *JAMS* 28 (1975), pp. 143–49.

15. *A General History of Music* (London, 1776); new ed. F. Mercer (London, 1935), vol. 2, pp. 350–56.

16. *Musica Britannica* has published three volumes of Blow's anthems: vol. 7, "Coronation Anthems," "Anthems with Strings," ed. Anthony Lewis & Harold Watkins Shaw (London, 1953); vol. 50, Anthems II: "Anthems with Orchestra," ed. Bruce Wood (London, 1984); vol. 64, Anthems III: "Anthems with Strings," ed. Bruce Wood (London, 1993). To date there is no published edition of the verse anthems with organ. But see Fredrick A. Tarrant, "John Blow's Verse Anthems with Organ Accompaniment" (Ph.D. diss., Indiana University School of Music, 2000).

17. *Musica Britannica,* vol. 7.

18. Ibid.

19. The complete corpus of English madrigals is published in *The English Madrigal School,* ed. E. H. Fellowes (1913–24), rev. ed. by T. Dart and others as *The English Madrigalists* (1956–88).

20. See the work of Joseph Kerman, *The Elizabethan Madrigal* (New York, 1962).

21. Their madrigals are published in *The English Madrigal School.*

22. For an excellent survey of the English song, see Ian Spink, *English Song: Dowland to Purcell* (New York, 1974).

23. See Diana Poulton's *John Dowland: His Life and Works* (Berkeley, 1972).

24. Dowland's and the lute songs by other composers are found in the series *The English School of Lutenist Song Writers,* ed. E. H. Fellowes (1920–32); partly revised by Thurston Dart as *The English Lute-Songs* (1959–66); further rev. with additional vols. (1959–69).

25. The list includes Thomas Greaves (fl. 1604), Robert Johnson (c. 1583–1633), Michael Cavendish (c. 1565–1628), Robert Jones (fl. 1597–1615), Philip Rosseter (1567 or 1568–1623), Francis Pilkington (c. 1570–1638), John Danyel (1554–c. 1626), Thomas Ford (d. 1648), John Bartlet (fl. 1606–1610), Alfonso Ferrabosco (c. 1575–1628), William Corkine (fl. 1610–1617), Robert Ramsey (fl. 1616–1644), Tobias Hume (?c. 1579–1645), Martin Peerson (1571/73–1651), John Hilton (1599–1657), and the last composer to publish lute songs (1622), John Attey (fl. 1622–c. 1640).

26. In vol. 33 of *Musica Britannica,* "English Songs, 1625–1660," Ian Spink has edited a selection of ayres that includes in addition to examples by these composers others by another twenty-four composers.

27. Ibid., this and the following examples, nos. 10.11 and 10.12.

28. John Wilson (ed.), *Roger North on Music* (London, 1959).

29. The entire example from which this excerpt is taken appears in Spink, *English Songs,* together with an analysis of the entire song.

30. All of these are found in *Musica Britannica,* vol. 33.

31. For detailed discussion and analysis of many of the songs written from the beginning of the Restoration, including those for plays, see Spink, *English Songs,* pp. 151–200.

32. Published in facsimile edition in the series *Music for London Entertainment, 1660–1800,* series A, vols. 5a and 5b (London, 1989).

33. Even in the critically well-balanced study by Spink, *English Songs,* he tends to judge Blow harshly for not achieving Purcell's breathtaking originality. Spink's conclusion, "that Blow as a song writer, fails at all levels. He either cannot or will not please with trifles, and though he aspires to something higher he just has not got what it takes," is unfair since it is not adequately supported by the few critical jabs he takes at Blow's song techniques.

34. *Amphion Anglicus* = "English Amphion." Amphion, the son of Zeus and Antiope, was known for playing a lyre given to him by Hermes with which he charmed the stones to create a wall around Thebes. Facsimile edition available (Ridgewood, N.J., 1965).

35. From the edition by Walter Bergmann (Mainz, 1962).

36. The *In nomine* is the plainsong "Gloria tibi Trinitas" that Tavener employed in his Mass of that name, where the In Nomine *à4* from the Benedictus of the Mass includes this plainsong. The earliest "In nomines" were transcriptions of this section of that Mass. For more concerning the history of this plainsong and its usage in other contrapuntal settings, see Reese, *Music in the Renaissance,* pp. 779–80.

37. Examples of consort music by most of these composers are found in *Musica Britannica,* vol. 9, ed. Thurston Dart and William Coates.

38. Ibid., fantasia in three parts, no. 8.

39. Ibid., no. 43.

40. All published in *Musica Britannica,* vol. 48, ed. John Harper.

41. Published in *Musica Britannica,* ed. John Irving, vol. 59.

42. The only general introduction to the life and works of William Lawes remains Murray Lefkowitz's *William Lawes* (London, 1960).

43. Edited by David Pinto (London and Bermuda, 1995).

44. For a detailed analysis of these works, see Andrew Ashbee, *The Harmonious Musick of John Jenkins* (London, 1992), vol. I, pp. 161–274. For the music, see *Consort Music of Six Parts*, ed. Donald Peart, *Musica Britannica*, vol. 39 (London, 1977); *Consort Music in Five Parts*, ed. Andrew Ashbee, *Musica Britannica*, vol. 26 (2d rev. ed., London, 1975).

45. See Frank Traficante, "Lyra-Viol Music? A Semantic Puzzle," in *John Jenkins and His Time: Studies in English Consort Music*, ed. Andrew Ashbee and Peter Holman (Oxford, 1996), pp. 325–52; and Traficante's edition of John Jenkins, *The Lyra Viol Consorts* (Madison, Wis., 1992).

46. The former belief that the violin was introduced into England at the court of Charles II is refuted by Peter Holman's *Four and Twenty Fiddlers: The Violin at the English Court, 1540–1690* (Oxford, 1993).

47. Published in *Musica Brittanica*, vol. 40, ed. David Pinto.

48. See Andrew Ashbee, "John Jenkins's Fantasia-Suites for Treble, Two Basses and Organ," *Chelys* 1 (1969), pp. 3–15; 2 (1970), pp. 6–17.

49. Edited and transcribed by Robert A. Warner, *John Jenkins: Three-Part Fancy and Ayre Divisions*, Wellesley Edition 10 (Wellesley, Mass., 1966).

50. Published in *Musica Britannica*, vols. 31 and 32, ed. Michael Tilmouth.

51. Ed. Hilda Andrews (London, 1926).

52. A small, oblong, single-manual keyboard instrument with plucked strings, a type of harpsichord. The term "virginals," however, was generally applied to all quilled keyboard instruments.

53. Published by J. A. Fuller Maitland and W. B. Squire (London and Leipzig, 1894–99; repr. 1964).

54. The complete keyboard works of Byrd, edited by Alan Brown, are published in *Musica Britannica*, vols. 27 and 28.

55. The complete keyboard works of Bull are in *Musica Britannica*. Vol. 14, edited by John Steele and Francis Cameron, is devoted primarily to organ music; vol. 19, edited by Thurston Dart, to secular works.

56. The Byrd Walsingham variations are found in *Musica Britannica*, vol. 27, no. 8; the Bull setting in *Musica Britannica*, vol. 19, no. 85.

57. The complete keyboard works of Farnaby, edited by Richard Marlow, are in *Musica Britannica*, vol. 24.

58. The complete keyboard works of Orlando Gibbons, edited by Gerald Hendrie, are in *Musica Britannica*, vol. 20.

59. The complete keyboard works of Thomas Tomkins, edited by Stephen D. Tuttle, are in *Musica Britannica*, vol. 5.

60. See Candace Bailey's edition of *Late-Seventeenth-Century English Keyboard Music* (Madison, Wis., 1997).

61. Complete edition by Barry Cooper in *Musica Britannica*, vol. 69.

62. This section is indebted to Matthew Spring's chapter "Solo Music for Tablature Instruments," in *Music in Britain: The Seventeenth Century*, ed. Ian Spink (Oxford, 1992).

63. See Richard T. Pinnell, *Francesco Corbetta and the Baroque Guitar, with a Transcription of His Works*, 2 vols. (Ann Arbor, 1980). Volume 2 contains transcriptions of Corbetta's lute music into staff notation, including *La guitarre royalle dediée au Roy de la grande Bretagne* (i.e., Charles II).

64. See *D. Bacheler: Selected Works for Lute,* ed. M. Long (London, 1972).

65. See *Complete Works for Solo Lute,* ed. A. Sundermann (London, 1970).

66. Oxford, Bodleian Library, MS Mus. Sch. b. 1. See Vincent Duckles, "The 'Curious' Art of John Wilson: An Introduction to His Songs and Lute Music," *JAMS* 7 (1954), pp. 93–112, with several examples from these lute pieces.

67. An important monograph regarding the court masque is by Peter Walls, *Music in the English Courtly Masque, 1604–1640* (Oxford, 1996).

68. For example, see Andrew Sabol, *Songs and Dances for the Stuart Masque* (Providence, R.I., 1959; rev. 1978 as *Four Hundred Songs and Dances for the Stuart Masque*).

69. Ed. Peter Walls, 3 vols., *English Instrumental Music of the Late Renaissance* (London, 1975–76).

70. Ed. B. Thomas, 3 vols. (London, 1974).

71. Ed. Murray Lefkowitz in *Trois masques à la cour de Charles Ier d'Angleterre* (Paris, 1970). See the detailed description of these masques together with many music examples in Wall, *Music in the English Courtly Masque,* pp. 159–205.

72. Ed. E. J. Dent, *Musica Brittanica,* vol. 2 (1951; rev. 1965).

73. See in particular "The Origins of English Recitative," in Wall, *Music in the English Courtly Masque,* pp. 86–103.

74. The preface to *Albion and Albanius* (1685), in *The Works of John Dryden,* ed. E. Miner, G. R. Guffey, and F. B. Zimmerman (Berkeley, 1976), vol. xv, pp. 6–7.

11. HENRY PURCELL (1659–1695)

1. A valuable study for the understanding of Purcell's musical style is Martin Adams's *Henry Purcell: The Origins and Development of His Musical Style* (Cambridge, 1995).

2. From *The Works of Henry Purcell,* vol. 31 (London, 1959), p. 41.

3. Z numbers refer to the catalogue by Franklin B. Zimmerman, *Henry Purcell 1659–1695: An Analytical Catalogue of His Music* (London, 1963).

4. Ibid., p. 10.

5. Ibid., p. 16.

6. For an excellent examination of this question, see Michael Tilmouth and Christopher D. S. Field, "Purcell and the Trio Sonata," in *Music in Britain: The Seventeenth Century,* ed. Ian Spink (Oxford, 1992), pp. 264–79.

7. From *The Works of Henry Purcell,* vol. 5: *Twelve Sonatas of Three Parts* (London, 1893), p. 36.

8. Ibid., p. 64.

9. From *The Works of Henry Purcell,* vol. 7: *Ten Sonatas of Four Parts* (London, 1896), p. 8.

10. Ibid., p. 27.

11. In *Ten Sonatas of Four Parts* (London, 1896), p. 57.

12. The anthems are published in *The Works of Henry Purcell* (London, 1878–1965), vols. 13, 14, 17, 28, 29, 32.

13. Ibid., vol. 13.

14. Concerning the mutual influences between Blow and Purcell, see Martin Adams, "Purcell, Blow and the English Court Ode," *Purcell Studies,* ed. Curtis Price (Cambridge, 1995), pp. 172–91.

15. The odes and welcome songs are published in *The Works of Henry Purcell,* vols. 1, 4, 8, 10, 11, 15, 18, 24, and 27.

16. Which some writers label a "pseudo-ostinato."

17. Purcell first used trumpets in the Yorkshire Feast ode, *Of old, when heroes Thought it base* (1690).

18. The enormous body of music contained in Restoration plays remains largely unknown to music historians and performers. It is astonishing that this substantial contribution by Purcell has been almost totally neglected by performers. The major work on this vital subject regarding music in England at the end of the seventeenth century is by Curtis A. Price, *Music in the Restoration Theatre: With a Catalogue of Instrumental Music in Plays, 1665–1713* (Ann Arbor, 1979). See also Price's important work *Henry Purcell and the London Stage* (Cambridge, 1984), to which the subsequent comments given here are indebted.

19. The hypothesis of Bruce Wood and Andrew Pinnock, that the performance of *Dido and Aeneas* at Priest's Chelsea school in 1689 was a revival of a performance some five years earlier at the court of Charles II, remains unproven. See their article in *Early Music* 20 (1992).

20. Ellen T. Harris, *Henry Purcell's "Dido and Aeneas"* (Oxford, 1987). This monograph includes considerable important material on the text and music, the manuscript source, and a performance history of the work.

21. Curtis Price, ed., Purcell, *Dido and Aeneas: An Opera,* Norton Critical Scores (New York, 1986), p. vii. Included is a new edition of the opera in full score.

22. For a detailed analysis of this work, see Ellen Harris, *Henry Purcell's "Dido and Aeneas,"* pp. 69–119.

23. Purcell's music in these and all the other plays to which he contributed is examined in Price, *Purcell and the London Stage.*

24. Ibid., pp. 290–95, where Price has sorted out the probable political references.

25. See Ellen Harris, "*King Arthur's* Journey into the Eighteenth Century," in *Purcell Studies,* ed. Curtis Price (Cambridge, 1995), pp. 257–89.

26. Ibid., p. 305.

13. BAROQUE MUSIC IN EASTERN EUROPE

1. Francis H. Eterovich and Christopher Spalatin, eds., *Croatia: Land, People, Culture* (vols. I–II, Toronto, 1964–70; reissued 1976; vol. III, Chicago, 1998), is accessible for the general reader. Cf. also Ivo Banac, "The Revived Croatia of Pavao Ritter Vitezović," in *Concept of Nationhood in Early Modern Eastern Europe,* vol. X, ed. I. Banac and F. E. Sysyn (Cambridge, Mass., 1986), pp. 492–507.

2. For general information on music in Croatia, cf. Josip Andreis, *Music in Croatia* (Zagreb, 1982); Lovro Županović, *Centuries of Croatian Music,* 2 vols. (Zagreb, 1984–89); and Ennio Stipčević, *Hrvatska glazba: Povijest hrvatske glazbe do 20. stoljeća* [Croatian Music: History of Croatian Music Before the 20th Century] (Zagreb, 1997).

3. Modern edition of *Parnassia militia* (Strasbourg, 1662) is prepared by Albe Vidaković (Zagreb, 1957); see also *Vincentius Jelić, Sechs Motetten aus Arion primus (1628),* ed. Albe Vidaković, Musik alter Meister 5 (Graz, 1957). A comprehensive comparative view of Jelić's music is given by Anne Kirwan-Mott, *The Small-Scale Sacred Concertato in the Early Seventeenth Century* (Ann Arbor, 1981), 2 vols.

4. See Giuseppe Radole, "Musica e musicisti in Istria nel Cinque e Seicento," *Atti e memorie della Societa Istriana di archeologia e storia patria,* n.s. XII (1965), 147–213; Ennio Stipčević, *Hrvatska glazbena kultura 17. stoljeca* [Croatian Musical Culture of the 17th Century] (Split, 1992).

5. See Dragan Plamenac, "Damjan Nembri of Hvar (1584–c. 1648) and his Vesper Psalms," *Musica Antiqua Europae Orientalis* VI (Bydgoszcz, 1982), pp. 669–85.

6. See L. Županović, *Centuries of Croatian Music,* vol. I.

7. See Eleanor Selfridge-Field, *Venetian Instrumental Music from Gabrieli to Vivaldi* (New York, 1994); Ennio Stipčević, "Francesco Sponga-Usper, compositore veneziano di origine istriana: Considerazioni preliminari," *Atti del Centro di Richerche Storiche di Rovigno* 16 (1985–86), pp. 165–231; Stephen Bonta, "The Use of Instruments in the Ensemble Canzona and Sonata in Italy, 1580–1650," *Ricercare* 4 (1992), pp. 23–43.

8. First pioneering studies on Croatian Renaissance and early Baroque music were those by Dragan Plamenac. See his essay "Music in the 16th and 17th Centuries in Dalmatia," *Papers Read by Members of the American Musicological Society 1939* (New York, 1944), pp. 21–51; idem, "Music in the Adriatical Costal Areas of the Southers Slavs," in Gustave Reese, *Music in the Renaissance* (New York, 1954), pp. 757–762. For further information, see Koraljka Kos, "Style and Sociological Background of Croatian Renaissance Music," *International Review of the Aesthetics and Sociology of Music* 13, no. 1 (1982), pp. 55–82, with an extensive bibliography. See also Ennio Stipčević, "La cultura musicale in Istria e in Dalmazia nel XVI e XVII secolo: Principali caratteristiche storiche, geopolitiche e culturali," *International Review of the Aesthetics and Sociology of Music* 23, no. 2 (1992), pp. 141–52.

9. Cf. Stanislav Tuksar, *Croatian Renaissance Music Theorists* (Zagreb, 1981); idem, "Sixteenth-Century Croatian Writers on Music: A Bridge between East and West," in *Essays in Honor of Claude V. Palisca,* ed. Barbara R. Hanning et al. (New York, 1992), pp. 129–42; Ivano Cavallini, *I due volti di Netuno: Studi su teatro e musica a Venezia e in Dalmazia dal Cinquecento al Settecento* (chapter "Le muse in Illiria: l'Accademia dei Concordi a Ragusa (Dubrovnik) e i ragionamenti sulla musica di Nicolo Vito di Goze e Michele Monaldi") (Lucca, 1994), pp. 45–80.

10. See Albe Vidaković, *Yury Krizanitch's "Asserta musicalia" (1656) and His Other Musical Works* (Zagreb, 1967); Ivan Golub, "Juraj Križanić's 'Asserta musicalia' in Caramuel's Newly Discovered Autograph of 'Musica,'" *International Review of the Aesthetics and Sociology of Music* 9, no. 2 (1978), pp. 219–78; idem, *Juraj Križanić glazbeni teoretik 17. stoljeca* [Juraj Križanić, musical theorist of the 17th century] (Zagreb, 1981).

11. See *Il teatro del Rinascimento e del Barocco tra Venezia, Regione Giulia e Dalmazia: Idée accademiche a confronto,* ed. Ivano Cavallini (Trieste, 1991); Bojan Bujić, "Pastorale o melodramma? Le traduzioni croate di 'Euridice' e 'Arianna' per le scene di Dubrovnik," *Musica e storia* 6, no. 2 (1998), pp. 477–99.

12. The best overview of the reception of Baroque librettos in Croatian literature is given by Slobodan P. Novak, *Povijest hrvatske književnosti* [History of Croatian literature], vol. 3 (Zagreb, 1997).

13. See Ivano Cavallini, "Il *San Giovanni* a Trau: Gli intermedi per una sacra rappresentazione di Girolamo Brusoni," in *I due volti di Nettuno . . . ,* pp. 81–92. In this context one should mention also Christophor Ivanovich, well-known Venetian librettist and writer; see Cavallini's essay in ibid.

14. Bartol Kašić, *Rituale Romanum Urbani VIII. Pont. Max. iussu editum Illyrica lingua / Ritual rimski istomačen slovinski* (Roma, 1640), reprint ed. Vladimir Horvat (Zagreb, 1993).

15. See Jerko Bezić, *Razvoj glagoljaškog pjevanja na zadarskom području* [The development of Glagolitic singing in the region of Zadar] (Zadar, 1973); idem, "Glagolitic Chant," in *Croatia and Europe,* vol. I: *Early Middle Ages* (London and Zagreb, 1999), pp. 569–76.

16. Last printed collection of Croatian Protestant songs was *Duševne pesne i psalmi* [Spiritual songs and psalms], 2 vols. (Sv. Kriz 1609–11) by Grgur Mekinić-Pythareus, church

writer from Burgenland (Austria) (reprint edited and prefaced by Alojz Jembrih (Zagreb, 1990), 3 vols.

17. See Ennio Stipčević, "Counter-Reformation, Jesuits and Music Culture in Croatia of the 17th and 18th Centuries," in *The Musical Baroque, Western Slavs, and the Spirit of the European Cultural Communion,* ed. Stanislav Tuksar (Zagreb, 1993), pp. 85–90. For more general information, see Hana Breko, "Music and Religious Orders in Dalmatia in the 17th Century," *Musica e storia* 8, no. 2 (2000), pp. 455–76.

18. Modern edition ed. Koraljka Kos, Antun Šojat, and Vladimir Zagorac (Zagreb, 1994). See also Koraljka Kos, "Volkstumliche Zuge in der Kirchenmusik Nordkroatiens im 17. und 18. Jahrhundert," in *Musica Antiqua Europae Orientalis,* vol. 3 (Bydgoszcz: Filharmonia Pomorska imienia Ignacego Paderewskiego, 1972), pp. 267–90.

19. For a reprint of the 3rd ed., cf. *Cithara octochorda,* 2 vols., ed. Lovro Županović (Zagreb, 1998).

20. See Ladislav Šaban and Zdravko Blažeković, "Izvještaj o dvogodišnjem sređivanju triju glazbenih zbirki u Osijeku i o pregledu glazbenih rukopisa i knjiga u franjevačkom samostanima u Slavoniji i Srijemu" [A report on the classification and the cataloguing of three musical archives in Osijek and an overview of musical manuscripts and books in Franciscan monasteries in Slavonia and Srijem], *Arti musices* 11, no. 1 (1980), pp. 47–95.

21. See Miho Demovič, *Musik und Musiker in der Republik Dubrovnik (Ragusa) vom Anfang des XI. Jahrhunderts bis zum Mitte des XVII. Jahrhunderts* (Regensburg, 1981); idem, *Glazba i glazbenici u Dubrovačkoj republici od polovine XVII. do prvog Desetljeca XIX. Stoljeća* [Music and musicians in the Republic of Dubrovnik from the beginning of the 17th to the first decade of the 19th century] (Zagreb, 1989).

22. See Giuseppe Radole, *L'arte organaria in Istria* (Bologna, 1969); Jagoda Meder, *Organs in Croatia* (Zagreb, 1992).

23. See Ladislav Šaban, "Contributo alla biografia di Don Pietro Nakić," *L'organo* 9, no. 2 (1971), pp. 257–65; idem, "Umjetnost i djela graditelja orgulja Petra Nakića u Dalmaciji i Istri" [The art and works in Istria and Dalmatia of the organ builder P. Nacchini], *Arti musices* 4 (1973), pp. 5–45.

24. See Ivano Cavallini, *Musica, cultura e spettacolo in Istria tra '500 e '600* (Florence, 1990); Bojan Bujić, "Taste and Style in Early 17th-Century Music," in *Glasbeni barok na Slovenskem in Evropska glasba / Baroque Music in Slovenia and European Music,* ed. Ivan Klemenčić (Ljubljana, 1997), pp. 61–70.

25. The most comprehensive study is still Dragan Plamenac, "Toma Cecchini, kapelnik stolnih crkava u Splitu i Hvaru u prvoj polovici XVII stoljeća: Bio-bibliografska studija [Tomaso Cecchini, chaplain of cathedrals in Split and Hvar during the first decades of the 17th century: A bio-bibliographical study], *Rad JAZU* 262 (1938), pp. 77–125. For more detailed stylistic analysis, see Bojan Bujić, "Patronage and Taste in Venetian Dalmatia: The Case of Tomaso Cecchino's *Amorosi concetti,*" *Revista de musicologia* 16, no. 3 (1993), pp. 1416–22; idem, "A 'Provincial' Musician and His Wider Circle: Some Aspects of Tomaso Cecchino's Secular Music," *Musica e storia* 8, no. 2 (2000), pp. 391–416.

26. Cf. Ivano Cavallini, "Feste, spettacoli popolari e una raccolta di mascherate a 3 voci," in *Musica, cultura e spetaccolo . . . ,* pp. 165–95.

27. Reprint ed. E. Stipčević (Zagreb, 1989).

28. For more about relations between Cecchini and Dalmatian clergy, see Ennio Stipčević, "Influssi veneziani nelle musiche dei maestri dalmati del Cinque e Seicento," *Musica e storia* 6, no. 1 (1998), pp. 227–36.

29. See Josip Torbarina, *Italian Influence on the Poets of the Ragusan Republic* (London, 1931).

30. See Bojan Bujić, "Cecchinijeve mise iz godine 1617" (Cecchini's Masses from 1617), *Arti musices* 1 (1969), pp. 195–214.

31. See Marco Di Pasquale, "Tomaso Cecchini's *Sonate per gl'istrumenti, bassi & soprani* from His Op. 23 (1628)," in *Zagreb 1094–1994: Zagreb i hrvatske zemlje kao most između srednjoeuropskih i mediteranskih glazbenih kultura / Zagreb and Croatian Lands as a Bridge Between Central-European and Mediterranean Musical Cultures,* ed. Stanislav Tuksar (Zagreb, 1998), pp. 105–25. A modern edition is *Tomaso Cecchini: Osam sonata /Eight Sonatas,* ed. Bojan Bujić (Zagreb, 1984).

32. See Ivan Lukačić, *Odabrani moteti (1620)* [Selected motets, 1620], ed. Dragan Plamenac (Zagreb, 1935, 1975). For a complete and critical edition, see Ivan Lukačić, *Sacrae sanctiones, Venezia 1620: Mottetti a 1–5 voci* (in *Corpus Musicum Franciscanum*), ed. Ennio Stipčević and Ludovico Bertazzo (Padova, 1986). Cf. also the reprint of *Sacrae cantiones* (ed. by E. Stipčević) (Zagreb and Šibenik, 1998).

33. For more about Jurjević, see Ennio Stipčević, *Glazba iz arhiva: Studije i zapisi o staroj glazbi* [Music from the archives: Studies and essays on early Croatian music] (Zagreb, 1997). About his literal work, see Slobodan P. Novak and Mirko Kratofil, *Povijest hrvatske književnosti . . . ,* vol. 3.

34. See Stanislav Tuksar, "Writers on Music in the Croatian Lands in the Period 1750–1820: A Preliminary Review of Personalities, Topics and Social Milieus," in *Off-Mozart: Glazbena kultura i "mali majstori" srednje Europe 1750–1820 / Musical Culture and the "Kleinmeister" of Central Europe 1750–1820,* ed. Vjera Katalinić (Zagreb, 1995), pp. 167–78.

35. For more details about Franciscan Baroque, see *Glazbeni barok u Hrvatskoj* [Baroque Music in Croatia], ed. Ennio Stipčević (Osor, 1989).

36. For a general introduction to the situation in Inner Austria, see Alexander Novotny and Berthold Sutter, eds., *Inner-Österreich 1564–1619* (Graz, 1967); Robert A. Kann, *A History of the Habsburg Empire 1526–1918* (Berkeley, 1977), pp. 45–53; and Jean Bérenger, *A History of the Habsburg Empire 1273–1700* (London and New York, 1994), pp. 232–33 and 238–39.

37. For an integral bibliography on this period in today's Slovenia, see Metoda Kokole, "The Baroque Musical Heritage of Slovenia," *The Consort* 51, no. 2 (1995), pp. 91–102, especially pp. 91–92, notes 2–5. See also Ivan Klemenčić, ed., *Glasbeni barok na Slovenskem in Evropska glasba: Zbornik referatov z mednarodnega simpozija 13. in 14. oktobra 1994 v Ljubljani / Baroque music in Slovenia and European music: Proceedings from the International Symposium held in Ljubljana on October 13th and 14th, 1994* (Ljubljana, 1997).

38. Adam Gottron, "Gabriel Plautz 1612–1641, Kapellmeister des Mainzer Erzbischofs Schweikard von Kronberg," *Kirchenmusikalisches Jahrbuch* 31–33 (1936–38), p. 58; idem, *Mainzer Musikgeschichte von 1500 bis 1800* (Mainz, 1959), pp. 43–56; Dragotin Cvetko, ed., *Skladatelji Gallus, Plautzius, Dolar in njihovo delo* [The composers Gallus, Plautzius, Dolar and their works] (Ljubljana, 1963), pp. xv–xvi; and W. Steger, *Gabriel Plautz: Ein Mainzer Hofkapellmeister im frühen 17. Jahrhundert* (Würzburg, 1991).

39. Andrej Rijavec, *Glasbeno delo na Slovenskem v obdobju protestantizma* [Music in Slovenia in the Protestant era] (Ljubljana, 1967); Jože Sivec, "Stilna orientacija glasbe protestantizma na Slovenskem" [Stylistic orientation of Protestant music in Slovenia], *Muzikološki zbornik* 19 (1993), pp. 17–29.

40. For general information on the Jesuit order in Ljubljana, see Vincenc Rajšp, ed.,

Jezuitski kolegij v Ljubljani (1597–1773) [The Jesuit College in Ljubljana (1597–1773)] (Ljubljana, 1998).

41. It is generally known that at least until 1619, when Archduke Ferdinand moved his court to Vienna after being elected Holy Roman Emperor, Graz was the leading center of sacred monody not only in Inner Austria but also in Austria as a whole. It is therefore not surprising that, for example, the few-voice motets from Ferdinand's court, especially those published in 1615 in the anthology *Parnassus musicus Ferdinandeus,* align themselves closely with contemporaneous works from northern Italy and that most of the salient features of these works follow Venetian practice. See the well-documented monograph by Steven Saunders, *Cross, Sword and Lyre: Sacred Music at the Imperial Court of Ferdinand II of Habsburg (1619–1637)* (Oxford, 1995), especially pp. 129–37; and also an earlier monograph by Hellmut Federhofer, *Musikpflege und Musiker am Grazer Habsburgerhof der Erzherzöge Karl und Ferdinand von Innerösterreich (1564–1619)* (Mainz, 1967).

42. For Hren, see August Dimitz, *Geschichte Krains,* vol. 3 (Ljubljana, 1876), pp. 235–409. For his patronage of arts, see also the well-documented study by Ana Lavrić, *Vloga ljubljanskega Škofa Tomaža Hrena v slovenski likovni umetnosti* [The role of Bishop Tomaša Hren of Ljubljana in the Slovenian fine arts], 2 vols. (Ljubljana, 1988). From the documents listed in vol. 2 of Lavrić's book, it is clear that Hren bought numerous *objets d'art* as well as *musicalia* through different tradesmen, most of whom were Venetians.

43. They all came from Hren's collection and are now preserved in the manuscript division of the Narodna in Univerzitetna Knižnica (NUK) in Ljubljana, R MS 339–44. For a detailed discussion and a list of contents, see Edo Škulj, *Hrenove korne knjige* [Hren's choirbooks] (Ljubljana, 2001).

44. This volume of litanies is by Bianco, Gatto, Rovigo, and Vecchi (NUK R MS 344). See also Janez Höfler, *Glasbena umetnost pozne renesanse in baroka na Slovenskem* [Late Renaissance and Baroque music in Slovenia] (Ljubljana, 1978), pp. 33–35; and Hellmut Federhofer, *Musikpflege und Musiker . . . ,* pp. 46 and 96.

45. For a general discussion of the *Inventarium,* see Dragotin Cvetko, "Ein unbekanntes *Inventarium musicalium* aus dem Jahre 1620," *Kirchenmusikalisches Jahrbuch* 42 (1958), pp. 77–80; and Janez Höfler, *Glasbena umetnost . . . ,* pp. 36–41 and 134–57.

46. Composers worthy of note are Josquin Desprez, Nicolas Gombert, Dominique Phinot, Johannes de Cleve, Jakob Regnart, Orlando di Lasso, Andrea and Giovanni Gabrieli, Cipriano de Rore, Claudio Merulo, Philipp de Monte, Jacobus Gallus, Luca Marenzio, and Carlo Gesualdo da Venosa.

47. Ballestra even composed a Mass for a celebration in Ljubljana. He remained in contact with this city also in succeeding years. See Janez Höfler, *Glasbena umetnost . . . ,* p. 17 and pp. 131–32.

48. Jerome Roche, *"Aus den berühmbsten italiänischen Autoribus:* Dissemination North of the Alps of the Early-Baroque Italian Sacred Repertory through Published Anthologies and Reprints," in *Claudio Monteverdi und die Folgen,* ed. Silke Leopold and Joachim Steinheuer (Kassel, 1998), pp. 13–28.

49. In the Bishop's chapel were engaged vocalists and instrumentalists. Also the Jesuits, who were actually practising stage performances, had a their own musicians. There was also an organised body of town (pipers and fiddlers) and provincial musicians (trumpeters and kettle-drummers), as well as musicians in the service of certain noblemen.

50. For documentation on Posch, see the monograph by Metoda Kokole, *Isaac Posch "diditus Eois Hesperiisque plagis—slavljen v deželah Zore in Zatona": Zgodnjebaročni skladatelj*

na Koroškem in Kranjskem [Isaac Posch "*diditus Eois Hesperiisque plagis*—Praised in the Lands of Dawn and Sunset": Early Baroque Composer in Carinthia and Carniola] (Ljubljana, 1999); and also idem, "The compositions of Isaac Posch—Mediators between the German and Italian Musical Idioms," in *Contributi musicologici del Centro Richerche dell'A.M.I.S.,* vol. 10, ed. Alberto Colzani et al. (Como, 1997), pp. 87–120; and idem, "Isaac Posch 'Crembsensis': Neue Angaben über die Jugend des Komponisten in Regensburg," *Die Musikforschung* 52/3 (1999), pp. 318–21.

51. Despite the zealous efforts of the Counter Reformation, however, many noble families—patrons of the arts—in Carniola and Carinthia actually remained until 1628 largely faithful to Lutheran teaching. Especially in Carinthia Protestantism took stronger root, both in the towns and the country, than in any other Slovenian region. Its most important center was Klagenfurt, which was from 1518 onward under the rule of the Provincial Estates, the assembly of local nobles. Even after 1600 the nobles, who were also the main musical patrons and promoters of music-making in their homes, maintained their Protestant services. The final and irreversible expulsion of the Inner-Austrian nobility in 1628 brought about—in respect of musical patronage and cultural life—a great impoverishment of these regions. About 280 wealthy families, numbering about 750 persons, left the Duchy of Carniola, taking all their property. For a more detailed discussion, see Andrej Rijavec, *Glasbeno delo na Slovenskem . . . ,* pp. 129–32; Dragotin Cvetko, *Slovenska glasba v evropskem prostoru* [Slovene music in its European setting] (Ljubljana, 1991), pp. 48–65; and Helmut Rumpler, "Sozialer Wandel und Gegenreformation in Klagenfurt," in *Katholische Reform und Gegenreformation in Innerösterreich 1564–1628,* ed. Werner Drobesch (Klagenfurt, 1994), pp. 573–97.

52. Isaac Posch, *Musicalische Ehrenfreudt* (Regensburg, 1618). Modern edition by Metoda Kokole, in *Monumenta artis musicae Sloveniae,* vol. 30 (Ljubljana, 1996).

53. Isaac Posch, *Musicalische Tafelfreudt* (Nuremberg, 1621). Modern edition by Metoda Kokole, in *Monumenta artis musicae Sloveniae,* vol. 31 (Ljubljana, 1996).

54. Isaac Posch, *Harmonia Concertans* (Nuremberg, 1923). Modern edition by Karl Geiringer, in *Series of Early Music,* vols. 1, 4, and 6 (Santa Barbara, 1968 and 1972); and by Metoda Kokole, in *Monumenta artis musicae Sloveniae,* vol. 35 (Ljubljana, 1998).

55. For a discussion of the dancing aspect of Posch's ensemble instrumental pieces of the collection *Musicalische Ehrenfreudt,* see Metoda Kokole, "Plesna glasba zgodnjega 17. stoletja: Inštrumentalne suite Isaaca Poscha" [Early-17th-century music for dancing: Isaac Posch's instrumental suites], in *Zbornik ob jubileju Jožeta Sivca / Essays in honor of Jože Sivec,* ed. Jurij Snoj and Darja Frelih (Ljubljana, 2000), pp. 87–104.

56. *Neue liebliche Paduanen, Intraden und Galliarden* (Nuremberg, 1609).

57. *Neue Padovan, Intrada, Däntz und Galliarda* (Nuremberg, 1611).

58. *Banchetto Musicale: Neuer anmutiger Padouanen, Gagliarden, Courenten und Allemanden* (Leipzig, 1617). Modern edition by Arthur Prüfer, in *Johann Hermann Schein, Sämtliche Werke,* vol. 1 (Leipzig, 1901).

59. For Simpson, see Peter Holman, *Four and Twenty Fiddlers: The Violin at the English Court 1540–1690* (Oxford, 1995), p. 253.

60. Hellmut Federhofer, "Graz Court Musicians and Their Contribution to the *Parnassus musicus Ferdinandeus* (1615)," *Musica disciplina* 9 (1955), pp. 167–244. For a more detailed discussion of this collection, especially the Italian elements of Posch's motets, see Metoda Kokole, "Venetian Influence on the Production of Early-Baroque Monodic Motets in the Inner-Austrian Provinces," *Musica e storia* 8 (2000), pp. 477–507.

61. In the original: ". . . Denn andere gelehrte Leute vnberührt was sind die jetzigen

Musicanten vnd absonderlich die *Concertisten* anders, als liebliche Nachtegallen, welche auß Welschland vnd Franchreich noch vor wenig Jahren in Teutschland ankommen, vnd hin vnd wieder mit ihren anmutigen *Compositionen* sich lassen hören? Wer weiß nicht vom *Viadana, Finetti* vnd *Poschio* wie sie so künstlich gegen einander *concertiren*? . . ."

62. The list is given in the monograph by Metoda Kokole, *Isaac Posch, "diditus . . . ,"* pp. 265–66.

63. For a general discussion on cultural life in Istria in the seventeenth century, see Giuseppe Radole, *La musica a Capodistria* (Trieste, 1990); Ivano Cavallini, *Musica, cultura e spettacolo in Istria tra '500 e '600* (Florence, 1990); and Ivano Cavallini, "Il libro per musica nel litorale istriano tra cinquecento e seicento," in *Libro nel bacino adriatico* (Florence, 1992), pp. 99–110.

64. Janez Höfler, "Glasbeniki koprske stolnice v 17. in 18. stoletju" [Musicians in the cathedral of Koper in the 17th and 18th centuries], *Kronika* 16 (1968), pp. 140–44.

65. For Puliti, see Ennio Stipčević, "Uvodna razmatranja o umjetnosti Gabriella Pulitija" [Introduction to the art of Gabriello Puliti], *Arti musices* 14 (1983), pp. 33–50; Ivano Cavallini, "Quelques remarques sur la musique sacrée en Istrie au XVII s. et les premiers essais monodique de Gabriello Puliti," in *Musica Antiqua Europae Orientalis* 8/1 (Bydgoszcz, 1988), pp. 233–47; and Ennio Stipčević, *Gabriello Puliti, ranobarokni skladatelj u Istri / Gabriello Puliti, compositore del primo barocco in Istria* (Zagreb, 1996).

66. For general information on music activities in the Jesuit college in Ljubljana, see Tomaž Faganel, "Glasbeno delo v ljubljanskem kolegiju: Poskus prikaza ustroja in njegove vsebinske zasnove" [Music endeavours of the Jesuit college of Ljubljana: An attempt at reconstruction of its organization and activities], in *Jezuitski kolegij v Ljubljani (1597–1773)*, ed. Vincenc Rajšp (Ljubljana, 1998), pp. 229–33.

67. For a discussion of earliest opera performances in Ljubljana, see Metoda Kokole, "Italian Opera in Ljubljana in the Seventeenth and Eighteenth Centuries," in *Il teatro musicale italiano nel Sacro Romano Impero nei secoli XVII e XVIII*, ed. Alberto Colzani et al. (Como, 1999), pp. 265–71; and Metoda Kokole, "Italijanske operne predstave pri Auerspergih sredi 17. stoletja: Drobtinica k slovenskemu glasbenemu zgodovinopisju" [Mid-seventeenth-century Italian opera performance(s) in Count Auersperg's palace in Ljubljana: A few additions to the Slovenian music historiography], *Muzikološki zbornik* 35 (1999), pp. 115–29.

68. Two exhaustive descriptions of the emperor's visit to his hereditary Duchy of Carniola were published in the seventeenth century: first in 1661 by Lorenzo de Churelichz, *Breve, e succinto Racconto del Viaggio* [. . .] (Vienna, 1661); and the second in the tenth book of Johann Weichard Valvasor's *Die Ehre des Herzogtums Krain*, vol. 3 (Nuremberg, 1689), pp. 307–96.

69. For general information, see Dragotin Cvetko, "Die Rolle der Musik bei dem Adel im Herzogtum Krain im 17. und zu Beginn des 18. Jahrhunderts," in *La Musique et le rite sacre et profane II: Proceedings of the 13th Congress of the International Society of Musicology,* ed. Marc Honegger and Paul Prevost (Strasbourg, 1986), pp. 533–41; Matej Klemenčič and Stanko Kokole, "Perception and Reception of the Italian Baroque Art in Ljubljana," in *Francesco Robba and the Highlights of Venetian Baroque Sculpture in Ljubljana* (Ljubljana, 1998), pp. 12–14 and 43–45 (bibliography).

70. For information on Dolar, see Dragotin Cvetko, *Skladatelji Gallus . . . ,* pp. xvi–xix; Janez Höfler, "Johannes Baptista Dolar: Beiträge zu seiner Lebengeschichte," *Die Musikforschung* 25, no. 3 (1972), pp. 310–14; Tomaž Faganel, "Zur Besetzung und Aufführungspraxis in den Messen von Joannes Baptista Dolar (um 1620–1673)," in *The Musical*

Baroque, Western Slavs and the Spirit of the European Cultural Communion (Zagreb, 1993), pp. 139–46; Jiří Sehnal and Jitřenka Pešková, *Caroli de Liechtenstein—Castelcorno episcope Olomuscensis operum artis musicae collectio Cremsirii reservata* (Prague, 1998).

71. The majority of the original transcriptions of Dolar's works are kept in the Liechtenstein archive at Kroměříž in the collection of Karl Liechtenstein-Castelcorn. Modern editions: Janez Krstnik Dolar, *Missa Villana,* ed. Mirko Cuderman, in *Monumenta artis musicae Sloveniae,* vol. 4 (Ljubljana, 1984); Janez Krstnik Dolar, *Missa sopra la bergamasca,* ed.Tomaž Faganel, in *Monumenta artis musicae Sloveniae,* vol. 22 (Ljubljana, 1992); Janez Krstnik Dolar, *Psalmi,* ed. Tomaž Faganel, in *Monumenta artis musicae Sloveniae,* vol. 23 (Ljubljana, 1993); Janez Krstnik Dolar, *Balletti—Sonate,* ed.Tomaž Faganel, in *Monumenta artis musicae Sloveniae,* vol. 25 (Ljubljana, 1994); Janez Krstnik Dolar, *Missa Viennensis,* ed. Uroš Lajovic, in *Monumenta artis musicae Sloveniae,* vol. 29 (Ljubljana, 1996).

72. For Tarsia, see Salvator Žitko, ed., *Antonio Tarsia: 1643–1722* (Koper, 1993); the articles by Edvilijo Gardina, Janez Höfler, Milko Bizjak, Ivano Cavallini, Tomaž Faganel, and others were first printed in *Muzikološki zbornik* 27 (1992), pp. 5–55.

73. Kajetan Gantar (ed.), *Academia operosorum* (Ljubljana, 1994); and Primož Simoniti, ed., *Academia operosorum Labacensium: Apes academicae* (Ljubljana, 1988).

74. For the Academia Philharmonicorum Labacensium, see Dragotin Cvetko, "Contribution à la question sur l'année de la fondation de l'Academia Philharmonicorum Labacensis," in *Festschrift für Walter Wiora zum 30. Dezember 1966,* ed. Ludwig Finscher and Christoph-Hellmut Mahling (Kassel, 1967), pp. 342–47; idem, "Leges Academiae Phil-Harmonicorum Labaci metropoli Carniolae adunatorum," *Acta musicologica* 2 (1967), pp. 106–15; idem, *Academia Philharmonicorum Labacensis* (Ljubljana, 1962); and Metoda Kokole, "Academia Philharmonicorum Labacensium: Zgledi, ustanovitev in delovanje" [Academia Philharmonicorum Labacensium: Prospects, founding and activities], in *Historični seminar II,* ed. Oto Luthar and Vojislav Likar (Ljubljana, 1997), pp. 205–22.

75. Metoda Kokole, "Italian Opera in Ljubljana . . . ," pp. 271–91 (including a catalogue of Italian opera libretti).

76. Claudio Sartori, *I libretti italiani a stampa dalle origini al 1800: Catalogo analitico con 16 indici,* 5 vols. and 2 index vols. (Cuneo, 1990–94).

77. Dragotin Cvetko, "Il Tamerlano de Giuseppe Clemente Bonomi," in *Essays Presented to Egon Wellesz,* ed. Jack Westrup (Oxford, 1966), pp. 108–13.

78. The most exhaustive study on the Italian theater in Ljubljana is Stanko Škerlj, *Italijansko gledališče v Ljubljani v preteklih stoletjih* [Italian theatre in Ljubljana in the past centuries] (Ljubljana, 1973).

79. The term "Muscovy" is generally used to describe the period of the Moscow-centered state, from around the fourteenth century until the foundation of St. Petersburg in 1703 by Peter the Great; it was preceded by the state centered around Kiev (Kievan Rus').

80. Olearius made four trips to Muscovy in the 1630s–1640s; his account of the burning of the instruments was probably based on information supplied by informants, as Olearius was not there in 1653. His account is in Samuel Baron, trans. and ed., *The Travels of Olearius in Seventeenth-century Russia* (Stanford, Calif.: Stanford University Press, 1967), pp. 262–63.

81. This observation is made by Miloš Velimirović in his commentary to the forthcoming English translation of Nikolai Findeizen, *Ocherki po istorii muzyki v Rossii* (Moscow: Gosudarstvennoe izdatel'stvo Muzsektor, 1928), in his introduction to the notes for Chapter 10. The population of Moscow during the course of the seventeenth century is estimated

at between one hundred thousand and two hundred thousand (see Martha Lahana, "Novaia Nemetskaia Sloboda: Seventeenth Century Moscow's Foreign Suburb" [Ph.D. diss., University of North Carolina in Chapel Hill, 1983], p. 2).

82. It is difficult to translate the names of the singing ensembles. The term *d'iak* refers to a cleric (as well as to an administrative clerk); a *pod"d'iak* is a subcleric. See the English language discussion of these ensembles in Morosan, *Choral Performance in Pre-Revolutionary Russia,* in Malcolm Brown, ed., Russian Music Studies 17 (Ann Arbor: UMI Research Press, 1986), Chapters 1 and 2, passim.

83. S. G. Zvereva, "O khore gosudarevykh pevchikh d'iakov v XVI v." [On the choir of the sovereign singers in the sixteenth century], *Pamiatniki Kul'tury: Novye Otkrytiia* [henceforth abbreviated as *PKNO*] *1987* (Moscow: Nauka, 1988), p. 125; see also her "Gosudarevye pevchie d'iaki posle 'Smuty' " [The sovereign singers after the "Time of Troubles"], in *Germenevitka drevnerusskoi literatury* 2 (Moscow, 1989), n. 2, on evidence from the late fifteenth century. See also N. P. Parfent'ev, *Professional'nye muzykanty rossiiskogo gosudarstva XVI–XVII vekov* [Professional musicians in the Russian state, sixteenth–seventeenth centuries] (Cheliabinsk: Kniga, 1991).

84. On the the musical implications of the conversion to Christianity in the tenth century, see basic references in *The New Grove Dictionary,* 2d ed. (henceforth abbreviated *NG2*), and in the excellent anthology by Vladimir Morosan, ed., *One Thousand Years of Russian Church Music,* series 1, vol. 1 of Monuments of Russian Sacred Music (Washington, D.C.: Musica Russica, 1991).

85. These figures are from Zvereva, "O khore gosudarevykh pevchikh d'iakov," n. 21.

86. Zvereva, "Gosudarevye pevchie d'iaki posle 'Smuty,' " esp. pp. 359ff.

87. On Gavrilov's career, see D. V. Razumovskii, "Gosudarevy pevchie d'iaki XVII veka" [The sovereign singers in the seventeenth century], *Sbornik obshchestva drevne-russkogo iskusstva* (1873), pp. 167 and 177, and documents in *Russkaia istoricheskaia biblioteka* [Russian historical library; henceforth abbreviated as *RIB*] 21and 23, kn. 3 (St. Petersburg: Arkheograficheskaia komissiia, 1904); see also the detailed summary in Parfent'ev, *Professional'nye muzykanty rossiiskogo gosudarstva,* pp. 172–73.

88. Zvereva, "Gosudarevye pevchie d'iaki posle 'Smuty,' " p. 367.

89. On Potap Maksimov, see documents from 1664–75 in *RIB* 23, kn. 3; Razumovskii, "Gosudarevy pevchie d'iaki XVII veka," pp. 173 and 179; and Protopopov, "Notnaia biblioteka Tsariia Fedora Alekseevicha" [Tsar Fedor Alekseevich's (notated) musical library], *PKNO 1976* (Moscow: Nauka, 1977), pp. 14 and 121.

90. See the discussions of these ceremonies in Robert O. Crummey, "Court Spectacles in Seventeenth-Century Russia: Illusion and Reality," in *Essays in Honor of A. A. Zimin,* ed. Daniel Waugh (Columbus, Ohio: Slavica, 1985), pp. 130–60; Paul Bushkovitch, "The Epiphany Ceremony of the Russian Court in the Sixteenth and Seventeenth Centuries," *Russian Review* 49, no. 1 (1990), pp. 1–17; and Richard Wortman, *Scenarios of Power: Myth and Ceremony in Russian Monarchy,* vol. 1: *From Peter the Great to the Death of Nicholas I* (Princeton, N.J.: Princeton University Press, 1995), p. 36.

91. Crummey, "Court Spectacles in Seventeenth-Century Russia," p. 133; also Findeizen, *Ocherki* 1:312, where he describes the visits of the patriarchs of Antioch and Alexandria.

92. The term *deistvo* literally means "action"; here we have translated it as "play"; Miloš Velimirović, "Liturgical Drama in Byzantium and Russia," *Dumbarton Oaks Papers* 16 (1962), pp. 349–85 is indispensable on this topic and is the source for information in this survey; see also Findeizen, *Ocherki* 1:280ff and Iu. V. Keldysh, O. E. Levasheva, and A. I. Kandinskii, general eds., *Istoriia russkoi muzyki v desiati tomakh* [A history of Russian

music in ten volumes] (Moscow: Muzyka, 1983–) 1:152ff (this series is henceforth abbreviated as *IRM*).

93. Morosan, *One Thousand Years of Russian Church Music,* xliv. Basic introductions to Russian chant and its theory and to the conversion to Christianity are available, in English, in *NG2* (articles by Miloš Velimirović); the introduction to Morosan's *One Thousand Years of Russian Church Music;* Johann von Gardner, *Russian Church Singing,* translated by Vladimir Morosan (Crestwood, N.Y.: St. Vladimir's Seminary Press, 1980–); and Nicolas Schidlovsky, "Sources of Russian Chant Theory," in *Russian Theoretical Thought in Music,* ed. Gordon McQuere, Russian Music Studies 10 (Ann Arbor: UMI Research Press, 1983), pp. 83–108. See also the forthcoming translation of Findeizen, *Ocherki.* One of the fundamental Russian language works is M. V. Brazhnikov, *Drevnerusskaia teoriia muzyki* [Early Russian music theory] (Leningrad: Muzyka, 1972).

94. Krestianin's works are published in M. V. Brazhnikov, *Fedor Krest'ianin: Stikhiry,* vol. 3 of Pamiatniki russkogo muzykal'nogo iskusstva [henceforth abbreviated as PRMI] (Moscow: Muzyka, 1974), and see also Morosan, *One Thousand Years of Russian Church Music,* pp. 20–22. On Kazan and Greek chant, see the summaries in *NG2* and Morosan, *One Thousand Years of Russian Church Music,* p. 731; see especially L. A. Igoshev, "Proiskhozhdenie grecheskogo rospeva (opyt analiza)" [The origins of Greek chant (an attempt at an analysis)], *PKNO 1992* (Moscow: Nauka, 1993), pp. 147–50, for the most recent thinking on the origins of Greek chant.

95. On *demestvennyi* chant, see the surveys in Morosan, *One Thousand Years of Russian Church Music,* 727; *IRM* 1:147–51; and *NG2.*

96. See Velimirović's articles on Russian chant in *NG2.*

97. N. P. Parfent'ev's important work is summarized in his article "Aleksandr Mezenets" in *Slovar' knizhnikov XVII v.* [A dictionary of writers of the 17th century] (St. Petersburg: Institut russkoi literatury, 1992), pt. 1, pp. 63–68, which includes additional bibliography; this is summarized in Miloš Velimirović's editorial remarks to the forthcoming publication of Findeizen, *Ocherki,* ch. 9. Mezenets's treatise was published by Stepan Vasil'evich Smolenskii, ed., *Azbuka znamennogo peniia (Izveshchenie o soglasneishikh pometakh) startsa Aleksandra Mezentsa (1668-go goda)* [Alphabet of *znamennyi* chant (report about the most agreeable markings) by the monk Aleksandr Mezenets in 1668] (Kazan: Tip. Imp. universiteta, 1888); a new edition is available by Zivar Guseinova and Nikolai Parfent'ev, eds., *Aleksandr Mesenets i prochie, Izveshchenie . . . zhelaiushchim uchitsia peniiu, 1670 g.* [Aleksandr Mezenets and others, the "Report . . . for those who want to learn singing," 1670] (Cheliabinsk: Kniga, 1996). On the *dvoznamenniki,* see the works cited in n. 95 above.

98. See the English-language summary of their activities in Morosan, *Choral Performance in Pre-Revolutionary Russia,* p. 42. The Ukrainian singers seem consistently to have been called *vspevaki* (singers); see the important discussion in K. V. Kharlampovich, *Malorossiiskoe vlianie na velikorusskuiu tserkovnuiu zhizn'* [Ukrainian influence on Russian church life] (Kazan: M. A. Golubev, 1914; rpt. Slavistic Printings and Reprintings 119, ed. C. H. van Schooneveld, The Hague: Mouton, 1968), pp. 317–29.

99. Quoted in Vladimir Morosan, "*Penie* and *Musikiia:* Aesthetic Changes in Russian Liturgical Singing during the 17th Century," *St. Vladimir's Theological Quarterly* 23, nos. 3–4 (1979), p. 163; he is quoting from a mid-century saint's life.

100. On these linguistic changes, which revolved around the pronunciation (or lack thereof) of certain vowels and half-vowels, see the summary in Gardner, *Russian Church*

Singing 1:140, Miloš Velimirović's commentary to Findeizen, *Ocherki,* ch. 3, and his articles in *NG2.*

101. Wortman, *Scenarios of Power,* p. 33.

102. Paul's observations are quoted in Claudia Jensen, "Nikolai Diletskii's 'Grammatika' (Grammar) and the Musical Culture of Seventeenth-Century Muscovy" (Ph.D. diss., Princeton University, 1987), p. 68, and see pp. 69–70 on the Uniate source and for related bibliography.

103. Simeon is quoted in N. P. Popov, "O poezdke v Smolensk k mitrop. Simeonu 'dlia velikikh del' " [The trip to Smolensk to Met. Simeon 'for important affairs'], *Chteniia v Imperatorskom Obshchestve Istorii Drevnostei Rossiiskikh pri Moskovskom Universitete* (1907): part 4, pp. 42–43. On the *bratstva,* see Morosan, *Choral Performance in Pre-Revolutionary Russia,* pp. 38–42; Jensen, "Nikolai Diletskii's 'Grammatika,' " pp. 57–58, and the bibliography cited in both sources. The 1697 inventory is published in *Arkhiv Iugo-Zapadnoi Rossii* [Archive of southwest Russia] (Kiev: Komissiia dlia razbora drevnikh aktov, 1904), 12, part 1, pp. 62–71.

104. See the summaries in Morosan, *One Thousand Years of Russian Church Music,* p. xlvi, and *NG2.*

105. Zvereva, "Gosudarevye pevchie d'iaki posle 'Smuty,' " p. 374.

106. A. S. Belonenko, "Pokazaniia arkhiereiskikh pevchikh XVII veka" [The testimony of the archiepiscopal singers in the 17th century], *Trudy otdela drevnerusskoi literatury Instituta russkoi literatury Akademii nauk SSSR* [henceforth abbreviated as *TODRL*] 36 (1981), pp. 320–28; and Zvereva, "Gosudarevye pevchie d'iaki posle 'Smuty,' " pp. 368ff., who analyzes the makeup of individual *stanitsy* to determine how they might have performed polyphonic music.

107. Russell Zguta, *Russian Minstrels: A History of the Skomorokhi* ([Philadelphia]: University of Pennsylvania Press, 1978) is the basic English language source; see also Findeizen, *Ocherki* 1, ch. 5.

108. Quoted in A. I. Rogov, ed., comp., and trans., *Muzykal'naia estetika Rossii XI–XVIII vekov* [Musical aesthetics in Russia in the eleventh through eighteenth centuries] (Moscow: Muzyka, 1973), pp. 53–54. The unhelpful answer reads: "At the time of a wedding, the *skomorokhi* and merry-makers are not allowed to come to the church, and the priest must forbid it forcefully so this kind of disorder does not occur."

109. [Guy Miege], *A Relation of Three Embassies from His Sacred Majestie Charles II to the Great Duke of Muscovie, the King of Sweden, and the King of Denmark* (London: J. Starkey, 1669), pp. 104–105. See also Velimirović, "Liturgical Drama in Byzantium and Russia," p. 373 on the *skomorokhi.*

110. See the discussion of instruments in the forthcoming English translation of Findeizen, *Ocherki,* ch. 3, p. 6, and elsewhere; other references on musical instruments are in *IRM* 1 and L. Roizman, *Organ v istorii russkoi muzykal'noi kul'tury* [The organ in the history of Russian musical culture] (Moscow: Muzyka, 1979), esp. ch. 1, and bibliography cited in these sources.

111. Isaac Massa, *A Short History of the Beginnings and Origins of These Present Wars in Moscow under the Reign of Various Sovereigns down to the Year 1610,* trans. with an introduction by G. Edward Orchard (Toronto: University of Toronto Press, 1982), pp. 133 and 140. See also Findeizen, *Ocherki,* ch. 8.

112. There are scattered references on this topic; see V. N. Sergeev, "Russkie pesnopeniia XVII v. na istoricheskuiu temu" [Russian songs of the seventeenth century on his-

torical themes], *PKNO 1975* (Moscow: Nauka, 1976), pp. 41–43; V. V. Danilov, "Sborniki pesen XVII stoletiia—Richarda Dzhemsa i P. A. Kvashnina" [Seventeenth-century song collections of Richard James and P. A. Kvashnin], *TODL* 2 (1935), pp. 165–80; and see the texts in V. I. Ignatov, comp., *Russkie istoricheskie pesni: Khrestomatiia* [Russian historial songs: A reader], 2d ed. (Moscow: Vysshaia shkola, 1985).

113. Miege, *A Relation of Three Embassies,* pp. 129–30. To be fair, it should be noted that others described Muscovite ceremonial music as being enjoyable and excellent; see, for example, Joseph Sebes, *The Jesuits and the Sino-Russian Treaty of Nerchinsk (1689): The Diary of Thomas Pereira, S.J.* (Rome: Institutum historicum S.I., 1961), pp. 231 and 287.

114. Miege, *A Relation of Three Embassies,* pp. 99–100.

115. Igor Vinogradoff, "Russian Missions to London, 1569–1687: Seven Accounts by the Masters of the Ceremonies," *Oxford Slavonic Papers,* n.s., 14 (1981), p. 55, and see further mention of the musicians on p. 56.

116. The basic source for organs in seventeenth-century Russia is Roizman's excellent *Organ;* see pp. 28–30 on Ivan Spasitel and pp. 69–82 for his careful discussion of Simeon Gutovskii. Horsey's comment is in Edward Bond, ed., "Russia at the close of the sixteenth century, comprising the treatise 'Of the Russe Common Wealth,' by Dr. Giles Fletcher; and the Travels of Sir Jerome Horsey, Knt," *The Hakluyt Society* 20 (1856), p. 217.

117. Baron, *The Travels of Olearius,* 263; the term *positiv* is in Adam Olearius, *Vermehrte Newe Beschreibung der Muscovitischen vnd Persischen Reyse,* ed. Dieter Lohmeier (Tübingen: Max Niemeyer Verlag, 1971), p. 302, a facsimile of the 1656 edition. On other instruments, see the examples cited in Jensen, "Music for the Tsar," p. 384. The illustrations in Istomin's work are widely reproduced; see, for example, Roizman, *Organ,* foll. p. 48, and V. I. Luk'ianenko and M. A. Alekseeva, eds., *Bukvar': Sostavlen Karionom Istominym gravirovan Leontiem Buninym otpechatan v 1694 godu v Moskve* [The alphabet compiled by Karion Istomin and engraved by Leontii Bunin, printed in 1694 in Moscow] (Leningrad: Avrora, 1981), which includes instruments illustrating the letters *A, B, G, Z, K, T,* and *Ps.* The illustration of the organ is at the letter *O.*

118. On the Foreign Quarter, see Lahana, "Novaia Nemetskaia Sloboda," and the sources cited there; see Philip Longworth, *Alexis: Tsar of all the Russias* (New York: Franklin Watts, 1984), ch. 9 on the cultural renaissance. On the multiple intellectual influences in late seventeenth-century Muscovy, see Max J. Okenfuss, *The Rise and Fall of Latin Humanism in Early-Modern Russia: Pagan Authors, Ukrainians, and the Resiliency of Muscovy,* Brill's Studies in Intellectual History 64 (Leiden: E. J. Brill, 1995).

119. These sources are discussed in Jensen, "Music for the Tsar," and in Claudia Jensen and John Powell, " 'A Mess of Russians Left Us but of Late': Diplomatic Blunder, Literary Satire, and the Muscovite Ambassador's 1668 Visit to Paris Theatres," *Theatre Research International* 24, no. 2 (1999), pp. 131–44.

120. The Orpheus production is discussed briefly in Jensen, "Music for the Tsar," pp. 373–75, and further in the forthcoming "Orpheus in Muscovy," to appear in the Velimirović Festschrift, edited by N. A. Gerasimova-Persidskaia. Many thanks to Dr. Martha Lahana for her generosity in sharing archival material on this production.

121. On the musical elements of the plays and for further bibliography, see Jensen, "Music for the Tsar," passim. Simon Karlinsky, *Russian Drama from Its Beginnings to the Age of Pushkin* (Berkeley: University of California Press, 1985) gives a general survey of the theater of this period. The texts of the plays are available in the series *Ranniaia russkaia dramaturgiia,* ed. O. A. Derzhavina, K. N. Lomunov, and A. N. Robinson (Moscow: Nauka, 1972–76).

122. On the characteristics and role of the bass lines in *kanty*, see Olga Dolskaya-Ackerly, "The Early Kant in Seventeenth-Century Russian Music" (Ph.D. diss., University of Kansas, 1983), pp. 136–40; a discussion of their origins is in Olga Dolskaya-Ackerly, *Spiritual Songs in Seventeenth-Century Russia*, in Hans Rothe, ed., Bausteine zur Slavischen Philologie und Kulturgeschichte, ser. B, n.s., vol. 4 (Cologne: Böhlau, 1996), pp. xviii–xxvi.

123. Polotskii's introduction is in Simeon Polotskii, *Izbrannye sochineniia* [Collected works], ed. I. P. Eremin (Moscow: Akademiia nauk SSSR, 1953), p. 213. Dolskaya-Ackerly, *Spiritual Songs in Seventeenth-Century Russia*, is an edition of a complete *kant* manuscript from the State Historical Museum in Moscow. See further the bibliographies in Dolskaya-Ackerly's edition and dissertation. The scholar Aleksandr Pozdneev has specialized in studies of the linguistic origins and manuscript circulation of these pieces in a series of Russian language studies; see the references in the bibliography of *Spiritual Songs in Seventeenth-Century Russia*.

124. On this piece, see Morosan, *One Thousand Years of Russian Church Music*, p. 686, and Dolskaya-Ackerly, *Spiritual Songs in Seventeenth-Century Russia*, pp. xxxvii–xl. From Dolskaya-Ackerly's edition in Morosan, *One Thousand Years of Russian Church Music*, pp. 121–28, where an English translation is provided as follows (first strophe only): "Today is the day of rejoicing and salvation/ this entire day is chosen in brightness for us,/ for Christ God, having trampled on the enemy,/ and having bound proud Satan with fetters,/ He Himself has heard the prayer of the wretched,/ [who were] all melting/ from the severe torments of hell." Note that the transliteration system used in the anthology differs from that used in this essay.

125. The issue of performance of the *kontserty* is complex and unresolved; see the discussions in Vladimir Morosan, *Choral Performance in Pre-Revolutionary Russia*, esp. pp. 50–51, 55, and see fig. 2.1; and Olga Dolskaya-Ackerly, "Vasilii Titov and the 'Moscow' Baroque," *Journal of the Royal Musical Association* 118, no. 2 (1993), p. 213.

126. Morosan, *One Thousand Years of Russian Church Music*, p. xlviii, reviews the patterns of wear and use in surviving *kontsert* manuscripts; see also Dolskaya-Ackerly, "Vasilii Titov and the 'Moscow' Baroque," p. 206, and, on Pekalitskii, V. V. Protopopov, *Muzyka na poltavskuiu pobedu* [Music for the Poltava victory], PRMI 2 (Moscow: Muzyka, 1973), p. 237.

127. Dolskaya-Ackerly, "Vasilii Titov and the 'Moscow' Baroque," p. 205; these works are available in Olga Dolskaya-Ackerly, *Vasily Titov and the Russian Baroque: Selected Choral Works*, in Vladimir Morosan, ed., Monuments of Russian Sacred Music, series 13, vol. 1 (Madison, Conn.: Musica Russica, 1995); see also the brief, informative discussion in Morosan, *One Thousand Years of Russian Church Music*, xlviii–xlix. Another extremely important work on *kontserty* has been carried out by N. A. Gerasimova-Persidskaia; although it has not been translated from Russian or Ukrainian, English-speaking readers will find her publications of scores invaluable; see especially her *Ukrains'ki partensni moteti pochatku XVIII stolitiia/Ukrainian Choral Motets of the Early 18th Century* (Kiev: Muzichna ukraina, 1991), with an English summary on pp. 37–42, and her collection of Nikolai Diletskii's *kontserty* in *Mikola Dilets'kii: Khorovi tvori* [Nikolai Diletskii: Choral works] (Kiev: Muzichna ukraina, 1981).

128. From Olga Dolskaya-Ackerly, *Vasily Titov and the Russian Baroque*, pp. 125–28, in which an English translation is provided as follows: "O Thou Joy of all the sorrowful!/ Intercessor for the oppressed,/ Nourisher of the hungry,/ Comfort of the travelers,/ Haven of the storm-tossed,/ visitation of the sick,/ Protection and Intercessor of the infirm,/ Staff

of old age!/ O Mother of God Most High,/ since Thou are most pure,/ hasten, we pray, to save Thy servants!"

129. See the commentary to Dolskaya-Ackerly, *Vasily Titov and the Russian Baroque.* This work has been recorded by Chanticleer, using a small ensemble (*Magnificat,* Teldec compact disc 8573-81829-2); recordings of other *kontserty* by Titov, Diletskii, and several anonymous composers use a full mixed choir (see Vladimir Minin, director, *Russkii partesnyi kontsert / A Concert of old Russian Polyphonic Choral Music,* performed by the Moscow Chamber Choir, Melodiia, phonograph 10-10909-10).

130. For a brief survey of Diletskii's work and its several editions, see *NG2;* the most recent edition is by V. V. Protopopov, ed., *Nikolai Diletskii: Idea Grammatiki Musikiiskoi* [Nikolai Diletskii: An Idea of Music's Grammar], PRMI 7 (Moscow: Muzyka, 1979), with substantial commentary and a full translation into modern Russian. On the theoretical background of the work and its long-lived vocabulary, see Claudia Jensen, "A Theoretical Work of Late Seventeenth-Century Muscovy: Nikolai Diletskii's *Grammatika* and the Earliest Circle of Fifths," *JAMS* 45, no. 2 (1992), pp. 305–31; and Jensen, "Nikolai Diletskii's 'Grammatika,'" chapters 1 and 4; for comparative sources from Western Europe, see Joel Lester, *Between Modes and Keys: German Theory 1592–1802,* Harmonologia Series 3 (Stuyvesant, N.Y.: Pendragon Press, 1989).

131. Razumovskii, *Patriarshie pevchie diaki i poddiaki,* pp. 55–56, and Morosan, *Choral Performance in Pre-Revolutionary Russia,* pp. 57–58.

132. The basic source in music printing in Russia is B. L. Vol'man, *Russkie pechatnye noty* [Russian printed music] (Leningrad: Gosudarstvennoe muzykal'noe izdatel'stvo, 1957); a brief English language summary of these experiments is in Jensen, "Nikolai Diletskii's 'Grammatika,'" pp. 79–81. The first printed liturgical book (staff notation) was the L'vov Irmologion of 1700; the first printed liturgical books appeared in Russia, published by the Synodal Press, in the 1770s.

133. See Keldysh's survey in *IRM* 2, pp. 29–64; on p. 43, he notes the relationship between these polyphonic, celebratory pieces and the liturgical tradition of the *mnogoletie* (many years, a series of prayers to the monarchs and high clergy), and see also the illustrations following p. 64.

134. I. V. Saverkina and Iu. N. Semenov, "Orkestr i khor A. D. Menshikova (K istorii russkoi muzykal'noi kul'tury)" [A. D. Menshikov's orchestra and choir (Toward a history of Russian musical culture)], *PKNO 1989* (Moscow: Nauka, 1990), pp. 162–63.

135. On Beliaev, see S. B. Butskaia, "Stefan Ivanovich Beliaev—gosudarev pevchii d'iak" [Stefan Ivanovich Beliaev, sovereign singer], *PKNO 1992* (Moscow: Nauka, 1993), pp. 151–56; on the other choirs and on Peter's travels, see the summary in *IRM* 2, pp. 57–58.

136. Protopopov, *Muzyka na poltavskuiu pobedu,* in which he discusses the ordering of the pieces on p. 204.

137. See Max J. Okenfuss, trans. and ed., *The Travel Diary of Peter Tolstoi: A Muscovite in Early Modern Europe* (DeKalb: Northern Illinois University Press, 1987); Bergholz's diary is the subject of an important forthcoming dissertation by Elizabeth Sander (University of Western Ontario). Another glimpse of the musical life of this period is provided by the memoirs of a young castrato singer who wrote of the several years he spent in St. Petersburg; see Daniel Schlafly, "Filippo Balatri in Peter the Great's Russia," *Jahrbücher für Geschichte Osteuropas* (Spring 1997), pp. 181–98. Findeizen, *Ocherki* 1, ch. 12 also surveys this period.

138. On Menshikov's ensemble, see Saverkina and Semenov, "Orkestr i khor A. D. Menshikova," p. 161; Robert Karpiak, "Culture of the Keyboard in 18th-century Russia,"

Continuo (December 1998), pp. 5–6, on aristocratic performers in the early eighteenth century, and see also his "Researching Early Keyboards in Russia," *Continuo* (February 1996), pp. 2–6. See also Findeizen, *Ocherki,* vol. 1, ch. 12 and vol. 2 passim.

139. L. M. Starikova, "Russkii teatr petrovskogo vremeni, Komedial'naia khramina i domashnie komedii tsarevny Natal'i Alekseevny" [Russian theater of the Petrine era, the Komedial'naia khramina [where the plays were performed], and Tsarevna Natalia Alekseevna's domestic plays], *PKNO 1990* (Moscow: Krug, 1992), pp. 50–51; see also the summaries in Karlinsky, *Russian Drama from its Beginnings; IRM* 2; and in another work by Starikova, "Dokumental'nye utochneniia k istorii teatra v Rossii petrovskogo vremeni" [Some specifics from the sources on the history of the theater in Petrine-era Russia], *PKNO 1997* (Moscow: Nauka, 1998), pp. 179–90. There is an edition of Dmitrii Rostovskii's Christmas play by E. Levashev, ed., *Rozhdestvenskaia drama, ili Rostovskoe deistvo* [Christmas drama, or the Rostov drama] (Moscow: Sovetskii kompozitor, 1989).

140. See Olga Dolskaya-Ackerly, "From Titov to Teplov: The Origins of the Russian Art Song," in *A Window on Russia: Papers from the V International Conference of the Study Group on Eighteenth-century Russia, Gargnano, 1994,* ed. Maria Di Salvo and Lindsey Hughes (Rome: La Fenice, 1996), pp. 197–213.

141. On these early operatic productions, see the comprehensive surveys in *IRM* 2 and 3; Richard Taruskin presents brief summaries in a series of articles in *NG2*. One of the most important early surveys is in Findeizen, *Ocherki* vol. 2, where the author mines the rich resources of contemporary newspapers from Moscow and St. Petersburg to construct a history of concert life in the cities.

142. See the listing of operas in *IRM* 3; Findeizen's lists will be updated and corrected in the forthcoming English translation of his work.

14. MUSIC IN ITALY

1. "The Baroque was the period of Italian supremacy in music. Italy's rise to the accomplishment of this historic mission took place suddenly, in the course of a single generation." Friedrich Blume in *Renaissance and Baroque Music,* trans. M. D. Herter Norton (New York, 1967), p. 153.

2. See Part I, Chapter 4.

3. Charles E. Troy, *The Comic Intermezzo* (Ann Arbor, 1979), p. 63. This is a fine study of the comic intermezzo, to which I am indebted.

4. Ibid., pp. 91–130 where the comic musical style is examined in some detail.

5. By Charles de Brosses, in *Lettres familières écrites d'Italie en 1739–1740,* 2nd ed. (Paris, 1858), vol. 1, p. 386, cited by Michael F. Robinson in his comprehensive study of *Naples and Neapolitan Opera* (Oxford, 1972), p. 1.

6. Donald J. Grout, with Hermine Weigel Williams, *A Short History of Opera,* 3rd ed. (New York, 1988), p. 213.

7. See Gloria Rose's succinct history of "The Italian Cantata of the Baroque Period," in *Gedenkschrift Leo Schrade* (Bern, 1973), pp. 655–77.

8. Smither, *A History of the Oratorio,* vol. 1, pp. 358–59.

9. The statistics regarding oratorios performed in Venice are taken from Denis Arnold and Elsie Arnold, *The Oratorio in Venice* (London, 1986), pp. 77–103.

10. *Sedecia,* which is published in facsimile in *The Italian Oratorio, 1650–1800,* vol. 6, is discussed briefly in Smither, *A History of the Oratorio,* vol. 1, pp. 310–41.

11. Newman, in *The Sonata in the Baroque Era,* p. 163, suggests thirty Italians contributed to the sonata repertory in the first half of the eighteenth century.

12. See the valuable discussions of Albinoni's life and music by Michael Talbot, *Tomaso Albinoni: The Venetian Composer and His World* (Oxford, 1990) especially pp. 85–114 regarding the early instrumental works (to 1700).

13. For another perceptive discussion of Albinoni's chamber music, see Eleanor Selfridge-Field's *Venetian Instrumental Music from Gabrieli to Vivaldi* (3rd rev. ed., New York, 1994), pp. 199–207.

14. See John Walter Hill, *The Life and Works of Francesco Maria Veracini* (Ann Arbor, 1979), esp. pp. 103–23, 153–71.

15. Regarding Tartini's sonatas, see Newman, *The Sonata in the Baroque Era*, pp. 189–92.

16. There is no major study of Locatelli in English. The two classic works are Arend Koole, *Leven en werken van Pietro Antonio Locatelli da Bergamo, 1695–1764* (Amsterdam, 1949), and Albert Dunning, *Pietro Antonio Locatelli: der Virtuose und seine Welt* (Buren, 1981). Dunning is the editor with others of *Pietro Antonio Locatelli: Opera omnia* (London, 1994).

17. Talbot, *Tomaso Albinoni: The Venetian Composer and His World*, p. 103.

18. Ibid., pp. 256–61 for a description of these concertos.

19. There are five catalogues of Vivaldi's works: Rinaldi, *Catalogo numerico tematico delle composizioni di A. Vivaldi* (Rome, 1945); Pincherle, *Inventaire-Thématique*, vol. 2 of *Antonio Vivaldi et la musique instrumentale* (Paris, repr. 1948); Antonio Fanna, *Catalogo numerico-tematico delle opere strumentali* (Milan, 1968), all three being variously unsatisfactory; and two by Peter Ryom, *Verzeichnis der Werke Antonio Vivaldis: kleine Ausgabe* (Leipzig, 1974; 2d ed. 1979); *Répertoire des oeuvres Antonio Vivaldi: les compositions instrumentales* (Copenhagen, 1986). All of Vivaldi's works are listed with their Ryom catalogue (RV) numbers in *The New Grove Dictionary*, 2d ed., vol. 26, pp. 824–38.

20. The full extent of Vivaldi's compositional output was realized only with the discovery of the so-called Turin manuscripts (also known as the Foà-Giodano collection), two large collections of Vivaldi's personal scores, the first purchased by the Turin National Library in 1926 with funding from Roberto Foà, the second half for the same library in 1930 with funding from Filippo Giordano.

21. See Selfridge-Field, *Venetian Instrumental Music*, pp. 225–31 and also Michael Talbot, *Vivaldi* (London, 1978), pp. 124–37.

22. For a detailed examination of Vivaldi's Op. 8, including the Four Seasons, see Paul Everett, *Vivaldi: The Four Seasons and Other Concertos, Op. 8* (Cambridge University Press, 1996).

23. Invaluable for its extensive study of the sacred works is Michael Talbot's *The Sacred Vocal Music of Antonio Vivaldi* (Florence, 1995).

24. Highly recommended is the extensive and informative analysis of *Juditha triumphans* by Talbot, ibid., pp. 409–47.

15. OPERA AT HAMBURG, DRESDEN, AND VIENNA

1. J. A. Scheibe, *Über die musikalische Composition* (Leipzig, 1773), p. liii.

2. J. Mattheson, *Das neu-eröffnete Orchestre* (Hamburg, 1713), p. 217.

3. J. Mattheson, *Grundlage einer Ehren-Pforte* (Hamburg, 1740), p. 133.

4. Ibid, p. 129.

5. Better known as "August the Strong," who in 1697 converted to Catholicism in order assume the dual titles of Elector of Saxony and King of Poland.

6. Concerning musical organizations at the court of August the Strong, see I. Becker-Glauch, *Die Bedeutung der Musik für die Dresdener Hoffeste* (Kassel, 1951), pp. 20–29.

7. The only work in English devoted to Hasse's operas is F. L. Millner, *The Operas of Johann Adolf Hasse* (Ann Arbor, 1979).

16. GEORGE FRIDERIC HANDEL (1685–1759)

1. Early in his career, Handel used various spellings of his name. However, after becoming a naturalized British subject (1727) he chose this spelling. German writers continue to use the form Georg Friedrich Händel, the spelling used at birth, even though this is contrary to the composer's own later usage.

2. Two accounts of Handel's life originated in the eighteenth century. The first is a biographical sketch by Handel's friend, Johann Mattheson, in the latter's *Grundlage einer Ehren-Pforte* (Hamburg, 1740; new ed. Max Schneider, Kassel, 1969). The second was written by Handel's contemporary John Mainwaring, *Memoirs of the Life of the Late George Frederic Handel* (London, 1760; repr. 1964, 1967). The best biography and critical study is by Donald Burrows, *Handel* (Oxford/New York, 1994). Another important biography and critical study is by Paul Henry Lang, *George Frideric Handel* (New York, 1966). Also useful is Christopher Hogwood's *Handel* (London, 1984).

3. These four operas are catalogued as HWV 1, 2, 3, and 4 in the *Händel-Handbuch*, vol. 1, ed. Berndt Baselt (Kassel, 1978). This thematic and systematic catalogue of all of Handel's works appears in three volumes: the first for the operas; the second for the oratorios, vocal chamber works, and sacred music (1984); and the third for instrumental works, pasticcios, and fragments (1986).

4. With a few exceptions all of Handel's music was published by Friedrich W. Chrysander, *G. F. Händels Werke: Ausgabe der Deutschen Händelgesellschaft* (Hamburg, 1858–94). Since 1955 a new edition has been in progress, *Hallische Händel-Ausgabe*.

5. Proof of this opera's performance in Florence was established by Reinhard Strohm in "Händel in Italia: Nuovi contributi," *Rivista italiana di musicologia* 9 (1974), pp. 152–74.

6. Significant evidence regarding Handel's Rome period was first discovered by Ursula Kirkendale, "The Ruspoli Documents on Handel," *JAMS* 20 (1967), pp. 222–73, 517. See also her "Orgelspiel im Lateran und andere Erinnerungen an Händel. Ein unbeachteter Bericht in 'Voiage historique' von 1737," *Mf* 41 (1988), pp. 1–9. Here Kirkendale proves that it was Handel who is referred to in a contemporary diary entry for 14 January 1707, which reports that a certain excellent Saxon composer and keyboardist had astonished by his organ virtuosity an audience gathered in the cathedral, St. John Lateran, in Rome.

7. A center for aristocratic intellectual activity in Rome was the Arcadian Academy. It originated in 1689 when a group of aristocrats wished to honor the memory of Queen Christina of Sweden who had died in exile in Rome. During Handel's Roman period the Academy usually met in the palace of Cardinal Pietro Ottoboni, but also at times in Ruspoli's palace. Members of this private circle assumed fictitious names as "shepherds." For example, Corelli was known as Arcimelo, Alessandro Scarlatti as Terpando. Support was given to poetry that emphasized the supposed naturalness and simplicity of pastoral life and reflected in various ways the pastoral masterwork by Guarini, *Il pastor fido*. Music played a central role in these academy gatherings.

8. The text as divided into movements (with an English translation) are:

I. Dixit Dominus Domino meo,	The Lord said unto my Lord:
Sede a dextris meis,	Sit thou on my right hand,
Donec ponam inimicos tuos	until I make thine enemies
scabellum pedum tuorum.	thy footstool.

II. Virgam virtutis tuae emittet Dominus ex Sion: dominate in medio inimicorum tuorum.	The Lord shall send the rod of thy power out of Sion: be thou ruler, even in the midst of thine enemies.
III. Tecum principium in die virtutis tuae in splendoribus sanctorum: ex utero ante Luciferum genui te.	In the day of thy power shall the people offer free-will offerings with an holy worship: the dew of thy birth is of the womb of the morning.
IV. Juravit Dominus, et non poenitebit eum:	The Lord did swear, and will not repent:
V. Secundum ordinem Melchisedech, Tu es sacerdos, in aeternum.	Thou art a Priest for ever after the order of Melchisedech.
VI. Dominus a dextris tuis; confregit in die irae suae reges. Judicabit in nationibus, implebit ruinas, conquassabit capita in terra multorum.	The Lord upon thy right hand; shall wound even kings in the day of wrath. He shall judge among the heathen; he shall fill the places with dead bodies; and smite asunder the heads over diverse countries.
VII. De torrente in via, in via bibet, Propterea exaltabit caput.	He will drink from the brook by the way; therefore he will lift up his head.
VIII. Gloria Patri et Filio Et spiritui Sancto, Sicut erat in principio et nunc et semper. Et in saecula saeculorum, Amen.	Glory be to the Father and the Son and to the Holy Spirit As it was in the beginning, is now, and ever shall be: world without end. Amen.

9. For a detailed discussion of this work, see Ellen Rosand, "Handel Paints the Resurrection,"*Festa musicologica: Essays in Honor of George J. Buelow* (Stuyvesant, N.Y., 1995), pp. 7–52.

10. Concerning Handel's opera *Agrippina* and its relationship to the Venetian opera scene, see Harris Sheridan Saunders, Jr., "Handel's 'Agrippina': The Venetian Perspective," in *Göttinger Händel Beiträge* III 1987 (Kassel, 1989), pp. 87–97.

11. John Mainwaring, *Memoirs of the Life of the Late George Frederic Handel* (London, 1760), p. 53.

12. See Buelow's examination of the borrowings in *Agrippina* in "Handel's Borrowing Techniques: Some Fundamental Questions Derived from a Study of *Agrippina* (Venice, 1709)," *Göttinger Händel Beiträge* 2 (Kassel, 1986), pp. 105–28.

13. The most informative examination of Handel's short stay in Hanover is by Donald Burrows, "Handel and Hanover," *Bach, Handel, Scarlatti, Tercentenary Essays,* ed. Peter Williams (Cambridge, 1985), pp. 35–59.

14. An especially helpful summary of events regarding Italian opera in London before Handel's arrival is found in Winton Dean and J. Merrill Knapp, *Handel's Operas, 1704–1726,* "The English Background: Italian Opera in London, 1705–1710," pp. 140–50.

15. Concerning Aaron Hill's part in creating the libretto for *Rinaldo,* see Curtis Price, "English Traditions in Handel's *Rinaldo,*" *Handel Tercentenary Collection* (Ann Arbor, 1987), pp. 120–37.

16. The numerous borrowings in *Rinaldo* are examined in detail by Reinhold Kubik, *Händels Rinaldo: Geschichte, Werk, Wirkung* (Neuhausen-Stuttgart, 1982).

17. See Burrows, "Handel in Hanover," pp. 40–46.

18. The operas of Handel from *Almira* through *Scipione* are discussed in penetrating detail in Dean and Knapp, *Handel's Operas* (Oxford, 1987).

19. A table of all the opera productions of the Academy, together with the number of repetitions for each work, is given in Dean and Knapp, *Handel's Operas,* pp. 308–09.

20. "Anti-heroic" is Winton Dean's term, as are "heroic" and "magic." This discussion of operatic categories is taken largely from his book *Handel and the Opera Seria* (Berkeley, 1969), chs. 5–7.

21. As an example, see Ariodante's aria at the opening of act II, in which the A section sets an angry tone as Ariodante threatens Duke Polinesso with death if the former learns the latter had lied about the unfaithfulness of Ginevra, Ariodante's betrothed. In contrast the B section is slow and totally contrasted in affect as Ariodante declares he would die should the accusation be true.

22. A seventh role for Odoardo (tenor) has no arias.

23. Donald J. Grout, *A Short History of Opera,* 3d edition (New York, 1988), p. 201, speaks eloquently of Handel's achievements in creating "ideal types of humanity" through the quality of his music: "This quality is more than the reflection of a certain musical style or a consummate technique; it is the direct emanation of Handel's own spirit, expressed in music with an immediacy that has no parallel outside Beethoven. It is the incarnation of a great soul."

24. Sir John Hawkins, *A General History of the Science and Practice of Music* (London, 1776), vol. V, p. 270.

25. Barthold Brockes (1680–1747) was a well-known German literary figure who may have met Handel already during the former's student days at Halle University. Brockes was a lawyer, diplomat, and distinguished member of the Hamburg Senate. He was a leading supporter of the arts in his city. Bach employed parts of his Passion text in the *St. John Passion,* and it was also set in its entirety by several lesser composers. J. S. Bach, with the assistance of his wife Anna Magdalena, made a complete copy of Handel's score. Handel also used poetry by Brockes for his other London composition to a German text, the *Neun deutsche Arien* (c. 1724–27).

26. Mainwaring, *Memoirs of the Life of the Late George Frederic Handel,* p. 95.

27. In John Macky, *A Journey Through England* (1722), as quoted in Hogwood, *Handel,* p. 72.

28. From a document in the Huntington Library, San Marino, California, quoted in the study of the Chandos Anthems by Graydon Beeks, *The Chandos Anthems and Te Deum of George Frideric Handel* (Ph.D. diss., University of California, 1981), p. 17. Beeks's ordering of the composition of the anthems presented in this study was subsequently altered in his article "Handel and Music for the Earl of Carnarvon," in *Bach, Handel, Scarlatti Tercentenary Essays,* ed. Peter Williams (Cambridge, 1985), pp. 1–20. These changes as given here reflect the more recent studies of the watermarks and other characteristics of Handel's manuscript papers by Donald Burrows and M. J. Ronish, *A Catalogue of Handel's Musical Autographs* (Oxford, 1994).

29. Paul Henry Lang had often spoken of the dynastic trait in Handel's English ceremonial music, but he apparently had not arrived at the term when writing his Handel biography. See, however, his introductory essay in the *Tercentenary Handel Studies, American Choral Review,* ed. Alfred Mann, vol. 27 (1985), p. 6.

30. Further concerning the coronation of King George and the role Handel played in it, see Donald Burrows, "Handel and the 1727 Coronation," *The Musical Times* 118 (1977), p. 469.

31. Vol. 3 of the *Händel-Handbuch,* ed. B. Baselt (Kassel, 1986), catalogues all of Handel's instrumental music: HWV 287–610, more than three hundred individual compositions.

32. The RISM volume of printed music before 1800, *Einzeldrucke vor 1800,* vol. 4 (Kassel, 1974), identifies more than fifteen hundred prints of Handel's music, vocal and instrumental, appearing before the end of the eighteenth century.

33. Terence Best, "Handel's Harpsichord Music: A Checklist," in *Music in Eighteenth-Century England: Essays in Memory of Charles Cudworth,* ed. C. Hogwood and R. Luckett (Cambridge, 1983), pp. 171–87. The checklist provides a complete and accurate listing of Handel's keyboard works together with approximate dates of composition and a summary of the interrelationships between various versions.

34. The borrowings used by Handel for the trio sonatas are listed in the *Händel-Handbuch,* vol. 3, pp. 182–95.

35. Information based on entries in the *Händel-Handbuch,* vol. 3.

36. "Hallenser Sonaten" is Chrysander's term, used in his edition of HWV 374, 375, 376, in the belief these were among the earliest sonatas composed by the young Handel in Halle. There is no evidence validating this theory.

37. The title refers to the Fitzwilliam Library, Cambridge, where the manuscript containing these sonatas was found. Thurston Dart was the first to publish them in an edition, *The Fitzwilliam Sonatas by G. F. Handel from the Autograph MSS in the Fitzwilliam Museum, Cambridge* (London, 1948).

38. This aspect of the organ concertos, as well as the most complete study of the organ concertos generally is found in William D. Gudger, *The Organ Concertos of G. F. Handel: A Study Based on the Primary Sources,* 2 vols. (Ph.D. diss., Yale University, 1973).

39. Further concerning the origins of Op. 3, see Hans Joachim Marx, "The Origins of Handel's Opus 3: A Historical Review," *Handel Tercentenary Collection* (Ann Arbor, 1987), pp. 254–70.

40. See the *Händel-Handbuch,* vol. 3, pp. 61–70, for these and the other sources within Handel's works for the various movements of these concertos.

41. James P. Malcolm, *Anecdotes of the Manners and Customs of London during the Eighteenth Century* (London, 1808), p. 145.

42. Report written by Bonet, the Prussian Resident, to Berlin and quoted (in translation) in Otto Erich Deutsch, *Handel, A Documentary Biography* (New York, 1955), p. 77.

43. The sources for the *Water Music* are given in the *Händel-Handbuch,* vol. 3, pp. 119–20, and also in the preface to the *Hallische Händel-Ausgabe,* series IV/13 (Kassel, 1962), ed. Hans Ferdinand Redlich. It was Redlich who first published the *Water Music* as a set of three suites grouped according to tonality.

44. From the *Gentlemen's Magazine,* as cited in Deutsch, *Handel, A Documentary Biography,* p. 668. See also on p. 641 a contemporary picture of Green Park with the structure built for the occasion.

45. The most important work on Handel's oratorios is Winton Dean's *Handel's Dramatic Oratorios and Masques* (London, 1959), which includes richly documented materials on the background of Handel's works as well as a definitive study of each of the "dramatic" oratorios.

46. Cited in Deutsch, *A Documentary Biography,* pp. 288–89.

47. See, for example, Dean's perhaps too critical viewpoint of *Deborah* in *Handel's Dramatic Oratorios,* pp. 225–36.

48. The distinction between these oratorios with a dramatically delineated plot and those without one determines the organization of Dean's study, *Handel's Dramatic Oratorios*

and Masques, in which he does not discuss in detail oratorios he considered nondramatic, for example, *Israel in Egypt* and *Messiah.*

49. An informative beginning for such an examination is Ruth Smith's "Intellectual Contexts of Handel's English Oratorios," in *Music in Eighteenth-Century England: Essays in Memory of Charles Cudworth,* ed. C. Hogwood and R. Luckett (Cambridge, 1983), pp. 115–33.

50. Regarding the history of opinions about Handel's borrowing practice, see the author's "The Case for Handel's Borrowings: The Judgment of Three Centuries," *Handel Tercentenary Collection,* ed. S. Sadie and A. Hicks (Ann Arbor, 1987), pp. 61–82. Many of Handel's borrowings in the oratorios are listed in Dean's *Handel's Dramatic Oratorios and Masques,* appendix E. Borrowings found in the operas are discussed in Dean and Knapp, *Handel's Operas, 1704–1726,* and appear in Appendix D.

17. JOHANN SEBASTIAN BACH (1685–1750)

1. See Christoph Wolff's *The New Grove Bach Family* (New York, 1983) for an informative family tree showing the male Bach lineage and also biographical data concerning these male members.

2. The earliest detailed biography of J. S. Bach, written with information supplied by Carl Philipp Emanuel and Wilhelm Friedemann Bach, was published in 1802 by J. N. Forkel. Among the many biographies to follow in the nineteenth century the most important was by Philipp Spitta, *Johann Sebastian Bach* (Leipzig, 1873–89; English trans. 1884–85, repr. 1951). These and all other Bach biographies are now superseded by Christoph Wolff's *Johann Sebastian Bach: The Learned Musician* (Cambridge, Mass., 2000).

3. *The New Bach Reader, A Life of Johann Sebastian Bach in Letters,* ed. Hans T. David and Arthur Mendel, rev. and enlarged by Christoph Wolff (New York, 1998), p. 300.

4. Wolff, *Bach: The Learned Musician,* p. 65.

5. Published in facsimile as *The Neumeister Collection of Chorale Preludes from the Bach Circle,* introduction by Christoph Wolff (New Haven, 1986).

6. BWV (Bach-Werke-Verzeichnis) refers to the systematic catalogue of all of Bach's works in Wolfgang Schmieder, *Thematisch-systematisches Verzeichnis der musikalischen Werken von Johann Sebastian Bach,* 2d ed. (Wiesbaden, 1990).

7. An alternative origin of this work is suggested by Wolff, *Bach: The Learned Musician,* pp. 74–75, who believes it was written earlier than 1704 and perhaps at Lüneburg for some kind of graduation party in honor of his friend Georg Erdmann.

8. For an important study of the *Orgelbüchlein,* giving a wide range of historical and analytical perspectives, see Russell Stinson, *Bach: The Orgelbüchlein* (New York, 1996).

9. See *The New Bach Reader,* pp. 100–109 for a series of documents by the Leipzig town council and also by Bach related to the affairs leading up to Bach's appointment as cantor.

10. Bach's *Christmas Oratorio* was performed in Leipzig on Christmas Day 1723, his first Christmas in Leipzig as Thomaskantor. This was the first of two distinct versions in the key of E flat. A second version in D major (BWV 243) is better known, and was prepared sometime between 1723 and 1735. Marshall believes it may have been performed on 1 July 1733 for the feast of the Visitation of Mary. See Robert Marshall, "On the Origin of the Magnificat" in his *The Music of Johann Sebastian Bach: The Sources, the Style, the Significance* (New York, 1989), pp. 161–73.

11. For the redating of Bach's instrumental music to the Leipzig period, see Christoph Wolff, *Bach: Essays on His Life and Music* (Cambridge, Mass., 1991), pp. 223–38.

12. "The World-famous Organist, Mr. Johann Sebastian Bach, Royal Polish and Elec-

toral Saxon Composer, and Music Director in Leipzig," obituary by Carl Philipp Emanuel Bach and Johann Friedrich Agricola, published in 1754. Given in English translation in *The New Bach Reader,* pp. 297–307. Further concerning Bach's unique genius and how to define it, see Christoph Wolff, " 'The Extraordinary Perfection of the Hon. Court Composer': An Inquiry into the Individuality of Bach's Music," in *Bach: Essays on His Life and Music* (Harvard, 1991), pp. 391–97.

13. For a valuable discussion regarding the chronology of the organ preludes, see George B. Stauffer's *The Organ Preludes of Johann Sebastian Bach* (Ann Arbor, 1980).

14. Wolff gives a detailed discussion of the Neumeister collection and its relationship to Bach's *Orgelbüchlein* in *Bach: Essays on His Life and Music,* pp. 107–27.

15. See Russell Stinson, *Bach: The Orgelbüchlein* (New York, 1996), for a detailed discussion of this work and an analysis of each of the chorale preludes.

16. For these comments on early chronology I am indebted to the article on Bach's organ music by Christoph Wolff in *The New Bach Family* (New York, 1983), pp. 144–48.

17. Wolff, in *Bach: The Learned Musician,* p. 94, suggests the Passacaglia may originate in Arnstadt.

18. An excellent commentary on Bach's harpsichord and clavichord music is found in David Schulenberg's *The Keyboard Music of J. S. Bach* (New York, 1992).

19. See especially Schulenberg, Chapters 3–7.

20. Further regarding types of fugues, see George Stauffer's article "Fugue Types in Bach's Free Organ Works," in *J. S. Bach as Organist,* ed. George Stauffer and Ernest May (Bloomington, 1986), pp. 133–56.

21. Two other suites are associated with Bach's French Suites. They are a suite in A minor, BWV 818 (and a revision, BWV 818a), and a suite in E flat, BWV 819 (and a revision, BWV 819a). These are discussed in Schulenberg, *The Keyboard Music of J. S. Bach,* pp. 257–62.

22. *The New Bach Reader,* p. 468.

23. The manuscript sources for the French Suites are numerous and Bach's many revisions often appear in copies made by students and others close to the composer. The complexities of the sources are discussed in detail in Schulenberg, *The Keyboard Music of J. S. Bach,* Chapter 14.

24. The title apparently refers back to Kuhnau's two collections of keyboard music entitled *Neue Clavier-Übung* (Leipzig, 1689 and 1692).

25. Schulenberg, *The Keyboard Music of J. S. Bach,* p. 277.

26. *The New Bach Reader,* p. 463. The recognition and fame of these keyboard compositions is underscored, perhaps, by the fact that Christoph Willibald Gluck borrowed the gigue of the first partita for the aria "Je t'implore et je tremble" which opens Act IV of his opera *Iphigénie en Tauride* (Paris, 1779). Further concerning this borrowing, see Buelow, "A Bach Borrowing by Gluck" in *Eighteenth-Century Music in Theory and Practice: Essays in Honor of Alfred Mann* (Stuyvesant, N.Y., 1994).

27. Schulenberg, however, suggests there are also influences from the concertos composed by younger contemporaries such as Quantz and the Graun brothers. See *The Keyboard Music of J. S. Bach,* p. 302.

28. *The New Bach Reader,* pp. 464–65.

29. An edition of the fourteen canons and their realization has been published by Christoph Wolff in *Bach: Fourteen Canons on the First Eight Notes of the Aria Ground from the "Goldberg Variations"* (Kassel, 1976). See also Wolff's article, Bach's *Handexemplar* of the Goldberg Variations," in *Bach: Essays on His Life and Music,* pp. 162–77. The careful

numbering of each canon by Bach suggests the special emphasis he placed on the number fourteen, which in the numerical-alphabetical translation of B-A-C-H (2 + 1 + 3 + 8) equals 14. Also significant, the thirteenth canon is borrowed from the portrait of Bach painted by Elias Gottlob Haussmann in 1746. Bach looks to his viewer and presents in his right hand a piece of manuscript paper on which he has written the canon and on it inscribed "Canon triplex á 6 Voc. Per J. S. Bach."

30. *The New Bach Reader,* p. 468.

31. An important discussion of the sources and what they reveal about the evolution of the work is presented in George F. Stauffer's " 'This fantasia . . . never had its like': On the Enigma and Chronology of Bach's Chromatic Fantasia and Fugue in D Minor, BWV 903." In *Bach Studies,* ed. Don O. Franklin (Cambridge, 1989), pp. 160–82.

32. Johann Gottfried Walther, *Musicalisches Lexicon* (Leipzig, 1732), p. 434.

33. See Westhoff's *Sechs Suiten für Violine solo* (Leipzig/New York, 1974).

34. *The New Bach Reader,* p. 472: "For a long series of years, the violin solos were universally considered by the greatest performers on the violin as the best means to make an ambitious student a perfect master of his instrument."

35. This aspect of the unaccompanied violin sonatas is convincingly demonstrated in Joel Lester's *Bach's Works for Solo Violin: Style, Structure, Performance* (New York, 1999).

36. Preserved in a manuscript written by Bach's student Johann Christoph Altnickol in Leipzig probably 1724–27, the title of these works is given as: *Sei Suonate à Cembalo certato è Violino Solo, col Basso per Viola da Gamba accompagnata se piace composte da Giov: Sebast: Bach.*

37. Movements 3 and 5 of the second version were from harpsichord Partita No. 6, movements 3 and 6. Movement 3 of the first version and movement 4 of versions one and two were original compositions. See BWV 1019a.

38. See Wolff, *Bach: Essays on His Life and Music,* pp. 324–31, for a discussion of the music. Analyses of the collection of compositions are found in Malcolm Boyd's *Bach,* pp. 196–201, and Hans T. David's monograph, *J. S. Bach's "Musical Offering": History, Interpretation, and Analysis* (New York, 1945), which despite its age, remains one of the most comprehensive studies of this work.

39. In 1871 by the distinguished German violinist August Wilhelmj (1845–1908).

40. In *The New Bach Reader,* p. 92.

41. The phrase is not absolutely clear as to meaning. It may mean "for several instruments" though "several different instruments" seems more precise.

42. In Manfred Bukofzer's *Music in the Baroque Era* (New York, 1947), p. 291.

43. For a more comprehensive study of these works, see Malcolm Boyd, *Bach: The Brandenburg Concertos* (Cambridge, 1993).

44. In *The New Bach Reader,* p. 304.

45. The so-called new chronology established by Alfred Dürr in *Zur Chronologie der Leipziger Vokalwerke J.S. Bachs,* in *Bach-Jahrbuch* xliv (1957), pp. 5–162, and Georg von Dadelsen in *Bemerkungen zur Handschrift Johann Sebastian Bachs, seiner Familie und seines Kreises,* in Tübinger Bach-Studien 1 (Trossingen, 1957), and also von Dadelsen, *Beiträge zur Chronologie der Werke Johann Sebastian Bachs* in Tübinger Bach-Studien, 4/5 (Trossingen, 1958).

46. See *Bach Compendium: Analytisch-bibliographisches Repertorium der Werke Johann Sebastian Bachs,* Part I, Vocal Works, by Hans-Joachim Schulze and Christoph Wolff (Frankfurt, 1986).

47. In *The New Bach Reader,* pp. 472–73.

48. *Bach Compendium,* Part I, p. 37.

49. Therefore, Cantata No. 1, *Wie schön leutchtet der Morgenstern,* is the first cantata published, not the first cantata composed by Bach. These numbers are retained in the *Bach-Werke-Verzeichnis* (BWV).

50. Bach was invited back to Mühlhausen for the two subsequent years to perform two additional cantatas for church services observing town council elections. These works are lost.

51. For a detailed discussion of cantata BWV 4's origin, musical content, and the history of the chorale *Christ lag in Todesbanden,* see Gerhard Herz, *Bach Cantata No. 4, Christ lag in Todesbanden,* Norton Critical Scores (New York, 1967).

52. Alfred Dürr, *Die Kantaten von Johann Sebastian Bach* (Kassel, 1971), vol. 2, pp. 611–12 (author's translation).

53. They include, grouped according to year: 1713–1714 (?): BWV Nos. 18, 21; 1714: BWV Nos. 63, 182, 12, 172, 54, 199, 61, 152; 1715: BWV Nos. 80a, 31, 165, 185, 161, 162, 163, 132; 1716: BWV Nos. 155, 70a, 186a, 147a.

54. It is not always possible to determine the Weimar form of cantatas that exist only in later Leipzig versions. Therefore, these are not included in this list.

55. The exception is Alfred Dürr's survey of all the cantatas, *Die Kantaten von Johann Sebastian Bach,* 2 vols. (Kassel, 1971). It, however, also does not attempt to give a comprehensive view or summary of Bach's achievement in the cantatas.

56. *Bach Compendium,* Part I, p. 37.

57. These works, preceded by BWV 22 and 23 composed for Bach's examination, include BWV 24, 25, 37, 40, 44, 46, 48, 59, 60, 64, 65, 66, 67, 69a, 73, 75, 76, 77, 81, 83, 86, 89, 90, 95, 104, 105, 109, 119, 134, 136, 138, 144, 148, 153, 154, 166, 167, 179, 181, 186, 190, 194.

58. They are BWV 1, 2, 5, 7, 8, 10, 20, 26, 33, 38, 41, 62, 78, 91, 92, 93, 94, 96, 99, 101, 107, 111, 113, 114, 115, 116, 121, 122, 123, 124, 125, 126, 127, 130, 133, 135, 139, 178, 180.

59. BWV 6, 42, 85, librettist uncertain; BWV 68, 74, 87, 103, 108, 128, 175, 176, 183, by von Ziegler of which 68, 108, and 128 are chorale cantatas.

60. Based on the assumption the cycle III ended in early 1727, the 34 cantatas would be, according to year, 1725: BWV 28, 79, 110, 137, 164, 168; 1726: BWV 3, 13, 16, 17, 19, 27, 32, 35, 39, 43, 45, 47, 49, 52, 55, 57, 72, 88, 102, 146, 151, 169, 170, 187; 1727: 58a, 82, 84.

61. However, Christoph Wolff has suggested that perhaps the eight-part BWV 225 and the five-part BWV 227 may have been composed by Bach for choral exercises to train his students in vocal techniques and genres. See *Johann Sebastian Bach: The Learned Musician* (New York, 2000), p. 249.

62. See Daniel R. Melamed, "Probleme zu Chronologie, Stil und Zweck der Motetten Johann Sebastian Bachs," in *Beiträge zur Bach-Forschung,* Heft 9/10 (Leipzig, 1991), pp. 277–83.

63. See Daniel R. Melamed and Reginald L. Sanders, "Zum Text und Kontext der "Keiser"-Markuspassion, *BJ* (1999), pp. 35–50, who suggest the composer may have been Friedrich Nicolaus Brauns (1685–1718).

64. See Wolff, *J. S. Bach: The Learned Musician,* p. 178.

65. The following comments about music in the *St. John Passion* are based on the edition by Arthur Mendel in the NBA (Kassel, 1975).

66. An account found in a book on the Divine Service in Saxony by church historian Christian Gerber (1732), though not thought to be related to church services in Leipzig,

included the following relevant passage: "when in a large town this Passion music was done for the first time, with twelve violins [strings], many oboes, bassoons, and other instruments, many people were astonished and did not know what to make of it. . . . But when this theatrical music began, all these people were thrown into the greatest bewilderment, looked at each other, and said, 'What will come of this?' An old widow of the nobility said, 'God save us, my children! It's just as if one were at an Opera Comedy'." See *The New Bach Reader*, pp. 326–27.

67. Simple recitative is employed here instead of the misleading and inaccurate common terminology of "recitativo secco."

68. Numbers according to the Urtext edition J. S. Bach, *Neue Ausgabe sämtlicher Werke*, Series II, vol. 5, ed. Alfred Dürr.

69. See *The New Bach Reader*, pp. 145–51.

70. Ibid., pp. 144–45.

71. For the complete letter, see ibid., pp. 151–52.

72. Translation from *The New Bach Reader*, p. 158.

73. The outstanding recent study of Bach's Mass is George B. Stauffer's *Bach, the Mass in B Minor* (New York, 1997). See pp. 34–37 for his suggestions as to possible performances of the *Missa*.

74. Ibid., p. 39.

75. First established by Yoshitake Kobayashi in "Zur Chronologie der Spätwerke Johann Sebastian Bachs, Kompositions- und Aufführungstätigkeit von 1736 bis 1750," in *Bach-Jahrbuch* 74 (1988), pp. 7–72.

76. It is important to note that Bach does not give a comprehensive title of "B minor Mass," which first received this widely recognized title only in the edition of the Bach Gesellschaft's *Bach-Gesamtausgabe* of 1856–57. Also important to note is that the work is not a Mass in "B minor," as this is only the key of the first Kyrie and one of several other keys used in the Mass, among which is the dominating tonality of D major.

77. See Stauffer, *Bach, the Mass in B Minor*, pp. 27–29.

78. Ibid., p. 49.

79. In addition to Stauffer's work, other significant books on the B Minor Mass include: Walter Blankenburg, *Einführung in Bachs h-moll Messe* (Kassel, 1950/1973); John Butt, *Bach: Mass in B Minor* (Cambridge, 1991); Helmuth Rilling, *Johann Sebastian Bach's B-Minor Mass,* trans. Gordon Paine (Princeton, N.J., 1984).

80. For an in-depth analysis for each of the movements of the B Minor Mass readers should consult Stauffer's monograph.

81. As has been suggested by Robert L. Marshall in "Bach the Progressive: Observations on His Later Works," in *The Musical Quarterly* 62 (1976), and reprinted in *The Music of Johann Sebastian Bach: The Sources, the Style, the Significance* (New York, 1989), p. 42.

82. It is worth noting that Bach's magnificent gift of the Kyrie and Gloria movements to the Saxon Elector consists of 1,040 measures, a symbolic reference to Bach's authorship in the number fourteen.

83. The subject of number symbolism in general and how it may determine aspects of Bach's compositional process is relevant to his music but also controversial. Although there are a number of articles and books that discuss number symbolism in music as well as in literary forms, it is not a subject that can be examined within the parameters of this book.

84. See Alfred Dürr, " 'Entfernet euch, ihr kalten Herzen.' Möglichkeit und Grenzen der Rekonstruktion einer Bach-Aria," *Die Musikforschung* 39 (1986), pp. 32–36.

85. See Wolff, "The Agnus Dei of the B Minor Mass: Parody and New Composition Reconciled," in *Bach: Essays on His Life,* p. 332.

86. See Stauffer, *The Mass in B-Minor,* p. 168.

87. Questions have been raised by some writers whether Bach's B Minor Mass is one work, or rather four separate works. This was the particular theory of Friedrich Smend, editor of the work for the Neue Bach Ausgabe. The question no longer seems valid, but overlooked, I believe, is a proof from Bach himself, a symbolic testimony expressed in number. One may remember that Bach's original composition, the *Missa* (Kyrie and Gloria), had 1,040 measures, an imprint that expresses symbolically Bach's authorship with his name given in its number equivalent. It should not be surprising, although actually it is, that the four parts making up the *Missa tota* also have a symbolically significant number of measures. They add up to 2,345, a perfect numerical series that Bach surely planned so that when one adds the digits together they equal fourteen!

18. GEORG PHILIPP TELEMANN (1681–1767)

1. Important albeit incomplete catalogues of Telemann's vocal and instrumental music are: *Thematisches Verzeichnis der Vokalwerke von Georg Philipp Telemann,* vols. I and II, ed. Werner Menke (V. Klostermann, Frankfurt am Main, 1982–83), and *Georg Philipp Telemann: Thematisch-Systematisches Verzeichnis seiner Werke* (TWV), vols. I, II, and III, ed. Martin Ruhnke (Kassel, 1984, 1992, 1999).

2. From Telemann's autobiography published in Johann Mattheson's *Grundlage einer Ehren-Pforte* (Hamburg, 1740), p. 361.

3. In a letter to Johann Friedrich Armand von Uffenbach, 31 July 1723. See *Georg Philipp Telemann, Briefwechsel,* ed. Hans Grosse and Hans Rudolf Jung (Leipzig, 1972), p. 213.

4. Telemann research by American scholars, as listed in Doctoral Dissertations in Musicology—Online (July 2001), includes only eight significant Telemann dissertations. Of particular importance is the dissertation by Brian D. Stewart, "Georg Philipp Telemann in Hamburg: Social and Cultural Background and Its Musical Expression" (Stanford University, 1985), unfortunately not published but available from University Microfilms International, 300 N. Zeeb Rd., Ann Arbor, MI 48106. In Germany, Telemann research has been supported almost entirely by the Zentrum für Telemann-Pflege und Forschung Magdeburg. For decades the Zentrum has published invaluable congress reports of the research papers read at the Magdeburger Telemann Festtage.

5. This data is drawn from Steven Zohn's excellent Telemann article and comprehensive Works List in *The New Grove Dictionary of Music and Musicians,* 2d ed., vol. 25, ed. Stanley Sadie (London, 2001), pp. 199–232.

6. Johann Mattheson, *Grosse General-Bass-Schule* (Hamburg, 1731), p. 170: "Singen ist das Fundament zur Music in allen Dingen. Wer die Composition ergreifft/muss in seinen Sätzen singen. Wer auf Instrumenten spielt/muss des Singens Kündig seyn. Also präge man das Singen jungen Leuten fleissig ein."

7. Johann Gottfried Walther, *Musicalisches Lexicon oder Musicalische Bibliothec* (Leipzig, 1732), pp. 596–97.

8. *Der General-Bass in der Composition* (Dresden, 1728), p. 10 (fn).

9. J. J. Quantz, *On Playing the Flute,* English trans. Edward R. Reilly (London, 1966), p. 341 from *Versuch einer Anweisung die Flöte traversiere zu spielen* (Berlin, 1752).

10. In his Telemann entry for *The New Grove Dictionary of Music and Musicians,* 2d edition, vol. 25, p. 204.

11. See the extensive article on "Galant" in *The New Grove Dictionary of Music and Musicians,* 2d ed., vol. 9, pp. 430–31, by Daniel Heartz and Bruce Alan Brown, and also David A. Sheldon, "The Galant Style Revisted and Re-evaluated," *Acta Musicologica* XLVII (1975), pp. 240–70.

12. In the textbook to Heinichen's opera *Lybischen Talestris.* According to Wolf Hobohm in "Zum Stil einiger Jugendwerke Telemanns," *Konferenzbericht der 3. Magdeburger Telemann-Festtage* (Magdeburg, 1969), p. 64.

13. Another set of six quartets, published in Hamburg in 1730, are often called the "Paris Quartets." To avoid confusing these with those from 1738, the latter are best referred to as the "Nouveaux quatuors."

14. *Grundlage einer Ehrenpforte,* p. 367.

15. Johann Scheibe, *Critischer Musikus* (Leipzig, 1745), p. 673.

16. This and subsequent critical comments about the reception of Telemann's music are excerpts, translated by this author from the German, contained in Christine Klein, *Dokumente zur Telemann-Rezeption, 1767–1907* (Oschersleben, 1998), pp. 25–27. All subsequent references to this book will be as Klein, *Telemann-Reception.*

17. Ibid., pp. 144–45.

18. Ibid., pp. 187–88.

19. Renate Federhofer-Königs, *New Grove Dictionary of Music and Musicians,* 2d ed., vol. 3, p. 637.

20. Klein, *Telemann-Reception,* pp. 228–30.

21. Ibid., p. 267.

22. Ibid., pp. 331–32.

23. *Grosse General General-Bass-Schule,* pp. 176–77: "Ein Satz der Hexerey in seine Zeilen fasst/ Ich meyne/ wann das Blat viel schwehre Gänge führet/ Ist musicirenden fast meistens eine Last/ Worbey man offtermahls genung Grimacen spühret./ Ich sage ferner so: Wer vielen nutzen kan/ Thut besser/ als wer nur für wenige was schreibet; Nun dient/ was leicht gesetzt/ durchgehends jedermann: Drum wirds am besten seyn/ dass man bey diesem bleibet.

Bibliography

Adami da Bolsena, Andrea. *Osservazioni per ben regolare il coro de i cantori della Capella pontificia: Tanto nelle funzioni ordinarie, che straordinarie.* Rome: Per Antonio de Rossi, 1711.

Adams, Martin. *Henry Purcell: The Origins and Development of His Musical Style.* Cambridge: Cambridge University Press, 1995.

Adlung, Jakob. *Anleitung zu der musikalischen Gelahrtheit.* Erfurt, 1758.

Adson, John. *Courtly Masquing Ayres, 1621.* Edited by Peter Walls. 3 vols. English Instrumental Music of the Late Renaissance, vols. 3–5. London: London Pro Musica Edition, 1976–1979.

Ahles, Johann Rudolph. *Ausgewählte Gesangswerke: Mit und Ohne Begleitung von Instrumenten.* Edited by Johannes Wolf. Denkmäler deutscher Tonkunst, 1st ser., vol. 5. Leipzig: Breitkopf & Härtel, 1901.

Albert, Hanns Bernard Anton Maria. "Leben und Werke des Komponisten und Dirigenten Abraham Megerle (1607–1680): Beitrag zur Geschichte der Bayerisch-österreichischen Kirkenmusik." Ph.D. diss., Munich, 1927.

Albert, Heinrich. *Arien.* Edited by Eduard Bernoulli with an introduction by Hermann Kretzschmar. 2 vols. Denkmäler deutscher Tonkunst, 1st ser., vols. 12–13. Leipzig: Breitkopf & Härtel, [1903–1904].

Albrecht, Christoph, ed. *Neue Ausgabe sämtlicher freien Orgelwerke,* by Dietrich Buxtehude. 5 vols. Kassel: Bärenreiter, 1994–1998.

Alegria, José Augusto. *História da Capela e Colégio dos Santos Reis Magos de Vila Viçosa.* Lisbon: Calouste Gulbenkian Foundation, 1983.

———. *História da escola de Música de Sé de Évora.* Lisbon: Calouste Gulbenkian Foundation, 1973.

———. *O ensino e prática da Música nas Sés de Portugal: Da Reconquista aos fins do século XVI.* Biblioteca breve (Instituto de Cultura e Lingua Portuguesa), vol. 101. Lisbon: Instituto de Cultura e Língua Portuguesa, 1985.

Allsop, Peter. *The Italian "Trio" Sonata: From Its Origins until Corelli.* Oxford Monographs on Music. Oxford: Clarendon Press, 1992.

Almeida, Renato de. *História de Música brasileira.* 2d rev. ed. Rio de Janeiro: F. Briguiet, 1942.

Andreis, Josip. *Music in Croatia.* Edited by Ivo Supicic. Translated by Vladimir Ivir. 2d enl. ed. Zagreb: Institute of Musicology, Academy of Music, 1982.

Anthony, James R. *French Baroque Music from Beaujoyeulx to Rameau.* Rev. and expanded ed. Portland: Amadeus Press, 1997.

———. "The French Opera-Ballet in the Early 18th Century: Problems of Definition and Classification." *Journal of the American Musicological Society* 18, no. 2 (1965): 197–206.

———, ed. *De profundis: Grand Motet for Soloists, Chorus, Woodwinds, Strings, and Continuo,* by Michel Richard de Lalande. Early Musical Masterworks. Chapel Hill: University of North Carolina Press, 1980.

Apel, Willi. *The History of Keyboard Music to 1700.* Translated and revised by Hans Tischler. Bloomington: Indiana University Press, 1972.

———. *Italian Violin Music of the Seventeenth Century.* Translated by Thomas Binkley. Music—Scholarship and Performance. Bloomington: Indiana University Press, 1990; originally published as *Die Italienische violinmusik im 17. Jahrhundert.* Beihefte zum Archiv für Musikwissenschaft, vol. 21 (Wiesbaden: F. Steiner, 1983).

———, ed. *Collected Keyboard Works,* by Johann Adam Reincken. Corpus of Early Keyboard Music 16. N.p.: American Institute of Musicology, 1967.

————. *Original Compositions for Organ [by] Delphin Strunck and Peter Mohrhardt.* Corpus of Early Keyboard Music 23. N.p.: American Institute of Musicology, 1973.

Arkhiv Iugo-Zapadnoi Rossi (Archive of southwest Russia). Kiev: Komissiia dlia razbora drevnikh aktov, 1859–1914.

Arnold, Denis. *Monteverdi.* The Master Musicians Series. London: J. M. Dent, 1963.

Arnold, Denis, and Elsie Arnold. *The Oratorio in Venice.* Royal Musical Association Monographs, no. 2. London: Royal Musical Association, 1986.

Arnold, Franck Thomas. *The Art of Accompaniment from a Thorough-Bass: As Practised in the XVIIth and XVIIIth Centuries.* London: Oxford University Press, H. Milford, 1931.

Ashbee, Andrew. *The Harmonious Musick of John Jenkins.* 2 vols. [Surbiton, Surrey]: Toccata Press, 1992.

————. "John Jenkins's Fantasia-Suites for Treble, Two Basses and Organ." Parts 1 and 2. *Chelys* 1 (1969): 3–15; 2 (1970): 6–17.

Ashbee, Andrew, and Peter Holman, eds. *John Jenkins and His Time: Studies in English Consort Music.* Oxford: Clarendon Press, 1996.

Auld, Louis E. *The Lyric Art of Pierre Perrin, Founder of French Opera.* 3 vols. Musicological Studies, vol. 16. Henryville, Penn.: Institute of Medieval Music, 1986.

Bacheler, Daniel. *Selected Works for Lute.* Edited and transcribed by Martin Long. Music for the Lute, bk. 5. London: Oxford University Press, 1972.

Bailey, Candace, ed. *Late-Seventeenth-Century English Keyboard Music.* Recent Researches in the Music of the Baroque Era, vol. 81. Madison, Wis.: A-R Editions, 1997.

Banac, Ivo, and Frank E. Sysyn, eds. *Concepts of Nationhood in Early Modern Eastern Europe.* Harvard Ukrainian Studies, vol. 10, no. ¾. Cambridge: Ukrainian Research Institute, Harvard University, 1986.

Barndt-Webb, Miriam W. "Andreas Hofer: His Life and Music (1629–1684)." Ph.D. diss., University of Illinois, 1972.

Baron, John H., ed. *Spanish Art Song in the Seventeenth Century.* Translated, with commentary, by Daniel L. Heiple. Recent Researches in the Music of the Baroque Era, vol. 49. Madison, Wis.: A-R Editions, 1985.

Barwick, Steven. "Sacred Vocal Polyphony in Early Colonial Mexico." 2 vols. Ph.D. diss., Harvard University, 1949.

Bataille, Gabriel. *Airs de différents autheurs mis en tablature de luth.* Vol. 3. Paris: Ballard, 1911.

Beaujoyeulx, Baltasar de. *Le balet comique de la royne.* Translated by Carlos and Lander MacClintock. Music transcribed by Carol MacClintock. Musicological Studies and Documents 25. N.p.: American Institute of Musicology, 1971.

Becker, Danièle, ed. *Las obras humanas de Carlos Patiño.* Cuenca: Instituto de Música Religiosa de la Diputación Provincial de Cuenca, [1987].

Becker-Glauch, Irmgard. *Die Bedeutung der Musik für die Dresdener Hoffeste: Bis in die Zeit Augusts des Starken.* Musikwissenschaftliche Arbeiten, no. 6. Kassel: Bärenreiter, 1951.

Beckmann, Klaus, ed. *Sämtliche Orgelwerke,* by Franz Tunder. 4th ed. Wiesbaden: Breitkopf & Härtel, 1985.

————. *Sämtliche Orgelwerke,* by George Böhm. Wiesbaden: Breitkopf & Härtel, 1986.

Beeks, Graydon. "The Chandos Anthems and Te Deum of George Frideric Handel." Ph.D. diss., University of California, Berkeley, 1981.

————. "Handel and Music for the Earl of Carnarvon." In *Bach, Handel, Scarlatti: Tercentenary Essays,* edited by Peter Williams, pp. 1–20. Cambridge: Cambridge University Press, 1985.

Béhague, Gérard. *Music in Latin America: An Introduction.* Prentice Hall History of Music Series. Englewood Cliffs, N.J.: Prentice Hall, 1979.

Belonenko, A. S. "Pokazaniia arkhiereiskikh pevchikh XVII veka" (The testimony of the archiepiscopal singers in the 17th century). *Trudy otdela drevnerusskoi literatury* 36 (1981): 320–28.

Benevoli, Orazio. *Missa salisburgensis, 1628.* Edited by Laurence Feininger. [Salzburg: S. Pustet], 1969.

Bérenger, Jean. *A History of the Hapsburg Empire.* Translated by C. A. Simpson. Vol. 1, *1273–1700.* London: Longman, 1994.

Bermúdez, Egberto. *La Música en el arte colonial de Colombia.* 2d ed. Música americana. [Bogotá, Colombia]: Fundación de Música, 1994.

Bernhard, Christoph. *Geistliche Harmonien (1665).* Edited by Otto Drechsler and Martin Geck. Das Erbe Deutscher Musik, 1st ser., vol. 65. Kassel: Bärenreiter, 1972.

———. *Geistliche Konzerte und andere Werke.* Edited by Otto Drechsler. Das Erbe Deutscher Musik, 1st ser., vol. 90. Kassel: Bärenreiter, 1982.

Besard, Jean-Baptiste. *Thesaurus harmonicus.* Cologne: G. Greuenbruch, 1603. Reprint, Geneva: Minkoff, 1975.

Best, Terence. "Handel's Harpsichord Music: A Checklist." In *Music in Eighteenth-Century England: Essays in Memory of Charles Cudworth,* edited by Christopher Hogwood and Richard Luckett, with a foreword by Stanley Sadie, 171–87. Cambridge: Cambridge University Press, 1983.

Bezić, Jerko. "Glagolitic Chant." In *Croatia in the Early Middle Ages: A Cultural Survey,* edited by Ivan Supicic, translated by Nina Key-Antoljak and Kresimir Sidor, pp. 569–76. Croatia and Europe, vol. 1. London: Philip Wilson, 1999.

———. *Razvoj glagoljaškog pjevanja na zadarskom području.* Djela, Institut Jugoslavenske akademije znanosti i umjetnosti u Zadru, no. 5. Zadar: Jugoslavenska akademija znanosti i umjetnosti, 1973.

Bianchi, Lino, ed. *Gli oratorii di Alessandro Scarlatti a cura e studio di Lino Bianchi.* 5 vols. Rome: Edizioni de Santis, 1964–.

Bianconi, Lorenzo. *Music in the Seventeenth Century.* Translated by David Bryant. Cambridge: Cambridge University Press, 1987.

Bittinger, Werner, ed. *Schütz-Werke-Verzeichnis (SWV).* Small ed. Kassel: Bärenreiter, 1960.

Bjurström, Per. *Giacomo Torelli and Baroque Stage Design.* 2d rev. ed. Acta Universitatis Upsaliensis, Figura, n.s. 2. Stockholm: Almqvist & Wiksell, 1962.

Blankenburg, Walter. *Einführung in Bachs h-moll Messe mit vollständigem Text.* Kassel: Bärenreiter, 1950; reprint, 1973.

Blow, John. *Amphion Anglicus: A Work of Many Compositions for One, Two, Three and Four Voices with Several Accompagnements of Instrumental Musick, and a Thorow-Bass to Each Song Figur'd for an Organ, Harpsichord, or Theorboe-Lute.* London, 1700. Reprint, Ridgewood, N.J.: Gregg Press, 1965.

———. *Anthems.* Edited by Anthony Lewis, Harold Watkins Shaw, and Bruce Wood. 4 vols. Musica Britannica, vols. 7, 50, 64, and 79. London: Stainer and Bell, 1953–2002.

———. *Complete Organ Music.* Edited by Barry Cooper. Musica Britannica, vol. 69. London: Stainer and Bell, 1996.

———. *Ode on the Death of Mr. Henry Purcell: For Two Countertenors (Contraltos), Two Treble Recorders, and Harpsichord (Piano) with Violoncello ad. lib.* Edited by Walter Bergmann. London: Schott, [1962].

Blume, Friedrich. *Renaissance and Baroque Music: A Comprehensive Survey.* Translated by M. D. Herter Norton. New York: W. W. Norton & Co., [1967].

Blume, Friedrich, et al. *Protestant Church Music: A History.* New York: W. W. Norton & Co., 1974. Major portion originally published in German in Blume, *Geschichte der evangelischen Kirchenmusik* (Kassel: Bärenreiter, 1965).

Bond, Edward A., ed. *Russia at the Close of the Sixteenth Century, Comprising the Treatise "Of the Russe Common Wealth," by Dr. Giles Fletcher; and the Travels of Sir Jerome Horsey, Knt.* The Hakluyt Society, no. 20. London, 1856.

Bonini, Severo. *Discorsi e regole sopra la musica de Severo Bonini.* Edited by Leila Galleni Luisi. Instituta et monumenta, ser. 2: Instituta, no. 5. Cremona: Fondazione Claudio Monteverdi, 1975.

———. *Discorsi e regole: A Bilingual Edition.* Translated and Edited by Mary Ann Bonino. Provo, Utah: Brigham Young University Press, 1979.

Bonta, Stephen. "The Use of Instruments in the Ensemble Canzona and Sonata in Italy." *Recercare* 4 (1992): 23–43.

———. "The Uses of the *Sonata da Chiesa*." *Journal of the American Musicological Society* 22, no. 1 (1969): 54–84.

————, ed. *La cetra: Sonata a due, tre e Quattro stromenti, libro quattro, opus 10, 1673.* Vol. 2 of *The Instrumental Music of Giovanni Legrenzi.* Harvard Publications in Music, vol. 17. Cambridge: Harvard University Press, 1992.

————. *Sonate a due e tre, opus 2, 1655.* Vol. 1 of *The Instrumental Music of Giovanni Legrenzi.* Harvard Publications in Music, vol. 14. Cambridge: Harvard University Press, 1984.

Bontempi, Giovanni Andrea Angelini. *Il Paride.* Facsimile ed. Bologna: Forni Editore, n.d.

Bordas, Cristina, ed. *The Spanish Guitar.* New York: Metropolitan Museum of Modern Art, 1992.

Borges, Armindo. *Duarte Lobo (156?–1646): Studien zum Leben und Schaffen des portugiesischen Komponisten.* Kölner Beiträge zur Musikforschung, vol. 132. Regensburg: Gustav Bosse Verlag, 1986.

Boyd, Malcolm. *Bach: The Brandenburg Concertos.* Cambridge Music Handbooks. New York: Cambridge University Press, 1993.

————. *Domenico Scarlatti: Master of Music.* London: Weidenfeld & Nicolson, 1986.

Boyd, Malcolm, and Juan José Carreras, eds. *Music in Spain during the Eighteenth Century.* Cambridge: Cambridge University Press, 1998.

Brade, William. *Newe ausserlesene liebliche Branden, Intraden, Mascharaden, Balleten, All'manden, Couranten, Volten, Auffzüge, und Frembde Täntze, 1617.* Edited by Bernard Thomas. 3 vols. London: Musica Rara, 1974.

Bradshaw, Murray C. "Cavalieri and Early Monody." *Journal of Musicology* 9, no. 2 (1991): 238–53.

————, ed. *Emilio De' Cavalieri: The Lamentations and Responsories of 1599 and 1600 (Biblioteca Vallicelliana MS o 31).* Miscellanea 5: Early Sacred Monody, vol. 3. Neuhausen-Stuttgart: American Institute of Musicology, Hänssler-Verlag, 1990.

Brasil, Hebe Machado. *A Música na cidade de Salvador, 1549–1900: Complemento da História das artes na ciadade do Salvador.* Evolução história ca cidade do Salvador 4a. Salvador: Prefeitura Municipal, 1969.

Brazhnikov, M. V. *Fedor Krest'ianin: Stikhiry.* Pamiatniki russkogo muzykal'nogo iskusstva 3. Moscow: Muzyka, 1974.

————. *Drevnerusskaia teoriia muzyki: Po rukopis. materialam XV–XVII vv.* (Early Russian music theory: According to 15–17th century manuscript materials). Leningrad: Muzyka, 1972.

Breig, Werner. *Die Orgelwerke von Heinrich Scheidemann.* Beihefte zum Archiv für Musikwissenschaft, vol. 3. Wiesbaden: F. Steiner, 1967.

————, ed. *Einzelne Psalmen,* by Heinrich Schütz. 2 vols. Neue Ausgabe sämtliche Werke, vols. 27–28. Kassel: Bärenreiter, 1970–1971.

————. *Orgelwerke,* by Heinrich Scheidemann. 3 vols. Kassel: Bärenreiter, [1970–1971].

Breko, Hana. "Music and Religious Orders in Dalmatia in the 17th Century." *Musica e storia* 8, no. 2 (2000): 455–76.

Brito, Manuel Carlos. *Estudos de História da Música em Portugal.* Imprensa universitária, no. 78. Lisbon: Editorial Estampa, 1989.

————. *Opera in Portugal in the Eighteenth Century.* Cambridge: Cambridge University Press, 1989.

Brito, Manuel Carlos, and Luisa Cymbron. *História da Música portugesa.* Lisbon: Universidade Aberta, 1992.

Brown, David. *Thomas Weelkes: A Biographical and Critical Study.* New York: F. A. Praeger, [1969].

Brown, Howard Mayer. *Music in the Renaissance.* Prentice Hall History of Music Series. Englewood Cliffs, N.J.: Prentice Hall, 1976.

Brunold, Paul, ed. *Pièces de clavecin de Louis Couperin.* New rev. ed. Edited by Davitt Moroney. Monaco: Editions de l'oiseau-lyre, 1985.

Brunold, Paul, and André Tessier, eds. *Oeuvres complètes de Chambonnières,* by Jacques Champion de Chambonnières. Les maitres français du clavecin. Paris: Editions M. Senart, 1925. Reprint, with an English translation and new preface by Denise Restout, New York: Broude Brothers, 1967.

Bryant, David. "The *cori spezzati* of St. Mark's: Myth and Reality." *Early Music History* (Cambridge) 1 (1981): 165–86.

Buck, Sir Percy Carter, and Edmund Horace Fellowes, eds. *Tudor Church Music.* 10 vols. London: Oxford University Press, 1922–1929.

Buelow, George J. "A Bach Borrowing by Gluck: Another Frontier." In *Eighteenth-Century Music in Theory and Practice: Essays in Honor of Alfred Mann*, edited by Alfred Mann and Mary Ann Parker, pp. 187–203. Stuyvesant, N.Y.: Pendragon Press, 1994.

———. "Die schöne und getreue Ariadne (Hamburg 1691): A lost opera by J. G. Conradi Rediscovered." *Acta Musicologica* 44, no. 1 (1972): 108–21.

———. "Handel's Borrowing Techniques: Some Fundamental Questions Derived from a Study of *Agrippina* (Venice, 1709)." *Göttinger Händel Beiträge* 2 (1986): 105–28.

———. "A Schütz Reader: Documents of Performance Practice." *American Choral Review* 27, no. 4 (1985): 3–35.

———. *Thorough-Bass Accompaniment according to Johann David Heinichen.* Rev. ed. Lincoln: University of Nebraska Press, 1992.

Bujić, Bojan. "Cecchinijeve mise iz godine 1617" (Cecchini's Masses from 1617). *Arti musices* 1 (1969): 195–214.

———. "Pastorale o melodramma? Le traduzioni croate di 'Euridice' e 'Arianna' per le scene di Dubrovnik." *Musica e storia* 6, no. 2 (1998): 477–99.

———. "Patronage and Taste in Venetian Dalmatia: The Case of Tomaso Cecchino's *Amorosi concetti.*" *Revista de Musicologia* 16, no. 3 (1993): 1416–22.

———. "A 'Provincial' Musician and His Wider Circle: Some Aspects of Tomaso Cecchino's Secular Music." *Musica e storia* 8, no. 2 (2000): 391–415.

———, ed. *Osam sonata* (Eight sonatas), by Tomaso Cecchini. Zagreb: Muzicki informativni centar Koncertne direkcije Zagreb, 1984.

Bukofzer, Manfred F. *Music in the Baroque Era: From Monteverdi to Bach.* New York: W. W. Norton & Co., 1947.

Bull, John. *Keyboard Music.* Edited by John Steele, Francis Cameron, and Thurston Dart. 2d rev. ed. 2 vols. Musica Britannica, vols. 14, 19. London: Stainer and Bell, 1967–1970.

Burney, Charles. *A General History of Music: From the Earliest Ages to the Present Period.* Edited by Frank Mercer. 2 vols. London: G. T. Foulis, 1935. Originally printed in London for the author 1776–1789.

Burrows, David, ed. *Cantatas*, by Antonio Cesti. The Wellesley Edition, vol. 5, The Italian Cantata, no. 1. Wellesley, Mass.: Wellesley College, 1963.

Burrows, Donald. *Handel.* Master Musician Series. Oxford: Oxford University Press, 1994.

———. "Handel and Hanover." In *Bach, Handel, Scarlatti: Tercentenary Essays*, edited by Peter F. Williams, pp. 35–60. Cambridge: Cambridge University Press, 1985.

———. "Handel and the 1727 Coronation." *The Musical Times* 118, no. 1612 (1977): 469–73.

Burrows, Donald, and Martha J. Ronish. *A Catalogue of Handel's Musical Autographs.* Oxford: Clarendon Press, 1994.

Bushkovitch, Paul. "The Epiphany Ceremony of the Russian Court in the Sixteenth and Seventeenth Centuries." *Russian Review* 49, no. 1 (1990): 1–17.

Bussey, William M. *French and Italian Influences on the Zarzuela: 1700–1779.* Ann Arbor: UMI Research Press, 1982.

Butskaia, S. B. "Stefan Ivanovich Beliaev—gosudarev pevchii d'iak" (Stephan Ivanovich Beliaev, sovereign singer). *Pamiatniki Kul'tury: Novye Otkrytiia* (1992): 151–56.

Butt, John. *Bach: Mass in B Minor.* Cambridge Music Handbooks. Cambridge: Cambridge University Press, 1991.

Buxtehude, Dietrich. *The Collected Works.* Edited by Kerala J. Snyder. 9 vols. to date. New York: Broude Trust, 1987–.

Byrd, William. *Keyboard Music.* Transcribed and edited by Alan Brown. 2d rev. ed. 2 vols. Musica Britannica, vols. 27–28. London: Stainer and Bell, 1976–1985.

———. *My Ladye Nevells Booke.* Edited, with an introduction and notes, by Hilda Andrews, with a preface by Sir Richard Terry. London: J. Curwen & Sons, 1926.

Caballero, Carmelo Fernandéz-Rufete. *"Arded, corazón, arded": Tonos humanos del barroco en la península ibérica.* Música española del barroca, vol. 1. Valladolid: Las Edades del Hombre, 1997.

Caccini, Giulio. *L'Euridice composta in musica in stile rappresentativo.* Florence, 1600.

―――. *Le nuove musiche.* Edited by H. Wiley Hitchcock. Recent Researches in the Music of the Baroque Era, vol. 9. Madison, Wis.: A-R Editions, 1970. Originally printed in Florence, 1601.

―――. *Nuove musiche e nuova maniera di scriverle: (1614).* Edited by H. Wiley Hitchcock. Recent Researches in the Music of the Baroque Era, vol. 28. Madison, Wis.: A-R Editions, 1978. Originally printed in Florence, 1914.

Caluori, Eleanor. *The Cantatas of Luigi Rossi: Analysis and Thematic Index.* 2 vols. Studies in Musicology, no. 41. Ann Arbor: UMI Research Press, 1981.

Cambert, Robert. *Les peines et les plaisirs de l'amour.* Edition conforme au manuscrit de la Bibliotèque du Conservatoire de Musique. Chefs-d'œuvre classiques de l'opera français, vol. 3. Paris, [1882].

―――. *Pomone.* Edition conforme au manuscrit de la Bibliotèque du Conservatoire de Musique. Chefs-d'œuvre classiques de l'opera français, vol. 2. Paris, [1881].

Campra, André. *Motets à I, II, et III voix avec la basse continue, livre premier.* Facsimilé Jean-Marc Fuzeau, La musique française classique de 1650 à 1800. Courlay, France: Editions J. M. Fuzeau, 1986.

Cardoso, José Maria Pedrosa. "O canto litúrgico da Paixão em Portugal nos séculos XVI e XVII: Os passionários polifónicos de Guimarães e Coimbra." Doctoral diss., University of Coimbra, Faculdade de Letra, 1998.

Carissimi, Giacomo. *Cantate.* Edited by Lino Bianchi. Monumenti/Istituto italiano per la storia della musica 3, vol. I. Rome: Istituto italiano per la storia della musica, 1960.

―――. *Ionas: Historia Ionae.* Edited by Lino Bianchi. Monumenti/Istituto italiano per la storia della musica 3, vol. II. Rome: Istituto italiano per la storia della musica, 1989.

Carreras, Juan José. *La Música sacra española en el siglo XVIII.* Zaragoza, 1986.

Carter, Tim. *Jacopo Peri, 1561–1633: His Life and Works.* 2 vols. Outstanding Dissertations in Music from British Universities. New York: Garland, 1989.

―――. *Music in Late Renaissance & Early Baroque Italy.* Portland, Ore.: Amadeus Press, 1992.

Carver, Anthony F. *Cori spezzati.* 2 vols. Cambridge: Cambridge University Press, 1988.

Casares Rodico, Emilio, ed. *Diccionario de la música española y hispanoamericana.* 7 vols. [Madrid]: Sociedad General de Autores y Editores, 2000.

Casares Rodico, Emilio, et al., eds. *España en la música de Occidente: Actas del Congreso Internacional celebrado en Salamanca, 29 de octubre–5 de noviembre de 1985: "Año Europeo de la Música."* 2 vols. Madrid: Instituto Nacional de las Artes Escénicas y de la Música, Ministerio de Cultura, 1987.

Castagna, Paulo. "Fontes bibliográficas para a pesquisa da pratica musical no Brasil nos séculos XVI e XVII." Master's thesis, University of São Paulo, Escola de Comunicação e Artes, 1991.

―――. "O estilo antigo na prática musical religiosa paulista e mineira dos séculos XVIII e XIX." Doctoral diss., University of São Paulo, Faculdade de Filosofia, Letras e Ciências, 2000.

Cauchie, Maurice, et al., eds. *Œuvres complètes de François Couperin: Publiées par un groupe de musicologues sous la direction de Maurice Cauchie.* 12 vols. Monaco: Éditions de l'oiseau-lyre, 1933.

Cavallini, Ivano. *I due volti di Nettuno: Studi su teatro e musica a Venezia e in Dalmazia dal Cinquecento al Settecento.* Musica ragionata 7. Lucca: Libreria musicale italiana, 1994.

―――. "Il libro per musica nel litorale istriano tra cinquecento e seicento." In *Il libro nel bacino adriatico, secc. XV–XVIII,* edited by Sante Graciotti, pp. 99–110, Civiltà veneziana: Studi 44. Florence: L. S. Olschki, 1992.

―――. *Musica, cultura e spettacolo in Istria tra '500 e '600.* Studi di musica veneta 17. Florence: L. S. Olschki, 1990.

―――. "Quelques remarques sur la musique sacrée en Istrie au XVII s. et les premiers essais monodique de Gabriello Puliti." In *Musica Antiqua 8,* vol. I, pp. 233–247. Bydgoszcz: Filharmonia Pomorska im. Ignacego Paderewskiego, 1988.

―――, ed. *Il teatro musicale del Rinascimento e del Barocco tra Venezia, regione Giulia e Damalzia: Idée accademiche a confronto.* Trieste: Circolo della Cultura e delle Arti, 1991.

Cesti, Marc Antonio. *Il pomo d'oro.* Edited by Guido Adler. Prologue and Act 1, Denkmäler der Tonkunst in Österreich, Jg. III/2, vol. 6; Acts 2–5, Denkmäler der Tonkunst in Österreich, Jg. IV/2, vol. 9. Graz: Akademische Druck- u. Verlagsanstalt, 1959.

Chafe, Eric Thomas. *The Church Music of Heinrich Biber.* Studies in Musicology, no. 95. Ann Arbor: UMI Research Press, 1987.

Charpentier, Marc-Antoine. *Pestis Mediolanensis* (The Plague of Milan: Dramatic motet for soloists, double chorus, woodwinds, strings, and continuo). Edited by H. Wiley Hitchcock. Early Musical Masterworks. Chapel Hill: University of North Carolina Press, 1979.

Chase, Gilbert. *A Guide to the Music of Latin America.* 2d rev. and enl. ed. Washington, D.C.: Pan American Union and Library of Congress, 1962.

Churelichz, Lorenzo de. *Breve e succinto racconto del viaggio, solenne entrate, & ossequiosi vasallaggi: Essibiti alla gloriosa maestà dell'augustissimo imperatore Leopoldo, dall'ecclesi Stati . . . dell'inclite ducale provincie di Stiria, Carinthia, Carniola, Goricia, Trieste, & c. . . . Con l'appendice di tutti l'atti publici, e notabili, accaduti minutamente nelli omaggi, etc.* Vienna, 1661.

Claro, Samuel. *Antología de la música colonial en América del Sur.* Santiago de Chile: Ediciones de la Universidad de Chile, 1974.

Conceição, Roque da. *Livro de obras de órgão.* Transcribed and edited by Klaus Speer. Portugaliae musica, ser. A, 11. Lisbon: Calouste Gulbenkian Foundation, 1967.

Corelli, Arcangelo. *Werke ohne Opuszahl.* Edited by Hans Oesch with an introduction by Hans-Joachim Marx. Historische-kritische Gesamtausgabe der musikalischen Werke/Arcangelo Corelli, vol. 5. Cologne: A. Volk Verlag, 1976.

Cotarelo y Mori, Emilio. *Orígenes establecimiento de la opera en España hasta 1800.* Madrid: Revista de arch., bibl., y museos, 1917.

Couperin, François. *Neuf motets.* Edited by Phillipe Oboussier. Le Pupitre 45. Paris: Heugel, 1972.

Cowart, Georgia. *The Origins of Modern Musical Criticism: French and Italian Music, 1600–1750.* Studies in Musicology, no. 38. Ann Arbor: UMI Research Press, 1981.

Croce, Benedetto. *Storia della èta barocca in Italia: Pensiero-poesia e letteratura vita morale.* Scritti di storia letteraria e politica, no. 23. Bari: G. Laterza, 1929.

Crummey, Robert O. "Court Spectacles in Seventeenth-Century Russia: Illusion and Reality." In *Essays in Honor of A. A. Zimin,* edited by Daniel Clarke Waugh, pp. 130–60. Columbus, Ohio: Slavica, 1985.

Crussard, Claude. *Un musicien oublié: Marc-Antoine Charpentier, 1634–1704.* Paris: Librairie Floury, 1945.

Culley, Thomas D. *Jesuits and Music.* Vol. 1, *A Study of the Musicians Connected with the German College in Rome during the 17th Century and of Their Activities in Northern Europe.* Sources and Studies for the History of the Jesuits, vol. 2. Rome: Jesuit Historical Institute; St. Louis: St. Louis University, 1970–.

Cvetko, Dragotin. *Academia Philharmonicorum Labacensis.* Ljubljana: Cankarjeva zalozba, 1962.

———. "Contribution à la question sur l'année de la fondation de l'Academia Philharmonicorum Labacensis." In *Festschrift für Walter Wiora zum 30. Dezember 1996,* edited by Ludwig Finscher and Christoph-Hellmut Mahling, pp. 342–47. Kassel: Bärenreiter, 1967.

———. "Die Rolle der Musik bei dem Adel im Herzogtum Krain im 17. und zu Beginn des 18. Jahrhunderts." In *La musique et le rite sacre et profane II: Proceedings of the 13th Congress of the International Society of Musicology,* edited by Marc Honegger and Paul Prevost, pp. 533–41. Strasbourg: University of Strasbourg Press, 1986.

———. "Leges Academiae Phil-Harmonicorum Labaci metropoli Carnioliae adunatorum." *Acta Musicologica* 39, nos. 3–4 (1967): 106–15.

———. *Slovenska glasba v evropskem prostoru* (Slovene music in its European setting). Ljubljana: Slovenska matica, 1991.

———. "*Il Tamerlano* de Giuseppe Clemente Bonomi." In *Essays Presented to Egon Wellesz,* edited by Jack Westrup, pp. 108–13. Oxford: Clarendon Press, 1966.

————. "Ein unbekanntes *Inventarium musicalium* aus dem Jahre 1620." *Kirchenmusikalisches Jahrbuch* 42 (1958): 77–80.

————, ed. *Skladatelji Gallus, Plautzius, Dolar in njihovo delo* (The composers Gallus, Plautzius, Dolar and their works). Ljubljana: Slovenska matica, 1963.

D'Accone, Frank A., ed. *Gli quivoci nel sembiante: Critical Notes,* by Alessandro Scarlatti. Vol. 7 of *The Operas of Alessandro Scarlatti,* edited by Donald J. Grout. Harvard Publications in Music, vol. 12. Cambridge: Harvard University Press, 1982.

Dadelsen, Georg von. *Beiträge zur Chronologie der Werke Johann Sebastian Bachs.* Tübinger Bach-Studien, nos. 4–5. Trossingen: Hohner, 1958.

————. *Bermerkungen zur Handschrift Johann Sebastian Bachs, seiner Familie und seines Kreises.* Tübinger Bach-Studien, no. 1. Trossingen: Hohner, 1957.

Daniels, David Wilder. "Alessandro Stradella's Oratorio *San Giovanni Battista*: A Modern Edition and Commentary." Ph.D. diss., State University of Iowa, 1963.

Danilov, V. V. "Sborniki pesen XVII stoletiia—Richarda Dzhemsa i P. A. Kvashnina" (Seventeenth-century song collections of Richard James and P. A. Kvashnin). *Trudy otdela drevnerusskoi literatury* 2 (1935): 165–80.

Dart, Thurston, ed. *The English Madrigalists.* Rev. ed. London: Stainer and Bell, 1956–1988. Original edition published as *The English Madrigal,* edited by Edmund H. Fellowes, London: Stainer and Bell, 1913–1924.

————. *The Fitzwilliam Sonatas: From the Autograph Mss. in the Fitzwilliam Museum, Cambridge,* by George Frederic Handel. Music for Recorder (Schott). London: Schott, [1948].

Dart, Thurston, and William Coates, eds. *Jacobean Consort Music.* 2d rev. ed. Musica Britannica, vol. 9. London: Stainer and Bell, 1966.

David, Hans T. *J. S. Bach's "Musical Offering": History, Interpretation, and Analysis.* New York: G. Schirmer, [1945].

David, Hans T., and Arthur Mendel, eds. *The New Bach Reader: A Life of Johann Sebastian Bach in Letters and Documents.* New ed. Revised and enlarged by Christoph Wolff. New York: W. W. Norton & Co., 1998.

Davison, Archibald T., and Willi Apel. *Historical Anthology of Music.* 2 vols. Cambridge: Harvard University Press, 1946–1950.

Dean, Winton. *Handel and the Opera Seria.* The Ernest Bloch Lectures 1. Berkeley: University of California Press, 1969.

————. *Handel's Dramatic Oratorios and Masques.* London: Oxford University Press, 1959.

Dean, Winton, and J. Merrill Knapp. *Handel's Operas, 1704–1726.* Oxford: Clarendon Press, 1987.

Dedekind, Constantin Christia. *Die Aelbianische Musen-Lust.* Edited and introduced by Gary C. Thomas. Nachdrucke deutscher Literatur des 17. Jahrhunderts, vol. 47. Bern: Lang, 1991.

Demovič, Miho. *Musik und Musiker in der Republik Dubrovnik (Ragusa) vom Anfang des XI. Jahrhunderts bis zur Mitte des XVII. Jahrhunderts.* Kölner Beiträge zur Musikforschung, vol. 114. Regensburg: G. Bosse, 1981. Simultaneously published as *Glazba i glazbenici u Dubrovačkoj republici od polovine XVII. do prvog Desetljeca XIX. Stoljeća* (Music and musicians in the Republic of Dubrovnik from the beginning of the 17th to the first decade of the 19th century). Zagreb: Jugoslavenska akademija znanosti i umjetnosti, 1981; reprint, 1989.

Dent, Edward Joseph. *Alessandro Scarlatti: His Life and Works.* Rev. ed., with additions by Frank Walker. London: E. Arnold, 1960.

Derzhavina, O. A., Konstantin Nikolaevich Lomunov, and Andrei Nikolaevich Robinson, eds. *Ranniaia russkaia dramaturgiia.* 5 vols. Moscow: Nauka, 1972–1976.

De Sanctis, Mila, ed. *Domenico Zipoli: Itinerarii iberoamericani della musica italiana del settecento. Atti del Convegno Internazionale, Prato, 30 settembre–2 ottobre 1988.* Quaderni della Rivista italiana di musicologia 31. Florence: L. S. Olschki, 1994.

Deutsch, Otto Erich. *Handel, a Documentary Biography.* New York: W. W. Norton & Co., [1955].

Dimitz, August. *Geschichte Krains von der ältesten zeit bis auf das jahr 1813: Mit besonderer Rücksicht auf Culturentwicklung.* 4 vols. in 2 bks. Laibach: Kleinmayer & Bamberg, 1874–1876.

Diniz, Jaime C. *Músicos pernambucanos do passado*. 2 vols. to date. Recife: Universidade Federal de Pernambuco, 1969–.

Dirksen, Pieter. *The Keyboard Music of Jan Pieterszoon Sweelinck: Its Style, Significance and Influence*. Muziekhistorische monografieën 15. Utrecht: Koninklijke Vereniging voor Nederlandse Muziekgeschiedenis, 1997.

———, ed. *Sämtliche Werke für Clavier (Cembalo)* [Complete harpsichord music], by Heinrich Scheidemann. Wiesbaden: Breitkopf & Härtel, 2000.

Dixon, Graham. "Progressive Tendencies in the Roman Motet during the Early Seventeenth Century." *Acta Musicologica* 53, no. 1 (1981): 105–19.

Doderer, Gerhard. *Orgelmusik und Orgelbau in Portugal des 17. Jahrhunderts: Untersuchen an Hand des MS 964 der Biblioteca Pública de Braga*. Würzburger musikhistorische Beiträge, vol. 5. Tutzing: Hans Schneider, 1978.

———, ed. *Obras selectas para órgão: Ms. 964 da Biblioteca Publica de Braga*. Portugaliae musica, ser. A, 25. Lisbon: Calouste Gulbenkian Foundation, 1974.

Dolar, Janez Krstnik. *Balletti-Sonate*. Edited by Tomaž Faganel. Monumenta artis musicae Sloveniae, vol. 25. Ljubljana: Slovenska akademija znanosti in umetnosti, 1994.

———. *Missa sopra la bergamasca*. Edited by Tomaž Faganel. Monumenta artis musicae Sloveniae, vol. 22. Ljubljana: Slovenska akademija znanosti in umetnosti, 1992.

———. *Missa Viennensis*. Edited by Urož Lajovic. Monumenta artis musicae Sloveniae, vol. 29. Ljubljana: Slovenska akademija znanosti in umetnosti, 1996.

———. *Missa Villana*. Edited by Mirko Cuderman. Monumenta artis musicae Sloveniae, vol. 4. Ljubljana: Slovenska akademija znanosti in umetnosti, 1984.

———. *Psalmi = Psalms*. Edited by Tomaž Faganel. Monumenta artis musicae Sloveniae, vol. 23. Ljubljana: Slovenska akademija znanosti in umetnosti, 1993.

Dolskaya-Ackerly, Olga. "The Early Kant in Seventeenth-Century Russian Music." Ph.D. diss., University of Kansas, 1983.

———. "From Titov to Teplov: The Origins of the Russian Art Song." In *A Window to Russia: Papers from the V International Conference of the Study Group on Eighteenth-Century Russia, Gargnano, 1994*, edited by Maria Di Salvo and Lindsey Hughes, pp. 197–213. Rome: La Fenice, 1996.

———. "Vasilii Titov and the 'Moscow' Baroque." *Journal of the Royal Musical Association* 118, no. 2 (1993): 203–22.

———, ed. *Spiritual Songs in Seventeenth-Century Russia*. With an editorial note by Hans Rothe. Bausteine zur Slavischen Philologie und Kulturgeschichte, ser. B, new ser., vol. 4. Cologne: Böhlau, 1996.

———. *Vasily Titov and the Russian Baroque: Selected Choral Works*, by Vasilii Polikarpovich Titov. Monuments of Russian Sacred Music, ser. 13, vol. 1. Madison, Conn.: Musica Russica, 1995.

Doni, Giovanni Battista. *Annotazioni sopra il Compendio de' generi e de' modi della musica. Con due trattati, l'vno sopra i tuoni e modi veri, l'alto sopra i tuoni é armonie de gl' antichi. Et sette discorsi sopra le materie più principali della musica, ò concernenti alcuni instrumenti nuoui praticati dall' autore*. Rome: A. Fei, 1640.

Dryden, John. *Plays: Albion and Albanius, Don Sebastian, Amphitryon*. Edited by Earl Miner, George R. Guffey, and Franklin B. Zimmerman. Vol. 15 of *The Works of John Dryden*. Berkeley: University of California Press, 1976.

Du Caurroy, Eustache. *Missa pro defunctis quinque vocum*. Edited by Michel Sanvoisin, with an introduction by François Lesure. Le Pupitre 65. Paris: Heugel; Représentation exclusive pour le monde entire, Alphonse Leduc, 1983.

Duckles, Vincent. "The 'Curious' Art of John Wilson (1595–1674): An Introduction to His Songs and Lute Music." *Journal of the American Musicological Society* 7, no. 2 (1954): 93–112.

Dufourcq, Norbert, ed. *Oeuvres de clavecin*, by Nicolas Lebègue. Monaco: Editions de l'oiseau-lyre, 1956.

Dunn, Thomas D. "The Sonatas of Biagio Marini: Structure and Style." *Music Review* 36, no. 3 (1975): 161–79.

Dunning, Albert. *Pietro Antonio Locatelli: Der Virtuose und seine Welt*. 2 vols. Buren: F. Knuf, 1981.

Dunning, Albert, et al., eds. *Opera omnia*, by Pietro Antonio Locatelli. 8 vols. to date. London: Schott & Co., 1994–.

Duprat, Régis. *Garimpo musical*. Coleção Ensaios 8. São Paulo: Editora Novas Metas, 1985.

———. *Música na Sé de São Paulo colonial*. São Paulo: Sociedade Brasileira de Musicologia, Paulus, 1995.

———, ed. *Música sacra paulista*. São Paulo: Editora Arte e Ciência, 1999.

Dürr, Alfred. " 'Entfernet euch, ihr kalten Herzen': Möglichkeiten und Grenzen der Rekonstruktion einer Bach-Arie." *Die Musikforschung* 39, no. 1 (1986): 32–36.

———. *Die Kantaten von Johann Sebastian Bach*. 2 vols. DTV Wissenschaftliche Reihe 4080–81. Kassel: Bärenreiter, 1971.

———. "Zur Chronologie der Leipziger Vokalwerke J. S. Bachs." *Bach-Jahrbuch* 44 (1957): 5–162.

Dürr, Alfred, ed. *Matthäus-Passion = St. Matthew Passion, BWV 244*, by Johann Sebastian Bach. Neue Ausgabe sämtlicher Werke: Johann Sebastian Bach, ser. II, vol. 5. Kassel: Bärenreiter, 1972.

Einstein, Alfred. *The Italian Madrigal*. Translated by Alexander H. Krappe, Roger H. Sessions, and Oliver Strunk. 3 vols. Princeton: Princeton University Press, 1949.

Eisen, Walter, and Margret Eisen, eds. *Händel-Handbuch: Gleichzeitig Supplement zu Hallische Händel-Ausgabe (Kritische Gesamtausgabe)*. 5 vols. to date. Kassel: Bärenreiter, 1978–.

Elías, Josep. "Tocata de contras quinto tono." In *Orgelmusik des spanischen Barock*, edited by James Wyly. Liber Organi, vol. 11. Mainz: Schott, 1966.

Eslava, Hilarion, ed. *Lira sacro-hispaña: Gran colección de obras de música religiosa, compuesta por los mas acreditados maestros españoles, tanto antiguos como modernos*. 10 vols. Madrid: M. Salazar, [1869].

Esses, Maurice. *Dance and Instrumental Diferencias in Spain during the 17th and 18th Centuries*. 3 vols. Dance and Music Series, no. 2. Stuyvesant, N.Y.: Pendragon Press, 1991–1994.

Estensoro, Juan Carlos. *Música y sociedad coloniales: Lima, 1680–1830*. Colección de arena. Lima: Editorial Colmillo Blanco, 1990.

Estève, Pierre. *L'esprit des beaux-arts*. 2 vols. Paris: C. J. B. Bauche, 1753.

Esteves, João Rodrigues. *Obras selectas*. Transcribed and edited by Cremilde Rosado Fernandes and Gerhard Doderer. Portugaliae musica, ser. A, 33. Lisbon: Calouste Gulbenkian Foundation, 1980.

Eterovich, Francis H., and Christopher Spalatin, eds. *Croatia: Land, People, Culture*. 3 vols. Vols. 1–2, Toronto: University of Toronto Press, 1964–1970; reissued, 1976. Vol. 3, Chicago: University of Chicago Press, 1998.

Everett, Paul. *The Four Seasons and Other Concertos, Op. 8*. Cambridge Music Handbooks. Cambridge: Cambridge University Press, 1996.

Expert, Henry. *Florilège du concert vocal de la Renaissance*. Paris: A la Cité des livres, 1928.

Fabbri, Paolo. *Monteverdi*. Biblioteca di cultura musicale: Autori e opera. Turin: EDT/Musica, 1985.

Fanna, Antonio. *Antonio Vivaldi (1678–1741): Catalogo numerico-tematico delle opera strumentali*. Milan: Edizioni Ricordi, 1968.

Farnaby, Giles. *Giles and Richard Farnaby: Keyboard Works*. Transcribed and edited by Richard Marlow. 2d rev. ed. Musica Britannica, vol. 24. London: Stainer and Bell, 1974.

Federhofer, Hellmut. "Graz Court Musicians and Their Contributions to the *Parnassus musicus Ferdinandaeus* (1615)." *Musica disciplina* 9 (1955): 167–244.

———. *Musikpflege und Musiker am Grazer Habsburgerhof der Erzherzöge Karl und Ferdinand von Innerösterreich (1564–1619)*. Edition Schott 5519. Mainz: B. Schott's Söhne, 1967.

Fellerer, Karl G. *Das Palestrinastil und seine Bedeutung in der vokalen Kirchenmusik des achtzehnten Jahrhunderts: Ein Beitrag zur Geschichte der Kirchenmusik in Italien und Deutschland*. Augsburg: D. B. Filser Verlag, 1929.

Fellowes, Edmund Horace. *English Cathedral Music from Edward VI to Edward VII*. London: Methuen, 1941.

Fellowes, Edmund Horace, ed. *The English School of Lutenist Song-Writers.* Revised and edited by Thurston Dart as *English Lute-Songs.* London: Stainer & Bell, 1920.

Fiebig, Folkert. *Christoph Bernhard und der stile moderno: Untersuchung zu Leben u. Werk.* Hamburger Beiträge zur Musikwissenschaft, vol. 22. Hamburg: Verlag der Musikalienhandl. Wagner, 1980.

Findeizen, Nikolai. *Ocherki po istorii muzyki v Rossii.* 7 vols. Moscow: Gosudarstvennoe izdatel'stvo Muzsektor, 1928–1929. English translation by Miloš Velimirović forthcoming.

Fortune, Nigel. "A Handlist of Printed Italian Secular Monody Books, 1602–1635." *R. M. A. Research Chronicle,* no. 3 (1963): 27–50.

———. "Italian Secular Monody from 1600 to 1635: An Introductory Survey." *Musical Quarterly* 39, no. 2 (1953): 171–95.

———. "Italian Secular Song from 1600 to 1653: The Origins and Development of Accompanied Monody." Ph.D. diss., Cambridge University, 1954.

Francisque, Antoine. *Le trésor d'Orphée.* Paris, 1600. Reprint, Geneva: Minkoff, 1975.

Franklin, Don. Review of *Complete Church Music, I–II,* by Peter Dennison. *Journal of the American Musicological Society* 28, no. 1 (1975): 143–49.

Franklin, Don, ed. *Bach Studies.* Vol. 1. Cambridge: Cambridge University Press, 1989.

Frescobaldi, Girolamo. *Il primo libro di Toccate d' intavolatura di cembalo e organo, 1615–1637.* Edited by Etienne Darbellay. Vol. 2 of *Opere complete Girolamo Frescobaldi.* Monumenti musicali italiani, no. 4. Milan: Suvini-Zerboni, 1977.

———. *Il primo libro di capricci fatti sopra diversi soggetti e arie: 1624.* Edited by Etienne Darbellay. Vol. 4 of *Opere complete Girolamo Frescobaldi.* Monumenti musicali italiani, no. 8. Milan: Suvini-Zerboni, 1984.

Froberger, Johann Jakob. *Orgel- und Klavierwerke.* Edited by Guido Adler. 3 vols. Denkmäler der Tonkunst in Österreich, Jg. IV/1, vol. 8; Jg. VI/2, vol. 13; Jg. X/2, vol. 21. Vienna, 1897; 1899; 1901. Reprint, Graz: Akademische Druck- u. Verlagsanstalt, 1959.

Fryer, Peter. *Rhythms of Resistance: African Musical Heritage in Brazil.* [Middletown, Conn.]: Wesleyan University Press, 2000.

Fuller-Maitland, J. A., and W. Barclay Squire, eds. *The Fitzwilliam Virginal Book.* 2 vols. London and Leipzig: Breitkopf & Härtel, [1894–1899]. Reprint, New York: Dover Publications, [1963].

Fux, Johann Joseph. *Sämtliche Werke.* Ser. 6, vol. 1, *Werke für Tasteninstrumente.* Edited by Friedrich Wilhelm Riedel. Kassel: Bärenreiter, 1964.

Gabrieli, Andrea. *Concerti di Andrea, et di Gio: Gabrieli organisti della Sereniss. Sig. Di Venetia. Contenti musica di chiesa, madrigali, et altro, per voci, et stromenti musicali à 6, 7, 8, 10, 12, et 16. Novamente con ogni diligentia dati in luce.* Edited by David Bryant. 2 vols. Edizione nazionale delle opera di Andrea Gabrieli, no. 11. Milan: G. Ricordi, 1989.

Gallico, Claudio, ed. *Cento concerti ecclesiastici: Opera duodecima, 1602,* by Lodovico da Viadana. Monumenti musicali mantovani, vol. 1. Mantova: Istituto Carlo d'Arco per la Storia di Mantova, 1964–.

Gantar, Kajetan, ed. *Academia operosorum.* Ljubljana, 1994.

Gardner, Johann von. *Russian Church Singing.* Translated by Vladimir Morosan. 2 vols. Crestwood, N.Y.: St. Vladimir's Seminary Press, 1980–2000.

Gaultier, Denis. *La rhétorique des dieux, et autres pièces de luth.* Edited by André Tessier. 2 vols. Publications de la Société française de musicologie, 1st ser., vols. 6–7. Paris: E. Droz, 1932–1933.

Gerasimova-Persidskaia, Nina Aleksandrovna, ed. *Khorovi tvori* (Choral works), by Mykola Pavlovych Dylets'kyi. Kiev: Muzichna ukraina, 1981.

———. *Ukrains'ki partensni moteti pochatku XVIII stolitiia = Ukrainian Choral Motets of the Early 18th Century.* Kiev: Muzichna ukraina, 1991.

Gianturco, Carolyn. *Alessandro Stradella, 1632–1682: His Life and Music.* Oxford Monographs on Music. Oxford: Clarendon Press, 1994.

———, ed. *The Italian Cantata in the Seventeenth Century: Facsimiles of Manuscripts and Prints of Works of Leading Composers Including an Edition of the Poetic Texts.* 16 vols. New York: Garland, 1985–.

Gibbons, Orlando. *Consort Music.* Transcribed and edited by John Harper. Musica Britannica, vol. 48. London: Stainer and Bell, 1982.

———. *Keyboard Music.* Transcribed and edited by Gerald Hendrie. 2d rev. ed. Musica Britannica, vol. 20. London: Stainer and Bell, 1974.

———. *Verse Anthems.* Edited by David Wulstan. Early English Church Music, vol. 3. London: Stainer and Bell, 1964.

Gilbert, Kenneth, ed. *Œuvres complètes de François Couperin.* Rev. ed. 11 vols. to date. Monaco: Éditions de l'oiseau-lyre, 1980–.

———. *Pièces de clavecin,* by Jean-Henri D'Anglebert. 2 vols. Le Pupitre 54. Paris: Heugel, 1975.

Glahn, Henrik, and Søren Sørensen, eds. *Musikhåndskrifterne fra Clausholm,* by Jacob Praetorius. Copenhagen: W. Hansen Musik-Forlag, 1974.

Glixon, Beth. "Recitative in Seventeenth-Century Venetian Opera: Its Dramatic Function and Musical Language." Ph.D. diss., Rutgers University, 1985.

Glover, Jane. *Cavalli.* London: Batsford, 1978.

Goldschmidt, Hugo. *Studien zur Geschichte der italienischen Oper im 17. Jahrhundert.* Vol. 1. Leipzig: Breitkopf & Härtel, 1901.

Golub, Ivan. "Juraj Križanić's 'Asserta Musicalia' in Caramuel's Newly Discovered Autograph of 'Musica.'" *International Review of the Aesthetics and Sociology of Music* 9, no. 2 (1978): 219–78.

———. *Juraj Križanić, glazbeni teoretik 17. stoljeca* (Juraj Križanić, musical theorist of the 17th century). Zagreb: Jugoslavenska akademija znanosti i umjetnosti, 1981.

González Quiñones, Jaime, ed. *Villancicos y cantatas mexicanos del siglo XVIII.* Monumentos de la música mexicana, ser. 1, nos. 3–9. Mexico: Universidad Nacional Autónoma de México, Escuela Nacional de Música, 1990.

Gottron, Adam. "Gabriel Plautz, 1612–1641: Kapellmeister des Mainzer Erzbischofs Schweikard von Kronberg." *Kirchenmusikalisches Jahrbuch* 31–33 (1936–1938): 58.

———. *Mainzer Musikgeschichte von 1500 bis 1800.* Beiträge zur Geschichte der Stadt Mainz, vol. 18. Mainz: Auslieferung durch die Stadtbibliothek, 1959.

Grgur, Mekinica. *Dusevne peszne psalmi.* 2 vols. N.p., 1609–1611. Reprint, with a preface by Alojz Jembrih, 3 vols. Biblioteka Bibliografska izdanja i reprint, Zagreb: Krscanska sadasnjost, 1990.

Grosse, Hans, and Hans Rudolf Jung, eds. *Georg Philipp Telemann, Briefwechsel: Sämtliche erreichbare Briefe von und an Telemann.* Leipzig: VEB Deutscher Verlag für Musik, 1972.

Grout, Donald J. *Alessandro Scarlatti: An Introduction to His Operas.* Berkeley: University of California Press, 1979.

———, ed. *The Operas of Alessandro Scarlatti.* 9 vols. Harvard Publications in Music, vols. 6–13, 15. Cambridge: Harvard University Press, 1974–1985.

Grout, Donald J., and Hermine Weigel Williams. *A Short History of Opera.* 3d ed. New York: Columbia University Press, 1988.

Gudger, William D. "The Organ Concertos of G. F. Handel: A Study Based on the Primary Sources." Ph.D. diss., Yale University, 1973.

Gustafson, Bruce. *French Harpsichord Music of the 17th Century: A Thematic Catalog of the Sources with Commentary.* 3 vols. Studies in Musicology, no. 11. Ann Arbor: UMI Research Press, 1979.

Gutiérrez de Padilla, Juan. *Mirabilia testimonia tua, Deus in adiutorium meum intende, and Salve Regina: For 8 Voices.* Transcribed and edited by Ivan Moody. Mapa Mundi: Renaissance Performing Scores, ser. F, Mexican Church Music, no. 1. London: Vanderbeck & Imrie, 1989.

Haas, Robert Maria. *Die Musik des Barocks.* Handbuch der Musikwissenschaft, vol. 3. Wildpark-Potsdam: Akademische Verlagsgesellschaft Athenaion, 1928.

Hammerschmidt, Andreas. *Ausgewählte Werke.* Edited and critically revised by Hans Joachim Moser. Denkmäler deutscher Tonkunst, 1st ser., vol. 40. Wiesbaden: Breitkopf & Härtel, 1958. First edition edited by Hugo Leichtentritt.

———. *Diagoli, oder Gespräche einer gläubigen Seele mit Gott I: Für Vokalstimmen mit Instrumentalbegleitung.* Edited by A. W. Schmidt. Denkmäler der Tonkunst in Österreich, Jg. VIII/1, vol. 16. Graz: Akademische Druck- u. Verlagsanstalt, 1959.

———. *Weltlich Oden oder Liebesgesänge (Freiburg 1642 und 1643, Leipzig 1649).* Edited by Hans

Joachim Moser. *Das Erbe deutscher Musik*, vol. 43 = Abteilung Oper und Sologesang, vol. 5. Mainz: Schott's Söhne, 1962.

Hammond, Frederick. *Girolamo Frescobaldi*. Cambridge: Harvard University Press, 1983.

—————. *Music and Spectacle in Baroque Rome: Barberini Patronage under Urban VIII*. New Haven: Yale University Press, 1994.

Handel, George Frederic. *Werke: Ausgabe der Deutschen Händelgesellschaft*. Edited by Friedrich W. Chrysander. 94 vols.; vol. 49 not published. Leipzig: Breitkopf & Härtel (vols. 1–18); Hamburg: Friedrich W. Chrysander (remaining vols.), 1858–1894, 1902.

—————. *Water Music*. Hallische Händel-Ausgabe, ed. Hans Ferdinand Redlich, ser. 4, Instrumentalmusik, vol. 13. Kassel: Bärenreiter, 1962.

Hanley, Edwin. "Alessandro Scarlatti's Cantate da Camera: A Bibliographical Study." Ph.D. diss., Yale University, 1963.

Hanning, Barbara Russano. *Of Poetry and Music's Power: Humanism and the Creation of Opera*. Studies in Musicology, no. 13. Ann Arbor: UMI Research Press, 1980.

Harrán, Don, ed. *Salamone Rossi, Complete Works*. 13 vols. in 5 bks. Corpus mensurabilis musicae 100. Neuhausen: American Institute of Musicology, 1995.

Harris, C. David, ed. *The Collected Works for Keyboard*, by Johann Kaspar Kerll. 2 vols. The Art of Keyboard 2. New York: Broude Trust, 1995.

Harris, Ellen T. *Handel and the Pastoral Tradition*. London: Oxford University Press, 1980.

—————. *Henry Purcell's "Dido and Aeneas."* Oxford: Clarendon Press, 1987.

Hassler, Hans Leo. *Sämtliche Werke*. Edited by C. Russell Crosby, Jr. 13 vols. to date. Wiesbaden: Breitkopf & Härtel, 1961–.

Hawkins, Sir John. *General History of the Science and Practice of Music*. London, 1776.

Hayes, Maurice, ed. *Bernardo Paquini (1637–1710), Collected Works for Keyboard*. 7 vols. Corpus of Early Keyboard Music 5. N.p.: American Institute for Musicology, 1964–1968.

Heinichen, Johann David. *Der General-Bass in der Composition*. Dresden, 1728.

Herz, Gerhard, ed. *Cantata No. 4, Christ lag in Todesbanden: An Authoritative Score, Backgrounds, Analysis, Views and Comments*, by Johann Sebastian Bach. Norton Critical Scores. New York: W. W. Norton & Co., [1967].

Hill, John Walter. *The Life and Works of Francesco Maria Veracini*. Studies in Musicology, no. 3. Ann Arbor: UMI Research Press, 1979.

—————. "Oratory Music in Florence." Parts 1, "*Recitar cantando*: 1583–1655," 2, "At San Firenze in the Seventeenth and Eighteenth Centuries," and 3, "The Confraternities from 1655 to 1785." *Acta Musicologica* 51, no. 1 (1979): 108–36; no. 2 (1979): 246–67; 58, no. 1 (1986): 129–79.

Hitchcock, H. Wiley. "The Latin Oratorios of Marc-Antoine Charpentier." *Musical Quarterly* 41, no. 1 (1955): 41–65.

—————. *Marc-Antoine Charpentier*. Oxford Studies of Composers 23. Oxford: Oxford University Press, 1990.

—————, ed. *Les œuvres de Marc-Antoine Charpentier: Catalogue raisonné* (The works of Marc-Antoine Charpentier). La vie musicale en France sous les rois Bourbons. Paris: Picard, 1982.

Hobohm, Wolf. "Zum Stil einiger Jugendwerke Telemanns." In *Konferenzbericht der 3. Magdeburger Telemann-Festtage vom 22. bis 26. Juni 1969*, edited by Gunter Fleischhauer and Walther Siegmund-Schultze, pp. 161–72. 2 vols. Magdeburg: Rat der Stadt, 1969.

Höfler, Janez. *Glasbena umetnost pozne renesanse in baroka na Slovenskem* (Late Renaissance and Baroque music in Slovenia). Ljubljana: Partizanska knjiga, Znanstevni tisk, 1978.

—————. "Glasbeniki koprske stolnici v 17. in 18. stoletju" (Musicians in the cathedral of Koper in the 17th and 18th centuries). *Kronika* 16, no. 3 (1968): 140–44.

—————. "P. Johannes Baptista Dolar (um 1620–1673): Beiträge zu seiner Lebengeschichte." *Die Musikforschung* 25, no. 3 (1972): 310–14.

Hogwood, Christopher. *Handel*. London: Thames and Hudson, 1984.

Holman, Peter. *Four and Twenty Fiddlers: The Violin at the English Court, 1540–1690*. Oxford Monographs on Music. Oxford: Oxford University Press, 1993.

Howard, John Brooks. "The Latin Lutheran Mass of the Mid-Seventeenth Century: A Study of

Andreas Hammerschmidt's Missae (1663) and Lutheran Traditions of Mass Composition." 2 vols. Ph.D. diss., Bryn Mawr College, 1983.

Hudson, Barton, ed. *Bernardo Storace, Selva di varie compositioni d'intavolatura per cimbalo ed organo.* Corpus of Early Keyboard Music 7. N.p.: American Institute of Musicology, 1965.

Humfrey, Pelham. *The Complete Church Music.* Edited by Peter Dennison. 2 vols. Musica Britannica, vols. 34–35. London: Stainer and Bell, 1972.

Ignatov, V. I. *Russkie istoricheskie pesni: Khrestomatiia* (Russian historical songs: A reader). 2d ed. Moscow: Vysshaia shkola, 1985.

Igoshev, L. A. "Proiskhozhdenie grecheskogo rospeva (opyt analiza)" (The origins of Greek chant (an attempt at an analysis). *Pamiatniki Kul'tury: Novye Otkrytiia* (1992): 147–50.

Isherwood, Robert M. *Music in the Service of the King: France in the Seventeenth Century.* Ithaca: Cornell University, 1973.

The Italian Oratorio: 1650–1800. Edited and introduced by Joyce L. Johnson and Howard E. Smither. 31 vols. New York: Garland, 1986–.

Jenkins, John. *Consort Music of Four Parts.* Transcribed and edited by Andrew Ashbee. 2d rev. ed. Musica Britannica, vol. 26. London: Stainer and Bell, 1975.

———. *Consort Music of Six Parts.* Transcribed and edited by Donald Peart. Musica Britannica, vol. 39. London: Stainer and Bell, 1977.

———. *The Lyra Viol Consorts.* Edited by Frank Traficante. Recent Researches in the Music of the Baroque Era, vols. 67–68. Madison, Wis.: A-R Editions, 1992.

———. *Three-Part Fancy and Ayre Divisions: For 2 Trebles and a Bass to the Organ.* Edited by Robert Austin Warner. Wellesley Edition 10. Wellesley, Mass.: Wellesley College, 1966.

Jensen, Claudia R. "Music for the Tsar: A Preliminary Study of the Music of the Muscovite Court Theater." *Musical Quarterly* 79, no. 2 (1995): 368–401.

———. "Nikolai Diletskii's 'Grammatika' (Grammar) and the Musical Culture of Seventeenth-Century Moscow." Ph.D. diss., Princeton University, 1987.

———. "A Theoretical Work of Late Seventeenth-Century Muscovy: Nikolai Diletskii's *Grammatika* and the Earliest Circle of Fifths." *Journal of the American Musicological Society* 45, no. 2 (1992): 305–331.

Jensen, Claudia R., and John Powell. " 'A Mess of Russians Left Us but of Late': Diplomatic Blunder, Literary Satire, and the Muscovite Ambassador's 1668 Visit to Paris Theatres." *Theatre Research International* 24, no. 2 (1999): 131–44.

Jensen, Niels Martin. "Solo Sonata, Duo Sonata and Trio Sonata: Some Problems of Terminology and Genre in 17th-Century Italian Instrumental Music." In *Festskrift Jens Peter Larsen 1902–14 VI–1972,* edited by Nils Schiørring, Henrik Glahn, and Carsten E. Hatting, pp. 73–101. Studier udgivet af Musikvidenskabeligt Institut ved Københavns Universitet. Copenhagen: Wilhelm Hansen Musik-Forlag, 1972.

Joachim, Joseph, and Friedrich Chrysander, eds. *Les oeuvres de Arcangelo Corelli.* 5 vols. Augener's Edition, no. 4963. London: Augener, 1888–1891.

Johnson, Martha N. "A Critical Edition of Ignatio Donati's Magnificat Sexti Toni (Salmi Boscarecci, 1623): With Introduction and Background." D.M. document, Indiana University, 1986.

Johnson, Robert. *Complete Works for Solo Lute.* Edited and transcribed by Albert Sundermann. Music for the Lute, bk. 4. London: Oxford University Press, [1970?].

Jonckbloet, Willem Josef Andries, and J. P. N. Land, eds. *Musique et musiciens au XVIIᵉ siècle: Correspondance et oeuvre musicales de Constantin Huygens.* Leiden: E. J. Brill, 1882.

Jung, Hermann. *Die Pastorale: Studien zur Geschichte eines musikalischen Topos.* Bern: Franke, 1980.

Junkermann, Hilde H. "The Magnificats of Johann Stadlmayr." 2 vols. Ph.D. diss., Ohio State University, 1966.

———, ed. *Selected Magnificats,* by Johann Stadlmayr. Recent Researches in the Music of the Baroque Era, vol. 35. Madison, Wis.: A-R Editions, 1980.

Kann, Robert A. *A History of the Hapsburg Empire, 1526–1918.* Berkeley: University of California Press, 1977.

Karlinsky, Simon. *Russian Drama from its Beginnings to the Age of Pushkin.* Berkeley: University of California Press, 1985.

Karpiak, Robert. "Culture of the Keyboard in 18th-Century Russia." *Continuo* 22, no. 5 (1998): 5–8.

———. "Researching Early Keyboards in Russia." *Continuo* 20, no. 1 (1996): 2–6.

Karstädt, Georg. *Thematisch-systematisches Verzeichnis der musikalischen Werke von Dietrich Buxtehude: Buxtehude-Werke-Verzeichnis (BuxWV).* 2d ed. Wiesbaden: Breitkopf & Härtel, 1985.

Kašić, Bartol, and the Catholic Church. *Ritval Rimski: Istomaccen slovinski po Bartolomeu Kassichiu Popu Bogoslovçu od Druxbae Yesusovae Penitençiru Apostolskomu.* Rome: Iz Vteisteniçae Sfet: Skuppa od Razplodyenya S. Vierrae, 1640. Reprint, *Ritval Rimski: Po Bartolomeu Kassichiu od Druxbae Yesusovae,* edited by Vladimir Horvat, Posebna izdanja Zavoda za hrvatski jezik, no. 3 = Bibliofilska izdanja: Niz Reprinti 26, Zagreb: Krscanska sadasnjost, Zavod za hrvatski jezik Hrvatskog filoloskog instituta, 1993.

Kastner, Macario Santiago. *Carlos de Seixas.* [Coimbra]: Coimbra Editora, 1947.

———. *Contribución al estudio de la música española y portuguesa.* Lisbon: Editorial Ática, 1941.

———. *Três compositors lusitanos para instrumentos de tecla: António Carreira, Manuel Rodrigues Coelho, Pedro de Araújo = Drei lusitanische Komponisten für Tastaninstrumente: António Carreira, Manuel Rodrigues Coelho, Pedro de Araújo.* [Lisbon]: Calouste Gulbenkian Foundation, 1979.

Kaufmann, Henry W. "Music for a *Favola Pastorale* (1554)." In *A Musical Offering: Essays in Honor of Martin Bernstein,* edited by Edward H. Clinkscale and Claire Brook, pp. 163–82. New York: Pendragon Press, 1977.

Keldysh, Iurii V., O. E. Levasheva, and A. I. Kandinskii, eds. *Istoriia russkoi muzyki v desiati tomakh* (A history of Russian music in ten volumes). 10 vols. Moscow: Muzyka, 1983–.

Keller, Hermann, ed. *Orgelwerke,* by Vincent Lübeck. York: C. F. Peters, 1940.

Kerman, Joseph. *The Elizabethan Madrigal: A Comparative Study.* American Musicological Society: Studies and Documents, no. 4. [New York]: American Musicological Society; distributed by Galaxy Music Corp., [1962].

Kharlampovich, Konstantin Vasil'evich. *Malorossiiskoe vlianie na velikorusskuiu tserkovnuiu zhizn'* (Ukrainian influence on Russian church life). Kazan: M. A. Golubev, 1914. Reprint, edited by C. H. van Schooneveld, Slavistic printings and reprintings 119, The Hague: Mouton, 1968.

Kinkeldey, Otto. *Orgel und Klavier in der Musik des 16. Jahrhunderts.* Leipzig: Breitkopf & Härtel, 1910.

Kirkendale, Ursula. "Orgelspiel im Lateran und andere Erinnerungen an Händel. Ein unbeachteter Bericht in 'Voiage historique' von 1737." *Die Musikforschung* 41, no. 1 (1988): 1–9.

———. "The Ruspoli Documents on Handel." *Journal of the American Musicological Society* 20, no. 2 (1967): 222–73.

Kirkpatrick, Ralph. *Domenico Scarlatti.* Princeton: Princeton University Press, 1953.

Kirwan-Mott, Anne. *The Small-Scale Sacred Concertato in the Early Seventeenth Century.* 2 vols. Studies in British Musicology. Ann Arbor: UMI Research Press, 1981.

Kiss, Georges, ed. *Ausgewählte Werke für Orgel (Cembalo),* by Hans Leo Hassler. Mainz: Schott's Söhne, 1971.

Klein, Christine. *Dokumente zur Telemann-Rezeption, 1767 bis 1907.* Schriftenreihe zur mitteldeutschen Musikgeschichte, ser. 2, vol. 1. Oschersleben: Ziethen, 1998.

Klemenčič, Ivan, ed. *Glasbeni barok na Slovenskem in Evropska glasba: Zbornik referatov z mednarodnega simpozija 13. in 14. oktobra 1994 v Ljubljani* (Baroque music in Slovenia and European music: Proceedings from the International Symposium held in Ljubljana on October 13th and 14th, 1994). Ljubljana: Znanstvenoraziskovalni center SAZU, 1997.

Klemenčič, Matej, and Stanko Kokole. "Perception and Reception of the Italian Baroque Art in Ljubljana." In *Francesco Robba in beneško barocno kiparstvo v Ljubljani = Francesco Robba and the Highlights of Venetian Baroque Sculpture in Ljubljana,* pp. 12–14, 43–45. Ljubljana: Narodna galerija, 1998.

Klenz, William. *Giovanni Bononcini of Modena: A Chapter in Baroque Instrumental Music*. Durham, N.C.: Duke University Press, 1962.

Knüpler, Sebastian, Johann Schelle, and Johann Kuhnau. *Ausgewählte Kirchenkantaten*. Edited by Arnold Schering. Denkmäler deutscher Tonkunst, 1st ser., vols. 58–59. Leipzig: Breitkopf & Härtel, 1918.

Kobayashi, Yoshitake. "Zur Chronologie der Spätwerke Johann Sebastian Bachs: Kompositions- und Aufführungstätigkeit von 1736 bis 1750." *Bach-Jahrbuch* 74 (1988): 7–72.

Köchel, Ludwig Ritter von. *Die kaiserliche Hof-Musikkapelle in Wien von 1543 bis 1867: Nach urkundlichen Forschungen*. Vienna: Beck'sche Universitäts-Buchhandlung, 1869.

Kokole, Metoda. "Academia Philharmonicorum Labacensium: Zgledi, ustanovitev in delovanje" (Academia Philharmonicorum Labacensuim: Prospects, founding and activities). In *Historični seminar II*, edited by Oto Luthar and Vojislav Likar, pp. 205–22. Ljubljana: Znanstvenoraziskovalni center SAZU, 1997.

———. "The Baroque Musical Heritage of Slovenia." *The Consort* 51, no. 2 (1995): 91–102.

———. "The Compositions of Isaac Posch: Mediators between the German and Italian Musical Idioms." In *Relazioni musicali tra Italia e Germania nell'età barocca: Atti del VI Convegno internationale sulla musica italiana nei secoli XVII–XVIII = Deutsch-italienische Beziehungen in der Musik des Barock: Beiträge zum sechsten internationalen Symposium über die italienische Musik im 17.–18. Jahrhundert*, edited by Alberto Colzanti et al., pp. 85–120. Contributi musicologici del Centro Richerche dell'A.M.I.S., vol. 10. Como: A.M.I.S., 1997.

———. "Isaac Posch 'Crembsensis': Neue Angaben über die Jugend des Komponisten in Regensburg." *Die Musikforschung* 52, no. 3 (1999): 318–21.

———. *Isaac Posch, "Diditus eois hesperiisque plagis/Slavjen v deželah zore in zatona": Zgodnjebaročni skladatelj na Koroškem in Kranjskem* (Isaac Posch, "diditus eois hesperiisque plagis—Praised in the lands of dawn and sunset"). Ljubljana: Slovenska akademija znanosti i umetnosti, Znanstvenoraziskovalni Centar, 1999.

———. "Italian Operas in Ljubljana in the Seventeenth and Eighteenth Centuries." In *Il teatro musicale italiano nel Sacro Romano Impero nei secoli XVII e XVIII*, edited by Alberto Colzani et al., pp. 263–91. Como: A.M.I.S., 1999.

———. "Italijanske operne predstave pri Auerspergih sredi 17. stoletja: Drobtinica k slovenskemu glasbenemu zgodovinopisju" (Mid-seventeenth century Italian opera performance(s) in Count Auersperg's palace in Ljubljana: A few additions to the Slovenian music historiography). *Muzikološki zbornik* 35 (1999): 115–29.

———. "Plesna glasba zgodnjega 17. stoletja: Inštrumentalne suite Isaac Poscha" (Early-17th century music for dancing: Isaac Posch's instrumental suites). In *Zbornik ob jubileju Jožeta Sivca* (Essays in honor of Jože Sivec), edited by Jurij Snoj and Darja Frelih, pp. 87–104. Ljubljana: Slovenska muzikološko drustvo, 2000.

———. "Venetian Influence on the Production of Early-Baroque Monodic Motets in the Inner-Austrian Provinces." *Musica e storia* 8, no. 2 (2000): 477–507.

Koole, Arend Johannes Christiaan. *Leven en werken van Pietro Antonio Locatelli da Bergamo, 1695–1794* [i.e., 1764]: *"Italiaans musycqmeester tot Amsterdam."* Amsterdam: Jasponers, 1949.

Kos, Koraljka. "Style and Sociological Background of Croatian Renaissance Music." *International Review of the Aesthetics and Sociology of Music* 13, no. 1 (1982): 55–82.

———. "Volkstumliche Zuge in der Kirchenmusik Nordkroatiens im 17. und 18. Jahrhundert." In *Musica Antiqua Europae Orientalis*. Vol. 3, pp. 267–90. Bydgoszcz: Filharmonia Pomorska imienia Ignacego Paderewskiego, 1972.

Kos, Koraljka, Anton Šojat, and Vladimir Zagorac, eds. *Pavlinski zbornik: 1644*. 2 vols. Djela Hrvatske akademija znanosti i umjetnosti. Razred za filološke znanosti. Razred za glazbenu umjetnost i muzikologiju, vol. 71, nos. 1–2. Zagreb: Hrvatska akademija znanosti i umjetnosti, 1991.

Krieger, Adam. *Arien*. Edited by Alfred Heuss. Denkmäler deutscher Tonkunst, ser. 1, vol. 19. Leipzig: Breitkopf & Härtel, 1905.

Kubik, Reinhold. *Händels "Rinaldo": Geschichte, Werk, Wirkung*. Neuhausen-Stuttgart: Hänssler, 1982.

Kuhnau, Johann. *Klavierwerke*. Edited by Karl Päsler. Denkmäler deutscher Tonkunst, 1st ser., vol. 4. Leipzig: Breitkopf & Härtel, [1901].

Kurtzman, Jeffrey G. *Essays on the Monteverdi Mass and Vespers of 1610*. Rice University Studies, vol. 64, no. 4. Houston: William Marsh Rice University, 1978.

Küster, Konrad. "Zur Geschichte der Organistenfamilie Scheidemann." *Schütz-Jahrbuch* 21 (1999): 99–113.

La Gorce, Jérôme de, and Herbert Schneider, eds. *Jean-Baptiste Lully: Actes du colloque Saint-Germain-en-Laye, Heidelberg 1987*. Neue Heidelberger Studien zur Musikwissenschaft, vol. 18. Laaber: Laaber-Verlag, 1990.

Lahana, Martha Luby. "Novaia Nemetskaia Sloboda: Seventeenth Century Moscow's Foreign Suburb." Ph.D. diss., University of North Carolina at Chapel Hill, 1983.

Laird, Paul R. *Towards a History of the Spanish Villancico*. Detroit Monographs in Music/Studies in Music, no. 19. Warren, Mich.: Harmonie Park Press, 1997.

———. "The Villancico Repertory at San Lorenzo el Real del Escorial, ca. 1630–ca. 1715." 2 vols. Ph.D. diss., University of North Carolina at Chapel Hill, 1986.

La Laurencie, Lionel de, Adrienne Mairy, and G. Thibault. *Chansons au luth et airs de cour Français du XVIᵉ siècle*. Publications de la Société française de musicologie, 1st ser., vols. 4–5. Paris: Heugel, 1976.

Lang, Paul Henry. *George Frideric Handel*. New York: W. W. Norton & Co., 1966.

Lange, Francisco Curt. *História da Música nas irmandades de Vila Rica*. Vol. 1, *Freguesia de Nossa Senhora do Pilar de Ouro Preto*. Publicaçãoes do Archivo Público Mineiro, no. 2. Belo Horizonte: Arquivo Público Mineiro, 1979.

———. *La música eclesiástica en Córdoba durante la dominación hispánica*. Córdoba: Imprenta de la Universidad, 1956.

Launay, Denise. *Anthologie du motet Latin polyphonique en France (1609–1661)*. Publications de la Société française de musicologie, 1st ser., vol. 17. Paris: Heugel, 1963.

———. "Church Music in France 1630–60." In *Opera and Church Music, 1630–1750*, edited by Anthony Lewis and Nigel Fortune, pp. 414–37. New Oxford History of Music, vol. 5. London: Oxford University Press, 1975.

Lavrić, Ana. *Vloga ljubljanskega Škofa Tomaža Hrena v slovenski likovni umetnosti* (The role of Bishop Tomaša Hren of Ljubljana in the Slovenian fine arts). 2 vols. Dela / Slovenska akademija znanosti in umetnosti, Razred za zgodovinske in druzbene vede. Umetnostnozgodovinski inštitut Franceta Steleta = Opera / Academia Scientiarum et Artium Slovenica, Classis I, Historia et Sociologia 32 = Institutum Historiae Artium 1. Ljubljana: Slovenska akademija znanosti i umjetnosti, 1988.

Lawes, William. *Fantasia-Suites*. Transcribed and edited by David Pinto. Musica Britannica, vol. 60. London: Stainer and Bell, 1991.

———. *The Royall Consort*. Edited by David Pinto. New version. London: Fretwork, 1995.

———. *Trois masques à la cour de Charles Iᵉʳ d'Angleterre: The Triumph of Peace, The Triumphs of the Prince d'Amour, Britannia triumphans*. Edited by Murray Lefkowitz. Le choeur des muses. Paris: Editions du Centre National de la Recherche Scientifique, 1970.

Le Cerf de la Viéville, Jean Laurent. *Comparaison de la musique italienne et de la musique française*. Brussels, 1704–1706.

Lefkowitz, Murray. *William Lawes*. London: Routledge and K. Paul, [1960].

Legrenzi, Giovanni. *X Sonate da chiesa [from] Op. 4 [and] Op. 8*. Edited by Albert Seay. Le Pupitre 4. Paris: Heugel, [1968].

Le Huray, Peter. *Music and the Reformation in England, 1549–1660*. Studies in Church Music. New York: Oxford University Press, 1967. Reprint, Cambridge Studies in Music, Cambridge: Cambridge University Press, 1978.

Lessa, Elisa. "Os mosteiros beneditinos portugueses, século XVI a XIX, centros de ensino e prática musical." Doctoral diss., Universidade Nova de Lisboa, 1998.

Lester, Joel. *Bach's Works for Solo Violin: Style, Structure, Performance.* New York: Oxford University Press, 1999.

———. *Between Modes and Keys: German Theory, 1592–1802.* Harmonologia Series, no. 3. Stuyvesant, N.Y.: Pendragon Press, 1989.

Lesure, François. "Le recueil de ballets de Michel Henry (vers 1620)." In *Les fêtes de la Renaissance: Études reunites et présentées par Jean Jacquot.* Vol. 1, pp. 205–19. Collections le Chœur des muses. Paris: Éditions du Centre national de la recherche scientifique, 1956.

Libby, Dennis. "Interrelationships in Corelli." *Journal of the American Musicological Society* 26, no. 2 (1973): 263–87.

Locke, Matthew. *Anthems and Motets.* Edited by Peter Le Huray. Musica Britannica, vol. 38. London: Stainer and Bell, 1976.

———. *Chamber Music.* Transcribed and edited by Michael Tilmouth. 2 vols. Musica Britannica, vols. 31–32. London: Stainer and Bell, 1971–1972.

———. *Cupid and Death.* Edited by Edward J. Dent. 2d rev. ed. Musica Britannica, vol. 2. London: Stainer and Bell, 1965.

Lockwood, Lewis, ed. *Pope Marcellus Mass: An Authoritative Score, Backgrounds and Sources, History and Analysis, Views and Comments,* by Giovanni Pierluigi da Palestrina. Norton Critical Scores. New York: Norton, 1975.

Lolo, Begoña. *La Música en la Real Capilla de Madrid: José de Torres y Martínez Bravo.* Colección de estudios 32. [Madrid]: Ediciones de la Universidad Autónoma de Madrid, 1988.

Longworth, Philip. *Alexis: Tsar of all the Russians.* New York: Franklin Watts, 1984.

López-Calo, José. *Historia de la música española.* Vol. 3, *Siglo XVII.* Alianza música 3. Madrid: Alianza Editorial, 1983.

Lovro, Županović, ed. *Cithara octochorda.* 2 vols. Zagreb, 1998.

Luisi, Francesco, ed. *Cantatas,* by Luigi Rossi. The Italian Cantata in the Seventeenth Century, vol. 1. New York: Garland, 1986.

Lukačić, Ivan. *Odabrani moteti (duhovni koncerti) iz djela "Sacrae cantiones" (1620).* Edited by Dragan Plamenac. Zagreb: Hrvatskog glazbenog zavoda, 1935. Reprint, 1975.

———. *Sacrae cantiones singulis, binis, ternis, quaternis, quinisque, vocibus concinendae.* Venice: Gardani, 1620. Reprint, edited by Ennio Stipčević, Hereditas musicae 1, Zagreb: Izdavaci, Muzicki informativni centar, 1998.

———. *Sacrae cantiones, Venezia 1620: Motteti a 1–5 voci.* Edited by Ennio Stipčević and Ludovico Bertazzo. Corpus musicum franciscanum. Padova: Messaggero, 1986.

Luk'ianenko, V. I., and M. A. Alekseeva, eds. *Bukvar': Sostavlen Karionom Istominym gravirovan Leontiem Buninym otpechatan v 1694 godu v Moskve* (The alphabet compiled by Karion Istomin and engraved by Leontii Bunin, printed in 1694 in Moscow). Leningrad: Avrora, 1981.

Magnificat: A Capella Works by Josquin, Palestrina, Titov, Victoria, and others. Chanticleer. Joseph Jennings. Teldec compact disc 8573–81829–2.

Mainwaring, John. *Memoirs of the Life of the Late George Frederic Handel: To Which is Added, a Catalogue of His Works, and Observations upon Them.* London: R. and J. Dodsley, 1760. Reprint, [Amsterdam: F.A.M. Knuf]: 1964.

Malcolm, James P. *Anecdotes of the Manners and Customs of London during the Eighteenth Century.* London, 1808.

Maniates, Maria Rika. *Mannerism in Italian Music and Culture, 1530–1630.* Chapel Hill: University of North Carolina Press, 1979.

Mann, Alfred, ed. *Tercentenary Händel Studies.* New York: American Choral Foundation, 1985; published as a special issue of the *American Choral Review* 27, nos. 2–3 (1985).

Mantica, Francesco, ed. *Prime fioriture melodrama italiano: Collezione diretta da Francesco Mantica.* 2 vols. Rome: Casa Editrice Claudio Monteverdi, 1912.

Mariz, Vasco. *História da música no Brasil.* 2d rev. ed. Coleção Retratos do Brasil, vol. 150. Rio de Janeiro: Civilizção Brasileira, 1983.

Marshall, Robert Lewis. "Bach the Progressive: Observations on His Later Works." *The Musical Quarterly* 62, no. 3 (1976): 313–57; reprinted in *The Music of Johann Sebastian Bach: The Sources, the Style, the Significance.* New York: Schirmer Books, 1989.

———. *The Music of Johann Sebastian Bach: The Sources, the Style, the Significance.* New York: Schirmer Books, 1989.

Martín Moreno, Antonio. *Historia de la música española.* Vol. 4, *Siglo XVIII.* Alianza música 4. Madrid: Alianza Editorial, 1985.

———. *La música en la corte española del siglo XVIII.* Zaragoza, 1986.

———. *El Padre Feijóo y las ideologies musicales del siglo XVIII en España.* Instituto de Estudios Orensanos Padre Feijóo 7. Orense: Instituto de Estudios Orensanos Padre Feijóo, 1976.

Marx, Hans-Joachim. *Arcangelo Corelli: Historische-kritische Gesamtausgabe der musikalischen Werke.* Supplementary volume, *Die Überlieferung der Werke Arcangelo Corellis: Catalogue raisonné.* Cologne: A. Volk Verlag, 1980.

Massa, Isaac. *A Short History of the Beginnings and Origins of These Present Wars in Moscow under the Reign of Various Sovereigns down to the Year 1610.* Translated and introduced by G. Edward Orchard. Toronto: University of Toronto Press, 1982.

Massenkeil, Günther. "Die oratorische Kunst in den lateinischen Historien und Oratorien Giacomo Carissimis." Ph.D. diss., Johannes Gutenberg–Universität zu Mainz, 1952.

———. "Die Wiederholungsfiguren in den Oratorien Giacomo Carissimis." *Archiv für Musikwissenschaft* 13, no. 1 (1956): 42–60.

Mathiesen, Thomas J. *Ancient Greek Music Theory: A Catalogue Raisonné of Manuscripts.* Réportoire international des sources musicales, ser. b, vol. 11. Munich: G. Henle Verlag, 1988.

Matthaei, Karl, ed. *Ausgewählte Orgelwerke: Für den praktischen Gebrauch,* by Johann Pachelbel. Vol. 1, *Praeludium, Fantasia, 5 Toccaten, 3 Fugen, Ricercar und Ciaconen in d und f.* 2d ed. Kassel: Bärenreiter, 1931.

Mattheson, Johann. *Critica musica.* 8 pts. Hamburg, 1722–1725.

———. *Grosse General-Bass-Schule, oder: Der exemplarischen Organisten-Probe.* 2d ed. Hamburg: J. C. Kissner, 1731.

———. *Grundlage einer Ehren-Pforte: Woran der tüchtigsten Capellmeister, Componisten, Musikgelehrten, Tonkünstler, &c. Leben, Werke, Verdienste, &c. erscheinen sollen.* Edited by Max Schneider. New ed. Berlin: Kommissionsverlag von L. Liepmannssohn. Reprint, Kassel: Bärenreiter, 1969. Original edition published in Hamburg, 1740.

———. *Das neu-eröffnete Orchestre, oder, Universelle und Gründliche Anleitung wie ein gallant homme einen vollkommenen Begriff von . . . der edl en Music erlangen . . . möge. . . .* 3 vols. Hamburg, 1713–1721.

———. *Der vollkommene Capellmeister.* Hamburg, 1739.

McGowan, Margaret M. *L'art du ballet de cour en France, 1581–1643.* Collection le Chœur des muses. Paris: Éditions du Centre national de la recherche scientifique, 1963.

Meder, Jagoda. *Orgulje u Hrvatskoj.* Photographs by Nino Vranic, with a summary in English and German. Biblioteka Likovne monografije. Zagreb: Globus, 1992.

Melamed, Daniel R. "Probleme zu Chronologie, Stil und Zweck der Motetten Johann Sebastian Bachs." In *Johann Sebastian Bach: Schaffenskonzeption, Werkidee, Textbezug: Bericht über die Wissenschaftliche Konferenz zum VI. Internationalen Bachfest der DDR in Verbindung mit dem 64. Bachfest der Neuen Bachgesellschaft, Leipzig 11.–12. September 1989,* edited by Andreas Glöckner et al., pp. 277–83. Beiträge zur Bach-Forschung, nos. 9–10. Leipzig: National Forschungs-und Gedenkstätten Johann Sebastian Bach, 1991.

Melamed, Daniel R., and Reginald L. Sanders. "Zum Text und Kontext der 'Keiser'- Markuspassion." *Bach-Jahrbuch* 85 (1999): 35–50.

Melgás, Diogo Dias. *Opera omnia.* Transcribed and edited by José Augusto Alegria. Portugaliae musica, ser. A, 32. Lisbon: Calouste Gulbenkian Foundation, 1978.

Mellers, Wilfrid Howard. *François Couperin and the French Classical Tradition.* New rev. ed. London: Faber and Faber, 1987.

Melli, Domenico. *Musiche . . . composte sopra alcuni madrigali di diversi. Per cantare enl chitarrone, clavicembalo & altri instromenti.* Venice, 1602.

Mendel, Arthur, ed. *Johannes-Passion = St. John Passion, BWV 245,* by Johann Sebastian Bach. Neue Ausgabe sämtlicher Werke: Johann Sebastian Bach, ser. II, vol. 4. Kassel: Bärenreiter, 1975.

Menke, Werner, ed. *Thematisches Verzeichnis der Vokalwerke von Georg Philipp Telemann.* 2 vols. Frankfurt am Main: V. Klostermann, 1982–1983.

Mersenne, Marin. *Harmonie universelle.* Paris, 1636–1637.

[Miege, Guy]. *A Relation of Three Embassies from His Sacred Majestie Charles II to the Great Duke of Muscovie, the King of Sweden, and the King of Denmark.* London: J. Starkey, 1669.

Migliorini, Bruno. *Profili di parole.* Florence: F. Le Monnier, 1968.

Millner, Fredrick L. *The Operas of Johann Adolf Hasse.* Studies in Musicology, no. 2. Ann Arbor: UMI Research Press, 1979.

Mompellio, Federico. *Lodovico Viadana: Musicista fra due secoli, XVI–XVII.* Historiae Musicae Cultores: Biblioteca, no. 23. Florence: L. S. Olschki, 1967.

Monosoff, Sonya. "Violinistic Challenges in the Sonatas Op. 5 of Arcangelo Corelli." In *Studi corelliani IV,* edited by Pierluigi Petrobelli and Gloria Staffieri, pp. 155–64. Florence: Olschki, 1990.

Monteverdi, Claudio. *The Letters of Claudio Monteverdi.* Translated and introduced by Denis Stevens. Cambridge: Cambridge University Press, 1980.

Morell, Martin. "New Evidence for the Biographies of Andrea and Giovanni Gabrieli." *Early Music History* (Cambridge) 3 (1983): 101–22.

Morosan, Vladimir. *Choral Performance in Pre-Revolutionary Russia.* Russian Music Studies 17. Ann Arbor: UMI Research Press, 1986.

———. "*Penie* and *Musikiia*: Aesthetic Changes in Russian Liturgical Singing during the 17th Century." *St. Vladimir's Theological Quarterly* 23, nos. 3–4 (1979): 149–79.

———, ed. *One Thousand Years of Russian Church Music, 988–1988.* Monuments of Russian Sacred Music, ser. 1, vol. 1. Washington, D.C.: Musica Russica, 1991.

Moser, Hans Joachim. *The German Solo Song and the Ballad.* Anthology of Music: A Collection of Complete Musical Examples Illustrating the History of Music, no. 14. Cologne: Arno Volk Verlag, 1958.

———. *Heinrich Schütz: His Life and Work.* Translated from the 2d rev. ed. by Carl F. Pfatteicher. St. Louis: Concordia Pub. House, 1959.

Mota, Jaime, Fernando Bessa Valente, and Jorge Alexandre Costa, eds. *La Giuditta,* by Francisco António de Almeida. Oporto: Fermata, 2000.

Murata, Margaret. *Operas for the Papal Court, 1631–1668.* Studies in Musicology, no. 39. Ann Arbor: UMI Research Press, 1981.

Nawrot, Piotr, ed. *Música de vísperas en las reducciones de Chiquitos-Bolivia, 1691–1767: Obras de Domenico Zipoli y maestros jesuitas e indigenas anónimos.* [Bolivia]: Archivo Musical Chiquitos Concepción, 1994–.

———. *San Francisco Xavier: Drama musical (opera edificante) para 2 voces, 2 violines, bajo y continuo (orquesta complementaria ad libitum).* Monuménta música in Chiquitórum reductiónibus Bolíviae. Drama musicum. Indígenas y cultura musical de las reducciones Jesuíticas, vol. 3. Cochabamba: Editorial Verbo Divino, 2000.

Nery, Rui Vieira. "The Music Manuscripts in the Library of King D. João IV (1604–1656): A Study of Iberian Music Repertoire in the Sixteenth and Seventeenth Centuries." Ph.D. diss., University of Texas at Austin, 1990.

———. "New Sources for the Study of the Portuguese Seventeenth-Century Consort Music." *Journal of the Viola da Gamba Society of America* 22 (1985): 9–28.

———, ed. *A música no Brasil colonial.* Lisbon: Calouste Gulbenkian Foundation, 2001.

Nery, Rui Vieira, and Paulo Ferreira de Castro. *História da música.* Sínteses da cultura portuguesa. Lisbon: Comissariado para a Europália 91, [1991].

The Neumeister Collection of Chorale Preludes from the Bach Circle: Yale University Manuscript LM 4708. With an introduction by Christoph Wolff. New Haven: Yale University Press, 1986.

Newman, Joel. Communication. *Journal of the American Musicological Society* 14, no. 3 (1961): 418–19.

Newman, William S. *The Sonata in the Baroque Era.* Chapel Hill: University of North Carolina Press, 1959.

Novak, Slobodan Prosperov, and Mirko Kratofil. *Povijest hrvatske književnosti* (History of Croatian literature). 3 vols. Biblioteka Antibarbarus, Biblioteka Historia. Zagreb: Izdanja Antibarbarus, [1996–1997].

Novotny, Alexander, and Berthold Sutter, eds. *Innerösterreich, 1564–1619.* Joannea, vol. 3. Graz: Universitötsbuchdruckerei styria, [1967].

Okenfuss, Max J. *The Rise and Fall of Latin Humanism in Early-Modern Russia: Pagan Authors, Ukrainians, and the Resiliency of Muscovy.* Brill's Studies in Intellectual History, vol. 64. Leiden: E. J. Brill, 1995.

———, ed. and trans. *The Travel Diary of Peter Tolstoi: A Muscovite in Early Modern Europe.* DeKalb: Northern Illinois University Press, 1987.

Olearius, Adam. *The Travels of Olearius in Seventeenth-Century Russia.* Translated and edited by Samuel H. Baron. Stanford, Calif.: Stanford University Press, 1967.

———. *Vermehrte Newe Beschreibung der Muscowitischen und Persischen Reyse.* Edited by Dieter Lohmeier. Deutsche Neudruck. Reihe: Barock 21. Tübingen: Max Niemeyer Verlag, 1971.

Osthoff, Helmuth. *Adam Krieger (1634–1666): Neue Beiträge zur Geschichte des deutschen Liedes im 17. Jahrhundert.* Leipzig: Breitkopf & Härtel, 1929. Reprint, with addenda and revisions by the author, Wiesbaden: Breitkopf & Härtel, 1970.

Pachelbel, Johann. *94 Kompositionen: Fugen über das Magnificat für Orgel oder Klavier.* Edited by Hugo Botstiber and Max Seiffert. Denkmäler der Tonkunst in Österreich, Jg. VIII/2, vol. 17. Graz: Akademische Druck- u. Verlagsanstalt, 1959.

Pacquier, Alain. *Les chemins du baroque dans le nouveau monde: De la terre de feu à l'embouchure du Saint-Laurent.* Les Chemins de la musique. [Paris]: Fayard, 1996.

Pagano, Roberto. *Scarlatti: Alessandro e Domenico, due vite in una.* Musica e storia. Milan: Arnoldo Mondadore, 1985.

Pagano, Roberto, Giancarlo Rostirolla, and Lino Bianchi. *Alessandro Scarlatti: Catalogo generale delle opera a cura di Giancarlo Rostirolla.* Collana di monografie per servire alla storia della musica italiana. Turin: ERI, 1972.

Pajerski, Fred M. "Marco Uccellini and His Music." 2 vols. Ph.D. diss., New York University, 1979.

Palisca, Claude V. "Aria in Early Opera." In *Festa musicologica: Essays in Honor of George J. Buelow,* edited by Thomas J. Mathiesen and Benito V. Rivera, pp. 257–69. Festschrift Series, no. 14. Stuyvesant, N.Y.: Pendragon Press, 1995.

———. *Baroque Music.* 3d ed. Prentice Hall History of Music Series. Englewood Cliffs, N.J.: Prentice Hall, 1991.

———. "The Beginnings of Baroque Music: Its Roots in Sixteenth-Century Theory and Polemics." Ph.D. diss., Harvard University, 1953.

———. *The Florentine Camerata: Documentary Studies and Translations.* Music Theory Translation Series. New Haven: Yale University Press, 1989.

———. *Humanism in Italian Renaissance Musical Thought.* New Haven: Yale University Press, 1985.

———. "Musical Asides in the Diplomatic Correspondence of Emilio De' Cavalieri." *Musical Quarterly* 49, no. 3 (1963): 339–355.

———, ed. *Letters on Ancient and Modern Music to Vincenzo Galilei and Giovanni Bardi: A Study with Annotated Texts,* by Girolamo Mei. 2d corr. ed., with addenda. Musicological Studies and Documents, no. 3. Neuhausen-Stuttgart: American Institute of Musicology, 1977.

———. *Norton Anthology of Western Music.* 2d ed. 2 vols. New York: W. W. Norton & Co., 1988.

Parfent'ev, N. P. "Aleksandr Mezenets." In *Slovar' knizhnikov i knizhnosti Drevnei Rusi* (Dictionary of early Russian writers and writings), edited by Dmitrii Sergeevich Likhachev, vol. 3, *XVII v.*, pt. 1, pp. 63–68. St. Petersburg: Dmitrii Bulanin, 1992.

———. *Professional'nye muzykanty rossiiskogo gosudarstva XVI–XVII vekov: Gosudarevy pevchie d'iaki i patriarshie pevchie d'iaki i pod'iaki.* Cheliabinsk: Kniga, 1991.

Perdomo Escobar, José Ignácio. *El archivo musical e la catedral de Bogotá.* Biblioteca de publicaciones del Instituto Caro y Cuervo 37. Bogotá: Instituto Caro y Cuervo, 1976.

Peri, Jacopo. *La musiche di Jacopo Peri, nobil Florentino, sopra L'Euridice del Sig. Ottavio Rinuccini, rappresentate nello sponsalizio della Christianisima Maria Medici, regina di Francia.* Florence, 1601.

Peuerl, Paul. *Neue Padovan, Intrada, Däntz und Galliarda.* Nuremberg, 1611.

Pincherle, Marc. *Antonio Vivaldi et la musique instrumentale.* Vol. 2, *Inventaire-Thématique.* Paris: Floury, 1948.

Pinho, Ernesto Conçalves de. *Santa Cruz de Coimbra: Centro de actividade musical nos seculos XVI e XVII.* Lisbon: Calouste Gulbenkian Foundation, 1981.

Pinnell, Richard T. *Francesco Corbetta and the Baroque Guitar: With a Transcription of His Works.* 2 vols. Studies in Musicology, no. 25. Ann Arbor: UMI Research Press, 1980.

Pirrotta, Nino, and Elena Povoledo. *Music and Theatre from Poliziano to Monteverdi.* Translated by Karen Eales. Cambridge Studies in Music. Cambridge: Cambridge University Press, 1982. Originally published as *Li due Orfei* (Turin: Eri, 1969).

Plamenac, Dragan. "Damjan Nembri of Hvar (1584–c. 1648) and his Vesper Psalms." *Musica antique* (Poland) 6 (1982): 669–85.

———. "Music in the 16th and 17th Centuries in Dalmatia." In *Papers Read by Members of the American Musicological Society 1939*, pp. 21–51. New York: Music Educators' National Conference, 1944.

———. "Toma Cecchini, kapelnik stolnih crkava u Splitu i Hvaru u prvoj polovici XVII stoljeća: Bio-bibliografska studija" (Tomaso Cecchini, chaplain of cathedrals in Split and Hvar during the first decades of the 17th century: A bio-bibliographical study). *Rad Jugoslavenske Akademije Znanosti i Umjetnosti* 262 (1938): 77–125.

Playford, John. *Choice Ayres, Songs, and Dialogues.* 2 vols. London, 1673–1684. Reprint, with an introduction by Ian Spink, Music for London Entertainment 1660–1800, ser. A, Music for Plays, vol. 5a and b, London: Stainer and Bell, 1989.

Pluche, Noël Antoine. *Spectacle de la nature: Ou, entretiens sur les particularités de l'histoire naturelle, qui ont paru les plus propes à rendre les jeunes-gens curieux, & à leur former l'esprit.* Vol. 7. Paris: Novelle edition, 1746.

Polotskii, Simeon. *Izbrannye sochineniia* (Collected works). Edited by I. P. Eremin. Literaturnye pamiatniki. Moscow: Akademiia nauk SSSR, 1953.

Popov, N. P. "O poezdke v Smolensk k mitrop. Simeonu 'dlia velikikh del' " (The trip to Smolensk to Met. Simeon 'for important affairs'). *Chteniia v Imperatorskom obshchestve istorii i drevnostei rossiiskikh pri Moskovskom universitete* (1907): 42–43.

Porter, William V. "Peri's and Corsi's *Dafne:* Some New Discoveries and Observations." *Journal of the American Musicological Society* 18, no. 2 (1965): 170–96.

Posch, Isaac. *Harmonia Concertans: 1623.* Edited by Karl Geiringer. 3 vols. Series of Early Music, vols. 1, 4, and 6. Bryn Mawr, Penn.: Theodore Presser, 1968–1972.

———. *Harmonia Concertans (1623).* Edited by Metoda Kokole. Monumenta artis musicae Sloveniae, vol. 35. Ljubljana: Slovenska akademija znanosti in umetnosti, 1998.

———. *Musicalische Ehrenfreudt (1618).* Edited by Metoda Kokole. Monumenta artis musicae Sloveniae, vol. 30. Ljubljana: Slovenska akademija znanosti in umetnosti, 1996.

———. *Musicalische Tafelfreudt (1621).* Edited by Metoda Kokole. Monumenta artis musicae Sloveniae, vol. 31. Ljubljana: Slovenska akademija znanosti in umetnosti, 1996.

Poulton, Diana. *John Dowland: His Life and Works.* Berkeley: University of California Press, 1972.

Praetorius, Jacob. *Choralbearbeitungen: Für Orgel.* Edited by Werner Breig. Kassel: Bärenreiter, 1974.

Praetorius, Michael. *Gesamtausgabe der musikalischen Werke.* Edited by Friedrich Blume in association with Arnold Mendelssohn and Wilibald Gurlitt. 21 vols. Wolfenbüttel: Möseler, 1928–1960.

————. *Syntagma musicum.* 3 vols. Wolfenbüttel, 1614–1618.

Price, Curtis Alexander. *Henry Purcell and the London Stage.* Cambridge: Cambridge University Press, 1984.

————. *Music in the Restoration Theatre: With a Catalogue of Instrumental Music in Plays, 1665–1713.* Studies in Musicology, no. 4. Ann Arbor: UMI Research Press, 1979.

————, ed. *Dido and Aeneas: An Opera,* by Henry Purcell. Norton Critical Scores. New York: W. W. Norton & Co., 1986.

————. *Purcell Studies.* Cambridge: Cambridge University Press, 1995.

Printz, Wolfgang Caspar. *Historische Beschreibung der edelen Sing- und Kling-Kunst.* Dresden, 1690.

Priuli, Giovanni. *Sacrorum concentuum, pars prima (1618).* Edited by Albert Biales. Concentus musicus, vol. 2. Cologne: A. Volk Verlag-H. Gerig, 1973.

————. *Vier Generalbassmotetten aus dem Parnassus musicus Ferdinandaeus (1615).* Edited by Hermann J. Busch. Musik alter Meister, vol. 23. Graz: Akademische Druck- u. Verlagsanstalt, 1970.

Protopopov, Vladimir Vasil'evich. *Muzyka na poltavskuiu pobedu* (Music for the Poltava victory). Pamiatniki russkogo muzykal'nogo iskusstva 2. Moscow: Muzyka, 1973.

————. "Notnaia biblioteka Tsariia Fedora Alekseevicha" (Tsar Fedor Alekseevich's [notated] musical library). *Pamiatniki Kul'tury: Novye Otkrytiia* (1976): 119–33.

————, ed. *Idea Grammatiki Musikiiskoi,* by Mykola Pavlovych Dylets'kiy. Pamiatniki russkogo muzykal'nogo iskusstva 7. Moscow: Muzyka, 1979.

Prunières, Henry, ed. *Oeuvres complètes de J. B. Lully.* 10 vols. Paris: Éditions de la Revue musicale, 1930–1939. Reprint, New York: Broude Brothers, 1966.

Puliti, Gabriello. *Armonici accenti: Opera 24.* Venice, 1621. Reprint, [Zagreb: Muzicka omladina Hrvatske, 1989].

Purcell, Henry. *The Works of Henry Purcell.* 32 vols. London: [Purcell Society], Novello, Ewer & Co., 1878–[1965; vol. 32, 1962].

Quantz, Johann Joachim. *On Playing the Flute: A Complete Translation.* Translated and introduced by Edward R. Reilly. London: Faber, 1966. Originally published as *Versuch einer Anweisung die Flöte traversiere zu spielen,* Berlin, 1752.

Quitin, José, ed. *Meslanges à II, III, IV et V parties avec la basse continue: Contenant plusieurs chansons, motets, magnificats, préludes et allemandes pour l'orgue et pour les violes et les litanies de la Vierge,* by Henry Du Mont. 2 vols. Publications de la Société liégeoise de musicologie, fasc. 4, 6. Werbomont: Société liégeoise de musicologie, 1983–1984.

Quittard, Henri. "Un musicien oublié du XVIIᵉ siècle français: G. Bouzignac." *Sammelbände der Internationalen Musikgesellschaft* 6, no. 3 (1905): 356–417.

Racek, Jan. *Stilprobleme der italienische Monodie: Ein Beitrag zur Geschichte des einstimmigen Barockliedes.* Opera Universitatis Purkynianae Brunensis: Facultas Philosophica, no. 103. Prague: Státní Pedagogické Nakladatelství, 1965.

Radole, Giuseppe. *L'arte organaria in Istria.* Biblioteca di cultura organaria e organistica, vol. 2. Bologna: R. Patron, 1969.

————. *La musica a Capodistria.* Trieste, 1990.

————. "Musica e musicisti in Istria nel Cinque e Seicento." *Atti e memorie della Societa Istriana di archeologia e storia patria,* new ser., 12 (1965): 147–213.

Radulescu, Michael, ed. *Orgelwerke,* by Nicolaus Bruhns. 2 vols. Diletto musicale 1171–72. Vienna: Doblinger, 1993.

Rajšp, Vincenc. *Jezuitski kolegij v Ljubljani (1597–1773): Zbornik razprav* (The Jesuit College in Ljubljana (1597–1773): An annual report). Redovništvo na Slovenskem 4. Ljubljana: Zgodovinski inštitut Milka Kosa, Provincialat slovenske province Druzbe Jezusove, Inštitut za zgodovino Cerkve Teološke fakultete v Ljubljani, 1998.

Rampe, Siegbert, ed. *Sämtliche freie Orgel- und Clavierwerke* (Complete free organ and keyboard works), by Matthias Weckmann. Kassel: Bärenreiter-Verlag, 1991.

Rampe, Siegbert, and Helen Lerch, eds. *Sämtliche Orgel- und Clavierwerke,* by Johann and Johann Philipp Krieger. 2 vols. Kassel: Bärenreiter, 1999.

Ray, Alice E. "The Double-Choir Music of Juan de Padilla, Seventeenth-Century Composer in Mexico." 2 vols. Ph.D. diss., University of Southern California, 1953.

Rayner, Clare G. *Christian Erbach: Collected Keyboard Compositions.* 5 vols. Corpus of Early Keyboard Music 36. N.p.: American Institute of Musicology, 1971–1977.

Razumovskii, D. V. "Gosudarevy pevchie d'iaki XVII veka" (The sovereign singers in the seventeenth century). *Sbornik obshchestva drevne-russkogo iskusstva* (1873).

Rebelo, João Lourenço. *Psalmi tum Vesperarum, tum Completorium, item Magnificat, Lamentationes et Miserere.* Transcribed and edited by José Augusto Alegria. 4 vols. Portugaliae musica, ser. A, 39–42. Lisbon: Calouste Gulbenkian Foundation, 1982.

Reese, Gustave. *Music in the Renaissance.* New York: W. W. Norton & Co., 1954.

Reiner, Stuart. "Vi sono molt'altre mezz'Arie . . ." In *Studies in Music History: Essays for Oliver Strunk,* edited by Harold Powers, pp. 241–58. Princeton, N.J.: Princeton University Press, 1968.

Rifkin, Joshua. *The New Grove North European Baroque Masters: Schütz, Froberger, Buxtehude, Purcell, Telemann.* Composer Biography Series. London: Macmillan, 1985.

Rijavec, Andrej. *Glasbeno delo na Slovenskem v obdobju protestantizma* (Music in Slovenia in the Protestant era). Razprave in eseji 12. Ljubljana: Slovenska matica, 1967.

Rilling, Helmuth. *Johann Sebastian Bach's B-Minor Mass.* Rev. ed. Translated by Gordon Paine, with a foreword by Howard S. Swan. Princeton, N.J.: Prestige Publications, 1984.

Rinaldi, Mario. *Catalogo numerico tematico delle composizioni di Antonio Vivaldi: Con la definizione delle tonalità, l'indicazione dei movimenti e varie tabelle illustrative.* Rome: Editrice Cultura Moderna, 1945.

Ripollés, Vicente. *El villancico y la cantata del segle XVIII a València.* Biblioteca de Catalunya, Publicaciones del Departmento de música 12. Barcelona: Institut d'estudis catalans, Biblioteca de Catalunya, 1935.

Robinson, Michael F. *Naples and Neapolitan Opera.* Oxford Monographs on Music. Oxford: Clarendon Press, 1972.

Robledo, Luis, ed. *Juan Blas de Castro (ca. 1561–1631): Vida y obra musical.* Publicación 1.201 de la Institución Fernando el Católico. Zaragoza: Institución Fernando el Católico, Sección de Música Antigua, Excma. Diputación Provincial, 1989.

Roche, Jerome L. A. " 'Aus dem berühmbstem italiänischen Autoribus:' Dissemination North of the Alps of the Early-Baroque Italian Sacred Repertory through Published Anthologies and Reprints." In *Claudio Monteverdi und die Folgen,* edited by Silke Leopold and Joachim Steinheuer, pp. 13–28. Kassel: Bärenreiter, 1998.

———. "The Duet in Early Seventeenth-Century Italian Church Music." *Proceedings of the Royal Musical Association* 93 (1966–1967): 33–50.

———. "Monteverdi and the *prima prattica.*" In *The New Monteverdi Companion,* ed. Denis Arnold and Nigel Fortune, pp. 159–82.

———. *North Italian Church Music in the Age of Monteverdi.* Oxford: Clarendon Press, 1984.

Rogov, A. I., ed., comp., and trans. *Muzykal'naia estetika Rossii XI–XVIII vekov* (Musical aesthetics in Russia in the eleventh through eighteenth centuries). Pamiatniki muzykal'no-esteticheskoi mysli. Moscow: Muzyka, 1973.

Roizman, L. I. *Organ v istorii russkoi muzykal'noi kul'tury* (The organ in the history of Russian musical culture). Moscow: Muzyka, 1979.

Rosand, Ellen. "Aria in the Early Operas of Francesco Cavalli." Ph.D. diss., New York University, 1971.

———. "Barbara Strozzi, *virtuossima cantatrice*: The Composer's Voice." *Journal of the American Musicological Society* 31, no. 2 (1978): 241–81.

———. "The Descending Tetrachord: An Emblem of Lament." *Musical Quarterly* 65, no. 3 (1979): 346–59.

———. "Handel Paints the Resurrection." In *Festa musicologica: Essays in Honor of George J. Buelow,* edited by Thomas J. Mathiesen and Benito V. Rivera, pp. 7–52. Festschrift Series, no. 14. Stuyvesant, N.Y.: Pendragon Press, 1995.

———. "Music in the Myth of Venice." *Renaissance Quarterly* 30, no. 4 (1977): 511–37.

————. *Opera in Seventeenth-Century Venice: The Creation of a Genre*. Berkeley: University of California Press, 1991.

————, ed. *Cantatas*, by Barbara Strozzi. The Italian Cantata in the Seventeenth Century, vol. 5. New York: Garland, 1986.

Rose, Gloria. "The Cantatas of Giacomo Carissimi." *Musical Quarterly* 48, no. 2 (1962): 204–15.

————. "The Italian Cantata of the Baroque Period." In *Gattungen der Musik in Einzeldarstellungen: Gedenkschrift Leo Schrade, I*, edited by Wulf Arlt et al., 655–77. Bern: Francke, 1973.

Rosow, Lois. "French Baroque Recitative as an Expression of Tragic Declamation." *Early Music* 11, no. 4 (1983): 468–79.

Rostovskii, Dmitrii. *Rozhdestvenskaia drama, ili Rostovskoe deistvo: V dvukh deistviiakh s prologom i epilogom* (Christmas drama, or the Rostov drama: In two acts, with prologue and epilogue). Moscow: Sovietskii kompozitor, 1989.

Rousseau, Jean-Baptiste. *Correspondance de Jean-Baptiste et de Brossette*. Edited and introduced by Paul Bonnefon. 2 vols. Paris: Édouard Cornély et cie, 1910–1911.

Rousseau, Jean-Jacques. *Oeuvres complètes de J. J. Rousseau: Mises dans un nouvel Ordre, avec des notes historiques et des éclaircissements*. Edited by Victor Donatien de Musset [Musset-Pathay]. 25 vols. Paris: P. Dupont, 1823–1826.

Ruhnke, Martin, ed. *Georg Philipp Telemann: Thematisch-Systematisches Verzeichnis seiner Werke, Telemann-Werkverzeichnis (TWV): Instrumentalwerke*. 3 vols. Kassel: Bärenreiter, 1984–1999.

Rumpler, Helmut. "Sozialer Wandel und Gegenreformation in Klagenfurt." In *Katholische Reform und Gegenreformation in Innerösterreich, 1564–1628*, edited by Werner Drobesch et al., pp. 573–97. Klagenfurt: Hermagoras-Mohorjeva, 1994.

Russell, Craig H., ed. *Santiago de Murcias' Códice Saldívar no. 4: A Treasury of Secular Guitar Music from Baroque Mexico*. 2 vols. Music in American Life. Urbana: University of Illinois Press, 1995.

Russkaia istoricheskaia biblioteka (Russian historical library). 39 vols. St. Petersburg (Leningrad, Petrograd): Arkheograficheskaia komissiia, 1872–1927.

Russkii partesnyi kontsert = A Concert of Old Russian Polyphonic Choral Music. Moscow Chamber Choir. Vladimir Minin. Melodiia phonograph 10–10909–10.

Ryom, Peter. *Répertoires desœuvres Antonio Vivaldi: Les compositions instrumentals*. Copenhagen: Engstrøm & Sødring, 1986.

————. *Verzeichnis der Werke Antonio Vivaldis (RV): Kleine Ausgabe*. 2d ed. Leipzig: Deutscher Verlag für Musik, 1979.

Šaban, Ladislav. "Contributo alla biografia di Don Pietro Nakić." *L'organo* 9, no. 2 (1971): 257–65.

————. "Umjetnost i djela graditelja orgulja Petra Nakića u Dalmaciji i Istri" (The art and works in Istria and Dalmatia of the organ builder P. Nacchini). *Arti musices* 4 (1973): 5–45.

Šaban, Ladislav, and Zdravko Blažeković. "Izvještaj o dvogodišnjem sređivanju triju glazbenih zbirki u Osijeku i o pregledu glazbenih rukopisa i knjiga u franjevačkom samostanima u Slavoniji i Srijemu" (A report on the classification and the cataloguing of three musical archives in Osijek and an overview of musical manuscripts and books in Franciscan monasteries in Slavonia and Srijem). *Arti musices* 11, no. 1 (1980): 47–95.

Sabol, Andrew J., ed. *Four Hundred Songs and Dances for the Stuart Masque*. Rev. ed. Providence, R.I.: Brown University Press, 1978. First ed. published in 1959 as *Songs and Dances for the Stuart Masque*.

Sachs, Curt. "Barockmusik." *Jahrbuch der Musikbibliothek Peters* 26 (December 1919): 7–15.

————. *The Rise of Music in the Ancient World, East and West*. New York: W. W. Norton & Co., 1943.

Sadie, Stanley, and Anthony Hicks, eds. *Handel: Tercentenary Collection*. Studies in Musicology, no. 99. Ann Arbor: UMI Research Press, 1987.

Saldívar, Gabriel. *Historia de la música en México: Épocas precortesiana y colonial*. Mexico: Editorial Cultura, 1934.

Sartori, Claudio. *I libretti italiani a stampa dale origini al 1800: Catalogo analitico con 16 indici*. 6 vols. in 7 bks. Cuneo: Bertola & Locatelli, 1990–1994.

Sas, Andrés. *La música en la cathedral de Lima en el virreinato*. 2 vols. Colección de documentos para la historia de la música en el Perú. Lima: Universidad Nacional Mayor de San Marcos, Casa de la Cultura del Perú, 1971–1972.

Sasportes, José. *História da dança em Portugal*. [Lisbon]: Calouste Gulbenkian Foundation, [1971].

Saunders, Harris Sheridan, Jr. "Handel's *Agrippina:* The Venetian Perspective." *Göttinger Händel Beiträge* 3 (1989): 87–98.

Saunders, Steven. *Cross, Sword, and Lyre: Sacred Music at the Imperial Court of Ferdinand II of Habsburg (1615–1637)*. Oxford Monographs on Music. Oxford: Clarendon Press, 1995.

———, ed. *Fourteen Motets from the Court of Ferdinand II of Hapsburg*. 3 parts. Recent Researches in the Music of the Baroque Era, vol. 75. Madison, Wis.: A-R Editions, 1995.

Saverkina, I. V., and Iu. N. Semenov. "Orkestr i khor A. D. Menshikova (K istorii russkoi muzykal'noi kul'tury)" [A. D. Menshikov's orchestra and choir (Toward a history of Russian musical culture)]. *Pamiatniki Kul'tury: Novye Otkrytiia* (1989): 160–66.

Sawkins, Lionel. "Lalande and the Concert Spirituel." *Musical Times* 116, no. 1586 (1975): 333–35.

Scarlatti, Alessandro. *Passio Domini Nostri Jesu Christi secundum Joannem*. Edited by Edwin Hanley. Collegium musicum, no. 1. New Haven: Yale University Press, 1955.

Scheibe, Johann Adolphe. *Critischer Musikus*. New ed. Leipzig: Bernhard Christoph Breitkopf, 1745.

———. *Über die musikalische Composition*. Leipzig: Schwickert, 1773.

Scheidemann, Heinrich. *Choralbearbeitungen*. Edited by Gustav Fock. Kassel: Bärenreiter, 1967.

———. *Magnificat Bearbeitungen*. Edited by Gustav Fock. Kassel: Bärenreiter, 1970.

———. *12 Orgelintavolierungen*. Edited by Cleveland Johnson. 3 vols. Wilhelmshaven: Heinrichshofen, 1990–1993.

Scheidt, Samuel. *Werke*. Edited by Gottlieb Harms and Christhard Marenholz. 16 vols. to date. Vols. 1–13, Hamburg: Ugrino/Ableitung Verlag, 1923–1962; Vols. 14–16, Leipzig: VEB Deutscher Verlag für Musik, 1971–.

Schein, Johann Hermann. "Banchetto Musicale: Neuer anmutiger Padouanen, Gagliarden, Courenten und Allemanden." In *Venuskräntzen un Banchetto musicale*. Vol. 1. of *Johann Hermann Schein, Sämtliche Werke*, edited by Arthur Prüfer. Leipzig: Breitkopf & Härtel, 1901.

———. *Opella nova*. Edited by Adam Adrio et al. 2 vols. Neue Ausgabe sämtlicher Werke, vols. 4–5. Kassel: Bärenreiter, 1973–1986.

Schelle, Johann. *Six Chorale Cantatas*. Edited by Mary S. Morris. Recent Researches in the Music of the Baroque Era, vols. 60–61. Madison, Wis.: A-R Editions, 1988.

Schenk, Eric, ed. *The Italian Trio Sonata*. Cologne: A. Volk Verlag, sole distributors for the U.S.A., Leeds Music Corp., 1955.

Schidlovsky, Nicolas. "Sources of Russian Chant Theory." In *Russian Theoretical Thought in Music*, edited by Gordon McQuere, pp. 83–108. Russian Music Studies, no. 10. Ann Arbor: UMI Research Press, 1983.

Schierning, Lydia. *Die Überlieferung der deutschen Orgel- und Klaviermusik aus der ersten Hälfte des 17. Jahrhunderts: Eine quellenkundliche Studie*. Schriften des Landesinstituts für Musikforschung Kiel, vol. 12. Kassel: Bärenreiter-Verlag, 1961.

Schlafly, Daniel, Jr. "Filippo Balatri in Peter the Great's Russia." *Jahrbücher für Geschichte Osteuropas* 45, no. 2 (1997): 181–98.

Schlager, Karl-Heinz, and Otto Edwin Albrecht, eds. *Einzeldrucke vor 1800*. Vol. 4. Répertoire international des sources musicales, ser. A, I/4. Kassel: Bärenreiter, 1974.

Schmidt, Carl B. "Antonio Cesti's *Il pomo d'oro:* A Reexamination of a Famous Hapsburg Court Spectacle." *Journal of the American Musicological Society* 29, no. 3 (1976): 381–412.

Schmidt, Gustav Friedrich. "Johann Wolfgang Francks Singspiel *Die drey Töchter Cecrops.*" *Archiv für Musikforschung* 4, no. 3 (1939): 257–316.

Schmieder, Wolfgang, ed. *Thematisch-systematisches Verzeichnis der musikalischen Werken von Johann Sebastian Bach: Bach-Werke-Verzeichnis (BWV)*. 2d ed. Wiesbaden: Breitkopf & Härtel, 1990.

Schmitz, Eugen. *Geschichte der Kantate und des geistlichen Konzerts*. Kleine Handbücher der Musikgeschichte nach Gattungen, vol. 5. Leipzig: Breitkopf & Härtel, 1914.

Schneider, Herbert. *Die Rezeption der Opern Lullys im Frankreich des Ancien Regime.* Mainzer Studien zur Musikwissenschaft, vol. 16. Tutzing: Herbert Schneider, 1982.

Schnoebelen, Anne. "Performance Practices at San Petronio in the Baroque." *Acta Musicologica* (Leipzig) 41, nos. 1–2 (1969): 37–55.

Schrade, Leo. *Monteverdi: Creator of Modern Music.* New York: W. W. Norton & Co., 1950.

Schreiber, Felix, ed. *Ausgewählte Werke des Nürnberger Organisten Johannes Erasmus Kindermann (1616–1655).* 2 vols. Part 1, with an introduction by Schreiber, Denkmäler der Tonkunst in Bayern, 2d ser., vol. 13. Leipzig: Breitkopf & Härtel, 1913; Part 2, with an introduction by Bertha Antonia Wallner, Denkmäler der Tonkunst in Bayern, 2d ser., vols. 21–24 (in 1). Augsburg: Dr. Benno Filser & Co., 1924.

Schulenberg, David. *The Keyboard Music of J. S. Bach.* New York: Schirmer Books, 1992.

Schulze, Hans-Joachim, and Christoph Wolff. *Bach Compendium: Analytisch- bibliographisches Repertorium der Werke Johann Sebastian Bach.* Vol. 1, *Vokalwerke.* Frankfurt: C. F. Peters, 1986.

Schütz, Heinrich. *Gesammelte Briefe und Schriften.* Edited by E. H. Müller von Asow. Deutsche musikbücherei, vol. 45. Regensburg: G. Bosse, 1931.

Sebes, Joseph. *The Jesuits and the Sino-Russian Treaty of Nerchinsk (1689): The Diary of Thomas Pereira.* Bibliotheca Instituti Historici Societatis Iesu, vol. 18. Rome: Institutum Historicum S. I., 1961.

Sehnal, Jiří, and Jitřenka Pešková. *Caroli de Liechtenstein—Castelcorno episcope Olomuscensis operum artis musicae collection Cremsirii reservata.* 2 vols. Catalogus artis musicae in Bohemia et Moravia cultae. Artis musicae antiquioris catalogorum series, vol. 5. Prague: Bibliotheca Nationalis Reipublicae Bohemicae, 1998.

Seiffert, Max, ed. *15 Praeludien und Fugen,* by Heinrich Scheidemann. Organum, 4. Reihe: Orgelmusik, no. 1. Leipzig: F. Kistner & C. F. W. Siegel, [1925].

———. *Gesammelte Werke von Friedr. Wilh. Zachow.* Denkmäler deutscher Tonkunst, 1st ser., vols. 21–22. Leipzig: Breitkopf & Härtel, 1905.

———. *Orgelkompositionen von Johann Pachelbel (1653–1706): Nebst beigefügten Stücken von W. H. Pachelbel (1686–1764).* Denkmäler der Tonkunst in Bayern, 2d ser., Jg. IV, vol. 1. Leipzig: Breitkopf & Härtel, 1903. Parts 1 and 2 republished in Seiffert, ed., *Organ Works,* by Johann Pachelbel (Mineola, N.Y.: Dover, 1994).

Seixas, Carlos. *80 Sonatas para instrumentos de tecla.* 2d ed. Vol. 2, transcribed and edited by Macario Santiago Kastner. Portugaliae musica, ser. A, 10. Lisbon: Calouste Gulbenkian Foundation, 1992.

Selfridge-Field, Eleanor. *Venetian Instrumental Music from Gabrieli to Vivaldi.* 3d rev. ed. New York: Dover, 1994.

Sepp, Antonio. *Viagem às missões jesuíticas e trabalhos apostólicos.* Translated by A. Reymundo Schneider. Coleção Reconquista do Brasil, new ser., vol. 21. Belo Horizonte: Editora Itatiaia, 1980.

Sergeev, V. N. "Russkie pesnopeniia XVII v. na istoricheskuiu temu" (Russian songs of the seventeenth century on historical themes). *Pamiatniki Kul'tury: Novye Otkrytiia* (1975): 41–43.

Sheldon, David A. "The Galant Style Revisited and Re-Evaluated." *Acta Musicologica* 47, no. 2 (1975): 240–270.

Simoniti, Primož, ed. *Akademske cebele ljubljanskih operozov, ali, Ustanova, pravila, smoter, imena in simboli nove akademije, zdruzene pod simbolom cebel v Ljubljani, izrocene slovstvenemu svetu z nastopnim govorom na prvem javnem zboru, govorjenim veljakom Emone = Apes academicae operosorum Labacensium.* Ljubljana: Slovenska akademija znanosti in umetnosti, 1988.

Sivec, Jože. "Stilna orientacija glasbe protestantizma na Slovenskem" (Stylistic orientation of Protestant music in Slovenia). *Muzikološki zbornik* 19 (1993): 17–29.

Škerlj, Stanko. *Italijansko gledališče v Ljubljani v preteklih stoletjih* (Italian theatre in Ljubljana in the past centuries). Slovenska akademija znanosti in umetnosti: Razred za filološke in literarne vede, Dele 26. Ljubljana: Slovenska akademija znanosti in umetnosti, 1973.

Škulj, Edo. *Hrenove korne knjige* (Hren's choirbooks). Ljubljana, 2001.

Smallman, Basil. *Schütz.* The Master Musicians. Oxford: Oxford University Press, 2000.

Smith, Ruth. "Intellectual Contexts of Handel's English Oratorios." In *Music in Eighteenth-Century England: Essays in Memory of Charles Cudworth,* edited by Christopher Hogwood and Richard

Luckett, with a foreword by Stanley Sadie, pp. 115–33. Cambridge: Cambridge University Press, 1983.

Smither, Howard E. *A History of the Oratorio.* 2 vols. Chapel Hill: University of North Carolina Press, 1977.

Smolenskii, Stepan Vasil'evich, ed. *Azbuka znamennogo peniia (Izveshchenie o soglasneishikh pometakh) startsa Aleksandra Mezentsa (1688-go goda)* [Alphabet of *znamennyi* chant (report about the most agreeable markings) by the monk Aleksandr Mezenets in 1668]. Kazan: Tip. Imp. universiteta, 1888.

Snyder, Kerala J. *Dieterich Buxtehude: Organist in Lübeck.* New York: Schirmer Books, 1987.

Solteri, Angelo. *Le origini del melodrama: Testimonian ze dei contemporanei.* Piccola biblioteca di scienze moderne, no. 70. Turin: Fratelli Bocca, 1903.

Spiess, Lincoln B., and E. Thomas Stanford. *An Introduction to Certain Mexican Musical Archives.* Detroit Studies in Music Bibliography 15. Detroit: Information Coordinators, 1969.

Spink, Ian. *English Song: Dowland to Purcell.* New York: C. Scribner's Sons, [1974].

———. *Restoration Cathedral Music, 1660–1714.* Oxford Studies in British Church Music. Oxford: Clarendon Press, 1995.

———, ed. *English Songs, 1625–1660.* Musica Britannica, vol. 33. London: Stainer and Bell, 1971.

———. *Music in Britain: The Seventeenth Century.* The Blackwell History of Music in Britain, vol. 3. Oxford: Blackwell Reference, 1992.

Spitta, Philipp. *Johann Sebastian Bach: His Work and Influence on the Music of Germany, 1685–1750.* Translated by Clara Bell and J. A. Fuller Maitland. 3 vols. London: Novello and Co., 1884–1885; reprint, 1951. Originally published in German, Leipzig: Breitkopf & Härtel, 1873–1880.

Staden, Sigmund Theophil. *Die älteste bekannte deutsche Singspiel Seelewig.* Edited by Robert Eitner. Monatshefte für Musikgeschichte, vol. 14, nos. 4–6. Berlin: T. Trautwein, 1881.

Starikova, L. M. "Dokumental'nye utochneniia k istorii teatra v Rossii petrovskogo vremeni" (Some specifics from the sources on the history of the theatre in Petrine- era Russia). *Pamiatniki Kul'tury: Novye Otkrytiia* (1998): 179–90.

———. "Russkii teatr petrovskogo vremeni, Komedial'naia khramina i domashnie komedii tsarevny Natal'i Alekseevny" (Russian theatre of the Petrine era, the Komedial'naia khramina [where the plays were performed], and Tsarevna Natalia Alekseevna's domestic plays). *Pamiatniki Kul'tury: Novye Otkrytiia* (1990): 137–56.

Stauffer, George B. *Bach, the Mass in B Minor: The Great Catholic Mass.* Monuments of Western Music. New York: Schirmer, 1997.

———. *The Organ Preludes of Johann Sebastian Bach.* Studies in Musicology, no. 27. Ann Arbor: UMI Research Press, 1980.

Stauffer, George B., and Ernest May, eds. *J. S. Bach as Organist: His Instruments, Music, and Performance Practices.* Bloomington: Indiana University Press, 1986.

Steger, W. *Gabriel Plautz: Ein Mainzer Hofkapellmeister im frühen 17. Jahrhundert.* Würzburg, 1991.

Stein, Louise K. "Music in the Seventeenth-Century Spanish Secular Theatre, 1598– 1690." 2 vols. Ph.D. diss., University of Chicago, 1987.

———. *Songs of Mortals, Dialogues of the Gods: Music and Theatre in Seventeenth-Century Spain.* Oxford Monographs on Music. Oxford: Clarendon Press, 1993.

Stenzl, Jürg. Introduction to *Historisch-kritische Gesamtausgabe der musikalischen Werke,* by Arcangelo Corelli. Edited by Hans Oesch. Vol. 2, *Sonate da Camera, Opus II and IV.* Laaber: Laaber-Verlag, 1986.

Steude, Wolfram, ed. *Der Schwanengesang: Des Königs und Prophetens David 119. Psalm in elf Stücken, nebst einem Anhang des 100. Psalms und eines deutschen Magnificats, für zwei vierstimmige Chör und Basso continuo, SWV 482–494,* by Heinrich Schütz. Neue Ausgabe sämtlicher Werke, vol. 39. Kassel: Bärenreiter, 1984.

Stevens, Denis. *Thomas Tomkins, 1572–1656.* Unabridged and corrected ed. New York: Dover Publications, 1967.

Stevenson, Robert M. *Music in Aztec and Inca Territory.* Berkeley: University of California Press, 1968.

————. *Music in Mexico: A Historical Survey.* New York: Thomas Y. Crowell Co., 1952.

————. *The Music of Peru: Aboriginal and Viceroyal Epochs.* Washington, D.C.: Pan American Union, [1959].

————, comp. *Renaissance and Baroque Musical Sources in the Americas.* Washington, D.C.: General Secretariat, Organization of American States, 1970.

————, ed. *Christmas Music from Baroque Mexico.* Berkeley: University of California Press, 1974.

————. *Antologia de polifonia portuguesa, 1490–1680.* Portugaliae musica, ser. A, 37. Lisbon: Calouste Gulbenkian Foundation, 1982.

————. *Vilancicos portugueses.* Portugaliae musica, ser. A, 29. Lisbon: Calouste Gulbenkian Foundation, 1976.

Stewart, Brian D. "Georg Philipp Telemann in Hamburg: Social and Cultural Background and Its Musical Expression." Ph.D. diss., Stanford University, 1985.

Stinson, Russell. *Bach: The Orgelbüchlein.* Monuments of Western Music. New York: Schirmer Books, 1996.

Stipčević, Ennio. "La cultura musicale in Istria e in Dalmazia nel XVI e XVII secolo: Principali caratteristiche storiche, geopolitiche e culturali." *International Review of the Aesthetics and Sociology of Music* 23, no. 2 (1992): 141–52.

————. "Francesco Sponga-Usper, compositore veneziano di origine istriana: Considerazioni preliminari." *Atti del Centro di Richerche Storiche di Rovigno* 16 (1985–1986): 165–231.

————. *Gabriello Puliti, ranobarokni skladaatelj u Istri = Gabriello Puliti, compositore del primo barocco in Istria.* Zagreb, 1996.

————. *Glazba iz arhiva: Studije i zapisi o staroj hrvatskoj glazbi* (Music from the archives: Studies and essays on early Croatian music). Mala knjiznica Matice hrvatske, new ser., vol. 28. Zagreb: Matica hrvatska, 1997.

————. *Hrvatska glazba: Povijest hrvatske glazbe do 20. stoljeca* (Croation music: History of Croatian music before the 20th century). Zagreb: Skolska knjiga, 1997.

————. *Hrvatska glazbena kultura 17. stoljeca.* Biblioteka znanstvenih djela 60. Split: Knjizevni krug, 1992.

————. "Influssi veneziani nelle musiche dei maestri dalmati del Cinque e Seicento." *Musica e storia* 6, no. 1 (1998): 227–236.

————. "Uvodna razmatranja o umjetnosti Gabriella Pulitija (oko 1575–iza 1641)" (Introduction to the art of Gabriello Puliti (ca. 1575–post-1641). *Arti musices* 14, no. 1 (1983): 33–50.

————, ed. *Glazbeni barok u Hrvatskoj* (Baroque music in Croatia). Osor, 1989.

Stribos, Stijn, ed. *Toccatas,* by Hans Leo Hassler. Corpus of Early Keyboard Music 45. Neuhausen-Stuttgart: American Institute of Musicology, Hänssler-Verlag, 1985.

Strohm, Reinhard. "Händel in Italia: Nuovi contributi." *Rivista italiana di musicologia* 9 (1974): 152–74.

Strunk, Oliver, comp. *Source Readings in Music History: From Classical Antiquity through the Romantic Era.* New York: W. W. Norton & Co., 1950.

Subirá, José. *Historia de la música española e hispano-americana.* Barcelona: Salvat Editores, 1953.

Suess, John. "Giovanni Battista Vitali and the Sonata da chiesa." 3 vols. Ph.D. diss., Yale University, 1962.

Sutkowski, A., ed. *Opere complète di Tarquinio Merula.* 4 vols. Institute of Medieval Music Collected Works, vol. 7. Brooklyn: Institute of Medieval Music, 1974–1978.

Sweelinck, Jan Pieterszoon. *Opera omnia: Editio altera quam edendam curavit Vereniging voor Nederlandse Muziekgeschiedenis.* 7 vols. in 10. Amsterdam, 1968–1990.

Szarán, Luís, and Jesús Ruiz Nestosa. *Música en las reduciones jesuíticas: Colección de instrumentos de Chiquitos, Bolivia.* Asunción: Fundación Paracuaria, 1996.

Talbot, Michael. *The Sacred Vocal Music of Antonio Vivaldi.* Studi di musica veneta, Quaderni vivaldiani 8. Florence: L. S. Olschki, 1995.

————. *Tomaso Albinoni: The Venetian Composer and His World.* Oxford: Clarendon Press, 1990.

————. *Vivaldi.* The Master Musicians Series. London: Dent, 1978.

Tapié, Victor Lucien. *The Age of Grandeur: Baroque Art and Architecture*. Translated by A. Ross Williamson. Books That Matter. New York: Praeger, 1961.

Tarrant, Fredrick A. "John Blow's Verse Anthems with Organ Accompaniment." Ph.D. diss., Indiana University, 2000.

Tello, Aurelio, ed. *Misas de Manuel Sumaya*. Tesoro de la música polifónica en México 8. Mexico: Instituto Nacional de Bellas Artes, 1996.

Thesselius, Johannes. *Neue liebliche Paduanen, Intraden und Galliarden*. Nuremberg, 1609.

Thomas, R. Hinton. *Poetry and Song in the German Baroque: A Study of the Continuo Lied*. Oxford: Clarendon Press, 1963.

Timms, Colin. "The Chamber Duets of Agostino Steffani (1654–1728) with Transcriptions and Catalogue." 2 vols. Ph.D. diss., University of London, 1976.

———, ed. *Twelve Chamber Duets*, by Agostino Steffani. Recent Researches in the Music of the Baroque Era, vol. 53. Madison, Wis.: A-R Editions, 1987.

Tinhorão, José Ramos. *Os negros em Portugal: Uma presence silenciosa*. Colecção universitária 31. Lisbon: Caminho, 1988.

Tintori, Giampiero, ed. *4 [i.e. Quattro] Cantate (inedite) per canto e pianoforte* (4 [i.e. four] cantatas (previously unpublished) for voice and piano), by Alessandro Scarlatti. [Milan]: Ricordi, 1958.

Tomkins, Thomas. *Consort Music*. Transcribed and edited by John Irving. Musica Britannica, vol. 59. London: Stainer and Bell, 1991.

———. *Keyboard Music*. Edited by Stephen D. Tuttle. 2d rev. ed. Musica Britannica, vol. 5. London: Stainer and Bell, 1964.

———. *Musica Deo sacra*. Transcribed and edited by Bernard Rose. 6 vols. Early English Church Music, vols. 5, 9, 14, 27, 37, 39. London: Stainer and Bell, 1965–1992.

Tomlinson, Gary. *Italian Secular Song: 1606–1636: A Seven-Volume Reprint Collection*. Vol. 3, *Rome and Naples*. New York: Garland, 1986.

———. "Madrigal, Monody, and Monteverdi's 'via naturale alla immitatione.' " *Journal of the American Musicological Society* 34, no. 1 (1981): 60–108.

———. *Monteverdi and the End of the Renaissance*. Berkeley: University of California Press, 1987.

———. "Twice Bitten, Thrice Shy: Monteverdi's 'finta' *Finta pazza*." *Journal of the American Musicological Society* 36, no. 2 (1983): 303–11.

Torbarina, Josip. *Italian Influence on the Poets of the Ragusan Republic*. London: Williams & Norgate, 1931.

Torrente, Álvaro J. "The Sacred Villancico in Early Eighteenth-Century Spain: The Repertory of Salamanca Cathedral." 2 vols. Ph.D. diss., Cambridge University, 1998.

Trede, Hilmar, ed. *Klavier-Übung, 1728*, by Vincent Lübeck. Leipzig: C. F. Peters, 1940; London, New York: Hinrichsen-Peters, 1941.

Troiano, Massimo. *Dialoghi di Massimo Trojano: Nozze dello . . . Prencipe Guglielmo . . . Duca di Baviera, e Renata di Loreno . . . .* Venice, 1569.

Troy, Charles E. *The Comic Intermezzo: A Study in the History of Eighteenth-Century Italian Opera*. Studies in Musicology, no. 9. Ann Arbor: UMI Research Press, 1979.

Tuksar, Stanislav. *Croatian Renaissance Music Theorists*. Translated by Sonja Bašic. Studies in Croatian Musical Culture: Collection of Translations 1. Zagreb: Music Information Center, Zagreb Concert Management, 1980.

———. "Sixteenth-Century Croatian Writers on Music: A Bridge between East and West." In *Musical Humanism and Its Legacy: Essays in Honor of Claude V. Palisca*, edited by Nancy Kovaleff Baker and Barbara Russano Hanning, pp. 129–42. Festschrift Series, no. 11. Stuyvesant, N.Y.: Pendragon Press, 1992.

———. "Writers on Music in the Croatian Lands in the Period 1750–1820: A Preliminary Review of Personalities, Topics and Social Milieus." In *Off-Mozart: Glazbena kultura I "mali majstori" srednje Europe 1750–1820: Radovi s medunardnog muzikološkog skupa odrzanog u Zagrebu, Hrvatska, 1.–3. 10. 1992 = Musical Culture and the "Kleinmeister" of Central Europe 1750–1820: Pro-*

ceedings of the International Musicological Symposium held in Zagreb, Croatia, on October 1–3, 1992, edited by Vjera Katalinić, pp. 167–78. Serija Musikološki zbornici, no. 3. Zagreb: Hrvatsko musikološko društvo, 1995.

———, ed. *The Musical Baroque, Western Slavs, and the Spirit of the European Cultural Communion: Proceedings of the International Musicological Symposium held in Zagreb, Croatia, on October 12–14, 1989*. Serija Muzikološki zbornici, no. 1. Zagreb: Croatian Musicological Society, 1993.

———. *Zagreb 1094–1994: Zagreb i hrvatske zemlje kao most između srednjoeuropskih i mediteranskih glazbenih kultura = Zagreb and Croatian Lands as a Bridge Between Central-European and Mediterranean Musical Cultures*. Serija Muzikološki zbornici, no. 5. Zagreb: Croatian Musicological Society, 1998.

Tunder, Franz. *Gesangswerke: Solocantaten und chorwerke mit instrumentalbegleitung*. Edited by Max Seiffert. Denkmäler deutscher Tonkunst, 1st ser., vol. 3. Leipzig: Breitkopf & Härtel, 1900.

Tunley, David. *The Eighteenth-Century French Cantata*. 2d ed. Oxford: Clarendon Press, 1997.

Valvasor, Johan Weichard. *Die Ehre des Herzogtums Krain*, vol. 3, bk. 10. Nuremburg: W. Moritz, 1689.

Vega, Carlos. *La música de un códice colonial del siglo XVII*. Buenos Aires: Imprensa de la Universidad, 1931.

Velmirović, Miloš M. "Liturgical Drama in Byzantium and Russia." *Dumbarton Oaks Papers* 16 (1962): 349–85.

Verchaly, André, ed. *Airs de cour pour voix et luth (1603–1643)*. Publications de la Société française de musicologie, 1st ser., vol. 16. Paris: Heugel, 1961.

Vereniging voor Nederlandse Muziekgeschiedenis. *Jan Pieterszoon Sweelinck: Opera omnia*. Amsterdam: G. Alsbach, 1957–1966.

Vetter, Walther. *Das frühdeutsch Lied: Ausgewählte Kapitel aus der Entwicklungsgeschichte und Aesthetik des ein- und mehrstimmigen deutschen Kunstliedes im 17. Jahrhundert*. 2 vols. Universitas-Archiv: Eine Sammlung wissenschaftlicher Untersuchungen und Abhandlungen, vol. 8. Münster i. W.: Helios-Verlag, 1928.

Vidaković, Albe. *Yury Krizanitch's "Asserta musicalia" (1656) and His Other Musical Works*. Edited by Josip Andreis. Zagreb: Yugoslav Academy of Sciences and Arts, 1967.

———, ed. *Sechs Motetten aus Arion primus (1628)*, by Vinko Jelic. Musik alter Meister, vol. 5. Graz: Akademische Druck- u. Velagsanstalt, 1957.

———. *Vinko Jelic (1596–1636?): i njegova zbirka duhovnih koncerata i ricercara "Parnassia militia" (1622)*. Jugoslavenska akademija znanosti i umjetnosti: Odjel za musicku umjetnost, no. 2 = Spomenici hrvatske musicke prolosti, no. 2. Zagreb: Izdavacki zavod Jugoslavenske akademije, 1957.

Vieira, Ernesto. *Diccionario biographico de musicos portuguezes*. 2 vols. Lisbon: M. Moreira & Pinheiro, 1900.

Vinogradoff, Igor. "Russian Missions to London, 1569–1687: Seven Accounts by the Masters of the Ceremonies." *Oxford Slavonic Papers*, n.s., 14 (1981): 36–72.

Vollen, Gene E. *The French Cantata: A Survey and Thematic Catalog*. Studies in Musicology, no. 51. Ann Arbor: UMI Research Press, 1982.

Vol'man, Boris L'vovich. *Russkie pechatnye noty XVIII veka* (Russian printed music from the 18th century). Leningrad: Gosudarstvennoe muzykal'noe izdatel'stvo, 1957.

Volpe, Maria Alice, and Régis Duprat, eds. *Recitativo e ária para José Mascarenhas*. São Paulo: Editora da Universidade de São Paulo, 2000.

Walker, D. P. "The Aims of Baïf's *Académie de Poésie et de Musique*." *Journal of Renaissance and Baroque Music* 1, no. 2 (1946): 91–100.

Walls, Peter. *Music in the English Courtly Masque, 1604–1640*. Oxford Monographs on Music. Oxford: Clarendon Press, 1996.

Walther, Johann Gottfried. *Musikalisches Lexicon, oder, Musicalische Bibliothec*. Leipzig: W. Deer, 1732.

Webber, Geoffrey. *North German Church Music in the Age of Buxtehude*. Oxford Monographs on Music. Oxford: Clarendon Press, 1996.

Weckmann, Matthias. *Choralbearbeitungen: Für Orgel.* Edited by Werner Breig. Kassel: Bärenreiter, 1979.

Weelkes, Thomas. *Collected Anthems.* Transcribed and edited by David Brown, Walter Collins, and Peter Le Huray. Musica Britannica, vol. 23. London: Stainer and Bell, 1966.

Welleck, René. "The Concept of Baroque in Literary Scholarship." *Journal of Aesthetics and Art Criticism* 5 (December 1946): 77–108.

Wessely, Othmar, comp. *Frühmeister des Stile nuovo in Österreich: Bartolomeo Mutis, Conte di Cesara, Francesco degli Atti, Giovanni Valentini.* Edited by Erika Kanduth. Denkmäler der Tonkunst in Österreich, vol. 125. Graz: Akademische Druck- u. Verlagsanstalt, 1973.

Westhoff, Johann Paul, and Manfred Fechner, eds. *Sechs Suiten für Violine Solo,* by Johann Sebastian Bach. Peters Reprints. Leipzig: Peters, 1974. Originally published in Dresden, 1696.

Whenham, John. *Duet and Dialogue in the Age of Monteverdi.* 2 vols. Studies in British Musicology, no. 7. Ann Arbor: UMI Research Press, 1982.

———, ed. *Claudio Monteverdi: "Orfeo."* Cambridge Opera Handbooks. Cambridge: Cambridge University Press, 1986.

Wilsdorf, Susanne, ed. *Drama, oder Musicalisches Schauspiel von der Dafne,* by Giovanni Andrea Angelini Bontempi and Marco Gioseppe Peranda. Denkmäler mitteldeutscher Barockmusik, 2d ser., vol. 2. Leipzig: Hofmeister, 1998.

Wilson, John, ed. *Roger North on Music: Being a Selection from His Essays Written during the Years c. 1695–1728.* London: Novello, 1959.

Witzenmann, Wolfgang. *Autographe Marco Marazzolis in der Biblioteca Vaticana.* 2 vols. in 1. Cologne: Böhlau-Verlag, 1969–1970. Originally published as articles. Part 1 in *Analecta musicologica,* vol. 7 = *Studien zur Italienisch-Deutschen Musikgeschichte,* vol. 6 (1969): 36–86; Part 2 in *Analecta Musicologica,* vol. 9 = *Studien zur Italienisch-Deutschen Musikgeschichte,* vol. 7 (1970): 203–94.

———, ed. *Sacrae concertationes,* by Domenico Mazzochi. Concentus musicus, vol. 3. Cologne: A. Volk-H. Gerig, 1975.

Wolff, Christoph. *Bach: Essays on His Life and Music.* Cambridge: Harvard University Press, 1991.

———. *Johann Sebastian Bach: The Learned Musician.* New York: W. W. Norton & Co., 2000.

———. *The New Grove Bach Family.* The Composer Biography Series. New York: W. W. Norton & Co., 1983.

———. *Der Stile antico in der Musik Johann Sebastian Bachs.* Beihefte zum Archiv für Musikwissenschaft, vol. 6. Wiesbaden: Steiner, 1968.

———, ed. *Vierzehn Kanons: Über der ersten acht Fundamentalnoten der Aria aus den "Goldberg-Variationen" = Fourteen Canons on the First Eight Notes of the Aria Ground from the "Goldberg Variations,"* by Johann Sebastian Bach. Bärenreiter 5153. Kassel: Bärenreiter, 1976.

Wolgast, Gesa, ed. *Sämtliche Werke,* by George Böhm. Rev. ed. 2 vols. Wiesbaden: Breitkopf & Härtel, 1952. Original edition edited by Johannes Wolgast.

Wood, Bruce, and Andrew Pinnock. " 'Unscarr'd by Turning Times'? The Dating of Purcell's *Dido and Aeneas.*" *Early Music* 20, no. 3 (1992): 372–90.

Worsthorne, Simon Towneley. *Venetian Opera in the Seventeenth Century.* Oxford: Clarendon Press, 1954.

Wortman, Richard. *Scenarios of Power: Myth and Ceremony in Russian Monarchy.* Vol. 1, *From Peter the Great to the Death of Nicholas I.* Studies of the Harriman Institute. Princeton, N.J.: Princeton University Press, 1995.

Yates, Frances Amelia. *The French Academies of the Sixteenth Century.* Studies of the Warburg Institute, vol. 15. London: Warburg Institute, 1947.

Zguta, Russell. *Russian Minstrels: A History of the Skomorokhi.* [Philadelphia]: University of Pennsylvania Press, 1978.

Zimmerman, Franklin B. *Henry Purcell, 1659–1695: An Analytical Catalogue of His Music.* London: Macmillan, 1963.

Zipoli, Domenico. *Cantos Chiquitanos: Arias, cantos eucarísticos y de acción de gracias, cantos devocionales, letanías, musica instrumental, para solo y orquesta, coro a capella y coro con violines y continuo*. Transcribed and edited by Piotr Nawrot. Monuménta música in Chiquitórum reductiónibus Bolíviae. Indígenas y cultura musical de las reducciones Jesuíticas, vol. 2. Cochabamba: Editorial Verbo Divino, 2000.

Žitko, Salvator, ed. *Antonio Tarsi: 1643–1722*. Koper, 1993.

Županović, Lovro. *Centuries of Croatian Music*. Translated by Vladimir Ivir. 2 vols. Studies in Croatian Musical Culture: Collection of Translations 3. Zagreb: Music Information Center, Zagreb Concert Management, 1984–1989.

Zvereva, Svetlana G. "Gosudarevye pevchie d'iaki posle 'Smuty' (1613–1649)" (The sovereign singers after the "Time of Troubles" [1613–1649]). In Vol. 2 of *Germenevitka drevnerusskoi literatury*, edited by A. S. Dëmin et al., pp. 355–83. Moscow: Institut Mirovoj Literatury imeni Gor'kogo, 1989.

———. "O khore gosudarevykh pevchikh d'iakov v XVI v." (On the choir of the sovereign singers in the sixteenth century). *Pamiatniki Kul'tury: Novye Otkrytiia* (1987): 125–130.

Index

References to tables and musical examples are italicized.

GEORGE J. BUELOW, Professor of Musicology at Indiana University (retired), is former President of the American Bach Society. His research and publications, including several articles in *The New Grove Dictionary of Music and Musicians*, focus on the music of the Baroque and the history of opera.

Contributors

Claudia Jensen is a specialist in Muscovite music. Her research, beginning with her doctoral dissertation from Princeton University, includes studies of the theorist Nikolai Diletskii and the Muscovite theater. Her research has appeared in the *Journal of the American Musicological Society*, *Musical Quarterly*, and *Theatre Research International*. She is currently co-editing Nikolai Findeizen's monumental study of early Russian music for Indiana University Press.

Metoda Kokole is a specialist in the music of Slovenia. She completed her doctorate in musicology at the Znanstvenoraziskovalni center SAZU with a dissertation on the Baroque composer Isaac Posch. Dr. Kokole has published several papers on Posch, both in Slovenia and abroad, and has edited several volumes of his music.

Rui Vieira Nery studied at the Academia de Música de Santa Cecília and the Conservatório Nacional de Lisboa before earning his doctorate from the University of Texas at Austin. His doctorate, completed with a Fulbright Scholarship, focuses on musical life in lusophone Brazil during the eighteenth century. He is Assistant Professor in the Departamento de Artes at the Universidade de Évora, and Adjunct Director of the Serviço de Música da Fundação Calouste Gulbenkian in Lisbon.

Ennio Stipčević received his doctorate in musicology from the Academy of Music in Zagreb. He is a senior researcher at the Institute for the History of Croatian Music, Croatian Academy of Sciences and Arts, and honorary professor at the Academy of Music in Zagreb and at the Studia Croatica in Zagreb. He has been a Fulbright visiting scholar at Yale University, and is an associate member of the Croatian Academy of Sciences and Arts.